History of American Presidential Elections

Volume I

History of American Presidential Elections
1789-1968

Arthur M. Schlesinger, jr.
Editor
Albert Schweitzer Chair in the Humanities
City University of New York

Fred L. Israel
Associate Editor
Department of History
City College of New York

William P. Hansen
Managing Editor

CHELSEA HOUSE PUBLISHERS
In Association With
McGRAW-HILL BOOK CO.
New York   Toronto   London   Sydney

Assistant to the Editor: Alice Sherman

Editorial Staff: Joan Tapper, Grace Corso,
Jeanne Brody, Susan Appleman, Janet Doeden, Betsy Nicolaus

Design by Connie Frey

Prefatory Note

In his preface to the first edition of *History of Presidential Elections* (1884), Edward Stanwood modestly noted that his 407-page volume "professes to be little more than a record of the circumstances of such elections, and of whatever had an appreciable influence upon the result." In the ensuing eighty-seven years, there have been abundant monographs dealing with presidential elections. The Library of Congress Card Catalogue lists hundreds of titles under the entry *Presidents - U.S. - Election*, and it would take a volume larger than Stanwood's just to list the scholarly articles on this subject.

Our four volumes do not profess to be the definitive study of American presidential elections — such a task would be impossible. Our goal has been to provide a comprehensive history, written by prominent historians and political scientists. In a sense, we have aimed at Edward Stanwood's goal — to record "the circumstances of such elections, and of whatever had an appreciable influence upon the result."

Our forty-five contributors had two assignments — to analyze a presidential election and to choose relevant documents illustrating their theses. These documents are included in an appendix at the end of each essay. (Except for long "f" changes in eighteenth- and early nineteenth-century documents, all spelling, grammar, and punctuation used in the original have been maintained.) We believe that these essays and documents comprise the most comprehensive history of American presidential elections ever published.

CONTENTS

Volume I

Election of 1892   *H. Wayne Morgan*   1703

Volume III

Election of 1952   *Barton J. Bernstein*   3215

Presidential Elections and the Party System

by *Arthur M. Schlesinger, jr.*

> For a long while before the appointed time has come, the election becomes the important and, so to speak, the all-engrossing topic of discussion. Factional ardor is redoubled, and all the artificial passions which the imagination can create in a happy and peaceful land are agitated and brought to light. . . . As the election draws near, the activity of intrigue and the agitation of the populace increase; the citizens are divided into hostile camps, each of which assumes the name of its favorite candidate; the whole nation glows with feverish excitement; the election is the daily theme of the press, the subject of every private conversation, the end of every thought and every action, the sole interest of the present.
>
> It is true that as soon as the choice is determined, this ardor is dispelled, calm returns, and the river, which had nearly broken its banks, sinks to its usual level; but who can refrain from astonishment that such a storm should have arisen?

So, with some wonder, Alexis de Tocqueville described the American system of elections, emphasizing the contrast between the sounds of crisis and the speed of reconciliation. If the nations of Europe had thus to choose their leaders, he noted, few "could escape the calamities of anarchy or of conquest every time they might have to elect a new sovereign." But the American democracy, rejecting the principle of hereditary succession, had invented a means by which, in spite of ominous hullabaloo, power peacefully passed from one head of state to the next, and Tocqueville was suitably impressed. How formidable an achievement this was we can well understand today when we consider the way the problem of succession torments and convulses so many of the nations of our own day.

1.

When Tocqueville made these observations, the United States of America was well established as a nation. Half a century earlier the American situation had been far more precarious. The new nation then faced the hard question whether, given localism at home and imperialism abroad, it could survive at all. Disputes over the devolution of power could become a threat to survival both by feeding division within the country and by offering foreign empires their chance, as James Madison put it at the Constitutional Convention, "to mix their intrigues & influence with the Election." The solution of the succession problem was therefore a vital part of the quest for stability.

Marcus Cunliffe in his essay on "The Elections of 1789 and 1792" recalls the complex debates which finally produced Article II, Section 1, of the Constitution. This article confided the choice of the President neither to the Congress, as some had proposed at Philadelphia, nor directly to the people, as favored by others, but to a group of "electors," designated in each state for this single, specific, and temporary purpose. The electors, exercising their independent judgment in their respective states, would cast their votes for President, a majority to prevail; and, since no one supposed that any individual (after General Washington) would easily obtain a majority, it was expected that the House of Representatives would ordinarily make the final choice from the five highest in the list they received from the Electoral College. The second man in the House vote would become Vice-President.

Defending this system in the *68th Federalist*, Alexander Hamilton laid particular stress on the importance of affording "as little opportunity as possible to tumult and disorder" in the election of the chief magistrate. Selection of the President by the Congress would be an invitation to "cabal, intrigue, and corruption . . . chiefly from the desire in foreign powers to gain an improper ascendant in our councils"; moreover, it was essential that "the Executive should be independent for his continuance in the office on all but the people themselves." But direct selection of the President by the people would expose the process to "heats and ferments" arising from mass emotion. While "the sense of the people" had to be expressed in the choice, Hamilton said,

> the immediate election should be made by . . . a small number of persons, selected by their fellow-citizens from the general mass, [who] will be most likely to possess the information and discernment requisite to such complicated investigations. . . . The choice of *several*, to form an intermediate body of electors, will be much less apt to convulse the community with any extraordinary and violent movements, than the choice of *one* who was himself to be the final object of the public wishes.

This "mode of appointment," Hamilton added, "is almost the only part of the system, of any consequence, which has escaped without severe censure, or which has received the slightest mark of approbation from its opponents."

His satisfaction turned out to be remarkably misplaced. The united desire of the electors to make Washington President at first concealed the defects of the process; but it really only worked once—in the election of 1796. Thereafter the electors stopped exercising independent judgment and began casting party votes; and, as Noble E. Cunningham, Jr., explains in his discussion of "The Election of 1800," the Jefferson-Burr imbroglio in the House of Representatives led to the first substantive modification of the Constitution when the 12th Amendment in 1804 required electors thereafter to vote separately for President and Vice-President.

2.

The original process got into trouble because of one of the few notable miscalculations by the Founding Fathers—their failure to realize that the competition for the Presidency would generate the formation of political parties; indeed, their larger failure to see that their splendid plan of government could hardly work at all without a party system.

This was an understandable failure. The eighteenth-century world was without experience of political parties in the modern sense. Burke was almost alone in defining party favorably—"a body of men united for promoting by their joint endeavors the national interest upon some particular principle in which they are all agreed"—and in contending that a party system could be a good thing. The American experience in particular had been from colonial days with family cliques or local juntos. Given the concern over national survival, the Founding Fathers saw such groupings as gratuitous sources of instability and condemned them as "factions." Washington summed up the feeling in his Farewell Address, where he warned, as he put it, " in the most solemn manner against the baneful effects of the Spirit of Party." While acknowledging that this spirit, "unfortunately," was inseparable from human nature and that it broke out in all forms of government, Washington said that in popular governments "it is seen in its greatest rankness and is truly their worst enemy."

Yet the very intensity of his language proceeded from his recognition that the spirit of party was already beginning to rise in American politics. The reasons for the appearance of the party system were manifold. Basically party competition reflected the economic diversity of the new republic and first appeared in the debate over Hamilton's fiscal program. Madison, in the *10th Federalist*, after the customary denunciation of factions, went on reluctantly to concede that "the various and unequal distribution of property" was "the most common and durable source of factions" and that the "regulation of these various and interfering [economic] interests . . . involves the spirit of party and faction in the necessary and ordinary operations of the government." Moreover, the commitment of the Fathers to the idea of a balanced government itself soon implied a role for parties; in 1792 Madison, while still determined to oppose the spirit of party, wrote that the evil could be mitigated "by making one party a check on the other, so far as the existence of parties cannot be prevented." The revolutionary government in France, to which the Hamiltonians and the Jeffersonians responded in sharply different ways, accelerated the political division; it "kindled and brought forward the two parties," Jefferson said in 1793, "with an ardour which our own interests merely, could never excite." The argument over foreign policy also helped insure that the party system, as it crystallized, would be a *two* party system (though this also corresponded with John Adams' view that in "every society where property exists, there will ever be a struggle between rich and poor" and Jefferson's view that "men by their constitution are naturally divided into two parties"—those who distrusted the people and those who had confidence in them). By 1794 John Taylor of Caroline could write a pamphlet entitled *A Definition of Parties*. "The existence of two parties in Congress," he said, "is apparent"; he then added, in the vein of the times, that this was "extremely perilous" because "truth is a thing, not of divisibility into conflicting parts, but of unity. Hence both sides cannot be right."

The Constitution, the Congress, and disputes over foreign policy thus created a *national* politics; the party distinctions arising in Congress made contact with political groupings in the states; and there developed rather quickly the first real party system known anywhere in the modern world. It was, as Walter Dean Burnham has emphasized, an "experimental" system. It had no models and no precedents; organization was rudimentary; the essential links in party communication were provided by the press. Because this was the first generation to have parties at all, the factor of traditional party loyalty, later to become so central in American politics, had little weight. And undercutting the whole enterprise lingered the conviction that a party system was somehow bad.

The great test of the American solution to the succession problem came in 1800. The thought of a Jefferson victory appalled many Federalists; but, when the horrid moment arrived, they accepted the result with astonishing equanimity, and power passed tranquilly from one side to the other. The Federalist party now entered a slow decline, compromised itself by toying with the idea of secession during the War of 1812, saw many of its policies taken over by its opponents after the war, and failed to come up with any new policies of its own. When it finally disappeared as a national party after the election of 1816, the restoration of a one party system seemed no more than a return to basic principle. "Now is the time to exterminate the monster called party spirit," General Andrew Jackson wrote President-elect James Monroe in 1816; and Monroe, presiding over the Era of Good Feelings, described parties to Madison in 1822 as "the curse of the country."

3.

But already the party system was moving into a new phase—a phase in which, ironically, Jackson was to be both beneficiary and master. The evolution of the party system registered changes in the nation itself. By the 1820's the equalitarian impulse was beginning the transformation of American politics. In 1824 nearly all adult white males could vote in seven-eighths of the states; and in three-quarters of the states presidential electors were now chosen by popular vote rather than by the state legislature. The deferential order of the early republic was fading away. The union was rushing on into the frontier west. New democratic energies were seeking expression.

And a new breed of political leaders now appeared to guide and exploit these energies. They were professional politicians; the party was their vehicle, their domicile, and almost their religion; and they were prepared to challenge fundamentally the old ideas about the baneful influence of party spirit. While such men could be found all across the country, they emerged in the most notable and articulate way in the state of New York. Here Martin Van Buren and the Albany Regency legitimized the political party as a democratic association ruled by its members, and defended it, in effect, as an end in itself, controlled by discipline and consecrated in loyalty. Moreover, Van Buren and his friends saw the strife between parties as absolutely proper and necessary in a democratic republic. In a certain sense, despite John Taylor of Caroline, both sides, they felt, could be right.

As usual, the presidential contest precipitated the crystallization of party divisions. In 1824 four candidates, all nominally Republicans, competed for the White House. Jackson led both popular and electoral vote but lost in the House of Representatives; and one consequence was a deep sense of political frustration. Moving into the vacuum, Van Buren assumed leadership of Jackson's campaign for 1828. Jackson's victory then, repeated in 1832 and confirmed in Van Buren's own success in 1836, gave the two party system its classical form.

The new system not only legitimized but democratized party conflict. Some of the democratization was symbolic, but much of it was real: the essence of the period was the incorporation of the mass of voters into the party system. In this undertaking the Democrats led the way; the National Republicans and their successors, the Whigs, resisted for a time but eventually went along. Jackson, of course, was peculiarly identified with the effort to include the people in national politics. His celebrated veto in 1832 of the bill to recharter the Bank of the United States was a deliberate (and successful) attempt to circumvent constitutional bodies and leaders and appeal directly to the voters. His lieutenants meanwhile devised the machinery to institutionalize this appeal.

The democratization effort ushered in the most inventive period in American history in the field of political structure and technique. The nomination of presidential candidates by congressional caucus was discredited after 1824; nomination by state legislatures proved an unsatisfactory substitute; and in the 1830's the politicians came up with the national convention to provide for popular participation in the nominating process. Conservatives resisted this innovation. "I find these assemblies dangerous," John Quincy Adams told Tocqueville. "They usurp the place of political bodies and could end by completely thwarting their action." Tocqueville himself, while regarding the convention as—at least for the French—"a dangerous and impracticable consequence of the sovereignty of the people," acknowledged that in such meetings "men have the opportunity of seeing one another; means of execution are combined; and opinions are maintained with a warmth and energy that written language can never attain." The first national conventions were improvised and unrepresentative gatherings; and the professional politicians soon became as adept at managing conventions—especially as a consequence of the two-thirds rule in the Democratic convention—as they had once been at managing caucuses. But nonetheless conventions became for a time the nerve center of the system, and they spawned a whole network of subsidiary structures.

For America, as Tocqueville so often remarked, was indeed the land of voluntary association. The political party rapidly provided the national genius for organization a major outlet. In 1840 the Democratic convention first adopted a national platform, an example followed by the Whigs four years later, and in 1848 the Democratic convention appointed the first national chairman, Benjamin F. Hallett of Massachusetts, and the first national committee. American politics was now acquiring an elaborate apparatus of conventions and committees at all levels, designed not only to mobilize voters but to raise funds and churn out party propaganda, the whole enterprise bound together by the glue of federal patronage.

The transformation of structure was accompanied by a transformation of style. Political campaigns now came into their uproarious own, above all at the time of presidential elections. The candidate himself was still expected to stay above politics, but he could make his presence felt, as Jackson so effectively did, by receiving delegations and sending out public letters. When, however, Jackson was rash enough to attend a barbecue in Kentucky in 1832, the opposition *National Intelligencer* in Washington expressed the repugnance of the older school: "This is certainly a new mode of electioneering. We do not recollect before to have heard of the President of the United States descending in person into the political arena." The ordinary citizen, however, suffered no such inhibition. "His concern for politics," said Tocqueville, "is his biggest concern and, so to speak, the only pleasure an American knows. . . . Even the women frequently attend public meetings and listen to political harangues as a recreation from their household labors. Debating clubs are, to a certain extent, a substitute for theatrical entertainment." In the absence of competing amusements, the political rally was rivaled only by the religious revival as a source of color and excitement amidst the monotony of daily life. And, as a man belonged to his father's church, so now he tended to belong to his father's party.

The statistics of voter turn-out, as compiled by W. D. Burnham, suggest the success of the Jacksonian two party system as an agency for political mobilization. In 1824, 27 per cent of those eligible voted in the presidential election; four years later the figure shot up to 58 per cent; by 1840 it was 80 per cent; in 1860 it was 81 per cent. But a party system must not only turn out the vote; it must also meet the problems of the country. In this regard the political order as reconstituted in the 1830's eventually got into trouble.

For a generation, indeed, one point of the new system was precisely to dodge the question of slavery. But the question could not be dodged for long, and the formation of the Liberty party in 1840 signalled the start of the attack on the two party system of the 1830's. When in another irony, Van Buren, the supreme political professional of the 1820's, broke with the system by becoming the Free Soil nominee in 1848, the major parties, like nearly every other national institution, began to disintegrate. The Whig party faded away after the Kansas-Nebraska Act of 1854. Then the emergence of the Republican party in 1856 expressed the frustration of a growing body of voters and foreshadowed, as so often in American history (as perhaps the Anti-Masonic party had in the late 1820's), the beginning of a new political era.

4.

If the Jacksonian period could be considered the time of the rise of the two party system, the period after the war was clearly that of the system's apogee. Voter turn-out continued at high levels; it did not fall under 70 per cent in a single presidential election between 1864 and 1900. In spite of the isolation of life on the farm, the rural voter displayed no symptoms of political apathy; and the urban machine reached its height of accomplishment in marshalling and suborning the voter in the city. Burnham estimates that two-thirds of the potential electorate were regular voters, only one-tenth were intermittent and peripheral, and about one quarter remained outside the process. Moreover, within the active electorate, the political party itself had probably never, before or since, commanded the continuing loyalty of so large a proportion of the voters. The system survived a major crisis in 1876, when Samuel J. Tilden, the Democratic candidate, won a bare majority of the popular vote but lost (after a special commission ruled on disputed states) by a single vote in the Electoral College. In 1888 Grover Cleveland received a plurality of the popular vote — 48.66 per cent — but Benjamin Harrison, with a popular vote of 47.86 per cent, had an electoral majority of 58 per cent. In each case, the losers accepted the result calmly.*

The period, however, saw few changes in political structure or style. Party organization, as inherited from pre-war years, underwent little development; only new and gaudier methods of manipulation and corruption strengthened the hold of the professionals on the process. The single striking experiment in campaign techniques was attempted early in the era when Stephen A. Douglas in 1860 introduced the notion that the presidential candidate should take an active role in his election. Desperate to hold the crumbling union together, he ignored public criticism and stumped large parts of the country. Horatio Seymour made a "swing around the circle" eight years later, and in 1872 Horace Greeley delivered almost two hundred speeches in eleven days. Probably because the pioneers were all losers, the innovation failed to catch on. While William Jennings Bryan travelled eighteen thousand miles up and down the nation in 1896, William McKinley stayed comfortably at home, read statements from his front porch to visiting delegations, and won the election.

*Fourteen Presidents have failed to receive a majority of the popular votes, though all but J. Q. Adams, Hayes in 1876, and Harrison in 1888 won a plurality. The others were Polk in 1844 (49.56 per cent), Taylor in 1848 (47.35 per cent), Buchanan in 1856 (45.63 per cent), Lincoln in 1860 (39.79 per cent), Garfield in 1880 (48.32 per cent), Cleveland in 1884 (48.53 per cent), Cleveland in 1892 (46.04 per cent), Wilson in 1912 (41.85 per cent), Wilson in 1916 (49.26 per cent), Truman in 1948 (49.51 per cent), and Kennedy in 1960 (49.71 per cent).

Though Theodore Roosevelt had campaigned actively as a vice-presidential candidate in 1900, he went into purdah as President four years later, complaining bitterly a few weeks before the vote, "Of course a President can't go on the stump and can't indulge in personalities, and so I have to sit still and abide the result." The inhibition apparently weighed less, however, on candidates than on incumbents; and in 1908 William Howard Taft, in spite of strong temperamental disinclination, campaigned extensively in the East and Middle West. Thereafter even Presidents were expected to play some personal role in the campaign.

Still, if there were few changes in structure or style, there were significant changes in the composition of the parties. The emergence of the Populists in 1890 foreshadowed a period of reshuffle; and the election of 1896 left Republican strength concentrated in the urban North and East, Democratic strength in the agricultural South and West. "Excluding the special case of 1912," Burnham writes, "84.5 per cent of the total electoral vote for Democratic presidential candidates between 1896 and 1928 was cast in the Southern and Border states." The sectional line-up produced a decline in two party competition in large areas of the country; and this development, along with the enlargement of the passive electorate through growth in the newly-naturalized immigrant sector and, later, through the 19th Amendment and votes for women, led to a marked reduction in voter turn-out. In no presidential election in the twentieth century has the proportion of turn-out exceeded 65 per cent.

The twentieth-century two party system thus suffered badly by comparison with the nineteenth century in terms of success in voter mobilization, and this in spite of spectacular improvements in transportation and communication. And the efforts of the parties to strengthen their support often led to a weakening of party structures. So the decline in two party competition meant that in one party areas conflict began to take place within rather than between the parties. This soon resulted in a demand for direct primaries and created new opportunities for the outsider to challenge the organization.

The primary movement quickly affected the system of presidential choice. A number of states in the Progressive period passed laws providing for presidential preference primaries or for the election of delegates to the national convention, either of which constituted an invitation to presidential candidates, or their backers, to enter the state. In 1912 Theodore Roosevelt became the first man to seek the presidential nomination via the primary routes. He carried nine of the twelve primary states (La Follette carried two of the other three); but Taft nevertheless controlled the Republican convention and became the candidate.

The primary enthusiasm was still high for another moment, and in 1913 Woodrow Wilson in his first annual message urged "the prompt enactment of legislation which will provide for primary elections throughout the country at which the voters of the several parties may choose their nominees for the Presidency." He added that this legislation "should provide for the retention of party conventions, but only for the purpose of declaring and accepting the verdict of the primaries and formulating the platforms of the parties." Wilson further suggested that the conventions should consist not of delegates chosen for this single purpose but "of the nominees for Congress, the nominees for vacant seats in the Senate of the United States, the Senators whose terms have not yet closed, the national committees, and the candidates for the Presidency themselves, in order that platforms may be framed by those responsible to the people for carrying them into effect."

This singularly imaginative proposal was too late, or perhaps too early. After TR's frustration in 1912, the primary movement began to lose its first momentum. Though twenty-six states had presidential primary laws in 1916, eight had repealed their laws by 1935. Only one state — Alabama — was added to the list between 1920 and 1949. Candidates, in the main, ignored the primary. In 1928, for example, Herbert Hoover and Alfred E. Smith allowed their supporters to enter their names in a few states but did not take primaries seriously enough to enter the states themselves (though by this time, once they had the nominations, they were prepared to stump in the general election). Franklin Roosevelt followed their example in 1932.

5.

If the two party system was measurably less effective in the early twentieth than it had been in the nineteenth century, it had nevertheless by 1930 beaten back the presidential primary, and the mode of presidential choice remained much as it had been three quarters of a century earlier. The composition of the parties, however, was once again in flux. The urban coalition of business and labor put together by McKinley and Mark Hanna in 1896 began to fall apart when the Republican party, after disgorging Theodore Roosevelt in 1912, concentrated thereafter on ministering to the whims of the business community. The character of the post-TR Republican policies gave Democrats their chance to split off the working class in the Republican urban strongholds, a tendency intimated by Wilson in 1916, greatly advanced by Smith in 1928 and, as the business cult collapsed into the rubble of the Great Depression, triumphantly concluded by Franklin Roosevelt in the 1930's.

The result was a new majority coalition, now based on classes rather than on sections. The Roosevelt era brought about a distinct resurgence in voter turn-out, if not to the levels of the late nineteenth century. And the ferment stirred by the New Deal led in time to an apparent revitalization of the two party system. This development, made possible by the commitment of the Democratic party to a militant civil rights program, nationalized political competition and by the 1970's practically abolished one party states. Yet it remained unclear whether this apparent revitalization represented a genuine resurgence of the two party system or only the hectic flush before a final illness. For a number of developments in the years since the New Deal had deprived the parties of many of their functions and threatened to weaken the very bases of the traditional political order. Indeed, if the 1870's could be said to have seen the maturation of the two party system, the 1970's might well be the period of the crisis of that system.

An enumeration of lost functions will suggest the contemporary dilemma of the parties. We have already seen how the parties had receded as instruments of voter mobilization. The waning of immigration ended the Ellis Island role as an agency of acculturation. The advent of the welfare state finished the party as the patron of the unemployed, sick, and old. The city boss was in many respects a casualty of the New Deal. In that classic novel of urban politics, Edwin O'Connor's *The Last Hurrah*, a character observes that it was Franklin Roosevelt who

> destroyed the old-time boss. He destroyed him by taking away his source of power. . . . The old boss was strong simply because he held all the cards. If anybody wanted anything—jobs, favors, cash—he could only go to the boss, the local leader. A few little things like Social Security, Unemployment Insurance, and the like—that's what shifted the gears, sport. No need now to depend on the boss for everything: the Federal Government was getting into the act. Otherwise known as a social revolution.

The more intelligent or younger bosses, sensing the drift of things, tapered off their old ties with businessmen and crooks and came to terms with the social revolution. But their status was diminished. They were no longer delivering the goods themselves; they were only claiming a free ride on a government process which delivered the goods in their stead. By the 1970's, the remaining city bosses—Mayor Richard Daley of Chicago was perhaps the last of the Mohicans—were anachronisms.

On the larger stage, the professional politicians began to lose control of vital parts of the political machinery. To this the abolition in 1936 of the two-thirds rule in the Democratic convention and, more especially, the revival of the presidential primary made important contributions. For thirty years after 1912 the primary had been a negligible factor in the presidential calculus. Then Wendell Willkie, who had won the Republican nomination in 1940 without entering a single primary, lost it in 1944 by running last in the primary in Wisconsin. This proved at least the veto power of the primary. Four years later Harold Stassen, beginning his perennial quest for the Republican nomination, demonstrated that the primary could become an effective recourse for candidates who lacked organization support; and Thomas E. Dewey was able to secure renomination only by showing he could beat Stassen in Oregon. Though neither Robert A. Taft, a Republican, nor Estes Kefauver, a Democrat, won nomination in 1952, the consequence of their impassioned primary efforts was to reawaken public interest in the primary system. New laws were passed. New states joined the primary rolls.

At the same time, changes in the means of communication, and especially the spread of television in the 1950's, reinforced this process. Television, for example, made the viewer an intimate and daily participant in primary contests. It fostered the expectation that candidates for the presidential nominations would be familiar faces, not distant "favorite sons" or unknown "dark horses"; otherwise the presidential choice would appear to have been conjured up by bosses out of smoke-filled rooms. By 1956 it seemed that only a sitting President, or his personally chosen candidate, could escape the primary test. Adlai Stevenson that year, John F. Kennedy in 1960, Barry Goldwater in 1964, Richard Nixon in 1968 — all settled the nomination in the primaries and, in effect, presented *faits accomplis* to the conventions. Not after 1952 did a convention require more than a single ballot to choose its candidate. And the probability of humiliating defeat in the Wisconsin primary in 1968 was unquestionably a major factor in Lyndon B. Johnson's decision to bow out of the presidential contest that year. By 1970 so many new states were rushing to join the primary parade that, to some observers, it seemed inevitable that the nation would have a *de facto* national primary system without knowing it. Sixty years later the conditions were becoming ripe to enact Wilson's vision of 1913.

The impact of television on the nominating process was only part of the deeper impact of the new electronic world on politics. Altogether television, the public opinion poll, and the computer began to devastate the traditional political structure. For a century a cluster of institutions — the political machine, the farm organization, the trade union, the ethnic federation — had mediated between the politician and the voter, interceding for each on behalf of the other and providing the links that held the party system together. The electronic age was severing these links. Television presented the politician directly to the voter; public opinion polls presented the voter directly to the politicians. The political brokers began to lose their jobs, and the mediating agencies, insofar as they had political functions, were confronted by obsolescence.

The parties, cut loose from old moorings, sailed vaguely on in uncharted waters. Reform movements arose to rescue them and, in trying to do so, further diminished the power of the professionals. Thus the reconstruction of the nominating process, proposed for the Democrats by the McGovern Commission after the disastrous Chicago convention of 1968, would increase citizen participation in the party but at the expense of the permanent party structure. The effort in 1970 to abolish that vestigial survival, the Electoral College, and choose the President by direct popular vote threatened further to enfeeble state organizations. In short, the political process the professionals once thought they owned had turned in their hands into a set of ceremonies. What had happened to the Electoral College in 1800 was now happening to the national convention: it was increasingly a forum, not for decision, but for ratification. Political competition in the future, as James David Barber remarked, would revolve increasingly around access to the electronic media. And, if advertising agencies did not quite practice the black arts their own mythology assigned to them, still American politics was entering a time when election specialists, hired out as mercenaries, would play a larger role in mobilizing the voters.

6.

The functional depletion of party organization was accompanied by changes in the character of the electorate. The fastest growing group in American society was the one defined by the Bureau of Labor Statistics as "professional, technical and kindred workers." In 1900 that group constituted 4 per cent of the labor force and as late as 1940 less than 8 per cent. By 1970 it was more than 12 per cent, and it was continuing to increase at more than twice the average rate for other fields of employment. If one added to this group those defined as "managers" and "officials" in the BLS category of "managers, officials and proprietors, excluding farm," the cumulative figure approached 20 per cent of the labor force.

This group, moreover, had a political zeal and sophistication which gave it influence far exceeding its numbers. Its members were predominantly college-educated—and by the middle 1970's, according to current estimates, more than 40 per cent of the electorate would have gone to college. They lived predominantly in the suburbs—and, as the 1920 census showed that the cities outnumbered the countryside, the 1970 census showed that the suburbs now outnumbered the cities. Although this professional-technical-managerial class was by no means unified in its views or values, its unprecedentedly high level of education and aspiration generated both an informed interest in issues and a formidable commitment to public affairs—and this at just the time that, as a consequence of the electronic revolution, the old politics of the mediating institutions was giving way to the new politics of instantaneous mass involvement.

The politicians, having lost their protective buffer of mediating agencies, now began to stand eyeball-to-eyeball with a diffuse, frustrated, and aggressive public opinion. The United States in the 1970's would never (at least since the 1790's) have so large a proportion of well-informed, independent, discriminating, and, to use the jargon, "issue-oriented" voters, or so many determined to influence the course of history. In his great work on *Public Opinion* half a century ago, Walter Lippmann had written that the power of opinion was "for all practical purposes the power to say yes and no." As Samuel Lubell emphasized, that had now drastically changed. People "are unwilling to be limited to 'yes' or 'no'; nor are they content to channel all their interests and emotions through the parties. Instead there has developed a sharp struggle for political visibility—by the voters to make themselves seen and felt, and by presidents and other managers of society to control or shape what should become visible."

The general competition for visibility was probably set off by the success of the black revolution. The civil rights movement stimulated a host of spin-offs and imitations, organizing women, students, Indians, Mexican Americans, Italian Americans, homosexuals in their own crusades of self-assertion. Even when the self-asserters stayed within the two party system, they operated through citizens' and volunteers' associations, which they formed with rapidity and skill, if sometimes with limited attention span; these, along with the mercenary specialists, were increasingly displacing the party organization as sources of publicity and manpower. But very often they regarded the old party system with automatic mistrust, rallied to candidates who inveighed against it, voted split tickets or for minor parties, and otherwise drove the old politics even more against the wall.

Compounding the crisis of the two party system was the evolution in the substance of political issues. Psephologists, in their preoccupation with quantity and structure, have tended to underrate the impact on politics of the policy choices forced upon the government. Yet such choices, as we have seen in the case of slavery in the 1850's and social justice in the 1930's, remain in the end the most powerful determinants of political development. A number of changes had taken place in the substance of political questions since the last great creative period in national policy during the 1930's and the two party system of the 1960's and 1970's showed few signs of a capacity to absorb and digest these new issues.

One such issue was the growing sense of the incipient fragmentation of the social order. A series of tensions had begun to strain the national fabric: tensions between young and old, between poor and rich, between black and white, between educated and uneducated. "Of all dangers to a nation," Walt Whitman once wrote "there can be no greater one than having certain portions of the people set off from the rest by a line drawn—they not privileged as others, but degraded, humiliated, made of no account." The urgent task of contemporary American politics—the task identified especially with John and Robert Kennedy and neglected since their murders—was surely to give the alienated groups a feeling of membership in the national process. The alienated groups consisted of two sorts—the estranged and the excluded. The estranged were those who in the past had formed part of the national community—the intellectuals, the young, the lower-middle-class whites, for example—and who were disaffected on recent and particular grounds: the intellectuals and the young because of the Vietnam war; the lower-middle-class whites because of student violence and the black revolution. The excluded were those—the structurally poor, the blacks, the Indians, the Chicanos, the Puerto Ricans—who had never been full members of the nation. The domestic imperative of the 1970's was to bring these groups into the national community.

For this mission, the two party system had thus far been inadequate. The rise of such anti-system movements as the George Wallace party of 1968 and the various black nationalist organizations might well foreshadow, as other third parties had in the past, the recombinations which usher in a new political era. In addition, the problems of government in the high-technology society were becoming, or at least were appearing, increasingly technical in nature and therefore inaccessible to traditional party policies or solutions. And world affairs, for the first time since the 1790's, were a continuous and sometimes decisive issue in domestic policy; and this too consistently eluded the two party system because of the power inexorably exercised, regardless of the party in office, by the foreign policy and military establishments.

The experience of a century and a half had left the popular impression that the two party system was ordained by Providence for Americans to elect their Presidents. Yet it was by no means clear that this system was permanent and irrevocable. A process formed in the relatively simple America of the 1830's might not necessarily meet all the needs of the diversified and explosive America of the 1970's. Much evidence confirmed the view that the two party system, if not in decay, was at least in crisis. Beginning in the Eisenhower Presidency, the voters showed an increasing tendency to use both parties for their purposes, as when in the 1950's they balanced off a Republican President and a Democratic Congress. Party lines and loyalties grew increasingly fluid. Political disaffiliation was high, especially among the young, who would, after all, be the voters of the future. A Gallup poll in 1970 reported that two-fifths of the electorate felt it made "no difference" which party was in power. The electronic world had sapped much of the vitality of the traditional political structures. The "tumult and disorder," the "extraordinary and violent movements," feared long ago by Hamilton now seemed an inseparable part of the public process. Tocqueville's river, instead of sinking back to its usual level after the electoral storm, seemed ever more likely to overflow its banks.

Presidential elections remained the moments of truth when the electorate had its chance to affirm or alter the direction of national policy. But, for the two party system to work, it had to present effective choices; the outcome had to make a difference; no vital group could feel unrepresented in the party duel. It had been a while since the two choices quadrennially presented to the people held out much hope of satisfying, or even containing, the energies of national frustration, rancor, and despair. Only the most extraordinary leadership, it appeared, was likely to save the two party system in its present form. Should such leadership not emerge, the United States could anticipate, at the least, extensive upheaval and realignment within the existing parties and, quite possibly, the multiplication of parties in response to the demanding diversity of public interests and concerns. Would the nation see the crystallization perhaps of a three or four party system as portended, for example, by the possible abolition of the Electoral College, or could there even be a gradual evaporation of parties in their traditional sense? The age of experimentation in political structure might well have come again.

"Before my term is over," John F. Kennedy said in 1961, "we shall have to test anew whether a nation organized and governed such as ours can endure. The outcome is by no means certain." The outcome seemed even less certain a decade later.

Elections of 1789 and 1792

MARCUS CUNLIFFE is Professor of American Studies at the University of Sussex. His chief publications are The Literature of the United States; George Washington: Man and Monument; The Nation Takes Shape, 1789 – 1837 *and* Soldiers and Civilians: The Martial Spirit in America, 1775 – 1865.

Elections of 1789 and 1792

by *Marcus Cunliffe*

The nature of the presidential office proved to be the most recalcitrant of all the issues that confronted the delegates at the Philadelphia convention in 1787. There were, James Madison reported to Thomas Jefferson, "tedious and reiterated discussions" on whether the executive should "consist of a single person, or a plurality of co-ordinate members, on the mode of appointment, on the duration in office, on the degree of power," and on whether the President should be eligible for reelection. True, a majority of the delegates fairly soon reached agreement on the need for a single executive. But the other problems concerning the office were more intractable. Within the whole tangle, as Madison later recollected, a key difficulty was that "of finding an unexceptionable process for appointing the Executive Organ of a Government such as that of the United States . . . ; and as the final arrangement of it took place in the latter stage of the Session, it was not exempt from a degree of the hurrying influence produced by fatigue and impatience in all such bodies."

The Philadelphia convention began on May 25, 1787. Within a week the delegates had declared themselves in favor of a single "Executive Magistracy" who was to be elected by the national legislature for a term of seven years and then to be "ineligible a second time." By July 26, having so far consumed the greater part of eight days in discussing the election and term of office of the President, the delegates were still on record (by the votes of seven states to three) as supporting the original broad method proposed in Edmund Ran-

3

dolph's resolution of May 29. Such harmony was, however, far more apparent than real; it signified that, for the moment, they could see no ideal solution to the complexities which they had explored.

Randolph's "Virginia plan" seemed to provide the only workable means of election. In 1787 only a few states, including Massachusetts, New Hampshire, and New York, relied upon the popular election of their governors. Arguing the point on July 17, Roger Sherman of Connecticut thought that "the sense of the Nation would be better expressed by the Legislature, than by the people at large. The latter will never be sufficiently informed of characters, and besides will never give a majority of votes to any one man. They will generally vote for some man in their own State, and the largest State will have the best chance for the appointment." In the same debate, George Mason of Virginia concurred: "It would be as unnatural to refer the choice of a proper character for chief Magistrate to the people, as it would, to refer a trial of colours to a blind man. The extent of the Country renders it impossible that the people can have the requisite capacity to judge of the respective pretensions of the Candidates." Charles Pinckney of South Carolina and Hugh Williamson of North Carolina were of the same opinion. Then and subsequently, certain delegates (Madison and Gouverneur Morris of Pennsylvania among them) preferred the idea of popular election. But they could not disguise their uneasiness at the prospect of an election on so diffuse a scale; their recommendation was not so much out of enthusiasm for the principle of popular suffrage, but rather out of resistance to other principles for which they felt still less enthusiasm.

Nor did alternative proposals immediately commend themselves. Elbridge Gerry of Massachusetts, for example, made no headway on June 9 with a resolution "that the National Executive should be elected by the Executives of the ⸴States whose proportion of votes should be the same with that allowed to the States in the election of the Senate." Replying to Gerry, Edmund Randolph of Virginia maintained that in such a method the big states would secure the appointment; that even so, bad appointments would result, "the Executives of the States being little conversant with characters not within their own small spheres"; that a President selected under state auspices would be unlikely to defend the national interest against state encroachments; and that state governors would not willingly support a national executive – "They will not cherish the great Oak which is to reduce them to paltry shrubs."

John Dickinson of Delaware found equally little support for a suggestion (July 25) that the people of each state should nominate a "best citizen. . . . [They] will know the most eminent characters of their own States, and the people of different States will feel an emulation in selecting those of which they will have the greatest reason to be proud – Out of the thirteen names thus selected, an Executive Magistrate may be chosen," either through the national legislature, or electors appointed by it. More attention was paid to sundry proposals for electors chosen by state legislatures. But these and other expedients failed to unite a convinced majority of delegates. "There are objections," said Madison (July 25), "against every mode that has been, or perhaps can be proposed." His fellow-Virginian, Colonel Mason, wearily echoed the observation (July 26): "In every Stage of the Question relative to the Executive, the difficulty of the subject and the diversity of the opinions concerning it have appeared. Nor have any of the modes of constituting that department been satisfactory."

At this phase of the convention, on the eve of a ten-day recess, the delegates revealed a sort of fatigued dullness — the dullness that comes when men feel that they have explored every possible alternative and are dissatisfied with all. To some extent, also, they seemed to have become the prisoners of the initial formulation: election by the national legislature for a single seven-year term. Every time the executive came up for discussion this basic premise was reiterated and voted on. One reason for the frustrating sense of impasse, as J. R. Pole explains, was that "the delegates wanted the new head of state to have some of the attributes of a prime minister but some of the attributes of a king; and they allowed themselves to be confused by their own terminology." British precedent both impressed and alarmed them. They did not fully understand the respective, and changing, roles of the Crown and the chief minister in the British system — in part because of their own sensitivity to the charge that they might, deliberately or otherwise, saddle the United States with a monarchy or an aristocracy, or both. They were groping for a means of establishing an executive element that was to be much more than a formal head of state.

Gradually, and thanks largely to the lucid interventions of James Madison, the logic of their wishes disclosed itself. One of Madison's most persuasive speeches was delivered on July 25. The President, he said, must be elected either by some existing authority under the national or state constitutions, or by some special authority derived from or directly exerted by the people of the United States. Under the national constitution the two existing authorities would be the legislature and the judiciary. The judiciary was clearly unsuitable. As for the legislature, Madison continued, summarizing views already expressed in the convention and adding some of his own, it too was an unsuitable agency. A major objection was that the election would seriously "agitate & divide the legislature." The effect upon a presidential candidate would be equally undesirable. He would "intrigue with" the legislators, would owe his appointment to "the predominant faction," and would be "apt to render his administration subservient" to the controlling faction. Moreover, as the cases of the Holy Roman Emperor and the elective Polish monarchy showed, such a claustrophobic method of election would encourage foreign powers to meddle: "No pains, nor perhaps expence, will be spared, to gain from the Legislature an [appointment] favourable to their wishes."

If appointment within the national sphere would be unsatisfactory, what of the state level? Neither governors nor the judiciary would be desirable. As for state legislatures, they were unreliable bodies with a propensity for "pernicious measures." One of the purposes of a national legislature was to offset this. And one of the objects of creating a national executive was to control the national legislature (through the veto power), "so far as it might be infected with a similar propensity." But such a check would be impossible if the executive were chosen by a legislative body, at whatever level.

There remained accordingly the mode of popular election, either "immediately" or by means of electors popularly chosen. Madison himself preferred the notion of a mass popular vote, though he admitted that there were snags — notably "the disposition in the people to prefer a Citizen of their own State," which would confer an advantage on the larger states. He was also responsive to the idea of selection by specially chosen electors. But he admitted that the device, having already been rejected by the convention, would probably not win approval.

On this occasion Madison's reasoning did not prevail. But he stimulated a fruitful discussion. Here was one of the days when instead of negating and perplexing each other the delegates seemed collectively to think their way forward. Some, it is true, reverted to the stale issue of whether ineligibility for reelection would be an adequate safeguard against undue legislative influence upon the President, or whether that would not excessively hamper the executive freedom of maneuver. But other delegates were more alertly constructive. Williamson suggested that if popular election were sanctioned, the claims of candidates from the smaller states could be recognized by allowing every voter to choose three names. One of the three would probably be a man from his own state; the other two might well be drawn from other states. Gouverneur Morris liked the idea, suggesting as an amendment that "each man should vote for two persons one of whom at least should not be of his own State." Madison also warmed to the amended suggestion. A plethora of favorite sons would be likely to yield the election to some universally admired second choice. There was the risk that each citizen might throw away his second vote on some obscure figure, in order to improve the chances of his favorite candidate. "But it could hardly be supposed," said Madison, "that the Citizens of many States would be so sanguine of having their favorite elected, as not to give their second vote with sincerity to the next object of their choice."

The decisive advance was still some way off. On August 24, when the delegates again scrutinized the executive provisions of their draft constitution, they were still committed to election through Congress (as it was to be called). They wrangled over the question of whether the President was to be chosen by one or both houses of Congress. Faced with the prospect of an interminable task, and increasingly restive, they agreed however to place all such unfinished business in the hands of a committee made up of one delegate from each state.

Now the leaven worked. The committee comprised some of the ablest members of the Philadelphia convention, and some of those most firmly persuaded of the need for a strong executive. On September 4 they introduced a set of proposals in almost the form with which we are familiar. They had concluded that the principle of a separation of powers made it impossible to elect the executive entirely in the legislature. Once this was affirmed, there was likewise no overriding need to limit the executive to a single term, since the

President would be immune to excessive congressional influence. Nor need his term of office be lengthy if he could be reelected: four years would be preferable to seven. The method of election recommended, in line with some of the previous suggestions of delegates, was via a body of presidential electors, to be chosen as each state legislature determined. The number of electors would equal the number of federal senators and representatives to which each state would be entitled. The electors would meet in their respective states (not in one central place, which might have exposed them to corruption, and which would have been a laborious and expensive procedure). They would vote for two persons, "one of whom at least shall not be an inhabitant of the same State with themselves." Their votes would be transmitted to the presiding officer of the Senate, under whose chairmanship the Senate—balloting among themselves if there were no clear majority—would decide the outcome. The person coming second in number of votes should become Vice-President, and would then act as President of the Senate.

An intricate debate followed, and continued next morning (September 5). "The greater part of the day," noted James McHenry of Maryland, whose appetite for constitution-making had become sated, was "spent in desultory conversation on that part of the report respecting the mode of chusing the President—adjourned without coming to a conclusion." He was too despondent. The delegates were very near to completing their task. Except for the few who were uneasy over the whole tenor of the convention, opposition to the committee's proposals focused mainly on the prominence given to the Senate. By September 6 the draft had been amended to meet the chief objections.

In the event of a tie, or the absence of a clear majority of votes, the House of Representatives (one vote per state) was to choose a President by ballot. At last the convention had a formula commanding the assent if not the enthusiasm of the majority of delegates. They probably assumed that the election would nearly always be determined in Congress; this had certainly been their contention when the plan was to let the Senate be the arbiters. Still, they had hit upon a pattern that would in theory allow the voice of the people to be heard. If all went well, the principal persons nominated ("candidates" is perhaps the wrong word) would be worthy characters, hopefully of nationwide repute; they would not have been picked by any small conclave or cabal; and Congress would thus be obliged to make its choice from among citizens chosen by the citizenry.

An additional comment should be made on the invention of the Vice-Presidency, an office not mentioned in the Philadelphia proceedings until the committee report of September 4. It had previously been implied that the President would also act as President of the Senate, hardly an acceptable provision if the separation of powers was to be observed. Yet this was not the main reason for creating a Vice-President; indeed Elbridge Gerry and George Mason were among those who complained that "the office of vice-President [was] an encroachment on the rights of the Senate; . . . it mixed too much the Legislative & Executive, which . . . ought to be kept as separate as possible." Roger Sherman of Connecticut defended the innovation by remarking that if the Vice-President were not to preside over the Senate he would have nothing to do; and—an argument with a shade more force—that if some senator were to preside, he would automatically be deprived of his voting rights: a deprivation that would as a result halve the voting strength of one state. The chief rationale for the Vice-Presidency was mentioned by Hugh Williamson, who thought it a superfluous office: it was "introduced only for the sake of a valuable mode of election which required two to be chosen at the same time." He was more or less correct. The genesis of the office appears to lie in Williamson's own proposal of July 25, as amended by Gouverneur Morris. They hoped to avoid jealousies between the states, and a sense of impotence among the smaller ones, by permitting more than one vote for the Presidency. Once the idea was implanted, duties could readily be found for the man who was runner-up; and there were equivalent figures (lieutenant-governors and the like) in the organization of state governments. At any rate the Vice-Presidency was established, belatedly, consequentially, and somewhat perfunctorily. Yet the comments of Madison and others on the niceties of plural voting indicated that American politicians would be quick to master the tactics appropriate to a dual vote.

Both at Philadelphia and in the ensuing months, Americans of every viewpoint seem to have assumed that there was only one man who could and would inaugurate the presidential office: General Washington. When the convention first broached the idea of a single executive on June 1, there was a "considerable pause" before the debate got under way. Among the reasons for this hesitation was no doubt a certain embarrassment at discussing the proposal in the presence of the presiding officer: George Washington. Three days later, on June 4, Pennsylvania's venerable delegate Benjamin Franklin offered some gloomy predictions as to the eventual aggrandizement of the executive branch. He conceded however that "the first man, put at the helm will be a good one." Such observations crop up again and again in private correspondence, in pamphlets and in the newspapers. The Philadelphian Dr. Benjamin Rush, not present at the convention but alert to catch stray rumors that filtered through its closed doors, was enthusiastic over the prospects. "The new federal government," he told Timothy Pickering on August 30, "like a new Continental waggon will overset our state dung cart . . . and thereby restore order and happiness to Pennsylvania. . . . General Washington it is said will be placed at the head of the new Government, or in the stile of my simile, will drive the new waggon." An unidentified correspondent, writing to Thomas Jefferson on October 11, 1787, also from Philadelphia, in the same general spirit as Rush, explained the reasons why the Constitution would and ought to be ratified. Thus, Washington was still vigorously alive, and "as he will be appointed President, jealousy on this head vanishes." The General's associates were writing to him in the same strain. David Humphreys, a Connecticut soldier-diplomat, and one of the General's most devoted admirers, wrote, "What will tend, perhaps, more than anything to the adoption of the new system will be an universal opinion of your being elected President of the United States and an expectation that you will accept it for a while." Washington's wartime friend Lafayette chimed in from Paris, "You cannot refuse being elected President."

Even those with deep misgivings on the "new system" concentrated their criticism upon other features of the Constitution, or—like Franklin—upon the hazards that would befall America after Washington had gone. The Virginian Richard Henry Lee, a one-time president of the Continental Congress, was convinced that the Philadelphia document was fraught with danger. A reeligible President, he argued in January, 1788, "will have no permanent interest in the government to lose, by contests and convulsions in the state, but always much to gain, and frequently the seducing and flattering hope of succeeding. . . . [This] will be the case with nine tenths of the presidents; *we may have, for the first president*, and, perhaps, one in a century or two afterwards . . . *a great and good man, governed by superior motives*; but these are not events to be calculated upon in the present state of human nature." Pierce Butler, a former delegate, admitted in May, 1788, that the considerable powers entrusted to the executive would not have "been so great had not many of the members cast their eyes toward General Washington as President; and shaped their Ideas of the Powers to be given to a President, by their opinions of his Virtue."

The expectation that General Washington would become President Washington was voiced in the press within a few days of the adjournment of the convention. Newspapers favoring the Constitution, such as the important *Pennsylvania Packet*, repeatedly sang his praises. Washington, they assured their readers, would not have lent his name to the convention if its intentions had been dubious; and with him at the head the new government's success was beyond doubt. The Fourth of July celebrations in 1788 came at the climactic moment of the struggle over ratification. Though the news took some time to reach every corner of the Union, the necessary nine states (including Washington's Virginia) had already ratified. At many places the national holiday was seized upon as an occasion to pay tribute to the future President. Toasts and songs embroidered the sentiment—

—Farmer Washington—may he like a second Cincinnatus, be called from the plow to rule a great people

—May the Saviour of America gratify the ardent wishes of his countrymen by accepting that post which the voice of mankind has assigned him.

—Great Washington shall rule the land/While Franklin's counsel aids his hand.

Whatever the nation expected of him, or friends urged upon him, George Washington was far from reconciled to the apparently inevitable. Well-informed Americans were worried by what Jefferson called Washington's "vast reluctance," though like Jefferson they clung to the conviction that Washington "will undertake the presidency if called to it." Alexander Hamilton was only the most persistent of several correspondents in pressing the General to signify his willingness. They appealed to his pertinacity, his patriotism, his personal sense of duty, his standing with posterity, the parlous state of the country. Hamilton was particularly subtle in his reading of Washington's psychology; he never resorted to such overblown statements as that of the General's old friend John Armstrong, who seemed to feel that divine providence was in charge of the impending election.

George Washington's hesitations were understandable. Fifty-six years old in 1788, he felt that he had already given up some of the best years of his life to the service of his country. After eight and a half years as Commander-in-chief he had, at the end of 1783, resigned his commission with unfeigned relief. His own affairs, above all the management of his Mount Vernon estate, absorbed his energies — energies which he felt to be waning. Moreover, in quitting public service he had stressed the finality of his retirement. If he now came back at the head of affairs he could, he wrote Alexander Hamilton, be accused of "inconsistency and ambition." He well knew from the tenor of the Philadelphia convention, and from the abundant subsequent criticisms of the Constitution, that Americans were highly suspicious of the corrupting effect of high office.

As he frequently remarked, he dreaded the "new fatigues and troubles" of undertaking an immense new responsibility for which he did not think himself properly equipped. Soldiering had been onerous enough; the entire weight of executive responsibility would be almost unendurable.

One aspect of his uneasiness was thus a matter of propriety. Even if he were firmly to decide that he was ready to stand, he could see no acceptable way of making this known without seeming presumptuous. Certainly he could not declare himself, or do more than make plain his support for the new Constitution as a whole, while its ratification remained uncertain: that would be to anticipate events to an unthinkable degree. And in the second half of 1788, when ratification had been assured (at least by eleven of the thirteen states: North Carolina and Rhode Island still held aloof), the delicacy of his position continued to preoccupy him. It was surely not his task to inform the nation that he would agree to be President, before or even after the meetings of the presidential electors in the various states. He may well have reflected that it would be egotistical even to announce in advance that he would *not* serve; for that would be to indicate that he saw himself as a likely occupant of the office. Other men might not have shown so much punctilio in his shoes. But from 1787 to 1789 no other men were remotely close to standing in his shoes; Washington's situation was unique, and therefore — for him — uniquely painful. He was neither running for office nor able to run away from it.

A second cause for uneasiness shaded from the first. Almost nine months elapsed between the close of the Philadelphia convention and the knowledge that the Constitution had passed muster, in some instances by a narrow majority in state ratifying conventions. Prominent citizens in his own state — George Mason, Edmund Randolph, Patrick Henry — were outspoken in criticism of the new instrument of government. Nine more months were to elapse before the results of the first presidential election would be formally announced, though they had been unofficially bruited about several weeks earlier. In this long, dragging period the extent of opposition was a source of increasing dismay to Washington. He confided to Hamilton that he found some consolation in the faint hope that "the Electors, by giving their votes in favor of some other person, would save me from the dreaded Dilemma of being forced to accept or refuse." It had become objectively apparent that Washington was the only person being spoken of for the Presidency. But the actual operation of the Electoral College was conjectural. No one could accurately predict whom the electors would be; they were not even to be chosen, so dilatory were the workings of the old moribund Congress, until the first Wednesday in January, 1789. Washington's anxiety shifted to the possibility that his consolation might instead prove a form of humiliation. In the same letter, he went on to ask:

> If the friends to the Constitution conceive that my administering the government will be a means of its acceleration and strength, is it not probable that the adversaries of it may entertain the same ideas? and of course make it an object of opposition? That many of this description will become Electors, I can have no doubt of . . . . It might be impolite in them to make this declaration *previous* to the Election, but I shall be out in my conjectures if they do not act conformably thereto—and from that the seeming moderation by which they appear to be actuated at present is . . . a finesse to lull and deceive. Their plan of opposition is systemised, and a regular intercourse, I have much reason to believe between the Leaders of it in the several States is formed to render it more effectual.

Such a development would obviously be humiliating if it led to a spread of votes in which some other man was preferred to Washington. That however was most unlikely, unless by some fluke distribution of electoral preferences; the only American who could be ranked with George Washington in universal esteem was Benjamin Franklin, but Franklin was eighty years old and in failing health. One gains the impression that, for Washington, any semblance of a contest between him and some other man or men would be extremely disagreeable. He did not want to be President. Yet if he must be President, he wanted to be chosen *nem.con.* In other words, he could not seriously have supposed that someone else would get more votes than he. What perturbed him was the possibility of any sort of competition. A challenge of that kind would stigmatize his good name, and indicate alarming dissensions within the country.

Washington's perplexity was aggravated by the sluggishness of the newly-elected Congress. The twenty-two senators and fifty-nine members of the House converged on New York (the temporary seat of the Federal Government) with agonizing slowness. The presidential electors duly met on the first Wednesday in February, 1789, and the presidential inauguration had been set for March 4. But the electoral votes could not be counted until there was a quorum of both houses. By March 4 only eight senators and eighteen representatives had shown up; and the last laggard legislator required to make the necessary quorum did not arrive in New York until April 5. Washington was still parrying the congratulations and importunings that each post delivered to Mount Vernon. In effect he had consented to stand, and to become President. He must have been cheered to learn that "Federalists" (i.e., men ready to defend the Constitution) had secured a commanding position in the elections for the Senate, and a sizeable share of the House of Representatives. But one of the few clues to his own acquiescence in the apparently inevitable came when his followers consulted him on a suitable person for the Vice-Presidency. His answer could be interpreted as a definite though hardly enthusiastic commitment on his own part. Washington intimated that any "true Foederalist" capable of commanding the votes of true American would not be "disagreeable" to him. Whoever the hypothetical person might be, "I would most certainly treat him with perfect sincerity and the greatest candor in every respect. I would give him my full confidence and use my utmost endeavors to cooperate with him, in promoting . . . the national prosperity; this should be my great, my only aim."

An assurance in a private letter was about the nearest that Washington came to a declaration of his readiness to serve if elected. Candidates in future presidential elections would make gestures toward the Washington style of stately, reluctant immobility. But never would a hat float so spectrally into the ring. Nor would any future putative President add, as Washington did in the same letter, his "fixed and irrevocable resolution of leaving to other hands the helm of the State, as soon as my services could possibly with propriety be dispensed with." He would serve, that is true; but he would not bind himself for a full term if a chance of escape came his way.

Since none of the Anti-Federalists made any move to deny the Presidency to General Washington, partisan calculations were confined to the Vice-Presidency. Even at this rudimentary stage of presidential electioneering, both sides were swift to see the utility of uniting around one name instead of allowing the scatter of choices envisaged by the Philadelphia delegates. (Perhaps this quick development owes as much to the primacy of Washington as to controversy over the Constitution and the means by which it had been introduced. If more than one man had appeared outstandingly qualified for the Presidency, it is at any rate conceivable that the electors, and politically active Americans, would not have drawn any sharp distinction between the two people whom they desired to see in executive office.) With Washington as the universal nominee for the first office, the situation of the second office engrossed attention.

Among the leading Federalists, the initial problem was to agree upon a suitable associate for General Washington. To name another Virginian would be to lose the 10 votes of the Virginia electors, who would be debarred from giving both their sets of votes to men of their own state. But in any case sectional strategy dictated the choice of a Northerner, presumably from the powerful state of Massachusetts (which also had ten electors), since the comparably powerful states of New York and Pennsylvania had no one of outstanding eligibility.

Massachusetts possessed an ample share of prominent citizens. Among those who had become associated with Washington during the Revolutionary War were Henry Knox and Benjamin Lincoln. Hamilton referred to both, though somewhat incidentally, in canvassing opinion.

Another man with a national reputation, Samuel Adams, was ruled out because of his brusque temperament and his supposed antagonism to the Constitution. He had remarked, on the occasion of the Massachusetts ratifying convention: "As I enter the building I stumble on the threshold. I meet with a National Government, instead of a Federal Union of Sovereign States." A more plausible candidate, certainly in his own eyes, was Governor John Hancock, who had appropriated much of the credit for his state's ratification. Hamilton seems to have been prepared at one point to back him. At length, though, Hamilton and his cronies concluded that John Adams was their best bet.

Adams had a long record of public service—a delegate to the First and Second Continental Congresses (1774–78), Commissioner to France (1778), delegate to the Massachusetts Constitutional Convention (1780); and under Franklin and Jay, a negotiator of the Paris Peace Pact (1783)—and a considerable if slightly equivocal reputation as a political theorist. The first volume of his *Defence of the Constitutions of the United States of America*, written while he was American minister in London, appeared just in time to be consulted by the Philadelphia convention. Returning home in 1788, Adams, now fifty-three years old, soon made it clear, in spurning an offer of election to the Senate, that he wished for either a high office or none at all. He had not displayed ecstatic admiration for the new Federal Constitution, and he could never be said to possess a lovable disposition. But his assets far outweighed his disadvantages.

Several scholars feel that Adams was the victim of complex machinations on the part of Hamilton. There is no doubt that Hamilton did express only a grudging readiness to recommend him, and that he did his best to reduce the vote for Adams. Replying to Theodore Sedgwick in October, 1788, Hamilton showed that he was not yet entirely willing to agree that Adams should be the man. He mentioned theories that Adams was "unfriendly in his sentiments to General Washington," and might form an alliance with the Virginia Lees that would greatly embarrass a Federalist executive.

Once the selection had narrowed to Adams, within the Hamiltonian circle, Hamilton worked busily to ensure that Adams would poll appreciably fewer votes than Washington. The reason he gave was "that defect in the constitution which renders it possible that the man intended for Vice-President may in fact turn up President." The probability, he said, was that Washington would be a unanimous choice. But so might Adams. Either through accident or "Anti-Foederal malignity," the transfer of a handful of votes could place Adams in the Chief Magistracy. It was therefore advisable to "throw away a few votes," say 7 or 8, that would have gone to Adams, and distribute them among "persons not otherwise thought of." Hamilton instructed at least two people along these lines—James Wilson of Pennsylvania and Jeremiah Wadsworth of Connecticut. The outcome was much as Hamilton had foreseen it. In later years Adams got wind of Hamilton's intervention, and complained bitterly of the "dark and insidious manner" in which Hamilton, "like the worm at the root of the peach," had intrigued against him.

Hamilton's inner motives can only be guessed at. There is no proof that he acted out of malice, though within a few years he and Adams were to become intensely suspicious of one another. Nor, on the scanty evidence, are we entitled to assert that his conduct was underhand, though it was certainly staged—as it had to be—under cover. In defense of Hamilton, one might note that he was not alone in doubting the suitability of John Adams. James Madison, at this juncture a staunch supporter of the Constitution, provided a similar estimate of vice-presidential candidates in October 1788:

> Hancock is weak, ambitious, a courtier of popularity, given to low intrigue, and lately reunited by a factious friendship with Samuel Adams. John Adams has made himself obnoxious to many, particularly in the southern states, by the political principles avowed in his book. Others, recollecting his cabal during the war against General Washington, knowing his extravagant self-importance, and considering his preference of an unprofitable dignity to some place of emolument . . . as a proof of his having an eye to the presidency, conclude that he would not be a very cordial second to the General, and that an impatient ambition might even intrigue for a premature advancement.

Such opinions suggest that Hamilton may merely have been voicing reservations shared by a number of Adams' contemporaries. It should also be added that Hamilton's own ambitions, while they included President-making, probably did not run to making himself President. In this respect he was not a rival to Adams. Madison's comments are a reminder of how deep were the distrusts of the day, and how sharp the memory remained of wartime "cabals." There is a further worry that may legitimately have concerned Hamilton, as it seemed to concern Madison. Washington's dream of an early retirement was presumably known to all of his associates. They may have indulged him in the idea that it might be feasible, in order to strengthen his resolve to submit to the electoral will. Suppose Washington, once in office, persisted in the idea? According to the somewhat hazy constitutional notions of succession held in 1788–1789, John Adams would then merely be acting President. But he might be difficult to dislodge. Madison's letter suggests that he contemplated the possibility; so perhaps did Hamilton. In a memorandum of May, 1792, describing a conversation with Washington concerning retirement from office, Madison noted that he had in 1788 "contemplated, & I believe, suggested" to the General "a voluntary retirement to private life as soon as the state of the Government would permit," in order to demonstrate the sincerity of previous announcements about remaining a private citizen.

On the matter of "losing" votes that would otherwise have gone to Adams, Hamilton's intentions may likewise not have been "dark and insidious," and the problem may have been anticipated by others. At Philadelphia, after all, Madison had speculated that in an undifferentiated two-vote system the second vote might be the winning one. Subsequent experiences revealed that Hamilton was quite correct in describing the two-vote mechanism as defective; the 12th Amendment recognized the fact. With so much at stake, and so much uncertain, there was a strong argument for making sure that Washington came first. If through mischance the General came second, the consequences might be appalling. Washington would clearly not consent to fill the role of Vice-President; whoever was installed as President would be regarded as an interloper, if not a usurper; and the new Federal Government might well collapse under the strain. It is perhaps significant that John Adams' son-in-law, William Stephens Smith, writing to Jefferson on February 15, 1789, showed no sign of believing that there had been any treachery: "It is Generally believed here [Boston] and in the middle states, that Mr. Adams will be the Vice President, he had the unanimous Vote of Massachusetts and New Hampshire and 5 out of 7 of the electors of Connecticut. That he had not the whole there, originated from an apprehension, that if the state of Virginia should not vote for General Washington that Mr. A. would be President, which would not be consistent with the wish of the country and could only arise from the finesse of antifoedral Electors with a view to produce confusion and embarrass the operations of the Constitution, against which many have set their faces, both in this and some of the other states."

While Hamilton and other Federalists were at work, the "Anti's" were equally though less masterfully preoccupied with their own exercises in electoral arithmetic. They too, accepting that General Washington would be President, wanted a northerner as Vice-President. The most conspicuous possibility was Governor George Clinton of New York, whose anti-Constitutional onslaught had gone down to a narrow defeat in the state ratifying convention. Like Governor Patrick Henry of Virginia, he talked of summoning a new national plenary convention to reopen the affair. "Mr. Henry," a Virginia correspondent told Madison in November, 1788, "is putting in agitation the name of Clinton for vice-president." The main activity on behalf of Clinton went on in New York and Virginia, with feelers put out to other areas. Early in the new year, St. John de Crèvecoeur, the author of *Letters from an American Farmer*, then in New York as French consul and in outlook a rather bewildered Federalist, reported to Jefferson: "'tis proposed in Virginia to Vote for Govr. Clinton as a President, some back Counties in Pensilvania Will unite as well as this State." Henry was one of Virginia's presidential electors, and in fact gave his second vote to Clinton, who also collected 2 other Virginia votes. But this meager total of 3 was all that Clinton garnered in the electoral college. His New York enemy Hamilton rightly discerned that Clinton's challenge was negligible. Clinton could nibble away a few votes in the South; a few more might have been forthcoming in New York, but a dispute over the method of selecting electors led to a failure to choose any, so that Clinton's own state had no say in the 1789 presidential election. Indeed, as Hamilton explained to Madison, Clinton's candidacy could actually benefit the federal cause: "if pains are taken the dangers of an Antifoedral vice President might itself be rendered the instrument of Union."

The New York electoral fiasco wrecked whatever hopes Clinton and his friends may have nourished. The "Federal-Republican" clubs they had founded and the circular letters they had sent counted for little at this juncture. Even with better fortune it is hard to see how the Anti-Federalism of 1788 – 1789 could have been organized into a coherent opposition. There was a real case against some aspects of the Constitution, mixed up with a miscellany of fears and grudges. In ratifying, six of the eleven states had submitted lists of proposed amendments, and two other states had withheld ratification. Clinton was presented as a plain, hearty Republican who inside the new government would speak for the dissatisfied. But as yet the situation supplied no leverage. The new government could not be attacked until it had been given a reasonable opportunity to display itself, and to honor the understanding that amendments would be incorporated in the Constitution. What could an Anti-Federalist Vice-President hope to accomplish, especially when he dare not, and had no reason to, impugn the good faith of the man destined to be President?

The first part of the process, the choosing of electors, passed off fairly smoothly in most of the states, though not without some excitements—not surprisingly, since at the same time elections for Congress were also under way. Only in New York was there a total fiasco. In part this reflected the Clintonian-Hamiltonian division, in part the weaknesses of a method involving a bicameral legislature, when the two houses were of two minds. For in New York, as in Connecticut, Delaware, Georgia, New Jersey, and South Carolina, presidential electors were to be chosen by the legislature. The Assembly, the lower house, was Clintonishly Anti-Federalist; the Senate, the upper house, was predominantly though not overwhelmingly Federalist in tone. The Assembly proposed a joint ballot, the Senate a concurrent one: in other words, an arguing match. The details are unimportant for our purposes; each house calculated that its own method might yield the desired results in the shape of a batch of faithful Federalist (or Anti-Federalist) electors. Since neither would agree to compromise, New York deprived itself of its presidential ballots—and, incidentally, also of its pair of senators during the first session of the new Congress.

A dispute of similar proportions threatened a similar outcome in New Hampshire. Here the nomination of electors was left to popular choice, but the actual appointment to the legislature. It had not been explained how the appointment should be determined. The lower house wanted a joint ballot; the upper house insisted on a veto power, on the same lines as its power to negate bills and resolutions emanating from the lower house. After prolonged contention the lower house gave way, under protest. New Hampshire ended up with five presumed Federalists for electors.

There was a certain electricity in the atmosphere of two other states, Pennsylvania and Maryland, where the choice of electors depended directly upon a popular vote. Citizens of those states feared or hoped, according to temperament, that there would be an Anti-Federalist majority. Two "tickets" were disclosed in Pennsylvania. That of Lancaster, representing the sentiment of eastern counties, listed ten men known to be staunch supporters of Washington and the Constitution. The Harrisburg ticket, representing the suspicions of the western counties, listed a phalanx of men who had resisted the ratification of the Constitution. The Lancasterians triumphed though: all 10 of the Pennsylvania electoral votes went to Federalists. In Maryland too there were rival tickets, addresses, accusations of fraud. A few electoral nominees in Baltimore, whose leanings were in doubt, issued cards declaring that if chosen they would cast their votes for Washington and Adams. The same thing was done in Philadelphia. As in Pennsylvania, Federalism—or at least Washingtonism—gained the victory.

There were some scuffles in Virginia, of the kind taken for granted on election day. Otherwise, the first Wednesday in January, 1789, went off tranquilly. No troubles were reported, for instance, in Massachusetts, where two electors were chosen at large, and the eight others were picked by the legislature from twenty-four names produced by the state's congressional districts. In the nation as a whole, sixty-nine electors were chosen: with New York the number would have been seventy-nine, and of course larger still if North Carolina and Rhode Island had come within the rubric.

The electors duly met a month later, cast their votes, and prepared to transmit the sealed figures to Congress as soon as there was an adequate Congress to count them. Their lips were less sealed. As we have seen, the verdict was accurately though unofficially tabulated long before the official announcement. The electors clearly did not feel that their ballots were secret, and indeed there was no reason why they should, except out of courtesy to Congress.

It goes without saying that none of the men who received an electoral vote had delivered himself of a manifesto, or of a promise as to how he would act if elected. General Washington had scrupulously declined to commit himself, not only to being a candidate but also to considering the claims of those who wrote to him about possible federal appointments. Naturally enough, though, those who labored in support of particular candidates allowed themselves to think that loyalty would not go unrewarded. Benjamin Rush, for example, was actuated by more than simple benevolence when he wrote to John Adams in January, 1789:

> You will perceive by the Philadelphia papers that your friends *here* have not been idle. You will I believe have every vote from this state, and pains have been taken to secure the same unanimity in your favor in several of the adjoining states. I assure you, sir, that friendship for you has had much less to do in this business . . . than a sincere desire to place a gentleman in the Vice-President's chair upon whose long-tried integrity, just principles in government, and firm opposition to popular arts and demagogues, such a dependence could be placed as shall secure us both from a convention and from alterations falsely and impudently called by some of our state governors *amendments*.

A month later, Rush had the embarrassment of accounting to Adams for something less than the "unanimity" of which he had boasted. Two of Pennsylvania's vice-presidential votes had gone to John Hancock, although Adams acquired the other 8. All of Delaware's 3 votes had been diverted from Adams to John Jay, and Maryland's 6 to Benjamin Harrison.

Rush turned the difficulty to advantage. The conduct of Delaware and Maryland in "throwing away their votes for a vice-president" was he suggested due in part to "a jealousy of the New England states, which has been revived . . . by their vote in favor of the meeting of the first Congress in

New York." Philadelphia was the true "headquarters of federalism." The setback to Adams was thus explained—and linked with a broad hint that his
friends had rallied to him in the belief that he would be their champion.
"There is an expectation here," Rush asserted, "that your influence will be
exerted immediately in favor of a motion to bring Congress to Philadelphia."

A foretaste of interest politics? But in 1789, so far as Adams was concerned, there was no deal. Pennsylvanians like Rush and William Maclay
supported him in the hope that he would use his weight to bring the national
capital to their state. Philadelphia did become the temporary capital, but this
was a mere sop. They were soon disabused. Like a second Washington, apparently, Adams supposed that votes would accrue to him as of right; he
would not bargain for them.

So came April 6, when the electoral votes were opened in Congress, in
the presence of both houses. The result amazed few men, though it gratified
George Washington and chagrined John Adams. Every one of the sixty-nine
electors, even the disaffected Patrick Henry, had given a vote to Washington.
While Adams had no serious rival, he had gathered only 34 votes (Henry's
other vote, it will be recalled, went to Clinton).

STATE	WASHINGTON	ADAMS	JAY	HANCOCK	OTHERS
New Hampshire	5	5			
Massachusetts	10	10			
Connecticut	7	5			2
New Jersey	6	1	5		
Pennsylvania	10	8		2	
Delaware	3		3		
Maryland	6				6
Virginia	10	5	1	1	3
South Carolina	7			1	6
Georgia	5	—	—	—	5
	69	34	9	4	22

A few of the also-rans—Jay, Hancock, John Rutledge of South Carolina (who
collected 6 of his state's 7 votes)—were men of some stature. Others such as
John Milton and Edward Telfair, whose fellow-Georgians gave 2 votes
and 1 vote respectively, were in no sense national figures. However the verdict was interpreted—and Adams thought his own treatment "scurvey . . . an
indelible stain on our Country, Countrymen and Constitution"—it was clear
that in 1788–1789 Washington was *hors de concours*, and that any who stood
against him would be ignominiously placed *hors de combat*.

The final stroke of the electoral mechanism consisted of notifying Washington and Adams that they had been chosen. A messenger brought the summons to Adams on April 12, as he fidgeted in his Braintree home, his bags
already packed. Charles Thomson, the elderly Secretary of Congress, had a
more difficult journey to Mount Vernon, and did not therefore arrive with the
news until April 14.

> I have now, sir, to inform you that the proofs you have given of your
> patriotism and of your readiness to sacrifice domestic separation and pri-
> vate enjoyments to preserve the liberty and promote the happiness of your
> country did not permit the two Houses to harbour a doubt of your under-
> taking this great, this important office to which you are called not only by
> the unanimous vote of the electors, but by the voice of America, I have it
> therefore in command to accompany you to New York where the Senate
> and House of Representatives are convened for the dispatch of public
> business.

The formal notification, which old Thomson also delivered, while it was brief-
er and reminded the General that the support he commanded was that of "a
free and enlightened people," was in the same mode of solemn compliment.
The vocabulary of such addresses suggested that the first President had received an "election" almost more in the religious than in the political sense of
the word.

Four years after his first qualms about undertaking the office of President, Washington found himself embroiled in the same cycle of painful uncertainties. The renewed demands upon him were to lead to the same conclusion:
reelection by a unanimous vote for a second term, and reelection by a divided
vote of Vice-President John Adams.

Much had, however, changed in the meantime; and the changes both increased and made more illusory Washington's desire to liberate himself from
the shackles of responsibility. He celebrated his sixtieth birthday in February,
1792, and felt older than his years. He had survived serious illnesses in
1790 and 1791. He was, he complained, growing deaf; his eyesight was dete-
riorating; and his memory was beginning to be defective. The detailed and far
from absentminded letters that he wrote on Sundays and sent to his agents at
Mount Vernon on points of farm management reveal that he was perhaps not
so much tired of life as tired of being President. The Federal Government had
moved headquarters from New York to Philadelphia in the autumn of 1790,
but though Washington was now less than a week's coach-ride away from
Mount Vernon, and managed to spend some time there in 1791 and 1792, it
was still too far away to suit him. His concern for his plantations increased; in
the summer of 1792 his nephew-manager George Augustine Washington fell
into a wasting illness (from which he was to die in February, 1793). Uncle
Washington knew that his nephew's decline and the decline of the estate
would go hand in hand.

He was concerned too for his own reputation. To judge from correspondence he had not yet overcome the scruples of four years before. In fact they
were augmented. If he had then fretted over the impropriety of taking office,
despite previous declarations of a final retirement, he now feared that he
might appear still more disingenous if he did not decisively honor his old
pledge. Moreover, the hope of resigning before the end of his first term had
proved illusory. But he had surely given enough of himself by enduring the
weight of one whole term?

Nor could this first term be regarded as pleasurable. There were solid
accomplishments in which he could take pride. Some Anti-Federalist griev-

ances had been removed by the ten amendments to the Constitution that formed the so-called Bill of Rights. North Carolina and Rhode Island had entered the Union and so had two new states—Vermont and Kentucky. He had drawn some of the country's most brilliant men into his Administration —notably Alexander Hamilton as his Secretary of the Treasury and Thomas Jefferson as his Secretary of State. Edmund Randolph, his Attorney-General, had become a firm supporter of the Constitution. The Secretary of War, Henry Knox, was staunchly loyal to his old military chief.

Yet there were fresh, bitter, and growing dissensions. Hamilton's financial measures—the funding and assumption of state and national debts, the establishment of a national bank under federal auspices, an excise tax—had generated fierce opposition, and indicated the persistence or the emergence of deep sectional and economic cleavages. His opponents maintained that the legislation he had pushed through Congress confirmed what they had suspected ever since 1787, or even earlier: the move toward a "consolidated" government was a move toward dictatorship by a selfish, "aristocratic" minority. Such assertions filled the columns of "Republican" newspapers. The most truculent of these, the *National Gazette*, had begun publication in 1791 in Philadelphia under the very nose of the national Government. Worse still for Washington's ease of mind, the controversy radiated from within his executive circle. Hamilton and Jefferson were, as Jefferson later remarked, pitted against one another like two fighting-cocks. Both men had a gift for friendship, and Jefferson in particular was temperamentally averse to personal quarrels. But their friends were more and more grouped in rival camps (they resorted to pseudonymous journalism to attack one another), and Jefferson was accused of having treacherously and improperly established the *National Gazette* in order to undermine the Administration. There was no denying that its editor, Philip Freneau, was on the payroll of Jefferson's State Department in a minor capacity.

Some of the most disagreeable feuding was still to come when in May, 1792, the President summoned James Madison on a confidential matter. Madison, a member of the House of Representatives, was already a critic of Hamilton's financial policy and was to develop into a leading Jeffersonian. Washington, however, still relied upon Madison's political acumen, and wanted to reopen a question on which he had hitherto sought Madison's advice: "the *mode* and *time*" for announcing to the nation that he would not again consent to be President. He had already consulted Jefferson, Hamilton, Knox, and Randolph, though apparently not John Adams. They had all "made pressing representations" to induce the President to reconsider his decision. What he wanted from Madison was a draft of a suitable Farewell Address, and an opinion as to how he should deliver it. As in 1788, Washington was fretted by a logical paradox. He could not retire without saying so; but if he said so, he might seem to be "arrogantly presuming" that he would be reelected. The timing also was difficult. The opening of the next session of Congress, in November, would be "an apt occasion" in itself. But it would be perhaps too close to the election, and the reply that Congress would make to his Farewell Address "might entangle him in further explanations."

Apart from such questions of protocol, Washington revealed to Madison something of the much heavier burdens that oppressed him. For example, popular discontents were showing themselves more and more; and while "the various attacks against public men & measures had not in general been pointed at him, yet in some instances it had been visible that he was the indirect object." In spite of Madison's counter-arguments, the President gave no indication that he had relented, or would do so.

As in 1788, a combination of gloomy reluctance and bashful *hauteur* inhibited Washington from making any direct statement, positive or negative, during the second half of this election year. His dismay at continuing in office was no doubt magnified by further evidence of the gulf between Hamilton and Jefferson, and of factions throughout the nation. The stirrings of a "whiskey rebellion" in western Pennsylvania at the end of the summer could be taken as a symptom of a widespread unruliness. Washington and his associates were ready to believe that disaffection was being fomented by the enemies of the Administration. Hamilton, in his pamphleteer-role, asserted that one of the principal enemies might be inside the Administration — the Secretary of State. Edmund Randolph, writing to Hamilton early in September, was perturbed enough to begin his letter: "Persuaded as I am, that the last effort for the happiness of the United States must perish with the loss of the present Government." The President, in correspondence with Randolph at about the same time, revealed his angry alarm at the effects of newspaper polemics — "those attacks upon almost every measure of government with some of the Gazettes are so strongly pregnated; & which cannot fail, if persisted in with the malignancy they now team, of rending the Union asunder. . . . In a word if the Government and the officers of it are to be the constant theme for Newspaper abuse . . . it will be impossible, I conceive, for any man living to manage the helm, or to keep the machine together." And while the abuse was only obliquely aimed at him (by comparison with the salvoes sent against John Adams, he was immune) he took it personally.

However, the worse things became, the more he was open to the insistence of his contemporaries that he alone could save the nation. Randolph had not meant to say in his lament to Hamilton that the United States was doomed, but only that it would be if the Federal Government allowed the situation to get out of hand. The men whom the President consulted about his retirement all returned the same answer: it would be a black day for the country, at the present juncture. They also, and perhaps inconsistently, attempted to reassure him that things were not so bad, and might with luck and good management soon vastly improve. One reason for this, no doubt, was a desire to convince the President that this time he might escape without having completed his term. The crisis was coming to a head, Jefferson told him in May, 1792, and must shortly be settled. If so, Washington might retire "without awaiting the completion of the second period of four years. I cannot but hope" — Jefferson added a flattering flourish — "that you can resolve to add one or two more to the many years you have already sacrificed to the good of mankind." Two months later, in almost identical language, Hamilton begged

the President to "make a further sacrifice. . . . I trust that it need not continue above a year or two more—And I think it will be more [eligible] to retire
from office before the expiration of the term of an election, than to decline a
reelection." But that there *was* a crisis Randolph direly insisted: "Should a
civil war arise, you cannot stay at home. And how much easier will it be, to
disperse the factions, which are rushing to this catastrophe, than to subdue
them after they shall appear in arms? It is the fixed opinion of the world"
—again an appeal to Washington's self-esteem—"that you surrender nothing
incomplete."

The condition of the outside world, especially in western Europe, was in
itself enough to demand continuity and stability in the American Government.
The ferment of militant French republicanism might have the gravest consequences for the United States. But in the midsummer of 1792, as Washington
sought the relative tranquility of Mount Vernon, domestic and personal factors were probably foremost in his imagination. One point developed by Madison may well have struck home. Eventually there would of course have to be
a successor to Washington; but who could succeed him at the moment? Madison reviewed the options, with a "Republican" emphasis that could be discounted to some extent but not entirely dismissed. The three likeliest successors were Jefferson, Adams, and John Jay (who in a close-fought election had
just been robbed of the governorship of New York by Clinton, in circumstances discreditable to Clinton). Of these, Jefferson wanted to quit public life
for the peace of his Monticello home; and in any case he could not command
enough support in the North. Adams was unacceptable because his views
were too "monarchical" and because he was unpopular in the South. "It
would not be in the power of those who might be friendly to his private character, & willing to trust him in a public one, notwithstanding his political principles, to make head against the torrent." As for Jay, he had succeeded in
becoming unpopular with groups throughout the Union; "his election would
be extremely dissatisfactory on several accounts." Washington might not feel
that such an estimate was altogether fair, but he could not deny that it was
essentially correct. There was no plausible alternative, or none to be risked at
a time of unrest. He was the only person who could command a national following.

This was reinforced by the remarkable harmony of viewpoint expressed
by Hamilton and Jefferson. Agreeing, it appeared, on almost nothing else,
they were at one in wishing Washington to remain in office. Could he though
expect that the rest of the nation would concur? Even if no one could come
near him in electoral votes, might there not be a contest of sorts, and of an
ugly character? Hamilton reassured him, exactly as in 1788: "The dread of
public indignation will be likely to restrain the indisposed few. If they can calculate at all, they will naturally reflect that they could not give a severer blow
to their cause than by giving a proof of hostility to you. But if a solitary vote or
two should appear wanting to perfect unanimity, of what moment can it be?"

Thus for Washington on this issue the wheel had come full circle. In 1792,
as in 1788, he yearned to avoid the inevitable, while friends implored him to

yield to it. Not knowing what else to do, he kept silent—though his friends fancied they could read between the lines. They and the nation took his silence for consent. By November, 1792, when Congress reassembled and the President offered no indication of impending withdrawal, it was taken for granted that next March would witness his second inauguration. As in 1788, the political horoscope then shifted to a subsidiary yet highly intriguing question: who would qualify as his Vice-President?

For those who were generally in sympathy with the development of American affairs, and approved of Hamiltonian policies, it seemed obvious that John Adams should remain as the President's deputy. Though his office was, as he complained, relatively insignificant, it made him known to every member of Congress. Even overshadowed by Washington, he was unquestionably a national figure. The warmest support not surprisingly came from his own section, New England. But he could count on the personal esteem of men throughout the Union, whether or not they shared his political opinions. He enjoyed for example a fluctuating but basically firm friendship with Thomas Jefferson, who thought that in the coming election "the strength of [Adams's] personal worth and his services will . . . prevail over the demerits of his political creed," and so actually recommended Adams to one of the Virginia electors. Leading Federalists such as Charles Carroll of Maryland, Oliver Wolcott of Connecticut, and Rufus King of New York, all gave him their imprimatur. Hamilton, perhaps a little ambiguously, also bestowed a blessing; certainly he did not contemplate any other candidate within the Federalist persuasion.

Jefferson himself held aloof from electioneering in 1792. Others in the Republican camp made fitfully strenuous efforts to turn the vice-presidential contest to their advantage. When the struggle was over, the Federalist Theodore Sedgwick observed that the "Opposition has been as busy as the Devil in a gale of wind." One tack was to denounce Adams for monarchical leanings. Undoubtedly he was a tempting target. He had made himself somewhat ridiculous in the first session of Congress by advocating semi-regal designations ("His Highness") for the President. His *Defence of the Constitutions*, written in 1786–87 and stretching to three volumes, made plain his conviction that the executive branch must be separate and powerful, and that there was much to be said for a hereditary instead of an elective chief of state. He argued on the same lines in his *Discourses on Davila*, which he regarded as a sequel to the *Defence*. The *Discourses* were written as a series of letters in John Fenno's Federalist newspaper the *Gazette of the United States* in 1791. They provoked so much "Jacobinical" complaint that Adams terminated the series before he had exhausted his argument—though not before he had trailed his coat in thirty-two issues of the *Gazette*. Freneau's rival publication, the *National Gazette*, thundered against "those monarchical writers on Davila, &c., who are armed with long wigs, long pens and caitiff printers ready to disseminate their poisoned doctrines." Admirers of Adams countered, sometimes in dinner-table exchanges, by asking his critics whether they had read his works, or merely heard about them. Patrick Henry was challenged in this way. So was the vehement Virginia Republican William Branch Giles, who was forced to admit that his knowledge of Adams' "monarchal" doctrines was confined to newspaper accounts and random extracts. Jefferson observed (in code) to Madison about Adams that the presidential title affair was "superlatively ridiculous. . . . It is a proof the more of the justice of the character given by Dr. Franklin of my friend, 'always an honest man, often a great one, but sometimes absolutely mad.'" In short, Adams' idiosyncratic and skeptical ruminations weakened his popular appeal; yet their very idiosyncrasy prevented them from doing fatal damage, since his attitudes were complex and hard to disentangle.

Thrusts at John Adams were merely incidental; the Republicans needed a candidate to set against him. As in 1788, George Clinton was the most obvious person. His reputation suffered in the unedifying dispute over the vote-count in the New York gubernatorial election of 1792 — an episode prefiguring in miniature the disputed presidential election of 1876. Jefferson feared that it might weaken "the cause of republicanism." There were subsequent rumors that if Clinton succeeded in ousting Adams he would continue to be Governor of New York while also acting as Vice-President — a pluralism calculated to cast contempt upon the Federal Government. The affair, again according to rumor, put Clinton at odds with New York's junior senator Aaron Burr, who together with Senator Rufus King was asked to adjudicate in the controversy.

Nevertheless by June it seemed certain that the Republicans were agreed on backing Clinton. "You are I presume aware," Hamilton told Adams, "that Mr. Clinton is to be your Competitor at the next election. I trust he could not have succeeded in any event, but the issue of his late election will not help his cause." Hamilton added "Alas! Alas!" with less than heartfelt sincerity. At the same time, of course, the Republicans were making a determined effort to run strong candidates in the forthcoming congressional elections.

Adams' own reaction, somewhat akin to that of Jefferson, was an unhappy (and incomplete) detachment. The news that reached him of maneuvers afoot heightened his old distaste for "electioneering" (a word which, incidentally, was already current). In his native Massachusetts, his cousin Samuel Adams and John Hancock were said to be promoting the Anti-Federalist interest. Fisher Ames, the Massachusetts Federalist — "the colossus of the monocrats and paper [money] men" in Jefferson's phrase — was being sharply challenged. Ames in turn, urging New Englanders to give "zealous support" to Adams, expressed his regret at the tone of anti-Adams propaganda; it was sad that "a life of virtue and eminent usefulness should be embittered by calumny." Adams, who in selfrighteous moments felt the same way about himself, decided to remain in seclusion on his Quincy farm, and not to expose himself to the factious atmosphere of Philadelphia until well after the beginning of the next session of Congress in November. Alarmed by the report, the tireless Hamilton, claiming it was "the universal wish of your friends," implored him to show himself "as soon as possible at Philadelphia."

> I fear that this will give some handle to your enemies to misrepresent — and though I am persuaded you are very indifferent personally to the . . . election, yet I hope you are not so as it regards the cause of good

> Government. The difference . . . is in my conception between the suc-
> cess of Mr. Clinton or yourself; and some sacrifices of feeling are to be
> made.

Others in Philadelphia, including the Vice-President's son Thomas Boylston
Adams, wrote in the same vein. But John Adams stayed put, and did not set
out from Quincy until the end of November. By the time he reached the federal capital the presidential electors had met and cast their votes. No one
would be able to say that John Adams had stooped to conquer.

In the meantime there had been a flurry of behind-the-scenes activity
among the Republicans, especially between key men in New York, Pennsylvania, and Virginia. Two busy personages in Pennsylvania were Dr. Benjamin
Rush, and John Beckley, the clerk of the House of Representatives, who in
recent years has been shown to be a significant agent in the formation of a
fully-fledged Republican party. Rush, previously a good friend of Adams, had
become temporarily hostile to what he thought Adams portended. Gripped in
the hectic emotions of a period when both America and Europe saw before
them a tremendous drama of choices, Rush opted for the side of liberty and
republicanism — as he interpreted it. With the knowledge of Madison and
Jefferson, Beckley traveled to New York at the end of September. He bore a
letter of introduction from Rush to Aaron Burr. Burr's own opinions had not
hitherto seemed to place him firmly in one camp or the other. He was not on
good terms with Clinton. On the other hand he could be presumed not to be in
collusion with Hamilton, since he had captured the Senate seat of Hamilton's
father-in-law Philip Schuyler. Apparently he was now reckoned to be a Republican, and a talented and promising one; for Rush wrote that his "friends
everywhere look to you to take an active part in removing the monarchical
rubbish of our government. It is time to *speak out* — or we are undone." Rush
also encouraged Burr to extend the network into New England: "The association in Boston augurs well. Do feed it by a letter to Mr. Samuel Adams."
Apart from pseudonymous printed polemics, it would seem most of the speaking out was done in private, almost conspiratorially.

Beckley, back in Philadelphia, informed Madison that Burr was ready to
"support the measure of removing Mr. A" and replacing him with Mr. C. But
a Philadelphia Republican, John Nicholson, had already suggested a better
candidate in the shape of Mr. B — namely, Senator Burr. "The people here,"
said Nicholson, understood that Clinton wished to withdraw. They thought
Burr might prove a more popular candidate in some areas. They would back
either man, and would like "a communication with their Southern Brethren on
the subject." Burr sent an emissary to Nicholson: and in the same crowded
interval a letter signed by two New York Republicans arrived in Virginia,
addressed to Madison and to James Monroe and delivered by hand to Monroe. The bearer, Monroe told Madison, "was intrusted with a similar [commu-
nication] for some [gentlemen] in Penn'a & elsewhere, particularly to the
south." The message was more or less that imparted by Nicholson. Monroe
was not enthusiastic. He thought Burr too young, and the scheme somewhat
presumptuous, and probably launched too late. It was difficult to know how
best to proceed; in a straight contest, he would not hesitate "to aid Burr in

opposition to Adams." Madison wrote back to express his general agreement, but proposed that he and Monroe should first meet in Fredericksburg, Virginia, and jointly "weigh the subject in every scale." When they were able to reply to the New Yorkers, they stated that "the Republican interest, so far as the voice of this State may be estimated, requires that things should be kept to the course which they have in a manner spontaneously taken." In short, Virginia preferred Clinton. "Warmly supported by sundry influential characters," he was more likely "to unite a greater number of electoral votes." When they wrote, a meeting had in fact already taken place in Philadelphia between Pennsylvania Republicans and one of the New York spokesmen, Melancton Smith. They had firmly decided to "exert every endeavor for Mr. Clinton and to drop all thoughts of Mr. Burr." Smith volunteered to make the decision known, and to take an immediate trip into New England to spread the word for Clinton. John Beckley, present at the meeting, begged Madison and Monroe to display similar energy in Virginia and other southern states. The chronology of the episode, which was squeezed into about a fortnight, indicates the sense of urgency of those involved, and their capacity to move swiftly despite the handicaps of distance.

So ended the brief flare of Burr's candidacy. Clandestine though it had been, it soon came to the ears of Rufus King. He wrote in alarm to Hamilton: "If the enemies of the Government are secret and united we shall lose Mr. Adams." Burr was "industrious in his canvass." In Connecticut Burr's uncle Pierpont Edwards, a prominent lawyer, was busy on his behalf; and maneuvers were in train elsewhere. The danger was not so much that Burr would win, but that he could get so many votes that Adams might out of pique "decline the Office." For a few weeks Hamilton seems to have been seriously worried. Or at least, he appears to have lost his usual coolness, perhaps out of the personal antipathy to Burr that was to grow with the years and eventually to cost him his life on the dueling ground at Weehawken. He conveyed the gist of King's letter to several correspondents, including Charles Cotesworth Pinckney, a leading citizen of South Carolina, John Steele, a congressman from North Carolina, and—perhaps the clearest indication of his loss of composure—to President Washington, who may have thought Hamilton's letter indiscreet and best left unanswered. In nearly identical phrasing Hamilton, in his other letters also, offered a ferocious assessment of Burr. Clinton was bad enough—"a man of narrow and perverse politics, . . . steadily opposed to national principles." Burr was potentially far more dangerous—a man "whose only political principle is, to *mount at all events* to the highest legal honours of the Nation and as much further as circumstances will carry him."

Hamilton revealed himself too to be in the grip of an oddly unrealistic conviction about Jefferson. In the course of his *nom-de-plume* newspaper onslaughts against the Republicans he had asserted that Jefferson was scheming to become President through jealousy of Hamilton. In so doing he seems to have given unwitting proof of his own jealousy of Jefferson. At any rate he speculated in this batch of letters as to whether Clinton or Burr, or both, might be run by the Republicans "as a diversion in favour of Mr. Jefferson." Perhaps he was genuinely mystified by the Republican tactics. Perhaps he honestly believed that votes might be steered to Jefferson, though such a plan would not have made much sense. Even more than the clash of personality, however, Hamilton's reaction points to the intensity of emotion and suspicion aroused by the political divisions of the era. Where so much was at stake, each group understandably assumed that the other group would act without scruple in order to secure an advantage. Hamilton and others of the Federalist "interest" watched their opponents like hawks. And Hamilton, for political as well as personal reasons, must have been vastly relieved when it was clear that the Burr candiacy had been abandoned. Once this was apparent, it could be seen as evidence of Republican confusion rather than collusion. And once Hamilton had regained his composure, he was convinced that Adams would be safely reelected.

In March, 1792, Congress approved a new law regulating the presidential succession, and the method of establishing the electoral vote. The electors were to be appointed in the month preceding the first Wednesday in December, on which day they were to meet in their states and vote by ballot for two men — making no mark on their papers to disclose which of the two they preferred for President or Vice-President. A certificate from each state was to be sent to the presiding officer of the Senate before the first Wednesday in January, 1793; and the votes were to be counted in Congress on the second Wednesday in February. No elector was pledged in advance. Each camp read the successive signs — the trend in congressional and state elections, the political coloration of the men chosen as presidential electors, the analyses published in the press or conveyed in private letters — and toted up provisional scorecards. The Republican interest gained appreciably in Congress, though they would not take their seats until the fall of 1793 and so could not influence the immediate pattern of events in Philadelphia. However, Republican morale was high, and Adams for one disclosed his uneasiness in a Christmas letter to his wife Abigail. The Burr following had swung behind Clinton; Burr's New England uncle Pierpont Edwards had turned up in Philadelphia and closeted himself with Jefferson. Ready for the moment to think the worst of his friend, Adams professed to be "really astonished at the blind spirit of party which has seized on the whole soul of this Jefferson. There is not a Jacobin in France more devoted to faction." The public seem to be carried away "with every wind of doctrine and every political lie." He believed that the Federalists must fight the enemy on every literary front: "reasoning must be answered by reasoning; wit by wit. . . ; satire by satire; . . . even buffoonery by buffoonery."

The war of pamphlets continued, with Hamilton as an army in himself. The votes came in slowly; corroboration of those from the new state of Kentucky apparently did not reach Philadelphia until March 1. But every sophisticated citizen knew before the close of 1792 that there would be no startling surprises. The only uncertainty was the exact margin of Adams' lead over Clinton. In mid-October Hamilton accurately forecast the outcome. Adams, he said, would have a "nearly unanimous vote" in New England. In New York, the Republican majority in the legislature would pick Clintonian electors. Adams would get all the votes of New Jersey, and probably sweep the board in Pennsylvania. Delaware and Maryland were fairly secure. Virginia and Georgia were Republican territory; North Carolina might be. Adams would get some votes in South Carolina, but Hamilton confessed he did not know how many. By December 18, he wrote of the election as a thing of the past. "The success of the Vice President," Hamilton informed John Jay, "is as great a source of satisfaction as that of Mr. Clinton would have been of mortification & pain to me." He protested that he would "relinquish my share of the command, to the Antifoederalists if I thought they were to be trusted — but I have so many proofs of the contrary as to make me dread the experience of their preponderancy." When the tally was complete, it confirmed a unanimous vote for Washington: 132 in all. Adams had 77 votes, Clinton 50. The ghost-candidacies of Jefferson and Burr were commemorated in a couple of eccentric gestures: 4 for the former, the product of Rhode Island's obscurely wayward practices; and a single stray South Carolina vote for Aaron Burr. Otherwise the scattering of 1789 had disappeared, giving way to a significantly more disciplined alignment. Each "interest" could draw some satisfaction from the result, although — a perhaps apocryphal story — Adams is said to have reacted to the news of the final vote with a furious "Damn 'em, damn 'em, damn 'em! You see that an elective government will not do." One Republican, writing to Madison on December 24, 1792, felt that their newspaper campaign against Federalist iniquities had started too late. A Massachusetts Federalist, David Cobb, described the result in his state in somewhat odd — perhaps jocular — language: "Our Elections are unanimous for the old King and his second." The Republicans had failed to make any real impact on Pennsylvania. On the other hand, they had swung obediently behind Clinton, for all the peculiarities of his candidacy; they had the makings of a solid southern bloc; and the link between New York and Virginia was emphatically pictured in the following voting table.

The two presidential elections of 1788–89 and 1792 possess an obvious fascination as the forerunners of a long and still flourishing sequence of such contests. They hold something of the pride of place, the nostalgic appeal that in the history of aviation is accorded to those few precarious seconds when the Wright brothers first became airborne over the dunes at Kitty Hawk. By analogy, we may say that in the first try-outs the federal electoral mechanism took wing. It *worked*, if not very well; optimists, of whom on the whole George Washington was one, could feel reasonably confident that with time the machinery would work a good deal better. The electors were chosen — apart from the New York muddle of 1789 — just as the blueprint prescribed. Having been chosen, the electors chose; and their choices were nationally accepted. No elector was assassinated or kidnapped or browbeaten, though a certain amount of psychological pressure was doubtless brought to bear upon them. In this respect the two Washington-Adams elections set the vital precedent.

Yet in other respects they furnish only a shadowy precedent. Seen in the perspective of later elections, they may appear strikingly different, even aberrant. The gap between them and subsequent campaigns is indicated indeed in that word, since the events of 1788–1792 were not "campaigns" in the familiar American understanding of the term. The lines were not clearly drawn, the performers were (by later standards) singularly reluctant and uncommunicative, their supporters secretive and maladroit. Absent were the characteristic features of a campaign in any modern sense: the prolonged search for candidates, the nationwide activities of professional politicians, the crowded and ritualized conventions, the banners and songs and slogans and processions, the convergence of a mass electorate on the polling stations on a specified day in November. The profound divisions that existed in 1788 – 1792 were not yet focussed and polarized. To the extent that they found a political outlet, they were expressed rather in state and congressional elections than in the presidential one. While this was most conspicuously evident in the states where the legislature picked the electors, it applied also in states where the electors had to submit to a popular vote. So we may argue that the subsequent presidential elections are linked to the first ones not so much by direct as by a kind of collateral descent. *Lucus a non lucendo*?

STATE	WASHINGTON	ADAMS	CLINTON	JEFFERSON	BURR
New Hampshire	6	6			
Massachusetts	16	16			
Connecticut	9	9			
New Jersey	7	7			
Pennsylvania	15	14	1		
Delaware	3	3			
Maryland	8	8			
Virginia	21		21		
South Carolina	8	7			1
Georgia	4		4		
New York	12		12		
North Carolina	12		12		
Rhode Island	4			4	
Vermont	3	3			
Kentucky	4	4			
	132	77	50	4	1

A major difference, as has been noted, was created by the unique situation of George Washington. This factor alone would be enough to explain much that was atypical in 1792. Though James Monroe was to be unopposed in 1820, and to receive every electoral vote except one, he owed his elevation to the temporary disappearance of the party system, not to any widespread belief that he was a second Washington. Washington was the automatic and universal nominee, *pater patriae*, the father of his people, even if some men grumbled privately at the dangers of excessive adulation, and if these murmurings found their way into print toward the end of his second Administration. Because he was above the battle, the Presidency did not yet become the principal strategic feature of the political battleground. Because of this, the Vice-Presidency likewise did not serve as a genuine symbol around which to rally; for the office in its nature lacked an autonomous reality. Its meaning was conditional upon the meaning attached to the Presidency. Adams understood this and once remarked, "I am nothing, but I may be everything." While Washington was President, Adams was a cipher, the occupant of what he termed "the most insignificant office that ever the invention of man contrived or his imagination conceived." No wonder that the effort to beat him in 1792 had a slightly half-hearted quality. He was blanketed, so to speak, by Washington's aura; while Washington was President, there was no great point in mounting a large-scale operation to capture the post of Vice-President.

Viewed thus, Washington inhibited and delayed the political evolution of the Presidency, like a man who will not allow a match to be put to a fire that has been laid. If such a parallel had been suggested to him, he might well have replied that he had indeed no intention of risking a conflagration before the house was fireproof. But leaving aside for the moment the question of party politics, it can be argued that Washington's mere presence may have inhibited the growth of highly undesirable forms of electioneering. If there had been a free-for-all contest, there might have been vicious wrangling over the methods of choosing electors, and an overwhelming temptation to buy and sell them. John Adams, culling his examples from the sadly corrupt history of mankind in all epochs, insisted that this was the inevitable tendency of government by the few. "Awful experience," he said in 1790, had convinced him "that Americans are more rapidly disposed to corruption in elections than I thought they were fourteen years ago." Adams nourished a belief, which became more and more heretical in the American context, that it would be safer to appoint an executive and an upper house for life than to plunge the country into the machinations of an elective system. "First magistrates [i.e., Presidents] and senators had better be made hereditary at once, than that the people should be universally debauched and bribed, go to loggerheads, and fly to arms regularly every year." One does need to accept the Adamsite thesis in order to concede that presidential elections were open to abuse. To the degree that Washington's reputation spared him such fevers, he may have provided his country with a beneficial lull, during which electioneering was muted. This, and the fact that the Presidency was not yet the major prize of political competition, may explain why there was so little discussion in the Washington era of the possibility that a handful of men would arrange the business between them, a point touched on, for instance, by historian James Schouler. The 1788–89 election, he writes, "showed that though [the] State colleges might act independently of the people, they were exposed to the yet greater danger of secret cabals among party leaders. In fact the machinery of this election, with all its simplicity of choice, was turned by a crank over which a few party Federalists presided."

Washington's primacy may also have minimized the serious inadequacy of the constitutional device of naming two men without separating the functions for which they were being named. True, the confusion was to produce an alarming deadlock in the 1800 election, that had to be resolved by the 12th Amendment. At any rate Washington's lead over all other potential candidates postponed the crisis for a few years, until Americans were more habit-uated to their new Government. Simply by being President, he may also have saved the United States from the divisive confusion that could have been caused by competition between a multiplicity of candidates. Such a competition had been envisaged when the Constitution was drawn up. But one can imagine the delay, bewilderment and dissatisfaction that would have followed if the first presidential elections had had to be decided in the House of Representatives.

Suppositions of this kind should not be taken too far, though; they ignore another equally crucial factor, the relative absence of national party politics during 1788 – 1792. The matter may be put the other way round: without Washington, party politics might have emerged earlier. Parts of the problem remain conjectural, though much has been clarified by the recent investigations of Joseph Charles, William N. Chambers, Noble E. Cunningham, and others. It is difficult to relate national to state considerations, and organization to ideology. It is difficult to make definite pronouncements about motivation in 1788 – 1792, except over the question of continuity of ideas and personnel between the anti-federalism of 1787 – 88 and the republicanism of the 1790's, on which most present-day writers seem to agree that essentially new elements underlay the rise of the Democratic-Republican persuasion. These difficulties are increased by the near impossibility of knowing what men of the period meant when they used a word like "party." What are we to make, for instance, of the following statement?

> In all public bodies there are two parties. The Executive will necessarily be more connected with one than with the other. There will be a personal interest therefore in one of the parties to oppose as well as in the other to support him. Much has been said of the intrigues that will be practiced by the Executive to get into office. Nothing has been said on the other side of the intrigues to get him out of office. Some leader of party will always covet his seat, will perplex his administration, will cabal with the Legislature, till he succeeds in supplanting him.

It occurs in a speech by Gouverneur Morris at Philadelphia in 1787. Is it remarkably prescient vision of the future course of presidential politics, or merely Morris's version of English parliamentary tactics, with their alternation of "ins" and "outs"? The latter seems more likely; Morris seems to confine his notion of party behavior to what goes on inside the government.

What is clear is that though many Americans of the era expected parties to emerge, few rejoiced in the prospect and fewer still could perceive the shape that they would take. If by a "party" we mean an interconnected structure operating at national, state, and local level, with a program of sorts, a self-conscious identity of name and sentiment, and a sustained determination to capture the federal executive branch, then obviously such a phenomenon did not exist in the period under review. "Opposition" claimed but was not granted legitimacy. Party labels tended to be anachronistic ("Anti-Federal"), and pejorative rather than honorific, terms of abuse rather than badges of identity. They have been loosely employed in this essay, but with the partial justification that they were loosely employed at the time. The word "interest" perhaps comes closest to conveying both the limited, manipulative nature of political groupings, and the conception that Madison, Hamilton, and others actually had of their own activities.

Yet such groupings—cliques, cabals, juntos, connexions, all with an eighteenth-century flavor of politics as a game played by family alliances —were not incompatible with a passionate if uneven and intermittent response to ideological issues. The presidential politics of the 1790's were, starting in 1793, to be powerfully swayed by ideology, though these heady emotions did not last. The elections of 1788–89 and 1792 mark a transitional zone. The elements that were to make the capture of the Presidency a central aim of party politics were already in being, but not as yet brought together. Washington could still endeavor to conduct himself as a "disinterested" *head of state*; most of his successors would owe their election and their subsequent fortunes to the fact that they had also been designated *head of a national party*. Perhaps the process was inevitable, once a federal government was a going concern. E pluribus unum: the many depended upon some single focus; in unity was strength. The differences between these two primordial elections and the style of a fully developed presidential system are substantial. Most of the enduring precedents set by Washington belong to quite other realms of statecraft. Yet there are continuities to be discerned, in the amorphous but coalescing affiliations between New York and Virginia, and even in the various things that Washington and Adams did *not* do.

A final analogy may help to summarize the situation: in children's drawing books there are pages made up of apparently miscellaneous dots, each dot with a number. They are transformed into recognizable pictures —say of a donkey or an elephant—by joining up the dots in numbered order. From 1788 to 1792, so far as presidential elections were concerned, the dots were all there. The diagram, however, had not yet been completed, and only some of the dots bore numbers; others were puzzlingly blank. So, within the scope of the diagram, a different though not totally different picture could have emerged.

Appendix

Correspondence between Alexander Hamilton
and General George Washington

*The necessary nine states had ratified the new Constitution by the end of June,
1788. New York, Hamilton's state, gave grudging assent (30 votes to 27) late
in July. Hamilton, a frequent correspondent of General Washington, lost no
time in urging him to signify his willingness to become the first President
under the Constitution.*

New York
August 13, 1788

Sir. I take it for granted, Sir, you have concluded to comply with what will no
doubt be the general call of your country in relation to the new government.
You will permit me to say that it is indispensable you should lend yourself to
its first operations — It is to little purpose to have *introduced* a system, if the
weightiest influence is not given to its firm *establishment*, in the outset.
 I remain with the greatest esteem Dr Sir Yr. Obed & hum servant

*In answering Hamilton, Washington revealed complex reasons for his reluc-
tance to put himself forward.*

Mount Vernon
August 28, 1788

Dear Sir: On the delicate subject with which you conclude your letter, I can
say nothing; because the event alluded to may never happen; and because, in
case it should occur, it would be a point of prudence to defer forming one's
ultimate and irrevocable decision, so long as new data might be afforded for
one to act with the greater wisdom and propriety. I would not wish to conceal
my prevailing sentiment from you. For you know me well enough, my good
Sir, to be persuaded, that I am not guilty of affectation, when I tell you, that
it is my great and sole desire to live and die, in peace and retirement on my
own farm. Were it even indispensable a different line of conduct should be
adopted; while you and some others who are acquainted with my heart would
acquit, the world and Posterity might probably accuse me [of] *inconsistency*
and *ambition*. Still I hope I shall always possess firmness and virtue enough
to maintain (what I consider the most enviable of all titles) the character of
an honest man, as well as prove (what I desire to be considered in reality)
that I am, with great sincerity and esteem, etc.

33

*In common with other men close to the General, Hamilton continued to argue
that Washington was "indispensable" to the nation.*

New York

September (n.d.), 1788

Dear Sir It cannot be considered as a compliment to say that on your acceptance of the office of President the success of the new government in its
commencement may materially depend. Your agency and influence will be
not less important in preserving it from the future attacks of its enemies than
they have been in recommending it in the first instance to the adoption of the
people. Independent of all considerations drawn from this source the point
of light in which you stand at home and abroad will make an infinite difference
in the respectability with which the government will begin its operations in
the alternative of your being or not being at the head of it. I forbear to urge
considerations which might have a more personal application. What I have
said will suffice for the inferences I mean to draw.

First — In a matter so essential to the well being of society as the prosperity
of a newly instituted government a citizen of so much consequence as yourself
to its success has no option but to lend his services if called for. Permit me
to say it would be inglorious in such a situation not to hazard the glory however great, which he might have previously acquired.

Secondly. Your signature to the proposed system pledges your judgment
for its being such an one as upon the whole was worthy of the public approbation. If it should miscarry (as men commonly decide from success or the
want of it) the blame will in all probability be laid on the system itself. And
the framers of it will have to encounter the disrepute of having brought about
a revolution in government, without substituting any thing that was worthy
of the effort. They pulled down one Utopia, it will be said, to build up another.
This view of the subject, if I mistake not my dear Sir will suggest to your mind
greater hazard to that fame, which must be and ought to be dear to you, in
refusing your future aid to the system than in affording it. I will only add that
in my estimate of the matter that aid is indispensable.

I have taken the liberty to express these sentiments to lay before you my
view of the subject. I doubt not the considerations mentioned have fully occurred to you, and I trust they will finally produce in your mind the same result,
which exists in mine. I flatter myself the frankness with which I have delivered
myself will not be displeasing to you. It has been prompted by motives which
you would not disapprove. . . .

Replying to Hamilton's skillful plea, Washington disclosed that while still reluctant he had not closed his mind. There is an interesting suggestion that he might, if elected, be able to retire before the end of the presidential term.

Mount Vernon
October 3, 1788

Dear Sir, In acknowledging the receipt of your candid and kind letter by the last Post; little more is incumbent upon me, than to thank you sincerely for the frankness with which you communicated your sentiments, and to assure you that the same manly tone of intercourse will always be more than barely wellcome, Indeed it, will be highly acceptable to me. I am particularly glad, in the present instance, you have dealt thus freely and like a friend. Although I could not help observing from several publications and letters that my name had been sometimes spoken of, and that it was possible the *Contingency* which is the subject of your letter might happen; yet I thought it best to maintain a guarded silence and to lack the *counsel* of my best friends (which I certainly hold in the highest estimation) rather than to hazard an imputation unfriendly to the delicacy of my feelings. For, situated as I am, I could hardly bring the question into the slightest discussion, or ask an opinion even in the most confidential manner; without betraying, in my judgment, some impropriety of conduct, or without feeling an apprehension that a premature display of anxiety, might be construed into a vain-glorious desire of pushing myself into notice as a Candidate. Now, if I am not grossly deceived in myself, I should unfeignedly rejoice, in case the Electors, by giving their votes in favor of some other person, would save me from the dreaded Dilemma of being forced to accept or refuse. If that may not be—I am, in the next place, earnestly desi[r]ous of searching out the truth, and of knowing whether there does not exist a probability that the government would be just as happily and effectually carried into execution, without my aid, as with it. I am *truly* solicitous to obtain all the previous information which the circumstances will afford, and to determine (when the determination can with propriety be no longer postponed) according to the principles of right reason, and the dictates of a clear conscience; without too great a referrence to the unforeseen consequences, which may affect my person or reputation. Untill that period, I may fairly hold myself open to conviction—though I allow your sentiments to have weight in them; and I shall not pass by your arguments without giving them as dispassionate a consideration, as I can possibly bestow upon them.

In taking a survey of the subject in whatever point of light I have been able to place it; I will not surpress the acknowledgment, my Dr Sir that I have always felt a kind of gloom upon my mind, as often as I have been taught to expect, I might, and perhaps must ere long be called to make a decision. You will, I am well assured, believe the assertion (though I have little expectation it would gain credit from those who are less acquainted with me) that if I should receive the appointment and if I should be prevailed upon to accept it; the acceptance would be attended with more diffidence and reluctance than ever I experienced before in my life. It would be, however, with a fixed and sole determination of lending whatever assistance might be in my power to promote the public weal, in hopes that at a convenient and an early period, my services might be dispensed with, and that I might be permitted once more to retire — to pass an unclouded evening, after the stormy day of life, in the bosom of domestic tranquility. But why these anticipations? — if the friends to the Constitution conceive that my administering the government will be a means of its acceleration and strength, is it not probable that the adversaries of it may entertain the same ideas? and of course make it an object of opposition? That many of this description will become Electors, I can have no doubt of: any more than that their opposition will extend to any character who (from whatever cause) would be likely to thwart their measures. It might be impolite in them to make this declaration *previous* to the Election, but I shall be out in my conjectures if they do not act conformably thereto — and from that the seeming moderation by which they appear to be actuated at present is neither more nor less than a finesse to lull and deceive. Their plan of opposition is system[at]ised, and a regular intercourse, I have much reason to believe between the Leaders of it in the several States is formed to render it more effectual.

With sentiments of sincere regard and esteem I have, the honor to be &c.

Letter from Alexander Hamilton to Theodore Sedgwick
October 9, 1788

Assuming that Washington's hesitation could be taken for consent, Hamilton and his associates turned their attention to the Vice-Presidency. Although initially unsure about John Adams, they were in agreement that a Massachusetts man was desirable, and were equally sure that Governor George Clinton of New York ("the other Gentleman") was not.

My Dear Sir, On the subject of Vice President, my ideas have concurred with yours, and I believe Mr. Adams will have the votes of this state. He will certainly, I think, be preferred to the other Gentleman. Yet, *certainly*, is perhaps too strong a word. I can conceive that the other, who is supposed to be a more pliable man may command Antifoederal influence.

The only hesitation in my mind with regard to Mr. Adams has arisen within a day or two; from a suggestion by a particular Gentleman that he is unfriendly in his sentiments to General Washington. Richard H Lee who will probably, as rumour now runs, come from Virginia is also in this state. The Lees and Adams' have been in the habit of uniting; and hence may spring up a Cabal very embarrassing to the Executive and of course to the administration of the Government. Consider this. Sound the reality of it and let me hear from you.

What think You of Lincoln or Knox? This is a flying thought.

Yrs. with sincere regard

Letter from Alexander Hamilton to James Wilson
January 25, 1789

In this letter to Wilson, a prominent Pennsylvania supporter of the Constitution, Hamilton exhibits both an equivocal attitude towards John Adams and an astute awareness of the potential hazards of the electoral mechanism.

My Dear Sir, A degree of anxiety about a matter of primary importance to the new government induces me to trouble you with this letter. I mean the election of the President. We all feel of how much moment it is that Washington should be the man; and I own I cannot think there is material room to doubt that this will be the unanimous sense. But as a failure in this object would be attended with the worst consequences I cannot help concluding that even possibilities should be guarded against.

Every body is aware of that defect in the constitution which renders it possible that the man intended for Vice President may in fact turn up President. Every body sees that unanimity in Adams as Vice President and a few votes insidiously witheld from Washington might substitute the former to the latter. And every body must perceive that there is something to fear from machinations of Antifoederal malignity. What in this situation is wise?

By my accounts from the North I have every reason to believe that Adams will run there universally. I learn that he is equally espoused in Jersey Pensylvania & Delaware & that Maryland is not disinclined to him. I hear of no persons thought of to the South, but Rutlege in South Carolina and Clinton in Virginia. As the accounts of the appointments of electors will satisfy the partisans of those Gentlemen in each of those States that they will have no co-adjustors elsewhere, it seems not improbable that they will relinquish the attempt in favour of their intended candidates. Here then is a *chance* of unanimity in Adams. Nothing [is] so apt to beget it as the opinion that the current sets irresistably towards him. Men are fond of going with the stream. Suppose personal caprice or hostility to the new system should occasion half a dozen votes only to be witheld from Washington — what may not happen? Grant there is little danger. If any, ought it to be run?

The votes from New Hampshire to Delaware inclusively & exclusive of New York are 41, South of Delaware 32. Here supposing equal unanimity on each side in a different candidate the chance is that there will be Eight votes to spare from Adams leaving him still a majority. Take the probability of unanimity in the North in Adams & of division in the South between different candidates and the chances are almost infinite in his favour. Hence I conclude it will be prudent to throw a few votes say 7 or 8; giving these to persons not otherwise thought of. Under this impression I have proposed to friends in Connecticut to throw away two to others in Jersey to throw away an equal number & I submit it to you whether it will not be well to lose three or four in Pensylvania. Your advices from the South will serve you as the best guide; but for God's sake let not our zeal for a secondary object defeat or endanger a first. I admit that in several important views and particularly to avoid disgust to a man who would be a formidable head to Antifoederalists – it is much to be desired that Adams may have the plurality of suffrages for Vice President; but if risk is to be run on one side or on the other can we hesitate where it ought to be preferred?

If there appears to you to be any danger, will it not be well for you to write to Maryland to *qualify* matters there?

Yrs sincerely & affecly

Letter from Jeremiah Wadsworth to Alexander Hamilton
February (n.d.), 1789

Hamilton was actively lobbying other cronies, including Wadsworth of Connecticut. Edward Carrington, a Virginia Federalist, had intimated that critics of the Constitution favored Clinton for the Vice-Presidency. The Hamiltonian maneuver succeeded. Washington received unanimous support from the electors (69 votes); Adams came second (34 votes) but so much in the rear that his innocent self-esteem was bruised.

My Dear Sir Your favor of the 25 Jany came in good time. Our Votes were given agreeably to your wishes Washington 7 — Adams 5. Governor Huntington 2. By letters from Carrington I learn that Clinton is the antifederal Vice President but I think we have nothing to fear. I believe N Hampshire will give Adams 4. Massachusetts 6 — Georgia 6 as letters from Georgia say he will have at least so many — which with ours makes 21, which is more than Clinton can get & we may certainly reckon on Nine Men for Adams in So Carolina Maryland Delaware Pensylvanea & N Jersey. We waved an answer to Your State & Virginia as you did not get my letter in Season to answer me on that Subject I feared we should not do any good by an answer — and as ye Antifederalists did not move it — I thot we had best let it Sleep. . . .

I am dear Sir your Affectionate friend

Presidential Power
1787; 1804; 1969

The portion of the 1787 Constitution dealing with presidential powers was not very explicit. It went into detail, however, to explain the electoral procedure; and these sentences were to be much studied (and worried over) until they were revised by the Twelfth Amendment (1804). One hundred and sixty-five years later Congress passed a proposed amendment providing for the direct popular election of Presidents.

Federal Constitution:
Article II, Section I

. . . The executive Power shall be vested in a President of the United States of America. He shall hold his Office during the Term of four Years, and, together with the Vice President, chosen for the same Term, be elected, as follows

Each State shall appoint, in such Manner as the Legislature thereof may direct, a Number of Electors, equal to the whole Number of Senators and Representatives to which the State may be entitled in the Congress: but no Senator or Representative, or Person holding an Office of Trust or Profit under the United States, shall be appointed an Elector.

The electors shall meet in their respective States, and vote by ballot for two persons, of whom one at least shall not be an inhabitant of the same State with themselves. And they shall make a list of all the persons voted for, and of the number of votes for each; which list they shall sign and certify, and transmit sealed to the seat of the Government of the United States, directed to the President of the Senate. The President of the Senate shall, in the presence of the Senate and House of Representatives, open all the certificates, and the votes shall then be counted. The person having the greatest number of votes shall be the President, if such number be a majority of the whole number of electors appointed; and if there be more than one who have such majority, and have an equal number of votes, then the House of Representatives shall immediately chuse by ballot one of them for President; and if no person have a majority, then from the five highest on the list the said House shall in like manner chuse the President. But in chusing the President, the votes shall be taken by States, the representation from each State having one vote; a quorum for this purpose shall consist of a member or members from two-thirds of the States, and a majority of all the States shall be necessary to a choice. In every case, after the choice of the President, the person having the greatest number of votes of the electors shall be the Vice President. But if there should remain two or more who have equal votes, the Senate shall chuse from them by ballot the Vice President.

The Congress may determine the Time of chusing the Electors, and the Day on which they shall give their Votes; which Day shall be the same throughout the United States.

No person except a natural born Citizen, or a Citizen of the United States, at the time of the Adoption of this Constitution, shall be eligible to the Office of President; neither shall any Person be eligible to that office who shall not have attained to the Age of thirty five Years, and been fourteen Years a Resident within the United States.

In Case of the Removal of the President from Office, or of his Death, Resignation or Inability to discharge the Powers and Duties of the said Office, the Same shall devolve on the Vice President, and the Congress may by Law provide for the Case of Removal, Death, Resignation or Inability, both of the President and Vice President, declaring what Officer shall then act as President, and such Officer shall act accordingly, until the Disability be removed, or a President shall be elected.

The President shall, at stated Times, receive for his Services, a Compensation, which shall neither be encreased nor diminished during the Period for which he shall have been elected, and he shall not receive within that Period any other Emolument from the United States, or any of them.

Before he enter on the Execution of his Office, he shall take the following Oath or Affirmation: — "I do solemnly swear (or affirm) that I will faithfully execute the Office of President of the United States, and will to the best of my Ability, preserve, protect and defend the Constitution of the United States."

Federal Constitution:
Twelfth Amendment

The Electors shall meet in their respective states, and vote by ballot for President and Vice-President, one of whom, at least, shall not be an inhabitant of the same state with themselves; they shall name in their ballots the person voted for as President, and in distinct ballots the persons voted for as Vice-President, and they shall make distinct lists of all persons voted for as President, and of all persons voted for as Vice-President, and of the number of votes for each, which lists they shall sign and certify, and transmit sealed to the seat of the government of the United States, directed to the President of the Senate; — The President of the Senate shall, in the presence of the Senate and House of Representatives, open all certificates and the votes shall then be counted; — The person having the greatest number of votes for President, shall be the President, if such number be a majority of the whole number of Electors appointed; and if no person have such majority, then from the persons having the highest numbers not exceeding three on the list of those voted for as President, the House of Representatives shall choose immediately, by ballot, the President. But in choosing the President, the votes shall be taken by states, the representation from each state having one vote; a quorum for this purpose shall consist of a member or members from two-thirds of the states, and a majority of all the states shall be necessary to a choice. And if the House of Representatives shall not choose a President whenever the right of choice shall devolve upon them, before the fourth day of March next following, then the Vice-President shall act as President, as in the case of the death or other constitutional disability of the President. — The person having the greatest number of votes as Vice-President, shall be the Vice-President, if such number be a majority of the whole number of Electors appointed, and if no person have a majority, then from the two highest numbers on the list, the Senate shall choose the Vice-President; a quorum for the purpose shall consist of two-thirds of the whole number of Senators, and a majority of the whole number shall be necessary to a choice. But no person constitutionally ineligible to the office of President shall be eligible to that of Vice-President of the United States.

Proposed Election Amendment
September 18, 1969

Section 1. The people of the several states and the district constituting the seat of Government of the United States shall elect the President and Vice President. Each elector shall cast a single vote for two persons who shall have consented to the joining of their names as candidates for the office of President and Vice President. No candidate shall consent to the joinder of his name with that of more than one other person.

Section 2. The electors of President and Vice President in each state shall have the qualifications requisite for electors of the most numerous branch of the state legislature, except that for electors of President and Vice President the legislature of any state may prescribe less restrictive residence qualifications, and for electors of President and Vice President the Congress may establish uniform residence qualifications.

Section 3. The pair of persons having the greatest number of votes for President and Vice President shall be elected, if such number be at least 40 per centum of the whole number of votes cast for such offices. If no pair of persons has such number, a runoff election shall be held in which the choice of President and Vice President shall be made from the two pairs of persons who received the highest numbers of votes.

Section 4. The time, place and manner of holding such elections and entitlement to inclusion on the ballot shall be prescribed in each state by the legislature thereof, but the Congress may at any time by law make or alter such regulations. The days for such elections shall be determined by Congress and shall be uniform throughout the United States. The Congress shall prescribe by law the time, place and manner in which the results of such elections shall be ascertained and declared.

Section 5. The Congress may by law provide for the case of the death or withdrawal of any candidate for President or Vice President before a President and Vice President have been elected, and for the case of the death of both the President-elect and Vice President-elect.

Section 6. The Congress shall have power to enforce this article by appropriate legislation.

Section 7. This article shall take effect one year after the 21st day of January following ratification.

Personal Memorandum of James Madison
May 25, 1792

In this personal memorandum, Madison reviews Washington's reasons for seeking retirement at the end of his first term.

Substance of a Conversation with the President 5th May, 1792.

In consequence of a note this morning from the President requesting me to call on him I do so; when he opened the conversation by observing, that having some time ago communicated to me his intention of retiring from public life on the expiration of his four years, he wished to advise with me on the *mode* and *time* most proper for making known that intention. He had he said spoken with no one yet on those *particular points*, and took this opportunity of mentioning them to me, that I might consider the matter, and give him my opinion, before the adjournment of congress, or my departure from Philadelphia. He had he said forborne to communicate his intention to any other persons whatever, but M[r] Jefferson, Col. Hamilton, General Knox & myself, and of late to M[r] Randolph. Col: Hamilton & Gen[l] Knox he observed were extremely importunate that he should relinquish his purpose, and had made pressing representations to induce him to it M[r] Jefferson had expressed his wishes to the like effect. He had not however persuaded himself that his continuance in public life could be of so much necessity or importance as was conceived, and his disinclination to it, was becoming every day more & more fixed; so that he wished to make up his mind as soon as possible on the points he had mentioned. – What he desired was to prefer that mode which would be most remote from the appearance of arrogantly presuming on his re-election in case he should not withdraw himself, and such a time as would be most convenient to the public in making the choice of his successor. It had, he said, at first occurred to him, that the commencement of the ensuing Session of Congress, would furnish him with an apt occasion for introducing the intimation, but besides the lateness of the day, he was apprehensive that it might possibly produce some notice in the reply of Congress that might entangle him in further explanations.

I replied that I would revolve the subject as he desired and communicate the result before leaving Philad[a], but that I could not but yet hope there would be no necessity at this time for his decision on the two points he had stated. I told him that when he did me the honor to mention the resolution he had taken, I had forborne to do more than briefly express my apprehensions that it would give a surprize and shock to the public mind, being restrained from enlarging on the subject by an unwillingness to express sentiments sufficiently known to him; or to urge objections to a determination, which if absolute, it might look like affection to oppose; that the aspect which things had been lat-

terly assuming, seemed however to impose the task on all who had the opportunity, of urging a continuance of his public services; and that under such an
impression I held it a duty, not indeed to express my wishes which would be
superfluous, but to offer my opinion that his retiring at the present juncture,
might have effects that ought not to be hazarded; that I was not unaware of
the urgency of his inclination; or of the peculiar motives he might feel to withdraw himself from a situation into which it was so well known to myself he
had entered with a scrupulous reluctance; that I well recollected the embarrassments under which his mind labored in deciding the question, on which he
had consulted me, whether it could be his duty to accept his present station
after having taken a final leave of public life; and that it was particularly in my
recollection, that I then entertained & intimated a wish that his acceptance,
which appeared to be indispensable, might be known hereafter to have been in
no degree the effect of any motive which strangers to his character might suppose. but of the severe sacrifice which his friends knew. he made of his inclinations as a man, to his obligations as a citizen; that I owned I had at that
time contemplated, & I believed, suggested as the most unequivocal tho' not
the proof of his real motives, a voluntary return to private life as soon as the
state of the Government would permit, trusting that if any premature casualty
should unhappily cut off the possibility of this proof, the evidence known to
his friends would in some way or other be saved from oblivion and do justice
to his character; that I was not less anxious on the same point now than I was
then; and if I did not conceive that reasons of a like kind to those which required him to undertake, still required him to retain for some time longer, his
present station; or did not presume that purity of his motives would be
sufficiently vindicated, I should be the last of his friends to press, or even to
wish such a determination.

He then entered on a more explicit disclosure of the state of his mind; observing that he could not believe or conceive himself anywise necessary to the
successful administration of the Government; that on the contrary he had
from the beginning found himself deficient in many of the essential
qualifications, owing to his inexperience in the forms of public business, his
unfitness to judge of legal questions, and questions arising out of the Constitution; that others more conversant in such matters would be better able to execute the trust; that he found himself also in the decline of life, his health becoming sensibly more infirm, & perhaps his faculties also; that the fatigues &
disagreeableness of his situation were in face scarcely tolerable to him; that
he only uttered his real sentiments when he declared that his inclination
would lead him rather to go to his farm, take his spade in his hand, and work
for his bread, than remain in his present situation; that it was evident moreover that a spirit of party in the Government was becoming a fresh source of
difficulty, and he was afraid was dividing some (alluding to the Secretary of
State & Secy. of the Treasury) more particularly connected with him in the
administration; that there were discontents among the people which were also
shewing themselves more & more, & that altho' the various attacks against
public men & measures had not in general been pointed at him, yet in some

instances it had been visible that he was the indirect object, and it was probable the evidence would grow stonger and stronger that his return to private
life was consistent with every public consideration, and consequently that he
was justified in giving way to his inclination for it.

I was led by his explanation to remark to him, that however novel or
difficult the business might have been to him, it could not be doubted that with
the aid of the official opinions & informations within his command, his judgment must have been as competent in all cases, as that of any one who could
have been put in his place, and in many cases certainly more so; that in the
great point of conciliating and uniting all parties under a Gov^t which had excited such violent controversies & divisions, it was well known that his services had been in a manner essential; that with respect to the spirit of party
that was taking place under the operations of the Gov^t I was sensible of its
existence but considered that as an argument for his remaining, rather than
retiring, until the public opinion, the character of the Gov^t and the course of
its administration sh^d be better decided, which could not fail to happen in a
short time, expecially under his auspices; that the existing parties did not appear to be so formidable to the Gov^t as some had represented; that in one party
there might be a few who retaining their original disaffection to the Gov^t
might still wish to destroy it, but that they would lose their weight with their
associates, by betraying any such hostile purposes; that altho' it was pretty
certain that the other were in general unfriendly to republican Gov^t and probably aimed at a gradual approximation of ours to a mixt monarchy, yet the
public sentiment was so strongly opposed to their views, and so rapidly manifesting itself, that the party could not long be expected to retain a dangerous
influence; that it might reasonably be hoped therefore that the conciliating
influence of a temperate & wise administration, would before another term of
four years should run out, give such a tone & firmness to the Government as
would secure it against danger from either of these descriptions of enemies;
that altho' I would not allow myself to believe but that the Gov^t would be
safely administered by any successor elected by the people, yet it was not to
be denied that in the present unsettled condition of our young Government, it
was to be feared that no successor would answer all the purposes to be expected from the continuance of the present chief magistrate; that the option
evidently lay between a few characters; Mr Adams, Mr Jay & Mr Jefferson
were most likely to be brought into view; that with respect to Mr Jefferson,
his extreme repugnance to public life & anxiety to exchange it for his farm &
his philosophy, made it doubtful with his friends whether it would be possible
to obtain his own consent; and if obtained, whether local prejudices in the
Northern States, with the views of Pennsylvania in relation to the seat of
Gov^t would not be a bar to his appointment. — With respect to Mr Adams, his
monarchical principles, which he had not concealed, with his late conduct on
the representation-bill had produced such a settled dislike among republicans
every where & particularly in the Southern States, that he seemed to be out of
the question. It would not be in the power of those who might be friendly to
his private character, & willing to trust him in a public one, notwithstanding

his political principles, to make head against the torrent. With respect to Mr Jay his election would be extremely dissatisfactory on several accounts. By many he was believed to entertain the same obnoxious principles with Mr Adams & at the same time would be less open and therefore more successful in propagating them. By others (a pretty numerous class) he was disliked & distrusted, as being thought to have opposed the claims of British Creditors at the expence of the reasonable pretensions of his fellow Citizens in debt to them. Among the western people, to whom his negociations for ceding the Mississippi to Spain were generally known, he was considered as their most dangerous enemy & held in peculiar distrust & disesteem. In this state of our prospects, which was rendered more striking by a variety of temporary circumstances, I could not forbear thinking that altho' his retirement might not be fatal to the public good, yet a postponement of it was another sacrifice exacted by his patriotism.

Without appearing to be any wise satisfied with what I had urged, he turned the conversation to other subjects; & when I was withdrawing repeated his request that I would think of the points he had mentioned to me, and let him have my ideas on them before the adjournment. I told him I would do so; but still hoped his decision on the main question, would supersede for the present all such incidental questions.

Wednesday Evening May 9, 1792

Understanding that the President was to set out the ensuing morning for Mount Vernon, I called on him to let him know that as far as I had formed an opinion of the subject he had mentioned to me, it was in favor of direct address of notification to the public in time for its proper effect on the election, which I thought might be put into such a form as would avoid every appearance of presumption or indelicacy, and seemed to be absolutely required by his situation. I observed that no other mode deserving consideration had occurred, except the one he had thought of & rejected, which seemed to me liable to the objections that had weighed with him. I added that if on further reflection I sh^d view the subject in any new lights, I would make it the subject of a letter tho' I retained my hopes that it would not yet be necessary for him to come to any opinion on it. He begged that I would do so, and also suggest any matters that might occur as proper to be included in what he might say to Cong^s at the opening of their next Session, passing over the idea of his relinquishing his purpose of retiring, in a manner that did not indicate the slightest assent to it.

Excerpts from a Letter from Thomas Jefferson to President George Washington
May 23, 1792

In this letter Jefferson urged Washington not to give up the Presidency.

I have determined to make the subject of a letter, what, for some time past, has been a subject of inquietude to my mind without having found a good occasion of disburthening itself to you in conversation, during the busy scenes which occupied you here. perhaps too you may be able, in your present situation, or on the road, to give it more time & reflection than you could do here at any moment.

When you first mentioned to me your purpose of retiring from the government, tho' I felt all the magnitude of the event, I was in a considerable degree silent. I knew that, to such a mind as yours, persuasion was idle & impertinent: that before forming your decision, you had weighed all the reasons for & against the measure, had made up your mind on full view of them, & that there could be little hope of changing the result. pursuing my reflections too I knew we were some day to try to walk alone; and if the essay should be made while you should be alive & looking on, we should derive confidence from that circumstance, & resource if it failed. the public mind too was then calm & confident, and there in a favorable state for making the experiment. had no change of circumstances supervened, I should not, with any hope of success, have now ventured to propose to you a change of purpose but the public mind is no longer so confident and serene; and that from causes in which you are in no ways personally mixed.

*   *   *

I can scarcely contemplate a more incalculable evil than the breaking of the union into two or more parts, yet when we review the mass which opposed the original coalescence, when we consider that it lay chiefly in the Southern quarter, . . .

*   *   *

. . . Who can be sure that these things may not proselyte the small number which was wanting to place the majority on the other side? and this is the event at which I tremble, & to prevent which I consider your continuance at the head of affairs as of the last importance. the confidence of the whole union is centered in you. your being at the helm, will be more than an answer to every argument which can be used to alarm & lead the people in any quarter into violence or secession. North & South will hang together, if they have you to hang on: and, if the first corrective of a numerous representation should fail in it's effect, your presence will give time for trying others not inconsistent with the union & peace of the states.

I am perfectly aware of the oppression under which your present office lays your mind, & the ardor with which you pant for retirement to domestic life. but there is sometimes an eminence of character on which society have such peculiar claims as to controul the predilection of the individual for a particular walk of happiness, & restrain him to that alone arising from the present & future benedictions of mankind. this seems to be your condition. & the law imposed on you by providence in forming your character, & fashioning the events on which it was to operate: and it is to motives like these, & not to personal anxieties of mine or others who have no right to call on you for sacrifices, that I appeal from your former determination & urge a revisal of it, on the ground of change in the aspect of things. should an honest majority result from the new & enlarged representation; should those acquiesce whose principles or interests they may controul, your wishes for retirement would be gratified with less danger, as soon as that shall be manifest, without awaiting the completion of the second period of four years. one or two sessions will determine the crisis: and I cannot but hope that you can resolve to add one or two more to the many years you have already sacrificed to the good of mankind.

The fear of suspicion that any selfish motive of continuance in office may enter into this sollicitation on my part obliges me to declare that no such motive exists.

*   *   *

Weighty motives for your continuance are to be found in our foreign affairs. I think it probable that both the Spanish & English negociations, if not completed before your purpose is known, will be suspended from the moment it is known; & that the latter nation will then use double diligence in fomenting the Indian war. — With my wishes for the future I shall at the same time express my gratitude for the past, at least my portion in it; & beg permission to follow you whether in public or private life with those sentiments of sincere attachment & respect, with which I am unalterably, Dear Sir,

Your affectionate friend & humble servant

Letter from Alexander Hamilton to
President George Washington
July—August, 1792

Alexander Hamilton advised Washington that his reelection would be unanimous and urged the President to serve another term.

Sir. I received the most sincere pleasure at finding in our last conversation, that there was some relaxation in the disposition you had before discovered to decline a reelection. Since your departure, I have lost no opportunity of sounding the opinions of persons, whose opinions were worth knowing, on these two points—1st the effect of your declining upon the public affairs, and upon your own reputation—2dly. the effect of your continuing, in reference to the declarations you have made of your disinclination to public life—And I can truly say, that I have not found the least difference of sentiment, on either point. The impression is uniform—that your declining would be to be deplored as the greatest evil, that could befall the country at the present juncture, and as critically hazardous to your own reputation—that your continuance will be justified in the mind of every friend to his country by the evident necessity for it. Tis clear, says every one, with whom I have conversed, that the affairs of the national government are not yet firmly established—that its enemies, generally speaking, are as inveterate as ever—that their enmity has been sharpened by its success and by all the resentments which flow from disappointed predictions and mortified vanity—that a general and strenuous effort is making in every state to place the administration of it in the hands of its enemies, as if they were its safest guardians—that the period of the next house of representatives is likely to prove the crisis of its permanent character—that if you continue in office nothing materially mischievous is to be apprehended—if you quit much is to be dreaded—that the same motives which induced you to accept originally ought to decide you to continue till matters have assumed a more determinate aspect—that indeed it would have been better, as it regards your own character, that you had never consented to come forward, than now to leave the business unfinished and in danger of being undone—that in the event of storms arising there would be an imputation either of want of foresight or want of firmness—and, in fine, that on public and personal accounts, on patriotic and prudential considerations, the clear path to be pursued by you will be again to obey the voice of your country; which it is not doubted will be as earnest and as unanimous as ever.

On this last point, I have some suspicion that it will be insinuated to you, and perhaps (God forgive me, if I judge hardly) with design to place before you a motive of declining—that there is danger of a division among the electors and of less unanimity in their suffrages than heretofore. My view of this matter is as follows:

While your first election was depending I had no doubt, that there would be characters among the electors, who if they durst follow their inclinations, would have voted against you; but that in all probability they would be restrained by an apprehension of public resentment—that nevertheless it was possible a few straggling votes might be found in opposition, from some headstrong and fanatical individuals—that a circumstance of this kind would be in fact, and ought to be estimated by you, as of no importance—since their would be sufficient unanimity to witness the general confidence and attachment towards you.

My view of the future accords exactly with what was my view of the past. I believe the same motives will operate to produce the same result. The dread of public indignation will be likely to restrain the indisposed few. If they can calculate at all, they will naturally reflect that they could not give a severer blow to their cause than by giving a proof of hostility to you. But if a solitary vote or two should appear wanting to perfect unanimity, of what moment can it be? Will not the fewness of the exceptions be a confirmation of the devotion of the community to a character, which has so generally united its suffrages, after an administration of four years at the head of a new government, opposed in its first establishment by a large proportion of its citizens and obliged to run counter to many prejudices in devising the arduous arrangements, requisite to public Credit and public Order? Will not those, who may be the authors of any such exceptions, manifest more their own perverseness and malevolence than any diminution of the affection and confidence of the Nation? I am persuaded, that both these questions ought to be answered in the affirmative; and that there is nothing to be looked for, on the score of diversity of sentiment which ought to weigh for a moment.

I trust, Sir, and I pray God that you will determine to make a further sacrifice of your tranquillity and happiness to the public good. I trust that it need not continue above a year or two more—And I think that it will be more eligibile to retire from office before the expiration of the term of an election, than to decline a reelection.

The sentiments I have delivered upon this occasion, I can truly say, proceed exclusively from an anxious concern for the public welfare and an affectionate personal attachment. These dispositions must continue to govern in every vicissitude one who has the honor to be very truly and respectfully
Sir Your most Obedt. & hum serv

Excerpts from a Letter from Edmund Randolph
to President George Washington
August 5, 1792

Edmund Randolph predicted dire consequences for the young republic if Washington did not accept a second term.

I have persuaded myself, that this letter, tho' unconnected with any official relation, and upon a subject to the decision of which you alone are competent, will be received in the spirit, with which it is written.

*   *   *

It is feared by those, who take a serious interest in the affairs of the U.S. that you will refuse the chair of government at the approaching election. If such an event must happen, indulge me at least in the liberty of opening to you a course of thought, which a calm attention to the federal government has suggested, and no bias of party has influenced.

*   *   *

In this threatening posture of our affairs, we must gain time, for the purpose of attracting confidence in the government by an experience of its benefits, and that man alone, whose patronage secured the adoption of the constitution, can check the assaults, which it will sustain at the two next sessions of congress.

*   *   *

The fuel, which has been already gathered for combustion, wants no addition. But how awfully might it be increased, were the violence, which is now suspended by an universal submission to your pretensions, let loose by your resignation. . . . The constitution would never have been adopted, but from a knowledge, that you had once sanctified it, and an expectation, that you would execute it. It is in a state of probation. The most inauspicious struggles are past; but the public deliberations need stability. You alone can give them stability. You suffered yourself to yield, when the voice of your country summoned you to the administration. Should a civil war arise, you cannot stay at home. And how much easier will it be, to disperse the factions, which are rushing to this catastrophe, than to subdue them, after they shall appear in arms? It is the fixed opinion of the world, that you surrender nothing incomplete.

I am not apprized of many disagreeable sensations, which have laboured in your breast. But let them spring from any cause whatsoever, of one thing I am sure (and I speak this from a satisfactory inquiry lately made) tho if a second opportunity shall be given to the people of showing their gratitude, they will not be less unanimous than before.

Reply from President George Washington
to Edmund Randolph
August 26, 1792

In his answer to Edmund Randolph, Washington expressed his desire to return to private life. The President was increasingly disturbed at newspaper critiscism directed at his Administration.

My dear Sir, The purpose of this letter is merely to acknowledge the receipt of your favors of the 5th & 13th inst', and to thank you for the information contained in both without entering into the details of either. —

With respect, however, to the interesting subject treated on in that of the 5th I can express but one sentiment at this time, and that is a wish—a devout one—that whatever my ultimate determination shall be, it may be for the best. — The subject never recurs to my mind but with additional poignancy; and from the declining state in the health of my Nephew, to whom my concerns of a domestic & private nature are entrusted it comes with aggrivated force — But as the allwise disposer of events has hitherto watched over my steps, I trust that in the important one I may soon be called upon to take, he will mark the course so plainly, as that I cannot mistake the way. — In full hope of this, I will take no measures yet a while, that will not leave me at liberty to decide from circumstances, & the best lights I can obtain on the subject. —

I should be happy in the mean time to see a cessation of the abuses of public officers—and of those attacks upon almost every measure of government with which some of the Gazettes are so strongly pregnated; & which cannot fail, if persisted in with the malignancy they now team, of rending the Union asunder. The seeds of discontent—distrust & irritations which are so plentifully sown—can scarcely fail to produce this effect and to mar that prospect of happiness which perhaps never beamed with more affluence upon any people under the Sun—and this too at a time when all Europe are gazing with admiration at the brightness of our prospects. — And for what is all this? — Among other things, to afford Nuts for our transatlantic—what shall I call them? —Foes!

In a word if the Government and the officers of it are to be the constant theme for News-paper abuse, and this too without condescending to investigate the motives or the facts, it will be impossible, I conceive, for any man living to manage the helm, or to keep the machine together — But I am running from my test, and therefore will only add assurances of the affect° esteem & regard with which I am always — Yours

Excerpt from a Letter from Alexander Hamilton
to John Steele
October 18, 1792

In this letter Alexander Hamilton endorses John Adams for Vice-President.

The late symptoms of acquiescence in the duty on distilled spirits, which you announce in your quarter are particularly satisfactory. If the people will but make trial of the thing, their good will towards it will increase. This has hitherto happened every where, where the law has gone into operation. There certainly can be no tax more eligible or less burthensome.

Though I impose on myself great circumspection on the subject of elections for the Fœderal Government, yet in relation to the characters you mention, I feel myself more at liberty, and my intire confidence in you will not permit me to affect reserve. I take it for granted that in all the Northern and Middle states, the present President will have an unanimous vote. I trust is will be so in the South also. A want of unanimity would be a blot in our political hemisphere and would wound the mind of that excellent character, to whom this Country is so much indebted.

For Vice President, Mr Adams will have a nearly unanimous vote in the Eastern States. The same thing would happen in New York, if the Electors were to be chosen by the People; but as they will be chosen by the Legislature, and as a majority of the existing assembly are Clintonians, the electors will I fear be of the same complexion. In Jersey Mr. Adams will have a unanimous vote and according to present appearances in Pennsylvania likewise. The parties have had a trial of their strength here for representatives, and though the issue is not finally ascertained, there is a moral certainty from the returns received that the Ticket supported by the Fœderal Interest will prevail by a large majority. The electors *nominated* by the same interest will all or nearly all favour Mr Adams. I believe the weight of Delaware will be thrown into the same scale. And I think it probable there will be votes for Mr. Adams in Maryland. I presume none in Virginia or Georgia. Of North Carolina you can best Judge. In South Carolina, he will have votes but I am at a loss to judge of the proportion.

This statement will inform you, that Mr. Adams is the man, who will be supported in the Northern & Middle States by the friends of the Government. They reason thus — "Mr. Adams like other men has his faults and his foibles. Some of the opinions he is supposed to entertain, we do not approve — but we believe him to be honest firm faithful and independent — a sincere lover of his country — a real friend to genuine liberty; but combining his attachment to that with the love of order and stable government. No man's private character can be fairer than his. No man has given stronger proofs than him of disinterested

& intrepid patriotism. We will therefore support him as far preferable to any one, who is likely to be opposed to him."

Who will be seriously opposed to him I am yet at a loss to decide. One while Governor Clinton appeared to be the man. Of late there have been symptoms of Col Burr's canvassing for it. Some say, one or both of these will be played off as diversion in favour of Mr. Jefferson.

I do not scruple to say to you, that my preference of Mr. Adams to either of these characters is decided. As to Mr. Clinton he is a man of narrow and perverse politics, and as well under the former as under the present Government, he has been steadily since the termination of the war with Great Britain opposed to national principles. My opinion of Mr. Burr is yet to form—but according to the present state of it, he is a man whose only political principle is, to *mount at all events* to the highest legal honours of the Nation and as much further as circumstances will carry him. Imputations not favourable to his integrity as a man rest upon him; but I do not vouch for their authenticity.

There was a time when I should have ballanced between Mr. Jefferson & Mr. Adams; but I now view the former as a man of sublimated & paradoxical imagination—cherishing notions incompatible with regular and firm government.

Thus have I opened myself to you with frankness. I doubt not that I am perfectly safe in doing it.

[For 1789 and 1792 Electoral Votes see pp. 18, 29.]

Election of 1796

PAGE SMITH is Professor of Historical Studies and Provost of Cowell College, University of California, Santa Cruz. Among his many publications is John Adams, *a two-volume biography awarded the 1962 Bancroft Prize.*

Election of 1796

by *Page Smith*

It might well be argued that the election of 1796 was the most important in our history. Washington's unanimous election to the Presidency in 1789 was, of course, a foregone conclusion, as was his reelection in 1792. In the aftermath of the framing of the Federal Constitution the country was united as it would seldom be again. The splendid and immaculate figure of the General seemed to many Americans only slightly less than divine. But the facade of unity soon showed cracks. While Washington retained the greater part of his prestige throughout his term of office, serious divisions appeared in the country, most notably between the adherents of Thomas Jefferson and those of Alexander Hamilton.

The central issue of the election of 1796 was a simple one: could the new republic survive what Fisher Ames, a prominent Federalist, called the "transmigration" of power? Could the office of President devolve from the god-like Washington to an ordinary mortal and do this in a time of bitter factionalism? Could the new nation weather the most crucial transition provided for by the Constitution—the passing of the Presidency from its first occupant to his successor?

To set the stage for the drama of the election of 1796 it is necessary to describe in some detail the "factions" which undertook to contend for the presidential succession. The Jeffersonians, whose strength lay principally in the South, aspired to a primarily agrarian order based on the independent yeoman farmer; they had a deeply ingrained suspicion of the city, of industry, and of finance, strong distrust of centralized government, and confidence in the people to govern themselves locally with a minimum of governmental interference.

The Federalists, on the other hand, were more skeptical of the claims of democracy, more committed to the development of commerce and industry, more favorable to the creditor interest, and more anxious to develop an effective financial structure within a national government with strong executive leadership. The strength of the Federalists lay, for the most part, in New England.

Behind the sectional differences lay opposing economic interests. The South, overwhelmingly agricultural, wished for free trade, low tariffs, and easy money. The North had a preponderance of farmers, of course, but they were small farmers as opposed to the big plantation owners of the South. The wealth and influence of the North were largely in the hands of the commercial class, merchants and traders, with a small but growing class of industrial entrepreneurs.

We can trace in a figure like James Madison the growing tendency toward a polarization of political attitudes based on an increased awareness of diverse economic interests. Madison, who by the early 1790's had emerged as Jefferson's principal lieutenant, had started out as a champion of nationalism, committed to a strong central government and a "national" system of finances. In this spirit he had initially supported tariff proposals, specifically a tonnage duty in 1789. But he had already displayed a sentimental preference for the French in the form of a discriminatory clause directed against foreign nations that had no commercial treaty with the United States. Since the French had such a treaty and the British did not, the clause clearly worked to the disadvantage of the latter. As the bulk of American trade was carried on by New England merchants with Great Britain, Madison was clearly prepared, by inhibiting that trade, to sacrifice the prosperity of the northern states in an effort to extract a commercial treaty from the British Ministry. Not unnaturally, the clause was strongly resisted in the Senate although Madison's version of the bill passed the House. To the argument of the northern merchants that they were being asked to bear the burden of disciplining England, the southerners replied that any tariff was in effect a tax paid for by the South for the protection of northern commerce and industry.

While the economic issue, focusing on the question of the tariff, became in time one of the principal bones of contention in the election of 1796, it was clearly overshadowed by ideological concerns. Historians of modern times have industriously sought (and, of course, have often succeeded in finding) a material basis for political ideas. It is very hard to trace such a connection between practical interests and ideologies in the 1790's. Of course most merchants favored Great Britain and wished for an active trade with that country. But there was, on the face of it, no particular reason why a Virginia planter should hate Britain and feel a passionate attachment to the French Revolution. He lived in a far more aristocratic, indeed feudal, society than did his Massachusetts compatriot. To be sure, he might owe money to a British factor dating from the days before the outbreak of the American Revolution, and he might be determined to resist all efforts to collect such a debt, but that could hardly account for his enthusiasm for the French version of the Rights of Man.

Furthermore it would, of course, be an error to suggest that French supporters were confined to the southern colonies. They were to be found in considerable numbers in every state. Where they were joined with pronounced sectional interests, such as the interest of the South in low tariffs, they predominated; where they found themselves opposed by such interests they ran a strong second. The ideological hard core of the Jeffersonians was made up of individuals who distrusted the infant capitalism that they professed to discern in the North. They did so not from the perspective of the agrarian reformer, but from the perspective of the traditional landholder, to whom merchants and bankers were a threat to an ancient order based on humane values and on relations between people rather than on relations between "pieces of paper." To the feudal southerner the only true property was "real" property, land. Money was suspect and such things as bills of credit were a patent fraud, designed to rob an honest man of his labors. To call a piece of paper "property" seemed to such gentlemen an offense against nature.

Southern planters were not the only ideologues, of course. There were many small farmers and businessmen in the North, and merchants as well, who were friends of the French Revolution because they understood it to be a rejection of all ideas of an elite, of a group entitled by birth, or indeed by education or wealth for that matter, to hold the reins of government under the pretense of a republican system. The new "establishment" which had appeared in the years immediately prior to the Revolution, and which had deepened and extended its power during the Revolution and in the years following, spoke of "an aristocracy of talents," a "natural aristocracy" of men who ruled because of superior gifts (Jefferson was one of the principal supporters of the notion of a natural aristocracy). The non-southern Democrats-Republicans-Jeffersonians (they were known by all three names while their Federalist enemies called them "Jacobins" after the radical French revolutionaries) were in fact searching for a way to express their resistance to a system of paternalism. Although they understood little of what it was about, the French Revolution provided the Jeffersonians with a rationale for aspirations which could not be adequately articulated within the then-accepted assumptions about the distribution and utilization of political power.

Democratic societies sympathetic to the ideals of the Revolution were founded in many parts of the country in the early 1790's. The naval war between France and England which broke out in 1793 added material grievances to ideological differences; the impressment of American sailors and the seizure of American vessels engaged in trade with the belligerents heightened animosities.

Hamilton's astute maneuvers, designed to establish the credit of the United States on a substantial basis and rally the support of the commercial interests by paying off the debts incurred in the War for Independence, further exacerbated feelings between the two factions.

Washington's efforts to preserve American neutrality in the war between France and England were particularly irritating to the pro-French faction, which believed that America's obligations to France represented by the treaties of 1778, if they did not require the active participation of the United States in the war against Great Britain, were at least inconsistent with a policy of neutrality. Supporters of the French cause fitted out privateers to prey on British shipping and to carry contraband. The British in turn issued Orders In Council in November, 1793, instructing the navy to seize all ships laden with French goods or goods intended for France or for any French colony.

In this atmosphere of deepening crisis, Washington dispatched Chief Justice John Jay to England to negotiate a treaty that would, it was hoped, resolve the principal causes of friction between the two countries and thereby lessen the danger of a war for which the United States was entirely unprepared. On the eve of Jay's departure a party of Philadelphia Republicans carried an effigy of the Chief Justice about the streets of the city, guillotined it, and blew it up with gunpowder. This act of symbolic savagery boded ill for any treaty Jay might obtain. In practical fact the Chief Justice, undermined by Hamilton, who assured the British minister that the United States had no intention of going to war, probably got about as good a treaty as could have been obtained under the circumstances. On the British side, George Grenville was forced to defend himself in the House of Commons against the charge that he was pro-American.

But Jay returned to face a storm of indignation by no means confined to the Jeffersonian Republicans. Burning Jay in effigy became a popular outdoor sport. Republicans wore tricolored cockades in their hats to indicate their support of the French, and partisans attacked each other in the streets. Republican newspapers even dared to attack the President himself. Benjamin Franklin's grandson, Benjamin Franklin Bache, editor of the *Aurora*, accused Washington of wishing to be a dictator; and Blair McClenachen, a prominent Philadelphia Republican, brandished a copy of the treaty above his head and shouted to a responsive crowd: "What a damn treaty! I make a motion that every good citizen in this assembly kick this damn treaty to hell." Impaling the treaty on a pole the mob marched first to the house of French Minister Pierre Adêt, and then on to the residence of British Minister George Hammond, where they smashed windows and burned the treaty on his doorstep.

Southern opposition focused on the fact that no indemnity had been secured for slaves carried off by the British during the Revolution. Northern merchants were disgruntled by Jay's failure to win any relaxation of the British regulations directed against neutral shipping. Through the winter of 1795 the country had little on its mind but the unfortunate Jay Treaty. What astonished and discomforted the Federalists was that the violence of the reaction seemed out of all proportion to the treaty's shortcomings. They could not see how the treaty, conceding its not inconsiderable faults, could be the cause of turning the country upside down and raising the spectre of anarchy and civil war. It is hardly surprising that they soon saw their tormentors as fiends and devils bent on destroying the infant republic.

It can be taken as a rule of social life that, when an action taken by those in authority produces a reaction out of all proportion to any conceivable grievance caused by that action, the real problems lie elsewhere and are not fully comprehended by either party. In many instances the most violent opponents of the treaty had not bothered to read it and had only the sketchiest notion of its contents or, indeed, of the issues with which most of its articles dealt. It was enough for them that it was a treaty with Great Britain, the enemy of France, negotiated by the Federalists who were aristocrats and enemies to the rights of man.

It is not going too far to say that the Jay Treaty, infuriating the Republicans and demoralizing the Federalists, posed the greatest threat to the unity of the country prior to the events which began with the Kansas-Nebraska Act and culminated in the Civil War. Today we can face alarms and disorders which, however disturbing, seem to be characteristic of a democratic society. The rancor among Americans generated by the issues of the Viet Nam War and the Black Power movement takes place, after all, against a background of almost 175 years of not merely survival but of remarkable growth and development. The Federal Union and the form of constitutional government which binds it together have provided a remarkably tough and adaptable political order.

The view from 1795 was very different. The framers of the Federal Constitution, indeed leaders of both political persuasions, Federalist and Republican, were only too well aware through their study of ancient history of the dangers that beset republics. They were acutely conscious of how easily the social fabric could be rent by violence, rancor, and public disorder, by, in the word they found most appropriate, "factionalism." Most of them had thus opposed the very notion of rival parties as tending to promote factionalism, and they watched in dismay as parties gradually emerged. Washington of course did his best to reconcile the opposing factions in his own Cabinet and prevailed on Jefferson and Hamilton to work in uneasy tandem long after they were inclined to go their separate ways.

Not only were factions much in evidence by 1795, and parties plainly taking form but political rivalry and personal animosities seemed to increase by the day. Tens of thousands of Americans openly opposed the declared policy of their government and attempted to frustrate its edicts. The Excise Tax was resisted by the farmers of the frontier and South and their resistance finally broke forth in armed rebellion—the Whisky Insurrection—which had to be put down by a force of federal troops.

Outside observers, having in mind classical precedents, were generally skeptical that the Union could survive. This was clearly the opinion of at least some of the ministers of George III. Any treaty with the United States was, in their view, premature. After the disintegration of the Union, advantageous treaties could be made with individual sovereign states. Each state, after all, had its particular interests; sectional differences were acute as well—North versus South, the frontier versus the seacoast, the manufacturing versus the commercial versus the agrarian interests. These differences were, as we have seen, compounded by ideological differences that cut across class and sectional lines. Although material interests, class attachments, and regional loyalties often determined party affiliation, decisions were frequently made on an intensely personal basis; even families were split. Fisher Ames and his brother Dr. Nathaniel Ames were such a family. When Washington signed the Jay Treaty, Nathaniel Ames noted in his journal: "Washington now defies the whole Sovereign that made him what he is — and can unmake him again. Better his hand had been cut off when his glory was at its height, before he blasted all his Laurels." And when Fisher Ames left his sick bed to give the dramatic speech in favor of the Jay Treaty which was judged to have secured its passage, Dr. Ames noted in his journal: "The Treaty fish swallowed, tail foremost, by Congress. The President [Washington] is a rebel against General Washington and United States. . . . Federal Government become near as arbitrary as any European; the worst Tories and Conspirators with English [are] caressed." To Fisher Ames, on the other hand, his brother's pro-French views were the result of "folly and passion."

The most revealing signs of the deterioration of trust, not only in the policy but the morals and good intentions of the government, were the attacks on Washington himself. Bache wrote in the *Aurora*: "If ever a nation was debauched by a man, the American Nation has been debauched by Washington. . . . If ever a Nation has been deceived by a man, the American Nation has been deceived by Washington. . . . Let the history of the Federal Government instruct mankind, that the masque of patriots may be worn to conceal the foulest designs against the liberties of a people."

Violence even invaded churches. During a church service in the town of Raynham, a Francophile took a seat in the gallery wearing a French cockade in his hat. An indignant Federalist knocked the hat off. It "fell from the gallery and the Federalists over benches, pews, etc., ran and caught it, from which they dismounted the detested 'ade. There was followed by clinching, swearing, and even by blows. The screechings of old women heightened the scene. Here were in view justices, lawyers, and even grand juries, all clinched by collars, hairs, and cheeks, until at last the Jacobins were thrust out of the house, some with no hats, others with bloody cheeks, and nearly all with dishevelled polls."

This then was the atmosphere in which the country faced the approach of the election year of 1796. Rumors had circulated since early in 1795 that Washington intended to retire, but Washington, characteristically, kept his own counsel, and John Adams, the man most likely to be affected by the General's decision to return to Mount Vernon, was left to speculate with others on the President's plans and on his own prospects. Adams, at sixty, although widely respected, was far from a popular political figure. Unlike Hamilton or Jay he had no personal following. Even his political principles were the subject of speculation. His enemies accused him of monarchial principles, quoting in proof passages from his *Defence of the Constitutions*, and his supporters found him hard to classify. Like his rival Jefferson he was known as an enemy to banks and banking with a sentimental affection for the northern version of Jefferson's yeoman farmer. But he was far too much his own man and far too reserved to be a successful political leader. There was in him, in addition, a streak of perversity that induced him to often go out of his way to make clear his opposition to popular prejudice or a favorite political nostrum.

In February, 1796, Adams undertook to analyze the probable effects of Washington's retirement. Although he himself had expressed anxiety about the difficulties involved in a transfer of power, on further reflection he decided that there would be "no more danger in the change than there would be in changing a member of the Senate." If Jay or even Jefferson "(and one or the other it certainly will be if the succession should be passed over) should be the man, government will go on as ever," he wrote. "Jefferson would not stir a step in any other system than that which is begun. Jay would not wish it." The office of the President was already, after a brief seven years, so clearly defined that its nature could not be substantially altered.

That, if true, was perhaps the most remarkable fact of all. The major credit was clearly due to Washington. The least flamboyance, the mildest excess of charismatic leadership would have blurred the nature of the office, confused its functions, and made vastly more difficult the problem of succession. Only Washington's extraordinary rectitude allowed the Presidency to emerge — one could hardly say independently of him because he in fact defined it — and acquire a character that could be separated from the personality of Washington himself. This was, in plain fact, an extraordinary and perhaps unique accomplishment.

Adams, continuing his analysis, was sure that the electoral votes would be split between himself, Jay, and Jefferson, with Jefferson clearly the most formidable rival. If Jefferson were elected President and Jay Vice-President, which Adams suggested was the most likely outcome of the election, he would retire "without a murmur of complaint to his farm, forever." On the other hand, if elected President he would serve out one term and then withdraw. Or so at least he professed.

As much as Adams aspired to the Presidency he wrote to his wife that he was unwilling to enter any contest for succession. Such an act would put him at the head of a party and he would quit the country before he would become the agent of party spirit and faction. In such a course he professed to see nothing but "vexation, disease, and death for myself, and nothing but poverty, pride, and a humiliating fall for my children." In Adams' view it would be best for the country if a successor to Washington could be generally agreed upon from among the most likely candidates and the choice, supported by Washington's prestige, made public. The idea was a naive one but it illustrates the anxiety aroused by the prospective dangers of party rivalry.

There was logic in the idea that the Vice-President should succeed the President. He was his successor in event of death or crippling disability and thus presumably chosen in the full knowledge that he might fall heir to the office. Since there was as yet no notion of a presidential "ticket" whereby the vice-presidential candidate was selected because of his appeal to some particular portion of the electorate, the Vice-President would normally be the candidate who was runner-up to the President. Yet the issue was clearly ambiguous. From the beginning there was certainly an awkwardness. In 1789 it was clearly the intention of the College of Electors to elect Washington unanimously. If the electors had cast a single ballot for Washington as President and Adams as Vice-President the two men would have technically tied in votes for the Presidency. It was therefore necessary to abstain by prearrangement from recording a certain number of votes for Adams so that he would fall to second place in the total votes. Such a system of course invited intrigue.

When Jefferson resigned as Secretary of State in Washington's Cabinet to return to his projects and experiments at Monticello, Adams was convinced that the move was a strategic withdrawal, the purpose of which was to give Jefferson an opportunity to plan and promote a campaign to make himself President should Washington step down. Jefferson, now fifty-three years old, strengthened this impression by statements which were interpreted by some as being intended to disarm his opponents and free himself of too close an association with the more extreme Jacobins. Adams believed that his old friend, surrounded by good advisers, "might do very well" as President; "yet," he added, "in such hands as will hold him, he would endanger too much."

James Madison at forty-two, Patrick Henry at fifty-nine, and Alexander Hamilton at thirty-eight were also spoken of as presidential candidates. Henry, as a conservative anti-Jefferson southerner, might draw off a few critical southern votes from Adams. And of course Hamilton, although there was doubt about his eligibility, would obviously be a serious contender.

Adams himself maintained, at least to the world, an attitude of aloofness. He professed to be above the battle—or, in a word which was especially precious to him, "disinterested." If he were called by the country to succeed Washington he would do his duty, but he would never seek the office or solicit the support of party leaders. Yet his constant assessment of his prospects —"Either we must enter upon ardors more trying than ever yet experienced; or retire to Quincy, farmers for life," he wrote Abigail—and his recurrent speculations about the President's intentions reveal clearly enough his own ambition to occupy Washington's office.

Indeed, as soon as it became clear that the presidential succession was a prize that would be warmly contended for, Adams took a perverse satisfaction in the impending contest. It was, after all, his principal prospective rival, Jefferson, who wished the Presidency to be a kind of cipher, who feared its powers and wished them as closely confined as possible, and it was Adams whose championing of a strong executive had exposed him to the charge that he favored monarchy. He wrote Abigail that the Presidency appeared "the great object of contentions—the center and main source of all emulation as the learned Dr. Adams teaches in all his writings, and everybody believes though nobody will own it."

Jefferson, like Adams, disclaimed all interest in being President. He was too devoted to the cultivation of his plantation, to his books and hobbies to be willing to expose himself again to the tumult of public office. So at least he told himself and others. Rumors, nonetheless, circulated of a bargain proposed by certain southerners whereby Adams, as a moderate Federalist, would be accepted as Vice-President if the top spot were to go to Jefferson. When the story reached Adams he rejected the notion out of hand. On one thing he was quite clear—he would not serve as Vice-President under Thomas Jefferson: "I will not be frightened out of the public service, nor will I be disgraced in it." He would, he assured Abigail, take his "resolutions with cool deliberation . . . watch the course of events with . . . critical attention." On the other hand, even if he should become President the chances were that Jefferson, as runner-up in the presidential balloting, would become Vice-President. Since Adams and Jefferson differed so radically on the general principles of government (they were, as Adams put it, "in different boxes"), such an event would, in Adams' view, produce "a dangerous crisis in public affairs."

Convinced that Jefferson would be a candidate, Adams undertook to sound him out. He wrote the Virginian a letter deploring the excesses of the French Revolution. "Passion, prejudice, interest, necessity has governed," he noted, "and a century must roll away before any permanent and quiet system will be established." In reply Jefferson disavowed any active interest in politics. It was "a subject I never loved and now hate." In response to Adams strictures on the French, Jefferson sought a countervailing assurance. "I am sure, from the honesty of your heart," he wrote, "you will join me in detestation of the corruption of the English government."

Jefferson's reply strengthened Adams' conviction that the Virginian would be a candidate for the Presidency, the same kind of candidate as Adams himself—apparently reluctant but open to persuasion and a call to serve his country, but actually, under the necessary cloak of disinterestedness, a determined seeker of the office.

Confiding in Abigail, Adams once again confessed that he considered himself "heir apparent" and expected the support and encouragement of the President, noting at the same time that "the French and the demagogues intended to set aside the descent. . . . I have no very ardent desire," he wrote, "to be the butt of party malevolence. Having tasted of that cup, I find it bitter, nauseous, and unwholesome." Although Adams professed to "hate speeches, messages, addresses and answers, proclamations, and such affected, studied, contraband things . . . levees and drawing rooms," and "speaking to a thousand people to whom I have nothing to say," he was quite capable of performing such duties and indeed seemed determined to do so.

If the prospective candidates were constrained by Washington's silence, the press was not. Benjamin Franklin Bache, editor of the *Aurora*, worked hard for Jefferson—"the good patriot, statesman, and philosopher" was the obvious choice of the people to succeed Washington. Encouraged by Bache and other Republican editors such as Benjamin Austin of Boston, the Democratic clubs began an active Jefferson-for-President campaign.

The Federalists, in turn, busied themselves organizing meetings and rallies in support of the Jay Treaty and the President. Such occasions provided an opportunity to drum up support for the Vice-President. At Ipswich a gathering offered a toast to "John Adams; may his virtues, genius, and knowledge long revolve, the first planet from our political sun." When the word reached

Adams he was pleased at this modest indication of popular support and drew encouragement from the practice reputedly favored by the College of Cardinals of choosing the oldest among them "because he cannot hold the papal chair long." "I am so old," he wrote Abigail, "that they all know they can make me miserable enough to be glad to get out of it as soon as Washington, if not in half the time." Adams' comment is revealing because it reminds us, through Adams' reference to the length of time a President may serve, that the Constitution imposed no limit and Washington or any of his successors might have served as many terms as they and the electorate wished. Adams saw that in the minds of rival politicians his age was an asset since it could reasonably be assumed that he would not seek more than a term or two in office. Since the framers of the Constitution hoped to avoid the rise of parties and factions, it was not unreasonable to assume that the President, presiding benignly over a contented people, might serve, as for example John Winthrop of Massachusetts had done as governor of Massachusetts, for fifteen or twenty years.

Yet Adams himself, confident at one moment of an easy transition, suffered periodic doubts, the more so as contention over the Jay Treaty flared up in the House of Representatives, where the Republicans, thwarted in the Senate, were determined to block the treaty by refusing to appropriate the money needed to give it effect. Adams spoke for many of the friends of the government when he wrote gloomily to Abigail, "What is to come next I do not know." If the House succeeded to undermine the Treaty "it will then be evident that this constitution cannot stand. . . . I see nothing but the dissolution of government and immediate war." There was such rancor of party, he wrote, "that the prospect of a change in administration quite cures me of all desire to have a share in it."

The talk of the possible dissolution of government was not confined to Adams. Federalists and Republicans alike freely predicted the imminent end of the brief experiment in popular government. Fisher Ames was convinced that the "spirit of jacobinism . . . will be a gymnasium in which the turbulent passions will be disciplined and grow strong by exercise. . . . If such a crisis can be produced . . . in the midst of prosperity, peace, and knowledge and while the government is administered with integrity, and with Washington at the head,—does it warrant very sanguine expectations for future tranquillity, when adversity, disturbance, and panic, shall prevail; when the hated head of one party shall exact obedience from the other; when the ruling party shall, as all ruling parties will, abuse its power sometimes and commit blunders at others?"

From early January until March the House wrangled bitterly over the treaty. Fisher Ames, trying to rally the pro-treaty forces, was convinced that the government was sick "and, many of the physicians say, of a mortal disease. A crisis now serious, the most serious I ever witnessed" Oliver Wolcott wrote in the same spirit to Jonathan Dayton a few months later, "I can say to you in *confidence,* that the President (Washington) will decline a reelection. We must therefore take all the risks of a change in the interesting situation that he now possesses. Your regrets on this occasion cannot excel my own. I fear the country is not sufficiently united to make a choice by the electors." And in October Oliver Wolcott Sr. wrote to his son that Washington's succession "will probably ascertain whether our system and union can be preserved."

The Republicans in the House of Representatives, led by Madison and Giles, who were determined to join the issue on the treaty, resembled a poker player who has placed his whole stake on the throw of one card. It was a desperation tactic and they had to succeed or go down. But the strategy was bad; despite their majority in the House they were on weak ground; the longer the debate dragged on the more apparent became the flaws in the Republican case. As strict constructionists, they contended for a complex and implausible interpretation of the Constitution by means of which it could be argued that the House was supposed to have a voice in the making of treaties despite the plain allocation of this responsibility to the President and Senate in the Constitution. (When Madison supported such an interpretation, Washington reminded him that he had argued the contrary position in the Federal Debates themselves.) Moreover, the Republicans were handicapped in their attacks on the good faith and judgment of the Administration by the fact that they did not have access to the official correspondence relating to the treaty. They requested that it be made available to them but Washington, after a week's reflection, refused. Another nice constitutional question! Did the President have the right to refuse such a request made by the legislative branch? The indignant protests of the Republicans had an air of futility about them. It was clear that Washington had no intention of surrendering the documents. The Republicans, compounding their initial error, felt their strength ebbing throughout the winter and early spring. It was reported that Madison appeared "worried to death, pale, withered, haggard," and Edward Livingston, Burr's lieutenant, looked "like horror."

By late spring the anti-treaty faction in the House had been defeated and there was a kind of "armed neutrality," as Fisher Ames called it, between the parties. It seemed clear that Adams would be the candidate of the Federalists while Jefferson would be put forward by the Republicans. Ames believed that events favored Adams. The intractability of the Republicans and their assaults on Washington had caused a reaction in favor of the Federalists as the champions of the Constitution and of reason as opposed to passion. The battle in the House which had kept public opinion in a turmoil for months had, at the same time, cleared the air. In Fisher Ames' view, "The People are calm, and reason has made herself understood. . . . Since the Treaty we see nothing but blue sky."

Throughout the summer of 1796 Washington remained silent about his own plans, his intention undoubtedly being to prevent open electioneering with its attendant divisiveness. In consequence everything had to be done backstage. Samuel Otis and other visitors from Philadelphia brought word to John Adams, tending his farm in Quincy, that Washington remained unshaken in his determination to retire. David Howell from Rhode Island sounded out Adams on the notion of having Hamilton as his Vice-President. Adams was cautiously noncommittal, but it is safe to assume that he had even less enthusiasm for Hamilton than for Jefferson.

It was September 17 before Washington announced publicly that he would not be a candidate. The vehicle of his announcement was his Farewell Address, a carefully articulated statement of Federalist principles, appealing in eloquent tones for peace at home and abroad. The strictures against faction were reinforced by Washington's recruitment of Madison and Hamilton to help frame the address. His warning against "excessive partiality for one foreign nation and excessive dislike of another" seemed, in light of the controversy over the Jay Treaty, to be directed against the Republicans. But the address as a whole bespoke a wise and humane spirit, and could be as appropriately quoted to those Anglophiles who abhorred the French as to the enthusiastic "Jacobins" who wished to have the United States take up arms against the English.

Bache hailed the news of Washington's retirement as a deliverance and castigated the President as "the source of all the misfortunes of our country . . . . Every heart in unison with the freedom and happiness of the people ought to beat high with exultation that the name of Washington from this day ceases to give currency to political iniquity and to legalized corruption."

The Farewell Address was, in the words of Fisher Ames, "a signal, like dropping a hat, for the party racers to start." It then became the task of the Federalists to secure, in the two months remaining, the election of men to the Electoral College known to be loyal to Federalist principles and, hopefully, favorable to the candidacy of John Adams.

In a move to draw southern support away from Jefferson, the Federalists prevailed on Thomas Pinckney to run on the ticket with Adams. Pinckney's name on the ballot might also attract some votes in Pennsylvania and Maryland.

With Thomas Pinckney, who was enjoying a modest fame as the author of an advantageous treaty with Spain, as Adams' running mate, the Republicans settled on Aaron Burr with the hope of capturing the electoral votes of New York plus those of a few disaffected New Englanders. The presidential candidates themselves did no campaigning, and it was left to their supporters to round up votes as best they could. Adêt, the French minister, worked actively on behalf of Jefferson. In November he published four proclamations in the form of letters to Secretary of State Timothy Pickering charging the Federalists with a catalogue of offenses against the French, and threatening action by the Directory if Washington's policies were not reversed. It is doubtful if Adêt's intervention aided the Republican cause.

A move to steal a vote from John Adams by putting up Sam Adams as a presidential elector in Massachusetts was defeated by the Federalists. Pamphlets and handbills circulated accusing Adams of monarchial principles. One such proclaimed: "Thomas Jefferson is a firm republican—John Adams is an avowed monarchist." In Pennsylvania voters were exhorted to support

Thomas Jefferson, "the uniform advocate of equal rights among citizens," rather than Adams, "the champion of rank, titles, and hereditary distinctions."

If Adams and Jefferson remained aloof, the same could not be said for Aaron Burr. He spent six weeks touring the New England states speaking on his behalf to potential electors and was credited with the notion of putting Sam Adams up as a Republican elector. Indeed, the Republicans were, for the most part, much more enterprising in carrying their message to the voters. While the Federalists were content to concentrate their attentions on those individual electors who might be persuaded to support the Federalist ticket, the Jeffersonians directed their efforts at the ordinary citizen. Handbills were printed and nailed to doors of houses and gate posts and men were hired to ride through the state scattering anti-Federalist broadsides. The message was a simple one: Adams was a monarchist who would rivet the chains of despotism on the republic; Jefferson, on the other hand, was a friend of the rights of man and a champion of democratic principles. While the Federalist's strategy was the more successful in the short run, the Republicans had hit upon the strategy of the future by working to create what came to be known as grass-roots sentiment for their party and their candidate.

Since the electors were not bound to vote for a particular candidate or ticket much of the electioneering went on after the electors had been chosen in November. The votes were to be counted in January, and meanwhile rumor ran rife. (The appointment of electors occurred at various times during November, 1796. Sixteen states took part in the election—in ten states the legislature chose the electors: Tennessee, Vermont, Rhode Island, Connecticut, New York, New Jersey, Delaware, South Carolina, Georgia, and Kentucky. Six states held popular elections for the electors: New Hampshire, Massachusetts, Pennsylvania, Maryland, Virginia, and North Carolina.)

The revived fortunes of the Federalists tempted Hamilton to a dangerous plot. Pinckney had, as we have seen, been added to the Federalist ticket to attack electors in borderline states and in hopes of picking up some anti-Republican votes in the South. Hamilton, who had reluctantly accepted Adams as Washington's successor, hit upon the notion of diverting a few electoral votes from the Vice-President to his running mate, thereby giving the election to Pinckney.

The plan called for the Federalist electors in New England to cast all their votes for Adams and Pinckney for President and Vice-President while the electors in South Carolina, Pinckney's home state, would throw away a few Adams votes and thus give the Presidency to the man plainly intended to be Vice-President, leaving Adams in that office. It was a reckless plan with unforeseen consequences. Had it succeeded and the Federalist candidate for Vice-President become President by a ruse, the Federalist party would have been split beyond hope of repair. Adams would almost certainly have resigned as Vice-President, leaving that office presumably to Jefferson or Burr. Equally likely was the election of Jefferson as President.

Word of the scheme leaked out and in the nick of time. A number of New England electors protected Adams by scratching Pinckney's name from their ballots but in South Carolina 8 votes went to Pinckney and 8 to Jefferson. Between the choice of the electors in November and the counting of the ballots in January endless rumors circulated.

By the middle of November Samuel Otis had compiled a preliminary count of the electoral vote based on the best available rumors. "By lies, abuse, and bribery," he wrote John Adams, "the disorganizers will carry their ticket through the state [Pennsylvania]." But Adams should get 51 votes from New England and New York, and some 17 votes south of the Mason-Dixon line, giving him a total of 76 with 70 needed for a majority. "I presume further," wrote Otis, "that these 76 contain 7/8ths of the honesty and property, and 4/5ths of the good sense of the nation."

Fisher Ames' calculations in early December credited Adams with 58 certain votes in New England. Delaware was prepared, the word was, to cast 3 votes for Adams, Maryland 6 or possibly 7. There would be 2, some said 4, sure Federalist votes from Virginia. North Carolina was expected to cast 1 vote for Adams. "Thus, you see," Ames wrote to Christopher Gore, "it is very close. Accident, whim, intrigue, not to say corruption, may change or prevent a vote or two. Perhaps some may be illegal and excluded. . . . Who can foresee the issue of this momentous election? Perhaps the Jeffs, foreseeing a defeat, may vote for Mr. Pinckney, in which case he might come in by two-thirds of all the votes. But they expect success, and therefore will not throw away their votes. Yet Mr. P. may have more than Adams; and of the three chances, his may be thought the most hopeful. That would be a subject of incalculable consequences. On the one hand, he is a good man; on the other, even a good President, thus made by luck or sheer dexterity of play, would stand badly with parties and with the country. It would war an ill aspect in Europe, as well as here."

A few days later Ames, still troubled by the report that the election would go to Pinckney by a fraud, observed to a friend, "Jefferson, I hope and trust, has the worst chance of the three. . . . His being Vice would be a formidable evil, if his pride would let him take it." However, by the middle of the month, it appeared to most close observers that Adams would receive enough votes to win the election. It was reported that even William Giles, the indefatigable Republican leader in the House, was ready to concede the election of Adams, remarking, "The old man will make a good President, too. . . . But we shall have to *check* him a little now and then. That will be all."

About a week later Fisher Ames calculated that Adams had 67 certain votes with 4 more due from Vermont. It seemed equally certain that Jefferson would secure enough votes, primarily because of Hamilton's strategem, to become Vice-President. "Combining the *antis*, and standing at their head," Ames wrote from Philadelphia to Nathaniel Gore, "he will balance the power of the chief magistrate by his own." And the "two Presidents, like two suns in the meridian, would meet and jostle for four years, and then the Vice would be first."

To Nathaniel Ames the case, of course, seemed much different. Writing in his journal on the last day of December the Doctor noted "a sharp conflict between the Lawyers or Aristocrats on one side, and the Democrats of '75 men (or Jacobins, as stigmatized) on the other, to get a new President. The first party strive for John Adams, who favors the Britons, our enemies; the second party strive for Thomas Jefferson, who is a friend to the French, who are friends to the Human Race, and helped us out of the paws of the British government. . . . It is confidently affirmed that Adams, an aristocratic lawyer, in favor of British dignities, manners and Government will be President, — and Jefferson . . . a firm supporter of the Rights of Man, and an admirer of the French Revolution, will be Vice-President."

As the conviction grew that Adams would be declared the winner, Republican editors began to find heretofore unperceived virtues in the Vice-President and indeed to use Adams as an excuse to belabor Washington. One Republican editor hailed the day when the country would be governed by "talents and science" rather than the "mysterious influence of a name." How little Adams' own sentiments were known is suggested by the fact that both the British and French ministers, Liston and Adêt, wrote their respective governments that Adams' election would be favorable to the interests of their countries.

With his election assured beyond reasonable doubt, Adams felt bolstered by his confidence "in the sense, spirit, and resources of this country, which few other men in the world know so well [or] have so long tried and found solid." Thus he wrote Abigail Adams in January. On February 8 the votes were counted and Adams declared the official winner with a bare margin of 71. Jefferson was second with 68, Pinckney third with 59. The margin of victory could hardly have been narrower. If the Federalists had managed matters more efficiently Pinckney would have come in second with 71 votes and a Federalist administration would have been assured.

In fact the country responded, as it was so often to do in the future, in a good spirit. Expressions of support and affection came spontaneously from many communities and from old friends and allies of past years and even from opponents. Jefferson symbolized the mood of reconciliation by visiting Adams and pledging his strong support. Even Jarvis, an ardent pro-Republican editor in Boston, pronounced himself reconciled to Adams' election on the grounds that it was impossible for the new President to be worse than Washington.

The Inauguration itself was a simple but impressive ceremony. Adams, well aware of the significance of the moment found himself more than once on the verge of tears. For the first time in the brief life of the Republic the position of Chief Executive was changing hands — "the sight of the sun setting full-orbed, and another rising (though less splendid), was a novelty," he wrote Abigail.

Chief Justice Oliver Ellsworth administered the oath of office and Adams stepped forward to deliver his Inaugural Address. Its mode was historical. Adams traced the development of the new nation from the outbreak of the struggle for independence, through the war itself and the trying years of the Confederacy, to the framing of the Constitution — "better adapted to the genius, character, situation, and relations of this nation and country than any which had ever been proposed or suggested." He attempted to put to rest the notion that he was an advocate of monarchy by declaring that "it was not then, nor has been since, any objection to it in my mind that the executive and Senate were not more permanent." The operation of the Constitution had equalled the most optimistic hopes of its friends. "From an habitual attention to it, satisfaction in its administration, and delight in its effects upon the peace, order, prosperity, and happiness of the nation—I have acquired an habitual attachment to it and veneration for it." Robes and diamonds could not be more respectable than the authority that sprang "fresh from the hearts and judgements of an honest and enlightened people. . . . It is their power and majesty that is reflected, and only for their good, in every legitimate government."

But the underpinning of a republic was free and honest elections and Adams warned his audience that the government would be in peril from the moment that a single vote could be influenced by "foreign nations, by flattery or menaces, by fraud or violence, by terror, intrigue, or venality." Then it would be foreign nations "who govern us, and not we, the people, who govern ourselves." (This for Adêt and those who had aided and abetted him.)

Adams was at pains to praise Washington and to identify himself and his Administration, so far as he could, with the General. Washington's conduct of the Presidency had "merited the gratitude of his fellow citizens, commanded the highest praises of foreign nations, and secured immortal glory with posterity." Adams would give proper regard to "the rights, interest, honor, and happiness of all the states in the Union without preference or regard to a Northern or Southern, an Eastern or Western, position." He wished to reconcile "various political opinions . . . and virtuous men of all parties and denominations." Further, he would support every rational effort to encourage schools, colleges, universities, academies, and every institution for propagating knowledge, virtue, and religion among all classes of the people, not only for their benign influence on the happiness of life in all its stages and classes and of society in all its form, but as the only means of preserving our constitution from its natural enemies—the spirit of sophistry, the spirit of party, the spirit of intrigue, the profligacy of corruption, and the pestilence of foreign influence which is the angel of destruction to elective governments. The reference to the major theme of Washington's Farewell Address was, of course, calculated. It was another way to bind together the two Administrations and to emphasize that the succession was a passing on of a policy and a spirit as much as of the machinery of government itself. The new President was determined to put into effect a "system of neutrality and impartiality among the belligerent powers of Europe." To placate the Francophiles he expressed his "personal esteem for the French nation" and "a sincere desire to preserve the friendship which has been so much for the interest of both nations." He then pledged himself to support the Constitution and to promote the peace and prosperity of his country.

The Republicans were perhaps more satisfied with the speech than the members of Adams' own party. Senator Mason of Virginia was reported to have said that America would lose nothing by the change in Administrations, "for he had never heard such a speech in public in his life," Bache was delighted with the address and hailed it in the *Aurora* as a model of wisdom and moderation, and its author as a man "of incorruptible integrity," a "friend of France, of peace, an admirer of republicanism, the enemy of party. . . . How characteristic of a patriot." Word reached Adams that the Federalist ultras had complained that the speech was too conciliatory to the Jacobins and that the Federalist editor and lexicographer Noah Webster saw evidence in the address that Adams had been seduced by the Francophiles.

Yet these were, for the moment, simply clouds on the horizon. The crucial thing in the minds of all friends of the Republic was that an orderly succession had taken place, unmarred by violence or disruption. The reins of government had passed from the hands of a figure of mythical power and potency into the hands of an able but lesser luminary and this in the midst of deep and bitter political divisions. Another landmark had been passed successfully, and Adams' euphoria was understandable and in a degree justified when he wrote to Abigail that the inauguration "taken together . . . was the sublimist thing ever exhibited in America."

A strong case can be made that Adams' election in 1796 was the best outcome from the point of view of restoring some measure of harmony to a badly divided nation. The transmigration of power was a risky business at best. To have it take place within the same party, thus assuring a degree of continuity, was very important. Simply the unseating of Federalist officials and their replacement by inexperienced and untried men would have had a demoralizing effect on the country and could hardly have failed to exacerbate party feeling.

Moreover, having Jefferson as Vice-President legitimated the Republican faction as a party within the government. This simple fact moderated the violence of Republican partisanship by keeping before the Republicans the expectation of Jefferson's succession. Since they were, at least to a degree, "in" the government, their sense of alienation was proportionately diminished. Furthermore, it somewhat inhibited Jefferson's own political activities; it reassured the French and perhaps made the British somewhat more cautious. It introduced a note of uncertainty about the character of the new government that, at least initially, disarmed attack from all quarters. What would happen in an administration in which the President and Vice-President were not only members of opposite parties but had, in fact, been rivals for the Presidency, it was impossible to tell. It was a situation that had certainly not been foreseen by the framers of the Constitution. There was nothing to do but wait and see.

It was left to John Adams to bear the double burden of a Vice-President in avowed opposition to his Administration as well as the relentless hostility of a party leader, Hamilton, who had already tried to rob him of the succession and whose agents were securely established in the Cabinet that Adams had inherited from his predecessor.

Had Pinckney become an accidental President as the consequence of Hamilton's plot, the spirit of partisan bitterness so apparent in the country would have increased with results that could hardly have been favorable to stability and good order. Adams Federalists and Jeffersonian Republicans would have shared at least one thing in common—a conviction that intrigue and manipulation had thwarted the popular will.

The consequences of Jefferson's election are equally conjectural, of course. If the Virginian had indeed tried to reverse Washington's foreign policy, he would have found himself in a severe contest with the Senate, which was still a Federalist stronghold. In such circumstances he could have acquiesced without enthusiasm in a foreign policy that was basically Federalist, in which case the powers of the President in the field of foreign affairs might have been seriously compromised, or, conversely, he might have looked to the Republican House for support, thus intensifying the split between the two branches of Congress, which at the time of the Jay Treaty seemed to many observers to threaten the survival of constitutional government.

The most likely outcome would have been, as Adams conjectured, that Jefferson would, under a smokescreen of mildly pro-French sentiments, have followed a foreign policy not very different from that of his predecessor. It was, after all, the charge of the Republicans not so much that the Federalists were hostile to the French but that they were subservient to the British. The responsibilities of office almost invariably have a moderating effect on those who have to pass from the relative freedom of the opposition to the severe limitations of a practical situation. If Jefferson had followed a substantially Washingtonian path, he would soon have fallen out of favor with the more radical among his supporters. The Federalists, as the opposition party, might have consolidated their strength under the leadership of Hamilton, while Adams, as the defeated candidate, withdrew to Quincy, leaving the moderate group of "Adams Federalists" leaderless and the party, in consequence, more conservative than ever. It is at least conceivable that the Federalists, under such circumstances, might have returned to power in 1800 with results difficult to calculate.

The strange trinity of Adams, Hamilton, and Jefferson perhaps served a purpose better than they knew. What was crucial was that neither Hamilton (in the form of a Pinckney who might have been his tool) nor Jefferson held the supreme executive power. Either eventuality could only have dangerously increased the polarization of American politics. Yet it was equally important, as we have suggested, that the Federalist ultras and the Republicans should have a continuing stake in the government. For the hopes of the Hamiltonian Federalists lay in the fact of a Federalist-dominated Senate, the predominantly conservative Federalist Cabinet inherited by Adams and finally, the at least nominal Federalism of the President himself. For the Republicans, as has been mentioned, the presence of their leader in the second place in the Administration, and a predominant if not decisive voice in the House itself, were sources of encouragement. On the other hand Adams' relations with the Republicans undoubtedly profited from the fact that he was as unsympathetic to the Hamiltonian wing of his own party as to the Republicans themselves. What was perhaps most important, ultimately, was that the general situation should remain complicated and obscure, thus confusing the protagonists while keeping their respective hopes alive. Time was needed above all, time for the new Republic, having given impressive evidence of its ability to create a resourceful and efficient government, to develop channels for dissent and the capacity to give wider segments of the population a sense of active participation in its processes. For this purpose the very awkwardness of the political situation served as no orderly and rational resolution could have.

There was a dialectic at work and the dialectic needed time. The Administration of John Adams gave it that time. Adams' genius was in his character — independent, suspicious, secretive, obdurate, and perverse enough to enjoy thwarting his adversaries in both camps and willing to pay the price for such intractability. If we trace the course of his Administration it becomes clear that Hamiltonians and Jeffersonians alike were baffled and occasionally enraged by his unpolitic as well as, occasionally, impolitic behavior. What a more subtle man might have accomplished by Machiavellian guile, Adams accomplished by keeping his own counsel and using Abigail as his only true confidant.

The armed conflict between Britain and the revolutionary French Government served, as we have seen, to polarize American opinion. Domestic issues were still poorly defined — the leading one was doubtless the charge of autocracy, of an excess of governmental authority represented by the considerable presidential powers, which were supported by a company of "aristocrats" indifferent to the real needs and concerns of the mass of common folk. In a certain sense no one yet knew what the critical domestic issues were; they remained to be defined and until they were defined it was obvious that the parties (as yet themselves unformed) could hardly take a stand on them.

If it had been possible to define genuine issues in the 1790's, the results would probably have been fatal to the young Republic. If one party or faction had really represented the interests of the New England merchants, another the interests of the frontier farmers, another the interests of the southern planters, another the tradesmen, artisans, and mechanics, and other fairly specific sectional issues, the country could hardly have survived. Fortunately the issues were ideological, but ideological on such a level of airy abstraction and overblown rhetoric, that the most diverse possible interests were able to rally around each heraldic emblem.

So the decade of the 1790's was a decade of frustration. Political impulses were seeking political forms and issues through which to express themselves. Theory which denied the validity of party activity increased frustration by treating opposition as a form of criminality, as a conscious assault upon the foundations of order itself, and thereby upon civilization and morality. Thus we have a generally familiar political phenomenon in an acute form — most of what was said in the 1790's by politicians and journalists bore very little relation to any identifiable reality. Since the initiative in *attacking* lay with the Republicans, the Federalists, as reasonable men, reacted from 1793 to the end of the decade with understandable resentment to charges which seemed to them to be not only entirely without foundation but not possible of being contained within any recognizable framework of political controversy.

There were further ironies. The attraction that the French Revolution, so different from its American predecessor, had for many citizens of the new republic was the result of certain currents in American thought. The Revolutionary period had been marked by a notably "universal" spirit which drew nourishment from the old Puritan dream of universal redemption. The American Revolution, as the Great Seal of the United States announced, was designed to inaugurate "a new series of ages" *(novus ordo seculorum)*, a new hope for oppressed and abused humanity everywhere in the world. The French Revolution was carried out in the name of that ideal and the Jeffersonians, attaching themselves to it, claimed to be the party of humanity. They thereby laid claim to the universalist and redemptive spirit of Puritan Christianity in secular form. That Virginia, rather than the stony soil of New England, should have been the stronghold of such sentiment was especially ironic. To complete the paradox it might be said that the rational spirit of the Enlightenment which had so long warred against the passionate zeal of Reformation Christianity, was appropriated by the Federalists; and it is certainly true that they had a legitimate claim to be the party of order and rationality, whereas the Republicans rallied the romantic utopians, the reformers, the enthusiastic democrats, the champions of universal redemption.

In terms of the dialectic of American history, the paradox proved a fruitful one. Through the impact of the French Revolution the redemptive passion of the Puritans became "politicized," that is to say it became a vital element in the American political tradition, which, in turn, reinfected evangelical Protestantism with an almost limitless zeal for social reform. The Americans who adored the French Revolution had as little notion of its reality (which, could they have understood it, would have shocked them beyond words) as did the Americans who more than a hundred years later idealized Stalin's Russia. They were, in a sense, much better than the Revolution they admired so inordinately. Through them the best ideals of the French Revolution entered the bloodstream of American political thought. The Federalists could hardly be blamed for not sufficiently appreciating this fact. All they saw were "enthusiastic zealots and ranting madmen" who seemed to be celebrating anarchy and disorder and lamenting the fact that peaceful America was not revolutionary France. There is usually some saving grace in every form of madness; certainly there was in that of the Jeffersonians.

The reforming passion of the Republicans, "the party of humanity," became in time "internalized" as the psychologists say, that is, it lost its universalist thrust. The dominant mood came to be that of "isolationism," a feeling that the rest of the world was fallen and corrupt and that America's mission was to save itself. The universal redemptive passion, although periodically stirred by such events as the revolutions of 1848, the appearance of a Bolivar in South America, or a Mazzini in Italy, or by a desire to make the world safe for democracy, became predominantly parochial.

Only partly obscured by the ideological identification of the Republicans with the French Revolution was a profound restlessness among the "lower orders" at the fact that the direction of the affairs of the nation was in the hands of an "aristocracy," a company of men of wealth and substance, highly educated, and, in most cases, "well-born." That there was little to distinguish between Federalist and Republican leaders in this regard was less important than the fact that the Jeffersonians adopted the rhetoric of the "have-nots" in their denunciations of the "aristocratic" Federalists. For men like Jefferson, Madison, Charles Pinckney, or Thomas Mifflin to attack Hamilton or Adams as "aristocrats" was absurd on the face of it. What *was* significant was that the word evoked such powerful emotions in a considerable portion of the electorate.

But there were subtler elements in the election of 1796. The most important was undoubtedly that of succession. The year 1796 marked the first time in modern history that the elected chief executive of an independent nation had surrendered office of his own volition in accordance with a preconceived plan (the Constitution) upon the election of his successor. It was thus one of the critical moments in the evolution of modern political institutions. (We need only note in how many present-day nations such changes are effected more often by violence than by constitutional procedures.) One had to go back to classical times for precedents and they were, for the most part, not particularly encouraging ones.

Too much emphasis can hardly be placed on the issue of succession simply because we are so inclined to take it for granted from the perspective of some forty subsequent elections. In the words of Lester Cohen, "Politically, institutions were at least once proven to bear the weight of atemporality; modes that contain their own 'inner time', in the form of steps directed toward a proper, that is legal, conclusion."

Tied to the notion of succession was the equally important concept of "tenure," a tenure specifically limited and controlled, a tenure that was an integument of Time. Heinrich Maurer has written of the Puritans, "Time had to become God's time before it could become Daylight Saving Time." In the same sense Americans had to possess time before the notion of dividing, apportioning, and, to a degree, controlling time could present itself to men's imaginations. Prior to the formation of the American government certain offices had been held for stated periods but it was a much more common practice to hold office for life, or at the pleasure of him in whose hands the right of appointment lay. The idea of setting a particular period of time for the exercise of the very considerable power of the chief executive officer in a republic was a major innovation.

The dividing of time into two, four, and six year segments for congressmen, Presidents and senators demonstrated a faith in the possibilities of ordering time that became the basis of the industrial process as well as of education and ultimately permeated every area of American life. As Lester Cohen has put it, "To create an extension or continuance of the present was to ground the future before it thrust itself uncontrollably upon one. . . . To predicate the direction of the future by creating institutions intended to provide for recurrence with order might be to diminish the risk for the future." But it did so at the cost of representing that risk at the point of every planned recurrence, i.e., every election. Washington's reelection in 1792 was of significance only in that it marked the unimpeded completion of the initial four-year integument of time and the beginning of the second through an orderly process of re-election. The deeper significance was overshadowed by Washington's enor-mous prestige. He was a figure so powerfully present in the minds of Americans that he entirely dominated the event itself — the reelection. Moreover, parties had not yet clearly defined themselves, so it was still possible to imagine peace-ful successions unmarred by the rancors of factionalism and party strife.

The man elected President in 1796 is not generally considered to have been one of our more distinguished Chief Executives, although I have argued elsewhere, and at some length, that he was a much better President than most historians have credited him with being. But good or bad, to dwell on the character and abilities of Adams and his supporters or, indeed, of Jefferson and the Jeffersonians, would be to distort seriously the issue. What was of crucial importantce was that *the election took place*, and the "transmigration" of power was accomplished without disaster, indeed with surprising facility, and to the positive benefit of the country.

For the first time parties clearly took form. In the words of Richard McCormick, "It was the contest for the presidency that was [to] exert the determining influence on the structure of the American party system. . . . The rivalry between John Adams and Thomas Jefferson in 1796 and again in 1800 served not only to dramatize and polarize the emerging partisan cleav-age: it also enlarged party strife beyond the bounds of congressional districts, bringing it to embrace entire states and, by extension, the whole nation."

More profoundly, the election expressed a new and characteristically American relationship between time and politics. The future, by being antici-pated *politically* in the form of four-year elections, was, as Lester Cohen has argued, robbed of much of its menace. The capacity of Americans to inno-vate and improvise was related to the ability to foresee at least this integument of the future. Succession, the development of political parties, and a new *political* relationship to time — these were the most prominent among the consequences of the election of 1796.

Appendix

The Jay Treaty
November 19, 1794

The Jay Treaty precipitated the first major foreign policy crisis in the new nation. It served to crystallize anti-Federalist sentiment in a decisive way and thereby furthered the formation of political parties.

Art. I. There shall be a firm, inviolable and universal peace, and a true and sincere friendship between his Britannic Majesty, his heirs and successors, and the United States of America; and between their respective countries, territories, cities, towns and people of every degree, without exception of persons or places.

Art. II. His Majesty will withdraw all his troops and garrisons from all posts and places within the boundary lines assigned by the treaty of peace to the United States. This evacuation shall take place on or before [June 1, 1796,] . . . : The United States in the mean time at their discretion, extending their settlements to any part within the said boundary line, except within the precincts or jurisdiction of any of the said posts. All settlers and traders, within the precincts or jurisdiction of the said posts, shall continue to enjoy, unmolested, all their property of every kind, and shall be protected therein. They shall be at full liberty to remain there, or to remove with all or any part of their effects; and it shall also be free to them to sell their lands, houses, or effects, or to retain the property thereof, at their discretion; such of them as shall continue to reside within the said boundary lines, shall not be compelled to become citizens of the United States, or to take any oath of allegiance to the government thereof; but they shall be at full liberty so to do if they think proper, and they shall make and declare their election within one year after the evacuation aforesaid. And all persons who shall continue there after the expiration of the said year, without having declared their intention of remaining subjects of his Britannic Majesty, shall be considered as having elected to become citizens of the United States.

Art. III. It is agreed that it shall at all times be free to his Majesty's subjects and to the citizens of the United States, and also to the Indians dwelling on either side of the said boundary line, freely to pass and repass by land or inland navigation, into the respective territories and countries of the two parties, on the continent of America (the country within the limits of the Hudson's bay Company only excepted) and to navigate all the lakes, rivers and waters thereof, and freely to carry on trade and commerce with each other. . . . The river Mississippi shall, however, according to the treaty of peace, be entirely open to both parties; and it is further agreed, that all the

81

ports and places on its eastern side, to whichsoever of the parties belonging, may freely be resorted to and used by both parties, in as ample a manner as any of the Atlantic ports or places of the United States, or any of the ports or places of his Majesty in Great-Britain. . . .

Art. IV. Whereas it is uncertain whether the river Mississippi extends so far to the northward, as to be intersected by a line to be drawn due west from the Lake of the Woods, in the manner mentioned in the treaty of peace . . . it is agreed, that measures shall be taken . . . for making a joint survey of the said river from one degree of latitude below the falls of St. Anthony, to the principal source or sources of the said river, and also of the parts adjacent thereto; and that if on the result of such survey, it should appear that the said river, would not be intersected by such a line as is above mentioned, the two parties will thereupon proceed by amicable negociation, to regulate the boundary line in that quarter, . . .

Art. V. Whereas doubts have arisen what river was truly intended under the name of the river St. Croix, mentioned in the said treaty of peace, and forming a part of the boundary therein described; that question shall be referred to the final decision of commissioners to be appointed. . . . The said commissioners shall, by a declaration, under their hands and seals, decide what river is the river St. Croix, intended by the treaty. . . . And both parties agree to consider such decision as final and conclusive, so as that the same shall never thereafter be called into question, or made the subject of dispute or difference between them.

Art. VI. Whereas it is alleged by divers British merchants and others his Majesty's subjects, that debts, to a considerable amount, which were bona fide contracted before the peace, still remain owing to them by citizens or inhabitants of the United States, and that by the operation of various lawful impediments since the peace, not only the full recovery of the said debts has been delayed, but also the value and security thereof have been, in several instances, impaired and lessened, so that by the ordinary course of judicial proceedings, the British creditors cannot now obtain, and actually have and receive full and adequate compensation for the losses and damages which they have thereby sustained. It is agreed, that in all such cases, where full compensation for such losses and damages cannot, for whatever reason, be actually obtained, had and received by the said creditors in the ordinary course of justice, the United States will make full and complete compensation for the same to the said creditors: But it is distinctly understood, that this provision is to extend to such losses only as have been occasioned by the lawful impediments aforesaid, . . .

Art. VII. Whereas complaints have been made by divers merchants and others, citizens of the United States, that during the course of the war in which his Majesty is now engaged, they have sustained considerable losses and damage, by reason of irregular or illegal captures or condemnations of their vessels and other property, under colour of authority or commissions from his Majesty, and that from various circumstances belonging to the said cases, adequate compensation for the losses and damages so sustained cannot now be actually obtained, had and received by the ordinary course of judicial proceedings; it is agreed, that in all such cases, where adequate compensation cannot for whatever reason, be now actually obtained, had and received by the said merchants and others, in the ordinary course of justice, full and complete compensation for the same will be made by the British government to the said complainants. But it is distinctly understood, that this provision is not to extend to such losses or damages as have been occasioned by the manifest delay or negligence, or wilful omission of the claimant. . . .

Art X. Neither the debts due from individuals of the one nation to individuals of the other, nor shares, nor monies which they may have in the public funds, or in the public or private banks, shall ever in any event of war or national differences be sequestered or confiscated. . . .

Art. XI. It is agreed between his Majesty and the United States of America, that there shall be a reciprocal and entirely perfect liberty of navigation and commerce between their respective people, in the manner, under the limitations and on the conditions specified in the following articles:

[Art. XII., relating to trade with the West Indies, was suspended.]

Art. XIII. His Majesty consents that the vessels belonging to the citizens of the United States of America, shall be admitted and hospitably received, in all the sea-ports and harbours of the British territories in the East-Indies. And that the citizens of the said United States, may freely carry on a trade between the said territories and the said United States, in all articles of which the importation or exportation respectively, to or from the said territories, shall not be entirely prohibited. . . . The citizens of the United States shall pay for their vessels when admitted into the said ports no other or higher tonnage-duty than shall be payable on British vessels when admitted into the ports of the United States. And they shall pay no other or higher duties or charges, on the importation or exportation of the cargoes of the said vessels, than shall be payable on the same articles when imported or exported in British vessels. But it is expressly agreed, that the vessels of the United States shall not carry any of the articles exported by them from the said British territories, to any port or place, except to some port or place in America, where the same shall be unladen, and such regulations shall be adopted by both parties, as shall from time to time be found necessary to enforce the due and faithful observance of this stipulation. It is also understood that the permission granted by this article, is not to extend to allow the vessels of the United States to carry on any part of the coasting-trade of the said British territories; but vessels going with their original cargoes, or part thereof, from one port of discharge to another, are not to be considered as carrying on the coasting-trade. Neither is this article to be construed to allow the citizens of the said states to settle or reside within the said territories, or to go into the interior parts thereof, without the permission of the British government established there. . . .

Art. XIV. There shall be between all the dominions of his Majesty in Europe and the territories of the United States, a reciprocal and perfect liberty of commerce and navigation. The people and inhabitants of the two countries respectively, shall have liberty freely and securely, and without hindrance and molestation, to come with their ships and cargoes to the lands, countries, cities, ports, places and rivers, within the dominions and territories aforesaid, to enter into the same, to resort there, and to remain and reside there, without any limitation of time. Also to hire and possess houses and warehouses for the purposes of their commerce, and generally the merchants and traders on each side, shall enjoy the most complete protection and security for their commerce; but subject always as to what respects this article to the laws and statutes of the two countries respectively.

Art. XV. It is agreed that no other or higher duties shall be paid by the ships or merchandize of the one party in the ports of the other, than such as are paid by the like vessels or merchandize of all other nations. Nor shall any other or higher duty be imposed in one country on the importation of any articles the growth, produce or manufacture of the other, than are or shall be payable on the importation of the like articles being of the growth, produce, or manufacture of any other foreign country. Nor shall any prohibition be imposed on the exportation or importation of any articles to or from the territories of the two parties respectively, which shall not equally extend to all other nations. . . .

The two parties agree to treat for the more exact equalization of the duties on the respective navigation of their subjects and people, in such manner as may be most beneficial to the two countries. . . . In the interval it is agreed, that the United States will not impose any new or additional tonnage duties on British vessels, nor increae the now-subsisting difference between the duties payable on the importation of any articles in British or in American vessels. . . .

Art. XVII. It is agreed, that in all cases where vessels shall be captured or detained on just suspicion of having on board enemy's property, or of carrying to the enemy any of the articles which are contraband of war; the said vessel shall be brought to the nearest or most convenient port; and if any property of an enemy should be found on board such vessel, that part only which belongs to the enemy shall be made prize, and the vessel shall be at liberty to proceed with the remainder without any impediment. . . .

Art. IX. And that more abundant care may be taken for the security of the respective subjects and citizens of the contracting parties, and to prevent their suffering injuries by the men of war, or privateers of either party, all commanders of ships of war and privateers, and all others the said subjects and citizens, shall forbear doing any damage to those of the other party, or committing any outrage against them, and if they act to the contrary, they shall be punished, and shall also be bound in their persons and estates to make satisfaction and reparation for all damages, and the interest thereof, of whatever nature the said damages may be. . . .

Art. XXII. It is expressly stipulated, that neither of the said contracting parties will order or authorize any acts of reprisal against the other, on complaints of injuries or damages, until the said party shall first have presented to the other a statement thereof, verified by competent proof and evidence, and

demanded justice and satisfaction, and the same shall either have been refused or unreasonably delayed.

Art. XXVI. If at any time a rupture should take place, (which God forbid)
between his Majesty and the United States, the merchants and others of each
of the two nations, residing in the dominions of the other, shall have the privilege of remaining and continuing their trade, so long as they behave peaceably, and commit no offence against the laws; and in case their conduct should
render them suspected, and the respective governments should think proper
to order them to remove, the term of twelve months from the publication of
the order shall be allowed them for that purpose, to remove with their families, effects and property; but this favour shall not be extended to those who
shall act contrary to the established laws; . . .

Art. XXVIII. It is agreed, that the first ten articles of this treaty shall be permanent, and that the subsequent articles, except the twelfth, shall be limited
in their duration to twelve years, . . .

President George Washington's Farewell Address
New York, September 17, 1796

Washington's Farewell Address is perhaps the most important single document in American history, the Declaration of Independence and the Constitution excepted. Among other things it helped to set the direction of Adams' Administration and became a touchstone of American foreign policy for generations to come.

Friends and Fellow-Citizens:

The period for a new election of a citizen to administer the Executive Government of the United States being not far distant, and the time actually arrived when your thoughts must be employed in designating the person who is to be clothed with that important trust, it appears to me proper, especially as it may conduce to a more distinct expression of the public voice, that I should now apprise you of the resolution I have formed to decline being considered among the number of those out of whom a choice is to be made. . . .

The impressions with which I first undertook the arduous trust were explained on the proper occasion. In the discharge of this trust I will only say that I have, with good intentions, contributed toward the organization and administration of the Government the best exertions of which a very fallible judgment was capable. Not unconscious in the outset of the inferiority of my qualifications, experience in my own eyes, perhaps still more in the eyes of others, has strengthened the motives to diffidence of myself; and every day the increasing weight of years admonishes me more and more that the shade of retirement is as necessary to me as it will be welcome. Satisfied that if any circumstances have given peculiar value to my services they were temporary, I have the consolation to believe that, while choice and prudence invite me to quit the political scene, patriotism does not forbid it. . . .

Here, perhaps, I ought to stop. But a solicitude for your welfare which can not end with my life, and the apprehension of danger natural to that solicitude, urge me on an occasion like the present to offer to your solemn contemplation and to recommend to your frequent review some sentiments which are the result of much reflection, of no inconsiderable observation, and which appear to me all important to the permanency of your felicity as a people. . . .

Interwoven as is the love of liberty with every ligament of your hearts, no recommendation of mine is necessary to fortify or confirm the attachment.

The unity of government which constitutes you one people is also now dear to you. It is justly so, for it is a main pillar in the edifice of your real independence, the support of your tranquillity at home, your peace abroad, of your safety, of your prosperity, of that very liberty which you so highly prize. But as it is easy to foresee that from different causes and from different quarters much pains will be taken, many artifices employed, to weaken in your minds the conviction of this truth, as this is the point in your political fortress against which the batteries of internal and external enemies will be most constantly and actively (though often covertly and insidiously) directed, it is of infinite moment that you should properly estimate the immense value of your national union to your collective and individual happiness; that you should cherish a cordial, habitual, and immovable attachment to it; accustoming yourselves to think and speak of it as of the paladium of your political safety and prosperity; watching for its preservation with jealous anxiety; discountenancing whatever may suggest even a suspicion that it can in any event be abandoned, and indignantly frowning upon the first dawning of every attempt to alienate any portion of our country from the rest or to enfeeble the sacred ties which now link together the various parts.

For this you have every inducement of sympathy and interest. Citizens by birth or choice of a common country, that country has a right to concentrate your affections. The name of American, which belongs to you in your national capacity, must always exalt the just pride of patriotism more than any appellation derived from local discriminations. With slight shades of difference, you have the same religion, manners, habits, and political principles. You have in a common cause fought and triumphed together. The independence and liberty you possess are the work of joint councils and joint efforts, of common dangers, sufferings, and successes.

But these considerations, however powerfully they address themselves to your sensibility, are greatly outweighed by those which apply more immediately to your interest. Here every portion of our country finds the most commanding motives for carefully guarding and preserving the union of the whole.

The *North*, in an unrestrained intercourse with the *South*, protected by the equal laws of a common government, finds in the productions of the latter great additional resources of maritime and commercial enterprise and precious materials of manufacturing industry. The *South*, in the same intercourse, benefiting by the same agency of the *North*, sees its agriculture grow and its commerce expand. Turning partly into its own channels the seamen of the *North*, it finds its particular navigation invigorated; and while it contributes in different ways to nourish and increase the general mass of the national navigation, it looks forward to the protection of a maritime strength to which itself is unequally adapted. The *East*, in a like intercourse with the *West*, already finds, and in the progressive improvement of interior communications by land and water will more and more find, a valuable vent for the commodities which it brings from abroad or manufactures at home. The *West* derives from the *East* supplies requisite to its growth and comfort, and what is perhaps of still greater consequence, it must of necessity owe the *secure* enjoyment of indispensable *outlets* for its own productions to the weight, influence, and the future maritime strength of the Atlantic side of the Union, directed by an indissoluble community of interest as one nation. Any other tenure by which the West can hold this essential advantage, whether derived from its own separate strength or from an apostate and unnatural connection with any foreign power, must be intrinsically precarious.

While, then, every part of our country thus feels an immediate and particular interest in union, all the parts combined can not fail to find in the united mass of means and efforts greater strength, greater resource, proportionably greater security from external danger, a less frequent interruption of their peace by foreign nations, and what is of inestimable value, they must derive from union an exemption from those broils and wars between themselves which so frequently afflict neighboring countries not tied together by the same governments, which their own rivalships alone would be sufficient to produce, but which opposite foreign alliances, attachments, and intrigues would stimulate and imbitter. Hence, likewise, they will avoid the necessity of those overgrown military establishments which, under any form of government, are inauspicious to liberty, and which are to be regarded as particularly hostile to republican liberty. In this sense it is that your union ought to be considered as a main prop of your liberty, and that the love of the one ought to endear to you the preservation of the other. . . .

Is there a doubt whether a common government can embrace so large a sphere? Let experience solve it. To listen to mere speculation in such a case were criminal. It is well worth a fair and full experiment. With such powerful and obvious motives to union affecting all parts of our country, while experience shall not have demonstrated its impracticability, there will always be reason to distrust the patriotism of those who in any quarter may endeavor to weaken its bands.

In contemplating the causes which may disturb our union it occurs as matter of serious concern that any ground should have been furnished for characterizing parties by *geographical* discriminations—*Northern* and *Southern*, *Atlantic* and *Western*—whence designing men may endeavor to excite a belief that there is a real difference of local interests and views. One of the expedients of party to acquire influence within particular districts is to misrepresent the opinions and aims of other districts. You can not shield yourselves too much against the jealousies and heartburnings which spring from these misrepresentations; they tend to render alien to each other those who ought to be bound together by fraternal affection. . . .

To the efficacy and permanency of your union a government for the whole is indispensable. No alliances, however strict, between the parts can be an adequate substitute. They must inevitably experience the infractions and interruptions which all alliances in all times have experienced. Sensible of this momentous truth, you have improved upon your first essay by the adoption of a Constitution of Government better calculated than your former for an intimate union and for the efficacious management of your common concerns. This Government, the offspring of our own choice, uninfluenced and unawed, adopted upon full investigation and mature deliberation, completely free in its principles, in the distribution of its powers, uniting security with energy, and containing within itself a provision for its own amendment, has a just claim to your confidence and your support. Respect for its authority, compliance with its laws, acquiescence in its measures, are duties enjoined by the fundamental maxims of true liberty. The basis of our political systems is the right of the people to make and to alter their constitutions of government. But the constitution which at any time exists till changed by an explicit and authentic act of the whole people is sacredly obligatory upon all. The very idea of the power and the right of the people to establish government presupposes the duty of every individual to obey the established government. . . .

Toward the preservation of your Government and the permanency of your present happy state, it is requisite not only that you steadily discountenance irregular oppositions to its acknowledged authority, but also that you resist with care the spirit of innovation upon its principles, however specious the pretexts. One method of assault may be to effect in the forms of the Constitution alterations which will impair the energy of the system, and thus to undermine what can not be directly overthrown. In all the changes to which you may be invited remember that time and habit are at least as necessary to fix the true character of governments as of other human institutions; that experience is the surest standard by which to test the real tendency of the existing constitution of a country; that facility in changes upon the credit of mere hypothesis and opinion exposes to perpetual change, from the endless variety of hypothesis and opinion; and remember especially that for the efficient management of your common interests in a country so extensive as ours a government of as much vigor as is consistent with the perfect security of liberty is indispensable. Liberty itself will find in such a government, with powers properly distributed and adjusted, its surest guardian. It is, indeed, little else than a name where the government is too feeble to withstand the enterprises of faction, to confine each member of the society within the limits prescribed by the laws, and to maintain all in the secure and tranquil enjoyment of the rights of person and property.

I have already intimated to you the danger of parties in the State, with particular reference to the founding of them on geographical discriminations. Let me now take a more comprehensive view, and warn you in the most solemn manner against the baneful effects of the spirit of party generally.

This spirit, unfortunately, is inseparable from our nature, having its root in the strongest passions of the human mind. It exists under different shapes in all governments, more or less stifled, controlled, or repressed; but in those of the popular form it is seen in its greatest rankness and is truly their worst enemy. . . .

It serves always to distract the public councils and enfeeble the public administration. It agitates the community with ill-founded jealousies and false alarms; kindles the animosity of one part against another; foments occasionally riot and insurrection. It opens the door to foreign influence and corruption, which find a facilitated access to the government itself through the channels of party passion. Thus the policy and the will of one country are subjected to the policy and will of another.

There is an opinion that parties in free countries are useful checks upon the administration of the government, and serve to keep alive the spirit of liberty. This within certain limits is probably true; and in governments of a monarchical cast patriotism may look with indulgence, if not with favor, upon the spirit of party. But in those of the popular character, in governments purely elective, it is a spirit not to be encouraged. From their natural tendency it is certain there will always be enough of that spirit for every salutary purpose; and there being constant danger of excess, the effort ought to be by force of public opinion to mitigate and assuage it. A fire not to be quenched, it demands a uniform vigilance to prevent its bursting into a flame, lest, instead of warming, it should consume.

It is important, likewise, that the habits of thinking in a free country should inspire caution in those intrusted with its administration to confine themselves within their respective constitutional spheres, avoiding in the exercise of the powers of one department to encroach upon another. The spirit of encroachment tends to consolidate the powers of all the departments in one, and thus to create, whatever the form of government, a real despotism. . . . If in the opinion of the people the distribution or modification of the constitutional powers be in any particular wrong, let it be corrected by an amendment in the way which the Constitution designates. But let there be no change by usurpation; for though this in one instance may be the instrument of good, it is the customary weapon by which free governments are destroyed. The precedent must always greatly over-balance in permanent evil any partial or transient benefit which the use can at any time yield.

Of all the dispositions and habits which lead to political prosperity, religion and morality are indispensable supports. In vain would that man claim the tribute of patriotism who should labor to subvert these great pillars of human happiness — these firmest props of the duties of men and citizens. The mere politician, equally with the pious man, ought to respect and to cherish them. A volume could not trace all their connections with private and public felicity. Let it simply be asked, Where is the security for property, for reputation, for life, if the sense of religious obligation *desert* the oaths which are the instruments of investigation in courts of justice? And let us with caution indulge the supposition that morality can be maintained without religion. Whatever may be conceded to the influence of refined education on minds of peculiar structure, reason and experience both forbid us to expect that national morality can prevail in exclusion of religious principle.

It is substantially true that virtue or morality is a necessary spring of popular government. The rule indeed extends with more or less force to every species of free government. Who that is a sincere friend to it can look with indifference upon attempts to shake the foundation of the fabric? Promote, then, as an object of primary importance, institutions for the general diffusion of knowledge. In proportion as the structure of a government gives force to public opinion, it is essential that public opinion should be enlightened.

As a very important source of strength and security, cherish public credit. One method of preserving it is to use it as sparingly as possible, avoiding occasions of expense by cultivating peace, but remembering also that timely disbursements to prepare for danger frequently prevent much greater disbursements to repel it; avoiding likewise the accumulation of debt, not only by shunning occasions of expense, but by vigorous exertions in time of peace to discharge the debts which unavoidable wars have occasioned, not ungenerously throwing upon posterity the burthen which we ourselves ought to bear. . . .

Observe good faith and justice toward all nations. Cultivate peace and harmony with all. Religion and morality enjoin this conduct. And can it be that good policy does not equally enjoin it? It will be worthy of a free, enlightened, and at no distant period a great nation to give to mankind the magnanimous and too novel example of a people always guided by an exalted justice and benevolence. Who can doubt that in the course of time and things the fruits of such a plan would richly repay any temporary advantages which might be lost by a steady adherence to it? Can it be that Providence has not connected the permanent felicity of a nation with its virtue? The experiment, at least, is recommended by every sentiment which ennobles human nature. Alas! is it rendered imposssible by its vices?

In the execution of such a plan nothing is more essential than that permanent, inveterate antipathies against particular nations and passionate attachments for others should be excluded, and that in place of them just and amicable feelings toward all should be cultivated. The nation which indulges toward another an habitual hatred or an habitual fondness is in some degree a slave. It is a slave to its animosity or to its affection, either of which is sufficient to lead it astray from its duty and its interest. Antipathy in one nation against another disposes each more readily to offer insult and injury, to lay hold of slight causes of umbrage, and to be haughty and intractable when accidental or trifling occasions of dispute occur. . . .

So, likewise, a passionate attachment of one nation for another produces a variety of evils. Sympathy for the favorite nation, facilitating the illusion of an imaginary common interest in cases where no real common interest exists, and infusing into one the enmities of the other, betrays the former into a participation in the quarrels and wars of the latter without adequate inducement or justification. It leads also to concessions to the favorite nation of privileges denied to others, which is apt doubly to injure the nation making the concessions by unnecessarily parting with what ought to have been retained, and by exciting jealousy, ill will, and a disposition to retaliate in the parties from whom equal privileges are withheld; and it gives to ambitious, corrupted, or deluded citizens (who devote themselves to the favorite nation) facility to betray or sacrifice the interests of their own country without odium, sometimes even with popularity, gilding with the appearances of a virtuous sense of obligation, a commendable deference for public opinion, or a laudable zeal for public good the base or foolish compliances of ambition, corruption, or infatuation. . . .

Against the insidious wiles of foreign influence (I conjure you to believe me, fellow-citizens) the jealousy of a free people ought to be *constantly* awake, since history and experience prove that foreign influence is one of the most baneful foes of republican government. But that jealousy, to be useful, must be impartial, else it becomes the instrument of the very influence to be avoided, instead of a defense against it. Excessive partiality for one foreign nation and excessive dislike of another cause those whom they actuate to see danger only on one side, and serve to veil and even second the arts of influence on the other. Real patriots who may resist the intrigues of the favorite are liable to become suspected and odious, while its tools and dupes usurp the applause and confidence of the people to surrender their interests.

The great rule of conduct for us in regard to foreign nations is, in extending our commercial relations to have with them as little *political* connection as possible. So far as we have already formed engagements let them be fulfilled with perfect good faith. Here let us stop.

Europe has a set of primary interests which to us have none or a very remote relation. Hence she must be engaged in frequent controversies, the causes of which are essentially foreign to our concerns. Hence, therefore, it must be unwise in us to implicate ourselves by artificial ties in the ordinary vicissitudes of her politics or the ordinary combinations and collisions of her friendships or enmities.

Our detached and distant situation invites and enables us to pursue a different course. If we remain one people, under an efficient government, the period is not far off when we may defy material injury from external annoyance; when we may take such an attitude as will cause the neutrality we may at any time resolve upon to be scrupulously respected; when belligerent nations, under the impossibility of making acquisitions upon us, will not lightly hazard the giving us provocation; when we may choose peace or war, as our interest, guided by justice, shall counsel.

Why forego the advantages of so peculiar a situation? Why quit our own to stand upon foreign ground? Why, by interweaving our destiny with that of any part of Europe, entangle our peace and prosperity in the toils of European ambition, rivalship, interest, humor, or caprice?

It is our true policy to steer clear of permanent alliances with any portion of the foreign world, so far, I mean, as we are now at liberty to do it; for let me not be understood as capable of patronizing infidelity to existing engagements. I hold the maxim no less applicable to public than to private affairs that honesty is always the best policy. I repeat, therefore, let those engagements be observed in their genuine sense. But in my opinion it is unnecessary and would be unwise to extend them.

Taking care always to keep ourselves by suitable establishments on a respectable defensive posture, we may safely trust to temporary alliances for extraordinary emergencies.

Harmony, liberal intercourse with all nations are recommended by policy, humanity, and interest. But even our commercial policy should hold an equal and impartial hand, neither seeking nor granting exclusive favors or preferences; consulting the natural course of things; diffusing and diversifying by gentle means the streams of commerce, but forcing nothing; establishing with powers so disposed, in order to give trade a stable course, to define the rights of our merchants, and to enable the Government to support them, conventional rules of intercourse, the best that present circumstances and mutual opinion will permit, but temporary and liable to be from time to time abandoned or varied as experience and circumstances shall dictate; constantly keeping in view that it is folly in one nation to look for disinterested favors from another; that it must pay with a portion of its independence for whatever it may accept under that character; that by such acceptance it may place itself in the condition of having given equivalents for nominal favors, and yet of being reproached with ingratitude for not giving more. There can be no greater error than to expect or calculate upon real favors from nation to nation. It is an illusion which experience must cure, which a just pride ought to discard. . . .

Though in reviewing the incidents of my Administration I am unconscious of intentional error, I am nevertheless too sensible of my defects not to think it probable that I may have committed many errors. Whatever they may be, I fervently beseech the Almighty to avert or mitigate the evils to which they may tend. I shall also carry with me the hope that my country will never cease to view them with indulgence, and that, after forty-five years of my life dedicated to its service with an upright zeal, the faults of incompetent abilities will be consigned to oblivion, as myself must soon be to the mansions of rest.

Relying on its kindness in this as in other things, and actuated by that fervent love toward it which is so natural to a man who views in it the native soil of himself and his progenitors for several generations, I anticipate with pleasing expectation that retreat in which I promise myself to realize without alloy the sweet enjoyment of partaking in the midst of my fellow-citizens the benign influence of good laws under a free government — the ever-favorite object of my heart, and the happy reward, as I trust, of our mutual cares, labors, and dangers.

John Adams' Inaugural Address
Philadelphia, March 4, 1797

John Adams' Inaugural Address established his claim as Washington's successor and struck the theme of continuity that was to characterize every subsequent inaugural address.

When it was first perceived, in early times, that no middle course for America remained between unlimited submission to a foreign legislature and a total independence of its claims, men of reflection were less apprehensive of danger from the formidable power of fleets and armies they must determine to resist than from those contests and dissensions which would certainly arise concerning the forms of government to be instituted over the whole and over the parts of this extensive country. Relying however, on the purity of their intentions, the justice of their cause, and the integrity and intelligence of the people, under an overruling Providence which had so signally protected this country from the first, the representatives of this nation, then consisting of little more than half its present number, not only broke to pieces the chains which were forging and the rod of iron that was lifted up, but frankly cut asunder the ties which had bound them, and launched into an ocean of uncertainty.

The zeal and ardor of the people during the Revolutionary war, supplying the place of government, commanding a degree of order sufficient at least for the temporary preservation of society. The Confederation which was early felt to be necessary was prepared from the models of the Batavian and Helvetic confederacies, the only examples which remain with any detail and precision in history, and certainly the only ones which the people at large had ever considered. But reflecting on the striking difference in so many particulars between this country and those where a courier may go from the seat of government to the frontier in a single day, it was then certainly foreseen by some who assisted in Congress at the formation of it that it could not be durable.

Negligence of its regulations, inattention to its recommendations, if not disobedience to its authority, not only in individuals but in States, soon appeared with their melancholy consequences — universal languor, jealousies and rivalries of States, decline of navigation and commerce, discouragement of necessary manufactures, universal fall in the value of lands and their produce, contempt of public and private faith, loss of consideration and credit with foreign nations, and at length in discontents, animosities, combinations, partial conventions, and insurrection, threatening some great national calamity.

In this dangerous crisis the people of America were not abandoned by their usual good sense, presence of mind, resolution, or integrity. Measures were pursued to concert a plan to form a more perfect union, establish justice, insure domestic tranquillity, provide for the common defense, promote the general welfare, and secure the blessings of liberty. The public disquisitions, discussions, and deliberations issued in the present happy Constitution of Government.

Employed in the service of my country abroad during the whole course of these transactions, I first saw the Constitution of the United States in a foreign country. Irritated by no literary altercation, animated by no public debate, heated by no party animosity, I read it with great satisfaction, as the result of goods heads prompted by good hearts, as an experiment better adapted to the genius, character, situation, and relations of this nation and country than any which had ever been proposed or suggested. In its general principles and great outlines it was conformable to such a system of government as I had ever most esteemed, and in some States, my own native State in particular, had contributed to establish. Claiming a right of suffrage, in common with my fellow-citizens, in the adoption or rejection of a constitution which was to rule me and my posterity, as well as them and theirs, I did not hesitate to express my approbation of it on all occasions, in public and in private. It was not then, nor has been since, any objection to it in my mind that the Executive and Senate were not more permanent. Nor have I ever entertained a thought of promoting any alteration in it but such as the people themselves, in the course of their experience, should see and feel to be necessary or expedient, and by their representatives in Congress and the State legislatures, according to the Constitution itself, adopt and ordain.

Returning to the bosom of my country after a painful separation from it for ten years, I had the honor to be elected to a station under the new order of things, and I have repeatedly laid myself under the most serious obligations to support the Constitution. The operation of it has equaled the most sanguine expectations of its friends, and from an habitual attention to it, satisfaction in its administration, and delight in its effects upon the peace, order, prosperity, and happiness of the nation I have acquired an habitual attachment to it and veneration for it.

What other form of government, indeed, can so well deserve our esteem and love?

There may be little solidity in an ancient idea that congregations of men into cities and nations are the most pleasing objects in the sight of superior intelligences, but this is very certain, that to a benevolent human mind there can be no spectacle presented by any nation more pleasing, more noble, majestic, or august, than an assembly like that which has so often been seen in this and the other Chamber of Congress, of a Government in which the Executive authority, as well as that of all the branches of the Legislature, are exercised by citizens selected at regular periods by their neighbors to make and execute laws for the general good. Can anything essential, anything more than mere ornament and decoration, be added to this by robes and diamonds? Can authority be more amiable and respectable when it descends from accidents or institutions established in remote antiquity than when it springs fresh from the hearts and judgments of an honest and enlightened people? For it is the people only that are represented. It is their power and majesty that is reflected, and only for their good, in every legitimate government, under whatever form it may appear. The existence of such a government as ours for any length of time is a full proof of a general dissemination of knowledge and virtue throughout the whole body of the people. And what object or consideration more pleasing than this can be presented to the human mind? If national pride is ever justifiable or excusable it is when it springs, not from power or riches, grandeur or glory, but from conviction of national innocence, information, and benevolence.

In the midst of these pleasing ideas we should be unfaithful to ourselves if we should ever lose sight of the danger to our liberties if anything partial or extraneous should infect the purity of our free, fair, virtuous, and independent elections. If an election is to be determined by a majority of a single vote, and that can be procured by a party through artifice or corruption, the Government may be the choice of a party for its own ends, not of the nation for the national good. If that solitary suffrage can be obtained by foreign nations by flattery or menaces, by fraud or violence, by terror, intrigue, or venality, the Government may not be the choice of the American people, but of foreign nations. It may be foreign nations who govern us, and not we, the people, who govern ourselves; and candid men will acknowledge that in such cases choice would have little advantage to boast of over lot or chance.

Such is the amiable and interesting system of government (and such are some of the abuses to which it may be exposed) which the people of America have exhibited to the admiration and anxiety of the wise and virtuous of all nations for eight years under the administration of a citizen who, by a long course of great actions, regulated by prudence, justice, temperance, and fortitude, conducting a people inspired with the same virtues and animated with the same ardent patriotism and love of liberty to independence and peace, to increasing wealth and unexampled prosperity, has merited the gratitude of his fellow-citizens, commanded the highest praises of foreign nations, and secured immortal glory with posterity.

In that retirement which is his voluntary choice may he long live to enjoy the delicious recollection of his services, the gratitude of mankind, the happy fruits of them to himself and the world, which are daily increasing, and that splendid prospect of the future fortunes of this country which is opening from year to year. His name may be still a rampart, and the knowledge that he lives a bulwark, against all open or secret enemies of his country's peace. This example has been recommended to the imitation of his successors by both Houses of Congress and by the voice of the legislatures and the people throughout the nation.

On this subject it might become me better to be silent or to speak with diffidence; but as something may be expected, the occasion, I hope, will be admitted as an apology if I venture to say that if a preference, upon principle, of a free republican government, formed upon long and serious reflection, after a diligent and impartial inquiry after truth; if an attachment to the Constitution of the United States, and a conscientious determination to support it until it shall be altered by the judgments and wishes of the people, expressed in the mode prescribed in it; if a respectful attention to the constitutions of the individual States and a constant caution and delicacy toward the State governments; if an equal and impartial regard to the rights, interest, honor, and happiness of all the States in the Union, without preference or regard to a northern or southern, an eastern or western, position, their various political opinions on unessential points or their personal attachments; if a love of virtuous men of all parties and denominations; if a love of science and letters and a wish to patronize every rational effort to encourage schools, colleges, universities, academies, and every institution for propagating knowledge, virtue, and religion among all classes of the people, not only for their benign influence on the happiness of life in all its stages and classes, and of society in all its forms, but as the only means of preserving our Constitution from its natural enemies, the spirit of sophistry, the spirit of party, the spirit of intrigue, the profligacy of corruption, and the pestilence of foreign influence, which is the angel of destruction to elective governments; if a love of equal laws, of justice, and humanity in the interior administration; if an inclination to improve agriculture, commerce, and manufacturers for necessity, convenience, and defense; if a spirit of equity and humanity toward the aboriginal nations of America, and a disposition to meliorate their condition by inclining them to be more friendly to us, and our citizens to be more friendly to them; if an inflexible determination to maintain peace and inviolable faith with all nations, and that system of neutrality and impartiality among the belligerent powers of Europe which has been adopted by this Government and so solemnly sanctioned by both Houses of Congress and applauded by the legislatures of the States and the public opinion, until it shall be otherwise ordained by Congress; if a personal esteem for the French nation, formed in a residence of seven years chiefly among them, and a sincere desire to preserve the friendship which has been so much for the honor and interest of both nations; if, while the conscious honor and integrity of the people of America and the internal sentiment of their own power and energies must be preserved, an earnest endeavor to investigate every just cause and remove every colorable pretense of complaint; if an intention to pursue by amicable negotiation a reparation for the injuries that have been committed on the commerce of our fellow-citizens by whatever nation, and if success can not be obtained, to lay the facts before the Legislature, that they may consider what further measures the honor and interest of the Government and its constituents demand; if a resolution to do justice as far as may depend upon me, at all times and to all nations, and maintain peace, friendship, and benevolence with all the world; if an unshaken confidence in the honor, spirit, and resources of the American people, on which I have so often hazarded my all and never been deceived; if elevated ideas of the high destinies of this country and of my own duties toward it, founded on a knowledge of the moral principles and intellectual improvements of the people deeply engraven on my mind in early life, and not obscured but exalted by experience and age; and, with humble reverence, I feel it to be my duty to add, if a veneration for the religion of a people who profess and call themselves Christians, and a fixed resolution to consider a decent respect for

Christianity among the best recommendations for the public service, can enable me in any degree to comply with your wishes, it shall be my strenuous
endeavor that this sagacious injunction of the two Houses shall not be without
effect.

With this great example before me, with the sense and spirit, the faith and
honor, the duty and interest, of the same American people pledged to support
the Constitution of the United States, I entertain no doubt of its continuance
in all its energy, and my mind is prepared without hesitation to lay myself
under the most solemn obligations to support it to the utmost of my power.

And may that Being who is supreme over all, the Patron of Order, the
Fountain of Justice, and the Protector in all ages of the world of virtuous liberty, continue His blessing upon this nation and its Government and give it all
possible success and duration consistent with the ends of His providence.

THE ELECTORAL VOTE IN THE 1796 ELECTION

STATES	John Adams	Thomas Jefferson	Thomas Pinckney	Aaron Burr	Samuel Adams	Oliver Ellsworth	George Clinton	John Jay	James Iredell	George Washington	Samuel Johnston	John Henry	C. C. Pinckney
New Hampshire.	6	—	—	—	—	6	—	—	—	—	—	—	—
Vermont........	4	—	4	—	—	—	—	—	—	—	—	—	—
Massachusetts...	16	—	13	—	—	1	—	—	—	—	2	—	—
Rhode Island...	4	—	—	—	—	4	—	—	—	—	—	—	—
Connecticut.....	9	—	4	—	—	—	—	5	—	—	—	—	—
New York......	12	—	12	—	—	—	—	—	—	—	—	—	—
New Jersey.....	7	—	7	—	—	—	—	—	—	—	—	—	—
Pennsylvania....	1	14	2	13	—	—	—	—	—	—	—	—	—
Delaware........	3	—	3	—	—	—	—	—	—	—	—	—	—
Maryland.......	7	4	4	3	—	—	—	—	—	—	—	2	—
Virginia........	1	20	1	1	15	—	3	—	—	1	—	—	—
North Carolina..	1	11	1	6	—	—	—	—	3	1	—	—	1
South Carolina..	—	8	8	—	—	—	—	—	—	—	—	—	—
Georgia........	—	4	—	—	—	—	4	—	—	—	—	—	—
Kentucky.......	—	4	—	4	—	—	—	—	—	—	—	—	—
Tennessee......	—	3	—	3	—	—	—	—	—	—	—	—	—
	71	68	59	30	15	11	7	5	3	2	2	2	1

Election of 1800

NOBLE E. CUNNINGHAM, Jr. is Professor of History at the University of Missouri, Columbia. He is the author of The Jeffersonian Republicans: the Formation of Party Organization, 1789–1801; The Jeffersonian Republicans in Power: Party Operations, 1801–1909; The Making of the American Party System, 1789–1809 *and* The Early Republic, 1789–1828.

Election of 1800

by *Noble E. Cunningham, Jr.*

Looking back on the election of 1800 Thomas Jefferson spoke of "the re-volution of 1800" and affirmed that it had been "as real a revolution in the principles of our government as that of 1776 was in its form; not effected in-deed by the sword, as that, but by the rational and peaceable instrument of reform, the suffrage of the people." Although Jefferson exaggerated when he spoke of a revolution, the election of 1800 was indeed one of the most signifi-cant elections in American history. The transfer of control over the executive and legislative branches of the national government from the Federalists to the Republicans in 1801 marked the first such transfer of power in the national government from one political party to another; that this was accomplished in a peaceful and orderly fashion demonstrated the maturity of the nation's first system of political parties. The election of 1800 was the first test of strength of the two national parties that had been formed in the course of the 1790's, and, more than any Presidential election that had preceded or would follow for at least a generation, it was a *party* contest for control of the national administra-tion and for determining the direction and the management of national policy.

The two principal candidates who faced each other in seeking the Presi-dency in 1800 were the same men who had stood in contest in 1796, but their situations had greatly altered in the four years since John Adams had won the office by a margin of three electoral votes over Thomas Jefferson. In 1796 Adams had been Washington's Vice-President, promising to follow in the first

President's footsteps; in 1800 he was the President with the record of his own Administration to defend. In 1796 Jefferson, beginning his third year in retirement at Monticello, was genuinely reluctant to have his name brought forward for the demanding office, and he remained inactive throughout the campaign. In 1800 Jefferson as Vice-President was deeply involved in politics, not as part of the Administration in which he was Vice-President but as the active leader of the Republican opposition seeking to remove Adams and the Federalists from command of the national government.

Adams and Jefferson had first met in Philadelphia in the summer of 1775 as delegates to the Continental Congress. The Massachusetts-born (1735) graduate of Harvard College (1755) was seven years the senior of the Virginian who had graduated from the College of William and Mary (1762) and read law under George Wythe. In 1800 Adams was sixty-four, Jefferson fifty-seven. Each had served his political apprenticeship as a member of his respective colonial assembly. In the wartime Congress, Jefferson and Adams found themselves on the same side of debates, and they served together on the committee to draft the Declaration of Independence. Alterations that Adams suggested in his own hand on Jefferson's draft of the famous document linked the two men together in a great moment of history, and neither could have then imagined the roles of antagonists into which their political futures would lead them.

In the postwar years both men served in key diplomatic posts in Europe, Adams as Minister to Great Britain and Jefferson as Minister to France. Both were at these European posts during the Constitutional Convention of 1787, but both returned in time to become members of the first Administration under the Constitution, Adams as Vice-President and Jefferson as Secretary of State. As the Republican interest emerged, Adams, who had attracted considerable unfavorable publicity during the first Congress by favoring titles for executive officers, became a symbol of aristocratic tendencies, and there was an organized but unsuccessful attempt in 1792 to unseat him as Vice-President. As early as 1791 Jefferson had expressed his opposition to the "political heresies" which he found in the writings of Adams, but it was Alexander Hamilton rather than Adams who most alarmed Jefferson; and in 1797 Jefferson considered the possibility of his Republican followers coming to some understanding with the newly elected President as to the best means of preventing Hamilton from getting into office in the future. The possibility of an accommodation with Adams, however, soon appeared only as a passing thought, and Jefferson as Vice-President almost immediately found himself assuming the leadership of the Republican opposition. He was to spend much of the next four years mobilizing the party for the campaign of 1800.

That Jefferson and Adams had developed different outlooks on government since they had stood together during the Revolution was clear by the time they joined Washington's Administration. In his three-volume *A Defence of the Constitutions of the Government of the United States of America* Adams emphasized the need for balance between the forces of aristocracy and democracy. "In every society where property exists, there will ever be a struggle between rich and poor," wrote Adams. "Mixed in one assembly, equal laws can never be expected. They will either be made by numbers, to plunder the few who are rich, or by influence, to fleece the many who are poor. Both rich and poor, then, must be made independent, that equal justice may be done, and equal liberty enjoyed by all."

On the other hand, Jefferson avowed an unqualified faith in the people. In addressing his neighbors in Albemarle County, Virginia, before leaving to take up his duties as Secretary of State, Jefferson spoke of "the holy cause of freedom" and affirmed, "It rests now with ourselves alone to enjoy in peace and concord the blessings of self-government, so long denied to mankind: to shew by example the sufficiency of human reason for the care of human affairs and that the will of the majority, the Natural law of every society, is the only sure guardian of the rights of man. Perhaps even this may sometimes err. But its errors are honest, solitary and short-lived. — Let us then, my dear friends, forever bow down to the general reason of the society. We are safe with that, even in its deviations, for it soon returns again to the right way."

In the heat of the first election contest between Jefferson and Adams in 1796 these differences were made to appear by Jeffersonian partisans as the differences between "a firm Republican" and "an avowed Monarchist" — a choice between "the uniform advocate of equal rights among citizens" and "the champion of rank, titles and hereditary distinctions," between "the steady supporter of our republican constitution" and "the warm panegyrist of the British Monarchical form of Government." While such bold contrasts of the political characters of Jefferson and Adams never disappeared from the campaign literature, by 1800 the Republicans had added to their arsenal of campaign ammunition a major new weapon — the record of the Adams Administration.

John Adams alone, of course, did not write the record of his Administration, for it was written in part by Congress, which did not always follow the President's lead, and in part by his Cabinet, which for most of Adams' Presidency was more loyal to Hamilton than to the President. But the record was that of the Federalist party, to which all members of the Cabinet claimed allegiance and which had a majority in Congress. The Republican opposition had no reason to draw distinctions between moderate Federalists and ultra-Federalists, between friends of Adams and backers of Hamilton, for Republicans were excluded from the Administration and from offices in the government. For the first time under Adams the nation experienced a party Administration, however divided that party may have been; and for the first time in 1800 a party would have to stand on the record of an Administration.

To a large extent the record of the Adams Administration was written in response to the pressures of foreign affairs growing out of the crisis in French relations which greeted him when he took office and which, before it was settled, led to decisions in domestic policy more controversial than those in foreign affairs. Soon after his inauguration Adams summoned a special session of Congress to deal with the French problem. In reaction to the United States' acceptance of the Jay Treaty with Great Britain, France had begun an aggressive campaign against American shipping and had refused to receive Charles Cotesworth Pinckney as Minister from the United States. While calling upon Congress to provide measures for defense, Adams announced the appointment of a commission (John Marshall, Elbridge Gerry, and Charles Cotesworth Pinckney) to attempt further negotiations. The outcome of this effort was the famous XYZ crisis which broke upon the country in April, 1798, when Congress released for publication the dispatches from the envoys to France. The immediate effect was a wave of anti-French feeling throughout the country, extensive measures for defense, and an undeclared naval war with France. Federalist popularity soared, and Federalists increased their majority in Congress in the congressional elections of 1798–99. At the same time, the Federalist response to the difficulty with France provided the basis for the major issues raised by the Republican opposition during the campaign of 1800.

In preparing for defense Congress created the Department of the Navy and began the building of a naval force. The regular army was expanded, and the President was authorized to raise a provisional army. These decisions extended beyond the immediate crisis with France and raised broad questions of policy in regard to naval power, standing armies, and reliance on the militia for defense. When Hamilton was appointed Inspector General, second to Washington in command of the army, questions were raised in the minds of Republicans as to the purposes of the increased military establishment. The clear preference given to Federalists over Republicans for commissions in the army created additional concern. The increased military expenditures required new measures of taxation and government loans, thus supplying other issues for political debate. Above all, the French issue provided the occasion for the passage of the most controversial domestic legislation of Adams' Presidency: the alien and sedition laws and the naturalization act of 1798. These laws raised the issue of whether they were necessary for the internal security of the United States or whether under the guise of patriotic purposes they were designed to cripple, if not destroy, the Republican opposition. The alien and sedition laws also took on increased significance in the political contest between Federalists and Republicans both in respect to the manner in which they were enforced against Republican newspaper editors and in regard to the basic constitutional and civil-liberties issues involved in the legislation. Moreover, the alien and sedition acts provided the occasion for the issuance of the Kentucky Resolutions, secretly drafted by Jefferson, and the Virginia Resolutions, secretly authored by Madison. These resolutions of 1798 not only posed fundamental questions of constitutional interpretation and state rights, but they also became campaign documents to be used in the Republican effort to dislodge the Federalists from their command of the national government.

The Presidential election of 1796 had been extremely close, and in examining the results of that contest Republican party managers had been struck by the fact that Adams' three-vote margin of victory in the electoral college could be attributed to 1 vote from Pennsylvania, 1 from Virginia, and 1 from North Carolina. In each of these states the Republicans had won an impressive victory, amassing in the three states a total of 45 electoral votes. The loss of 3 votes in these strongly Jeffersonian states was due to the district method of electing Presidential electors. In looking for ways to improve their chances for victory in the next presidential election, Republican managers thus turned their attention to state election laws. No uniform system of selection of presidential electors prevailed. In some states electors were chosen by the state legislature; in others they were elected on a general ticket throughout the state; in still others they were elected in districts. This meant that the party which controlled the state legislature was in a position to enact the system of selection which promised the greatest partisan advantage. Thus, in January, 1800, the Republican-controlled legislature of Virginia passed an act providing for the election of presidential electors on a general ticket instead of by districts as in previous elections. By changing the election law, Republicans in Virginia, confident of carrying a majority of the popular vote throughout the state but fearful of losing one or two districts to the Federalists, insured the entire electoral vote of the Union's largest state for the Republican candidate.

When Virginia Federalists protested the change, Republicans replied that "the same game is playing off in New England, and some other Eastern States." And, indeed, it was. In Massachusetts, Federalists feared that Jefferson might carry as many as two districts in that state under the system previously employed. Thus, the Federalist-controlled legislature of Massachusetts changed the laws of that state to provide for the selection of presidential electors by the state legislature in place of popular election by districts. In New Hampshire a general ticket was similarly replaced by a legislative choice of electors. In New York, Republicans introduced a measure to move from legislative choice to election by districts, but the proposal was defeated by the Federalists, an outcome which ultimately worked to the advantage of the Republicans when they won control over the legislature in the state elections of 1800. In Pennsylvania, a Republican House of Representatives and a Federalist Senate produced a deadlock over the system to be used to select electors, and the vote of that state was eventually cast by the legislature in a compromise division of the 15 electoral votes, eight Republican and seven Federalist electors being named. This solution essentially deprived Pennsylvania of a voice in the presidential election of 1800.

When all changes in electoral procedures had been completed, in only five of the sixteen states were presidential electors popularly elected: Rhode Island, Maryland, Virginia, North Carolina, and Kentucky. With the naming of Presidential electors in the hands of the state legislatures in approximately two-thirds of the states in 1800, the elections of members to the state assemblies became a major aspect of the presidential election. "It is perfectly well understood," wrote Thomas Boylston Adams to his brother John Quincy Adams in Berlin, "that the tiral of strength between the two Candidates for the chief magistracy of the Union is to be seen, not in the choice of electors by the people, but in the complextion and character of the individual legislatures." These elections coming at various times during the year meant also that the campaign of 1800 would extend throughout the year and that the results of an election in one state might influence later elections in other states.

The organization of political parties was incomplete in 1800, and in contrast with later refinements party machinery was still rudimentary. But a system of competing national parties did clearly prevail in 1800, a condition which had not existed when Washington took office little more than a decade earlier. Formal party machinery was most extensive in 1800 in those states in which Republicans and Federalists were most evenly balanced and party competition was keenest. The Middle Atlantic States best displayed these conditions. New York and Pennsylvania had the most extensive networks of party committees, with systems of county committees, township committees, and city ward committees. The Republican party was better organized than the Federalist party and tended to take the initiative in devising party machinery and new campaign techniques. As the party in power, the Federalists enjoyed advantages which the Republicans sought to overcome through better organization and more effective campaigning. Federalists commonly attempted to duplicate Republican machinery wherever it appeared and, in fact, had more machinery than they were willing to admit, since they tried to leave the impression that they were superior to such devices.

The presidential election of 1800 led to the introduction of formal party machinery for the first time in several states. Virginia offers the best example of this and also illustrates the type of party organization developed by this early date. When, in January, 1800, the Virginia legislature changed the state presidential election law from a district system to a general ticket, the state was faced for the first time with a statewide election, since the governor was chosen by the legislature and congressmen and assemblymen were elected in districts. Under the new law each voter, who in the past had voted for 1 presidential elector from his district, was now required to vote for 21 electors from the state at large. To conduct such a statewide campaign demanded party machinery. In January, 1800, Republican machinery to meet this need was initiated by what was reported in the newspapers to have been "a meeting of ninety-three members of the Legislature and a number of other respectable persons." This was a party caucus, composed primarily of state legislators but also open to other Republican party leaders. The machinery created by this caucus consisted of a central committee of five members in Richmond and county committees, also usually of five members, in nearly every county in the state. The central committee, headed by a state chairman, coordinated the campaign throughout the state, publicized the slate of electors in the press, and kept up regular correspondence with the county committees, supplying them with copies of the ticket and information to be used in the campaign. Federalists in Virginia in 1800 copied the Republican organizational structure and formed a similar, though less extensive, network of committees. In other states where formal party machinery had been introduced by 1800, similar patterns of committees of correspondence and campaign committees tended to be followed. But although parties, especially the Republican party, had made major strides in building formal machinery by 1800, party organization in many states still depended upon the informal direction of party leaders and small groups of party activists.

National party organization rested primarily on the informal association of party leaders and particularly on the members of each party in Congress. By 1800 both Federalists and Republicans had instituted the congressional nominating caucus. As will be described below, a caucus of Republican members of Congress in 1800 decided that Aaron Burr should be supported as the Republican vice-presidential candidate to be run on the ticket with Jefferson, and the results of the election would demonstrate how effective this caucus had become. The Federalist members of Congress also held a caucus in 1800 in which they agreed to support John Adams and Charles Cotesworth Pinckney as the Federalist candidates.

In 1800 the congressional nominating caucus was vigorously attacked. "If any thing will rouse the freemen of America," exclaimed one political commentator, "it must be the arrogance of a number of members of Congress to assemble as an *Electioneering Caucus*, to control the citizens in their constitutional rights. Under what authority did these men pretend to dictate their nomination? Did they receive six dollars a day for the double purpose of *caucussing* and *legislating*? Do we send members to Congress to *cabal* once in four years for President?" But, though denounced in 1800 and repeatedly challenged as long as it survived, the caucus system of nominating presidential candidates introduced in 1800 was employed by the Republican party until 1824, and until 1824 every presidential candidate nominated by the Republican caucus would win election. Thus, by 1800 the Republican party had instituted the basic mechanism of party organization on the national level.

When the Philadelphia *Aurora* announced in its issue of January 20, 1800, that "the electioneering campaign has already commenced," this was hardly news to the members of Congress who had been sitting since early December. While Federalists charged Republicans with "canvassing for the Election of Mr. Jefferson at the expense of $1,000 per day," the Speaker of the House was counseling Federalist friends that "in all our measures, we must never lose sight of the next election of President." Indeed, as one contemporary observed, Congress appeared as "a conclave of cardinals, intriguing for the election of a Pope." The President's son Thomas Boylston Adams called the session "altogether and exclusively, an Electioneering Cabal and Conspiracy."

During the campaign of 1800 national attention shifted from one state to another as critical elections determining the electoral votes of key states were held at widely separated times. By April all eyes were focusing on the election in New York, where the control of the legislature which would cast that state's electoral vote was at stake. A victory there would give an important psychological boost to the successful party. Republicans were particularly anxious to win in New York, since Adams had carried that state's 12 electoral votes in 1796, and an early Republican victory there might be of great influence on elections elsewhere. Besides, Republican leaders were not at all sure that they could win without New York. Jefferson calculated that if the Federalists carried New York the Republicans would have to carry both New Jersey and Pennsylvania and "we could not count with any confidence" on doing that. In March, 1800, Jefferson thus regarded a Republican victory in New York as essential to his election. The key to success in New York, party leaders on both sides agreed, was to win in New York City. The strength of the two parties throughout the rest of the state indicated the election of a legislature so nearly balanced that the thirteen members from New York City could be expected to give a majority to whichever party carried the city. Thus, both Federalists and Republicans concentrated their greatest efforts on the city election.

The initial advantage appeared to rest with the Federalists, since they had elected their entire slate in the state election of the previous year. Moreover, the Federalist effort was being directed by Alexander Hamilton, who had greatly impressed Republicans as a campaign manager in a recent election by attending "*all* the polls of this city, *daily* and *hourly*." To counteract Hamilton's leadership, Republicans relied on more broadly organized party machinery, consisting of party committees in each ward of the city and a general committee composed of deputies from the respective ward committees, and on the management of Aaron Burr. At the height of the 1800 campaign in New York, Burr was described by a close associate as "a man whose intrigue and management is most astonishing." What appeared to many contemporaries as "intrigue and management" was in fact skillful planning, organization, and effective campaign direction. Burr in 1800 was not some devious plotter, but an aggressive, practical party organizer.

Burr's basic plan for victory in New York City rested upon maintaining Republican unity and framing a slate of candidates that would represent all elements of Republican strength and at the same time present a list of distinguished and influential candidates. What Burr had in mind was for the Republican ticket to contain the names of such prominent persons as former Governor George Clinton, General Horatio Gates, and Judge Brockholst Livingston—all as candidates for the state assembly. None of these men wished to be nominated, and it required Burr's best persuasive efforts to get their agreements. "But for the matchless perseverance of Colonel Burr," said one of the Republican committeemen who called on Clinton, "the ticket, as it stood, never could have been formed." In arranging for Republicans to nominate a number of influential and well-known persons whose names alone would attract votes, Burr was following the example of Virginia Republicans who had nominated a slate of presidential electors including such prominent figures as George Wythe, James Madison, and Edmund Pendleton. Having formed the ticket, Burr was careful to keep his strategy a secret until after the Federalists had announced their ticket. The Federalist slate was published in the New York newspapers on March 29. On April 16 notices appeared in the papers calling a Republican meeting on April 17 to make nominations. This "numerous meeting of Republicans" placed a ticket in nomination, and from the newspaper reports it appeared to be the spontaneous action of a party meeting. But the slate of candidates named was that which Burr had carefully put together and for which he had already secured the backing of other party leaders.

Burr's accomplishment in framing a strong ticket inspired the lesser party leaders to greater effort. "Never," said one of them, "have I observed such an union of sentiment; so much zeal and so general a determination to be active." In marshaling support for the Republican ticket, Burr worked through the network of party committees linked together by the general committee, rather than through the Tammany Society as frequently assumed. Some Republicans thought that Burr's leadership was indispensable. "If we carry this election," wrote Matthew L. Davis to Albert Gallatin, "it may be ascribed principally to Col. Burr's management and perseverance." Burr's success depended on mobilizing the regular party machinery into an effective campaign organization. This Burr was able to do.

The Republicans, Abigail Adams thought, "laid their plan with much more skill than their opponents," while the Federalists nominated "men of no note, men whol[l]y unfit for the purpose; only two names of any respectability graced their list." Federalists, nevertheless, were extremely active in the campaign. Hamilton's dislike of Adams did not lessen his efforts to defeat the Republicans, though some men were later to make that charge. One friend of Adams felt that Hamilton "was as industrious at the Election as was consistent with his Rank" and assured Mrs. Adams that he had heard Hamilton at a public meeting denouncing Jefferson as "an atheist, a modern french Philosopher, overturner of Government, etc.," while speaking most respectfully of President Adams.

Electioneering by both parties continued until the final hours of voting. When the polls opened on April 29, both parties were predicting victory, but neither side was prepared to relax its efforts. The polls remained open for three days, and considerable last-minute campaigning took place at or near the polling places. Although candidates themselves did not campaign at the polls, party leaders on both sides went from ward to ward, while other party activists stationed themselves at the various voting places. Both Hamilton and Burr were active throughout the three days of voting and were reported to have engaged in some brief public debates when they accidently met at polling places. On the last day of the voting, Burr was reported to have remained at the poll of the seventh ward for ten hours without interruption, and one of his lieutenants was kept so busy that he went without eating for fifteen hours. Hamilton's supporters were equally vigorous. "I have been night and day employed in the business of the election," wrote Federalist Robert Troup after the close of the polls. "I have not eaten dinner for three days and have been constantly upon my legs from 7 in the morning till 7 in the afternoon."

The New York polls closed at sunset on May 1. By midnight enough votes had been counted to indicate a Republican victory, and Republicans quickly dispatched letters to Philadelphia announcing the victory. "We have labored hard but the reward is great," wrote Edward Livingston to Jefferson. The final returns showed that the Republicans had carried their entire ticket for the assembly in New York City, and a Republican majority in the legislature appeared to be assured. Most knowledgeable New York Republicans were willing to give Burr the principal credit. James Nicholson, a leading New York Republican, confided to his son-in-law Albert Gallatin that the election "has been conducted and brought to issue in so miraculous a manner that I cannot account for it but from the intervention of a Supreme Power and our friend Burr the agent. . . . His generalship, perseverance, industry, and execution exceeds all description, so that I think I can say he deserves anything and everything of his country."

Burr's reward was not long in coming. As soon as the news of the New York victory reached Philadelphia, jubilant Republican members of Congress commissioned Gallatin to obtain "correct information of the wishes of the New York Republicans" in regard to the vice-presidential nomination, which had not yet been determined. Republican consensus made Jefferson the party's presidential nominee in 1800, as it had in 1796, but some means of formal nomination was required to concentrate Republican electoral votes on a second candidate. Republican members of Congress in 1796 had attempted to decide on the vice-presidential nomination in a party caucus, but they had failed, and as a result the second ballots of Republican electors were widely scattered. Republicans in 1800 were thus anxious to avoid the difficulties of 1796, and party members in Congress hoped to make a nomination for the second office that would enable Republicans to elect both the President and the Vice-President. After the New York victory, there was general agreement that the vice-presidential nomination should go to a New Yorker. The most likely candidate appeared to be either George Clinton or Aaron Burr. Which did New York Republicans prefer? After conferences with Clinton, Burr, and other Republican leaders, Nicholson reported back to Gallatin that Clinton declined being considered and that Clinton and all of the Republicans with whom he had consulted agreed that "Burr is the most suitable person and perhaps the only Man." Their confidence in Burr, Nicholson concluded, was "universal and unbounded."

This was all that the Republicans in Congress needed to know, and soon after the report reached Philadelphia a Republican caucus was held. Forty-three Republican members were reported to have attended the caucus that met on May 11, and they unanimously agreed to support Burr for Vice-President. This first congressional nominating caucus established the method by which the Republican party would nominate the party's presidential and vice-presidential candidates down to 1824, and it demonstrated as early as 1800 the dominant role which Republican members in Congress played in providing national organization for the party.

If the New York election had a powerful effect on the Republican party, it also had a similar effect on the Federalists. "Yesterday they were arrogant and certain of our defeat," Republican Edward Livingston wrote on the day after the election. "Today, there is a most auspicious gloom on the countenances of every tory and placeman." So despairing were New York Federalists that at least two of them wrote to Federalist Governor John Jay urging him to call a special session of the legislature before the terms of the Federalist majority ended on July 1 in order to change the election law from a choice of electors by the legislature to election by districts. One of these Federalists was Alexander Hamilton; the other was his father-in-law, General Philip Schuyler. Hamilton argued that "in times like this in which we live, it will not do to be overscrupulous. It is easy to sacrifice the substantial interest of society by a strict adherence to ordinary rules . . . . They ought not to hinder the taking of a *legal* and *constitutional* step, to prevent an *atheist* in Religion, and a *fanatic* in politics from getting possession of the helm of State." Jay, who had resigned from the Supreme Court of the United States to become governor of New York, was not persuaded by Hamilton's reasoning and endorsed Hamilton's letter: "Proposing a measure for party purposes, which I think it would not become me to adopt." Thus, the newly elected Republican majority in the New York assembly could be expected to choose electors pledged to Thomas Jefferson.

Shortly after the Federalist defeat in New York, Hamilton also sent off an urgent appeal to Federalist members of Congress to resolve to support Charles Cotesworth Pinckney as a Federalist candidate on an equal basis with John Adams. "To support *Adams* and *Pinckney* equally is the only thing that can possibly save us from the fangs of *Jefferson*," he wrote on May 4 to Theodore Sedgwick, the Federalist Speaker of the House of Representatives. "It is, therefore, essential that the Federalists should not separate without coming to a distinct and solemn concert to pursue this course *bona fide*." Hamilton's proposal was based upon the fact that the Constitution did not provide for separate balloting for President and Vice-President but specified that each elector cast two ballots without distinguishing between the two offices. The candidate with the highest number of votes, provided it was a majority, became President; the second highest candidate became Vice-President. The success of Hamilton's plan rested upon the expectation that the vote of South Carolina would be cast for Jefferson and Pinckney, a native son, just as in 1796 the South Carolina vote had gone to Jefferson and to Thomas Pinckney, another native son. In 1796 the second ballots of Federalist electors had been widely scattered, so that Jefferson had become Vice-President; but it was expected that in 1800 both parties would give more attention to the second office. If Federalist electors in all states except South Carolina voted for Adams and Pinckney, and South Carolina electors voted for Jefferson and Pinckney, Pinckney rather than Adams would be the highest Federalist candidate. In all probability he would also be higher than Jefferson and thus be elected President.

It seems clear that Hamilton had already discussed this plan with other Federalists leaders, since the Federalists in Congress met in a caucus immediately after the news of the New York defeat was received and before the arrival of Hamilton's letter. Sedgwick reported a few days later: "We have had a meeting of the whole federal party, on the subject of the ensuing election, and have agreed that we will support, *bona fide*, Mr. Adams and General Pinckney." The leading Federalist to oppose this scheme in the caucus was Samuel Dexter of Massachusetts, who argued that whatever opinion Federalist leaders might have of Adams, "as he is viewed by the great majority of federalists, he is the most popular man in the United States, and deemed best qualified to perform the duties of President." Dexter reasoned that should Pinckney be elected over Adams it would "crumble the federal party to atoms." But many Federalists in Congress agreed with Timothy Pickering that "the only chance of a federal President will be by General C. C. Pinckney," and all except Dexter reportedly consented to support the scheme "as far as their advice and influence would go." Theodore Sedgwick privately stated that at the time of the caucus the Federalist members form South Carolina gave assurances that, whatever electors were chosen in that state, the popularity of Pinckney was such that the vote would be either for Adams and Pinckney or for Jefferson and Pinckney.

In May, 1800, Hamilton was not prepared publicly to oppose Adams' reelection, but privately he made it clear that he would "never more be responsible for him by my direct support, even though the consequence should be the election of *Jefferson*. If we must have an *enemy* at the head of the government," he wrote, "let it be one we can oppose, and for whom we are not responsible, who will not involve our party in the disgrace of his foolish and bad measures." By May, 1800, it was also clear that Adams was prepared to seek reelection without Hamilton's support. Indeed, the decisiveness with which Adams moved after the Federalist defeat in New York suggests the reaction of a shrewd politician, which Adams himself would never have admitted being and which some historians are reluctant to concede. In this connection, a review of the sequence of events following the defeat of the Federalist ticket in New York is instructive.

The news of the outcome of the New York election arrived in Philadelphia on Saturday morning, May 3. On Saturday evening the Federalist caucus met and agreed to support Pinckney equally with Adams. On Monday, May 5, President Adams summoned Secretary of War James McHenry, one of the Hamiltonian clique in the Cabinet, and demanded his resignation, which McHenry presented the following day. On Saturday, May 10, Adams sent a letter to Secretary of State Timothy Pickering, the leading Hamiltonian in the Cabinet, requesting his resignation by the following Monday morning so that he could send the nomination of his successor to the Senate before Congress adjourned. Pickering's reply was in Adams' hands early on Monday morning, May 12, for Adams in his own hand endorsed the letter "Rec'd at 9 O'Clock, May 12, 1800." Pickering's letter was a lofty refusal to resign, and Adams immediately sent him a note informing him that he was "hereby discharged from any further service as Secretary of State." The nomination of John Marshall to be Secretary of State was sent to the Senate the same day; his appointment was confirmed the following day, and Congress adjourned on May 14.

The speed with which Adams moved after the New York election seems significant. The split between Adams and the key members of his Cabinet was not a sudden development. By retaining Washington's Cabinet in taking office, Adams had begun his Administration with subordinates who gave first loyalty to Hamilton, and tensions between Adams and his department heads had increased as time passed. The split in the Administration came out into the open early in 1799, when Adams decided, over the objections of the Hamiltonians, to send a second peace mission to negotiate with France. Yet, despite the fact that as early as 1799 there was an irreparable breach between Adams and Hamilton's supporters in the Cabinet — Timothy Pickering, Oliver Wolcott, and James McHenry — Adams was apparently unwilling to risk the political consequences of the further alienation of the Hamiltonian leaders that would follow the dismissal of Hamilton's friends from the Cabinet. After the Federalist defeat in New York, Adams no longer felt compelled to deal gently with Hamilton, who could no longer deliver the New York vote either for or against him. The best hope for political success would therefore appear to have been for Adams to seek to win support among moderate Federalists in such states as Maryland and North Carolina, where the electors would be popularly elected. The appointments of John Marshall, a moderate Virginia Federalist, as Secretary of State, and of Samuel Dexter, who opposed the movement to support Pinckney, as Secretary of War, were well designed to make such an appeal.

Republicans were quick to see the implications of Adams' moves and charged him with electioneering, a charge against which Mrs. Adams was prompt to defend her husband, arguing in private letters that "if popularity had been his object, he would not have sought it by a measure that must create two Enemies to one friend." But, it might be asked, after New York was lost would those enemies be in a position to cost Adams the votes that he might lose by maintaining an alliance with the ultra-Federalists? The ultras might attempt to get Federalist electors in New England to throw away votes from Adams to favor Pinckney, but unless Adams could pick up sufficient votes south of New York to balance the New York loss he had no chance of winning. Mrs. Adams might deny that any political considerations were involved in the Cabinet dismissals, and the President himself would never have admitted, even to himself, that he was acting like a politician, but a political interpretation seems a more reasonable conclusion than the explanation that Adams simply lost his temper when he fired McHenry. It is undoubtedly true, from McHenry's report on his interview with Adams, that the President lost his temper. But what triggered this? The news of the New York election, followed by the meeting of the Federalist caucus, must surely explain why Adams no longer felt compelled to maintain the patience with which he had for so long tolerated the obstruction of McHenry and Pickering. Adams' only hope for victory after the loss of New York was to seek support from moderate Federalists and to win votes south of New York; his actions suggest that he saw this as clearly as did his Republican opponents.

In contrast to his role in 1796 when he made no effort to promote his own election, Jefferson in 1800 worked systematically to bring about a Republican victory. In drafting the Kentucky Resolutions of 1798 to protest against the Alien and Sedition laws, Jefferson not only raised issues for constitutional debate but also launched the Republican campaign to drive the Federalists from power. Early in 1799 he explicitly set down the Republican platform for the election of 1800 in a letter to Elbridge Gerry (quoted below), and as the year advanced Jefferson's political activities quickened. In February, 1799, he wrote to Madison suggesting that "this summer is the season for systematic energies and sacrifices. The engine is the press. Every man must lay his purse and his pen under contribution. As to the former, it is possible that I may be obliged to assume something for you. As to the latter, let me pray and beseech you to set apart a certain portion of every post day to write what may be proper for the public. Send it to me while here, and when I go away I will let you know to whom you may send, so that your name shall be sacredly se- cret."

During the campaign of 1800 Jefferson appealed to other political friends to write political tracts and pieces for the newspapers, though he himself adhered faithfully to an earlier resolve not to write anonymously for publication. Jefferson also aided Republican newspaper editors who supported the Republican cause, including financial aid to James Thomson Callender, probably the most abusive opponent of John Adams in the country. Jefferson later indicated that his gifts to Callender were meant as charities rather than as encouragement to his writings, but on at least one occasion he suggested that Callender's *The Prospect Before Us* "cannot fail to produce the best effect." When Republican newspaper editors were indicted under the sedition law in prosecutions that appeared to the Republicans to be carefully timed to coincide with the election campaign, Jefferson came to their aid. "I as well as most other republicans who were in the way of doing it, contributed what I could to the support of the republican papers and printers," he recalled in 1802, "paid sums of money for the Bee, the Albany Register, etc. when they were staggering under the sedition law, contributed to the fines of Callender himself, of Holt, Brown and others suffering under that law."

Jefferson was also active in helping the Republican party in the distribution of political pamphlets. In sending a dozen such tracts to James Monroe in February, 1799, he suggested: "I wish you to give these to the most influential characters among our country-men, who are only misled, are candid enough to be open to conviction, and who may have the most effect on their neighbors. It would be useless to give them to persons already sound. Do not let my name be connected with the business." In the course of the campaign of 1800 Jefferson made considerable use of this method of campaigning. In April, 1800, he sent to the chairman of the Republican state committee in Virginia eight dozen copies of Thomas Cooper's *Political Arithmetic*, a pamphlet protesting against commercial expansion and well suited to the farmers and planters of Virginia. Jefferson requested that one copy of the pamphlet be sent to each county committee in the state. "I trust yourself only with the secret that these pamphlets go from me," he wrote to the Virginia chairman. "You will readily see what a handle would be made of my advocating their contents. I must leave to yourself therefore to say how they come to you."

Throughout the campaign of 1800 Jefferson took special precautions to guard against the possibility of any of his private letters falling into Federalist hands for use against him. Convinced that "the postmasters will lend their inquistorial aid to fish out any new matter of slander they can gratify the powers that be," he avoided the discussion of political subjects in correspondence except when writing to trusted friends in letters sent by private conveyance. He left many of his letters to close political associates unsigned. But, although guarded in writing any letter that might reach the public, Jefferson had made clear his position on the issues before the public, and his party kept his platform before the voters.

It is interesting to note that Vice-President Jefferson in the spring of 1800 considered making a public visit to Governor James Monroe of Virginia. Although he disapproved of "pomp and fulsome attention by our citizens to their functionaries," he was concerned about the reports of "a great deal of federalism and Marshalism" in Richmond and thought "republican demonstrations" might help to counteract it. "Sometimes it is useful to furnish occasions for the flame of public opinion to break out," he suggested. Governor Monroe, however, advised against the visit, and Jefferson abandoned the idea. Could it be that Jefferson had heard that President Adams was planning to visit the new capital at Washington after the adjournment of Congress?

Adams was not so active as Jefferson in 1800 in the types of campaign activities in which Jefferson engaged—letter-writing, circulating political pamphlets, urging friends to write pieces for the press, assisting Republican newspaper editors, and encouraging Republican followers throughout the country to assist in the party cause. But Adams enjoyed the advantages of being the President of the United States, and, whether consciously or not, he allowed his candidacy to benefit from these advantages. After the adjournment of Congress in May, 1800, Adams did make a trip to Washington to inspect the new capital to which the offices of government were to be moved by June 15. He journeyed to Washington by way of Lancaster and York, Pennsylvania, and Fredericktown, Maryland, receiving along the way the attention that his station commanded. "How is it he has taken the route . . . *fifty* miles out of the strait course?" asked the Republican Philadelphia *Aurora*. After inspecting the new capital, Adams went to pay his respects to Mrs. Washington at Mount Vernon, where six months before General Washington had died. On his return trip northward, Adams stopped at Baltimore, before speeding home to Quincy for the summer. If Adams did not recognize the political advantages of such a trip, his Republican opponents did, as did also the anti-Adams Federalists within his own party. "The great man has been south as far as Alexandria, making his addressers acquainted with his revolutionary merits," wrote Fisher Ames, "and claiming almost in plain words at New London, office as the only reward."

Spending the summer in Massachusetts in the center of Federalist infighting, Adams noted that the Boston Federalist leaders did not make their accustomed calls at Quincy; and those party leaders noticed that at a dinner in Faneuil Hall in July Adams volunteered a toast to "the proscribed Patriots Hancock and [Sam] Adams." "It is evident Mr. Adams calculates upon engaging the passions and prejudices of the populace on his side, and with this reinforcement to overcome or beat down his federal opponents," observed George Cabot, in noting that Adams "has lately toasted men he has hated or despised these fifteen years." Fisher Ames thought that "no measures will be too intemperate that tend to make the Citizens revolutionary enough to make the man of 1775 the man of 1800." So many opponents of Adams called attention to the efforts of Adams and his friends to recall his revolutionary service that it is impossible not to consider such tactics as campaign strategy. Whether or not the tactics originated with Adams, he lent himself to the efforts. There can be no doubt that Adams wanted to be reelected in 1800, and, as a man active in politics all of his life, he could hardly have been unaware of the political consequences of his movements and actions during the campaign of 1800. If, as Adams' biographer Page Smith has concluded, Adams "often threw away political advantage quite deliberately," there is little evidence that he did so during the election of 1800.

"Never was there a more singular and mysterious state of parties," wrote Fisher Ames in July, 1800. "The plot of an old Spanish play is not more complicated with underplot." The underplot to which Massachusetts Federalist Ames referred was the struggle within the Federalist party over whether or not to dump John Adams and openly to try to elect Charles Cotesworth Pinckney. Publicly, the Federalist party was committed to support the reelection of Adams for President, but privately many of the most influential leaders of the party were opposed to Adams' reelection. When the Federalist caucus in Philadelphia in May, 1800, agreed to recommend the support of Adams and Pinckney equally, it was the intention of Hamilton and other anti-Adams Federalists that this scheme would promote the election of Pinckney and the defeat of Adams. The public argument, however, was that this was the best plan to insure a Federalist President and prevent the election of Jefferson, and it was on this ground that Adams' friends had agreed to the caucus decision. In private letters the ultra-Federalist leaders freely avowed their opposition to Adams, but they hesitated publicly to denounce their party's nominee, who in the public mind was the Federalist candidate for President and who was also the President of the United States. "Of those who forsee the exclusion of [Adams]," wrote Ames in June, 1800, "few yet dare, and fewer think it prudent or necessary, to avow their desire of such an event of the election."

Massachusetts was the center of much of the Federalist plotting and counterplotting. Some believed that the transfer of the choice of presidential electors from a popular vote to the legislature was designed to insure that all electors would vote for both Adams and Pinckney, but neither side was certain that this was true, or satisfied, in any case, to accept it. As early as June, 1800, Secretary of the Treasury Oliver Wolcott, a Hamiltonian, was urging his ultra-Federalist friends in Massachusetts to work to obtain electors who would vote *only* for Pinckney. "If General Pinckney is not elected," he wrote, "all good men will find cause to regret the present inaction of the federal party." On the other hand, George Cabot reported in July that "great efforts are making to persuade our people that they ought to throw away votes at the election, lest Mr. P[inckney] should be made President." Cabot suggested that "there are even men among the federalists who prefer Jefferson to a *federal* rival of Mr. A[dams], and there are some certainly who prefer Mr. J[efferson] to Adams."

In June Hamilton returned from a trip to Massachusetts, New Hampshire, and Rhode Island convinced that there would be Federalist electors in these states but that there was "considerable doubt of perfect union in favour of Pinckney." As the summer advanced, Hamilton moved further and further in the direction of an open break with Adams and an all-out public effort to elect Pinckney. He was strongly supported in this by Oliver Wolcott, who felt that the Federalists "ought in the first place to decide on one object and then avow and pursue it in an open and explicit manner." But Hamilton's closest followers in Massachusetts argued against any last-minute effort to drop Adams. "We shall be greatly embarrassed, if at this late period, after our sentiments are extensively known, there should be a new or different ground taken," George Cabot wrote to Hamilton; and to Wolcott, Cabot explained, "I am, and have long been, as fully convinced as you are, that Mr. Adams ought to have been abandoned by the federal party, whom he has sacrificed. But it seems a majority were not brought to this opinion in season, and the present half-way system was the consequence . . . . but still I do not see how it will be practicable to discard Mr. Adams as a candidate at this period without confounding us in this quarter, and consequently exposing the whole party to a defeat."

Throughout the summer of 1800 as anti-Adams Federalist leaders debated in their private letters the course which they should take, the wisdom of an open attack on Adams was widely questioned. From New Jersey, Richard Stockton reported that a "public avowal of a design to drop and oppose" Adams would endanger the chance of Federalist success. It was impossible to expect the Federalist members of the state legislature suddenly to drop the man that they had for four years been holding up "as one of the wisest and firmest men in the United States." "But if we use a prudent silence we shall get in our ticket of electors, and if I am not deceived, they will be men who will do right in the vote; they will go on the basis of securing a federal president. Mr. P[inckney] will be the man of their choice. They will act, at all events, in conformity with the plan proposed, in Philadelphia, and if the eastern states will unite in a more direct and decisive system, they will not desert them. But they will not be prepared to say that they prefer J[efferson] to A[dams]; they would effectually destroy themselves in public estimation if they did."

Although most of the advice that reached Hamilton from party workers active in key states opposed an open avowal of the movement to elect Pinckney, Hamilton by August confessed, "I have serious thoughts of giving to the public my opinion respecting Mr. Adams, with my reasons, in a letter to a friend, with my signature." By the end of September such a letter had been drafted. Printed for private circulation among Federalist leaders, a copy fell into Republican hands, and near the end of October it was before the public.

In the *Letter from Alexander Hamilton, Concerning the Public Conduct and Character of John Adams, Esq., President of the United States*, Hamilton attacked Adams more devastatingly than any Republican had ever done. Adams "does not possess the talents adapted to the *administration* of government," said Hamilton, and "there are great intrinsic defects in his character, which unfit him for the office of chief magistrate." "He is a man of an imagination sublimated and eccentric; propitious neither to the regular display of sound judgment, nor to steady perseverance in a systematic plan of conduct; and . . . to this defect are added the unfortunate foibles of a vanity without bounds, and a jealousy capable of discoloring every object." Hamilton did not publicly advise that votes be withheld from Adams, but he suggested that if the Federalists who shared his opinion of Adams were willing to vote equally for Adams and Pinckney, the least they could expect would be for the friends of Adams not to withhold any votes from Pinckney, especially since by voting for both men "they will increase the probability of excluding a third candidate, of whose unfitness all sincere Federalists are convinced." Hamilton's letter appeared too late in the campaign to be of much help to the Republicans, but they made the most of it in the time that remained. Its publication was a sensational event in an election year filled with dramatic developments.

The campaign of 1800 was conducted both at the level on which issues were discussed and alternatives provided and at the level where parties appealed to the emotions, prejudices, sectional attachments, and selfish interests of the voters. Although these two levels of argument were often inseparable in the partisan literature of the campaign, it is useful for the purposes of analysis to separate them. At the same time, since there is no way to determine whether a voter made up his mind through a reasonable evaluation of the issues or an emotional response to the campaign, or a combination of both influences, all levels of campaign rhetoric must be examined.

The Republican party did offer the voters a platform in 1800. Although the term *platform* was not used nor was any statement officially adopted by any agency of the Republican organization, a clearly defined party program was formulated and repeatedly presented to the electorate. The basic principles of the Republican platform were well understood by Jefferson, who stated them precisely in letters to a number of correspondents as the election of 1800 approached and reiterated them as the campaign continued. With the election won, he would repeat this same broad statement of principles in his first Inaugural Address. In a letter to Elbridge Gerry in January, 1799, Jefferson provided his best expression of the Republican platform. He began by affirming his attachment to the Constitution and continued:

> I am for preserving to the States the powers not yielded by them to the Union, and to the legislature of the Union its constitutional share in the division of powers; and I am not for transferring all the powers of the States to the general government, and all those of that government to the Executive branch. I am for a government rigorously frugal and simple, applying all the possible savings of the public revenue to the discharge of the national debt; and not for a multiplication of officers and salaries

merely to make partisans, and for increasing, by every device, the public debt, on the principle of its being a public blessing. I am for relying, for internal defence, on our militia solely, till actual invasion, and for such a naval force only as may protect our coasts and harbors from such depredations as we have experienced; and not for a standing army in time of peace, which may overawe the public sentiment; nor for a navy, which, by its own expenses and the eternal wars in which it will implicate us, will grind us with public burthens, and sink us under them. I am for free commerce with all nations; political connection with none; and little or no diplomatic establishment. And I am not for linking ourselves by new treaties with the quarrels of Europe; entering that field of slaughter to preserve their balance, or joining in the confederacy of kings to war against the principles of liberty. I am for freedom of religion, and against all maneuvres to bring about a legal ascendancy of one sect over another: for freedom of the press, and against all violations of the constitution to silence by force and not by reason the complaints or criticisms, just or unjust, of our citizens against the conduct of their agents.

"These, my friend," Jefferson affirmed, "are my principles; they are unquestionably the principles of the great body of our fellow citizens."

The summary of the Republican position which Jefferson here offered in a private letter corresponded to the public positions that Republicans took in response to the measures of the Adams Administration. A series of resolutions adopted by Republicans in Dinwiddie County, Virginia, in November, 1798, and published in the Richmond *Examiner*, December 6, 1798, placed emphasis on many of the same points. These resolutions may serve as an example of the public statement of Republican arguments against Federalist policies, which Republicans made the principal issues of the election of 1800. The major points of these resolutions were:

(1) Opposition to standing armies. "A militia composed of the body of the people, is the proper, natural, and safe defence of a free state," it was declared in resolving "that regular armies, except in case of an invasion, or the certain prospect of an invasion, are not only highly detrimental to the public welfare, but dangerous to liberty. . . . Military establishments are in their nature progressive, the vast expense attending them, producing discontent and disturbances, and these furnishing a pretext for providing a force still more formidable; thus finally occasioning the oppression, the ruin, the SLAVERY of the people."

(2) Opposition to great naval armament "because it enlarges still more the fund for increasing executive influence: because the expense is incalculable . . . because this country cannot hope to protect its commerce by a fleet . . . or to guard from invasion a coast fifteen hundred miles in extent. . . . When therefore the navy of the United States is competent to the protection, not of our extensive coast, nor of our commerce throughout the world, but of our sea ports and coasting trade, from privateering and piratical depredations, it has attained the point, beyond which it ought not to go."

(3) Opposition to "an alliance with any nation on earth." Republicans "reprobate therefore the practice of maintaining ministers resident in foreign countries, in the extent to which it is carried by the executive of the United

States; because it adds still more to the already enormous mass of presidential patronage; because every important political view might be accomplished by a single minister advantageously stationed, and every valuable commercial purpose might be effected under the ordinary consular establishments; and because at a time like this, when money is borrowed to supply the deficiency of the taxes, every expense not absolutely necessary ought to be avoided."

(4) Opposition to increasing the national debt on the grounds that "the only proper way to raise money for national purposes, is by taxes, duties, excises and imposts, and that the power of borrowing money, ought not to be exercised except in cases of absolute necessity; that if money be really wanted, the people ought to be taxed to pay it; if not wanted, it ought not to be raised."

(5) Opposition to the alien act as "unnecessary, repugnant to humanity, and contrary to the constitution."

(6) Opposition to the Sedition Act as "a daring and unconstitutional violation of a sacred and essential right, without which, liberty, political science and national prosperity are at an end." "Freedom of the press is the great bulwark of liberty and can never be restrained but by a despotic government."

Various versions of this platform were published during the course of the campaign in party leaflets and in the press. The Philadelphia *Aurora* printed a popularized version listing the alleged Federalist record and the proposed Republican program in parallel columns, urging voters to "Take Your Choice" between "Things As They Have Been" and "Things As They Will Be."

In answer to the question "What do the republican interest want by so zealously attempting a change of men?" Charles Pinckney, who managed the Jeffersonian campaign in South Carolina, explained in a pamphlet: "Never to have such acts as the alien and sedition laws; or unnecessary embassies; or too intimate a connexion with any foreign power; but a just and impartial conduct to all — so that peace may be established, and wars avoided, with all their dangerous and expensive armaments and consequences — the public expense reduced, so that our revenue may be employed in paying and lessening the public debt, and an end put to heavy additional yearly loans, at the rate of eight per centum — no direct tax on the landed and agricultural interests only, but strict economy in all our expenditures . . . these are among the objects of the republican interest in endeavouring to place men in power in whom they can confide to accomplish them effectually."

While the Republicans thus presented a clearly identifiable platform, the Federalists essentially ran on their record, and in this they took pains to link together the Administrations of Washington and Adams and to lay a party claim to the accomplishments of the first President. Federalist literature stressed the "present prosperous situation" of the nation as a result of "the sage maxims of administration established by the immortal Washington, and steadily pursued by his virtuous successor," and argued against change. "An unvarying course of prosperity, like the even tenor of health, makes no impression, while we betray a quick sensibility to the slightest misfortune or pain," declared the Federalist state committee of Virginia. "We forget that our government has preserved us from two impending wars, the foundation of which was laid before its existence, with the two most powerful nations of the world, armed to the full extent of their powers; and that, without any sacrifice of the national interest, or of the national honor. We forget that we have been preserved from a close alliance with either of those nations, which would have been the worst, and the most inevitable, consequences of a war with the other; and that we remain, if we will, completely free and independent. But the fleet, the army, the taxes, all the little evils which were necessary to the attainment of these great and invaluable objects, make a strong impression, and are attributed as crimes to the government."

In a similar vein, a Federalist address to Rhode Island voters argued: "The land tax has afforded a topic of declamation to the opponents of government. It has been charged upon the administration when it ought to have been charged to the war in Europe, and the depredations which have been committed on our commerce by the powers at war. A Navy has become indispensable to the existence of our commerce, and the prosperity of our agriculture." Repeatedly, Federalists defended their record, and they expected voters to "value the blessings of good government too well to risque a change."

However clearly and reasonably the two parties presented their positions, as they did on numerous occasions, neither party rested its case on the restrained presentations of policy differences. Both parties appealed to the voters' emotions and prejudices, to their hopes and fears, and to their personal, class, and sectional interests. Although there was a note of restraint in most official party publications, whether Republican or Federalist, an emotional appeal rang through many campaign handbills, leaflets, and endless columns of newspaper print. "We ought . . . to bring our arguments home to their feelings," advised one Republican; while a Federalist urged his party to "sound the tocsin about Jefferson," arguing that "the hopes and fears of the citizens are the only source of influence, and surely we have enough to fear from Jefferson."

"*Is it not high time for a CHANGE?*" asked a Republican campaign leaflet addressed to the voters of New Jersey. And throughout the country Republicans painted a shocking picture of the state of the nation: "Our agriculture is oppressed by taxation. Our manufactures are superceded by British productions. Our commerce subjected to the spoliations of foreign cruisers. . . . We are struggling under a direct tax, with heavy imposts; raising money on loan at *Eight* per cent. — And our expenditures are encreasing, while our national debt is accumulating." On the outcome of the election, voters on Long Island were told, "will depend whether the present system of war, debt, and encreasing taxation shall continue to be pursued, or a new line of conduct shall be adopted." Republicans published long lists of figures showing governmental expenditures and the increase in the national debt. They compared the six-and-a-half-million dollar appropriation for the Army and Navy in 1800 with the total expenditure of nine hundred thousand dollars during Washington's first year in office and suggested that "if we want to return to the best days of Washington's presidency, let us elect Jefferson, who was his principal minister in those days." A New Jersey Republican committee urged voters to vote against "the present administration, under which your *taxes* and *public debt* have been greatly increased, in a time of peace; under which the number of federal officers hath been greatly increased, and mercenary armies attempted to be raised; which is not barely an unnecessary expense upon the people, but highly alarming and dangerous to their liberties."

A New England Federalist observed that the Republicans "have a certain number of sounds, thrown into the form of regular and well connected sentences, which they can on all occasions utter with the utmost facility and volubility. In these sentences the words British Influence—Standing Army—Direct Taxes—Funding System—Expensive Navy—Commerce can support itself—Congress have too high wages—Aristocracy—and Washington's Grave Stones, are ever and anon distinctly heard." Although Republicans directed their campaign rhetoric primarily against the record of the Federalist Administration rather than against Adams personally, there were charges of monarchist leveled against the President. One Republican writer, hoping that Americans "will never permit the chief magistrate of the union to become a *King* instead of a president," attempted to prove "that there is a monarchical party in the United States, and that Mr. Hamilton and Mr. Adams belong to that party." Republicans also tried to picture Administration leaders as British sympathizers. "We have seen with regret," declared a Republican state convention in September, 1800, "*British subjects* raised to posts of honor and profit, to the exclusion of *honest Americans*, who braved the perils of a long and bloody war. We have seen old tories, the enemies of our revolution, recommended as the guardians of our country."

Campaign literature frequently appealed to local prejudices and sectional attachments. Federalists in New England suggested that "the great and powerful State of Virginia seems to take the lead in the present opposition to the measures of administration. The plausible and specious cry that the liberties of the people are in danger, and that aristocracy is creeping into our government, originates in and emanates from that State. But will New-England-men, with arms in their hands, ever confess that they are in danger of slavery?" In a similar vein the *Connecticut Courant* insisted that the freemen of Connecticut should not stoop "to learn the principles of liberty of the slave-holders of Virginia." And one reader agreed: "We want no *Southern lights* in these parts: We have northern lights,—we have gospel light, and political light, sufficient to exterminate Jacobinism."

Republicans likewise shaped their appeals to the particular interests and sentiments of the voters addressed. "Why should you hear any more of the Alien Law?" they asked Pennsylvania Germans. In Rhode Island, they called particular attention to Jefferson's devotion to religious toleration and attacked Adams as a champion of established religion. In Pennsylvania, Republicans proclaimed that "to religious men, Mr. Jefferson has indisputably been the most useful character, since *William Penn*," and as President he would promote "the sound *practical Equality* of the Quaker" and "the *equal Brotherhood* of the Moravian, the Mennonist, and the Dunker." In New Jersey, Republicans accused Federalists of attacking Jefferson on religious grounds simply "because he is not a fanatic, nor willing that the *Quaker*, the *Baptist*, the *Methodist*, or any other denominations of Christians, should pay the pastors of other sects; because he does not think that a catholic should be banished for believing in transubstantiation, or a jew, for believing in the God of Abraham, Isaac, and Jacob."

In some regions, Republican campaign literature frequently referred to Jefferson's agrarianism, and a passage was widely quoted from his *Notes on the State of Virginia* in which he had written that "those who labor in the earth are the chosen people of God." The farmers of Rhode Island were told, "He has not fawned on great cities for support. He has declared, that 'if ever God has a chosen People, it is the cultivators of the soil.' Cultivators of the Soil—friends of peace, humanity, and Freedom: give him your support. He will not betray you." At the same time, Republicans in the cities appealed to the "mechanics" and other city dwellers, and Jefferson was held up as the "friend of the people." An editorial in the New York *American Citizen*, April 3, 1800, concluded that "*Thomas Jefferson* is the enlightened citizen, the patriot, the philosopher, and the friend of man, to whom the republican attachment and affections of this country ought to be directed." Republicans in the cities thus found ample ground for praising Jefferson without calling attention to his agrarianism.

Everywhere Republicans pointed to Jefferson as the author of the Declaration of Independence. "Let us therefore," urged one campaign broadside, "taking the Declaration of Independence in our hands, and carrying its principles in our hearts, let us resolve to support THOMAS JEFFERSON, whose whole life has been a comment on its precepts, and an uniform pursuit of the great blessings of his country which it was first intended to establish." Republicans also praised Jefferson for his "talents as governor of his native state, as an ambassador abroad, as legislator and secretary of state," and lauded him as "the adorer of our God; the patriot of his country; and the friend and benefactor of the whole human race." Concluded the Republican state committee of Virginia in its official address to the voters: "As a friend to liberty, we believe Jefferson second to no man, and the experience of no man has afforded better lessons for its preservation."

The Federalist picture of Jefferson was, of course, quite different. "You have been, Sir, a Governor, an Ambassador, and a Secretary of State," a writer in the *Gazette of the United States* addressed Jefferson, "and had to desert each of these posts, from that weakness of nerves, want of fortitude and total imbecility of character, which have marked your whole political career, and most probably will attend you to your grave."

One recurring theme in much of the anti-Jefferson literature was that his election would bring to the United States the disorders that the French Revolution had brought to France. Wrote "A North Carolina Planter": "Against the dangerous principles of Mr. Jefferson's philosophy . . . to warn you, my fellow citizens, I have only to direct your view to that ill fated country France, and bring to your recollection the history of the horrid government of their philosophers, who professed similar principles. . . . From the government of such philosophers, may the beneficent father of the universe protect us." A writer signing himself "A Christian Federalist" warned in *A Short Address to the Voters of Delaware*: "Can serious and reflecting men look about them and doubt, that if Jefferson is elected, and the Jacobins get into authority, that those morals which protect our lives from the knife of the assassin—which guard the chastity of our wives and daughters from seduction and violence—defend our property from plunder and devastation, and shield our religion from contempt and profanation, will not be trampled upon and exploded. Men are the same in their natures in different countries and at different times. . . . Let these men get into power, put the reins of government into their hands, and what security have you against the occurrence of the scenes which have rendered France a cemetery, and moistened her soil with the tears and blood of her inhabitants?"

The issue that received most attention in newspapers and pamphlets was Jefferson's religion. "The Grand Question Stated," as the Philadelphia *Gazette of the United States* repeatedly proclaimed, was: "At the present solemn and momentous epoch, the only question to be asked by every American, laying his hand on his heart is 'shall I continue in allegiance to

GOD—AND A RELIGIOUS PRESIDENT;

Or impiously declare for

JEFFERSON—AND NO GOD!!!' "

In newspapers, pamphlets, and handbills, Jefferson was charged with being a deist, an atheist, and an enemy to religion. The accusations were often voiced in the most vehement language. In the widely circulated pamphlet *Serious Considerations on the Election of a President: Addressed to the Citizens of the United States*, the Reverend William Linn of New York charged Jefferson with "disbelief of the Holy Scriptures" and the "rejection of the Christian Religion and open profession of Deism." Citing passages from *Notes on the State of Virginia*, Linn concluded that "the election of any man avowing the principles of Mr. Jefferson would . . . destroy religion, introduce immorality, and loosen all the bonds of society. . . . The voice of the nation in calling a deist to the first office must be construed into no less than a rebellion against God." Federalist editors reprinted long passages in their papers; the pamphlet, said the editor of the *Gazette of the United States*, "convicts Mr. Jefferson of scepticism, deism, and disregard of the holy scriptures."

It is evident from the number of replies to Linn's pamphlet that the Republicans were sensitive about this issue. They countered with their own passages from Jefferson's *Notes on the State of Virginia*, which offered abundant proof, they suggested, that Mr. Jefferson was not a deist. One Republican pamphlet argued "that the charge of deism, contained in such pamphlet, is false, scandalous and malicious—That there is not a single passage in the Notes on Virginia, or any of Mr. Jefferson's writings, repugnant to christianity; but on the contrary, in every respect favourable to it." Republicans also stressed Jefferson's authorship of the act for establishing religious freedom in Virginia and his efforts to promote toleration in religion. "Religious liberty, the rights of conscience, no priesthood, truth and Jefferson," promised the Philadelphia *Aurora's* version of the Republican platform.

"Jefferson is pretty fiercely attacked in different parts of the Continent on the ground of his religious principles," wrote Federalist Robert Troup of New York in September 1800. "It is not probable, however, that all that has been, or will be, written on this subject will deprive Jefferson of a single vote, so irrevocably bent is his party on forcing him into the President's chair." Republicans were, however, taking no chances, and they saturated the country with defenses of their candidate's religious principles.

Most of the campaign issues were debated within the context and procedures of state elections for members of the legislatures which would choose the presidential electors in two-thirds of the states. While presidential electors were popularly elected in only five of the sixteen states in 1800, the evidence is overwhelming that state elections were dominated by the presidential contest.

In Maryland, where under existing legislation presidential electors were popularly elected, a simultaneous campaign went on for members of the legislature. The election for the legislature was to be held on the first Monday in October, and Federalists campaigned on the promise to transfer the choice of electors to the state legislature before the election of presidential electors would be held on the second Monday in November. "We deem it a sacred duty to pursue every *proper and constitutional* measure to elect John Adams president of the United States," a group of Federalist candidates for the assembly announced in a joint statement.

There was more open campaigning in Maryland than in any other state in 1800. It took place wherever people gathered, "at a horse race, a cock-fight, or a Methodist quarterly meeting," explained one observer. "Here, the Candidates for political honors or preferment, assemble with their partizans —they mount the Rostrum, made out of an empty barrel or hogshead, Harrangue the Sovereign people—praise and recommend themselves at the expence of their adversary's character and pretentions." The Baltimore *Federal Gazette* on July 28, 1800, reported two large meetings where "the different candidates for elector of president and members of assembly attended and harangued the voters. . . . After panegyrising the character of Mr. Jefferson, and defending it against the charges of pusillanimity and deism," the Republican candidate for the assembly "discanted on the official conduct of Mr. Adams. He declared several acts of congress unconstitutional and offered himself as a member of the next assembly, to forward the election of the former and to oppose the re-election of the latter." A Republican candidate for elector also attempted "to prove the necessity of turning Mr. Adams out of the presidency and of electing Mr. Jefferson in his place." He was answered by a Federalist spokesman who solemnly replied "that the measures of the present administration were conceived in wisdom, and executed with firmness, uprightness and ability—that the path laid down by Washington had been faithfully pursued by Adams—and that the latter had done all that could be done, and no more, to ensure *justice* from abroad and *tranquillity* at home."

While Federalists attempted to associate Washington's name in the popular mind with Federalism, Republicans were unwilling to permit an exclusive claim to the young nation's greatest hero. "Consummate your reverence for the memory of Washington," suggested the Republican state committee of Virginia, "not by employing it as an engine of election, but by declaring, that even his name shall not prevent the free use of your own understandings." And the title page of a Republican pamphlet containing extracts from Jefferson's writings on religion ran a quotation from Washington: "The path of true piety is too plain to want political direction."

In private letters during the summer and fall political leaders on both sides arrived at similar conclusions about the outcome of the election. They agreed that, except for uncertain Rhode Island, the New England states would be Federalist, though whether they would be unanimous for Adams and Pinckney even Hamilton could not predict. New York would be Republican; Pennsylvania probably would not cast a vote; Delaware would be Federalist; New Jersey would be close. "We think we have an equal claim with the federalists, to the whole of New Jersey," Burr wrote in July. "The republicans of that State speak most confidantly of a republican legislature at the approaching election in October." From the Federalist side, Hamilton wrote in August: "The State of New Jersey is more uncertain than I could wish. Parties will be too nicely balanced there. But our friends continue confident of a favorable result."

Maryland was uncertain. If the district system prevailed, the 10 electoral votes would be divided. Burr in July claimed 4 certain, and 2 possible, Republican districts. Federalist James A. Bayard in August would concede but 3 Maryland districts to Jefferson. All agreed that Virginia would be unanimous for Jefferson; or, as Bayard expressed it, "Virginia is sold, and past salvation." North Carolina, where electors would be elected by districts, would be divided. Nathaniel Macon, who, a friend noted in passing along his prediction, was "too proud to promise on slight grounds," reported that Republicans could be sure of 8 votes out of 12 from that state. Bayard advised Hamilton to count 7 North Carolina votes for Jefferson. Kentucky, Tennessee, and Georgia were counted in Jefferson's column, but South Carolina had everyone guessing.

Burr predicted in July that if Pennsylvania did not vote Jefferson would have 63 votes, or a majority of 2. Hamilton refrained from an exact prediction but concluded in August that "there seems to be too much probability that Jefferson or Burr will be President." Bayard, however, predicting South Carolina for Pinckney and Jefferson, thought there was still "no reason to despond, unless the Eastern states play a foul game." At the end of November, Jefferson calculated that, excluding Pennsylvania, Rhode Island, and South Carolina, the Republicans would have 58 electoral votes and the Federalists 53. "Both parties count with equal confidence on Rhode Island and South Carolina," he said. "Pennsylvania stands little chance for a vote. . . . In that case, the issue of the election hangs on South Carolina." From Washington, D. C., two days earlier, Oliver Wolcott had written in much the same vein to a Federalist friend: "The issue of the election of a President, is, at this time, as uncertain as ever; all depends on the vote of South Carolina, and this is claimed and expected by both parties."

As elections in various states were decided and the party complexion of the electoral vote determined, it became clear that the election was, indeed, to be finally settled by South Carolina. Without that state's vote, the last to be reported, the Federalists had all of the New England electoral votes. They also won New Jersey and Rhode Island, carried 5 of 10 districts in Maryland, and elected 4 of the 12 electors in North Carolina. In Pennsylvania a compromise was reached on December 1 by which the Republicans secured 8 electors and the Federalists named 7 — a net gain of but 1 for the Republicans. These victories gave the Federalists 65 votes. On the other side, the Republicans won the entire vote of New York, Virginia, Georgia, Kentucky, and Tennessee, which together with 8 electors from Pennsylvania, 5 from Maryland, and 8 from North Carolina, gave the Republicans a total of 65 votes also. Thus, with South Carolina unrecorded, Republicans and Federalists stood equal. Some Federalist editors now began to predict a Federalist victory, though all agreed that the outcome rested upon South Carolina.

One person who had been convinced all along that "the choice of a President would in a great measure depend upon this States vote" was Charles Pinckney, Republican senator from South Carolina who had devoted himself to winning the state for Jefferson since returning home after the adjournment of Congress. Since June, Pinckney had been actively "sprinkling," as he put it, "all the southern states with pamphlets and Essays and every thing I thought would promote the common cause against what I well knew must be the Consequence if the federalists succeeded." Despite Pinckney's efforts, Federalists carried 11 out of the 15 seats from Charleston, and the composition of the state legislature appeared so doubtful that Pinckney himself, not a member of the assembly but a United States senator, decided to go to the capital at Columbia for the climactic meeting.

The assembly convened on the last Monday in November (November 24), and Presidential electors were to be chosen on the first Tuesday of December (December 2). In a week of political maneuvering Pinckney worked frantically to get a slate of electors for Jefferson and Burr. The presence of a native son, General Charles Cotesworth Pinckney, the Federalist candidate and a member of the state senate, further complicated the situation. At two evening caucuses Republicans named their slate. In a report to his partner and co-editor Seth Paine of the Charleston *City Gazette*, Peter Freneau described the situation in Columbia on November 27, three days after the opening of the session. "There have been two meetings of the republicans at the School House," he wrote, "and 69 have signed their names to support the Jefferson and Burr Ticket, and it is believed that there are 12 to 20 more who will Vote for it. It is the general opinion of the republicans here that all will go right, and this is my opinion if some arts are not successful between this and tuesday; every thing that can be done by the other party will be attempted. There is to be a meeting at the Presidents of the Senate this evening. There are 142 members present, we suppose there will be 150, of course 75 is equal, we count from 84 to 86, some say 90. I hope we are not mistaken still I am not confident as there are some of this number which do not like to give up P[inckney]. I have heard that the drift of the meeting this night is to offer a compromise, while others say that the General will not suffer his name to be run with Mr. Jefferson. At any rate I think things look favorable."

When Republicans caught wind of a Federalist plan to send speakers to the final Republican caucus the night prior to the balloting, they canceled the meeting. As Republicans understood the scheme, Federalist spokesmen hoped to appeal to state loyalty and propose a compromise ticket of Jefferson and Pinckney. If this were the case, no Federalist ever admitted it, and Federalists repeatedly claimed that General Pinckney had firmly resisted all attempts to form a ticket with Jefferson.

On December 2 the legislature elected all the Republican candidates by majorities of from 13 to 18 votes. Freneau hurriedly sent the news to Paine in Charleston: "Our Electors are chosen . . . rejoice and let the good news be known. Our Country is yet safe. The vote tomorrow will be Jefferson 8. Burr 7. Clinton 1. This I am told—it is not the wish to risque any person being higher than Jefferson. I know not what I am writing I am so rejoiced." Freneau gave much of the credit for the victory to Charles Pinckney; and from Pinckney's own letters to Jefferson written immediately after the South Carolina victory the clear implication was that Pinckney had made some promises of patronage. While the report went out that 1 vote would be withheld from Burr in South Carolina, the electors met in Columbia and cast 8 votes for Jefferson and an equal number for Burr.

In New York, Federalist Robert Troup wrote on December 4 to Rufus King in London: "This is the day appointed for the election of President and Vice President. The calculations now are that Adams and Pinckney will outrun Jefferson and Burr. . . . This opinion is based upon the votes of the States, now known, and, that, in South Carolina, all our accounts agree that the last election of members of the Legislature terminated in the triumph of the federalists, and that the electors appointed by them will of course be decidedly federal. General Pinckney who wrote to General Hamilton after the election, and before the event was certainly known, puts much confidence in the appointment of federal electors and says that they would vote honorably according to the agreement in Philadelphia for Adams and himself. It is this success in South Carolina that determines the event of the election."

Troup's optimism was shared by numerous Federalist editors, one of whom announced that "the non-election of (*Citizen*) Jefferson is now certain." The news of the actual South Carolina vote thus came as a blow to many Federalists. "I have never heard bad tidings on anything which gave me such a shock," a New England clergyman confided in his diary. The Republicans, too, got a jolt when the outcome in South Carolina was known and all the votes were tallied. The final count was Jefferson 73, Burr 73, Adams 65, Pinckeny 64, and Jay 1. The shock was not that the Republicans had won, but that Jefferson had not actually been elected President. Instead, the equal vote given to Burr forced the election into the House of Representatives, in the first of only two such occasions in American history.

PRESIDENTIAL AND CONGRESSIONAL ELECTIONS, 1800

	Electoral Vote					Members Elected to House of Representatives	
	Jefferson	Burr	Adams	Pinckney	Jay	Republicans	Federalists
New Hampshire			6	6			4
Vermont			4	4		1	1
Massachusetts			16	16		7	7
Rhode Island			4	3	1	2	
Connecticut			9	9			7
New York	12	12				6	4
New Jersey			7	7		5	
Pennsylvania	8	8	7	7		10	3
Delaware			3	3			1
Maryland	5	5	5	5		5	3
Virginia	21	21				18	1
North Carolina	8	8	4	4		5	5
South Carolina	8	8				3	3
Georgia	4	4				2	
Kentucky	4	4				2	
Tennessee	3	3				1	
	73	73	65	64	1	67	39

(*Italics* indicates states in which presidential electors were elected by popular vote.)

In analyzing the election returns, historians have frequently pointed to the fact that outside New York Adams received 7 more votes in 1800 than in 1796. That is true, but 6 of those 7 votes came from Pennsylvania, where the deadlocked legislature prevented an actual test of strength and divided the state's electoral vote 8 for Jefferson and 7 for Adams. Jefferson had carried 14 of the 15 electoral votes of Pennsylvania in 1796; in 1799 the Republicans won the governorship of the state, and in 1800 Republicans carried 10 out of the 13 districts in the congressional elections. It is thus evident that the Pennsylvania vote in 1800 did not reflect the true strength of parties, and no significance should be attached to the increase in Adams' electoral vote in that state. The observation that Jefferson could not have won without New York should not be used to suggest that Jefferson's victory reflected no real nationwide strength and that it resulted merely from the Republican success in New York City. This overlooks the clear evidence that Jefferson's strength in Pennsylvania was not reflected in the electoral vote, and it also ignores the impressive proof of Jeffersonian strength displayed in the congressional elections.

Any analysis must take into consideration the congressional elections, which, because of the manner in which the electoral system operated in 1800, more adequately reflected the preferences of the electorate. Congressional returns demonstrated that the Republican party was stronger in 1800 than the presidential electoral vote indicated and that there was a clear popular verdict in favor of the Republican party and its candidates. While the margin in the electoral vote between Jefferson's 73 and Adams' 65 electoral votes was narrow, in the elections for Congress the Republicans won 67 out of 106 seats in the House of Representatives.

The congressional vote also showed that the operation of parties and the basis of support of both parties were more national in scope than the electoral returns suggested. In New England (New Hampshire, Vermont, Massachusetts, Rhode Island, and Connecticut) where the entire electoral vote of 39 went to the Federalists, Republicans elected 10 of the 29 representatives. In the middle states (New York, New Jersey, Pennsylvania, and Delaware) the electoral vote was divided, 20 Republicans and 17 Federalists; and the congressional vote was divided, 21 Republicans and 8 Federalists. In the South (Maryland, Virginia, the Carolinas, and Georgia) the electoral vote was 46 Republicans to 9 Federalists, while the congressional representation was 33 Republicans to 12 Federalists. In the two western states (Kentucky and Tennessee) both the electoral vote of 7 and the congressional membership of 3 were unanimously Republican.

In assessing the outcome of the election, Federalists put a great deal of emphasis on the split in the Federalist party. Adams himself suggested that he sacrificed his chances for reelection by alienating the Hamiltonian leaders when he decided to send a second peace mission to France. An analysis of the election returns, however, fails to reveal that the Federalist split was in fact responsible for Adams' defeat. The divisions in Federalist ranks were the most serious in New England, but Adams lost not a single electoral vote in any New England state. The loss of New York cannot be attributed to Hamilton's opposition, for Hamilton worked to maintain Federalist control over the New York assembly. If Federalist control had been maintained, it might then have been used to promote Pinckney over Adams; but a Republican legislature would offer no hope, as Hamilton's frantic appeal to Governor Jay indicated. Adams carried New Jersey and Delaware, and the vote of Pennsylvania was determined by the deadlock in the legislature between the Republican house and the Federalist senate. In the southern and western states there is reason to believe that Adams was helped more than he was hurt by his repudiation of the ultra-Federalists. In Maryland, where Adams had won 7 electoral votes in 1796, he received 5 in 1800; in North Carolina, Adams' vote went from 1 in 1796 to 4 in 1800. In these two states, then, Adams had a net gain of 1. In Virginia, where Adams had received 1 electoral vote in 1796, there was no chance of winning any in 1800 because of the change in the method of electing presidential electors. Elsewhere in the South and the West Adams had won no votes in 1796. The best hope for increasing his vote in 1800 was in South Carolina, which had voted for Thomas Pinckney and Jefferson in 1796. It was Hamilton's hope that South Carolina might vote for Charles Cotesworth Pinckney and Jefferson in 1800 and give Pinckney the Presidency, but this, of course, did not occur. Still, there is no reason to conclude that Federalist divisions or Hamilton's opposition to Adams kept South Carolina from going either to Adams and Pinckney or to Jefferson and Pinck-

ney. Although one New York Federalist reported that letters from "respectable federalists in South Carolina" asserted that Hamilton's letter attacking
Adams had "accomplished the democratical majority in the South Carolina
Legislature," it is clear from surviving records that the events in South Carolina were not so easily explained.

A comparison of the presidential electoral vote in 1800 with that of 1796
suggests the acceptance of two-party competition in American politics by
1800 and a tightening of party discipline and control. In 1796 thirteen candidates received votes, though most of the scattering of electoral votes was in
the second ballots (for Vice-President). In 1800, with the exception of one
Rhode Island elector, all Presidential electors cast their votes for the Republican ticket of Jefferson and Burr or the Federalist slate of Adams and Pinckney.

The possibility of a tie vote between Jefferson and Burr had been considered by Republican leaders during the campaign, but no definite plans had
been completed to insure that it did not occur. James Madison, one of the
Virginia electors, recalled that "it was with much difficulty that a unanimous
vote could be obtained in the Virginia College of Electors for both [Jefferson
and Burr] lest an equality might throw the choice into the House." But he
"had received assurances from a confidential friend of Burr that in a certain
quarter votes would be thrown from B[urr] with a view to secure the majority
for Jefferson." Thus, Virginia electors were persuaded to vote for Jefferson
and Burr in order to strengthen the New York-Virginia alliance within the
Republican party. In 1796 Burr had received only 1 vote in Virginia, and he
had indicated in 1800 that "after what happened at the last election . . . it is
most obvious that I should not choose to be trifled with." Both Jefferson and
Madison worked to secure an unanimous vote for Burr in Virginia, relying on
the withholding of votes in some other state. This expectation rested more
upon reports, assurances, and rumors than on clear arrangements, and none of
the rumored plans to withhold votes from Burr materialized. Instead, there was
an unprecedented display of party regularity. As a result, the election was left
to the House of Representatives—and not the newly elected body that the
Republicans were sweeping into power but the Federalist-controlled House
elected in 1798 at the height of Federalist popularity following the XYZ
incident. "The Federalists in the legislature have expressed dispositions
to make all they can of the embarrassment," wrote Jefferson, "so that after
the most energetic efforts, crowned with success, we remain in the hands of
our enemies by the want of foresight in the original arrangements."

In the election by the House of Representatives, voting was by states,
with each state casting one vote. Although the Federalists had a majority,
they did not control a majority of the state delegations; but neither did the Republicans. Two state delegations were equally divided, and the Republicans
needed 1 of these to command the 9 states necessary for a majority. The Federalists were thus in a position to block the election of Jefferson or prevent a
decision before Adams' term of office ended on March 4. From the beginning of
the contest, Hamilton urged the Federalists to support Jefferson rather than
Burr, whose "public principles have no other spring or aim than his own ag-

grandisement." But the Federalists in Congress ignored Hamilton's advice and threw their support to Burr. They did not have the votes to elect Burr, but by supporting him persistently enough they might persuade some Republicans to switch from Jefferson to Burr in order to decide the election before Adams' term expired.

Burr early issued a statement declaring that anyone who knew him ought to know that he would utterly disclaim any competition with Jefferson and that he would never be an instrument in counteracting the wishes and expectations of the people of the United States. He publicly maintained this position throughout the contest, but he never clarified it, and he never issued the one statement that would have ended all Federalist hopes. Burr never declared that if elected he would refuse to accept the Presidency. Federalists thus circulated the word that Burr's statement was to be ignored and that he was willing to accept the office. Just what Burr was attempting to do behind the scenes cannot be fully determined. But it seems clear that Burr did not need to resort to intrigue to obtain Federalist support; this he already had. What Burr needed was Republican support. By not issuing a statement promising to resign if elected, Burr, many Republicans concluded, was actually seeking the Presidency for himself.

The election law required that the certificates of the electors be opened in a joint session of the two houses of Congress on the second Wednesday in February, and thus the election could not be decided before February 11, 1801. As soon as the returns were counted by Congress on February 11, balloting by states began in the House of Representatives. On the first ballot Jefferson received the votes of 8 states: New York, New Jersey, Pennsylvania, Virginia, North Carolina, Georgia, Kentucky, and Tennessee. Burr had the votes of 6 states: New Hampshire, Massachusetts, Rhode Island, Connecticut, Delaware, and South Carolina. Two states, Vermont and Maryland, were divided. This vote differed from the breakdown by states of the vote in the electoral college. There Jefferson had carried 8 states but had not carried New Jersey and had won South Carolina; Vermont's electoral vote had gone to Adams, and Maryland's vote had been equally divided.

By midnight of February 11, the first day of balloting, nineteen ballots had been taken. On each the result was the same. Balloting continued for nearly a week with no changes except for a few within state delegations that did not alter any state's vote. With the end of Adams' term only two weeks away, the deadlock was creating a major crisis. Governor James Monroe of Virginia assured Jefferson that if any unsurpation were atempted, he would immediately convene the Virginia assembly. There were rumors in Virginia that the Federalists planned to turn over the Presidency by legislative act to Secretary of State John Marshall until another election could be held. "If that party wish to disorganize, *that* is the way to do it." said Monroe. "If the union could be broken, that would do it." As Monroe implied, what was being tested by this crisis was nothing less than the peaceful transfer of political power in the national government from one party to another.

As tensions mounted, the Federalists yielded. On February 17, on the thirty-sixth ballot, Jefferson received the votes of 10 states and was elected President. This resulted from the Federalist members from Vermont and Maryland either not voting or putting in blank ballots so that those 2 states which had been divided went to Jefferson. The votes of Delaware and South Carolina were cast as blank ballots, so that no Federalist-controlled delegation actually voted for Jefferson. On the final ballot, Burr thus received only the votes of 4 New England states. The manner in which the Federalist vote was cast in this final ballot was arranged only a few minutes before the vote was taken, but the crucial decision was made when James A. Bayard, who as the only member from Delaware cast that state's vote, announced to a Federalist caucus that he was prepared to throw his vote to Jefferson to end the deadlock. That Bayard, who had been under pressure from Hamilton to support Jefferson from the beginning, did not reach this decision until all efforts to elect Burr had failed destroys the common assertion that Hamilton's influence was decisive in throwing the election in the House to Jefferson.

Why did the Federalists finally decide to give up Burr? Jefferson thought the Federalists saw the impossibility of electing Burr and "the certainty that a legislative usurpation would be resisted by arms, and a recourse to a convention to re-organize and amend the government." "The very word convention gives them the horrors," he wrote, "as in the present democratical spirit of America, they fear they should lose some of the favorite morsels of the constitution." On the other hand, some Federalists later indicated that they had secured guarantees as to future policy from Jefferson before permitting his election. Five years after the election Bayard testified that he had received assurances on certain points of policy and in regard to officeholders from Samuel Smith of Maryland on the authority of Jefferson. When questioned, Smith affirmed that he had given Bayard assurances and that he had conferred with Jefferson. However, Smith insisted that he had not acted on Jefferson's authority and that there had been no bargains. Indeed, he later affirmed that he had conferred with Jefferson "without his having the remotest idea of my object."

While there is no reason to question Smith's testimony that he did not tell Jefferson he was seeking assurances to be passed on to the Federalists, it seems unlikely that Jefferson did not realize that his discussions with Smith might be shared with others. At the same time, it is evident that Jefferson did not regard Smith as an emissary seeking to negotiate a contract. During the balloting Jefferson wrote Monroe that "many attempts have been made to obtain terms and promises from me. I have declared to them unequivocally that I would not receive the government on capitulation, and that I would not go into it with my hands tied." There is no reason to doubt Jefferson's declaration, and it is clear that, regardless of whatever satisfaction the Federalists may have obtained from Smith's reports, Jefferson in no way entered office with his hands tied.

"I hope you will have the cannon out to announce the news," said a message dispatched by express from Washington to Richmond reporting the final ballot in the House, and Republicans throughout the country were soon caught up in a wave of festivities celebrating the inauguration of Jefferson as President on March 4. For the moment, Burr, who was elected Vice-President, was still in Republican favor; but as Republicans reviewed the contest their confidence in him evaporated, and Burr was soon, in effect, read out of the Republican party. After the victory celebrations faded away, Republicans also remembered the anxiety of the months of crisis that resulted from the Jefferson-Burr tie, and this concern brought about the adoption of the 12th Amendment in 1804, prior to the presidential balloting of that year. Providing for the separate balloting by presidential electors for President and Vice-President, this amendment was a clear recognition of the existence of the party system in American politics.

The election of 1800 was truly a critical election in American history. It not only tested the operation of the political mechanisms that the Constitution and political parties had created, but also produced a meaningful change in the management of the national government. When Republicans replaced Federalists in control of the federal administration, they brought both new men and new policies. Although the campaign of 1800 was no pure contest of principles, there is ample evidence to conclude that voters had general conceptions of what to expect if the Federalists continued in office and what changes to anticipate if the Republicans were victorious. Above all, the election demonstrated that control of the vast political power of the national government could pass peacefully from one political party to another. Subsequent repetition of this accomplishment cannot diminish the significance of this first success.

Appendix

Republican Campaign Literature
1800

The following address To the People of New-Jersey* *was adopted at a Republican state convention in Princeton, New Jersey, September 30, 1800, two weeks before the election of the state legislature that would choose that state's presidential electors. It illustrates the concentrated Republican attack on the record of the Federalist Administration under Adams and the laudatory heights reached in campaign rhetoric in praise of Jefferson.*

Friends Countrymen and Fellow Citizens;

The Deputies from the several republican county-meetings of this state, met at Princeton, have endeavoured to execute the duties assigned them with candor and fidelity. We are aware that the time alotted us is disproportioned to the list of objects which demanded our attention; but as we need not the aid and despise the subterfuge, of sophistry and declamation, you can pardon our brevity, and reflect maturely on the subject submitted to your consideration.

The present period of our national concerns is as important in its nature, and as eventful in its consequences, as the memorable epoch when the American people revolted from the oppressions of the British monarch. We are now called upon to elect a chief magistrate of this extensive country; and on this election depends the future happiness of America. When freed from foreign oppression, and privileged to choose our own rulers, it was presumed that the people of America would remain the peaceable cultivators of their fields, uninfluenced by the politics of European courts, and regardless of their destinies. But the experience of a few years has removed the pleasing delusion.

Our agriculture is oppressed by taxation.

Our manufactures are superceded by British productions.

Our commerce subjected to the spoliations of foreign cruisers: and

Our national councils agitated by a faction, declared to be formed by England.

Mr. Lyman, a representative in congress from Massachusetts, and an avowed partizan of administration, has informed his constituents—"that the federal interest is divided in the national councils—and that A PARTY believe a few BOLD STROKES would silence all opposition to government:"—A serious question thence presents itself—Why do a party wish to destroy all opposition and enquiry—Are there men in our councils who wish to enslave us—whose conduct will not bear the test of examination?—And *who wish to*

*Reprinted from the Broadside Collection, courtesy of the Historical Society of Pennsylvania.

close the mouths of five millions of people, so lately freed from foreign despotism? But lest we should decide prematurely on this extraordinary declaration of Mr. Lyman, let us calmly review the conduct of our executive, and endeavour to obtain a dispassionate conclusion.

Our connections, by expensive agencies, &c. with foreign courts; undefined hostilities with the French Republic, with whom the British ambassador, Mr. Liston, says

"WE HAVE ENDEAVOURED TO PROVOKE A WAR!"

We are paying an enormous tribute to the petty tyrant of Algiers.

We have had an Alien and still have a Sedition law; by which many citizens have been deprived of their rights, and native Americans consigned to loathsome prisons for exercising the constitutional right of public enquiry.

We are struggling under a direct tax, with heavy imposts; raising money on loan at *Eight* per cent.—And our expenditures are encreasing, while our national debt is accumulating.

We have supported an army in time of peace, while our militia is neglected. The latter, said our beloved *Washington,* "IS THE NATURAL DEFENCE OF A COUNTRY."

We have an expensive and ineffectual navy, to support the interest of foreign merchants at the sacrifice of naval, agricultural, and mechanical interests.

We have a variety of stock-jobbing acts which have given birth to a system of speculation, fraud, and bankruptcy.

We have witnessed the effects of presidential patronage, we have seen with regret, *British subjects* raised to posts of honor and profit, to the exclusion of *honest Americans,* who braved the perils of a long and bloody war.

We have seen old tories, the enemies of our revolution, recommended as the guardians of our country.

We have seen injustice but time is not sufficient, to recapitulate the abuses of our constitution.—This catalogue contains only a *few* facts, facts serious in themselves, woefully notorious, and in principle demanding the strictest scrutiny. If they be not consistent with our national compact, the *Constitution,* that sacred archive of American liberty, you must then suspect that there is something wrong; and if you will only divest yourselves of prejudice, and cast off those inglorious veils which have obscured your understandings, you must of necessity decide in the affirmative. You will plainly see and feel that your present rulers have monopolized unauthorised power and exercised undue influence over us.

Believing, as we do, that there can be but one general voice in America, and that this voice must be, the preservation of our rights as freemen; we are bold to declare, that many of our fellow citizens, who have opposed us in political profession, have been grossly deceived by artful designing men; and nearly robbed of their liberties, before they awoke from the delusion.

As a branch of the American family we are bound to perform the relative duties existing between us and our sister states, and to endeavour to cultivate the reviving spirit of freedom in our own department.

We are now called upon by the constitution, to provide for the appointment of electors of President and Vice President of the nation.

The electors of President and Vice President are to be chosen "*in such manner as the Legislature of the state may DIRECT;*" so says the constitution. But, it must be observed, that the legislature of this state has uniformly *assumed the power of election*; has deprived you of this great national privilege, when it is merely authorised to DIRECT the mode in which YOU SHOULD CHOOSE THEM. And we regret that it is now too late, to remedy the evil previous to the ensuing appointment of electors.

The people of New Jersey must therefore determine, whether they will re-elect men as state representatives, who have been guilty of the most flagrant usurpation, or choose those who will regard the obligations of their oaths, and refer to the people the constitutional choice of electors. Their ordinary functions of enacting laws, are trifles, compared with the great national object of the due appointment of electors.

When we reflect on the precarious tenure by which we hold our liberties; when we consider the artifices which have been employed by foreign influence, to bring us back to a state of vassalage, we cannot but commiserate the fortune of misguided Americans, and reject the wiley agents who have endeavoured to effect our ruin. But with joy we see our brethren in our sister states, casting off the men who have misled them; many of our fellow-citizens are openly avoiding their delusion, and are ready to meet us in the exercise of our elective right, and the manly restoration of our freedom.

We have been told by Mr. Adams that "*the finger of Heaven points to war,*" – but we differ from our present chief magistrate, and discredit the declaration. *Benignant Heaven has not made such a decree.* The People of America are averse to carnage. They revolt from the bloody conflict, and are resolved to cherish the blessings of peace, while they disdain the intrigues of foreign despots.

Let us then recommend to you, our fellow citizens, to consider moderately and temperately, the serious truths here laid before you. The common resorts of wicked men are *violence* and *detraction*. We pray you to avoid the snares of the *cunning* and the *corrupt*, and to guard yourselves with temper becoming sober men, and worthy of freemen. Let not the *example of those who* are hostile to you lead you aside from the paths of truth, and the great principles for which so much American blood was shed.

Look up to that man, whose whole life, from the day on which he immortalised himself, by drawing up the Declaration of Independence to the present, has not given to his enemies a single cause of reproach; who cannot be impeached of immorality nor of vice: whose hands and whose coffers have never been soiled by speculation or gambling: whose domestic character is uncontaminated by the reproaches of any one debauchery: whose talents as a governor in his native state, as an ambassador abroad, as legislator and secretary of state, and whose pursuits have been from first to last, to promote toleration in religion and freedom in politics: to cultivate the arts and the virtues at home, and to shun the vices and depravities of corrupt foreign governments in a word, a man against whom falsehood has raised its voice, under the garb of religion, only because he has banished tythes and an established church from his native state, and who would brand him with the name of Infidel because he is not a fanatic, nor willing that the *Quaker*, the *Baptist*, the *Methodist*, or any other denomination of Christians, should pay the pastors of other sects; because he does not think a catholic should be banished for believing in transubstantiation, or a jew, for believing in the God of Abraham, Isaac, and Jacob.

It is not to the man, but to that confidence which his character and virtues, his talents and experience inspire, we call you. Let us therefore, taking the Declaration of Independence in our hands, and carrying its principles in our hearts, let us resolve to support THOMAS JEFFERSON, whose whole life has been a comment on its precepts, and an uniform pursuit of the great blessings to his country which it was first intended to establish—Bearing these resolutions in our hearts, and seeing that it is by his administration of his own precepts we are to be saved from further afflictions, abuses and dangers, let us also support no men at our elections who are so blind as not to discern the danger which we have escaped, and the injuries we suffer—because such persons are unfit to guard against those future dangers which it was the design of our revolution and the end of our government to prevent.

Signed by order.

Joseph Bloomfield,
　　　　　　　Chairman.

John Morgan,
　　　　　　　Secretary.

There were no official party platforms in 1800, but the following summary of Republican campaign arguments published in the Philadelphia Aurora, *October 14, 1800, was a popularized newspaper version of the Republican program.*

ATTENTION

Citizens of Philadelphia

Take Your Choice

FEDERAL	REPUBLICAN
Things As They Have Been	Things As They Will Be
1. The principles and patriots of the *Revolution* condemned and stigmatized.	1. The Principles of the *Revolution* restored; its Patriots honored and beloved.
2. *Republicanism*, a badge for persecution, and federalism a mask for monarchy.	2. *Republicanism* proved to mean something, and Federalism found to mean nothing.
3. The *Nation* in arms without a foe, and divided without a cause.	3. The *Nation* at peace with the world, and united in itself.
4. *Federalists* graduating a scale of "*hatred and animosity*," for the benefit of the people; and aiming "*a few bold strokes*" at political opposition, for the benefit of themselves.	4. *Republicanism* allaying the fever of domestic feuds, and subduing the opposition by the force of reason and rectitude.
5. The reign of terror created by false alarms, to promote domestic feud and foreign war.	5. Unity, peace, and concord produced by republican measures and equal laws.

6. Systems of rapine, fraud, and plunder by public defaulters under countenance of public servants.

7. Priests and Judges incorporated with the Government for political purposes, and equally polluting the holy altars of religion, and the seats of Justice.

8. Increase of Public Debt
   Additional Taxes
   Further Loans
   New Excises.
   Higher Public Salaries, and
   Wasteful Expenditure of public money.

9. Quixotish embassies to the Turks, the Russians, Prussians, and Portuguese, for Quixotish purposes of holding the balance of Europe.

10. A Sedition Law to protect corrupt magistrates and public defaulters.

11. An established church, a religious test, and an order of Priesthood.

6. Public plunderers and defaulters called to strict account, and public servants compelled to do their duty.

7. Good government without the aid of priestcraft, or religious politics, and Justice administered without political intolerance.

8. Decrease of Public Debt
   Reduced Taxes
   No Loans
   No Excises
   Reduced Public Salaries, and a system of economy and care of the public money.

9. The republican maxim of our departed Washington, "Not to intermeddle with European politics."

10. The Liberty of the Press, and free enquiry into public character, and our constitutional charter.

11. Religious liberty, the rights of conscience, no priesthood, truth and Jefferson.

Federalist Campaign Literature
1800

In A Candid Address to the Freemen of the State of Rhode-Island on the Subject of the Approaching Election, from a Number of Their Fellow Citizens,* *the Federalists argued against change in a period of crisis and at the same time appealed to sectional feelings in New England.*

The present most interesting crisis in the affairs of the United States, demands the dispassionate consideration of every individual citizen. It is now no time to trifle with interests so pressingly important as those which are at this moment at stake: it is no time to be governed, in our selection of public functionaries, by party or favouritism; it is even no time to be governed by an adherence to any mere system of administration, however plausible or demonstrable as a theory. In times less critical and turbulent, we might indulge our love of novelty, and our propensity to look for better in other circumstances, by making experiments on the administration of our government. But the present crisis forbids all such dangerous tampering. It demands that for the present, at least, and until the cloud has passed over and brighter prospects open, we venture not into the immeasurable field of change and certain confusion, but wait in our present attitude till we see the issue, and our way clear. Upon political subjects, men have always differed in opinion, and always will differ. But they have not always, and we hope they have not now, suffered their reason to desert them in the warmth of controversy. A false step at this time may never be retrieved. The occasion demands an exercise of your good sense and moderation, proportioned to its magnitude. It is not by the prevalence of this or that faction or system that nations have been found to thrive; but they, as well as individuals, have generally prospered according as they have followed the dictates of sound reason, and avoided hasty and inconsiderate conclusions, which only afford work for repentance.

These considerations are addressed to you by men whom you have honoured with your good opinion, and of whose sincerity and love of country you have never doubted. They are addressed to you by men enjoying, valuing, and feeling at stake, the same country, the same liberty, and the same constitution, as yourselves; who value as highly, and who will contribute and have contributed as liberally, to the support, soundness and continuance of those enjoyments. They are addressed to you under a solemn impression of their applicability to the present situation of affairs, and under a firm persuasion that our peace and constitutional government are in danger, from a party active, powerful and indefatigable, guided by craft and unprincipled ambition, and managed in the subordinate operations by weak and deluded engines. They

*Reprinted from Broadside, Special Collections, Brown University Library.

are addressed to you as principles which ought to govern you in whatsoever you may think your duty or privileges require or authorize you to do, with respect to the choice of Electors of President and Vice-President of the United States, at the ensuing election. The indefatigable industry and union of the party alluded to, render the like industry and union necessary on the side of the government. Accordingly, a number of gentlemen from all parts of the State, most of whom were members of the Legislature, or had the honour of serving you in other important stations, have offered you a list of persons to whom the office of Electors might be confided—Governor GREENE, Mr. CHAMPLIN, Mr. MANTON, and Mr. DAVIS. These persons unite in themselves the qualities proper for Electors. They are men of property, and of landed property, who must stand or fall with their country. They were supposed to be excelled by none in the knowledge of the interests of the Union, and of the State; and their disposition to consult and preserve those interests can never be doubted. For these men, or for the Federal ADAMS TICKET, your votes are solicited. Another, a Democratic and JEFFERSONIAN TICKET, is also offered to your consideration. Between these two it is probable you will choose. It is now too late to attempt a discussion of the merits of the two questions which divide the United States: and if time even permitted, how few could find the leisure or the patience to pursue the voluminous enquiry. What credit or confidence can we repose in the knowledge or good intentions of those who make it their business to calumniate the government, and sow discontents among the people? Upon other than political subjects, we should despise their judgment, and distrust their sincerity. Upon the whole, is it probable that the choice will be decided by every individual upon his own particular knowledge of the numerous and intricate circumstances on which a just opinion must at last be founded? There is a shorter mode of deciding between the two classes of candidates, by which if the people are not safe, all hopes of safety must hereafter be abandoned; and this is a mode to which, in a greater or less degree, we at last must always resort, and have always resorted. This mode is, to choose the best men. If we cannot confide in good men, it is certain that we cannot confide in any. The mere concurrence of our opinion with that of a man in no other respect to be selected, and of an opinion in which we may both be mistaken, is at last but a miserable reason for preference.

But although we shall wave a comparison between the merits of the two great political questions, yet we should be deficient in our duty, if we neglected to consider a few points, which have had an influence in causing us to prefer the present order of things to the uncertain event of a change.

The United States, under the administration of the great and excellent Washington, pursued the same system of policy which has been pursued, and is now pursued, under his successor. During the continuance of this system, they have flourished in spite of all the opposition which faction could throw in their way; they have become rich and powerful, in spite of the depredations of two powerful rival nations, and at this moment enjoy a greater portion of civil and political happiness, than was ever enjoyed by any nation of which we have any account. If our expences have been necessarily great, our means have always been equal to the support of them. Perhaps we may compare such a nation, complaining of and discontented with its condition, to a man who has never felt sickness or pain; he knows not how to prize the blessing of health, till disease has taught him its value.

Reflections and recriminations of one State upon another ought to be made only upon strong necessity. The great and powerful State of Virginia seems to take the lead in the present opposition to the measures of administration. The plausible and specious cry that the liberties of the people are in danger, and that aristocracy is creeping into our government, originates in and emanates from that State. But will New-England-men, with arms in their hands, ever confess that they are in danger of slavery? Will such men, celebrated as they always have been for their knowledge of the true principles of Liberty, and their spirit in asserting them, take lessons upon those subjects from the State of Virginia? From a State where a powerful aristocracy not only exists, but is openly professed and vindicated; — where the equality among the northern citizens is professedly a subject of derision; and where slavery constitutes a part of the policy of the government! The very great importance of that large and respectable State, and the eminent and patriotic characters which she has nursed and brought forward, entitle her to high consideration, and an elevated standing among the States of the Union. But when she appears as the advocate of liberty and equality, and the enemy of aristocracy, we may be excused if we doubt her sincerity, and suspect that some other object, more agreeable to her prejudices and ambition, lies under the covering of the veil.

It is well known that Virginia, sensible of her importance, and claiming pre-eminence among the States, has always complained of that part of the Constitution which restricts her to an equal representation in the Senate of the United States, and has asserted her right to a representation in both branches of the legislature proportioned to her population. It is also well known that it was not without a struggle of the small States that the representation was settled as it now stands. It is moreover apparent that an equal representation in both branches would reduce the small States to the rank of the governed, while the affairs of the nation would be absolutely under the management of the great States. Now if by any convulsions the present Constitution should be overthrown, we cannot in future expect the privileges which we enjoy at present. This constitution ought emphatically to be cherished by the small States. It is all their hope and dependence. The loss of it would be attended with the mortifying reflection that we had blown the coals which set fire to and consumed the house over our head. We should become the laughing stock of our good friends the advocates of democracy and equality.

The land tax has afforded a topic of declamation to the opponents of government. It has been charged upon the administration when it ought to have been charged to the war in Europe, and the depredations which have been committed on our commerce by the powers at war. A Navy has become indispensible to the existence of our commerce, and the prosperity of our agriculture. But without considering whether that tax is proper, equal or politic, the

Journals of Congress will prove to you that while the tax on Sugar and Snuff was under consideration, the democratic party in Congress proposed this very land tax as a substitute, and that the federal party opposed it, and finally prevailed. It may be also made to appear, that after the exigencies of the United States had increased the expences incurred for our protection, and the land tax was resorted to and adopted, this very democratic party threatened the federalists that they would make use of the land tax to throw odium on the government, and carry the points at which they were aiming. And faithfully have they fulfilled their promise.

We shall conclude by observing, that the present of all times is the most unfit for convulsion; that there is now a prospect of peace, when our public burthens will be diminished — when the rage of party will in a measure subside, and we shall have more leisure and opportunity to enquire into the grounds of the controversy. For the present, let us decide without prejudice or favour, and with the coolness which becomes us as New-England-men; as freemen who have every thing precious depending, and are not to be terrified by clamour, or influenced by those whose opinion upon most subjects is not equal to our own. Let us regard those who attempt to render us dissatisfied either as our enemies, or the tools of our enemies. Let us, as we value our country, its peace, its constitution, and the privileges of our State, choose as our only course men who possess a knowledge of our interest, and a disposition to maintain it. For the same reason let us reject the ignorant and insincere, whose only qualification is a disposition to follow whither their leaders choose to conduct them. Let us divest ourselves of every predilection in favour of any foreign country, and pursue the interest of our own. Let us remember that the monarchical form of the British government, and the real despotism of the government of France, are alike repugnant to the form and spirit of our own government, republican in form and free in substance. Those two powers are striving to acquire or to preserve, the one the empire of the sea, and the other that of the land; and equally hold cheap the peace or liberty of any other nation. Above all, let the result of your deliberations terminate as it may, let it be made with impartiality, and a constant eye to the good of our country.

We cannot however conclude this address, without asserting our belief that the object of the democratic ticket is to bring in Mr. Jefferson, to the exclusion of Mr. Adams; and our sincere conviction that the only object of the supporters of the federal ticket is to secure the election of Mr. ADAMS, in preference to *all* other candidates.

Official Communications of the Republican Party in Virginia, 1800

The Republican party was well organized in Virginia by 1800. The state central committee provided instructions to county committees, publicized the party ticket, and issued the following address To the Citizens of Virginia,* *which appeared in the Richmond* Virginia Argus, *July 11, 1800. This address was reprinted at regular intervals up to the election. Following the address is a circular which the central committee in Richmond also sent to all county Republican committees.*

I

We had presented to you, for your consideration, at the next choice of electors, a ticket, which we thought uncensurable; — founded on a law which we believed to be constitutional and wise. But the committee intrusted with the ticket prepared by the minority of the late assembly, have not hesitated to impeach the one, as being an invasion of ancient usages and established rights; and the other, as an attempt to influence your votes by great and imposing names.

It is not for us to detail the reasons, which produced the law. These, we presume, have been already explained by its makers, who are now daily with you whose conduct has been recently submitted to your approbation or displeasure; and most, if not all of them, so far as their inclination led them to a re-election, have again received the suffrages of their county or district; or are succeeded by patriots, not less distinguished by their attachment to that law. The free and unbiassed sense of the *people* confers the highest sanction on the act of their servants.

But we discern not, what ancient usage has been violated; what established right overthrown. By the federal constitution it is consigned to the discretion of each state to prescribe the mode of choosing electors, and thrice Virginia has preferred elections by districts, while several other states have either adopted a general ticket, or through their legislatures have appointed electors. The unanimity known to exist in favor of him, who filled the executive chair, for the first eight years, created an indifference to the mode. The third and last election discovered that Virginia, whose weight on such in occasion, ought to be proportioned to her population, might, against the will of a majority of her citizens, be reduced, through the means of district elections, to that of states, greatly inferior on the scale of representation, but more judicious in the concentration of their power. Where then is the ancient usage which thwarts this arrangement? What established right is impaired, when a constitutional discre-

*Reprinted from Broadside, Library of Congress.

tion is exercised by following "the example" (which is avowed by the committee to be a just motive) of those, who seek an advantage over Virginia? Is not the objection to this law of national self defense although unintentionally indeed, yet directly a branch of that system, which would prostrate Virginia at the feet of any combination of the other states, if a combination can be conceived? Upon this head she has candidly and amply unfolded her views in the subjoined preamble: "Whereas until some uniform mode for choosing a President and Vice-President of the United States, shall be prescribed by an amendment to the constitution, it may happen under the law of this commonwealth for appointing electors for that purpose that a choice may take place contrary to the will of a majority of the United States, and also contrary to the will of a majority of the people of this state, which would be inconsistent with the true intent and meaning of the constitution of the United States; and although this commonwealth is willing to accede to any reasonable and proper amendment of the said constitution to remedy the said evil, yet forasmuch as it ought in the mean time to be counteracted by every constitutional regulation within the power of the legislature until it shall be so removed."

The mere act of recommending electors is so obviously the right of every citizen, and a recommendation from those, to whom the people have confided their interests and are best acquainted with the candidates, is so plainly fit in itself, that the imputation of an attempt to influence, must exist if any where, in the names which our ticket exhibits. There is indeed an influence in their names: an influence, which we dare to avow: an influence, in which we glory. It is derived from that republican seal, which delights to honor those who deserve well of their country. If among them be men, who have been foremost in the political career; they have struggled to keep alive the flame of republicanism; if their objects have been "vast,' it is, because they have embraced the rights of the people; not the arrogant pretensions, or usurpations of individuals; if their passions have been roused, their enthusiasm was dignified by the course which it pursued; but it never was degraded by any irritation unbecoming free and submissive citizens. We thank Heaven that the "highest state employments" have now for the first time only been converted into topics of reproach; but if it were true, that they generate jealousy and hatred to the *rival* authorities (as they are called) of the union, the danger of those rival authorities, hating the *states*, is much nearer at hand; and it is the more incumbent upon the people of the states, to provide by the exercise of powers, referred to them by the constitution, for the support of the rights of the states. But who are the few, (for they are but few) thus alluded to? Men, tried and approved for half a century in public service; unsurpassed in talents, and in knowledge; unquestioned and unquestionable in virtue; independent in fortune and place; too happy to profit from confusion, and unambitious, except to retain the favor of their fellow citizens, which has followed them through a long life. Can *their* voices be gained, but by evidences of genuine excellence? Can they have an interest distinct from that of the people?

We insinuate nothing against the opposite ticket. Let the contest be considered as it really is, between Thomas Jefferson and John Adams. The former you know to be a sincere and enlightened republican; whose greatness has been promulgated through the unavailing calumnies of his enemies, though he stands unshielded by a sedition law. Strenuous then ought to be your solicitude at the approaching election of a chief magistrate. Unbounded ought it to be, if fleets, armies, taxes, and the destinies of the federal government depend so much upon him, as the committee are pleased to intimate. Under these impressions, ask yourselves for whom you ought to vote? Consummate your reverence for the memory of Washington, not by employing it as an engine of election, but by declaring, that even his name shall not prevent the free use of your own understandings. As a friend to liberty, we believe Jefferson second to no man, and the experience of no man has afforded better lessons for its preservation. If the sense of Virginia be with him, the mode which shall draw it forth deserves praise, and the meaning of language must be perverted if the will of the majority constitutionally expressed, upon a subject of expediency, and tending to give Virginia her constitutional weight by means formerly and at this moment practised by other states shall be deemed persecution. The committee complain not that the privilege of voting has been wrested from them; but that they are deprived of an opportunity of wielding it in such a manner, as to destroy the effect of the like privilege in the majority.

II

Richmond
August 9th, 1800.

Sir, We have taken the liberty to advise you, to have the Tickets for Electors of President and Vice-President of the United States written; and have thought proper to recommend to you the following form. We think it adviseable that the Committees in the different Counties should procure to be written, a sufficient number of Tickets to be distributed among the Freeholders. In the formation of the Ticket, particular attention should be paid, in discriminating between the Republican Candidate William H. Cabell, and the Federal Candidate William Cabell.

We are happy to inform you, that we have received positive assurances from Colonel Ellzey, that he will with pleasure serve as an Elector, if he should be honored by the suffrages of a majority of his fellow citizens.

We are Sir, very respectfully, Your fellow citizens,

> *P. N. Nicholas,* Chairman.
> *Meriwether Jones,*
> *Samuel Pleasants, Jun.* ⎫
> *Joseph Selden,*   ⎬ Committee.
> *Gervas Storrs,*   ⎭
> *John H. Foushee,* Secretary.

FORM OF THE REPUBLICAN TICKET.

The following persons are selected by the Voter, whose name is written on the back of this Ticket, for Electors of President and Vice-President.

George Wythe,	of the City of Richmond.
William Newsum,	of Princess Anne.
Edmond Pendleton, sen.	of Caroline.
William H. Cabell,	of Amhurst.
James Madison, jun.	of Orange.
John Page,	of Gloucester.
Thomas Newton, jun.	of Norfolk Borough.
Carter B. Harrison,	of Prince George.
General Joseph Jones,	of Dinwiddie.
William B. Giles,	of Amelia.
Creed Taylor,	of Cumberland.
Thomas Read, sen.	of Charlotte.
George Penn,	of Patrick.
Walter Jones,	of Northumberland.
Richard Brent,	of Prince William.
William Ellzey,	of Loudoun.
Andrew Moore,	of Rockbridge.
General John Brown,	of Hardy.
General John Preston,	of Montgomery.
Hugh Holmes,	of Frederick.
Archibald Stuart	of Augusta.

Official Communications of the Federalist Party in Virginia, 1800

Virginia Federalists duplicated in large part Republican party machinery. They prepared a party appeal to voters and instructed local committees on campaign methods. The official Federalist appeal, An Address to the Voters for Electors of President and Vice-President of the United States in the State of Virginia,* *issued in Richmond, May 26, 1800, is reprinted here, followed by a circular† sent by the Federalist state committee to county committees on September 22, 1800.*

I

The minority of the late Assembly, after an unavailing struggle for the ancient usages of elections, and for your established rights, were constrained at last to yield to the measure of a General Ticket. They saw with regret, that the first effect of this innovation would be an attempt to influence your votes; which, upon the truest principles of republicanism, they wished to remain free and unbiassed. But the Assembly, by compelling you to vote for twenty one Electors, dispersed through every district of the state, all of whom, except the resident in your own district, must be generally unknown to you, might suppose they acquired the right to enlighten, and direct your choice. Immediately there appeared what is styled the Republican Ticket, sanctioned by a majority of the state legislature, containing great and imposing names, and calculated, in every respect, to confine, by the weight of authority, your hitherto unlimited freedom of election.

To unite the friends of our government, it became necessary to follow, in some measure, this example. But the minority have chosen for their Ticket, not those men, who, as leaders of a party, with vast objects in view, have had their passions roused, and their tempers soured by the conflict; nor yet such as, enjoying the highest state employments, have been accustomed to regard the rival authorities of the union with a jealousy, too apt to degenerate into hatred; but men, who, bearing like yourselves only the common evils of government, and partaking only of its common advantages, are most likely to appreciate it justly. If this new fangled mode of election had not been adopted, you would have seen them, generally, among the candidates in your several districts.

The reasons we have to be satisfied with our present government, it would be long, and we hope unnecessary, to detail. The uncorrupted feelings of every American should make it unnecessary; nor need he learn from foreigners the increasing prosperity of our happy country, while the severest calam-

*Reprinted from Broadside, Library of Congress.
†Reprinted from Broadside, Virginia Historical Society.

148

ity afflicts almost the whole of the civilized world, and has nearly ruined the fairest portion of it. To the adoption of our constitution, to the sage maxims of administration established by the immortal WASHINGTON, and steadily pursued by his virtuous successor, may fairly be ascribed our present prosperous situation. The man who calmly contemplates, and can wish to change it, may be compared to the great enemy of mankind surveying maliciously the first abodes of happiness and peace.

But, an unvarying course of prosperity, like the even tenor of health, makes no impression; while we betray a quick sensibility to the slightest misfortune or pain. We forget that our government has preserved us from two impending wars, the foundation of which was laid before its existance, with the two most powerfull nations of the world, armed to the full extent of their power; and that, without any sacrifice of the national interest, or of the national honor. We forget that we have been preserved from a close alliance with either of those nations, which would have been the worst, and the most inevitable, consequences of a war with the other; and that we remain, if we will, completely free and independent. But the fleet, the army, the taxes, all the little evils which were necessary to the attainment of these great and invaluable objects, make a strong impression, and are attributed as crimes to the government.

In the eager desire of change, even the meaning of language is perverted, in order to justify it. Thus the free, peaceful, and flourishing condition of the United States, under the guidance of WASHINGTON, the father of his country, is called "the calm of despotism." Shall we then embark, with this writer, on "the tempestuous sea of liberty?" When tired of the voyage, vainly may we strive to regain our present peaceful haven. We must endure the unceasing storms, and deeply drink the bloody waves, and find no refuge at last, but in the calm of real despotism. Let us be content to take a lesson, on this head, from the French republic, rather than from our own experience.

We are apt to fancy ourselves called as citizens of the United States, to vote for the highest officers of the government of these states. But the late Assembly has separated us from our fellow-citizens of the union, and compels us to speak the voice of Virginia only. Our zeal for the Union, however increases with state persecution; and believing, as the conduct of the minority on this occasion demonstrates, that our principles are the most purely republican; we unite these traits of our political character, in the style of the American Republican Ticket; which by your sacred regard to the constitution, and all those blessings of which it is the source, the peace, freedom and happiness of yourselves, and of your posterity, we now solicit you to support.

II

Richmond
September 22, 1800.

Sir, Whether we shall succeed, or even (which is very important) appear a respectable minority, in the ensuing election, will depend almost entirely upon the active zeal of the county committees. They are relied upon for furnishing the written tickets, which may be required in their several counties; the distance, and shortness of time, precluding all assistance from us in this matter. By their exertions too, it is expected that all, who are disposed to vote favorably, will be induced to attend the election.

To effect these essential purposes, it may be necessary to convene the most influential federalists in your county, and in conjunction with them to divide the same into several precincts; to each of which should be alloted such characters as can be confided in, to prepare, and distribute, our ticket amongst their neighbours; and to bring forward all the federalists within their precinct, to vote on the day of Election.

I am your most Obedient Servant.

William Austin,
Secretary.

By order of the committee entrusted ⎫
with the Ticket of the Minority.   ⎭

In A Short Address to the Voters of Delaware,* *on September 21, 1800, a writer signing himself "A Christian Federalist" attempted to associate Republicans with the excesses of the French Revolution and in so doing drew a frightening picture of the consequences of a Jefferson victory.*

Fellow-Citizens,

The importance of the approaching election does not appear to be sufficiently felt by those on whom the cause of *Federalism* depends. They seem not to perceive that great national interests are at stake, as well as those essential principles, on which the immediate peace and security of society, and also the hopes of future happiness rest.

Can serious and reflecting men look about them and doubt, that if Jefferson is elected, and the Jacobins get into authority, that those morals which protect our lives from the knife of the assassin—which guard the chastity of our wives and daughters from seduction and violence—defend our property from plunder and devastation, and shield our religion from contempt and profanation, will not be trampled upon and exploded. Men are the same in their natures in different countries and at different times. Operated upon by the same causes, they are impelled in the same courses. A Frenchman bred from early infancy, and habituated to the customs of this country, would resemble in temper and manners, an American; under like circumstances, a similar effect would be produced on an American in France.

Under a regular government, we have seen the French the most polite, polished and humane people in Europe. We have seen them without a government, more ferocious than savages, more bloody than tygers, more impious

---

*Reprinted from the Pamphlet Collection, Rare Book Division, Library of Congress.

than demons. Recal the scene of the revolution for a moment. You have seen relations acting as spies and informers against each other, brothers shouting at the execution of their brethren, and children boasting of having led their parents to the scaffold. You have seen multitudes shut up in boats with false bottoms, and afterwards sunk in an instant to the bottom of rivers. You have seen hundreds planted in rows, and thus exposed to the mouths of devouring cannon. You have seen large cities pillaged, their inhabitants massacred and their habitations erased from the earth. You have seen a most dreadful war carried on against the temples of the most high, and those who were devoted to his service; and have seen the banishment or cruel death of those who refused to apostatize their faith and renounce the hope of their salvation. In short, you have seen a rich flourishing and happy nation become a scene of bloodshed, rapine and devastation, and deluged with all the crimes and miseries which spring from the ungoverned passion of wicked men.

These things we at first saw with astonishment and horror; but their continuance rendering them familiar, we at last viewed them with simple apathy. Will you pause, Fellow-Citizens, and enquire what produced these afflicting and wonderful events in France, and will you then ask do causes exist in this country capable of producing the same effect? In France, it was the suffering men of false and wicked principles to get into power, *men who taught that there was no God — no Saviour — no future rewards and punishments, but that death was an eternal sleep* — Men who could publicly set up a strumpet decorated in the garments of a religious form, and in the face of a people of a great capital, under the name of the goddess of Reason, worship her as the image of the only true Supreme Being. Such men easily believed, that crimes were mere inventions of priestcraft, and that when they had power they possessed the right of gratifying their ambition, or of indulging their passions at the expence of torrents of blood, and the indiscriminate miseries of thousands of their fellow creatures. I will not disgust you with an enumeration of the catalogues of crimes, which cast so black a mantle over the licentious periods of the French revolution. And now my fellow-citizens do you not believe that there are men in the United States, as unprincipled and profligate as any who existed in France? In France, Danton, Marat, and Robespierre, were flaming patriots — staunch democrats, and great sticklers for the rights of man. *Such was the mask they wore*, and do you not see that mask, which even French impudence is at present ashamed to wear, now covering the hypocrisy of our pretended republicans? Trace the history of the furious and bloody demagogues of the revolution, and then remark the correspondence with the acts of demagogues at home. By the same affected atttachment to the rights and interests of the people, they endeavour to gain their affections and confidence, in order to use them as the instruments of their ambition. Let these men get into power, put the reins of government into their hands, and what security have you against the occurrence of the scenes which have rendered France a cemetery, and moistened her soil with the tears and blood of her inhabitants?

What consolation was it to France, that Marat was dispatched with a dagger; or that Danton and Robespierre fell under the axe of the guillotine? It did not restore to widows and children their husbands and parents, nor repair the devastation and ravages of cities and provinces.

Remember that the reign of anarchy may create more evil in a year, than the order of government can eradicate in a century. What is it that your modern philosophers hold sacred in society? The name of religion is odious to them, and in order to extinguish the remembrance of the sabbath, the day of worship, they have converted the week into the decade, and they adopted generally the principle which the Spartans confined to theft—that a man commits no crime unless he is detected.

This, my fellow-citizens, is a true but imperfect view of the grounds of our political disputes and parties. Our government is as free as it is capable of being—the country as happy as a government can make it. What more do you want? Will you grasp at a shadow, and lose the substance?

When they talk of a violation of the constitution, is there a man among you who can say he *ever saw it or felt it*; will you believe such things before you *see* or *feel them*? Will you be governed by your *own eyes and feelings*, or *those of other people*? Others have an interest to deceive you; you have none to deceive yourselves. Trust yourselves, therefore, before others.—What is all the cry about republicanism? Do any of you know a man who is an enemy to republicanism? Did you hear him say so? Or what did you see him do which would lead to such an opinion? This is the 12th year of our government, and it has been in the same hands, and is it not as free and republican as it was the first year? If the *Jeffersonites* wish more republicanism, what must it result in? Not in the freedom of equal laws, which is true republicanism; but in the licentiousness of anarchy, which in fact is the worst of tyranny. Let me press this question upon you, are not the offices of the government open to all, and do not the laws rest equally on the shoulders of all?

This they say is not republicanism; and indeed, fellow-citizens, it is not what they mean by republicanism. The short system of their republicanism is the possession of all power, by the new sect of Philosophers; and in the extermination of all principle, which can bridle their passion in the enjoyment of it. A feeling heart which perceives an honest man, deluded by the hypocritical noise about republicanism, must weep over the frailty of human nature, so dangerous to its interest and peace.

Jacobinism is a new name for an ancient principle. Since the fall of the Angels, there have always been Jacobins. Like the prince of darkness, they are capable of assuming every shape. By Jacobinism I understand an essential want of integrity, and an unprincipled pursuit of whatever promotes the interests, or gratifies the passions of the individuals. Under a monarch, a Jacobin is a courtier; in a democracy, he is a demagogue; while in pursuit of power, he fawns and flatters; when his object is attained, he is imperious and oppressive. The people of Sussex and Kent have *seen and felt* the exercise of Jacobin power. They must know, that by Jacobin liberty is meant a right to confiscate, plunder and prosecute. Can they expect, if Jacobin power is re-established, they will be objects of more favour or commiseration than formerly? Let me beg them to read the following extracts from the Aurora of the 8th and 9th of October, 1799, from a letter written by a person in Wilmington, and they will judge —

Extract of a Letter from Wilmington, Delaware,
dated the 5th (Oct.) instant.

Our annual Election for Senators, Assembly, &c. came on last Tuesday, and I think the result in this County, (Newcastle) must prove ominous of the fate of your election in Pennsylvania. The combined Tory, British and Aristocratic interest has for several years past, predominated in every branch, both of our State Government, and, in our spite, at the General Government; in fact, we have had to submit to machinations and contrivances, that nearly pushed us to the brink of ruin. But, thank God, the nefarious party discovered their cloven foot, in time to rouse us to save ourselves from their harpy claws. The Republicans rallied to a man, and were joined by several of their former brethren, who had, under the influence of alarm, lately been induced to apostatize to the old Whig principles. Our bands thus recruited, gave us a complete victory. We carried the Republican, that is, the true Democrat Ticket, equal to three for one. And I have no doubt, but before the end of the month, I shall hear that you have been equally successful, not only as to your *Governor*, (of which there is no doubt entertained here) but likewise of your Senators and Assemblymen too.

Then shall we see the whole host of his Satannic, alias Britannic Majesty's imps, devils, and porcupines, like clouds of locusts and herds of swine, driven from our shores, to perish in the Atlantic.

Those of you, my Fellow-Citizens, who profess the religion of Christ, and believe that the Christian faith is not merely a creditable distinction in life, but the essential medium of present peace and future happiness, let me beg to pause, and consider the tendency of another Extract, which I have taken from the *Aurora* of the 13th instant —

It is proper, I think, that the subject be discussed — that we may find out whether Christ is a *Monarchist*, a *Republican*, a *Jacobin* — or WHAT!!

Do these publications present no serious views? Are we contending merely for the promotion of our favourites, or is not the stake the security of society, and the boon of Heaven's kindness to man? — Under such impressions, will you suffer your strength to be wasted in paltry disputes about personal preferencies, while your enemies are associated in a body, and advancing to attack you? If you should be surprized, and defeated, how great will your shame be — that in insisting upon some small pretensions capable of producing no consequences, you rendered principles, and the promoters of principles, triumphant, which reason and religion unite in teaching us to abhor?

A Christian Federalist.

Kent County,
Sept 21, 1800

Letter of Alexander Hamilton on John Adams
1800

The divisions in Federalist ranks during the campaign of 1800 reached a high point when Hamilton openly attacked the candidacy of Adams in a pamphlet which appeared late in the campaign. Excerpts from this pamphlet are printed below.

Some of the warm personal friends of Mr. Adams are taking unwearied pains to disparage the motives of those Federalists who advocate the equal support of General Pinckney at the approaching election of President and Vice-President. They are exhibited under a variety of aspects equally derogatory.

*   *   *

. . . I ought to premise that the ground upon which I stand is different from that of most of those who are confounded with me in pursuit of the same plan. While our object is common, our motives are variously dissimilar. A part, well affected to Mr. Adams, have no other wish than to take a double chance against Mr. Jefferson. Another part, feeling a diminution of confidence in him, still hope that the general tenor of his conduct will be essentially right. Few go as far in their objections as I do. Not denying to Mr. Adams patriotism and integrity, and even talents of a certain kind, I should be deficient in candor, were I to conceal the conviction that he does not possess the talents adapted to the *administration* of government, and that there are great and intrinsic defects in his character, which unfit him for the office of chief magistrate.

To give a correct idea of the circumstances which have gradually produced this conviction, it may be useful to retrospect to an early period.

I was one of that numerous class who had conceived a high veneration for Mr. Adams, on account of the part he acted in the first stages of our revolution. My imagination had exalted him to a high eminence, as a man of patriotic, bold, profound, and comprehensive mind.

*   *   *

But this did not hinder me from making careful observations upon his several communications, and endeavoring to derive from them an accurate idea of his talents and character. This scrutiny enhanced my esteem in the main for his moral qualifications, but lessened my respect for his intellectual endowments. I then adopted an opinion, which all my subsequent experience has confirmed, that he is a man of an imagination sublimated and eccentric; propitious neither to the regular display of sound judgment, nor to steady perseverance in a systematic plan of conduct; and I began to perceive what has been since too manifest, that to this defect are added the unfortunate foibles of a vanity without bounds, and a jealousy capable of discoloring every object.

*   *   *

. . . This statement, which has been made, shows that Mr. Adams has committed some positive and serious errors of administration; that in addition to these, he has certain fixed points of character which tend naturally to the detriment of any cause of which he is the chief, of any administration of which he is the head; that by his ill humors and jealousies he has already divided and distracted the supporters of the government; that he has furnished deadly weapons to its enemies by unfounded accusations, and has weakened the force of its friends by decrying some of the most influential of them to the utmost of his power; and let it be added, as the necessary effect of such conduct, that he has made great progress in undermining the ground which was gained for the government by his predecessor, and that there is real cause to apprehend it might totter, if not fall, under his future auspices. A new government, constructed on free principles, is always weak, and must stand in need of the props of a firm and good administration, till time shall have rendered its authority venerable, and fortified it by habits of obedience.

Yet with this opinion of Mr. Adams, I have finally resolved not to advise the withholding from him a single vote. The body of Federalists, for want of sufficient knowledge of facts, are not convinced of the expediency of relinquishing him. It is even apparent, that a large proportion still retain the attachment which was once a common sentiment. Those of them, therefore, who are dissatisfied, as far as my information goes, are, generally speaking, willing to forbear opposition, and to acquiesce in the equal support of Mr. Adams with Mr. Pinckney, whom they prefer. Have they not a claim to equal deference from those who continue attached to the former? Ought not these, in candor, to admit the possibility that the friends who differ from them act not only from pure motives, but from cogent reasons? Ought they not, by a co-operation in General Pinckney, to give a chance for what will be a *safe* issue, supposing that they are right in their preference, and the best issue, should they happen to be mistaken? Especially, since by doing this they will increase the probability of excluding a third candidate, of whose unfitness all sincere Federalists are convinced. If they do not pursue this course, they will certainly incur an immense responsibility to their friends and to the government.

*   *   *

THE ELECTORAL VOTE IN THE 1800 ELECTION

STATES	Thomas Jefferson	Aaron Burr	John Adams	C. C. Pinckney	John Jay
New Hampshire.....	—	—	6	6	—
Vermont..........	—	—	4	4	—
Massachusetts.......	—	—	16	16	—
Rhode Island.......	—	—	4	3	1
Connecticut........	—	—	9	9	—
New York..........	12	12	—	—	—
New Jersey........	—	—	7	7	—
Pennsylvania........	8	8	7	7	—
Delaware..........	—	—	3	3	—
Maryland	5	5	5	5	—
Virginia...........	21	21	—	—	—
North Carolina.....	8	8	4	4	—
South Carolina.....	8	8	—	—	—
Georgia...........	4	4	—	—	—
Kentucky..........	4	4	—	—	—
Tennessee.........	3	3	—	—	—
	73	73	65	64	1

Election of 1804

MANNING DAUER is Professor of Political Science at the University of Florida. He is the author of Adams Federalists.

Election of 1804

by *Manning Dauer*

In 1804, when Thomas Jefferson won reelection to the Presidency in a land-slide, he and his vice-presidential running-mate George Clinton received 162 electoral votes and carried fourteen states. Their Federalist opponents Charles Cotesworth Pinckney and Rufus King received 14 electoral votes and carried but two states. These results stand in sharp contrast with the election of 1800, in which Jefferson and Aaron Burr each received 73 electoral votes and the Federalist candidate John Adams received 65. In that election Jefferson won the Presidency only after the House of Representatives chose him over Burr.

Why were the results so close in 1800 but so one-sided in 1804? The answer is the overwhelming popular support built up by Jefferson. An understanding of this support requires a comprehension of Jefferson's program —what he and his party stood for in the eyes of the voters.

By 1804 the sixty-one-year-old Jefferson, best known as the author of the Declaration of Independence, had made many important political contributions to the history of the new nation. As a Virginia legislator and governor he had led the fight for the disestablishment of the Church of England and for the passage of the Virginia Statute of Religious Freedom. He had drafted the legislation abolishing primogeniture and entail in Virginia, which thus ended laws protecting large-scale hereditary estates. In addition he sponsored legislation to create public schools and a publicly supported university. Although the education bills were unsuccessful in Virginia, similar ones were adopted by

Georgia, New York, and North Carolina. In Virginia, Jefferson had sponsored legislation to open up western lands for settlement, and in the Continental Congress he had written the Northwest Ordinance, which set up self-governments in the western lands ceded by the states to the new union. Both measures aided in making public lands available on easy credit terms. During his first Administration, the President negotiated the Louisiana Purchase, which doubled the land area of the United States and opened still more western territory for settlement, especially in the Mississippi Valley.

In the context of an expanding agrarian society, new measures constituted a positive program for the average American and his family, 80 per cent of whom were engaged in farming. To these people the Jeffersonian program offered land, education, social mobility, and individual opportunity — social, economic, and political. Reinforcing these measures were local and state legislation to encourage canals, roads, and offer internal improvements. Moreover, by 1800 Jefferson had lessened his opposition to commerce and manufacturing; in fact, in the state legislatures the Republicans pursued policies which often aided business.

At the national level Jefferson and his Secretary of the Treasury Albert Gallatin made no opposition to continued operation of the Bank of the United States under a national charter. After the acquisition of New Orleans, for example, a branch of the bank was opened there. So, while Jefferson had been sharply opposed by Federalists in 1800 as the enemy of trade and commerce, by 1804 he had disarmed many of his critics — at least the more moderate ones.

In other national areas the Jeffersonians could point to equally successful and popular programs. The Alien and Sedition Acts were permitted to expire, and pardons were issued to those convicted. By 1803 the Jeffersonians reduced Army and Navy expenditures to one-third the level they had been in 1800. Total federal spending was out by 30 per cent, and the national debt declined from $83 million in 1800 to $77 million in 1803. Federal internal revenue taxes were virtually eliminated, leaving customs duties as the principal source of government income. These yielded an annual surplus of $2 million over expenditures. In addition, the federal payroll was reduced, the number of judges cut, and matters such as bankruptcy legislation returned to the states.

In foreign policy the dispute with France came to an end, and although Adams had negotiated the settlement of the 1798 crisis, Jefferson reaped the rewards. Furthermore, Napoleon delayed other colonial adventures because of the Black Rebellion in Santo Domingo and a renewed continental war. While Jefferson followed a pacific policy toward France and England, he took a strong line against the Barbary States of North Africa. Although the Federalists had charged Jefferson with abandoning commerce and dismantling the Navy, the existing naval vessels produced spectacular victories and wide public acclaim.

The success of his policies was reinforced by his personal popularity. Jefferson stood six feet two-and-a-half inches tall, and his hair, originally reddish, had turned gray. A horseman and outdoorsman, the President maintained an active physical schedule. He was somewhat angular, and loose-jointed, but his fair, freckled face seemed almost handsome. Although he was limited as an orator, Jefferson's written statements were lucid and eloquent. Since no stump speeches were required in the early 1800's, the press printed Jefferson's public papers as he wrote them — to his benefit.

At Monticello and in the White House Jefferson lived simply but well. His social style was more informal than most of the Federalists; he abolished the stuffy weekly levees of his predecessors as well as the custom of delivering an address in person at the opening of each congressional session. He even refused to reveal the date of his birth, not wishing to encourage public celebrations in his honor. This simple and direct manner appealed to the voters.

Intellectually Jefferson was a person of tremendous curiosity and flair, and his accomplishments attest to his many skills. In France, where he had served as ambassador, he was deemed a worthy successor to Benjamin Franklin. Moreover his *Notes on Virginia*, containing a great deal of historical, social, and political information, had gained him repute as a natural philosopher. He also maintained a broad correspondence with intellectual leaders in England and on the Continent. On occasion these letters appeared in the newspapers, revealing a speculative and active intellect in many fields. As an architect Jefferson designed buildings in the Greek Revival style. He enjoyed music and played the violin. To his friends and to the Republicans he was an attractive person with a lively intellect; to the Federalists he was tricky, impractical, and, because he speculated on religion, was wrongly believed to be an atheist. His liking for France and for liberalism was as admired by the Republicans as it was detested by the Federalists.

Jefferson's renomination came early in 1804, because in six states presidential electors were chosen by the state legislatures, and several of these states had spring elections for state offices. The Republicans were determined to replace Vice-President Aaron Burr, who had not withdrawn in the 1800 electoral tie nor had aided Jefferson in office. A congressional caucus on February 25, 1804, unanimously renominated Jefferson. For the Vice-Presidency the vote was as follows: George Clinton, New York, 67; John Breckenridge, Kentucky, 20; Levi Lincoln, Massachusetts, 9; John Langdon, New Hampshire, 7; Gideon Granger, Connecticut, 4; Samuel Maclay, Pennsylvania, 1. Burr received no votes. Earlier some consideration had been given to Thomas McKean of Pennsylvania but he had dropped out by February 25.

Born July 26, 1739, in Ulster, New York, George Clinton was now sixty-five. Unlike Jefferson, the intellectual, Clinton was a man of powerful physique, whose mere presence commanded respect. He had read law but chiefly was occupied in business and farming when not engaged in politics. At the age of thirty he was elected to the New York Assembly. Not a member of the aristocratic families who had previously dominated New York State's politics, Clinton soon achieved great popularity among farmers, as well as legislative leaders. With the growing opposition to England, he moved to the forefront and was elected to the Second Continental Congress. Next, he was chosen as a brigadier general of militia and then commissioned as a brigadier general in the Continental Army. In 1777 Clinton was elected first governor of New York, as well as lieutenant governor. He declined the second office and served for six sucessive terms as governor. Later he served a seventh. During the Revolution he continued in the army, ultimately achieving the rank of major general. By the end of the revolution, Clinton had become the leading popular figure in his state.

He opposed the Constitution and in 1788 received three second-choice votes for the Presidency. While continuing as governor of New York, he received fifty second-choice votes for President against John Adams in 1792. Shortly after, Clinton was replaced by Jefferson as the Republican candidate. Though still an imposing figure, he had aged noticeably by 1804 when DeWitt Clinton informed Jefferson of his uncle's interest in the Vice-Presidency. The old man's political principles, however, conformed with Jefferson's, and as leader of the New York Republicans he was a logical choice for the nomination.

On the Federalist side a unique situation developed. There was no caucus nor a Federalist candidate. In fact, between March and November, 1804, the question of Federalist candidates was hardly discussed. In March, several Federalist newspapers urged Charles Cotesworth Pinckney and Rufus King to run but after that silence prevailed. The authoritative Federalist paper, the Boston *Columbia Centinel*, flatly declared on October 3, "the proper personages to be voted for as President will be the inquiry of electors after they are chosen. The Federal Republicans believe it to be their duty to select the wisest and most patriotic citizens for electors. . . . They are not tied down to two candidates." This enigmatic attitude was maintained until the end. Most probably this contributed to the Federalists, loss of Massachusetts, although earlier in the year they had won the governorship and other major Massachusetts state offices.

Privately, the Federalists had agreed as to where their electoral ballots should go. Their presidential candidate, Pinckney, was born at Charleston, South Carolina, on February 25, 1746, the son of a wealthy plantation family. He had journeyed to England when he was twelve to be educated by private tutors until he entered Westminister School, and then Christ Church College, Oxford. Afterward he was admitted to the Middle Temple and the English Bar in 1769. He also attended the Royal Military Academy in France. In addition to his law practice, Pinckney had commercial and planting interests. He was chosen to the South Carolina provincial assembly in 1769 and when the revolution began he enrolled in the colonial militia as a lieutenant. By 1776 he was a colonel and aide to General George Washington. He was captured by the British in Charleston, exchanged in 1782, and completed his Revolutionary War service as a brigadier general.

A member of the Federal Convention of 1787, Pinckney vigorously supported the new constitution. Between 1791 and 1795 he was offered command of the Army and the posts of Secretary of War and Secretary of State but declined all three. In 1796 he did accept the ministry to France and, in 1797, took part in the special XYZ mission along with Eldridge Gerry and

John Marshall. A tough bargainer, his response to Tallyrand's demand for a bribe was, "No! No! Not a sixpence." Upon his return to the United States his reply was associated with the slogan "Millions for Defense, Not one cent for Tribute," and he and Marshall became popular heroes. In 1800 when he ran for the Vice-Presidency on the ticket with John Adams, Alexander Hamilton attempted to convince Federalist electors to favor him over Adams. A wealthy man of imposing personal appearance, Pinckney displayed considerable political ability. In 1803, his tour of New England received extensive newspaper coverage, and he continued to correspond with Hamilton deploring the administrative program of the Jeffersonians.

Rufus King of New York was the Federalist candidate for Vice-President. Born in Maine (then part of Massachusetts) in 1755, he was forty-nine in 1804. He graduated from Harvard in 1777, read law under Theophilus Parsons in Massachusetts, and was admitted to the bar in 1780. To fulfill his military obligations King enlisted in the Revolutionary Army, and from 1783–85 he served in the Massachusetts general court where his oratorical skills won him considerable renown. He served in the Continental Congress and, later, in the Philadelphia convention. Moving to New York after the establishment of the new government, he was elected senator, largely due to the support of George Clinton. However, King soon became a close supporter of Hamilton, defended Jay's Treaty, and was joint author with Hamilton of a newspaper series defending that treaty. He was made a director of the Bank of the United States, and in 1796 shortly after reelection to the Senate he succeeded Thomas Pinckney, brother of Charles Cotesworth Pinckney, as minister to England. King remained a close associate of Hamilton and while minister to England maintained a private correspondence with Hamilton and followed his advice. He resigned in 1803. Returning to New York, King was received cordially by the Federalists, who honored him with dinners and made him a key figure in their political celebrations.

The method of choosing the electors in 1804 can be seen in Table 1. During the first presidential elections formulas of selection had varied from state to state, and much of the electoral maneuvering arose over how the electors should be chosen. In 1804 the Federalists, who controlled the Massachusetts legislature, felt compelled to continue popular voting for electors but amended the state law so that all nineteen electors would be chosen at large. They erroneously believed that this winner-take-all approval would help the Federalists. The general picture can be summarized as follows: (1) six states provided for choice by the legislature; (2) seven states provided for popular vote to choose electors, all of whom ran at large; and (3) four states' electors were chosen by popular vote from districts.

The 12th Amendment, ratified by three-quarters of the states, became effective in September, 1804, just in time for the presidential election. Its object was to avoid an impasse like the one which had resulted in the Jefferson-Burr contest of 1800. It did so by changing the procedure in the Electoral College so that each elector, instead of voting for two persons without indicating which he wanted as President, would cast separate votes for

TABLE 1
METHOD OF CHOICE OF PRESIDENTIAL ELECTORS, 1804

STATE	NUMBER OF ELECTORS	HOW CHOSEN
Massachusetts	19	Popular vote, state at large
Connecticut	9	Legislature
New Hampshire	7	Popular vote, state at large
Vermont	6	Legislature
Rhode Island	4	Popular vote, state at large
New Jersey	8	Popular vote, state at large
Pennsylvania	20	Popular vote, state at large
New York	19	Legislature
Delaware	3	Legislature
Maryland	11	Popular vote by district. Nine districts, seven chose one each, two chose two each.
North Carolina	14	Popular vote by districts, fourteen districts
South Carolina	10	Legislature
Georgia	6	Legislature
Virginia	24	Popuoar vote, state at large
Kentucky	8	Popular vote, two districts
Tennessee	5	Popular vote, five districts
Ohio	4	Popular vote, state at large
	176	

President and Vice-President. There was overwhelming demand for the amendment, but bitter Federalist opposition to the plan had made the campaign for its ratification part of the presidential campaign as well.

A Republican campaign committee made up of one congressman from each state was named at the February 25, 1804, congressional caucus. In the states where there was opposition, state committees were set up, and in many of these one could find county and town committees. In Boston there even were ward committees. Supplementing the work of the committees were celebrations of patriotic days. Some of these, such as July 4, were celebrated by both parties. But the Jeffersonians also observed March 4 as the anniversary of Jefferson's inauguration. Other celebrations were held on muster and militia assembly days. In many areas of the country militia units had party affiliations.

Celebrations of a completely partisan nature, such as the March 4 celebration, usually started with a parade, in which there were Republican militia units, Republican local and state officials, occasionally organizations of professional men and workers (called mechanics), and benevolent societies. In celebration of the Louisiana Purchase, a May 11, 1804 Philadelphia parade, as reported in the Republican *Aurora*, included organizations like the St. Patrick's Society, the United Germany Benefit Society, the Cordwainers, the Victuallers, the Union Society, the Provident Society, and the "Young Men of Democratic Principles" bearing an emblematic flag. Such parades often concluded with a high-spirited dinner, where there could be as many as twenty-five toasts. The first toast to start off the dinner after the Philadelphia parade was to Jefferson. Then there followed toasts to leading Republicans and to Republican principles: to economy, peace, the Louisiana Purchase, Stephen Decatur, and so on.

Another important feature of Republican campaigning was the party press. By 1804, strong Republican dailies existed in most of the leading cities, with weeklies or twice-a-week papers in the towns. There were no press associations, but Jefferson had persuaded Samuel Harrison Smith to move from Philadelphia to Washington and establish the *National Intelligencer*, a paper which provided a ready forum for long series of articles defending the Administration. Smith had access to the White House, and his articles were immediately copied in other Republican papers from Georgia to Maine. The Republican papers were more popular in tone than the Federalist papers, although they were fewer in number and carried less advertising. Their style was lively and the news was directed to the average person, while the Federalists catered to shipping, to the professions, and to the established families. Printed circulars, called broadsides, containing announcements of meetings, parades, and important political speeches, supplemented the newspapers.

The issues of the Republican campaign centered on the Administration record: simplicity and frugality in government and measures at the state and Federal Government level to assure opportunity to land, to education, and to political office. Support for canals, roads, and other measures which would help develop the country was also stressed. Taxes had been reduced, the national debt was being cut back, there was peace, and the Louisiana Purchase had doubled the size of the country. If the campaign in 1804 was well-organized for the Republicans, it was not for the Federalists. In fact, in some states there was simply no Federalist campaign whatsoever. With the election of Jefferson, Adams had retired from politics. Almost immediately, except in New England, Delaware, Maryland and South Carolina, the Federalist party disintegrated at the state level and lost much of its strength in Congress. By 1804 it had less than a third of the membership in each house. At the same time the admission of new states in the West still further discouraged the Federalists since the party which stressed aristocratic leadership never had strength in the frontier territories.

Under these circumstances many of the leaders, like Fisher Ames of Massachusetts, former leader in the House of Representatives, gradually withdrew from politics. Hamilton, on the contrary, urged democratization of the party. He wanted it to follow the Republican plan of appealing to a broad spectrum of voters, to form participant societies and clubs. Specifically, he urged the founding of the Washington Benevolent Society. Some Federalist leaders, like James A. Bayard, agreed that the party's base should be broadened. But in Congress party leadership fell into the hands of Senator Timothy Pickering of Massachusetts. Pickering had been Adam's Secretary of State until the President dismissed him, after which he turned to farming. A Massachusetts group called the Essex Junto then placed him in the Senate. This group, headed by Ames, George Cabot, and Stephen Higginson, all wealthy commercial leaders, had been close to Hamilton. In Pickering they selected an ambitious lieutenant whose leadership was limited by narrow vision and restricted intelligence. Although vindictive and extremely conservative, he did have great energy. By now Pickering considered the Union hopeless, though he saw opportunity for himself in the Republican repudiation of Burr in February, 1804. Burr had returned to New York, and with the retirement of George Clinton from the governorship, hoped to split the Republicans, secure Federalist support, and succeed Clinton as governor. Pickering attempted to convince the Federalists that they should support Burr as a prelude to larger things. Burr should lead New York to join with New England in secession from the Union, and then the northeastern states could form a new confederation. Pickering convinced other New England congressmen, including William Plumer of New Hampshire, that this plan should be pursued, and also attempted to enlist the Essex Junto and, of course, the New York Federalists.

Hamilton's response was to oppose Burr with all his strength, and Burr was defeated by a wide margin in the gubernatorial election in April. In the process, however, Hamilton's statements about Burr's character incited Burr to challenge Hamilton to a duel. This was postponed until July, and at that time Hamilton was killed. His last political letter, written on the eve of the duel, urged his New England friends not to follow the secession plan which Pickering was still advocating.

Pickering had no interest in a national Federalist campaign. Wanting to end the compromise of the Constitution which permitted the southern states to count slaves as three-fifths in determining population ratios for distribution of House of Representatives' seats, Pickering attacked the southern states and the slaveholders there. His effort to preserve the sectional influence of New England, and a Pinckney-King ticket aroused no enthusiasm in Pickering and his cohorts. The Federalist press solved the problem by not mentioning the candidates. On one thing the Federalists could, however, readily agree: Jefferson was unfit to be President. In those states where electors were chosen by popular vote, the Federalists concentrated on attacking Jefferson. Organized slates of electors were entered only in Massachusetts, New Hampshire, and Maryland.

Federalist criticism of Jefferson started with the honest belief that none but Federalists was suitable to govern. The Federalists feared popular rule and democracy. In their view, all Republicans were "demagogues" who manipulated the press, raised false issues, and brought in foreigners like William Duane, editor of the Philadelphia *Aurora*, to corrupt America. The Federalists felt that inequality of property therefore had to be defended. They considered Jefferson an infidel who traveled on Sunday. They even claimed he had not written the Declaration of Independence, but only wrote down what others told him. Moreover, he was considered a deadbeat, who refused to pay his private debts. Jefferson had no judgment; his fiscal policy, conceived by Gallatin, was notoriously unwise. His repeal of the Judiciary Act and the weakening of the Army and Navy showed his desire to dismantle the government.

But the Federalists made themselves vulnerable by committing serious errors in their discussion of foreign policy. First, they had introduced a resolution in Congress demanding seizure of Louisiana. Then when Louisiana was purchased, charges were made that the cost was too great, that no power existed in the Federal Government to add territory, and that the proposed government of the Louisiana Territory was patterned after Napoleonic conquests in Europe. It was obvious to the Federalists that Jefferson was risking war with England by his favoritism to France. After having insulted the British minister and his wife by not paying attention to "the etiquette of our court," he had left the coast defenseless. Instead of building a real navy, he had followed the ridiculous policy of constructing gunboats.

Jefferson's ultimate goal of building a dictatorship became apparent when the Federalists analyzed his policy of federal appointments and his solicitation to Congress to impeach Judge Pickering and Justice Samuel Chase. Jefferson's power drive, it seemed, reminded the Federalists of Caesar, Robespierre, and Napoleon.

Like the Republicans, the Federalists held celebrations. One of the most festive took place on Washington's Birthday. The toasts showed what they wished to emphasize:

1. The Day . . . for the memory of Washington (seventeen cannons);
2. The People of the United States (Music: *Hail Colombia*);
3. The Friends of the People — not their Flatterers (Music: Yankee Doodle);
4. The Legislative and Executive Authorities — with constitutional powers — not more powerful than the constitution;
5. The Judiciary — as free from *persecution* as from *patronage*;
6. The Army and Navy — altho few in number, yet prevalent in Valour;
7. To the true *Seamen* of the United States — Protection at sea and relief on shore; but not to fugitives who assume the character and abuse it;
8. *A Free Press* — the publication of truth protected — not punished;
9. *Honesty*, *Capacity* and *Fidelity* to the Constitution — titles to approbation if not to Favoritism;
10. The Heroes and Statesmen of the Revolution — meritorius associates of WASHINGTON (Music: The Heroes Return);
11. Washington — he never deserted his post — animated by his examples we will never desert his Principles (Music: Washington's Grand March).

VOLUNTEERS

By Mr. Pickering — Religion and Morality — Effective supports of a free government.

Judge Marshall — that rare Patriotism which prefers public *interest* to public *favor*.

Judge Chase — The man who dares to be honest in the worst of *times*.

There were some Federalist efforts to confuse the Republicans. In New York, for example, the Federalist press called on electors to use their discretion and to vote for Clinton for President. Although this caused some Republican alarm, it soon proved not to have any weight with the electors, and indeed may have been the type of maneuver which caused the Federalists to oppose the 12th Amendment.

The biggest handicap which the Federalists faced in states choosing electors by popular vote was that they did not pledge their electors to specific candidates. This probably accounted for the loss of Massachusetts, where the Republican campaign again and again emphasized that the voter could not know who the electors would vote for. The Federalist explanation of their unpledged electoral slate proved unsatisfactory to the voters.

When the election was held, even Massachusetts and New Hampshire went for Jefferson; in Rhode Island the Federalists did not bother to name an electoral slate. Jefferson and Clinton carried fourteen states with 162 electoral votes; the Federalists received 2 electoral votes in Maryland and 12 more in Connecticut and Delaware for an inglorious total of 14. Where electors were chosen by popular vote Jefferson carried every state except for the two Maryland electors. In Massachusetts the December returns showed a Republican total of 29,310 and a Federalist one of 25,777. There was no Federalist slate in New Jersey and the Jeffersonians polled 13,039 to 19. New Hampshire went 9,088 to 8,386 for Jefferson, and no returns were given for Virginia in the absence of an official Federalist slate. The same situation prevailed for North Carolina. In Pennsylvania a few counties had a write-in Federalist slate, but the results were: Republican, 22,103, Federalists, 1,179. In Kentucky and Tennessee there is no record of Federalist electors; in Ohio the three Republicans on the official slate received votes of 2,593, 2,502, and 2,475. There were scattered votes for other candidates ranging from 364 to 76 votes.

One of the Virginia electors complained to Jefferson about the President's failure to appoint him to a federal position or even to answer his letters. Jefferson replied:

> You observe that you are, or probably will be appointed as elector. I have no doubt you will do your duty with a conscientious regard to the public's good and to that only. Your decision in favor of another would not excite in my mind the lightest dissatisfaction towards you. On the contrary I should honor the integrity of your choice. In the nominations I have to make, do the same justice to my motives. Had you hundreds to nominate instead of one, be assured they would not compose for you a bed of roses. You would find yourself in most cases with one loaf and ten wanting bread.

Jefferson was delighted by the result and even concluded that party divisions might be nearing an end. To his friend C. F. C. deVolney in France he wrote: "The two parties which prevailed with so much violence when you were here, are almost wholly melted into one. . . . I have received one hundred and sixty-two votes against fourteen only. Delaware is still on poise, as she has been since 1775, and will be until Anglomany with her yields to Americanism. Connecticut will be with us in a short time. Though the people in mass have joined us, their leaders have committed themselves too far to retract." In his exhilaration, however, the President underestimated the resistance of the American party system. The Federalist party was indeed dying; but before his second term was over Jefferson, by his own policies, would give it the final lease on life.

Appendix

Republican Platform
1804

Although no formal platform was ever issued, Republicans were in general consensus on basic issues:

In his first Message to Congress on December 8, 1801, President Jefferson advocated that all aspects of the economy should be equally supported by laws enacted by Congress:

Agriculture, manufacture, commerce and navigation the four pillars of our prosperity, are the most thriving when left most free to individual enterprise. . . . If in the course of your observations or inquiries they should appear to need any aid within the limits of our constitutional powers, your sense of their importance is sufficient assurance they will occupy your attention. . . .

Moreover, naturalization and immigration should be encouraged:

I cannot omit recommending a removal of the laws on the subject of naturalization. Considering the ordinary changes of human life, a denial of citizenship under a residence of fourteen years is a denial to a great proportion of those who ask it . . . And shall we refuse the unhappy fugitive from distress that hospitality which the savages of the wilderness extended to our fathers arriving in this land? Shall oppressed humanity find no asylum on this globe?

Collection of all internal taxes has been suspended, Jefferson declared, and the tax collectors dismissed:

The collection of internal taxes having been completed in some of the states, the officers employed in it are of course out of commission.

Jefferson advised the repeal of the Judiciary Act establishing additional federal courts:

The Judiciary system of the United States, and especially that portion of it recently erected will of course present itself to the contemplation of Congress. . . .

He recommended reduction in the size of the army and navy:

A statement has been formed by the Secretary of War on mature consideration of all the ports and stations where garrisons will be expedient and of the

171

numbers of men requisite for each garrison. The whole amount is considerably short of the present establishment. For the surplus no particular use can be pointed out. . . .

With respect to . . . our naval preparations . . . some difference of opinion may be expected. . . . A small force will probably continue to be wanted for actual service in the Mediterranean. . . .

Primary dependence for defense should be placed on the citizen militia:

Uncertain as we must ever be of the particular point in our circumfrence where an enemy may choose to invade us, the only force which can be made ready at every point and competent to oppose them, is the body of neighboring citizens as formed into a militia. On these, collected from the parts most convenient, numbers proportioned to the invading foe, it is best to rely. . . .

. . . The provision of military stores on hand will be laid before you, that you may judge, of the additions still requisite. . . .

Economy and decreased expenditures, Jefferson states in his October 16, 1803, message soon would provide for payment of the national debt, while also meeting government operating expenses from current annual tax revenues:

. . . the amount paid into the treasury [for 1803] has been between eleven and twelve million dollars . . . the revenue accrued during the same term exceeds . . . our current expenses. . . . [This will permit us] . . . to extinguish the public debt within the period heretofore proposed. . . .

Peace with major countries has been maintained while Europe is at war:

We have seen with sincere concern the flames of war lighted up again in Europe, and nations with which we have the most friendly and useful relations engaged in mutual destruction. While we regret the miseries in which we see others involved, let us bow with gratitude to that kind Providence which . . . guarded us from hastily entering into the sanguinary content. . . .

Jefferson recommended ratification of the Louisiana Purchase and anticipated great benefit to the United States. His message to Congress on October 17, 1803 stated:

The [acquisition] of the property and sovereignty of the Mississippi and its waters secure an independent outlet for the produce of the western states, and as uncontrolled navigation through their whole course . . . the fertility of the country, its climate and extent, promise in due season important aids to our treasury, an ample provision for our posterity, and a widespread field for the blessings of freedom and equal laws.

Treaties with Indian tribes open up more western lands to settlement, Jefferson declared in his October 17, 1803, message to Congress:

Another important acquisition of territory has also been made since the last session of Congress. The friendly tribe of Kaskaskia Indians, with which we have never had a difference, reduced by the wars and wants of savage life to a few individuals unable to defend themselves against the neighboring tribes, has transferred the country to the United States, reserving only for its members what is sufficient to maintain them in an agricultural way. . . .

Republicans appealed to rank and file citizens. Witness this particular meeting to endorse Massachusetts state candidates in 1804. The quotation is from the Boston Independent Chronicle *of April 2, 1804:*

At a large meeting of Shop-Keepers, Traders and Mechanics at Vila's on Saturday every man agreed to support the following ticket.

In Republican newspapers Democracy was defended. The Wilmington *[North Carolina]* Gazette *on September 5, 1803, termed the "elective democracy" a good form of government responsive to the people. "A DEMOCRACY has the same honor to defend, and a Republic or elective Democracy has as strong power to defend it as a monarchy or aristocracy has."*

Federalists were attacked in the Raleigh Register *of November 19, 1804, for monarchism and aristocracy, and a class appeal was stated:*

Fellow Citizens: Permit me once more to make a few remarks on the condition of those aristocrats who still continue to make a tool of religion to bend the minds of our Americans to their evil designs which undoubtedly is to overset our present government in favor of that which would establish luxury and dissapation by making the rich despot master, and the poor labourer a slave. . . .

Jefferson's religion was defended against Federalist attacks in the Raleigh Register, *November 14, 1803:*

The cavils against Mr. Jefferson are answered by an extract from his Notes on Virginia [Jefferson's one published book at this time.]

That the people of North Carolina, and others who have been imposed upon by false representations of Mr. Jefferson's religious opinion may be undeceived, I have sought to publish, in your Register, what is said by him on the topic of Religion . . . David R. Robinson.

The failure of the Federalists to name candidates was attacked as insulting to the voters, or so thought the Philadelphia Aurora *of November 6, 1804:*

The contempt for the judgement of the people, entertained by the federal leaders of the Hamiltonian school, has been seldom so strongly manifested as in the nominations for electors, without informing the voters whom the electors were to choose for president and vice president. In New England a caucus is held, an electoral ticket is formed, and the citizens are called upon to vote for it; such is the case in New Jersey—but in no instance have the people been told whether Jefferson or Pinckney, Clinton or Ellsworth were to be supported. Whilst the knowledge the intention of the republicans to vote for Jefferson and Clinton, enables the Federalists to slander and abase them, an opportunity is not afforded to the Republicans to examine the pretensions of those who are to be the federal candidates—the names are cunningly and cowardly concealed. This concealment, however, marks the weakness of the federalists as a party, and the little weight which the names of any of their leaders has with the people.

In the Massachusetts campaign the same complaint was made in two articles in the Boston Independent Chronicle *of September 20 and October 11:*

In answer to the question who are the candidates proposed by the Federalists, it has shrewdly been answered that the citizens must leave the choice to the electors. The people therefore, by their doctrines are not to have any voice in the important decision. The several districts are to assemble and vote for the federal ticket without having the characters contemplated by the Exxes Junto for President and Vice President. Nineteen men are the sole judges, on this interesting occasion and we are to insist implicitly their choice. This is a new system. . . . This may be called a federal trick. If the Junto are honest why do they not say explicitly that they intend to promote the election of Gen. *Pinckney* in opposition to Mr. *Jefferson.* . . . The Federalists christen their ticket 'Washington and Adams' when every boy in the street knows the fallacy of this profession. Will the Junto vote for Adams whom they constantly abuse, will the friends of Hamilton vote for Adams, when they recollect the calumny against him by the declared opponent? This truth may deceive idiots but freemen despise the *men* who practice such inconsistencies. . . .

The Independent Chronicle *again returned to the theme of no Federalist candidates after the Federalist press explained that the electors should make the choice:*

Messrs. Adams and Rhoades, Why do the Federal Party forbear to inform the public of the person they mean to support in the next Presidential election? Do they intend to run for *Mr. John Adams* or do they mean to pursue their old game of deception to sense the election of their General Candidates under his name, and then back desert him by voting for Mr. Pinckney? The Republicans have no wish to conceal their views on this occasion—They hesitate not to declare that their exertions to secure the success of the Republican. list proceeds from a desire to serve the re-election of *Thomas Jefferson*, for President, and *George Clinton* for Vice President. Let the Federalists come forward with the like frank declaration of their views—or the conclusion in the public mind must be that they have designs which they dare not present for public scrutiny.

Newspapers such as the National Intelligencer, *the Philadelphia* Aurora, *and the* Raleigh Register *continued to espouse the Republican cause.*

The right to vote should be extended to include universal manhood suffrage. Property, will be secured by interesting all in voting.

Slavery should be abolished. The New Jersey House has voted its abolition.

Internal improvements by Republican State legislatures are advocated. The Delaware and Chesapeake Canal has been surveyed. The Raleigh, North Carolina Republican newspaper also urged canal subscriptions.

Republican Banks and land companies should be established. As much as $60,000,000 in capital for development should be created.

Public roads should be constructed.

Common schools and universities should be established. Acadamies and state universities are supported.

A summary statement of Republican Principles, appearing in the Raleigh Register *October 24, 1803, states:*

The following published as the Political Creed of a New Jersey Republican, is not unworthy of general adoption.

1st. We believe that God created all men free and equal.

2nd. We believe that all power exists originally in the people, and is by them delegated to their representatives.

3rd. We believe that the will of the majority, constitutionally expressed, is the supreme law of the land.

4th. We believe, that the minority have a right to decent remonstrance and investigation.

5th. We believe, that opinion however erroneous, is not punishable at law.

6th. We believe, that religious establishments and religious tests are contrary to reason and the genius of liberty.

7th. We believe that every man who supports government is free to elect, and to be elected.

8th. We believe that virtue and knowledge are the basis of a Republic.

9th. We believe that peace is the duty and interest of all nations.

10th. We believe that navies and armies are the seminaries of war.

11th. We believe that the right of feeding a friend is prior and superior to the right of starving an enemy.

12th. We believe that trade and prices are their own best regulators.

13th. We believe that if seventeen sovereign and independent states can exist under one general government, so might all the nations of the earth, if they are properly informed and rightly disposed.

14th. We believe that the world will yet become one confederate republic.

15th. We believe that the fowls of the air will fly away with kings, and that then the nations will learn war no more.

16th. We believe that when a matter of difference arises between two nations, then it should be settled by enlightened and disinterested referees, and that the world as a confederate power should oblige them to abide the decision.

17th. We believe that if other nations will go to war, our duty is to preserve a strict neutrality.

18th. We believe that the powers at war have no right to search, detain or capture our vessels, even if there was enemy property on board.

19th. We believe that if they should do so under the specious pretense of the law of nations, that our best work of redress is *embargo* and *sequestration*.

20th. We believe that other nations should not dictate the law to America; and their duty is to learn wisdom from our example.

Federalist Platform
1804

The Federalists, like their Republican opposition, had no official party plat-
form from which to campaign. Nevertheless, all segments of the party, led by
Alexander Hamilton, were in agreement on certain basic principles, which
were reflected in contemporary Federalist writings.

On foreigners, Hamilton wrote:

We proceed to trace still farther, the consequences that must result from a too
unqualified admission of foreigners to an equal participation in our civil and
political rights.

The safety of a republic depends essentially on the energy of a common national sentiment, on a uniformity of principles and habits; on the exemption
of the citizens from foreign bias, and prejudice; and on that love of country
which will almost invariably be found to be closely connected with birth,
education and family.

Too great economy by Jefferson and the repeal of the Judiciary Act were also
attacked by Hamilton:

In the rage for change, or under the stimulus of a deep rooted animosity against
the former administrations, or for the sake of gaining popular favor by a profuse display of extraordinary zeal for economy, even our judiciary system
has not passed unspoiled.

The Jeffersonian fiscal program for abolishing internal revenue taxes was
opposed by Hamilton and the Federalists:

It is a matter of surprise to observe a proposition to diminish the revenue,
associated with intentions which appear to contemplate war . . . respecting
the Barbary States.

Jefferson's alleged pro-French and anti-British policy was attacked. The
speech of the President on the opening of Congress showed, according to the
Charleston Courier:

that party feelings can blind the reason and pervert the sentiments of the
greatest man. . . . To such men the democrat or the despot, the sanguinary
insanity of Robespierre, or the Turkish tyranny of Bonaparte are alike dear,
provided they are ardently embarked against the administration of this
country.

The Charleston Courier *also reported that Louisiana was given up by France only to avert the hostility of America so as not to impede her fight against Great Britain:*

To Great Britain more than to France is America indebted for that cession; though, in truth, it owes it to neither, but to the accidental circumstances in which Europe has been placed.

The Baltimore Federal Gazette *charged that should Mr. Jefferson unwisely plunge us into a war with Great Britain, his decision would remain a monument of weakness, ignorance. and rashness for the latest posterity:*

To the People of the United States: The Federalists have for a long time charged the Jacobin party in this country with a wish to subject this country to France. This they have argued from their continually harping on the exploded subject of *gratitude* to that nation from the artifices that have been used to draw us into the European war; from the mighty affection which they profess to feel for France.

The impeachments of judges and attacks on the Judiciary by Jefferson and the Republicans, reported the Charleston Courier, *were sharply opposed by the Federalists:*

. . . By destroying the independence of the judges the barrier which the constitution has raised to guard us from the ambitious views or unconstitutional measures of the executive is removed, and consequently the safety of the nation endangered.

Anti-religion was charged against Jefferson, in the Connecticut Courant:

The Jacobins of the country believe that children should grow up without any acquaintance with religious truths. This is all wrong. Children should, must, read the Scriptures. None but a Jacobin with a most fixed hatred to Christianity and its Author, will question the propriety of the mode, or the importance of the end.

Jefferson was attacked again as a would-be dictator. From the Washington Federalist:

To Thomas Jefferson, President of the United States, Emperor of Louisiana, Lord High Admiral of the Navy, MY LORD.

The Federalists did not specify candidates for the Presidency and Vice-Presidency in 1804. Newspapers had named Charles Cotesworth Pinckney and Rufus King as the likely candidates, but there was no designation by party caucus, and after March discussion was dropped until the electors acted in December. The first Federalist statement, quoted in the New London Connecticut Gazette, *naming candidates follows:*

It is reported that the federalists, for the middle and eastern states, propose holding up Mr. King and Mr. Pinckney for Presidency and Vice Presidency at the next election. If this be true their choice will be equally acceptable to the federalists of the southern states, the Carolinas in particular. There is no citizen of the United States, the integrity of whose political character is better established than that of Mr. King's. Having also been absent from this country in those late years in which faction and party spirit have so much prevailed, he appears better calculated than almost any other individual for harmonizing the minds of our citizens and restoring that peace and mutual concord which ought to be the basis of every well regulated government. Mr. King also, from his residence in Europe, during the most critical period in foreign politics is better versed and acquainted with the real designs of foreign courts, on this country than any other man. Mr. Pinckney is universally acknowledged to be both a soldier and a diplomat. Even the most daring among his opponents have never impeached his honor, his integrity or his talents. To the deep knowledge of the politician, he writes the most pleasing address, equally fascinating the courtier and the honest republican. We have no doubt that if the northern states continue in the idea of supporting Mr. King and Mr. Pinckney that they will prove successfull, and finally triumph over their enemies.

The Federalists attacked the value of the Louisiana Purchase and its possible benefits. They combined this attack with a ridicule of the scientific pretensions of Jefferson. In listing expected benefits Jefferson spoke of a mountain of salt in the territory. This led to the following in the Boston Columbian Centinel *and* Massachusetts Federalist, *Saturday, February 4, 1804:*

Mr. Russell, By the communication in your last, signed Inquiry, my doubts have again returned concerning that wonderful Mountain of Salt, and this more from the evidence, attempted to be adduced, than from the absolute impossibility of the thing, however strange. The Frenchman's evidence has no weight with me, and the Indians but little. The former amused the people, with the presentations of nature the better to conceal his designs of arts. — My suspicions have revived on noticing the use that has been made of the opinion of Dr. Waterhouse in this matter. It has exceedingly tickled some people at Washington, and has been published in many of the democratic papers. No man has a higher opinion of Dr. Waterhouse's knowledge of NATURAL HISTORY than myself. His high reputation as a teacher of it in our University is universally known and acknowledged. Often have I heard remarked that it is impossible to bring together a greater number of more courious and important facts in so few lectures, and that Harvard never had a teacher so eminent for perspicuity. But however knowing and accurate he may be, as it respects things he has seen and examined, he may for all that have been deceived as to the existence of a fact at a distance.

As miracles have ceased, and as the phenomena of nature are all the result of fixed laws, I would beg leave to ask the Professor one question, viz., as it is the nature of all salt to dissolve in water, and when supersaturated to precipitate to the bottom, how has it happened that a body of salt, so vast as to form a mountain, has been found above the earth's surface, contrary to the laws of chemistry and gravitation? So here the precipitate is on top and the heavy body under the lighter. By what peculiar power has this last lump of salt, resisted the solvent power of water for ages? These things stagger the faith of a man, and puzzle a simple INQUIRER.

Federalists also criticized Jefferson for corrupting the people. Here the Gazette of the United States *takes aim:*

It is a remark of Machiavel, and it is true that no scheme of government concentrates power into *so few* hands as a democracy. The *many* are indeed amused, and to borrow a vulgar phrase, humbugged with the notion that *they* rule. . . . We have in the United States, besides Mr. Jefferson, ten or twenty very adroit *dupe makers* — and *the people*, meaning always as the Jacobins do, the *rabble*, work as kindly, we must confess, as clay in the hands of the potter. . . . In form then, as well as in fact we are in the power of an oligarchy, a fate to which every Democracy is destined. In the first stage in the journey — the few govern a short time — then *one* — one counsul for life, and his sword in his scepter, We have got on beyond Rolandism almost to Robespierreism, and what remains of our role we shall soon run. . . .

The Federalists criticized the Republicans as being excessively democratic. This was leading to anarchy, as in France. Corruption of Democracy increases, stated the Gazette of the United States, *May 29, 1804:*

We have often expressed a confidence that the present delusion which infatuates our countrymen cannot possibly last long; that a day must soon arrive when the people will spurn and turn from their decievers with abhorrence. And that the nation must at no distant period once more learn to distinguish between honest friends and judicious flatterers, between tried patriots and treacherous pretenders, between the followers of Washington whom Washington trusted and approved of, and the followers of Jefferson, by whom Washington has been slandered and belied. . . . We begin to fear that we have calculated too much on the good sense and the virtue of the land we live in. . . . We begin to fear that her foster sons, that the foreign outcasts she has received . . . understand the disposition of our country much better than we do. We begin to fear that the [William] Duanes [1] the [James] Cheethams [2], the Paines [3], pestilent dregs of another clime, vomited on our shores have not so greatly mistaken the public temper.

[1], [2] Editors of Philadelphia and New York Republican papers; [3] is Thomas Paine.

On the danger of democracy the New London Connecticut Gazette *had this to say:*

LIBERTY AND EQUALITY

Deplorable indeed must be the state of society, where the principles of democracy bear unlicensed sway; and indifferent to his country's welfare must that man be, who views with calmness its approach.

From that fanatical spirit of liberty and equality which among democrats is the order of the day, we have everything to fear. Its ferocious nature knows no principle of justice, no guide but passion and no end but selfishness. With savage malignity, under the specious pretext of *Reformation* it attackes every institution of wisdom and antiquity, and alike dooms to destruction, our learning our laws and religion. — If there be any who think this description too highly coloured, let them peruse the following bill some years since introduced by a democratic member into the Legislature of Rhode Island, bearing in mind that the same Jacobincal spirit which dictated that Bill, is now amongst us employing every means, which wickedness can suggest to overthrow our state government and erect on its ruins the fabric of confusion.

An Act for more equal distribution of Happiness.

Whereas the God of Nature made all men equal. From whence it is evident that the different conditions among mankind have arisen from ambition, avarice, and the lust of domination, and whereas the great objects of the late war were the rights of equality. . . .

Wherefore it be enacted by the General Assembly and by the authority thereof, That all debts, dues, and demands of whatever nature or kind be forever abolished, exterminated and discharged.
And be it further enacted, that an equal distribution of all property, both real and personal, within this state be made by 1st day of May next making as many allotments as there are heads of families. . . . That forever hereafter at the end of thirteen years, respectively, there shall be a general abolition of debts, and an equal distribution of property.

THE ELECTORAL VOTE IN THE 1804 ELECTION

STATES	PRESIDENT		VICE-PRESIDENT	
	T. Jefferson	C. C. Pinckney	George Clinton	Rufus King
New Hampshire	7	—	7	—
Vermont	6	—	6	—
Massachusetts	19	—	19	—
Rhode Island	4	—	4	—
Connecticut	—	9	—	9
New York	19	—	19	—
New Jersey	8	—	8	—
Pennsylvania	20	—	20	—
Delaware	—	3	—	3
Maryland	9	2	9	2
Virginia	24	—	24	—
North Carolina	14	—	14	—
South Carolina	10	—	10	—
Georgia	6	—	6	—
Kentucky	8	—	8	—
Tennessee	5	—	5	—
Ohio	3	—	3	—
	162	14	162	14

Election of 1808

Election of 1808

by *Irving Brant*

Portents of political primacy confronted James Madison long before his own thoughts turned toward the Presidency—indeed, even before that office came into existence. As early as the days of the Continental Congress, when Madison was still in his early thirties, French minister Chevalier de la Luzerne said of him: "He is regarded as the man of the soundest judgment in Congress."

Since the proceedings of the Convention of 1787 remained secret for decades, Madison's leadership in framing the Federal Constitution was but vaguely known to the general public. In the Congress of the United States, however, his 1789 break with Alexander Hamilton over the funding of the public debt produced, in the public mind, a division of congressmen into "Madisonians" and "Hamiltonians." To those who supported Madison, it was a contest between the defenders of unpaid Revolutionary veterans and greedy speculators who had acquired their holdings for a few cents on the dollar under the duress of soldiers' poverty. Pay the whole debt, Madison argued, but divide it between the two groups with profit to both. Pay it all to present holders, urged the Secretary of the Treasury. To him, it was a method of binding the moneyed men of the country to the Federal Government for future stability and their protection. Hamilton won, and thereby created the Federalist party of "the wise, the rich, the good."

Madison was a "conservative radical" who believed in representative government by "the great body of the people," with checks and balances against arbitrary rule. His position in Congress was so fully recognized that the Hamiltonian leader Fisher Ames wrote about him in 1789: "He is our first man." But at the height of the conflict with Hamilton, Thomas Jefferson returned from his diplomatic post in Paris and became Secretary of State. His genius for political leadership transferred the focal point of controversy from Congress to the Cabinet. The "Madisonians" gradually turned into "Jeffersonians" and the Republican party emerged as their political instrument.

By 1794, Jefferson and Madison were pushing each other toward the Presidency. Jefferson began it on the occasion of Madison's marriage to Mrs. Dolley Payne Todd. "The political ship," he wrote in December, "would soon go onto a windward tack." Madison must not retire from his congressional position "unless to a more splendid and a more efficacious post. There I should rejoice to see you; I hope I may say, I shall rejoice to see you." This brought a reply that the most insuperable and obvious reasons shut Madison's mind "against the admission of any idea such as you seem to glance at." Jefferson, however, should prepare himself "to hear truths which no inflexibility will be able to withstand."

The reality was that the gathering forces of democracy could rise rapidly to full strength only under the guiding genius of Jefferson. The latter, however, merely iterated his appeal to Madison to seek the Presidency. "I expressed it with entire sincerity," he affirmed (with a slight lapse in diction), "because there is not another person in the U.S. who, being placed at the helm of our affairs, my mind would be so completely at rest for the fortunes of our political bark."

Widely circulated in Washington during Jefferson's 1801–09 Presidency was an explanation he gave for taking that office. French minister Turreau recorded a conversation in which Jefferson alledgedly told him that he would never " have accepted such a place, if he had not found in the best of his friends, all the talents necessary to help him fill it." This infatuation for "*un homme mediocre*" (Turreau completely altered his estimate of Madison later) perplexed the minister. But, he wrote, "it is beyond doubt that the Secretary of State entirely directs the cabinet at Washington. . . . His influence on the head of government is all the more powerful because the latter courts it."

One month earlier (April, 1806) Republican Senator Adair of Kentucky affirmed that Madison had acquired "a complete ascendancy" over President Jefferson, and Federalist Senator Gilman of New Hampshire agreed with him. With such reports and opinions spreading in Congress (totally contrary to the general public impression) there was no need for Jefferson to broadcast his desire that Madison should succeed him in the Presidency.

In addition to this symbiotic relationship with Jefferson, Madison was thrust headlong into the presidential picture by the Napoleonic Wars, which made foreign affairs the focal point of Administration policy and political contention. The early period at which he began to stand out as Jefferson's "inevitable" successor made him, at the same time, a clear target for Federalist hostility and Republican rivalry. The campaign to keep him out of the Presidency began hardly later than the first overt maneuver to open his way to it, which was incidental to the campaign of 1804.

To succeed Vice-President Aaron Burr (discredited by his 1800 intrigue to gain the Presidency), a congressional caucus wholly devoted to Jefferson nominated Governor George Clinton of New York. Few disputed the assertion of Senator Plumer that Clinton was zealously put forward by Virginians who wished "to elect an old man who is too feeble to aspire to the Presidency."

No such device could protect Madison from the jealous hatred of John Randolph, the shrill-voiced Virginia congressional orator who, deposed in 1805 – as the House's chief Administration spokesman, vented on Madison all the bitter rancor he dared not openly direct at Jefferson. Randolph realized that an alternative candidate would have to be found if Madison was to be defeated, and he saw that candidate in the person of James Monroe, who, after taking an incidental part in the acquisition of the Louisiana Territory from France, was shuttling between London and Madrid as an American envoy. "The satellites of government at Washington," wrote Randolphite Larkin Smith to Monroe in 1805, "are in favor of Mr. Madison, but the great body of your countrymen [probably meaning Virginians] have more confidence in you." Monroe himself disclaimed ambition, telling London friends that he would "sooner be a constable" than oppose Madison.

In October, 1805, Randolph informed Treasury Secretary Gallatin that he intended to spend the next few years in Europe, and added with seeming casualness that he hoped Monroe would be the next President. A few weeks later one of Randolph's congressional followers urged Madison to make Randolph Minister to England. That would have brought Monroe home but would have eliminated his only effective supporter. In any event, the Secretary of State replied that Randolph was unfitted for diplomacy.

The story swept through Congress. Randolph countered with a two-and-one-half hour diatribe (described by Senator Samuel Smith of Maryland, an auditor, as "replete with invective, the most severe that the English language can furnish") against Madison's conduct of foreign affairs. Senator John Quincy Adams recorded the next day in his diary what he considered Randolph's motives – "to prevent Mr. Jefferson from consenting to serve again, and Mr. Madison from being his successor."

To arouse Monroe, Randolph wrote to him that everything was being made "a business of bargain and traffic, the ultimate object of which is to raise Mr. Madison to the Presidency." To this the "old Republicans" [Randolph's adherents] would never consent. "Need I tell you that they are united in your support?" Randolph followed this with a new and even more violent assault on Madison in Congress. The Emperor Napoleon, having reduced Spain to tribute-paying vassalage, had lately offered to bring about a sale of the Floridas to the United States. President Jefferson, in a secret message, asked Congress to appropriate $2 million as an initial payment to Spain. Randolph discussed the President's request with Madison, who told him there were two ways of obtaining the territory, either by purchase from Spain through the influence of France, or by war with both France and Spain. He preferred purchase.

Randolph in committee advocated acquisition of the Floridas by force but said nothing about his talk with Madison. The committee approved the

$2 million installment. Taking the floor against the bill on April 5, 1806, Randolph accused Madison of having told him "that France would not permit Spain to come to any accommodation with us . . . and that we must give her money." That, said he, was "a base prostration of the national character . . . and from that moment, and to the last moment of my life, my confidence in the principles of the man entertaining these sentiments, died, never to live again."

Randolph's silence in committee stamped his horror as fictitious and his version of the story as false. Accusation there would have killed the bill unless disproved, as it would have been. The attack was denounced on the floor as "an outrage on decency." Madison ignored it. Politically, however, the speech passed into the campaign of 1808 as a ten-word blend of bribery and subserviency: "France wants money and we must give it to her."

Jefferson and Madison now had to decide what to do about Monroe. To keep him in London would unfairly choke off his political potential. To recall him might seem a reflection on his competence. The problem was both complicated and simplified by a conclusion that after more than two years of failure to reach an accord with England on great outstanding problems—impressment of American seamen into the British navy and seizure of American merchant vessels—Monroe needed a coadjutor. The decision was made to appoint William Pinkney, a leading Baltimore lawyer and mercantile expert, as special envoy under joint powers, and bearing a commission to succeed Monroe as minister whenever the latter should reach a decision to come home.

The President wrote to Monroe warning him to be on his guard against new friends who were attacking his old ones in a way to render Monroe great injury. Jefferson intended to observe "a sacred neutrality" in coming political events but suggested that Monroe come home before Congress met again in December. This letter was mislaid in Norfolk and came back to Jefferson six months later. All that Monroe received from Madison was the authorization of his return. To him, this looked alternatively like an ungracious recall, a scheme to keep him working on a treaty while Madison won the Presidency, or a device for transferring credit to Pinkney if the mission succeeded. Randolph heightened that feeling by ascribing the recent strange and injurious "amalgam of men and principles" in late government measures to Madison's "great and acknowledged influence" over the President.

Bound by mandatory orders to enter into no treaty that did not end impressments, Monroe and Pinkney signed one that said not a word on the subject. Jefferson and Madison pigeonholed the treaty and Monroe came home in December, 1807, convinced that the rejection was designed to damn him in the eyes of the American electorate. That belief was reinforced by Randolph's words: "The friends of Mr. Madison have left nothing undone to impair the high and just confidence of the nation in yourself." He did not read the offsetting words of impartial ex-Speaker Macon that the published extract of the treaty "has injured Monroe more than the return of it by the President."

Spurred by Randolph and his "Quids," Monroe decided to run for President on the treaty issue and foreign policy in general. (Quid, derived from the Latin for "what?", was a newly-popular political appellation not confined to the Randolphites. Applied to a political faction, explained the New York *Public Advertiser* after using the term a hundred times, "it inquires *what* are they? *What* are their principles?" The answer, said the editor, was that "A *Quid* is one who has no *fixed principles*," but is fixed in one characteristic: "A *Quid* is always in the minority, and the art of the game is to make the smaller number overcome the greater.") He wrote but did not publish a disclosure "by friends" that in reply to their query he "was not a candidate" but had put it beyond doubt that he would serve "should his fellow citizens be disposed to give him so high a proof of their confidence."

Under the laws of political survival, quiddism could menace the Republican party only in states where that party was in power. There was not a trace of it in Federalist Connecticut, for example. There, in Jefferson's second administration, the Republican minority was superbly organized under state, county, township, and district managers. Harmony prevailed in all Republican campaigns — and the Federalists won all the elections.

Far different was the situation in New York, where three Republican factions tore each other to pieces and one or another of them won every election. The state of affairs in New York was explained to Madison by special counsel Pierrepont Edwards in connection with the embarrassing episode of General Francisco Miranda's abortive filibustering expedition to free Venezuela from Spanish colonial rule. In 1806 Miranda came to the United States with a letter from British Privy Councilor Vansittart to Federalist Senator Rufus King, former minister to England. It suggested American financial aid, to be joined in later by England, for the Venezuelan foray. King sent the Vansittart letter to Madison, Miranda following. As Madison described their talk, he told Miranda that although the government was free to listen to him, there would be no departure from amity, and any transaction involving hostility toward Spain would be punished. Miranda raised money and men by saying he received assurance that "although the government would not sanction, it would wink at the expedition." The armed ships sailed, the Spanish minister screamed, and Miranda's two American partners were held for trial in New York.

The trial of holdover Port Collector William S. Smith (President Adams' son-in-law) and shipowner Samuel G. Ogden became a two-years-in-advance campaign against Madison for President. In congressional petitions presented by Federalists, Smith and Ogden charged government connivance. The Senate and House overwhelmingly rejected the charges, but publicity did its work. Defense lawyers subpoenaed the entire Cabinet. Its members ignored the subpoenas. Acquittal was assured in the choice of a partisan jury by a Burrite federal marshal.

Special counsel Edwards described the political background to Madison. The State of New York was divided into four parties — Clintonians, Lewisites, Burrites, and Federalists. The first three claimed to be Republican, but the Burrites were hostile to the Jefferson administration; the Lewisites (followers of former Governor Morgan Lewis) were friendly to it; the Clintonians were cultivating the Randolph faction, believing that its attempt to place Monroe in the Presidency would also "aggrandize DeWitt Clinton."

The Smith-Ogden trial made it clear that of the four New York parties and factions, all except the Lewisites were bent on keeping Madison out of the Presidency. The Clintonians left it uncertain whether they would seek the elevation of Vice-President (former Governor) George Clinton, or push the ambitious DeWitt, who had succeeded his uncle as the ruling figure in state politics. New York Federalists hardly counted except as ineffectual enemies of the faction in power.

Nationally, neither the Republicans nor the Federalists possessed a systematic, organized structure. Federalist candidates for President and Vice-President popped out of a shadowy no man's land—the product, apparently, of a self-assembled conclave of party leaders from various states. Republican candidates, beginning with Thomas Jefferson, were nominated in a caucus of the Republican members of Congress. These were national conventions in embryo, but they had the defect of excluding states which had no Republican representation in the national legislature. The caucus served to prevent the splitting of Republican electoral votes among the "favorite sons" of a dozen states—a course that would convert every Republican electoral college victory into a deadlock to be broken by the House of Representatives.

Back of Republican caucus and Federalist conclave was a more potent informal political force—the power of the press. Candidates for the nation's highest offices did no overt campaigning. Addresses or signed communications from them promoting their own candidacies would have given the public a terrible shock. Newspapers were filled with partisan assaults and eulogies, mostly signed with pseudonyms from classical literature, some written by genuine contributors, others concealing the editor's authorship. Since the Federalists were out of power, their press had but a single target and a single aim—to break the Democratic-Republican succession. The opposition press contributed not to unity but to strife. Every faction nursed and was nursed by its own organs. For better or worse, the campaign of 1808 would be fought *through* and to a great extent *by* the American press.

At the beginning of Jefferson's second term, Alexander J. Dallas of Philadelphia predicted to Secretary Gallatin that unless cohesion were brought into both public councils and elections, "the empire of republicanism will moulder into anarchy." Genuine Republicans must rally to the standard of reason, law and order: "At present we are the slaves of men whose passions are the origin and whose interests are the object, of all their actions. I mean your Duanes, Cheethams and Leibs, &c, &c. They have the press in their power; and though we may have virtue to assert the liberty of the press it is too plain that we have not spirit enough to resist the tyranny of the printers."

William Duane's newspaper, the Philadelphia *Aurora*, was the country's foremost Republican journal, with nationwide circulation and influence. Duane, at the time Dallas wrote, was engaged in a relentless crusade against Gallatin, with Madison, on account of presidential politics, as his greater but indirect target. This began after both cabinet members rejected Duane's request that State and Treasury printing be transferred from Washington to his plant in Philadelphia. U. S. Senator Leib was Duane's proxy intrigant. James Cheetham was publisher of the New York *American Citizen* and the *Republican Watch Tower*, whose daily praise of George and DeWitt Clinton was coincidentally followed by pages and pages of official printing furnished by the Clinton state machine. Cheetham was not renowned for factual accuracy. Thomas Paine was reported to have said of him: "He can not tell the truth without lying."

When the Clintonians, Burrites, and Federalists united to give Madison a black eye in the Smith and Ogden trial, it was a virtual proclamation of a Clinton presidential candidacy, either of George or DeWitt. Madison's campaign managers, Senators Wilson C. Nicholas and William B. Giles, thought of a way (a candidate was supposed to do no thinking) to strike down both possibilities — renominate sixty-eight-year-old George Clinton in spite of his age and mental state. These were described by Senator Plumer: "He is old, feeble, and altogether incapable of presiding over the Senate. He has no mind — no intellect — no memory." The perfect candidate.

Neither of the Clintons had ever challenged Jefferson's foreign policy, which Madison was expected to continue. That left them at the outset with but one issue — too many Virginians in the Presidency. Foreign policy, however, was almost certain to be dominant in the campaign. National welfare, security, and honor were wrapped up in it. Normally, the Federalists would have come boldly forward with a challenge of the whole Jeffersonian record and direction. But the Federalist party was in a state of near coma from its presidential and congressional defeats and loss of power in state governments. The challenge of foreign policy came initially from Monroe, whose first visit to Washington after his return from London left no doubt about the sharpness of his break with the Administration on the intensity of his ambition. Wrote Federalist Congressman Barent Gardenier of New York in the wake of that visit: "Clinton cannot compete successfully with Madison. The latter it begins now to be thought will find a much more powerful antagonist in Monroe, who is said to have a majority of the Virginia legislature in his favor. The Federalists here feel a strong partiality for him."

Federalist Senator Pickering of Massachusetts saw no choice for Federalists except to support the least evil Republican. Madison was the worst of them. As visionary as Jefferson, he would be ruled in every movement "from the top of Monticello." If George Clinton became President, DeWitt would rule both the nation and New York. Monroe was "inferior in learning and discernment to Mr. Madison" but more upright than either rival, and "being also thoroughly cured of his French attachment we greatly prefer him."

"French attachment" was the Federalist explanation of every American foreign policy move adverse to England: President Jefferson and Secretary of State Madison, if not in the pay of Napoleon, were completely under his thumb. In pre-Napoleonic days, the same attitude in them had been charged to undue sympathy for the French Revolution and a yearning for an American counterpart. Actually, Madison set the future Republican course in 1789, before the first mob struck at the Bastille, with his call in Congress for counter-discrimination against British navigation laws designed to hold down the American merchant marine. In 1794, after the wars of the French Revolution had led to British impressment of American seamen and seizures of American ships, Madison brought affairs to a crisis with his retaliation resolutions. The Washington Administration, by that time under Federalist sway, responded by negotiating Jay's treaty with England. This made the United States a silent partner of England in wartime trade and stimulated French reprisals which led to President Adams' naval war with France.

During the remainder of the Adams Administration American Secretaries of State, including Timothy Pickering, made ineffective protests against the claimed British right to search American vessels at sea and remove actual or alleged British subjects. Madison as Secretary of State intensified the protests and vainly sought relief by treaty. As the Anglo-French struggle mounted, England instituted "paper blockades" against uninvested French seaports, seizing ships en route to them. France retaliated with unenforceable decrees blockading the entire British Isles, with seizures to correspond. Arrogant British naval commanders carried their impressments to the American coast and harbors. This culminated in 1807 with a devastating surprise attack on the 36-gun American frigate *Chesapeake* by the 50-gun *Leopard*, with twenty-one American sailors killed or wounded and four men forcibly removed from the crew.

President Jefferson demanded reparations and, by proclamation, ordered all British ships of war to stay out of American seaports. Congress, responding to public clamor, began to prepare for war. England disavowed the attack on the *Chesapeake* but stalled on reparations and return of the seized men. Impressments, insults, and ship seizures increased. France ordered the capture of all vessels bound to or from the British Isles. England retaliated with the most stringent of her Orders in Council, forbidding American trade with French-held Europe *except under British licenses*. That was trade war with the United States, not national defense.

President Jefferson and his Cabinet, faced with a choice of war, submission, or some form of commercial pressure, asked Congress to place a universal embargo on the departure of American ships from American harbors. Congress instantly did so, while retaining a non-importation act just going into effect.

The triple purpose of the embargo was to avoid war, save American ships from capture, and put pressure on England (correspondingly on France, in theory) to modify her restrictive policies in order to obtain much-needed American goods for the British Isles and West Indies. The public response was partly patriotic, principally political. Republicans (except Quids) approved the embargo both out of party loyalty and hope that it would work and avert war. Federalists hailed it as the road to Republican downfall and their own triumph. Jefferson, they insisted, imposed it "to please France, and to beggar us." America, cried John Randolph, was crouching "to the insolent mandate of Bonaparte 'that there should be no neutrals.' "

The embargo, hitting both imposers and targets of it, was of necessity a temporary instrument. The only question was whether the resulting privations would bring Great Britain to terms before accumulating American commercial losses produced a domestic political convulsion. Although American aversion to war and Republican devotion to Jefferson produced strong initial acceptance, time was on the other side. Madison, as co-author of the embargo, was dangerously tied to a changeable public opinion.

In electoral mechanics, Madison's immediate need in 1808 was to win a Virginia endorsement over Monroe and a congressional endorsement over both competitors. Randolph had been spreading word that the Virginia legislature favored Monroe by a great majority. Clintonian newspapers, hoping to profit from the *Chesapeake* war scare, built up George Clinton as a great military figure in the Revolution ("though without military talents," remarked Robert Livingston). Madison must therefore step forward, Livingston told him, "to save us not only from foreign aggression but from the disgrace of falling into the hands of ignorant dotage at home."

Cheetham's *American Citizen* glorified Clinton as "the hero of the Revolution" and assailed Madison for retaining Federalists in the State Department: "Woe be to him who . . . is not a determined party man." The editor accused Madison, whose "influence over the President is known," of excluding Vice-President Clinton from Cabinet meetings. The Madison-Monroe rivalry was played up by the Clintonian press as proof that Virginians believed their state had a monopoly of presidential talent.

This last factor — a dangerous imponderable — was carefully studied by Madisonian managers Wilson and Giles. The Virginia legislature, they concluded, ought to hold back its expected endorsement of Madison until after the congressional caucus, which under the 1804 precedent would be held some time in February. A Madison victory in Congress would strengthen him in Virginia, whereas a prior endorsement in the state would intensify the attacks on "the Virginia Dynasty."

Concluding that Monroe could not win in Congress, his supporters assailed the caucus system. Said the Richmond *Virginian*: "If no person with safety can be held up as President without the approbation of the members of Congress, then the sovereignty of the states and the will of the people in relation to the election of President are but mere empty sounds."

In former elections, the *Virginian* argued, the caucus had a valid place because the conflict was between two great contending parties, with "no difference of opinion as to the *man* which each party should support." That had changed. With three candidates contending, on what ground "shall the members of Congress undertake to dictate to their constituents which of those characters they shall support? . . . It is a dangerous, irresponsible influence which ought to be checked in the bud."

This was total fallacy. A caucus, when all were agreed on a presidential candidate, was surplusage except as to Vice-President. In the face of presidential rivalries, it was the only existing agency to make national party strength effective. As the Monroeites saw it, state legislators were to dictate to their constituents on national preferences; congressmen were powerless to establish a national party majority.

Clintonians at this time were divided on the caucus. The *American Citizen* reprinted the *Virginian*'s attack on it, but gave space a few days later to a reply to it from the pen of "Lysias," a Clinton advocate later identified as Tunis Wortman, clerk of the City and County of New York. Lysias supported the congressional caucus in principle, as designed to embody the will of the greatest number. It was desirable from time to time "for ascertaining and combining the sentiments of the REPUBLICAN PARTY THRO-OUT THE UNION, for *suppressing factions*, for *preventing schisms*, and for *maintaining that harmony* which is so essential to the preservation of public liberty."

With the Virginia legislature speeding toward adjournment, a February congressional caucus would be too late. Wilson and Giles persuaded Senator Stephen Bradley of Vermont, chairman of the 1804 caucus, to exercise the power given him by that body and summon a meeting for January 23. Two days' printed notice was given. John Randolph's Quids boycotted the meeting. So did the New York delegation, but both New York senators and some representatives let it be known that they favored Madison. In the caucus no speeches were made. The vote: For President: Madison 83, George Clinton 3, Monroe 3, not voting 5. For Vice-President: George Clinton 79, John Langdon 5, Henry Dearborn 3, John Quincy Adams 1. Ten absentees sent in their names as supporters of Madison. Thus he was formally supported by 93 out of 150 Republican senators and representatives, and was opposed by less than half of the remainder.

A few days later news came that the Virginia legislature had acted on January 21, two days ahead of Congress. Separate caucuses were held on the same evening, one at the Bell Tavern, to which members "friendly to the election of James Madison" were invited; the other at the Capitol, open to the entire assembly. The results: At the Bell Tavern: Madison 123, Monroe 0, with three names added later to the Madison list. At the Capitol: Monroe 57, Madison 10.

The Bell Tavern gathering was limited to supporters of Madison in order to ensure the selection of a loyal slate of candidates for the Electoral College. Monroe's supporters attributed his overwhelming defeat to intrigue, but it was construed in Washington (said Congressman Burwell of Virginia) as solid evidence of Madison's supremacy in his own state.

The Monroeites now joined the Clintonians in denunciation of the caucus system, which either group would have hailed as holy if their candidate had come out on top. The caucus itself anticipated this attack. In their resolution *recommending* Madison "as a proper person to fill the office of President," the members declared that they acted in their private capacity, as citizens, and had "been induced to adopt this measure from the necessity of the case; from a deep conviction of the importance of union to the Republicans throughout all parts of the United States, in the present crisis of both our external and internal affairs; and as being the most practicable mode of consulting and respecting the wishes of all."

With this decision made, the Republican campaign entered its next phase: reaction of the congressional minority, action by state legislators and county and city conventions; and, most important of all, a choosing of sides by the Republican press. Totally undecided, as yet, was the course to be pursued by the Federalist party. And what would George Clinton do about his nomination for Vice-President when he wanted the highest office?

At the outset, Clinton's New York City organ set the course cautiously but clearly. Disregarding Monroe, Cheetham's *American Citizen* on January 25 said the country was *threatened* with two candidates for President. "I use the word *threatened*, since to have *two* would endanger the integrity of the party." The members of Congress were "*unhappily*" divided into two parties, one favoring "our venerable and patriotic CLINTON; the other, Mr. Madison, Secretary of State." As both were of the same party, "we must deal candidly and equitably with both."

To emphasize this seeming departure from past extremism, Cheetham republished a glowing eulogy of Madison by "Franklin" in the Washington *Expositor*, extolling his contributions to the country, such as the framing of the Constitution, the establishing of national credit, and the championing of national and personal rights and liberties. "But," said Franklin, "he is a Virginian! There's the rub." Was it a crime to be born in Virginia? If that thought prevailed, "then indeed we may with justice lay claim to the federal compliment,———."

The blank stood for "jackasses," "imbeciles," or something equally flattering. Cheetham took up Franklin's "angry invective in favor of Virginia" with a veneer of fairness. Real patriots could make no distinction for or against a state when there was none. But if other states had men equally fit "the ground of choice must be rotation," to obviate state jealousies. He could endorse what Franklin said about Madison and the Constitution:

> In the closet he is a correct and able statesman. . . . But in case of war, is a closet philosopher and statesman, however wise and skilful, fitted to 'ride on the whirlwind and direct the storm'! Our venerable Clinton is not inferior to Mr. Madison in all the advantages of theory, and to them, he adds a practice which commands the admiration and gratitude of this state, and I am much mistaken if not of the union. In war he has been a "thunderbolt," and would really be Commander in-Chief. He is now Vice President. Shall he be crossed to his advantage to the first office in the gift of the people, without good and sufficient cause?

Franklin, Cheetham noted, referred to Clinton's age. At sixty-eight, the editor replied, he resembled the immortal Benjamin Franklin, whose vigorous mind grew stronger with the increase of years. Furthermore, the President "has in fact but few *details* of office to perform." These Governor Clinton, if elected, would see were well performed, and he would give the country the benefit of his watchfulness and his understanding.

These four themes—exclusion of any Virginian from the Presidency on the score of rotation, Clinton the "thunderbolt of war" (in which he surrendered two forts) against Madison the closet statesman, the natural elevation of a Vice-President to the Presidency, the trivial nature of nonmilitary presidential duties – clearly pointed to Clintonian strategy if the Vice-President rejected the caucus decision and entered the presidential race. Not a word on that subject came from George Clinton or his nephew during the next six weeks.

As everybody expected, the nomination of Madison was heartily applauded by the Washington *National Intelligencer*, semi-official mouthpiece of the Jefferson Administration on public policy but professedly independent in partisan affairs. The *Intelligencer* put the stamp of regularity on the caucus action, as a step taken by those "who heretofore have been accustomed to take the lead in the nomination of candidates." To avoid stirring biases and prejudices, the editor had previously refrained from publicly expressing his decided conviction. Now it was time to speak out, fearlessly but with tolerance. If there was to be a division among the republicans, "let it be candid, honorable, magnanimous. Let no good man's character be traduced to brighten that of another." Let every consideration be banished except "the maintenance of those principles, which have established among us the empire of reason," and would if firmly adhered to extend it over the globe. Madison, the *Intelligencer* believed, was best fitted to guide the nation through the storm without sacrificing those principles:

> Whether we contemplate his irreproachable morals, or solid talents, we are supplied with the strongest reason for approbation. While in private life he has invariably sustained the unassuming character of modest merit, his discharge of public duty has been no less distinguished by intelligence, fidelity and zeal. And above all, we consider him best fitted for the highest honors in the gift of his country, because amidst the various public scenes in which he has been engaged, and in the exercise of the high function devolved upon him, he has invariably displayed a dignity and moderation, which are at once the best evidence and the surest preservative of republican principles.

More in doubt was the decision to be made by William Duane of the influential Philadelphia *Aurora*. For years he had been venting his passions on Madison for nonrecognition of his importance and his right tangible rewards. But Duane was a pragmatist: the choice was easy for him between a disliked but assured winner and a preferred loser. Reporting the results of the congressional caucus, he said the only real need was to continue the policies pursued under Jefferson, and it was no time to bicker about the choice of the man to do it. "The democracy will not divide – they will support the choice made in the usual manner, since no other or better manner has been provided by the constitution."

This reluctant but firm endorsement of Madison by a powerful personal enemy smote the Monroe forces with dismay. "Hortensius" (George M Hay, head of Monroe's campaign committee and engaged to marry his daughter) assailed Duane with the charge of hidden intrigue. Duane was stung into a lengthy reply in the *Virginia Argus*. His position, he said, was simply that the will of the majority should be respected by the minority. If his own vote could have decided the choice, or his own judgment have influenced it, his first choice would have been George Clinton, his second James Monroe, "as truly noble a man as breathes beneath the firmament."

However, Duane went on, "I am willing to sink my *personal predilection* in the voice of the greater number," the vital principle of government, where men alone were concerned. Many other things reinforced his determination to support the caucus choice — the state of our foreign relations, the necessity of adhering to wise existing policies, and "the great convulsion *which is at this moment impending, and menaces a revolution in the affairs of the universe, more extraordinary and eventful* than has, even in these *eventful times, yet happened.*" Here spoke the Duane whose insights could overcome passion and his self-interest, a quality that helped make him the outstanding publicist of the period. From this low-key, reluctant beginning he would throw his energies into the support of Madison.

Among Virginians, friends of Monroe unallied with Randolph were beseeching him to withdraw his candidacy. "For the public good and your future prospects," urged Congressman Matthew Clay, "put a stop to the contest." "Do not sever old, sincere and tried friendships," pleaded Congressman Walter Jones. John Taylor of Caroline, a virtual godfather to Monroe's political ambitions, warned him that all he would gain was "a personal and lasting enmity from all or most of Mr. Madison's friends and probably from himself." An unsuccessful attempt would probably "close upon you forever the avenue to the presidency."

Publisher Thomas Ritchie, whose editorial voice was the most potent in Virginia, contented himself for a time with opening the Richmond *Enquirer* to communications, most of them strongly for Madison. "Tullus" addressed the people on the "strange infatuation" of the Monroe people, who first predicted that both the Virginia legislature and the congressional caucus would support him, but "now rail at caucuses in general," and tell the people that the elective franchise is wrested from them. Most damaging to Monroe was the steady stream of notices in the *Enquirer* signed by members of the Monroe electoral slate and county campaign committees, withdrawing their names.

At length, on February 2, Ritchie announced "My Own Opinions." He considered both Madison and "Munroe" (*sic*) to be eminently qualified for the office of President, but under existing circumstances "the best interests of the republican cause, and of our common country call upon the citizens of Virginia to support James Madison." Next to monarchical government or disunion, the greatest evil that could befall the country was the division of the republican party. Its union and indivisibility was the great pillar of prosperity and should not be jeopardized. He added: "I believe that the collision of Madison and Monroe is calculated to produce mutual accusation and unfriendly recrimination; a schism that is not to be healed — and a division that is never to be removed."

He firmly believed that Monroe stood "little or no chance of being the next President," deriving this belief from Madison's triumphant ascendancy in the Virginia and congressional caucuses "and from concurrent information from all quarters of the union." This view was fortified, Ritchie went on, by the unfounded aspersions that were being cast on Madison's integrity, and "by the strange, unfortunate and surely accidental co-operation between the friends of Mr. Munroe (*sic*) and the enemies of the administration." A division of the Republican party would have a most unfortunate effect upon American relations with Great Britain. Consequently, a Monroe candidacy at this time was calculated "to inflict the severest calamities upon our country." The caucus was liable to some objections, "but where is there a *better* plan?"

This final observation hit at the core of the matter. The caucus was an imperfect but workable device to offset the failure of the framers of the Constitution to foresee the swift rise of the party system in America. More persuasive to Monroe were the siren voices of John Randolph and his double-octet congressional chorus. Monroe ignored the glee with which Federalist newspapers republished Virginia Congressman Edwin Gray's savage attack on "Dictator" Bradley for "usurpation of power" in summoning his abhorrent caucus for *midnight intrigues.* The *National Intelligencer* combated this and similar attacks with its usual calm analysis. The Constitution, it noted, provided two modes of electing a President: through the Electoral College or by the House of Representatives. The second method had a direct tendency to produce intrigue, faction, and abuse of power; the first accorded perfectly with American political institutions.

There were three ways of commencing the electoral process. "First. It may be left to the unconcerted movements of the people at large, in each state." That would produce so many candidates as to destroy all reasonable hope that any one candidate would ever achieve a popular majority. It would constantly give the House of Representatives the dangerous power of election.

Second. Selection of candidates might commence with nominations by state legislatures. "This scheme would open new sources of intrigue and discord in each state, or between several states," and would be equally likely to throw the election into the House of Representatives.

Third. "The members of Congress may assemble as mere private citizens, may compare their several opinions, and may endeavor, with all possible unanimity, to agree on fit characters, to be presented to the general view, for the offices of President and Vice-President."

The Constitution forbids members of Congress to become presidential electors, but members in their private capacity, the *Intelligencer* asserted, had the same right as others to express their *opinions* on public affairs. They came from all quarters of the union and were competent to form judgments. The persons recommended might or might not be acceptable to the people. "No authority is assumed, no coercion is attempted." The people could overrule the caucus at will.

As political logic, this was unanswerable. It left no effectual alternative to Randolph except to accuse the Republican members of Congress of recommending an unfit candidate for President. This Randolph proceeded to do, without giving up his objections to the caucus system. On February 28 Randolph and sixteen other members of Congress signed their address "To the People of the United States." This extraordinary caucus, wrote Randolph, was summoned by a senator under the pretext that the power to do so had been vested in him by a former convention. If true, that implied a right in the Congress of 1804 to direct their successors in the mode of choosing the chief magistrate—an assertion never before advanced. Not all who attended were Republicans. (That is, John Quincy Adams at this moment shifted parties.) Candidates were nominated without discussion or debate. The determinations of "this conclave" had been published as the act of the Republican party, binding on all members.

It was true, the seventeen protesters admitted, that there had been such actions before. But these were at times when the Federalists presented a formidable phalanx, and when the Constitution permitted a vice-presidential candidate to be elected President. Now all was changed. The Federalists would control only two state delegations in an election by the House. Alteration of the Constitution prevented intrigue to put an intended Vice-President in first place. No good reason existed, therefore, why a congressional nomination should be attempted.

All this was a sophistical veneer. The Constitution was changed before 1804, when President Jefferson was renominated in a congressional caucus. Randolph was arguing that congressmen of both parties should make a final choice between Republican candidates after absence of a caucus threw the contest into the House of Representatives.

These sophistries were useful, however, as a prelude to Randolph's main objective—the discrediting of Madison. He found the text for that in a resolution of the caucus asserting that it took its action out of necessity, from a deep conviction of the importance of Republican unity "in the present crisis of both our external and internal affairs." It was true, the Randolph protest conceded, that the aspect of foreign affairs was unpromising. The United States was perhaps on the brink of war with one of the great powers of Europe. This created no real need of Republican unity in favor of one individual, but if such necessity did exist, the choice of a President "should be directed to a man, eminently calculated by his tried energy and talents, to conduct the nation with firmness and wisdom, through the perils which surround it."

"[The choice should go] to a man who had not in the hour of terror and persecution, deserted his post, and sought in obscurity and retirement, a shelter from the political tempest, to a man not suspected of undue partiality or enmity to either of the present belligerent powers; to a man who had not forfeited his claim to public confidence, by recommending a shameful bargain with the unprincipled speculators of the Yazoo companies, a dishonorable compact with fraud and corruption."

Was "James Madison such a man"? Randolph paraphrased carefully chosen selections from the *National Intelligencer's* endorsement of Madison's candidacy:

> We ask for energy, and we are told of his moderation; we ask for talents, and the reply is his unassuming merit; we ask what were his services in the cause of public liberty, and we are directed to the pages of the Federalist, written in conjunction with Alexander Hamilton and John Jay, in

which the most extravagant of their doctrines are maintained and propagated. We ask for consistency as a republican, standing forth to stem the torrent of oppression, which once threatened to overwhelm the liberties of the country; we ask for that high and honorable sense of duty, which would at all times turn with loathing and abhorrence from any compromise with fraud and speculation; we ask in vain.

The address concluded with an argument for rotation in office. This would be a mockery, the dissenters said, unless it brought in a man not immediately connected with his predecessor and not, therefore, in a position to review his policies and abandon mistaken ones. This argument implied that even though the people approved President Jefferson's policies, they should not elect a successor who helped formulate them.

The whole assault was a typical Randolphian blend of half-truths and misleading innuendoes. The qualities he *called for* were those the *Intelligencer* said Madison *possessed*. The charge that Madison deserted his post "in the hour of terror and persecution" referred to his retirement from Congress *a year before the Sedition Act was thought of*. The assertion that he did nothing to stem a threatened "torrent of repression" harked back to the nonsensical charge that President Adams' expansion of the Navy was designed to subject the South to Northern tyranny.

The accusation of compromise with Yazoo speculators concerned the joint report of Madison, Gallatin, and Attorney General Levi Lincoln, as presidential commissioners on Georgia's land cession to the Union. They held that the claims of the Yazoo companies for compensation were legally insupportable, but the great number of innocent holders made a partial payment expedient for the sake of national tranquillity. Their proposed settlement, which Randolph blocked in Congress, would have saved the government vast sums that ultimately went to the speculators through the Supreme Court's dicision in *Fletcher* v. *Peck*.

Ritchie's *Enquirer* took the lead in rebutting the seventeen. How had Madison shown lack of energy? Was it in casting aside the feeble threads of the Confederation and substituting that energetic bond of union, the Federal Constitution? Was it in the courage and firmness with which, in Virginia's ratifying convention, he "vanquished that boasted prodigy of nature, Patrick Henry?" If true energy was evinced by calm and dignified, yet steady, zealous and persevering pursuit of an object, Madison's whole conduct during that period was honorably marked with energy. And that energy "rested on the most solid and durable basis—conscious rectitude: supported by the most profound and extensive information . . . and an eloquence, chaste, luminous and cogent."

Except on the score of "energy" the protest needed no rebuttal. Former Speaker Macon remarked that it would put New England Yazoo claimants (there were thousands of innocent ones) behind Madison. Duane wrote to Jefferson that the violence of it fixed the wavering on Madison's side.

Five New Yorkers were among the seventeen signers. Josiah Masters of that state, citing Monroe's poor showing in Virginia, worked on the latter's friends to induce him to take second place on a Clinton ticket. Writing to "Citizen" Edmond Genet (the ousted French minister who stayed in America and married George Clinton's daughter) Masters said this arrangement was "perfectly understood" in the Monroe camp. He did not report the reason for receptivity chronicled by British Minister Erskine—that Clinton was thought to be too old and infirm to live out his first term.

Monroe himself certainly gave no countenance to this scheme. He was confidentially displaying a recent letter from Jefferson, which, he told his friends, gave them warrant to declare that the President was not hostile to his ambition. "I see with infinite grief," wrote Jefferson, "a contest arising between yourself and another, who have been very dear to each other, and equally so to me." Public duty prescribed neutrality, and "my sincere friendship for you both will insure its sacred observance. . . . The object of the contest is a fair and honorable one, equally open to you all; and I have no doubt the personal conduct of all will be so chaste, as to offer no grounds of dissatisfaction with each other. But your friends will not be as delicate." One piquing remark would lead to another until all restraint was thrown off, and it would be difficult for the principals to stay clear of the passions stirred up by their friends. Anybody familiar with the past relations of the three men could see that Jefferson's neutrality cloaked the strongest kind of wish that Monroe would avert impending evils by withdrawing.

In faction-ridden Pennsylvania the Madison forces were having some trouble. Late in February Congressman James Sloan of New Jersey, who had voted for Madison in caucus, switched to Clinton and moved to transfer the national capital to Philadelphia. The purpose, wrote General Henry Lee to Madison, was "to draw Pennsylvania to the support of Clinton." The strong backing and lingering life of this fantastic maneuver led Senator Pickering to predict Madison's defeat.

Early in March a Pennsylvania "harmony convention" in Lancaster nominated a slate of presidential electors carefully chosen from the two domestic factions, but no opinion was expressed on presidential candidates. Retired Admiral Thomas Truxton briefed Madison on the meeting. Chairman Thomas Leiper told Truxton that when Madison's name came up they "were inundated with objections arising from letters traducing him." Endorsement of him was omitted because it would not have been unanimous. Leiper (himself on the electoral ticket) entertained a hope, he told Truxton, that on election day they would "bring about a unanimous vote for Mr. Madison." The principal complaint was that the Secretary of State had kept Federalist clerks Wagner, Brent, and Forrest in office—no trivial matter, since the entire State Department personnel, outside the foreign service, consisted of Madison and six clerks.

Monroeites and Clintonians promptly claimed Pennsylvania's votes. George Clinton, silent in public, revealed his rage over the caucus in letters to nephew DeWitt and Philip Van Cortlandt. This "illtimed and corruptly managed" offspring of Quiddism, he wrote to the latter on February 20, had created jealousies that never could be healed. He intended to notify the public that his own "spurious nomination" for Vice President was without his knowledge or approbation. Virginia, he was assured, would support Monroe. Even at Washington, "this sink of Quiddism and corruption," the Administration candidate was losing support day by day.

To DeWitt Clinton, on February 18, the Vice-President had written in a much milder tone, phrased for publication, but likewise repudiating the caucus. Deeply impressed with the need of united wisdom and patriotism to avert external dangers, he had determined at the convening of Congress to avoid any conversation touching the presidential election, and to say nothing that might tend to disunity. From this resolution he was now forced to make a partial departure "in order to remove the false impressions which it seems my silence has occasioned." He wished to assure his friends, through DeWitt, "that I never have been directly or indirectly consulted on the subject, either before or since that nomination was made," nor was he ever apprised of the meeting except by accidentally seeing a notice of it. He concluded with a denunciation of the caucus: "The objections which you have stated against this procedure are in my opinion correct and forcible."

This by implication rejected the vice-presidential nomination without putting Clinton into the field for President. DeWitt Clinton redated his uncle's (February 18) letter March 5 and published it in the *American Citizen* of March 10, as to an unnamed person. But he altered the concluding paragraph to this: "However correct and forcible the objections you have stated against this procedure may be, yet as it is a business in which I had no agency or participation, and over which I can have no control; it might be considered improper in me, situated as I am, to make any comment on it."

This left Clinton's friends free to support him for President, but kept him on the regular ticket as Madison's running mate for Vice-President. That, in turn, estopped the Madison forces from any attack on him as unqualified for the higher office. It was a finesse unprecedented and subsequently unparalleled in American history.

Federalists rejoiced at the Republican schism, but publisher Coleman of the New York *Evening Post* could not refrain from jabbing at Clinton. It was laughable, he wrote, to observe the coyness with which the letter was introduced into Clintonian newspapers as merely private, not intended for publication. "As to the *caucus* itself, the old Fox thinks it would be improper, situated as he is, to make any comments on it, but he takes good care to observe that the objections to that procedure are both *correct* and *forcible*." Coleman did not know that the foxiness came from a younger Fox.

Clinton's followers charged that Madison personally intrigued for his nomination. Editor Ritchie replied that no man "ever observed a more decorous or profound reserve towards his most confidential friends" than Madison did before and during that period. Madison's supporters assailed Clinton for not speaking out plainly concerning himself. If he should offer himself for the Presidency, predicted a Washington correspondent of the Baltimore *American*, it would unite the Republican party and defeat "the vain attempts of ambitious schismatics." This letterwriter offered a forecast of electoral votes:

For Madison, 107; uncertain or divided, 50; unclassified, New York 19.

Duane, republishing the Baltimore article, challenged the listing of Pennsylvania's 20 votes as uncertain or divided. If his observation and information were correct, Pennsylvania's vote would be cast solidly for Madison, raising his predicted total to 127 and leaving perhaps 40 in genuine doubt. The *Aurora* then casually offered a seemingly original suggestion: "To promote a completely unanimous vote, as the vice president appears disinclined to serve again in that station, would it not be both wise and proper to hold up Mr. *Dewit Clinton* as the republican candidate for vice president. We suspect no measure would be more effectual in allaying angry passions."

Duane apparently had heard a report, about which the Madison campaign managers were saying nothing, that friends of DeWitt Clinton, *before the caucus*, told them all opposition to Madison for President would cease if DeWitt instead of George Clinton were made his running mate. George Clinton's close friends were left in no doubt about his presidential candidacy. On the day his letter of "no comment" was published he wrote to Van Cortlandt that the Republican cause could not much longer exist "under the present visionary, feeble, and I might add corrupt management of our national affairs." It was disgusting their best friends and a shift from Jefferson to his "meditated successor will . . . make our situation still worse if possible."

That line of thought spread at once, presumably by extrasensory perception, throughout the Clintonian press, which almost monopolized the New York State journalistic field. James H. Main, hoping (unsuccessfully) for backing in establishing a friendly newspaper, told Madison how the Clintonian forces were operating: "By intrigue and slander they have completely subjugated this state and DeWitt manages all its affairs in his own way. His hired libellers are again set upon the scent to defame; and you are the victim they wish to sacrifice because you stand in the way of their overweening ambition."

Deviating decidedly from the Cheetham pattern was the Albany, New York *Register*, which took no position until March 25, then declared itself for Clinton provided he could be elected by fair and honorable means. "We disapprove of the decision of the CAUCUS at Washington," said the *Register*, "—but if that decision cannot be counteracted, without laying the foundation of a ruinous schism in the republican interest of the union, we shall be for acquiescing in it."

The Clintonian monopoly of the New York City press was intermittent because of the strange fluctuations of the *Public Advertiser*, which at the outset declared itself for Madison. An anonymous New Yorker (who later identified himself as Dr. J. H. Douglass) kept Madison informed of its chameleon shifts between support of Madison and extravagant adulation of Clinton. The publisher, "a very needy man" (wrote Douglass) was drawn from Madison by DeWitt Clinton's state printing, then was pulled back by ex-Burrite Matthew L. Davis, whose influence cut him into the official printing of the acts of Congress. Clintonian moneylenders hauled him back by calling their loans and threatening debtors' prison.

Matters stood thus when unidentified Madisonians visited the poor man and demanded that he *publish and answer* this question: "whether you shall continue to publish whatever malice, venality or aspiring profligacy may invent against Mr. Madison; yet refuse to his friends an opportunity of shielding his fair fame, and of hurling disgrace upon his accusers?" The demand had a bright lining of solid silver. If his answer was "no," all his debts would be taken up. The publisher ate his dish of crow in public, and, remarkably enough, became one of the most forceful and effective commentators in the Madison camp.

The Federalists during this shaking-down period mixed slight hope with deep despair but were united in condemnation of Madison as a conductor of foreign affairs. From January 16 of that election year through February 16 Madison negotiated with a special British envoy, Dr. "Young George" Rose, on reparations for the *Chesapeake* attack. The settlement offered was satisfactory, but the talks broke down because of an ironclad demand by Canning for humiliating disavowals of the (proper) conduct of the American frigate's commander.

A week later, while Madison and Rose were preparing final papers, the New York *Evening Post* quoted an alleged exchange between them. Rose, it was said, asked Madison whether President Jefferson, after satisfactory reparations were offered and accepted, would withdraw his proclamation excluding British warships from American harbors. "No, Sir," Madison was quoted as replying, "I tell you frankly the President would not." There were other grievances and "the proclamation is, therefore, not to be rescinded till all cause of complaint is removed."

This, if truly reported, was an unwarranted rejection of a fair offer to remove the principal threat of war. Political ethics did not permit a personal denial, but the *National Intelligencer* was allowed to "state, upon respectable authority," that the reported conversation "did not take place." That killed the canard, and the written exchanges between the two diplomats, published later in the campaign, turned those negotiations into a major asset for Madison.

Slanders were not lacking nearer home. The *Virginia Gazette* printed a story that Madison sold his 1807 wheat crop to a neighbor who, when dunned, replied that he would pay for the wheat if "Mr. Madison . . . will take off the embargo." John Strode, buyer of *all* Madison's wheat, denied the "malicious fabrication." Madison had told him personally, after the embargo depressed prices, that he would "be among the last who would ask for his payment."

Constructive Federalist policy in the campaign was totally undecided when New York City adherents of that party held an overflow meeting at Mechanics Hall on March 28. As reported in the *Evening Post*, Cadwallader Colden told them their "former huge majorities" furnished a prospect of success, but candidates should be put up only if bad government had brought us "to our present calamitous circumstances." It was clear now that the embargo, temporarily legitimate, was to be perpetual—a device to put the country's most interesting affairs entirely into the hands of the Executive. "Honest and firm men might yet save the nation."

Here at least was recognition of the economic foundation of the political conflict. David B. Ogden, following Colden, gave the contest a "classes and masses" aspect without a class conflict. When he saw ruin and distress "stalking among us, the rich about to be reduced to poverty, and the poor already experiencing absolute want and misery; when he saw our liberty and independence in danger of being laid prostrate at the feet of a foreign power"—all due to want of honesty or capacity in their rulers—" it was impossible, he thought, for federalists to remain silent and inactive spectators."

With Monroeites, Clintonians, and Federalists all accusing Madison of bias against England and charging subserviency to France, that issue had to be met. Before confirming William Pinkney, the Senate in February asked for his correspondence. The President at Madison's suggestion sent a few letters, notably his latest protest against the Orders in Council. Vice-President Clinton failed to notice the words "in confidence" and the dispatches were read before crowded galleries. The publicity gave Senator Pickering an opening to address an alarmist open letter to Governor Sullivan of Massachusetts.

"Why, in this dangerous crisis," he exclaimed, "are Mr. Armstrong's letters to the Secretary of State absolutely withheld . . . Has the French emperor required that *our ports*, like those of his vassal states in Europe, *be shut against British commerce?*" Was the embargo a milder substitute for full compliance with Napoleon's naked and insulting demand?

Pickering's letter had a devastating effect in London, but nothing could have suited Madisonian election strategy better than this call for complete publicity in foreign relations. Its Federalist origin saved Madison from the charge of electioneering when the President sent Congress a British and French diplomatic file running to a hundred thousand words, from 1804 into 1808. For six days the reading went on in both houses, while Vice-President Clinton sputtered against wasting time on papers "of no significance." Madison fixed the order of delivery, leading John Randolph to complain that the Secretary put his own position on the Monroe-Pinkney treaty ahead of the treaty itself. Randolph himself took over the reading and put all his eloquence into it when they reached Monroe's prodigious twenty-four-thousand-word defense of this treaty. This was not a genuine part of the diplomatic record but a campaign document written by him as a private citizen only four weeks before it was read.

When all was finished the members of Congress looked at each other with one common thought: the candidacy of James Monroe was dead. Madison had drafted a good treaty project; Monroe had made a bad one. That was all there was to the great conflict between the two men.

For two months this diplomatic correspondence filled American newspapers of all political complexions, while Madisonian editors exulted and opponents searched for details open to attack. "Never since the birth of Machiavel has this game of politics been played so dexterously and so knavishly," exclaimed the baffled New York *Evening Post*. The conduct of the American government in the *Chesapeake* affair had been "but a series of chicanery." Far different was the opinion of the Richmond *Enquirer*: "A more valuable body of dissertation on the rights of neutrals and the interests of the U. S. was never before condensed in the same space."

Particularly helpful to Madison was the controverted exchange between himself and Dr. Rose. The Trenton *True American* proclaimed that Madison had met the most celebrated British diplomats and "completely vanquished, disarmed and disgraced them." Even Cheetham admitted, as would "every man of sense and candor . . . that there was no just ground for suspicion" of an American desire to provoke war with England. Burwell voiced the reaction in Virginia: "Upon the subject of the next President there is literally no division."

Pickering was disappointed in his hope that the dispatches from Paris would disclose either a cringing before Napoleon or aid and comfort for him. Minister Armstrong, notoriously lazy, was a skimpy writer but savagely cynical in what he did write. The proof he offered of French violations of the 1800 treaty (which ended the naval war) left no room for the charge of subserviency. Jacob Wagner, the Federalist chief clerk whom Madison kept in office despite party protests, had resigned to launch a newspaper in Baltimore. As often happens when partisanship overwhelms gratitude, he placed no limit to the virulence of his attacks on his former chief. It was beyond his belief that "those wretched shreds of dispatches" put before Congress were all that came from the minister to France. The *long concealment* of them suggested "partiality to one nation, and hatred to another," perhaps personal intrigue. As former chief clerk, Wagner knew that Madison had violated diplomatic propriety in the speed with which they were made public.

The advantage Madison gained from this publicity was soon reduced by Napoleon's characteristic blundering. Armstrong had entered a vigorous protest against the emperor's Milan Decree of December 17, 1807. Countering British Orders in Council, France declared every ship of every nation, if forced into a British port or searched at sea, to be denationalized and subject to confiscation. Napoleon dictated Champagny's reply to Armstrong's protest. Reciting British aggressions *against the United States*, the foreign minister said the emperor expected a declaration of war by the American government against England. In fact, "war exists" between them "and His Majesty considers it as declared from the day on which England published her decrees." This arrogant letter reached Washington almost on the day the British minister delivered his government's newest Orders in Council hitting at American commerce.

Within a week of their receipt, President Jefferson sent both the French and British documents to Congress, in confidence, with the comment that they furnished good reason to stand by the embargo. Federalists, Clintonians, and Monroeites clamored for publication. Three times the House voted to observe the injunction of secrecy, but the agitation for disclosure became so menacing to Madison politically that the President withdrew the limitation on both the French and British papers.

Madison's rejoinder to Champagny's letter had not yet been made. Still kept secret, to preserve diplomatic amenities, were other strong protests by the Secretary against recent French conduct. Thus Champagny's letter stood alone and was instantly seized on by the political opposition. "The TRUTH is out at last," exclaimed Wagner in his Baltimore *North American*, the "at last" referring to a document made public with unseemly haste. The New York *Evening Post* averred that a single question presented itself: "Are we ready, in compliance with the wishes of a base and degenerate FACTION, to make a hunble surrender of our liberties at the feet of Bonaparte?" The Federalist county committee at Troy, New York, called on honest electors to put men in office "who are superior to foreign influence or to bribery and corruption."

These Federalist attacks on Madison virtually duplicated those by Clinton's leading organ, Cheetham's *American Citizen.* There the tone and content were set on March 3 with a portrait of Madison "as emblazoned by his eulogists." He was described as a former Federalist, a patron of Quids. He lacked energy and firmness. He was educated at Princeton, where he displayed promise "of a very fine genius, but of a very timid man." On May 30, *as* or *through* "Gustavus," Cheetham focused the assault. Great as Madison's diplomatic skill might be, "there is in these rough times an insuperable objection to his being placed in the Presidential chair. . . . It is an *incurable indecision of character.*" That defect could not be offset by his erudition, his urbanity, or the purity of his morals.

It was not until this same day, May 30, that Cheetham openly and formally declared himself opposed to the election of Madison and put forward his own ticket: "the venerable George Clinton" for President and "the patriotic James Monro' (*sic*) for Vice-President. Said Cheetham: "My opinion is . . . that if Mr. Madison, who by surprise if not by collusion has been nominated for the Presidency, be elected, the external commerce of the U. States will be annihilated, and that nothing short of a miracle can save the republican party from destruction."

The cry about commerce was that of the Federalists against the whole Jefferson Administration, and Clinton began to be called "the stalking horse of federalism." John Binns switched the Philadelphia *Democratic Press* from Clinton to Madison on that issue. The political shift reflected the outcome of the New York spring elections, in which, wrote Morgan Lewis to Madison, the Federalists had risen nearly to an equality with the Republicans in the next Congress, and with the Clintonians in the state assembly. Lewis blamed this on "uncandid representations respecting the embargo and the charge of French influence." Gallatin likewise termed it a reaction against the embargo and predicted that the pressure against that measure would increase.

The intensified feeling against the embargo was actually a protest against the enforcement measure passed by Congress in April, in response to President Jefferson's call. Congress also authorized the President to suspend the embargo against any belligerent that stopped molesting American commerce. Madison, by invitation of the Senate committee, wrote its report on this bill. In it he put forward, as committee opinion, two significant prospective changes of national policy:

    1. In case of a protracted adherence of the belligerent powers to their destructive course, an entire suspension of foreign commerce might not improperly take the place of the embargo.

    2. It was not for the committee to say when aggravated injuries

and sufferings might make the calamities of war preferable to the greater distresses of further forbearance.

This pointed decisively toward a deviation from Jefferson's policy if Madison became President. It was the first official step toward the War of 1812. But it did nothing to save him from the consequences of the new embargo enforcement act, which, by cutting off smuggling to the West Indies, struck at small Republican law-evaders as well as rich New England Federalists. Cheetham took full advantage of this, combining embargo unrest with "French influence" and avoiding direct calumniation by hurling anathema upon Madison in the persons of nameless supporters: "Who perceive nothing in the insolent note of Champagny but the disinterestedness of a friend and the tenderness of a lover? the friends of Mr. Madison." (Duane had condoned the letter.) "Who wish to ruin commerce by a permanent embargo — to destroy our fiscal resources so as to justify the imposition of a land tax by the plea of necessity — to multiply offices . . . and to carry the 'strong arm' of the law . . . to every man's fireside . . . ? the friends of Mr. Madison. Who . . . while endeavoring to destroy an Essex Junto, have been engaged in building up a Virginian aristocracy equally detestable? the friends of Mr. Madison."

The onslaughts on Administration policy hit in both directions. They came just as the powerful propagandist Tunis Wortman began a series of "John Milton" articles in the *American Citizen*, designed to prove that Madison's caucus nomination was long preconcerted and wholly improper. A week later, in the *Public Advertiser*, he abruptly switched to support of Madison (and thereby risked his livelihood as city clerk). He did so, he explained, after learning from Washington observers of the highest repute that the caucus was conducted with perfect fairness. Equally influencing him (apparently the decisive factor) were Cheetham's attacks on the policies of the national Administration. They made it apparent that the opposition to Madison "*if not connected to an actual understanding with the federal party*, was coupled with a *no less real* hostility to the government."

Cheetham turned with fury upon Wortman and characterized him as a traitorous ingrate who yielded to seduction or threats. Wortman (as Marcus Porcius Cato) became the foremost supporter of Madison in the *Public Advertiser* and joined with Col. Henry Rutgers (for whom Rutgers University was renamed) and A.B. Marling in rallying the city and blocking endorsement of Clinton by the New York legislature.

John B. Colvin of the pro-Madison Washington *Monitor*, who matched Cheetham in invective and excelled him in acumen, pointed out the weakness of the campaign being waged by the Clintonians. If they deluded the people into defeating Madison by persuading them that existing measures were wrong, "the federalists must be thought right; and . . . the people . . . will support a federalist for president in preference to Mr. Clinton."

The Federalists were in fact rousing from their lethargy, thanks both to Republican factionalism and the New York election. They stepped up their attacks on the embargo and "French influence" and began to talk hopefully of General Charles Cotesworth Pinckney of South Carolina and Rufus King of

New York as a national ticket. This had a counter-effect. Federalist revival and Clintonian adoption of Federalist policies rallied Republicans to Madison. More state legislative caucuses endorsed him, along with innumerable county committees. And who had nominated Clinton, jibed a Madisonian editor shortly before election — only his own newspaper organ.

The Madisonian press flayed Cheetham for his anti-Madison diatribes. There was no need, said the Trenton *True Republican*, for him to openly avow what his hypocrisy had been vainly laboring to conceal, that he and his coadjutors were opposed to the election of Mr. Madison. "We saw this factious spirit in his insinuations against the administration — in his clamors about French influence," in the conduct of New York congressmen. Would the Republicans of New York be deceived by the lies and sophistry of "this renegado"? No, they would unite with those of the rest of the country, nine tenths of whom, "we might say nineteen twentieths," would give their voices for James Madison.

New Yorkers who felt that way met in Marling's "long room" (which held 650) and resolved that the present opposition to the nomination of Mr. Madison "has a tendency to prostrate the dignity of the state — to excite disorder — to destroy the respect of the community for its public functionaries." (DeWitt Clinton had become mayor of the city.) It was resolved also that owing to their "base and infamous calumnies," James Cheetham's *American Citizen* and *Republican Watch Tower* "ought not any longer be esteemed as organs of republican opinion." The proceedings were circulated throughout the United States.

In all this tumult, the one calm, dispassionate voice was that of the Washington *National Intelligencer*, which alone among American newspapers was considered to reflect the spirit of Madison himself. On June 10, under the guise of "A Farmer," editor Samuel Harrison Smith (who owned a small farm) refused "to derogate from the well earned characters of other candidates," but gave six reasons for electing Madison. The fair and usual expression of public opinion had been decided in his favor. His election would unite Republicans, destroy party schisms, promote satisfactory foreign relations, and ensure adherence to Jeffersonian measures. "Sixthly, because his virtues and talents are equal, to say no more, to those of either of the candidates."

On that day the *Intelligencer* printed the *Aurora's* comment on conflicting election predictions by the *American Citizen* and the *Public Advertiser*. Cheetham gave Clinton 90 electoral votes (one more than a majority), Madison 15, Federals 22, doubtful 48. The *Public Advertiser* assigned 108 to Madison and 12 to Clinton, 8 of these from Pennsylvania. The *Aurora* challenged this. At no time, said Duane, were *more than two* electoral nominees "partial to Mr. Clinton; and it is well known that these will abide by the sentiments of their constituents."

Late in June, son-in-law "Citizen" Genet crowned the Clinton campaign with an expected knockout blow, delivered in the Albany *Register*. Writing as "A Citizen of New York" with subsequent identification, he first sharpened the campaign along existing lines. The embargo, which produced a ruinous stagnation of New York trade, was "the undisputed property of a few southern systematic politicians." These men (i.e. Madison) were conspiring with former Governor Lewis to bring the "quiddical" party to power and divide New York into two states, one half to be ruled by emigrant Virginians.

Genet ridiculed the idea that either England or France could be brought to terms by an embargo backed by speeches and river gunboats. The whole attempt was so obviously futile as to indicate that *"There is something else under the rose. Let us try to find it out."* The motive for the embargo, said Genet, ran back to 1793, when the French ambassador (himself, as he made clear elsewhere) presented Jefferson and Madison with decrees of the French National assembly, *naturalizing them both French citizens*!

Mr. Jefferson, "an older fox," took care of his own answer, but "the written answer of Mr. Madison, expressive of his gratitude, his admiration, and his devotion, was transmitted to France by the same minister, and the bloody Robespierre, who opened that memorable letter, was very much pleased at his civism."

Some of the principal actors in the national assembly of 1793, Genet observed, were now high in the imperial government and had a chance to renew their acquaintance with Gallo-American citizens Jefferson and Madison. It was not improbable that the embargo was concocted between them to comply with the imperious wishes of Napoleon, without displaying a manifest partiality. Out of this, Virginia hoped to get a southern acquisition to the United States, building up southern influence. Their purpose, with the embargo as its initial instrument, was to convert merchants into farmers and their wives into dairy women. This great "moral revolution without scaffolds" would leave "the maritime states humbled and impoverished." Virginia, "resting on the arm of slavery," would rule the union in peace, with Jefferson transferring his Confucian mantle to "his devoted servant" Madison.

There was of course a germ of truth in Genet's naturalization tale. On August 24, 1792, late in the libertarian period of the French Revolution, the National Assembly conferred French citizenship on eighteen world figures, including Washington, Madison, and Alexander Hamilton (not Jefferson). Washington and Hamilton ignored the action. Madison's acceptance of the "honorable adoption," written a year before Robespierre came to power, was addressed to Interior Minister Roland, who escaped the guillotine by committing suicide after his wife (immortalized by her dying words "O Liberty! What crimes are committed in thy name!") was beheaded by "the bloody Robespierre."

Madison treated the Genet story with silence and furnished no explanatory material. To most Americans, the accusation savored too much of grand opera to produce genuine shudders. The Albany *Register*, giving credence to the charges "for the sake of argument," disparaged their importance. "When Madison is called a Frenchman, an enemy to commerce, and a corrupt adherent of the Yazoo company of fraudulent conspirators, [the Republicans] view these charges as the offspring of prejudice or of a distempered zeal."

The Federalist press hailed the citizenship charge with joy, Jacob Wagner building it up on the strength of his former high position in the State Department. The Baltimore *American* asked, "Is the unsolicited declaration of a French National Convention" any proof that Madison and Jefferson were naturalized? French law required an oath of allegiance. Replying in his *North American*, Wagner said the tender of citizenship to men "always signalized by an undeviating adherence" to French wishes was probably made in a form to render the oath unnecessary. The *fiat* of a revolutionary government superseded the permanent laws of the country, and acceptance "finished the conversion of the aspirant to a French Sansculotte." Election of Madison, after exposure of his French citizenship, would cause America to "be devoured by the 'Beast,'" Napoleon, who had fattened on so many other nations.

Cheetham, avoiding direct reference to the Genet story, became "A Pennsylvanian" in describing its alleged political effect. The people of that state were turning away from "the French hireling" and would "give their suffrages to the war-worn Clinton; the friend of Washington and Jefferson." A few days later the charge was condensed to: "In politics, Mr. Madison is a *Frenchman*."

Cheetham followed this by calling a July 28 mass meeting of Old School Republicans in his newspaper offices. The chairman was James Cheetham, who also was secretary, platform writer, and deliverer of what he recorded as an "elegant address." It was resolved unanimously "That an American citizen should have neither foreign attachments nor foreign aversions." All of the country's troubles—the annihilation of commerce, the discouragement of agriculture, the *forced* desertion of seamen to the British fleet—were caused by excessive attachments to France and aversions from England.

So it was "Resolved unanimously, That GEORGE CLINTON . . . our Saviour in war, and our ornament in peace, is entitled," by his great services and exact fitness, "to be our next President." With like unanimity it was resolved that "Mr. Madison is *not fit* to be President." Because, declared the Old School Republicans, he is a disciple of Confucius, a Quid, opposed to commerce and therefore unfriendly to agriculture, opposed to defense of seaports, perniciously hostile to England and "inordinately attached to Napoleon. '*France wants money, and she must have it.*'" The next day Cheetham accused the "Bonaparte . . . Imperial Republicans" of poisoning the public mind by immoderate and merciless attacks on "the venerable Clinton, the hero of the Revolution."

If the Washington *Monitor* heard it correctly (which is unsure), the two Clintons began to disclaim any connection with Cheetham, DeWitt calling his conduct intemperate and deserving of condemnation. But the fact remained that two words from DeWitt "Stop it"—would have worked an instantaneous reform. Moreover, there was perfect suitability to George Clinton in Cheetham's presentation of a commercial platform in the resolutions of the Old School Republicans: "*Resolved, unanimously,* That all attempts to introduce manufacturing amongst us, by *national excitement and trick*, to the curtailing and detriment of our agriculture and commerce, are *dangerous and delusive.* . . . *Resolved*, That manufacturing, *gradually* and *individually* introduced, should be cordially patronized by our citizens."

This took account of a nationwide surge toward manufacturing, stimulated by the curtailment of overseas trade by the European wars and its temporary extinction by the embargo. On June 15 the mayor of Washington called on citizens to meet to consider "organizing a plan for the encouragement of *Domestic Manufactures*." The *Intelligencer* on the same day rejoiced "to hear that the pulse of Virginia beats high in favor of manufactures," utilizing "the injustice of the belligerent nations, to make us truly independent." This movement did not center in New England, heavily committed to maritime commerce, but was largely peripheral, extending in a broad sweep along the frontier from western New York and Ohio through Tennessee to Georgia. It reduced the sting of the embargo. Clinton could not assail that law effectively if he went all-out for manufactures, so his supporters struck a middle course, advocating slow development by individual effort.

Crucial to Madison were county and city proceedings in Pennsylvania, where Clinton was making his heaviest bid outside of New York. Republican electoral nominees, lacking statewide instructions, needed guidance from below. In county after county, resolutions followed a pattern—cordial endorsement of Madison for President and Clinton for Vice-President, approval of the caucus as the instrument of national party unity, and support of the embargo as the sole means of prolonging the blessings of peace. A Philadelphia ward added that the embargo turned American thoughts to "their own internal and inexhaustible resources." Those who opposed it were "enemies of our independence, friends to the British government, and unworthy of the name of American citizens."

Logically, that struck straight at Clinton, yet the same convention approved both him and Madison on the caucus ticket, expressing "the fullest confidence in their firmness, patriotism, love of our national unity and independence." These sentiments were echoed in an August circular of the Pennsylvania State Committee of Correspondence to the citizens of the state. The committee denied, on the personal authority of six members, the Clintonian claim that the Lancaster convention's failure to instruct the Electoral College nominees denoted hostility to Madison. No candidate's name was even glanced at there. The committee entertained "just reverence and respect" for Mr. Clinton, "but we now submit to the nomination of Mr. Madison because the choice has been made in the usual manner, and because the choice itself is good." Madison in his recent transactions with foreign nations had "displayed a vigor of mind worthy of the nation and the station for which he is proposed." Resolutions like those of the Pennsylvania counties, asserted the *National Intelligencer*, were being adopted "by the Republicans in every quarter of the union."

This blend of firm support and mollification did nothing to reduce the violence of the Clintonian assault, nor did praise of the embargo offset the growing repugnance to it. These two factors united to build up Federalist hopes, which received a further spur in a speech by Foreign Secretary Canning defending British policies. Since the return of Mr. Rose, he said, "no communication has been made by the American government, in the form of complaint, or remonstrance, or irritation," concerning the Orders in Council. So, exclaimed the Federalist Boston *Gazette*, despite "the groanings of the democratic presses against the British orders . . . our own administration . . . have *never preferred a complaint* against them, or required a repeal." The unseen hand of Napoleon was in this business, Congressman Gardenier suggested.

Material for the *National Intelligencer's* prompt reply was furnished by Chief Clerk John Graham of the State Department. President Jefferson the previous February had sent Congress "the spirited and argumentative remonstrance" of Minister Pinkney against the orders, made only twelve days after they were promulgated. And Rose himself carried Madison's "full reply or remonstrance" against them back to England — a protest still unanswered.

Graham appealed to Madison, at Montpelier, to refute another dangerous misstatement by Canning — that Rose brought satisfactory terms for reparation of the *Chesapeake* attack only to have the offer fail because the United States refused to revoke the proclamation excluding British warships from American harbors. The *Intelligencer's* ensuing corrective editorial — saying that the United States offered to act on both matters at the same time — included almost verbatim wordage from Madison's personal memoranda of his talks with Rose. It was, therefore, the presidential candidate himself who ended with the statement that "but for the equal injustice of both the great belligerents," the indignation of government and people over failure of the negotiations "would inevitably have issued in war against Great Britain." There were many other indications that Madison, who kept his lips sealed throughout the campaign, guided political strategy on all points affecting his own work as Secretary of State.

Madison spent the summer of 1808 on his Virginia farm but he probably spent more time reading hostile newspapers and pamphlets than overseeing his overseers. Clintonian Saunders Cragg of New York put him first among men, "deadly as the adder," who would spend money to avert French anger. Awful was the danger, with Napoleon ruling Spain, Mexico, and Florida. "O my countrymen," place brave and energetic Clinton at your head "and you are safe;" but should French citizen Madison rule, "war with England will immediately ensue," and America will "bow at the foot of the conqueror."

A Federalist writer who took the name "Samuel Adams" claimed to have sat with Madison in the Continental Congress, where in 1782 he displayed an "excessive attachment to France." The Richmond *Enquirer* shot back that Madison's enemies, unable to find firm ground of complaint in modern times, "have substantially confessed the impotency of their cause, by going back to the darkness of antiquity." During the Revolution "it was no sin to be a friend of the French," whose treasures and troops were supporting the cause of American independence.

The Madison forces were now more worried by the Federalist revival than by Clinton or Monroe. The *Intelligencer* in mid-August quoted the Charleston *Courier's* call: "Citizens of the union! Look around you and determine whether there is a man more fit to be your President" than General Charles Cotesworth Pinckney. "He has wisdom to plan and firmness to pursue, ways and means to extricate you from your present difficulties without committing the national honor." That appeal, commented the chief Madisonian organ, must be considered in connection with "the grand secret caucus now holding or about to be holden, about the region of New-York, by those to whom caucusing was but lately a crime of the deepest die. It behooves the yeomen of the United States to be on their guard."

The New York *Public Advertiser* seemed unworried. Every day, it said, exhibited fresh proof that the Federalists were "elate" over their prospects. "Vain hope of a deluded faction." It was true that a few hare-brained New York editors had produced some little ferment. "But in the state generally, and indeed in almost every quarter of the union, the republican party remains calm, firm and united."

The Federalist ticket of Charles Cotesworth Pinckney and Rufus King was put forward early in September with no public statement about the who, when, or where of the nominating gathering. However, Senator Timothy Pickering told a friend all about it. "Respectable men" from all states from Pennsylvania northward gathered in New York. The great question was not whom to nominate but whether to nominate anybody. That was settled decisively by information that in New York State, Madisonians and Clintonians were "disposed to unite to the abandonment of Clinton."

Election of Pinckney and King, said Pickering, would serve the true interests of the country. At the same time, "if their election were hopeless and by uniting with one portion of Democrats the federalists could have secured the chair of state to a northern Democrat of practical talents and energy of character, a friend to commerce, sound policy would have required them to give such a man their votes for the reason you mention—of two evils to choose the least."

Quite different was the account given by the Baltimore *North American*. To prevent Madison from fastening "the chains of Bonaparte upon us," there had been a spontaneous turning to "Gen. Charles C. Pinckney of South Carolina, a hero of our revolution," unattached to any country but his own. This gentleman, of unsullied fame, "has been brought before the public, not by a congressional caucus, but by the public voice, as a fit person to fill the high office of president."

This was fair praise of Pinckney's qualities as a citizen. He was a patriotic, upright, conservative Carolinian, who devoted himself in the Federal Convention of 1787 to protection of slavery and advocacy of government by the wealthy. Revolutionary France refused to receive him as minister, but as a member of President Adams' peace commission he joined in repelling Talleyrand's XYZ bribe solicitation. A remark attributed to him on that occasion, and probably sharpened in historical mythology, lifted him above the much better qualified Rufus King and made him a suitable rallying figure in this election.

A report spread from Philadelphia (quite naturally, in the light of Pickering's statement) that the Federalists actually intended to coalesce with Clinton, contenting themselves for the present with Pinckney as Vice-President. Predicting failure of this if attempted, John B. Colvin expressed disbelief that Clinton would ever connive at such an arrangement. His friends, to be sure, might reach an agreement with the Federalists, each faction winning all the electoral votes it could for its candidate, and then uniting the two interests for Clinton and Pinckney. By this method, Clinton could receive the Federalist electoral votes "without apparent criminality on his part." But if the Federalists should defeat Madison by this crafty course, they would have to rely entirely on "the feelings of gratitude in Mr. Clinton's bosom for remuneration."

Clinton and Monroe stayed in the race, the former and his friends remaining silent on a Federalist coalition. Not so the Monroe campaign committee, now pushing a virtually one-state candidacy. Late in September son-in-law (as he had become) Hay and associates put out a paper listing "unanswerable" objections to the election of Mr. Madison. Every crucial item was taken from the Federalist credo: "Our foreign commerce is totally suspended, our ships are rotting, our seamen dispersed and gone, and our produce shut up in our ware houses, our public revenue is cut off, and the deficiency resulting from that cause, must be supplied by recourse to the expensive system of internal taxation."

The committee hoped it was mistaken, "but if Mr. Madison is elected, we see at present, no alternative for the United States, but WAR, or an EMBARGO of indefinite duration." Madison could not adjust differences with foreign powers because he "stands fixed and committed" upon every question involved in foreign relations. The Richmond *Enquirer* instantly challenged Hay and his associates to state what points and facts they had in mind. This, said Ritchie after waiting more than a week, "they have not done. They dare not do it. Mr. Madison stands committed upon no point or fact, in which he will not be supported by the whole republican strength and influence throughout the United States." Hopes of Monroe's success "are placed entirely upon federal support."

The Federalist Norfolk *Herald* thought so too. The Monroe Committee's address, it said, may be considered "as pledging Mr. Monroe upon some leading points, particularly the cruel measure of the embargo, and upon our future intercourse with foreign nations." Virginia Federalists should reflect on the evident impossibility of succeeding with their own ticket. The *Herald* hoped "that the result of their reflections will produce a determination to give their *unanimous* suffrages for the ticket of Mr. Monroe." A Virginia Federalist party gathering gave this the seal of approval.

Explaining the action to candidate Pinckney, Chief Justice Marshall (still an ardent Federalist) said his party formed "a small and oppressed minority of our state" and had no love for any of the rival democratic candidates. "The superior talents of Mr. Madison would probably have placed us in his scale" had not has prejudices with respect to foreign relations lately become "still more inveterate and incurable" than those of Monroe or Clinton. A meeting was in session, to decide whether or not to put up Federalist electors, when advice came from the party committees in Washington and Georgetown to back Monroe. That was followed by the "unpleasant intelligence" that Republican Simon Snyder was elected governor of Pennsylvania. His triumph, in a campaign fought on national issues, created doubt whether the Federalist national ticket would be pressed. Combined, these factors produced the decision to support Monroe.

Colvin renewed his effort to shatter the projected realignments. "It is reduced to a certainty," said the *Monitor*, "that if either Governor Clinton or Mr. Monroe *could* succeed, it must be by a *combination* of *federal* and *republican* votes." Federalists who voted for either of them would violate principles and probity to defeat Madison. Even if they succeeded, the Republicans joining them would be contemptible in numbers. The winner, Clinton or Monroe, would have to satisfy the Federalists. Such a coalition would be nothing more than an aggregation of conflicting minorities, united to gratify bad passions — "an unprincipled intrigue, which would operate to the destruction of the liberties of the United States."

Meanwhile the Georgetown, South Carolina *Gazette*, hailing the Federalist ticket, set the initial tone of the party campaign by coupling the legendary utterance of Pinckney with the fictitious remark ascribed to Madison: "Millions for defence — not a cent for tribute." — CHARLES COTESWORTH PINCKNEY. "France wants money, and we must give it." — JAMES MADISON

Randolph's canard about money for France had lately been expanded into a charge that the $2,000,000 appropriated by Congress (for Spain) had actually been remitted to Napoleon. New York State Treasurer David Thomas (quietly friendly to Madison) inquired of the Secretary of the Treasury whether any part of that sum had been drawn from the Treasury, and if so, for what purpose. Official documents already published, Gallatin replied, "sufficiently shew that not a single cent of that money has ever been expended." The appropriation, he added in order to explode the underlying insinuation, "was made in order to enable the President to acquire Florida by treaty." That negotiation failing, no part of the money was drawn.

The mildly Clintonian Albany *Register* published Gallatin's letter along with a surprising comment. "Check not the impulse of honest hearts " in execrating the calumniators who, to answer the sinister purposes of faction, are willing not only to deceive and betray you — but are desperate enough to risk the perdition of their own souls." This was as much a repudiation of Clintonian tactics as a condemnation of the Federalists and Randolphian Quids. Behind it was recognition that the presidential contest no longer lay between Madison and Clinton, but between Madison and Pinckney, with Clinton and Monroe serving as conscious or unconscious allies of the latter.

With "the two million dollars" knocked out, the contest settled into the line made logical by Federalist entry into it — the embargo and Madison's management of foreign diplomacy as Secretary of State. "You have heard that New England is lost," wrote Gallatin to Madison after the September state elections. The people, he said, had been taught that the embargo, instead of being a shield against foreign aggressions, was the cause of the stagnation of commerce actually caused by the war. It was the boldest measure ever undertaken in a popular government, but must be abandoned. "There is not patriotism and union sufficient to bear with patience, where there is no stimulus."

One offset to the anti-embargo agitation needed no expression—the dread of war as its alternative. Far different were the incessant allegations of "French influence," bias against England, mismanagement in the conduct of foreign relations. These were susceptible of proof or disproof. There had been disproof of laggard conduct in the *Chesapeake* negotiations, the Rose mission, and resistance to the Orders in Council. But the less specific accusations persisted and were stepped up with the Federalist revival. On this score the *National Intelligencer* addressed Madison's adversaries on September 12.

Allegations of animosity to England, said Editor Smith, had been vamped for seven years in every form in which a fertile imagination could make them. At the last session of Congress the whole field of controversy with England was exposed to view; the gound taken by the American government laid down; its principles exhibited; its general disposition set forth. The means of establishing the truth of every charge were now before the public.

"But instead of drawing upon them you are silent as the grave. With all the disposition *to find proofs* of a repugnance to a reasonable settlement with England, *the whole mass of proceedings now in print has not produced a single specific charge.* Why not? Because not a solitary charge can be maintained without exposing the folly of those who should prefer it."

To check the growing shift from Clinton to Madison, "Citizen" Genet became once more "A Citizen of New York" and made a bold disclosure in the press: "As some Republicans have dreamt that if Governor Clinton declined, Mr. DeWitt Clinton would be made vice president, under Mr. Madison, and that such a disposition would harmonize the party, I state upon the authority of Josiah Masters, Esq., representative in Congress, from New York, that *such an arrangement* was treated with contempt by Mr. Madison's friends, at Washington, last winter."

This was what Duane, without proof, had hinted at. Now it was disclosed as fact by Clinton's son-in-law. The source was a convincing indication that George Clinton himself had sanctioned the attempted shift to DeWitt. The revelation turned the Clintonian declamations against the caucus into self-serving pretense. It enabled "Aristides" to say, in the *Public Advertiser*, that the "shameful division" in the Republican party, and the "clamorous attacks on the administration," did not result from the caucus preference for Madison over George Clinton, but from the refusal of Madison and his friends to buy support by ousting the Vice-President and putting his nephew in his place.

Had "such an arrangement" been agreed to, said Aristides, the magic of it "would have made Madison the first of men. The measures pursued by the government would have been wise and energetic. The talisman of French influence would have been dispelled in a moment" and the country's honor and glory made secure—all this "without the assistance of Governor Clinton to guide the helm of state."

Monroe's acceptance of Federalist support gave him kindred troubles. The Washington *Monitor*, late in October, reported that the Monroe Committee, "to prevent a total desertion . . . came forth and declared they would receive no resignations." In a final effort to reverse the current, Monroe asked Jefferson for permission to publish their correspondence of the previous spring concerning his candidacy. The President consented, but his declaration of neutrality in those letters was hardly strengthened by his assumption of full personal responsibility for the rejection of Monroe's treaty.

In New York, the slippage from Clinton became more pronounced. Morgan Lewis informed Madison on September 7 that the General Republican Committee of New York switched from Clinton to Madison because anti-embargo feeling was building up Federalist strength. The General Committee advertised a September 14 mass meeting in Marling's "long room." Responding to the suggestion of the *American Citizen*, Clintonians attempted to rush in and seize control but were overwhelmed as 2,500 Madisonian Republicans overflowed the huge room, the house, the yard, and the street. Resolutions approved the embargo, denounced opposition to administration measures and endorsed the "caucus ticket" of Madison and Clinton. The moves were aimed at the New York legislature, then in recess, which had final power to appoint the state's presidential electors without a vote of the people.

The *National Intelligencer* followed with an admonition to New York Republicans. Surveying the situation state by state, it found that omitting Pennsylvania as doubtful, Madison was fairly certain of 73 electoral votes— 16 short of a majority. There was a *possibility* that Pinckney would win 84 not including New York. In such a division, New York could elect Pinckney or Madison, or elect Clinton with full Federalist aid. What kind of an Administration could Clinton furnish if raised to power by Federalists? Every attempt to unite New York Republicans "in any other candidate than Mr. Madison will be mischievous, and may be fatal."

To James Cheetham, such reckoning was an admission of defeat. "Madison is in despair," proclaimed the *American Citizen*. He would have no more and perhaps less than 61 electoral votes. A few days later New York's Seventh Ward Republicans, with Colonel Rutgers in the chair, called on Alderman Mott to answer reports "derogatory to his political character." Mott replied that he was "a genuine Republican . . . favorable to the nomination of Mr. Madison" and to his election.

The doubt about Pennsylvania resulted from the rivalry of two Republican electoral slates overlapping in membership—that of the Lancaster Convention, friendly to Madison but uninstructed; the other put up later and instructed for him by a legislative caucus. To avert a possibly fatal division of Madisonian votes, a meeting of "Constitutional Republicans" in Philadelphia presented a "harmony slate" of electors chosen from the two lists. The convention warned that foreign nations were looking for proofs of weakness in American policy. "The election of Mr. Madison as President will stamp the principles he has so ably maintained with the seal of public approbation, and speak to the world in the most impressive manner, the language of patriotic determination."

An opposite picture was painted by the New York *Evening Post*. Election of Pinckney and King would entrust national affairs to men of probity and patriotism—men "blinded by no *foreign* attachments—biased by no *secret influence*." Under their fostering care, we could hope "to see our commerce once more revive from the paralyzing experiments of non-importation and embargo acts, and our nation, *extricated from the snares and shackles of Bonaparte and his emissaries*, resume that dignified stand which it once possessed under the enlightened administration of a WASHINGTON."

Congress reconvened on November 7, three days after the New York legislature met to appoint presidential electors. From returning members the *National Intelligencer* put together a forecast of election results. Madison was assured of 106 electoral votes, 17 more than were necessary to elect. He would carry Tennessee, Kentucky, Ohio, Georgia, South Carolina, Virginia, Pennsylvania, New Jersey, and Vermont—also picking up 16 (elected by districts) in North Carolina and Maryland. Probably for Madison were Rhode Island, New Hampshire and New York, adding 30 votes. Federalists were sure of 34 votes in the remaining states.

Madisonian hope for solid New York support was quickly dashed. Bidding for a divided delegation, Clintonians assured Madison's "milk and water" friends (so wrote Morgan Lewis to him) that Clinton had given up his presidential aspirations. They accepted thirteen Clintonians in the nineteen electors. With other uncertainties, this left room for a sliver of doubt about the national outcome.

Throughout the campaign, the most impressive pull for Madison had come from his own words as Secretary of State, disclosed from time to time by President Jefferson in messages to Congress. Before the long recess began, every attack had been answered by the documents of diplomacy except the charge that Madison cravenly swallowed the arrogant declaration of Napoleon, through Champagny, that war existed between the United States and England and he expected a declaration of it.

Jefferson took care of that on November 7, submitting to Congress the whole sheaf of 1808 diplomatic correspondence. Once more—at the very climax of the campaign—all the newspapers in the United States had their columns flooded with Madison's protests and instructions, defending American rights and interests against both belligerents. Voters read, for the first time, Madison's declaration that the emperor's Berlin Decree, as interpreted, violated both international law and treaty rights. They read his reply to the insolence of Champagny, that "no independent and honorable nation" could be guided by demands that meant "bending to the views of France against her enemy." That, commented Duane, put an end to delusions created by artful insinuations about connivance with France. Spread out also was Madison's "manly and honorable vindication," as the *Aurora* called it, of American rights and independence against the British Orders in Council. Republican newspapers republished Duane's comment on that letter of March 25, 1808: "The man who can read this able and spirited paper, without feeling his pride increased and his indignation excited, ought to suspect his head of imbecility, and his heart of insensibility to virtue or patriotism."

For good measure, Madison inserted a passage in Jefferson's message, congratulating the country on the conversion, "far beyond expectation," of industry to internal manufactures. The *American Citizen*, the day after it published Madison's reply to Champagny, virtually threw in the sponge by reprinting the *National Intelligencer's* comment on the whole French and British series:

"Never has any government made a disclosure more lucid, satisfactory or honorable. They manifest the most strenuous and persevering efforts of the administration to preserve the peace of the country as well as to maintain its rights: and refute every calumny cast upon them by their adversaries. . . . They prove that the tone of our government has been as strong and earnest to France as to England. Let us then hope to hear no more of the submission of our government to the mandate of Napoleon, or of its hostility to England."

The returns came rolling in, as the states held successive elections or completed legislative appointments of electors. On November 25 the *National Intelligencer* tabulated the party affiliations of electors from ten out of the seventeen states: Republican 89; Federalist 33. Even deducting from this New York's 19, Madison was sure of enough votes in three absent states (North Carolina, Kentucky and Tennessee) to make his election certain. With New York's action in doubt, and some states appointing electors belatedly, there could be no final tabulation of results until after the Electoral College met in the several states on December 7 and galloping or struggling horses brought in the returns over frozen or muddy roads. Not until January 4, 1809, were the totals announced in the press. With Kentucky losing 1 vote through absenteeism, the count stood: For President: James Madison 122 electoral votes; Charles Cotesworth Pinckney 47; George Clinton 6.

Six die-hard Clintonians rejected the appeal of thirteen colleagues to make the state's vote unanimous. For Vice-President, these six divided their votes between Madison and Monroe, and nine other electors defected to John Langdon, leaving Clinton with 113. Where popular elections were held Pinckney carried his states (Delaware and New England except Vermont) by narrow margins; Madison swept the others.

"Thus gloriously," rejoiced the *National Intelligencer*, "has terminated an election which has, not incorrectly, been said to have decided the destinies of the United States." The enemies of the Republican cause had been reinforced by personal, local and temporary causes of defection. "The patriotism of the nation has triumphed over all these sources of influence, and has lifted to power a man, *pledged* to the same political course . . . with him, who now guides the helm amidst the benedictions of millions."

The election, declared the Administration organ, marked more than a personal preference. "It is the pledge of an injured and insulted nation of free men, that they will expend their last cent, and spill their last drop of blood, before they will become the victims of an oppression, which, once submitted to, would be as inexorable as fate, and co-eval with time." The great election, moreover, had been conducted by Republicans with a calmness, decorum and dignity, worthy of its importance, and the response of the people had repelled the calumny that a continuance of existing policy would be the signal for tumult and rebellion.

This reaction illumined a striking evolution in national policy — that although one source of Madison's strength was the Jefferson Administration's success in keeping the country out of war, a greater one was the determination to maintain the country's rights against the European belligerents even if it had to be done by fighting. It was a prelude to the War of 1812.

Contributing in great measure to Madison's victory was his concentration on maintenance of national commercial rights and development of internal resources. Denounced as an enemy of commerce, he actually stood for the country's permanent commercial interests, which Federalists were willing to sacrifice for immediate profit by reducing the United States to a wartime trade appendage of Great Britain. Added to all this was the conspicuous contrast between the decent and orderly conduct of the Madison campaign and the vicious personal onslaughts upon him by the adherents of all three adversaries. Finally, the prestige of President Jefferson (vanishing in Congress) still was high among the people and carried over to a successor so closely affiliated with him as to need no endorsement.

Madison was fortunate in his competitors. Monroe, who started strongly, faded like a ghost on the same diplomatic record that built up Madison's prestige. Clinton had nothing to offer but personal ambition, the ground-out eulogies of a sycophantic political machine, and the slanderous pen of the Cheetham press. Pinckney was the sacrificial offering of a disorganized party — a figurehead out of the dead political past — as unassailable and as potent as a tombstone.

The Federalists, at all stages of the campaign, seemed to be living in a dream world of their own creation. Unlike the Clintonians, they believed what they were saying about Madison being the slave of Bonaparte. The American people pierced sham, penetrated fallacies and rejected slanders. They responded to blended appeals — personal well-being as bound up in national policy, belief in the fundamental morality of Republican principles, a new sense of direction in world affairs, an expanding concept of American destiny. To cap it, they had confidence in James Madison's qualifications for national leadership. The campaign as it was conducted against Madison represented American politics at its worst. The response of the people exhibited democratic self-government at its best.

Appendix

Editorial from the Washington *National Intelligencer*
January 25, 1808

The National Intelligencer, *published by Samuel Harrison Smith, was the semi-official organ of the Jefferson Administration. Its endorsement of Madison's candidacy gave him the implied backing of the President.*

The great question "who shall be our next President," is at length brought fully before the public. Those, who heretofore have been accustomed to take the lead in the nomination of candidates, have proposed James Madison for President and George Clinton for Vice President for the four years subsequent to the current Presidential term. We have, until this moment, refrained from publicly expressing any opinion on this momentous subject, not from the want of a decided conviction upon it; but from a strong, an anxious wish, that the public sentiment should be collected, from a calm and dispassionate consideration of the subject, without those biasses and prejudices but too likely to flow from a premature discussion. Aware, too, that it might possibly produce extensive collisions, perhaps local irritations, among those who on the great principles and the leading measures of our republican institutions are undivided, we have thought it advisable not unnecessarily to precipitate a discussion, that might embarrass or frustrate the important measures of defence and protection called for by the crisis.

But the season has now arrived for every independent man to speak out; and to exercise this prerogative of a freeman without fear, and, it is to be hoped, likewise without reproach. While, however, this right is asserted with fearlessness, let its exercise not be sullied by intemperance. Let it be uniformly accompanied by a tolerant spirit, that in asserting its own rights, knows how to respect those of others.

If there be a division among the republicans, let it be candid, honorable, magnanimous. Let no good man's character be traduced to brighten that of another. Let the virtues and talents of the respective candidates be spoken of as they really are. While we "*nothing extenuate, let us set down naught in malice.*"

The nominations made by the republican Representatives and Senators have our decided approbation; they are the nominations which we have long confidently anticipated, and which we believe the great body of the people have expected.

In forming this opinion we have strove to form an honest and impartial opinion; and in forming it, we are sensible of no biasses personal, local, or political, not directly and necessarily emanating from a regard of our country;

from that regard, which should at all times direct the judgment of a good citizen, & which ought at this time to banish every consideration unconnected with the maintenance of those principles, which have established among us the empire of reason, & will finally, if firmly adhered to by us, extend it over the globe. He, who is the best fitted to guide us through the impending storm, without sacrificing these principles, ought to be the man of our choice. Such, we believe, to be James Madison. Whether we contemplate his irreproachable morals, or solid talents, we are supplied with the strongest reasons for approbation. While in private life he has invariably sustained the unassuming character of modest merit, his discharge of public duty has been no less distinguished by intelligence, fidelity and zeal. And above all, we consider him best fitted for the highest honors in the gift of his country, because amidst the various public scenes in which he has been engaged, and in the exercise of the high functions devolved upon him, he has invariably displayed a dignity and moderation, which are at once the best evidence and the surest preservative of republican principles.

Letter from James Monroe to Secretary
of State James Madison
February 28, 1808

The following is part of a twenty-four-thousand-word letter written by Monroe, ostensibly as a diplomatic dispatch but actually composed for political purposes after his retirement as minister to England.

* * *

Sir: It appears by your letter of May 20, 1807 . . . that you had construed several articles of the treaty which we had signed with the British commissioners on the 31st December, 1806, in a different sense from that in which they were conceived by us. . . .

The impressment of seamen from our merchant vessels is a topic which claims a primary attention from the [?] which it holds in your letter, but more especially from some important considerations that are connected with it. The idea entertained by the public, is, that the rights of the United States were abandoned by the American commissioners in the late negotiation, and that their seamen were left, by tacit acquiescence, if not by formal renunciation, to depend for their safety on the mercy of the British cruisers. I have, on the contrary, always believed, and still do believe, that the ground on which that interest was placed by the paper of the British commissioners of November 8, 1806, and the explanations which accompanied it, was both honorable and advantageous to the United States; that it contained a concession in their favor, on the part of Great Britain, on the great principle in contestation, never before made by a formal and obligatory act of the Government, which was highly favorable to their interest; and that it also imposed on her the obligation to conform her practice under it till a more complete arrangement should be concluded to the just claims of the United States. To place this transaction in is true light, and to do justice to the conduct of the American commissioners, it will be necessary to enter at some length into the subject.

The British paper states that the King was not prepared to disclaim or derogate from a right on which the security of the British navy might essentially depend, especially in a conjuncture when he was engaged in wars which enforced the necessity of the most vigilant attention to the preservation and supply of his naval force; that he had directed his commissioners to give to the commissioners of the United States the most positive assurances that instructions had been given, and should be repeated and enforced, to observe the greatest caution in the impressing of British seamen, to preserve the citizens of the United States from molestation or injury, and that immediate and prompt redress should be afforded on any representation of injury sustained by them. It then proposes to postpone the article relative to impressment, on account of the difficulties which were experienced in arranging any article on that subject, and to proceed to conclude a treaty on the other points that were embraced by the negotiation. As a motive to such postponement and the condition of it, it assures us that the British commissioners were instructed still to entertain the discussion of any plan which could be devised to secure the interests of both States, without injury to the rights of either.

By this paper it is evident that the rights of the United States were expressly to be reserved, and not abandoned, as has been most erroneously supposed; that the negotiation on the subject of impressment was to be postponed for a limited time, and for a special object only, and to be revived as soon as that object was accomplished; and, in the interim, that the practice of impressment was to correspond essentially with the views and interests of the United States. . . .

In our letter to you of November 11th, which accompanied the paper under consideration, and in that of January 3d, which was forwarded with the treaty, these sentiments were fully confirmed. In that of November 11th, we communicated one important fact, which left no doubt of the sense in which it was intended by the British commissioners that that paper should be construed by us. In calling your attention to the passage which treats of impressment, in reference to the practice which should be observed in future, we remarked that the terms "high seas" were not mentioned in it, and added, that we knew that the omission had been intentional. It was impossible that these terms could have been omitted intentionally, with our knowledge, for any purpose other than to admit a construction that it was intended that impressments should be confined to the land. I do not mean to imply that it was understood between the British commissioners and us, that Great Britain should abandon the practice of impressment on the high seas altogether. I mean, however, distinctly to state, that it was understood that the practice heretofore pursued by her should be abandoned, and that no impressment should be made on the high seas, under the obligation of that paper, except in cases of an extraordinary nature, to which no general prohibition against it could be construed fairly to extend. . . .

*   *   *

Without relying, however, on the explanations that were given by the British commissioners of the import of that paper, or of the course which their Government intended to pursue under it, it is fair to remark on the paper itself, that as by it the rights of the parties were reserved, and the negotiation might be continued on this particular topic, after a treaty should be formed on the others, Great Britain was bound not to trespass on those rights while that negotiation was depending, and in case she did trespass on them in any the slightest degree, the United States would be justified in breaking off the negotiation and appealing to force in vindication of their rights. . . . We were, therefore, decidedly of opinion that the paper of the British commissioners placed the interest of impressment on ground which it was both safe and honorable for the United States to admit; that, in short, it gave their Government the command of the subject for every necessary and useful purpose. Attached to the treaty, it was the basis or condition on which the treaty rested. Strong in its character in their favor on the great question of right, and admitting a favorable construction on others, it placed them on more elevated ground in those respects than they had held before, and, by keeping the negotiation open to obtain a more complete adjustment, and administration was armed with the most effectual means of securing it. By this arrangement the Government possessed a power to coerce without being compelled to assume the character belonging to coercion, and it was able to give effect to that power without violating the relations of amity between the countries. The right to break off the negotiation and appeal to force could never be lost sight of, in any discussion on the subject, while there as no obligation to make that appeal till necessity compelled it. . . . Had we refused to proceed in the negotiation, what was the alternative which such a refusal presented to our view? The negotiation would have been at an end, after having failed in all its objects: for if this interest was not arranged, none others could be. . . .

*   *   *

. . . The attitude would become, in fact, what the exterior announced it to be- hostile; and it was difficult to perceive how it could be changed, and peace be preserved, with honor to the United States. They could not recede from the ground which they had taken, or accept, by compulsion, terms which they had rejected in an amicable negotiation. War, therefore, seemed to be the inevitable consequence of such a state of things; and I was far from considering it an alternative which ought to be preferred to the arrangement which was offered to us. When I took into view the prosperous and happy condition of the United States, compared with that of other nations; that, as a neutral Power, they were almost the exclusive carriers of the productions of the whole world; and that in commerce they flourished beyond example, notwithstanding the losses which they occasionally suffered, I was strong in the opinion that those blessings ought not to be hazarded in such a question. Many other considerations tended to confirm me in that sentiment. I knew that the United States were not prepared for war; that their coast was unfortified, and their cities in a great measure defenceless that their militia in many of the States were neither armed nor trained; and that their whole revenue was derived from commerce. I could not presume that there was just cause to doubt which of the alternatives ought to be preferred.

*   *   *

Letter from Vice-President George Clinton to DeWitt Clinton
March 5, 1808

Vice-President George Clinton wrote this letter in February to his nephew DeWitt Clinton, a New York political boss who published it the following month with important alterations.

Dear Sir, Yesterday I had the honor to receive your letter of the 1st inst, and am not surprised to learn that some of my friends in your city are induced to infer from my silence on the subject of the nomination of candidates for the offices of President and Vice-President, made some time ago at this place, and since published in the newspapers, that my name was mentioned for the latter, with my knowledge and approbation. The inference is a natural one, although in the present instance incorrect.

Viewing with great anxiety the critical and alarming situation of our national affairs, and deeply impressed with a belief that it would require the united wisdom and patriotism of the different branches of the government to avert the dangers which threaten our country, I formed a resolution at the commencement of this important session, not to participate in any conversation touching the ensuing Presidential election, or to express any sentiment or determination respecting it, that might have a tendency to disunion, or any baneful effect on our public deliberations. This resolution I have hitherto scrupulously observed, and now regret the necessity I feel myself under, of a partial departure from it, in order to remove the false impressions which it seems my silence has occasioned, by assuring my friends, through you, that I never have been directly or indirectly consulted on the subject, either before or since that nomination was made; nor was I ever apprised of the meeting held for the purpose, otherwise, than by having accidentally seen a notice or summons to one of the members to attend, from S. R. Bradley, Esq.

However correct and forcible the objections you have stated against this procedure may be, yet as it is a business in which I have had no agency or participation, and over which I can have no control; it might be considered improper in me, situated as I am, to make any comments on it.

I am with great respect and esteem, Your most obedient servant.

Protest Against the Caucus
March 7, 1808

In this public letter, to which seventeen members of the House affixed their signatures, John Randolph of Virginia protested the caucus method of choosing presidential candidates.

To the People of the United States:

Fellow-citizens, in the course of the events which have marked the conduct and characters of those, to whom you have at different periods, intrusted by your suffrages, the power of making laws for your government, few measures have occurred, since the adoption of the present constitution, more extraordinary, than the meeting lately held for the purpose of nominating a President and Vice-President of the United States.

Our alarm is equally excited, whether we advert to the mode in which the meeting was summoned, or the proceedings after it was convened. The Senator who assumed the power of calling together the members of Congress, did it under the pretext of that power being vested in him, by a former convention; this pretext, whether it be true or not, implies an assertion of a right in the Congress of 1804, to direct their successors in the mode of choosing the chief magistrate; an assertion which no man has ever before had the hardihood to advance. The notices were private; not general to all the members of the two houses; nor confined to the republican party; a delegate from one of the territories was invited and attended, a man who in elections has no suffrage, and in legislation no vote. The persons, who met in pursuance of this unprecedented summons, proceeded without discussion or debate, to determine by ballot the candidates for the highest offices in the union. The characters of different men, and their pretensions to the public favor, were not suffered to be canvassed, and all responsibility was avoided by the mode of selection. The determination of this conclave has been published as the act of the republican party; and with as much exultation as the result of a solemn election by the nation. Attempts are making to impress upon the public mind, that these proceedings ought to be binding upon all the republicans, and those who refused to attend, or disapproved of the meeting, are denounced as enemies of liberty, and as apostates from the cause of the people. In this state of things, we think it our duty to address you, and we deem ourselves called upon to enter our most solemn protest against these proceedings.

It is true that at former periods, when the election of a President, and Vice-President approached, it was customary to hold meetings of the members of Congress, for the purpose of recommending candidates to the public. But these meetings, if not justified, were palliated by the necessity of union. The federalists presented a formidable phalanx; and either to succeed at all, or to prevent them from placing the candidate for the Vice-Presidency in the Presidential chair, it was necessary to exert the combined efforts of the whole republican party. But it is equally true that in those instances, the nominations for the Presidency were mere matters of course. In the first and second elections under the constitution, the eyes of all were turned upon General Washington, and since the expiration of the two periods, during which he filled the supreme executive office, there has not until now been any difference of opinion among the republicans, as to the candidate for the first magistracy. The real object of all former meetings, was to produce such a co-operation as would secure the election of a republican Vice-President.

The circumstances, which might be urged in extenuation of such a measure heretofore, do not now exist. The federalists are comparatively few in number, and form but a feeble party; they cannot give to any one candidate, more than sixteen or seventeen votes out of one hundred and seventy six; no federalist can therefore be elected by the Electors; and should no person have a majority of all the electoral votes, the choice of the President will devolve on the members of the present House of Representatives, in which the federalists have the votes of only two states, Connecticut and Delaware. The alteration of the constitution prevents the danger of any intrigue, by which the intended Vice-President might be elected President. No good reason can therefore now be assigned, why an union of the republicans in favor of any particular person should be attempted by a measure in itself so exceptionable, as a nomination by the Senators and Representatives in Congress.

We do not say that a consultation among the members of Congress, respecting the persons to be recommended as candidates for the two highest offices of the nation, may not in some extraordinary crisis, be proper. But the propriety must arise from absolute necessity. Even then, we doubt whether it can be completely justified. — The people ought to exercise their right of election without any undue bias; and is it not the evident intention of such consultations, to produce a bias? . . .

So conscious were the members who attended the late meeting, of the weight of objections which might be urged against their proceedings, that they have thought it proper to publish an exculpatory resolution, proposed by Mr. Giles, of Virginia, and unanimously adopted. They have declared, that in "making their nominations, they have acted only in their individual characters as citizens;" this is very true, because they could act in no other, without a breach of their oaths, and a direct violation of the letter of the constitution. But was it not intended that those nominations should be enforced by the sanction of congressional names? They proceed to assert "that they have been induced to adopt this measure from the necessity of the case, from a deep conviction of the importance of union to the republicans thro'out all parts of the United States, in the present crisis of both our external and internal affairs." We trust we have shewn that no such necessity exists, and that an union among the republicans, in favor of any individual, is not important.

*   *   *

Letter from Secretary of State James Madison
to British Minister David M. Erskine
March 25, 1808

Madison's remarks to British Minister Erskine on London's rejection of their Anglo-American settlement perfectly illustrated Madison's political maxim, "Put your enemy in the wrong."

Sir: Having laid before the President your letter of the 23d of February, explaining the character of certain British orders of council issued in November last, I proceed to communicate the observations and representations which will manifest to your Government the sentiments of the President on so deep a violation of the commerce and rights of the United States.

These orders interdict to neutral nations, or rather to the United States, now the only commercial nation in a state of neutrality, all commerce with the enemies of Great Britain, now nearly the whole commercial world, with certain exceptions only, and under certain regulations, but too evidently fashioned to the commercial, the manufacturing, and the fiscal policy of Great Britain; and, on that account, the more derogatory from the honor and independence of neutral nations.

The orders are the more calculated to excite surprise in the United States, as they have disregarded the remonstrances conveyed in my letters of the 20th and 29th March, 1807, against another order of council, issued on a similar plea, in the month of January, 1807. To those just remonstrances no answer was indeed ever given; whilst the order has been continued in its pernicious operation against the lawful commerce of the United States, and we now find added to it others instituting still more ruinous depredations, without even the addition of any new pretext; and when, moreover, it is notorious that the order of January was of a nature greatly to overbalance in its effects any injuries to Great Britain that could be apprehended from the illegal operation of the French decree on which the order was to retaliate, had that decree in its illegal operation been actually applied to the United States and been acquiesced in by them.

The last orders, like that of January, proceed on the most unsubstantial foundation. They assume for fact an acquiescence of the United States in an unlawful application to them of the French decree; and they assume for a principle that the right of retaliation, accruing to one belligerent against a neutral, through whom an injury is done by another belligerent, is not to have for its measure that of the injury received, but may be exercised in any extent and under any modifications which may suit the pleasure or the policy of the complaining party.

The fact, sir, is unequivocally disowned. It is not true that the United

States have acquiesced in any illegal operation of the French decree; nor is it even true that, at the date of the British orders of November 11, a single application of that decree to the commerce of the United States on the high seas can be presumed to have been known to the British Government.

The French decree in question has two distinct aspects; one clearly importing an intended operation within the territorial limits as a local law, the other apparently importing an intended operation on the high seas.

Under the first aspect, the decree, however otherwise objectionable, cannot be said to have violated the neutrality of the United States. If the governing Powers on the Continent of Europe choose to exclude from their ports British property or British productions, or neutral vessels proceeding from British ports, it is an act of sovereignty which the United States have no right to controvert. The same sovereignty is exercised by Great Britain at all times, in peace as well as in war, towards her friends as well as her enemies. Her statute book presents a thousand illustrations.

It is only, therefore, under the other aspect of the decree, that it can have violated neutral rights, and this would have resulted from its execution on the high seas, whether on the pretext of nominal blockade, or with a view to enforce a domestic regulation against foreign vessels, not within the domestic precincts, but under the authority and protection of the law of nations.

Has, then, the French decree been executed on the high seas against the commerce of the United States with Great Britain? and have the United States acquiesced in the lawful and injurious proceeding?

I state, sir, on undeniable authority, that the first instance in which that decree was put in force against the neutral rights of the United States was that of the Horizon, an American ship, bound from Great Britain to Lima, wrecked within the territorial jurisdiction of France, but condemned under an exposition of the decree, extending to the high seas its operation against neutrals. This judicial decision took place as late as the 16th day of October, 1807, and was not officially known to the Minister Plenipotentiary of the United States at Paris until some time in November. At the date, therefore, of the first order of Great Britain, no injury whatever had been done to her, through an aggression on the commerce of the United States. . . .

I state, with equal confidence, that at no time have the United States acquiesced in violations of their neutral rights, injurious to Great Britain, or any other belligerent nation. So far were they in particular from acquiescing in the French decree of November, 1806, that the moment it was known to the Minister at Paris, he called for explanations of its meaning, in relation to the United States, which were favorable, and uncontradicted by the actual operation of the decree; that he steadily watched over the proceedings under it, with a readiness to interpose against any unlawful extension of them, to the commerce of the United States; that no time was lost, after the decree came to the knowledge of the Government here, in giving him proper instructions on the subject; that he was equally prompt, on receiving the decision of the court in the case of the Horizon, in presenting to the French Government a remonstrance in terms which can never be censured for a defect of energy; and that by the first opportunity after that decision reached the President, the particular instructions required by it were forwarded to that Minister. . . .

What more could have been required on the part of the United States to obviate retaliating pretensions of any sort on the part of Great Britain? Retaliations are measures of right in all cases. Where they are to operate through a third and involuntary party, they will never be hastily resorted to by a magnanimous or a just Power, which will always allow to the third party its right to discuss the merits of the case, and will never permit itself to enforce its measures, without affording a reasonable time for the use of reasonable means for substituting another remedy. What would be the situation of neutral Powers, if the first blow levelled through them by one belligerent against another was to leave them no choice but between the retaliating vengeance of the latter, and an instant declaration of war against the former? Reason revolts against this as the sole alternative. . . .

Retaliation is a specific or equivalent return of injury, for injury received; and where it is to operate through the interests of a third party, having no voluntary participation in the injury received, the return ought, as already observed, to be inflicted with the most forbearing hand. . . .

What, then, is the extent of the injury experienced by Great Britain from the measures of her enemies, so far as the operation of those measures through the United States can render them in any sense responsible?

A mere declaration by a belligerent, without the intention or the means to carry it into effect, against the rights and obligations of a neutral nation, and thence against the interests of another belligerent, could afford no pretext to the latter to retaliate at the expense of the neutral. The declaration might give just offence to the neutral, but it would belong to him alone to decide on the course prescribed by the respect he owed to himself. No real damage having accrued to the belligerent, no indemnity could accrue.

For the same reason, a declaration of a belligerent, which he is known to be either not in a situation, or not to intend to carry but partially into execution against a neutral, to the injury of another belligerent, could never give more than a right to a commensurate redress against the neutral. All remaining unexecuted, and evidently not to be executed, is merely ostensible, working no injury to any, unless it be in the disrespect to the neutral, to whom alone it belongs to resent or disregard it.

. . . Now, sir, it never was pretended that at the date of the first British order, issued in January, 1807, any injury had accrued to or was apprehended by Great Britain from an execution of the French decree against the commerce of the United States, on the theatre of their neutral rights. . . .

Such are the pretexts and such the principles on which one great branch of the lawful commerce of this country became a victim to the first British order, and on which the last orders are now sweeping from the ocean all its most valued remains.

Against such an unprecedented system of warfare on neutral rights and national independence, the common judgment and common feelings of mankind must forever protest. . . .

"Madison as a 'French Citizen' " by Edmond C. Genêt in the *New York Register* June 26, 1808

"Citizen" Genêt, ousted as French minister to the United States in 1793, and fearing execution by Robespierre, remained in this country, purchased a farm on Long Island, and married George Clinton's daughter.

. . . I don't believe that the embargo was any more calculated to prevent the usual loss of some of our property at sea, than to oblige the king of England and the Emperor of France to come to our terms; *There is something else under the rose.* Let us try to find it out. It cannot be denied that Mr. Jefferson made in France his entry on the diplomatic stage; he studied, at the court of Louis, the art of Machiavel, and from a courtier of the king become a courtier of the people; when the fire of the revolution first broke out, the most profuse doses of adulation and flattery were lavished upon him by the leading characters at that period; those marks of respect and confidence have been continued since, and the French ambassador brought to him and to Mr. Madison in 1793, decrees of the national assembly, (4) naturalising them both French citizens; the written answer of Mr. Madison, expressive of his gratitude, his admiration, and his devotion, was transmitted to France by the same minister, and the bloody Robespierre, who opened that memorable letter, was very much pleased at his civism. Mr. Jefferson, an older fox, took care himself of his answer. Some of the principal actors of the national assembly, who escaped murder by a timely emigration, occupying now high stations under the Imperial government, have had a chance to renew their correspondence with those Gallo-American citizens, for whose elevation they have felt some interest, and it is not altogether beyond the bounds of probability that when the French Emperor blockaded England and annulled her trade with his decrees, the Embargo, which effectually does not hurt France a great deal, was dexterously contrived to comply, as much as possible, with his imperious wishes, without incurring the local dangers of a manifest partiality. It appears, however, by some expressions which have leaked out *in the published part* of the letter written by the French minister of foreign affairs, Champagny, to our minister, that a little more than the embargo is wanted to give up to the United States the Floridas, lately kidnapped from Spain. *But here is the rub.* Our cabinet, it is conjectured, is willing to increase as much as possible the importance of the southern states, but they don't want our northern states to be strengthened by the acquisition of Canada, Nova-Scotia and the fisheries, which would of course take place if war was declared between America and England. . . .

* * *

Our aggrandisement to the southward is unquestionably the darling object, the notes on Virginia witness it, and when the penury of France has offered an opportunity to favor it, the money of the states, who are more hurt than benefitted by it, has not been spared.—It appears from these remarks, that there are in all state affairs pretexts brought forward to deceive the vulgar and secret motives which are dissimulated. . . .

*   *   *

The French . . . have cut off the heads of their richest merchants, taken their property, destroyed several of their seaports, burnt the opulent city of Lions and all their manufactures of luxuries, wore humespun and planted potatoes in the elegant garden of the Thuileries. But as those energetic measures would not do here, don't it seem to be likely enough that we proceed to the same end by a different course; And that an embargo, so cunningly introduced that it is not perhaps now in the power of congress to repeal it, will much sooner compel our merchants to turn to the plough, and their wives to the care of a dairy, and the labor of the loom, than England to acknowledge the modern principles of neutrality, and France to respect them? What a glory it will be to have accomplished such a useful and moral revolution without scaffolds, without bloodshed, and with the help alone of a few messages and letters. The maritime states humbled and empoverished, Virginia, resting on the arm of slavery, ruling the union in peace, Philosophy triumphant, and the sage of Monticello having modestly thrown his mantle on his devoted servant, proclaimed by his disciples far superior to Confucius the legislator of China!

Editorial from the New York *American Citizen*
July 24, 1808

American Citizen, the leading Clintonian organ, passed out of existence when deprived of public printing rights after the 1808 election.

The spirit of the Constitution, if not the letter, *forbids* the Members of Congress to nominate a President and Vice-president.

To prevent intrigue, as far as constitutions and laws can prevent it, and to exclude undue influence from the election of President and Vice-president, as much as may be, Art. 2 sec. 1 of the Constitution ordains, that "no Senator or Representative, or person holding an office of trust or profit under the United States shall be an elector."

This wise exclusion has a two-fold view. — "Persons holding offices of trust or profit," who are not members of Congress, are not to be electors, lest those official considerations, which are obvious to all, should warp the judgment, and pervert to sinister ends the freedom of elections.

Members of Congress are not eligible to be electors, since the House of Representatives chuses the President; and the Senate the Vice-president of the United States. The Constitution of the United States intends that Congress, when thus ultimately appealed to, shall be as free from a *previous* commitment or pledge, express or implied, as is the Court of Errors of this state, when appealed to from the inferior tribunals. Such are the free, the excellent principles of the constitution.

And yet, in violation of these principles, what do we witness, what applaud? We see Members of Congress, who cannot be Electors, and who, in the case of no choice by the electors, are the last appeal; we see them formally and solemnly assemble in caucus, at the seat of government, to nominate a President and Vice-president of the U. States! And such is the pernicious absurdity of party doctrine and the force of party discipline, that a nomination is equivalent to an election.

"Constitutionality of Congressional Recommendation" by Tunis Wortman in the New York *Public Advertiser* July 28, 1808

Tunis Wortman, a New York lawyer and county clerk who wrote as "Cato" and under other pseudonyms, switched his support from Clinton to Madison.

May not every elector if he pleases, *propose* a candidate? By what perversity in reasoning will you deny to public representatives, a *privilege* which is actually executed by every man who has money to purchase a printing press and abilities to write a clumsy paragraph? Who will doubt a general right of recommending? Who will not rather wish that it should be exercised by *those who possess the most correct opportunities of judging*? While we smile at the absurdity of such objections, we cannot but pity the imbecility of their framers.

But there still exists a remaining plea. It is said that the *advice* of congress will be tantamount to a *command*, and thus in reality controul the independence of electors. I grant that the council of so respectable a body will possess considerable weight; but deny its obtaining an undue ascendancy. The electors will embrace or reject the advice with an unshackled discretion, and if they pursue it, they will be actuated by a conviction of its cogency, or by the true policy they may perceive in observing it.

There is therefore no room for the pretence that a congressional recommendation is in any shape repugnant to the constitution. The clause which renders members of congress ineligible to the office of electors, was intended to deprive them of an opportunity to acquire *a real elective power* in the *first instance*. It was introduced to prevent an actual *coercive authority*; but it was never contemplated to deprive them of that *advising privilege* which they possess in common with every other citizen.

237

"Address to the Citizens"
Philadelphia, August 8, 1808

This Pennsylvania pamphlet, appealing for support of Madison on the basis of party regularity and unity, was circulated throughout the United States.

We think it incumbent on us to state, upon the *personal knowledge of six of the members of this committee*, that the subject of a candidate, or the name of a candidate for the presidency, or vice-presidency of the United States, was never brought before the convention at Lancaster, nor any question or topic touched or discussed during the whole period of its sittings, in which the name of Mr. Madison or Mr. Clinton, nor of any other person, was used or glanced at. . . .

For the venerable Mr. Clinton, this committee, and we believe, the whole people of Pennsylvania, entertain that just reverence and respect, which his early services and virtues inspire; from republicans this tribute is due; and is as cheerfully given; but we now submit to the nomination of Mr. Madison in preference to Mr. Clinton; because the choice has been made in the usual manner, and because the choice itself is good; because not to accord with that choice would subject us to the reproach of being *veering politicians* and faithless to our country and to our principles.

In like manner, the virtues, services and character of Mr. Monroe, we hold in the most respectful and sincere estimation; and for the same reasons we do not prefer him to Mr. Clinton as vice-president; and moreover because we cannot suppose that either of them would willingly become instruments of division and distraction — or at this period endanger that union of national sentiment, which is so requisite to deter foreign enemies from using our divisions to our utter destruction.

Beside these motives arising out of the fundamental principles of representative government, and which alone would outweigh all other considerations; we have motives cogent, rational and irrefragable. Mr. Madison, besides being the candidate regularly selected, has displayed a vigor of mind worthy of the nation and the station for which he is proposed, in the very recent transactions with foreign nations.

Mr. Monroe, by common consent, is out of the question as president; and the considerations for the people to make, are now reduced to the *question of principle*, as it regards the choice made in the usual way — from which we cannot deviate without deviating from our principles.

The state of the world at the present time, requires not only great previous knowledge of political relations, but faculties ripe and quick to act upon events that may arise; we very much question if any man coming newly into the chair of state, at this period, could with the best and most perfect faculties of mind, in a short time, completely possess himself of the necessary knowledge for the station which Mr. Madison already possesses; and we believe no other man so likely to pursue that wise and virtuous policy which Mr. Jefferson has pursued, and in which Madison has so honorably participated. As to the aspersions thrown out against Mr. Madison, they merit no good man's attention; the like have been for years reiterated against Mr. Jefferson, and the world has seen with what contrary effect — his virtues have triumphed in the triumphs of his country over enmity and calumny — and we entertain a confident hope that those of Mr. Madison will.

Letter from Tunis Wortman to James Cheetham
in the New York *Public Advertiser*
September 8, 1808

Wortman's defection to Madison made him the target of slanderous personal accusations, which he rebutted at length while reaffirming his legal argument.

To Mr. James Cheetham: In a very irregular and immethodical publication, intended to attack M. P. Cato, rather than refute his doctrines, you have taken two grounds, which possessing the semblance of *something like argument*, may warrant a reply.

You have said that the meeting and proceedings at Washington were *uncontitutional*; and you have assailed the principle which teaches that the *majority of a party ought to govern*. Upon both of those points I could have confuted you by your own words, but you are perfectly welcome to the whole force of Seneca's apology: your new friends undoubtedly must think you have grown vastly wiser. . . .

There exists no *express* prohibition; if there does, let it be produced. But you say there is a clause which *implies one*. *What is* that clause? It is the article which prevents a member of congress from being *chosen an elector*; but does that render it unlawful for him to *express his opinions*? You cannot believe so. There exists no manner of connexion between the premises and your conclusion. I defy you to unite the subjects in a *regular syllogism*. . . .

All that the constitution intends to secure is the *independence of the electors*, the *power of chusing without controul*. Does Cato's principle impair that right? Has Cato questioned their authority to elect with perfect freedom? Sir, there is not substance in the dispute to bear an argument.

*　　*　　*

240

Editorial from the Washington *National Intelligencer*
September 14, 1808

The emergence of General Charles Cotesworth Pinckney as Federalist nominee for President intensified the call for Republican unity behind Madison.

A number of the leading federal prints have at length come forward with the nomination of *General Pinckney* for the Presidency. For a long time these prints affected a fastidious neutrality, or satisfied themselves with expressing a preference of one republican candidate to the others named. Whether this change in their tone arises from any hope entertained of succeeding in the choice of a federal man, or from an entire hopelessness of dividing the republicans, or from an insidious attempt to throw the republicans off their guard, it is not easy to say. It is, however, immaterial which of these is their object, as they ought all of them to have the same influence. It is highly probable, indeed, that, according to circumstances, the federal votes will be given to a federal man, or to a republican, in such a way as shall best subserve federal ends.

For a while the federal party flattered themselves with the hope of a serious division among the republicans. While any circumstances occurred to favor this hope, they perceived and yielded to the policy of keeping themselves as much as possible out of view. Fortunately, however, for the nation, it has spoken on this head the most unequivocal language, and there is not a republican state in the union that has not declared itself in favor of Mr. Madison. Even New York with a patriotism that reflects upon her the highest honor, has sacrificed local to national motives, and manifested her purpose not to be separated from her sister states.

If there be a hope entertained by the federalists of carrying a federal man into the Presidency, we may rest satisfied that every exertion in the power of man will be made to effect so great an object. It will be endeavored to effect it, not from the superior talents or virtues of their candidate, not from the prediliction of the people of the U. States for federalism, but by producing the impression that the great measures of the last session of Congress, and more especially the embargo, are impolitic, and that the good of the country requires that these steps should be retraced. Heaven and earth will be moved to produce this conviction; the people will be loudly appealed to on this head, and they will be called upon to overlook every other consideration. As a large portion of every community are prone to sacrifice their ultimate interests to those of the moment, the low price of produce and the stagnation of commerce will be copiously dwelt upon, and ascribed, not to the unjust conduct of foreign powers, but the embargo.

To counteract these false impressions on the public mind, it will be the duty of the republicans to be vigilant and assiduous. Let them realise the present crisis as all-important. On its issue truly depend the great interests of the nation; not those of a day, but those of many years, and perhaps of ages. The election of Mr. Madison can no longer be considered in any degree as a personal contest. He is the republican candidate, and the only republican candidate. The other republicans named, however, sincere their political sentiments may be, must derive their support from the federalists. Can there, under such a state of things, any longer exist a division among the republicans? Are they not called upon by the most powerful motives of patriotism to sacrifice their personal or local predilictions on the altar of patriotism? Who among them, that is a republican at heart, that will forgive himself should his apathy or vote throw the affairs of the country into the hands of the federalists, or justify the impression of foreign governments that the people of the U. States do not possess the fortitude to adhere to the present system of measures?

*   *   *

Under every view, then, in which this subject can be presented, the republicans of the U. States are admonished to vigilance and exertion. Never has there been a period in the annals of nations in which there was a stronger claim on the virtue of a community. They have more to preserve than any nation that ever existed. On the maintenance of their independence, on their resistance of oppression, on their union, depend their future fate, their individual felicity and the true glory of their country. A foreign power, co-operating with the mercenary spirit that actuates a portion of our fellow-citizens, has flattered itself with the hope of subverting our present happy system of measures, and thus paving the way for an entirely new political era. If they can succeed in frustrating the republican wishes of the people by raising some man to the Presidency, who will undo all that has lately been done, they will have taken a bold step towards the attainment of their object; and, still further profiting themselves of our divisions, they may indeed flatter themselves with turning us from the *error of our ways.*

Editorial from the New York *Public Advertiser*
September 28, 1808

The Public Advertiser *was one of the few newspapers in the state of New York which supported Madison.*

Of Two Evils, Choose the Least—This maxim is the polar star of the federalists during the next presidential election. Their votes will be given to Clinton, to Monroe or Pinckney, or to any other candidate, in preference to the man who will be supported by the great majority of the republican party. "Any other man than Madison," is their creed; their cry; their rallying point. Their impression is, that with any other man in the chair, there will be a change of measures. Of course their votes will receive that disposition which is best calculated to effect this object. Though the federal prints of the south have nominated C. C. Pinckney as their president, yet the probability is, that the federalists are playing a deep game. That those in the north, and the federal electors in the south, will ultimately vote for Mr. Clinton. The Clintonians of New York cannot be guilty of such a palpable abandonment of principle as to vote for a federal candidate. The federalists, therefore, if they discover no great probability of their electing Mr. Pinckney, will concentrate their votes upon Mr. Clinton.

It is probable, however, that their course is not yet definitively marked out. The elections in New Hampshire and Rhode Island have raised their tone and elevated their crest: And if the late election in Vermont, that in New Jersey, and the gubernatorial election in Pennsylvania should correspond with their expectations, that then they will encounter every risk, and run Mr. Pinckney. Should New Jersey and Pennsylvania disappoint them, then they will in all probability pour their ballots into the urn of Mr. Clinton.

Editorial from the Norfolk *Ledger*
October 14, 1808

This editorial did much to bring about the remarkable decision of Virginia's Federalists to abandon Pinckney in favor of Monroe.

. . . The address from Mr. Monroe's friends is plain, and may be considered as pledging Mr. Monroe upon some leading points, particularly the cruel measure of the embargo, and upon our future intercourse with foreign nations. War or perpetual embargo; peace and commerce are the questions? To avoid the two former, and to secure the two latter our exertions must be directed. If there was a hope, that a federal ticket could prevail in this state, it cannot be supposed that the editor of this paper would permit local state partiality or personal respect, to govern him in declining his co-operation with his federal brethren. Believing as we most sincerely do believe, that if the present course of measures are not arrested, that even the UNION, that rock of our political safety, will cease to exist twelve months longer — we must be allowed to pursue a course for ourselves. As every calamity which could befal us as a nation, is included in the separation of the states, we shall enumerate no others. The impossibility of succeeding with a federal ticket is to us so evident, that we think any calculation upon the subject would be thrown away. In conclusion, we hope that the federalists of this state will reflect seriously upon the present crisis; and that the result of their reflections will produce a determination to give their *unanimous* suffrages for the ticket of Mr. Monroe.

Editorial from the Baltimore *North American*
October 17, 1808

Jacob Wagner, publisher of the North American, *had been chief clerk of the State Department under Federalist Secretary Timothy Pickering. Although retained in office by Madison, he broke with the Administration when he was offerred a political sinecure.*

Presidential Election—The federalists have never, as a body intended to interfere in the existing disputes of their variegated adversaries. But they are sensible of the nearer approximation of some individuals of the democratic party, to their own opinions and principles, than others. For example, they are apprehensive of no deadly hostility to commerce from Mr. George Clinton; and they would expect from Mr. Monroe a patriotic impartiality towards other nations, as well as a protecting solicitude for the real Independence of the Union. From both they would expect greater reverence for the legal and constitutional provisions in favor of liberty, than from any member of the present administration, which has repeatedly and flagrantly violated them.

In states or districts, where the contest lies exclusively between two persons of the party opposed to the federalists we agree with the Norfolk Ledger, that the federalists ought not to remain inactive. Every freeman is bound to give his opinion by his suffrage. It does not often happen, that he can have a choice between perfection and its contrast. His judgment is more frequently required to make a difficult choice between various degrees of imperfection. This duty is exemplified and enforced by what is to take place in Virginia, early in next month, with respect to the Presidential Election. There will be but two candidates offered, Mr. Monroe and Mr. Madison. Both of them have stood in the foremost ranks of opposition to federalists; but in the present state of things, there is room for a decided preference between them. Mr. Madison has had a conspicuous share in that ruinous system of policy, which has reduced us to greater distress, and sunk us deeper in the estimation of an impartial world, then any merely accidental complication of events could possibly have produced, if counteracted by a very moderate share of circumspection and skill. Mr. Monroe and his friends, on the contrary, have in their writings and speeches, publicly condemned the most prominent of those measures, the maturity of which has at length overwhelmed us. They were opposed to the tribute to France, in the shape of settling the boundaries between us and Spain; they were opposed to the act restricting the intercourse with England; they were in favor of a treaty with her; and above all, they are averse to the continuance of the embargo.

THE ELECTORAL VOTE IN THE 1808 ELECTION

STATES	PRESIDENT			VICE-PRESIDENT				
	James Madison	George Clinton	C. C. Pinckney	G. Clinton	J. Madison	J. Langdon	J. Monroe	Rufus King
New Hampshire..	—	—	7	—	—	—	—	7
Vermont........	6	—	—	—	—	6	—	—
Massachusetts....	—	—	19	—	—	—	—	19
Rhode Island....	—	—	4	—	—	—	—	4
Connecticut.....	—	—	9	—	—	—	—	9
New York.......	13	6	—	13	3	—	3	—
New Jersey......	8	—	—	8	—	—	—	—
Pennsylvania.....	20	—	—	20	—	—	—	—
Delaware........	—	—	3	—	—	—	—	3
Maryland.......	9	—	2	9	—	—	—	2
Virginia.........	24	—	—	24	—	—	—	—
North Carolina...	11	—	3	11	—	—	—	3
South Carolina...	10	—	—	10	—	—	—	—
Georgia.........	6	—	—	6	—	—	—	—
Kentucky*......	7	—	—	7	—	—	—	—
Tennessee.......	5	—	—	5	—	—	—	—
Ohio...........	3	—	—	—	—	3	—	—
	122	6	47	113	3	9	3	47

* One Kentucky elector did not vote.

Election of 1812

NORMAN K. RISJORD is Associate Professor of History at the University of Wisconsin. He is the author of The Old Republicans: Southern Conservatism in the Age of Jefferson *and the editor of a collection of essays on* The Early American Party System.

Election of 1812

by *Norman K. Risjord*

The presidential election of 1812 took place within five months after the declaration of war against Great Britain, and the justice of the war, as well as the President's methods of conducting it, were the central issues of the campaign. Wartime elections—often referred to in the twentieth century as "khaki elections"—usually redound to the benefit of the President and the party in power. In a military emergency the nation tends to rally around its President as a symbol of unity, and the regime in power often profits from reluctance to change Administrations in the midst of a crisis. But this was not the case in 1812. Campaign rhetoric focused almost exclusively on the war issue, making the election a virtual referendum on the wisdom of continuing a war with the mightiest naval and military power in the world. In regions where the war was generally unpopular—particularly in the northeastern states—President Madison lost a substantial number of votes which, in calmer times, he might have expected to receive.

In 1812 most eastern states still restricted the suffrage with property qualifications, but the intensity of the party conflict had tended to bring increasing numbers of voters to the polls. In states where the parties were almost evenly divided and elections closely contested, the number of voters often approached 60 to 80 per cent of the adult male population. Reflecting increasing concern for public image, party labels were rather fluid in 1812. The supporters of President Madison generally adhered to the name Republican because it was well established and appealing. Adopted initially by the

Jeffersonian party in the early 1790's, the label gave them the image of being supporters of the Republic, while their opponents, by implication, were incipient "monarchists." The opposition party had willingly assumed the name Federalist in the 1790's because it meant that they were the supporters of the federal system of government created by the Constitution. But after 1800 Republican propaganda made the name unpopular by associating it with aristocracy and elitism. By 1812 the Federalists were generally calling themselves "federal republicans," or occasionally just "Republicans," while referring to their opponents as "Democrats," a term that continued to carry its eighteenth-century connotations of demagoguery and mob rule. In states where the war was particularly unpopular, the Federalists sought bipartisan support by calling themselves the Peace party, while labeling their opponents the War party.

Despite the fluidity of party names, partisan organizations in 1812 were better developed than at any earlier time. In an organizational sense the election of 1812 was the pinnacle of the first party system. The demise of the Federalist party after the war removed the necessity for highly structured electoral machinery, and not until the 1830's would party organizations again reach the level of sophistication achieved in 1812. The crude party machinery of the 1790's was organized in hierarchical fashion from the top down, with matters of national policy and presidential nominations determined by the congressional caucus. After 1800 this organizational structure was gradually expanded. In an effort to build party support in New England the Republicans initiated state nominating conventions. Their tiny minorities in the New England legislatures made the caucus system impractical, and, in any case, the convention appeared more democratic. The idea soon spread into the middle states, and the success of the Republicans at the polls through Jefferson's Administrations forced the Federalists to emulate their methods.

By 1812 both parties had evolved organizations based on loose confederations of local groups. County meetings of the party faithful, summoned by newspaper notices, nominated assembly candidates and elected delegates to state conferences. These state conventions in turn chose party candidates for Congress and nominated slates of presidential electors. Since the evolution of this machinery was largely the result of party competition, it was most mature in those states where the parties were evenly balanced. In regions of one-party rule partisan organization was still quite primitive. In New England the Federalists, who controlled the state assemblies, continued to use the caucus system of nomination. Among the southern states only Virginia possessed a semblance of a state organization. There, a Republican central committee in Richmond made the key decisions on nominations and policy, and these were usually ratified by legislative caucus. The committee numbered only a half dozen men, and its continuity in membership earned it the nickname "Richmond Junto."

At the county level throughout the South nominating procedures were quite informal. Ambitious members of the gentry announced their candidacy for seats in the assembly through the newspapers, usually taking care to note that their availability was a reluctant surrender to the pleas of numerous friends. Occasionally these self-projected nominations were ratified by county meetings, particularly in areas where the Federalists retained some support. In much of the South, however, the Federalists were quite weak, and Republican candidates often ran unopposed.

Because formal machinery was the product of competition, it reached its highest development in the middle states, where the parties were evenly divided. In presidential elections, the Middle Atlantic states held the balance of power, since New England was generally Federalist and the South remained Republican. These states were the target of intense electioneering by both sides. As a result, New Jersey possessed what may have been the most sophisticated electoral machinery in the nation. In 1812, both parties in that state held nominating conventions where delegates were elected by county meetings open to all voters. These meetings nominated candidates for Congress, drew up slates of presidential electors, and drafted statements of principles that resembled modern platforms. In the use of such devices, however, New Jersey was well in advance of most other states. Even in hotly contested New York the legislature clung to the caucus system of nominating a presidential candidate.

New York, however, did pioneer the development of semi-secret fraternal societies, whose partisan activities complemented those of the county organizations. The most successful of these was the Tammany Society, a social organization dating from pre-Revolutionary times, which Aaron Burr had made into an appendage of the Republican party during the 1790's. By 1812 the "Marling Men" of Tammany virtually controlled New York city elections, and they helped enforce party discipline and regularity in the state. Their success encouraged imitation, and after 1800 "Sons of Tammany" appeared in cities and towns from New England to Ohio. The Federalists at first denounced these organizations as subversive, but they were eventually forced to form their own fraternal orders. The most durable of the Federalist associations were the Washington Benevolent Societies. The first of these was founded in New York on February 22, 1809, and by 1812, similar societies were functioning in nearly every northern state, and as the organization spread, its charitable functions became subordinate to its political operations.

The fraternal societies used by both parties played an important role in mobilizing the electorate. By making membership easy and dues minimal they sought to appeal to a broad spectrum of voters. Their secrecy and ritual appealed to a nation of joiners. On public holidays they organized parades and barbecues to reinvigorate the party faithful. Funds that they collected were turned over to county leaders during election campaigns to finance broadsides, the distribution of printed tickets, and refreshments for voters. In an age when the "ward heeler" was unknown and local party organizations relatively primitive, these voluntary associations helped integrate the common man into the electoral process.

The democratization of nominating procedures through the use of conventions, the evolution of county organizations, and the use of voluntary societies to interest voters were all pretty much confined to the North. In the southern states, the Republicans generally held unchallenged control and felt little need to abandon the traditional caucus method of nomination. Southerners, moreover, dominated the Republican party in Congress, and it was generally assumed that President Madison would be renominated when the party caucus met, as it usually did, toward the end of the congressional session in May. The opposition to Madison within the party was less personal than sectional, the result of northern jealousy over Virginia's stranglehold on the Presidency. For eight years Vice-President George Clinton of New York had been the center of this anti-Virginia sentiment, but his prospects of mounting a challenge to Madison were dimmed by age and ill health (indeed, he died on April 20, 1812). By the early weeks of 1812 the anti-Madison feeling was already focusing on the Vice-President's nephew DeWitt Clinton, lieutenant governor of New York.

Hoping to forestall a Clintonian rebellion, the Republicans in the Virginia assembly caucused in February and nominated a slate of twenty-five electoral candidates pledged to Madison. They had used the same tactic in undermining the Monroe candidacy four years before, and for the moment it seemed to work again. On March 7 the Republican caucus in Pennsylvania endorsed the Madison nomination and published a slate of loyal electors. But if these state endorsements were to have much influence on the congressional caucus, unanimity was required; hence much depended on the response of New York. In that state Governor Daniel D. Tompkins was loyal to Madison, but there was considerable doubt as to whether he could control the Clintonians in the legislature. To avoid a rupture several Republican congressmen dropped hints that DeWitt Clinton might be considered for the Vice-Presidency if his uncle should decline, but the young politician, after a secret meeting with his legislative followers in Albany on March 16, declined to commit himself until he had sounded out his prospects for the top office. He hoped to secure the endorsement of the New York assembly, but that body was prorogued by Governor Tompkins late in March. The governor's excuse was a bribery scandal involving a bill to charter a bank, in which Federalists and some Clintonians had an interest. By the time the New York legislature reassembled in late May the congressional caucus had already met.

The caucus of Republican members of Congress met in the Senate chamber on the evening of May 18. Madison was the unanimous choice of the eighty-two senators and representatives present, although one Clintonian observer did not vote. The surface unanimity, however, masked considerable opposition both to the President and to the caucus system. Fifty-one congressmen failed to attend the meeting, though many of these were out of town. For second place on the ticket the caucus selected John Langdon of New Hampshire, but the Revolutionary War veteran declined because of his age — seventy. The caucus thereupon reassembled and nominated sixty-seven-year-old Elbridge Gerry of Massachusetts. An old friend of John Adams and a former governor, Gerry could be expected to draw some New England votes, yet he was too old to threaten the Virginia succession in 1816. At this second caucus ten more Republicans declared for Madison, giving him the support of more than two-thirds of the congressional party.

On May 29 ninety out of ninety-five Republicans in the New York legislature voted in caucus to nominate DeWitt Clinton. The apparent unity disguised serious misgivings on the part of many who feared the action might disrupt the party. In the midst of the discussion a letter arrived from Postmaster General Gideon Granger, a Connecticut Republican who shared Clinton's aversion to Virginians. Denouncing the Administration for leading the country into war, Granger demanded energetic leadership and firm policies that would shorten the conflict. The letter evidently tipped the balance in favor of Clinton. Waverers were induced to support the nomination for the sake of unity, and the meeting closed with a blast at the whole system of nominating candidates by presidential caucus. The action of the legislative caucus projected Clinton onto the national political stage, but it left the Republican party in New York in shambles. The nomination was denounced by many of the leading Republicans in the state, including Governor Tompkins, Robert R. Livingston, Judge Ambrose Spencer (Clinton's brother-in-law), John Armstrong (soon to be Madison's Secretary of War), and the "Marling Men" of Tammany Hall. It was an inauspicious beginning for a presidential candidacy.

In his early forties, DeWitt Clinton was a rugged, strong-willed politician and an able executive. Historians have often denounced him as unprincipled, but he appears that way only when contrasted with the dogmatic Virginians who had elevated politics into a theology. Clinton was, by nature, an opportunist and a pragmatist, perhaps the first such in our national history to run for President. Though a man of integrity, he lacked profound ideological commitment. The Erie Canal, constructed with government aid in an age of laissez faire, is a fitting monument to his initiative and practicality. Yet amidst a generation that venerated principle above policy and often preferred ideological consistency to progress, Clinton seems oddly out of place, and he was never able to resolve the basic dilemma of his candidacy. Nominated by Republicans who hoped he could shorten the war by firm measures that would force England to the peace table, he had no hope of winning without the support of the Federalists, who demanded an immediate cessation of hostilities. In trying to appeal to both war hawks and pacifists, Clinton earned the distrust of contemporaries and the scorn of historians. The irony is that he probably would have made a better war President than James Madison.

The nomination of Clinton placed the Federalists in a quandary. Uncertain of his attitude toward the war, mistrusting his political principles, the Federalists also realized that they could not hope to defeat Madison without the aid of dissident Republicans. Timothy Pickering, arch-enemy of Jeffersonianism, expressed the Federalist dilemma: "I am far enough from desiring Clinton for President of the United States. I would infinitely prefer another Virginian—if Judge Marshall could be the man. But I would vote for any man in preference to Madison."

Pickering was by no means alone in desiring a Marshall candidacy. The Chief Justice possessed impeccable credentials as a Federalist, and he had the advantage of being a Virginian. The Marshall boomlet appears to have centered in Maryland where Benjamin Stoddert, former Secretary of the Navy under Adams, spent much of the summer writing letters in behalf of the Chief Justice. Stoddert's argument was that any Federalist could carry New England, New York, New Jersey, and Delaware (with 95 electoral votes). The remaining 15 electoral votes needed for victory had to come from Virginia and North Carolina, and the only man able to win support in those two states was Marshall. Robert Smith of Maryland, maverick Republican whom Madison had dismissed as Secretary of State the previous year, wrote to the Chief Justice to sound his views on a potential candidacy. Marshall responded with a denunciation of the conflict and suggested that the old party rivalries be subordinated to the single issue of peace or war. It was a guarded reply that did not completely shut the door on his candidacy, but it also seemed to endorse the idea of fusion with dissident Republicans, such as Clinton.

In the end, the fusion idea won out. Marshall was too valuable to the Federalists as a fixture on the Supreme Court to be sacrificed on the presidential altar, and it seemed likely his candidacy would be just that. The Chief Justice might take a few southern votes away from Madison, but it was very doubtful whether he could carry New York. That state held the key to the election and DeWitt Clinton held the key to New York.

Overtures to Clinton began as early as July when Federalist agents visited the lieutenant governor and received encouragement. Clinton hinted that he was contemplating a complete break with the Administration, even to the extent of making Federalist appointments and relying on the Federalists for advice. These initial soundings culminated on August 5 in a meeting at Morrisania, baronial home of Gouverneur Morris, between Clinton and the Federalist leaders of New York: John Jay, Rufus King, and Morris. The Federalists read aloud a series of resolutions that called for a convention to a peace party. Clinton replied that he agreed with their sentiments but suggested delay. New York Republicans were badly divided on the war issue, and if the military campaigns went badly, peace sentiment in the state would increase. If delayed for four or five weeks, the peace convention would have a better chance of attracting Republican support. In the meantime it would be best, Clinton thought, if his incipient break with the Administration were not publicized, lest it alienate certain key Republicans.

The Federalists came away from the Morrisania meeting only partially satisfied, although they apparently agreed with Clinton that the alliance ought to be kept secret for the time being. Over the next month Clinton remained silent on political affairs, even when news of General Hull's cowardly surrender of Detroit offered the opportunity he had been seeking for an open break with the Administration. At length, the Federalists decided to go ahead with their peace convention, even if it was unlikely that any Republicans would attend. The meeting was decided upon in correspondence among the leaders, and the 1808 convention provided a natural precedent.

With the experience of 1808 to guide them, the meeting was well-planned and shrewdly organized. Delegates were selected by Federalist committees of correspondence in each state, and there was a genuine effort to make it a representative national meeting. The central committee in Philadelphia explained the procedures to a North Carolina Federalist: "The number of delegates is left entirely to yourselves, but it is desirable that the representation from each state should be as weighty as possible in point of talent and influence — comprehending characters from different parts of the state and of different professions."

On September 15, 1812, sixty-four delegates from eleven states assembled in New York City for the convention. Two states that were not represented (Virginia and North Carolina) sent letters of support, and the remainder were southwestern states with no organized Federalist party. It was generally understood that the purpose of the meeting was to endorse Clinton's candidacy; Harrison Gray Otis and the Massachusetts delegates threatened to stay home if any other object were contemplated. Even so, there was much lingering suspicion of Clinton. Rufus King argued that fusion with anti-war Republicans would divide the Federalist party and shatter its independence and integrity. Denouncing Clinton as unprincipled and unscrupulous, King predicted that the Federalists would only be trading a Madison for a Borgia. For two days the delegates contemplated the possible nomination of Marshall or Jay until an impassioned appeal by Harrison Gray Otis carried the day for fusion. In the end, the convention did not formally endorse Clinton; it merely agreed not to put forth a Federalist candidate and to recommend that Federalists throughout the country exert themselves to secure presidential electors who would bring about a change. The rationale, evidently, was that a formal endorsement would only damage Clinton's prospects in the predominantly Republican middle states. Moreover, if the Federalists happened to win an electoral majority, they could then drop Clinton and bring forth a Federalist candidate in the Electoral College.

The Federalist meeting was the closest approximation to a modern party convention prior to the 1830s. It was national in scope, and it met for the purpose of nominating a candidate, or at least agreeing on a party stance. It differed from a modern convention only in its irregular method of selecting delegates and the attempted secrecy of its proceedings. The meeting closed on September 17 after appointing a committee to collect and disseminate information. Composed of Pennsylvania Federalists and quartered in Philadelphia, this committee offered a semblance of a national party organization.

Rufus King's aggressive opposition to Clinton might have opened the way for his candidacy on a strict party ticket, but the only echo came from Virginia. There, plans were well under way for a state party convention even before the New York meeting. Since the Federalists lacked a central committee in Virginia, it was necessary to summon a general convention in order to nominate a slate of twenty-five presidential electors. Federalist newspapers in the state spread the word, and on September 21 a total of thirty-two delegates from eighteen counties assembled in the Shenandoah Valley town of Staunton. It is unlikely that the results of the New York convention had reached Virginia by that date, but the Staunton meeting would not have endorsed the unpopular Clinton in any case. There was, however, substantial disagreement over whether the meeting ought to make any endorsement, other than a slate of electors. A resolution supporting a formal nomination was adopted by the slender margin of 16 to 15. That issue decided, the convention then proceeded without further recorded vote to nominate Rufus King for President and William R. Davie of North Carolina for Vice-President. The meeting then adopted an address which accused the Administration of pro-French bias in the conduct of foreign affairs. The war was unnecessary, but, what was worse, the nation entered it totally unprepared. Hull's surrender of Detroit was a typical example of the Administration's incompetence, for it left "the western wilderness . . . howling with the exulting cry of a savage foe." The meeting closed with a suggested campaign slogan: "Peace, Union and Commerce, and no Foreign Alliance."

The only effect of the Staunton nomination was that Virginians who cast Federalist ballots voted for King, rather than Clinton. In every other state the Federalists supported Clinton, although opposition to the alliance continued to simmer. In late October an exchange of correspondence among New York Republicans was widely printed in the newspapers. Judge Ambrose Spencer (Clinton's brother-in-law) and John W. Taylor (candidate for Congress) wrote to Clinton's chief defender Richard Riker to suggest that Clinton withdraw in favor of King. Clinton's candidacy, they suggested, only served to divide the peace forces and would destroy his future political prospects. In reply, Riker pointed out that Clinton was the choice of the people of New York and any deal with King would be as underhanded and undemocratic as Madison's nomination by congressional caucus. Riker went on to suggest that Clinton was the one chance for preserving the Republican party, since if Madison were reelected the northern wing of the party was likely to break away. It is doubtful that this highly publicized exchange of letters swayed many Republicans; to most people, even in New York, Clinton was the Federalist candidate.

It had long been anticipated that the war would be the primary issue of the campaign, and the alliance between Federalists and Clintonians confirmed it. In New England, where the war was generally unpopular, Federalist support of Clinton was open. Throughout the autumn the Federalist press in the region printed letters that projected Clinton as the one hope for peace. But in the crucial, and evenly divided, middle states more artful methods were necessary.

Among these states New York was the most vital, and it was a committee of New York Clintonians that assumed the direction of the campaign. On August 17 they issued an "Address to the People of the United States" which functioned, for all practical purposes, as Clinton's platform. The cleverly devised document skirted the war issue and sought a broad popular appeal in the North and West. Denouncing the caucus system as "hostile to the spirit of the federal constitution," the address suggested that the method by which Madison was nominated amounted to intervention by the legislature in the executive branch and left the selection of a President to a "junto of Congressmen," instead of the people. Moreover, because the nomination was performed in secret by a small minority, it was subject to possible foreign influence, an accusation that was tailored to the long-standing Federalist fear that Madison was a tool of France.

The address also sought to appeal to the northern jealousy of Virginia, noting that Virginians had controlled the Presidency for twenty out of the twenty-four years since the Constitution was adopted. One result was that the agricultural and commercial states were beginning to be arrayed against each other, and only a candidate from a middle state could hold the balance even and conciliate all interests. Besides being a middle state, New York was also a frontier state, bordering on both Canada and the Ohio valley, and therefore shared with the West the brunt of the fighting. Thus only a New Yorker, such as Clinton, could understand the military needs of the West and conduct the war effectively.

Although the address refrained from denouncing the war in principle, it accused Madison of leading the nation into war completely unprepared, with an untrained, ill supplied army. It also charged that Madison's military advisers were totally inept, and that his policy of financing the war by floating loans rather than raising taxes was utterly irresponsible. Clinton, in contrast, offered the promise of new leadership—"from his energy we anticipate vigor in war, and a determined character in the relations of peace." A change in Administrations would also enable the new President to find "the best talents in the nation to fill the high stations of government." Moreover, since Clinton was not partial to any foreign power, he would be able to negotiate an honorable peace, and peace would benefit the commercial interests and restore national unity. On the whole, it was an effective document, and it formed the text for Clintonian appeals throughout the country. In New York, however, the assembly still retained the power to choose presidential electors, so the outcome in that state depended less on popular appeals than on legislative management.

New Jersey and Pennsylvania chose electors by popular vote; the first was generally hostile to the war, the other enthusiastically supported it. In New Jersey the Federalists seized the initiative in the campaign by summoning a Peace party convention at the end of June. Hoping to attract dissident Republicans, they adopted an address that denounced the caucus system and included on their slate of congressional candidates three Republicans who had voted against the declaration of war. Taken by surprise, the Republicans, who normally held their nominating convention in the autumn, hastily assembled one hundred delegates at Burlington on July 10. This meeting drafted a public address and made arrangements for a formal convention to meet at Trenton in October. To build up party morale and call attention to the democratic nature of the device the Republican meeting at Trenton was publicized as the largest ever held in the state. Over a hundred delegates were formally elected by county meetings open to all voters. When they met at Trenton the Republicans set up a committee consisting of two delegates from each county to draw up a list of nominees for Congress and a slate of presidential electors, while another committee drafted a statement of principles.

Despite this well-organized response, the Federalists retained the initiative in the New Jersey campaign, capitalizing on the antiwar sentiment in the state by disseminating peace tracts and pamphlets attacking Madison. The unpopularity of the President was manifest. In 1808 ten Republican county meetings had endorsed Madison, in 1812 only two named him specifically. To counter this sentiment the President ventured into the campaign by addressing a letter to the New Jersey convention, which was widely circulated in the Republican press. Madison defended the war in general terms and promised an honorable peace. Praising New Jersey's role in the Revolution, he ended the letter with the implied hope that the state would exhibit equal patriotism in the present emergency. It was a dignified but far from stirring appeal.

In Pennsylvania, where the war was generally popular, the Clinton forces had to change their tune. Instead of attacking the war in principle and promising peace, they focused on the Administration's strategy and management of the war. One writer complained that the western armies had been sent into battle "without tents or clothing, ammunition, arms, or money." The surrender of Hull at Detroit in early August sent a shiver of alarm across western Pennsylvania, and Clintonian agents seized the opportunity to make political capital by flooding the mountain counties with pamphlets blaming the Administration for the debacle. On August 26 a secret meeting in Lancaster, presided over by Republican Congressman Joseph Lefever, agreed to support Clinton and adopted an address for distribution across the state. The address denounced the caucus system, criticized the Administration for mishandling the war, and demanded a greater role for Pennsylvania in national councils. It invited county meetings to nominate a slate of Clintonian electors and a vice-presidential candidate. The Lancaster meeting's nominee for Vice-President was Jared Ingersoll, the Federalist attorney general of the state. The few county meetings that responded to the Lancaster appeal seemed to concur in the choice of Ingersoll. Clinton let the nomination stand because it strengthened his chances in the state.

Except for the nomination of Ingersoll, the Clintonian Republicans in Pennsylvania steered clear of the Federalists and refused to denounce the war. The Federalist organization in the state was quite weak. They possessed only one seat out of Pennsylvania's eighteen in the national House of Representatives, and they were active only in Philadelphia and the lower Delaware counties. The Federalist opposition to the war won support among Philadelphia Quakers and merchants whose trade was disrupted, but this was hardly a strong foundation for electoral victory. With Federalist support assured in any case, the Clintonians concentrated on the Administration's handling of the war. A Clintonian meeting in Pittsburgh demanded that the war be "prosecuted with vigour, until the honour of our common country is retrieved, her rights established, and reparation made for the injuries she has sustained." For this a change in Administration was required, for only Clinton could overcome the sectional jealousies provoked by Virginia rule, expunge the foreign influence on our policies, and prosecute the war with energy.

To this novel assault the Madison forces in Pennsylvania had ready answers. The Clintonian slogan of "peace and commerce" was just exactly what the Administration was fighting for; the obstacle to both was not Madison, but Britain. The Madisonians pointed out that Clinton had made no pledges on the war one way or another; his campaign was a combination of sectional jealousy and "artful appeals" on the mode of nomination. The Madison forces were well-organized and active. The Republican correspondence committee in the state issued a steady stream of campaign material that was disseminated by county organizations. On September 16, John Binns, publisher of the *Democratic Press*, issued an eight column reply to the New York Clintonian committee's "Address to the People." Refuting the charge of insufficient preparation, Binns pointed out that no genuinely republican government could effectively prepare for war in time of peace. To preserve a state of constant military readiness would undermine the spirit of the Constitution. Moreover, "to impute to Madison the failure of every military expedition" was to place a burden on his shoulders that even President Washington could not have supported.

In neighboring Ohio the Clinton forces virtually ignored the war issue, though there were scattered complaints that the Administration had left the state badly exposed by failing to construct a navy on the lakes. Instead, Clinton was promoted as the first and ablest advocate for the Erie Canal, which promised great benefit to Ohio in opening new markets and increasing land values. The Clintonian cry of "too much Virginia" also had some appeal among the New England migrants in the state. But Ohio, like the rest of the West, was Republican country, and party regularity kept it in the Madison fold. As one Ohio Republican observed, the Great Canal could not be constructed until the war was over, and the incumbent Administration had a better chance of securing a proper peace.

The farther the Clinton campaign ventured from the centers of antiwar sentiment the more inverted it became. In the South it was positively belligerent. One South Carolina Federalist argued that it was the Federalists who had continually supported military and naval preparations before the war, while the Republicans had rejected armament and then plunged the nation into war. It was a half-truth at best but he insisted that the Federalists did not oppose the defense of American rights: "Far from it, we deplore the existence of this war principally on account of the weakness, the folly and the vices of those men who have dared to engage the country in it, unprepared for defense and totally incapable of offense." The "Peace party," this South Carolinian suggested, was more competent to bring an honorable end to the war because it was not hampered by bias against Britain. And if negotiations failed, it could prosecute the war more effectively because "War brings with it many exigencies, which we are convinced will require more practical wisdom than is to be expected from these speculatists and experimentalists."

In his inimitable style Henry Adams summarized the inconsistencies in the Clinton campaign:

> No canvass for the Presidency was ever less creditable than that of De-Witt Clinton in 1812. Seeking war votes for the reason that he favored more vigorous prosecution of the war; asking support from peace Republi-

cans because Madison had plunged the country into war without preparation; bargaining for Federalist votes as the price of bringing about a peace;
or coquetting with all parties in the atmosphere of bribery in bank
charters, – Clinton strove to make up a majority which had no element of
union but himself and money.

There is much justice in Adams' indictment, but Clinton was in a difficult position. He doubtless felt that the war should never have been undertaken, but,
once begun, it should be prosecuted with efficiency. Convinced that the Administration was unreasonably biased against Britain and subservient to
France, Clinton was certain that only a change in the government could bring
prompt peace negotiations. He was by no means the last wartime candidate to
offer such promises. Unprincipled though his campaign appeared, in the regions where the war was already unpopular it was effective.

In the face of this aggressive campaign on Clinton's behalf, Madison's
efforts seemed languid and desultory. The President relied on the Republican press, led by the *National Intelligencer* to expound his program, but
the newspapers seemed more intent upon exposing the inconsistencies of
Clinton than defending the Administration. To his credit, Madison refused to
curry public favor by dismissing his Secretary of War William Eustis, even
though the incompetent Eustis would have been a convenient scapegoat for
the military disasters of the summer. To Madison the election was a referendum on his foreign policy, the *"experimentum crucis"* as he put it to Jefferson,
and he was convinced that his party would rally around his defense of the nation's honor. Besides his letter to the New Jersey convention, the President's
only foray into the campaign was a letter addressed to the South Carolina
assembly in September. Replying to the assembly's address of August 28 in
support of the war, Madison acknowledged their "Fidelity to the national
rights and sensibility to the national character. It is a war worthy of such a
determination," he continued. "Having its origin neither in ambition or in vain
glory, and for its object neither an interest of the Government distinct from
that of the People, nor an interest of part of the people in opposition to the
welfare of the whole." Implying that the Clintonian opposition was hampering
his conduct of the war and efforts toward peace, the President informed South
Carolina that if its loyalty and patriotism were emulated by other states it
would help speed "the blessings of a just and Honourable peace."

The campaign rambled on through the autumn of 1812, as each state
appointed its own date for balloting. The method of choosing presidential
electors varied widely. In five states (New Hampshire, Rhode Island, Pennsylvania, Virginia, and Ohio) electors were chosen by popular ballot on a statewide basis, with the winner taking the entire electoral vote of the state. In
four states (Massachusetts, Maryland, Tennessee, and Kentucky) the electors
were chosen by districts, and thus the vote in those states could be divided
between the candidates. In the remaining nine states the legislatures chose
electors, although in several the legislature was elected in the course of the
presidential campaign and hence presumably reflected the attitude of the voters toward the national election.

Antiwar New England went to Clinton, with the exception of Vermont. Even in the 1790s Vermont had exhibited Jeffersonian tendencies that disturbed Federalists elsewhere in New England, and by 1812 Republicans controlled both the legislature and the executive. On the declaration of war the state's congressional delegation divided along party lines, the three Republicans supporting the war and the lone Federalist (from the northern district that had been trading with Canada) opposing it. The war was generally popular in Vermont, and in the state elections held in September, 1812, the Republicans won a decisive victory. The new legislature met in October and promptly delivered the state's 6 electoral votes to Madison. It was well that they acted quickly, for the war fever in Vermont waned rapidly as the populace began to feel the pinch of the wartime restrictions on their trade with Canada. In the elections the following year the Federalists returned to power.

Because presidential electors were chosen by the legislature, it is difficult to analyze the vote in Vermont. Moreover, the statistics for the legislative election are incomplete; hence, the best barometer of voter sentiment was perhaps the gubernatorial election of September, 1812. The incumbent governor was a Republican, Jonas Galusha, who firmly supported both the war and the Administration; he was opposed by Martin Chittenden, the Federalist congressman who had cast Vermont's only vote against the war. It is difficult to determine the extent to which the contest revolved upon national issues, but the war does not seem to have hampered Galusha. He defeated Chittenden by a vote of 19,158 to 15,950, a greater plurality than he had received when he beat Chittenden in 1811. Except for Windham County in the southeast corner of the state along the Connecticut River, the Federalist majorities were in the counties that bordered Canada and Lake Champlain. The people of this region disliked the war because it wrecked their profitable trade with Canada and exposed them to attack.

A similar pattern emerged in New Hampshire where Federalist/Clintonian support was strongest in the border counties of the north and on the seacoast. Republicans had controlled the state (with the exception of the embargo years) since 1806, and there was an all-Republican delegation in the Twelfth Congress. Opposition to the embargo had induced New Hampshire to give its electoral votes to the Federalist Charles Cotesworth Pinckney in 1808, and popular disapproval of the war gave the Federalists a new lease on life in 1812. The gubernatorial election held in March of that year was so close that it ended up in the state legislature where the Republican majority installed its candidate William Plumer. Detecting the drift of public sentiment, two of the state's Republican congressmen broke ranks and voted against the declaration of war in June. The Federalists in the state sent two delegates to the New York convention in September, and during the autumn they campaigned hard for the "peace party" ticket. In an effort to attract antiwar Republicans they distributed pamphlets and handbills claiming that prominent Republicans in Pennsylvania and New York were supporting Clinton.

In the presidential canvass held in November New Hampshire balloted on a statewide basis. Of 34,800 votes cast the eight Clintonian electors won with votes that varied from 20,386 to 18,839. A comparison with the vote in the gubernatorial election of the preceding spring reveals the impact of the war. The total popular vote increased by about 8 per cent, reflecting a heightened interest in the national election, but the Federalist increase was half again as great as the Republican. Madison carried only two counties (Hillsborough and Cheshire in the southwest quarter of the state), both by about the same margin as the Republican governor Plumer. The populous seacoast county of Rockingham went to Clinton by the same margin that it had gone Federalist in the spring election. The big Federalist gain was in the three counties that composed the northern two-thirds of the state, and in northernmost Coos county in the White Mountains the Republican vote actually declined from spring to fall. Remote, provincial, deeply religious, and traditionally Federalist, these interior counties had little interest in a war for "free trade and sailors' rights" and probably shared the Vermonters' fear of invasion. Confirming the peace party victory in the fall elections was a complete turnover in the state's congressional delegation. All six Representatives elected to the Thirteenth Congress were Federalists, including an articulate young lawyer named Daniel Webster.

While an interesting regional pattern of voting appeared in northern New England, southern New England was solidly Federalist. The Republican party had not made any substantial inroads into either Connecticut or Rhode Island, and both states opposed the war because it disrupted their trade. Clinton carried both handily. Massachusetts, on the other hand, possessed a strong Republican party, but it was decimated by the election. The Republicans had made steady inroads in Massachusetts since the 1790s. They managed to survive the temporary setback of the embargo, and in the state elections of 1811 they elected Elbridge Gerry governor, won control of the assembly, and claimed half the state's congressional delegation. But as war approached, Republican fortunes began to decline. In the spring election of 1812 Josiah Strong defeated Gerry (though by the narrow margin of 1,370 votes out of a total of 104,000) and the Federalists regained control of the state House of Representatives. Hoping to salvage something in the presidential contest, the Republican-controlled Senate insisted on passing a new electoral law. Under the general ticket law in effect the Federalists were almost certain to capture the entire electoral vote of the state. After much haggling, the legislature in October, 1812, divided the state into six districts and apportioned the twenty-two electors among them.

The Republican strategy of dividing the state's electoral vote failed to work, for the Federalists swept every district in the November balloting. The most significant feature of the Massachusetts canvass was the decline in the number of voters from April to November. Despite intense campaigning by both sides and the importance of national issues, there were 26,765 fewer voters in November. Several factors help account for this, one being that in the April gubernatorial election there was an unusually high voter turnout — 68 per cent of the adult males (compared with 55 per cent in the previous year). And a suffrage qualification of one year's residence was required for the national election but not for the state election. Nonetheless, it is clear that the most important factor accounting for the decline in voter participation was the war. In Massachusetts the war was almost the only issue in the election. Though six of the state's congressmen voted for the declaration, the war was generally unpopular, even among Republicans (all six congressmen were defeated in the fall election). The fusion between Federalists and Clintonians was more solid than in any other state, the old party labels being replaced by "peace party" and "war party" on the published tickets.

In the course of the decade since Jefferson's election the Republicans had built a strong party in Massachusetts, based upon the small farmers of the interior, many of them religious dissenters, and the rising merchants of the seaboard. Geographically they were strongest in the mountainous west, in Maine, and on the seaboard south of Boston (Norfolk, Plymouth, and Barnstable counties). And it was precisely in these counties that the Republican vote declined most drastically from April to November, 1812. In the mountain counties of Berkshire and Hampden, and in populous Middlesex in the east, all of which Gerry won by substantial majorities in April, the Republican vote declined by half in the national election. There was no corresponding increase in the peace vote, however, which suggests that many Republicans, unable to stomach Clinton, expressed their distaste for the war by staying home. In the Southeast, on the other hand, the Clinton vote increased in rough proportion to the Republican decline. One Cape Cod Republican explained the success of Clinton's fusion candidacy to a Boston correspondent:

> You express surprise at our votes. We are not changed in principle — we are still Republicans. . . .
> It is not a question, whether the war is just or unjust. — We all agree in one point, viz. '— That our present rulers are not the men to carry it on. — We want energy in War — or honorable Peace — we believe that respectable Republican DeWitt Clinton, equal to effect either. Certainly a more advantageous Peace can be made by a third man, than by the first parties in a war.

Traditionally Republican Maine was closely divided, but the only county Madison won was tiny Oxford on the Canadian border. Most of the interior towns remained Republican, but the exposed seacoast voted for peace. In the state as a whole Clinton's total of 50,254 was not far from the 52,696 Federalist votes garnered by Strong the previous spring, but Madison's 27,003 was a long way short of Governor Gerry's 51,326. For the President the war was a political disaster in Massachusetts.

While Clinton was winning handily in the New England states where presidential electors were chosen by popular vote, he had much more difficulty controlling his own home state of New York where the choice was still in the hands of the legislature. Elections for a new assembly were held in April, 1812, and it was a close contest. The Federalists benefited from the rising sentiment against the war, and the Republicans were hampered by poor organization and internal differences. When the new assembly met in late October, the Republicans had a slim majority of 74 to 67 on a joint ballot of the two houses. Pursuant to their agreement to avoid public support of Clinton, Federalists put up their own slate of electoral candidates. If they won it was possible that they would abandon Clinton and support a Federalist in the Electoral College. To overcome the Federalist challenge required Republican unity, but, unhappily for Clinton, about twenty of the Republican assemblymen favored Madison. Worse yet, the Madisonians threatened that they would refuse to vote unless Madison were given a fair share (at least a third) of the Republican electoral slate. This would have divided the New York vote and ruined Clinton's prospects. But a Madisonian defection would have permitted the Federalists to win. To preserve Republican unity, defeat the Federalists, and install a solidly Clintonian slate of electors required a high order of political craft. Luckily for him, Clinton found the manager he needed.

Among the new members of the legislature was Senator Martin Van Buren, twenty-nine-year-old lawyer from Kinderhook. In October, shortly before the legislative session opened, Clinton appointed Van Buren his floor manager for the Republican caucus. It seemed a choice born of desperation, for Van Buren lacked any sort of legislative experience, though he brought with him a reputation for political guile. For Van Buren, a supporter of Madison and a proponent of the war, the decision to aid Clinton was even stranger. Van Buren's rationale was that Clinton was the nominee of the New York caucus, and party regularity was the essence of his politics. No doubt the young senator was also quite flattered at Clinton's offer, and the lieutenant governor was the biggest power in the state. Van Buren realized that Clinton could not win this presidential election, but he felt him a good prospect for the contest of 1816. An alliance with Clinton was a good political bet.

The Republican caucus met on the eve of the legislative session in early November. Van Buren sought to soothe the dissidents by nominating a Madison supporter to chair the meeting. He then offered a resolution that the caucus support the entire Clinton slate of electors. Outraged, the Madison men demanded minority representation, and the chairman stomped out of the hall. Van Buren calmly replaced him with a Clintonian, cut off debate by moving the previous question, and pushed through his resolution by majority vote. He then insisted that the decision of the caucus be followed in the name of party unity. In the end, he was only able to persuade the angry supporters of Madison to cast blank ballots. This would have been disastrous had a number of Federalists not broken party ranks (possibly after talks with Van Buren) and voted for the Clintonian slate. The final tally in the legislature was 74 votes for the Clinton electors, 45 for the Federalists, and 22 blanks. It won Clinton New York and it helped earn for Van Buren the title of "little magician."

The same sort of underhanded tactics helped Clinton win in New Jersey. The state was a Republican stronghold which Madison had carried easily in 1808. In the state elections of 1811 the Federalists managed to win only one county, Burlington, in the center of the state. But by the summer of 1812 the situation was reversed. The Federalists seized the initiative by holding a party convention in June, and they maintained their momentum through the autumn campaign. They capitalized on popular suspicion of Virginia, they appealed to the democratic hostility toward the caucus system of party nominations, and they flooded the state with antiwar literature. Fusion between Federalists and Clintonians was more complete than in any state except Massachusetts, and the "peace party" conducted a clever campaign, focusing its efforts on those counties that were evenly divided.

The New Jersey election was conducted in two stages. The legislative election was held in October and the popular balloting for presidential electors took place in November. In the state elections the Federalists won a narrow victory. The Republicans had a statewide popular majority of about 4000, but their vote was concentrated in two large counties in the North, Essex and Sussex. The Federalists carried most of the rest of the state (except for Salem and Cumberland on the lower Delaware) and emerged with a majority in the legislature. They controlled the Council, or upper house, by 7 to 6 and the assembly by 23 to 17. In a joint sitting of the two houses Federalists outnumbered Republicans 30 to 23. When the new assembly met, just a week before the scheduled presidential election, the Federalists altered the electoral law, placing the choice of electors in the hands of the legislature. This assured the choice of a Clintonian slate of eight electors. They then proceeded to rearrange the congressional districts to give maximum advantage to Federalist candidates, and added insult to injury by dropping two of the three antiwar Republicans they had endorsed in June. In the November election the Federalists won four of New Jersey's six seats in the House of Representatives.

The change in New Jersey from popular to legislative selection of electors prohibits analysis of the vote in the presidential contest. However, the state election of October, 1812, was fought largely on national issues and hence provides a fair barometer of public attitudes. The following table lists the vote in four counties for which records are available. The vote for the legislative council in 1812 is compared with the popular vote in the presidential election of 1808:

		Federalist	Republican	Per cent of eligibles voting
Essex County (Newark	1808	378	2744	61%
vicinity)	1812	0	2282	42%
Sussex County	1808	1747	2085	76%
(Northwest)	1812	1426	2460	73%
Hunterdon County (Trenton and upper	1808	2043	2123	88%
Delaware Valley)	1812	2208	2257	88%
Middlesex County	1808	1590	1280	74%
(Raritan valley)	1812	1776	1423	79%

Even though the sample is quite limited, it covers the major geographical regions of the state, and it does offer some instructive figures. The most striking feature is the extremely high percentage of eligible voters who turned out at the polls. This suggests the intensity of public interest, even in the legislative contest of 1812, and it testifies to the sophisticated level of party organization and propaganda. Yet the level of voter participation varied widely. In Republican Essex and Sussex counties there is a marked decline in voters, indicating that substantial numbers of Republicans preferred to express their dissatisfaction with the war by staying home, a phenomenon also noted in Massachusetts. In Hunterdon County, where the two parties were almost evenly divided, voter participation remained at a fantastically high level. In that area both parties evidently made strenuous efforts to mobilize the electorate. Although the Republicans won the race the Federalists showed the greatest increase in votes from 1808 to 1812, again suggesting the unpopularity of the war. In contrast to the decline in voter participation in the Republican counties, there was a significant increase in Federalist Middlessex County. Since both parties increased their vote totals by similar margins, it does not appear that there was any crossover by dissident Republicans, but it does confirm the polarizing effect of the war issue.

The campaign in New Jersey was a complex one. The Federalists were able to garb themselves in a mantle of democracy by denouncing the caucus system and utilizing nominating conventions. Moreover they obscured the war issue by promising to do their constitutional duties toward national defense if elected. Although antiwar sentiment in the state seriously hampered Republicans, it is highly probable that Madison would have carried the state had the Federalists not altered the electoral law. In doing so, Federalists violated their own democratic promises and compromised their future prospects. Moreover, their peace platform proved to be of only short-term value, for New Jersey soon rallied to the war effort. In the legislative elections of 1813 the Federalists were turned away, never again to be an important factor in the politics of the state.

Pennsylvania, like New Jersey, held its canvass in two stages—a state and local election on October 13 and popular balloting for presidential electors on October 30. Both parties regarded the state as crucial and campaigning was intense. The state's congressional delegation voted 16 to 2 in favor of the declaration of war (one of the opponents was a Clintonian Republican and the other a Federalist), and the war was generally popular in the state. Clinton, however, was able to capitalize on the military disasters of the previous summer and anti-Virginia sentiment. In the state elections of October 13 the Federalists scored modest gains, increasing their seats in the assembly from eleven to eighteen (out of a total of ninety-five) and retaining their one congressional seat. A few days later the Clintonians published their slate of electoral candidates. The list included a number of prominent Republicans, including former governor Thomas McKean. On October 17 a Federalist party committee announced its support of Clinton. That induced several Republicans to refuse to serve on the Clintonian electoral slate, and the committee had to revise its ticket periodically down to the eve of the election.

In the presidential balloting of October 30 Madison won a decisive victory. Of the forty-five counties in the state only five gave majorities to Clinton, and four of those were in the formerly Federalist southeastern part of the state. The electors pledged to Madison averaged 48,946 votes, while the Clinton electors averaged only 29,056. In percentage terms Madison's majority was a resounding 63 per cent. Yet even in Pennsylvania the war was a liability for the Administration. Madison's total was about 10,000 fewer votes than he had obtained in 1808, when he carried every county but one.

In Pennsylvania Madison's margin was slimmest in the mountain counties of the west, a region which for two decades had been a stronghold of Republicanism. The support for Clinton reflected dissatisfaction with the course of the war in the west and the hope that a change in administrations might infuse new energy into the army. The same feeling gave Clinton an opportunity in predominantly Republican Ohio, a state that had entered the war with considerable misgivings. One of its two senators voted against the declaration on the grounds that it would expose the frontier to Indian raids. Many in Ohio felt that war should have been delayed until the nation was better prepared, and the military reversals of the summer confirmed their worst fears. Clinton catered to this sentiment by promising a more vigorous prosecution of the war. He also managed to receive the endorsement of the state's tiny Federalist party, which put up a slate of Clintonian electors.

To add to Republican woes the party in Ohio was internally divided between supporters and opponents of the local Tammany societies. Each faction put up its own slate of electoral candidates, though both were pledged to Madison. Ohio's eight presidential electors were chosen by statewide voting on November 11. The ticket representing the Tammany Republicans received votes varying from 7,420 to 5,732, with the average about 6,300. On the anti-Tammany ticket Madison picked up an additional 1,051 votes. The leading Clintonian elector received 3,301 votes; the lowest got 3,111. Both parties trailed their vote totals of 1808, though the Republicans showed the biggest decline. In Ohio it was apparently a case of countervailing liabilities — the war hanging over Madison's head and Clinton's inconsistencies discouraging the Federalists. Even so, the President's majority — 72 per cent of the vote for the leading electoral candidates — was impressive enough.

The results of the Ohio canvass trickled in through the month of November, and in the meantime attention focused on the upper South. After failing to carry Pennsylvania, Clinton had to capture Delaware, Maryland, and North Carolina to win because Madison had a firm hold on the rest of the South. Of these three states he could count only on Delaware. With the exception of a Republican governor elected in 1810, the state had been in the grasp of the Federalists since 1804. Commercial New Castle County in the north was marginally Republican, but the remainder of the state was a land of prosperous, intensely religious farmers who voted more by habit than by interest or issues. Clinton had little difficulty winning the state, though Madison carried New Castle.

Maryland was more evenly divided, and the campaign there was further confused by local issues. The political division of the state tended to follow geographical lines. The eastern shore of Chesapeake Bay and the Potomac

Valley was traditionally Federalist, while the remainder of the state was generally Republican. Since 1800 Republicans had made steady progress in expanding their control. The state chose its presidential electors by districts, and in 1808 Madison won by 9 to 2. By 1812 the Republicans controlled both houses of the assembly, the governorship, and possessed a 6 to 3 majority on the state's congressional delegation. Madison could anticipate another comfortable margin in the presidential election. But then disaster struck. On July 27 a Republican mob in Baltimore attacked the newspaper office of Alexander C. Hanson's *Federal Republican*. Hanson was one of the Federalist leaders in the state and a violent opponent of the war. While Republican city officials stood by helplessly, the rioters murdered a Revolutionary War hero, General James M. Lingan, and seriously injured other prominent Federalists. Hanson himself escaped only by pretending to be dead.

The result of the Baltimore riot was a public reaction of sympathy toward the Federalist martyrs. Also involved in the issue was planter suspicion of city mobs and rural hostility to the influence of Baltimore in the politics of the state. Resolutions condemning the riot were passed by meetings in almost every county. The *Federal Republican* (temporarily reestablished in Georgetown) kept the issue boiling for months by publishing personal accounts from suffering Federalists. The political impact was soon evident. In the state elections held in October the Federalists won control of the House of Delegates by the substantial majority of 54 to 26.

The victory in the state elections improved the prospects for the Federalists in the presidential canvass of November, but they threw away much of their advantage by extremism and internal bickering. The Maryland Federalists were never enthusiastic supporters of Clinton. They much preferred a southern candidate such as Marshall on the grounds that the only way Madison could be "dethroned" was by "breaking in upon his stronghold, the Country south and west of the Potomac." The moderates were also annoyed by Hanson's unnecessarily provocative editorials and tended to blame him for the Baltimore fracas. When the state's delegates to the New York Federalist convention, headed by Congressman Robert Goodloe Harper, agreed to support Clinton, a number of moderate Federalists, led by young Roger B. Taney, bolted from the Hanson-Harper leadership. The refusal of the moderates to endorse Clinton weakened the Federalist campaign and left the party permanently divided.

The state's eleven presidential electors were chosen by popular vote in nine electoral districts (the Baltimore-Annapolis district and the western district each chose two electors). In the November balloting Maryland was the only state to divide its electoral vote: 6 for Madison, 5 for Clinton. The use of the district system permitted a certain amount of gerrymandering that distorts the picture. (Madison picked up 2 electoral votes on the predominantly Federalist eastern shore by building heavy majorities in two counties.) But if viewed by counties rather than districts, the popular vote reveals an interesting sectional pattern. The lower eastern shore and the entire Potomac Valley were Federalist/Clintonian, while the upper part of Chesapeake Bay (on both eastern and western shores) was Republican. The decline in Republican support in direct ratio to distance from Baltimore and Annapolis probably reflected rural distrust of the city in the wake of the summer's riots. Moreover, the eastern shore and the mountainous west were traditional strongholds of Federalism, partly out of sectional jealousy over western shore domination of the state. The Federalist gains in the previously Republican lower western shore may also have resulted from dissatisfaction with the war and the loss of grain markets.

The vote in Virginia, though overwhelmingly Republican, evidenced a regional pattern similar to Maryland's. Virginia Federalism was a sectional phenomenon, confined almost exclusively to the eastern shore and the upper Potomac and Shenandoah Valleys. But, despite the domination of both state and national governments by Virginia Republicans, it had proved surprisingly durable since 1800. In 1808 the Virginia Federalists divided their vote between Charles Cotesworth Pinckney and the dissident Republican candidate, James Monroe. The remainder of the state—lower Tidewater, Piedmont, and mountainous southwest—was solidly Republican, though the Republicans seemed divided among themselves by John Randolph's continued course of opposition in Congress. On the declaration of war Randolph joined the four valley Federalists in opposition, while thirteen Republicans supported it (with four abstentions).

Virginia's twenty-four electors were chosen on the basis of statewide voting, which took place on November 2. Because of the vast distances in the state, however, it was three weeks before the results were completely tabulated. As a result of the Staunton meeting in September, the Federalist slate of electors was technically pledged to Rufus King, though it is likely that if they had won they would have swung to Clinton in the Electoral College. Of the seventy-nine counties and three boroughs which reported election results (there are no exact returns for two counties), King carried only thirteen. He received a sizable minority vote, (more than 40 per cent) in three others, but in the remainder his support was miniscule. In thirty-two counties, or nearly half the state, Madison received 90 to 100 per cent of the vote. The total popular vote stood at 15,050 for Madison and 4,650 for King.

When the Chesapeake region is viewed as a unit, the sectional pattern of voting becomes clear. The peninsula between the Delaware and Chesapeake Bays (composed of Delaware and the eastern shores of Maryland and Virginia) was predominantly Federalist. Indeed, it had been the center of Federalism ever since ratification of the Constitution. In its economy and social structure this region did not differ materially from the counties on the western shore of Chesapeake Bay; hence, its voting pattern must be attributed partly to sectional jealousy. It voted Federalist because its rivals across the bay, who dominated the state governments in both Virginia and Maryland, were Republicans. The other major center of Federalism was the Potomac-Shenandoah watershed. This region was bound into a commercial and political unit by the Potomac, which provided a channel of communication and an outlet for the export of its cereal grains. The commercial hub of this region was Alexandria,

Virginia, and Georgetown, Maryland, and both cities possessed strong Federalist organizations. In addition, the counties along the Allegheny in Maryland and Virginia, as well as the Shenandoah Valley, shared with the eastern shore a sectional rivalry with the "low country" Republican planters who governed the state.

The center of Republicanism in both Maryland and Virginia was the Tidewater counties on the western shore and the tobacco-growing Piedmont. In Virginia the Ohio River counties and the mountainous southwest were also heavily Republican. This was a region of small, remote farms, many outside the market economy, and their outlook was traditionally western, provincial, and Jeffersonian.

The fact that voting in the Chesapeake region followed sectional patterns that had persisted with fair consistency since the 1790's suggests that party regularity and voting habits were more important in 1812 than immediate issues. The issues of the campaign did have some effect, however. Federalist strength in both Virginia and Maryland had been declining since 1800. The increased Federalist vote in 1812, particularly on the eastern shore and lower Potomac, indicated hostility to the war in an area exposed to amphibious attacks. In Maryland it was also the product of anti-urban feeling resulting from the Baltimore riots. This sentiment may also have affected northern Virginia, since one of the Federalist "martyrs" at Baltimore was a Virginia war hero, Henry Lee.

North Carolina was similarly divided by persistent regional patterns of partisan interest. The state was predominantly Republican, from the tobacco-growing Roanoke Valley to the wheat and cattle farms of the western hills. The center of Federalist strength was the Cape Fear River Valley, a region populated originally by Highland Scots. Like the Potomac watershed, the Cape Fear was a land of prosperous plantations producing timber and naval stores for an export market. On the declaration of war the state divided along partisan lines. Six Republican congressmen voted for war (with three absent or abstaining), while the two Federalists opposed it. One maverick Republican, Richard Stanford, whose district included Federalist Fayetteville, voted against the war.

Neither partisan allegiance nor the war issue had much effect on the state's vote in the presidential election, however, for the Republican assembly abolished the popular choice of electors in 1811. Since 1803 the state had voted for presidential electors under the district system, but that method had given the Federalist Pinckney 3 of the state's 14 electoral votes in 1808. To prevent such Federalist inroads, the Republican-controlled legislature in 1811 abolished the district system and placed the selection of presidential electors in its own hands. The tactic was not uncommon, but in North Carolina such blatant and undemocratic partisanship created a popular furor. The electoral issue dominated the state elections in the summer of 1812, and more than half the assembly was turned out of office. Benefiting from the popular reaction, Federalists made substantial gains in the August election, and the two parties seemed almost evenly balanced in the new assembly. It was this body, meeting in November, which would choose the state's presidential electors.

Federalist tactics in the presidential contest were designed to capitalize on their sudden and unfamiliar popularity. At the end of August the North Carolina Federalists committed themselves to Clinton's candidacy in the hope of attracting dissident Republicans in the legislature. To further this end they suggested that the Federalist campaign committee in Philadelphia suspend the nomination of a vice-presidential candidate until they sounded out prominent North Carolina Republicans for the post. The targets of this Federalist effort at fusion were Governor William Hawkins and Congressman Nathaniel Macon. Neither man was notably close to Madison and both, at one time or another, had been at odds with the Administration. The effort was doomed to failure, however, for Hawkins was an ardent war hawk and Macon was more devoted to Jeffersonian principles than even the President himself. The northern supporters of Clinton recognized this and proceeded with the nomination of the Pennsylvanian Ingersoll.

The Federalist effort at fusion in North Carolina was coupled with demands that the governor summon the assembly into special session to repeal the 1811 law. By returning to the district system they hoped to capture a portion (at least 3 and possibly 6) of the state's electoral vote. Governor Hawkins, however, demonstrated his party loyalty by refusing to call the session, thereby letting the 1811 alteration stand until after the presidential election.

While Pennsylvania and Ohio were still in doubt, the possibility of taking North Carolina greatly improved Clinton's chances of winning the election. And the uncertain balance of parties in the new assembly made the possibility a very real one. Through the early autumn the Clintonian forces in the north had hopes of capturing the state, but unfortunately they overplayed their hand. By early November rumors were circulating in Raleigh about an attempt to bribe fourteen members of the legislature in Clinton's behalf. The rumors were sparked by two suspicious characters, who arrived in Raleigh from New York and then departed mysteriously. Whether any money changed hands mattered little; the rumors seriously embarrassed the Federalists.

When the assembly met on November 16, the House of Commons selected a Republican speaker by the narrow vote of 64 to 59. The Federalist candidate doubtless received some support from Republicans unhappy with the electoral law, but the vote nonetheless suggested the close division of the lower house and boosted Clintonian hopes. It was thus a great surprise when the legislature in joint session on November 21 chose a Republican slate of fifteen electors by the substantial margin of 130 to 60. The Raleigh *Minerva*, a Federalist paper, complained that a secret Republican caucus had forced the dissidents into line. Probably more important was Federalist embarrassment over the bribery rumors. About twenty Federalists voted for the Republican slate on the grounds "that as agents were at hand to buy their voices, they must, to prove their incorruptibility, vote for Madison."

With news of North Carolina's decision coming on the heels of slowly accumulating returns from Ohio, Madison's reelection was assured. The lower South was firmly Republican. South Carolina was the most warlike state of all, and the Federalist party there had been moribund for a decade. In the October assembly elections the Republicans carried previously Federalist Charleston by a substantial margin, and elsewhere the Federalists were decimated. In many parishes they did not even bother to run candidates. On December 1 the legislature appointed a slate of eleven presidential electors, who met the following day and voted unanimously for Madison and Gerry. In Georgia, Kentucky, Tennessee, and Louisiana, the people were loyal to the President and supported the war enthusiastically. In none of the four states did Clinton receive more than a few scattered votes. The final tally was 128 electorial votes for Madison, 89 for Clinton.

It was the closest presidential contest since 1800, and it is clear that the war was a liability for the Administration. If Clinton had carried just one more state—Pennsylvania—he would have won. It is equally clear that the effort at fusion between Federalists and antiwar Republicans was a success. In 1808, when Madison was saddled with the unpopular embargo, he defeated a regular Federalist candidate, Charles Cotesworth Pinckney, by the substantial margin of 112 to 47. It is true that in the legislative and gubernatorial elections the Federalists won more states than Clinton did, but Clinton helped assure them the crucial vote of New York. Had Madison faced a regular Federalist candidate in 1812 it is likely that New York, despite substantial antiwar sentiment, would have gone Republican. At the state level, fusion with dissident Republicans helped the Federalists to carry Massachusetts and New Jersey, and it made them a threat in Pennsylvania and North Carolina.

The other significant feature of the 1812 election was its sectional character. Madison got only 6 electoral votes (Vermont's) north and east of the Delaware River; Clinton got only 9 votes in the south (all in Delaware and Maryland). It was the most sectionally oriented presidential election prior to 1860. The division of the nation reflected the division in popular sentiment toward the war, and it was thus a temporary phenomenon. On the other hand, it was the sectional nature of their support that ultimately contributed to the demise of the Federalists. Despite their experiments in popular appeal during the election campaign, the Federalists became increasingly tied to New England regionalism. Their opposition to the war made them vulnerable to the accusation of disloyalty, and their states' rights provincialism ran contrary to the surge of nationalism fostered by the war. As a result, the Federalist party withered rather quickly after the war, and the nation experienced a period of one-party rule under the triumphant Republicans.

Appendix

The Clinton Platform
1812

The closest approximation to a "platform" for the Clintonian campaign appeared in an "Address to the People of the United States," dated August 17, 1812, and drafted by the New York Committee of Correspondence for Clinton.

Fellow-Citizens

The most important interest of the United States are interwoven with the acts of their chief magistrate. Every citizen has, therefore, a deep concern in the choice of that high officer, and an undeniable right to lay his reflections on that subject respectfully, but with freedom, before the community, of which he is a member. — On that broad basis we might perhaps justify this address, and trust to the correctness of the principles we maintain, for vindication with our countrymen; but we are induced to present ourselves by another, and we think a sufficient consideration.

The state of New York has, by an open nomination of a candidate for the presidency, entered its formal protest against the practice of congressional nominations. Convinced as we are of the superior worth and qualifications of Mr. Clinton, we are also impelled by the sincerest respect to the federal constitution; by our desire to preserve the sovereignty of the states, as guaranteed and marked out by that instrument; by a regard to the rights of the people and to the freedom of election, to maintain her in the stand she has taken.

The general committee of correspondence on the part of the state, have appointed us a select committee to explain and vindicate the grounds on which the nomination has been made, and to aid in carrying it into effect. We have accepted the trust, and shall perform it at least with fidelity. The fear of criticism and censure shall not overawe the sense of duty, nor silence the strong convictions of our judgements. Our interests and obligations, whether as citizens of this state, or of this confederation, have, we know, a reciprocal relation; and we cannot be true to the one, without diligently discharging the other.

Nevertheless, we feel much restraint and embarassment in thus appearing before the American nation; we are sensible of the delicacy of the undertaking, and enter upon it with diffidence and solicitude. While most anxious to avoid blame, and to obtain consideration only through the purity of our motives, and the soundness of our opinions, we anticipate harsh animadversions: we shall be held up to the scrupulous as rash, and to the formal as innovators: our appeal to your tribunal will be stigmatized as presumptuous: our sincere

273

persuasions on subjects of national concern will be imputed to unworthy motives; will be treated with levity by some, and opposed with bitterness by many.

We are, however, convinced that those will be loudest in their invectives, whose interests are engaged, or whose prejudices have been enlisted against the cause we espouse, and in favor of the doctrines we conceive our duty to dispute. — Does the Mussulman who venerates the Koran, and bows before the crescent, abide the scrutiny of the understanding, or weigh the force of argument, when he reviles the christian infidel that rejects the Mahometan faith?

Free citizens of America, be not deceived by such as, wrapping themselves up in the mantle of infallibility, disdain to inquire after truth by the sober light of reason, or to learn wisdom in the school of experience: distrust those who shrink from investigation, because it is their interest to maintain prevailing tenets, and to continue existing practices; examine national questions for yourselves: decide upon them according to the counsel of your own unbiassed judgments.

We have said that the state of New York has entered its protest against congressional nominations. In doing so, it has acted wisely. *The nomination of a candidate for the presidency of the United States by an association of members of Congress, convened at the seat of government, is hostile to the spirit of the federal constitution, dangerous to the rights of the people, and to the freedom of election.*

Whoever examines that constitution with attention, will perceive that the election of the president is intended to be made, not by the *people* of the United States, in the sense in which they may be said to choose the members of the house of representatives; but by the *states composing the union, in their separate sovereign capacities,* each state voting in the ratio of its population.

The unbiassed exercise of this invaluable right of state sovereignty has been guarded in that instrument with jealous care. "No senator or representative, or person holding an office of trust or profit under the United States, shall be appointed an elector." Even a state, in delegating its own *sovereign right,* is restrained from confiding its power to any person connected with the congress of the general government.

Permit us now to ask, did this pointed exclusion of the individuals composing congress, or interested in the general government, from participating in the election of president merely contemplate the averting of corrupt influence? Even if that were its only object, no evasion of it should be tolerated; but we believe it further and more particularly aimed, at maintaining the authority and rights of the individual states; and we are confirmed in that opinion by observing that where the members of the house of representatives are, from necessity, permitted to interfere in the election, they are compelled to vote *by states.* The constitution thus, in every case, maintaining the principle that the chief magistrate is to be chosen by the states, in their separate, sovereign capacities.

It is perfectly manifest, therefore, that those who compose a congressional caucus are, except in one event, and that in the last extremity, excluded by the express words of the constitution, from intermedding in the election of a president. Can their attempt then in the first instance, to nominate the candidate for that office, be consistent with its spirit? Who should nominate? Some among the states which enjoy the constitutional right to elect. Surely none of those persons whose interference is cautiously prohibited as teeming with danger, and who are therefore made subject to an incapacity imposed upon no other citizen; and yet, these prohibited and disqualified characters, are to stand forth and designate the president with an authority so conclusive, that to differ from them, and exercise an independent right, agreeably to the letter and spirit of the constitution, is stigmatized as nothing short of political heresy!

The very power possessed by congress of selecting among the different candidates, where a choice has failed through a division of the electoral votes, *although it may be, and we believe has been the motive and ground-work of congressional nominations*, ought in all delicacy and fairness, to be an insuperable bar against them. The bias of that nomination is certain of influencing the result of that selection. The connection between a nomination originated through members of congress, and an eventual choice by them conformably thereto, is obvious and has, we fear been contemplated. But is it consistent with the spirit of the constitution, or the principles of justice, that those should decide in the last appeal, who had made themselves partizans in the first resort, and had committed themselves by previous engagements?

We are aware of the distinctions made by members of congress. When making those nominations, they affect to act in the capacity only of private citizens. Is it possible that the good sense of the community can be deceived by such a shallow artifice? If in good faith they mean to act only as private citizens, let them do so in their respective states, to which the right of election, and the consequent right of nomination belong. There (if anywhere) their influence would be correctly exercised. But at the very seat of government, on forbidden ground, that almost all the disqualified persons in the union should assemble, and designate a presidential candidate, seems to us something like an indecent infringement of the rights of the states, and an open contempt of the provisions of the constitution. If the members of the house of representatives were to assemble and point out to the president and senate, a foreign ambassador or a judge, would it not be considered as monstrous arrogance? How then are we to characterize the act of the same men, and of the senate, who, notwithstanding their personal disabilities, presume to nominate to the respective states, the officer whom they are required to choose? Suppose the two houses, by a concurrent resolution, recommended a candidate for the chief magistracy, who would hesitate to say it was a violation of the constitution? If then, such an act by them in the forenoon, would be *a violation*, is not the very same act by the very same men in the afternoon, at least *an evasion of the constitution*? Are not the mischiefs to which we have already alluded, and those we are about to suggest, as likely to result from their vote in caucus, as from their vote in congress? Indeed, of two evils, let us choose the least. If they are to interfere let them do it in such a way, as that their conduct may be fairly cognizable by their constituents. If they must act, let them act at least under their official responsibility.

If we are not mistaken, we have demonstrated that a nomination to the presidency, by members of congress is repugnant to the constitution; we shall now vindicate that instrument, by shewing that the measure, if it shall grow into usage, will also be dangerous to the rights of the people, and to the purity and freedom of election. "If it shall grow into usage:" and has it not already grown into usage? Is it not engrafting itself upon our constitution, and acquiring strength after the manner of all other successful usurpations? Even now, acquiescence in *the regular nomination at Washington*, is by many considered as the touchstone of republicanism. The individuals, or the states that dare to exercise the right of independent choice, are denounced as schismatics and factionists; and if already an innovation so recent, and so flagrant, be called *the regular nomination*, what will be its influence, should time and repetition give it additional sanction? Let the encroachments of constituted authorities, upon every free government that has been undermined, furnish the answer. Should the practice become inveterate we do not hesitate to say, *that to promulgate a nomination will be to decree the election.* The congress will appoint the president, and the constitutional electors will be mere officers, to register its edicts.

Would this change in our system produce beneficial results? At best it would endanger the independence of the executive, by giving to congress an influence over the measures of government never contemplated by the constitution, and calculated to diminish the responsibility of the president, the people's only security for his faithful conduct in office. The chief magistrate of the union would owe his elevation and continuance in office to a junta of congressmen and not to the nation. A sovereign right of the states would be absorbed in congressional influence, or sacrificed to executive patronage; and an inestimable control, provided by the constitution over the measures of the federal administration, and vested in the states, would be thus defeated and destroyed. But in truth, the general government would be made to depend upon itself and upon its skill in generating a cabal through intrigue, and intriguing through a cabal.

If the heads of departments, with their clerks and the other persons holding offices of trust or profit under the United States, were to assemble *in their individual capacities*, at the capitol at Washington, and nominate a presidential candidate, would you not be disgusted and shocked? And yet do you believe that they are passive spectators of a *regular caucus nomination*? Mark the danger at least, that on some future occasions, men whose station and standing, nay, whose very bread may depend upon the continuance of the same administration will cultivate the opportunities of private friendship, of official intercourse, of familiar hospitality, of public magnificence; will bias the understanding, engage the hearts, work upon the weakness, and perhaps tamper with the purity of your representatives, collected as they will be in the very focus of executive influence; and having made them fitting instruments, will remain in the back ground, but in fact promulgate the nomination of their own peculiar patron and protector, or perpetuate the succession, if not in the same family, at least in the same dynasty!

How far the germ of these evils is already observable, we do not wish to enquire; but rather proceed to indicate another danger which would grow out of this change of system; and become daily more imminent from the increasing importance of this country. As yet, we hope, no foreign power has attempted to influence the elections of our chief magistrate. The thing is impossible, so long as the provisions of the constitution are observed in spirit as well as letter. While the choice of that officer is in truth made by the states, no foreign agents can approach them or bias their suffrages; and thus a calamity that has harassed Poland, Venice, Genoa, the Papal See, almost every other people having an elective executive, is effectually guarded against. But as we rise in the scale of nations, should we concenter the real electors (or at least those whose nomination is to be received as the first regular step to an election) in the one place, and that to the residence of foreign ministers, whose diplomatic office it often is to conciliate and corrupt, can we be so foolish as to suppose, that the opportunity would be neglected by them of obtaining a hold in our councils, and a control over our government?

These are our convictions respecting the unconstitutionality and dangers of our congressional nominations. Were we not restrained by respect for many of the individuals concerned in them, we would expatiate on them as a public offence; and did we not hope that general reprobation would henceforward abolish their use, we should urge their prohibition by law. Very different indeed is the nomination by individual states. Though not enjoined by the constitution, it is perfectly consistent with its principles, and can never produce any inconvenience but the number of candidates; which would at least be accompanied with the advantage of affording a greater opportunity for judicious selection. The inconvenience, however, is merely imaginary, and would never have practical existence. Mutual forebearance, reciprocal intercourse, and good understanding, would be established by the common interests. Circumstances would almost always decide which state should nominate. The acknowledged celebrity or worth of some prominent character; the propensity to rotation; the importance of some members of the confederation, and other similar considerations, would combine to indicate the state from which the chief magistrate, for a term, should be taken. If any one among them should be perpetually urging pretentions and claiming superiority or should seek, to retain to itself a monopoly of honors or power, the spirit of independence, equality, and participation in the other states, would check its pretensions and teach it moderation.

The state of New-York has now, for the first time, put forward its claim; and examine, we request you, whether some considerations do not strongly mark the propriety of its giving the next president to the union.

The state of Virginia has, for twenty out of the twenty-four years of our present government, enjoyed that honor; she seems desirous of possessing it for another term, and perhaps for as many more as the patience of her sister states will permit. We cheerfully acknowledge the worth and services of the magistrates she has produced; nor do we doubt her competency to furnish a brilliant succession for many years to come; but may be permitted to suggest, that the patriotism and wisdom of the union are not entirely confined within her precincts. If her pretensions be founded on exclusive, or even superior talents, they are offensive to her compeers, and we think unjust. If other states then, can furnish able and intelligent chief magistrates, there are reasons of no light moment, why she should for a time, retire from the competition.

Perhaps if the original framers of our constitution, had inserted a provision for the practical restoration of the presidential office, in the different states, and in some proportion to their population or importance, they would have given an additional proof of their wisdom and foresight. If they had done so, we should not now have occasion to allude to jealousies, the existence of which it is vain to deny, however deeply they may be lamented, as gradually undermining the habitual attachment of many for our confederation. We will abstain from enquiring into their justice; it is unnecessary; since to render them dangerous to our prosperity, it is not essential that they should be well founded; it is sufficient if they exist. They will in that case equally rankle in the heart, bias the understanding, and alienate the affection of whoever feels them. To what are they chiefly owing? Why is *Virginia influence,* a bye-word in the eastern states, while no one talks of South Carolina or Pennsylvania influence? We are not disposed to facilitate our success, by encouraging those jealousies against Virginia influence. The best interests of the union require that they should be allayed; but we are convinced they never will cease, while the cause or pretext for them remains. Virginia herself, as she values the confederation, should abdicate a situation, which she cannot retain without wounding the feelings of her associates and weakening their attachments for our union.

Another evil has resulted from the protracted continuance of power in the same quarter. The agriculture and commercial states are beginning to be arrayed against each other, and to feel as if they were not connected by a common bond of interests. The errors of this sentiment we disclaim; but the practical merchants and farmers are prone, in every country, to regard each other as rivals; nor will either party ever patiently submit to be long and exclusively governed by the other, or regulated by its peculiar views or tenets. The population and resources of this state place it in the first rank, while its local situation makes it one of the fit depositories of power, until the distrust and suspicions alluded to shall have subsided, or the evils they complain of shall be remedied. It is a middle state, not deeply tinged with either northern or southern prejudices: it is eminently commercial, and most extensively agricultural: it would be likely to hold the balance even, and to conciliate the interests and good wishes of all.

These considerations would be weighty, even in times of profound peace; but the existence of a war furnishes another and a most powerful argument. New-York is, indeed a *middle*, but she is also emphatically a *frontier state*. Whatever disasters may be produced by the war, she will share them as a common calamity, and probably she will also feel them with peculiar severity, as inflicted on herself. We do not utter this in the spirit of querulous repining;

nature has placed us in the post of danger, and our hearts and principles determine us to defend it as the post of honor. But if our borders are to be harrassed, and, peradventure, our territory invaded; if our opulent and defenceless capital seems to invite the foe, does not the welfare of the union at large, require that its resources should be directed to the protection of those exposed places, by a statesman to whom their wants are perfectly known, and who would guard them with affectionate zeal? If to this argument of general concern, we added somewhat of personal gratification, should we do wrong? If we said—now that our fortitude is to be peculiarly tried; that our population is to be poured out; that our property may be laid waste; that our individual happiness is put at risque; we offer you a chief magistrate whose republican principles you cannot doubt; of whose competency and talents to discharge the duties of that station, you are well convinced; gratify us in his election. He enjoys our utmost confidence; he inherits the blood, the principles and firmness of that hero, whom ourselves and our fathers long delighted to honor —who was the guide and guardian of his native state, when the same enemy desolated our lands and burnt our towns; who was never appalled in its utmost difficulties, and whose valor and wisdom eminently contributed to the ultimate triumph of America.—If we even urged a persuasive like this, is there an American heart, susceptible of feeling or gratitude, that would repel our claim?

There remains to us another subject, which we most reluctantly enter upon, and which we shall endeavor to discuss with candor and forbearance. We are not enemies to Mr. Madison, and should regret exceedingly if we were considered as disparaging his reputation. Much as we esteem Mr. Clinton, and desirous as we are of his success, we should reject it, if it could only be accomplished by villifying his competitor; but the merits of the one do not require to be set off by censuring the other. Mr. Madison has passed through a life of honor and public services, and has been already exalted to the first office in the union. His friends are desirous of his enjoying it for another term, and allege something like usage in the re-election of his predecessors.——It is true Washington, the idol of all parties, was so exalted; it is true Jefferson, the idol of the republicans, obtained the same distinction; but a magistrate may be very meritorious, without deserving the honors conferred upon Washington and Jefferson.

We are not aware of any advantage that can result by establishing the rule, that every president, who is not extremely disapproved of, shall be re-elected. The next step will be, that some favorite public servant, as a proof of our peculiar esteem, will be continued in office for three successive terms; and soon three times will be the ordinary period of a president whom it is not intended to disgrace: thus we shall imperceptibly slide into an election for life and perhaps towards an hereditary succession. Eight years are not an uncommon length of time, as a reward for uncommon services: but there is no reason why they should become the ordinary tenure of office. Nevertheless, had there been no sufficiently countervailing motives; and had the times been more tranquil, we should not, perhaps, object to the re-election of Mr. Madison, if that honor were deemed necessary to fill the measure of his fame. But, much as we respect the feelings of that gentleman we cannot consent to offer them that tribute under existing circumstances. The present situation of our country excites the deepest anxiety, and renders the choice of its first public officer more important and interesting than ever. This choice involves in effect a question of administration, the appointments of heads of departments, and the institution of principles of policy for conducting our public affairs, of the utmost consequence to the union.

It is a sacred provision of our government, that the president is the responsible officer under the constitution. The prerogative maxim of Britain cannot be applied to him, *that he can do no wrong.* He is answerable to the nation not only for the general system of administration, but also for the prominent public acts and omissions of his secretaries. The officers are to act under his direction, and cannot be admitted to stand in the same capacity with the ministers of the king of England, interposed between the chief magistrate and the people, to bear the burden of public censure, and screen him from public observation. A severe enforcement of this essential rule, which makes the president responsible to the nation for the acts of his secretaries, has become indispensable for the restoration of the republic to a healthy condition.

The mode of conducting the war in which we are embarked, is intimately and essentially connected with a satisfactory adjustment of our differences, with the best interests of our country, and with the honor of the American name.

The probability of its taking place could not but have been anticipated; the resources it would require, should have been maturely considered, and the means of providing them directed and arranged; the preparations to wage it with effect ought to have been reasonably made. Have those things been done? We do not wish to enter into a minute detail, that might present a disheartening picture to our country, but we are compelled to ask, where are the marks of system and preparation? Our armies have entered upon military service; which of them is properly provided for the present, or when and where have arrangements been made for securing to it the necessary supplies for the future? We fear it will not be found in the army under general Hull; we are sure it is not in the force collected to defend New York; nor that organizing on our western border. Supplies for the first should have been furnished through the lakes, and collected before the British had notice of the war: it is now impossible: and that the last is even as yet provided with tents, is entirely owing to the uncommon and unremitted exertions of the governor of this state. — Indeed the very impossibility of furnishing our armies by the lakes, is in itself a striking proof of incompetency or inattention. We think no administration, possessing either foresight or vigor, would have omitted strengthening our naval force upon those extensive inland waters, so as to ensure to us the naval superiority in them. The facility of doing this is nearly equal to its importance: and in time of war that superiority is of the last importance to the U. States, particularly if an attack upon the Canadas be contemplated; besides, the augmentation of our naval force there, is not subject to the same objection frequently made against a similar measure in our Atlantic ports, that it would tend to involve us in the maritime conflicts of Europe.

It is vain to say that these are the errors of the heads of departments. The just and salutary rule of our constitution compels us to place them to the account of our present executive.——The secretaries of the navy and of war, are bound to execute the orders given them by the president, on all naval and military affairs: either he directed the necessary preparations to be made, or he did not. If he directed them, he is responsible for continuing incapable men in office: if he did not, the blame attaches personally on himself.

But wherefore this lingering preparation, and final inadequacy of the means employed in the contest our government has undertaken? Appropriations were made, in preceding sessions of congress, for the timely provision of munitions of war, in the apprehension that hostilities would grow out of the infringements of our neutral rights. Why has the application of them been neglected, till the conflict was at hand? Do not our raw recruits and vulnerable points in the most valuable and important quarters, declare that recourse has been had to hostilities without a digested system either of defensive or offensive operations? Neither advice of the declaration of war, nor instructions or orders were received by the commanding officer of our squadron at New-York, till general publicity afforded sufficient time for the enemy, most exposed to his operations, to avoid attack and elude pursuit. An opulent fleet of merchantmen sailed from Jamaica, exactly in time to have been easily intercepted, if the orders of government had been prompt and decisive: but they escaped caputre by some negligent delay at Washington; and we should even wish to know, was commodore Rodgers informed of that fleet by our government, or did he accidentally hear of it at sea?

If this country be competent to carry on the war, and we are sure it is—if our executive sufficiently foresaw the approach of hostilities, and informed themselves as the best means of conducting them with effect, and shortening their duration by a vigorous commencement, we should have expected to see, not ten or twelve hundred men collecting in the vicinity of Albany, but forces formed, organized and disciplined; an army invading Nova Scotia to wrest from England her best naval station on our seas; another acting against the Canadas, and a third, attacking the Floridas at the same time.

How shall we characterise the uninterrupted permission to carry on trade with Spain and Portugal? Is it a measure of electioneering policy, or a further proof of the absolute inefficiency that pervades our councils? It undoubtedly affords to England the amplest means of supplying her armies with provisions of every kind, of which they would otherwise be destitute; and therefore gives the most effectual *aid and comfort* to the enemy. It is a trade which cannot be carried on under the American flag; for that will necessarily be excluded by the superiority of the British power in the seas that wash those coasts. It may easily be carried on by British vessels, covered by subjects of Spain and Portugal. It affords them to the foe, the means of prolonging the war against us, and promotes the prosperity of British and foreign tonnage, to the ruin of our own ships and merchants. Had the parliament of England legislated for us on this subject, from its policy, its wisdom, and its hatred to our shipping and trade, this arrangement might, perhaps, have been expected; proceeding from our own rulers, it seems almost incomprehensible.

But money has been aptly called the sinews of war, and what system of procuring it has been furnished by our present administration? Where is the republican who is not astonished and confounded at the scheme of taxation proposed through the department of the treasury? It almost seemed intended to damp the public spirit of the country: objects of revenue were presented, odious to the feelings of the citizen, and which, under similar circumstances, formerly occasioned the reprehension of the very person who now revives them. It was not found expedient to adopt this plan; perhaps it was judged cunning to postpone it till after the presidential election. The credit of the nation is therefore put to the test, by a call for a very large loan, without a specification of security, and impaired, by placing at the disposal of the administration, for instant expenditure, and in order to avoid the immediate resort to direct taxes, monies appropriated to the sinking fund, for the purpose of buying unredeemed debt at a price under par. This injudicious use of that fund, heretofore held sacred by all administrations, cannot fail most injuriously to affect the credit of the other loans at market.

The expenses incident to our situation must, we know, be incurred, and we think that the administration have insulted the patriotism of the people, by declining to take the necessary steps for meeting them; but indeed, considering the conduct hitherto pursued, we are seriously apprehensive lest an immense public debt should be accumulated, without the attainment of any equivalent advantage. The service of the next year may be expected to call for twenty millions, without having made any serious impression on the enemy, or any advance towards the favorable adjustment of our disputes.

The nomination of De Witt Clinton for the presidency, by the state of New-York, proposes to the Union, as we firmly believe, a relief from the evils of an inefficient administration, and of an inadequately conducted war. His patriotic and inflexible principles guarantee a firm and unyielding maintenance of the sovereign rights of the United States.————Nevertheless, he is not engaged, through any effect of foreign diplomacy, as to the controverted claims of the belligerents of Europe upon each other, in the new and outrageous species of hostility introduced into the present war.

His qualities, as they have been proved by a long trial in public life, assure us of an able and upright conduct of our national affairs. From his discernment, we infer an excellent selection of the best talents in the nation, to fill the high stations of government, and aid the republic with their counsel and services.

From his energy we anticipate vigor in war, and a determined character in the relations of peace. We believe him to be, in this respect, formed on the model of his venerated uncle, whose decisions of mind, constancy and firmness, were almost unequalled.

His attachment to the commercial interests of the union, is founded upon an intimate acquaintance with their beneficial results, and a persuasion of the national advantage accruing from commercial pursuits.

His administration would, we believe, aim at reviving the almost expiring commerce of the country, and extending to it a naval protection proportioned to its value, and to the revenue poured by it into the national coffers. In fine, we believe, that to maintain the rights of his country, would be his unalterable resolution; to regain peace would be his study; to retain it would be his desire; and to restore the republic to health and prosperity, his highest ambition.

We therefore earnestly recommend him to the support of the other states, and to the suffrages of the electors for the next president of the union.

William W. Gilbert,
Matthias B. Tallmadge,
John McKesson,
Preserved Fish,
Pierre C. Van Wyck,
Gurdon S. Mumford,
Jacob De La Montaigne
Benjamin De Witt,
Silvanus Miller,
Thomas Addis Emmett,
Benjamin Ferris,
R. Riker,
Elbert Herring
P. Wilson
John H. Sickles,
Samuel Harris,

Address from the South Carolina Assembly
to President James Madison
Charleston, September 1, 1812

As a Virginia gentleman, Madison considered it unseemly to "run" for public office, and in the election of 1812 he doubtless felt the public was sufficiently aware of the issues. Thus the "Address of the South Carolina Assembly," September 1, 1812, the ideas of which President Madison approved, constituted one of the few Republican campaign pronouncements.

I

We have the honor of transmiting to you An Address Which was unanimously adopted by both branches of the Legislature of this state, at an Extra Session.

At the sametime, we avail ourselves of this occasion, to express individually, the high opinion we entertain of your public and private virtues; and the satisfactory manner in which you have in a time of peril and great difficulty, discharged the various duties of the high station to which you have been called by the voice of your Country.

> We have the honor to be,
> with great respect and Esteem
> your most obedient
>
> *Samuel Warren,*
> President of the Senate

John Geddes, Speaker of the House of Representatives of
the State of South Carolina.

II

Sir: In a government like ours, which, emanating from the will of all, is strong or weak in proportion to the current of public opinion in its favor, it cannot but be deeply interesting to the servants of the people, to know the light in which their Conduct is considered by those who have invested them with power. Under this impression, and influenced by the consideration that those who have the right to censure where censure is deserved, ought not to pass over with the silence of indifference the merit of their agents, where that merit is conspicuous; the Legislature of South Carolina, called together by the late change in our political relations, cannot separate without expressing the lively approbation they feel at the dignified and decisive appeal to arms, adopted by the President and a majority of Congress, in vindication of our long outraged rights, and violated Sovereignty as a Nation.

In other governments, it has been the constant effort of the real friends of the people, to Curb the angry passions of their rulers; to interrupt the vain dreams of National glory and foreign conquest, by the melancholy exhibition of ruined Husbandmen and starving Manufacturers; and to shade the deceitful picture of splendid victories and triumphal arches, held up to dazzle and mislead a giddy populace, by introducing on the canvass the more faithful and certain representation of individual misery. It was reserved for the United States to present the spectacle, so consolatory to distressed humanity, of a government uninfatuated by the illusions of National aggrandizement, or the glory of conquest; anxious only to promote the true Happiness of the People, and in deciding on the great question of Peace or War, weighing every drop of blood likely to be shed in the last resort, with the same caution, the same solicitude, as tho' each drop were to be drawn from the veins of those themselves, on whom rested the decision. If the signal for battle can be supposed to have been ever registered in "Heaven's Chancery," with any other emotions than those of horror or contempt for human wickedness or folly, it was on the Eighteenth Day of June, 1812. Influenced by no lust of dominion, no unjust spirit of encroachment; but impelled to arms by wanton and continued violations of our best rights, out vital Interests—if ever a war deserved to be denominated Holy, it is this. It is a war of right against lawless aggression, of Justice against perfidy and violence. Thus driven to Hostilities, it is in vain that Faction would repress the energy and spirit of the Nation, or disaffection depreciate the resources of our Country.

The glory of the issue will be commensurate with the righteousness of our cause. If we cannot at this moment, contend with our enemy for the empire of the Ocean, Individual valour and enterprize at length, permitted to be exerted, will ensure to our Citizens no inconsiderable indemnity forthe spoliations so long practiced upon their fair and peaceful commerce. If the acquisition of Canada be of little value in a territorial point of view, in other respects it will not be unimportant. It will remove from us a treacherous and barbarous Neighbor, who at the very moment her envoys ever loudest in protestations, of conciliation and friendship, was secretly fomenting by her emissaries, divisions and factions among us; and who has at no time ceased to direct the tomahawks and scalping knives of her fellow savages, the indians against the defenceless women and Children of our frontier. From the inconveniences and privations incident to a state of war, we affect not to expect an exemption; but be are willing and able to support them. We shall support them with the more cheerfulness, as they will not fail to be accompanied with more than correspondent advantages. A Commercial, as well as political Independence, predicted upon the improvement and advancement of domestic Manufactures; the extermination of the spirit of faction; a cordial Union of all parties for the common welfare; a happy amalgamation of the various, and in some instances, discordant materials, which, to a certain degree, compose our population; in a word, the formation of a National Character—these are some of the benefits confidently anticipated from the present contest. When to these on one hand, are added, on the other, the accumulated insults and wrongs sustained from Great Britain — wrongs which, if tamely submitted to, must have reduced us to worse then colonial Slavery; we do not hesitate to believe the war in which we have engaged, wise, necessary and Just.

Under this conviction, Sir, the Legislature of South Carolina, have deemed it expedient and right not to withhold the full expression of their feelings and opinions —

Therefore,

Resolved, that the energy, the patriotism and wisdom of James Madison, President of the United States, manifested in his communication to Congress upon the question of war, give him new claims to the confidence and support of the people of South Carolina.

Resolved, that in the opinion of this Legislature, the Majority of Congress have consulted the true interests and honor of their Country in declaring war, against Great Britain.

Resolved, that this Legislature highly approve of the Conduct of the delegation of this State, in the present Congress.

In the House of Representatives
August 28, 1812

Resolved that this House do agree to the same unanimously.

Ordered that the same be sent to the Senate for their concurrence.

By order of the House

(signed,) —

> *Richard Gantt.*
> Clerk of the
> House of Representatives, of the
> State of South Carolina

In the Senate
August 29, 1812

Resolved, that this House do concur Unanimously, with the House of Representatives in the foregoing address.

Ordered, that the same be returned to the House of Representatives.

By order of the Senate

(signed,) —

> *John Murphy,*
> Clerk of Senate.

Letter from Rufus King to Christopher Gore
September 19, 1812

A number of older Federalists feared the effects on their party of fusion with the "peace Republicans." Rufus King of Massachusetts, formerly a member of the Federal Convention of 1787, described to a friend the meeting at which Federalist leaders came to terms with DeWitt Clinton and listed his own objections to the scheme.

My dear Sir: I balanced much whether I would attend the meeting in New York respecting the approaching Presidential Election.* I had understood as well from the declaration made in the Boston Town Meeting, as from the Echo of the same opinion from other quarters, that it would be deemed inexpedient to name a federal Candidate, and project to co-operate with the views of Mr. Clinton: as I differed in opinion on both these points, and as (certainly without desire or gratification on my part) my name had been mentioned amongst others, I felt the difficulty that I should place myself in by becoming a member of this meeting.

Some of our friends in the ctiy pressed me to attend, and altho' from all I had heard, I was fully persuaded that the Gentlemen who should meet would entertain and adopt opinions and measures, wholly repugnant to my Judgment, I nevertheless after full Reflexion, determined not to absent myself, chiefly because I was unwilling that my absence should by any possibility be construed to mean, what is not true in respect to my personal views.

I accordingly attended the meeting, which was composed of more than sixty Gentlemen, assembled from So. Carolina and the States east of Virginia. After receiving from the members the best information in their power to afford respecting the Character of the Electors likely to be chosen within their

*J. Radcliff to R. King.

New York, Sept. 12, 1812.

Dr Sir: Since I had the pleasure of seeing you the Corresponding Committee of the Federal Republicans of this city have directed me particularly to request the favor of your attendance at the meeting to be held here on the 15th instant; the objects of which have already been mentioned as far as my information extends.

It is not only the wish and expectation of our friends in this State, but Gentlemen from Connecticut & I believe from other States have expressed an anxious desire that you and Mr. Jay should attend this meeting. Questions of primary importance will no doubt be made and perhaps be decided, and we hope you will not fail to afford us your counsel and advice.

On behalf of the Corresponding Committee, I have the honor to be with great regard, your most obed.

Jacob Radcliff

The meeting referred to is thus spoken of by Hildreth, *United States History*, vi., p. 376: "For the purpose of deciding what course their party should take, a convention of Federalists from all the States North of the Potomac, with delegates also fom South Carolina, assembled in New respective States, it was resolved "that from the information so received, it was in the opinion of the meeting impracticable to elect a fedl. President, and that it would be inexpedient to name a fedl. Candidate. 2nd that it should be recommended to the Federalists to co-operate in the election of a President, who would be likely to pursue a different course of administration from that of Mr. Madison; and that a Committee should be appointed to collect the earliest information of the character and views of the Electors, and to communicate the same to the Federalists throughout the States."

I disapproved of the first Resolution, because I would have nominated a candidate, a respectable federalist from any quarter, not in the expectation, nay without the desire, of succeeding in his Election; but for the purpose of keeping the federal body as entire in numbers and as unbroken in principle as possible, to the end that their character and influence may be reserved for the occasion which, in the present course of affairs, cannot fail to arrive.

I disliked the second Resolution, because it did not speak out and name the person, whom every one had in view, and because there was no evidence exhibited that Mr. Clinton, with the aid of the federalists, can be elected, and, if elected, that he will pursue a better system than that of Mr. Madison.

I stated my sentiments to the meeting, a great majority of whom thought them incorrect. Time, wh. reveals truth, must decide between us.

I think the question who shall be President, a secondary one and quite unimportant in comparison with the attempt which we are bound to make, to preserve the freedom and Independence of the nation by reforming the Constitution. I know that our political adversaries will say that we aim at a Monarchy; perhaps some of our friends even may suspect our views. I am and shall always be ready to purge myself from this suspicion; I would lessen, sooner than increase, the presidential power. But it is idle to go into explanations upon a Subject that is now so little likely to call for attention. I am convinced that things cannot remain where they are if the war continues; a great change must happen, the signs of its approach are not equivocal. I have earnestly hoped, and thought that I had grounds for doing so, that by a prudent course we should be able to direct the change and to turn it to the advantage

---

York. They met privately, with closed doors, and three days were consumed in eager debates. The adoption of Clinton as their candidate was very eagerly opposed by King and others, who denounced him as a mere ambitious demagogue, a second Aaron Burr. That course was, nevertheless, finally agreed upon, principally through the urgency and eloquence of Otis, on the ground that the defeat of Madison would speedily lead to a peace, for which the door stood open in the repeal of the orders in council. The Clintonians in their turn agreed to adopt as their candidate for the vice-presidency Jared Ingersoll, a Pennsylvanian of New England origin."

Henry Adams, in *History of the U. S.*, vi., p. 410, after justly characterizing the canvass for the Presidency in New York on behalf of De Witt Clinton as being most discreditable, and giving his reasons for this opinion, says:

"Federalists held a conference at New York in September and in spite of Rufus King, who was said to have denounced Clinton as a dangerous demagogue in almost the words used by Hamilton to denounce Aaron Burr ten years before, after three days' debate, largely through the influence of Harrison Gray Otis, the bargain was made which transferred to Clinton the electoral votes of the federal States. No one knew what pledges had been given by Clinton and his friends; but no man of common-sense who wished to preserve the government and the Union could longer refuse to vote for Madison."

of the Country. These hopes have been the result of an impartial estimate of the tendency of the measures of Government, and of the most anxious solicitude to discover the duty of good and disinterested men at the present Crisis. I deprecate, and, above all other evils, fear the interposition of the Sword as the umpire of our difference. Should a civil war break out, we have no occasion in future for caucusses respecting Presidential Electors. Things will then be ordered in a different way. One chance, and only one, in favor of reform without violence has seemed to me to exist, and above every other consideration to be worthy of the deliberate attention of the Federalist — Offer a federal Candidate for the Presidency; acquiesce in Mr. Madison's re-election. He cannot in four years ruin the Country; but, if I am not egregiously mistaken, unless Peace be made, he will in that time so disgust and degrade it, that the federalists at its expiration will come into the possession of the Government, and with as great support by the People, as Jefferson had, when he succeeded Adams. Grant this, and if the Federalists should not then so reform the Constitution as to protect the Country in future from the Evils it now feels and fears, they and their posterity will deserve to suffer the ills, which, without such reform, must crush them to the earth.

Recollect what never must be forgotten in a popular Government, that next to the power of the Sword is that of a depressed party when risen to be a triumphant one.

But Mr. Madison may make a French Alliance. If he dare, I fear he would: the country will not now bear it, and the course of his disastrous administration will render the Country still less inclined to bear it. But come the worst, let the French Alliance be made, and French troops introduced; the certain, and I think the immediate, consequence will be a civil war and the introduction of English troops. No Event would be more calamitous, none so perilous to the public Liberties; but this event will occur, tho' perhaps not immediately, unless the Constitution be reformed.

A new president from the Democracy would perhaps adopt measures that for the moment might mitigate present evils; tho' I have seen no evidence that he will be either willing or able to do so. But neither a democratical nor a federal President could in the actual State of parties do anything to remove our present evils, or to prevent their recurrence. All palliatives, such as the mere change of President among Democrats, or between them and federalists, will have the effect, not only to postpone the chance of reform, but to weaken the faculty of making it, should the opportunity occur. They would have this effect by the more complete conversion of political parties into political factions; by the inevitable progress of corruption and by the difficulty which daily increases of confining the young men of the Country to a political Creed, which is sure to prevent them from sharing in public distinctions.

No fact seems to be more fully established than that a nation may, and that too in a short period, become so debased by corruption and the agency of faction, that the Sword alone can put an end to the public misery. The Roman Empire, as we are told, was *once* offered to the highest bidder at a public sale — but our Country is in danger to be so sold at every successive Election.* If the practice of corruption has heretofore been more prevalent among our advesaries than among ourselves, I fear that this distinction is henceforth at an end, enough was disclosed in our meeting to make me apprehend that those who possess the greatest means, will hereafter become the greatest corrupters. The consequence is unavoidable—there must be a speedy end of our political systems or the public Liberties will sink with them.

Against so great an evil, I have thought that we are bound to struggle; and I had persuaded myself, tho' I have been unable to persuade others, that the re-election of Mr. Madison would produce a more favorable opportunity for a peaceful effort at Reform, then can hereafter be expected to occur.

I have believed it due to our long and uninterrupted friendship to write this letter; especially as we were informed by one of yr. Delegates, that you† approve of the co-operation of the Feds. to elect Mr. Clinton; and I ask the favor of you to shew this letter to Mr. Cabot, Mr. Parsons & Mr. Strong from whose opinions, as they were stated in our meeting, I feel the deepest concern in being obliged to dissent.‡

*Montesquieu observes "that it is impossible for the leading men to be knaves and the inferior sort to be honest, and for the former to be cheats, and the latter to rest satisfied with being only dupes."

†Observation, the Representation was wholly incorrect, and that respecting Cabot, Strong, and Parsons ill-founded.

‡Among Mr. King's papers is the following account of the meeting of Federal delegates in New York, Sept. 15, 16, and 17, 1812:

"Harper moved a Resolution, wh. was adopted by a majority, that from the information received from all parts of the Union, the election of a Fedl. Pr. now appeared to be impracticable, & that it was inexpedient to nominate Fedl. Candidates.

"It was on the 2nd day agreed to committ to a member from each State the propositions respecting the support of Dmo. Candidates for Pr. & V. P. On the third day their Report was made and accepted by a large majority, viz.:

"That it is recommended to the Federalists to support such Candidates for Pr. & V. P. at the ensuing election as would be likely to pursue a difft. course of measures from that of the now Presidt.

"And that a Comtee of 5 persons (Pennsylvanians) be appointed to ascertain the result of the elections for Electors, and the Candidates whom they wd. be inclined to support, and to communicate the same as expeditiously as practicable to the Electors of the several States.

"I opposed every part of these measures, and attempted to prevent the adoption of the first Resolution, and afterwards to amend the second so as that it should express what it means, namely to support Mr. D. Clinton. This was objected to as likely to prove injurious to Mr. C.

"In conclusion I observed that I regarded the Resolution as a recommendation of the election of Mr. Clinton—added that the practicability of such election shd. appear probable, and moreover if chosen, that we shd. have reason to expect he would pursue different and better measures; that no information was communicated respecting his views; that he was educated and practised in the principles of Democracy; that no man in the country was more unequivocal in his character. As evidence of the course he wd. be likely to follow, we should remember that he disapproved the Embargo, then receded from his opinion, and in speech made in the Senate, wh. he published, restored himself to the confidence of the Demos by a tirade of abuse poured out upon the Feds., and that this was so directed as to bear particularly upon the Genn. of B. who must have magnanimity more than belongs to our nature, to be afterwards Mr. C.'s advocate.

"That personally I could feel no dislike to Mr. Clinton on any acct. other than that wh. arose from his political character & views; that I had had no individual intercourse with him, but that I feared, if we succeeded in promoting his election, that we might place in the chair a Cæsar Borgia instead of a James Madison—intimated however that the treatment by Madn. of the Genn. of Boston had been such in the charge of the Henry Mission that I could suppose their resentment implacable; that were I in the situation I never would forgive the injury.

"A letter from Genl. Pinckney to the Corresponding Comtee of Philadelphia declines explicitly being a candidate for the Presidency: recommends Jay or King.

"A letter from B. Stoddart, Maryland, recommends Marshall (C.J.S.) as the only man for wh. any probability existed of the vote of Virginia, and Strong V. P.: that if Virginia shd. succeed in an electoral ticket Marshall or K. shd. be the Candidate – the former preferable on acct. of his great popularity in Virginia.

"A letter from John Hopkins recommends Marshall and states that if Virga. is fedl. she wd. support Jay, King, Strong, Griswold, Pickering or any other respectable Fedst, and that Clinton cd. obtain no better support than Madn.

"A letter from Judge Washington to the N. Jersey Com. of Correspondence, who applied to him to become a Candidate, declines in a modest manner, disqualifying his abilities, and preferring his present peaceful office of a judge – Clinton rather than Madison.

"A letter from Dexter, Boston, about Piso's conspiracy agt. Cæsar: the object to shew that a Fed. Cand. shd. not be named.

"A letter from Pierson, No. Carolina, Legislature fedl.; if convened will district the State."

Editorials from the *Columbian Centinel*
Boston, October 28, 31, 1812

For the Federalists in 1812 the main issue of the presidential campaign was the declaration of war on Great Britain. The following editorials from the Boston Columbian Centinel *entitled "The Clintonian, No. 1," October 28, 1812, and "The Clintonian, No. 2," October 31, 1812, summarize the arguments in favor of fusion with antiwar Republicans on a peace platform.*

THE CLINTONIAN, No. I.

While the Federalists throughout the Union, except in the State of *Virginia*, have studiously avoided the nomination of a Candidate for the Presidency from their own party, there seems to be among them a general assent to the project of supporting by their voices, a rival to the present Chief Magistrate of the opposite party, whose competition may probably be attended with success. As the correctness of this determination may not be obvious to all, I propose to examine, in a very cursory manner, those reasons which justify it in the minds of many of our most firm and distinguished friends.

That high and honorable sentiment of dignity which disdains compromise, and will be satisfied with nothing less than a complete victory over our political opponents is entitled to respect, and should constitute the principle of action so long as any hope of success remains in the open field of controversy. It is this success alone which can enable great and virtuous statesmen to confer upon the community the *greatest possible good* by an exclusive control of public measures. But something short of this may render them instrumental in preventing the *greatest possible evil*. If we are not committed to adopt a course of policy which we feel assured would save the State, it is not the less our duty to assist in warding off the dangers which menace it with *certain ruin*. So long as factions can be prevented or repressed by great and virtuous Magistrates, these alone should receive our suffrages. But when this experiment has failed, and the ascendency of any one faction becomes decisive and dangerous, it is in vain to affect to be idle or contemptuous spectators of the struggle between rival demagogues. We *must* interfere and endeavor to maintain a balance of power. We must ally ourselves to the least dangerous faction, and aid in breaking down the power of that which is the most formidable and pernicious. To repine at a condition which, first or last, becomes inseparable from every Republic is merely to lament over the infirmities of nature. Few are the situations which allow us to select either the employments, the pleasures or the companions which we should prefer beyond all others.

We are generally doomed in our ordinary concerns, to choose between things, of which none are perfectly agreeable; and when we can no longer ride in our carriage, it is best to choose that stage coachman who is least likely to break our bones, and we must pursue our journey by the best means in our power.

As the morbid state of the body politic forbids all hope of succeeding in the choice of a *Federal President*, our party must decide upon one of the following alternatives. They must either make an attempt, knowing it will prove abortive, to elect a Federalist; thus concentrating the opposition and hostility of all the Democratic factions; — or they must forbear all agency in the election; thus confessing their own impotence and disheartening their adherents — Or they must promote the election of MR. CLINTON. The universal abhorrence of MADISON's administration places the support of him out of the question. It is very difficult to imagine any good reason in favor of sporting with a Federal Candidate, or in favor of retiring from the contest altogether, *unless it were possible that the election of Mr. Clinton might make bad worse*. But this is confidently denied. No condition of colonial dependance can be more humiliating than that we now endure — No depression by foreign conquest more complete and degrading than that which must befall us under MADISON. The commercial States are wantonly deprived of their only resource, with a view to build up a Southern Dynasty upon its ruins. Our navigation and commerce are ruined. Our cities are impoverished, our merchants made bankrupt. Our ships rot in the docks while the produce of the southern States finds its way to market in neutral bottoms. The declaration of war is a signal deliberately made by our government, inviting and authorizing the capture and plunder of our vessels on the ocean. The best men of our country, the proprietors of the soil, and the monied interest; all the learned of all professions; whatever can be found of virtue, talent and real interest in the country, with inconsiderable exceptions, are excluded from all participation in the government, and are placed under the controul of upstart placemen, and ordinary, unprincipled sycophanis and miuions of the executive. All regular occupations are suspended — all steady pursuits deranged, all innocent pleasures banished. Income fails. — Taxes increase. — The avenues to the advancement and establishment of the rising generation are closed. We are obliged to contribute towards making war upon ourselves. We are condemned to hopeless and ruinous crusades against the *loghouses* of *Canada* which we are unable to take, and our brethren and children are hurried into the wilderness to be sacrificed by savages, for the mere purpose of affording to our government new means of exasperating the public sensibility. We are plunged into a war with the British, with the Algerines, with the Indians. The designs of government on *Florida* expose us to a war with *Spain* and the tendency of these measures is to an alliance with *France*, which will inevitably be followed by a civil war. For this deplorable system of policy discovering men can perceive no motive but fear of *France* and hatred to Commerce, nor can any termination of it be rationally expected, so long as the present Frenchified administration keeps in power. This power, it is their plan to perpetuate, either in their own person or in *Virginians* of their own nomination. Now it is believed that no change can be more disastrous, than the present posture of affairs. The principal objects of civil society, protection, liberty and the free pursuit of the innocent means of subsistence and happiness are at end. The relations which create a preference for country, the sources of national pride and attachment are impaired, and those who are versed in the history of nations are ready to despair of the republic. The real interests of the Eastern States are no more represented in Congress than they are in the local Legislature of *Virginia.* — The voice of complaint and the freedom of debate are stifled by the arbitrary will of a majority, and the reign of terror which was planned and threatened during the last session of Congress, will be resumed as the only practical mode of enforcing obedience, extorting money and prosecuting war. Such is our situation at this juncture. — I repeat that *no condition can be worse*, and will endeavor to shew in another number that, under the administration of DEWITT CLINTON, a change may rationally be expected for the better, though Federalists may not be called to aid in its formation, and though he may still continue to be in heart a democratic republican.

THE CLINTONIAN, No. II.

Having shewn, as I trust, that our present unhappy condition *cannot* be aggravated by the election of a new democratic President, it is not difficult to maintain the position that great benefit to our country may be expected from the change, though inferior in degree to that which would result from the restoration of power to Federal hands. Two or three obvious propositions which are nearly self-evident will lead to this conclusion. It must be admitted, that the *Peace Party*, by whose aid MR. CLINTON's election will be effected, however discordant may be the materials of which it is composed, are nevertheless agreed in some essential particulars, or they could not act in unison. They undoubtedly desire a change in the principal features of the Madisonian policy. They are weary of the War, and still more disgusted with the improvidence and weakness manifested in its prosecution. They are anxious to seek for Peace in the spirit of peace, and if unobtainable, to prosecute the war by practicable and vigorous means. — They are hostile to the system of Commercial Restrictious, and State-Supremacy. And they look to an alliance with *France* as an abomination.

Again, Should this party succeed in effecting their object, the event will demonstrate them to be in fact a majority of the people. These points being incontrovertible, it may be conceded for the moment, that while CLINTON's moral character is unimpeachable in all the private and social relations of life, his political conscience is under the dominion of ambition; — that he has been a zealous persecutor of Federalism, and is at heart a Democrat. This is the sum of all the objections urged by his most vindictive opponents.

If then MR. CLINTON upon coming into power, should promote those objects of the party that elevates him, in which the individuals composing it are agreed, our principle will be established, namely, That the change will have meliorated the condition of the country. Will he then promote those objects? Now it is quite inconceivable, *how he should have the inclination or the power to do otherwise.* Let us consider what would be the state of Parties upon his accession to the chair. We have already shewn that the Peace Party would have on its side strength and success. The Madisonian or War Party would be in a state of defeat and disgrace. Between these MR. CLINTON must choose, if indeed he had the power of election. But what inducement could be presented to his mind, to desert a great triumphant party by whose zeal and exertions his ambitious and aspiring views should have been accomplished, and attempt to form a new league with a fallen party, whose resentments against him as the instrument of their ruin must of necessity be implacable? Interest, ambition, self-love, every principal incentive which impels the mind to action would render this apostacy impossible — Mere instinct would teach any man not absolutely imbecile the expediency of cultivating and strengthening the party which was at once the source of his power and his hopes. *He could take no other course.* He could find no party among his adversaries. The controversy between them would be in its own nature irreconcileable. — There is but one Presidency. The supreme Executive Power is not an estate which admits of partition. — Nothing can satisfy the Virginian Party but the power of crippling the Commercial States and thus ruling the Confederacy. A successful rival would be the last man to be admitted into their confidence. — Already he is assailed by the Madisonian Retainers, with every variety of invective. Already the gauntlet is formed from *Maine* to *Orleans*, and every great and little parasite of the Ancient Dominion who can twirl a switch, from Generals down to Pettifoggers and Postmasters, stands ready to scourge the *Pretender.*

As such would be the relation of MR. CLINTON to the respective parties upon his elevation, he could support himself in no other mode than by favoring the views, and promoting the objects of those who shall have made him great. Those objects have been just enumerated, and as they would consist with the honor and prosperity of the nation, and with the peculiar interests of his native State; as they would also conduce to the success and splendor of his administration; it is reasonable to believe that inclination and a sense of duty would concur with other motives, in their influence upon his measures. No honorable Federalist will deny that this consummation would be in a high degree beneficial to our country, and a relief to the distressing anxiety of good men, although he or his friends should not be employed in effecting the immediate objects of the reformation. This ought not to be expected. The claims of CLINTON's political friends will be importunate, and probably deemed paramount to all others. But the pressing concern with every honest man is to save and not to govern the falling state. In process of time, however, Federalists might reasonably expect to participate in the offices of government, under a new order of things, should returning peace and prosperity be the fruit of this new experiment, mutual jealousies and animosities would subside, and those who shall have combined their efforts successfully for one object, will become insensibly disposed to a further concert for promoting the common good. The present party distinctions might be gradually blended and lost, and the *Virginia* aristocracy might, as MR. ADAMS once recommended for all *Nobility*, be placed "in a hole by itself."

Some worthy and intelligent friends have expressed their apprehensions that by this compromise, the federal party will be degraded and disabled from rallying upon future emergencies. But if after an incessant effort for twelve years, to promote to power those only who were the objects of our predilection and confidence, we find ourselves at a greater distance than ever from success; how can it be derogatory to the honor of our party, *at least to suspend* these unavailing efforts, until we have rescued ourselves from dangers which threaten to render them *forever abortive*? It may be a subject of regret, that one is compelled to choose between CAESAR and POMPEY. But if such is our destiny it is unmanly to complain, and foolish to be sulky. We must adhere to him who will do the least mischief, and if neither is the man of our heart, it is consolation that we are not in a worse condition than every other people, who are obliged to acquiesce in the dominion of those in whose appointment they have no part.

Nor is there any just ground to dread the annihilation of the Federal party. The principles of Federalism are original, founded in Patriotism and Public Virtue. The alliance of its friends is the result of sympathy, not of combination. The conviction of mutual purity is the source of unwavering confidence, and as their object is always the public good, they form a *high and distinct CAST in the community which can never be mistaken or confounded.*

THE ELECTORAL VOTE IN THE 1812 ELECTION

STATES	PRESIDENT		VICE-PRESIDENT	
	James Madison	De Witt Clinton	Elbridge Gerry	Jared Ingersoll
New Hampshire....	—	8	1	7
Vermont..........	8	—	8	—
Massachusetts......	—	22	2	20
Rhode Island.......	—	4	—	4
Connecticut........	—	9	—	9
New York.........	—	29	—	29
New Jersey.........	—	8	—	8
Pennsylvania.......	25	—	25	—
Delaware..........	—	4	—	4
Maryland..........	6	5	6	5
Virginia...........	25	—	25	—
North Carolina.....	15	—	15	—
South Carolina.....	11	—	11	—
Georgia...........	8	—	8	—
Kentucky..........	12	—	12	—
Tennessee..........	8	—	8	—
Louisiana..........	3	—	3	—
Ohio..............	7	—	7	—
	128	89	131	86

Elections of 1816 and 1820

LYNN W. TURNER is the President of Otterbein College and the author of William Plumer of New Hampshire.

Elections of 1816 and 1820

by *Lynn W. Turner*

The most conspicuous casualty of the War of 1812 was a noncombatant—the Federalist party. This was an ironic twist of fate, for almost until the end of hostilities it appeared that the miserably conducted and humiliating conflict should redound to the benefit of those who, from its beginning, had labeled it "premature and inexpedient."

The unpopular war, preceded by a long series of commercial restrictions imposed by Republican Administrations upon the ports and mercantile interests of the nation, had, in fact, led to a Federalist revival in those parts of the country most dependent upon foreign trade. Congressmen from every state north of the Potomac had voted against the declaration of war, and there had been negative votes as well from Virginia and North Carolina. In the new House of Representatives, elected during the early months of hostilities, the Federalist contingent had been doubled, and some of the war hawks had been repudiated at the polls. By 1814, Federalist governors and legislative majorities had once more taken control of all New England, Maryland, and Delaware. Strong Federalist minorities had also reappeared in the state legislatures of New York, Pennsylvania, and New Jersey.

Except for a few spectacular naval victories, little had occurred during the first twenty months of the war to bring cheer to President Madison and the Republicans. Delay, indecision, blundering, and defeat had characterized most of the fighting on the Canadian border. The army could not be raised to full strength, little money could be borrowed, trade with the enemy could not be prevented, and party discipline could not be enforced. Finally, in the summer of 1814, came the ultimate indignity—the capture of Washington and a helter-skelter flight of Republican politicians across the Potomac. In the fall elections Federalist revival reached full strength. It appeared to the exultant Federalists as well as to their discouraged opponents that the two-party system, which Jefferson had almost extinguished in 1804–1807, was, a decade later, in the process of flourishing recovery. That is to say, it would so have appeared to them had early nineteenth-century Americans thought of politics in such terms as a party in power and a party in loyal opposition. They were not yet accustomed to such ideas. Parties in power, in those days, assumed that they alone had the right to rule and equated opposition almost with treason, while parties out of power did not scruple to demand fundamental changes in the form of government or even a dissolution of the Union in order to recover their position. It was generally assumed, therefore, that when representatives from the five New England states met in secret conclave at Hartford in the autumn of 1814 they would require extreme concessions from the Federal Government as the price for remaining in the Union.

Even while the Hartford Convention was in session, however, President Madison's Administration was rescued by an apparent intervention of divine providence. It was a remarkable turnabout. After Macdonough's brilliant naval victory on Lake Champlain, General Prevost withdrew his invading British army from before the slender defenses of Plattsburg and marched back into Canada. One day later, General Ross, the incendiary of Washington, was killed by the spirited defenders of Baltimore and his marauding expedition cleared out of Chesapeake Bay. Early in February, Washington received news of General Jackson's still more incredible victory at New Orleans, the death of another British general, and the ignominious retreat of another army of European veterans from American soil. In apparently logical sequence, dispatches came from Ghent, including a copy of the treaty which brought the war to an end without the surrender of a single inch of American territory or a single iota of sovereignty, after it had appeared in the earlier negotiations that these disasters were inevitable.

The effect on the American people of this spectacular series of events was electric. Suddenly, Madison's aggressive policies seemed vindicated and his mistakes were forgotten. America had not only re-won, but confirmed her independence. A wave of patriotic fervor and nationalism swept the land, drowning the particularists and separatists—in other words, the Federalists. Even though seven not at all extreme demands had been carried to Washington by the Hartford Convention delegates, they dared not present them to Congress. In the tense days of December it had not seemed extraordinary that a body of dissident Americans should resort to the essentially revolutionary but well-tried device of an extralegal assembly to give voice to their grievances and to exert pressure upon the regular organs of government. In the brilliant February light of New Orleans and Ghent, however, the procedure appeared to be not only exceptionable but treasonable. No fulcrum remained upon which the Hartford commissioners could rest the lever of their seven demands; they discreetly aborted their mission and slipped back to New England.

Although the immediate cause of Federalist collapse was the fatal stain of "Hartford Conventionism," which no amount of explanation would ever wash away, the party disappeared in the long run because it had no platform on which to stand. Federalism's first principles, formulated by Hamilton and given sanctity by the immortal name of Washington, had been quietly appropriated by its political opponents. After 1800 the Jeffersonian Republicans increasingly became the party of nationalism and centralization, while the Federalists became the champions of sectionalism and particularization. Old John Adams described this phenomenon pretty well in 1813 when he said, "Our two great parties have crossed over the valley and taken possession of each other's mountain." The Republicans were indeed entrenched upon the heights of nationalism in 1814, but the Federalist position was no longer a mountain—it was a morass.

The Fourteenth Congress, which assembled in December, 1815, consisted of 159 Republicans from fourteen of the eighteen states, and sixty-two Federalists, elected from twelve states. For sheer individual ability, few Congresses in American history have matched the Fourteenth. Majority leadership rested in the hands of the younger Republicans—Henry Clay, who was again chosen Speaker of the House, John C. Calhoun, William Lowndes, John Forsyth, Samuel Ingham, Peter Porter, and Richard M. Johnson, the slayer of Tecumseh. Their ablest opponents were young Daniel Webster, sent to Congress by the Federalists of New Hampshire, Rufus King, the Federalist senator from New York, and John Randolph, the eccentric Virginian who thought of himself as the sole remaining repository of Republican virtue, and bitterly denounced the backsliding of his former friends.

To this Congress, on December 5, 1815, President Madison presented his seventh annual message, therewith providing his followers with the early nineteenth-century equivalent of a party platform. He confirmed, in somewhat hesitant language, what his younger colleagues were ready to shout from the housetops—that the Republicans were now willing to exert the economic powers of the central government, in the words of a newspaper critic, "far beyond what was ever contemplated by the federal administration." He had already abandoned Jefferson's reliance upon a citizen militia and a gunboat fleet in favor of a strong, permanent army and navy—now he advocated the reestablishment of a national bank, the enactment of a protective tariff, and a program of federally financed internal improvements. Congress was eager to carry out the President's suggestions. Led principally by Calhoun and Clay, it chartered the Second Bank of the United States, passed the Tariff Act of 1816, and enacted into law a bill to devote the bonus paid into the national treasury by the new bank to the building of roads and canals. This question of constitutionality in all of these startling measures was either assumed to be noncontroversial, argued on broad bases of loose construction, or ignored—except by Madison, who suffered a final attack of Republican conscience and vetoed the Bonus Bill the day before he retired from office. John Randolph, viewing this record of the Fourteenth Congress with acerbic sarcasm, proclaimed it as nothing but "old Federalism, vamped up into something bearing the superficial appearance of Republicanism."

What is really significant, however, is that these were not party measures, but policies of economic interest, and congressmen voted according to the dictates of their constituencies rather than the demands of their leaders. Federalists supplied 28 per cent of the votes which carried the Tariff Act of 1816, and 42 per cent of those opposed to it; Federalist Rhode Island voted overwhelmingly in its favor and Federalist New Hampshire voted solidly against it. The Bonus Bill elicited an almost purely sectional vote, with New England, New Jersey, Delaware, and Maryland nearly unanimously opposed; the South and West almost evenly divided; and New York and Pennsylvania furnishing the overwhelming support which carried the measure. By 1816, even before they had ceased to influence presidential elections, party distinctions in Congress were almost completely at an end.

One of the functions assumed by the Fourteenth Congress but not delegated to it by the Constitution, or by anything other than expediency, was the nomination of presidential and vice-presidential candidates to be elected in the autumn of 1816. In spite of the Constitution's jealous insistence upon a separation of the legislative and executive functions, members of the respective parties in Congress had, since 1796, assumed the task of "recommending" to the country persons suitable to perform the duties of the principal executive offices. On the tenth of March (in the midst of the House debate on the national bank bill), an unknown person posted an invitation to Republican members of both houses to meet on the twelfth in the Representatives' chamber for the purpose of making the necessary nominations. At the appointed time, only fifty-eight of the 141 Republican members appeared. This was obviously too small a number to give respectability even to a pre-determined choice, and Jeremiah Morrow of Ohio, chairman of the rump session, was persuaded to issue a more official call for a Republican caucus on March 16. With only twenty-two of the eligible members absent, the caucus proceeded to business in spite of resolutions offered by Henry Clay and John W. Taylor that it was inexpedient to do so.

This rather strange series of maneuvers was due in part to growing dissatisfaction with the caucus system of nomination and the reluctance of presidential aspirants to be identified with it. The *National Intelligencer*, which spoke for the Administration, declared in April that James Monroe would have been content to have had no caucus at all, and that caucuses did not truly represent public opinion. No doubt a certain number of congressmen stayed away from both caucuses in 1816 out of the conviction that the procedure was evil. However, the principal factor behind the caucus history of 1816 was undoubtedly a jockeying for position between the followers of the two foremost Republican candidates, James Monroe and William Crawford. Monroe, as the Administration candidate, had every reason to avoid a caucus if possible, especially since Crawford's followers in Congress might very well capture it. "Every day thins the ranks of Mr. Monroe's friends," reported an observer from Georgia in February. "The fact is," he continued, "that an overwhelming majority is in favor of Mr. C. and that he can be the next president if he wishes." A statement from Senator Bibb of Georgia, printed in the *Intelligencer* of February 2, declaring that Mr. Crawford "did not consider himself among the number of those from whom the selection ought to be made," seemed to have no effect in slowing down the Crawford bandwagon. It would have been logical enough, therefore, for Monroe's adherents to have tried to avoid a showdown, and for Crawford's friends to take the lead by making the anonymous call for a caucus on March 12. Monroe's followers would have ignored the call, thus accounting for the poor attendance, but since their hands had been forced they would have attempted to rally all their strength for the second caucus. Its outcome confirms the reliability of this hypothesis.

This is also the way the newspapers interpreted events. Far out in Ohio, the *Muskingum Messenger* wondered in March why the caucus was so late in being called. The *National Intelligencer* asserted that no one knew who had issued the call for the first caucus, but that it certainly had not come from Monroe's friends because they would not attend. Later it stated categorically that the first caucus had been arranged by Monroe's opponents. Finally, the *Intelligencer* approved the second caucus and hopefully assumed that "the prominent candidate" would "in the end, unite the suffrage of the whole Republican party." The *Washington City Weekly Gazette* opined that Crawford would have won if the caucus had been held four weeks earlier, but that Monroe's majority would be larger if it were held four weeks hence. "The cause of this, for the honor of republicanism. it is better to leave to conjecture, than to attempt to portray."

William Harris Crawford is a man of mystery in American annals, principally because so little evidence has survived to explain his great eminence and popularity. It is altogether probable that he could have become President of the United States in 1816 had he chosen to assert his claims, yet few even well-informed Americans today know anything about him. He was deaf to opportunity when first she knocked, and his later attempt to woo the Fickle Goddess ended in tragedy.

Descended from an early Scot emigrant to Virginia. William Crawford was born in the shadow of the Blue Ridge in 1772. but moved with his family a few years later to the Georgia frontier. As Andrew Jackson, at almost the same time, cast his lot with the western settlements. Crawford became the spokesman and champion of the southern upland planter, making his permanent home at "Woodlawn," a plantation near Lexington in the Georgia Piedmont. Again, like Jackson, he established a reputation for pure Republicanism while actually allying himself with the conservative, financially orthodox Savannah merchants and lawyers. He killed his opponent in one duel and suffered a shattered wrist in another, in the best tradition of frontier politics. He denounced the perpetrators of the Yazoo frauds in the state legislature and built his alliances so shrewdly that in 1807 he was elected to the United States Senate.

Crawford's career in national government was one of steady advancement. He was elected President *pro tempore* of the Senate when Vice-President George Clinton died in 1812. A year later he succeeded Joel Barlow as the American minister to France and was carried to his new post by the United States sloop *Argus*, which subsequently destroyed two million dollars worth of British shipping in the Irish Sea. During his voyage home from Paris in 1815, Crawford was elevated to President Madison's Cabinet as Secretary of War and promptly became Secretary of State Monroe's chief rival for the Presidency. With his "gigantic stature, handsome face, studious disposition, clear judgment, native sagacity, engaging affability and fund of anecdotes," he was a formidable opponent.

James Monroe, however, was the heir apparent, the chosen successor to the mantle of the Virginia Dynasty, and his nomination, according to the *National Intelligencer*, was expected by the country at large. Although as far as we know, President Madison had never committed his personal predilections to paper or to another ear, he had brought his Virginia neighbor into his Cabinet in 1811 as Secretary of State—the recognized stepping stone to the Presidency. Monroe fulfilled the other indispensable qualification by having been from his youth a friend and protege of Thomas Jefferson. He had duly emphasized the relationship by purchasing a country estate on the outskirts of Charlottesville, only a few miles from Monticello. His Republicanism had never been questioned and his integrity had been certified by Jefferson himself who had said of him in 1786 that his "soul might be turned wrong side outwards without discovering a blemish to the world."

Monroe's less intimate acquaintances, however, had discovered several blemishes, not the least of which was that he came from Virginia and the country was growing weary of Virginia Presidents. Querulous John Adams, who, of course, believed that there was "not a more fit man in creation for the Presidency" than his son, had concluded that John Quincy would be kept in Europe waiting his turn "till all Virginians shall be extinct." Contemporary newspapers were full of objections to another Virginia President. The *Raleigh Minerva* reported that a rebel electoral ticket "not subservient to Virginia" was being formed by Federalists and dissident Republicans in North Carolina. After the nomination of Monroe, the *New-York Patriot* promised its support but admitted being "averse to the nomination of another citizen from Virginia." The *Charleston Courier* of May 29 printed a lengthy diatribe which charged that "a few leading men in Virginia, have outrageously violated republican principles."

Equally dangerous was a strong feeling in New York that it was time for one of its citizens to advance from second fiddle to concert master in the Republican orchestra. Governor Daniel Tompkins, who had just been re-elected over Rufus King by 60 per cent of the voters, was selected as a favorite-son candidate and the state legislature passed certain "Resolutions, advancing the pretensions of New York and reprehending the assumptions of Virginia." Although Tompkins took himself seriously, it is difficult to believe that anyone else did. He had a good record as a war governor, but he was hardly known outside his own state and even there was supported by only one faction of the Republican party. Peter B. Porter tried to persuade Monroe that all the political maneuvering going on really signified no opposition to him, and Jabez Hammond, another New York congressman, believed that Martin Van Buren, then a state senator, stage-managed the operation in order to divert votes from Crawford to Monroe. In view of the fact that the New York delegation subsequently voted almost unanimously in the caucus for Crawford, it might be easier to take the action at its face value and assume that New York was simply not reconciled to a continuation of the Virginia Dynasty.

The threat represented by William H. Crawford was serious. It served to remind citizens of another blemish in Monroe's record—namely, that he had listened for some time in 1808 to the siren song of revolt as piped by John Randolph and the other "Quidites" against the dynastic succession of Madison. He could therefore hardly complain now that dissident Republicans in New York and the South were rallying behind the vigorous and younger Georgian. Sentiment for Crawford was so strong in the winter that those who yearned for harmony in the Republican ranks expressed alarm at "the measures resorted to, to divide the friends of the late war." One of Monroe's correspondents voiced the hope "that you and William Crawford will be both so truly great, as not to suffer your friendships to be impaired thereby."

Perhaps there did exist such an element of true greatness in Crawford's composition, although more cynical observers were convinced that he was induced to withdraw from the race in 1816 by the promise of support for the succession in 1824. A Monroe supporter, Senator Abner Lacock of Pennsylvania, later admitted to a newspaper publisher that he had voluntarily called upon the Secretary of War in early March and asked him to renounce his candidacy. Lacock had argued for party loyalty but had also pointed out that Crawford was a young man with plenty of time for a later turn at the Presidency. The Georgian, Lacock reported, had replied that his own feelings would not permit him to oppose Monroe for office. Before the second caucus met on March 16, Senators Charles Tait and William Bibb of Georgia, friends of Crawford, spread the word that the Secretary of War could not run against so venerable a figure as the Secretary of State. This statement was a little condescending perhaps, but capable of translation into a spirit of loyal and noble forbearance. Unfortunately, the friends of Crawford bungled the rest of the job. They were supposed to have attended the caucus, made a formal statement of Crawford's renunciation, voted for Monroe, and explained the whole heroic procedure in the Government press. Instead, they absented themselves from the caucus, which proceeded to nominate Monroe by 65 votes, a narrow majority of 11 over the 54 cast by stubborn Crawford partisans from New York, New Jersey, North Carolina, Georgia, and Kentucky. Had all of the Georgian's supporters from among the twenty-two absent Republicans been present and voted, James Monroe might never have become President of the United States.

The caucus finished its work by nominating Daniel Tompkins for the

Vice-Presidency, giving him 85 votes to 30 for Governor Simon Snyder of Pennsylvania. The New Yorker may have taken some comfort in the 20-vote margin by which he exceeded the presidential nominee. Four days later, a committee headed by Congressman Samuel Smith of Maryland, a Republican who was harldy more than lukewarm toward Monroe, informed the Secretary of State that he had been "recommended to the people of the United States by a General Meeting of the Republican members of both houses of Congress as a proper person to fill the office of President."

Smith's committee did not inform Monroe that only 46 per cent of the Republicans in Congress had seen fit to join in the recommendation, but the new candidate could read this fact for himself. A Federalist newspaper, the *Charleston Courier*, printed on May 29 what purported to be a copy of a pamphlet published by the "fifty-four Democrats" who had voted for Crawford, entitled "Exposition of the Motives for opposing the nomination of Mr. Monroe for the office of President of the United States." This may have been an unusually audacious forgery, but if the document was genuine, its authors were men of extraordinary courage, for they could never again have made their peace with the incoming President. They had voted against Monroe, they said, because he continued the Virginia succession, to which all the genuine talent in the country had been sacrificed. John Armstrong, John Quincy Adams, and De Witt Clinton had been effectively blocked, isolated or disgraced by the Virginia manipulators. "As to all the endowments which should belong to the chief magistrate of this country," they declared, "strength of mind, knowledge of character, decision, literacy, legal and philosophical attainments, there is no comparison between [Monroe] and Mr. [De Witt] Clinton." In further consideration of Monroe's lack of qualifications, the apologists emphasized particularly his "slowness of comprehension, and want of penetration and decision." Finally, they reported that they had voted for Crawford "because they knew him to be independent, virtuous, and able. Had it not been for the discouraging delicacy of that respectable gentleman . . . he would, beyond all question have been nominated for the presidency."

It is hard to imagine American history without a President Monroe and a Monroe Doctrine, yet the Virginian had come perilously close to losing the nomination. Jabez Hammond, from New York, who voted for Crawford in the caucus, regarded him as far superior to Monroe. The latter, he thought, was "not distinguished for vigor of intellect, or for decision of character, independence of action, or indeed for any extraordinary public services." Had the canvass of 1816 been conducted in anything like the glare of today's publicity, and particularly if there had been any television exposure, the hearty, bluff and handsome Georgian would have enjoyed a tremendous advantage over the colorless and unimpressive Virginian. Crawford represented the "new politics" of the day while Monroe was almost a relic of the old; but the predetermined pattern withstood the assault of novelty and the party closed ranks behind it. "We were averse to the nomination of another citizen from Virginia," wrote the editor of the *New York Patriot*, but now that "*the decision has taken place*" he promised to support it and called for united backing of Monroe and Tompkins.

From distant Ohio, John McLean wrote that he heard nothing but approval of Monroe's nomination. "I am now more fully convinced than I was last winter, that a different nomination could not have turned the current of public opinion, in the Western Country," he declared, "I anticipate an expression at the ensuing election, more unanimous than has heretofore been given on any similar occasion." William Pinkney, from still more distant Naples, expressed his confidence that "before this reaches you it will be known that your fellow Citizens think you entitled by a Life of unsullied Honour and enlightened patriotism to be preferred to all others as their Chief Magistrate." The accolade which Monroe undoubtedly prized most, however, came from the venerable Sage of Monticello. "I shall not waste your time in idle congratulations," Thomas Jefferson wrote simply. "You know my joy in the commitment of the helm of our government to your hands."

From the other side of the political fence, Rufus King, the Federalist senator from New York, predicted that "the opposition which favored Mr. Crawford will submit." He was obviously unaware at the time (March) that he himself was to be remembered in American history as the last symbol of Federalist resistance to the Republican juggernaut. In fact, King's unawareness may have extended to the week after the meeting of the Electoral College in which he won 34 votes for President. There is nothing in his correspondence to indicate that he was a candidate for the office. There is no record of a Federalist caucus having been held in Washington, nor was there any agreement upon a candidate among Federalist newspapers. On December 3, just before the meeting of the Electoral College, the *Boston Daily Advertiser* claimed not to know for whom the Federalist electors would vote. Although Federalists in their private correspondence had mentioned such possibilities as General Howard of Maryland and had even toyed with the idea of supporting Crawford, they really had little choice other than to vote for King or abandon the field. As a native New Englander, a member by marriage of the New York aristocracy, an unwavering but not fanatical Federalist from the days of the Constitutional Convention, the party's vice-presidential candidate in 1808, and a prominent senator able to win election from a powerful and predominantly Republican state, Rufus King was the only candidate still acceptable to Federalists throughout the nation.

The New York Federalists, however, had failed to rally behind King for governor in the spring of 1816, and his friends did almost nothing to make him a winner in November. Three of the four Federalist electors chosen by the voters in Maryland and one of the three named by the legislature in Delaware did not even bother to attend the Electoral College. Although the Federalists controlled the state government in Rhode Island, they did not present an electoral ticket to the voters, nor did they contest the election in Vermont, New Jersey, Ohio, or in any state south of the Potomac. Some measure of their strength was exerted in New Hampshire where their general electoral ticket won 46.4 per cent of the popular vote, and in the New York assembly where thirty-five of the 126 members voted for a Federalist ticket, but it was obvious, elsewhere, that there had been the customary lack of coordination, from top to bottom. Even King, commenting on the election to his Massachusetts

Federalist friend, Christopher Gore, as late as November 5, observed, "nobody except Duane [the maverick editor of the Philadelphia *Aurora*] seems to take any concern about it, and so certain is the result . . . that no pains are taken to excite the community on the subject. It is quite worthy of remark, that in no preceding election, has there been such a calm respecting it; and it is equally so, that the Candidate does not possess the full respect and confidence of either party." It is significant that King wrote "Candidate" in the singular—and he was not referring to himself!

The archaic and unwieldy system devised by the Constitutional Convention for choosing Presidents of the United States is under justifiably heavy attack today, but it is far more rational and democratic now than it was in 1816. Nineteen states chose a total of 221 electors in this particular quadrennial exercise. A bare majority of ten permitted their citizens some share in the process, but only three of these, Maryland, Kentucky, and Tennessee, chose their thirty-one electors by popular vote in districts, which is a reasonably democratic system. Unfortunately, these popular votes went unrecorded, even in the newspapers. The seven states which chose their electors on general tickets (as all states do today) cast 93 electoral votes for Monroe, thus depriving the Federalist minority which existed in every one of them (New Hampshire, Rhode Island, New Jersey, Pennsylvania, Virginia, North Carolina, and Ohio) of any weight in the election. In the remaining nine states the electors were chosen by the legislatures—again on the all or nothing basis determined by the political majority. Thus, Massachusetts, Connecticut, and Delaware chose Federalist electors who cast 34 votes for King and none for Monroe, although probably 47 per cent of the voters in these states were Republicans. The Vermont, New York, South Carolina, Georgia, Louisiana, and Indiana legislatures appointed sixty-two electors who voted for Monroe. It is ironic that at least four of these were frontier states where democracy was supposed to flourish. Altogether, Monroe and Tompkins received 183 well-disciplined votes while King was given 34. The Federalists exercised exemplary self-determination in voting for a vice-presidential candidate, Massachusetts giving 22 votes to General Howard, Delaware 3 to Robert G. Harper of Maryland, and the Connecticut electors splitting, 5 for James Ross of Pennsylvania and 4 for John Marshall of Virginia. In the light of so overwhelming a Republican victory and so ignominious a Federalist defeat, it was generally recognized that the Federalists had played their last role on the national stage.

In local politics, Federalism persisted in isolated areas for various lengths of time after 1816, but even on this level the erosion of strength was rapid. Vermont Federalists never recovered from the crushing defeat in the state elections of 1816, although they continued to elect some representatives from the Connecticut River towns. Led by a former Federalist, William Plumer, and making a political issue out of a nasty quarrel between the President and the trustees of Dartmouth College, Republicans regained control of every branch of the state government of New Hampshire in 1816, even purging the judiciary of its Federalist judges. Federalist opposition diminished rapidly thereafter; by 1820 they had no gubernatorial candidate nor any representatives in the legislature.

The success of the Republicans in New England was due, in part, to their championship of religious liberty and their attacks on the state churches. In 1817 for the first time, they won control of the principal bastion of orthodoxy, Connecticut, by uniting with a group of liberal Federalist dissenters to disestablish the Congregationalist Church. Their successful candidate for governor was Oliver Wolcott, the former Secretary of the Treasury in the Cabinets of Presidents Washington and Adams. Federalists, combining now with dissatisfied Republicans, tried to stage comebacks in 1819 and 1820 but failed. After this their efforts virtually ceased. In Rhode Island they held on a little longer; in 1822 they still elected half of the state legislature, but had lost control of all state offices. The Massachusetts Federalists were clever enough to offer General John Brooks, a highly respected Revolutionary veteran, as their candidate for governor in 1816. His mild and conciliatory policy was so generally acceptable that the Republicans did not oppose him seriously, although they regained control of the legislature in 1819. When Brooks decided to retire in 1823, the Federalists commited a major blunder by running Harrison Gray Otis, of Hartford Convention infamy, as their gubernatorial candidate. He was soundly beaten in 1824, and again in 1825, after which the Federalists made no further effort to organize a ticket. Nothing illustrated their death wish more clearly than their determination to commit political suicide with Otis.

Outside New England, the Federalists maintained their greatest local strength in the Middle Atlantic states, where, by combining with the "peace Democrats" they had won the electoral votes of New York, New Jersey, Delaware, and nearly half of Maryland in 1812. However, the New Jersey Federalists were unable to cement their alliance with any of the Republican factions, and they were almost exterminated in the elections of 1820. The Federalist party in Maryland maintained control of the state government until 1819, when it lost the governorship, and was disastrously beaten in the legislative elections of 1820. Although there was a slight Federalist revival in all of the Middle Atlantic States in 1822-23, the Federalists of Maryland never again captured their state government. It was, strangely enough, in rural, isolated Delaware that Hamilton's party survived for the longest period of time. Due to Federalist divisions, a Republican congressman was elected from Delaware in 1816, a governor in 1820, a Republican legislature in 1821, and a senator in 1822. These were aberrations, however; by 1824 everything was back to normal, and Delaware was again a Federalist state—the only one in the Union. Delaware Federalism merged into Whiggism almost without a break.

Although the Federalists in New York and Pennsylvania were numerous, influential and diligent, they had never, since the advent of Jeffersonian Republicanism, been able to recover the governments of their own states. However, the inevitable schisms among the triumphant Republicans had served to keep the Federalist apparatus alive, in the hope of holding the balance of power and selling its support to the highest bidder. De Witt Clinton won the governorship of New York in 1817 with Federalist help, although he did little to reward his coadjutors. Martin Van Buren's faction, the Bucktails, wooed Federalist support by helping to reelect Rufus King to the Senate in 1820. In like manner, the Pennsylvania Federalists allied themselves with the "Old School Republicans" to support a German politician, Joseph Heister who was defeated in 1817 but won the governorship in 1820. Unfortunately, even when in the minority, the Federalists could not repress their internecine feuds which placed the kiss of death upon any Republican faction willing to acknowledge their support. By 1824, Federalist influence in the two largest states of the Union had dwindled to negligible proportions.

In the South, long before 1816, Federalism had ceased to be more than a petty annoyance to Republican governors, and in the new western states it offered only token resistance, although there were prominent individual adherents of the faith in both of these areas. By 1816, a Federalist editor in Ohio expressed the probable sentiments of his party when he wrote that it was "high time for the Federalists to give up an opposition which only serves to heighten the asperities of party spirit, and exhibit the thinness of their ranks." Christopher Gore echoed this feeling in the exaggerated pessimism affected by the eastern Federalists when he wrote, in 1822, that the party had "died long since by Suicide." The collapse of local resistance and local organization left no basis on which a national campaign could be mounted and practically assured the reelection of James Monroe in 1820.

The fifth President of the United States was not quite fifty-nine years of age when, on March 4, 1817, he took his oath of office from Chief Justice John Marshall and delivered the first outdoor inaugural in the history of the republic to "an immense concourse of officers of the government, foreign officers, strangers (ladies as well as gentlemen) and citizens." The long and turgid address was in many respects a repetition of President Madison's last annual message to Congress. The "highly favored condition of our country," said the new President, "must be protected by adequate land and naval forces, a well trained militia and an extensive system of coastal fortifications. . . . We shall bind the Union more closely together . . . by roads and canals. . . . Our manufacturers will likewise require the systematic and fostering care of the Government." Monroe struck a slight note of novelty by promising to civilize the Indian tribes, extinguish the national debt, and hold the public fiscal agents to strict accountability. But most of his speech dwelt upon the glories of republican government and "the increased harmony of opinion which pervades our Union. Discord does not belong to our system," declared the complacent President. "The American people . . . constitute one great family with a common interest. . . . To promote this harmony in accord with the principles of our republican Government and in a manner to give them the most complete effect, and to advance in all other respects the best interests of our Union, will be the object of my constant and zealous exertions."

Monroe's appearance was in harmony with the seriousness of his discourse. He was a decidedly old-fashioned looking gentleman, dressed in somber black broadcloth tail-coat and knee breeches, long white stockings, buckled shoes, a powdered wig, and tricorn hat. These fashions had gone out of style with the French Revolution, but Monroe was a product of the earlier American Revolution—one of its last still in public life. In fact, he vaguely reminded contemporaries, and those of us today who compare the Stuart portraits, of General Washington, but without the firm jaw and commanding eye. There were, indeed, some similarities of character—a strong sense of public duty, a reputation, at least, for integrity, and an unwavering patriotism. By no stretch of the imagination, however, could it be said that Monroe was "first in the hearts of his countrymen."

On the other hand, unlike many of our contemporary aspirants, Monroe had "earned" his turn at the Presidency by a lifetime of public service, including an honorable wound at the Battle of Trenton, election to the Virginia House of Burgesses, service in the "old Congress," a term in the United States Senate, a series of diplomatic missions, both regular and extraordinary, three terms as governor of his state, and the unusual experience of directing, for a time, both the War and State Departments in Madison's Cabinet. While he had always been prudent, diligent, and conscientious, Monroe had not distinguished himself in any of these offices. He lacked the intellectual firmness of Washington, the vigor of Adams, the acumen of Jefferson, or the subtlety of Madison. He was, in fact, the weakest man who had thus far been elevated to the Presidency. In comparison with his predecessors, his Administration might well have been labeled the Era of Mediocrity.

It has actually gone down in history, however, as the Era of Good Feelings, and this is appropriate, if only for the reason that Monroe himself, at this stage of his career, was overflowing with good will for his fellow men. He wanted to unite all sections of the country by bringing a representative from each of them into his Cabinet. In this laudable ambition he was thwarted by the refusal of any eligible westerner to join him, although he offered the War Department in turn to Henry Clay and Isaac Shelby. The President showed a considerable degree of courage by appointing John Quincy Adams, a former Federalist, to head the State Department. By accident, rather than design, Monroe's Cabinet finally became not a model of geographical balance, but a collection of rare abilities—of men superior, in most instances, to the President himself. Adams proved to be one of our most distinguished Secretaries of State; Crawford was an exceedingly able head of the Treasury; and Calhoun brought the War Department to a peak of efficiency hitherto unknown.

In only one respect did the new President betray any vindictiveness: he refused to take an actual Federalist into his official family, although he was urged to do so by no less a partisan than Andrew Jackson. "Now is the time to exterminate the monster called party spirit," wrote the Tennessean. "By selecting characters most conspicuous for their probity, virtue, capacity and firmness, without any regard to party, you will go far to . . . eradicate those feelings, which, on former occasions, threw so many obstacles in the way of government; and perhaps have the pleasure of uniting a people heretofore divided." Monroe agreed with him "decidedly, in the principle, that the Chief

Magistrate of the country, ought not to be the head of a party, but of the nation." He went on to say what almost any American would have said in those days, that "the existence of parties is not necessary to free government," but his formula for extinguishing party spirit was not to accommodate Federalists, but to wait for them to see the error of their ways and become Republicans.

It must have appeared to Monroe, in the next few months, that this was exactly what was happening. When he made his celebrated tour of the northern states in the summer of 1817, he was received nowhere with such open-handed hospitality and marks of official respect as he was in Boston, the very citadel of Federalism. It was here, from the least likely source, namely, the columns of the arch-Federalist *Columbian Sentinel*, that the Administration of the fourth Virginia President was hailed as the "Era of Good Feelings." Governor Brooks entertained the President in his own home, and Federalist leaders all over the North called upon him with pledges of support. In Washington, John Quincy Adams read the newspaper accounts of these phenomena with astonishment. "Party spirit has indeed subsided throughout the Union to a degree that I should have thought scarcely possible," he reported to his son-in-law in London. Crawford reported his own faintly envious astonishment with a touch of sarcasm. "If the bondmen and bondwomen were not set free, and individual debts released, a general absolution of political sins seems to have been mutually agreed upon."

The euphoria persisted until after the 1820 election, which was virtually uncontested. Conflict and change are the essence of history, and where they both appear to be absent for a period of eight years we are bound to have the dullest period in America's political annals. Historians unite in pointing out that the surface calm was only superficial, and that the forces of bitter personal antagonism and renewed sectional strife were gathering for future explosions, but no one has ever explained satisfactorily why these were not released until 1824. James Monroe was not a very effective President, and it is difficult to understand why there did not develop within his own party a strong movement against his renomination and reelection.

When the period for thinking about the selection of candidates arrived in the early months of 1820, the country was in the throes of an economic depression, resulting from wild speculation in public lands and private banks, and precipitated by a sudden contraction of credit on the part of the Bank of the United States, a quasi-federal agency. State banks had reduced their note issues from a hundred million in 1817 to forty-five million in 1819, and dozens of them in the South and West were forced to close their doors. Purchasers of government land fell more than twenty-two million dollars in arrears in their payments to the Treasury, which also suffered, at the same time, a drastic curtailment in revenue duties. For the first time since the end of the war, the Government finished the year 1819 with a deficit, and Congress had to borrow three million dollars early in 1820. With most of the western landholders delinquent in their payments to the Government and most of the western businessmen mortgaged to the national bank, foreign trade in the doldrums, the price for cotton, wool, wheat, and tobacco depressed, and many of the factories that had sprung up during the war forced into bankruptcy by foreign competition, the entire country was suffering on the eve of the election. In 1820, Monroe faced roughly the same kind of dilemma which was to confront Herbert Hoover in 1932.

Neither Congress nor the President, however, suggested any immediate measures to relieve the people from their distress. In 1819, the third branch of the Government had displayed what seemed to be an equal indifference to the interests of poor Americans in the form of two celebrated Supreme Court decisions. The *Dartmouth College Case* put chartered monopolies beyond the reach of legislative regulation and *McCullough vs Maryland* specifically protected branches of "the Monster," the Bank of the United States, from state taxation. A dozen states protested against these decisions, and in Ohio agents of the state treasurer forcibly collected a hundred thousand dollars in taxes from the Chillicothe branch of the national bank, six months after John Marshall had declared such acts unconstitutional. This kind of defiance alarmed the men in Washington. Secretary of War Calhoun, in agreement with Secretary of State Adams, stated that there had been "an immense revolution of fortunes in every part of the Union; enormous numbers of persons utterly ruined; multitudes in deep distress; and a general mass of disaffection to the Government not concentrated in any particular direction, but ready to seize upon any event and looking out anywhere for a leader."

In the area of foreign relations, Adams had succeeded in negotiating a treaty by which Spain relinquished Florida but the Spanish court had refused to ratify it. Jackson's high-handed occupation of Florida and execution of two British subjects had stirred up an international storm. Henry Clay had not only attacked the Administration on this score, but had vigorously criticized Monroe's refusal to recognize the revolutionary governments in South America. Few Administrations have stayed in office when a popular and powerful Speaker of the House opposed their policies.

Finally, the Sixteenth Congress, which had the generally recognized responsibility for making the usual caucus nominations, had before it in the winter and spring of 1819-20 the "Missouri Questions," potentially the most explosive issue that had faced the National Government since the War of 1812. The proposal, by a New York Republican, to force an anti-slavery constitution upon the state of Missouri had won almost unanimous approval in the North and unanimous condemnation in the South. Senator Rufus King's vigorous speeches in defense of the exclusion principle had led Jefferson and many other Republicans in the South to believe that he was seeking to revive the Federalists as a northern, anti-slavery party, and vault into the Presidency perhaps at the expense of the Union itself. George Hay, a member of the Virginia legislature who had married one of Monroe's daughters, warned his father-in-law that any indication of doubt or hesitation in dealing with the issue would be fatal. "The members have gone up to the caucus [where they would nominate and instruct their Presidential electors]," he wrote, "under a conviction that you will put your veto on the infamous Cabal and intrigue in all its forms and shapes." As a matter of fact, when it learned that Monroe might sign the Compromise Bill passed by the House on March 2, the caucus adjourned without nominating electors, but subsequently reassembled and decided to support its fellow Virginian.

Modern historians agree that the crisis created by the Missouri question can hardly be exaggerated, and contemporaries were fully aware of its significance. Jefferson's famous "fire bell in the night" metaphor was echoed in many letters and newspaper essays. In the delightful correspondence which former Presidents Adams and Jefferson had begun in their old age, Adams had mentioned "the Missouri Slavery" as one of a dozen issues which threatened "thunder and lightening" when the new Congress assembled in November. Jefferson replied that all of the others, including the depression, were nothing — they, "like waves in a storm, will pass under the ship." But the Missouri issue could well bring the ship of state upon the rocks. To President Monroe, native of a slave state, avowed friend of the West, but anxious that nothing ruin his prospects for a second term, the clause in the Missouri Bill prohibiting slavery in the northern Louisiana Territory presented serious problems. "Should the bill pass, it will place the President in a sad dilemma," wrote a young congressman from New Hampshire. "If he rejects it . . . he loses all the North, where his best friends now are — if he approves it, he is at open war with Virginia and the South." Since his first instinct was certainly to avoid open war, Monroe originally drafted a veto message, stating that "the proposed restriction to territories which are to be admitted into the Union, if not in direct violation of the Constitution, is repugnant to its principles." A better idea occurred to him, however — he would seek the advice of his Cabinet. He found these able men as sharply divided on the issue as the Congress, but a little judicious modification of the President's questions finally enabled them to arrive at their own compromise and provide him with the opinion that the Enabling Act, even with the Thomas Amendment, was not inconsistent with the Constitution. With this support, Monroe signed the Missouri Bill on March 2, 1820.

While the question was still pending in February, there were rumors in Washington that a caucus of congressmen from the non-slaveholding states would nominate "some person in opposition to Mr. Monroe," but no such move materialized. The leader for whom Calhoun thought the "general mass of disaffection" was searching failed to appear within the ranks of the Republicans, nor did Rufus King, the only Federalist with any stature, have the political ambitions which the South ascribed to him. So James Monroe won a second term by default, in a general atmosphere of indifference.

It is not for the historian to speculate on what might have been, but the philosopher might be willing to devote a minute's thought to the effect which instant communication might have exerted on Monroe's political fate. If television news commentators, armed with instantaneous press releases embellished by photographs, were bringing nightly reports of bankruptcies all over the country, of bank wars in Maryland, Ohio, and Kentucky, of angry debates in Congress threatening disunion over slavery in Missouri, of apoplectic Tennesseans asking why Florida was still closed to them after they had seized it under Jackson three years earlier, of interviews with John Taylor of Caroline, the acidulous critic of the Supreme Court, or with Henry Clay, Speaker of the House and equally passionate critic of the Administration's foreign policy, it is hard to believe that the general discontent would not have coalesced into political opposition to Monroe. The forces of democratic nationalism and of economic sectionalism were only slowly gathering, however, in 1820. It was over Monroe's Secretary of State and successor in the executive mansion that the storm was to burst.

In summation then—it is reasonably clear that the apparent extension of the Era of Good Feelings to cover Monroe's reelection in 1820 is a species of optical illusion, induced by the nineteenth-century time-lapse between the perception of political pain and the physical reaction to it, and that the unanimity with which the country favored him was indeed, as John Randolph expressed it, "the unanimity of indifference, and not of approbation." Monroe was not even formally renominated. General Samuel Smith, chairman of the 1816 caucus, did invite *all* members of Congress to a meeting early in April, for the usual purpose of settling upon suitable candidates, but it proved to be a fiasco. A heavy rainstorm and an even heavier blanket of indifference kept all but forty congressmen securely in their boarding houses. The abbreviated caucus voted that it was inexpedient to make any nominations and adjourned.

Although newspapers in every section of the country assumed that Monroe would be reelected, there was a small flurry of excitement over the Vice-Presidency. This came in part because Tompkins had entered the lists against De Witt Clinton for the governorship of New York and a small army of "Pretenders to the throne" hoped to succeed him. Pre-eminent among these was Henry Clay, who was certain that the caucus would have nominated him, had it acted at all. This would indeed have presented an interesting ticket; an incumbent for whom there was little enthusiasm and his most virulent critic as running mate. Tompkins, however, simplified matters by losing the New York election and retaining his claim upon party loyalists for another four years in Washington.

Had there been any genuine contest in 1820, it would have been labeled more democratic than the election of 1816. Five new states with a total of 21 electroal votes had been added to the Union; and two of them, Maine and Illinois, chose their electors by districts, while Mississippi used the general ticket system. The frontier states of Alabama and Missouri, however, deprived their citizens of direct vote for the Presidency by allowing the legislatures to choose their electors. Two of the older states added to the democratic trend, Massachusetts by changing from the choice of electors by the legislature to a district system, and Connecticut to a general ticket. One hundred and sixty-three of the 235 electors in 1820 were chosen by direct suffrage of the people—105 of them in nine states on general tickets and fifty-eight in six states by districts—leaving only seventy-two in nine states to be chosen by the legislatures. In spite of the increased opportunity, however, the nearly total lack of incentive accounted for one of the smallest popular votes on record. Probably less than 1 per cent of the male population went to the polls in 1820.

The actual process of choosing electors began in state legislative caucuses early in 1820 — we have already seen how the Virginia caucus came to its reluctant decision to recommend Monroe electors. As the Missouri controversy died down and the summer advanced, it became clear that little opposition to Monroe would develop. "There appears no great excitement in any quarter, concerning the next presidential election." declared the *Ohio Monitor* (Columbus) in April. "In most of the States the elections occur with great quietness, too great, perhaps, for the general safety of the Republic." However, even though Federalists showed no disposition to struggle for the safety of the Republic, there were a few dissident Republicans who took up the cudgels. In New York, the hotbed of anti-slavery political sentiment, rival slates of electoral candidates were presented to the legislature by Clinton's and Tompkins' supporters. The latter, labeled the *Slave Ticket* by the newspapers, was elected by a majority of 72 – 54 in the legislature.

Only in Pennsylvania did opposition to Monroe express itself in the popular vote, and this was due exclusively to William Duane, the caustic Philadelphia publisher. Denouncing the President, not only for being a Virginian but for having accepted the Missouri Compromise, Duane offered his own electoral ticket, pledged to vote for De Witt Clinton and to throw off the shackles of the slave-holding South. This act of defiance enabled a third of the citizens who came to the polls in Philadelphia to vote against Monroe, but it had negligible effects elsewhere. The twenty-five electors chosen by the voters in Pennsylvania were pledged to Monroe, as were those chosen in every other state.

It is worth noting that the only opposition to Monroe came from his own party. The Federalists offered none whatever. Even the thirteen identifiable Federalists among the 235 electors, eight from Massachusetts, four from Delaware (the two states still under Federalist control), and one from Maryland, all voted for Monroe. In the strict sense, party politics was dead in 1820. "Now if voting for Mr. Monroe be the touchstone of Republicanism," declared the *Boston Intelligencer and Evening Gazette*, a moderately Federalist newspaper, "we suspect that [after the election, people] will be puzzled to find any but Republicans in the Union."

While Federalists were willing enough to tolerate Monroe for another term, they balked at voting again for Tompkins. "There will be a number of us, *of course*, in this state," wrote Daniel Webster, one of the Federalist electors from Massachusetts, "who will not vote for Mr. Tompkins, and we must therefore look up somebody to vote for." The Bay Staters went far afield for their "somebody," finally lighting upon Richard Stockton, a New Jersey Federalist. The four Delaware electors cast their vice-presidential votes for Daniel Rodney, from their own state, and one Marylander also voted for a Federalist colleague, Robert G. Harper. Tompkins, therefore, received only 218 of the 231 votes cast by the Electoral College.

Daniel Webster's search for "somebody to vote for" as Vice-President probably led to the most bizarre and newsworthy incident in the otherwise lusterless history of the election of 1820. Webster's first impulse was to direct the Federalist votes toward John Quincy Adams, the only New Englander in Monroe's Cabinet and himself a former Federalist. Adams, however, was regarded by most Federalists as a despicable apostate, and there were few channels through which Webster could communicate with him. One of these was Adams' friend, William Plumer of Epping, New Hampshire, a former senator and governor, and also a former Federalist. Webster wrote to a mutual friend, Jeremiah Mason of Portsmouth, New Hampshire, asking him to solicit Plumer's intervention with Adams to gain support for the project.

Plumer, in turn, wrote to his son, a congressman, in Washington, and William Plumer, Jr. subsequently called upon the Secretary of State to outline the plan which Webster had in mind. Adams' reaction was strongly negative—he obviously felt that such a vote would embarrass his relations with the Administration and create unnecessary hostility among the Tompkins men in New York. The young congressman's conveyance of this discouraging message did not reach Epping, however, until after William Plumer, Sr. had set out for Concord to perform his own duties as an elector. He had been nominated to this honorific office as a token of respect by his fellow Republicans and elected to it by a desultory vote of New Hampshire citizens, every one of whom undoubtedly expected him to vote for Monroe and Tompkins. Plumer's political career, however, had been independent to the point of eccentricity, and he had retired from the governorship of New Hampshire in June, 1819, with the avowed intention of never accepting another political post. Since he had neither solicited the office of elector, nor given any pledges in order to obtain it, he was in a favorable position to exercise a personal choice, a freedom rarely encountered by electors in American history.

Plumer admired John Quincy Adams immensely but had little respect for James Monroe. The best thing that the latter had done as President, he thought, was to appoint the former to his Cabinet. Plumer's correspondence during the years 1817-20 is laden with criticism of President Monroe, primarily of his economic policies. Many of his contemporaries were aware, therefore, of his opinion that Monroe's Administration had been weak, extravagant, and undisciplined. Nevertheless, none of them would have anticipated the length to which his opposition would go.

The evidence in Plumer's writings is not conclusive, but it suggests rather strongly that Webster's proposal led him to conceive a still bolder plan—to cast his own vote for Adams, not for the Vice-Presidency but for the first office itself. Characteristically, he did not reveal his intention to anyone, not even to his son in Washington, nor to Webster, nor to Adams himself. He first announced his plan to his fellow New Hampshire electors on December 5 when they assembled in the Capitol at Concord. In so doing, he explained his motivation clearly and fully. He reviewed the shortcomings and misdeeds of Monroe and Tompkins in detail, then stated that in the face of such incompetence he simply could not vote for their continuance in office. John Quincy Adams and Richard Rush were fully qualified, he declared, and they would receive his vote. On the following day, he voted as he had said that he would, and returned to his home supremely satisfied with himself. He subsequently summarized his action in a straightforward and pithy sentence: "I was compelled, not only from a sense of duty, but respect to my own character, to withhold my vote from Monroe and Tompkins; from the first because he had discovered a want of foresight and economy; and from the second, because he grossly neglected his duty." There is no room for misunderstanding in these words.

Although Plumer recognized the possibility that his electoral vote might be the only one not given Monroe, he could not be sure of the fact until several days afterward when the newspapers were reviewing the nationwide results and in some cases rather acidly referring to the probability that Plumer's vote would be "the only one throughout the United States in opposition to the reelection of the present incumbent, and thus to prevent a unanimous election will be pronounced sheer folly." This uncertainty of communication in pre-telegraph days makes utterly absurd the legend that a New Hampshire elector voted against Monroe in order to maintain for George Washington the sole distinction of having been elected unanimously to the Presidency. Plumer could not possibly have known, at the time he voted, how the 227 electors outside his own state were exercising their franchise.

Not only is the Washington myth patently ridiculous—it has no basis whatever in historical evidence; there is not the faintest suggestion of it in any of Plumer's voluminous correspondence or diaries, in the writings of any of his contemporaries, in the newspaper columns of the day, or in the earliest histories of this period. Not until 1885, in fact, a whole generation later, did the story first appear in print. James Schouler then gave it immortality in these words, "One New Hampshire elector, . . . threw away . . . the vote which belonged like those of his colleagues to Monroe, determined, so it is said, that no later mortal should stand in Washington's shoes."

By whom "it" was "said," Schouler did not disclose, but one may speculate that this retired Boston lawyer picked up the story as oral legend circulating among the gossips of New Hampshire, where Schouler had a summer home. Charles H. Bell, a former New Hampshire governor, judge, and amateur historian had, in fact, included the tale in his collection of sketches entitled *Bench and Bar of New Hampshire* which was published posthumously in 1894. He had heard it many times, he wrote, from Judge George Y. Sawyer "who remembered the occurrence well." This eminent judge had died in 1882 and had been fifteen years of age in 1820. Judge Sawyer may, indeed, have possessed a remarkable memory, but his gifts as a raconteur were probably even better. At any rate, he left behind him, as his contribution to the centennial celebrations of his country, another addition to the Washington legend.

Schouler's fanciful account of Plumer's vote was followed almost immediately by Edward Stanwood in the first edition of his *History of Presidential Elections,* and subsequently by John Bach McMaster, David H. Montgomery, Josephus Larned, Henry Elson, Jacques Redway, and James W. Woodburn in their popular volumes. Stanwood printed a correction in his second edition(1898) and, in 1916, Charles O. Paullin found in the Plumer letters in the

Library of Congress evidence which completely refuted the legend. Nevertheless, during the last half century, college textbooks in which the Washington-Monroe-Plumer myth is firmly embedded have continued to be written by reputable historians. The most recent example, probably, is the little booklet entitled "How We Elect Our President," prepared by the editors of the *Reader's Digest Almanac and Yearbook* in 1968 as a guide to our most recent election. "William Plummer," it says (note the misspelled name) "of New Hampshire voted against Monroe, believing that only Washington's election should be unanimous." Historical legends never die, but neither do they fade away.

Neither the near-unanimity of the election of 1820 nor Plumer's defiance of it created much of a contemporary stir. Since the former had been expected there was little left to say about it. The unexpectedness of the latter did stimulate some comment in the newspapers, but nothing like that which greeted Dr. Lloyd Bailey in 1968 when he switched from Nixon to Wallace. Curiously enough, Plumer's vote against the Republican President was criticized by Federalist newspapers in New Hampshire, and defended by a Republican journal (Clintonian, of course) in New York. William, Jr. reported that his father's "independence" had been praised by several congressmen, who wished that other electors had displayed the same courage. The vote brought chagrin to John Quincy Adams and some anxiety to William, Jr., but Monroe apparently paid no attention to it. And this, until many years later, was the general reaction.

In fact, the normally routine business of counting the electoral votes in Congress precipitated far more conflict than had the election itself. Missouri had been authorized to form a constitution and apply for admission to the Union under the terms of the compromise Enabling Act approved on March 6 by President Monroe. The constitution created in July by Missouri's convention, however, contained clauses regarding slavery and free Negroes which were in clear contravention of the Federal Constitution and which the restrictionist members of Congress were determined not to accept. When the two houses assembled on February 14, 1821, therefore, to count the electoral ballots. Missouri had not yet been admitted to the Union. Her legislature, nevertheless, had appointed electors; they had cast their votes for Monroe and their ballots had been carried to Washington to be tallied. Whether Congress accepted them or not was completely immaterial to the election of Mr. Monroe, but it was painfully relevant to the question of Missouri's legal status.

The joint committee appointed to arrange for the vote-counting procedure proposed to solve this dilemma by a simple evasion. The President of the Senate was to announce the total number of votes for Monroe if Missouri's three were counted, then announce the total if they were not counted, then declare happily that in either event Mr. Monroe was elected President. After lengthy debates in both houses, surprisingly passionate on such a humorous abstraction, this resolution was adopted.

The actual counting of the vote did not, however, proceed harmoniously under this resolution. No sooner had John Gaillard, the President of the Senate, announced the vote from Missouri than Arthur Livermore, a congressman from New Hampshire, objected that there was no such state in the Union. This disconcerted Gaillard so much that he and the other senators retired, leaving the House to indulge in an acrimonious dispute in which John Randolph outdid himself in constitutional nit-picking and threats of anarchy. Henry Clay, resigned from the Speakership but returned as a private number, finally persuaded his colleagues that the matter had already been settled by the resolution and that the Senate should be recalled to get on with the counting. After the final vote had been tallied in the either/or fashion prescribed by the resolution, and the Senate had once more retired, John Randolph rose again to insist that Missouri's votes were legal and that they had not been declared agreeable to the provisions of the Constitution. But the house had finally wearied of the farce and adjourned without allowing Mr. Randolph to give his resolutions to the clerk.

Thus, on a note of burlesque following a dull comedy of manners, ended the ninth presidential election in American history. The successful candidate received the usual messages of congratulation; among them, one reminded him of his imminent retirement and expressed the hope that nothing would happen during his second term to "prevent your name from being handed down to posterity, a model of persevering integrity and in other respects an ornament to your country." It is more likely that a newspaper writer in New Jersey expressed the feelings of most Americans in looking forward to a new day "after the present wearisome and threadbare Presidential incombent retires from office."

In all fairness to Monroe, it must be acknowledged that he was becomingly modest about his overwhelming reelection. His second inauguration took place on Monday, March 5 (postponed a day since March 4 fell on Sunday), a typical March day in Washington: cold, muddy, sleeting. Consequently, the ceremony was held inside the chamber of the House of Representatives, which was so suffocatingly crowded that the Right Honorable Stratford Canning, British minister to the United States, could not push his way to a seat. His only consolation was that the newly reelected President was equally pressed and jostled by the *hoi-polloi*. Dressed, as usual, in his old-fashioned black broadcloth knee breeches and buckled shoes, Monroe finally succeeded in delivering his speech, admitting that he had "no pretensions to the high and commanding claims of [his] predecessors. . . . I consider myself," he continued, "rather as the instrument than the cause of the union which has prevailed in the late election."

Few historians would quarrel with this analysis. It was convenient in 1820 to have a candidate such as Monroe who was not too closely identified with any of the country's economic interests, who had avoided the controversies in Congress, who had usually arranged to be on the winning side in every situation, and who symbolized a national unity which was already fast disappearing but to which even the disunionists wished to cling a little while longer. As John Quincy Adams said of Monroe, tranquillity was "the pole-star of his policy," and Americans were happy to settle for four more years of tranquillity before the storm was to burst in 1824. It is reasonably safe to predict that if ever another American President comes virtually uncontested to the White House, it will not be because of his popularity, his charisma, his strong-armed disposal of all opposition, or his superb political adroitness; it will be because fate has fitted him, as it did Monroe, for the role of stand-in.

Appendix

Resolutions Adopted by the Hartford Convention
Hartford, December 15, 1814

These resolutions would probably have been submitted by the New England Federalists to the platform committee of their party had such a practice existed at the time and had there been an election in 1814. They represented the strong opposition to "Mr. Madison's War" felt by most Federalist politicians, and they also helped to destroy the Federalists as a national party after the Treaty of Ghent.

Therefore resolved—that it be and hereby is recommended to the Legislatures of the several States represented in the Convention, to adopt all such measures as may be necessary effectually to protect the citizens of said States from the operation and effects of all acts which have been or may be passed by the Congress of the United States, which shall contain provisions, subjecting the militia or other citizens to forcible drafts, conscriptions, or impressments, not authorized by the Constitution of the United States.

Resolved, That it be and hereby is recommended to the said Legislatures, to authorize an immediate and earnest application to be made to the Government of the United States, requesting their consent to some arrangement, whereby the said States may, separately or in concert, be empowered to assume upon themselves the defence of their territory against the enemy; and a reasonable portion of the taxes, collected within said States, may be paid into the respective treasuries thereof, and appropriated to the payment of the balance due said States, and to the future defence of the same. The amount so paid into the said treasuries to be credited, and the disbursements made as aforesaid to be charged to the United States.

Resolved, That it be, and it hereby is, recommended to the Legislatures of the aforesaid States, to pass laws (where it has not already been done) authorizing the Governours or Commanders in Chief of their militia to make detachments from the same, or to form voluntary corps, as shall be most convenient and conformable to their Constitutions, and to cause the same to be well armed, equipped and disciplined, and held in readiness for service; and upon the request of the Governour of either of the other States, to employ the whole of such detachment or corps, as well as the regular forces of the State, or such part thereof as may be required and can be spared consistently with the safety of the State, in assisting the State, making such request to repel any invasion thereof which shall be made or attempted by the publick enemy.

Resolved, That the following amendments of the Constitution of the United

States, be recommended to the States represented as aforesaid, to be proposed by them for adoption by the State Legislatures, and, in such cases as may be deemed expedient, by a Convention chosen by the people of each State.

And it is further recommended, that the said States shall persevere in their efforts to obtain such amendments, until the same shall be effected.

First. Representatives and direct taxes shall be apportioned among the several States which may be included within this union, according to their respective numbers of free persons, including those bound to serve for a term of years, and excluding Indians not taxed, and all other persons.

Second. No new State shall be admitted into the union by Congress in virtue of the power granted by the Constitution, without the concurrence of two thirds of both Houses.

Third. Congress shall not have power to lay any embargo on the ships or vessels of the citizens of the United States, in the ports or harbours thereof, for more than sixty days.

Fourth. Congress shall not have power, without the concurrence of two thirds of both Houses, to interdict the commercial intercourse between the United States and any foreign nation or the dependencies thereof.

Fifth. Congress shall not make or declare war, or authorize acts of hostility against any foreign nation, without the concurrence of two thirds of both Houses, except such acts of hostility be in defence of the territories of the United States when actually invaded.

Sixth. No person who shall hereafter be naturalized, shall be eligible as a member of the Senate or House of Representatives of the United States, nor capable of holding any civil office under the authority of the United States.

Seventh. The same person shall not be elected President of the United States a second time; nor shall the President be elected from the same State two terms in succession.

Resolved, That if the application of these States to the government of the United States, recommended in a foregoing Resolution, should be unsuccessful, and peace should not be concluded, and the defence of these States should be neglected, as it has been since the commencement of the war, it will in the opinion of this Convention be expedient for the Legislatures of the several States to appoint Delegates to another Convention, to meet at Boston, in the State of Massachusetts, on the third Thursday of June next, with such powers and instructions as the exigency of a crisis so momentous may require.

Resolved, That the Hon. George Cabot, the Hon. Chauncey Goodrich, and the Hon. Daniel Lyman, or any two of them, be authorized to call another meeting of this Convention, to be holden in Boston, at any time before new Delegates shall be chosen, as recommended in the above Resolution, if in their judgment the situation of the Country shall urgently require it.

President James Madison's Seventh
Annual Message to Congress
Washington, December 5, 1815

Madison here announced, in an early nineteenth-century equivalent of a party platform, the Republican party's shift to a strong nationalist position.

Fellow-Citizens of the Senate and of the House of Representatives:

I have the satisfaction on our present meeting of being able to communicate to you the successful termination of the war which had been commenced against the United States by the Regency of Algiers. The squadron in advance on that service, under Commodore Decatur, lost not a moment after its arrival in the Mediterranean in seeking the naval force of the enemy then cruising in that sea, and succeeded in capturing two of his ships, one of them the principal ship, commanded by the Algerine admiral. The high character of the American commander was brilliantly sustained on the occasion which brought his own ship into close action with that of his adversary, as was the accustomed gallantry of all the officers and men actually engaged. Having prepared the way by this demonstration of American skill and prowess, he hastened to the port of Algiers, where peace was promptly yielded to his victorious force. In the terms stipulated the rights and honor of the United States were particularly consulted by a perpetual relinquishment on the part of the Dey of all pretensions to tribute from them. The impressions which have thus been made, strengthened as they will have been by subsequent transactions with the Regencies of Tunis and of Tripoli by the appearance of the larger force which followed under Commodore Bainbridge, the chief in command of the expedition, and by the judicious precautionary arrangements left by him in that quarter, afford a reasonable prospect of future security for the valuable portion of our commerce which passes within reach of the Barbary cruisers.

It is another source of satisfaction that the treaty of peace with Great Britain has been succeeded by a convention on the subject of commerce concluded by the plenipotentiaries of the two countries. In this result a disposition is manifested on the part of that nation corresponding with the disposition of the United States, which it may be hoped will be improved into liberal arrangements on other subjects on which the parties have mutual interests, or which might endanger their future harmony. Congress will decide on the expediency of promoting such a sequel by giving effect to the measure of confining the American navigation to American seamen—a measure which, at the same time that it might have that conciliatory tendency, would have the further advantage of increasing the independence of our navigation and the resources for our maritime defense.

In conformity with the articles in the treaty of Ghent relating to the Indians, as well as with a view to the tranquillity of our western and northwestern frontiers, measures were taken to establish an immediate peace with the several tribes who had been engaged in hostilities against the United States. Such of them as were invited to Detroit acceded readily to a renewal of the former treaties of friendship. Of the other tribes who were invited to a station on the Mississippi the greater number have also accepted the peace offered to them. The residue, consisting of the more distant tribes or parts of tribes, remain to be brought over by further explanations, or by such other means as may be adapted to the dispositions they may finally disclose.

The Indian tribes within and bordering on the southern frontier, whom a cruel war on their part had compelled us to chastise into peace, have latterly shown a restlessness which has called for preparatory measures for repressing it, and for protecting the commissioners engaged in carrying the terms of the peace into execution.

The execution of the act for fixing the military peace establishment has been attended with difficulties which even now can only be overcome by legislative aid. The selection of officers, the payment and discharge of the troops enlisted for the war, the payment of the retained troops and their reunion from detached and distant stations, the collection and security of the public property in the Quartermaster, Commissary, and Ordnance departments, and the constant medical assistance required in hospitals and garrisons rendered a complete execution of the act impracticable on the 1st of May, the period more immediately contemplated. As soon, however, as circumstances would permit, and as far as it has been practicable consistently with the public interests, the reduction of the Army has been accomplished; but the appropriations for its pay and for other branches of the military service having proved inadequate, the earliest attention to that subject will be necessary; and the expediency of continuing upon the peace establishment the staff officers who have hitherto been provisionally retained is also recommended to the consideration of Congress.

In the performance of the Executive duty upon this occasion there has not been wanting a just sensibility to the merits of the American Army during the late war; but the obvious policy and design in fixing an efficient military peace establishment did not afford an opportunity to distinguish the aged and infirm on account of their past services nor the wounded and disabled on account of their present sufferings. The extent of the reduction, indeed, unavoidably involved the exclusion of many meritorious officers of every rank from the service of their country; and so equal as well as so numerous were the claims to attention that a decision by the standard of comparative merit could seldom be attained. Judged, however, in candor by a general standard of positive merit, the Army Register will, it is believed, do honor to the establishment, while the case of those officers whose names are not included in it devolves with the strongest interest upon the legislative authority for such provision as shall be deemed the best calculated to give support and solace to the veteran and the invalid, to display the beneficence as well as the justice of the Government, and to inspire a martial zeal for the public service upon every future emergency.

Although the embarrassments arising from the want of an uniform national currency have not been diminished since the adjournment of Congress, great satisfaction has been derived in contemplating the revival of the public credit and the efficiency of the public resources. The receipts into the Treasury from the various branches of revenue during the nine months ending on the 30th of September last have been estimated at $12,500,000; the issues of Treasury notes of every denomination during the same period amounted to the sum of $14,000,000, and there was also obtained upon loan during the same period a sum of $9,000,000, of which the sum of $6,000,000 was subscribed in cash and the sum of $3,000,000 in Treasury notes. With these means, added to the sum of $1,500,000, being the balance of money in the Treasury on the 1st day of January, there has been paid between the 1st of January and the 1st of October on account of the appropriations of the preceding and of the present year (exclusively of the amount of the Treasury notes subscribed to the loan and of the amount redeemed in the payment of duties and taxes) the aggregate sum of $33,500,000, leaving a balance then in the Treasury estimated at the sum of $3,000,000. Independent, however, of the arrearages due for military services and supplies, it is presumed that a further sum of $5,000,000, including the interest on the public debt payable on the 1st of January next, will be demanded at the Treasury to complete the expenditures of the present year, and for which the existing ways and means will sufficiently provide.

The national debt, as it was ascertained on the 1st of October last, amounted in the whole to the sum of $120,000,000, consisting of the unredeemed balance of the debt contracted before the late war ($39,000,000), the amount of the funded debt contracted in consequence of the war ($64,000,000), and the amount of the unfunded and floating debt, including the various issues of Treasury notes, $17,000,000, which is in a gradual course of payment. There will probably be some addition to the public debt upon the liquidation of various claims which are depending, and a conciliatory disposition on the part of Congress may lead honorably and advantageously to an equitable arrangement of the militia expenses incurred by the several States without the previous sanction or authority of the Government of the United States; but when it is considered that the new as well as the old portion of the debt has been contracted in the assertion of the national rights and independence, and when it is recollected that the public expenditures, not being exclusively bestowed upon subjects of a transient nature, will long be visible in the number and equipments of the American Navy, in the military works for the defense of our harbors and our frontiers, and in the supplies of our arsenals and magazines the amount will bear a gratifying comparison with the objects which have been attained, as well as with the resources of the country.

The arrangements of the finances with a view to the receipts and expenditures of a permanent peace establishment will necessarily enter the deliberations of Congress during the present session. It is true that the improved condition of the public revenue will not only afford the means of maintaining the faith of the Government with its creditors inviolate, and of prosecuting successfully the measures of the most liberal policy, but will also justify an immediate alleviation of the burdens imposed by the necessities of the war. It is, however, essential to every modification of the finances that the benefits of an uniform national currency should be restored to the community. The absence of the precious metals will, it is believed, be a temporary evil, but until they can again be rendered the general medium of exchange it devolves on the wisdom of Congress to provide a substitute which shall equally engage the confidence and accommodate the wants of the citizens throughout the Union. If the operation of the State banks can not produce this result, the probable operation of a national bank will merit consideration; and if neither of these expedients be deemed effectual it may become necessary to ascertain the terms upon which the notes of the Government (no longer required as an instrument of credit) shall be issued upon motives of general policy as a common medium of circulation.

Notwithstanding the security for future repose which the United States ought to find in their love of peace and their constant respect for the rights of other nations, the character of the times particularly inculcates the lesson that, whether to prevent or repel danger, we ought not to be unprepared for it. This consideration will sufficiently recommend to Congress a liberal provision for the immediate extension and gradual completion of the works of defense, both fixed and floating, on our maritime frontier, and an adequate provision for guarding our inland frontier against dangers to which certain portions of it may continue to be exposed.

As an improvement in our military establishment, it will deserve the consideration of Congress whether a corps of invalids might not be so organized and employed as at once to aid in the support of meritorious individuals excluded by age or infirmities from the existing establishment, and to procure to the public the benefit of their stationary services and of their exemplary discipline. I recommend also an enlargement of the Military Academy already established, and the establishment of others in other sections of the Union; and I can not press too much on the attention of Congress such a classification and organization of the militia as will most effectually render it the safeguard of a free state. If experience has shewn in the recent splendid achievements of militia the value of this resource for the public defense, it has shewn also the importance of that skill in the use of arms and that familiarity with the essential rules of discipline which can not be expected from the regulations now in force. With this subject is intimately connected the necessity of accommodating the laws in every respect to the great object of enabling the political authority of the Union to employ promptly and effectually the physical power of the Union in the cases designated by the Constitution.

The signal services which have been rendered by our Navy and the capacities it has developed for successful cooperation in the national defense will give to that portion of the public force its full value in the eyes of Congress, at an epoch which calls for the constant vigilance of all governments. To preserve the ships now in a sound state, to complete those already contemplated, to provide amply the imperishable materials for prompt augmentations, and to improve the existing arrangements into more advantageous establishments for the construction, the repairs, and the security of vessels of war is dictated by the soundest policy.

In adjusting the duties on imports to the object of revenue the influence of the tariff on manufactures will necessarily present itself for consideration. However wise the theory may be which leaves to the sagacity and interest of individuals the application of their industry and resources, there are in this as in other cases exceptions to the general rule. Besides the condition which the theory itself implies of a reciprocal adoption by other nations, experience teaches that so many circumstances must concur in introducing and maturing manufacturing establishments, especially of the more complicated kinds, that a country may remain long without them, although sufficiently advanced and in some respects even peculiarly fitted for carrying them on with success. Under circumstances giving a powerful impulse to manufacturing industry it has made among us a progress and exhibited an efficiency which justify the belief that with a protection not more than is due to the enterprising citizens whose interests are now at stake it will become at an early day not only safe against occasional competitions from abroad, but a source of domestic wealth and even of external commerce. In selecting the branches more especially entitled to the public patronage a preference is obviously claimed by such as will relieve the United States from a dependence on foreign supplies, ever subject to casual failures, for articles necessary for the public defense or connected with the primary wants of individuals. It will be an additional recommendation of particular manufactures where the materials for them are extensively drawn from our agriculture, and consequently impart and insure to that great fund of national prosperity and independence an encouragement which can not fail to be rewarded.

Among the means of advancing the public interest the occasion is a proper one for recalling the attention of Congress to the great importance of establishing throughout our country the roads and canals which can best be executed under the national authority. No objects within the circle of political economy so richly repay the expense bestowed on them; there are none the utility of which is more universally ascertained and acknowledged; none that do more honor to the governments whose wise and enlarged patriotism duly appreciates them. Nor is there any country which presents a field where nature invites more the art of man to complete her own work for his accommodation and benefit. These considerations are strengthened, moreover, by the political effect of these facilities for intercommunication in bringing and binding more closely together the various parts of our extended confederacy. Whilst the States individually, with a laudable enterprise and emulation, avail themselves of their local advantages by new roads, by navigable canals, and by improving the streams susceptible of navigation, the General Government is the more urged to similar undertakings, requiring a national jurisdiction and national means, by the prospect of thus systematically completing so inestimable a work; and it is a happy reflection that any defect of constitutional authority which may be encountered can be supplied in a mode which the Constitution itself has providently pointed out.

The present is a favorable season also for bringing again into view the establishment of a national seminary of learning within the District of Columbia, and with means drawn from the property therein, subject to the authority of the General Government. Such an institution claims the patronage of Congress as a monument of their solicitude for the advancement of knowledge, without which the blessings of liberty can not be fully enjoyed or long preserved; as a model instructive in the formation of other seminaries; as a nursery of enlightened preceptors, and as a central resort of youth and genius from every part of their country, diffusing on their return examples of those national feelings, those liberal sentiments, and those congenial manners which contribute cement to our Union and strength to the great political fabric of which that is the foundation.

In closing this communication I ought not to repress a sensibility, in which you will unite, to the happy lot of our country and to the goodness of a superintending Providence, to which we are indebted for it. Whilst other portions of mankind are laboring under the distresses of war or struggling with adversity in other forms, the United States are in the tranquil enjoyment of prosperous and honorable peace. In reviewing the scenes through which it has been attained we can rejoice in the proofs given that our political institutions, founded in human rights and framed for their preservation, are equal to the severest trials of war, as well as adapted to the ordinary periods of repose. As fruits of this experience and of the reputation acquired by the American arms on the land and on the water, the nation finds itself possessed of a growing respect abroad and of a just confidence in itself, which are among the best pledges for its peaceful career. Under other aspects of our country the stongest features of its flourishing condition are seen in a population rapidly increasing on a territory as productive as it is extensive; in a general industry and fertile ingenuity which find their ample rewards, and in an affluent revenue which admits a reduction of the public burdens without withdrawing the means of sustaining the public credit, of gradually discharging the public debt, of providing for the necessary defensive and precautionary establishments, and of patronizing in every authorized mode undertakings conducive to the aggregate wealth and individual comfort of our citizens.

It remains for the guardians of the public welfare to persevere in that justice and good will toward other nations which invite a return of these sentiments toward the United States; to cherish institutions which guarantee their safety and their liberties, civil and religious; and to combine with a liberal system of foreign commerce an improvement of the national advantages and a protection and extension of the independent resources of our highly favored and happy country.

In all measures having such objects my faithful cooperation will be afforded.

James Monroe's Inaugural Address
Washington, March 4, 1817

In this message Monroe's heavy-handed emphasis on peace, prosperity, harmony, and the continuance of strong nationalist measures ushered in the Era of Good Feelings.

I should be destitute of feeling if I was not deeply affected by the strong proof which my fellow-citizens have given me of their confidence in calling me to the high office whose functions I am about to assume. As the expression of their good opinion of my conduct in the public service, I derive from it a gratification which those who are conscious of having done all that they could to merit it can alone feel. My sensibility is increased by a just estimate of the importance of the trust and of the nature and extent of its duties, with the proper discharge of which the highest interests of a great and free people are intimately connected. Conscious of my own deficiency, I cannot enter on these duties without great anxiety for the result. From a just responsibility I will never shrink, calculating with confidence that in my best efforts to promote the public welfare my motives will always be duly appreciated and my conduct be viewed with that candor and indulgence which I have experienced in other stations.

In commencing the duties of the chief executive office it has been the practice of the distinguished men who have gone before me to explain the principles which would govern them in their respective Administrations. In following their venerated example my attention is naturally drawn to the great causes which have contributed in a principal degree to produce the present happy condition of the United States. They will best explain the nature of our duties and shed much light on the policy which ought to be pursued in future.

From the commencement of our Revolution to the present day almost forty years have elapsed, and from the establishment of this Constitution, twenty-eight. Through this whole term the Government has been what may emphatically be called self-government. And what has been the effect? To whatever object we turn our attention, whether it relates to our foreign or domestic concerns, we find abundant cause to felicitate ourselves in the excellence of our institutions. During a period fraught with difficulties and marked by very extraordinary events the United States have flourished beyond example. Their citizens individually have been happy and the nation prosperous.

Under this Constitution our commerce has been wisely regulated with foreign nations and between the States; new States have been admitted into our Union; our territory has been enlarged by fair and honorable treaty, and with great advantage to the original States; the States, respectively protected by the National Government under a mild, parental system against foreign dangers, and enjoying within their separate spheres, by a wise partition of power, a just proportion of the sovereignty, have improved their police, extended their settlements, and attained a strength and maturity which are the best proofs of wholesome laws well administered. And if we look to the condition of individuals what a proud spectacle does it exhibit! On whom has oppression fallen in any quarter of our Union? Who has been deprived of any right of person or property? Who restrained from offering his vows in the mode which he prefers to the Divine Author of his being? It is well known that all these blessings have been enjoyed in their fullest extent; and I add with peculiar satisfaction that there has been no example of a capital punishment being inflicted on anyone for the crime of high treason.

Some who might admit the competency of our Government to these beneficent duties might doubt it in trials which put to the test its strength and efficiency as a member of the great community of nations. Here too experience has afforded us the most satisfactory proof in its favor. Just as this Constitution was put into action several of the principal States of Europe had become much agitated and some of them seriously convulsed. Destructive wars ensued, which have of late only been terminated. In the course of these conflicts the United States received great injury from several of the parties. It was their interest to stand aloof from the contest, to demand justice from the party committing the injury, and to cultivate by a fair and honorable conduct the friendship of all. War became at length inevitable, and the result has shown that our Government is equal to that, the greatest of trials, under the most unfavorable circumstances. Of the virtue of the people and of the heroic exploits of the Army, the Navy, and the militia I need not speak.

Such, then, is the happy Government under which we live—a Government adequate to every purpose for which the social compact is formed; a Government elective in all its branches, under which every citizen may by his merit obtain the highest trust recognized by the Constitution; which contains within it no cause of discord, none to put at variance one portion of the community with another; a Government which protects every citizen in the full enjoyment of his rights, and is able to protect the nation against injustice from foreign powers.

Other considerations of the highest importance admonish us to cherish our Union and to cling to the Government which supports it. Fortunate as we are in our political institutions, we have not been less so in other circumstances on which our prosperity and happiness essentially depend. Situated within the temperate zone, and extending through many degrees of latitude along the Atlantic, the United States enjoy all the varieties of climate, and every production incident to that portion of the globe. Penetrating internally to the Great Lakes and beyond the sources of the great rivers which communicate through our whole interior, no country was ever happier with respect to its domain. Blessed, too, with a fertile soil, our produce has always been very abundant, leaving, even in years the least favorable, a surplus for the wants of our fellow-men in other countries. Such is our peculiar felicity that there is not a part of our Union that is not particularly interested in preserving it. The great agricultural interest of the nation prospers under its protection. Local interests are not less fostered by it. Our fellow-citizens of the North engaged in navigation find great encouragement in being made the favored carriers of the

vast productions of the other portions of the United States, while the inhabitants of these are amply recompensed, in their turn, by the nursery for seamen
and naval force thus formed and reared up for the support of our common
rights. Our manufactures find a generous encouragement by the policy which
patronizes domestic industry, and the surplus of our produce a steady and
profitable market by local wants in less-favored parts at home.

Such, then, being the highly favored condition of our country, it is the interest of every citizen to maintain it. What are the dangers which menace us? If
any exist they ought to be ascertained and guarded against.

In explaining my sentiments on this subject it may be asked, What raised
us to the present happy state? How did we accomplish the Revolution? How
remedy the defects of the first instrument of our Union, by infusing into the
National Government sufficient power for national purposes, without impair-
ing the just rights of the States or affecting those of individuals? How sustain
and pass with glory through the late war? The Government has been in the
hands of the people. To the people, therefore, and to the faithful and able
depositaries of their trust is the credit due. Had the people of the United
States been educated in different principles, had they been less intelligent, less
independent, or less virtuous, can it be believed that we should have maintained the same steady and consistent career or been blessed with the same
success? While, then, the constituent body retains its present sound and
healthful state everything will be safe. They will choose competent and faithful representatives for every department. It is only when the people become
ignorant and corrupt, when they degenerate into a populace, that they are incapable of exercising the sovereignty. Usurpation is then an easy attainment,
and an usurper soon found. The people themselves become the willing instruments of their own debasement and ruin. Let us, then, look to the great cause,
and endeavor to preserve it in full force. Let us by all wise and constitutional
measures promote intelligence among the people as the best means of preserving our liberties.

Dangers from abroad are not less deserving of attention. Experiencing the
fortune of other nations, the United States may be again involved in war, and
it may in that event be the object of the adverse party to overset our Government, to break our Union, and demolish us as a nation. Our distance from
Europe and the just, moderate, and pacific policy of our Government may
form some security against these dangers, but they ought to be anticipated
and guarded against. Many of our citizens are engaged in commerce and navigation, and all of them are in a certain degree dependent on their prosperous
state. Many are engaged in the fisheries. These interests are exposed to invasion in the wars between other powers, and we should disregard the faithful
admonition of experience if we did not expect it. We must support our rights
or lose our character, and with it, perhaps, our liberties. A people who fail to
do it can scarcely be said to hold a place among independent nations. National
honor is national property of the highest value. The sentiment in the mind
of every citizen is national strength. It ought therefore to be cherished.

To secure us against these dangers our coast and inland frontiers should be
fortified, our Army and Navy, regulated upon just principles as to the force of

each, be kept in perfect order, and our militia be placed on the best practicable footing. To put our extensive coast in such a state of defense as to secure our cities and interior from invasion will be attended with expense, but the work when finished will be permanent, and it is fair to presume that a single campaign of invasion by a naval force superior to our own, aided by a few thousand land troops, would expose us to greater expense, without taking into the estimate the loss of property and distress of our citizens, than would be sufficient for this great work. Our land and naval forces should be moderate, but adequate to the necessary purposes—the former to garrison and preserve our fortifications and to meet the first invasions of a foreign foe, and, while constituting the elements of a greater force, to preserve the science as well as all the necessary implements of war in a state to be brought into activity in the event of war; the latter, retained within the limits proper in a state of peace, might aid in maintaining the neutrality of the United States with dignity in the wars of other powers and in saving the property of their citizens from spoliation. In time of war, with the enlargement of which the great naval resources of the country render it susceptible, and which should be duly fostered in time of peace, it would contribute essentially, both as an auxiliary of defense and as a powerful engine of annoyance, to diminish the calamities of war and to bring the war to a speedy and honorable termination.

But it ought always to be held prominently in view that the safety of these States and of everything dear to a free people must depend in an eminent degree on the militia. Invasion may be made too formidable to be resisted by any land and naval force which it would comport either with the principles of our Government or the circumstances of the United States to maintain. In such cases recourse must be had to the great body of the people, and in a manner to produce the best effect. It is of the highest importance, therefore, that they be so organized and trained as to be prepared for any emergency. The arrangement should be such as to put at the command of the Government the ardent patriotism and youthful vigor of the country. If formed on equal and just principles, it can not be oppressive. It is the crisis which makes the pressure, and not the laws which provide a remedy for it. This arrangement should be formed, too, in time of peace, to be the better prepared for war. With such an organization of such a people the United States have nothing to dread from foreign invasion. At its approach an overwhelming force of gallant men might always be put in motion.

Other interests of high importance will claim attention, among which the improvement of our country by roads and canals, proceeding always with a constitutional sanction, holds a distinguished place. By thus facilitating the intercourse between the States we shall add much to the convenience and comfort of our fellow-citizens, much to the ornament of the country, and, what is of greater importance, we shall shorten distances, and, by making each part more accessible to and dependent on the other, we shall bind the Union more closely together. Nature has done so much for us by intersecting the country with so many great rivers, bays, and lakes, approaching from distant points so near to each other, that the inducement to complete the work seems to be peculiarly strong. A more interesting spectacle was perhaps never seen than is exhibited within the limits of the United States — a territory so vast and advantageously situated, containing objects so grand, so useful, so happily connected in all their parts!

Our manufacturers will likewise require the systematic and fostering care of the Government. Possessing as we do all the raw materials, the fruit of our own soil and industry, we ought not to depend in the degree we have done on supplies from other countries. While we are thus dependent the sudden event of war, unsought and unexpected, can not fail to plunge us into the most serious difficulties. It is important, too, that the capital which nourishes our manufacturers should be domestic, as its influence in that case instead of exhausting, as it may do in foreign hands, would be felt advantageously on agriculture and every other branch of industry. Equally important is it to provide at home a market for our raw materials, as by extending the competition it will enhance the price and protect the cultivator against the casualties incident to foreign markets.

With the Indian tribes it is our duty to cultivate friendly relations and to act with kindness and liberality in all our transactions. Equally proper is it to persevere in our efforts to extend to them the advantages of civilization.

The great amount of our revenue and the flourishing state of the Treasury are a full proof of the competency of the national resources for any emergency, as they are of the willingness of our fellow-citizens to bear the burdens which the public necessities require. The vast amount of vacant lands, the value of which daily augments, forms an additional resource of great extent and duration. These resources, besides accomplishing every other necessary purpose, put it completely in the power of the United States to discharge the national debt at an early period. Peace is the best time for improvement and preparation of every kind; it is in peace that our commerce flourishes most, that taxes are most easily paid, and that the revenue is most productive.

The Executive is charged officially in the Departments under it with the disbursement of the public money, and is responsible for the faithful application of it to the purposes for which it is raised. The Legislature is the watchful guardian over the public purse. It is its duty to see that the disbursement has been honestly made. To meet the requisite responsibility every facility should be afforded to the Executive to enable it to bring the public agents intrusted with the public money strictly and promptly to account. Nothing should be presumed against them; but if, with the requisite facilities, the public money is suffered to lie long and uselessly in their hands, they will not be the only defaulters, nor will the demoralizing effect be confined to them. It will evince a relaxation and want of tone in the Administration which will be felt by the whole community. I shall do all I can to secure economy and fidelity in this important branch of the Administration, and I doubt not that the Legislature will perform its duty with equal zeal. A thorough examination should be regularly made, and I will promote it.

It is particularly gratifying to me to enter on the discharge of these duties at a time when the United States are blessed with peace. It is a state most consistent with their prosperity and happiness. It will be my sincere desire to preserve it, so far as depends on the Executive, on just principles with all nations, claiming nothing unreasonable of any and rendering to each what is its due.

Equally gratifying is it to witness the increased harmony of opinion which pervades our Union. Discord does not belong to our system. Union is recommended as well by the free and benign principles of our Government, extending its blessings to every individual, as by the other eminent advantages attending it. The American people have encountered together great dangers and sustained severe trials with success. They constitute one great family with a common interest. Experience has enlightened us on some questions of essential importance to the country. The progress has been slow, dictated by a just reflection and a faithful regard to every interest connected with it. To promote this harmony in accord with the principles of our republican Government and in a manner to give them the most complete effect, and to advance in all other respects the best interests of our Union, will be the object of my constant and zealous exertions.

Never did a government commence under auspices so favorable, nor ever was success so complete. If we look to the history of other nations, ancient or modern, we find no example of a growth so rapid, so gigantic, of a people so prosperous and happy. In contemplating what we have still to perform, the heart of every citizen must expand with joy when he reflects how near our Government has approached to perfection; that in respect to it we have no essential improvement to make; that the great object is to preserve it in the essential principles and features which characterize it, and that that is to be done by preserving the virtue and enlightening the minds of the people; and as a security against foreign dangers to adopt such arrangements as are indispensable to the support of our independence, our rights and liberties. If we persevere in the career in which we have advanced so far and in the path already traced, we can not fail, under the favor of a gracious Providence, to attain the high destiny which seems to await us.

In the Administrations of the illustrious men who have preceded me in this high station, with some of whom I have been connected by the closest ties from early life, examples are presented which will always be found highly instructive and useful to their successors. From these I shall endeavor to derive all the advantages which they may afford. Of my immediate predecessor, under whom so important a portion of this great and successful experiment has been made, I shall be pardoned for expressing my earnest wishes that he may long enjoy in his retirement the affections of a grateful country, the best reward of exalted talents and the most faithful and meritorious service. Relying on the aid to be derived from the other departments of the Government, I enter on the trust to which I have been called by the suffrages of my fellow-citizens with my fervent prayers to the Almighty that He will be graciously pleased to continue to us that protection which He has already so conspicuously displayed in our favor.

Address in Behalf of the Citizens of Hartford
to President James Monroe, June 23, 1817

This and the following two addresses were presented to President Monroe as part of the welcoming ceremonies staged by the New England towns during the President's celebrated northern tour in the summer of 1817. John Morgan, the Federalist mayor of the town in which the quasi-treasonable Hartford Convention had met only three years earlier, evidenced in stilted language the remarkable change in political sentiment which had occurred in New England.

Sir—The pleasing duty has devolved on us of presenting you the congratulations of the citizens of Hartford, on your arrival in this city. It is with sentiments of regard for private worth, no less than respect for official dignity, that the personal presence of the first Magistrate of our Nation is associated.

The endearing relation which subsists between the people of a free country and their political father and guide, is peculiarly fitted to cherish and ennoble these sentiments.

It is no less our happiness, sir, than yours, that your administration has commenced at a period gilded by the recent exploits of our Army and Navy, and at the same time enjoying the tranquillity and security of peace; when full scope is given to the enterprize, industry and skill of our citizens, in the employments of agriculture and manufactures; when the pursuits of science, and the cultivation of the arts of civilized life are encouraged by their appropriate rewards; and when the spirit of party, with its concomitant jealousies and misrepresentations, no longer "render alien to each other, those who ought to be bound together by paternal affection." We anticipate in your administration, commenced under such auspices, and blessed with the smiles of Him, "whose dominion is an everlasting dominion;" a period of glory to our country, and of honour to yourself.

The State of Connecticut, as she was among the first to adopt the Constitution of the United States, so will she always be among its most firm and zealous supporters.

The people of this State, while they cherish a high spirit of freedom, are, from the force of our institutions and habits, distinguished also for their love of order and submission to the laws. In pursuing a policy, which, as we confidently expect, will give the best effect to the principles of our government; establishing commerce upon a permanent basis; render us strong and independent; confer on us a distinct and elevated national character; and secure to our country those high advantages, which seem destined for her by Providence, you may be assured of an hearty support.

May Heaven grant, Sir, that your life may be long and happy; and that the freedom and independence of our country may be perpetual.

Address by President of Harvard College John T. Kirkland
to President James Monroe
Cambridge, July 7, 1817

The words of the president of Harvard College to the heir of Jeffersonian Republicanism are especially interesting coming as they did from the very citadel of Federalism.

Sir — The President and Fellows of Harvard College, are happy in an opportunity of presenting their respectful salutations to the Chief Magistrate of the nation. It is peculiarly grateful to us, that a visit to this University, has not been found inconsistent with those objects of public concern, which engage the attention of the President of the United States, in the course of his itinerary progress.

We take satisfaction in this notice of our seminary as evincing your estimation of liberal studies, and your interest in the education and character of American youth. Our Academic functions cannot fail to derive dignity and effect from the countenance of the civil authorities; and our pupils to find incitements to excellence, in all the demonstrations of sympathy in their pursuits and destination, given by those who fill exalted stations.

We bid you welcome, sir, to an establishment, coeval with the foundation of the State, and the object of public and individual favour through many successive generations. While, however, its connexion with the history of past times, and the number of sons which, in the lapse of nearly two centuries, it has annually dismissed from its care, are circumstances which naturally excite a degree of interest, we are sensible, that antiquity alone, tho' venerable, is an inadequate basis of respect from men of intelligence and reflection. We would hope, that this cherished seminary has other and stronger claims to complacent regard from every friend to the best interests of man, every patron of intellectual and moral excellence.

With the rudiments of good literature, and the elements of science, it has been the constant and elevated aim in this institution, to inspire the minds of youth with those principles of virtue and piety, with those manly sentiments, and with that pure love of truth and duty, which are the most valued ingredients of character, and which are best calculated to form the man and the citizen.

By pursuing such a course, this ancient school has sought to preserve, in close alliance, the interests of religion and learning, of faith and charity, of liberty and order.

Desiring to train those who are under our charge for the whole public and for mankind, we deem it an essential part of our office, to endeavour to temper the prejudices and feelings incident to particular attachments and geographical divisions; to exhibit the evidence and authority of our common faith

338

with a due moderation in respect to pecularities of opinion and mode; and to encourage free enquiries into the nature, the value, the dangers, and the pre- servatives of our republican institutions, with a just reserve upon those con- troverted questions which tend to inflame the spirit of party.

We present to your view, sir, that portion of the youth of our country, now resident within these walls; and are happy to bear testimony to the many pledges they give of their regard to the interesting objects of literary pursuit, and to those attainments on which their future usefulness must depend.

May they, and all the sons of this University, ever cherish those generous affections, and aim at those solid acquirements which shall bind and endear them to their country, and render them approved instruments in advancing the interests and honour of our nation, and strengthening and protecting its pre- cious institutions.

In these indications of the purposes of public education, we are persuaded, sir, that we refer to objects which you deem worthy of high regard.

We congratulate you on the auspicious circumstances which attend the com- mencement of your administration. Accept our wishes and prayers for its happy course and issue; and indulge the expression of our desire, that whilst you, by the favour of Heaven, upon the exercise of the appropriate duties of your high station, obtain the happiness of seeing the associated communities over which you preside, safe and prosperous, it may be our privilege, by fidelity and zeal in our allotted sphere, under the smile of the same good Provi- dence, to co-operate in the work of patriotism, by diffusing the light of knowl- edge, and the saving influence of religion and morals.

Address in Behalf of the Citizens of Portsmouth
to President James Monroe
July 12, 1817

Portsmouth was a small but bustling seaboard metropolis in New Hampshire. Although it was a Republican town, the Federalist minority consisted of wealthy and influential merchants, landowners, clergymen, and lawyers. Jeremiah Mason, a skillful attorney and politician, was one of the foremost Federalists in the state. Although his address contained subtle overtones about the protection of commerce, his consistent flattery of the President shows how completely the Federalists had succumbed to the general Era of Good Feelings.

Sir—The presence of the Chief Magistrate, selected for his eminent virtues and public services, to preside over and direct the councils of a great nation, must always excite feelings of the highest interest. The inhabitants of the town of Portsmouth, remote from the seat of general government, can expect few opportunities of witnessing such a gratifying scene. We therefore eagerly embrace this fortunate occasion, to present our ardent and sincere congratulations.

Engaged chiefly in the business of commerce and navigation, we know that our destinies are, in a peculiar manner, dependent on the measures of the government, to which the protection of those important objects, is exclusively confided. These enterprising pursuits, which have always been greatly contributory to the general welfare, are now suffering under a temporary depression. But we have entire confidence, that the wisdom and justice of government, will extend to them all the protection and support, that shall be in its power.

To superintend and conduct the national concern has always, in free governments, been the favorite employment of the best and greatest men. By no other means can an individual of distinguished talent so eminently promote the public good. The successful performance of such duties must, at all times, constitute a sure claim to the gratitude of a generous people. Thus, Sir, is the arduous and honourable service, which is entrusted to you, by the citizens of the United States.

Sensible how greatly the national prosperity depends on the due administration of the government we recall to our recollection, with much satisfaction the numerous pledges of attachment to the public interest, furnished by the history of your past life. It is our earnest and confident hope that your administration, by perfecting our valuable institutions, and by uniting public sentiment, and wisely directing it to proper national objects, may fulfil the present happy anticipations, and thus establish, on a firm basis, your own and your country's happiness, honour and glory.

Letter from Governor William Plumer
to President James Monroe
July 18, 1817

One of the political curiosities of President Monroe's northern tour was that while the Federalist governors of Connecticut and Massachusetts vied with each other to honor him, the Republican governor of New Hampshire, William Plumer, failed to meet the President personally or to order a militia escort. The letter reproduced here gives Plumer's explanation. The Federalist papers of the day ridiculed it as specious, and in 1820, when Plumer registered the lone electoral vote against Monroe, his conduct in 1817 was recalled as further evidence of a stubborn prejudice.

Dear Sir—It is to me a subject of much regret that in your Tour through New-Hampshire, I have been unable to pay you that respectful attention, and those personal civilities, which I consider due both to your private character and official station. You were verbally informed, while at Portsmouth, of my severe indisposition: and I am now obliged to add, that I am still confined to my chamber and bed, by an attack of the typhus fever, which has not yet, I fear, reached its crisis. This unfortunate event has deprived me of the satisfaction of a personal interview with you; and prevented me from receiving a visit at this place with which I had flattered myself you would have honoured me.

A military escort having been called out by the Governours of some of the States, to accompany you through those parts of the country, I was desirous that the same tribute of respect should be paid you on your passage through New-Hampshire. The power to call out such an escort seemed, at first view, incident to the nature of my office as Commander in Chief of the militia; yet so accurately is this command defined, and so cautiously restricted, by the prudence, or the jealousy of our State constitution, that I have authority at no time to order out the militia, except for certain known objects particularly designated in the constitution and by the laws enacted under it. I have thought proper to make this statement, both in justice to myself, and to the state over which I preside; a state which yields to none in the Union, either in attachment to the General Government, or in respect to the distinguished individual, who with its full consent and approbation, has been raised to the first office in the gift of the nation.

This letter will be delivered to you, by the Secretary of State. Had my health permitted, I should have taken great pleasure in waiting upon you in person during the time you remained in this State, and in suggesting some objects of inquiry, which might perhaps have merited your attention in this part of our common country. But in my present condition I can only add my sincere congratulations, and my best wishes for the success of your administration, which has commenced under circumstances peculiarly favourable to yourself, and our beloved country. . . .

Excerpt from William Plumer Papers
(Library of Congress)

Here Plumer narrates his duties as a presidential elector in 1820 and explains his motives for voting against Monroe.

Dec 5| At ten o'clock in the morning I met all the other electors two of whom, Ezra Bartlet & Samuel Dinsmore, hold offices (collectors of taxes) under the United States, & are therefore ineligible to the office of electors; but as there is not provision for the board or any other tribunal to settle that question, I was silent, & they took their seats & acted as electors. The board unanimously elected me there president,; & having notified the legislature of our having all met, & accepted our appointments, we adjourned to the afternoon.

After having met, we agreed upon the form of our return & conver/sed upon the subject of appointing a messenger to carry our votes to Washington. We had letters from thirty six persons soliciting that appointment, some of them respectable men, & most of [them] present in town.

I observed to the electors that I was appointed against my will, that when I first heard I was a candidate I thot I would decline, but could not assign reasons that were satisfactory to my own mind, & when elected I thot myself bound to attend & accept, but I have maturely resolved that this shall be the last act of my public life. That this afternoon I wished to have a free confidential conversation upon the question to whom we shall give our votes to be president & vice president.

After stating the importance of the election of a chief majestrate for the nation, I observed I should vote for John Quincy Adams to be president, & not for James Monroe. My acquaintance with Mr. Adams has been long & intimate. I know he is in every respect qualified for that high trust. Mr. Monroe during the last four years has, in my opinion, conducted, as president, very improperly. He cut off one of the sources of public income by recommending the repeal of the internal taxes & duties; & at the same time unnecessarily augmented those of expenditure, by granting pensions to a vast amount, increasing the pay of congress, & the salaries of civil officers — & locating the army, in several instances, in a most injudicious manner. In this state of affairs, & in consequence of his errors, the government has been compelled, in a season of profound peace, instead of paying the public debt to resort to a loan of three million of dollars on interest, which is not to be repaid short of twelve years. These facts cannot be denied. I must therefore withhold my vote from him.

That Daniel D. Tompkins whose duty consists in presiding over the senate — for which he receives annually a salary of five thousand dollars; during the last three years he was absent from the senate during their session nearly three fourths of the time, & thereby occasioned an extra-expence to the nation of nearly twenty five hundred dollars. He has not that weight of character which his office requires — the fact is he is grossly intemperate. I cannot vote for him to be again Vice president — my vote will be given to Richard Rush, whom I have every reason to believe is well qualified for that office.

I made this statement with great calmness, & fully illustrated every idea in a very particular manner, taking half an hour. The board listened with fixt attention, but appeared surprized, & were perfectly silent. After sitting a few minutes, I observed, I had made those observations not to influence their decision, but to justify the votes I should give tomorrow — & that I thot it was a respect due to them to disclose the reasons & motives that would govern my conduct. The gentlemen discovered neither passion or opposition, but declined conversing on the subject.

Dec 6/ The Electors met, I gave my votes for Adams & Rush; & the other seven electors voted for Monroe & Tompkins. I have acted according to my own judgement; & shall have no cause to regret it tho no other elector should vote for the same men.

THE ELECTORAL VOTE IN THE 1816 ELECTION

STATES	PRESIDENT		VICE-PRESIDENT				
	James Monroe	Rufus King	D. D. Tompkins	John E. Howard	James Ross	John Marshall	Robert G. Harper
New Hampshire....	8	—	8	—	—	—	—
Vermont...........	8	—	8	—	—	—	—
Massachusetts......	—	22	—	22	—	—	—
Rhode Island.......	4	—	4	—	—	—	—
Connecticut........	—	9	—	—	5	4	—
New York..........	29	—	29	—	—	—	—
New Jersey.........	8	—	8	—	—	—	—
Pennsylvania.......	25	—	25	—	—	—	—
Delaware...........	—	3	—	—	—	—	3
Maryland..........	8	—	8	—	—	—	—
Virginia...........	25	—	25	—	—	—	—
North Carolina.....	15	—	15	—	—	—	—
South Carolina......	11	—	11	—	—	—	—
Georgia............	8	—	8	—	—	—	—
Kentucky..........	12	—	12	—	—	—	—
Tennessee..........	8	—	8	—	—	—	—
Louisiana..........	3	—	3	—	—	—	—
Ohio..............	8	—	8	—	—	—	—
Indiana............	3	—	3	—	—	—	—
	183	34	183	22	5	4	3

THE ELECTORAL VOTE IN THE 1820 ELECTION

STATES	PRESIDENT		VICE-PRESIDENT				
	James Monroe	J. Q. Adams	D. D. Tompkins	R. Stockton	R. G. Harper	R. Rush	D. Rodney
Maine..............	9	—	9	—	—	1	—
New Hampshire.....	7	1	7	—	—	1	—
Vermont...........	8	—	8	—	—	—	—
Massachusetts.......	15	—	7	8	—	—	—
Rhode Island.......	4	—	4	—	—	—	—
Connecticut.........	9	—	9	—	—	—	—
New York..........	29	—	29	—	—	—	—
New Jersey.........	8	—	8	—	—	—	—
Pennsylvania*.......	24	—	24	—	—	—	—
Delaware..........	4	—	—	—	—	—	4
Maryland..........	11	—	10	—	1	—	—
Virginia............	25	—	25	—	—	—	—
North Carolina.....	15	—	15	—	—	—	—
South Carolina......	11	—	11	—	—	—	—
Georgia............	8	—	8	—	—	—	—
Alabama...........	3	—	3	—	—	—	—
Mississippi*........	2	—	2	—	—	—	—
Louisiana...........	3	—	3	—	—	—	—
Kentucky..........	12	—	12	—	—	—	—
Tennessee*........	7	—	7	—	—	—	—
Ohio..............	8	—	8	—	—	—	—
Indiana...........	3	—	3	—	—	—	—
Illinois............	3	—	3	—	—	—	—
Missouri...........	3	—	3	—	—	—	—
	231	1	218	8	1	1	4

* In each of these states, one elector died before the meeting of the electoral college.

Election of 1824

JAMES F. HOPKINS has been a member of the Department of History of the University of Kentucky since 1940. He is the author of two books on Kentucky history and is editor of The Papers of Henry Clay *(3 vols. to date; 1959-).*

Election of 1824

by *James F. Hopkins*

The presidential campaign of 1824 stood in sharp contrast to the ones preceding it, for in no previous contest had so many men indicated a willingness to become candidates for the nation's highest office nor, for almost a generation, had an election stirred such emotion. Since no candidate won a majority in the Electoral College, the victor was not named until more than three months after the voters had gone to the polls. It was then that the United States House of Representatives performed, for the second and perhaps last time, its constitutional function of naming the President.

Popular interest in the 1824 campaign began to develop even before President James Monroe was elected to his second term. A galaxy of talented and ambitious men, each commanding a loyal following, appeared on the political horizon and became the subject of widespread speculation.

The appearance of this large number of serious contenders resulted from the breakdown of the political system that had arisen after the adoption of the Constitution. Under that system, the Federalists and Republicans had each chosen a champion to battle for the Presidency. After the War of 1812, however, the Federalist party was no longer an effective force in national politics, and all who wanted to succeed James Monroe in March, 1825, claimed to be Republicans. The issues between the old parties had disappeared or had diminished in importance, while new issues had not yet proved divisive enough to bring about the formation, on a national scale, of clearly defined, opposing political groups.

Political competition now took place within the surviving national party. Factions clustered around individual leaders and tended to be sectional in nature although they were based to some extent on national questions like slavery, tariff, internal improvements, banking, and public land policy. The Missouri Controversy of 1820-21 had stirred men's passions on the slavery issue in a foreboding manner for the future. Moreover, the Panic of 1819 and the ensuing depression had aroused forces not clearly understood nor easily handled by the politicians. Candidates might disagree with one another on specific issues, yet not one could claim that his stand on any matter of national importance was exclusively his. Each man represented what he thought to be the paramount interests of his own section of the country but if he expected to win a national election he had to cultivate support in areas outside his own.

In the absence of an opposition party the Republicans felt no need to publish a platform. Each candidate stood on his record, without presenting the voters with a statement on the questions of the day or outlining a program for the future. John C. Calhoun and Henry Clay did develop some programs but not even Clay's "American System," conceived to serve the interests of both his section and the nation as a whole, constituted a formal platform in the modern sense. Furthermore, the views of other contenders coincided with some aspects of Clay's and Calhoun's policies.

In any case, it was apparent that one of the new generation of leaders would win the election of 1824. The elder statesmen who had held the reins of power since the adoption of the Constitution were passing from the political scene, and younger politicians were replacing them. Tradition dictated that the incumbent President should not seek a third term and Monroe seemed to accept this. According to another, younger tradition, the Secretary of State could then be expected to move into the Presidency, although the mantle of office had fallen twice to the Vice-President. A third tradition, violated only once, pointed to a Virginian as Monroe's successor, or, since no resident of Virginia entered the race, at least indicated that the successful candidate would enjoy the backing of the traditional New York-Virginia alliance.

It was impossible to fulfill the latter two conventions in 1824, since the Secretary of State was a New Englander and was therefore not acceptable to the leaders of the New York-Virginia coalition. A change in what had become the usual order of succession was inevitable. Also working against the old order were new political forces, new issues, and the disappearance of old alignments. Since the War of 1812 the Union had been enlarged by the admission of six new states, five of them in the West and Southwest. These sections, which included the older states of Kentucky, Tennessee, and Louisiana, were highly conscious of the fact that no westerner had yet been seriously considered for the Presidency.

Seven prominent political figures were most often and most seriously mentioned as candidates. Three of them, however, were no longer in contention by the time of the election: DeWitt Clinton of New York was elected governor of his state in 1824; William Lowndes of South Carolina died shortly after his candidacy had been announced; and John C. Calhoun, also of

South Carolina, found it expedient to withdraw before the end of the contest. In the fall of 1824, four candidates were still in the running: John Quincy Adams of Massachusetts, Henry Clay of Kentucky, William Harris Crawford of Georgia, and Andrew Jackson of Tennessee.

All four were well known throughout the country and had attracted followers beyond their own sections. Adams and Crawford were members of President Monroe's Cabinet; Clay and Jackson both returned to Congress in 1823, the former as a member of the House of Representatives, the latter as a senator; Clay, Crawford, and Jackson were slaveholders; the same three were also duelists. All, save Jackson, had served their country abroad in the field of diplomacy, while Jackson was the only military hero of the group. Their educational background was widely varied, but all four had been trained in the law. Adams was a New Englander, Crawford represented the South and appeared to be the beneficiary of the New York-Virginia alliance, and both Clay and Jackson may be termed westerners.

Before and during much of the campaign, William H. Crawford seemed to hold a tactical advantage over his competitors. Born February 24, 1772, in Virginia, as a child he had migrated with his parents to South Carolina and a few years later to the area now included in Columbia County, Georgia. His formal education, interspersed with labor on the farm, was received in rural schools and in a local academy conducted by the Reverend Moses Waddell. Ambition, as well as a desire for learning, led him to the study of law, and after having been admitted to the bar, he began practice at Lexington, Georgia, in 1799. He established his estate "Woodlawn" nearby a few years later. Crawford was a highly successful attorney and he attracted a great deal of favorable notice as one of the compilers of the first published digest of the laws of his adopted state. At an early date he became aligned with one of the two factions contending for political control of Georgia and in his rise to leadership fought two duels. He killed a man in 1802 and in 1806 was himself severely wounded by John Clark, leader of the opposing political group and his inveterate enemy.

Crawford's public career began in 1803, when he was elected to the state legislature. Four years later he was chosen to fill a vacancy in the United States Senate, where he voiced Republican principles while maintaining a considerable amount of independence. He opposed enactment of the Embargo in 1807 but a year later opposed its repeal; in both instances he favored strong measures to protect American neutrality rights. Reelected to the Senate without opposition in 1810, Crawford fought a losing battle against many of his fellow Republicans to renew the charter of the Bank of the United States. He saw his cause triumph in 1816 when many who had earlier opposed the bank now joined in reestablishing it. Respect for his ability and leadership was manifested in 1811, when, upon the death of Vice-President George Clinton, Crawford was elected president pro tempore of the Senate. After the declaration of war against England, he declined the offer of a Cabinet post (Secretary of War) preferring to remain in the Senate.

Crawford's legislative experience came to an end in 1813, when President James Madison appointed him to the difficult post of United States minister to France, a position he held throughout the War of 1812. In the summer of 1815 he resigned from the diplomatic service, returned home, and almost immediately accepted appointment as Secretary of War. Crawford's achievements in this office and his interest in sound fiscal policy led Madison, in October, 1816, to promote him to Secretary of the Treasury.

Although he was urged by many Republicans to become a candidate for the Presidency in 1816, Crawford refused to oppose James Monroe. Nevertheless, in the Republican congressional nominating caucus he received 54 votes, only 11 fewer than Monroe, who became the Republican nominee and the next President. At Monroe's request he remained in the Cabinet as Secretary of the Treasury for the next eight years. The esteem shown to Crawford by both caucus and the President augured well for the future. Long in the public service, heir to the Virginia tradition, supported by the old states rights Republicans, and heading an executive department which controlled much patronage throughout the country, Crawford was in an excellent position to launch a campaign. On the other hand, his prominence made him the target of all other contenders.

If the Presidency should elude Crawford, the most logical successor to Monroe would be Secretary of State John Quincy Adams, who was better fitted for high office by family background, education, and experience than any of his rivals. Five years older than Crawford, he was born at Braintree, Massachusetts, July 11, 1767, the eldest son of John Adams (President of the United States, 1797-1801). John Quincy received most of his early schooling at home. Later he accompanied his father abroad and attended schools in France and the Netherlands, including the University of Leiden. In 1781 he went to St. Petersburg as private secretary to Francis Dana, who had been sent by Congress on a fruitless mission to the court of Catherine the Great, and after fourteen months in Russia, Adams returned to Paris to serve as his father's secretary, until 1785. In the spring of that year he came home and in March, 1786, entered the junior class at Harvard College. He was admitted to Phi Beta Kappa before the year was out and in July, 1787, graduated from the college. Three years of additional study prepared him for admission to the bar and in 1790, at the age of twenty-three, he began his law practice in Boston.

In recognition of the young man's experience and ability, President George Washington in 1794 appointed him minister to the Netherlands, one of only five diplomatic posts maintained abroad by the United States. Two years later Washington named him minister to Portugal, but before departing for his new assignment in July, 1797, the young man learned that he had been appointed by his own father, now President of the United States, as minister to Prussia. This phase of Adams' diplomatic career ended early in 1801, when his father, defeated in his bid for reelection and approaching the end of his term as President, ordered him home.

Returning to law practice, Adams soon entered politics and became a successful Federalist candidate for a seat in the Massachusetts senate. In 1802 he lost a close race for election to the United States House of Representatives but was chosen United States senator for the term beginning March 4, 1803.

Young Adams was too independent ever to be a partisan politician, and he soon lost favor with the more conservative wing of the Federalist party. As United States senator he aroused the fury of Federalist colleagues by supporting Republican measures and, in 1808, by attending the Republican caucus. Rebuked by the Massachusetts legislature, which chose his successor long before the expiration of his term, Adams resigned from the Senate on June 8, 1808, and retired to a Harvard professorship to which he had been appointed in 1806.

Private life did not hold him long, for he was now adopted by the Republicans and named by President James Madison a minister plenipotentiary to Russia in 1809. He remained there for approximately five years, declining at one point an appointment to the United States Supreme Court. In 1813, together with Albert Gallatin and Senator James A. Bayard, he was named to a commission, established prematurely as it turned out, to negotiate a peace with Great Britain to end the War of 1812. Months later, when England finally agreed to direct discussion with American representatives, the same commissioners, joined by Henry Clay and Jonathan Russell, negotiated the Treaty of Ghent which was signed December 24, 1814. The Americans presented a united front to their British counterparts, but certain disagreements among themselves broke out later during the campaign of 1824. Following the end of the war, Adams became minister to the Court of St. James, arriving there in time to join Clay and Gallatin in signing a commercial treaty which, with modifications, is still in effect.

Appointment as Secretary of State by President James Monroe in 1817 provided the opportunity for a highly successful climax to Adams' career as a diplomat. Serving brilliantly during both of Monroe's terms, Adams' most notable achievements were the treaty with Spain, the acquisition of East Florida and the Spanish claim to the Pacific coast of North America above the forty-second parallel, recognition of the independence of the Latin American republics, and collaboration with the President in the formulation of the Monroe Doctrine.

Highly intelligent, well-educated, and widely experienced in statesmanship, Adams appeared to have the qualities needed in a national leader. However, he was reserved and even cold in manner, averse to the operations of partisan politics, and lacking in the common touch. He was considered an apostate by the Federalists and viewed by the old Republicans, especially in the South, with suspicion and distaste; he had no large popular following. Nevertheless, despite the dislike of the more conservative Federalists for him (and for his father), he was more acceptable to New England than any of the other candidates. He was also respected, though not popular, in other sections of the country, mainly because of his diplomatic achievements. By appointing him Secretary of State President Monroe had not only chosen the best-qualified man available for the position but, at the same time, had called attention to the availability of John Quincy Adams as a candidate for the Presidency.

The third presidential hopeful in Monroe's Cabinet was young, brilliant, and ambitious John Caldwell Calhoun. Born on March 18, 1782, to a prosperous farm family at Abbeville, South Carolina, Calhoun received his early education at home. At the age of thirteen he was sent to Georgia to attend the academy conducted by his brother-in-law, the Reverend Moses Waddell, at which William H. Crawford was a pupil. The deaths of his sister, Mrs. Waddell, and his father forced young Calhoun to leave the academy in 1796 to resume the life of a farmer, but his mother and two brothers agreed to finance his education for seven years and he returned to Waddell's academy. In 1802 Calhoun enrolled in the junior class at Yale College and in 1803 was initiated into Phi Beta Kappa. In the next year, at the age of twenty-two, Calhoun graduated from the college.

Calhoun then turned to the study of law. During the winter of 1804-05 he read in the office of a prominent attorney of Charleston, South Carolina, after which he returned to New England to enroll in the famous law school conducted by Judge Tapping Reeve at Litchfield, Connecticut. Upon receiving his diploma from that institution, he came back to South Carolina for additional study in Charleston and in an attorney's office at Abbeville. Exceptionally well prepared for a legal career, he was admitted to the bar in 1807 and began an immediately successful practice in his home town.

Despite the time and effort he had devoted to his legal training and the extensive practice he rapidly acquired, Calhoun had never really liked the law. Politics was more to his taste, and he lost little time, once his studies had been completed, entering the political arena. He was elected to the South Carolina legislature in 1808 and served quietly for two sessions. The opportunity to distinguish himself arose when the state Republican caucus met to nominate possible candidates for the next presidential election. Indignant at British violations of American rights, Calhoun spoke out against the policies of the national Administration and opposed the renomination of Vice-President George Clinton. Calhoun emerged from this caucus as the leader of the young war hawks of his state and, at the same time, assured himself nomination as a candidate for Congress.

Calhoun was elected to the House of Representatives in 1810 and found a group of kindred spirits when he reached Washington for the first session of the Twelfth Congress. They were young, resentful of British actions, and impatient with the leadership of their own nation for its failure to protect the rights of Americans. Speaker Henry Clay, leader of the war hawks in the House of Representatives, appointed Calhoun to the important Committee on Foreign Affairs, of which he frequently served as acting chairman and was unquestionably the leader. It was Calhoun who, on June 3, 1812, presented to the House the report recommending a declaration of war. At that time the report was taken as his own work but long afterward was proven to have come from the pen of James Monroe.

Once the decision for war had been reached, Calhoun became "the young Hercules," striving, as he had done even before the declaration, to find ways to provide the money, men, ships, and supplies needed to pursue the conflict.

In appreciation of his efforts, his constituents reelected him without opposition in 1812 and 1814. When the war ended, he was convinced that the peace was only temporary and urged preparation for a third bout with England. An ardent nationalist, Calhoun set forth proposals for a strong army and navy, a second Bank of the United States, internal improvements, and a protective tariff. His ideas were close to those of Clay; Calhoun the sectionalist had not yet emerged.

Although he was not President Monroe's first choice for the position, Calhoun accepted appointment as Secretary of War in 1817. The burdens of this office were heavy, but the young man who had exhibited brilliant logic in debate and a mastery of legislative procedures now seized the opportunity to demonstrate his talents as an administrator. His conduct of the department was, on the whole, highly successful, even though Congress refused to put into effect his scheme for the defense of the country.

Though younger than other potential candidates, Calhoun nevertheless decided early in Monroe's second Administration to enter the presidential contest. There was a great deal in his favor: he had distinguished himself in Congress and in the Cabinet: he could expect support from his own state; his nationalistic program appealed to Pennsylvania and other areas; and the department over which he presided had wide influence. The rivalry for political advantage was intense, both within Monroe's Cabinet and without, but in view of the successes he had already enjoyed, Calhoun had no cause to doubt his own genius.

Outside the Cabinet, by his own choice, was Henry Clay, whose ambition and cheerful optimism were to make him a perennial candidate for the Presidency. Clay was born on April 12, 1777, in an area of Virginia called "the Slashes." His father, a Baptist preacher, farmer, and slave owner, died in 1781, and his mother remarried. The boy's early education consisted of instruction obtained at home, plus three years of more formal schooling in a local academy. Somehow he learned to write a neat, clear script, but he had little opportunity to acquire the classical knowledge prized by the public men of his time.

In 1792 the family moved to Kentucky, leaving the lad, now fifteen years old, in Richmond, employed as a deputy clerk in the Virginia High Court of Chancery. There he attracted the attention of the chancellor, George Wythe, signer of the Declaration of Independence and distinguished lawyer and judge, who made Clay his amanuensis. Tall and awkward, but bright, ambitious, and eager to please, the youth not only performed the duties of copyist but also, under the direction of the chancellor, began to read the classics and law. In 1796 he seriously entered law study in the office of Virginia's attorney-general Robert Brooke and, on November 6, 1797, obtained a license to practice. Clay then joined his mother and stepfather in Versailles, Kentucky, where they operated a tavern. Soon thereafter he after decided to cast his lot with the West.

In Lexington, Kentucky, the young lawyer found an environment congenial to his temperament and abilities. Litigation over land titles and debt collection for local and eastern merchants placed him on the road to financial well-being, while his oratorical ability, self confidence, and quick wit brought success as a criminal lawyer. Lexington had passed the frontier stage by the time Clay arrived and took pride in its position as a commercial, social, and educational center. The town and young lawyer formed a warm attachment for one another; they, and the West, matured together.

An ambitious young attorney turned naturally to politics. As early as 1798 Clay's speech attacking the Alien and Sedition Acts called attention to his Republicanism. In 1803 he won his first election to office, as a member of the state house of representatives, and in 1806 the legislature chose him to fill the remaining few months of an unexpired term in the United States Senate. The fact that he had not yet reached the constitutional age of thirty apparently raised no doubts in the legislature, the United States Senate, or his own mind. In spite of his youth and brief tenure in the office, he was an active member of the Senate, introducing and speaking for measures beneficial to the West and supporting proposals to aid internal improvements.

Back in Kentucky in 1807, Clay was again elected to the state house of representatives, where he soon became Speaker. He distinguished himself in that position and also by a duel with Federalist Humphrey Marshall. Returned to the United States Senate in 1809 to complete another unexpired term, Clay firmly established himself as an eloquent spokesman for the West and began laying the foundation for the nationalistic economic and political program which he advocated all his life, and which came to be known as "the American System."

Elected to the United States House of Representatives in 1810, he entered that body as the leader of the group of able, impatient young men known as the war hawks. He was immediately chosen Speaker, an office which, during his long tenure, was highly partisan and more powerful than it had ever been before. With utmost practicality Clay used his power of appointment to fill House committees with members favorable to the measures he advocated. In control of the House machinery, Clay and the war hawks ended the policy of temporization, overrode the opposition of Federalists and Old Republicans, and pressed successfully for war with England.

In 1814 President Madison astutely added Clay to the commission appointed to negotiate for a peace that had proved unattainable in battle. That commission was successful in ending the war, but the Treaty of Ghent contained none of the objectives which Clay and his followers had hoped to secure. Nevertheless, after stopping in London to help negotiate the commercial treaty of 1815 with England, he returned home to a warm welcome and to reelection both to Congress and as the Speaker.

During most of the following decade Clay was a powerful figure in Washington, where he brought his ideas of political and economic nationalism to full bloom. Preferring to remain in Congress, he refused President Madison's offers of diplomatic and Cabinet posts. He was disappointed in his apparent desire to be Secretary of State, and rejected opportunities to become United States minister to England and Secretary of War. He remained in the House until 1821, an outspoken critic of the Administration. Clay urged expenditures for internal improvements and he warmly advocated recognition of the new republics in Spanish America long before the Administration was ready to take that step. However, he opposed Adams's treaty with Spain ending the Florida question because it relinquished United States claims to Texas. In one notable three-day speech he attacked the conduct of the war against the Seminole Indians and thereby incurred the displeasure of the Administration and the lasting enmity of General Andrew Jackson. Clay's efforts in engineering the Missouri Compromises in 1820 and 1821 demonstrated his political skill and his fervent desire to calm sectional passions. Financial difficulties caused him not to run for reelection in 1820, and for two years he served as attorney for the Bank of the United States in the West. He returned to the United States House of Representatives again in 1823 and was again elected Speaker.

Without the patronage enjoyed by a Cabinet member, Clay was nevertheless a serious candidate for the Presidency. His education could not compare to that of Adams or Calhoun, nor even that of Crawford, but he possessed a quick mind, a charismatic personality, great oratorical ability, daring, and a sanguine outlook on political life. He was a Republican, but different from the old party type, for he had adopted much of the Hamiltonian economic program. He represented the new West and the viewpoint of men in all sections who were interested in roads, canals, manufacturing, banking, and national defense. His greatest strength, however, lay in the House of Representatives. His best chance for the Presidency at this time was based on two conditions: that he win enough electoral votes to place him among the top three candidates, and that the election be thrown into the House.

Also outside the Cabinet (and excluded from early speculation) was Andrew Jackson, who proved to be one of the most astute politicians of his time. He was born on March 15, 1767, shortly after the death of his father, in the Waxhaw settlement, a backwoods area in South Carolina claimed also by North Carolina. Although he could read by the age of five, his education was meager. During the Revolutionary War, when the battles moved into the back country of South Carolina, the thirteen-year-old boy fought against the British and Tories and in 1781 was captured by the British and wounded when he refused to clean an officer's boots. The death of his mother shortly afterward left him with few restraints on his high spirits and love of excitement.

In 1784 Jackson began the study of law in the office of a prominent Salisbury, North Carolina, attorney and, despite an active and wild social life, he was admitted to the bar three years later. At the invitation of a friend, John McNairy, newly appointed judge of the Western District of North Carolina, Jackson crossed the mountains in 1788 to serve as public prosecutor. A bloodless duel with the most prominent lawyer at the superior court at Jonesboro helped introduce him to the West. Later in the year Jackson, followed shortly by Judge McNairy, reached the frontier village of Nashville, the seat of their court.

The high-strung, strong-willed young attorney found life in the West much to his liking. He was immediately successful as prosecutor and in the private practice of law. He rapidly acquired large land holdings, became prosecuting attorney of the Mero District of the Southwest Territory (created in 1790, when North Carolina ceded her western lands to the United States), and in 1792 received his first military appointment, as judge advocate of the Davidson County Militia. Marriage to Mrs. Rachel Donelson Robards brought alliance with the influential Donelson family connections and lasting embarrassment to the young couple, who learned, two years after they had been wed, that the bride's first husband had not obtained a divorce from her until after her union with the second. Following this mortifying discovery, the Jacksons were rewed.

Jackson quickly established a strong political base during his eight years in Nashville. In 1796 he was elected to the first Tennessee constitutional convention, and, after the state had entered the Union, he was sent to the United States House of Representatives. The next year, when William Blount, his political ally, was expelled from the United States Senate, Jackson resigned from the lower house and was chosen to fill the Senate vacancy. Business difficulties and a dislike for the Senate led to his resignation from Congress, however, and on his return home, in 1798, he was immediately elected one of the judges of the superior court of Tennessee. Another election, in 1802, made him major-general in the Tennessee militia.

Retiring from the judgeship in 1803, he managed to straighten out his tangled financial affairs and establish his home on a plantation near Nashville, where he later built the famous Hermitage. His hospitality was extended to many guests, including Aaron Burr.

The War of 1812 prompted Jackson's offer to raise and lead troops into battle, but, to his disappointment and anger, his services seemed unwanted by the federal authorities. Empowered by his own state to command an expedition against the Creek Indians in 1813, he waged war so savagely and so effectively that he crushed the power of the Creek nation and dictated a peace on his own harsh terms. The importance of his campaigns was recognized by the national government, which sent reinforcements and appointed him a major-general in the United States Army; his brilliant successes made him the hero of the entire frontier region. As commander of the military district embracing the southwestern part of the country, he was called on in 1814 to meet the threat of British invasion from the south. The Battle of New Orleans, fought on January 8, 1815, made Andrew Jackson nationally famous.

With the return of peace the United States Army was reorganized into two parts; Jackson was placed in command of the southern division, with headquarters at his own home. Routine tours of inspection and the management of his plantation and business affairs were interrupted in 1818 by a war against the Seminole Indians on the southeastern border. Jackson took the field on orders whose nature and extent have been disputed since that time, pursued the Indians across the international boundary into Florida, executed two British subjects, seized the province in the name of the United States, ousted the Spanish governor, and returned home a greater hero than before.

His high-handed actions, however, worried his own government over possible international repercussions. Florida was returned to Spain, and in both the Cabinet and Congress proposals were made for the censure of Jackson's conduct. The Administration eventually accepted the advice of Secretary of State John Quincy Adams and supported the General; the House of Representatives listened to Henry Clay's plea against "a triumph of the principle of insubordination—a triumph of the military over the civil authority— . . . a triumph over the Constitution of the land" but defeated resolutions of disapproval. Jackson's journey home from Washington, after his vindication, was a triumphal tour.

In 1821, after the acquisition of Florida by the United States, Jackson resigned his military commission and accepted appointment as governor of the new territory. He had the satisfaction of receiving the territory from the Spanish governor. he established local and territorial governments but before the year was out he resigned his post and returned to the Hermitage. Two years later, in October, 1823, the "Nashville Junto," having launched Jackson's campaign for the Presidency, succeeded in having him elected to the United States Senate.

Though well-known and popular throughout the country, Jackson appeared to have few of the attributes expected of a presidential candidate. He was no orator, he had held no Cabinet post, and his earlier services in Congress had been brief and without distinction. His principles, thought to be Jeffersonian, were not well known, perhaps even to himself. Though he was a lawyer and judge, he was not well-educated, even for his day. He was a duelist several times over and a gambler. His military successes had been characterized by cruelty to the Indians, autocratic and independent action, extremely severe punishment of insubordination in others, and a settled conviction that he was always in the right. Imperious and intolerant of opposition, he tended toward enmity to those who crossed him, though this characteristic was tempered somewhat during his campaigns for the Presidency. Often irascible, he was said to use his temper deliberately, as a means of silencing an opponent or an importunate seeker of patronage.

In the campaign of 1824 Jackson's initial strength, outside his own home grounds, rested in his military successes. Harsh treatment of the Indians endeared him to the frontier; the Battle of New Orleans made his name a household word throughout the country. Politicians in all parts of the nation seized on his popularity to gain support for themselves. Jackson responded by accepting the role of the democrat, the man of the people. He accepted the plaudits that were rightfully his and, without announcing himself as a candidate for the Presidency, expressed his willingness to do what the people demanded of him. Meanwhile, his letters and public statements contributed to a type of well-organized, grass roots campaign that was new in the 1820s.

Politicians were beginning to consider the question of Monroe's successor as early as 1820. Crawford, who had unexpectedly come close to the Republican nomination in 1816, would assuredly be a strong contender. A group of Clay's friends, in April, 1820, considered recommending him to the congressional caucus as a candidate for the Vice-Presidency, but the meeting was sparsely attended and adjourned without making any nominations. Clay considered the outcome partially the result of "the efforts of every Pretender to the throne, to defeat my recommendation, lest it should place me abreast with them if not in their advance." Later in the year certain New England electors sounded out Adams on the possibility of their voting for him instead of the Republican nominee, Daniel R. Tompkins, of New York, for Vice-President. Adams rejected the idea, probably because he hoped for Tompkins' support in New York in the next presidential election. In the Electoral College, however, one New England elector cast his vote for Adams for President, thus depriving Monroe of the honor of unanimous reelection.

Monroe retained his Cabinet for his second Administration, in spite of the rivalry already apparent among three of its members. Adams was on friendly terms with Calhoun until the Secretary of War became an avowed candidate himself. Adams was suspicious of Crawford, however, whom he considered a spoilsman. Ill will between Calhoun and Crawford came into the open, and all three viewed Clay with suspicion and jealousy because of his influence with the House of Representatives, which as early as 1820 seemed likely to decide the election.

When Congress assembled in December, 1821, its members naturally found politics a fascinating topic of conversation. Hezekiah Niles, visiting Washington early in January, 1822, professed astonishment at finding "so great a buz [sic] about the person who should succeed Mr. Monroe" but concluded after a few days "that the whole noise was to be traced to an inconsiderable number of persons." By the end of the session, in May, he had revised his opinion and deplored the amount of time wasted by the legislators "in electioneering for the next President of the United States."

Closely associated with this electioneering was the question of the caucus, which was heatedly discussed in Washington and throughout the country until early 1824. In the past era when the two-party system had existed, the congressional caucus, composed of senators and representatives loyal to a specific political party, had operated satisfactorily in nominating that party's candidates for President and Vice-President. As the strength of the Federalists dwindled, however, party unity became less important to the Republicans. The congressional caucus lost its importance and was attacked as a device for the politicians in Washington to dictate to the people the choice of candidates for the highest national offices.

Since all candidates in the campaign of 1824 were members of the same party, only the one—in this case, Crawford—who expected to be chosen by the caucus favored convening it. All his rivals and their supporters naturally opposed the caucus and looked elsewhere for their own nominations. Not one, however, dared be so crass as to announce publicly his intention of running and to work openly for his own nomination and election.

Nominations for local and state offices in some parts of the country were customarily made by party conventions, of varying degrees of formality, on the county or district level. Elsewhere such nominations were made by legislative caucus. In some previous presidential campaigns, recommendations of favored candidates had been made by legislative resolutions and by legislative caucus. All these methods of nomination were now employed, and, in addition, the more democratic practices of endorsement of candidates by mass meetings and by straw votes became popular.

The first candidates to become formally and openly committed to the race were the two South Carolinians, Lowndes and Calhoun. A legislative caucus in their home state met on December 18, 1821, to consider ways of blocking the Crawford movement. It was decided then and there by a small margin, to nominate a candidate for the Presidency, and the group unanimously endorsed Lowndes. Ten days later in Washington Calhoun received an evening call from a group of congressmen and somewhat hesitantly accepted their support in the forthcoming contest. Upon learning of his own nomination, Lowndes conferred with his friend Calhoun and both agreed to remain in the race. Their common opposition to Crawford and Lowndes' declining health doubtless contributed to their decision.

Adams, who had been friendly toward Calhoun, then reassessed his own position. From his ally Representative William Plumer, Jr. of New Hampshire Adams heard that Calhoun was serious about his candidacy, although, in Plumer's opinion, if his prospects should dim, he would be willing to withdraw. Adams now let it be known that, if his friends thought proper, he would not be averse to accepting a nomination for himself, preferably from a caucus of the Republican members of the Massachusetts legislature. In late January, 1822, he learned, however, that although the great majority of the Republicans of his state favored him, formal action was not considered advisable at that time.

Interest in the campaign was also evident in Tennessee, where in November, 1821, at a public dinner for Governor William Carroll, a toast was drunk to an unnamed "next President." Henry Clay confidently counted on the support of leaders in both factions of Tennessee politics, while William H. Crawford also had many friends in the state. Andrew Jackson, on the other hand, detested both these men and instead favored Adams and Calhoun. Jackson himself had been mentioned from time to time in connection with the Presidency, but the talk had never been taken seriously.

The Jackson movement, launched in Tennessee early in 1822, was prompted less by the thought actually of making Old Hickory President of the United States than for the sake of political objectives within the state. Carroll's election to the governorship in 1821 had been a blow to the Blount faction, with which Jackson had been long aligned, and had set its leaders scheming for a return to power. A group of politicians from Nashville and East Tennessee, including Judge John Overton and Felix Grundy (hitherto friends of Clay), United States Senator John H. Eaton and Willian B. Lewis (later strategists of Jackson's campaigns), Judge Hugh Lawson White, and state representative Pleasant M. Miller hit upon the idea of nominating Jackson for the Presidency and using his popularity to advantage in the subsequent elections of United States senators and representatives from the state.

Consequently, on July 20,1822, during a special session of the Tennessee legislature, the members of the house of representatives in recess unanimously adopted the following preamble and resolutions:

> The members of the general assembly of the state of Tennessee, taking into view the great importance of the selection of a suitable person to fill the presidential chair at the approaching election for the chief magis-

tracy of the United States, and seeing that those who achieved our independence, and laid the foundations of the American republic, have nearly passed away; and believing that moral worth, political acquirements and decision of character, should unite in the individual who may be called to preside over the people of the United States, have turned their eyes to *Andrew Jackson*, late major general in the armies of the United States.

In him they behold the soldier, the statesman, and the honest man; he deliberates, he decides, and he acts; he is calm in deliberation, cautious in decision, efficient in action. Such a man we are willing to aid in electing to the highest office in the gift of a free people. The welfare of a country may be safely intrusted to the hands of him who has experienced every privation, and encountered every danger, to promote its safety, its honor, and its glory: Therefore,

Resolved, As the opinion of the members composing the general assembly of the state of Tennessee, that the name of major general ANDREW JACKSON be submitted to the consideration of the people of the United States, at the approaching election for the chief magistracy.

Although politicians recognized the purpose of the maneuver, state pride suppressed overt opposition to these sentiments, and, after a delay of two weeks, the members of the senate voted their approval of the nomination. Faithful Clay adherents explained to the Kentuckian that the immediate object of the action appeared to be the defeat of the incumbent United States Senator, John Williams, who was disliked by the Blount-Overton faction. Recognizing the injury to Clay's chances by the appearance of another western candidate, his friends reassured him by asserting that the Jackson effort was not to be taken seriously. Ever the optimist, Clay informed a close friend in October that Jackson's name would be withdrawn.

Meanwhile Clay and his friends had been considering the proper time to announce his own candidacy. In June he agreed "that the name of any individual ought not to be prematurely thrust on the public notice," but, he confided, "On the other hand, one's friends ought not to delay bringing his pretensions into public view so long as to expose them to the danger of being forgotten or obscured." The following winter appeared early enough for "legislative nominations," and it was thought best that the first recommendation come from Ohio, a state considered favorable to him. In June, Clay also announced his candidacy for Congress, confidently expecting to win his seat without opposition. The August election turned out as he had predicted.

Ohio proved less eager to act than had been anticipated, and instead his first nomination came in Missouri on November 7, 1822. Clay was popular there because of his efforts to bring the state into the Union, and Senator Thomas Hart Benton, a kinsman of Mrs. Clay, worked in his behalf. Almost immediately a second nomination came from a legislative caucus in his own state. On November 18, following adjournment for the day, the members of both houses of the Kentucky general assembly met in the hall of the house of representatives and unanimously resolved that Clay "be recommended as a suitable person to succeed *James Monroe* as President" of the United States. In an accompanying address the Kentuckians expressed "a warm affection for, and a strong confidence in, their distinguished fellow-citizen" and a belief that the time had come "when the people of the West may, with some confidence, appeal to the magnanimity of the whole Union, for a favorable consideration of their equal and just claim to a fair participation in the executive government of these states."

A corresponding committee of the Kentucky legislators invited Ohio to follow Kentucky's lead in naming Clay, but at a meeting on December 10 the Ohio lawmakers decided by a margin of three votes "that it was inexpedient to go into any nomination, at that time." Clay's Ohio friends convened a second legislative caucus on January 3, 1823, at which slightly more than half of the members of the general assembly were present. In the balloting for a nominee Clay received fifty votes, Clinton seven, and Adams and Calhoun one each. On March 15,1823, members of the Louisiana legislature also adopted resolutions nominating Clay, but anticipation of similar action in Illinois and Indiana proved unjustified. Clay had many friends in the West, but it was apparent, even before the Jackson movement caught fire, that he could not count on the unanimous support of his own section.

In New England Adams' friends concluded that the name of their favorite should be placed before the public. A caucus "of most of the members" of the Maine legislature, held January 16, 1823, led the way by adopting the following preamble and resolutions:

> Whereas, it has been represented that the people of this state are in favor of the honorable William H. Crawford for the next president, and it being proper to correct any false impression on this subject; Therefore,
> *Resolved,* That this convention entertained the highest respect for the distinguished talents and public services of the honorable *John Q. Adams,* and do fully believe that no man possesses better qualifications for the important office of president of the United States; but as the election of president will not take place for a considerable time to come, this convention do not deem it expedient to make a formal nomination of any person as a candidate for that station.

A week later, on January 23, "a meeting of the Republican members of both branches of the legislature of the commonwealth of Massachusetts, and of Republican delegates from various towns of the commonwealth not represented in the legislature, held . . . in the city of Boston," adopted a resolution expressing "unlimited confidence in the republican principles of JOHN QUINCY ADAMS."

All the major candidates save Crawford, who could expect nomination by the congressional caucus, were thus launched into the campaign. Nominations and resolutions of approval continued as the election drew nearer. After the death of Lowndes in October, 1823, members of the South Carolina legislature resolved to support Calhoun and recommended him to the consideration of the people of the country. Early in the next month a convention of citizens of Jefferson County, Ohio, met at Steubenville and recommended DeWitt Clinton for President and Andrew Jackson for Vice-President.

In the spring of 1822, long before the last of the nominations, a journalist observed that the "electioneering begins to wax hot." Noting the prevalence of personal attacks, he urged moderation: "It cannot be supposed that Messrs. Adams, Crawford, or Calhoun, Mr. Clay and others spoken of as fitted to succeed to the chief magistracy of the United States, are cold enemies of their country, destitute of talents, or without moral principle." In a campaign lacking basic issues and party loyalties, however, personal considerations were highly important and attacks inevitable: Adams' habits of dress and conduct were criticized; Calhoun was pictured as a young man consumed with ambition; Clay was by some accounts a drunkard and gambler; Crawford's honesty was questioned; and Jackson was to his opponents a mere military chieftain.

An early effort to injure the reputation of Adams began in January, 1822, when John Floyd of Georgia introduced, and the United States House of Representatives adopted, a resolution calling on the President to lay before the house "all the correspondence which led to the Treaty of Ghent, which has not yet been made public. . . ." In the tangled series of events which followed, a letter written by Jonathan Russell in February, 1815, critical of Adams' stand at Ghent on the question of navigation of the Mississippi River could not be found at the State Department. Russell delivered a duplicate of his original letter to that department but when the original turned up, in Monroe's private papers, discrepancies were noted between it and the "duplicate." Adams then proceeded in a communication to Congress, published by newspapers and in pamphlet form, to demolish Russell.

The attack obviously had been intended to stir resentment against Adams in the West; his defense had been written with an eye to solidifying support for himself in his own section of the country. To his diary he grumbled: "Mr. Calhoun's friends had countenanced Russell's attack upon me, though Calhoun himself had disclaimed it." The Secretary of State was more bitter toward another rival: "Russell will be disappointed, and have the public voice against him; but Clay, for whom Russell has performed the part of the Jackal, will so far gain his point that it will form a theme for prejudice in the Western and Southern country against me." Nevertheless, shortly before writing that statement, Adams, pursuing what he considered "a generous policy towards" Clay, proposed that the President appoint the Kentuckian as minister to Colombia.

Clay had no desire to be eliminated from the presidential race by accepting a foreign mission. However, he was placed in an embarrassing position by the Adams-Russell controversy. In reply to an appeal from Russell, he was critical of "the variance between" the two versions of the letter in question and expressed a hope that a satisfactory explanation would be forthcoming. Later in the year, in a letter published in a Washington newspaper, Clay expressed regret at the "unhappy controversy" that had arisen and said there were, he thought, some errors in Adams' publication. He stated his intention "at some future period more propitious than the present to calm and dispassionate consideration," to make a statement on the subject of the negotiations at Ghent, and he denied knowledge of Congressman Floyd's intention to call for the correspondence. On the following day, the same paper carried an acid, self-righteous letter from Adams, in which he insisted that whatever he had "said, written, or done . . . , has been in the face of day, and under the responsibility of my name."

The second of the major efforts to tarnish the reputation of a candidate was directed at Crawford and involved the notorious "A. B. Plot." As early as January, 1822, Daniel Pope Cook, representative from Illinois, had introduced resolutions in the lower house of Congress calling for an investigation of Crawford's handling of land offices and of deposits of public money. Though Secretary Crawford defended himself in reports to Congress, charges against him continued in the following year through letters signed "A.B.," published in the Washington *Republican*, a Calhoun organ, and through House committee testimony given by Cook's father-in-law Ninian Edwards. In April, 1824, Edwards admitted authorship of the "A.B." letters and made detailed charges of malfeasance in regard to Crawford's administration of the Treasury Department. A committee investigation resulted in a report in June, exonerating Crawford. Shortly afterwards, when a committee planning a public dinner in Washington on July 4 was prevailed on by Crawford's friends to exclude Edwards from the affair, Adams, Calhoun, and Postmaster General John McLean published a joint letter announcing withdrawal of their own subscriptions.

It is difficult to assess the effect of these charges and countercharges. The importance of other factors in the outcome is less open to speculation. Most noteworthy were the rise in Jackson's popularity, the Calhoun withdrawal, Crawford's illness, and Clay's inability to hold the strength he appeared to have at the beginning of the contest.

The nomination of Jackson by the Tennessee legislature had elicited no response from him and had appeared to stir little immediate interest outside his own state. Early in November, 1822, a Philadelphia newspaper published a report "that the hero of New Orleans has resolved to withdraw from all public employments." Almost two months later, however, a meeting at Greensburg, Pennsylvania, established a correspondence committee to launch a movement for Jackson's nomination, and in February, 1823, the *Nashville Gazette* firmly declared that there was "not the least foundation in the assertion" that his name had been withdrawn from consideration for the Presidency. His rejection of an appointment as minister to Mexico heartened those who wished him to accept the role of candidate.

Jackson's reply to a letter in January, 1823, showed that he was becoming receptive to the idea. His statement was similar to those he had written earlier to a very few friends but up to this point he had taken no public notice of presidential talk. The wording in this instance was highly effective: "The office of chief magistrate . . . is one of great responsibility. As it should not be sought, . . . so it cannot, with propriety, be declined. . . . My political creed prompts me to leave the affair . . . to the free will of those who have alone the right to decide." With the words, "The committee of Dauphin county," substituted for the name of the addressee, this letter was published in the Harrisburg, Pennsylvania *Commonwealth* and copied widely by papers over the country. There was no mistaking its import.

The desire to throw a stumbling block in the paths of Clay and Crawford undoubtedly played an important part in Jackson's decision. He had been angered by Governor Carroll's continued support of Clay and he declared to a friend his intention of confronting Carroll with a letter from the Governor's pen, which had stated "that Clay will get the unanimous vote of Tennessee." Wrathfully, Jackson wrote: "His friends shall also see it, and I suppose the individuals of Tennessee will inquire by what right he attempted to give lie to the expression of the Legislature of the state." More to the point in regard to his own ambitions, he added: "Should the people take up the subject of my nomination in the south and west, as they have in Pennsylvania they will soon undeceive Mr. Clay's friends. If the people of Alabama, Mississippi, and Louisiana, follow the example of Pennsylvania, they will place Clay and Crawford where they ultimately will be *Dehors the political combat.*"

Having acknowledged his candidacy, Jackson proceeded with great astuteness. He occupied high ground, bowing only to the will of the people, while the Nashville Junto and their allies managed his campaign with enormous skill. Though a southern planter, a slave owner, and a conservative, he became the idol of the common man, who in militia musters, mass meetings, and local conventions pledged his support to the hero. Jackson also appealed to a different class through his correspondence, and he placed himself on record as favoring encouragement of domestic manufactures. Elected to the United States Senate in October, 1823, he reached Washington in time to be the center of attention at an anniversary celebration of the Battle of New Orleans and, over the next several weeks, he managed to demonstrate that he was more than an Indian fighter. Friend and foe alike were impressed with his suave and dignified bearing.

Jackson had the satisfaction of seeing his burgeoning campaign injure the chances of Crawford for the Presidency and ultimately stifle those of Clay. More immediately, however, it caused the downfall of another candidate, Calhoun. Pennsylvania was the key state in this connection; it was there that the Jackson campaign received its greatest impetus outside Tennessee, and it was there that the aspirations of the Secretary of War were dashed.

Calhoun counted heavily on winning the support of Pennsylvania, where his nationalistic views were applauded. Unfortunately, however, the ground swell in favor of Jackson spread from the western part of the state. By October, 1823, it had reached Philadelphia, where attendants at a court house meeting adopted, "as democrats," resolutions strongly favoring Jackson as the next President of the United States. The reasons given for their action helped create the image that attracted the support of common men everywhere:

> Because, he has always been a uniform and consistent democrat.
> Because, he is eminently qualified, both as a statesman and a warrior, to govern the nation wisely, in peace, and to conduct her triumphantly through war.
> Because, as a patriot, we have full confidence in his moderation, his virtue and his firmness; being a friend to the *rights of man* and *universal suffrage.*

Having declared its support for a legendary hero, the meeting adopted highly practical campaign procedures, setting up a committee of correspondence and recommending that the friends of Jackson throughout the state "hold meetings and organize their strength in their several districts, thus taking a firm stand in defence of their country, the constitution, and the glorious principles of *seventy six*."

The nomination of the state Republican convention at Harrisburg in March, 1824, was at stake. Calhoun's lieutenants worked hard but there was no mistaking the growing popularity of Old Hickory. George M. Dallas, a leading Calhoun supporter, warned the South Carolinian early in February "that he thought the cause was lost in Pena," and his foresight was soon confirmed. The crowning blow was struck on February 18 at a meeting in Philadelphia, where Dallas himself, bowing to the popular will, presented a resolution urging that the local delegates to the Harrisburg Convention support the candidacy of Andrew Jackson.

Calhoun was unaccustomed to defeat, and for the moment found it hard to accept. Any faint hope that may have remained in his own mind was shattered, however, when the Pennsylvania convention nominated Jackson for the Presidency, with only one dissenting vote. Calhoun's popularity as the second choice was evidenced in the nomination for the vice-presidential candidate: he received eighty seven votes, Clay and Albert Gallatin ten each, and three other nominees a combined total of seventeen.

Having been eliminated from the presidential race, Calhoun now became the leading contender for the Vice-Presidency. There his base of support was larger than it had been when he sought the higher office, for now he was unmistakably a national candidate. The Jackson followers favored him, as did a great many of the Adams men. He could, in a sense, be considered the running mate of both of these candidates, with an excellent prospect of election. Moreover, he was young, he could afford to wait and, as heir apparent to the next President, he could still look forward to fulfilling his ambition for the Presidency.

By the time of Calhoun's withdrawal, Crawford, the early favorite, had also suffered a series of setbacks. As the candidate of the "Radicals," the old, Jeffersonian Republicans of the South, he had enlisted little support outside his own section except in New York, where he had been supported by the Van Buren faction. Even in the South Crawford's position had been weakened by the efforts of Calhoun and the grass roots popularity of Jackson. In addition, in September, 1823, he fell dangerously ill, either from a paralytic stroke or from an overdose of a drug administered for the relief of erysipelas. Paralyzed and blind, he retained a hold on life, and as his condition slowly began to improve, he declared his determination to continue his campaign. His followers agreed and struggled in a losing cause to ultimate defeat.

The fact of Crawford's illness became well known, but the nature and seriousness of the ailment were kept from the public. Rumors, of course, abounded, and in some quarters his case was said to be hopeless. By the beginning of 1824, however, he was able to take care of some official business, and his backers pictured him as well on the road to recovery. Although his condition gradually improved, he never fully recovered. A Kentuckian who saw him at Fredericktown, Maryland, in September, 1824, reportedly said "that his gait, articulation, and general appearance indicated most clearly the paralysis under which he has labored; and that he appeared to be much more infirm than Mr. Jefferson, at the age of eighty-two, whom he also saw."

The state of Crawford's health appears to have intensified his supporters' desire for his nomination by the caucus of Republican members of Congress. In spite of endorsements of candidates in meetings on state and local levels, the national caucus retained some importance. Should it be held, should it be well attended, and should it make a choice, its nominee could justifiably claim to be the choice of the Republican party. Consequently, the friends of Adams, Calhoun, Clay, and Jackson sought to prevent the caucus. Newspapers, legislative caucuses, and public gatherings participated in the controversy, and the debate, which had begun earlier, grew heated in 1823.

In April, United States Senator Martin Van Buren, leader of the anti-Clinton faction in New York politics and a determined supporter of Crawford, appeared in Albany and attempted to obtain a nomination of his favorite from a caucus of the Republican members of the legislature. The effort failed, but he did succeed in getting unanimous approval of the following resolutions from the group:

> That although a nomination by the republican members of congress is not entirely free from objections, yet that, assembled as they are from the different quarters of the union, — coming from the various classes of the community; elected during the pendency and discussion of the question, and in a great degree, with reference to it; they bring into one body as perfect a representation as can be expected of the interests and wishes of all and of each; and that a nomination made by them in a manner which has heretofore been usual, is the best attainable mode of effecting the great object in view which has yet been suggested:
>
> That we fully believe that a convention thus constituted, will be less liable to be influenced by those sectional jealousies, against which the father of his country has so solemnly and justly cautioned us — more likely to cherish those purely national feelings, which it is the interest, and should be the pride, of every state to protect — and better calculated to preserve unbroken those political ties which bind together the republicans of the north and of the south, the east and the west, and are consecrated by the recollection of times and events dear to the democracy of the nation, which triumphed in the election, and prospered under the administration of the illustrious Jefferson . . . .

The statement only added fuel to the discussion being carried on over the country. By September, according to one editor, there had been enough talk, and "The people are beginning to act." The action he had in mind occurred in Cecil County, Maryland, where, in response to a call issued by "a meeting of democratic republicans" a month earlier, "a numerous meeting of the citizens . . . . convened at the court house, in Elkton . . . for the purpose of instructing their representative in congress, upon the subject of the next presidential election." A resolution expressing opposition to a caucus was adopted, and the group further "*Resolved*, That, our representative in congress be, and hereby is, instructed not to enter into any congressional caucus on the subject of the presidential election, during his term of service."

Early in October the Tennessee legislature, "believing that the true spirit of the constitution will be best preserved by leaving the election of president and vice president to the *people themselves*, through the medium of electors chosen by them, uninfluenced by any previous nominations, made by members of congress," adopted a series of resolutions offered by Felix Grundy. Included were a summons to the state's senators and representatives in Washington "to use their exertions to prevent a nomination" by congressional caucus; a statement of legislative intention to "divide the state into as many districts, in convenient form, as this state is entitled to electoral votes, for the purpose of choosing an elector in each, to vote for president and vice president of the United States"; and a directive to the Tennessee governor to transmit to the executives of other states copies of these resolutions "with a request that the same be laid before each of their respective legislatures."

Only in Maryland and Alabama did legislatures follow the lead of Tennessee in officially expressing disapproval of the congressional caucus. In states favorable to Crawford the Tennessee resolutions were rejected. In New York, local meetings endorsed the caucus, the state senate formally recorded its disagreement with the Tennessee action, and the legislative caucus, reaffirming its own earlier stand, requested that the United States senators and representatives from that state join the Republican caucus in Washington. The Georgia legislature adopted resolutions favoring Crawford, and at the same time expressed its willingness to yield to "the clearly expressed voice of the republican majority." A legislative caucus in Virginia, in January, 1824, approved the New York resolutions of the previous year, and recommended that the Virginia members of Congress cooperate in procuring the nomination of suitable candidates. Caucuses in two of the New England states indicated their preference for Adams, but at the same time stated their willingness to abide by the results of a congressional caucus. In other states either the legislatures or legislative caucuses considered the question but took no action. On the local level a small number of meetings of Republicans expressed approval of Crawford and the caucus but, as the Jackson campaign picked up strength, more and more public meetings endorsed him and condemned nominations by caucus.

The agitation reached Congress, where, according to Henry Clay, "What engrosses most of the conversation . . . is the Presidential Election." Though he was not an unbiased observer, Clay had reason for writing in a letter on January 3,1824: "The Cause of a Caucus is on the decline, and I do not think there will be one, unless in a state of despair the friends of Mr. Crawford determine to hold one of a minority of the republicans." Shortly afterward, fourteen members of the Pennsylvania congressional delegation issued a statement declaring their intention to refuse to attend a caucus and proposing a national convention of the Republican party. Crawford leaders continued, nevertheless, to work toward a caucus, while on the other hand Samuel

D. Ingham of Pennsylvania led the effort to form an anti-caucus organization. By the end of January Clay could write: "It has been, I understand, *ascertained* that there are 181 members against a Caucus, sixty-eight for one, and the residue doubtful."

The Washington *Daily National Intelligencer* carried two highly interesting notices on February 7, 1824. One, reflecting the desperate state of the Crawford cause, invited all democratic members of Congress to assemble in the chamber of the House of Representatives on the evening of February 14 "to recommend Candidates to the People of the United States for the Offices of President and Vice-President of the United States." Appended to the document were the names of eleven Crawford supporters, each from a different state. The other announcement, signed by twenty-four members of Congress, representing fifteen states, declared that 181 of the 261 members "deem it inexpedient, under existing circumstances, to meet in Caucus, for the purpose of nominating Candidates for President and Vice-President . . . and they have good reasons to believe, that a portion of the remainder will be found unwilling to attend such a meeting."

When the caucus assembled at the appointed time, it was found that only sixty-six members were in attendance. They represented fourteen states, but forty-eight of the delegates were from only four states—New York, Virginia, North Carolina, and Georgia. Five states furnished one member each, and ten states were not represented. In view of the small attendance, a motion was made to adjourn for six weeks, but Van Buren prevailed on the gathering to continue. Balloting for a presidential candidate resulted in sixty-four votes for Crawford (two of them by proxy from absentees), two for Adams, one for Jackson, and one for Nathaniel Macon. Turning to the nomination of a candidate for Vice-President, the caucus cast fifty-seven votes for Albert Galatin and scattered nine among eight other persons, including one for John Quincy Adams. Having settled on its ticket, the caucus drew up an address to the people, stressing the regularity of its procedures and warning of threatened "dismemberment of the party to which it is our pride to be attached."

The meeting was a fiasco. Instead of launching a strong movement for its nominees, it demonstrated the weakness of the Crawford candidacy. Gallatin's nomination was a gesture toward Pennsylvania, his home state, but the futility of the campaign became so obvious that in September he withdrew from the race. An estimate of Crawford's strength in mid-February allowed him the electoral votes of only four states, three that had supported him in the caucus—Virginia, North Carolina, and Georgia—and Delaware, represented in Congress by Federalists. Supporters of the other presidential candidates managed to place the caucus in such bad repute that it never again assembled as a nominating body. Subsequently Crawford was nominated by the Virginia legislative caucus, although an earlier meeting had narrowly decided against a nomination.

These events led Clay, who had not yet realized the seriousness of the Jackson movement, to be extremely sanguine in regard to his own candidacy.

The caucus nomination, he thought, "must inevitably destroy all" Crawford's prospects, and he expected to profit from the destruction. Confident of western support, he also had hopes of New York and, should Crawford be abandoned, even of Virginia. He corresponded freely with friends in both these crucial states, while his agent, Senator Josiah Stoddard Johnston of Louisiana, worked zealously in his behalf, principally in New York and Pennsylvania. A search for a New York running mate who could help garner support in that state resulted in the choice of Nathan Sanford, chancellor of the state of New York, who had previously served in the state legislature and the United States Senate.

From early spring, 1824, until the election, Clay's campaign was beset by a rumor, or a series of rumors, that he had withdrawn from the race. At one time ill health was cited as the reason for the alleged decision; at another, he would accept a cabinet post; again, his friends and Crawford's had decided to unite; or, his supporters had simply abandoned him. At first he scoffed at "the idle report," which was "too ridiculous to merit a serious contradiction," but repeatedly his friends found it necessary to issue addresses and circulars denying that he had any intention of dropping out. After the November election, when disappointing returns reached him from states he had expected to carry, he blamed "fabrications of tales of my withdrawal" as a partial cause of his defeat.

As the year wore on there was no doubt that Adams and Jackson were the leading candidates, with the latter gaining support despite some southern dissatisfaction over his votes for the tariff and internal improvements. Campaign biographies of both men were published and circulated. That of Adams lauded his patriotic ancestry; that of Jackson, by Senator John Henry Eaton, left no doubt of the general's heroic qualities. Crawford attempted, by returning to his duties at the Treasury Department and by public appearances, to demonstrate the extent of his recovery, but not even the magic of Van Buren could conceal the true condition of his health. Clay, meanwhile, had lost hope of carrying the election but expected, as he assured friends in different parts of the country, to be one of the three receiving the highest number of electoral votes. Once his name was placed before the House of Representatives, he had no doubt of the outcome.

The results were determined, of course, by presidential electors, chosen in the manner prescribed by each state for itself: they were named by legislatures in Vermont, New York, Delaware, South Carolina, Georgia, and Louisiana; elsewhere they were chosen by popular vote, either by districts, as in Maine (where two were elected by the state at large), Maryland, Tennessee, Kentucky, and Illinois, or by state-wide ticket, as in the remaining thirteen states.

There was little reason to doubt that Adams would carry New England. The Federalists were still strong in some parts of that section, but without a presidential candidate of their own they either voted for the Secretary of State or stayed away from the polls. Crawford had some support, mainly from the "regular" Republicans, who considered him the logical successor to Monroe.

Clay also had friends in the area but they were unable to stir enthusiasm for his cause. Although Adams once suggested Jackson as a vice-presidential candidate, the suggestion aroused little interest in that part of the country.

Largely because there was no real contest in New England, where voters appeared apathetic, a majority of the eligible voters did not bother to cast their ballots in any northeastern state. In Massachusetts, with 15 electoral votes, the electors had previously been chosen by districts (two by the state at large). Some interest, however, was generated during the early summer of 1824 by a barely successful legislative effort, supported by the Adams faction, to adopt a general ticket method of election. Adams's opponents then nominated "an Opposition Ticket without reference to Candidates," which, however, failed to accomplish their purpose. In the election the Adams slate won an overwhelming majority of the ballots cast.

Opposition tickets were also nominated with similar results in Maine (nine electoral votes), Connecticut (eight), and Rhode Island (four). Adams met no opposition in New Hampshire (eight votes); and in Vermont (seven), where the legislature still named the electors, there were few votes against the slate pledged to him. The New Englander was thus solidly backed by his own section with fifty-one votes in the Electoral College.

Elsewhere, the race was more hotly contested. Two of the Middle States, New York and Pennsylvania, with thirty-six and twenty-eight electoral votes respectively, were especially important, and without a favorite son in the race, the section offered hope and opportunity to all the candidates. They therefore expended a great effort in trying to win support there. In New York local issues, political cross currents, and intrigue added complexity to the campaign. Two factions fought one another for control of state politics: the followers of DeWitt Clinton, and the "Bucktails," whose leaders were known as the "Albany Regency." After the state election of 1822, the Regency gained control and, under the leadership of Martin Van Buren, joined the effort to elevate William H. Crawford to the Presidency.

Adams and Clay also had friends in New York, and to some degree they worked together to block the delivery of the state to Crawford. Opposition to the Regency could unite in a common campaign to place in the hands of the people the power to choose the state's presidential electors. The People's party, created in 1823, was unable to bring about the desired change before the election in the next year, but it placed the Regency in an unpopular light and threatened to challenge the Bucktails for control of the state. Meanwhile, in April, 1824, the Bucktails committed an outrageous blunder by ousting Clinton from the office of canal commissioner, a position he had filled for over a dozen years. This created such popular sympathy for him that he was returned to the governorship of the state in the elections that fall. The electoral bill won approval in a special session of the state house of representatives in the summer of 1824, but the senate adjourned without even considering it.

Faced with public disapproval and with internal divisions as a result of the events of the past few months, the Bucktails were not able to control the legislature in its selection of electors in November. Adams had become the favorite of the People's party, and Clay received assurances of enough votes to support the belief that his name would be among the three placed before the United States House of Representatives. When the balloting began, under a complicated legislative procedure, no candidate had a majority. The Crawford ticket led in the senate, the supporters of Adams in the house. The Crawford vote combined was larger than that of either of the other candidates, and the Clay slate was running a rather poor third. However, neither of the two leaders could win without acquiring at least some of the support given to Clay.

Little change occurred during three days of balloting, but combination and intrigue began to make an appearance. Thurlow Weed, a journalist later famed as a political manipulator, worked out a scheme that was eventually adopted. On the final vote the legislature chose twenty-five electors for Adams, seven for Clay, and only four for Crawford. Although Clay clung to the hope that he would "receive about one half of" what he termed "the 11 uncertain votes," when the electors met, he was deserted by three of those who had been chosen in his behalf. In the balloting for President New York cast twenty-six votes for Adams, five for Crawford, four for Clay, and one for Jackson. It may be noted that if Clay's electors had all remained loyal, his total national electoral vote would have equaled that of Crawford.

A lively contest also developed in New Jersey, where Adams, Clay, and Crawford each had friends and where Jackson gained support rapidly, especially after the Pennsylvania decision in his favor. By August, Adams appeared to be the leading candidate, and there was some consideration of a combination of Clay and Crawford forces to block him. Toward the end of September it was obvious that Adams was being successfully challenged, not by Clay and Crawford, however, but by Jackson. A combination of Jackson and Crawford forces was able to control the state Republican convention, which met October 19, and choose a ticket composed of five Jackson electors and three pledged to Crawford. The Adams men, finding themselves outnumbered, had attempted to adjourn the meeting without forming a ticket. When that stratagem was unsuccessful they withdrew and, in a separate gathering, nominated their own electors. During the following week, still another convention assembled, named a "People's Ticket" pledged to Jackson, and launched a vigorous campaign for the hero. The voters responded by giving him all the state's eight electors.

In Pennsylvania the action of the Harrisburg convention in nominating Jackson, and a slate of electors pledged to him, proved conclusive, although the three remaining candidates did not allow him to win the state by default. In separate gatherings during the following months friends of Crawford, Clay, and Adams nominated tickets of their own. The Crawfordites attempted to strengthen their cause by promoting Clay for the Vice-Presidency. The Kentuckian, on the other hand, expected that his program of internal improvement and tariff would awaken Pennsylvanians to the advantages of supporting him for President. In September, a group of Philadelphians nominated electors favorable to Clay, formed a committee of correspondence, and adopted an address which was described as "appropriate — manly — & popular." At about the same time the Philadelphia *Aurora* joined the Clay campaign. Nevertheless, in the election the Jackson ticket won easily over the combined opposition.

The Federalist party held sway in Delaware, which had three electoral votes. Some months before the election Crawford appeared strong enough among the legislators to carry the state, although friends of other contenders attempted to push their favorites. When the two houses of the legislature met in joint session to choose the presidential electors, one Adams man was named on the first ballot, two on the Crawford ticket missed election by one vote each, and none of the remainder came close. Through a strange and unexpected interpretation of the state law governing tie votes, the presiding officer of the senate cast an additional vote for each of the Crawford men, both of whom were declared elected.

Maryland apparently inclined toward Adams, although the method of choosing electors by districts invited all candidates to try for at least a part of the state's eleven votes. As in other areas, Jackson's strength increased as the election approached, and he won the lion's share of the electors without, however, quite matching the popular vote attained by Adams. Seven of the state's electors were pledged to Jackson, three to Adams, and the remaining one to Crawford. The hope expressed by Clay's friend Josiah S. Johnston in August, 1824, that two of the districts would support the Kentuckian, proved ill-founded.

Although Virginia, with twenty-four electoral votes, and Georgia, with nine, were Crawford strongholds, Adams had friends in the former state, and Jackson picked up some support. After Crawford fell ill, Clay hoped that the Georgian would withdraw or be dropped. In that case, he himself might claim the electoral vote of his native state. But Crawford remained in the race and his ticket prevailed. In Georgia the legislature was under the control of the Troup faction, with which Crawford was aligned, and it chose electors favorable to the state's favorite son as a matter of course.

In the remainder of the South, Jackson eventually won the fifteen electoral votes of North Carolina and the eleven of South Carolina. Adams had friends in both states, particularly in the former. Crawford also had substantial strength in the ranks of the Republican planter class. On Christmas eve, 1823, a legislative caucus in North Carolina had nominated a ticket in favor of the Georgian, and some of the congressional delegation from the state participated in the congressional caucus. Calhoun's influence, felt in both states, was dominant in South Carolina, but after the events of early 1824, that state moved into the Jackson fold. Calhoun had also harbored hopes of winning North Carolina, and early in 1824 his friends combined with other opponents of Crawford to form a "People's Ticket." After Calhoun's withdrawal from the race, Jackson became the beneficiary of the "People's Ticket," although cooperation with friends of the other candidates continued. That ticket defeated the Crawford slate and, in the presidential election cast all the state's electoral votes for Jackson.

After Jackson became a serious contender, there was no doubt of his winning at least two of the states of the South. Alabama gave him her five electoral votes by an overwhelming margin, as did Mississippi her three, even though Adams had influential friends in the latter state. Only in Louisiana was there a contest. Clay was the early favorite there owing to his personal ties with prominent men in New Orleans, to his endorsement of protection for Louisiana sugar, and to his western residence. However, as the Jackson movement became serious, it cut into Clay's strength, and by the time the legislature was to choose presidential electors, Old Hickory's prospects almost equalled Clay's. The situation lent itself to intrigue. Before the balloting began, the Jackson forces bargained with Adams' friends to defeat Clay and divide the electors between themselves. According to Clay, accident also played a role in the outcome: two of his friends in the legislature failed to arrive in time for the session; two who had been present "went to the Country and having got overturned from a gig were unable to attend"; and "Three deserted in consequence of false rumors." Even then the opposing coalition defeated his ticket by only two votes; the outcome ratified the prearranged division of electors between Jackson and Adams: three for the former and two for the latter.

Kentucky and Tennessee each remained constant in support of its own favorite son. Clay remained officially aloof from the struggle in his state between the Old Court-New Court factions, which had grown out of the depression following the panic of 1819. His sympathies lay with the Old Court, although he had friends on the other side. Toward the end of the campaign, in 1824, the Relief, or New Court, party began to turn to Jackson. Clay, however, captured Kentucky's fourteen electoral votes by a large margin. His hopes in Tennessee evaporated as a result of Jackson's continued candidacy, and the general captured his own state's eleven electors without difficulty.

From the beginning of the campaign Clay had counted heavily on winning the four western states, Ohio, Indiana, Illinois, and Missouri, but he found himself faced by serious challenges in all but the last. His friends in Ohio gave him early encouragement and in January, 1824, agreed upon a slate of electors in his behalf. Supporters of Crawford tried shortly afterward to launch a movement in favor of the Georgian, but their meeting broke up amid dissension. In July, however, "conventions" were held in Columbus for Jackson, Adams, and Clay. In each of these meetings an electoral ticket was adopted and committees set up to carry on the various campaigns. Clay had the advantages of an early start and influential friends, including William Henry Harrison and Charles Hammond, a newspaper editor, but he had also made some enemies as counsel for the Bank of the United States before his return to Congress in 1823. He triumphed in the election, gaining Ohio's sixteen votes, but Jackson was close behind in the returns.

Majorities in both houses of the Indiana legislature were said to be favorably disposed toward Clay early in 1824. A slate of electors was formed by his friends in the legislature, while an opposing list was drawn up by supporters of Adams. The issue was not to be decided by the legislature, however, but by the people, and during the summer a Jackson campaign was organized.

In the election, which apparently stirred little excitement, Jackson won Indiana's five votes. Clay ran second, and Adams far behind. Illinois was divided into three districts, and in each one a slate of electors for each of the four candidates was placed before the public. Jackson won two of the districts, and Adams the third. In Missouri, where Thomas Hart Benton managed his campaign, Clay won the state's three electoral votes.

An air of uncertainty prevailed in all camps as the election returns from state after state were publicized. Not until after the Congress had reassembled in December were the Louisiana results announced, eliminating Clay from the race. Jackson was the leader, with ninety-nine electoral votes, Adams had eighty-four, Crawford was a poor third with forty-one, and Clay brought up the rear with thirty-seven. The election had not yet been decided, and under the Twelfth amendment to the United States Constitution, it remained for the House of Representatives to choose the next President of the United States from the three candidates with the highest number of electoral votes. Calhoun had easily won the Vice-Presidency, with 182 electoral votes. His nearest competitor, Sanford, received only thirty. Virginia gave Nathaniel Macon twenty-four, a scattered thirteen went to Jackson, Georgia gave nine to Van Buren, and Clay had two from Delaware.

The electors met according to law, in their respective states in early December. Their ballots were forwarded to Washington, where Congress assembled on December 6. On January 18, 1825, the House of Representatives adopted a resolution providing for the appointment of a committee "to prepare . . . rules . . . to be observed by this House in the choice of a President of the United States, . . . if, on counting the votes given in the several states . . . , it shall appear that no person has received a majority of the votes of all the Electors of President and Vice President." The plan reported by the committee was similar to that used in the election of 1801. A Senate resolution, proposed on February 1, resulted in the appointment of a joint committee to count the votes according to the procedure fixed by the Constitution. February 9 was the date set for the tally.

Members of the House of Representatives, making their choice among the three candidates before them, were not bound by the popular or electoral votes that had been cast. The delegation from each state, regardless of size, had one vote; in this instance the lone representative from Illinois or from Delaware exercised as much power as the entire group of thirty-four from New York or twenty-six from Pennsylvania. A state legislature might attempt to instruct the representatives from that state, but it had no power to enforce its instructions. The practical politicians in the House had complete freedom to select from the three men whose names were before them the next President. One frightening possibility, which had some weight in the decision reached on February 9, was that, should the first ballot fail to resolve the matter, a deadlock might ensue.

Now that he had been rejected by the electorate, Clay became the center of attention in Washington. He could not, of course, turn his electoral vote over to another candidate, nor did he have the power to compel the House delegations, from the three states that had supported him, to cast their ballots in accordance with his wishes. He was credited, however, with having great influence in the House, perhaps with more than he actually possessed. As early as May, 1824, an announcement was released from Washington by "The friends of Mr. CLAY," who had foreseen that the election would go to the House of Representatives. It stated their determination "to *adhere* to" their favorite, in the expectation that if he "should not be returned to the House, his friends . . . will be able, by concentration, to control the event — they will hold in their hands the balance — they will determine between the opposing and conflicting interests, and secure to the country a republican administration." In December, an Adams supporter had discussed with a member of the Ohio congressional delegation the division of sentiment within that group and had come to the conclusion that it was "very much in Mr. Clay's power to make the President."

Before the election Clay himself had referred optimistically to his chances of victory if his name should be among those before the House. His election as Speaker for many years had attested to his popularity among his fellow congressmen, and in his hands that office wielded great power. Yet there were limits to the influence he could exert, even among the members of the Kentucky delegation, and in the long weeks preceding February 9 much pressure was exerted on him and his colleagues in the House.

For a time Clay was assiduously courted by the friends of each of the candidates. He wrote to his son-in-law that the Crawford supporters "now feel their error and are full of professions to me and express great regrets that a different direction had not been given to their exertions. This resembles the eulogiums which are pronounced upon a man after his death." Apparently he came to enjoy the attentions bestowed on him and wrote lightheartedly to a Kentucky friend: "My position in relation to the friends of the three returned candidates is singular enough and often to me very amusing. . . . they all beleive [*sic*] that my friends have the power of deciding the question, and that I have the power of controling [*sic*] my friends." Jackson partisans reminded him "how much we want a western President"; Crawford's adherents considered him and their favorite "the only genuine Republican candidates"; and friends of Adams noted the New Englander's "admiration" for Clay's "talents — There is no station to which they are not equal." "Really," said Clay, "the friends of all the three Gentlemen are so very courteous, and affectionate, that I sometimes almost wish that it was in my power to accomodate [*sic*] each of them."

Back in October Clay had for a moment faced up to the possibility that he would be placed in the position in which he now found himself. At that time he had objected to Crawford because of the Georgian's nomination by caucus, "the state of his health," and "the principles of administration which there is reason to fear will be adopted by him." In regard to the two other candidates he also had noted, but did not list, "strong if not decisive objections." After the electoral returns were in he still held the same opinions. Crawford was out of the question, and Clay considered the choice between Adams and Jackson a selection of the lesser of two evils.

Though he asked the advice of friends and professed difficulty in determining which of the candidates to favor, it is extremely doubtful that the Kentuckian ever seriously considered giving his influence to Jackson. Aside from the fact that he and the general would be rivals for western support and that, if one westerner were made President, the other would stand small chance of succeeding him, there were other considerations to be weighed. Jackson was a military man, noted for his high temper and unbending will. He had not distinguished himself in the United States Senate, and had not held public office in Tennessee since the early part of the century. He put forth no program of government, and his undeniably increasing popularity was based on military exploits and the carefully nurtured legend, born after his entrance into the campaign, of his concern for the common people. He had, of course, led all others in both popular and electoral votes in the recent election.

On the other hand, there were good reasons to support Adams though Clay had little liking for him. There was no doubt of the New Englander's intellectual attainments, experience in government and diplomacy, and ability to perform the duties of the presidential office. The two men were not far apart in their views of the issues that made up Clay's "American System," and Clay could feel, if Adams were President, that the country was in safe hands. Also, though this particular aspect of the matter was left unstated, a westerner might hope to succeed an easterner in the Presidency.

It is not certain when Clay definitely made up his mind to throw his influence to Adams. According to a later account, he told friends in Kentucky, before leaving for Washington in November, 1824, that he could not vote for Jackson and made a similar statement to a companion while en route to the capital. Thomas Hart Benton, who cast his lot with Jackson after the defeat of Clay, afterward recalled that, about mid-December, the Kentuckian had expressed to him a preference for Adams. On December 28, Clay responded to an inquiry from a New York friend by writing that he had "long since decided in favor of Mr. Adams, in case the contest should be between him and General Jackson," adding "unequivocally" that he could not "support a military man." Whatever the date of his decision, it did not become public knowledge until the fourth week in January, 1825.

Since early December the attention of the members of Congress was focused mainly on the decision to be made by the House. The candidates' friends, with or without the knowledge of their favorite, talked of possible combinations and trades to influence the outcome. Daniel Webster, who had his eye on the mission to England, was cautious in his relations with the Jackson camp until he learned, from an Adams lieutenant, that his fellow Bostonian might fulfill his wishes. After that he worked to bring the Federalist congressmen from New York, Delaware, and Maryland into the Adams fold. In late December or early January, Representative James Buchanan of Pennsylvania, a Jackson supporter, approached the general with an unauthorized proposal of a trade by which Clay would become Secretary of State in return for his support. Old Hickory indignantly rejected the idea and did not understand, or refused to believe, that it did not emanate from Clay himself.

Earlier in December Robert P. Letcher of Kentucky approached Adams to ascertain his opinion of Clay and, finding it favorable, pointed out during a later visit that Adams could not expect to win without the support of the West. Clay's friends in that area, suggested Letcher, would be pleased if their favorite should be given a cabinet post. Adams made no promises (writing in his diary "*Incedo super ignes*"), but he left the way open for further conversations. On New Year's Day Letcher obtained Adams' agreement to hold a conference with Clay, an arrangement confirmed that night when Adams and Clay sat together at a dinner for Lafayette. On the evening of January 9, Clay called at Adams' home, where they held a long conversation. From this meeting the two men emerged as allies.

That Clay had already made up his mind in this connection is obvious in a letter he wrote to Francis Preston Blair of Frankfort, Kentucky, on the preceding day. In that communication he stated that he would "with great regret" give his support to Adams, because his "friends entertain the belief that their kind wishes" toward him would be "more likely to be accomplished by so bestowing their votes." He added that he had, "however most earnestly entreated them" not to consider him in reaching their decision, "& be guided solely by the public good." Clay did not yet know that on January 11 the Kentucky legislature had adopted resolutions instructing the delegation from that state to vote for Jackson. He refused to be governed by the instructions and worked to hold as much of the delegation as possible for Adams.

During the last weeks of January, and on into the next month, the fierce competition continued. In the Adams camp Clay, Webster, and the candidate himself were especially active. Clay had been writing his friends of the decision he had reached since about the middle of January, but the full impact of that decision seems not to have been realized until the majority of the Kentucky and Ohio delegations announced, on January 24, their intention of voting for Adams. Almost immediately there was a shrill outcry from the Jackson forces and charges of sale and intrigue. A few days later the Philadelphia *Columbian Observer*, a Jackson paper, carried an anonymous statement, purportedly from a member of Congress, accusing Adams of buying Clay's support with the offer of appointment as Secretary of State. Outraged, Clay impetuously published a "Card" challenging the anonymous writer, "a base and infamous calumniator, a dastard and a liar," to identify himself and prepare to satisfy the Kentuckian's honor. To Clay's consternation and to the amusement of his opponents, a Pennsylvania congressman, George Kremer, noted for his eccentric dress rather than for any semblance of literary skill, acknowledged authorship of the earlier statement and offered to prove the allegations in it.

Clay demanded an investigation of the charges and Kremer offered to testify before a committee to substantiate them, but once the committee had been appointed, the Pennsylvanian refused to appear. Clay believed that the Jackson forces were behind the whole affair, and that John H. Eaton had composed the original statement. The matter could hardly have been managed better for the injury of Adams and Clay. A corrupt bargain could not have been proved against them, but since no investigation was held, they had no opportunity to vindicate themselves. The charge proved especially injurious to Clay, following him for the rest of his life — and haunting his memory afterward. It appears to have had little effect at the moment, however, for the Adams-Clay coalition held firm through the election in the House.

"At twelve o'clock, precisely," on February 9, the United States Senate filed into the hall of the House of Representatives, and its presiding officer, president pro tempore John Gaillard, called both houses to order. "The certificates, forwarded by the electors from each state," were opened and the ballots counted, with results already known; the senators filed out again, and the House began the serious business of the day. Clay, as Speaker, "directed the roll of the house to be called by states, and the members of the respective delegations to take their seats in the order in which the states should be called." With one exception, "every member of the house was present." From the sergeant-at-arms each delegation received a box in which the ballots were to be deposited to determine the delegation's choice, after which the state's ballot would be recorded on two slips of paper and placed in the hands of tellers sitting at two tables. Webster and John Randolph were appointed to announce the results.

Thirteen states constituted a majority. The six New England states, as expected, declared for Adams. The decision of New York was eagerly awaited, for it was known that the delegation was divided — seventeen of the representatives had declared for Adams, fourteen for Crawford, two for Jackson, and one, the aged Stephen Van Rensselaer, had encouraged all sides. An earlier conference with Adams concerning possible treatment of Federalists in an Adams Administration appears to have caused the elderly gentleman to believe, somewhat vaguely, that he had committed himself. That belief was undoubtedly reinforced in a secluded conversation with Clay and Webster on the morning of the House balloting. Years later, however, Van Buren remembered Van Rensselaer telling him that as his turn came to vote, he bowed in prayer and opened his eyes to see on the floor an Adams ballot, which he picked up and dropped in the box. In any case, his vote gave Adams a majority of the New York delegation, and the state's ballot.

Thanks to Webster's work with Maryland delegates, Adams carried that state, although the electoral vote had gone to Jackson. Clay undoubtedly aided in delivering Louisiana, Kentucky, Ohio, and Missouri to the New Englander, and Adams' personal friendship with Representative Daniel Pope Cook took Illinois from the Jackson column. Jackson held the other states he had carried in the election, except for North Carolina, whose delegation deserted him for Crawford. The first ballot proved sufficient. Thirteen states voted for Adams, seven for Jackson, and four for Crawford.

At noon the next day a committee of the House of Representatives, chaired by Daniel Webster, called upon Adams at his home to give formal notice of his election. There, according to one account, the group found him greatly agitated. The unpleasant necessity of being a politician during the past few weeks and the strain of waiting for the results of all the conferences that had been held, the agreements that had been reached, and the promises that had been made showed in his nervous demeanor. Citing the course adopted by Thomas Jefferson on "the only preceding occasion since the establishment of the Constitution of the United States upon which a similar notification had been made from the House of Representatives," he produced a written acceptance, which he read and handed to Webster.

Shortly afterward the President-elect offered the appointment as Secretary of State to his ally, Henry Clay. The Kentuckian, realizing that the outcry against him would not be stilled regardless of his decision, made up his mind to join the Adams Cabinet and thereby demonstrate his approval of the Administration he had helped bring into power. The implicit bargain, hardly corrupt, was thereby consummated.

With the action of the House of Representatives on February 9, 1825, and John Quincy Adams' acceptance, the campaign of 1824 at long last had come to an end. But politics was not laid aside, and the next presidential campaign had already begun.

Appendix

John Quincy Adams, *Memoirs*

In his Memoirs *John Quincy Adams commented on the other presidential candidates and revealed something of his own efforts to win the election.*

June 2, 1822

I said I believed that Mr. Calhoun was too sanguine in his calculations of success as a candidate for the next Presidency. There were in Congress three parties — one for Mr. Crawford, one for Mr. Clay, and one for Mr. Calhoun. They embraced indeed almost the whole. But the party for Mr. Crawford was the strongest, and that of Mr. Calhoun the weakest, of the three. And I had little doubt that the parties of Crawford and Clay would finally coalesce together.

*　　*　　*

June 20, 1822

. . . I proposed to the President that the mission to the republic of Colombia, whether to be appointed now or at the meeting of Congress, should be offered to Mr. Clay. I thought it doubtful whether he would accept it — very probable that he would make no delicate or generous use of it — and that the comments upon the offer, both of his partisans and of others, would be various, and in many cases invidious. But, upon the whole, the effect upon the public would be favorable. He wanted the offer. The Western country wished it might be made to him. His talents were eminent; his claims from public service considerable. The republic of Colombia, and particularly Bolivar, with whom he has been in correspondence, will be flattered by his appointment, or even by information that he had the offer of it. In the relations to be established between us and that republic, Mr. Clay's talents might be highly useful; and I did not apprehend any danger from them.

The President appeared to be well disposed to take this course. He said that Mr. Clay's conduct towards him and his Administration had not been friendly or generous, but he was disposed entirely to overlook that. He stood upon ground quite independent of Mr. Clay, and as he had never needed his support, he had never felt the want of it. He would consider of the proposal to offer him the mission, and was not indisposed to it.

*　　*　　*

July 8, 1822

The relations in which I now stand with Calhoun are delicate and difficult. At the last session of Congress he suffered a few members of Congress, with an Irishman named Rogers, editor of a newspaper at Easton, Pennsylvania, at their head, to set him up as a candidate for the succession to the Presidency. From that moment the caballing in Congress, in the State Legislatures, in the newspapers, and among the people, against me, has been multiplied tenfold. The Franklin Gazette, of Philadelphia, under the direction of R. Bache, G. M. Dallas, T. Sergeant, and Ingham, in concert with Rogers, opened immediately upon me, and has kept up ever since an insidious fire against me. Calhoun's partisans have countenanced it, and have been as busy as those of Mr. Crawford in their efforts to degrade me in the public opinion. Meanwhile, Calhoun has always professed to be a friend and admirer of mine, and to persons whom he knows to be my friends has said that he did not mean to be a candidate against a Northern man, and that he himself was decidedly for a Northern President. There was a time during the last session of Congress when so large a proportion of members was enlisted for Calhoun that they had it in contemplation to hold a caucus formally to delcare him a candidate. But this prospect of success roused all Crawford's and Clay's partisans against him. The administration of his Department was scrutinized with severity, sharpened by personal animosity and factious malice. Some abuses were discovered, and exposed with aggravations. Cavils were made against measures of that Department in the execution of the laws, and brought the President in collision with both Houses of Congress. Crawford's newspapers commenced and have kept up a course of the most violent abuse and ribaldry against him, and his projected nomination for the Presidency has met with scarcely any countenance throughout the Union. The principal effect of it has been to bring out Crawford's strength, and thus to promote the interest of the very man whom he professes alone to oppose. Calhoun now feels his weakness, but is not cured of his ambition. My personal intercourse with him now is necessarily an intercourse of civility, and not of confidence.

*   *   *

August 3-4, 1822

There is in the Argus of Western America, a newspaper published at Frankfort, Kentucky, under date of the 18th of July, an article, apparently editorial, headed "The Ghent Mission," which, both from its style and contents, I take to have been written by Mr. Clay; but, it not, certainly from him indirectly. It is bitter upon "the Secretary," and apologizes for Clay's having agreed to the Mississippi proposition upon the plea of the new instructions. It abandons all Russell's pretences, and says that Clay thought the Government ought not to have given the instructions. Clay's conduct throughout this affair towards me has been that of an envious rival—a fellow-servant whispering tales into the ear of the common master. He has been seven years circulating this poison against me in the West, and I have now no doubt that Russell's letter was brought forth upon suggestions originating with him. Russell has all along performed for him the part of a jackal. Clay seems to have fancied that I should have no means of self-vindication if Russell's letter should be brought before Congress, and this article in the Argus evidently betrays his vexation and disappointment at the result.

4th. There is in the Richmond Enquirer of the 2d instant, which came this day, a Jesuitical and most insidious article upon the diplomatic controversy. It begins by copying from the Charleston (South Carolina) Courier an article upon it, very severe upon Russell, with which it expresses concurrence in part, but cavils at some comment in it upon Floyd, and instigates Floyd to come out against it. Then it pronounces Russell decidedly in fault in the quarrel about the duplicate, and with the same dogmatism pronounces that the proposition made to the British at Ghent seems to defy all justification; extracts all the part of the sham editorial article in the Frankfort Argus which charges the "Secretary," and calls upon me to answer it but omits all that part of the same article which contains Clay's admissions of his having assented and subscribed to the proposition. The main object of the Richmond Enquirer's instigators in this affair is to blow the coals. They want to bring in Floyd and Clay to fall upon me and help out Russell, for, considering him as already disgraced before the nation, they wish to uphold him just enough to assist him in his notable attempt to disgrace me. At the first explosion of this affair they could not suppress their exultation at the prospect of two distinguished Massachusetts men afoul of each other, and sure both to lose character by the result. But the burst of public sentiment was so quick and so strong against Russell, on the publication of his duplicate letters and my remarks, that in a few days the Richmond Enquirer gave out that I had seized with great ability upon this occasion to make myself a party for the next Presidential election; for which it declared I was before quite out of the question. The Richmond Enquirer is the organ of a great and predominating political party in Virginia. It is the mainspring for Mr. Crawford's election in that State, and indeed throughout the Union. It is the very Mrs. Candor of newspapers, and, under an affectation of impartiality and liberality, has been, and will be, managed with the most inverterate hostility to me. I have concluded to publish the papers of this controversy in a pamphlet and have prepared a paper to be published in the National Intelligencer announcing this intention.

*   *   *

August 26-27, 1822

The Washington City Gazette has this day come out for the first time with the Treasury stamp unequivocal upon its face. It has long been at market, apparently between Mr. Crawford and me; really, sold to him years ago, but wishing also to make its price with me. Wyer told me not long since that Elliot, the editor, had asked him if I was *his* friend; complained that I had given him no jobs of printing lately to do; said that my objections to his account for printing papers relating to the census had been only a misunderstanding; hinted that he could not afford to be my friend for nothing; boasted that he had entirely put down Mr. Calhoun's pretensions to the Presidency, and considered himself as thereby serving me; with a distinct intimation that he could serve me as he had served Mr. Calhoun. I told Wyer that I had been obliged to cut down Elliot's account for the census papers for its extortion, and had then told him that I should give him no more work at the public charge; that he had not put down Mr. Calhoun, and if he had, it was not for the purpose of serving me; and that I should not purchase the services of any printer, either with public money or my own.

This was but a few days since; and this day the Gazette shows its flag. It enumerates also the other newspapers which it considers as pledged to the same cause; which is obviously to give them a signal of mutual intelligence. The organization of newspaper support for Mr. Crawford throughout the Union is very extensive, and is managed with much address. Democracy, Economy, and Reform are the watch-words for his recruiting service — Democracy to be used against me, Economy against Calhoun, and Reform against both. Calhoun is organizing a counter-system of newspaper artillery, and his Washington Republican is already working powerfully in his favor. These engines will counteract each other, but I shall be a mark for both sides, and, having no counter-fire upon them, what can happen but that I must fall? This fall may be the happiest event that could befall me, and I but fervently ask that my mind may be disciplined to whatever may betide me, and supported to the level of higher aims than any political fortune can reach.

Mr. Calhoun called to make enquiries. He noticed the decisive manner in which the Washington City Gazette came out yesterday in favor of Mr. Crawford, and against me. He has long considered the Gazette as edited from the Treasury Department, and all the articles in it against him as coming almost directly from Mr. Crawford himself. He says the course Crawford is now pursuing is precisely the same as he kept in 1815 and 1816, which he had great opportunities of then observing, as he was of the same mess with two or three of Crawford's managing partisans. He says that Crawford is a very singular instance of a man of such character rising to the eminence he now occupies; that there has not been in the history of the Union another man with abilities so ordinary, with services so slender, and so thoroughly corrupt, who has contrived to make himself a candidate for the Presidency. He thinks it, however, impossible that he should succeed.

Mr. George Graham was at the theatre; he has just returned from a long visit to Kentucky, and says that the people there have got into excessive ill humor with the General Government, and a universal passion for Mr. Clay to be the next President; though they are at the same time in a flame of internal combustion, with stop laws, paper money, and hunting down Judges, in which Clay is on the unpopular side, which at this time is the side of justice. At the late election, a decided majority of the State Legislature has been chosen for removing the Judges who pronounced the relief laws unconstitutional; and in the elections for Congress the candidates opposed to the Administration were everywhere elected. Clay himself is one of them.

*   *   *

November 30, 1822

. . . He said Mr. Clay was coming to the next Congress with the intention of making the Speaker's chair a step for his own promotion to the Presidency; as on the very probable contingency that the election would fall to the House of Representatives, his influence in the House, and the "esprit de corps" in favor of their own Speaker, would operate strongly upon the members in his favor. But, he said, he had lately seen Mr. Shaw, formerly a member of Congress from Berkshire, Massachusetts, and a very particular friend of Mr. Clay, with whom he is in correspondence, who told him that he believed there had been some understanding between Mr. Clay and me, or between our friends, who would move in concert. He said he did not wish to draw from me anything I might wish not to disclose, but his own views at present might in some sort be influenced by the knowledge of the facts.

I told him that I had no motive for concealment or hesitation with him. There was no understanding or concert between Mr. Clay and me on the subject, and never had been. When Mr. Clay left Congress, two years ago, we parted upon friendly terms, and although Mr. Clay's political course as a member of the House had not been remarkably friendly to me, I had never been unfriendly to him. As to the next Presidential election, I had no concert or understanding with any one.

*   *   *

January 25, 1824

I told Taylor that my mind was made up. I was satisfied there was at this time a majority of the whole people of the United States, and a majority of the States, utterly averse to a nomination by Congressional caucus, thinking it adverse to the spirit of the Constitution, and tending to corruption. I thought it so myself; and therefore would not now accept a Congressional caucus nomination, even for the Presidency. And of course a nomination for the Vice-Presidency, in cooperation with one for Mr. Crawford as President, could have no charms for me. Not that I despised the Vice-Presidency, or wished peevishly to reject the second place because I could not obtain the first; but because the people disapproved of this mode of nomination, and I disapproved of it myself. I added that in opposition to such nomination I wished my friends to take any measures in concert with others opposed to it as might be proper. In effecting this concert, I wished them to dispose of me as they should think best for the public service. I was entirely prepared to consider the election by the people of another person to the Presidency as an indication of their will that I should retire to private life.

*   *   *

April 22, 1824

T. Fuller, member from Massachusetts, called late in the evening. He asked if I had seen a piece in the New York Patriot signed "Mercury." I had. It asserts that while my friends are boasting of my purity and exemption from intrigue, and pretending that I rejected with indignation a proposal from Mr. Crawford's friends to support me for the Vice-Presidency, I had been guilty of the same corruption; for that Fuller more than a year since had stated that I had authorized him to offer the Vice-Presidency to Mr. Clay. Fuller was excessively incensed at this paltry electioneering squib, and said he would compel the publisher of the Patriot to give up the author of it or would prosecute him for a libel. He said it was not only false, but there never had been anything which could give rise to it; that I had never said one word to him about supporting Clay for the Vice-Presidency—nor he to any human being.

I advised him to be cool; to cause to be published an explicit contradiction of the falsehood, and if, upon demand, the author would not avow himself, that would be enough; but that political prosecutions for anything published in the newspapers against a public man were, in this country, desperate remedies. The juries always favored the slanderer.

Fuller said this way a charge of *corruption*. That, I said, if he prosecuted, would be explained away. It would be said to have been used only with reference to my supposed fastidious purity. It would be said the fact charged, if true, was no evidence of corruption; that if I had authorized him to propose to Mr. Clay's friends to support him for the Vice-Presidency, there would have been no corruption in it, and that, therefore, there was no libel in the charge, although the matter stated as fact was not true. I further said that although I never had authorized any man to make such a proposal to Clay, yet friends of mine, and friends of Clay too, had often suggested it to me as desirable; nor is there anything in it unconstitutional, illegal, or dishonorable. The friends of every one of the candidates have sought to gain strength for their favorite by coalition with the friends of others; and to deny very indignantly an imputation of that which is not wrong in itself, is giving the adversary the advantage of fastening upon you a consciousness of wrong where there is none. Fuller seemed still to think he could get the author or publisher of the piece indicted; but I suppose he will not attempt it.

*   *   *

December 17, 1824

Letcher wished to know what my sentiments towards Clay were, and I told him without disguise that I harbored no hostility against him; that whatever of difference there had been between us had arisen altogether from him, and not from me. I adverted to Jonathan Russell's attack upon me, which, I said, I believed Mr. Clay had been privy to and countenanced. But, having completely repelled that attack, I felt no animosity against any person concerned in it.

Letcher said Clay's friends thought he had been wrong in his letter against me concerning that affair. It was written in a moment of excitement. He was sure Clay felt now no hostility to me. He had spoken respectfully of me, and was a man of sincerity. Of the fourteen electors of Kentucky, seven voted for Calhoun as Vice-President; and this vote I thought, and Letcher fully concurred in the opinion, was more hostile to Clay than any vote for Jackson as President could be. It held up Calhoun as a future competitor against Clay, and thereby postponed all his prospects indefinitely. The drift of all Letcher's discourse was much the same as Wyer had told me, that Clay would willingly support me if he could thereby serve himself, and the substance of his *meaning* was, that if Clay's friends could *know* that he would have a prominent share in the Administration, that might induce them to vote for me, even in the face of instructions. But Letcher did not profess to have any authority from Clay for what he said, and he made no definite propositions. He spoke of his interview with me as altogether confidential, and in my answers to him I spoke in mere general terms.

*   *   *

December 22, 1824

Visit from Mr. James Barbour, Senator from Virginia, with whom I had a confidential conversation of more than two hours upon the prospects of the Presidential election. He spoke at first of papers relating to the piracies, which I had sent him as Chairman of the Committee of Foreign Relations of the Senate, and for copies of which there is now a call by resolution of that body. He soon, however, introduced the other topic, and freely stated to me his own impressions, and what he believed to be those of a majority of the Virginia delegation in the House of Representatives. Their first choice had been Mr. Crawford. The electors of the State had voted for him, and a majority of the people of the State were favorable to him. The representation of the State in the House would vote at first for him, and adhere to him as long as they could hope for success; but, if they should find that impracticable, their next preference would be for me. He had no doubt this was the feeling of the people of the State; that I was much more popular there than General Jackson, or even than Mr. Clay, though he was one of their own natives. He said he thought it would be treason to the Constitution to hold out and prevent an election by the House until the 4th of March, so as to give the actual Presidency to the Vice-President. He asked if I thought my friends in the House would not, if they must make a choice, prefer Mr. Crawford to General Jackson. I said I believed they would not make an option, but would adhere to me until they should obtain a majority of States, or that one should be made against them. He said something about a moral majority of votes in New York for Mr. Crawford; but he did not press much this argument, nor did I think it deserved waste of time in refuting it.

*   *   *

January 9, 1825

Note from H. Clay. Heard Little, from Ecclesiastes vii. 23: "I said, I will be wise; but it was far from me." And in the afternoon at Mr. Baker's, a son of Dr. Mason, formerly of New York, from Hebrews xi. I: "Now faith is the substance of things hoped for, the evidence of things not seen." This discourse was not ineloquent, but the learning and morality and instructiveness of Mr. Little's sermon were more satisfactory to me. In the interval between the two services, I visited J. W. Taylor and A. H. Tracy. They are speculating upon the approaching event, still without conclusive materials for judgment. I received a letter from James Tallmadge, now Lieutenant-Governor of New York, at Albany. Mr. Clay came at six, and spent the evening with me in a long conversation explanatory of the past and prospective of the future. He said that the time was drawing near when the choice must be made in the House of Representatives of a President from the three candidates presented by the electoral colleges; that he had been much urged and solicited with regard to the part in that transaction that he should take, and had not been five minutes

landed at his lodgings before he had been applied to by a friend of Mr. Crawford's, in a manner so gross that it had disgusted him; that some of my friends
also, disclaiming, indeed, to have any authority from me, had repeatedly applied to him, directly or indirectly, urging considerations personal to himself
as motives to his cause. He had thought it best to reserve for some time his
determination to himself: first, to give a decent time for his own funeral solemnities as a candidate; and, secondly, to prepare and predispose all his friends
to a state of neutrality between the three candidates who would be before the
House, so that they might be free ultimately to take that course which might
be most conducive to the public interest. The time had now come at which he
might be explicit in his communication with me, and he had for that purpose
asked this confidential interview. He wished me, as far as I might think proper,
to satisfy him with regard to some principles of great public importance, but
without any personal considerations for himself. In the question to come before the House between General Jackson, Mr. Crawford, and myself, he had no
hesitation in saying that his preference would be for me.

*   *   *

January 21, 1825

Morning visits from R. P. Letcher, of Kentucky, J. Scott, of Missouri,
J. Reed, of Massachusetts, J. McKim, of Maryland, and W. C. Bradley, of
Vermont, members H. R., and from B. O. Tayloe and P. Force.

Letcher brought me a letter from G. Robertson, formerly a member of the
House, now in the Kentucky Legislature; and he told me that Scott would call
upon me this morning, and he mentioned the proceedings in the Kentucky
delegation after they received what they call their instructions.

Scott came, and gave me the list of the printers whom he wished to have
appointed for printing the laws in Missouri. They were the same that had been
appointed last year. Scott explained to me his causes of complaint against me,
which consisted only in my having appointed several years since one newspaper to print the laws in Missouri, which was politically opposed to him. He
appeared to be satisfied with the assurances that I gave him, that I had not in
that, or any other instance, acted with intentions unfriendly to him. He spoke
of the application to the President for the removal of his brother as a Judge in
the Territory of Arkansas, for having killed in a duel his colleague on the bench.

I told him there was such an application, which had been made as long since
as last summer. But as the President had not acted upon it hitherto, I thought
he would not.

Scott then proceeded to speak of the approaching election, and said that he
had made up his mind to vote with the other Western delegations, but intimated
that he should incur great opposition for it in his own State. He spoke of himself as being entirely devoted to Mr. Clay, and of his hope that he would be a
member of the next Administration.

I told him that he would not expect me to enter upon details with regard to
the formation of an Administration, but that if I should be elected by the
suffrages of the West I should naturally look to the West for much of the
support that I should need.

He parted from me apparently satisfied.

Reed came to speak about Webster, Louis McLane, and the federalists. His own disposition is favorable to me; but Webster is specially apprehensive that the federalists will be excluded from office by me.

I told Reed that I should exclude no person for political opinions, or for personal opposition to me; that my great object would be to break up the remnant of old party distinctions, and bring the whole people together in sentiment as much as possible.

*   *   *

January 29, 1825

On my return home, Mr. Clay came in, and sat with me a couple of hours, discussing all the prospects and probabilities of the Presidential election. He spoke to me with the utmost freedom of men and things; intimated doubts and prepossessions concerning individual friends of mine, to all which I listened with due consideration. He was anxious for the conciliation of Webster and Louis McLane, and expressed some jealousy as from Webster of the persons by whom he supposed me to be surrounded.

I told him the sources of Webster's anxieties, and my own earnest desire to conciliate him; the manner in which my overtures had been received by him, and my own high opinion of his talents and capacities for service.

*   *   *

February 3, 1825

Webster's talk was about the election. He read to me a letter from Warfield, of Maryland, to him, concerning the election, and asking advice of him with regard to his vote; and the draft of an answer which he had prepared; and said he would send it or not, as I should think proper. He said that J. Lee, also of Maryland, had consulted him too, and was under impressions similar to those of Warfield. Their concern was lest, in the event of my election, the federalists should be treated as a proscribed party. Webster's answer to Warfield expressed entire confidence that I should be governed by no such considerations, and said that he should show this confidence by his vote. It intimated a hope that the object of the Administration would be to promote harmony among the people, and that the disposition would be marked by conferring some one prominent appointment upon a person of that party.

I observed that if that referred to the formation of an Administration, it would imply more than I could confirm.

He said it did not—but to an appointment perhaps of a Judge.

I said I approved altogether of the general spirit of his answer, and should consider it as one of the objects nearest to my heart to bring the whole people of the Union to harmonize together. I must, however, candidly tell him that I believed either General Jackson or Mr. Crawford would pursue precisely the same principle, and that no Administration could possibly succeed upon any other.

He said that General Van Rensselaer entertained similar sentiments to his own, and by his advice would call on me at eleven o'clock to-morrow morning.

Recommendation of Henry Clay for the Presidency
Frankfort, November 18, 1822

Kentucky legislators, in caucus, recommended their fellow citizen for the Presidency and appealed to the country to give just consideration to a westerner.

At a meeting of the members of the senate and of the house of representatives, composing the general assembly of the state of Ky. convened after the adjournment of the respective houses in the hall of the house of representatives, agreeably to a previous notice, for the purpose of taking into consideration the propriety of recommending to the people of the United States some suitable person to fill the office of the president of the United States, after the expiration of the present presidential term. *William T. Barry* was called to the chair, and *Thomas Speed* appointed secretary to the meeting, when the following resolution and address were offered for consideration by *George Robertson:*

Resolved, That *Henry Clay*, late speaker of the house of representatives of the United States, be recommended as a suitable person to succeed *James Monroe* as president thereof.

In respectfully inviting the attention of the people of the United States to a citizen of Kentucky, as a fit person to fill the highest office in their gift, that portion of the citizens of Kentucky now assembled, will not conceal that they entertain a warm affection for, and a strong confidence in, their distinguished fellow-citizen whom they have ventured to propose; nor deny that they think the time has arrived, when the people of the west may, with some confidence, appeal to the magnanimity of the whole union, for a favorable consideration of their equal and just claim to a fair participation in the executive government of these states. Sectional motives they are ready freely to admit, ought not to have a predominant influence in the choice of a chief magistrate: But it cannot be disguised that they ever must have some weight, until that sentiment shall be eradicated from the human breast, which attaches man most to those whom he knows best, and to the objects which are nearest and dearest to him. It is not, however, alone, nor principally, upon considerations merely local or personal, but on those of a much more liberal and elevated character, that they rest the pretensions of the individual whom they now recommend: For they believe, without disparaging, in the smallest degree, the very great and acknowledged merits of the other illustrious men, to whom public attention has lately been directed, that, throughout his whole public career, no American statesman has been less actuated by narrow or selfish impulses, and that he yields to none in eminent services, in distinguished ability, in political rectitude and virtue, nor in liberal and enlarged views of national policy.

In presenting him, therefore, to the consideration of their fellow-citizens, they think they are authorized to believe, that they have consulted the best interests of the whole union, as well as the feelings and interests of the west, and that they may be allowed to hope that his strong claims to the confidence and approbation of his country, will be properly appreciated, and his talents and public services justly rewarded.

And, on the question being put thereon, the said resolution and address were unanimously adopted.

W. T. Barry,
Chairman.

Presidential Nomination of John Quincy Adams
Boston, January 23, 1823

Massachusetts Republicans, both legislators and delegates from "towns . . . not represented in the legislature," placed before the people the name of their favorite son.

At a meeting of the republican members of both branches of the legislature of the commonwealth of Massachusetts, and of republican delegates from various towns of the commonwealth not represented in the legislature, held at the old court house, in the city of Boston, on Thursday evening, Jan. 23, 1823, the following report was unanimously adopted—

The committee consisting of one member from each congressional district in the commonwealth, appointed to consider whether any, and, if any, what measures ought to be adopted by the republican citizens of Massachusetts in relation to the next election of president of the United States, have had that subject under consideration and respectfully report:

That the time for electing a successor to the present illustrious chief magistrate of the United States is so far distant that it cannot now be ascertained what then will be the condition of the country, or who among its citizens can be most usefully called to that arduous and responsible station. But the great importance of the office then to be filled, and the momentous consequences of deciding who shall be the person to fill it, have commanded attention in every part of the union, and in various forms and by various authority, eminent men are holden forth for the approbation and suffrage of the people.

Your committee are not inclined to favor the practice of nominating a candidate for the presidency by assemblies in the states, for this, among other obvious reasons, that the tendency of such nomination is to throw the election into the house of representatives, where, as experience has proved, it is liable to manifold abuse. In their view it is desirable that the attention of our fellow citizens should be drawn to a candidate, rather by the commanding influence of his character than by any local or sectional feelings arrayed in his support.

But as unanimity, to a good degree, is most desirable on this great occasion, and as the opinion of one section of the country must be made known to others, that a common sentiment and feeling may, in the end, be produced, the committee see great propriety in the public expression of such opinion as prevails among their fellow citizens, with a view, not as partizans, to contend for the election of a favorite, but to dissemminate information that may be necessary for an intelligent decision by the people.

The republicans of Massachusetts, actuated by a national spirit, have always avoided, as the greatest national evil, any measures which would bear a local or sectional construction. They have, with pleasure, given their undivided support to elevate to office those illustrious citizens of the south, who have, for the last twenty-two years, so ably conducted the destinies of the nation, convinced that they were worthy to sustain, and justly entitled to receive, the highest honors and utmost confidence of the people.

Among the candidates, now before the public, is a citizen of this commonwealth, and the committee believe it is not only due to his high character, but that it is respectful to their republican brethren throughout the United States, to declare the opinion which our political friends in this commonwealth entertain of his qualifications for the high office of president of the United States. By making such declaration, no determination is expressed to support the individual in question, at all events and under all possible circumstances. Such inflexibility of opinion might destroy that common principle of action from which is to be expected an harmonious and useful result.

By declaring to our friends, in other parts of the United States, our opinion and feelings, at the present time, we mean to convey information which may influence their deliberations, and are not precluded from receiving and examining, with candor, their sentiments and wishes, in the hope that, by the interchange of opinion, the minds of the whole people may be eventually fixed on that man, who, in all his official relations, will most worthily sustain the character of an American patriot.

The committee, therefore, recommend the following resolution to be adopted:

Resolved, That we have unlimitted confidence in the republican principles of *John Quincy Adams*: That we hold in the highest respect the uniform integrity of his public and private character: That we consider his exalted talents, his various and eminent services, his political experience, and his profound knowledge of the great interests of the nation, as pledges of the ability with which, as the chief magistrate of the American people, he would promote their prosperity and honor.

Jonas Sibley
Chairman.

Letter from General Andrew Jackson
to the Dauphin County Committee
February 23, 1823

Old Hickory revealed his availability as a candidate.

Gentlemen—Your letter of the 3d inst. with the Harrisburg paper entitled the "Commonwealth," containing the address you have alluded to, has been this day received. The complimentary manner in which my fellow citizens of Pennsylvania have been pleased to notice my military services, and their voluntary expressions of respect and confidence in me, has excited, on my part, a proper sense of gratitude. As a committee, appointed to draft an address to the people of the United States, on the subject of the next presidential election, you ask to be informed "whether I can, or do approve of my name being used at this time as a candidate for the presidency of the United States."

I should have consulted my own feelings by continuing to avoid speaking on the subject, but the respectable source from whence the inquiry emanates, prohibits any but a candid notice of your communication.

My undeviating rule of conduct through life, and which I have and ever shall deem as congenial with the true republican principles of our government, has been, neither to seek or decline public invitations to office. For the services which I may have rendered, and which have, it is hoped, proved in a degree beneficial to my country, I have nothing to ask. They are richly repaid with the confidence and good opinion of the virtuous and well deserving part of the community. I have only essayed to discharge a debt which every man owes his country when her rights are invaded; and if twelve years' exposure to fatigue and numerous privations, can warrant the assertion, I may venture to assert, that my portion of public service has been performed; and that, with this impression, I have retired from the busy scenes of public life, with a desire to be a spectator merely of passing events.

The office of chief magistrate of the union, is one of great responsibility. As it should not be sought by any individual of the republic, so it cannot, with propriety, be declined, when offered by those who have the power of selection. It is interesting to the American people alone, and in the election, they should exercise their free and unbiassed judgment. It was with these impressions, I presume, and without any consulation with me, that the members of the legislature of the state of Tennessee, as an additional testimony of their confidence in me, thought proper to present my name to the American community. My political creed prompts me to leave the affair uninfluenced by any expression on my part, and to the free will of those who have alone the right to decide.

Declaration of New York Republican Caucus
April 22, 1823

A caucus of Republican members of the New York legislature recommended continuation of the practice of nominating presidential candidates by congressional caucus.

At a meeting of the republican members of both branches of the legislature of the state of New York, held at the assembly chamber in the city of Albany, on the 22d day of April 1823 — the hon. Walter Bowne, of the senate, was called to the chair, and James Mullett, jr. esq. of the assembly, appointed secretary.

On motion of the lieutenant-governor, it was

Resolved, That a committee be appointed by the chair, to prepare and report resolutions expressive of the sense of this meeting, in regard to the approaching presidential election; and thereupon, the hon. Erastus Root, the hon. Messrs. Redfield and Dudley, of the senate; the hon. Peter R. Livingston, speaker of the assembly, and Messrs. Gardiner, Goodell, Seaman, Birdseye and Hager, of that body, were appointed such committee.

The following resolutions, being reported by the committee, were, after discussion, unanimously adopted:

Whereas, the period fixed for the election of a chief magistrate of the United States has so nearly approached, that the members of the legislatures of several of our sister states have already thought it advisable to express their feelings upon the occasion, and have thereby rendered it proper that those who have been elected, in a similar capacity, to represent the state of New York, should leave no reason for supposing that this state is more insensible than other members of the confederacy to the importance of such a question: Therefore,

Resolved, That we consider an explicit avowal of our sentiments in the matter, as not only called for by the occasion, but due to the commendable solicitude which is felt by our republican brethren in other parts of the union:

That it is highly essential to the interests of those who have the happiness to live under a republican form of government, that its administration should be committed to persons whose opinions and feelings are in coincidence with its fundamental principles, and whose lives and conduct furnish the most unequivocal evidence of their entire devotion to the preservation of those principles:

That, the practice of making nominations for the office of president by individual states, has a tendency to disturb the harmony of the great republican family, by creating and strengthening individual predilections and local feelings, and thereby preventing that concert of action which has heretofore crowned their exertions with success:

That although a nomination by the republican members of congress is not

397

entirely free from objections, yet that, assembled as they are from the different quarters of the union; coming from the various classes of the community; elected during the pendency and discussion of the question, and, in a great degree, with reference to it; they bring into one body as perfect a representation as can be expected of the interests and wishes of all and of each; and that a nomination made by them in the manner which has heretofore been usual, is the best attainable mode of effecting the great object in view which has yet been suggested:

That we fully believe that a convention thus constituted, will be less liable to be influenced by those sectional jealousies, against which the father of his country has so solemnly and justly cautioned us — more likely to cherish those purely national feelings, which it is the interest, and should be the pride, of every state to protect — and better calculated to preserve unbroken those political ties which bind together the republicans of the north and of the south, the east and the west, and are consecrated by the recollections of times and events dear to the democracy of the nation, which triumphed in the election, and prospered under the administration of the illustrious Jefferson:

That we feel an unhesitating confidence, that, when the proper time for making such nomination shall arrive, the republican members of congress will select as a candidate, for an office of general supervision over the great political, agricultural, manufacturing and commercial interests of the nation, one who is not only a sound democratic republican in principle and practice, but who will labor with equal assiduity for the just promotion of all those great interests; and to whom the republicans of New York can give their willing support.

Resolved, That the proceedings of this meeting be signed by the chairman and secretary, and published.

Walter Bowne,
Chairman.

Declaration of Support for General Andrew Jackson
Philadelphia, October, 1823

This document illustrates the zeal and organization that turned Pennsylvania to Jackson and ended Calhoun's 1824 presidential hopes.

A meeting was held at the county court house, in Philadelphia, on the 5th instant, *Jacob Holgate* chairman, and *Z. Philips* secretary — at which, after a spirited preamble, which says that "the star of Jackson's glory first emerged to brightness from the clouds and darkness of our revolutionary tempest," the following resolutions were adopted:

Resolved, That we hold it to be the imperative duty of the people, as well as a sacred right secured to us by the constitution, to select our own candidate for the presidency of the United States, independent of all interference, and aloof from all dictation.

Resolved, That, as *democrats*, we maintain the right to think and act for ourselves, and never will surrender to a self constituted aristocracy, that freedom of opinion, which is, at once, the source of our greatness and the preserver of our liberties.

Resolved, That, in accordance with these principles, we will support *general Andrew Jackson* as the next president of the United States.

Because, he has always been a uniform and consistent democrat.

Because, he is eminently qualified, both as a statesman and a warrior, to govern the nation wisely, in peace, and to conduct her triumphantly through war.

Because, as a patriot, we have full confidence in his moderation, his virtue and his firmness; being a friend to the *rights of man* and *universal suffrage*.

Resolved, That we consider Andrew Jackson as having claims to the gratitude of this republic, for this distinguished station. which no other candidate can prefer, and which we are bound to grant, by our love of country, our devotion to liberty, and our admiration of patriotism.

Resolved, That this meeting pledge themselves solemnly to one another, to devote all their exertions to promote the election of general Andrew Jackson to the presidency of the United States.

Resolved, That James Thackara, John Goodman, Stephen Simpson. Jacob Holgate, Jacob Shearer, Thomas Lieper, James Ronaldson, Nathan Jones, (Blockley), and John M. Taylor, constitute a committee of correspondence, to hold communication with similar committees throughout the state, and for the purpose of an interchange of sentiment with similar committees throughout the union.

Resolved, That this meeting do, earnestly, recommend to the *friends of Jackson* throughout the state, to hold meetings and organize their strength in their several districts. thus taking a firm stand in defence of their country, the constitution, and the glorious principles of *seventy six*.

Presidential Nomination of Secretary of War John C. Calhoun
Columbia, November 29, 1823

The South Carolina legislative caucus resolved to support John C. Calhoun and recommended his election.

In conformity with previous notice, a meeting of the members of the legislature of South Carolina was held in the representative chamber.

The hon. *Jacob Bond I'on* was called to the chair, and *Robert Anderson* appointed secretary.

The following preamble and resolution, submitted by Mr. *Pinckney*, were considered and adopted:

Whereas, in the opinion of this assembly, the period has arrived when it is proper and expedient that the sentiments and feelings of every section of the union should be known and promulgated, in relation to the approaching election of chief magistrate of the nation; and whereas it is the opinion of this assembly also, that the distinguished talents and public services of Mr. *Calhoun*, together with his devotion to the general administration, his superiority to local views and sectional principles, his zeal and energy in promoting the declaration and prosecution of our late war with Britain, and his pure and incorruptible integrity, eminently entitle him to the favor and approbation of the people:

Therefore, be it resolved, that we will support *John C. Calhoun* for the office of president of the United States, at the ensuing election, and that we recommend him to our fellow citizens throughout the United States, as a suitable person to fill the same.

Ordered, that the foregoing preamble and resolution, signed by the chairman and secretary, be published in all the newspapers in this state.

Jacob Bond I'on,
Chairman.

Address by Senator Benjamin Ruggles
to the Republicans of the United States
Washington, February 21, 1824

A defense of the action of the congressional caucus was joined with a warning ing that divisions in Republican ranks would lead to a resurgence of the Federalists.

Fellow citizens:

Pursuant to notice, and conformable to usage, the republican members of both houses of congress, whose names are stated to you, have proceeded to recommend suitable persons to fill the offices of president and vice-president of the United States, for the term ensuing the expiration of the present. Existing circumstances will justify, if they do not require, a brief exposition of the grounds of this proceeding. In its adoption, and submission to your consideration, we have acted as members of the republican party, pursuing the footsteps of those who have gone before us, from the important revolution in the politics of the country, resulting in the choice of Mr. Jefferson, to the period of the first election of the present chief magistrate. That this course has not been sanctioned by all our republican colleagues, is a subject for regret. Others, with whom we wished to associate and unite in measures of conciliation and concord, have, though respectfully invited, declined to co-operate with us. We have been ready and anxious, in a general meeting of all the republican members, to submit our preferences to the will of the majority. Those who differ with us in opinion have refused their concurrence. It is your right, and becomes your duty, to decide between us. We intend no impeachment of the conduct or motives of others. We speak for ourselves only, without affecting to conceal our expectation of obtaining your approval of the course of proceeding we have adopted. It is now twenty four years since the great political revolution to which we have alluded was effected, and the power which was then acquired by republicans in the government of the union is still retained. Their enjoyment of this ascendancy has not, however, been undisturbed; on the contrary, they have had an unwearied struggle to maintain with the same adversary over whom their triumph was achieved. It is not to be doubted that it was by union and concert of action that the strength of the republican party was consolidated, and its success in the decisive controversy *effected*. It is as little to be doubted, that it is by adherence to the same principle and policy of action that its unbroken force and continued ascendancy can be preserved. The reasons for adhering to this policy of efficiency and safety derive, in our judgment, peculiar force from the circumstances which characterize the existing period. The correctness of this opinion is demonstrated by a revision of the grounds which have been assigned for a deviation from that policy. Those grounds we understand to be, the supposed obliteration of party distinctions, the change of opinion on the subject, which is apprehended to have taken place in the republican body, and the improbability that a general attendance of the republican members could be obtained. In relation to the correctness of the first of these grounds, the supposed obliteration of party distinctions, your ability to decide can derive little aid from any observations of ours. That, in some parts of the union, where the federal party have always been weaker and less violent, the fact is, in some degree, as stated, and that, since the late war, their exertions have no where been as efficient as formerly, we admit. But that danger is not to be apprehended from this source, in connexion with the pending divisions in the republican party, and the angry dissentions they are likely to engender, we deny. That our adversaries have not lost their disposition to avail themselves of those divisions, to regain their ascendancy, is confirmed by a reference to the past, and ought not to be doubted. There is not an instance to be found in the history of the politics of the different states, for the last twenty years, in which serious and continued divisions among republicans have not led to a temporary success of their opponents. The same cause will produce a more extended effect on a larger scale of operations, and, we are persuaded, that all calculations, of a different result, will, in the end, deceive and disappoint those who shall be so indiscreet as to indulge them. As it respects the supposed change of sentiment among the republicans of the union, on the question of the fitness of conventions of this character, the proceedings of the last twelve months have strongly impressed our minds with a different conclusion. Heretofore conventions of the republican members of congress, for the nomination of candidates for president and vice president, have been held upon the *presumed* approbation of their constituents *only*. The question now, however, stands upon a very different footing. Resolutions, expressive of their dissent to meetings of this character, have, during their last session, been passed by the legislature of the state of Tennessee, and transmitted to the executives of the other states, for the purpose of being laid before their legislatures for concurrence. No mode could have been adopted better devised to ascertain the state of public sentiment. It is known that those resolutions have been acted upon by the legislatures of Maine, New York, Virginia, Georgia, North Carolina, Rhode Island, Ohio, Pennsylvania and Indiana; which states are entitled to one hundred and forty-six out of the *two hundred and sixty one votes* to be given in the United States. By the republican members of the legislatures of the four states first named, and entitled to seventy-eight votes, resolutions have been passed, with great unanimity, approving, in the warmest terms, such a meeting as has been held. In the remaining states mentioned, the resolutions of Tennessee have been postponed, in some instances indefinitely, and in others disposed of in a manner evincive of a determination not to act upon them. In no state, except Maryland, entitled to eleven votes, has there been an expression of concurrence, by the legislature, in the views of the legislature of Tennessee. In South Carolina, entitled to the same number of votes, one branch of the legislature, in opposition to the opinion of the other, has expressed such concurrence. Nor have the members of the legislature of any state, in their individual capacity, expressed similar views.

From reference to these facts, we feel authorized in the belief, that a large majority of the republicans of the union have desired and expected the adoption of the course which, under the influence of those impressions, we have felt it our duty to pursue. On the remaining subject of review, we have a word only to offer. The circumstance of the absence of so many republicans from our meeting has already been stated as a subject for regret. It is neither our privilege nor disposition to exercise any right of judgment on their conduct. We have been uniform in the expression of our readiness to abide by the sentiment of a general convention of our republican brethren, and to renounce our predilections in obedience to its award. Various causes have combined to reduce the number of those who have attended. Several, who were friendly to the candidates nominated, had objections, which they conceived to be founded in principle; other circumstances have co-operated. Without detaining you by an enumeration, we content ourselves with a reference to the striking fact, that, although the states of New York, Virginia and Maine have, with unusual unanimity, recommended to their members, in express terms, to attend this meeting, only thirty-four persons have represented the sixty-nine votes to which they will be entitled in the election.

We will not attempt to conceal the anxiety with which we are impressed by the present conjuncture. To our minds, the course of recent events points to the entire dismemberment of the party to which it is our pride to be attached. The admission, unreservedly made, that, on the question of the expediency of a convention, the entire amalgamation of parties has been assumed, is, of itself, sufficient ground of solicitude. Other considerations justify apprehensions of the same character. The injurious consequences likely to be produced by a departure, at this time, from the ancient usages of the party, will not be confined to the election of president and vice president. Exertions are every where making, to break up the entire system of conventions for the nomination of candidates, in reference to state as well as federal elections. It is submitted, then, whether an abandonment of the practice here will not involve the ultimate prostration of the system wherever it prevails, and with it the securities of the republican ascendancy. It is from an apprehension of such results, in the event of the abandonment of established principles and of the usage of the party, that we have adopted the proceedings now submitted to your consideration. *The question is, in our best judgment, one touching the dismemberment or preservation of the party.* This question it is your province to decide. The office we have sought to discharge has been to place the subject before you for this decision. The limits allotted to this address will not permit us to dwell on the many and pressing considerations of a more general nature, urging to union among republicans, with a view to the decision of the approaching election of the first officers of the government by the people, and the avoidance of the unalleviated mischiefs of an election by the house of representatives. Among the most striking of these considerations, is to be ranked the inevitable inefficiency, as it respects the measures, both of domestic and foreign character, of an executive administration having to rely for its support on the cooperation of a legislature distracted by angry and implacable divisions. Of the persons recommended to you as candidates, it has not been usual to speak. No motive exists to depart from the established usage in this respect. Known to you by a long course of public life, by their uniform devotion to the best interests of the nation, in stations of the highest responsibility, in which their zeal, integrity and capacity have been amply proved, we are satisfied that we have only anticipated your wishes by giving them our recommendation. Without intending to derogate from the merits of others, for whom your confidence may be solicited, it is just to remind you that the candidate we recommend for the first office in your government, has established a peculiar claim to the esteem of the republican party, by his manly and disinterested conduct upon a former occasion, under the strongest temptation to become the instrument of compromising its integrity.

Letter from Speaker of the House Henry Clay
to Francis Preston Blair
January 8, 1825

Clay jested concerning the attention showered on him after his elimination from the race.

My dear Sir. My position in relation to the friends of the three returned candidates is singular enough and often to me very amusing. In the first place they all believe, that my friends have the power of deciding the question, and that I have the power of controling my friends. Acting upon this supposition in the same hour, I am sometimes touched gently on the shoulder by a friend (for example) of Genel. Jackson, who will thus address me. "My dear Sir, all our dependence is on you; don't disappoint us; you know our partiality was for you next to the Hero; and how much we want a western President — Immediately after a friend of Mr. Crawford will accost me "The hopes of the Republican party are concentrated on you   For God's sake preserve it — If you had been returned instead of Mr. Crawford every man of us would have supported you to the last hour. We consider him & you as the only genuine Republican Candidates." Next a friend of Mr. Adams comes "with tears in his eyes." "Sir Mr. Adams has always had the greatest respect for you, & admiration for your talents — There is no station to which they are not equal — Most undoubtedly you were the second choice of New England. And I pray you to consider seriously whether the public good & your own future interests do not point most distinctly to the choice which you ought to make — " How can one withstand all this disinterested homage & kindness? Really the friends of all the three Gentlemen are so very courteous, and affectionate, that I sometimes almost wish that it was in my power to accommodate each of them. But that being impossible we are beginning to think seriously of the choice which we must finally make. I will tell you then, that I believe the contest will be limited to Mr. Adams & Genl. Jackson; Mr. Crawford's personal condition precludes the choice of him; if there were no other objection to his election. As to the only alternative which is presented to us, it is sufficiently painful, & I consider whatever choice we may make will be only a choice of evils — To both those Gentlemen there are strong personal objections — The principal difference between them is that in the election of Mr. Adams we shall not by the example inflict any wound upon the character of our institutions; but I should much fear hereafter, if not during the present generation, that the election of the General would give to the Military Spirit a Stimulus and a confidence that might lead to the most pernicious results — I shall therefore with great regret, on account of the dilemma in which the people have placed us, support Mr. Adams — My friends are generally so inclined. What has great weight with me is the decided preference which a majority of the delegation from Ohio has for him over the Genl. Jackson — If therefore Kentucky were to vote for the Genl. it would probably only have the effect of dividing our friends, without defeating ultimately the election of Mr. Adams. Three of the four States, favorable to Mr. Crawford are believed to prefer Mr. Adams to the General. Virginia is one of them —

I am inclined to think that nearly three-fourths of our delegation have yeilded [*sic*] to the influence of these views, and will vote for Mr. Adams — My friends entertain the belief that their kind wishes will, in the end, be more likely to be accomplished by so bestowing their votes — I have however most earnestly entreated them to throw me out of their consideration in bringing their Judgements to a final conclusion and to look, & be guided solely by the public good — If I know my self that alone has determined me — Your representative is inclined to concur with us in these sentiments and views; and if they should meet your approbation, as I know that he has great respect for your Opinions, I would be glad if you would by the return mail address a letter to him to strengthen him in his inclination. Be pleased to show this letter to Crittenden alone.

I remain faithy, Your friend

Letter from Speaker of the House Henry Clay
to Francis Preston Blair
January 29, 1825

Clay explains his decision to support Adams and comments on the reaction to it.

My Dear Blair, I received this morning your very agreeable favor of the 17th Inst. A letter from you is always refreshing, and I wish that I could entitle myself to expect them more frequently, by more punctuality & diligence, on my part, in our correspond [ence].——My last letter informed you of the unction that was unceasingly applied to me by all the returned Candidates for the Presidency, or rather their friends. Since then I have avowed my intention to support Mr Adams, under actual circumstances, and thereupon the oil has been instantly transformed into vinegar. The friends of (——) (The devil knows who else for I think if he does not preside in their councils he must be quite conversant with them) have turned upon me and with the most amiable unanimity agree to vituperate me. I am a deserter from Democracy: A Giant at intrigue; have sold the West — sold myself — defeating Genl Jacksons election to leave open the Western pretentions that I may hereafter fill them myself — blasting all my fair prospects &c &c &c   To these are added a thousand other of the most gentle and kind and agreeable epithets and things in the world.————who are themselves straining every nerve to elect Jackson that the claims of the West may be satisfied and I be thereby pretermitted, are accusing me of acting on their own principles. The Knaves cannot comprehend how a man can be honest. They cannot conceive that I should have solemnly interrogated my Conscience and asked it to tell me seriously what I ought to do? that it should have enjoined me not to establish the dangerous precedent of elevating, in this early stage of the Republic, a Military Chieftain, merely because he has won a great victory? that it should have told me that a public man is undeserving his station who will not regardless of aspersions and calumnies, risk himself for his country? I am afraid that you will think me moved by these abuses. Be not deceived. I assure you that I never in my whole life felt more perfect composure, more entire confidence in the resolutions of my judgment and a more unshakeable determination to march up to my duty. And, my Dear Sir, is there an intelligent and unbiased man who must not sooner or later, concur with me? Mr Adams, you know well, I should never have selected, if at liberty to draw from the whole mass of our citizens for a President. But there is no danger in his elevation now or in time to come. Not so of his competitor, of whom I cannot believe that killing 2500 Englishmen at N. Orleans qualifies for the various, difficult and complicated duties of the Chief Magistracy. I perceive that I am unconsciously writing a sort of defence, which you may possibly think imp[lies] guilt. What will be the result? you will ask with curiosity, if not anxiety. I think Mr Adams must be elected. Such is the prevailing opinion. Still I shall not consider the matter as certain until the election is over. With my best respects to Mrs Blair and Mr Crittenden,

I remain truly Your friend

THE VOTE IN THE 1824 ELECTION

STATES	POPULAR VOTE				ELECTORAL VOTE			
	Andrew Jackson	John Quincy Adams	William H. Crawford	Henry Clay	Andrew Jackson	John Quincy Adams	William H. Crawford	Henry Clay
Maine............	—	10,289	2,336	—	—	9	—	—
New Hampshire...	—	9,389	643	—	—	8	—	—
Vermont†........	—	—	—	—	—	7	—	—
Massachusetts	—	30,687	6,616	—	—	15	—	—
Rhode Island.....	—	2,145	200	—	—	4	—	—
Connecticut......	—	7,587	1,978	—	—	8	—	—
New York†.......	—	—	—	—	1	26	5	4
New Jersey.......	10,985	9,110	1,196	—	8	—	—	—
Pennsylvania......	36,100	5,441	4,206	1,690	28	—	—	—
Delaware†........	—	—	—	—	—	1	2	—
Maryland........	14,523	14,632	3,364	695	7	3	1	—
Virginia.........	2,861	3,189	8,489	416	—	—	24	—
North Carolina....	20,415	—	15,621	—	15	—	—	—
South Carolina†...	—	—	—	—	11	—	—	—
Georgia†.........	—	—	—	—	—	—	9	—
Alabama.........	9,443	2,416	1,680	67	5	—	—	—
Mississippi........	3,234	1,694	119	—	3	—	—	—
Louisiana†.......	—	—	—	—	3	2	—	—
Kentucky.........	6,455	—	—	17,331	—	—	—	14
Tennessee.........	20,197	216	312	—	11	—	—	—
Missouri..........	987	311	—	1,401	—	—	—	3
Ohio.............	18,457	12,280	—	19,255	—	—	—	16
Indiana..........	7,343	3,095	—	5,315	5	—	—	—
Illinois..........	1,901	1,542	219	1,047	2	1	—	—
	152,901	114,023	46,979	47,217	99	84	41	37

† In these six states electors were appointed by the legislature.
It is the first time in the history of presidential elections that the popular votes were preserved, though no great reliance can be given to these figures.

Election of 1828

ROBERT V. REMINI is Professor of History at the University of Illinois, Chicago Circle. He has written Martin Van Buren and the Making of the Democratic Party; The Election of Andrew Jackson; Andrew Jackson; *and* Andrew Jackson and the Bank War.

Election of 1828

by *Robert V. Remini*

When the presidential contest of 1824–25 ended in the election of John Quincy Adams, the defeated candidate, Andrew Jackson, took his loss with all the grace and dignity one might expect from this enormously self-assured and imposing westerner. At a reception given by President Monroe on the night of the election in the House of Representatives, Senator Jackson stepped up to the President-elect and without the slightest trace of disappointment in his voice, said, "How do you do, Mr. Adams. I hope you are well, sir."

"Very well, sir," replied Adams, "I hope General Jackson is well!" And with that the two men parted. About the election, there was not a word, not even one of congratulations from the defeated candidate. Jackson accepted his loss and seemed to pay no further heed to it. He might never have said much more about it had not Adams, shortly after their meeting, announced his intention of appointing Henry Clay his Secretary of State. The news convulsed Jackson. His well-known temper blazed up in all its terrible fury. He was transfixed with anger and soon convinced himself that he had been cheated of the Presidency by Adams and Clay. He, who had won a popular and electoral plurality in the fall election, he declared, had been swindled in the House by conniving politicians who would not hesitate to set aside the popular will to satisfy their ambitions. In Jackson's mind, and indeed in the minds of many other politicians, the selection of Adams had been arranged prior to the House election by a "deal" in which Clay promised to throw his enormous support among the representatives to Adams in return for an appoint-

413

ment as Secretary of State, a position which historically led straight to the Presidency. There had been rumors of such a "deal" but no proof. Now, with Clay's appointment, Jackson claimed he had all the evidence he needed to prove that a "corrupt bargain" had been struck to prevent his election as President. He returned to his home in Tennessee, resigned from the Senate and poured out his wrath in a series of letters to politicians all over the country about how the people's will had been thwarted and how chicanery and fraud now ruled in Washington. With uncanny skill and instinct he had touched upon the one issue his friends could use to attack and embarrass the new Administration. It was the issue they would superbly develop to elect Jackson President in 1828.

In Congress the "corrupt bargain" cry was taken up by the General's followers and rung through a thousand changes. Clay was accused of seeking out several candidates until he finally found the one who agreed to give him what he wanted. John Randolph of Roanoke, the eccentric senator from Virginia, fired off a speech in the upper chamber which amused the Jacksonians but horrified the friends of the Administration. He described the coalition of Adams and Clay in terms of two notorious characters from Fielding's novel *Tom Jones.* Said he: "I was defeated, horse, foot, and dragoons—cut up—and clean broke down—by the coalition of Blifil and Black George—by the combination, unheard of till then, of the Puritan and the black-leg."

Clay, understandably sensitive to the charge since he had indeed arranged the election and his own appointment, though not by fraud or corruption, challenged Randolph to a duel in the hope of silencing his critics. The two men met on the southern shore of the Potomac River and exchanged single shots. Both shots missed. At that point Senator Thomas Hart Benton of Missouri, who had been watching the duel, tried to intervene and bring the fight to a halt. Clay brushed him aside. He insisted on a second shot. Randolph airily agreed to the demand but whispered to Benton that he would not return the fire. On the second exchange Clay put a bullet through the senator's coat, while Randolph blithely discharged his pistol into the air. Randolph then came forward, hand outstretched, which Clay readily grasped. "I trust in God, my dear sir, you are unharmed," said Clay. "After what has occurred I would not have harmed you for a thousand worlds." "You owe me a coat, Mr. Clay," came the reply. "I am glad the debt is no greater," said the Secretary.

So ended this ridiculous duel, but it silenced neither Randolph nor other Jacksonians in their efforts to discredit the Administration. Indeed, it served as a reminder of how the election had been decided and of Clay's inordinate need to stifle all reference to it. Rumbling throughout the entire campaign of 1828 was the charge of a "corrupt bargain" along with Jackson's impassioned cry that the "will of the people" had been thwarted.

Apart from creating the leading issue of the campaign, the announcement of Clay's appointment produced an immediate political effect. No sooner did the President indicate his selection for the State Department than the new Vice-President, John C. Calhoun, along with a number of his friends, marched straight into the camp of General Jackson. Obviously, the Adams-Clay coalition would now block the road to the Presidency for many years, perhaps as long as sixteen; so the impatient Calhoun, who could not wait that long for his own turn to come around, decided to abandon his neutral position and join forces with Jackson in the expectation that he would succeed to the Presidency four or possibly eight years hence. Even before Jackson left Washington for Tennessee, Calhoun and "other members of the South Carolina delegation" dined with him and agreed to form a party "to oppose Mr. Adams' administration."

The initial formation of an opposition party inaugurated with Clay's appointment was accelerated by the President's first annual message to Congress delivered on December 6, 1825. In a bold and forthright assertion of the Government's responsibility to develop the country and its resources, Adams outlined a program of public works that showed his personal commitment to Henry Clay's American System, a system which advocated protective tariffs, internal improvements, stable currency, distribution of federal surpluses to the states, and a sound banking system. "The great object of the institution of civil government," Adams contended, "is the improvement of the condition of those who are parties to the social compact, and no government, in whatever form constituted, can accomplish the lawful end of its institution but in proportion as it improved the condition of those over whom it is established." Accordingly, he proposed the building of roads and canals, the establishment of a national university as well as an astronomical observatory, the exploration of the western territories and northeastern coastline, the building of a naval academy similar to West Point, and the adoption of a uniform standard of weights and measures—all at government expense. "The spirit of improvement is abroad upon the earth," he proclaimed, and the United States must take the lead in furthering it." Unfortunately, in closing his message, Adams committed the unpardonable political blunder of telling Congress not to give the rest of the world the impression "that we are palsied by the will of our constituents."

The message, when read to Congress, produced quite a jolt, particularly among those of the Republican party who supported the candidacy of William H. Crawford in the presidential election of 1824. This faction was known as the party of "Old Republicans" or "Radicals" because of its deep commitment to a highly conservative interpretation of the Constitution and their equally conservative approach to a definition of governmental powers. The Old Republicans advocated states rights; by the same token they opposed a strong central government in Washington; they called for rigid economy in budgeting national expenditures; they opposed protective tariffs and internal improvements; in fact they opposed virtually everything the American System espoused. To them, therefore, Adams' entire message was a declaration of war and they agreed almost at once to do everything in their power to wreck the President's legislative program.

Because Crawford suffered a paralyzing stroke during the 1824 campaign the Old Republicans were now led by the junior senator from New York,

Martin Van Buren, known to some as the "Little Magician" because of his unparalleled skill as a political manipulator and compromiser. Van Buren had been raised in the rough and tumble school of New York politics where he learned how to survive in an arena of cutthroat politicians. After a long, hard fight with De Witt Clinton for control of the New York Republican party, Van Buren won out and forced Clinton into retirement. He then created a state-wide machine, called the Albany Regency, to govern New York while he was absent in Washington. Basically, this machine was a governing council of approximately half a dozen adroit politicians, operating out of Albany and dispensing patronage and instilling discipline among party regulars.

To someone like Van Buren, who was intellectually committed to the Jeffersonian philosophy of states rights and who was also the political leader of a state involved in the expensive building of the Erie Canal, it is no wonder that he and his "Radical" friends objected to President Adams' call for a national program of internal improvements. But apart from these "philosophic" considerations was Van Buren's own extremely shrewd appraisal of the developing political scene. He knew that the election of 1828 would be limited to Adams and Jackson, and of the two men he certainly preferred Jackson. Not only was the President's policy offensive to the Old Republicans, but Adams himself was devoid of popular appeal and seemingly indifferent to his public image. To many, he was an unattractive, intellectual, hard-nosed Puritan; and while he had enjoyed a distinguished career as minister to the Russian Court, as commissioner who assisted at Ghent in writing the peace treaty that ended the War of 1812, and as Secretary of State under Monroe, he was not the man to attract politicians to his cause. Professional politicians measure the size of a man's coattails. And Van Buren reckoned that Adams had no coattails at all.

Jackson, on the other hand, was obviously popular with the voting masses, as seen in the election results of 1824. Much of his popularity was based on his extraordinarily successful military record. After an interesting but by no means outstanding civilian career as a lawyer, judge, storekeeper, and legislator in Tennessee, where he emigrated from the Carolinas, Jackson took up soldiering just prior to the outbreak of the War of 1812. Elected general of the Tennessee militia he was sent against the Creek Nation in the South and won a tremendous victory that forever crippled Creek power. He then proceeded to New Orleans where he repelled a British invasion and inflicted on the invaders a devastating defeat. It was the greatest victory of the war and gave the American people a sense of national pride they had rarely experienced before. Known to his men as "Old Hickory," Jackson now became the affectionate "Hero of New Orleans" who proved to the world that independence was something the United States had earned and could keep.

In 1818 Jackson added to his reputation by defeating the Seminole Indians and seizing Florida from the Spanish. Though his actions brought a demand by nearly all the members of Monroe's Cabinet to censure him, they eventually led to the purchase of Florida by the United States. This was due mainly to the efforts of John Quincy Adams, the only member of the Cabinet to defend Jackson. Adams convinced the President to stand behind his General and press the Spanish to sell Florida.

Jackson's appearance on the national scene in larger-than-life size was indeed fortuitous. He arrived just as the country was undergoing profound economic and political changes, when a new generation of men was coming forward to seize leadership from an older social and political elite. These men saw in Jackson a symbol of their own ambitions; they also saw in him a living example of the self-made man. Surely if an orphan boy from the backwoods could make good, there was no reason why they too could not aspire to wealth and social status by relying on their own talents to get what they wanted.

Furthermore, this was an age of developing professionalism in all fields — including politics. In the 1820's, men were hard at work perfecting the techniques of winning elections. They built machines to manage the popular vote; they believed in organization; and they were determined to rule. As sharp-nosed professionals, like Van Buren, they were quick to sense the response the General's popularity produced among the "rising" classes of Americans and to realize that association with Jackson might be crucial to their future position in politics, both nationally and locally. Small wonder, then, that Van Buren decided in the winter of 1826–27 to move into the Jackson camp and to bring with him as many of the Old Republicans as he could influence. "If Gen Jackson & his friends will put his election on old party grounds," Van Buren wrote to one Radical, "preserve the old systems, avoid if not condemn the practices of the last campaign we can by adding his personal popularity to the yet remaining force of old party feeling, not only succeed in electing him but our success when achieved will be worth something."

Since Jackson had resigned his Senate seat after his House defeat and was therefore not in Washington, Van Buren went to Vice-President Calhoun, who was now openly allied to the General, and offered him Radical support for the election of Jackson in 1828. Van Buren promised to swing over the Richmond Junto, the Virginia political machine, through his influence with Thomas Ritchie, editor of the Richmond *Enquirer* and a leader of the Junto. He also promised to tour the South and do everything possible to bring the entire Old Republican faction into the new coalition, even to the extent of seeing Crawford and winning his support. During their conversation about this alliance, Calhoun and Van Buren also discussed the possibility of holding a national nominating convention to replace the outmoded caucus system, but nothing definite was decided at this time.

In a subsequent letter to Ritchie, Van Buren clearly stated that his concern for the political scene went further than a single election. He urged the Radicals to join him in this new coalition, not simply to defeat Adams but to achieve "what is of still greater importance, the substantial reorganization of the Old Republican party." He called for a revival of the two-party system and for a renewal of Jefferson's old North-South alliance, between what he termed the "planters of the South and the plain Republicans of the North." For Van Buren, like many other politicians of the day, recognized that the political system of the 1820's had failed to respond to a changing society and that unless something were done right away it might collapse altogether.

Because of the efforts of many men to restructure the system, the election of 1828 witnessed the reemergence of the two-party system in American politics. The Jackson-Calhoun-Van Buren coalition eventually became known as the "Democratic" Republican party, or simply the Democratic party, while the Adams-Clay combination was called the "National" Republican party. With respect to party principles—not that they were much discussed in the campaign of 1828—the Democrats tended, when prodded, to restate the doctrines of Jefferson, particularly those emphasizing the rights of the states and the importance of the ordinary citizen. The National Republicans, on the other hand, affirmed the need for a strong central government in advancing the material well-being of the nation. Although there continued to be personal factions and cliques operating within the system, and while party organization did not advance in every state with equal rapidity, still in 1828 there was the beginning of a genuine, nationally organized, two-party system, a system that came of age in the 1830's.

The work of Calhoun and Van Buren—particularly Van Buren—was essential to the creation of the Democratic party, but it should be remembered that their efforts were efficacious only insofar as Jackson's primacy within the party was acknowledged. This was so obvious that for a long time the new coalition was called simply the "Jackson party." Not until 1832 was "Democratic party" used regularly as a substitute. Indeed, the General by his own actions proved that he regarded himself as the head of the emerging party. After his renomination for the presidency by the Tennessee legislature in October, 1825, he toiled relentlessly for the next three years to win the Presidency. He supervised the establishment and direction of a central committee in Nashville, composed of such loyal friends as John Overton, William B. Lewis, Alfred Balch, and George W. Campbell. They corresponded with other Jackson committees in the different sections of the nation. The General also engaged in an enormous personal correspondence with party leaders in every state; moreover, he directed the activities of a small band of men, such as John Eaton and Major Henry Lee, who travelled about the country eagerly campaigning for him.

In Washington a cadre of congressmen committed to the General started holding regular caucus meetings to map strategy for defeating the National Republicans. Soon a wide channel of communication between Nashville and Washington was opened through an exchange of letters between the leading Jackson congressmen and the Nashville Central Committee. And the Hero himself took great care that the factions merging into his party would have no difficulty in adjusting their principles to his political views. Displaying ever improving qualities of political skill, he exercised extreme caution in defining his position on leading issues. He acknowledged himself a friend of the states but he warned against interpreting his words as hostile "to domestic manufactures or internal works." While he frowned on public works sponsored by the Federal Government, he did think surplus revenues could be distributed to the states to permit them to undertake their own improvements. With respect to the tariff, he placed himself on the side of a "careful Tariff," one that pursued a "middle and just course" — wherever that was. Similarly he did not disclose his strong prejudice against banks and paper money or his highly conservative views about credit and specie. On one point, however, he was emphatic. As President, if elected, he would "purify the Departments" and "reform the Government." He informed Amos Kendall, one of his most important supporters in Kentucky and the editor of the *Argus of Western America,* that all men in office "who are known to have interfered in the election as committeemen, electioneers or otherwise . . . would be unceremoniously removed." Furthermore, he would remove "all men who have been appointed from political considerations or against the will of the people, and all who are incompetent." During the campaign the Jackson newspaper editors assured their readers that the General's political headhunting was in fact a crusade to purge the Federal Government of corruption and privilege.

The importance of party newspapers during this campaign cannot be over-emphasized. The creation of a vast nationwide newspaper system to inform the electorate of political affairs was one of the most important accomplishments of the two parties. On the Democratic side, it was understood that a congressional caucus had agreed to sponsor "a chain of newspaper posts, from the New England States to Louisiana, and branching off through Lexington to the Western States." So rapid was the appearance of these newspapers that Hezekiah Niles, editor of *Niles Weekly Register,* reported that by 1828 there were six hundred newspapers published in the country, fifty of them dailies, one hundred fifty semi-weeklies and four hundred weeklies. The cost of publication for all these papers, approximating one thousand of each, was placed at a half-million dollars a year.

Among Democratic sheets the most influential was the *United States Telegraph* edited by Duff Green. Green, a close friend of Calhoun's, had been brought from St. Louis to run the paper. He turned it into a slashing, hard-hitting, vigorous newspaper whose influence extended to every Democratic organization within the states. Also important were the Richmond *Enquirer,* edited by Thomas Ritchie; the Albany *Argus,* the mouthpiece of the Albany Regency, edited by Edwin Croswell; the *Argus of the West,* edited by Amos Kendall; and the New Hampshire *Patriot,* edited by that state's most energetic organizer Isaac Hill. These newspapers barraged the public with cries against the "corrupt bargain" that had cheated Old Hickory in 1825. At the same time they insisted that "Andrew Jackson is the *candidate of the People,*" the candidate of the ordinary citizen in opposition to the candidate of the aristocracy. Democrats contended that the contest was basically a struggle for "free principles and unbiased suffrage," between the few and the many, the rich and the poor. "The Aristocracy and the Democracy of the country are arrayed against each other," pontificated one New Yorker.

John Quincy Adams, on the other hand, was rapped as the darling of the rich who believed that the will of the majority counted for nothing and that the "few should govern the many." Democrats feigned horror at his "kingly pretensions." As President, they said, he strolled about the White House like a ruling monarch. Nor was Henry Clay any better. He pretended devotion to his "American System," but in the State Department he used fancy English writing paper in all his communications. "O fie, Mr. Clay," mocked Duff Green in the *Telegraph*, "—*English* paper, *English* wax, *English* pen-knives, is this your *American* System?"

In their efforts to capture votes, Democratic newspaper editors even stooped to invoking religious bigotry or national prejudice. They trifled with minority groups by concocting lies about Adams and they intimidated recent immigrants by playing on their fears. For example, the Administration was accused of speaking rudely of the Dutch, "calling them *'the Black Dutch,' 'the Stupid Dutch,' 'the Ignorant Dutch'* and other names equally decorous and civil." At another time immigrants were warned that John Adams, the father of the incumbent, was the "author" of the Alien and Sedition Acts, a series of laws aimed specifically at hobbling an immigrant's progress toward naturalization. To please the Irish and Scotch-Irish it was pointed out that Jackson was "the son of honest Irish parents. . . . That natural interest which all true-hearted Irishmen feel in the fame of one who has so much genuine Irish blood in his veins, has drawn upon the head of that devoted people, the denunciations of the partisans of Messrs. Adams & Clay."

On the religious issue, Duff Green was not loath to accuse John Quincy Adams of anti-Catholicism. "Mr. Adams denounced the Roman Catholics as bigots, worshippers of images, and declared that they did not read their bibles." Or Adams was lambasted as a "Unitarian," which in some parts of the West was as good as calling a man an "atheist." Isaac Hill criticized him in New England for "travelling through Rhode Island and Massachusetts on the Sabbath. . . ." It was bad enough that he desecrated the holy day by touring but it was worse because he was seen "in a ridiculous outfit of a jockey." Jackson, of course, was praised for his firm adherence to the Christian faith and the diligence with which he performed his devotions regularly with his family at a Presbyterian Church. "Does the old man have prayers in his own house," asked Martin Van Buren of a friend visiting the General. "If so, mention it modestly." Isaac Hill was not so discreet in telling his readers about the Hero's religious practices. He assured them that Jackson said prayers "every morning and night, also table prayers."

In addition to creating a large and effective press which poured out all kinds of propaganda to blacken the reputation of the Administration and its friends, the Jacksonians developed and improved techniques for raising money to pay for the campaign. As in most elections, the regular costs incurred in the 1828 campaign were absorbed at the local level. Large contributions were solicited and, in addition, fund raising committees were established in many counties to pay for expenses. Also, delegates to conventions and local meetings were taxed a fixed amount to meet printing costs. One county in Ohio requested each ward within the county to "appoint a fund committee . . . for the purpose of receiving . . . contributions . . . and that the same be paid over to the treasurer of the general committee of the county." Elsewhere, public dinners and banquets were held to defray costs. But one of the most burdensome items—the expense of mailing newspapers and other propaganda —was deftly shifted to the Federal Government through the franking privilege. The cost of mailing, running to the hundreds of thousands, was easily disposed of by Jacksonian congressmen who franked anything and everything that had to go out in the mails. Thomas Ritchie even noted that Democrats were franking wrapping paper which was then distributed to committees to be used as needed. Hezekiah Niles figured that something like $2,250,000 a year was involved in the privilege.

It has been estimated that to win election to the House of Representatives from a western state in 1828 cost somewhere in the neighborhood of three thousand dollars, exclusive of mailing expenses. In the East, especially New York and Pennsylvania, the amount was higher by a thousand dollars or so. Because of the unusual efforts to stir popular interest in the candidates exerted in this campaign, and the resulting expenses connected with these efforts, the cost of a presidential election soared appreciably. Estimating roughly, and including the franking expense in the estimate, it probably cost close to one million dollars to elect Jackson President of the United States.

Campaign costs were high because this was the first presidential election in which the great mass of American people were encouraged to express their preference at the polls. From 1824 to 1828 the number of persons eligible to vote soared because many states removed the last remaining restrictions to the suffrage, mainly property qualifications. Moreover, most states had terminated legislative selection of presidential electors. By 1828, only two states —South Carolina and Delaware—had failed to provide popular selection of electors. With these changes politicians recognized the necessity of changing with the time. They sensed a need to bring the people closer to the Government and its operation, to root the party not simply in sectional alliances or alliances between states or economic interests but in the great mass of the American electorate. In adjusting to a new and essentially more popularistic society they reckoned their political future depended on their ability to bring the national party into a closer relationship with the people. "Our true object," said Duff Green, "is to . . . induce all aspirants for office to look to the people . . . for support." "Contending as we are against wealth & power," wrote one Kentucky politician, "we look for success in numbers."

The necessity of building a party based on numbers forced politicians to concern themselves with convincing the masses to vote the party ticket. What they did was to improve and perfect the committee system which managed the details of a campaign, details such as raising money, providing party propaganda, arranging parades and dinners, and corresponding with committees in other parts of the state and outside the state. A vast number of these committees were set up at all political levels, from the local ward to the state central committee. Normally, the central committee directed the functions of local groups within the state and communicated with central committees in other states for purposes of coordination and cooperation. The extensiveness of these committees can be seen in a report written by one politician to Andrew

Jackson. "I therefore originated," he wrote, "and with the cooperation of half a dozen, intelligent and zealous friends, carryed into full and successful operation last year, a plan, or System of Committees, from a Principle or Central Committee . . . down to Sub Committees into every ward of the Town, and Captains Company in the Country."

Also important in the development of party organization were the state conventions. These conventions were especially useful in generating party discipline and loyalty. They were usually called to name the state ticket and endorse the national candidate. But they were also important in dictating the party line for the campaign. "As party spirit increased more and more," wrote one man, "the necessity of some mode of concentrating the party strength became more and more apparent. . . . An attempt at this was early made . . . by introducing the convention system of nominating candidates."

The directions of the state convention were most effectively carried out by the local ward committees, which, during the 1828 campaign, were frequently called "Hickory Clubs." These clubs were principally concerned with exciting voter interest in the candidates and in getting them to the polls to register their interest. The techniques normally employed to build mass support included rallies, barbecues, town meetings, parades, hickory pole raisings, and street demonstrations. In the 1828 campaign the raising of a hickory pole in the town square was particularly popular with the local ward committees. These ubiquitous monuments appeared "in every village," reported one, "as well as upon the corners of many city streets. . . . Many of these poles were standing as late as 1845, rotten momentoes /sic/ of the delirium of 1828." One "Grand Barbecue" for Jackson held in Baltimore was arranged by Roger B. Taney to climax a celebration commemorating the successful defense of the city against British attack during the War of 1812. "I am told by a gentleman who is employed to erect the fixtures," Jackson was informed, "that three Bullocks are to be roasted, and each man is to wear a Hickory Leaf in his hat by way of designation." At this celebration there was also a parade, the firing of cannons, speeches, and the singing of songs in praise of Old Hickory. These scenes of enthusiasm for the party's candidate supposedly helped to build popular majorities. At least the leading Democratic politicians seemed to think so. "Van Buren has learned you know," said an Administration man, "that the *Hurra Boys* were for Jackson . . . and to my regret they constitute a powerful host."

To encourage the "Hurra Boys" and whip up even greater excitement for Jackson, some politicians even toyed with the idea of bringing the General himself to their meetings, although this clearly violated tradition and ran the risk of provoking resentment. "You *must*, yes I say, you *must* visit us next autumn in person," wrote an Ohio organizer to Jackson. But Old Hickory vetoed all such proposals — all, that is, except one. He chose to accept an invitation of the Louisiana Central Committee to attend a ceremony in New Orleans on January 8, 1828, to commemorate his victory over the British in 1815. Although the celebration was ostensibly "non-political" there were representatives from many state delegations along with a group of leading national Jacksonians. The occasion, widely reported in the press, was "the most stupendous thing of the kind that had ever occurred in the United States," said one man. It served to remind the American people the debt they owed General Jackson. The welcoming ceremony, the speeches, parades, and dinner were unlike anything ever seen before. "The World has never witnessed so glorious, so wonderful a Celebration," exclaimed a participant, "—never has *Gratitude & Patriotism* so happily united, so beautifully blended—& it will form a bright page in American history."

In comparison to the Jackson party, the National Republican party of Adams and Clay was sadly deficient in such essentials as organization and leadership. Only in the matter of program and principles was the party superior. Its goals were relatively clear, straightforward and unambiguous. Supporting the American System, the National Republicans called for a federal program of aid to all partners of the social compact. Such support included public works, the establishment and development of cultural and intellectual institutions, aid to domestic manufactures, and higher tariffs.

But a party needs more than a program and so the labor of erecting a national organization behind Adams fell mainly to Henry Clay. Unfortunately, Adams would do nothing to assist his reelection, not even help his friends in purging the Government of those appointees who actively opposed his Administration. He admitted he had been "reproached" by his supporters "because I will not dismiss, or drop from Executive offices, able and faithful political opponents to provide for my own partisans." Nor would he abandon the candidate's traditional silence, adopt the role of President as party leader, and encourage popular support. A brooding introvert, he reacted coldly to any public display of affection, as though he could hardly care less whether the electorate approved of him or not. "I am a man of reserved, cold, austere and forbidding manners," he wrote in a deadly accurate self description. "My political adversaries say, a gloomy misanthrope, and my personal enemies an unsocial savage. With the knowledge of the actual defects of my character, I have not the pliability to reform it."

Under the circumstances, Clay and other National Republican organizers such as Daniel Webster of Massachusetts worked as best they could to amalgamate a party behind the President which would be responsive to the changing times. They raised money to subsidize a favorable press, recognizing its propaganda value. Said Clay, "The course adopted by the Opposition, in the dissemination of Newspapers and publications against the Administration and supporting presses leaves to its friends no other alternative than that of following their example, so far at least as to circulate information among the people." And, by and large, the National Republicans had an excellent press. In Washington they were supported by the *National Intelligencer* edited by Joseph Gales and William W. Seaton, and the *National Journal* edited by Peter Force. Elsewhere they received the strong backing of the New York *American*, Cincinnati *Gazette*, Virginia *Constitutional Whig*, the Baltimore *Weekly Register*, the Massachusetts *Journal*, and the Missouri *Republican*.

Like the Democrats, the National Republicans held local rallies, county meetings, and state conventions. "Political meetings are continually taking place in the different Towns of the State" [New Jersey] explained one Administration man, "where Resolutions are passed and Delegates appointed to attend at Trenton to fix on the Electoral Ticket." At the conventions central committees and correspondence committees were appointed. In addition, an address to the public was usually written to extol the virtues of Adams and urge his reelection. At several such conventions Richard Rush of Pennyslvania was selected to run with Adams. Rush had had a very respectable diplomatic career, serving as Secretary of State *pro tem* when the Rush-Bagot agreement was signed neutralizing the Canadian border, and as minister to Great Britain when the English first suggested a joint resolution to prohibit foreign influence into Latin America. Although Rush seemed to have the support of most National Republicans, some state conventions left the second slot vacant and simply instructed their electors to vote for that man most acceptable to the majority of Adams men within the state.

Despite the efforts of many politicians to erect a national organization the results were woefully uneven throughout the country. In some states the Adams supporters were exceedingly slow in setting up party machinery, resulting occasionally in no machinery at all. When Clay sent out a detailed paper on the necessity of large committees of vigilance he received an acknowledgement from one state leader that questioned the advisability of such a committee. "It was apprehended by some," the letter read, "that the appoint. of such a comm. would excite the animadversions of our adversaries." No wonder the party suffered from organizational deficiencies in the West and South when such politicians feared to arouse the "animadversions" of the Democrats.

Still, as a party with a specific course of action to offer the people — one united behind a man of proven talent and experience — the National Republicans reckoned they had a fighting chance to win the election, despite weaknesses. For example, in calculating the electoral vote, they believed they had a slight edge over the Democrats. By counting all of New England as reasonably safe for Adams, they began with 51 electoral votes. Then they added Kentucky, Ohio, and Missouri, all won by Clay in 1824, which brought the total to 84. Thus if they could pick up a substantial number of votes from New Jersey, Delaware, and Maryland — all of which were leaning heavily toward Adams — the election could be successfully concluded in New York and Pennsylvania, two states highly susceptible to the tariff argument. Unfortunately, this extremely important and useful issue was lost to the National Republicans by the aggressiveness and astuteness of the Jacksonian leaders in Congress.

When the Twentieth Congress convened in December, 1827, the friends of the General had won control of both houses. The previous fall elections had gone to the Jacksonians largely because of their superior organization.

For their part, the National Republicans were still unable to match their opponents in this vital political sector. "We are in the same disjointed state here as formerly," wrote one Administration man from the middle states, "a great many well wishers . . . but no organization." Out West, an Adams man reported the Democrats as "an organized corps, active and well disciplined," while in the South one of Clay's advisers predicted, the "organization of the other side . . . *will be* stronger than all." All of this was reflected in the fall elections of 1827, resulting in Jacksonian control of Congress. So complete was that control that one senator remarked, "The opposition party constitute in fact the *administration*. Upon it rests the responsibility of all legislative measures."

For the next several months of the session the Democratic leadership in Congress addressed itself to a single difficulty, that of providing electorally important states with substantial reasons for voting for Jackson in 1828. Nothing was more indicative of their efforts at political brokerage than the passage of the Tariff of 1828, more popularly known as the Tariff of Abominations.

One major difficulty respecting protection was the sharp sectional difference it automatically triggered. In the North there was strong demand for increased rates from most manufacturers, but in the South such action was regarded as ruinous. The problem was complicated by the opposition of certain northern commercial groups to the tariff; furthermore, westerners required protection for their raw materials which not all manufacturers approved. Thus, it was a tricky business to put together a tariff schedule that could operate to the credit of the sponsoring party and win electoral votes. The astuteness and cynicism with which the Democrats managed this feat was a remarkable performance of political legerdemain.

What they did was to draw up a bill that laid heavy duties on imported raw materials, particularly hemp, iron, and sail duck. All of these items struck most heavily against New England commercial interests; at the same time they pleased the agrarians in the West. In addition, a duty of ten cents per gallon was levied against molasses, while that on distilled spirits was raised ten cents — again injuring New England by penalizing her distillery industry. In order to attract Pennsylvania's support, a high duty was placed on iron products. But the most important schedules in the bill related to raw wool and woolen products. In effect, the Democrats safeguarded the producers of raw wool, but only offered token protection to the manufacturers of woolen commodities. Thus the tariff was "arranged" to appeal to western voters, particularly those in Kentucky, Ohio, and Missouri, who had voted for Clay in 1824, and secure the favor of the protectionist farmers in New York and Pennsylvania. Only New England distillers, shipbuilders, and woolen manufacturers were discriminated against, for New England was written off as unalterably attached to President Adams. Unfortunately, the high protectionist rates also offended southerners, but the Democratic leadership felt they could afford this offense because the southerners could not retaliate and vote for Adams since the President was regarded as the "acknowledge leader" of all manufacturing interests. Southerners would support Jackson under any circumstance, high tariff or no.

The bill passed the House of Representatives despite strong opposition by New England and southern congressmen. However, in the conservative Senate the opposition had proportionately greater strength, and was prepared to kill the tariff unless altered. To prevent this, the Democratic leadership, in a cynical move, agreed to a single amendment which raised the tax on all woolen manufactures to a 40 per cent ad valorem rate with a 5 per cent increase each year until it reached 50 per cent. This change was just enough to satisfy some New England senators to win their votes and in so doing squeeze the bill through. Now farmers from the middle and western states had protection for their raw materials, Pennsylvania had its duty on iron, and New York the duty on raw wool. Hopefully, they would reciprocate this Democratic generosity by voting the Jackson ticket in 1828. As one senator feared, the tariff was "changed into a machine for manufacturing Presidents, instead of broadcloths, and bed blankets."

Southerners were outraged by the passage of the message and some of them threatened secession if their demands continued to go unheeded. John C. Calhoun returned home and wrote an "Exposition and Protest" which enunciated the doctrine of nullification. It was the Vice-President's argument that a state enjoyed the privilege of voiding a federal statute if that law was deemed injurious to the state. But despite this near-violent reaction the South stayed with Jackson, believing that as President he would redress the wrong and lower the tariff. Even so, a number of southerners loudly criticized the Democratic leadership in Congress for having stooped to deception to get the tariff passed. Senator Littleton W. Tazewell of Virginia supposedly cornered Van Buren one day immediately after the passage of the tariff and said: "Sir, you have deceived me once; that was your fault; but if you deceive me again the fault will be mine."

Regrettably, there was a great deal of deception in this election. There were double-dealing and gutter tactics. Indeed, the election of 1828 was probably the "dirtiest," coarsest, most vulgar election in American history. Jackson, on the one hand, was publicly labeled an adulterer, murderer, and traitor; Adams, on the other, was called a pimp and a gambler. The charges against Jackson had been cited before, but in this election they were given greater publicity and sharpened to a finer political point. The charge most often discussed concerned his marriage to his wife Rachel.

Rachel Donelson Jackson was previously married to Lewis Robards, from whom she separated after a series of bitter quarrels. A neurotically suspicious man, Robards believed he had been cuckolded by Jackson, who, for a time, lived in the same house with Robards and his wife. Whether Jackson was guilty of the charge is impossible to say; in any event Rachel could stand the accusations no longer and fled with Jackson to Natchez, chaperoned by the elderly Colonel John Stark. Later, when the couple heard that Robards had begun legal proceedings to obtain a divorce on the grounds of adultery and desertion, they waited a decent interval and then were married in August, 1791. Unfortunately, at the time of their marriage Robards had not yet received the divorce. All he had was an enabling act from the legislature permitting him to bring suit against his wife in a court of law. Not until September, 1793 did Robards actually go through with his suit and win a divorce. A few months later, on January 17, 1794, Jackson and Rachel married a second time.

In the 1828 campaign, Charles Hammond, editor of the Cincinnati *Gazette* spent a great deal of time "researching" the curious circumstances of the marriage. Then, in lurid detail, he spread the results of his investigation in the pages of his newspaper and did not hesitate to use such words as "bigamist" and "adulterer" to make his points. "Ought a convicted adultress and her paramour husband to be placed in the highest offices of this free and christian land?" he asked. The shocking manner in which Jackson's marriage was described forced the Nashville Central Committee to issue a detailed report on the circumstances of the technical bigamy to explain how it had accidentally occurred. Both Jackson and Rachel were deeply injured by this publicity — and Rachel mortally so, according to her friends, for she died of a heart attack shortly after the election. The General himself believed that Henry Clay was behind the attack, had subsidized Hammond's "research" trip, and supplied him with evidence. This was denied several times by the Clay's allies but Jackson remained unconvinced. Later, when the story was reprinted in the Washington newspapers, he blamed the President for doing nothing to prevent its publication. He felt the Administration could have intervened had it not wanted to take full advantage of the scandal. Jackson never forgot how the newspapers had abused him, and blamed much of the abuse on Clay and Adams.

The depth to which this campaign sunk in repeating or creating stories to vilify the candidates is best exemplified by the indecent assault on Jackson's mother. "General Jackson's mother was a COMMON PROSTITUTE," said one piece, "brought to this country by the British soldiers! She afterwards married a MULATTO MAN, with whom she had several children, of which number GENERAL JACKSON IS ONE!!" It is reported that when the Hero read this story he broke down in tears and his body shook with grief. Seeing his distress, Rachel asked him what was wrong. Jackson pointed to the offending newspaper and said, "Myself I can defend. You I can defend; but now they have assailed even the memory of my mother."

Jackson's reputation as a duelist and gunfighter was also given considerable play in the newspapers. He was maligned as a bully and a ruffian, a street brawler, cockfighter, and gambler. His famous gunfight with the Benton brothers and his duel with Charles Dickinson were narrated in great detail and with much distortion, necessitating a full and "accurate" account of the incidents by the Nashville Central Committee. Also noticed, were the military executions that took place under his command, especially the six militiamen shot during the Creek War in 1813. These men were charged with mutiny, desertion, inducing others to desert, and stealing military supplies. They were tried, found guilty, and executed. But the Administration newspapers in 1828 saw the incident as savage brutality. The men, declared the newspapers, had legally completed their military service and desired to return home. Instead of their being returned home, as was their right, they were murdered by Jackson. John Binns, editor of the Philadelphia *Democratic Press*, printed a handbill to dramatize the incident. The names of the six "victims" were printed at the top, and under each name a picture was drawn of a large, black coffin. Below that came a narrative account of the "murders." The entire handbill was enclosed in a black border. Called the "Coffin Hand Bill," it proved to be a very effective propaganda tool which the National Republicans believed would convince the American people that Jackson was a wild man under whose charge the Government would collapse.

Jackson was also criticized for his involvement in Aaron Burr's western conspiracy. Indeed, the impression was distinctly given that his participation was suspiciously treasonous. It was claimed that he had levied troops for Burr by calling on governors of the several states to supply militiamen. It was documented that he built flat boats for Burr to carry soldiers down the Mississippi River. It was also contended that these soldiers meant to attack New Orleans, and that Jackson was therefore a chief officer in the conspiracy. Finally it was noted that the General testified for Burr at his treason trial despite clear evidence that Burr was guilty of a major crime. Naturally the Democrats vigorously denied the charges and insisted that the first tangible evidence that President Jefferson received about a western conspiracy came from Andrew Jackson. And, inasmuch as Henry Clay had defended Burr concerning his western activities before a grand jury in Kentucky, the Democrats were able to counter any accusation against Jackson in this matter with equally fraudulent accusations against Clay.

The mudslinging that typified this election was not confined to the National Republicans. The Democrats gave as good as they got. One of the nastiest (if not funniest because it is so absurd) stories circulated at the time was the accusation that John Quincy Adams once procured an American girl for the Czar of Russia when he was minister to that country. The charge was certainly untrue, but some men chose to repeat it, adding that the reasons for Adams' fabulous success as a diplomat had at last been uncovered. Adams' wife was also attacked for having indulged in premarital relations with the President, but the charges brought against her in no way compared to those leveled at poor Rachel.

Democrats were especially effective in repeating the charge that Adams was an aristocrat. They accused him of assuming the manner of a monarch, with the White House as his palace. "We disapprove the kingly pomp and splendour that is displayed by the present incumbent," editorialized several newspapers. To prove the charge of "royal extravagances," a report was published that public funds had been expended to equip the East Room with gambling furniture, in particular a billiard table, cues and balls, and a set of expensive chessmen made of ivory. Something like twenty-five thousand dollars was supposedly spent on the gambling equipment, cried the Democrats, an expenditure unheard of in a republican country.

But the most telling accusation against Adams was the "corrupt bargain" charge. This was repeated over and over and no amount of denials by Clay or the National Republicans could hush the story. Even Jackson took to repeating it regularly to the many politicians who visited him at his home in Tennessee. He said he received the details of the notorious deal from "a congressman of high respectability." This congressman turned out to be James Buchanan of Pennsylvania, who, when pressed, was unable to produce substantiating evidence.

Clearly the election of 1828 devolved into a contest of personalities. No real national issue was discussed. It seemed as though politicians believed the people preferred scandalous stories to intelligent debates on the important issues. However, there were two movements that appeared toward the end of the campaign which tried to force a discussion of several important questions. These movements began in New York and Philadelphia and had long-range effects.

In New York there was a sudden release of violence in the western counties of the state as a result of the disappearance and reported death of a man named William Morgan. Morgan was a stonemason who settled in Batavia, New York, and joined the order of Freemasonry. He was not an especially personable man and in time got into a heated quarrel with his fellow Masons. Swearing revenge for the injury he believed he had suffered, Morgan set about writing a book revealing the secrets of the order. He talked David C. Miller, editor of the Batavia *Advocate*, into publishing the manuscript, at the same time refusing to listen to the pleas of other Masons that he abandon his project and destroy the manuscript. Since Morgan was deaf to their entreaties his former friends decided to teach him a lesson. They had him arrested for allegedly stealing a shirt and a tie, seized the page proofs of his book, and set fire to Miller's establishment.

But Morgan was a stubborn man and not easily intimidated. The charge against him was not sustained, so he was released. Since Morgan had every intention of pursuing his project he was rearrested almost immediately after his release for a debt owed to another Mason. Then someone paid his bail. As Morgan emerged from the jail he was seized, hustled into an awaiting carriage, and taken to Fort Niagara, where, according to one account, he was held captive for several days and then drowned in the Niagara River. However the only source which attempts to account for Morgan's death is open to some doubt, so it will probably never be known what really happened to him, or how and when he met his death.

Even so, there was no question that Morgan had disappeared, and to most New Yorkers the Masons were guilty of a ghastly crime. Within weeks, the western counties of the state were ablaze with demands to apprehend the kidnappers and obliterate the Masonic Order. Westerners convinced themselves that the fraternity was a conspiracy against ordinary citizens. It was an elitist group, made up of aristocrats, they said, to control everything—the government, the courts, and business. If anyone opposed them, like poor Morgan, they did not hesitate to exterminate him.

Sensing the dimension of this outburst, the governor of the state, De Witt Clinton, ordered an investigation of Morgan's disappearance. Soon there were public meetings calling for the dismissal of every appointed Mason in office and the defeat of those who held their positions at the hands of the electorate. As one man, a judge of the court of appeals, said: "Believing that the shocking oaths, which the members of the Masonic fraternity took, on entering it, were subversive of good order, impediments in administering justice and enforcing execution of the laws, and also encouraged and even enjoined the commission of murder, I became an anti-Mason, and did what I could to put an end to Masonry in this country." Because the Masons denied equal opportunity to other citizens, the order had to be eliminated, said its attackers. New Yorkers seemed willing—nay anxious—to use their vote to rid society of this "aristocratic" institution. All of which said something about the desire of most people in 1828 to remove any obstacle which seemed to militate against the equality of all.

Not long after the disappearance a body was washed up on the shores of Lake Ontario. Morgan's widow inspected the remains and to her horror she recognized her late husband because of the "double teeth all around." However, several more bodies were later fished out of the lake—usual around election time—and all were identified as the decomposed Mr. Morgan. "Some dead body is always dug up and examined," complained one man, "two or three times, in order to excite into activity all the old prejudices against the masons and masonry."

While it is very difficult to understand the sudden and explosive outbreak of anti-masonry, it would appear that it was partially caused by the "disturbed and unsettled state of the public mind" during a period of rapid economic and political transition. It was a spontaneous release of violence in which deep pyschological and perhaps religious forces were at work. Most of the initial "infection" was concentrated in the western parts of the state where Bible-oriented, pious Yankees had recently moved from New England. Perhaps their unsettled state and their deep commitment to the Puritan ethic had something to do with the severity of the explosion.

In any event, it did not take long for sharp-eyed politicians to see an opportunity to direct this agitation, particularly since it seemed naturally bent on entering the political arena. Thurlow Weed, for example, took advantage of the movement and established the Anti-Masonic *Enquirer* in Rochester and soon had the assistance of an able young lawyer by the name of William H. Seward. These and other men began to direct the emerging state party by calling a convention and nominating candidates for state offices, including the gubernatorial office. Since Andrew Jackson was a Mason of very high rank, Weed tried to move the new party into the Adams camp, particularly since the President had categorically denied any association with Freemasonry. "I state that I am not, never was, and never shall be a freemason," wrote Adams. However, some of the political advantage of the President's disclaimer was lost because his Secretary of State, Henry Clay, was known to be a high-ranking Mason.

As the Anti-Masonic party expanded it soon spilled over the borders into neighboring states; and as it grew it turned more and more toward demanding freedom of opportunity for the individual and the elimination of all institutions and practices which impeded, threatened, or denied that freedom.

Another movement advocating wide social reforms that began during the campaign of 1828 centered around the demands of the laboring man. The Mechanics Union of Trade Associations founded in Philadelphia in 1827 and the Workingmen's party which appeared late in 1828 in that city were two expressions of this important new movement. These organizations consisted of a wide range of social and professional classes, from laborers, physicians, intellectuals, and merchants to speculators, lawyers, and politicians. One of their most insistent demands called for the restriction of the power of the state legislature to create corporations by special charter. Such action, in the minds of these Workingmen, tended to concentrate the "wealth producing powers of modern mechanism" in the hands of a few and thereby injure the small businessman who could not compete under this increasingly monopolistic system. The Workingmen were particularly concerned about the granting of bank charters. As hard money men (as most of them were) they objected to the bank-issued paper currency whose value was frequently unstable. Moreover, banks were less willing to lend money to small capitalists because of high risk; yet it was the small businessman who was most in need of financial support.

In addition, the Workingmen urged the passage of mechanics lien laws which would force employers who went bankrupt to recognize the legitimate claims of workers, just as they did other creditors, and pay them a portion of their wages out of whatever funds were available. They also demanded laws to prevent employers from declaring themselves bankrupt in order to avoid paying workers' salaries. Furthermore, the mechanics were most forceful in urging the abolition of imprisonment for debt. They argued rather logically that it helped no one to imprison a debtor and thereby keep him from earning the money he needed to pay his debt. The practice hurt both debtor and creditor. Besides, the practice was seen as having its cruelest impact on the poor and served to lock them in a perpetual state of poverty.

The Workingmen also advocated improvements in general education in order that their children might acquire a free, public education without the parents having to humiliate themselves by openly acknowledging their indigence. The improvement and expansion of public education was just beginning in the United States at this time, and it would take several more decades before free education was generally available at both the primary and secondary levels. Moreover, the mechanics urged the reform of the auction and lottery systems and an end to the issuance by banks of large amounts of paper money. They also opposed the "excessive distillation of liquor."

While the Workingmen's movement attracted considerable support from middle-class capitalists, it did include a bona fide labor group contending for the interests of the wage earner. Late in 1828 the movement developed into a political party in Philadelphia and soon spread to other large cities, most notably New York, Boston, and Baltimore. Although more a local phenomena than a unified national movement, the party was most effective in urging social and economic reform during the Jacksonian era. Whenever necessary to gain approval for its reforms, the Workingmen's party shifted its support within the states from the Democrats to the National Republicans, crossing political lines at will.

In Philadelphia in 1828 all the candidates of the Workingmen's party who also ran on the Jackson ticket were elected. Indeed, the Democrats proved quite strong in many cities, not simply Philadelphia. Of course they had an extremely popular figure as their candidate. But they also had an energetic and aggressive party machine that knew how to go after the popular vote. However, the organization was not evenly developed in all the states. Such states as New York, Pennsylvania, New Hampshire, Virginia, North Carolina, Ohio, Kentucky, and Indiana had the most effective organizations. Many others had already made notable starts in erecting the party apparatus. All were exhorted to turn out the vote and see to it that those "who can get to the polls, shall go there, and vote /for Jackson/." One southern politician described the extent of party activity to get the masses to the polls. "Considerable pains were taken to bring out the people," he said; "flags were made and sent to different parts of the country, and the people came in in companies of fifty or sixty with the flag flying at their head, with the words, 'Jackson and Reform' on it in large letters." In the *Telegraph*, Duff Green pleaded for a massive turnout. "To the polls," he cried. "To the Polls! The faithful sentinel must not sleep — Let no one stay home — Let every man go to the Polls — Let not a vote be lost — Let every Freeman do his duty; and all will triumph in the success of

JACKSON, CALHOUN AND LIBERTY."

Balloting in the election extended from September to November. In most states, voting occurred over a period of several days. The states did not provide an official ballot; instead, the parties printed their own ballots, distributing them to friends and employing high-pressure party hacks at the polls to get the voter to accept the ticket. It was not unusual for a person to be accosted by several hawkers at once and threatened with bodily harm unless he accepted the proffered ballot.

The procedures for voting varied considerably throughout the twenty-four states. Delaware and South Carolina were the only states whose legislatures chose the electors. In all other states, they were chosen from a general or district ticket by an electorate that was roughly equivalent — except in Louisiana, Virginia, and Rhode Island — to the adult, white male population. Maryland, Maine, Illinois, Tennessee, and New York were the states using the district system, which meant that their electoral votes could be split between the candidates on a proportional basis. In all other states where the general ticket was employed, the candidate with the highest popular vote received all the electoral votes. Only Rhode Island and Virginia continued to restrict suffrage with property qualifications, and Louisiana maintained tax payments as a voting requirement.

When the election ended and the ballots were counted, it was clear that Jackson had won a stupendous victory. Out of a total of 1,155,022 popular votes cast, John Quincy Adams received 507,730; Andrew Jackson won 647,292 or just a little better than 56 per cent of the entire vote. This was an extraordinary achievement by Jackson, a veritable landslide. In percentages it was unequalled in any presidential election during the nineteenth century. And his total represented substantial support from all sections of the country, including New England.

The total popular vote in the election represented an increase of nearly eight hundred thousand over the previous election in 1824. In Pennsylvania alone, the number rose from forty-seven thousand to 152,000 four years later. There were several reasons for this spectacular rise. In the first place, the two-party system had been reestablished, if unevenly, and where in 1824 there were several candidates running for the Presidency there were only two in 1828. Second, there was considerable interest in the election generated to a large extent by an exciting, if not scurrilous, campaign initiated by both the Democratic and National Republican parties. Third, there was a concerted effort on the part of many politicians to get out the vote at election time; and finally, four states, representing a considerable electorate, changed their laws and transferred the selection of electors from the legislature to the people.

In the Electoral College, Jackson's victory was even more impressive. He won a total of 178 electoral votes to 83 for Adams. He swept everything south of the Potomac River and west of New Jersey. Adams carried New England (except for a single electoral vote in Maine), Delaware, New Jersey, and most of Maryland. Adams and Jackson shared New York, with the General taking 20 of the state's 36 electoral votes. All the remaining states went to Old Hickory. The election was relatively close in New Hampshire, New York, New Jersey, Maryland, Kentucky, Louisiana, Ohio, and Indiana. In the final analysis, what made the difference in virtually every one of these states was superior party organization.

In the Vice-Presidential race, Calhoun won an easy reelection over Richard Rush, but received 7 fewer electoral votes than Jackson, because Georgia, which resented Calhoun's treatment of William H. Crawford when they sat in Monroe's Cabinet together, awarded 7 votes to Senator William C. Smith of South Carolina.

Aside from the importance of party in producing Jackson's triumph there was also his own popularity and charisma. He was a living, authentic legend, the victor of New Orleans, the man who won over the British the greatest feat of arms in American history. Moreover, there was a dignity and bearing about him that bespoke leadership and authority. He was "presidential-looking," more so than any other public figure of the day. He inspired confidence among the largest mass of voters despite his lack of education and his reputation as an untamed westerner. In that sense Jackson himself was the essential issue in the campaign, just as he would be again in 1832, and the people in "vast numbers" crowded to his side.

Recently, however, some historians have questioned the vastness of the 1828 victory. Comparing the statistics of this election with previous state elections and future presidential elections, one historian has raised serious doubts as to whether the people poured out to the polls to express their confidence in Jackson. Perhaps it is possible to make meaningful comparisons between a presidential election and a state election for local officers held at different times or two presidential elections separated by a dozen or more years. And perhaps not. But in any event the fact remains that no matter how the statistics are analyzed or interpreted the people themselves who lived at the time believed that Jackson's election represented a great surge of popular support for the General. They believed that the ordinary citizen, the so-called "common man," who were farmers, workers, frontiersmen, and the like, had seized the opportunity to express their political opinion by voting for Jackson. And what is believed by the electorate is frequently more important than the objective reality. Many Democratic politicians, of course, saw the contest as one between "farmers & mechanics of the country" on one hand and the "rich and well born" on the other, "between the *aristocracy* and democracy of America." Thus when they read the returns from such states as Pennsylvania, Virginia, North Carolina, Ohio, and elsewhere they were astounded by the figures and therefore convinced of the truth of their own propaganda.

Not only did the Democrats see the election as a victory produced by the "vast numbers" of American people, but the National Republicans thought so too. That is what is even more astonishing. "Well," sighed one of them, "a great revolution has taken place. . . . This is what I all along feared but to a much greater extent." "It was the howl of raving Democracy," wrote another, "that tiped /sic/ Pennsylvania & New York & Ohio—and this will be kept up here after to promote the ends of the /Democratic party./" "All our efforts," said one of Clay's friends, "have not withstood the Torrent." Hezekiah Niles in his newspaper credited Jackson's "triumphant victory" to the "ardor of thousands." And Edward Everett of Massachusetts, one of Adams' most dedicated supporters in Congress, explained to his brother that the General won "by a majority of more than *two* to *one*, an event astounding to the friends of the Administration and unexpected by the General himself and his friends. . . . /They/ are embarrassed with the vastness of their triumph and the numbers of their party."

Generations of historians, therefore, have interpreted Jackson's election in 1828 as the beginning of the "rise of the common man" in American history. Of course, such an easy and sweeping generalization does not take into consideration the fact that the "common man" had been rising for generations, and had made notable political advances long before Jackson appeared on the scene. Yet this election seemed to symbolize the people's arrival to political responsibility. Whether or not this was objectively true hardly mattered; what mattered was an expressed sense of participation in the electoral process experienced by ordinary citizens and that because of it a true "man of the people" had at last been elected President of the United States.

The notion of a popular "uprising" in Jackson's favor was strengthened by the scenes that occurred during his inauguration as President on March 4, 1829. Some twenty thousand people from all parts of the country converged on Washington to witness the triumph of their candidate. It was "like the inundation of the northern barbarians into Rome," wrote one, "save that the tumultuous tide came in from a different point of the compass." Daniel Webster was dumbfounded at the scene. "I never saw such a crowd here before," he said. "Persons have come five hundred miles to see General Jackson, *and they really seem to think that the country is rescued from some dreadful danger."*

The ceremony itself was staged out-of-doors and the people massed themselves in front of the Capitol to see for themselves the "inauguration of popular government." The press of the crowd was so great that a ship's cable had to be stretched about two-thirds of the way up the flight of stairs leading to the portico. "Never can I forget the spectacle which presented itself on every side," said one observer, "nor the electrifying moment when the eager, expectant eyes of that vast and motley multitude caught sight of the tall and imposing form of their adored leader, as he came forth between the columns of the portico." As Jackson appeared, the mob began to scream and shout, and shake the very ground beneath them. Then, "as if by magic," the "color of the whole mass changed. . . all hats were off at once, and the dark tint which usually pervades a mixed map of men was turned. . . into the bright hue of ten thousand upturned and exultant human faces, radiant with sudden joy."

When the ceremony ended, the throng rushed through the streets and avenues to get to the White House, where a reception was scheduled to permit the people to meet their new President. But what was planned as a function of proper decorum turned into a wild mêlée. The mob poured through the White House looking for Jackson and the refreshments that had been promised them. They were "scrambling, fighting, romping" from one room to the next. "The President," wrote Mrs. Samuel H. Smith, "after having been *literally* nearly pressed to death & almost suffocated & torn to pieces by the people in their eagerness to shake hands with Old Hickory, had retreated through the back way or south front & had escaped to his lodgings at Gadsby's." It was a "regular Saturnalia," said one congressman who watched the scene. The mob "broke in, in thousands. . . in one uninterrupted stream of mud and filth." The danger to the White House—to say nothing of life and limb—grew so great that the liquor was taken outside to the garden to draw the crowd from the house. Men jumped through the windows in their haste to reach the alcohol, thus instantly easing the pressure inside the mansion. So began the Administration of the "people's President," an Administration baptized by the screams and shouts of a wildly enthusiastic public.

The election of 1828 was in some respects the first modern presidential election. Democrats launched a national campaign of song, slogan, and shouting to attract the largest possible number of votes. It was the first campaign which witnessed a concerted effort to manipulate the electorate on a mass scale. Hereafter the major parties sought presidential candidates with wide popular appeal — frequently war heroes — then backed them with an engine of ballyhoo in order to create the numbers which would provide success. In the 1828 election, barbecues, parades, tree plantings, and the like were extensively used as part of the popular entertainment. Such techniques had been employed in previous elections but not on such a lavish scale. When they proved so effective by virtue of Jackson's extraordinary victory they became standard techniques in subsequent elections, receiving their biggest display in 1840.

But Jackson's impressive showing was not so much the result of the campaign ballyhoo as it was the organization that provided it, plus the General's widespread popularity based on his military exploits. The organization in time became an elaborate party machine through which the ordinary citizen could control the operation of Government and shape public policy. But the major importance of Jackson's election was the conscious and concerted effort of many politicians to organize an effective popular majority. In the process, the two-party system slowly reemerged after a hiatus of nearly sixteen years. So ended the political disorder of the Era of Good Feelings. A new party system had begun.

Appendix

Editorials from the *National Intelligencer*
March-April, 1827

Nothing was more influential in the 1828 election of Andrew Jackson than the structuring of a national party by such professional politicians as Martin Van Buren. The National Intelligencer, *a Washington newspaper, noticed Van Buren's activity and tried to alert the electorate to what was going on. The series, eleven articles in all, appeared during March and April, 1827, and was headed "Signs of the Times." The most interesting and important sections from the editorials are reproduced herewith.*

March 7, 1827

It is known, we believe, to our readers, that we have never accorded in the doctrine, that party spirit, in a free Government, is dangerous to the public interest. It has always been our opinion, on the contrary, that the existence of party spirit, to a certain extent, is greatly to be preferred to the calm of despotism, whether that despotism be one of opinion or of physical strength. An opposition to the measures of a Government, when founded upon principle, is entitled to respect and consideration, even from the Administration to which it is opposed. When founded upon different principles, or rather upon no principle at all, but that of a combination to obtain possession of the offices and patronage of a Government, it is still useful; because it induces caution, and a regard for public opinion, on the part of those who administer the Government, which cannot fail to serve and protect the public interest. We must have good reasons, however, before *we* engage in an opposition to an existing Administration, of the nature first above stated, and we never will, under any circumstances, engage in one of the nature last described.

With respect to the present Administration of the Government, it will be remembered by all who read this Journal, that, at the time of its induction to office; on its subsequent organization; and at a later date, we have expressed our conviction that the election of the President had been honestly made, and that the President had acted wisely, and with exclusive regard to the public interest, and to the circumstances of his election, in the appointment of the Officers, who preside over the different Departments of the Government, and represent our country abroad. More recently, we have had occasion to say, that, judging the Administration by its measures, we believed, for any thing that we could see, that the election of President by the House of Representatives resulted beneficially to the country, there being more to approve than to disapprove in the measures of this Government. We have yet seen nothing to change this opinion. "Unwarped by party rage," or even by personal attach-ments; wholly unconnected with the executive Administration of the General Government: free from any engagement, understanding, or alliance, with any party, or party men, this is the unbiassed dictate of our deliberate judgment.

This sentiment, such as we have heretofore expressed it, we now repeat, with entire deference to the opinions of others. We have not sought to seduce others to our opinions: still less have we denounced those who have come to different conclusions, or acted upon different principles, from us.

Recent circumstances, however, have disclosed the existence of an organ-ized Opposition to the present Administration, the object of which is to put it down, right or wrong. The first open application of this principle having been made, contemporaneously with its avowal, to us personally, occasioned us no little surprise. It is with pain, indeed, we find ourselves obliged to direct the attention of our readers to some features of the scheme, by which the Machia-velian priniciples of a very few individuals are sought to be made the rule of action for a great People—of the scheme, in the prosecution of which, public utility, faithful services, and acknowledged integrity, are to be sacrificed to the Moloch of party—of the scheme, by the successful operation of which this Administration is, in the language of a highly respectable member of the party, to be "put down, though it be as pure as the Angels which stand at the right hand of the throne of God! . . ."

With these preliminary remarks, we invite the attention of our readers to the vote, in the Senate of the United States, on Thursday last, for a Printer to that body. The occasion was in itself an unimportant one, wholly unworthy of special notice, and to which we certainly should never have invited the atten-tion of our readers, but for the organization which it for the first time dis-closed, and for the principles openly avowed on that occasion by the Honora-ble Martin Van Buren, an eminent Senator from the State of New York, who has earned the distinction of being brought into this bold relief, by presenting himself, on that day, as the spokesman of the party of which we shall take the freedom to consider him the head and representative, if he be not both its par-ent and its guardian. Of that Senator, we should be the last to speak with per-sonal disrespect. With talents enough to be a great man, he has the manners of a gentleman, and an enviable private character. It is only of his political prin-ciples, his notions of party discipline, and the manner in which he has brought them both to bear upon the present state of public affairs, that we mean to speak.

On the occasion to which we have already referred, Mr. Van Buren made the following remarks, which were carefully noted down by our Reporter, and will not be denied or retracted:

"He had long been of opinion (he said) that the public interest might be promoted, *the condition of the Press, as well here as throughout the country, improved,* and respect for the Senate, and accuracy in the publication of the Proceedings of the Senate, better secured, by a judicious revision of the laws relative to the public printing at large." "At a more convenient season, he hoped the subject would be revised, and he promised himself the best results from such provision as the nature of the subject was susceptible of."

Now, to "the revision of the laws," &c. we have not the slightest possible objection; nor do we care how the Senate shall think proper to have its printing done for the future, so it be decently done. It is to the *avowed object* of this proposed revision, that we take exception. We throw out of view the "accuracy in the publication of the Proceedings," as a motive for the proposed revision, because every one, who knows any thing about it, knows that this suggestion is thrown in to make up light weight: we pass by also the "respect for the Senate," in which every man of sense knows, and every man of candor will acknowledge, we have never been in any manner deficient: and, leaving such arguments to those who can swallow them, we enter our protest against the doctrine embraced in the other part of his remarks, that the *condition of the Press* is to be regulated, not only here, but throughout the United States," by any vote of the Senate, or by any legislation of both Houses of Congress combined. We protest against this revival of the odious principle of the old Sedition Law, vz: the right of a party to protect itself by or from the Press through the agency of legislation by Congress. . . .

The honorable Senator ought to be well aware of the utter futility of all attempts to *organize* the public press. Its conductors are made of sterner stuff than to be brought down upon their knees with one accord, to worship any idol of party which he may choose to set up. There are a thousand of these individuals, many of whom would not only part with the paltry profit flowing from party patronage, but even with liberty, or life itself, sooner than with the right of private judgment, of which *his* notion of party discipline requires the absolute surrender. Nor can the press be chastised, any more than it can be bought or sold. The idea of thus operating upon the press cannot live in the pure atmosphere of public opinion, however it may be cherished by passion or prejudice. Much may be effected, we know, in regard to the press, by party organization within the limits of a single State: we have seen examples of that, as we have recently of the effect of similar organization in the particular department of the Government to which the honorable Senator belongs. But, in the nation, such consentaneousness of sentiment and language can have no duration, either among the conductors of the press, or the body of the People, independently of reason and conviction. Public opinion turns upon and *resists* every attempt to dragoon it. It *resents* every attempt, by an organized party, to bend the press by bribery to its selfish purposes. Of the first of these operations, we have seen an example in the case of the old sedition law: of the other, we shall see it again whenever Mr. Van Buren succeeds in his notable project of *improving* the condition of the press "throughout the country," by means of the Public Printing, whether it be bestowed as a boon for obsequiousness, or taken away as a punishment for independence and integrity of conduct.

The observations of Mr. Van Buren would not have been considered entitled to the consequence we have given to them, in these few remarks, but for the vote by which they were followed up and sustained, which exhibited an organized strength of two and twenty votes in favor of a measure, which, we say without reserve or hesitation, we do not believe the *reason* of a single individual of the whole number approved. Not desiring to be thought to speak disrespectfully of any of these gentlemen, we must explain that we confine our application of the word "reason" to the merits of the thing actually to be disposed of, viz: the printing of the Senate. In a political or party sense, it is true, we *can* conceive how some gentlemen should think it very reasonable to give consequence, by their votes, to a print established here to rail at the Administration, right or wrong, and which must be admitted to have been true to its vocation. But even in that sense, it was lamentable to see such men as our old friend Dickerson, the incorruptible Macon and Smith of South Carolina, Benton, of capacious mind, the Chandler, of blunt honesty, not to speak of others, ranging themselves under the standard of a new cabalistical party organization, the first object of which, when brought to a head, was to "improve the condition of the press" by proscribing *the National Intelligencer*, and identifying the Senate of the United States with *the Telegraph!* The intention might have been disclaimed, had not the vote been preceded by the observations of Mr. Van Buren. They gave to that vote its true character, and to Mr. Van Buren's remark its right interpretation. The force of party could no further go. Ancient connections, recent associations, personal attachments, all melted into thin air before the wand of the great magician! It is really a lamentable subject of contemplation. For their own sakes, it grieved us to see such men yielding all the inclinations of their hearts, along with the convictions of their reason, to the grand political scheme, by which the vote of New York is to be secured to the newly organized party, and, as the price of it, Mr. Van Buren is to be—any thing he pleases. This, of course, the reader will be good enough to understand to be our opinion, but, for that opinion we shall, another day, give what appear to us to be very substantial reasons.

To Mr. Van Buren's elevation to higher office than he now holds, on proper principles, we should have had no objection. In the last Presidential Election he acted throughout with firmness and consistency: we should have been very willing to have seen him elected Vice President at that time, and would, indeed, if we could, have promoted his elevation to the honorable station now occupied by his friend and successful competitor. Mr. Calhoun. But when he comes forward with the Shibboleth of a new party in his mouth, the first utterance of which is to strike at the independence of the press, we must be excused if we treat him, as he has treated us, downrightly, and without knowing or caring how our exposition may affect his feelings or his ambitious projects.

Let no one suppose, that our views of his projects, and those of the small party which he is endeavoring, with practised art, to form into a large one, are founded on the single incident in the Senate, plainly as that speaks. We have other and much higher matter to place before our readers hereafter. But this exposition, which has been forced upon us by considerations not to be disregarded without a sacrifice of every political principle we have ever professed, involves too much matter to be disposed of at a single sitting.

March 12, 1827

Of Caucuses, pretending to *an authority* over public sentiment we have never been either the advocates or defenders. As a mode of setting forth the opinions of those who assemble to consult, we have supposed caucus recommendations of persons for high public stations unobjectionable, on the score of principle. We believe that opinions, expressed by such assemblies, are entitled to all the respect that is due to the characters and standing of those by whom they are expressed, and to no more or higher respect. In this light, we highly approved the open and frank nomination of Mr. Crawford and Mr. Gallatin, for the Presidency and Vice Presidency, previous to the last election, as one of the most honorable and virtuous acts of public duty ever performed by an assembly of individuals. Considered in this aspect, a Caucus is but another term for a Public Meeting, whose proceedings are of greater or less authority, according to the character and standing of those who compose it.

To the principle of Caucus recommendations or resolutions, intended *to control majorities* by the force of political combinations, we are, and ever have been, decidedly averse. There is a species of Caucus, however, which we regard in a much more serious light than even those last mentioned.

We refer to that description of Caucus which is held, whether at stated times or periodically, to determine the fate of great public concerns, not upon their merits, but upon other principles; which is composed of persons self-appointed, of whom some individual must always be "the master-spirit," to give impulse and direction to the whole; which is held under the cover of night, and obligations of secrecy; whose fist is felt before it is revealed; whose influence is visible at noon-day, without any one being able to tell whence it cometh, or whither it goeth. . . . Intrigues are on foot to place the election of President and Vice President of the United States within the control of a Central Junta in Washington, of which Mr. Van Buren's happy genius is the ascendant influence—of a Junta whose plan has been deliberately concerted, during the past Winter, for the Summer campaign. In pursuance of this plan, we find ground broken in the State of New York, where most is to be effected, and where success is most important. The whole scheme is founded on the presumption that the vote of New York is at the disposal of Mr. Van Buren: and the object of these labored productions is to prevent any "committals" at Albany, where the Legislature is now in session, which may stand in the way of this hopeful speculation.

March 29, 1827

The "organization" of a party opposed to the present Executive Administration, right or wrong, has been admitted, by the confidential organs of that party, so far as regards the Senate of the United States—not in terms, but in effect. *Admitted*, did we say? It has been *exulted in* by the most influential of those prints, at the same time that, failing in that object at the last session, a similar organization is predicted in *the other branch* of the Legislature at the next session. The Ohio Republican, of the 13th, holds the following language on the occasion of the vote in the Senate for a Printer to that body: "This appointment, *we* "*are informed*, tested the force and influence of "the Administration." "We had previously "been *informed*, that no measure *could be carried* "through the Senate without the aid of the 'factious opposition.'" The

Richmond Enquirer, it has been seen, was *informed* by its correspondents in Congress exactly to the same effect. Confident of their strength, they took pains to make it known to those who were co-laborers with them: and they determined to "punish" those who would not labor along with them. So at least says the Charleston Mercury, always the true barometer of the feelings of that party, and particularly sensitive as well as exact at the present moment, for a reason we need hardly mention. It was in that print, even before the inauguration of Mr. Adams as President, that it was predicted, from Washington, that a determination already existed to "hurl Artaxerxes from his throne," referring, by this figure of speech, to the President and the old armchair in his study. Since the visitation of Mr. Van Buren and his illustrious friends, to Charleston, the same print has been fired with fresh zeal in its vocation. . . .

April 10, 1827

We have had occasion already to notice, as one of the "Signs of the Times," the extraordinary conjunction of interest and purpose between certain persons at Richmond, and certain persons at Albany, as indicated by the cooing and billing of the Enquirer representing the one party, and the Argus representing the other.

A still more remarkable conjunction, however, is that which has apparently been effected between the heretofore rival stars of the hemisphere of New York — Governor Clinton and Mr. Van Buren. The extent of that conjunction we cannot pretend to describe; nor can we say whether the approximation has been on the part of the former or the latter; whether it is accidental or concerted; whether it be personal or merely political; or whether it be for permanent or temporary purposes. We should have doubted the reality of this combination of rival powers, against the existing Administration of the General Government, if the assertion, by the organ of "the concentration here," of the concurrence of Governor Clinton in Mr. Van Buren's projects, had not been silently submitted to by the prints friendly to Governor C. in the State of New York. We should have doubted it, because, within the State of New York, we have considered them irreconcileably hostile to each other's pretensions, individually and politically. The effect, however, of a common antipathy, is very powerful. We have seen it illustrated in the Senate of the United States, where those are ranged side by side against the Administration (and against every one suspected of not being hostile to it) who agree upon scarcely any one point of either constitutional interpretation or of national policy. What identity of feeling or principle, for example, can there be between Col. Hayne, of South Carolina, and Mr. Randolph, of Virginia — the one the advocate of Internal Improvement; of a liberal bankrupt law; the patron of the Navy; the friend of the Army — the other, hostile to every one of these objects? Equally singular would be the alliance between the rival leaders of the State of New York, in any political contest. . . .

But it is to the case of Mr. Van Buren, particularly, that we desire to direct the attention of our readers, and even his own attention, should he find our crude suggestions worth the reading. In his Speech at the Charleston Dinner,* an account of which is copied on the preceding page, Mr. Van Buren, associated by a complimentary toast with State Sovereignty, (a very indefinite idea, as it is expressed, but the intention of which may be guessed at,) acknowledges the application of the sentiment to his present opinions. The festive board, he said, was not the place for political essays. [If he had been allowed to follow the bent of his inclination, instead of the example of the talented gentleman who preceded him, we should have had some rare "Signs of the Times." Our word for it, he would have denounced the National Intelligencer at the dinner table, as he had before done at the councilboard.] But, though not the place for political essays, Mr. Van Buren contrived to make one, sufficiently significant, and quite adapted to the meridian of South Carolina, where, we are told, "construction construed" is becoming so popular, that, for any thing we know, we shall have the Legislature of that State, ahead even of Virginia, voting the forts in Charleston harbor to be unconstitutional, and the light houses in the bays and rivers to be gross usurpations upon State Rights. It has even been whispered that the present Governor of the State is infected with a horror of the General Government, and was elected partly on that ground—a thing that we will not believe upon any authority short of his own oral testimony : for we well remember the time, fifteen years ago, when he, in one House of Congress, contemporaneously with Mr. Crawford in the other, ridiculed all such straight-laced notions of the Constitution as are now coming in vogue. We should be sorry to hear him confirm what has been told to us, because, if wrong, his errors not being political, or the result of cool calculation, but conscientious, the fact would show that the prevailing disease is deeper rooted in the body politic than we wish to believe.

In Mr. Senator Van Buren's letter, of recent date, to the Senate of the State of New York, to which we have heretofore had occasion to allude, he says: "and to justify their confidence, it shall be my constant and zealous endeavor to protect the *remaining* rights reserved to the States by the Federal Constitution; to *restore* those of which they have been divested by construction," &c.

In the same spirit in which he delivered himself at the Charleston dinner, he alleges that the States have been deprived of some of their rights, and that their restoration, and the preservation of what is left, shall be his constant and zealous endeavor. This is a serious charge, and such as no one ought to make on light grounds. It is to be regretted that it has not been conveyed in more specific terms.

April 19, 1827

Recurring to the proposition with which we set out, that the existence of parties is not in itself an evil, we are of the belief that there is a description of party to which a man may attach himself, to which we never will belong. We mean a party merely *personal*, whether in reference to its aversion to a man, or set of men, or to the aggrandizement of those who form and lead the party.

That there were individuals who entertained sufficient hostility to the Administration, and particularly to Mr. Adams and Mr. Clay, to be willing to fall into the ranks of such a party, if not to place themselves at the head of it, we had long known. We had seen it promulged through the Charleston Mercury, by letters from this City, which the Editor of that print will not deny to have been written by distinguished public men, immediately after the choice of Mr. Adams by the House of Representatives, that, whatever might be the measures of the President, he should be hurled from his seat, at the end of four years.

Here and there, we saw and heard, in the following Summer, indications of the existence of a similar sentiment in other individuals and public prints. During the first session of the last Congress, being the first after the induction of Mr. Adams to the Presidency, instances were familiarly addressed to us by personal friends, that we should go with them in opposition to this Administration: to which our answer was, usually, that we saw nothing in the course of the Administration to oppose; that this Administration appeared to be steadily following the policy of preceding Administrations, which had been almost unanimously approved by the People; and we did not see how we could reconcile it to consistency or propriety, to oppose a system of policy which we had always decidedly approved — and, further, that, in his appointments to office, the President appeared to us to have been even more fortunate than his predecessors, and especially to have surrounded himself with a Cabinet in whose ability and zeal for the public good we had the greatest confidence. If any reply was made to this, it was, probably, that the election of the President, and the appointment of Secretary of State, were the result of a bargain or previous understanding, and therefore they must be put down. To which we generally rejoined, that he who used this argument was doubtless sincere in his belief of its truth, but that *belief* is a matter not communicable from one to another, and we must therefore be excused for dissenting from his premises as well as his conclusions; that the opinion expressed by us, a day or two after the election of President was consummated, in the entire purity of that election, had been confirmed, rather than weakened, by all our subsequent observation. Discovered to be thus untractable, we were left to go our way, or perhaps were told, that it was perfectly immaterial how well the Government was administered, or how pure the Administration was — it should be put down if they who professed this opinion could effect the object. We have already stated the terms in which this sentiment was understood to have been expressed by one of the Senators of the United States: we did so, not out of the slightest disrespect to him, whom we did not name, and for whose personal character and private virtues early association and long observation had inspired us with the highest regard; but merely to place in the strongest light, of which it was susceptible, a sentiment which we had often heard freely expressed by individuals. This sentiment was, about that time, proclaimed as a principle of action, by a print established here, under the patronage of Members of Congress, being the same to which the person lately voted for by the Opposition, in the Senate, was subsequently attached as Editor. We perfectly recollect marking the sentiment when we met with it, as one would a counterfeit coin, that no one might be taken in by it.

Though we were aware of the opinions thus entertained by individuals, we supposed they were rare, and never would be made the basis of a party organization; and, agreeing entirely in opinion with the Sage of Monticello, that error of opinion may be safely tolerated where reason is left free to combat it, we contented ourselves with pursuing our own way, leaving others to pursue theirs undisturbed. This was a course prescribed by courtesy to the opinions of others, and that spirit of toleration which has always ruled this press, and ever shall do so.

The proceedings towards the close of the late Session of Congress, however, and especially the vote for a Printer to the Senate, developed a new state of things, which required a departure from the reserve it would have been more agreeable to us to have continued to maintain, and obliging us to speak out plainly to our readers.

Respecting this matter of the Printing for the Senate, it is but justice to ourselves to say that it is a subject on which we have never introduced conversation to any Senator—much less have we ever condescended to solicit a vote for it, either in that body, or the other House. We have contented ourselves with discharging, to the best of our ability, the duty which the appointment of printers to both Houses devolved upon us, and that we supposed to be all the duty which was required of us. We knew that no member of the Senate (one perhaps excepted) had any ground of personal hostility to us, or betrayed in his personal deportment, any the least symptom of such hostility—it was therefore undoubtedly not without astonishment that we beheld, on the first of March, the array of three and twenty Senators against us, on the grounds avowed by Mr. Van Buren, and with feelings indicated by other gentlemen on that day. That astonishment was not lessened by the information which we received on the day following, that the vote against us was the result of a party determination. The state of the vote against the amendment of the House of Representatives to the Colonial bill in the Senate, the next day but one afterwards, and its exact correspondence with the vote for the editor of the Opposition paper here, left us no longer a loop to hang a doubt upon, as to the existence of an organized opposition, in the existence of which, although we had begun to suspect it, we were extremely unwilling to believe.

Next came the rumor that, during the late session, a regular Caucus, or Club, had been held here, composed of members of Congress, by whom questions were decided before they came upon the floor of Congress, and that the corresponding votes of the Senate were to be traced to the decisions of this irresponsible tribunal. Then we received from New York the information, contemporaneously divulged there, that "a concentration of sentiment" had taken place among the members of Congress at Washington, and that it was understood that old usages were to be restored by a Caucus nomination, to be made next Winter, of candidates for the Presidency and Vice Presidency. It was not possible to shut our ears or our eyes to these sounds and signs, or to resist the conviction that a party was organized in Congress, upon principles different from those of any party that has ever before existed in our Government, and whose main object was, to put down this Administration without reference to its measures—that is, to put it down, right or wrong.

We were slow to believe that a Caucus had been held here, at which the fate of public measures and of public men was decided, and before which we were arraigned and sentenced to proscription because we appeared to be indisposed to become instruments in the hands of those who composed it. The outgivings of the National Advocate, however, satisfied us at once that there was some foundation for the rumor; and that Mr. Van Buren was to derive credit at home, to be converted into power there, and reflected in his favor here, by being made out to be "the Master Spirit" by whose agency this machinery had been established, to substitute the regular operation of the Government, and to control the popular elections by means of organized clubs in the States, and organized presses every where. The reader cannot have forgotten that the re-election of this gentleman was the signal for triumph here, at Richmond, and elsewhere, because it indicated his strength at home; and that the importance of that strength lay in the face, boasted in the Advocate, that the control of the State of New York over the Presidential Election was absolute and certain. Nor did we any injury to Mr. Van Buren in thus interpreting the oracles of the Advocate: the reputation of this sort of influence and intrigue is valuable where these caucus "usages" determine every thing. Indeed, the New York Enquirer, received only yesterday, informs us that "Mr. Van Buren likes these attacks: they place him in a more conspicuous position than he occupies, and he himself cannot but smile complacently when he is told that the vote of New York is in his hands." This is completely in the Caucus-party spirit, which regards political power as every thing—the public interest as nothing.

At length these rumors of Caucus Proceedings, here, under the veil of profound secrecy and under the mantle of night are confirmed to us from authority in which we have implicit confidence. We assert, without fear of contradiction, that such a Caucus was held; that it was composed of materials the most incongruous and heretofore discordant—of Federalists, of Quids, of Democrats of divers sorts—that it was therefore convened, not upon the ground of a common sentiment on great fundamental *principles*, such as heretofore has been held to justify caucuses, but upon the ground of a common *object*, stronger even than the repugnance of those who composed it to one another, (and Heaven knows how strong must have been the attractive influence to counteract the natural repulsion between some of them.) We have the names of most of these gentlemen, but we shall drag no names unnecessarily before the Public. We should not have used even Mr. Van Buren's in this discussion, had he not himself placed himself conspicuously in the van, and had it not been that he evidently deserved the honor, which the Advocate claimed for him, of being "the Master Spirit" by whose agency this caucus machinery was put in operation.

The operations in regard to the public press began here, by the proscription of the National Intelligencer, by a political inquisition. They are carried on elsewhere by different means. In some cases by direct menace, as in the case of the Harrisburg Intelligencer; in others, by an operation of a different sort, which sometimes succeeds, and sometimes does not. In other instances, we find presses rising like exhalations, blazing for awhile, and which, expiring for lack of aliment, will soon leave nothing but an offensive odour by which to remember their existence.

Our object, however, is not at this time to fatigue our readers by asking them to go over again all the ground we have already trodden with them, but to place before them, in a few words, the conclusions to which we have been led by our investigations, which are as follow:

That there exists an organised Opposition to this Administration, right or wrong, which, though chiefly observable in Congress, is connected extensively with the public Press.

That public measures have consequently been decided, in Congress, upon the principle of party expediency, and with reference to the Presidential Election, rather than to the respective merits of those measures.

That an influence has been visible in the Senatorial Branch of Congress, different from the influence of purely Constitutional considerations.

That rumor imputes that influence to the decisions of a small Caucus or Junta, occasionally held in this City, whose proceedings have been wrapt in the profoundest privacy.

That contemporaneous publications in New York and communications to journalists in Richmond, make a boast of this organization.

That, though the main purpose of this Combination here is the regulation of the Presidential Election, it has other and subsidiary purposes.

That one of these purposes is the subjugation of the press by means unknown to the law and inconsistent with principle.

That the effect of the success of these operations would be to place the Government of the United States in the hands of an organized and disciplined party, instead of the hands of the legitimate sovereign, the People.

That the Hon. Martin Van Buren, a Senator from New York, represents this party, and is necessarily the life and soul, and bone and sinew of it.

That the success of this organization would be, therefore, necessarily, to place the whole of the routine of the high public offices, and all the important legislation of the country, under the absolute control of that distinguished citizen.

That such success would be an usurpation of the rights of the People, and a tyranny of odious complexion.

Whether our deductions are just or otherwise, is for our readers to decide, and for the present we willingly leave the question with them. Whether the concerns of this great nation are to be placed under the control of a National Caucus, anticipating and superseding the ordinary forms of legislation, as well as the process of free popular election, is a grave question which we call upon the People of the United States to examine and decide. That the attempt has been made to introduce this system into the General Government, there can be no doubt. Emboldened by partial success, the Senate of the United States, subjected to the dominion of this system, has been exultingly proclaimed the controlling power of the Government, and even the examination of the Speech of a member of the boasted majority of that body has been pronounced a dangerous breach of privilege. We shall see, in the result, whether these corruptions of our political system—these high-toned aristocratic principles—this combination of secret purposes with boasted power and asserted privilege, will be countenanced by the approbation of an intelligent People, or will receive their indignant condemnation.

Editorial from the *United States Telegraph*
May 4, 1827

The claim that John Quincy Adams was an aristocrat who advocated the establishment of a monarchy in the United States was repeatedly argued by the Jacksonian press. The following article belabored the point.

> "Train up a child in the way he should go, and when he is old he will not depart from it."

   Mr. John Quincy Adams was trained up in anti-republican principles, and has given many proofs in his old age that he has not departed from them. His father, whatever he might have been during the war of the revolution, was poisoned with monarchy and aristocracy during his embassy in London, in 1786 – 7 – 8, and wrote three books to convert the American people to the same doctrine. Mr. John Q. Adams was born to the inheritance of those principles, had them inculcated upon him by education, enforced by parental authority, and confirmed by a foreign residence in the courts of Europe. His earliest writings and latest acts bear the impression of this early training, and it becomes a serious question with the *republican* part of the American people, whether they can safely trust the preservation of our *republican* institutions with such a man. For the information of the candid and patriotic republicans, I propose to submit some proofs upon this point, and invoke their serious attention to them. I will draw chiefly upon the elder Mr. Adams' work, miscalled a defence of the American constitutions, and which many citizens are badly enough informed to suppose, to be, in reality, a work in defence of our present constitution, when, in fact, it was written before that constitution was adopted, and for the avowed purpose of procuring a convention, to be called for the purpose of establishing a monarchial government – a government of kings, lords, and commons, in the United States – The late republican patriot, Col. John Taylor of Caroline, in his new views of the constitution, has shown that this was the object of Mr. Adams's work, and that Mr. Gouveneur Morris openly brought forward the kingly plan in the convention, . . . and that it was favored by a powerful party, and only not adopted, because it was dreaded that the people would resist it with arms! It is a subject of the greatest regret to *republicans*, that the proceedings of the convention of '78, were wrapped in secrecy, and not revealed until a few years ago; but that veil being now removed, a universal inquiry should be set on foot to learn its proceedings, as from this knowledge will be learnt the reason why that vital phrase, in the old articles of confederation, the words "EXPRESSLY *enumerated*," should have been left out in the new constitution, and the Congress thereby left at liberty to exercise *implied* powers, instead of being confined to those EXPRESSLY *granted.*

449

But to proceed with the proofs which will show, that Mr. J. Q. Adams by his birth imbibed, and by his early education was taught to believe in, anti-republican doctrines; the whole three volumes of his father's work abound with these, and the reader is earnestly requested to refer to the books themselves wherever it is impracticable.

At the tender age of eleven, he was sent to *Eton*, in England, to be educated among the children of the British nobility and aristocracy. Before he was sixteen he had been carried through half the courts of Europe, over as far as Russia, and fed his eyes daily upon the magnificence of kings and emperors. The influence of such an education could not be lost upon a son, the hope and pride of his family, and destined by his father to succeed to the chief magistracy of his country. Accordingly, we find him immediately upon his return from Europe, as early as the year '93, giving proofs of his anti-republicanism, in a series of monarchial essays, entitled *Publicola*. He was sent out as an ambassador, at the age of 24, and lived in the court of the most despotic king in Europe, the king of Prussia, at which time he wrote his Silesian Letters; a work which was pronounced by the Edinburgh Review in 1804, to be the production of a monarchist. During the Administration of his father, he supported all the anti-republican measures of his Administration; and upon his return, after the downfall of his father, he was taken up by the federal party in Boston, upon the true hereditary principle, as their future leader. They first offered him to the *people* as a candidate for Congress, in opposition to Dr. Eustis, the *republican* candidate, in which contest he shared his usual fate before the people, being rejected by a great majority. He was then offered by them to the State Legislature, a majority of which was federal, for the Senate of the United States, and was elected by the federal party, after four ballotings. As this election has been misrepresented, &, bold and impudent assertion has lately been put forth, that Mr. Adams was elected on this occasion by a union of the *republicans* and *moderate federalists*, I herewith submit a detailed statement of the ballotings, which will show that the republicans stood together from first to last, and voted for a candidate of their own, and that the federalists after a struggle between Timothy Pickering and Mr. John Quincy Adams, finally gave the preference to the latter, and immediately after the sitting member having resigned, also elected Mr. Pickering; so that the Senate of the United States, in the year 1803, saw Mr. Pickering and Mr. John Quincy Adams arrive together in that body as the legitimate representatives of the Mass. federalists! In the Senate Mr. A. and Mr. P. voted together for *four* years, when Mr. A. quitted his colleague and crossed over to the republican ranks upon the principle, as declared by his father in the Cunningham letters, that it was the only way for an illustrious family of declining popularity to recover their lost power! But he did not deceive Mr. Jefferson in this transit. That great republican *used* the new convert but did not *trust* him! *He never gave him an office*, and never approved the policy of Madison and Monroe, who did, and who could only urge in their defence the necessity of breaking and dividing the federal party. But Mr. J. Q. Adams took care not to forget the confidence of his old federal friends. In 1809 he refused to be polled as a *re-*

publican candidate for governor of the State, upon the ground, as declared by his father in the Cunningham letters, that *"it would occasion an eternal breach with the federalists."* So far from breaking with them, that he got all the federal electoral votes at the late election for President, and will get them again. That party still gives many votes. In 1803, it gave 47 to R. King and C. C. Pinckney; in 1812 it gave De Witt Clinton the better half for the 89 votes which he got. In 1816 it gave 34 to R. King, in opposition to Mr. Monroe, and would have given its whole strength, about 50 votes, to Mr. Crawford, if that Roman republican would have consented to receive them, and to have been elected by the joint efforts of all the federalists and a part of the republicans. In 1824 the federalists for the first time since 1801 carried the election.

They gave their entire vote, about 50 in number, to Mr. J. Q. Adams, which, added to about 34 republican votes made 84, and put him into the House of Representatives, where he gained the election, by the means designated by his father in vol. 3, p. 275 of the work on the American Constitutions, as herein before quoted. This election was hailed in Boston as the *restoration* of the old federal party. A royal salute of 100 guns was fired, morning, noon, and night, as was done in Paris at the restoration of the Bourbons. A grand entertainment was given at which Mr. Josiah Quincy, the cousin and old fellow-federalist of Mr. Adams presided, and gave for a toast, which was received with enthusiasm, the following sentiment:"The political regeneration: —*Those who* fell *with the* first Adams, rise *with the* second." And so it has been. The old federalists have risen. Mr. King, though superannuated and unfit for service, immediately went forth to the court of London; all the departments of government are filled with them. The House of Representatives is placed under the immediate management of Mr. Webster, a man whose federalism sublimated by the doctrines of the Hartford convention, and displayed during the war in a thousand acts in opposition to his country, and who even carried his opposition to what he called *"a weak or wicked administration,"* so far as to vote against the customary resolution of thanks to Mr. Speaker Clay, when he quit the chair to go to Ghent in pursuit of peace,—that Mr. Clay whose faithful organ and submissive coadjutor he now is! Two years only have elapsed, and pregnant proofs of ultra federalism flow from Mr. Adams' administration. The people are not to be palsied by the will of their constituents; the authority of the Senate is to be set aside in the institution of embassies—the constitution is to be construed, not by its terms, but by its effects; speculative scruples are to be dissolved in practical blessings: the general welfare is to be the object and the limit of action—and in the meditated civil war with Georgia, the divine right of kings is obscurely alluded to! An authority above the laws is openly appealed to!

Can republicans behold these *signs of the times*, and not feel the necessity of rallying against the son in 1828, as they did against the father thirty years ago!

Editorial from the Steubenville, Pennsylvania, *Leger*
May 17, 1827

A general catalogue of John Quincy Adams' misdeeds as President appeared regularly in the Jacksonian press prior to the 1828 campaign. The following excerpt is typical.

What sign was it, when, immediately on the ascension of Mr. Adams to power, the first call of those who forced him into office, was, *come—come —unite within—*amalgamate—don't say a word against us—don't talk of the manner of our elevation—cast that into oblivion; and judge us by our great public acts—don't "palsy" our exertions! What would have been the language of upright, honest men, who had acquired power by honest means? It would have been this: We are your servants—the power we possess is entrusted to use for your good—freely examine, and freely decide—if we do not *do your will,* and satisfy your utmost expectations, it is your right and your duty to discharge us.

What sign was it, that a *Billiard Table*—an instrument used by genteel and fashionable gamblers in high-life to play, and sport their money and time with: an instrument seen at European courts and in the palaces of the "nobility" and wealthy cormorants of the public treasuries, but never seen in a President's House, or in the Secretary's mansion, in this moral and republican country until the year 1825? What sign was it, to see the *President of the United States* indulging either his taste for gentility, or for gambling, in expending the money, which is taken from the pockets of the people, in the purchase of *Tables and Balls, which can be used for no purpose but for gambling?*

What sign was it, when the *new* President, in his first Message to the representatives of the people, wherein he is expected, for such is the duty the constitution imposes upon him, to recommend such measures as the situation and circumstances of a great and moral people may require, and as would tend to relieve their wants, and advance their interests, especially in the economy of public expenditures, so as not to take from the "mouth of labor" its hard-earned pittance—what sign was it, to see a President recommending to the active consideration of the agents and servants of the people, wild and extravagant scientifical projects, to equal the "gigantic strides" in European powers, in building "lights in the skies," and such gullible schemes, and at the same time, as if a conscientiousness of his own high bearing was "weighing him down," exhorts those very servants of the people, *"not to be palsied by the will of their constituents"*—their masters! *Palsied by the will of the people!* What! a President of the United States dare to say to the servants of the people in public employ —Don't mind what your employers, the *people,* say—they are an ignorant "swinish multitude"—you ought to rise above popular feeling and popular sen-

452

timent—*European* politicians will laugh at you, if you talk about the will of your constituents—it is *"unparliamentary!"* What's the sign reader?

What is the sign—(we ask gentlemen of the *Turf* specially)—when you see the owners of two celebrated nags keeping and training them for a long season for the track, encouraging others to risk their *valuables* on the beasts, and when the day arrives, the track being in prime order, each horse *apparently* does his best; but, much to the disappointment of the spectatars and all others, but the two owners and their particular friends, the *slowest* horse of the two takes the purse, and the *owners* in the face of the world divide its contents between them. What is the sign! *Booty* or no *booty?* What say you gentlemen of *the Turf?*

What is the sign, when former enemies strike hands over a purse of money about which they have long contended?

What is the sign, when a Secretary of State of the United States, which possesses the only really pure republican government on earth, challenges a Senator of that government, and tries to take his life, because he spoke of him in debate on national concerns?

What is the sign, when the friends of that Secretary, and that Secretary himself, blamed the said Senator for speaking, as he and they thought the Senator did, in his place in the Senate, *of his private life*, where, by the Constitution the utmost freedom of debate is allowed and protected; and justified the Secretary for challenging him for so speaking . . . what is the sign, we ask, when these same justifiers of duelling for remarks of that character, hold it correct and blameless, nay, commendable, to traduce in public prints not only the private character of a distinguished private citizen, merely because he is a candidate for office, but "drag" his *wife* before the public, and lacerate the Senator of sensibility, piety, and virtue, to injure the standing of the candidate? What say you reader, does this sign indicate?

What is the sign, when a Secretary of State, in the highest confidence with the President, and the whole administration partly, *fights a duel* in coolblood—retains his office and influence with the *party;* yet, that same party call public meetings of pious people, and roundly and solemnly resolve, that it is ungodly, impious and immoral, and destructive to the peace and happiness of society, to encourage duelling, or countenance it in any shape. —What, say you does this sign indicate, that the friends of the party are coming to their senses, or that they wish to shake off Mr.————Secretary?

What is the sign, when the rulers in a free government, who ought always to consider themselves, what they really are, the servants of the people, proscribe. all who do not think and act in concert with them?

What is the sign, when these rulers, or any of them, say the Secretary of State, dismisses from the employment and service of the *People*, the Prioters of the laws, who are no more his servants or agents than the people who made him master, are his servants, or agents, merely because they do not think *him* a Saint, and laud him and his patron: because they dare as *Americans* to think and speak for themselves? And, forsooth, because they dare think and speak their own free sentiments of public men and public measures, they must be proscribed—must be dismissed from the service of *the People*, and told, in a haughty and imperious manner, that *Mr. Clay*—yea, verily, *Mr. Clay*, will have no *neutrals!* True imperial style—and all the benefits—all the honors, and all the emoluments of office are to be bestowed, not on *Mr. Jefferson's* rule—"Is he honest is he capable, is he faithful to the constitution,"—but on the tyrant's doctrine—*Is he for me!* If he is not, he shall be "palsied" *by my arm!* let the people say what they will! What is the sign reader?

What is the sign, when you see the administration party, throughout the country, trembling in their shoes, and, fearing the popularity of an upright and long tried patriot, who, from the serene shades of private life, is brought before an enlightened and grateful people, and, like the tide of the *Mississippi*, is moving on in a current of public opinion irresistible: and knowing, as they well do from the *prince* down to the shoe black of their party, that his virtues, public services, talents, and unrivalled qualifications, place himself beyond the reach of slander and corruption, they attack *his wife!* Should it prove to be the fact, that Gen. ANDREW JACKSON, whose life has been devoted in youth and in age to his country's service and glory, and whose virtues, as well in private as in public, have even stilled the rankling malice of envious minds, is unfortunately connected with a woman, who, for upwards of thirty years, has been the partner of his bosom, the comforter of his happiest as of his most afflictive hours, yet that she has in former periods of her life been indiscreet —been unfaithful to one to whom she had made the most solemn vows. Suppose all this be true;—which, by the bye, is INFAMOUSLY FALSE—but suppose it true; What is the sign, to see the administration, through all its affiliated presses, "dragging," as one press boasts its willingness to do, a female into public discussion—not for any good it will do him—not for any good it will do the public—not for any injury it will do Gen. Jackson; but with the hope that it will add credit and honor to Mr. *Adams!* Such laurels he may deserve at the hands of such friends! But may Heaven preserve the people from such public guardians! What say you of the sign, reader? IS THE SHIP SINKING OR NOT?"

Open Letter from the Nashville Central Committee
Reprinted in the *United States Telegraph*
June 22, 1827

What made the election of 1828 particularly acrimonious was the discussion in the campaign of Jackson's marriage. Charles Hammond, editor of the Cincinnati Gazette, *claimed that Jackson had prevailed upon Rachel Donelson to desert her husband and "live with him in the character of a wife." The Nashville Jackson Committee was asked to refute this charge and in June, 1827, the committee issued this rejoinder.*

In reply to your note published in the Nashville Republican, under date May 12th, 1827, calling our attention to certain newspaper charges against General Jackson and his lady, and particularly the charge made in one newspaper of Cincinnati, that, "in the summer of 1790, General Jackson prevailed upon the wife of Lewis Robards, of Mercer county, Kentucky, *to desert* her husband and live with himself in the character of a wife," and having also seen the evidence by which the Editor attempts to support this charge; we now submit to you a succinct statement of the facts attending the separation of Lewis Robards and his wife, and the subsequent marriage of Mrs. R. with Gen. Jackson, and also such evidence and documents as will probably be sufficiently satisfactory to the public.

Before we proceed, it may be proper to know something of the persons whose testimony is subjoined, alluded to, or quoted.

The character of Gen. James Breckenridge, of Fincastle, Va., is, no doubt, well known to you; it is said to be high and unspotted; he was a member of the Virginia Legislature when Capt. Robards applied for a divorce, and one of the committee appointed to examine his application and report a bill, as stated in the Cincinnati paper.

Judge M'Nairy, whose letter is subjoined, is the district judge of the Federal Court, a man of high and unblemished reputation, whose statements may be relied on as most accurate and incontrovertible: those who know him, know, that no considerations could induce him to give the slightest coloring to any part of his testimony.

Mrs. Elizabeth Craighead is the widow of the late Rev. Thos. B. Craighead, and sister to James Brown, our present Minister to France, a lady of the purest character, with a mind highly intelligent and cultivated.

Mrs. Sally Smith, widow of General Daniel Smith, formerly a Senator in Congress, a lady of unblemished character, and of excellent good sense.

Mrs. Mary H. Bowen, widow of Capt. William Bowen, sister of Gen. Russell and the late Col. Russell, of Fayette county, Ky., a most respectable and sensible lady.

Mr. Thomas Crutcher, the treasurer of West Tennessee, whose character for honesty and veracity is as high and unquestioned as that of any man in the State.

Of Mr. A. Foster, it is only necessary to say that he was, for many years, President of the Board of our Land Commissioners—one of the most honorable and correct men of our country.

Of Judge Overton's character, we need say nothing; the testimony of no person has been resorted to, where there could be any, the slightest, question raised as to their characters.

In making the investigation you wished, we have met with some difficulty and delay on account of the great length of time since the facts occurred, and that the public mind, for a great many years, in this country, had ceased to think on this subject. At the time when Mr. Robards separated from his wife, applied for a divorce, obtained it, and General Jackson married her; when all the facts were fresh and distinct, public opinion was formed, and the cotemporaneous judgment of the society in which those persons resided, came to a clear and decisive result in their favor. There did not exist even an injurious suspicion with regard to their previous conduct; to the justice of this judgment thirty-seven years of domestic peace and useful virtue, have given a sanction which must operate upon every candid and generous mind, with irresistible power. But notwithstanding all these difficulties, we believe that we are able to present to you a correct history of those transactions.

In the summer or fall of 1788, Mrs. Robards was compelled by her husband, Capt. Robards, who then resided in Mercer county Ky to leave him, and to seek a home with her mother, Mrs. Donelson, a widow lady, living about ten miles from Nashville, in Tennessee. That Mrs. Robards was *compelled* at this time, by her husband to leave him, is proven by Judge Overton's testimony, by Gen. Ray and by Mr. John McGinnis; that she was an injured and innocent woman, of most irreproachable character and conduct, is proven by the same persons, and by Maj. Thomas Allen and Capt. John Meaux; Capt. Robards himself acquits her, and admitted that his suspicions were unjust.

In the spring or summer of 1789 Judge Overton and Gen. Jackson became boarders at Mrs. Donelson's when Gen. Jackson first saw Mrs. Robards; in the same spring or summer, Capt. Robards and his wife became reconciled, and lived together at her mother's (Mrs. Donelson.)

In the summer or fall of this year, Capt. Robards became jealous of Gen. Jackson; upon this part of the subject we will quote the statement of Judge Overton, as giving the most authentic account of the several facts which transpired about that time. He says, "not many months elapsed before Robards became jealous of Jackson, which I felt confident was without the least ground. Some of his irritating conversation on this subject with his wife, I heard amidst the tears of herself and her mother, who were greatly distressed. I urged to Robards the unmanliness of his conduct, after the pains I had taken to produce harmony, as a mutual friend of both families, and my honest conviction that his suspicions were groundless. These remonstrances seemed not to have the desired effect; as much commotion and unhappiness prevailed in the family, as in that of Mrs. Robards in Kentucky. At length I communicated to Jackson, the unpleasant situation of living in a family where there was so much disturbance, and concluded, by telling him, that we would endeavor to get some other place; to this he readily assented, but where to go we did not know. Being conscious of his innocence, he said, that he would talk to Robards. What passed between Capt. Robards and Jackson I do not know, as I was absent some where, not now recollected, when the conversation and results took place, but returned soon afterwards. The whole affair was related to me by Mrs. Donelson (the mother of Mrs. Robards) and as well as I recollect, by Jackson himself. The substance of their account was, that Mr. Jackson met Capt. Robards near the orchard fence, and began mildly to remonstrate with him, respecting the injustice he had done his wife as well as himself. In a little time Robards became violently angry and abusive, and threatened to whip Jackson; made a show of doing so, &c. Jackson told him, he had not bodily strength to fight him, nor should he do so, feeling conscious of his innocence, and returned to his cabin, telling him at the same time, that if he insisted on fighting, he would give him gentlemanly satisfaction, or words to that effect. Upon Jackson's return out of the house, Capt. Robards said, that he did not care for him nor his wife, abusing them both — that he was determined not to live with Mrs. Robards. Jackson retired from the family, and went to live at Mansker's station. Capt. Robards remained several months with his wife, and then went to Kentucky, in company with Mr. Thomas Crutcher, and probably some other persons."

So far as we have been able to ascertain by inquiry, this is the only altercation that ever took place between Gen. Jackson and Capt. Robards; Mr. Crutcher says, "I never heard of Gen. Jackson and Capt. Robards having any quarrel or misunderstanding but the one, nor do I believe they ever did."

This difference or quarrel, was in assertion of the injustice, (as declared by Gen. Jackson,) of Capt. Robards, suspicions against him: Gen. Jackson seems immediately to have left Mrs. Donelson's; Capt. Robards and his wife lived together several months afterwards, in apparent harmony.

In the month of May or June, 1790, Captain Robards left Mrs. Donelson's to go to Kentucky in company with Mr. Thomas Crutcher, with the *avowed* intention of returning and settling in Mrs. Donelson's neighborhood, which had been made one of the terms of reconciliation by Mrs. R, though *really* his determination appears to have been never to return or live with his wife again, but to desert her forever; and, in fact never did return or see her again. For this part of the testimony we refer you to Mr. Crutcher's statement.

Mrs. Robards lived at her mother's during the whole of the summer and fall of 1790, or perhaps occasionally at Col. Hays' who had married her sister. In December, 1790, (while Mrs. Robards was living at her mother's, where Capt. Robards left her on his departure for Kentucky,) Capt. Robards applied to the Legislature of Virginia for a divorce, upon the allegations that his wife had deserted him, &c. upon which, the Legislature authorized a judicial inquiry, and a divorce, if found true.

Whether the suspicions of Capt. Robards at this period were just, and whether Gen. Jackson had injured Capt. Robards in the manner which his jealousies suggested, are facts, as to which, we will present you with such circumstances, testimony and conclusions, as we can obtain or arrive at.

Here we will remark, that if true, it is a charge which should be affirmatively proven by clear evidence of specific facts. Those who make the charge, rely on the act of the Legislature of Virginia, the legal proceedings in Kentucky, with the subsequent acts of General and Mrs. Jackson. The decree of Mercer county court, and what occurred subsequent to the act of the Legislature of Virginia, shall be considered presently.

That Capt. Robards was jealous or suspicious, would probably weigh but little, as he was predisposed that way, and seems to have entertained those feelings long before, in a most violent degree, most unjustly. That the Legislature of Virginia passed the act, which has been referred to, will not probably be considered in any degree as tending to prove the justice of the charge against Mrs. R. by her husband, because the Legislature clearly was not satisfied of the truth of any charge made, and referred it to further inquiry by a court; but of this you will be satisfied by recurrence to General Breckenridge's letter, of which we will here quote a part. "I was a member of the Virginia Legislature in the session of 1790, when a petition was presented in behalf of a Mr. Robards for a divorce. He was said to be resident in one of the counties of the district of Kentucky, then a part of Virginia. It was, I believe, the second instance of an application for a divorce that had been made to the Legislature; very certainly the second, that I had been called upon to vote. I was a young man at that time, and the deep impression made on my mind was, the novelty and importance of the case, combined with the interest which I felt in behalf of the female concerned — remain with great distinctness. Mr. Robards was represented to be a man of vile, wild habits, and harsh temper; his wife lovely and *blameless* in her disposition and deportment; so cruelly treated by her husband as to make a separation necessary to her happiness. It was under impressions produced by a state of facts like these, that I voted for a judicial inquiry on the subject, which I always understood eventuated in a divorce.

"If Mr. Robards alleged incontinency in his wife as a ground of divorce, and I rather think that he did, I am very sure that I thought her *innocent*, and that my vote was intended to liberate her, as the injured party."

In addition to which, we will now call your attention to such positive testimony as we have collected, as to the injustice of Capt. Robard's suspicions, and the charge made against Gen. Jackson.

Judge Overton, who lived in the same room with Gen. Jackson during all the period in question, slept with him, held the strictest and most confidential intimacy with him, states, as his solemn, clear belief, that Mrs. R. was innocent, and most unjustly suspected, that such was the result of his own observations, and such were, at all times, the solemn asseverations of General Jackson during that period, and at all times since. Mrs. Craighead, Mrs. Smith, and Mrs. Bowen had the best opportunities of judging correctly: in speaking of Mrs. R.'s conduct during the period which elapsed from the time she came from Kentucky, and of the injustice of R.'s suspicions, Mrs C. says, "I have no hesitation in stating it as my firm belief, that his (Capt. R.'s) suspicions were entirely groundless; no lady ever conducted herself in a more becoming manner, during the whole of that period; I have lived within a few miles of Mrs. Jackson's ever since that time, (with the exception of about two years,) and have been intimate with her, and can say, that no lady maintains a better character, or is more exemplary in her deportment, or more beloved by her friends and neighbors."

Mrs. Smith says, "all the circumstances attending this rupture, I cannot attempt to state with much particularity at this late day; but it is hardly possible, considering the free and unreserved intercourse that prevailed amongst all the respectable classes of people here at that time, that an incident of this kind should occur without being fully and generally known; and that every person should concur in the same views upon its character, without the best reasons. In this transaction, Mr. Robards alone was censured, and I never heard a respectable man or woman intimate, that the conduct of his wife differed from that of the most prudent and virtuous female. Gen. Jackson boarded at the time in the house of Mrs. Donelson, and it was the common belief that his character and standing, added to his engaging and sprightly manners, were enough to inflame the mind of poor Robards, addicted, as he was, to vicious habits and the most childish suspicions."

Mrs. Bowen says, "in this transaction, (refering to the jealousy of Robards and his last separation from his wife,) I can safely say from my intimacy with both Mrs. Donelson and her daughter, Mrs. Robards, as well as Gen. Jackson, that not the least censure ought to be thrown upon any person but Mr. Robards. When the circumstances happened this was the language of all the country, and I never heard until now, that there was any person living who had, *from a knowledge of the facts*, entertained a different opinion, except Mr. Robards himself, in whose weak and childish disposition I think the whole affair originated."

From this testimony, concurring with the testimony of all the other persons whose statements are subjoined for your examination, there seems to be but one possible conclusion—that the charge made on Gen. Jackson was unfounded, and Mrs. Jackson perfectly innocent; but of this, you and the public will judge; and perhaps more satisfactory upon seeing the further progress of this affair and the testimony connected with it.

Some time in the month of January, 1791, Mrs. Robards descended the river, to Natchez, under the protection of Col. Stark, an old and respectable gentleman; Gen. Jackson accompanied Col. Stark and Mrs. Robards to Natchez, and so soon as Gen. Jackson saw them safely landed at Natchez, he immediately returned to Nashville—was at the May Superior Court, and attended to business, as Attorney General. Mrs. Robards, during her residence in the neighborhood, lived principally in the family of Col. Tho. Green, and Col. Bruen, families as highly respectable as any in that country. The causes of this journey by Mrs. Robards, and the reasons which induced Gen. Jackson to accompany Col. Stark, we will give literally in the language of the testimony of Judge Overton and Mr. Crutcher. Judge Overton says, "some time afterwards, during the winter of 1791, Mrs. Donelson told me of her daughter's intention to go down the river to Natchez, to some of her friends, in order to keep out of the way of Capt. Robards, as she said he had threatened to "*haunt*" her. Knowing, as I did, Capt. Robards, unhappy, jealous disposition, and his temper growing out of it, I thought that she was right to keep out of his way; though do not believe that I so expressed myself to the old lady, or any other person.

"The whole affair gave Jackson great uneasiness—and this will not appear strange to one as well acquainted with his character as I was; continually together during our attendance on wilderness courts, whilst other young men were indulging in familiarities with females of relaxed morals, no suspicion of this kind of the world's censure, ever fell to Jackson's share.—In this—in his singularity delicate sense of honor, and in what I thought, his chivalrous conceptions of the female sex, it always occurred to me, that he was distinguishable from every other person with whom I was acquainted.

"About the time of Mrs. Donelson's communication to me respecting her daughter's intention of going to Natchez, I perceived in Jackson symptoms of more than usual concern. I determined to ascertain the cause, when he frankly told me, that he was the most unhappy of men, in having innocently, and unintentionally, been the cause of the loss of the peace and happiness of Mrs. Robards, whom he believed to be a fine woman. In this I concurred with him, but remonstrated upon the propriety of his not giving himself any uneasiness about it. It was not long after this before he communicated to me his intention of going to Natchez with Col. Stark, with whom Mrs. Robards was to descend the river—saying that she had no friend or relative that would go with her, or assist in preventing Stark, his family, and Mr. Robards from being massacred by the Indians; then in a state of war, and exceedingly troublesome. Accordingly, Jackson in company with Mrs. Robards and Col. Stark, a venerable and highly esteemed old man, and friend of Mrs. Robards, went down the river from Nashville to Natchez, some time in the winter or spring of 1791. It was not, however, without the urgent entreaties of Col. Stark, who wanted protection from the Indians, that Jackson consented to accompany them, of which I had heard, before Jacksons' conversation with me, already alluded to." Mr. Crutcher says, "Capt. Robards, never, to my knowledge, returned to West Tennessee, or what was then called Cumberland. It was reported, however, that he threatened to come and take his wife to Kentucky, and compel her to live there. She, as well as all her friends, was very much opposed to this, and in order to place herself beyond his reach, as I understood at the time, determined to descend the river under Col. Stark's protection to Natchez. It was in December, or perhaps January, before Col. Stark could get off with his family; Gen. Jackson also went along; but after they landed at Natchez, the General returned to this country."

In the winter or spring of 1791, information was received at Nashville that Capt. Robards had obtained a divorce from the Legislature of Virginia: This was the belief of all persons in the country. Mr. Crutcher says, "I do not know how the information reached the country, but it was generally, indeed, I believe, universally, relied on as being correct." Judge Overton's account is substantially the same, and further, that in the summer of 1791, he was in Kentucky, remained part of his time at old Mrs. Robards, and never understood otherwise than that Capt. Robards' divorce was final until the latter part of the year 1793. Of the strength and universality of this opinion, there can be no doubt. Upon the receipt and general belief of this information, Gen. Jackson, in July or August, 1791, returned to Natchez in company with Mr. David Deadrick — married Mrs. Robards, and returned in September 1791, to Nashville with her.

These transactions, would seem, under the circumstances accompanying them, to require no comment, and could not fairly be subject to misconstruction, when the character of Gen. Jackson and the conduct and character of Mrs. Jackson are in the slightest degree understood and appreciated; but we will again call your attention to such testimony, as will be entitled to the greatest and most conclusive weight in public estimation.

We cannot do justice to Judge M'Nairy's testimony, but by using his own words — "Gen. Jackson and myself have been acquainted more than forty years, I think 44 or 45 years; part of the time we lived together, and the balance in the immediate neighbourhood of each other. We moved together from North Carolina to this State, and arrived at Nashville in October 1788.

"Not long after we came here, I was informed that Mrs. Jackson and her then husband had been separated in the State of Kentucky. I knew Gen. Jackson had never seen her until this time, and I do not think for some time afterwards. About this time I was informed that Robards and his wife were living very unhappily at her widowed mother's. The public report and impression, I know, was, that Robards was treating her cruelly, by charges found in his own jealous imagination alone.

"As to the particular facts, which took place, that produced the second separation I have no knowledge of my own — I can only speak of what was the prevailing opinion at the time. But this much, I can say, with as much positiveness as any man can, when speaking of another, that from my particular acquaintance with him, I believe General Jackson was, at any period of his life, incapable of seducing any man's wife from him.

"I have known Mrs. Jackson for nearly forty years. No woman, for that time, has sustained a more irreproachable character than she has; hospitable, kind, and charitable. The evening of her days was hastening to a close, in much peace and comfort."

We will also trouble you with quoting from the testimony of Mrs. Smith, on account of its own weight, and more particularly as giving the sentiment and opinions of the Rev. Thos. B. Craighead, known to most literary divines as one of the ablest and most enlightened clergymen in the United States; known to all his acquaintance as a most pious and good man, and one who had the best opportunity to judge correctly of the true character of those transactions, and of Gen. Jackson and Mrs. Jackson. Mrs. Smith states, "Mr. Robards had not been long gone from Tennessee when information was received here, that he had obtained a divorce from his wife. Whether this information came by letter, or by a newspaper from Virginia, addressed to my husband, I cannot now say with certainty, but I think by the latter. It was after this information came, that Gen. Jackson married Mrs. Robards; and I recollect well the observation of the Rev. Mr. Craighead in relation to the marriage; it was, that it was a happy change for Mrs. Robards, and highly creditable to Gen. Jackson, who, by this act of his life, evinced his own magnanimity, as well as the purity and innocence of Mrs. Robards; and such was the sentiment of all my acquaintances.

"Since this period, I have lived within a few miles of Mrs. Jackson, and have never been acquainted with a lady more exemplary in her deportment, or one to whom a greater share of the respect and regard of friends and acquaintances can be awarded."

The testimony of Judge Overton, Mr. Crutcher, Mr. Anthony Foster and others, accompanying this letter, proves substantially the same.

In the fall of 1793, Gen Jackson, for the first time, understood that the act of the Legislature of Va. only authorized a judicial inquiry and decree of divorce; and that such proceedings had been taken in the Mercer quarter session court, and that a divorce had been granted in Sept. 1793. He was then, in January, 1794, married again to Mrs. Jackson.

Of this judicial proceeding and decree, it will only be necessary to remark, that we have given you such evidence as will satisfy you of the true state of the facts, and the innocence of Mrs. Jackson; such as shows that this proceeding was entirely exparte, and without any knowledge of it by Mrs. Jackson or Gen. Jackson; that at the time when the offence was charged in the petition to have taken place, viz: July 1st 1790, Mrs. Robards was living at her mothers, where Robards had left her, and where he had promised to return to her. But in addition to all this, we have the strongest reasons to believe that Hugh M'Gary, the only witness who seems to have been introduced on that inquiry, never saw Gen. and Mrs. Jackson together, until the month of Sept. 1791, after their marriage at Natchez, when they were living together as married persons, in the most fair, honest, and innocent belief that they were lawfully joined in wedlock. Hugh M'Gary came through the Indian country from Natchez to Nashville at the same time and in the same company in which General and Msr. Jackson came, in Sept. 1791, and circumstances then occurred calculated to excite in M'Gary a stronger feeling of dislike towards Gen. Jackson, which it is unnecessary to detail, as they related solely to a meditated attack by the Indians.

The petition for divorce seems not to have been filed until the fall of 1792 —tried at Sep. 1793, and there is much greater probability upon an exparte hearing, that the testimony of Hugh M'Gary was not very accurately applied or confined to the allegations in the declaration, than that he swore that which was untrue; which must have been the case had his evidence agreed with the declaration.

We have now, gentlemen, laid before you the facts connected with General Jackson's marriage—his own conduct, and the character of his lady. Much more testimony could have been produced, if necessary, proving the same facts substantially, but in our inquiries we have met with none conflicting with this, which we presented. The necessity for this course, the members of this Committee have felt with deep regret. Those who reside here, cannot be surprised that this regret should exist in our bosoms—since some of us have associated with General Jackson and his family for more than thirty years—no one of us for less than twelve. During these periods we and our families have met our distinguished countryman, and his pious, charitable and amiable lady, in the most elevated ranks of society. In this protracted series of years, we have seen *him* commanding the respect of all men, and the enthusiastic attachment of his friends; *her*, we have seen, deserving and enjoying the kindest attentions of her female acquaintances, and the unqualified and exalted regard of the honorable, moral and religious men of our country.

The result of this inquiry must place the character of Mrs. Jackson upon that basis where it has rested for nearly forty years, in the society where she has lived and been best known. It must show Gen. Jackson in this part of his history, sustaining that high character for honor and magnanimity, which has distinguished his course through life.

To the honorable and high-minded political opponents of Gen. Jackson, this result will be received with great pleasure—such persons must, at all times, have viewed this attack with pain and dissatisfaction.

> *R. C. Foster,*
>   Chairman pro tem.
> *G. W. Campbell,*
> *Robt Whyte,*
> *J. Wharton,*
> *T H Claiborne,*
> *Will. White,*
> *Jo Philips,*
> *Daniel Graham,*
> *Will. L Brown,*
> *Alfred Balch,*
> *Edward Ward,*
> *Wm. B. Lewis,*
> *Felix Robertson,*
> *Jno. Shelby,*
> *Josiah Nicol,*
> *Jn. Catron,*
> *Nelson Patterson,*
>   Secretary

The undersigned has not signed or acted on this subject for the obvious reason that his testimony has been given and used.

> *John M'Nairy*

I have not signed it for the same reason.

> *Jno. Overton.*

National Republican Campaign Statements
Reprinted in the *National Intelligencer*
January — November, 1828

The following appeals issued by the National Republicans widely reprinted in Virginia, New York, and Maryland emphasized John Quincy Adams' unique qualifications for the Presidency and Andrew Jackson's spectacular lack of them. All agreed that Jackson's sole claim on the American people was his military victory over the British at New Orleans.

ADDRESS TO THE PEOPLE OF VIRGINIA

January 17, 1828

Having been delegated, by those who oppose the election of Andrew Jackson as President of the United States, and having assembled in the City of Richmond, pursuant to our appointment, and formed an Electoral Ticket, we feel it due to ourselves, to those who departed us, and to our country, to submit a brief exposition of our views, on the very interesting subject which has brought us together.

It is no ordinary occasion, which, at this inclement season of the year, has brought so many of us from our business and our homes. We believed that the dearest interests of our country were at stake; that her character, her peace and happiness, and even the permanence of her free institutions, were in peril. We feared the most pernicious consequences from the election of General Jackson, and we have come to consult about the means of averting this calamity from our country. We believe that the only means of effecting this great object in the re-election of the present Chief Magistrate, and have formed an Electoral Ticket for that purpose, which we earnestly commend to the support of the People of Virginia.

We know that many of you strongly disapprove some of the leading measures of the present Administration, — have not confidence in it, and would be exceedingly unwilling to sanction the principles of construction applied by the present Chief Magistrate to the Constitution of the United States. But we do not perceive, in these circumstances, any sufficient reason for withholding your support from the ticket we have recommended. We ourselves are not agreed upon these subjects. While some disapprove these measures, want confidence in the Administration, and are unwilling to sanction the principles of construction adopted by the President, — most of us approved the general course of the Administration, have confidence in its virtue, its patriotism, its wisdom, and see nothing to condemn in the President's interpretation of the Federal Constitution. Yet we do not discuss among ourselves, and we will not discuss before you, the grounds of this difference. We waive such discussion, as wholly inappropriate, and postpone it to the time when there may be some choice offered us, that might be influenced by it. Now there is none such. We are left to the alternative of choosing between Jackson and Adams; and however we may differ in opinion as to the merits of the latter, we heartily concur in giving him a decided preference over his competitor. The measures which some dissapprove in the present Administration, none would hope to see amended under that of General Jackson: the distrust in the present Chief Magistrate entertained by some, is lost in the comparison with that which all feel in his competitor; and the Constitution, which we would preserve from the too liberal interpretation of Mr. Adams, we would yet more zealously defend against the destroying hand of his rival.

While, however, we decline a discussion of those subjects, on which we differ in opinion, and pretermit any general indication of the Chief Magistrate, his Cabinet, or his measures, we cannot pass unnoticed some topics connected with the last election, and some acts of the Administration in relation to which, we think, the public mind has been greatly abused.

The friends of General Jackson have confidently held him up, as the favorite of the People — have insisted that, in the last election, his plurality of votes proved him to be the choice of the nation — and have bitterly complained, that that choice was improperly disappointed by the Representatives in Congress.

Never was there a more direct appeal to those prejudices and passions, which, on all occasions, the good should disdain, and the wise should repress: never was a complaint more utterly ungrounded; and never one more characteristic of that disregard for the Constitution, which has been manifested on more occasions than one, when its provisions stood in the way of General Jackson's march.

Whether General Jackson is the People's favorite, is to be tested by the event, not assumed as the basis of the pending election. That his plurality of votes proved him to be the choice of the nation at the last election, we confidently deny. It may, perhaps, be found, upon examination, that, while General Jackson had a plurality of electoral votes, Mr. Adams had a plurality of voice at the polls; and we are confident, that if Mr. Crawford and Mr. Clay had been withdrawn from the canvass, and the contest had been single-handed between General Jackson and Mr. Adams, the election would have resulted as it has done, in the choice of Mr. Adams.

But this is not the light in which this question deserves consideration. The minds of the People ought not to be influenced by such extraneous considerations; and above all, the principles of our Constitution ought not to be abused, by admitting, for a moment, that the plurality of voice given to General Jackson, should have governed the choice of the House of Representatives. We do not mean to say, that a proper respect for the wishes of the nation, fairly ascertained, ought not always to be observed by its Representatives. But we do say, that the present Chief Magistrate holds his seat by the will of the People of the United States, regularly expressed, in the only way in which an expression of that will has any authority. They have willed, in the most solemn form — in the form of a Constitution, which they declare shall be the supreme law of the land — that a plurality of votes shall not constitute an election; that, when there is such plurality, the Representatives shall elect, voting by States — thus withdrawing from the People that equality of influence which is given them in the first vote, and transferring it to the States in the second. This provision of our Constitution is in the true spirit which pervades the whole of it, and which marks it the result of a conference between States, surrendering in part, and retaining in part, their political equality. Shall this spirit be appealed from, on every occasion in which it was intended to soothe and to conciliate, and the spirit of faction be invoked, to expose our magistrates, to unjust prejudice, and bring our institutions into discredit? These things are revolutionary in their tendency, and ought to be discouraged.

Of like character is the complaint against the Kentucky delegation, for disregarding the instructions of their Legislature. We have too much respect for the Legislature of Kentucky to suppose that they meant to bind the delegation by an instruction. We can only suppose that they meant to furnish the best information in their power, of the opinions on the People on a question which had never been submitted to them. Such information was entitled to the respect due to intelligent opinion, and to more. It was not the constitutional organ through which the will of the People was to be conveyed to the Representative. The Representatives in Congress were directly responsible to their Constituents, not to the Legislature. And an attempt of the Legislature to control the immediate Representatives of the People, would be usurpation upon the rights of the People — an act, which, instead of deserving obedience, or even respect, rejected resistance and even reprobation. The faithful Representative will obey the instructions of his constituents whenever constitutionally given. He will pay a respectful attention to their wishes, and every evidence of their wishes. But, when not bound by instruction, he will look beyond the imperfect evidences of their will, informally conveyed: he will rest upon the conclusions of his own mind, formed from the best lights he can obtain; will consult his country's good, and firmly meet the responsibility of those acts, he deems proper for its attainment. This we believe the Kentucky delegation did. They were not instructed — they did not choose to shelter themselves from responsibility, under the cover of a legislative recommendation: consulting their own judgments, they preferred the man thought most capable of advancing the interest of his country; and there is no question, that Virginia then concurred in the opinion, and approved the act.

This vote, which, if honestly given, is an affair chiefly between the Representative and his Constituents, would not have been obtruded on your attention, had it not been connected with a charge of grave import, made upon the punity of the election, impeaching the integrity of the Chief Magistrate of the Nation, and the first member of his Cabinet. This charge, in it strongest form, imports, that, at the last election, the vote of the Kentucky delegation was in the market, for the highest bidder; that it was offered to one candidate, and, being refused by him, was sold to the other; and that the consideration of the vote, was the office of Secretary of State, bestowed on Mr. Clay. If this were true, we should not hesitate to affirm, that it stamps infamy on the characters of the guilty, and renders them forever unworthy of public trust.

This charge, not so strongly, however, as has been here stated, was made, for the first time, pending the Presidential election. It was promptly met, and challenged by M. Clay, and deserted by its supporters. They rallied again, after the election, gave it a form somewhat varied, drew to its aid some imposing circumstances, and, at last, gave it the public sanction of Gen. Jackson's name. Mr. Clay again publicly denied it, called for the proof, and challenged inquiry. No proof has appeared to sustain it, no inquiry has been instituted, and now, in all its phases, it stands reprobated, by body of proof. So strong and so convincing, as to require from the least charitable, its open disapproval, and from the most suspicious,, a candid acknowledgment, that they have done injustice in even thinking it probable.

It may not be unworthy of notice, as one of the means by which the public mind has been prejudiced and inflamed, that opinions, the most offensive to a Republican People, have been unwarrantably and uncandidly inferred from some of the President's communications to Congress, and gravely imputed to him, as doctrines in his political creed. He has, on one occasion, not perhaps with strict rhetorical propriety, used the expression, "pulsed by the will of our constituents" — in reference to duties enjoined by the Constitution.

This phrase has been torn from its context, misinterpreted, and used as the authority upon which the President is charged with the heresy, that a Representative owes no obligation to the will of his constituents. On another occasion, incautiously taking it for granted that every one would understand that the high obligation of an oath was derived from Heaven, he has again, perhaps, without much felicity of phrase, made an obvious, though not avowed reference to his oath of office, as imposing an obligation above all human law — and this reference is tortured into a public avowal of the odious doctrine, that his political power was *jure divino*. If these had been the taunts and the railing of anonymous newspaper scribblers, they would have been deemed unworthy of this public notice. But when such charges are seriously made and reiterated, by men holding high stations in the Government, and exercising some influence over public opinion, they cannot be too strongly condemned.

Mr. Adams, it is said, is friendly to a regulation of the tariff of duties, with a view to the encouragement of American manufactures, and this is clamorously urged against him, as a serious objection, by those who support the election of Gen. Jackson.

This objection seems to have been treated, before the public, as if Mr. Adams were the founder of a new and odious doctrine, and the father of the measures to which it had given birth. Nothing can be further from the truth. Not a single act of the Government, on this subject, has its date within his administration. And so far is he from being the founder of the doctrine, that it is traced to the earliest and purest times of the Republic, avowed and acted upon from the foundation of the Government, when the Father of his Country presided over its destinies. Before the adoption of the Federal Constitution, the power of regulating commerce, and imposing duties on imports, belonged to the State Governments, and such of them, as deemed it expedient, so regulated their tariff of duties as to give encouragement to their manufactures. The

Constitution transferred to the Federal Government, by express provision the power of regulating commerce, and of imposing duties. An act, passed at the first session of the first Congress, held under the Constitution, advocated by James Madison, and signed by George Washington, on the 20th of July, 1789, contains the first tariff of duties on imported goods laid by the General Government, and its preamble recites, that it was "necessary for the support of Government, for the discharge of the debts of the United States, *and the encouragement and protection of manufactures.*" This doctrine was acted upon, by every succeeding Administration, by the elder Adams, by Jefferson, by Madison, and Monroe.The policy of protecting and encouraging manufactures was recommended by them all. The tariff was increased from time to time, with a view to that object; and yet, no champion of the Constitution, though many and bold and able there were, always at their posts, ever challenged the authors of these measures, as invaders of constitutional ground; until, during the administration of the last President, when the fathers of the Constitution, having most of them retired from the field of action, a member from Virginia suggested, in Congress, the want of constitutional power to give protection to manufactures.

On this question we forbear to enter the field of argument; and content ourselves with saying, that the power of Congress to regulate the tariff of duties, so as to give protection and encouragement to agriculture, manufactures, commerce, and navigation, cannot be denied, without denying to the letter of the Constitution its plain import, and to its spirit its most obvious essential attributes; without affirming that those who have administered the Government, from its foundation to the present day, have either misunderstood the charter of their powers, or wantonly and habitually violated it without coming to the extraordinary conclusion, either that a power which existed in the State Governments, and was frequently exercised by them, before the adoption of the Federal Constitution, was annihilated by the secret and magical influence of that instrument, or that such power does not properly pertain to the Legislature of any free People.

The exercise of this power is necessarily referred to the sound discretion of Congress, to be justly and impartially employed for the common benefit of all—not to be perverted to the purpose of advancing the interest of one class of the community, or of one part of the country, at the expense of another; and, whatever some of us may think as to its abuses under a former administration, or of the danger of such abuses under the present, all must concur in the opinion, that the remedy is not to be found in the election of General Jackson; but, if sought at all should be looked for in the vigilance and exertions of faithful and able Senators and Representatives in Congress.

The opinions of Mr. Adams, and his recommendations to Congress, in relation to internal improvement, are unpopular in Virginia, and have been urged against him with much earnestness, and perhaps with some effect, even though it cannot, with any color of reason, be contended, that his competitor, Gen. Jackson, is not exposed to precisely the same objection. We do not vindicate these opinions, or discuss them, because they fall within the intraduct we have imposed on ourselves — we differ in opinion concerning them. But we will remind you, that these opinions, whatever may be their merit, have produced but few and unimportant acts, during the present Administration; and we will avail ourselves of the occasion to appeal to the good sense and good feeling of Virginia and invoke its influence in tempering the asperity of politics, and in securing to every subject of national interest, a deliberate and candid consideration. We beg leave also to remind them, that the questions of Constitutional law, and State policy, connected with this subject, are important, delicate, and of acknowledged difficulty; that there are arrayed on either side of them. Statesmen of approved patriotism and talent, whose opinions should be examined with great consideration, and whose gestures, if deemed wrong, after being judged with candor, should be opposed with reason, not with passing — with firmness, not with violence, — that those among us, who deny the Constitutional power, and comdemn the policy, should entitle our doctrines to respect, by the fairness of our views, and the force of our reasoning, and give weight to our opposition, by its temper and its dignity; while those who affirm the power, and approve the policy should observe the most respectful deference for the opinions of the many and the wise, who differ from them; should consult the public interest and tranquillity, by confining their measures to objects of acknowledged and general interest, by infusing into them a spirit of the most exact justice; and by observing, in all things, scrupulous care in the exercise of a power so delicate, and so much controverted.

Thus far, we have endeavored to correct error and disarm prejudice, that reason might be left free to estimate fairly the present Administration, and its principal measures. We have offered no panegyric on the present Chief Magistrate — we cheerfully have you to estimate the value of his long and varied public services, his great experience, his talent, his learning, and his private virtues, — and to set off against them, whatever your fancy or your judging it may find to blame, in his private or public life. When you have done this — reflect on the character of the office you are about to fill — inquire what feelings, what temper, what talent, what acquirements, what habits, are best suited to the discharge of its high duties; and then carefully conpare John Q. Adams with Andrew Jackson, in reference to the great question. Which of them is best qualified for the first office in the nation — which most likely to preserve to us the distinguished blessings we enjoy — from which is most danger to be apprehended to our personal happiness, our lives and liberties.

It is not in wantonness that we speak; but, in the sadness of our hearts, we are compelled to declare, that, while we yield our confidence to the present Chief Magistrate in very different degrees, we are unanimous and unhesitating in the opinion that Andrew Jackson is altogether unfit for the Presidency, and that his election would be eminently dangerous; that, while we cheerfully accord to him his full share of the glory which renders the anniversary of the 8th of January a day of joy and triumph to our land, we must, in the most solemn manner, protest against a claim to civil rule, founded exclusively upon military renown; and avow that nothing has occurred in the history of our country so much calculated to shake our confidence in the capacity of the People for self-government, as the efforts which have been made and are yet making, to elevate to the first office in the nation, the man, who, disobeying the orders of his superiors, trampling on the Laws and Constitution of his country, sacrificing the liberties and lives of men, had made his own arbitrary with the rule of his conduct.

In stating an opinion so unfavorable to a distinguished man, who has rendered valuable services to his country, a proper respect for ourselves and for you, requires that we should declare the reasons which compel us to withhold our confidence from him.

Capacity for civil affairs, in a country like ours, where the road to preferment is open to merit, in every class of society, is never long concealed, and seldom left in retirement. General Jackson has lived beyond the age of 60 years, and was bred to the profession best calculated to improve and display the faculties which civil employments require; but the history of his public life, in these employments is told in a few brief lines — on a single page of his biography. He filled, successively for very short periods, the office of Member of the Tennessee Convention, which formed their State Constitution: Representative and Senator in Congress; Judge of the Supreme Court of Tennessee, and again, Senator in Congress of the United States. Here was ample opportunity for distinction, if he possessed the talent, taste, and application, suited for civil eminence. But he resigned three, and passed through all of these stations acknowledging his unfitness in two instances — manifestly feeling it in all — and having no single act, no trace, behind, which stamps his qualifications above mediocrity.

For civil government — and in no station more emphatically than in that of President of the United States — a well-governed temper is of admitted importance. General Jackson's friends lament the impetuosity of his, and all the world has evidence of its fiery misrule.

To maintain peace and harmony in the delicate relations existing between the Government of the Union and the various State Governments in our Confederacy, requires a courtesy and forbearance in their intercourse, which no passion should disturb. Let the spirit of domination displayed in General Jackson's celebrated letter to Governor Rabun, warn us of the danger of contributing to his keeping this precious deposite — sacred to the Union of our Republics, and to the freedom of mankind.

Military men should never be allowed to forget, that the obligation to obey being the sole foundation of the authority to command, they should inculcate subordination, not by precept only, but by example, that profound respect for the laws and Constitution of their country, is an indispensable guarantee of their worthiness to be entrusted with the sword which is drawn to defend them; that they should lose no fit occasion for manifesting that respect, by practical illustrations of the principle, sacred in every well ordered Republic, which proclaims the military subordinate to the civil power; that mercy even to the guilty, and humanity always to the conquered and the captive, are part of the law of God and man, found in every civilized code, written in every human heart, and indispensable to the true glory of the Hero.

General Jackson has been unmindful of these truths. Though he has enjoined subordination by precept, and enforced it by authority, he has not recommended it by example. He has offered indignity to the Secretary of War, in the very letter which assigned his reasons for disobeying an order to disband his troops, he has placed his own authority in opposition to that of the War Department, by a general order forbidding the officers of his command to obey the orders of that Department, unless they passed through the channel which he had chosen to prescribe; and he disobeyed the orders of the Government in his military operations in the Spanish territory.

He has been unmindful of the subordination of military to civil power, and has violated the law and the Constitution, by declaring martial law at New Orleans, and maintaining it, of his own arbitrary will, for more than two months after the enemy had been beaten and repulsed, and all reasonable apprehension of their return had ceased by surrounding the hall of the Louisiana Legislature with an armed force, and suspending their deliberations, by seizing the person of Louaillier, a free citizen of Louisiana, and member of their Legislature, and bringing him to trial before a military tribunal, for having the boldness to denounce, through the public press, the continued arbitrary reign of martial law; by disapproving the acquittal of Louaillier upon his trial, when, to have condemned and executed him, would have exposed the actors in the fatal tragedy to the legal pains of death; by suspending of his own arbitrary will, the writ of *habeas corpus* when the Legislature of Louisana had refused to suspend it on his application, when no law of Congress authorized it, and no imminent danger pleaded its apology; by arresting and imprisoning Judge Hall for issuing the writ of *habeas corpus* to relieve Louaillier from illegal confinement, and arresting and imprisoning two other officers of the law, for appealing to civil process against his tyranic rule, by the arrest, trial, and execution, of six men, who were guilty of no other offence than the assertion of their lawful right to return home, after their legal term of service had expired by organizing a corps of volunteer militia and appointing its officers, without any warrant for so doing, and against the provisions of the Constitution which expressly reserve the appointment of the officers of the militia to the States respectively and by making war upon the Spanish Territory, seizing and holding Spanish posts in violation of the order of his Government and whilst peace existed between Spain and the United States.

That mercy and humanity may unite with the offended Law and Constitution in accusing General Jackson of being unmindful of their voice, and in refusing to his laurel crown the rays of true glory, will be acknowledged by impartial posterity, when they review the history of his Indian campaigns and especially when they read the stories of the cold-blooded massacre at the Horseshoe, of the decoyed and slaughtered Indians at St. Mark's, of the wanton and unexampled execution of Ambrister, an Englishmen, found fighting it is true, in the ranks of the Seminoles, but taken prisoner, tried, doomed to a milder punishment, and executed by order of the commanding General, against the sentence of the tribunal appointed by himself and of the still more injured Arouthnot, another Briton, not burning arms at all, only found among the warring Indians, a trader, and an advocate for peace.

We have done with this sickening catalogue. You have now a brief summary of the evidence, on the authority of which we regard General Jackson as wholly disqualified for the Presidency, and look to the prospect of his election with the most gloomy forebodings.

You think, perhaps, we pay a poor compliment to the virtues of our People, and the strength of our institutions, by indulging in apprehensions of danger from the encroachments of military power, in the youth and vigor of our Republic, and in the midst of profound peace. We should, indeed, do great injustice to the virtue of our People, the circumstances of our country, and the value of our Government, if we indulged in the idle fear, that an open attack upon our liberties, made with any military force, which General J. could probably command in the course of his administration, would bring us under the yoke of his power. These are not our apprehensions; we would bid a proud defiance to his power, if he should so dare our liberties. Nor will we do him the injustice to charge his ambition with any designs, at present, on the liberties of his country, or withhold our acknowledgment, that, if they were assailed by others, we believe he would promptly and boldly draw his sword to defend them.

But we have no security for the continuance of peace, in whatsoever hands the Government may be placed; and it is not unreasonable to think, that, in the hands of a man of military pride and talent, and of ungovernable temper, the danger of war will be increased. A foreign war may come, may rage with violence, and find General Jackson at the head of the civil government, and commander-in-chief of the land and naval forces. Dissentient views among the States may arise, controversies grow up between the State and Federal authorities, as dissensions and controversies have heretofore arisen; and who, then, we pray you, can answer for the consequences of that spirit which said to Governor Rabun, *When I am in the field, you have no authority to issue a military order*! Reflect on this question, we beseech you—on the peculiar structure of our Government; on the collisions of opinion, and the threatened collisions of action, both in peace and war, which have already occurred between the State and Federal authorities and then tell us, whether the fear is altogether visionary, that the first foreign war, seriously waged against the United States, with General Jackson their chief, would bring danger of civil discord, dissolution of the Union, and death to the hopes of every free government in the world.

We say nothing of the danger of civil discord, even when no foreign war should afflict us—though the retrospect of a few short years would teach us that such danger is not imaginary—and that the slightest want of tact, in its management, the least indulgence of temper, on the part of the Chief Magistrate, might inflame the whole nation, and light the funeral pile of freedom.

There are dangers of another kind. If we are correct in the detail of offences committed by General Jackson, against the most sacred principles of our Government, what will be the moral effect of the direct sanction given for these offences, by rewarding the offender with the first honor of the nation? Can we preserve our love and reverence for institutions which we suffer to be violated, not only without censure, but with applause? Will not our affections and our veneration be transferred from the despised Laws and Constitution to the honored Hero who has abused them—from republican simplicity and virtue, to military pomp and glory? Will you not, in time, by such example, lay the sure foundation of that moral depravity, and admiration of arms, which must soon reduce us to the condition in which Greece was enslaved by Alexander: Rome, by Caesar: England, by Cromwell: France, by Bonaparte: and in which we will assuredly find some future Jackson, not too fastidious to accept the proffered crown, and erect a military despotism on the ruins of the last Republic.

We appeal to the People of Virginia, to say what there is in the present party politics, so alluring on the part of the Opposition, so frightful on the part of the Administration, as to seduce them to the fraternal embrace, or drive them under the protection, of such a man as Andrew Jackson? We ask an answer to this question, not from their offended pride, nor from the prejudice which attachment to party never fails to beget; but we ask it from their love of country, their love of truth and virtue; we ask it, after a deep and dispassionate consideration of the true state of the question; after a candid estimate of the little to be possibly gained by the rejection of Mr. Adams, the incalculable mischiefs which may probably attend the success of his rival. If you indulge the faint hope, that, under the Administration of General Jackson, the tab to which agriculture will pay for the encouragement of domestic industry and enterprise, will be somewhat lighter than at present — we ask you, first, whether the hope is not groundless? and next, whether it is wise to insist on enjoying the profits of your estates in the uttermost farthing of their fancied value, at the risk of having your free allodial lands converted into military tenures or fiefs of the crown? If you are fighting the battles of General Jackson, in this political contest, with the vain hope that victory will conquer from your adversaries some barren spot of constitutional ground — we ask whether you will wage such a war with your countrymen, at the hazard of laying all your conquests, and all your former possessions — the Constitution itself, and the freedom it was intended to protect — at the feet of a despot? This does not become the character of Virginians!

In the ancient state of political parties, when federalists and republicans contended for ascendency, there was something in the great questions of foreign policy, in the leading principles of construction applied to the Constitution, bearing strongly on the essential character of the Government, and worthy of a generous struggle between the statesmen, who, on the one hand, sought to guard against a dissolution of the Union, by strengthening the Federal bond, and, on the other, endeavored to avert consolidation, by establishing more firmly the State authorities. But this state of things has passed away, and the feelings and doctrines to which it gave rise, though not entirely forgotten, are almost unknown in the party distinctions of the day. Federalists and republicans mingle together in the ranks of the Opposition — and, together, rally around the standard of the Administration. There will be no great principle of political doctrine to distinguish them, unless the Opposition, following too closely the footsteps of those who trample on the Laws and Constitution of the country, should give to the supporters of the Administration some claim to be the champions of civil rule and constitutional law. Shall our parties be hereafter founded on local interests, and marked by geographical boundaries, arraying the North against the South, the East against the West — losing the generous enthusiasm which is always inspired by a contest for principle, for honorable distinction, for pre-eminence in the service of our common country; and acquiring the bitterness of spirit, acrimony of feeling, narrow policy, and sordid views, which ever characterise the contests of men, striving, not for the promotion of the common good, but for the advancement of their own peculiar interests — and which must lead, inevitably, to the entire subjugation of the weaker party, or a dissolution of the Union?

We know well, that the People of Virginia will never countenance any such distinction. Their generous sacrifices in the cause of their country, their uniform devotion to civil liberty, and their noble daring in the defence of freedom, from whatever quarter assailed, is the sure guarantee that they will not be slow to follow where the path of duty leads; and on that guarantee we repose with confidence, that, in this hour of danger, sacrificing all minor considerations, they will go forth in their strength, and save the Temple of Liberty from pollution.

1. *Resolve*, That JOHN QUINCY ADAMS, of Massachusetts, be recommended to the People of the United States, as a fit person to be supported for the Office of President.

2. *Resolved*, That this Convention approve the nomination of RICHARD RUSH, of the State of Pennsylvania, for the Office of Vice President, made by the Convention at Harrisburg, and recommend him to the People of Virginia as a fit person to be supported for that office.

3. *Resolved*, That the President of this Convention be requested to transmit a copy of the proceedings and address of this Convention to each of the gentlemen who have been nominated on the Electoral Ticket, and inform them of their several appointments.

4. *Resolved*, That the following persons be appointed a Central Corresponding Committee, with the authority to fill any vacancies which may occur within their own body, or in the Electoral Ticket in favor of the election of John Quincy Adams as President of the United States, and Richard Rush as Vice President, vis: Judge William H. Cabell, Judge Dabney Carr, Judge John Coalter, Mr. Robert Stanard, Reverend John Kerr, General J. B. Harvic, Mr. Peyton Randolph, Mr. John H. Pleasants, Mr. Charles Copland, Mr. Thomas Brockenbrough, Mr. F. W. Rootes, Mr. J. H. Eustace, Dr. Thomas Nelson.

5. *Resolved*, That the Corresponding Committees, which have been appointed by the meetings opposed to the election of General Jackson as President of the United States, in the various Counties and Corporations of this Commonwealth, constitute the Corresponding Committees of said Counties and Corporations, with authority to add to their numbers, and fill any vacancies which may occur in said Committees.

6. *Resolved*, That the Central Corresponding Committee be authorized to appoint corresponding committees in the several counties and corporations which have not appointed them, which committees shall have authority to exercise the same powers as those which have heretofore been appointed.

7. *Resolved*, That it be recommended to the Convention that each member should pay the sum of five dollars to the Secretaries, to be deposited in the Bank of Virginia to the credit of the Chairman of the Central Committee, to defray the expenses of printing and circulating the documents directed to be published by the Convention, and such other publications as may be thought advisable by the said Central Committee for the purpose of distribution among the citizens of the Commonwealth, and all other incidental charges.

8. *Resolved*, That at least thirty thousand copies of the proceedings and address of this Convention be printed and circulated, under the direction of the Central Committee, through the several counties and corporations of the Commonwealth.

9. *Resolved*, That the Central Corresponding Committee be requested to publish, in pamphlet form, as many copies of the address of the Hon. Henry Clay, with the accompanying documents, as they may deem expedient, and that they cause to be published such other documents, as, in their opinion, will sustain the facts and principles set forth in the address of this Convention.

10. *Resolved*, That the Central Committee be requested to make to the officers of the Senate and House of Delegates who have attended upon this Convention during its session, such compensation as they may deem proper, to be paid out of the fund provided by this Convention.

11. *Resolved*, That this Convention entertain feelings of unfeigned gratitude for the facilities offered, and the spirit of accommodation manifested, by both Houses of the Virginia Assembly and their officers, to this Convention, in the prosecution of their duties, and that the President be requested to tender the thanks of this Convention to both branches of the Assembly and their officers, for their kindness and liberality.

13. *Resolved*, That the Editors of the several newspapers printed in Virginia be requested to publish the proceedings of the Convention, together with their address to the People of Virginia, in their respective papers.

ADDRESS TO THE PEOPLE OF NEW YORK

June 23, 1828

"If intellectual powers of the highest grade, and cultivated with almost unexampled assiduity and success, contribute to fit a man for the first office in our Nation, then, it must be admitted, that the choice of Mr. Adams, so far considered, was eminently proper: for Mr. Adams had shone too long, and to brightly in public life, and the elegant and powerful productions of his pen were too universally admired, to leave the superiority of his mind at all questionable. If unblemished morals, no less than talents and learning, should distinguish our President—if his example, as influential as his station is elevated, should be such as to rebuke vice and encourage virtue—then, the sober chaste, religous life of Mr. Adams forms another, and, by no means inconsiderable, argument in favor of his election. And here, if we were writing the eulogy of Mr. Adams, we might expatiate on those simple, unostentatious, abstemious, and laborious habits, which, whilst they constitute him a pattern for all public men, do, at the same time no little honor to his country, in their practical and flattering illustrations of the genius of her institutions. The vitious constitution of Royal Governments is no more apparent from their lazy, sensual, star-spangled monarchs, than are the simplicity and excellence of republicanism, from the President of the habits of Mr. Adams. If too, our President should be a statesman — and this seems to be indispensible, in view of even the *ordinary* duties of his great office — then does the election of Mr. Adams answer well to this requirement also: for, besides his superior capacity for becoming a great statesman, few men have enjoyed his opportunities to educate themselves in this character. All who are aware of the inquiring and reflecting case of Mr. Adams' mind, will agree, that, in his thirty years of public service, he must have exended his knowledge of our national affairs to an unsurpassed degree, and that, during his residence at most of the courts of Europe, his quick sagacious, studious observations, upon her social and political structures must have contributed largely to fill up the measure of a statesman's education.

The fact, that Mr. Adams had passed through a longer graduation of political honors than any other man in the nation was, in itself, no small evidence of his fitness to be President; but this evidence is peculiarly magnified by looking at the sources from when he received the most distinguished of these honors.

His first appointment, as Foreign Minister, he received from President Washington; and we have no less than Washington's testimony of his able performance of its duties. "I give it," said that discriminating man, in the year, 1797, "as my decided opinion, that Mr. Adams is the most valuable public character we have abroad, and there remains no doubt on my mind that he will prove himself the ablest of our diplomatic corps." It will be recollected that our foreign Ministers, at that period, were no less than Rufus King, Chief Justice Marshall, Chas. Gatesworth Pinckney, and Elbridge Gerry.

The subsequent reputation and services of Mr. Adams realized the bright promises of his youth.

The honors with which the "Father of his Country" invested him, were increased at the hands of the immortal Jefferson; and the estimation in which he was held by Madison and Monroe, best appears from the pre-eminent stations which these venerable patriots assigned him, throughout their administrations. Comment is unnecessary on the fact, that these great and good men all tokened their high esteem of Mr. Adams; that no one administration of our Government has failed to seek the aid of his distinguished abilities. The bare fact goes very far to vindicate his present elevation, and to outweigh, in every candid mind, all the inventions of malice against his unsullied fame."

The opponents of the Administration, dispairing of success to their cause by any appeals it can make to the sober judgment of the People, and, withal, distrusting the sufficiency of their cunning falsehoods to work this success, are seeking to associate and even to identify that unrighteous cause with the military glory of the nation; and are busily invoking to its aid the popular enthusiasm, which that spirit-stirring subject is so capable of exciting. It is with this object, and this only that they have selected Andrew Jackson for the candidate against Mr. Adams. We fear not to submit it to the candor of all men, whether this nomination of Gen. Jackson is susceptible of any other explanation than that which we have here given it: — whether it could have proceeded from any other motives than the single one we have here ascribed to it. We fear not to ask any of our constituents, whether it is for Andrew Jackson the Statesman, or for Andrew Jackson the Soldier, that they find their votes solicited; whether the trumpeters of the General's merits desire dispassionate comparisons of the fitness of the two men for civil office, or, whether they are not incessantly displaying their Hero to the passions and imagination, so as most effectually to swell the tide of popular admiration, on which the Victor of New Orleans is bearing down the unobtrusive and noiseless merits of Mr. Adams. "Our enemies themselves being judges," the nomination of General Jackson has not proceeded from any sense of his *fitness* to be President: for the leaders of the party, opposed to the Administration, before submitting to the necessity of taking him up, and whilst they were free to speak of him, as they thought, expressly classed his election amongst the greatest curses that could befal our country. We need not go into all the particulars, they would make up the completest proof of the truth of this assertion. A reference to the files of some of the newspapers which are the prominent organs of this party, will sufficiently establish it. The newspapers of this class, with which the People of this State are most familiar, are the "Richmond Enquirer," New York Evening Post," and "Albany Argus." We do not refer to these papers to expose the inconsistencies of their Editors. That would be beneath the dignity of this Convention. But, inasmuch as these papers are the channels through which the leaders of the Opposition have elected to communicate with the public mind, they are certainly useful records of the remarkable changes experienced by those leaders. These mercenary papers have changed with their masters, and then columns are now as crowded with the praises of General Jackson, as, but four years ago, they were with the reproaches and denunciations of him. In how little favor the General stood with these papers, at that time, is manifest from such paragraphs as the following:

"We cannot consent," says the Richmond Enquirer, "to lead a hand towards the electon of such as man as General Jackson. He is too little of a Statesman — too rash — too violent in his temper — his measures too much inclined to arbitrary government, to obtain the humble support of the Editors of this paper. *We would deprecate his election as a curse upon our country.*"

"General Jackson," says the New York Evening Post, "from the moment he was entrusted with command, has avowedly and systematically made his own will and pleasure the sole rule and guide of all his actions. He has suspended the executive, legislative, and judicial functions, with military sway. He has insulted the Executive of the United States; spurned its authority; disregarded and transcended its orders. He has usurped the high prerogative of peace and was entrusted by all nations to the sovereign power of the State, and, by our Constitution, to Congress alone! He has abrogated the known laws of nations, and promulgated a new code of his own—conceived in madness of folly, and *written in blood!* He has, in fine, violated all laws, human and divine." The same paper, after stating that General Jackson "Ordered the unhappy Ambrister to instant execution, without any sentence at all," adds: "In doing so, I assert he committed, in the eye of the law of his country, Murder with malice prepense."

The columns of the Albany Argus sum up their objections to General Jackson in the conclusion, that, "He stands, in the minds of the People of this State, at an *immeasurable distance* from the Executive Chair; that *his habits*, aside from his politics, are *quite too summary for that.*"

It is obvious, then, whatever may now be pretended to the contrary, that General Jackson has not been brought forward for the Presidency, on the score of his fitness for it. The charms of a successful Soldier are relied on to captivate our imaginations, and to hide the want of that fitness—and his distinguished services to his country are to make their irresistible appeal to our gratitude, for the highest reward we can confer on him. It is, in short, to recompense his part in the defence of New Orleans, that we are called on to make General Jackson President: for it was on that occasion that his character acquired all the splendor, which makes him so imposing a candidate for popular honors. No one, indeed, presumes to say, that Gen. Jackson would ever have been thought of for President, but for the victory of New Orleans. The glories of that victory comprise all his pretensions to the honor.

Such, then, is the candidate for President, supported by the Opposition: a man who, confessedly, from the lips and presses of their own leaders, is utterly unqualified for the office, and altogether, the most dangerous man that can be placed in it. Here, too, is the further expedient to overthrow the Administration, to which we last invited your attention; which deserves your unmeasured reprehension, and which, by all the love you bear your country, you must defeat.

To associate in the hand of a brilliant and elevated soldier, who has never exhibited the qualifications of an eminent Statesman, the highest civil power of the nation, with the still greater power of his military glory, is, certainly, to neglect and despise the verdict of experience and the voice of history. This union has accelerated the ruin of every Republic that has preceded us. The public safety is so deeply interested in confining the ambitious soldier within the limits of his usefulness, as to require us to make his profession and the utmost success in it, altogether foreign to the ways and means of civil preferment. Least of all can we tolerate the idea, which is now so sedulously inculcated, that the Presidency of the Nation is a suitable reward for distinguished military services; and that Gen. Jackson, for his part in the defence of New Orleans, richly merits it. We conjure you, fellow-citizens, do not so cheapen this honor. It is the greatest that mortal hands were ever permitted to bestow. It is too precious to weave in the garland of any soldier. Keep it for such virtuous Statesmen and Soldiers, as you have hitherto adorned with it. When military merit has once bought it, it will have lost all its worth. It will then have fallen into the same process of degradation, which reduced the soveriegnty of Imperial Rome to the mere game and plaything of her successful and ambitious Generals.

On this subject of filling your highest civil office with a military man, what language can we hold to you, that will, at once, be so instructive, and enforce itself with so high authority, as Thomas Jefferson's? The words of his political wisdom, to every genuine and intelligent Republic, are "like apples of gold in pictures of silver." This great Apostle of Republicanism, after the last Presidential Election, addressing himself to several gentlemen, including his intimate friend Governor Coles, said, that, during long public life, he had attentively watched the progress of events in the United States, with the particular view of satisfying his mind that mankind were competent to self-government, to believe which his principles inclined him; and that during his whole political observation, the disposition of the American People to elect General Jackson President, was the single circumstance, that had shaken his faith, and made him fear that the American Republic was soon to follow the fate of all others, and to fall under military rule.

The great and boasted argument, then, for the election of Gen. Jackson, founded on his splendid military achievements, gives way before the obvious conclusion, that his martial lame, so far from entitling him to the Presidency, would make him, in the absence of conspicuous civil qualifications, a peculiarly unsafe depository of its extensive powers.

ADDRESS TO THE PEOPLE OF MARYLAND

November 6, 1828

A struggle is at hand, fraught with more than ordinary importance. On the *tenth of November*, you will be called upon to settle the most august question which has ever agitated this country since the Revolution. You will then be called upon to decide, by your votes, whether our present happy form of Government shall be placed on a firm and solid foundation by the re-election of John Quincy Adams—whether that system in the Administration of the affairs of our country, founded by Washington, pursued by every subsequent President, and which has conferred so many blessings on us all, individually and collectively, is to be continued—or whether, by the elevation of an unlettered, though successful soldier, to the Chief Magistracy of this Nation, you will place on the ruins of the Republic, a Government based in despotism, and founded alone in the headlong passions and will of, one who has never yet regardeᴏ the Constitution or Laws of his country, as being barriers to the gratification of his own capricious whims. In presenting the case, in this strong light, to your consideration, we do not do it with a view of alarming your fears, unnecessarily, or of exciting your prejudices against General Jackson. Our object is of a higher order—the preservation of those liberties achieved by the blood and consecrated by the wisdom of the patriots and sages of the Revolution is the only aim we have in view. Let it not be said that they are not to be endangered by the elevation of General Jackson to the Presidency; for the experience of his past conduct shows, most conclusively, that there is great cause of apprehension. Let us look back upon the whole history of his official conduct, whether acting in the character of a Republican General or as Governor of Florida, as we shall have presented to our sight a continued scene of violence and outrage. At one moment we behold General Jackson, in defiance of the plainest provisions of law, urging Governor Blount to order out the militia for twice the legal time of service, and pledging himself to be held accountable for the consequences. At another time, we find him absolutely refusing to obey the orders of the President, who had peremptorily directed the discharge of the militia under his command—at another, we find him ordering the trial of two hundred militiamen for desertion, whom he had illegally and unjustly detained in service—and, as if to cap the climax of cruelty in this soul-rending catastrophe, we find him, the day after he had been to the temple of the Almighty to return thanks for the victory vouchsafed to the American arms, deliberately consigning six of the victims of his own oppression to an ignominious death, and upwards of *one hundred and eighty* others to a most disgraceful punishment—a punishment never before inflicted upon any except the culprits of Penitentiaries and State Prisons. At another time we behold him opposing the meeting of the Legislature, by causing the bayonets of his soldiers to be directed against their breasts. At another time we behold him restraining the liberty of the press and speech—suspending the writ of *habeas corpus*—trying citizens by military courts, thereby jeopardizing the lives of those who, in fact, had committed no offence whatever. Again, while Governor of Florida, we behold him usurping the powers of all the other branches of the Government—practising the most odious tyrannies upon all descriptions of persons, from the Judge down to the private citizen; brow-beating and abusing the former, and imposing burthensome and illegal taxes upon the latter.

We have thus hastily sketched a few of the many disqualifying and arbitrary acts of General Jackson; sufficient, however, to convince all reasonable men, that the man who, when fulfilling subordinate stations could thus abuse the trust reposed in him, would, if placed in possession of the chief executive power, go still further. People of Maryland! we ask you to reflect seriously upon the ills which would befall our country, under the guidance of such an impetuous and uncontrollable man. His partisans need not tell us he would call to his aid, in the Cabinet, able advisers—who are his advisers? Are they not those Southern Hotspurs, who have been threatening to dissolve the Union, rather than the industry of American manufacturers, artisans, and mechanics, should be protected? These are the men whom he would call to his aid—men but little (if any) less rash than himself.

We appeal to you, men of Maryland, to save your country from such a calamity as would ensure the election of General Jackson. We call upon you, friends of religion, and of good morals, young and old, rich and poor, to turn out on the 10th of this month, and enter your solemn protest against a measure so pregnant with evil—so threatening to liberty itself. Let no man stay at home; but let each set an example worthy of the emulation of his neighbors: let the young and healthy assist the aged and sick in reaching the polls. If the re-election of Mr. Adams should be secured by one vote, what a pleasing reflection will it be to him who gave that vote; but on the other hand, if by one of the friends of order remaining at home, General Jackson should succeed, and establish a despotism, how corroding the thought, that, because he had not energy enough to quit his home, and discharge his duty as a good citizen, he had lost to his country its liberties, and unconsciously bound himself, his countrymen, and posterity, in the chains of slavery.

Friends of peace! Lovers of liberty! We invoke you one and all, to make one great and glorious, effort, and *Preserve your country!* Recollect that the heritage we enjoy is a rich and precious one, and cost our fathers many years of sacrifice, of toil, and of danger—that it has been handed down to us to preserve inviolate. The trust is a sacred one—as its conservators we conjure you by the blood of our Fathers!—by every tie endearing to man!—by the blessings of free Government!—Not to stay at home *on the 10th of November. The eyes of happy America are upon you*—Justify the expectations of patriotism and virtue. Go to the polls and vote for John Quincy Adams and Richard Rush. In doing so, you will entitle yourselves to the thanks—to the grateful thanks, of the present and future generations, for having rescued the destinies of the Republic from the ruin and desolation consequent on military misrule.

Editorial from the *United States Telegraph*
September 11, 1828

The following article, printed in what was commonly known as a "Jackson mouthpiece," is typical of the general argument and logic aimed at the incumbent President, John Quincy Adams.

Among a people like that of the United States, who recognize no difference between political and social morals, and who believe that, he who would be false to one engagement would not be true to any, no quality is more highly estimated than party fidelity. They consider parties, and very justly, essential to the political health of a republic; for, viewing these parties as spies on each other, they consider their mutual distrust the best restraint against any improper courses. But besides the utility of parties in a republic, every member of the Democratic Republican party must feel that, to him in common with his associates, is confided the great cause of the many against the few, of equal rights against privileged orders, of democracy against aristocracy. Therefore every member of this party must feel that, John Quincy Adams must be an object of particular distrust to Democratic Republicans.

Mr. Adams was educated among the Federal party, and indebted to Federalists for his first appearance in public employment. He afterwards abandoned this party, and joined that of the Democratic Republicans. Federalists have believed that he deserted and calumniated them. If this be true, he deserves no confidence from Democratic Republicans for having violated the principle of party fidelity, which, in this country, all parties do or ought to respect, he can justly claim the confidence of no party. Other Federalists maintain that, he joined the Democratic Republican party for the purpose of destroying it. If *this* be true, I need not say what he deserves from this party. In a former number, I endeavored to show, by the testimony of a witness who could not be impeached, who, as a Federalist viewed with just indignation the desertion of his own party, and as an honorable man, with equal indignation the attempt to destroy its opponent party by dishonorable means, that, Mr. Adams had associated himself with the Democratic Republican party, for the purpose of compassing its ruin.

1st. He is devoid of sincerity. To some politicians, who separate public from private morals, and believe that to obtain votes, any course or expedient is justifiable that may influence public opinion, want of sincerity in a candidate for public employment may seem a venial infirmity. But this class, it may be hoped, is not numerous in this land. The great majority of the American people, honest themselves, selecting agents to transact their most important business, the management of their institutions, will certainly — deem the honesty of such agents an important consideration. And how can they deem that agent honest, who holds one language to the world and another to the few; one to those whom he professes to have abandoned, and another to those whom he pretends to have joined? All mankind join in expressing veneration for truth and detestation of falsehood. This sentiment is not more general than necessary, for how can society be held together in peace, unless its members can confide in the statements and declarations of each other? Then as sincerity consists in strictly adhering to truth, and detesting the odious vice of falsehood, and as, in republic, honesty and fidelity in public agents are vitally important, with what propriety can we say that, want of sincerity affords no objection against a candidate for public office? — Admitting this, what citizen of honest feelings can approve the character of Mr. Adams, so far as it has been evinced by insincere professions to the Democratic party?

2d. He is regardless of means in seeking his object. Fraud, deceit, artifice, circumvention, seem, to him, excusable if not justifiable means of compassing a political design. What could be more deceptive, more fraudulent, than to join a party for the purpose of destroying it? Such conduct involves both espionage and treachery, and must meet the unqualified condemnation of all honorable minds. To compass this design, he must seem a traitor to his early friends and associates; for he could not, with any hope of success, confide his scheme to the whole Federal party. Such disclosure would publish it to the whole community, and put his opponents on their guard. He must, therefore, in pursuit of his design, necessarily deceive the majority of his Federal friends, and subject himself, in their estimation, to the charges of perfidy and ingratitude. In seeking admittance at the door of the Democratic party, he must assign some satisfactory or plausible reason for denouncing his old friends, or incur the imputation of changing to gratify personal ambition. Accordingly, he accused the Federal party of plotting against the Union and institutions of their country.

This charge was true or false. If true, Mr. Adams sought the destruction of the Democratic party, for the purpose of restoring to power those whom he knew to be a band of traitors. If false, Mr. Adams stands before the world as a calumniator of his old friends, as a pretender to principles he contemns, and a promoter of policy he disapproves, and for the purpose of subverting the liberties of his country. In either case, his course is marked by double fraud, and should prepare for him a niche in the Temple of Fame, as a character which none can mistake.

3d. He is an aristocrat. Why should he be so solicitous about expelling the Democratic party frm public trust, and restoring Federalism to power? He has assigned the reason; and to every Democrat, that reason *ought* to be *satisfactory*. His object was to change the democratic institutions of his country, and replace them by some more resembling the aristocratic institutions of England. On this point, comment is needless, for every Democratic Republican will know what sentence to pronounce.

4th. He is a moral traitor. To seek the destruction of the government, has, in all countries, been denommated *treason*, though in all cases, the epithet is not applied correctly. Our revolutionary fathers sought the destruction of a colonial tyranny, for the purpose of restoring to a people their plundered rights. They were not *traitors*, but *patriots*. But to seek the destruction of the liberty which they established, and for the purpose of restoring the tyranny which they overthrew, would be *treason*, and of the darkest hue, in one who had been nurtured and educated amid that liberty, and who saw and felt that, to its salutary influence must be ascribed the happiness, the prosperity, the security of his country. General Henry Lee, who aided Washington and La Fayette in fighting the battles of liberty, was no *traitor*, though an Englishman by birth, and for years an officer in the British military service. Yet Arnold was a traitor, though in drawing his sword against his native country, he followed the example of General Lee. What constitutes the difference? One abandoned an unjust and the other betrayed a righteous cause. In the estimation of every Democratic Republican, Mr. Adams has followed the example of Arnold, and not of General Lee; for he did not abandon an unjust in order to aid a righteous cause, but falsely pretended to abandon an unjust, for the purpose of betraying a righteous cause. A pretended disciple of liberty, he sought its ruin for the sake of arbitrary power; and therefore, in the estimation of all who deem liberty valuable, he must be pronounced a *traitor*.

The Coffin Handbill

The Coffin Handbill was a powerful propaganda instrument employed by the anti-Jackson forces during the 1828 presidential contest. It originated with John Binns, editor of the Philadephia Democratic Press, *and was widely reprinted. The handbill was bordered in black; across the top were depicted six large black coffins over which were affixed the names of the militia men Jackson had allegedly executed "in violation of the laws of the country and the usages of civilized society."*

SOME ACCOUNT OF SOME OF THE BLOODY DEEDS
OF GENERAL JACKSON.

A brief account of the Execution of the Six Militia Men

As we may soon expect to have the official documents in relation to the Six Militia Men, arrested, tried, and put to death, under the orders of General Andrew Jackson, this may not be an improper time to give to the public some of the particulars of their execution, as we have them from "An Eye Witness", who appeals to Col Russell, for the truth of every word he relates.

Harris was a Baptist preacher, with a large family. He had hired as a substitute for three months. This was the case with most of them. They were ignorant men, but obstinate in what they believed right, and what they had been told by their officers was right. — They were all sure they could not be kept beyond three months, and they gave up their musquets, and had provisions dealt out to them, from the public stores, before they left the camp. — This confirmed their convictions that they were right and doing what was lawful.

Col. Russel commanded at the execution. The Militia men were brought to the place in a large wagon. The military dispositions being made, Col. Russell rode up to the wagon and ordered the men to descend. Harris was the only one who betrayed feminine weakness. The awfulness of the occasion; his wife and nine children; the parting with his son; and the fear of a quickly approaching ignominious death! quite overcame him, and he sunk in unmanly grief. No feeling of military pride could brace him up.

Col. Russel, doubtless, felt as a man, but he felt also for the pride of the army, and desired to animate the men with fortitude.

You are about to die, said he, by the sentence of a Court Martial — die like men; *like soldiers.* You have been brave in the field — you have fought well — do no discredit to your country, or dishonour to the army, or yourselves, by any unmanly fears. Meet your fate with courage."

Harris attempted to make some apology for his conduct, but while he spoke, he wept bitterly. The fear of death, the idea that he should never again behold his wife and little ones, and his son weeping near him, had taken such entire possession of his mind that it was impossible he should rally.

Lewis, the gallant Lewis, said in a clear and manly tone, "Colonel, I have

485

served my country well. I love it dearly, and would, if I could, serve it longer and better. I have fought bravely—*you know* I have, and here, I have a right to say so myself. I would not wish to die in this way"—here his voice faltered, and he passed the back of his right hand over his eyes—"I did not expect it: But, I am now as firm as I have been in battle, and you shall see that I will die as becomes a soldier, you know I am a brave man". "Yes, Lewis, said the Colonel, you have always behaved like a brave man". Other sentences were uttered, other declarations were made, and words of comfort spoken, but they were lost on me: my attention, says an Eye Witness, being chiefly directed to Lewis.

Six coffins were ranged as directed, and on each of them knelt one of our condemned American Militia Men—Such a sight was never seen before! I trust to God it never will be seen again! Six soldiers were detailed and drawn up to fire at each man. What an awful duty! Their white caps were drawn over the faces of the unhappy men.—Harris evidently trembled, and I could almost persuade myself that the heart of Lewis was enlarged, and that his bosom rose with manly courage to meet death. The fatal word was given and they all fell.

As we approached the scene of blood and carnage, Lewis gave signs of life; the rest were all dead—he crawled upon his coffin. After the lapse of a few minutes he said—I give his very words: "Colonel"—the Colonel was close to him—"Colonel, I am not killed, but I am sadly cut and mangled". His body was now examined and it was found that but four balls had wounded him. "Colonel", said he, "did I behave well". "Yes, Lewis"—said the Colonel in the kindest tone of voice—"like a man". "Well sir", said he, "have I not atoned for this offence? *Shall I not live?*" The Colonel was much agitated, and gave orders that the Surgeon should, if possible, preserve his life. They did all that skill and humanity could do—it was all of no avail. Poor Lewis expressed a great desire to live—"not", said he at one time, "that I fear death, but I would repent me of some sins, and I desire to live yet a little longer in the world". He suffered inconceivable agony, from his wounds, and died on the fourth day.

Many a soldier has wept over his grave. He was a brave man and much beloved. He suffered twenty deaths.—I have seen the big drops chase each other down his forehead with pain and anguish. There was much sensibility and sympathy throughout the camp.—I would not have, unjustly and unnec-essarily, signed this death warrant for all the wealth of all the Indies. The soldiers detailed to shoot Lewis had, from strong feelings of sympathy, or mistaken humanity failed to shoot him—but four balls had entered his body.

"An Eye Witness" appeals to Col. Russell, who he thinks now lives in Ala-bama, for the perfect truth of this sketch. He does not fear but the Colonel will keenly recollect and faithfully depict the horrors of the day on which six Americans were shot to death under his command—but not by his orders.

The order bears date the very day after *General Jackson* returned in triumph to New Orleans, and the day before he joyfully went, under triumphal arches, to the Temple of the living God; where, says the historian, "they *crowned* their adored General with laurels". The order for the execution of these six unhappy men bears date January 22, 1815. His crown of laurels had not yet withered, when blood, the life's blood of his countrymen, of his fellow soldiers, flowed plentifully by his order. May that order and its consequences, sink deep into the hearts of the American people and steel them against him who had no flesh in his obdurate heart; who did not feel for Man; in the midst of Joy and Revelry, almost in the more immediate presence of his Creator, who issued the fatal order to put his fellow creatures to death, and to make their wives and children, widows and orphans.

MOURNFUL TRAGEDY;

Or, the death of Jacob Webb, David Morrow, John Harris, Henry Lewis, David Hunt, and Edward Lindsey — six militia men, who were condemned to die, the sentence approved by Major General Jackson, and by his order the whole six shot.

O! did you hear that plaintive cry
   Borne on the southern breeze?
Saw you John Harris earnest pray
   For mercy, on his knees?

Low to the earth he bent, and pray'd
   For pardon from his chief;
But to his earnest prayer for life
   Jackson, alas! was deaf.

"Spare me" — he said — "I mean no wrong,
   "My heart was always true:
"First for my county's cause it beat,
   "And next, great Chief, for you.

"We thought our time of service out —
   "Thought it our right to go:
"We meant to violate no law,
   "Nor wish'd to shun the foe.

"Our officers declared that we
   "Had but three months to stay;
"We served those three months faithfully,
   "Up to the latest day.

"No one suspects intended wrong;
   "The judgment only erred:
"In such a case, O noble Chief,
   "Let mercy's voice be heard.

"At home an aged mother waits
   "To clasp her only son;
"A wife, and little children — this arm
   "Alone depend upon.

"Cut me not off from those dear ties;
   "So soon from life's young bloom;
"O 'tis a dreadful thing to die,
   "And moulder in the tomb!

"Sure mercy is a noble gem
   "On every Chieftain's brow;
"More sparkling than a diadem —
   "O exercise it now. — "

'Twas all in vain, John Harris' pray'r,
   'Tis past the soul's belief!
Hard as the flint was Jackson's heart;
   He would not grant relief.

He order'd Harris out to die,
   And five poor fellows more!
Young, gallant men, in prime of life,
   To welter in their gore!!

Methinks I hear the muffled drum,
   And see the column move;
— Lo here they come — how sad their looks:
   Farewell to life and love!

See six black coffins rang'd along —
   Six graves before them made;
Webb, Lindsey, Harris, Lewis, Hunt,
   And Morrow kneeled and prayed.

They kneel'd and pray'd, and tho't of home,
   And all its dear delights,
The deadly tubes are levell'd now —
   The scene my soul affrights!

Sure he will spare! Sure Jackson yet
   Will all reprive but one —
O hark! those shrieks! that cry of death!
   The deadly deed is done!

All six militia men were shot;
   And O! it seems to me
A dreadful deed — a bloody act
   Of needless cruelty.

II. A short time before the execution of the militia-men, seven regular soldiers were shot near Nashville, by a band of regulars scarcely sufficient to guard the prisoners. — They were confined in a house, and taken out and executed one at a time, there being scarcely enough men for the purpose of executing and guarding at the same moment. An eighth soldier was to have been executed at the same time. He was a young man, who had deserted one month before his time had expired. General Jackson doomed him to die with the others. He was saved by a writ of habeas corpus from Judge M'Nairy, who fell under Jackson's displeasure for snatching this one victim from his blood-stained hands. If Jackson's army had been at hand, no doubt M'Nairy would have shared the fate of Judge Hall and Judge Fromentin. Capital punishments in an army, are designed for example as well as for penalty; but in this case it was a transaction of horror to peaceful citizens: no army was there to witness the bloody tragedy. He has ever been a man of "blood and carnage".

III. Poor John Woods; he was a generous hearted, noble fellow as ever lived, who had volunteered in the service of his country. He was on guard one day at Fort Strother—the officer of the guard had permitted him to go to his tent, and snatch a hasty breakfast; whilst disposing of his scanty meal, seated on the ground beside his skillet, an upstart little officer, who was not Woods' equal at home, ordered him to pick up and carry off some bones that lay scattered about the place—Woods refused, and the little officer attempted to compel him. At this instant, Gen. Jackson, having heard the dispute, came out of his tent, and without knowing any thing of the merits of the case, repeatedly vociferated—*"Shoot the damn'd rascal!—Shoot the damn'd rascal"*. For this offence, the unfortunate, the gallant Woods, was tried, condemned and shot. Before his trial, Gen. Jackson used this language to the court-martial. *"By the immortal God! if you find him guilty I will not pardon him!"* And he kept his promise; though he did offer a pardon provided he would enlist in the regular service—Thus perished as noble a fellow as ever lived, for as trifling an offence as ever took the life of man!!!

IV. On the 27th day of March, 1814, General Jackson had found at an Indian village, at the bend of the Tallapousie, about 1000 Indians, with their *squaws* and *children*, "running about among their huts". The following is an account of the sanguinary massacre which took place;—it is Gen. Jackson's own, and therefore must be received as sufficient evidence against himself. He says:—"Determining to exterminate them, I detached Gen. Coffee with the mounted men, and nearly the whole of the Indian force, early on the morning of yesterday, to cross the river about two miles below the encampment, and to surround the bend in such a manner as that none of them should escape by attempting to cross the river." The result he then details:—*"Five hundred and fifty seven were left dead on the Peninsula, and a great number of them were killed by the horsemen in attempting to cross the river;* it is believed that no more than ten escaped.* We * continued * to destroy many of them who had concealed themselves under the banks of the river, until we were prevented by the night.* This morning we killed 16 which had been concealed."

We ask you to pause and reflect that the above tragic narration of cold-blooded and merciless cruelty, is taken from an official communication made by General Andrew Jackson.

The General, after sleeping (with what composure, we cannot say) thro' the night ensuing the tragedy we speak of, awoke in the morning surrounded by the corpses of "five hundred and seventy" fellow creatures, to cause, by way of worthy afterpiece, sixteen others to be dragged from their concealments, and put to death in cold blood. We cannot boast of more than common sensibility, but we must think that to witness such an act, would make ours a little cold also. What are the general's words?—these: "this morning we killed sixteen which had been concealed"—and the man who acts and speaks thus; who has half as much blood upon his conscience, as he has upon his hands,

—he, forsooth, is to be called the peer and *like* of Washington, the happy warrior,—

———————— "he
Whom every man at arms could wish to be."

But it is time to have done with the unpleasant subject. We will observe in addition to the details already given, that the village was burnt, and several women and children killed. In conclusion, we ask our fellow citizens, whether Genl Jackson though he has contributed largely to the military reputation of our country, has not done enough to disqualify him, in the eyes of the people as virtuous as they are free, for the office he seeks at their hands.

Franklin, Tenn.,
September 10, 1818.

V. A difference which had been for some months brewing between Gen. Jackson and myself, produced on Saturday, the 4th inst. in the town of Nashville, the most outrageous affray ever witnessed in a civilized country. In communicating the affair to my friends and fellow-citizens, I limit myself to the statement of a few leading facts, the truth of which I am ready to establish by judicial proofs.

1. That myself and my brother, Jesse Benton, arriving in Nashville on the morning of the affray, and knowing of General Jackson's threats, went and took lodgings in a different house from the one in which he staid, on purpose to avoid him.

2. That the General and some of his friends came [to] the house where we had put up, and commenced the attack by levelling a pistol at me, when I had no weapon drawn, and advancing upon me at a quick pace, without giving me time to draw one.

3. That seeing this, my brother fired upon General Jackson, when he had got within eight or ten feet of me.

4. That four other pistols were fired in quick succession; one by General Jackson at me; two by me at the General; and one by Col. Coffee at me. In the course of this firing, General Jackson was brought to the ground; but received no hurt.

5. That daggers were then drawn. Col. Coffee and Mr. Alexander Donelson made at me, and gave me five slight wounds. Captain Hammond and Mr. Stokeley Hays engaged my brother, who being still weak from the effect of a severe wound he had lately received in a duel, was not able to resist two men. They got him down; and while Capt. Hammond beat him on the head to make him lie still, Mr. Hays attempted to stab him, and wounded him in both arms, as he lay on his back parrying the thrusts with his naked hands. From this situation a generous hearted citizen of Nashville, Mr. Summer, relieved him. Before he came to the ground, my brother clapped a pistol to the breast of Mr. Hays, to blow him through, but it missed fire.

6. My own and my brother's pistols carried two balls each; for it was our intention, if driven to arms, to have no child's play. The pistols fired at me were so near that the blaze of the muzzle of one of them burnt the sleeve of

my coat, and the other aimed at my head at a little more than arms length from it.

7. Capt. Carroll was to have taken part in the affray, but was absent by the permission of General Jackson, as he has proved by the General's certificate, a certificate which reflects I know not whether less honor upon the General or upon the Captain.

8. That this attack was made upon me in the house where the Judge of the District, Mr Searcy, had his lodgings! Nor has the civil authority yet taken cognizance of this horrible outrage.

These facts are sufficient to fix the public opinion. For my own part, I think it scandalous that such things should take place at any time; but particularly so at the present moment, when the public service requires the aid of all its citizens. — As for the name of *courage*, God forbid that I should ever attempt to gain it by becoming a bully. — Those who know me, know full well that I would give a thousand times more for the reputation of Croghan in defending his post, than I would for the reputation of all the duellists and gladiators that ever appeared upon the face of the earth.

Thomas Hart Benton, *Lieut. Col. 39th Infantry.*
And now a member of the Senate of the United States.

VI. Do not be startled, gentle reader at the picture before you. It is all true and every body ought to know it. Gen. Jackson having made an assault upon Samuel Jackson, in the streets of Nashville, and the latter not being disposed to stand still and be beaten, stooped down for a stone to defend himself. While in the act of doing so, Gen. Jackson drew the sword from his cane and run it through Samuel Jackson's body, the sword entering his back and coming out of his breast. — For this offence an indictment was found against Gen. Jackson by a grand jury, upon which he was subsequently arraigned and tried. But finding means to persuade the petit jury that he committed the act in self-defence, he was acquitted. Gentle reader, it is for you to say, whether this man, who carries a sword cane, and is willing to run it through the body of any one who may presume to stand in his way, is a fit person to be our President.

VII. Gen. Jackson, detailing his progress among the Indians, in the course of which, men, women, and children, were indiscriminately "exterminated", their towns burnt and their country laid waste, with the utmost complacency and *sang froid*, says, in his letter dated, "Camp before St. Marks, April 9, 1818" — "Capt. M'Ever having hoisted English colours on board of his boats, Francis *the Prophet,* Hocomochemutcho and *two others*, were *decoyed* on board. *These have been hung today!*" Reader, mark the perfect indifference with which Gen. Jackson shoots, hangs or stabs his fellow beings, with or without trial, and the more than callous, aye, even exulting composure, with which he details his horrid and bloody deeds! If the Indians, according to the customs of their nation, put to death a prisoner, all the feelings of our nature rise into indignation against them. With what feelings then should we contemplate the *decoying* and the cold-blooded murder of prisoners by a civilized man in the face of the laws and customs of his country!

THE VOTES IN THE 1828 ELECTION

| STATES | POPULAR VOTE FOR PRESIDENT | | ELECTORAL VOTES FOR | | | | |
| | Andrew Jackson | John Q. Adams | PRESIDENT | | VICE-PRESIDENT | | |
			A. Jackson	J. Q. Adams	J. C. Calhoun	Richard Rush	William Smith
Maine.........	13,927	20,733	1	8	1	8	—
New Hampshire.	20,922	24,134	—	8	—	8	—
Vermont.......	8,350	25,363	—	7	—	7	—
Massachusetts..	6,016	29,876	—	15	—	15	—
Rhode Island...	821	2,754	—	4	—	4	—
Connecticut.....	4,448	13,838	—	8	—	8	—
New York.....	140,763	135,413	20	16	20	16	—
New Jersey.....	21,951	23,764	—	8	—	8	—
Pennsylvania....	101,652	50,848	28	—	28	—	—
Delaware*......	—	—	—	3	—	3	—
Maryland......	24,565	25,527	5	6	5	6	—
Virginia........	26,752	12,101	24	—	24	—	—
North Carolina.	37,857	13,918	15	—	15	—	—
South Carolina*	—	—	11	—	11	—	—
Georgia........	19,363	No opp.	9	—	2	—	7
Alabama.......	17,138	1,938	5	—	5	—	—
Mississippi.....	6,772	1,581	3	—	3	—	—
Louisiana......	4,603	4,076	5	—	5	—	—
Kentucky.......	39,397	31,460	14	—	14	—	—
Tennessee......	44,293	2,240	11	—	11	—	—
Missouri.......	8,272	3,400	3	—	3	—	—
Ohio..........	67,597	63,396	16	—	16	—	—
Indiana........	22,257	17,052	5	—	5	—	—
Illinois.........	9,560	4,662	3	—	3	—	—
	647,276	508,064	178	83	171	83	7

* In these two states electors were appointed by the legislature.

Election of 1832

ROBERT V. REMINI is Professor of History at the University of Illinois, Chicago Circle. He has written Martin Van Buren and the Making of the Democratic Party; The Election of Andrew Jackson; Andrew Jackson *and* Andrew Jackson and the Bank War.

Election of 1832

by *Robert V. Remini*

Andrew Jackson's first Administration was marred by a long, running duel between his Secretary of State Martin Van Buren and his Vice-President John C. Calhoun over the presidential succession. At the beginning of the Administration it appeared that Calhoun would easily succeed Jackson in four years, but the situation changed rapidly after Jackson took office, and the turn of events did not favor Calhoun. Eventually the Vice-President's enemies decided that the only way to stall his ambitions was to prevail upon Old Hickory to run for a second term. In view of the strained relations that had developed between Jackson and Calhoun, their task did not prove too difficult.

The first indication of friction appeared with the appointment of John H. Eaton as Secretary of War in 1829. Calhoun resented the choice because he feared Eaton's influence over Jackson and because he wanted to dominate the Cabinet in order to protect his own presidential interests. In addition, Eaton was Calhoun's critic and had repeatedly tried to drive the Vice-President off the Democratic ticket prior to the 1828 election. Certainly he would not now hesitate to use his influence to Calhoun's disadvantage. What made matters worse was that no one from South Carolina had been selected for the Cabinet; Calhoun's friends had made a special effort to prevent Eaton's appointment and have Robert Y. Hayne or James Hamilton, Jr., both of South Carolina, chosen in his place. The failure, therefore, was twofold: not only was Eaton chosen to head the War Department but his influence was clearly visible in the appointment of several other men. With the selection of Van Buren for the State Department—a man of considerable political skill, and one obviously intent on winning the Presidency for himself—Calhoun became increasingly fearful. His position and future jeopardized, Calhoun decided he must force the appointment of a new Cabinet or see Van Buren replace him as Jackson's successor.

The method of assault proved as easy as it was unfortunate. The Secretary of War had just married the daughter of a Washington innkeeper —the pretty Margaret (Peggy) O'Neale, who frequently served as barmaid in her father's establishment. Peggy's first marriage to John Timberlake, a U.S. Navy purser, ended with Timberlake's suicide, probably caused by the knowledge of his wife's misconduct with Eaton. When Eaton married Peggy he did so with Jackson's approval and encouragement. But the marriage soon brought on the indignant disapproval of the wives of other Cabinet officers, wives led by Mrs. Floride Calhoun, who objected to Peggy's presence among them because of her notorious past. The women refused to associate with her at social functions and in fact did everything possible to humiliate and embarrass both Peggy and her husband.

Because his own wife had suffered such abuse, Jackson angrily defended Mrs. Eaton. He would not listen to the evidence several clergymen amassed to "prove" the charges of misconduct rumored against Peggy. Nor could he understand the reactions of his Cabinet and the war waged by their wives against "a helpless and virtuous female." And what deeply hurt the President was the refusal of his nephew's wife, Emily Donelson, to call on Peggy as her duty required. Emily, who served as mistress of the White House because of the recent death of Jackson's wife, said she would receive the lady in the executive mansion as her uncle's guest, but she would not return the courtesy. Visibly shocked and angered by her decision, Jackson ordered Emily back to Tennessee.

Van Buren played a part in this unsavory business by doing everything possible to widen the rift between Jackson and Calhoun. He himself went out of his way to be courteous to Peggy, and since he was a widower with no daughters to embarrass him, he could be as kind, as sociable, and as courteous to the Eatons as he pleased. Van Buren encouraged the foreign ministers from Great Britain and Russia to give dinner parties which he knew the wives of the other Cabinet members would pointedly refuse to attend, thus infuriating Jackson even more.

The initial estrangement between Jackson and Calhoun soon worsened because of their sharply differing interpretations of the nature of the Union. The Webster-Hayne debate in the Senate during December and January, 1829-30, focused at length upon Calhoun's doctrine of nullification, a doctrine Jackson found abominable. Jackson believed in states rights only as long as the states acknowledged their bond within an indestructible Union. Let any state threaten that bond and Jackson would teach it the meaning of treason. The President expressed his feelings on the matter at a meeting of Democrats held on April 13, 1830, commemorating the birthday of Thomas Jefferson. After dinner, Jackson was called upon to propose a toast. Reportedly he looked straight at Calhoun and said, "Our Federal Union. It must be preserved."

The final break between the two men occurred with the disclosure of Calhoun's wish during the Monroe Administration Calhoun to censure Jackson for his invasion of Florida in pursuit of the Seminole Indians. Jackson thought he had Monroe's approval for the venture — indeed that he had been urged to violate the Florida border — and was therefore outraged at the attempts of both the Cabinet and the Congress to punish him for his actions. Almost all the members of the Cabinet, including Calhoun who was then Secretary of War, urged the President to repudiate the general's action and punish him for his misconduct. Only John Quincy Adams, the Secretary of State, defended Jackson, and finally convinced Monroe that the general's actions had been required to subdue the Seminoles. Eventually, through Adams' skillful diplomacy, Florida was purchased from Spain, and all efforts to censure Jackson collapsed.

At the time Jackson believed Calhoun had defended him. Calhoun "has professed to be my friend," he wrote, and "approves my conduct and that of the President." Some of Jackson's advisers disagreed. Men like Sam Houston and William B. Lewis tried to convince him that Calhoun had been one of his critics, and unsuccessfully sought to prevent Calhoun's selection as Jackson's running mate in 1828. Not until 1830 did Jackson learn directly from William H. Crawford, Monroe's Secretary of the Treasury, what actually happened inside the Cabinet. As soon as he received this evidence, Jackson asked Calhoun for an explanation. Responding in fifty-two pages, the Vice-President desperately tried to explain away what was now perfectly obvious. Jackson curtly answered this dissertation with the comment that "no further communication with you on the subject is necessary."

Calhoun then committed the unpardonable error of going to the newspapers and publishing his version of the affair. He ended the account by accusing Van Buren of engineering a plot to bring about his downfall. This public disclosure of the feuding that had been going on within the Cabinet for the past two years was the final piece of evidence Jackson needed. He was now convinced that Calhoun had been his enemy all along and was trying to destory his Administration through scandal. Thus when Van Buren cleverly suggested that he resign from the Cabinet, thereby forcing the resignations of the other members, the President quickly agreed. Jackson readily saw that he could remake his Cabinet and in the process entirely eliminate the influence of John C. Calhoun. But before consenting to this agreement, however, the President insisted that Van Buren must not sacrifice himself in the process for, if nothing else, it would only give Calhoun a measure of satisfaction. Instead he prevailed upon his Secretary to accept the post of minister to Great Britain. Van Buren agreed and shortly thereafter resigned his post. The Cabinet was remade in the spring of 1831 and the Calhoun faction was excluded. That fall Van Buren sailed for England.

Calhoun did squeeze out one small measure of revenge. When Van Buren's nomination came before the full Senate for confirmation late in January, 1832, a tie vote resulted, 23 to 23, with the friends of the Vice-President joining the National Republicans opposing confirmation. The deciding vote belonged to Calhoun and with great appetite he voted to reject the nomination. Immediately after the vote, he turned to a friend and said, "It will kill him, sir, kill him dead. He will never kick, sir, never kick."

Naturally the rejection enraged the President. He regarded it as sheer spitefulness on the part of the Vice-President. "I have no hesitation in saying that Calhoun is one of the most base hypocritical and unprincipled villains in the United States," he wrote. "His course of secret session, and vote in the case of Mr. Van Buren, has displayed a want of every sense of honor, justice, and magnanimity. His vote has dam'd him by all honest men in the Senate, and when laid before the nation, and laid it will be, will not only dam (sic) him and his associates, but astonish the American people."

Jackson viewed the "plot" against Van Buren as something more than an act of personal revenge. Characteristically, he saw the rejection as an attack upon himself, just another vicious attempt to embarrass him and his Administration. "The people will properly resent the insult offered to the Executive," he wrote to Van Buren, "and the wound inflicted on our national character, and the injury intended to our foreign relations, in your rejection, by placing you in the chair of the very man whose casting vote rejected you." By replacing Calhoun with Van Buren, Jackson, in a single stroke, could punish one as he rewarded the other. He planned to have Van Buren nominated as his running mate in the presidential election of 1832.

Despite the personal vendetta that formed the background to this election, and despite the fact that any election involving Jackson was certain to reflect a strong personal tone, the presidential contest of 1832 revolved around a most important political issue—the Second Bank of the United States. The question arose because of Jackson's contention that the Bank was unconstitutional and had failed to establish a uniform and sound currency. He proposed to do away with it and finally took the matter to the people for resolution.

The dispute had been growing a long time. As a young land speculator in Tennessee, Jackson suffered financial disaster when he accepted promissory notes from a man who subsequently defaulted. He soon developed extremely conservative ideas about money, credit, and banks. Not only did he disapprove the paper issued by banks but he argued that hard money—specie—was the only coin honest men used in their business transactions. He also condemned credit because it encouraged speculation and indebtedness. Thus, it was the note-issuing, credit-producing aspects of banking that disturbed Jackson and eventually led him to attack the Second Bank of the United States. But he frankly admitted to Nicholas Biddle, the president of the Bank, that his prejudice was not confined to only one institution. "I do not dislike your bank any more than all banks," he said. Jackson also admitted to another bias. He was committed to a states' rights philosophy, and denied that the Constitution authorized the Bank's existence.

The Second National Bank of the United States had been chartered by the Federal Government in 1816 when President James Madison signed the necessary legislation. It was established with a capital stock of $35 million, one-fifth of which was owned by the national Government, the rest sold to the public. It served as a depository for Government funds as well as an agent for the collection of taxes. The Bank issued notes, redeemable in specie and acceptable in the payment of taxes. In 1823, Biddle became president of the Bank and within a few years converted what was essentially a multi-branched banking operation handling federal money into a bona fide central bank, capable of creating and destroying the circulating media.

Shortly after Jackson became President he told his friend John Overton that he planned to change "the present incorporated Bank," not simply because of his economic views, but because he believed the Bank had used its influence against him in the presidential election. Indeed, Jackson thought it had exerted its massive financial power to control the political process. He had recently learned, he said, "of the injurious effect . . . the Bank had in our late election which if not *curbed* must destroy the purity of the right of suffrage."

In order to curb the Bank's operation and "prevent our liberties [from being] crushed by the Bank," Jackson went before Congress in December, 1829, and raised several serious questions about the Bank's charter, which was due to expire in 1836. He referred to the question of constitutionality, an issue that had haunted the Bank since its inception, and he insisted that the institution had really "failed in the great end of establishing a uniform and sound currency." He asked the Congress to modify the present charter and devise alternatives that would avoid the constitutional problems and yet secure all the advantages the country enjoyed under the present Bank.

The controversy dragged on for several years as Jackson turned to other more pressing problems, such as the Eaton affair and the dissolution of his first Cabinet. Then, because he had decided to run for reelection in 1832 and would face the combined opposition of the National Republicans and the Calhoun faction, he backed away from the Bank issue since he realized it could profoundly disturb the electorate and threaten his reelection. Moreover, because of the scandals of his first Administration, he was extremely anxious to pile up a decisive popular majority and this, he felt, was impossible if he became locked in a savage struggle with the Bank. Pennsylvania, where the parent institution was located, would probably slip from the Democratic column because of the issue, and several other states seemed certain to follow.

For this very reason Henry Clay and other National Republicans were anxious to bring the question out into the open and force Jackson to either sign the bill for recharter—even though it had four more years to go—or veto it and face possible defeat at the polls in 1832. Clay, the obvious presidential nominee of the National Republicans, was instrumental in convincing Nicholas Biddle to ask Congress for immediate recharter. And although Biddle was warned by several Democrats that a challenge to Jackson would surely mean a veto, he chose to disregard the advice. The necessary legislation was introduced into Congress early in 1832 and both sides lined up for a head-on clash.

After a six-month debate that was particularly acrimonious in the Senate, the bill for recharter passed both houses of Congress and came to Jackson for his signature. Furious at Biddle for having challenged him, the President reacted with characteristic stubbornness. When Martin Van Buren returned from Great Britain after his Senate rejection, he visited Jackson at the White House and was startled to find the old man lying on a couch looking very pale and worn. As Van Buren walked into the room the President grasped his friend's hand. "The bank, Mr. Van Buren, is trying to kill me," he said, *"but I will kill it."* Convinced that the Bank was a political agency ready at any time to tamper with the electoral process to get what it wanted Jackson prepared to veto the Bank bill. He no longer wished to compromise with the institution, simply curb its power, or alter the provisions of its charter to dispose of his constitutional reservations. Now he talked only of destroying the Bank outright.

The veto message written by Jackson and several advisers was sent to Congress on July 10, 1832. In it the President claimed the Bank enjoyed exclusive privileges which gave it a monopoly of foreign and domestic exchange. An inordinate percentage of its stock, he contended, was owned by foreigners who thereby reaped a disproportionate profit from the Bank's operation. Jackson again questioned its constitutionality, despite the favorable decision handed down in *McCulloch* vs. *Maryland* by the Supreme Court in 1819. Then at the very end of the message, Jackson let fly a verbal thunderbolt. He said it was to be "regretted that the rich and powerful too often bend the acts of government to their selfish purposes." The Federal Government must not be discriminatory, he declared. "Every man is equally entitled to protection by law; but when the laws undertake to add to these natural and just advantages artificial distinctions, to grant titles, gratuities, and exclusive privileges, to make the rich richer and the potent more powerful, the humble members of society – the farmers, mechanics, and laborers – who have neither the time nor the means of securing like favors to themselves, have a right to complain of the injustice of their Government. There are no necessary evils in government. Its evils exist only in its abuses. If it would confine itself to equal protection, and, as Heaven does its rains, shower its favors alike on the high and the low, the rich and poor, it would be an unqualified blessing."

Because there were only a few months before the nation would go to the polls, Jackson, in writing his veto, laid the Bank issue squarely before the American people for decision. This was the first time a Chief Executive had taken a strong stand on an important issue, challenging the electorate to do something about it if they did not approve his position. The people could vote him out of office if they disapproved his action, thus insuring the renewal of the Bank's charter. In one of the rare instances in American history, the people were given a real opportunity to decide an important issue. And the alternatives were clear: Jackson or the Second Bank of the United States.

The election of 1832 was also unique in that it was the first contest in which the major parties held national nominating conventions to select the presidential candidates. Moreover, it marked the emergence of the first third party in American politics: the Anti-Masonic party.

Ever since William Morgan's death in 1826, allegedly at the hands of

Masons, the agitation against members of this secret society had gathered momentum. Directed in New York by such astute politicians as Thurlow Weed and William H. Seward, the Anti-Masonic movement soon spread across the border of New York into Pennsylvania and Vermont and finally into the rest of New England and parts of the Midwest. By the early 1830's party machinery existed in enough states to encourage the Anti-Masons to challenge the national candidates for office. Since Jackson and Clay, the prospective nominees of the two major parties, were both high-ranking Masons, a decision was made to enter the presidential contest in 1832 and run an Anti-Masonic candidate against them. To select the candidate and unite support behind him, a national nominating convention was summoned to meet in Baltimore on September 26, 1831.

There was nothing especially novel about the convention technique for the selection of candidates. States had been using it for years when naming nominees for local offices, but it had never been employed before in a presidential election. Because the caucus system had been discredited, and because so many more people participated in presidential contests than heretofore, there was a need to experiment with something different and the simplest, most available, and most obvious device was the convention system. In the 1828 election some Democratic leaders had explored the possibility of holding a convention to name a candidate. Nothing came of these talks, perhaps because of fear that a fight would develop between the Calhoun faction and the Old Republicans over the vice-presidential nomination. In any event Jackson and Calhoun were placed on the Democratic ballot in a rather haphazard way through a series of nominations in state conventions. This only emphasized the fact that some more appropriate system was needed to name the national candidates. Thus when the Anti-Masons decided to put forward a presidential candidate, the most natural thing for them to do was call a nominating convention on the national level.

Delegates to the Anti-Masonic convention meeting in Baltimore, selected by conventions or caucuses, represented New Hampshire, Maine, Massachusetts, Rhode Island, Connecticut, Vermont, New York, New Jersey, Pennsylvania, Ohio, Maryland, Delaware, and Indiana. When they arrived in Baltimore they chose as their convention site the saloon of the Athenæum, a building located in the southwest corner of St. Paul and Lexington Streets. In all there were 116 members in attendance, including such distinguished public figures as Thurlow Weed, William H. Seward, Thaddeus Stevens, John C. Spencer, Samuel A. Foot, Henry Dana Ward, Nicholas Devereux, John Rutherford, William Sprague, and Jonathan Sloan. Only New York, Pennsylvania, and Massachusetts had delegations of any appreciable size; consequently these states tended to dominate the proceedings.

On Monday, September 26, the first day of the convention, the delegates started organizing themselves by appointing John C. Spencer of New York as president. They then chose four vice-presidents, four secretaries, and a group of committees to prepare statements on finance, "masonic penalties," judicial proceedings in the Morgan case, and an address to the people. The Chief Justice of the United States, John Marshall, and the former Attorney General, William Wirt, were invited to attend the convention; both accepted and took their seats by the side of the president to watch the proceedings. Charles Carroll of Carrollton, the last surviving signer of the Declaration of Independence and a most revered man, was also invited, but age prevented him from attending.

The following day the committee reports, except for the address to the people, were submitted and read. Then on Wednesday, September 28, the convention nominated the party's presidential candidate. At first delegates hoped that former President John Quincy Adams or John McLean of Ohio, an associate justice of the Supreme Court, would accept the nomination. However, Adams was unenthusiastic about the honor the Anti-Masons wished to thrust upon him. He said he "had not the slightest desire for the nomination, nor for the office of President of the United States itself; that I would not reject the nomination of the Convention if made." But apart from Adam's own indifference, some of the younger delegates to the convention "felt that [the party] could derive no strength or prestige" from Adams' nomination; they said the organization "needed a new name, not before identified with its history."

John McLean fitted that description, and unlike Adams, he had already indicated to Albert Tracy and Thurlow Weed that he was interested in the Anti-Masonic nomination and would accept it if offered. Then, just weeks before the convention met, he changed his mind. McLean shrewdly guessed that 1832, when he would have to face Jackson and Clay, was no year to run for President. So he wrote the delegates that he did not think it proper for a Supreme Court justice to enter the political lists at this time; his nomination would only "distract" the public mind. He added, "This I do not wish to see, as I fear it would be injurious to the best interests of the country."

His refusal jolted the convention, which was already prepared to nominate him. Men like Weed and Seward had been counting on McLean; now they were without a candidate. Seward said the letter of refusal, when read to the convention, "fell as a wet blanket upon our warm expectations." So the hunt for an acceptable candidate had to begin all over again. Dejected, the leaders looked around the convention for a possible substitute. As Weed's eye roamed around the saloon it fell on the massive and very dignified William Wirt, sitting near the president. Weed's interest stirred as he watched his man during the proceedings. When the convention adjourned for the day, he caught hold of Spencer, Albert Tracy, and Dr. Abner Phelps of Boston and together they visited Wirt at his home outside the city. The exploratory conversation began well enough, until Wirt disclosed that he had once been a Mason. Although he had since given up his membership, the hard, unfortunate fact remained. As the discussion continued however this disquieting information was soon discounted because the group found Wirt "in cordial sympathy with our principles." They finally concluded that his past association with Freemasonry would not seriously damage the party or hurt his candidacy. Because they were getting desperate, because Wirt was willing to allow his name to be offered to the convention, and because he was a man of national reputation and prestige, they quickly decided they had located their candidate.

Wirt was born in Maryland in 1772. He studied law and was admitted to the bar in Virginia where he took up residence. Interested in litetature, he wrote *The Letters of the British Spy* in 1803, a book which had a large popular success. But his great reputation was built on his law practice. As a result he was appointed Attorney General by President Monroe and retained by John Quincy Adams. Wirt added to his reputation by his participation in such famous Supreme Court cases as *McCulloch* vs. *Maryland*, *Gibbon* vs. *Odgen*, and the *Dartmouth College* case. In 1826 he was appointed president of the University of Virginia.

When the interview between Wirt and the Anti-Masonic delegation ended it appeared that the question of the nomination was settled. Weed and company returned to the city "in high spirits to announce the result of the visit to our anxious and impatient colleagues, "most of whom rejoiced to learn that a gentleman so distinguished had consented to become our standard bearer." But not everyone rejoiced. Thaddeus Stevens, the leading Anti-Mason in Pennsylvania, objected strenuously to Wirt, not simply because of his past membership in the Society of Freemasons but because Stevens thought his conversion too "sudden and interested." Wirt was obviously an opportunist, said Stevens, who cared nothing about Anti-Masonry. All he wanted was a crack at the Presidency.

To convince Stevens that he was mistaken and, more important, to get him to agree to Wirt's nomination, Weed assigned Seward to talk with the crusty Pennsylvanian in private caucus. The session lasted for hours, both men arguing, debating, pleading, and gesticulating. Seward was saddened and furious at how "unreasonable and impracticable" Stevens could be in maintaining his point of view, and by midnight the two men were exhausted. It was so late that Seward decided against returning to his own lodgings and stayed in Stevens' room. He fell asleep convinced he had failed in his mission and "that the convention would explode the next day by a refusal to nominate Mr. Wirt, or a fatal division on that question."

Seward was still troubled and agitated when he awoke the next morning. To his surprise he found Stevens "entirely calm and undisturbed." Seward immediately renewed the debate, pouring out all the arguments he had recited the evening before. Calmly, Stevens heard him out once more and when the harangue ended, he quietly informed Seward that if Wirt should be the choice of the convention he would not object. In the interest of harmony he would keep his peace. This sudden change of mind was as unexpected as it was welcome. The two men concluded their talk in a spirit of "cordiality and cooperation" and returned to the hall where the principal business of the convention was about to begin.

No nominating speeches were offered when the delegates started to choose their candidates, but it was decided that a three-fourths vote of the entire body was necessary for nomination. On the first ballot, which was written by each delegate and deposited in an open box, William Wirt received 108 votes, Richard Rush received 1 and there were 2 blanks. On a motion by Thaddeus Stevens, Wirt's nomination was made unanimous. For the Vice-

Presidency, the convention selected Amos Ellmaker of Pennsylvania, a respectable lawyer and a friend of Thaddeus Stevens.

A letter of acceptance written by Wirt was then read to the delegates, producing quite a shock; although Wirt had accepted the nomination, he did it in poor form, as though it were for recognition of his talents and accomplishments, not for his principles or abiding distaste for Masons and their practices. Indeed, he said he had "continually regarded Masonry as nothing more than a social and charitable club, designed for the promotion of good feeling among its members, and for the pecuniary relief of their indigent brethren." Although he was outraged by William Morgan's murder, he could not believe that this was Masonry as generally understood by some of its most notable members, among them George Washington. "Nor can I believe that in the quarter of the union with which I am best acquainted, intelligent men of high and honorable character, if they have been drawn in to take these shocking and impious oaths, can consider them as paramount to their duties to God and to their country." The delegates were appalled by parts of this letter, and a few of them contended that Weed had made a ghastly mistake in selecting this over-inflated former Mason. Still the choice had been made and there was nothing they could do now but live with it.

After the nominations were over, the delegates held a night session to hear the "Address to the People," which had been prepared by a special committee. The address took over an hour to read but was heard "with the most profound attention by the audience." It first listed the qualities a President should possess: intelligence, honesty, independence, vigilance, wisdom, prudence, and patriotism. This was followed by a general statement of principles which should guide any Administration: equal and exact justice for all; peace; commerce and honest friendship with all nations; no entangling alliances; support of states' rights; political equality, "implying general suffrage and eligibility of office," and majority rule. These principles were now in danger. "Their foe is rich, disciplined, and wily." Their foe is Freemasonry.

The fact that the first President of the United States, George Washington, had been a Mason, was neatly disposed of. Authors of the address maintained that he was only admitted to three degrees, visited a lodge once or twice after 1768, and never presided in one. "He afterwards in effect renounced it." So much for George Washington.

After detailing the crimes and dangers of Freemasonry the address called for an "enlightened exercise of the suffrage" by the electorate to "remove the evils" and "produce reforms." "After diligent inquiry and mature deliberation we have selected, and now nominate, for your support" William Wirt and Amos Ellmaker, men possessing the qualifications for office and committed to the principles enunciated in the address.

When the reading ended, the delegates resolved to meet in Washington in September, 1835, a year before the next presidential election, unless otherwise ordered by their Central Committee of Correspondence. Then the convention adjourned.

Wirt's nomination was generally regarded as a boost to Jackson's campaign because it split off votes that would have gone to the National Republicans. There was even some effort to unite the Anti-Masons and National Republicans to form a strong anti-Jackson ticket, but this did not work out. The National Republicans were intent on nominating Henry Clay, who, like Jackson, was a high ranking Freemason. And, in 1832, there was no denying Clay's right to stand as his party's presidential nominee.

Henry Clay was born in Virginia in 1777, studied law there, and then moved to Kentucky. He was elected to the United States Congress where he soon became Speaker of the House and leader of the War Hawks faction, advocating war with Great Britain in 1812. Later he participated in the peace negotiations at Ghent. Returning to the House of Representatives, Clay became the leading critic of the Monroe Administration and tried unsuccessfully to bring about congressional censure of Jackson for his invasion of Florida. His support of John Quincy Adams in the House election of 1825 brought about his appointment as Secretary of State. After Jackson's election to the Presidency, Clay retired to Kentucky, but in 1831 he was elected to the United States Senate. A forceful and articulate spokesman of anti-Administration forces in Congress, he preached an "American System," a program of protective tariffs, internal improvements, stable currency, distribution of federal surpluses to the states, and a sound banking system.

On December 12, 1831, the National Republicans met in the same saloon the Anti-Masons had occupied several months earlier. Because of the bad weather and roads, only 130 members arrived by opening day, but with each succeeding day the number increased until it finally reached 155. In all, eighteen states were represented: Maine, New Hampshire, Vermont, Massachusetts, Connecticut, Rhode Island, New York, New Jersey, Pennsylvania, Delaware, Maryland, Virginia, Ohio, Kentucky, North Carolina, Indiana, Louisiana, and Tennessee as well as the District of Columbia. Abner Lacock of Pennsylvania was immediately chosen temporary chairman and Thomas P. Ray of Virginia secretary. The following day delegates elected James Barbour of Virginia as permanent president of the convention, together with four vice-presidents and two secretaries. Barbour delivered a short address to the delegates, after which the members promptly proceeded to the business of nominating a presidential candidate.

Peter R. Livingston of New York, a former Democrat, rose and supposedly delivered the first nominating speech in presidential nomination history. Unfortunately his words were not reported, but his reputation as a persuasive orator probably justifies a reporter's comment that he spoke with "great eloquence and power." At the end of his speech he placed Henry Clay's name in nomination, and the delegates broke out "with loud and repeated plaudits." The National Republicans voted by roll call, and each of the 155 members rose from his seat and declared his candidate. Clay's unanimous nomination brought "repeated cheers from a great crowd of spectators" in the hall. The business of the day ended with the appointment of a committee, chaired by Alexander H. Everett, to write an address to the people.

The following day, John Sergeant of Pennsylvania, nominated by Boyd McNairy, the sole delegate from Tennessee, and seconded by Walter Jones of the District of Columbia, was nominated as the vice-presidential candidate. Later the convention adopted a resolution "that a central state corresponding committee be provisionally appointed in each state where none are now appointed. And that it be recommended to the several states to organize subordinate corresponding committees in each county and town, in their several respective states." This concern for organization was again apparent when additional committees were either formed or proposed the next day. Then, in the afternoon, the delegates laid aside their business to visit Charles Carroll and pay their respects. With the delegations arranged alphabetically by states, and led by the president and other officers of the convention, the members walked to Carroll's home where they were each greeted personally by the venerable patriot. Barbour offered "the homage of the national republican convention," and after refreshments, the delegates departed.

On the final day of the convention — Friday, December 16 — the delegates listened to the "Address to the People" prepared by Everett's committee, later approving its publication and the distribution of ten thousand copies. Because of the importance of the present crisis, began the Address, "a numerous portion of our fellow citizens residing in all parts of the country, and who have acted together in political affairs for some years past, under the name of National Republicans, have directed us to meet together and deliberate upon the course which they ought to pursue, and the persons whom they ought to support for the great offices of the Government at the approaching election." The Address then went on to excoriate Jackson for his failures as President. His use of the spoils system, his conduct of foreign affairs, his policies on the tariff and internal improvements, his treatment of the Indians, and his attitude toward the Second National Bank were all faulted. The Address carried a particularly strongly worded denunciation of his Bank policy. "This great and beneficial institution, by facilitating exchanges between different parts of the Union, and maintaining a sound, ample, and healthy state of the currency, may be said to supply the body politic, economically viewed, with a continual stream of life-blood, without which it must inevitably languish, and sink into exhaustion." If Jackson is reelected President, the Address continued, "it may be considered certain that the Bank will be abolished."

Jackson had to go if the country was to be spared further disaster. In his place the National Republicans offered Henry Clay, an "ardent, fearless, and consistent friend of liberty and republican institutions." As one of the founders of the "American System," he deserved the support of every citizen who favors domestic industry and internal improvements, said the Address. His "signal success" as Secretary of State under John Quincy Adams demonstrated his capacity for administration. The "generous frankness and captivating warmth of his manners" eminently fitted him for the presidency where it is necessary to "Conciliate the public favor." Compare these qualities with those of the incumbent, concluded the Address, "and may the goodness of Providence so enlighten your choice, [fellow citizens], that it may tend to promote the security and permanency of our excellent political institutions, and the true greatness and glory of our beloved country." On that note of prayerful guidance the convention adjourned.

A few months later, on May 7, 1832, a National Republican convention of young men met in Washington, D. C. to name their candidate. Some 316 delegates participated, but what made this convention unique was the nominee's appearance at the meeting to accept the nomination. On May 11, after receiving the announcement, Clay presented himself before the delegates to "express the deep and grateful sense which I entertain for the distinguished proofs which you have. . .given to me of your esteem and confidence." "If elected President," he said, it would be his "earnest endeavor. . .to maintain, with firmness and dignity, [the people's] interest and honor abroad; to eradicate every abuse and corruption at home; and to uphold with vigor and equality, and justice, the supremacy of the constitution and the laws." Liberty was the country's great possession, continued Clay, and could only be preserved and transmitted to posterity by "vigilance, virtue, and intelligence." Next in importance was the Union, inseparably linked with liberty. Clay ended by telling the delegates that the entire civilized world was watching, and "that the fate of liberty, throughout the world, mainly depends upon the maintenance of American liberty." When the speech ended Clay was introduced to each member of the convention.

Another unusual aspect of this Washington meeting was the decision to draw up a party platform. On May 11, a committee previously appointed to draft a statement on "such subjects as shall be deemed proper to be acted upon by this convention" reported on ten separate resolutions. They were relatively short and to the point, calling for the "adequate protection of American industry," a "uniform system of internal improvements," and support of the Senate of the United States against the efforts of the President and a partisan press to "overawe its deliberations." The resolutions also condemned the spoils system, called for acceptance of the King of Holland's advice as a settlement of the northeast boundary controversy, and denounced the manner in which the Anglo-American treaty settling the problem of West Indian trade had been reached. Several of the resolutions were discussed on the floor before their adoption by the full convention. The meeting ended with the young men paying their respects at the tomb of George Washington.

The Democratic party held its convention last—on May 21, 1832—in Baltimore. The delegates were appointed by legislative caucus or state conventions, or, in some instances, chosen in city and county elections. A vast number of party managers showed up at the convention, including Isaac Hill of New Hampshire, John Overton and John Eaton of Tennessee, Simon Cameron of Pennsylvania, and Silas Wright and Azariah Flagg of the New York Regency. The convention opened in the Athenæum, but the size of the meeting—it totaled 334 delegates from every state but Missouri—forced a move to the Universalist Church on St. Paul Street. Like the National Republicans, the Democrats started each meeting with a prayer of invocation led by a local clergyman.

As usual, organization occupied the first day of the convention. John Overton of Tennessee, Jackson's longtime friend, was suggested as chairman *pro tem*, but Eaton announced that Overton was ill and successfully named Robert Lucas of Ohio as a replacement. In establishing convention rules, the delegates decided to require a two-thirds vote for nomination of the Vice-President. This was done to indicate general agreement by the convention on its choice and to give the candidate an appearance of solid support. Because of the size of some state delegations, and because it permitted better management by the leaders, the convention also adopted the unit rule, authorizing the majority of each delegation to cast the entire vote of the state. The eastern delegations were the largest and the most efficiently managed groups. Their members were sometimes amused, sometimes appalled, by the way their southern and western colleagues wanted to conduct business. "They debate every question and point," chortled one easterner, "with as much zeal and eloquence as tho (sic) the fate of the union was at stake." On the whole, however, the members were in full agreement as to their purpose and objective; only Congressman William Gordon of Virginia and two Calhoun men ruffled the serenity of the proceedings.

In the afternoon session of the second day the delegates got down to the essential business. Without speeches or nominations they proceeded immediately to vote, and on the first ballot gave 208 votes to Van Buren; 49 to Philip P. Barbour of Virginia (representing votes from North Carolina, Virginia, Maryland, South Carolina, and Alabama); and 26 to Richard M. Johnson of Kentucky (from Illinois, Indiana, and Kentucky). The delegates then unanimously agreed on Van Buren's selection. Interestingly enough, no formal nomination of Jackson took place. As Congressman William King of Alabama said, "with regard to the candidate to be supported for the Presidency, there was no diversity of sentiment among the members of the Convention—all concurring in the propriety and importance of the reelection of our present worthy and venerable Chief Magistrate, Andrew Jackson." The convention simply "concurred" in the nominations the President had already received from many states.

On Wednesday, May 23, the members of the convention were told that instead of the usual address to the people, the delegations themselves were to "make such explanations by address, report, or otherwise to their respective constituents. . .as they may deem expedient." The convention then established a general corresponding committee for each state and a general central committee to reside in Washington. The delegates adjourned in high spirits, confident they had chosen a ticket certain of electoral success.

Compared to the other conventions, the Democratic meeting was virtually cut and dried. There was no great address, no statement of principles, no exalted declaration of Jackson's achievements. Undoubtedly the delegates felt no need for such expressions. To a large extent they sensed their strength, a strength based on the popularity of their candidate and the virtuosity of their organization. Indeed, it was the extraordinary vitality of the organization that built many of the impressive majorities for the President in every section of the nation. Organizational meetings were held at every level: state, county, and local, and a wide range of committees was established to drum up support for Jackson and find the necessary money to sustain a presidential campaign. The central committee in Washington capped this pyramid and attempted some semblance of coordination for the work undertaken at the state level.

One technique of organization began with the newspaper summons of Administration friends to a meeting to pass resolutions and arrange the necessary committees. An already existing, local group might do the same. In Philadelphia, for example, the "Democratic Hickory Club, No. 1" met and unanimously passed resolutions extolling Jackson's determination to guard "our institutions from the first approaches of foreign and moneyed influences" and adding that his veto "upon the Bank leaves our highest confidences unimpaired in the wisdom and patriotism of the President." In the West meetings were sometimes spontaneous. As one man wrote, "We are up and doing. The Veto was received. . .last evening. Many citizens from different sections of the State were in town, in attendance upon the Circuit and District Courts of the United States, now in session. The roaring of cannon announced that some important occasion had called forth that token of national, patriotic feeling. . . . Immediately. . .a meeting of the Democratic Republicans of this town, together with a number of our friends from different sections of the State, assembled at one of our public hotels, where the objections of the President on returning the bill, were read and considered. Spirited resolutions, approving of the course of the President were adopted and a feeling was imparted among the friends and supporters of the Administration seldom witnessed in this place on any public occasion." These resolutions were later published in the newspapers and sent to neighboring communities and states. After July, 1832, most, if not all, of these resolutions hammered away at the Bank issue. Jackson was uniformly lauded for saving "the people from becoming enslaved by the corruptions of a moneyed aristocracy and desperate politicians." The veto message itself was praised as "a document worthy of the purest days of our Republic. It brings us back nearer to the original principles which pervaded, and the spirit which animated the fathers of our country, than anything which emanated from the Executive since the days of Jefferson. It is the final decision of the President between the Aristocracy and the People—he stands by the People."

As these resolutions indicate, the Democrats constantly widened the scope of their attack on the Bank to include the broader questions of democracy and liberty. Taking their cue from the veto they described the presidential contest as a struggle between Jackson and the people on one hand, and Clay and the aristocracy on the other. "The Jackson cause," they wrote, "is the cause of democracy and the people, against a corrupt and abandoned aristocracy." "Will you desert him," asked one newspaper, "because those men who have enjoyed the exclusive profits of the stock for *twenty years*, will now be compelled to let other men have a share? Will you desert him to gratify *British Dukes and Lords*, who hold *one-third* of the whole stock of this mammoth institution? Every sound Republican from Maine to Georgia, answers, No." Jackson's newspaper, the Washington *Globe*, (ably edited by Francis

Blair), kept up a steady fire at the Bank for fostering inequality and privilege within the country. "From time immemorial to the present date," reported the *Globe*, "the great mass of mankind have been struggling to preserve their conventional rights against the usurpations of a *few*, who, from the circumstances of birth, fortune, or money, have been enabled to seize the reins of Government and ride them, 'rough shod,' as their interests or caprice dictated. This governing party has been denominated the Aristocracy. . . . The newfangled name 'National Republican,' is a *ruse de guerre*."

Jackson himself was delighted with this splendid propaganda about democracy and aristocracy, and of course, he credited it all to the strength of his Bank message. "The veto works well," he said, "instead of crushing me as was expected and intended, it will crush the Bank." Martin Van Buren agreed. "The Veto is popular beyond my most sanguine expectations," he wrote, "I will be greatly disappointed if its effect is not very considerable with the great body of people at the election."

In order to broadcast this propaganda and thereby produce a "considerable popular effect," these newspaper tirades were circulated around the country, as far as the remotest towns in Maine. "Extra *Globes*," reported the Maine *Advocate*, "are sent in bundles by the Administration and its officers, into every town where a Jackson man can be found to distribute them. Letters are written and *franked* by the different officers at Washington, and sent out in all directions, soliciting 'names and money', and it is avowed to be their intention to introduce them into every house in the State, if possible. . . . At what former period have we seen the government officers, and even the President himself. . .writing electioneering letters, and circulating papers filled with political trash and the vilest falsehoods?"

Much of the Democratic "trash and falsehoods" dealt with the Second Bank. But there were other questions debated in the public prints. The so-called spoils system received a round of attention because of Jackson's expressed desire to establish the principle of rotation. "In a country where offices are created solely for the benefit of the people," he wrote in one message to Congress, "no one man has any more intrinsic right to official state than another. Offices were not established to give support to particular men at the public expense. No individual wrong is, therefore, done by removal, since neither appointment to nor continuance in office is a matter of right." Despite the clear intention of his language Jackson actually removed far fewer officials than his critics contended. During his first eighteen months in office he replaced 919 persons out of 10,093, which is approximately one in ten. This is hardly the record of a spoilsman, particularly when these figures are seen in the light of normal replacements due to resignations and death, plus those dismissed for dishonesty or incompetence. Nevertheless, the principle of rotation, which he clearly supported, gave Jackson a bad name, one the National Republicans were able to capitalize on both during and after the election. He was charged with fostering the worst form of political pay-offs and attacked for encouraging such men as William L. Marcy, one of Van Buren's lieutenants, who had arrogantly announced in a Senate speech: "To the victor belong the spoils of the enemy."

Besides spoils, the quarrel with Calhoun and the old dispute over the Seminole problem also captured newspaper attention. Even more frightening were the references to the tariff and the undisguised threats coming out of the South. The Congress had just passed the Tariff of 1832 in an effort to ameliorate the worst features of the Tariff of Abominations. However, the South still resented the very high schedule rates which were retained on many products. The steady decline of the price of cotton plus the feeling that southern planters and farmers were subsidizing northern manufacturers partially explained the intense opposition raised by the question of protection. What helped to build the crisis, in view of abolitionist attacks and such Negro uprisings as the *Denmark Vesey* and *Nat Turner* rebellions, was the growing southern concern over the future of slavery. During the summer of 1832 there were fears that South Carolina might nullify the tariff or even secede from the Union. A number of meetings were held in that state, where the most extreme form of political action was threatened in order to get the tariff lowered. Democratic newspapers played down the controversy, but some National Republican journals insisted the country must not be blackmailed by the demands of extreme southerners. Jackson himself watched events very carefully during the summer, ready at a moment's notice to dash back to Washington from his home in Tennessee if the situation became critical.

For their part, the National Republicans tried to match the Democrats both in organizational strength and effectiveness of propaganda. Committees were established, meetings held, resolutions passed and publicized. At one such meeting in a large city ten thousand people allegedly attended. "We looked around," wrote one reporter, "and we saw the mariner and the merchant, the storekeeper and the mechanic, the manufacturer and the day laborer — all glowing and gratified at the eloquence of the orators." The meeting turned out to be a particularly "glorious one for our cause. It reanimated our friends, added warmth to their patriotism — and has given fresh ardour to their exertions."

At a "great meeting of naturalized Irish citizens" held in Philadelphia and described as a "bumper," Jackson was repudiated by the overwhelming sentiment of the crowd. "Thousands upon thousands were there," reported one man, and "we consider this meeting as a death blow to the administration in this quarter. . . . It is evident that the mass of the people — the bone and sinew of the city and county — the patriotism and purity of the community, are opposed to the re-election of Andrew Jackson."

In attacking the President, the National Republicans faulted him for his assault upon the Bank and the country's currency; they maligned him for seizing power unauthorized by the Constitution; they blamed him for heading a miserable Administration, one wracked with incompetence and scandal; and they lashed him for "introducing the spoils system" into the Federal Government. They were especially effective in labeling him a dictator or monarch. This was their principal theme and the one that had the greatest effect. "THE KING UPON THE THRONE: *The People in the Dust*!!!" read one newspaper headline. Andrew Jackson "has set at utter defiance the will of the people as strongly expressed by their Senators and Representatives. . . .he has exercised a power that no Monarch in Europe dared attempt. . . .he has, by his frequent exercise of power which should never be ventured upon but in the most extreme cases, proved himself to be the most absolute despot now at the head of any representative government on earth."

One Ohio newspaper catalogued the "pernicious measures of the present National Executive." The editors singled out "his system of favoritism and proscription—the incessant attacks of his devoted partisans upon those safeguards with which our excellent Constitution has surrounded our free institutions—his repeated encroachments on the legitimate powers of the coordinate branches of the Government—and his rapid advances towards an unlimited despotism." But there was still time to save the Republic. "One more opportunity—*perhaps the last*—is yet afforded us, of strangling the monster of despotism before it shall have attained its full growth, and checking the full tide of corruption before it shall have become too strong to be resisted. The power still remains in our hands. Let us so use it as men who are to render an account to our God, to our country, to the world—and all will be well."

Despite the importance of the Bank issue, the National Republicans recognized that the really important element in the campaign was Jackson himself and his conduct of the Government. To their mind he was out to wreck the constitutional system. The Bank issue simply reaffirmed the President's desire to annul every institution he could not control. "His rejection of the Bank Charter, however injurious," said one newspaper, "might have been tolerated, had he not chosen to couch it in such offensive and arrogant language, and to mix up, with the rejection, opinions the most dangerous and unconstitutional, on the most important subjects."

The National Republicans also benefited from the tremendous financial resources of the United States Bank in conducting their campaign against the President. Along with many thousands of dollars contributed by the Bank, Biddle distributed thirty thousand copies of Jackson's veto message around the country because he was convinced it would serve his cause. "The U.S. Bank is in the field," worried one Democrat, "and I cannot but fear the effect of fifty or one hundred thousand dollars expended in conducting the election in such a city as New York." Others agreed. "I fear the Bank influence more than anything else," said one, "I have no doubt that the Bank managers will expend a large sum of money." It has been estimated that the Bank contributed something close to $100,000 to prevent Jackson's reelection.

The overt activities of the Bank in the campaign gave the Democrats much of their best propaganda and served to prove that the institution did indeed interfere with the process of government just as Jackson had charged. At the same time Democrats hit hard at the "foreign influence" issue resulting from the sale of Bank stock to British "lords and noblemen." Perhaps responding unwisely, the National Republicans chose to ridicule this argument. "General Jackson says that foreigners shall not buy or sell American stocks," the Albany *Daily Advertiser* editorialized. "Suppose the English say Americans shall not buy our goods, would we not say *they* were fools? The cases are precisely similar; and Jackson is as absurd to prevent our selling them our stocks, as they would be in prohibiting the sale of their goods to us."

Despite the strength of the Bank and "foreign influence" questions, the Democrats did not rely on issues to win the election. As professional politicians in an age of rising professionalism they knew the importance of exciting the voter, entertaining him, and turning him out at the polls on election day. This was best accomplished with parades and barbecues — especially parades, which had become increasingly important by the 1832 election. Michael Chevalier, a Frenchman traveling through the United States, later described one of these demonstrations in his book *Society, Manners and Politics in the United States.* "It was nearly a mile long," he wrote. "The Democrats marched in good order, to the glare of torches; the banners were more numerous than I had ever seen them in any religious festival; all were in transparency, on account of the darkness. On some were inscribed the names of the democratic societies or sections: *Democratic young men of the ninth* or *eleventh ward;* others bore imprecations against the Bank of the United States; *Nick Biddle* and *Old Nick* here figured largely. Then came portraits of General Jackson afoot and on horseback; there was one in the uniform of a general, and another in the person of the Tennessee farmer, with the famous hickory cane in his hand. Those of Washington and Jefferson, surrounded with Democratic mottoes, were mingled with emblems in all tastes and of all colors. Among these figures an eagle, not a painting, but a real, live eagle, tied by the legs, surrounded by a wreath of leaves, and hoisted upon a pole, after the manner of the Roman standards. The imperial bird was carried by a stout sailor, more pleased than ever was a sergeant permitted to hold one of the strings of the canopy, in a Catholic ceremony. From further than the eye could reach, came marching on the Democrats. I was struck with the resemblance of their air to the train that escorts the *viaticum* in Mexico and Puebla. The American standard-bearers were as grave as the Mexican Indians who bore the sacred tapers. The Democratic procession, also, like the Catholic procession, had its halting-places; it stopped before the homes of the Jackson men to fill the air with cheers, and halted at the doors of the leaders of the Opposition, to give three, six or nine groans."

In addition to parades, the Democrats believed in barbecues as an important technique in winning the voter's favor. Even when they lost local elections, as they did in Kentucky, the Democrats seemed to think a barbecue was in order — or so the Louisville *Journal* reported. "There seems to be no way of convincing these fellows that they are fairly beaten. They have one sort of answering for every thing. If we show them that we have elected our Lieutenant Governor by a majority of nearly 30,000, *they reply by swallowing a pig.* If we show them that we have gained great strength in the Senate, and added to our superiority, *they reply by devouring a turkey.* If we show them that we have obtained a majority of two-thirds in the House of Representatives, *they reply by pouring off a pint of whiskey or apple-toddy.* There is no withstanding such arguments. We give it up."

If the Democrats were expert at parades and barbecues as a means of generating mass support, the National Republicans showed a remarkable flare for political cartooning, and it is very probable that that art came of age in this campaign. One of the most striking cartoons entitled "Uncle Sam in Danger" showed the good Uncle sitting in a chair, his arm lanced, with blood and specie flowing from the wound into a basin held by Amos Kendall. "Dr." Jackson stands over the victim, a scalpel in his hand. "Hold the Bason [*sic*] Amos," says Jackson, "this is merely an Experiment but I take the Responsibility." To one side of the picture Van Buren comments that he cannot take a stand on the operation, while on the other side stands a citizen who laments: "Twixt the Giniril (since He's taken to Doctring) and the little Dutch Potercary, Uncle Sam stands no more chance than a stump tailed Bull in fly time."

Many of the cartoons involved the Jackson-Van Buren relationship. One depicted Van Buren as an infant in Jackson's arms, being spoon-fed by the general; another showed the President receiving a crown from Van Buren and a scepter from the devil; still a third portrayed Jackson, Van Buren, and others attired as burglars, aiming a large battering-ram at the Bank's front door. One popular caricature depicted Jackson as Don Quixote, tilting at one of the marble pillars of the Bank and breaking his lance against it. But perhaps the cartoon that was most widely reprinted showed Jackson and Clay dressed as jockeys, riding a race to the White House, with Clay half a length ahead.

The ingenuity of the National Republicans in developing cartooning as a campaign technique indicates their concern with the need to widen their appeal among the masses. More and more they tried to match the Democrats in those tactics and gimmicks which would prove attractive to the largest number of voters. As the Ohio editor said: "There is no withstanding such arguments." A striking pamphlet can influence voters, remarked one commentator, "and so does a well-conducted newspaper; but a hickory pole, a taking cry, a transparency, a burst of sky rockets and Roman candles (alas! that it should be so!) have a potency over a large third of our voters that printed eloquence can not exert."

The National Republicans, at least some of them, were also conscious of their organizational deficiencies. The weaknesses became apparent in many states during the congressional elections and several newspapers called attention to them. "With regard to the congressional elections," observed the Ohio *State Journal*, "it must be remarked that the Jackson party owe their temporary advantage to the want of concert among our political friends. . . . All that is necessary, therefore, to insure a successful result at the final struggle. . .is a cordial union among those of our fellow-citizens of Ohio who concur in the opinion that the best interests of the state imperiously require that General Jackson should not be re-elected."

Because they were in an up-hill fight, the National Republicans were also aware of the need to attract Anti-Masonic votes, despite Clay's membership in the fraternity, and in several states a determined effort was made to initiate cooperation between the two parties. However, the results were very uneven since so many National Republicans were Masons themselves. The Democrats became alarmed at this maneuver and tried to alert the Anti-Masons to the "game" being played on them. It was pointed out that Wirt, a former Mason, was obviously a stalking horse for Clay. "*Be not deceived*," said Blair in the *Globe. All* the candidates are *Masons*. In this respect, they are on equal footing. The object of running Mr. Wirt, is to enable the *leaders* to transfer the votes you give to him—to Henry Clay."

Although New York cast an anti-Jackson vote for Clay, representing a coalition between the National Republican and Anti-Masonic parties, this technique did not work in any other state. And even if it had worked, the coalition could not approach the level of Jackson's popular appeal around the country, an appeal which was overwhelmingly registered in the fall election. When all the ballots were counted the results showed that Jackson received 688,242 popular votes, while Clay took 473,462 votes and Wirt 101,051. In the electoral college Jackson won 219 votes against 49 for Clay and 7 for Wirt. Clay carried Massachusetts, Rhode Island, Connecticut, Delaware, Kentucky, and a majority of the Maryland vote while Wirt took the single state of Vermont. Jackson captured all the rest except South Carolina, now verging on nullification, which gave its 11 votes to John Floyd of Virginia. In the vice-presidential contest Van Buren won handily by receiving 189 votes to Sergeant's 49 and Ellmaker's 7. South Carolina awarded its 11 votes to Henry Lee of Massachusetts, while Pennsylvania gave 30 to its favorite son, William Wilkins.

Besides Vermont, Wirt showed strength in Connecticut, Massachusetts, New York, and Pennsylvania; he also attracted a few hundred votes each from the states of Maryland, New Jersey, Ohio, and Rhode Island. Clay did relatively well in New England, the Middle Atlantic states, and some parts of the West such as Ohio and Kentucky. Jackson gathered his greatest support from the West and the South; he did fairly well in the Middle Atlantic states, but less so in New England, although he won the states of Maine and New Hampshire where the Democratic party had a strong organization. He had no opposition in Alabama, Georgia, and Mississippi. In Maryland, where the electoral vote was cast by district, Jackson took 3 of the 10 electoral votes at stake and Clay 7. However, two of the Clay electors did not cast their ballots in the election.

The final totals of this election are extremely inexact. For one thing it is impossible to distinguish the relative performance of Clay and Wirt because some states registered their tallies as either "Jackson" or "anti-Jackson." For another, Clay's Tennessee vote is suspiciously small; it is almost half the amount John Quincy Adams received in 1828. Moreover, the Missouri vote for Clay is non-existent. Some historians have argued that there was no opposition to Jackson in that state, but it is more probably that the final figure reported simply represents Jackson's majority over Clay in Missouri.

However the votes are examined and analyzed one thing is clear. Jackson won a smashing victory. Of the total votes cast he received 54.5 per cent, an achievement rarely attained in presidential elections. Yet, although the total number of votes cast in 1832 rose more than 100,000 over the 1828 contest, the percentage of Jackson's popular majority declined by more than 1.5 per cent from what he received four years earlier. Jackson is the only President in American history whose reelection to a second term registered such a decline. Perhaps, too much can be made of this fact, considering the trifling extent of the decline and the inexactness of the total figures of votes cast.

Still it has been suggested that Jackson may have been hurt by the Bank issue, which, because of the possible consequences to the country's financial life, probably frightened some Americans, and accounts for the decrease in the President's overall majority. It is strikingly clear that he owed his victory to his enormous popularity with the electorate, a popularity skillfully managed by an active political party. The only real issue in the campaign was Jackson himself; most voters trusted Jackson, loved him, and rallied to his cause, a cause which they believed to be democratic. With Jackson at the head of the Government they believed the artificial obstacles preventing the rise of ordinary citizen would be removed, and equality would be advanced throughout the country. "Who but General Jackson would have had the courage to veto the bill rechartering the Bank of the United States," asked one man, "and who but General Jackson could have withstood the overwhelming influence of that corrupt Aristocracy?"

Clay did not possess Jackson's charisma, nor did he have the party organization to match that of the Democrats. Wirt undoubtedly diverted some of Clay's strength, but it is clear that the existence of the third party in no way shaped the final results of the election. The Bank issue was as powerful an issue as Clay could have wished; still it was not potent enough to unseat Jackson.

Even so, that question had another important significance. Jackson had taken the issue to the people for decision. Since he was overwhelmingly reelected he could, and later did, declare that he had a mandate from the people to rid the country of the monster Bank. As he battled Congress in the next session to achieve this result, Jackson claimed his power to act had been enhanced by his great electoral victory, thus including all the people within the area of presidential responsibility. He also claimed he was the sole and direct representative of the people, a contention that brought howls of protest from Congress. Henry Clay was one of the first to see that Jackson, instead of acknowledging his obligations to Congress, was now seeking a new relationship and new supports from the people. "Sir," said Clay on the Senate floor, "I am surprised and alarmed at the new source of executive power which is found in the result of a presidential election. I had supposed that the Constitution and the laws were the sole source of executive authority. . .that the issue of a presidential election was merely to place the Chief Magistrate in the post assigned to him. . . . But it seems that if, prior to an election, certain opinions, no matter how ambiguously put forth by a candidate, are known to the people, those loose opinions, in virtue of the election, incorporate themselves with the Constitution, and afterwards are to be regarded and expounded as parts of the instrument!"

Although Clay overstated the case it is clear that Jackson believed the relationship between the electorate and the presidential office had been reconstituted as a result of the election. He also believed the election had increased executive power to act in destroying the Second National Bank. Thus the contest of 1832 was an important turning point in party history, not only because of the many political innovations introduced at this time, but because it also marked a new departure in the growth and development of the presidential office.

Appendix

Report on the Anti-Masonic Convention
in the *Niles' Register*, October 8, 29, 1831

The first national convention to nominate a candidate for the office of President of the United States was held by the Anti-Masons in Baltimore in September, 1831. The Anti-Masons were also the first third party in American history.

Sept. 26, 1831.

At 12 o'clock, M. the delegates to the national antimasonic convention assembled in the saloon of the Athenaeum, and were called to order by the hon. judge Burt, of New York, when the hon. John Ratherford was called to the chair, and the following officers being nominated were unanimously chosen: —

JOHN C. SPENCER, of New York, President.
JOHN RUTHERFORD, New Jersey, 1st V. P.
JONATHAN SLOAN, Ohio, 2d V. P.
THOMAS ELDER, Penn. 3rd V. P.
JOHN BAILEY, Mass. 4th V.P.

Benjamin F. Hallet,
Edward D. Barber, ⎫
S. C. Leavitt, ⎬ secretaries.
Caleb Emery, ⎭

On taking the chair, Mr. Spenser addressed the convention as follows: —

Gentlemen — I return you my thanks for the distinguished honor you have conferred in calling upon me to preside over your deliberations. While I distrust my ability to discharge the duties of the chair, I have yet learnt in the school of anti-masonary to decline no duty to which I may be called in the promotion of our great and growing cause. But my reliance, gentlemen, will be on your patriotism and urbanity, to render the duties of the station light and easy. I ask your indulgence for any errors that may be committed, assuring you that nothing offensive to any member shall proceed from the chair, or be permitted in the deliberations of the convention.

On motion of Mr. Phelps, of Mass. voted, that the credentials of the delegates be now received and examined; upon so doing it appeared that there were present, from

New Hampshire	1	New York	31
Maine	2	New Jersey	4
Massachusetts	13	Pennsylvania	19

517

Rhode Island	4	Ohio	5
Connecticut	6	Maryland	1
Vermont	5	Delaware	1

On motion of *Mr. Walker*, of Mass. voted, that a regular roll of the members of this convention be now made, and that the state, country and town, in which they reside, be fully designated.

On motion of *Mr. Morris*, of N.Y. voted, that a committee of three be appointed to invite the hon. Charles Carroll, of Carrollton, to take a seat in this convention. Messrs. Rutherford, of N.J. Burt, of N.Y. and Elder, of Pa. were appointed said committee.

Voted, on motion of *Mr. Phelps*, that a committee of one from each state be appointed to report upon the business of this convention, viz:

Phelps, of Mass.	Terry, of Connecticut,
Ward, N. Y.	Barber, Vermont,
Jones, Penn.	Vanderpool, N. Jersey,
Hallett, R. I.	Sloan, Ohio,
Cram, Maine	Gibbons, Delaware,
Emery, N. H.	Shriver, Maryland.

Voted to adjourn to meet again at 4 P.M. Met agreeably to adjournment. Mr. Phelps from the committee reported on the business to be adopted by the convention, which was unanimously accepted.

On motion of *judge Hopkins*, of New York, voted, that Messrs. Hopkins, of N. York, Jones, of Pa. and Walker, of Mass. be a committee to wait on his hon. chief justice Marshall, now in this city, and request his attendance on the sitting of this body.

Mr. Ward, from the committee, at the call of the convention, submitted a report which was read and laid apon the table.

The president of the convention announced the appointment of the following committees:

On masonic penalties — Hallet, of R.I. Larned, of Maine, Morris, of N.Y. Grimshaw, of Pa. and Warner, of Ohio.

On judical proceedings in the case of Morgan — J. C. Spencer, of N.Y. Ogle, of Pa. Walker, of Mass. Gibbons, of Del. Russell of N. York.

On the address to the people — Holly, of N.Y. Denny, of Pa. Leavitt of Connecticut.

On publishing the proceedings — Phelps, of Mass. Hopkins, of N.Y. and Foote, of N.Y.

On finance — Irwin, of Pa. Boynton, of Conn. Beckman, of N.Y. Jenkins, of Ohio, Shriver, of Md.

The committee appointed to wait on *judge Marshall*, reported by their chairman that they had seen that gentleman, and that, in reply to their invitation, his honor politely stated that he should leave the city at 6 o'clock, tomorrow morning, and therefore be unable to attend, although it would afford him great pleasure to do so.

On motion of *Mr. St. John*, of N.Y. voted to adjourn till 10 o'clock, to-morrow morning.

* * *

Tuesday, Sept. 27, 10 o'clock, A.M.

Met pursuant to adjournment.

The proceedings of yesterday were read by the secretary.

Messrs. Oliver, of Mass. *Harvey, Heister, Rugle, Burrowes, Waters* and *Stevens*, of Pa. *Baker*, of Ohio, and *Strong* of N.Y. appeared and took their seats.

A letter directed to the president of the convention from *Samuel Stevens*, a delegate from N.York, was presented and read to the convention, and on motion of *Mr. Seward* of N. Y. was ordered to be entered at large on the journal of the convention.

Mr. Hopkins, of N.Y. announced that chief justice Marshall having been unexpectedly prevented from leaving the city, would soon be in the hall, to attend the deliberations of the convention.

Mr. Rutherford, of N.J. from the committee appointed to wait on the venerable Charles Carroll, of Carrollton, and invite him to be present at the deliberations of the convention, reported,

"That the committee have seen the secretary of Mr. Carroll, and are informed that Mr. Carroll left this city in the month of June last, for his country residence on the manor of Carrollton, sixteen miles from Baltimore, and that he is not expected to return until the month of October next; that he is in good health, but is desirous to avoid the fatigue of journies to and from the city. The committee, therefore, did not proceed to Carrollton yesterday, more especially as the weather was inclement, and the visit and journey would occupy part of two days.

On motion of *Mr. Phelps*, of Mass.

Voted, That the time appointed to make nominations of president and vice president of the United States, be postponed till to-morrow at 10 o'clock, A.M.

Mr. Davis, of Vermont, submitted the following resolution:

Resolved, That this convention will adjourn without day on Wednesday next, the 28th inst.

Ordered to lie on the table.

On motion of *Mr. Hallett*, of R.I.

Resolved, That the resolution of this convention inviting the venerable Charles Carroll, of Carrollton, to be present at the proceedings of this convention, together with the report of the committee appointed on that resolution, be transcribed and certified by the officers of this convention, and communicated to Mr. Carroll.

Mr. Burt, of N.Y. called for the reading of the rules and orders of this convention, which were accordingly read.

Chief justice Marshall, introduced by Mr. Hopkins, of N.Y. appeared in the hall, in pursuance of the invitation given him, and took a seat to attend the deliberations of the convention.

Mr. Hallett, from the committee appointed to report on the construction of masonic penalties, &c. made a report, which was read and laid on the table.

The president from the committee appointed to prepare a brief history of judicial proceedings, &c. made a report, which was read and laid on the table.

Convention adjourned to four o'clock, P.M.

Four o'clock, P.M. Convention met pursuant to adjournment.

Messrs. Pike and *Fowler*, from Ohio, appeared and took their seats.

The reports of the committees on the construction of masonic penalties, and on the history of judicial proceedings, being under consideration, a debate ensued in which *Messrs. Foote*, of N.Y. *Hallett*, of R.I. *Ward*, of N.Y. *Morris*, of N.Y. *Seward*, of N.Y. *Walker*, of Mass. and *Harvey*, of Pa. took part.

Mr. Northrop, of N.J. appeared and took his seat.

The reports on the construction of masonic penalties and on the history of judicial proceedings, were ordered to be printed.

On motion of *Mr. Jones*,

Resolved, That a committee of five be appointed to report on the extent to which the principles of free masonry are political, and opposition to them by an organised political party.

Messrs. Jones, of Pa. *Seward*, of N.Y. *Sloane*, of Ohio, *Bailey*, of Mass. *Emery*, of N.H. were appointed said committee.

The convention adjourned to nine o'clock to-morrow morning.

Wednesday, Sept. 28.

Met pursuant to adjournment.

Mr. Wm. Vanderpool, of N.J. appeared and took his seat.

Mr. Seward, of N.Y. submitted the following preamble and resolution, which were read and passed.

Whereas, Wm. G. Verplanck, of Ballston, Saratoga county, N.Y. a delegate originally appointed by the state convention of the state of New York, has since the last adjournment, arrived in this city, having been detained by accident on his journey. And

Whereas, The place of said delegate has been supplied as a vacancy.

Resolved, That said Wm. G. Verplanck be admitted to a seat as an honorary member with the privilege of participating in the debates, but not in the votes of this convention.

Mr. Samuel J. Packer, of Pa. was also admitted to a seat in the convention in accordance with the aforegoing resolution.

On motion of *Mr Phelps*, of Mass.

The resolution relative to the nomination of president, &c. was re-considered and amended, so as to strike out that part requiring the convention to go into committee of the whole for that purpose.

On motion of *Mr. Walker*, of Mass.

Voted, To proceed to ballot for candidates for the offices of president and vice president of the United States.

Messrs. Phelps, of Mass. and Stevens, of Pa. were appointed by the president tellers to receive and count the votes.

The convention then proceeded to ballot for president.

Mr. Hambly, of Pa. being absent, on motion of Mr. Irwin, of Pa. Mr. Packer was admitted to vote in his stead.

Mr. Phelps, one of the tellers, reported as follows: —

```
Whole number of votes ..............................111
Necessary to a choice .............................. 84
William Wirt, of Maryland  ..........................108
Richard Rush, of Pennsylvania ......................  1
Blank ..............................................  2
```

The president announced the result, and declared William Wirt, of Md. duly nominated as the anti-masonic candidate for the presidency of the United States.

On motion of *Mr. Stevens*, of Pa.

Resolved unanimously, That William Wirt, of Md. be nominated as the anti-masonic candidate for the office of president of the United States at the ensuing election.

Resolved, That a committee of three members be appointed to communicate the preceding resolution to Mr. Wirt, and to request his acceptance of the above nomination. Messrs. Rutherford, of N. J. Sloane, of Ohio, and Elder, of Pa. were appointed said committee.

The convention then proceeded to ballot for vice president.

Mr. Stevens, one of the tellers, reported as follows:

```
Whole number of votes given ....................... 110
Necessary to a choice ............................. 83
Amos Ellmaker, of Penn. ........................... 108
John C. Spencer, of New York ...................... 1
Blank ............................................. 1
```

The president announced the result and declared Amos Ellmaker, of Pa. duly nominated as the anti-masonic candidate for vice president of the United States.

On motion of *Mr. Phelps*, of Mass.

Resolved, unanimously, That Amos Ellmaker, of Pa. be nominated by the convention, as the anti-masonic candidate for vice president of the United States, at the ensuing election.

Resolved, That a committee of three members be appointed to communicate the resolution above to Mr. Ellmaker, and request his acceptance of the above nomination. Messrs. Baily, of Mass. Lyman, of N.Y. and Shriver, of Maryland, were appointed said committee.

On motion of *Mr. Morris*, of N.Y.

Resolved, unanimously, That a committee of three members be appointed to express, by written communication, to the hon. Richard Rush, of Pa. the profound sense of this convention, of the patriotism, principle and firmness which dictated his eloquent exposition of the evils of free masonry, and their high appreciation of the beneficial results which it cannot fail to produce. Messrs. Morris, of N.Y. Denny, of Pa. and Gibbons, of Delaware, were appointed said committee.

Mr. Rutherford, from the committee appointed to wait on Mr. Wirt, &c. reported that the committee had performed that duty, and that he would send a written communication to the convention at 8 o'clock, P.M.

On motion of *Mr. Hopkins*, of N.Y.

Resolved, unanimously, That the thanks of this convention, he presented to these citizens of Baltimore at whose expense the convention has been accommodated with the use of the splendid hall of the Athenæum, and that this convention have felt peculiar pleasure in receiving such a proof of hospitality from the inhabitants of this elegant and polished city, and that the president of this convention be requested to transmit a copy of this resolution to the mayor of this city.

On motion of *Mr. Turner*, of R. I.

Resolved, That the president of this convention be requested to present a copy of the printed proceedings of this, and of the anti-masonic convention held at Philadelphia last year, to the president and vice president of the United States, to the ex-presidents of the United States, to the heads of the several departments, to the hon. John Marshall, chief justice, and to each of the justices of the supreme court of the United States, to the governors of the several states of the union, to gen. Lafayette, to the venerable Charles Carroll, of Carrollton, to the mayor of the city of Baltimore, to the trustees of the Athenæum of Baltimore, and to such other distinguished individuals of this country, as he may deem expedient.

On the consideration of this resolution a debate ensued, in which *Messrs. Turner*, of R.I. *Vanderpool*, of N. J. *Hallett*, of R.I. *Phelps*, of Mass. *Denny*, of Pa. and *Miller*, of Pa. took part.

Mr. Bailey from the committee to wait on Mr. Ellmaker reported that the committee had performed the duty assigned them, and that Mr. Ellmaker would shortly make a communication to the convention.

Adjourned to 5 o'clock, P.M.

September 28, 5 o'clock, P.M.

Met pursuant to adjournment.

Mr. Ward, from the committee on resolutions, made a report which was trice read and unanimously adopted.

Messrs. Foote, Fuller and *Hopkins*, of N.Y. *Hallett*, of R.I. and *Stevens*, of Pa. severally addressed the convention in support of the resolutions.

Mr. Seward, of N.Y. submitted the following resolutions, which were read and passed unanimously.

Resolved, That the committee of finance be authorised to pay over any surplus funds which may remain in their hands, towards the expenses of the national corresponding committee to be distributed by the publishing committee.

Resolved, That the thanks of this convention be returned to the national corresponding committee for the faithful discharge of their duties during the past year, and that this convention entertain a profound conviction that the results of their labors must be eminently beneficial to the cause of anti-masonry.

The report of the national corresponding committee was called up and ordered to be printed.

Adjourned to 8 o'clock this evening.

*   *   *

ADDRESS OF THE ANTI-MASONIC CONVENTION.

To the American People

A large and growing political party, through us, respectfully addresses you. Numerous bodies of enlightened and honest freemen, in states containing more than half the electors of our union, have openly and fairly delegated us to represent them, in the performance of duties, which cannot fail to affect your essential rights. And believing that your rights are inseparably blended with theirs, we seek, most earnestly, so to perform these duties, as to produce effects equally and extensively beneficial upon the rights of all. These duties consist in nominating citizens to be supported, as candidates for the offices of president, and vice president, of the United States, at the next election, and in setting forth the grounds, on which you are invited to sustain the nomination.

The concurrence of millions of men, in any act of deliberation or decision, for objects, in which they have a common interest, presents to the mind a magnificent and exciting spectacle. If the men be intelligent, patriotic, and free, and the object be that of appointing the most suitable of their number, to guard the rights, and advance the prosperity, of the nation, which they constitute, human life can rarely exhibit a spectacle of equal interest and sublimity. Scarcely any approach towards such an exhibition has ever been witnessed, in any country, but ours. Let it be our ambition, so to continue and improve the exhibition, in all its stated recurrences, and shall more and more commend it to be approbation and esteem of the great brotherhood of communities, to which we belong, and most effectually tend to the establishment and support of free principles, in every community of our fellow men.

In selecting candidates for the highest offices, in the gift of the people, it is essential to consider — the peculiar frame and objects of our government — the personal qualifications of the candidates — the principles, which should govern their administration — the sources at danger to these principles — and the means of removing that danger. On each of these considerations, we wish to offer our opinions with that ingeniousness, fullness, and earnestness, which become freemen, in addressing their equals and brethren, upon subjects involving their dearest hopes, and most imperative duties.

Government has always been a business of the highest importance. In every form, it has exercised a mighty influence upon the individual and collective condition of its subjects. In most countries, it has generally been the prey of crafty and fortunate violence; and wielded for partial and selfish objects. With such an origin and such an object, it was impossible that it should not be the parent of innumerable mischiefs. But bad as it has been, it has not been without its advantages; and these have greatly outweighed its evils. Without government, there could have been no extensive associations among men. Their conflicting interests and passions, would have produced universal collisions, so fierce and frequent, as to have prevented much increase; and the human face would have existed, at this day, only in the condition of a few scattered, ignorant, indigent, feeble, ferocious, and insecure families. To raise them above this condition, government was absolutely, indispensable.

The great use of government is to secure rights — all the rights of those, who unite in its formation. These are comprehended in the liberty, and the pursuit of happiness. To the security of these, order is essential. Order cannot be maintained without a common and definite arbiter of the differences, that may arise between the individuals composing a nation, and a power to protect the whole against external agression. Such an arbiter and power is government; which, to be perfect, should be just, intelligent, free from the bias of self interest, and effective, as to all the objects for which it is constituted. But such a government never existed. And so long as men are ignorant, selfish, and passionate, never will exist among them. The nearest possible approximation to such a government is a republic.

A republic acknowledges the rights of all, and seeks to avail itself of the wisdom and power of all, to promote their common welfare. Its theory is perfect. It is bounded upon the proper basis, pursues the proper end, and employs the proper means. And by the principles of elective representation and accountability, it may be so extended as ultimately to combine all nations — if not into one family — into a friendly association of several peaceful, prosperous, and numerous families. If right, duty, wisdom, and power, can contribute to the real exaltation and happiness of man; and if government can combine and apply them most comprehensively and beneficially to the regulation of human conduct, then republicanism offers a more majestic and reverend image of substantial glory, than can otherwise result, from the labors, and sufferings, and virtues of our race. It is a practical scheme of universal benevolence, sure to be approved, embraced, and sustained, by all men, in proportion to the just prevalence, in their minds, of intelligence, truth, and philanthropy. Such a government is the one, under which, it is our privilege to live.

Where it is the distinctive object of government to bring the public wisdom to the direction of the public will, for the public good; and the people understand their rights, their duties, and their interests, a designation to fill the high places of its administration, by a majority of their free voices, is the most precious reward, of earthly origin, which can be bestowed upon intellectual and moral merit; and imposes an accountability exactly proportioned to its value.

No step should be taken towards its bestowment, without a lively and generous solitude.

The qualities, which should be possessed, by every president of the U. States, are the most estimable, that can adorn a man. He should be industrious. No great end of human life can be obtained without great effort. Everything, which is good in the character and condition of man, is progressive, and cannot be otherwise. Knowledge, virtue, safety, happiness, are attainments, not gifts, nor inheritances. They are the slowly maturing, but precious fruits of exertion; not the capricious or unsought bounties of earth, or heaven. Free government, the most complicated and expansive good, that can spring from human effort, has not been acquired, and cannot be preserved, without perpetual and strenuous exertion. The chief magistrate of this government must therefore, be willing and accustomed to labor. Honest labor is always honorable. In the president of the U. States, it is most honorable, because his labor is consecrated to the noblest purposes that can be advanced by human means, and requires the employment of the highest qualities, that can animate the soul.

He should be intelligent. The objects and provisions of our government, in all its relations both foreign and domestic—the sources of its power, and the means of its support—the history of its origin, its establishment, and its fruits, are topics of inquiry and meditation more pregnant with valuable instruction to the genuine friends of man, than all others supplied by civil records. They are themes of enlightened examination, discussion, and admiration, every where. And the most respectable nations of the old world are now agonising to disabuse themselves of their ancient, burthensome, and unequal institutions, for the sake of following our example. To understand these topics, will well repay the efforts, it may cost, to every mind. It is an essential part of the education of every freeman. In him, who is entrusted with the most responsible application of all the knowledge they infold, to the holy purposes of rightful order and social advancement, it is equally the dictate of duty, self-respect, and honorable ambition, to understand them familiarly, and in all their details. Such understanding can be obtained, only by diligent study, deep reflection, candid observation, wise intercourse, and practical experience.

He should be honest. His conduct should be a perfect exemplification of the solemn claims of truth and right, in all his communications and influences, and of the strictest fidelity to the prescribed duties of his office. His manners should be plain, direct, and cordial, both in his official and private relations—the transcript of an upright, pure and benevolent mind, and suitable to aid in the accomplishment of all his grave and exalted functions. The greatest crime, which can be committed against freemen is the usurpation of power. It should be deemed the unpardonable sin of republics. It has been the unfathomable deep in which all the footsteps of liberty, in other countries, have been swallowed up, in all ancient and modern times. To it, the highest place of delegated powers affords both the most temptation, and the most probable means of success. Whoever fills that place should, therefore, be strong in honesty. If he yields to the temptations, and seeks to employ the means, entrusted to him only for the benefit of his fellow citizens, in endeavors, to raise himself upon their ruin, he should be branded like another Cain. His memory should be held in the most intense and immortal detestation.

He should be independent, following his own convictions of right, and not shrinking from any of his appropriate responsibilities. He should be swayed by no private and illegitimate influences, and never seek to cast his burthens upon others. In every act of the power lawfully assigned him, he should stand forth, as the personal agent of the public will, and answerable to all its just demands.

He should be vigilant. Our freedom, though well secured, may be invaded. In all other countries, freedom has been successfully invaded. Ours is too valuable, and has been too dearly purchased, to omit any means of its preservation. Without eternal vigilance, in all its sentinels, no means will be sufficient. With an awakened eye to every part of his charge, he who occupies the highest watch-tower of the nation, should carefully mark all the indications of good or evil, which may affect it, and weigh them well, the better to secure the objects of his care.

He should be wise in judgment. To this end, patient examination, cool deliberation, and impartial affections are requisite. Accordingly, he should be in the customary use of them. His judgment is the great hinge of good or evil to millions. It should not therefore be hasty, wavering, or weak; but well informed, faithful and firm.

He should be prudent. This quality refers more to action than to speculation, but includes both; and consists in a sagacious foresight of evils, and an effective application of means to avoid them, as well as in an enlightened anticipation of benefits, and adequate efforts to secure them. It is an exalted merit; not often brilliant in its means, because they are such as common sense enjoins, and therefore excite no wonder; but blessed in its effects, because under all circumstances it leads to the utmost attainable good. Prudence obtains less praise than it deserves, because it is often confounded with the partial and sordid purpose, to which it may be made subservient.

He should be disinterested and patriotic. Yielding himself to the wishes of his fellow citizens for the momentous task of their leading civil service, he should in all its specifications and labors, lose himself in them. Their rights, their safety, their happiness, should be his undeviating aim. Regarding them as his political brethren and principals, he will be intent upon promoting their interests. In this way, he will secure his own. And grateful to them for his elevation to the noblest and widest sphere of beneficent exertion, to which wisdom and virtue can aspire, in this world, he will labor, unceasingly, for the good of his country. With a country distinguished above all others—for its exemption from time-honored abuses either civil, ecclesiastical or military —for the self-directing, and self-relying habits of its people—for its ingenuity and enterprise, in all the walks of productive industry—for its force and steadiness of resolve, in pursuit of practical utility—for its just distribution of social respect and honor—for its high and equal valuation of individual rights—for its anxiety and ability to disseminate useful knowledge, among all its children—for the spirit of improvement incorporated in its frame of government, exciting to the discovery, and inviting to the adoption, of every new and useful principle, and method of operation—for its unparalleled advancement in wealth, numbers, and strength—for its facilities of enlargement over half a continent, and of influence over all the world—for the adaptation of its employments, purposes, and institutions, to the rights of man—for its large and increasing enjoyment of the esteem and favor of nations—and for its glorious hopes of perpetuity, it would be as natural as it would be necessary, that he should be a patriot. It would seem impossible for him to be otherwise. Penetrated with a just sense of the dignity and importance of his great trust, he should endeavor to discharge it, with parental and equal regard to every section and member of the national family.

What should be the principles of his administration? Such certainly as are found in the fundamental doctrines of the republic, and are best calculated to harmonise order and right. As drawn from our constitutions and illustrated by the writings and examples of our sages, they are chiefly the following—equal and exact justice to all men of whatever state, condition, or persuasion, religious or political—peace, commerce and honest friendship with all nations, entangling alliances with none—the support of the state governments, in all their rights, as the most competent administrations for our domestic concerns, and the surest bulwark against anti-republican tendencies—the preservation of the general government in its whole constitutional vigor, as the sheet anchor of our peace at home and safety abroad—a sacred regard to the principles and spirit of our union, which make us one people, and have been the essential means of our national power, honor, prosperity and freedom, as much as they were of the successful assertion of our national independence—acquiescence in the decisions of the majority, even if deemed wrongful, till they can be lawfully changed, by the influence of intelligence and patriotism; such acquiescence being the vital principle of republics, from which there is no appeal but to force, the vital principle and immediate parent of despotism—a well organised militia, our best reliance in peace, and for the first moments of war, till regulars may relieve them—the supremacy of the civil over the military authority—economy in the public expense, that labor may be lightly burthened—the honest payment of our debts and careful preservation of the public faith—encouragement of the great interests of agriculture, commerce and manufactures, that every branch of productive industry may be profitable, protected and respected—the diffusion of information, by the reasonable patronage of elementary schools, and scientific establishments, as well as by the publicity of all governmental transactions, with those temporary exceptions only, which are dictated by prudence, in relation to foreign intercourse, and the initiatory steps in prosecuting crime—the arraignment of all abuses at the bar of the public reason—the strict accountability of placement and frequent rotation in office—the unbroken dominion of the laws over all men, whether private citizens, public officers, or associations of both—the prompt and lawful application of all the necessary powers of government to secure the liberty and life of any citizen from criminal invasion, when it is known to be threatened, and the most strenuous and persevering exertion, on all occasions, to disclose and bring to legal punishment, the perpetrators of crime; government is unwilling, or unable, to withstand the enterprises of faction and crime, whether proceeding in secret or in public; confine each member of the society, and association of members, within the limits prescribed by the laws, and to maintain all, in the secure and tranquil enjoyment of the rights of person and property. There are yet other rights of the people of which his administration should manifest a zealous care—that of political equality, implying general suffrage, and eligibility to office—of the independent and safe application of the right of voting to all cases, which the people shall think proper, as in this way it may become the mild and safe corrective of abuses, which must be lopped by the sword of revolution where peaceable remedies are unprovided—of freedom of religion; freedom of the press, and freedom of person, under the protection of the habeas corpus; of trial by juries and judges impartial in their obligations and impartially selected; and of security in person, house, papers, and effects, against unreasonable searches and seizures. These seem to us the essential principles of our freedom. They have been raised out of the precious mine of human rights, by the labors of ages; and having disengaged them from the rubbish and dross, under which all the workings of ignorance, faction and tyranny, would keep them eternally buried, by the post pure-hearted, arduous, and sagacious exertions, our political fathers have combined and set them up, for our shelter and guidance. Let us never be unmindful of them. We can have nothing of so much worth. They are the most brilliant jewels of our nation already rich and renowned. We cannot overvalue them. But, unlike the shining baubles of ostentatious and unrighteous power, they are valuable in their use. In that alone are they good; and their most important use is, to be made the touchstone of the merits of those we trust.

Are these principles in danger? Every candid man, who will enquire, must think so. They were never in danger so imminent. Their foe is rich, disciplined, and wily. He obeys no rules of civilized warfare, no restraint of truth, no injustice, no pleadings of humanity. He already occupies the principal posts heretofore relied on, as the chief defence of our liberty; every where lies in wait to deceive; endeavors to poison the springs of resistance to him; seduces the unwary, disloyal, and sordid, by flattery, lucrative employment, and offers of preferment; intimidates the irresolute and weak, by haughty exhibitions of his power, and assails by a thousand ambuscades, and by all sorts of weapons the most envenomed and condemned, the watchful, thoughtful, steadfast, and unconquerable friends of free principles. Such a foe is freemasonry.

This appears incredible to honest unreflecting men, till they fairly understand the character of freemasonry, and ascertain its conduct. Whenever they do this, the incredibility vanishes; they join the great rally of antimasons, and work with one mind and untiring zeal, in all the way of law and honor, for its abolition. The disinclination to take up impressions of evil against it arises, almost wholly, from the fair characters of some men, who have been connected with it, and from the support of it, by interested politicians, and the presses under its control.

Honorable men have joined it, in early life. Incited by unsuspected representations of its purity and value, and by curiosity to explore a mystery, they surrendered themselves to the wish of its members, and offered to be conducted into its dark chambers. Of these we know some stopped at the threshold; some, in the first degree; some in the second; and more, in the third. None of them knew any thing of its peculiar ceremonies, oaths, or objects, till they had sworn to conceal them. They have often praised the virtues it claimed, for they loved virtue, and hoped the claim was just. But they never imbibed its spirit, or knowingly approved its principles. From the first step of their initiation, they always suspected both. If they did not, we should have heard from some of the ten thousand conscientious and patriotic seceders, who have opened the door upon all its proceedings, of fathers leading their sons to the masonic altar. Among them all, the seceders have probably witnessed admissions into nearly every lodge in the union. No one has told you, that he ever assisted at the initiation of his own son, or knew any other father do so, in relation to his son. Is not this a most honest, legible, and fatal condemnation of the order, derived from witnesses the most competent and credible though unwilling — even from the very hearts of its adhering members? What! would not a father initiate his son, the pride of his life, the hope of his age, the object of his prayers, into an association of honorable men most exclusively designed, and most wisely adapted, to the inculcation of science, charity, religion? How have good fathers done, who have become freemasons? Let each one look around among his acquaintances, and recall his past observation, for the answer. They have discontinued attendance upon the lodges. They have preferred other schools of science, for their children. They have resorted to better means of impressing the love and practice of charity upon their hearts. They have looked higher for their religion. Either the best of fathers, who had joined the lodge, were anti-masons in the bottom of their hearts, knowing the institution to be a base imposture; or they hated their children.

But how have members, who were most distinguished for public honor and private virtue out of the lodge, conducted, in relation to it? Franklin is said to have replied to his brother, who asked his advice about joining the society, "one fool is enough in a family." When the reputable and benevolent Jeremy Gridley, was grand master of the Massachusetts masons, before the most criminal degrees of the order were known in our country, he was enquired of, by a young friend, whether it was worth his while to become a mason? and he answered NO — with this pregnant addition, "by aggregation to the society a young man might acquire a little *artificial* support, but that *he* did not need it; and there was *nothing* in the masonic institution *worthy of his seeking to be associated with it.*" The enquirer, afterwards, by his bold and freedom-freighted thoughts, and the high bearing of his devoted expression of them, was the most prominent agent in carrying the declaration of independence, in the illustrious congress of '76.

But, Washington, and his brother officers of glorious memory, were masons.

True. They were admitted to three degrees. None of them went higher, in the early days of our independence. Washington never visited a lodge but once or twice after 1768; and never presided in one. He afterwards in effect, renounced it; and so did a large majority of the officers before alluded to, in their voluntary determination to extinguish the Cincinnati society. To this society they were bound by stronger ties than masonry can offer to uncorrupted minds — by those of a natural and general and generous sympathy, of which the golden links were struck out and forged, in the welding fires of our revolutionary war.

The origin of this society was innocent; its objects were laudable; its laws were published; its meetings were not secret; it administered no oaths, imposed no bloody penalties, had no division into degrees, and its members were respected and honored as the benefactors of their country; but it introduced distinctions between its members and other citizens; its associates wore badges, a ribbon and eagle; it was hereditary; admitted honorary members; and had funds for charity. Thus constituted all the whigs of the country, in civil life, as soon as it was known to them, opposed it, as eminently dangerous to liberty. It had no political objects. The conduct of its members, and the true purpose of the association were excellent. But it was liable to abuse. Political means were resorted to, for its abolition. Governors of states denounced it; legislative bodies expressed their opposition to it, by resolutions; assemblies of private citizens reprobated it; the press sternly and universally rebuked it; the whole country was excited to a flame against it.

Washington soon became sensible that it might produce political evils, which the pure and strong motives, in which it originated, had hidden from the observation of its members. And he attended its first annual meeting determined to exert all his influence for its suppression. He did so exert it. And the order was on the point of being annihilated by the vote of *the great majority* of its members. Its complete annihilation was prevented, only by a sense of courtesy and consistency towards their foreign brother officers, whom the members had officially and formally invited to join it, before they had well considered the abuses of which it was susceptible, and the political tendencies, which it might foster. They did destroy its essential features, by resolving that the order should be no longer hereditary, and that no new members should be admitted. They discontinued wearing its badges, in this country; and left nothing of its existence, but its name, its meetings, which were changed from being annual to triennial, and its charitable funds, which were ordered to be deposited with the state legislatures. This fundamental modification, with the well known cause of its continuance, in the shape it was made to assume by its own members, appeased the public; though Jefferson, and many others, expressed a decided disapprobation of its continuance at all.

Compare this society with freemasonry, in its motives, its origin, its degrading ceremonies, its accumulation of titles, its numerous expressive though fantastic badges; its exacting obedience in the lower degrees, and irresponsible authority in the higher; its secrecy; its oaths; its penalties; its claims of exclusive allegiance; its long list of degrees; its means of private recognition, command, and universal concert; its affiliation with members in all foreign countries; its numbers; its boasted power; its crimes, and the pertinacity with which it is sustained, by its adhering members; and it is impossible not to be convinced, that it is exceedingly dangerous; and that those, who were willing to renounce the Cincinnati society, would be compelled, by the same patriotic motives, which controlled them, in that act, if they had lived till now, to renounce freemasonry. They would have insisted upon its total abrogation. It must be abrogated.

The unavoidable inference drawn by every prudent man, from observing the conduct of its best members, in all past time, is, that its character is bad. This inference is greatly strengthened, by the intelligible hints and friendly advice of the most trust worthy among them. It should be ripened into unhesitating conviction by a consideration of the secrecy which it enjoins. *Standing secrecy always implies shame and guilt.* It is utterly inconsistent with social improvement, confidence and happiness. All the decendants of Adam inherit his nature. While he was innocent, he was ingenuous, communicative, without the need, or the desire, of concealment. For the first crime he committed, even before the sentence of banishment from Paradise, was pronounced upon him, he sought concealment.

But we are not left to our own reasonable inferences, or to hints, and a few honest but guarded expressions, from its members, to decide upon the character of freemasonry. That character has been revealed, under oath, by its adhering members, and by a great band of seceders. And how does it stand? Infamous beyond all parallel in human annals. Its principles are vicious, murderous, treasonable; and so far as they prevail fatally hostile to those of our government.

In the first degree, the candidate pledges himself under oath, and upon forfeiture of his life if he does not redeem the pledge, to ever conceal and never reveal the secrets of freemasonry, which he has then received, is about to receive, or may thereafter be instructed in. Among the secrets, which the candidate may, and must be instructed in, if he takes the second degree, is that of his pledge of passive obedience to the laws of the lodge, and all regular summonses sent him by a brother of that degree. If he takes the third degree, among those secrets are pledges to fly to the relief of a brother of that degree, when masonically required so to do, at the risk of life, should there be a great probability of saving the life of the brother requiring, than of losing his own to apprise a brother of all approaching danger if possible — and to conceal the secrets of a brother master mason when communicated to him as such, murder and treason only excepted, and they left at his discretion. And if he takes the royal arch degree, among those secrets are pledges — to extricate a brother of that degree from danger, if he can, whether that brother be right or wrong — to promote his political preferment before that of all others of equal qualifications — and to conceal his secrets, murder and treason not excepted. Thus is the concealment of crimes made a masonic duty; and the candidates expressly disclaim all equivocation, mental reservation, or evasion of mind, both in the first degree, and in the last.

How do these parts of masonry affect the moral character of its members?

In the first degree, and every other, no man knows any of its obligations, till after he has sworn to conceal them. It is a first principle in morals, that there is no accountability without knowledge and free will. Such oaths, therefore, are not binding, and no forms, or objects, or solemnities, can make them so. But what is the purpose of the order, in the ceremony of imposing them? Can it be good? It is certainly such as can be accomplished only by men divested of all sense of accountability. The less of this sense the better, for all the purposes of fraud and crime — and the more of it the better, for all the purposes of integrity and virtue. These are truths, which nobody can gainsay. All the history of piety, on the one hand, and of sin on the other, asserts them. They are obvious to the common sense of all men. This proceeding of freemasonry, is, therefore, obviously in hostility to good morals. It is more than that. To take such an oath deliberately and with an intent to perform it, is an attempt at the voluntary extinguishment of the highest rights of the soul, and a complete foreclosure of the source of every duty. It is not possible to imagine a more aggravated crime. Rape, murder, treason, may be repented of, and their perpetrators reclaimed. But to forego the rights of knowledge and volition, in regard to every proposition, which can be offered to a moral agent, amounts to a desperate erasure of the image of God from the breast. It would necessarily preclude repentance, reformation, pardon, hope; and be death, in its most unutterable horrors. It would be as much worse than common suicide, as the value of the immortal spirit is greater than that of the corruptible body.

In the degrees, higher than the royal arch, the members swear to oppose the interest, derange the business, and destroy the reputation, of unfaithful brethren, through life, — to prefer the interests of a companion of the order; and of a companion's friend, for whom he pleads, to those of any mere man of the world, in matters of difference submitted to them — never to engage in mean party strife, nor conspiracies against the government or religion of their country, *whereby their reputation may suffer*, nor ever to associate with dishonorable men, for a moment, except *it be to secure* the interest of such person, his family, or friends, to a companion, whose necessities require this *degradation* at their hands — to follow strictly every command of the illustrious knights, and grand commander, and especially to *sacrifice the traitors of masonry*.

Have these points of masonic obligation any political bearing? All the rights of man are founded in his moral nature. It is the intention of free government to secure him in the possession of these rights. Whatever is hostile to good morals is therefore opposed to the civil policy of freemen. We have seen large numbers of the most intelligent, wealthy, and respectable freemasons in New York, deliberating in their lodges and elsewhere, on the means of suppressing a written disclosure of their secrets, by one of their number — we have seen notices of a slanderous character, simultaneously printed, a few days before the seizure and murder of Morgan, in newspapers a hundred miles apart, warning the public against the designs of the author of this disclosure and especially directed to the masonic brotherhood — about the same time we have seen masons set fire to a building prepared by them with peculiar care for sudden combustion, because it was supposed to contain this disclosure in manuscript — we have seen them employ a masonic printer, who was a stranger and an alien, to go into the office where it was printing, with the offer to aid in that work by labor and money, for the sole purpose of stealing the manuscript — we have afterwards seen them kidnap the writer of it, carry him hoodwinked and bound, with the greatest secrecy and caution, through a great extent of populous country, to a fort of the United States — unlawfully and forcibly imprison him there — collect together in frequent deliberation, upon the means of his final disposition — communicate, while in this situation, with several members of a chapter of their body, then numerously attended in the neighborhood — and resolve unanimously, though with painful reluctance, on the part of some, that their masonic obligations required them to murder him; not for any offence against the state, but for the sole cause of his attempting to publish the secrets of the order, which he had a lawful right to do, and which, considering their character, he was bound to do, by every consideration of private morality and fidelity to his country. On the night of the 19th of September, 1826, they accordingly murdered him. To this tearful consummation none were privy, but those who had as masons, sworn to assist each other, right or wrong, and to conceal each other's murder and treason. After the murder, all the precaution possible was taken for concealing it; but this not being wholly successful, and legal prosecutions being threatened, the criminals frequently met and consulted together, for their mutual safety. The most influential among them insisted, that if called by the legal authorities of our country to testify, they one and all must swear they knew nothing of the matter; otherwise they would be forsworn to masonry and might lose the life they would thus forfeit. As witnesses, as magistrates, as sheriffs, as grand jurors, as petit jurors, as legislators, these masons and others with whom they were intimate, *would* know nothing of it. In all their civil relations they violated their oaths and the most sacred duties. They flew to each other's assistance knowing their criminality. They gave each other notice of the approaching danger of legal prosecution. They spirited away witnesses who, they feared, would disclose too much. They perjured themselves in court. They contumaciously refused to answer questions decided to be legal. They declined to answer, on the ground, that if they should, they would criminate themselves in relation to the murder. They prevented the judicial ascertainment, and punishment of the foulest criminals. They made common cause in behalf of these criminals, against the rights of the citizen, and the laws of the land. Thousands of them were acquainted with some of the steps of these crimes against the state. Hundreds of them know the leading malefactors.

A good citizen cannot look on with indifference and see a fellow freeman kidnapped and murdered. He cannot know that such crimes are successfully protected, by an extensive, artful, and powerful conspiracy, without being excited against it. The sympathies of a patriot embrace his whole country. The poorest man, the most defenceless woman, the weakest child in it, cannot be assailed with unlawful violence, without quickening his pulse, and stiffening his sinews, with indignation. His blood is up in every case of high crime; and it keeps up against the aggressor, till the law performs its office upon him. To the law he is willing to submit, because he knows it is the deliberate expression of the public will for the public good; the great shield spread by the hands of all, over the rights of all.

Individual rights are, separately considered, of immeasurable and indefinable worth. They partake of the infinitude of moral existence and responsibility. As contemplated by our government, a single individual, and one as much as another, is an august being, entitled to inviolable reverence, and bearing upon him the badges of a most majestic origin, and the stamp of most transcendant destinations. His safety, his liberty, his life, his improvement, his happiness, it designs, at all times and places, faithfully to protect, by the application of all its delegated means. The law is the beneficial instrument of this protection, and should be appreciated by every reflecting man as the sacred, living, and most venerable expression of the national mind and will. Break this, and the nation has but one right left, which it can peaceably enforce, the right of suffrage.

The masonic institution is answerable for the crimes to which we have referred. They were committed in obedience to its prescribed and specific oaths, and in fear of its penalties. The man-stealing and murder, were for no other than a masonic offence. The whole array of its frightful crimes, out of court, and in court, were no other than necessary means of carrying into effect the obligations it has deliberately and universally exacted of its members. All who uphold the obligations, uphold the crimes. No adhering mason has afforded the least willing assistance to the exposure and punishment of them. No lodge or chapter has called the criminals to account. Many of them are known to the public. Cheseboro, and Sawyer, and Lawson, and Bruce, and Whitney, have been convicted of the conspiracy to kidnap, and have been condemned and suffered infamous punishments, and the very murderers are known with moral, though not with strict judicial certainty. Not one of these men have been expelled. The grand lodge or grand chapter of which they were members, has the power of expulsion, but has declined to exercise it in relation to them; and such of them as are still living, are, in masonic estimation, worthy members of the order.

But the fraternity have gone much farther to make that crime their own. In 1827 the grand lodge gave 100 dollars to one of its members then under public accusation for kidnapping Morgan, and afterwards convicted of that offence; and the grand chapter, by its vote, placed 1,000 dollars at the control of another of its members, ostensibly for charitable uses, of which a part has been proved, in a court of justice, to have been applied for the benefit of other kidnappers; and the trustee of the charity has never been called to an account by the grand chapter, for any part of the sum, though in all other cases such accountability is enforced by the chapter. The records of this last body, apparently relating to this transaction, have been produced in court, and were seen to be mutilated.

The fraternity have also employed and paid able counsel to defend the criminals.

In this way, while the chief magistrate of the state of New York was, by proclamation, offering money, for the conviction of the offenders, the highest masonic bodies, in that state, were offering, and in their associate capacity actually paying money to protect and support them. Can it be justly thought surprising, then, that so few convictions have followed upon such enormous offences, and that no more of the facts have been ascertained in legal form?

The criminals, in all these atrocities, testified their devotion to the institution, and by its own laws are only the more entitled to its guardian care, by all the hazards they involved. That care has been extended to them in every term of expression tending to their relief and comfort. Besides the exertions of their brethren already alluded to, adhering masons have, at great expense, established and circulated newspapers to vilify all who were engaged in exposing the crimes, and to call into action the entire resources of the fraternity, in behalf of those who committed them. These newspapers have, with the most unblushing hardihood, asserted the innocence and praised the virtues of the convicts, several of whom they knew to have confessed their offences. They have commended the most stubborn refusal in court to reveal the truth by masonic witnesses, *as manly firmness*. They have in every form of misrepresentation, which they could devise, labored to darken all knowledge of the facts relating to the outrages; and to blot out the moral sense of the community.

Hundreds of the brethren in different counties in the state of New York, have published addresses, under their names, in which they have deliberately contradicted facts established judicially, by many of their adhering brethren and by many seceding masons; and which, under the sanction of a lawful oath, and subject to cross examination before the public, they would be compelled to admit. Similar falsehoods have been published in an address of a committee of the grand lodge of Rhode Island — and the grand secretary of the grand lodge of New York has recently issued an official letter, in which he represents that body as extending its dependants, confident in its strength, and determined to outbrave all the consequences of their detected guilt, and the public indignation. Nothing could account for this universal course of falsehood, but the unhappy truth, that the men who are engaged in it, have sworn, under the penalty of death, to conceal the secrets of freemasonry, a most essential branch of which consists in the crimes of its members. This course is countenanced by the president of the U. States, who is a mason, and who has recently appointed as heads of the departments in the national government, a majority of distinguished masons. One of these heads of departments — the post master general, the only one retained of the late cabinet, has removed a large number of his most competent and faithful deputies, in New York, for the sole cause of the zeal and patriotism with which they sought to bring into just disrepute the crimes and institution of freemasonry.

The course of these transactions is rapidly corroding and wearing away the very basis of all public and private virtue in our country; and eradicating that mutual confidence, upon which the business of life, its peace, and its enjoyments essentially depend. When men refuse to bear testimony in court, to public offences, of which they know the perpetrators, and are praised for it

—when they perjure themselves, and are not disgraced—when they are convicted of a conspiracy to kidnap a free citizen, and are applauded as victims to the prejudices of their countrymen—when the distinctions between right and wrong are practically superseded, by the systematic and solemn injunctions of a wealthy, intelligent, numerous and powerful society, diffused and sustaining itself in all the places of social influence and honor—when in pursuance of this injunction, the laws of the land, in the solemn places of their judicial application for the admonition and punishment of the most flagrant offences, are foully baffled, set aside and scorned—then, the social fabric is trembling—then there can be but one alternative, that of reform or ruin—then, looking beyond, but not forgetting, all the considerations of attachment to the policy of encouraging this or that branch of national industry—this or that scheme of financial management,—this or that exposition of the principles of our political organization—this or that object of all our foreign and domestic policy, the considerate friend of his country will govern himself primarily, by the obvious necessity to which he is reduced of preserving for his country the power of determining for itself upon any course of policy, and of disengaging the heart of the body politic from the fangs of a monster more blood thirsty, remorseless and insatiable, than any, which has ever come to prey upon the hopes of man.

There is a bearing of freemasonry, not yet embraced in this address, which is replete with the most distressing apprehensions. There is located, in Boston, a masonic body denominated the African grand lodge, which dates its origin before the American revolution, and derived its existence from a Scottish duke. This body acknowledges no allegiance to any of the associations of American masonry. Its authority is co-extensive with our union. It has already granted many charters to African lodges. We are afraid to intimate their location, to look in upon their proceedings, to count their inmates, or to specify their resources.

What are the means of removing these dangers? The dangers are confined to no one place, in our country, and to no one department of our social interests; but extend to all places, and infect every department. Common prudence demands, that the means should be capable of reaching them, wherever they exist, and susceptible of a safe application, in their utmost extent. Such means we have; and we are familiar with their use. They consist in the honest exercise of the right of suffrage, and the most patriotic employment of official patronage. The evils of freemasonry operate upon the moral and political condition of the nation, and can be removed only by moral and political means. It is the exalted excellence of our political institutions, that they are especially designed and adapted to secure our rights, all of which pertain to us as moral beings. In voting, every elector should always be governed by a knowledge of his rights, and the desire of preserving them. There can be no higher political duty than this.

But the use of our right of suffrage against freemasonry is termed proscription. Proscription cannot be imputed to a party, because it justly opposes what is wrong. It is not proscription to be resolute and active in detecting and denouncing opinions of which the obvious tendency is to unhinge society; or to resist, by every lawful means, the influence of men, who commit crimes, and confederate to support each other in their commission. To call such detection, denunciation and resistance, proscription, could never satisfy an honest mind. It would be like stigmatising, with an opprobrious epithet, those public benefactors, who teach men, that all violations of duty are criminal and disreputable, and make their best exertions to discourage them. Proscription can apply only to those, who oppose and lessen the influence of their fellow citizens, because they innocently and with good motives, think and act differently from themselves. Such proscription deserves reprehension, because it invades the equal rights of others, and is averse to the improvement and happiness of all.

The offences of freemasonry upon our individual and national rights, if they had been committed by a foreign nation would, by the law of nations, have justified a public war to avenge them. Shall we fall in love with crime because those who commit it are near us? Shall we spare the destroyer because we can subdue him peaceably? Freemasonry can be destroyed by the votes of freeman, and by nothing else. All who are truly opposed to it, will always vote against it. And they deceive nobody but themselves, who profess opposition to it, and yet dare not express that opposition by their vote.

No good reason has been rendered, or can be rendered, who a freeman, who is opposed to freemasonary, should not vote against it. The application of the right of suffrage against it is just, peaceable, effective and may be as comprehensive as the evils which alarm us. And no other means can be described, or imagined which unite these characteristics. Voting is the only decisive means by which public opinion can be distinctly ascertained upon the subject. And since many persons not initiated into the society, openly connect themselves with its fortunes, and make every exertion in their power to sustain it, by their votes, we cannot safely, if we would, betake ourselves to any other resort but the ballot boxes for its destruction. These persons affect to consider themselves as entitled to the praise of all candid and unexcited minds, by the course which they adopt; and profess to be neither masons nor anti-masons; claiming the respect of the community for their indifference to its rights and welfare. If it has not been for the support of the order, by interested and profligate politicians, who were not members, the forfeiture of public confidence justly incurred, by its crimes, would have been so carried home to the minds of its most worthy members, as long ago to have induced its entire dissolution. It is an undoubted fact, that the men, who are neither masons nor anti-masons, are answerable for the continuance of the order. They have kept it from sinking into annihilation by its sins, and are thus equally censurable with its members. No association of men, however impudent and hardened, can withstand, for years, the indignant, well founded, universal rebuke of their fellow citizens. So treated, the worst members would be driven from the face of the sun, and from public observation, into the fastnesses and caves of the earth, to take upon themselves the skulking habits, along with the flagitions purposes, of felons; and the best would be compelled to abandon it.

It is attempted to make anti-masonary odious, because it is political. But these attempts must recoil upon those with whom they originate. None but tyrants can think the use of political means degrading. And there seems to be peculiar effrontry required to impeach it, in a country where every thing most memorable, in its history has been inseparably connected with political movement, and every thing most animating in its prospects, is dependent upon political action and superversion. The exertions of our fathers to establish our independence, were political exertions. Even the revolutionary war and the war of 1812, were waged for political objects. The constitutions, by which our civil and religious rights are secured, are political constitutions. And this independence, these constitutions, and rights, can be preserved and perpetuated only by political means.

Voting for our public servants is the highest exercise of sovereign power known in our land. It is the paramount distinctive privilege of freemen. In countries where only a small minority of the people are authorised to vote, if oppressive measures are adopted, by their rulers, they must either submit, or fight. In countries where all the citizens are authorised to vote, if they are oppressed, they can throw off the oppression, by their votes. And if the frowns of power, or the calumnies of malefactors have force to dissuade them from using their votes to throw it off, they are fit for slaves, and can be only slaves. The highest functionaries of the general and state governments are amenable to the people, for the proper discharge of their duties. But a freeman, when he votes for a candidate, exercises the right of selecting, among those who are eligible, subject to no authority under heaven. For his choice, he is accountable only to his conscience and his God. And who should he not, in the most sovereign act he can perform, do himself the great justice of giving expression to the honest conviction of his soul? If having the will, he cannot do it, he is a slave. If having the power, he will not do it, he is corrupt.

An enlightened exercise of the right of suffrage is the constitutional and equitable mode adopted by the antimasons to remove the evils they suffer, and produce the reforms they seek. But this mode, to be availing, must include a judicious selection of candidates. After diligent inquiry and mature deliberation we have selected, and now nominate, for your support, as a candidate for the office of president of the United States, at the next election,

WILLIAM WIRT, of Maryland;

And for vice president,

AMOS ELLMAKER, of Pennsylvania.

These citizens we deem eminently possessed of the qualifications before set forth, as most essential for the offices, with which they have associated their names — and confident of their devoted attachment to the principles of administration contained in this address, and their concurrence in our views of the crimes of freemasonry, and the necessity of their removal, by directing against them the sovereign and the free remedy of public suffrage, and the bestowment of official favors, we earnestly recommend them to your support. Their election would be a great step towards the rescue of our republic from the odious and formidable power which endangers it; and we will labor to accomplish it, in the spirit of freemen. In this labor we invite you to participate.

Our free principles cannot be preserved without constant vigilance, and a continuance of the same disinterested and determined action, by which they were established. They are the best possession of the rich, and the only wealth of the poor. They are the common and peculiar property of the nation, embracing all its rights, its virtues and its fortunes.

Neither the price of our liberties nor their fruits will permit them to be regarded without emotion, by any intelligent mind. They have been purchased by ages of just, and earnest thought, of brave and generous effort, of vicissitude, and suffering, and blood. Nor have they been purchased in vain. They have taught man to form a just estimate of his own worth, and of that of his fellow beings, to estimate the value of a reasonable and responsible creature, not by the place which he may hold in an artificial and unnatural state of society, but solely by the faculties conferred upon him, by his Maker, and the intelligence and virtues of his character. And while they have abased the proud from his stilted and haughty elevation, they have brought up the poor to the exalted standard of human rights and human hopes; and thus opened the way for the whole family of man, "to run the great career of justice." We have set out first in this career. Let us remove every impediment, which would obstruct our progress in it, and by the attractions of our success invite all nations to embrace it. If we are true to ourselves, our institutions, our fathers and our posterity, this is to be our glorious destiny. — The influence of our example is already great. In our foreign conflicts and negotiations, our vigor, prudence, and wisdom, have made us respected and illustrious. Let not these qualities be wanting in their proper domestic applications, that the value of our example may be enhanced, and its influence increased. Providence has manifestly cast upon us the high responsibility of determining the most interesting problem of social life, that of man's capacity for self-government. If we suppress all unsocial conspiracy and selfish faction, from within, as we hitherto have done all dictation and tyranny from without, we shall determine it in favor of liberty. Such a determination the great and good of every nation expect from us; and they are beginning, in the face of all their foes, to hazard upon it, their possessions, their honor and their lives. Let us neither disappoint them, nor betray ourselves. A disinterested and faithful adherence to the principles which we inculcate, and to the modes of sustaining them, which we recommend, becomes both our cause and our responsibility; and irresistably commending itself to the honest and the free, it will give that cause success. If it fails, then, right, duty, improvement, self-government, happiness, are phantoms. We shall be compelled to repudiate the memory of our immortal sires, and forego the great inheritance they have bequeathed us. But it will not fail. Freedom is not more the friend of man, than the favorite of heaven. It is equally our highest glory, our most sacred duty, our most assured hope and our promised possession.

Report on the Republican Convention
in the *Niles' Register*, December 24, 1831

In December, 1831, just a few weeks after the Anti-Masons held their convention, the National Republicans gathered in Baltimore and nominated their presidential candidate, Henry Clay. The following May a second convention of National Republican Young Men met in Washington, D.C., at which time a party platform of sorts was adopted and Clay accepted the party's nomination.

Monday, Dec. 12.

The national republican convention met in the city of Baltimore, this day at 12 o'clock.

Mr. Peter R. Livingston, of New York, rose after the members had taken their seats, and remarked that he should beg leave to name a gentleman, as a temporary chairman of the convention, preparatory to its more perfect organization, distinguished for his talents, and applauded for his integrity and principles, throughout a long life of public service. He then moved that general Abner Lacock, of Pennsylvania be appointed chairman *pro tem.* of the convention. The motion was unanimously adopted.

Mr. James Barbour, of Va. moved that *Thomas B. Ray*, be appointed secretary of the convention, which motion was adopted, *nem. con.*

Mr. Livingston then rose, and after a few remarks, respecting the delay of members on the way occasioned by the inclement state of the weather and the extensive prevalence of the rising epidemic, which prevented as full an attendance this day as was desirable, offered the following resolution:—

Resolved, That the delegations of the several states represented in this convention be requested to examine the credentials (or the evidence of appointment) of the members of their respective states, and report a list of their names to-morrow at 12 o'clock.

Mr. Stone, of New York, observed, that in order to afford every possible facility to the gentlemen of the press, he availed himself of the present early moment to offer the following resolution:—

Resolved, That the editors of the several newspapers published in this city, together with all others in attendance from abroad, with their reporters, be invited to take seats to be appropriated for their accommodation.

Mr. Breck, of Kentucky, moved to strike out the word "*invited*," and insert "permitted," and expressed a hope that the gentleman offering the resolution, would assent to the modification.

Mr. Stone replied, that he would not consent to the motion. It was no compliment to the gentlemen of the press, merely to be *permitted* to enter the convention. And a precedent for the phraseology was to be found in the proceedings of the late tariff convention in New York, where the resolution upon this subject was offered in the old form of giving *permission* only, but was amended by substituting the word *invited*. Mr. S. said, that, being himself a representative, in part, of the public press, he had some feeling upon this subject, and he could not listen for a moment to the proposed amendment.

The resolution was withdrawn by *Mr. Breck*, and *Mr. Blunt*, of New York, thereupon suggested that the resolution had best be laid over until the convention should be completely organised.

A motion to lay it on the table was then made. *Mr. A. H. Everett*, Boston, opposed this motion. If the doings of the convention were to be reported at all, the incipient proceedings might be as interesting as those to follow.

This motion was therefore withdrawn, and the resolution unanimously adopted.

Mr. Combs, of Kentucky, then moved that when the convention adjourns, it will adjourn to meet to-morrow at 12 o'clock; which was agreed to.

The convention then adjourned.

[There were between 130 and 140 members in attendance this day.]

Tuesday, Dec. 13.

At 12 o'clock, the convention was called to order by A. Lacock, esq. and the proceedings of yesterday having been read, the secretary called over the names of the delegates, according to the order of the several states, when it appeared that there were 156 members in attendance, and representing seventeen states and the District of Columbia, viz: Maine, New Hampshire, Vermont, Massachusstts, Connecticut, Rhode Island, New York, New Jersey, Pennsylvania, Delaware, Maryland, Virginia, Ohio, Kentucky, North Carolina, Indiana, Louisiana, and the District of Columbia.

Mr. Holmes, of Maine, reminded the convention that the organization of yesterday having been merely temporary, it would be necessary to make a permanent organization. He then moved the following resolution:

Resolved, That a committee of five be appointed to organize the meeting, by selecting a president, &c., and report what further proceedings they might deem necessary.

Which being read was adopted, when the chair appointed Messrs. Holmes, Sergeant, Thomas, Dearborn, and Denny, the said committee. The committee retired, and after a short time returned and reported that it was deemed expedient that the officers of the convention should consist of a president, four vice presidents, and two secretaries; and recommended the following gentlemen as the officers to fill those stations:

For president—James Barbour of Virginia.

For vice presidents—Allen Trimble of Ohio, Joseph Kent of Maryland, Peter B. Porter of New York, and Robert Temple of Vermont.

For secretaries—Joseph L. Tillinghast of Rhode Island and Henry Bacon of Ohio.

The report having been agreed to

Governor Barbour took the chair, and addressed the convention as follows: "Fellow citizens:—I beg you to be assured that I most highly appreciate the distinguished and unexpected honor you have just conferred upon me. The approbation of such a body as this, under any circumstances, could not but be highly acceptable. To me, it is more precious, when I cast my eye over the assembly, even on many with whom it was my good fortune to be associated, in the public councils, in the better days of the republic. Every effort will be made, within the reach of my capacity, to justify this mark of your confidence. I may be permitted to add, that we have convened together for an object, always an important one, but now peculiarly so, from the times in which we are called to act. The auguries proclaimed at the commencement of our political career, that the burden of our experiment would be found in the executive branch of our government, are, I fear, in a rapid course of fulfilment. As yet, we may confide in the peaceful and sure remedy of republican recurrence to the people, a majority of whom I sincerely believe, would hail with joy, the redemption of the pledge so often given by the present incumbent of the chief magistracy, to retire to private life at the expiration of his present term of service. The union and co-operation of this majority is all that is necessary to enforce, whether voluntary or involuntary, the fulfilment of his promise. I am aware that large calculations are made on our divisions; but I will not believe that there is any individual whose ambition is so unchastened as to permit himself to be the instrument of fomenting these divisions, or that the people of the United States will become the dupes of their personal predilections or prejudices. I continue to repose confidence in their virtue and intelligence, and on that Providence who has so frequently manifested his protecting kindness to this people. It was here that the great scheme of human emancipation was first opened on an admiring world. It cannot be that it has been decreed summarily to pass away, "like the baseless fabric of a vision," leaving "not a wreck behind." Let us then, coming directly from the people, the great source of all authority, and animated by an exclusive regard to their interests, set an example of the harmony so essential to success, and indulge a hope that its influence will reach the extremities of the republic."

My ardent prayer is, that your deliberations may be conducted in that spirit—that your decision may be made with wisdom, and that the result thereof, may be propitious to the best interests of our beloved country.

On motion of *Mr. Sergeant*, it was ordered that an invitation be sent to *Charles Carroll* of *Carrollton*, and *Messrs. Howard* and *Thomas*, to take seats within the bar of the convention.

Mr. Holmes, as chairman of the committee appointed on the subject of the officers and business of the convention, rose to make a further report, in the shape of a motion, which he was sure, would entirely satisfy the impatience and delight the hearts of all. He then moved—"that the convention do *now* proceed to nominate a candidate for the office of president of the United States, to be supported by those who are opposed to the re-election of Andrew Jackson."

The motion was agreed to.

On motion, the hon. Jonathan Roberts of Pennsylvania and governor Sprigg of Maryland, were invited to take seats within the bar of the convention.

In this stage of the proceedings, the chair laid before the convention the following letter from Mr. Clay.

Washington, 10th Dec. 1831

My dear sir: I was extremely glad to learn that you had accepted the appointment of a member of the Baltimore convention, which is to assemble next week, to nominate, for the consideration of the people of the United States, candidates for their president and vice-president; and that notwithstanding the extraordinary inclemency of the weather, you had proceeded to the city where the important trust is to be performed. It is to be sincerely hoped that the acknowledged patriotism and intelligence of that convention, aided by the purity of intention and practical good sense by which I have so often witnessed you to be guided in public affairs, may conduct your deliberations to results satisfactory to the community. I must have been entirely regardless of passing events, if I had not observed that my name has been repeatedly mentioned as being likely to be brought before the convention, and that, in some instances, delegates have been instructed by their constituents to yield support to it, as a candidate for the presidency. This restriction, or any restriction upon the prefect freedom of deliberation and decisions of the conventions, is inexpedient. It would have had a more happy constitution if it had embodied the will of all who are desirous of rescuing the executive government of the union from the misrule which threatens to subvert established institutions and systems of policy, long and deservedly cherished, and to bring disgrace and ruin upon the country. So constituted, the convention could have made a comparative estimate of the many citizens of the United States who are competent to discharge the duties of chief magistrate, and selected from among them that one, who, possessing the requisite principles, would probably unite, to the greatest extent, the public confidence and the public support. For one, I anxiously wish that the convention, dismissing every feeling of previous attachment or predilection, will now make impartially such an estimate and selection; and should their choice fall upon any individual other than myself, it shall have, not only my hearty acquiescence and concurrence, but my cordial and zealous co-operation.

I have been very desirous to lay these sentiments before the convention, but it has appeared to me that I could not formally do it without incurring the imputation of presumptuousness or indelicacy. Will you then, my dear sir, with whom I have so often had the happiness to be associated in the public councils, consent to be the organ of making them known, if necessary, to the convention. Should my name not be presented to its consideration for the presidency, it will not be proper or necessary to make the communication; but if it should be, I confide the manner of doing it to your judgment and sense of propriety.

With fervent wishes to the prevalence of good feelings and harmony in the convention, I am cordially and constantly your friend.

H. Clay.
James Barbour, esq.

After the letter had been read, *Mr. Livingston*, of New York, rose, and, after some pertinent and eloquent remarks, nominated *Henry Clay*, which was received with loud and reiterated plaudits.

Mr. Dearborn, of Massachusetts, proposed that when the sense of the convention was taken on the nomination, that each member, as his name was called by the secretary, should rise and name the candidate to which he was most favorable. Mr. Livingston having accepted this amendment, it was agreed that the sense of the convention should be taken in that manner.

Accordingly, the secretary called over the names of the members, and each rising from his seat, avowed himself in favor of *Henry Clay*. *Mr. F. H. Shuman*, of North Carolina, (who was understood to say that his mind was not made up on the subject) was excused from nominating his candidate.

The chair announced that Henry Clay had been unanimously nominated by the convention as the most suitable person to be recommended to the people as a candidate for the office of president of the United States.

Here the plaudits were enthusiastically reiterated.

On motion of *general Dearborn*, it was ordered that a committee of seven members be appointed to prepare an address to the people, and the chair announced the following as the names of the committee, *Messrs. A. H. Everett*, of Massachusetts, *Stanard*, of Virginia, *Dodd*, of New Jersey, *Howk*, of Indiana, *Johns*, of Delaware, *Cummins*, of Maine, and *Wilson*, of New Hampshire.

On motion of *Mr. Sergeant*, of Penn. the president was requested to invite one or more of the clergymen of Baltimore to open the session of the convention with prayer.

Mr. Everett, of Mass. moved that the president and secretaries inform Mr. Clay of his nomination by the National Republican Convention, as a candidate for the office of president of the United States. This motion was withdrawn, and a resolution substituted, that a committee of one member from each state be appointed for that purpose. At the suggestion of the chair, the delegates from the several states appointed each their member of the committee, which consisted of the following gentlemen: — Maine, *Henry Warren*: New Hampshire, *Leonard Jarvis*; Vermont, *William Jarvis*; Massachusetts, *H. A. S. Dearborn*; Connecticut, *John A. Rockwell*; Rhode Island, *C. E. Robbins;* New York, *P. R. Livingston*; New Jersey, *Job S. Halsted*; Pennsylvania, *Thomas Burnside*; Delaware, *E. I Dupont*; Maryland, *William Price*; Virginia, *William Breckenridge*; Ohio, *John Sloan*; Kentucky, *Daniel Breck*; North Carolina, *F. H. Shuman*; Indiana, *John H. Neely*; Louisiana, *H. A. Bullard*; District of Columbia, *R. S. Coxe*.

Some conversation having arisen relative to the wish of the convention as to the manner in which the communication should be made to Mr. Clay, the matter was left entirely to the discretion of the committee.

On motion of *Mr. W. L. Stone*, of New York, the convention adjourned until to-morrow at 12 o'clock.

[The committee of one delegate from each state, appointed to inform Mr. Clay of his nomination by the convention, remained after the adjournment, and resolved to address him a letter, to be delivered to him by a sub-committee of five of their body. — Accordingly the sub-committee started for Washington in the afternoon at four o'clock.]

The president having taken his seat and called to order, it was

Resolved, That *gov. Coles*, the *honorable Daniel Webster*, of Massachusetts, and the *hon. E. F. Chambers*, of Maryland, of the senate of the U.S. be invited to take seats within the bar.

On motion of *Mr. Holmes*,

Resolved, That the names of such members as may have arrived since yesterday's session, be called that they may give their vote to the candidate whom they may prefer.

The following gentlemen answered to their names.

Virginia — P. J. Cohen, A. B. Spooner, James Carr.

Ohio — J. Morrow, E. Stone, R. A. Thruston, S. W. Davis.

Tennessee — Boyd McNairy.

North Carolina — John Hamilton.

New York — W. J. Bacon, J. H. Pierson.

The proceedings of Tuesday were then read.

Mr. Somerville, from the committee appointed to wait on the *hon. Charles Carroll*, of Carrollton, and to invite him to a seat in the convention, presented the following answer to the invitation:

Wednesday morning, Dec. 14, 1831

Gentlemen — The severity of the weather, and the apprehensions of my family on that account, admonish me to be cautious in venturing abroad at this season. I must therefore claim the privilege of advanced age, and apologise for not accompanying you this morning to the Athenaeum according to the promise of yesterday.

I request, gentlemen, that you will have the goodness to convey my apology to the distinguished individuals by whom you were deputed, to propose to me so flattering a compliment, and to accept, on their behalf, and for yourselves, an assurance of the regard and respect with which I am, gentlemen, respectfully, yours,

C. Carroll, of Carrollton.

Mr. Dearborn, from the committee appointed to wait upon *Mr. Clay*, and acquaint him with his unanimous nomination to this office of president of the United States, by the convention, laid before the meeting the following correspondence;

Baltimore, Dec. 13, 1831.

Hon. Henry Clay:

Sir, — The undersigned have been appointed a committee, by the convention of national republican delegates now assembled in this city, to announce that you were this day unanimously nominated as a candidate for the office of president of the United States.

Entertaining the most exalted opinion of your eminent talents, enlarged patriotism, and distinguished public services, we have the fullest confidence that you will receive the united, cordial, and zealous support of every friend to the constitution, the integrity of the union, all the great branches of national industry, and the prosperity of the general weal; and we pledge to you, in behalf of the convention, the assurance of an ardent determination to use all honorable means to insure your elevation to the chair of chief magistrate of this republic. With the highest consideration, we have the honor to be, sir, your most obedient servants,

Peter R. Livingston,	of New York.
Henry Warren,	Maine.
Leonard Jarvis,	New Hampshire.
William Jarvis,	Vermont.
Henry A. S. Dearborn,	Massachusetts.
Christ'r E. Robbins,	Rhode Island.
John A. Rockwell,	Connecticut.
Job S. Halsted,	New Jersey.
Thomas Burnside,	Pennsylvania.
E. I. Dupont,	Delaware.
William Price,	Maryland.
James Breckenridge,	Virginia.
J. Sloane,	Ohio.
Daniel Breck,	Kentucky.
Frederick H. Shuman,	N. Carolina.
John J. Neely,	Indiana.
H. A. Bullard,	Louisiana.
Richard S. Coxe,	D. Columbia.
	Committee.

Washington, 13th Dec. 1831.

Gentlemen—I have the honor to acknowledge the receipt of the note which, as a committee of the convention of national republican delegates now assembled in Baltimore, you addressed to me, stating that I had been this day unanimously nominated by the convention as a candidate for the office of president of the United States.

This manifestation of the confidence of a body so distinguished, is received, gentlemen, with lively sensibility and profound gratitude. Although I should have been glad if the convention had designated some citizen of the U. States more competent than myself to be the instrument of accomplishing the patriotic objects to which they have in view, I do not feel myself at liberty to decline their nomination. With my respectful and cordial acknowledgments, you will be pleased to communicate to the convention my acceptance of their nomination, with the assurance that, whatever may be the event of it, our common country shall ever find me faithful to the union, and the constitution, to the principles of public liberty, and to those great measures of national policy which have made us a people, prosperous, respected, and powerful.

Accept, gentlemen, of my thanks for the friendly manner in which you have conveyed the act and sentiments of the convention. I am, with high respect, your obedient servant,

H. Clay.

Messrs. P. R. Livingston, Henry Warren, Leonard Jarvis, Wm. Jarvis, H. A. S. Dearborn, C. E. Robbins, John A. Rockwell, Job T. Halsted, Tho. Burnside, E. I. Dupont, William Price, James Breckenridge, J. Sloane, Daniel Breck, F. H. Shuman, John J. Neely, H. A. Bullard and Richard S. Coxe, &c. &c.

The letter was received with immense applause, both by the members of the convention, and a crowded audience.

On motion of *Mr. Bradish*, of New York,

Revolved, That this convention do now proceed to nominate a candidate of the national republican party to fill the office of *vice president* of the United States.

Mr. Boyd McNairy, of Tennessee, then nominated JOHN SERGEANT, of Pennsylvania, as a suitable candidate for that important station, remarking that Mr. S. was too well known to require any eulogy from him.

The nomination of *Mr. Sergeant*, was seconded by gen. Jones, of Washington, in a speech of considerable length.

On motion of *Mr. William Halsted*, of New Jersey, the same course was directed to be pursued in nominating for the vice presidency, as was done yesterday in nominating for president: whereupon,

The delegates were all called over by name, and each one rose as he was called, and signified his preference for *John Sergeant*, of Pennsylvania.

So, JOHN SERGEANT, *of Pennsylvania*, was nominated by the convention for vice president of the U. States, with the same unanimity which had already attended the nomination of *Henry Clay* for the presidency — 160 persons this day answering to their names.

On motion of *Mr. Marshall*, of Virginia, a committee of five persons was ordered to be appointed by the chair, to inform *Mr. Sergeant* of his nomination. The committee appointed consisted of *Mr. Lacock*, of Pennsylvania, *Mr. Stanard*, of Virginia, *Mr. Jones*, of the District of Columbia, *Mr. Stone*, of New York, and *Mr. Morrow*, of Ohio.

Mr. Burke moved for the appointment of a committee to ascertain what would be the probable expenses incurred by the convention, and to make provision for paying them. Upon which,

Mr. John B. Morris, of Baltimore, rose, and stated, that so far as the place of meeting and other accommodations of the convention were concerned, no provision was necessary, the citizens of Baltimore having, so far as in their power, made all the necessary arrangements for reimbursing expenses.

On motion of *Mr. Livingston*, it was

Resolved, That the thanks of the convention be presented to those gentlemen who had prepared the accommodations, and for the very hospitable manner in which they had been treated, and that the president be the organ of the communication.

Mr. Everett stated that he thought the resolutions just adopted did not supercede the necessity of a committee, as certain expenses, such as printing, &c. were not taken into view. He therefore moved that a committee be appointed which motion was adopted.

The following gentlemen were named members of the committee:

Messrs. Burke, Somerville, Talliaferro, James, and Combs.

On motion of *Mr. Livingston*, it was

Resolved, That a committee of one member from each state, and one from the District of Columbia, be appointed to wait upon the hon. Charles Carroll, of Carrollton, the surviving patriot who signed the Declaration of Independence, to know at what time and place it would be agreeable to him to receive the members of the national republican convention, who wish to tender to him their best feelings and high sense of gratitude for his patriotic services.

The delegations of the respective states having consulted together, the following gentlemen were named as members.

Messrs. Mussey, of Maine: Wm. A. Kent of New Hampshire; A. H. Everett, of Massachusets; N. F. Hickson, of Rhode Island; Joseph Trumbull, of Connecticut; W. A. Griswold, of Vermont; A. R. Lawrence, of New York; Wm. Halsted, of New Jsersey; Josiah Randall, of Pennylvania; Wm. W. Morris, of Maryland; Robert Stanard, of Virginia; R. H. Alexander, of North Carolina; L. White, of Kentucky; Boyd McNairy, of Tennessee; Jeremiah Morrow, of Ohio; H. A. Buliard, of Louisiana; J. J. Neely, of Indiana; Walter Jones, of District of Columbia.

Mr. Combs, of Ky. stated he had just received a letter from two of his colleagues, *Messrs. Johnson* and *Morehead*, now on their way, and who would probably be here this evening, who had been reluctantly detained by the inclemency of the weather. His chief reason for mentioning the circumstance, however, was that they both assured him they were decidedly in favor of the nomination of *Henry Clay*, for the presidency.

On motion of *Mr. Randall*, of Pa. it was ordered that when the convention adjourn this day, it will adjourn to meet to-morrow, at 10 o'clock.

The convention then adjourned.

Thursday, Dec. 15.

The convention met this day pursuant to adjournment, and the throne of grace was addressed by the rev. Mr. Nevins, of the presbiterian church.

The president having taken the chair, and called the convention to order, the proceedings of yesterday were read.

The following additional delegates appeared to-day, viz: from Kentucky, *Francis Johnson*, and *James T. Morehead*, who severally recorded their votes in favor of the nomination of *Henry Clay* and *John Sergeant*.

On motion of *Mr. Fairfax*, of Va. the following resolution was agreed to:

Resolved, That a central state corresponding committee be provisionally appointed in each state where none are now appointed. And that it be recommended to the several states to organize subordinate corresponding committees in each county and town, in their several respective states.

Mr. Blunt, of New York, submitted the following resolution, which was agreed to:

Resolved, That it be recommended to the young men of the national republican party to hold a convention in the city of Washington, on the first Monday of May next.

In offering this resolution, *Mr. Blunt* stated that the young men of the national republican party had it in contemplation to assemble in convention at Washington, and he thought it right that their proposition should receive the countenance of this convention. With that view he submitted the resolution.

It was proposed that a convention of delegates appointed by the mechanics of the national republican party, to meet at Washington in May next, should be recommended, but on its being suggested that the present convention was, in fact, composed of delegates from the mechanics, as well as other classes of the party, and that, therefore, there existed no necessity for such a convention, the motion was withdrawn.

Governor Morrow, of Ohio, from the committee yesterday appointed to wait upon Mr. Carroll, reported that they had performed the duty assigned them, and that Mr. Carroll would be happy to receive the members of the convention at his house, this day, at 4 o'clock.

The *president* having intimated a wish to know whether it was the intention of the convention to proceed in a body to the residence of Mr. Carroll.

Mr. Dearborn, of Massachusetts, moved the following resolution, which was unanimously adopted:

Resolved, That the members of the convention will meet at the saloon of the Athenaeum, this afternoon, at a quarter before 4 o'clock, and proceed thence in a body to the residence of the venerable Mr. Carroll, to pay him their respects.

Mr. Lacock, from the committee yesterday appointed to wait upon John Sergeant, of Pennsylvania, and inform him that he had been unanimously nominated to the office of vice-president, by this convention, presented the following correspondence; which was read.

Baltimore, Dec. 14, 1831.

Hon. John Sergeant.

Sir: The undersigned, a committee appointed by the national republican convention for the purpose, inform you that you have this day been unanimously nominated by the said convention as a candidate for the office of vice president of the United States.

It gives them much pleasure to make this communication, having the strongest assurances, from a view of your political character and conduct, heretofore, that, if elected, you will be found an able and efficient auxiliary to the enlightened statesman recently nominated for the office of president; and that you will cheerfully co-operate with him in maintaining the supremacy of the laws and constitution of the United States, and defending the primary and important interests of the people. Under these impressions, the committee are extremely solicitous that you should accept the nomination thus unanimously and spontaneously tendered you by the convention; in which event, the committee are warranted in pledging you the hearty and zealous support, not only of their colleagues and themselves, but of the great constitutional party of the United States, by whom they have been delegated by this convention.

Accept, sir, the assurances of our respectful consideration.

> *A. Lacock,*
> *Wm. L. Stone,*
> *Jeremiah Morrow*
> *Robert Stanard,*
> *Walter Jones.*

Baltimore, December 14, 1831.

Gentlemen—I have received your note of this date, informing me that the national republican convention, now sitting in this city, have unanimously nominated me as a candidate for the office of vice president of the United States.

The nomination by a body so enlightened and patriotic, for one of the highest trusts of the republic is felt to be a very great honor, and is appreciated accordingly. It is the more gratifying, as it associates me in their estimation and support with that distinguished citizen, whose public life and character, marked by undeviating devotion to the best interests of our country, and a spirit as generous as it is elevated, are a sure pledge that an administration under his guidance would be comprehensive and national, aiming unceasingly to preserve the union, to maintain the supremacy of the constitution and laws, to keep unbroken the public faith and honor, and to regard, with becoming indulgence and respect, the honest differences of opinion among our fellow citizens, which our republican institutions permit and invite. To co-operate with him, to the extent of whatever means I possess, in thus promoting the welfare and happiness of the nation, and rescuing the freedom of opinion and conduct from unconstitutional oppression, would be no less my pleasure than my duty.

Be pleased, gentlemen, to make known to the convention my acceptance of their nomination, and with it, to express to them the unaffected sensibility with which I have received this distinguished proof of their confidence.

I beg you to accept my thanks for the kind and flattering terms of your communication to be assured of the high respect of, gentlemen, your most obedient servant,

John Sergeant

Messrs. Abner Lacock, &c. &c.

The acceptance of the nomination by *Mr. Sergeant*, was hailed with enthusiasm, and drew forth three very distinct rounds of applause.

On motion of *Mr. Halsted*, of New Jersey, it was unanimously

Resolved, That the thanks of the national republican convention be tendered to *Luke Tiernan, Hezekiah Niles, Nathanial F. Williams, William H. Freeman, Charles F. Mayer, Joshua Medtart*, and *James Harwood*, members of the national republican committee, and to *John B. Morris, Henry V. Somervill, N. F. Williams* and *James Harwood*, the committee of arrangement on the part of the numerous citizens of Baltimore, for the extensive accommodations they have provided for its sittings, and the attentions and courtesies they have extended to its members, and the facilities they have afforded to the objects of the convention.

[In submitting the foregoing resolve, Mr. H. said, that in adopting the resolution of yesterday the tender of thanks was too general and indefinite. The names of the national republican committee of Baltimore were now known, and it was due to them, and every member of this convention, he was confident, would be proud of the opportunity, to tender the thanks of this body to those very respectable gentlemen who had spontaneously come forward and provided for the accommodation of the conventions.]

Mr. Livingston, of New York, stated he was requested by the committee appointed to draft the address, to say that they would require a little more time for that purpose. He therefore moved that a recess be taken until one o'clock, P. M. which was carried, and the convention adjourned until that hour.

One o'clock, P. M.—The convention having assembled, a letter was read from *Mr. Samuel Parnell*, of Virginia, regretting the necessity of his absence, and hoping that Henry Clay would be nominated by the convention as the candidate for the presidency. The letter enclosed ten dollars to be appropriated to the incidental expenses of the convention. The letter was ordered to be recorded on the minutes of the proceedings.

After having agreed to assemble at four o'clock this afternoon, to pay their respects in a body to Charles Carroll of Carrollton, the convention adjourned until 12 o'clock on Friday.

At 4 o'clock in the afternoon of Thursday, the convention again assembled, when a procession was formed at the saloon of the Athenæum, headed by the president and other officers, the delegates being arranged in the geographical order of the states which they represent, which proceeded to the mansion of the venerable *Charles Carroll*, where each delegate was introduced to that distinguished patriot, who stood to receive them.

After the introduction was over, the president of the convention, James Barbour, of Virginia, advanced and tendered to Mr. Carroll the "homage of the national republican convention." He made a very handsome allusion to the patriotism of Mr. Carroll in the days of the revolution, spoke on the ven-

eration in which his name was held by a grateful people, as the last survivor of
that illustrious band of patriots who had signed the charter of our liberties;
and said that our infants were taught to lisp his name, as one of the benefactors of the republic. He concluded by observing that the prayers of the free
citizens of this highly favored land were daily offered to heaven in hearty sup-
plication that that life might be long preserved which had been freely devoted
to the sacred cause of liberty in the days of trial.

After partaking of some slight refreshment, which had been plentifully prepared at the hospitable mansion of the revolutionary worthy, the delegates
severally withdrew to their respective places of abode.

Mr. Carroll appeared to be pleased with the attention shown him, and conversed with several of the delegates for some time. When asked of his health,
he replied, "I enjoy *very good health.*" The epidemic which so generally prevails has affected the family of Mr. Carroll, as well as other; but that venerable
individual has entirely escaped.

Friday, Dec. 16.

The convention assembled this day at 12 o'clock; when the rev. Mr. Finley,
of the Baptist church, delivered a very appropriate prayer.

The record of yesterday's proceedings was read.

Mr. Everett, from the committee appointed to prepare an address to the
people of the United States, on the subject of the election of a president and
vice president of the United States, reported a draft as agreed upon by the
committee; which was read, and unanimously adopted.

On motion of *Mr. Coxe*, of Washington.

Resolved, That ten thousand copies of the proceedings of the convention,
and of the address just adopted, be printed, under the direction of a committee to be appointed by the chair.

On motion of *Mr. Rockwell*, of Connecticut,

Resolved, That it be recommended to the delegates from the several states to
promote among their constituents a zealous support of the principles of the
national republican party, and of the candidates nominated by this convention.

Mr. Morrow, of Ohio, said the duty had been assigned to him of offering to
the convention a resolution tendering a vote of thanks to the officers which
had been appointed to preside over its deliberations. That duty was the more
gratifying to him, as he had had the pleasure to associate with those individuals in other times—in times when the dark cloud of war lowered over the
land, and when it became the duty of every patriot to stand forward for his
country's safety and honor. The country was now at peace with all the
world—yet, he had again been permitted to take counsel with those same individuals, at a moment of great interest, and when the talents and moral powers
of every friend to the nation were required to be exerted for the security of its
best interests. He would not take up more of the time of the meeting, but
submit for its adoption the following resolution:

Resolved, That the thanks of this convention be presented to *James Bar-*

bour, the president; and *Allen Trimble, Joseph Kent, Peter B. Porter*, and *Robert Temple*, vice presidents, of this convention, for the able and dignified manner in which they have presided over its deliberations.

The resolution was unanimously agreed to.

On motion of *Mr. Dearborn*, it was

Resolved, unanimously, That the thanks of this convention be presented to *Joseph L. Tillinghast* and *Henry Bacon*, for the diligent and attentive manner in which they have discharged their duties as secretaries.

On motion of *Mr. Bradish*, it was

Resolved, That the thanks of this convention be presented to *Abner Lacock*, the chairman, and to *Thomas P. Ray*, the secretary, who officiated on the temporary organization of the convention.

Mr. Barbour then rose, and addressed the convention, in behalf of himself and his colleagues, for about twenty minutes, in a most able and eloquent manner, during which he was repeatedly interrupted by the cheers of the assembly.

On motion, it was

Resolved, That the committee this day appointed to superintend the printing of the address, be directed to have also printed and subjoined at the end thereof, the names of the members of the convention, and their respective places of residence.

On motion,

Resolved, That the thanks of this convention be presented to those clergymen of the city of Baltimore who have so kindly officiated at its several meetings.

On motion,

Resolved, That the president be requested to furnish for publication a copy of the address this day delivered by him, and that it be appended to the proceedings of this convention.

The convention then adjourned, *sine die*.

*   *   *

ADDRESS OF THE NATIONAL REPUBLICAN CONVENTION

To the people of the United States.

Fellow citizens: — The period will soon arrive when you will be called upon to exercise a right, which, of all the independent nations of considerable power on the globe, you alone possess — that of electing, by your own free choice, and from among yourselves, the person who is to be entrusted with the high functions of your chief executive magistrate. It is sometimes said that it is of little importance what individual is clothed with that character: that a president of the United States has no great personal influence either for good or evil, and that, in the present prosperous condition of the country the public affairs would be transacted just about as well under one president as another. Such opinions can only be entertained by persons who have reflected very little on the theory or the practical operation of our government. The whole course of the public affairs depends, in a very considerable degree, upon the direction which is given to the influence belonging to the office of president. It is no doubt true that the political machine may continue to move on a while with apparent success under very unskilful direction by the effect of a favorable impulse received at other times; but it is obvious, that if such a state of things continues long, the favorable impulse will be lost, and the principle of prosperity destroyed, perhaps forever. It is generally acknowledged that the pure and lofty character of Washington contributed more than any other cause to carry our institutions into successful operation, and that the eminent virtues and acknowledged talents of his successors in the presidency, have aided very powerfully in sustaining and perfecting the work which he began. It is equally apparent, that if the chief magistracy should ever be committed for any great length of time to persons of an opposite character, the condition of the country must undergo, in one way or another, a disastrous, perhaps a fatal revolution.

Such being the importance of the right which you will soon be called upon to exercise, you owe it to yourselves, to your children, to your country, to the cause of humanity, which is so deeply involved in the issue of the political experiment that is now making among us, to exercise it with full and mature deliberation — without any bias from party feeling or mere personal advantage, and with a single view to the public good. You owe this, not only to the interest, but to the honor of the nation. It is important to the preservation of the fair fame which we have already acquired throughout the world, that the seat of Washington, and his successors, should be worthily filled: that persons should be chosen to succeed these illustrious men, who shall be able, like them, to do honor, by their manner of discharging its duties, even to the high office of president of the United States: that the personal conduct of the head of the executive department should be marked, as it always was in former days, with dignity, judgment, good temper, discretion, and moderation; that the youth of our government should not be sullied by the foul stains of immortality that disfigure the antiquated and corrupt institutions of other countries, and that our citizens and the world at large should be able to look up to the high places of this union for examples of public and private virtue.

Under these impressions of the importance of the crisis, a numerous portion of our fellow-citizens residing in all parts of the country, and who have acted together in political affairs for some years past, under the name of National Republicans, have directed us to meet together and deliberate upon the course which they ought to pursue, and the persons whom they ought to support for the great offices of the government at the approaching election. In preparing to exercise this delicate trust, we have been naturally led to take a careful and deliberate survey of the political condition of the country, and of the manner in which the public affairs have been conducted by the present administration. This survey has resulted in a full conviction that the public good imperiously requires a change; and in proposing to you as candidates for the presidency and vice presidency the distinguished citizens whose names accompany this address, we have deemed it our duty to lay before you a concise statement of the principle circumstances which have led us to this conclusion.

No president ever entered on the duties of his office under circumstances more favorable to a successful discharge of them than the present incumbent. The country, thanks to Providence and to the ability and good fortune with which the public affairs had been carried on by preceding administrations, was in a high state of prosperity. — All the public establishments, and all the great branches of private industry were in the most flourishing condition. Agriculture was rapidly extending itself in all directions, and particularly through the wide and fertile regions of the west — manufactures were advancing with unprecedented rapidity — commerce, internal and foreign, was animated with a corresponding vigor — our relations with foreign powers were of the most amicable character — at home, tranquilty and general contentment pervaded every corner of the union — the parties that formerly divided the citizens and distracted the country, had in a great measure become extinct under the operation of time — the growing prosperity of the nation, and the judicious and liberal conduct of the government. In the pride and pleasure which we all felt in claiming the character of citizens of the United States, we were ready to forget that our fathers had been classed as republicans and federalists. The name of American had, by a sort of common consent taken the place of all other political distinctions. American principles had become the common creed of the high minded and patriotic adherents of all the former parties. In a word, the best friends of the country had little more to wish or hope, in regard to our political situation, than that we might proceed in the course which we were then pursuing, and remain, in every thing belonging to character and principles of government, substantial as we were.

This state of things, afforded, of course, the best evidence that could possibly be had in favor of the administration under which it had grown up. Much of it could be traced directly to the character and opinions of the leading members of that administration. It was, however, under these circumstances, that a vigorous, and, as has been shewn by the issue, successful effort was made to effect a change, and to place in the chair of the chief magistracy the present incumbent. Of the comparative qualifications of the president and his predecessor, for the high station which they have successively filled, we will not here speak. We cheerfully resign a task so ungrateful in one of its divisions, to the impartial and unshrinking hand of history. Nor will we here enlarge on the means by which the change in question was accomplished — the reckless and persevering calumny, which was constantly poured forth from hundreds of presses, on the best and the purest men in the nation, — the false pretentions to exclusive republicanism — the factious clamor which was kept up in congress — the artful combination of conflicting personal and party interests for a common object, and the various other unworthy arts, that were brought into action on this occasion. — Suffice it to remark, that the change was effected — in form, at least — in a legal and constitutional way; and, however, justly offensive the circumstances that brought it about, might and must have been to the friends of the last administration, however deficient the present incumbent might have been supposed to be in the qualities most requisite for the station to which he had been raised, it is believed that when he entered on his office, there was no disposition in any portion of the people to commence a premature or factious opposition to his measures.—It was alarming enough to prudent and well meaning men, that the government of the country had fallen into such hands, and far from attempting to perplex or embarrass the administration, they would rather have lent all the aid in their power to carry the country safely through so dangerous a crisis.—On the other hand, the military successes of the president had gained him an extensive personal popularity, which would have enabled him, had he known how to turn it to account, to carry on the government with extraordinary facility. Under this combination of circumstances, it is believed, that had the public affairs been managed with tolerable prudence and discretion, general Jackson might have gone through his term of official life without a show of opposition, and have been re-elected, had he been so inconsistent as to desire it, by a very unanimous vote.

Nor were the friends of the country without strong hopes that such a result would follow. Deficient as the president was known to be in the qualities and accomplishments most essential to a civil magistrate, it was yet anticipated that he might be found to possess the courtesy, the generous feelings, the high sense of decorum and propriety which form the appropriate ornaments of the military character, and would have secured him from any open offence against the dignity of his office. After the letter to the venerable patriot Monroe, in which he had so emphatically recommended the oblivion of the old party distinctions, it was confidently expected that nothing would be done by himself that should tend to revive them. He had given, on several public occasions, opinions on points of administration which—however at the time incorrectly applied—would have served excellently well as guides for his own conduct in office; and it was perhaps not unreasonable to hope that his actions would correspond, in some imperfect degree at least, with his previous professions. Had this been the case, his administration would have given complete satisfaction to the country. Whether its complete and acknowledged failure has been owing to defects in his own character, or to the influence of evil counsels on his mind and measures, is a point which it is unnecessary, and would be ungrateful, to discuss. We should regret to visit with too severe censure the last days of one who, in another line of duty, has done the state much service, and whom nothing but the imprudence of injudicious friends, or rather the efforts of political partisans, who found it convenient to make use of his name and popularity for their own selfish purposes, has prevented from going down to posterity with a high military reputation, and filling an honorable place in our history. We are rather willing to believe that, placed in a situation for which he was by education and character wholly unfit, worn out by toils, infirmities, and the natural progress of age, he acted under influences which, morally speaking, he could not well control. However this may be, it is certain that the expectations and hopes which some persons may have been disposed to indulge of the success of his administration, have been signally disappointed, and that his failure has been more complete than even his enemies could have possibly anticipated. The political history of the union for the last three years exhibits a series of measures plainly dictated in all their principal features by blind cupidity or vindictive party spirit, marked throughout by a disregard for good policy, justice, and every high and generous sentiment, and terminating in a dissolution of the cabinet under circumstances more scandalous than any of the kind to be met with in the annals of the civilized world. The voluntary dissolution of the cabinet authorises the remark which we have made above, that the failure of the administration of gen. Jackson was not only signal and complete, but *acknowledged*; and it is remarkable that, after this public acknowledgment of his incapacity to execute the duties of his office, through agents appointed by himself, even to his own satisfaction, he should deem it expedient to offer his services to the nation for a second term.

The first official act of the president indicated, in a striking and painful manner, in how small a degree any favorable anticipations, that might have been formed of his conduct were likely to be realized. We allude to his inaugural address to the people, in which he levelled against the admininistration of his predecessor a sweeping charge of incapacity and corruption. A charge of incapacity to conduct the civil affairs of the country preferred by Andrew Jackson against such men as Mr. Adams, Mr. Clay, and their distinguished colleagues in office, was of course merely ludicrous; but the imputation of corruption was of a more serious character. Had there been the least foundation for it in fact, it is obvious that the last person who ought to have made it his business to denounce it to the public was the president of the U. States, who has no other constitutional agency in regard to such offences but the power of pardon. The indecorum of this denunciation was hardly less glaring than its essential injustice, and can only be parallelled by that of the subsequent denunciation of the same administration, on the same authority, to a foreign government.

This proceeding awakened in the mind of every good citizen very painful forebodings as to the consequences which were to follow upon such a commencement.

These forebodings were too soon realized. The next act of the administration was a general removal of such of the public agents as were not recommended by attachment to the person or party of the president. The extent to which this system was carried is strikingly evinced by the fact, that within a month after the inauguration of gen. Jackson, more persons were removed from office than during the whole forty years that had elapsed since the adoption of the constitution. The motive which led to this policy is illustrated by the fact, that it was applied principally in states where the majority of the people were opposed to the administration, while in the others there were comparatively few removals. Such was the practical comment on the text of the inaugural address which denounced the preceding administration as having brought the patronage of the government into conflict with the purity of elections. The foreign ministers were abruptly recalled at large expense to the country, in some instances before they had reached their destination, and in all, without the observation of the common forms of civility towards them, or the governments near which they were accredited. Among the victims of prescription at home were some of the most respectable and interesting persons in the community — veterans who, after fighting the battles of the war of independence, had been placed by the justice of the government in the offices they held, and were now rudely thrust out of them to endure, at an advanced age, the miseries of actual want, as a reward for the devotion of their whole lives to the public service. This was not all. This universal proscription, taken in connection with the tenor of the inaugural address, amounted to a charge of universal corruption. Common justice required that the individuals against whom such a charge was brought should have opportunity to defend themselves. None was given. No enquiry was ordered. No specifications were made. No examination was had. When a public servant of unblemished character, now a member of congress, demanded of the late secretary of state an explanation of this implied charge of corruption, under which he had been removed from his place as a clerk in the department of state, he was coolly informed that no harm was meant, and that no explanation would be given. Even this was not the worst. Attempts were made in more than one instance, under pretext of a stricter control of the public accounts, to deprive these victims of persecution of the scanty remnant of their means of subsistence. A public servant of most respectable character and venerable years, was not only removed and thrown upon the world, at the age of more than eighty, but actually had his furniture seized, under a treasury warrant of distress, upon a false pretence of peculation, at a time when, as appears from a subsequent decree of the competent tribunal, the United States owed him more than twelve thousand dollars. Other cases occurred of a precisely similar character. Can there possibly be any thing behind more revolting then this? There is. In the case of the assistant post master general, there is too much reason to fear that there occurred in the post office department an actual alteration of the public accounts, for the purpose of fixing, upon that most meritorious public servant, the blame of some supposed malversation in office, which had really been committed by his successor. We cannot but hope, for the honor of the country, that some explanation will yet be given of this transaction, consistent with the probity of the individuals at the head of the post office.

The history of the administration of civilized governments presents no parallel to this scene. Many of the partizans of gen. Jackson have shrank from the task of defending it and taken refuge in a bold denial of the fact. Public writers of some respectability did not scruple to affirm that there had been no removals on account of political opinions, as if — to use the indignant language of a Roman historian — they thought they could blot out the record of their doings from the memory of the human race. After a while, the charge of corruption seems to have been abandoned, and in his first message to congress the president justified himself on the principle of *rotation in office;* affecting to suppose that the public would derive an advantage from employing new agents, as fast as the old ones acquired, by experience, the capacity for performing their duties with ability and success. This doctrine, which, if applied to practice in private life, would be thought to argue a degree of imprudence, equivalent, in its effects, to insanity, and would immediately ruin the most prosperous establishments—was gravely announced as an acknowledged truth. It was affirmed that the natural effect of possessing an office was to create negligence and corruption in the person holding it; that the public lost more in this way than was gained by the additional experience and dexterity resulting from the same cause—that frequent changes in office were highly expedient—that all offices should be held for short terms, and, in particular, that the constitution ought to be so amended, that no person be eligible a second time for that of the president of the United States.

These principles, whether true or false, are irrelevant to the subject, because the removals from office by gen. Jackson were not made, either really or professedly, for the purpose of change or rotation, but, professedly, because the incumbents were incapable or corrupt, and really for the purpose of "rewarding his friends and punishing his enemies." No disposition has been shewn to apply this wholesome principle of rotation to the president's partizans, and the best illustration of the real meaning of the language used on this occasion, is to be found in a letter written from the president's house, under the president's frank, to a member of the Pennsylvania legislature, requesting him to use his influence to procure from that legislature a nomination of the president for re-election. The doctrine of rotation in office had, therefore, nothing to do with the matter. The motives assigned, in the first instance, by the president, viz: the incapacity and corruption of the incumbents, would have been sufficient had they been founded in fact: but it was felt that no removal for such reasons would be tolerated by the public, unless the supposed incapable or corrupt functionary was first put upon his trial, and allowed an opportunity of defending himself against the specific charges, whatever they might be, which has been preferred against him. It was therefore, found necessary to abandon this ground, and for want of a better, resort was had by the president's counsellors to the stale sophistry of rotation in office.

On the appointments which were made to fill the numerous vacancies occasioned by these removals we shall not enlarge. Among them are to be found the names of some persons very honorably known to the public; but they were made, in general, almost avowedly for no consideration but that of party, and in many instances, with so little discretion that they were rejected, in one or two cases, almost unanimously, by the senate. An occurrence of this kind is, we believe, without a parallel at any previous period of our history, and would be sufficient of itself to throw discredit on the administration. Of the persons so rejected, some were recommended anew, under circumstances amounting to an attempt by the president to force them into office against the known opinion of his constitutional advisers. On this occasion was also exhibited a striking example of the inconsistency between his professions before his election, and his subsequent practice. Although he had himself signalized the appointment of members of congress to office as a great abuse, he selected four of the five heads of department from that body, and appointed its members to other places to an extent which had never been known before. Although he had inveighed with warmth against the supposed corruption of the public press under the preceding administration, and in his inaugural address had even denounced his predecessor for having brought the patronage of the government into conflict with the purity of elections, partizan editors were now among the most favored classes of pretenders to employment. Under these circumstances the first year of the present administration presented little else than an eager and tumultuous scramble for place. The offices which were instituted for the public service and ought to be conferred with a view to no other object, were apparently, and even avowedly, treated as prizes to be distributed among the conquerors in the struggle of parties. What have we been fighting for — was the language of some of the leading administration prints — if the public offices are not to be the spoils of victory?

Such were the auspices under which the present administration commenced their career. They were not of a kind to create very high expectations from the result of their labors. The subsequent progress of events has shewn very clearly that the least favorable expectations that could possibly have been formed of their policy were yet too sanguine — that our most important institutions are now seriously threatened, and that a continuance in the course that we are pursuing, will probably plunge the country, at no distant period, into dangerous — perhaps irremediable confusion.

In the conduct of the foreign affairs, there has been, however, an appearance of success, in consequence of the fact that several arrangements with foreign powers which had been matured, and in some instances concluded, under the preceding administration have been made public under this. Such was the case with the treaties with Austria, with Brazil, with Denmark, and with Turkey. In announcing the conclusion of these arrangements, a president of an elevated and generous disposition would have taken delight in doing complete justice to the merits of a political competitor. General Jackson took to himself, without scruple or ceremony, the whole credit of these negotiations, and on this and other occasions affectedly avoided to mention the name of his predecessor. In the recent treaty with France the principle adopted by the last administration in the arrangements with Denmark were proposed as the basis of a compromise and in consequence of a favorable change in the internal policy of the former power, was assented to. The treaty with Great Britain, supposing it even, which may well be doubted, to have been the best arrangement which circumstances rendered practicable, was obtained by concessions derogatory to the honor of the country and the dignity of the government.

The administration have, in other respects, mistaken the leading principles in the true foreign policy of the country. With Russia, our most important, powerful, and useful political ally, our relations have been wholly neglected. At a critical moment in the political affairs of Europe, when our influence with the emperor of Russia might have been turned to the best account in favor of the cause of free government, when the breaking out of a general war may render his influence in Europe of the highest importance to ourselves, a distinguished citizen, who had for many years represented the country with extraordinary credit and success at St. Petersburgh, and who was known to be personally agreeable to the imperial family, is abruptly recalled, and the affairs of the legation left in a wholly uncertain state.

On the great subjects of internal policy which have given rise to conflicting opinions and adverse feelings among the citizens, the course of the president has been so inconsistent and vacillating that is impossible for any party to place confidence in his character, or to consider him as a true and effective friend. By avowing his approbation of a judicious tariff, and at the same time recommending to congress precisely the same policy which had been adopted as the best plan of attack by the opponents of that measure: by admitting the constitutionality and expediency of internal improvements of a national character, and at the same moment negativing the most important bills of this description which were presented to him by congress, the president has shewn that he is either a secret enemy of the system, or that he is willing to sacrifice the most important national objects in a vain attempt to conciliate the conflicting interests or rather adverse party feeling and opinions, of different sections of the country. How can the president be regarded at the north and west as the friend of the tariff and internal improvements, when his only recommendation at the south is the anticipation that he is the person through whose agency the whole system is to be prostrated? With a chief magistrate who acts upon so temporising and uncertain a policy it is obviously impossible that any abatement can take place of the excitement that prevails upon these disturbing topics. It is only through the intervention of a statesman, in whose known sentiments and elevated character all parties can place confidence, that a hope can be entertained of so regulating these delicate subjects as to extend a fair and impartial protection to all the great branches of industry, whether agricultural, commercial, manufacturing, or mechanical, without exciting the just apprehensions of any sincere and enlightened friend of the constitution and the union.

Next to the great measures of policy which protect and encourage domestic industry, the most important question, connected with the economical policy of the country, is that of the bank. This great and beneficial institution, by facilitating exchanges between different parts of the union, and maintaining a sound, ample, and healthy state of the currency, may be said to supply the body politic, economically viewed, with a continual stream of life-blood, without which it must inevitably languish, and sink into exhaustion. It was first conceived and organized by the powerful mind of Hamilton. After having been temporarily shaken by the honest though groundless scruples of other statesmen, it has been recalled to existence by the general consent of all parties, and with the universal approbation of the people. Under the ablest and most faithful management it has been for many years past pursuing a course of steady and constantly increasing influence. Such is the institution which the president has gone out of his way in several successive messages, without a pretence of necessity or plausible motive, in the first instance six years before his suggestion could with any propriety be acted upon, to denounce to congress as a sort of nuisance, and consign, as far as his influence extends, to immediate destruction.

For this denuciation no pretext of any adequate motive is assigned. At a time when the institution is known to all to be in the most efficient and prosperous state—to be doing all that any bank ever did or can do, we are briefly told in ten words, that it has not effected the objects for which it was instituted, and must be abolished. Another institution is recommended as a substitute, which, so far as the description given of it can be understood, would be no better than a machine in the hands of the government for fabricating and issuing paper money without check or responsibility. In his recent message to congress, the president declares, for the third time, his opinion on these subjects, in the same concise and authoritative style as before, and intimates that he shall consider his re-election as an expression of the opinion of the people that they ought to be acted on. If, therefore, the president be re-elected, it may be considered certain that the bank will be abolished, and the institution which he has recommended, or something like it, substituted in its place.

Are the people of the United States prepared for this? Are they ready to destroy one of their most valuable establishments, to gratify the caprice of a chief magistrate, who reasons and advises upon a subject, with the details of which he is evidently unacquainted, in direct contradiction to the opinion of his own official counsellors? Are the enterprising, liberal, high-minded, and intelligent merchants of the union willing to countenance such a measure? Are the cultivators of the west, who find in the bank of the United States a never-failing source of that capital, which is so essential to their prosperity, and which they can get no where else, prepared to lend their aid in drying up the fountain of their own prosperity? Is there any class of the people or section of the union so lost to every sentiment of common prudence, so regardless of all the principles of republican government, as to place in the hands of the executive department the means of an irresponsible and unlimited issue of paper money—in other words, the means of corruption without check or bounds? If such be, in fact, the wishes of the people, they will act with consistency and propriety in voting for general Jackson, as president of the United States; for, by his re-election all these disastrous effects will certainly be produced. He is fully and three times over pledged to the people to negative any bill that may be passed for re-chartering the bank, and there is little doubt that the additional influence which he would acquire by a re-election, would be employed to carry through congress the extraordinary substitute which he has repeatedly proposed.

It may be said, instead, that the President's counselors do not agree with him on this subject, and may perhaps over-rule his opinion before the time of action shall arrive. In his recent report to congress, the secretary of the treasury has, in fact, undertaken an apology for the bank, which, coming from him, can be viewed in no other light than as a formal defence of that institution against the attack made upon it by the president, although he concludes with the intimation, that his views may be modified in compliance with those of the executive; as if he were not himself the head of the financial branch of that department. It is one of the singularities of our present political situation, that while we are told on the one hand, by the president's partizans, that his acknowledged incapacity may and will be remedied, by the employment of an able cabinet, we are now told, on the other hand, by this "able cabinet," that they cannot control the president's conduct, and that their sounder notions must be modified so as to meet the views of the executive. In what we are apt enough to consider as the corrupt and servile courts of Europe, a cabinet minister who cannot prevail upon the "executive" from whom he holds his commission to adopt his views, resigns his commission. He deems it improper to modify his opinions, in order to suit them to the views of the executive—in other words, to make himself responsible for a scheme of policy which he does not approve. But supposing that the present secretary of the treasury, if continued in place, would be able, when the time of action should arrive, to over-rule the president's opinion, substitute his own views for those of the executive, and stay this great mischief—what security can the country feel that he will be so continued? Who can assure us that some explosion, resulting from causes too frivolous to be even made, with propriety, the subject of distinct allusion in a serious political document will not scatter the present cabinet, like the last, to the four winds of heaven, and introduce into the councils of the nation a new set of advisers, still more ready than those who now occupy that place, to accommodate their opinions to the views of the executive? The only security which the country can have for the proper discharge of the duties of the executive, as of every other branch of the government, is the capacity, fidelity, and industry of the individual who is by law responsible for that department—that is, the president; and experience has amply shown, that an individual who is unfit for the office himself, is equally unfit to select those who are to assume his responsibility, and be virtually presidents under him.

The judiciary department, an institution still more important than any one can be that merely affects the economical interests of the union, seems also to be seriously threatened by the perverse policy of the present administration. The great improvement made by the adoption of the present constitution in the political system of the old confederation, was the extension of the power of the union over the persons of the individual citizens, through the action of the federal courts, including, as a necessary ingredient, a right of appeal to these courts from the decisions of those of the states. The adoption of this single salutary provision raised us from the situation of a cluster of poor, imbecile, and, for all substantial purposes, mutually dependent states, oppressed with debts, disturbed by insurrections, and on the verge of absolute anarchy, into our subsequent condition of one great, powerful, prosperous, glorious, free and independent federal republic. The rejection of this wholesome principle would bring us back again to the same situation in which we stood before. Notwithstanding this, a powerful party, represented by several important states, and by a large and respectable portion of the people seem to consider the union, and the principles on which it is founded, positive evils. Much is said of the sovereignty and independence of the states, and of their right, as separate states, to annul the laws; while threats are held out, which have not in all cases proved to be mere empty words, that this is to be immediately exercised, and the union of course virtually dissolved.

Under those circumstances, it was to have been expected that the president, as the head of the executive department, and natural guardian of the rights and powers of the federal government, would have exerted his influence to check this dangerous spirit. Instead of this, we find him openly encouraging it, and acting under its influence. When a proposition to repeal, without a substitute, the section of the judiciary act which authorises the appeal from the state to the federal courts, and forms the foundation of the jurisprudence of the union in this respect, was made in congress, it was favored by the immediate friends of the president, and by the journals under his control; and at the recent organization of the house of representatives, the member proposing the repeal was placed at the head of the judiciary committee. These proceedings seem to indicate a settled intention in the administration to shake the independence and destroy the efficiency of this most important branch of the government.

The last point which we shall notice in the conduct of the administration, as relates to the internal policy of the country, and it is, perhaps the most important of all, as far as concerns the principles involved, is that of our relations with the Indian tribes, and particularly that portion of the Cherokees situated within the territorial limits of Georgia. A series of solemn treaties concluded successively by all the administrations of the general government since the period of its establishment, guaranteed to these Indians the possession of their lands without interference or intrusion from any quarter, their right of governing themselves according to their own laws within those limits, and their character of sovereign states. An act of congress passed in the year 1802, authorised and required the president to protect the Indians in the rights guaranteed to them by those treaties, if necessary, by the employment of the military force. In open violation to all these solemn engagements the state of Georgia has extended her jurisdiction, over the territory and persons of the Cherokees situated within her limits, interrupted them in the possession of their dwellings and plantations, and attempted to deprive them of the character of distinct communities; while the president, instead of protecting the Indians against these acts of wholly unauthorised violence, has openly countenanced the pretentions of Georgia, and, instead of employing the armed force of the United States, in their defence, has actually withdrawn that force at the instance of the offending party, from the scene of action, and left the unoffending natives entirely at the mercy of their enemies.

The recent inhuman and unconstitutional outrages committed under the authority of Georgia upon the persons of several unoffending citizens heretofore residing as missionaries within the territory of the Cherokees, constitutes, perhaps, the most unjustifiable portion of these proceedings. They have received, like the rest, the countenance and approbation of the general executive. Few examples can be found, even in the history of barbarous communities, in which the sacred character of a minister of religion has furnished so slight a protection against disrespect and violence to the persons invested with it. We rejoice to learn that this subject will shortly be presented to congress and to the people, in full detail, and in a form fitted to excite the attention which it so well deserves.

It appears from this concise survey of the present situation of the union, as regards the principle branches of our foreign and domestic policy, that it is the duty of all patriotic citizens not only not to aid in the re-election of the present incumbent to the chief magistracy of the union, but to use their efforts to effect a change in the national administration: and in order that such efforts may be made with success, the time has now arrived when it is necessary to designate a candidate for the succession, whose name may be a rallying point and a principle of union among the citizens who are opposed to the re-election of Andrew Jackson.

In looking around the country for such a person, it is almost superfluous to say, that the eyes of all are instinctively directed towards that illustrious citizen, who, after occupying the most distinguished places in the gift of the people; and in all the departments of the administration, has dwelt for some years past in tranquil retirement in the bosom of the west. The qualifications and services of Henry Clay are too well known to require the aid of our testimony. As a statesman, advocate and orator, he has been from his youth upward the pride of our courts and legislative halls. As an ardent, fearless, and consistent friend of liberty and republican institutions, he has endeared himself to their friends throughout the world. His devotion to this great cause, furnishes the surest guaranty that he will, on all occasions, assert the supremacy of the laws, and that executive power in his hands, will be their faithful auxiliary. As one of the principal founders, and supporters of the American system, he is entitled to the warm support of all who desire the prosperity of the great cause of domestic industry and internal improvement. The signal success with which he conducted the affairs of the department of state, evinces his capacity for the actual business of administration; while the generous frankness and captivating warmth of his manners, eminently fit him for a station, where in order to be useful, it is necessary to conciliate the public favor as well as transact with ability the public business. He has already been designated in various ways, and in all quarters of the country, as the candidate of the opposition, and we consider it the duty of all good citizens to use all the means in their power for the purpose of securing his election.

In proposing, in connexion with the name of *Henry Clay,* as a candidate for the presidency, that of *John Sergeant* as a candidate for the vice presidency of the United States, the convention offer to your suffrages a citizen of acknowledged talents, various accomplishments, large experience in the highest and most honorable public trusts, unblemished reputation, and the most ardent and unwearied zeal for the honor and interest of the country. Pennsylvania has long looked up to him as one of her chief ornaments, and the citizens of other parts of the union, in placing him in the second office in the executive department of the government, will be happy to shew their concurrence in sentiment with that great and patriotic state.

Without meaning to encourage an undue confidence, which would only generate inactivity, we believe that, with proper exertion, the success of the good cause is beyond the possibility of doubt. The present administration has for some time past been justly discredited in public opinion. — General Jackson has been gradually losing, ever since the commencement of his official term, the popularity with which he entered it. Whole sections of the union have been alienated from him by his strange and inconsistent course upon the tariff and internal improvement. Extensive interests have been thrown into opposition by his reckless and unaccountable denunciation of the bank. Many of his ablest partisans among the public writers have deserted him, and if any considerable portion of reflecting men still adhered to his standard, the wanton attacks upon the judiciary department must have driven them from it in disgust. — The unity of his party is completely broken up, the open rupture between the friends of the vice president and the late secretary of state; and at this moment the citizens opposed to his re-election, constitute a large majority of the whole population of the U. States. Under these circumstances it is quite apparent, that nothing is wanted but zeal, activity and concert, to ensure success.

The aspect of this convention — the unanimity and spirit which have marked its proceedings — and the favorable results which may be expected from its influence upon the community, afford ample security that these requisites will not be deficient.

Such, fellow citizens, is the character of the present administration — such are the motives for changing it, and such are the persons whom we recommend to you for the chief executive officers. Compare their qualifications with those of their competitors; and may the goodness of Providence, so enlighten your choice, that it may tend to promote the security and permanence of our excellent political institutions, and the true greatness and glory of our beloved country.

James Barbour, President.

Allen Trimble,
Joseph Kent,
Peter B. Porter, } Vice Presidents.
Robert Temple,

Jos. Tillinghast, } Secretaries.
Henry Bacon.

Report on the Democratic Convention in the *Niles' Register*, May 26, 1832

The last party convention held before the election of 1832 was called by the Democrats in order to nominate Martin Van Buren for the Vice-Presidency. It should be noted that Andrew Jackson, the party's presidential candidate, was not formally renominated. The convention simply concurred in the numerous nominations he had already received from states throughout the Union.

Monday May 21, 1832.

The convention met at the Athæneum at 11 o'clock, when *Mr. Summer*, of New Hampshire, addressed the meeting as follows:

Gentlemen—The proposition for calling a general convention of delegates, to act on the nomination of a candidate for president, and to select a suitable candidate for the office of vice president of the United States, originated in the state of New Hampshire, by the friends of democracy in that state; and it appears that the proposition, although opposed by the enemies of the democratic party, has found favor in nearly and perhaps all the states in the union; so that we find collected at this time and place a greater and more general delegation from the people than was ever before assembled upon an occasion of the sort.

The object of the representatives of the people of New Hampshire who called this convention was, not to impose on the people, as candidates for either of the two first offices in this government, any local favorite; but to concentrate the opinions of all the states. They believed that the great body of the people, having but one common interest, can and will unite, in the support of important principles; that the operation of the machinery of government confined within its legitimate sphere is the same in the north, south, east and west; that although designing men, ever since the adoption of the constitution, have never ceased in their exertions to excite sectional feeling and sectional interest, and to array one portion of the country against another, the great and essential interests of all are the same. They believed that the coming together of representatives of the people from the extremity of the union, would have a tendency to soothe, if not to unite, the jarring interests, which sometimes come in conflict, from the different sections of the country.

They considered the individuals, who might be selected as candidates for office, to be of much less consequence than the principle on which they are designated; they thought it important to ascertain the fact, whether the people themselves, or those who would frustrate the voice of the people, should succeed in our elections.

They believed that the example of this convention would operate favorably in future elections; that the people would be disposed, after seeing the good

567

effects of this convention in conciliating, the different and distant sections of the country, to continue this mode of nomination. And for the purpose of leading to a proper organization of this assembly, I would propose that the hon. *judge Overton,* of Tennessee, officiate as chairman pro tem.

Mr. Eaton, of Tennessee, remarked that judge Overton, although in town, was this morning confined to his room by indisposition. He thanked the convention, on behalf of the Tennessee delegation for the honor that had been rendered to their venerable colleague, and concluded by moving that *gen. Robert Lucas*, of Ohio, be substituted for judge Overton, as chairman *pro tem.* which motion was unanimously concurred in.

Gen. Lucas, was accordingly conducted to the chair, and returned thanks in a brief and pertinent address.

On motion of *Mr. Burke*, of Ohio, *John A. Dix,* of New York, was appointed secretary.

On motion of *Mr. Hubbard,* of New Hampshire it was

Resolved, That a committee of one from each state be appointed to report to the convention the names of the delegates in attendance.

The following persons were then named members of the said committee, by their respective delegations:

Maine—John D. McCrate; *New Hampshire*—John Langdon Elwyn; *Massachusetts*—Ebenezer Sever; *Vermont*—Stephen Haight; *Connecticut*—John N. Niles; *Rhode Island*—Elisha R. Potter; *New York*—Azariah C. Flagg; *New Jersey*—Edward Condict; *Pennsylvania*—Simon Cameron; *Delaware*—George Reed; *Maryland*—Upton S. Heath; *Virginia*—Philip N. Nicholas; *North Carolina*—Wm. S. Williams; *South Carolina*—Daniel E. Huger; *Georgia*—Wylie Thompson; *Alabama*—Clement C. Clay; *Louisiana*—Henry Carleton; *Mississippi*—Jas. C. Wilkins; *Tennessee*—John H. Eaton; *Kentucky*—Samuel Davis; *Ohio*—John J. Keith; *Indiana*—Samuel Milroy; *Illinois*—John M. Robinson.

The convention then took a recess till 1 o'clock.

At 1 o'clock the convention re-assembled and was called to order by the president pro tem.

The committee appointed in the morning reported, that in the progress of their investigation a difficulty had presented itself, which they did not feel themselves authorized to settle, in relation to the admission of delegates to the convention from the District of Columbia, and concluded to report the facts of the case, with the opinion of the committee in relation to it. The proceedings of the meeting was then read, which had been held at Alexandria, at which delegates were appointed to this convention, and the committee proposed that they should be admitted as members, under such regulations as the convention should deem proper.

The names of the delegates were then read over in order by states, whereupon it was found that some of the names of delegates appointed from some of the states had been omitted.

The report of the committee was adopted, and then, on motion, it was resolved that the lists of delegates be amended by the members of the convention, whose names were omitted in the report, severally applying to the secretary, and having their names inserted.

A resolution proposed by the committee for the appointment of a committee to prepare rules for the government of the convention, the committee to consist of one delegate from each state, to be selected by each state delegation, was then taken up and adopted, with directions to the committee to report to-morrow morning at 9 o'clock.

The following resolution, on motion of *general Robert McAffee*, was unanimously adopted:

Resolved, That the venerable *Charles Carroll,* of Carrollton, the only survivor of that devoted band of patriots who made and signed the Declaration of Independence, be invited to take a seat in this convention, during its deliberations, and that a committee of three members be appointed to present this invitation.

In pursuance of which resolution the following persons were appointed by the chair to compose the committee, viz: *gen McAffe* and *Messrs. Renner* and *Gherhart.*

The convention then adjourned till 9 o'clock to-morrow.

Tuesday, May 22. The convention met in the Universalist church, at 9 o'clock, A.M.

Mr. King, of Alabama, from the committee to nominate officers, &c. made a report, and the result was that the following appointments were made.

> *Gen. Robert Lusas,* of Ohio, president;
> *Peter V. Daniel,* of Virginia, 1st vice president.
> *James Fenner,* of Rhode Island, 2d vice president.
> *John M. Barkley,* of Penn. 3d vice president.
> *A. S. Clayton,* of Georgia, 4th vice president.
> *John A. Dix,* of New York, ⎫
> *Stacy G. Potts,* of New Jersey, ⎬ secretaries,
> *Robert J. Ward,* of Kentucky, ⎭

The committee proposed the following resolution.

Resolved, That each state be entitled, in the nomination to be made of a candidate for the vice presidency, to a number of votes equal to the number to which they will be entitled in the electoral colleges, under the new apportionment, in voting for president and vice president; and that two-thirds of the whole number of the votes in the convention shall be necessary to constitute a choice.

Also the following, which were agreed to—

Resolved, That in taking the vote, the majority of the delegates from each state designate the person by whom the votes for that state shall be given.

Resolved, That the meetings of the convention be opened by prayer, and that the rev. clergy of this city be respectfully invited to perform the duty.

Mr. King stated that, with the permission of the convention, a further report would be made by the committee, and asked leave for them to sit again, which was granted.

The convention took a recess till 12 o'clock.

12 o'clock. The convention met pursuant to adjournment.

In accordance with the last resolution, adopted this morning, the meeting was opened with prayer by the rev. *Mr. Skinner.*

The committee appointed to wait upon the venerable *Charles Carroll of Carrollton*, reported that they had performed that duty, and that he had desired the committee to express his grateful acknowledgments, and to inform the convention that owing to the state of his health, he would be unable to attend this day.

Mr. Van Ness protested against the exclusion of the District of Columbia, as to a participation in the nomination. He said that delegates had been admitted from states which would not, in all probability, give their support to the ticket of the party — and he thought it due to the zeal of the citizens of the District, that they should not be excluded, &c. *Mr. Laussat* explained the grounds upon which the rule had been adopted. He admitted the zeal and abilities of the citizens of the District, but could not consent to give up a correct principle because it might appear to operate oppressively in some instances.

The question was taken and the right of voting refused to the delegates from the District of Columbia — 126 for and 153 against the proposition.

The committee on rules and regulations reported the following additional resolution:

Resolved, That the candidate for the vice presidency shall be designated by the ballot or ballots of the person or persons selected for this purpose, by the respective delegations, without nomination in convention — and that if a choice is not had upon the first ballotting, the respective delegations shall retire and prepare for a second balloting, and continue this mode of voting, until a selection is made. Which resolution was adopted.

On motion it was

Resolved unanimously, That the convention now proceed to ballot for the nomination of a candidate for the vice presidency.

Whereupon the several delegations proceeded to deposit their ballots at the secretary's table — and the balloting having been concluded, it appeared upon the count, that Martin Van Buren had received the following votes: — From Connecticut 8 votes; Illinois 2; Ohio 21; Tennessee 15; North Carolina 9; Georgia 11; Louisiana 5; Pennsylvania 30; Maryland 7; New Jersey 8; Mississippi 4; Rhode Island 4; Maine 10; Massachusetts 14; Delaware 3; New Hampshire 7; New York 42; Vermont 7; Alabama 1 — being in all 208.

That *Richard M. Johnson* had received the following votes: — From Illinois 2 votes; Indiana 9; Kentucky 15 — being in all 26 votes.

That *Philip P. Barbour* had received the following votes: — From North Carolina 6 votes, Virginia 23; Maryland 3; South Carolina 11; and Alabama 6 votes — being in the whole 49 votes.

It appearing, therefore, that *Martin Van Buren* had received a majority of more than two-thirds of all the votes given, he was declared to be selected as the candidate nominated by this convention for the vice presidency.

On motion of *Mr. Archer*, of Virginia, the convention then adjourned, to meet again at 4 o'clock this afternoon.

Four o'clock P.M. The convention met pursuant to adjournment.

Mr. Archer, of Virginia, presented to the convention the following resolution, which had been adopted by the delegation of that state, during the recess, and asked that it might be placed upon the records of the convention, viz: —

Resolved, That the delegation from Virginia to the convention, concur in, and approve, the nomination of a vice president which has been made by that body, and will recommend the cordial support of it to their constituents.

Ordered, unanimously, That the same be placed upon the records of the convention.

Mr. Jefferson Phelps, of Kentucky, offered the following: —

Whereas, Martin Van Buren, of New York, has received, upon the first ballot, more than two-thirds of all the votes given, for the purpose of selecting a candidate for the vice presidency of the United States — therefore:

Resolved, That this convention *unanimously concur* in recommending him to the people of the United States, for their support, for that office, at the ensuing election.

Which preamble and resolution were adopted unanimously.

On motion, *resolved*, That a committee, consisting of one member from each state, be appointed to draft an address to the people of the United States, and that such committee be appointed by the president.

The resolution being carried, a committee was appointed accordingly.

A resolution was then passed granting the privilege to the delegates from the District of Columbia of recording their votes for vice president.

On motion of *C. C. Clay*, of Alabama,

Resolved, That the convention repose the highest confidence in the purity, patriotism and talents of Andrew Jackson, and that we most cordially concur in the repeated nominations which he has received in various parts of the union, as a candidate for re-election to the office which he now fills with so much honor to himself and usefulness to his country.

On motion of *Mr. Sheppard,* of Ky.

Resolved, That the president and vice presidents of this convention be a committee to inform Martin Van Buren of his nomination to the office of vice president.

On motion *Messrs. Joel R. Poinsett, William R. Johnson* and *John Speed Smith*, were appointed a committee to ascertain the expenses incurred by the convention.

The following communication was received and read:

On behalf of the delegation of the state of Indiana in this convention, I am authorised to declare to the delegates of the several states: That the nomination of Martin Van Buren, as a candidate for the vice presidency, has their approbation, and will have their cordial support, and although col. Richard M. Johnson, of Kentucky, received their vote, so soon as the will of a majority of the convention was indicated, they were disposed cheerfully to yield their preference, for the favorite son of the west, whose claims to the rewards of this country, they believe, to be second to those of none, and unite with the elder states of the union in support of Mr. Van Buren, who, hesitate not to say, will receive the electoral vote of Indiana, in pursuance of his nomination by this convention,

Sam'l. Milroy, D.S.I.

Ordered, That the same be entered on the minutes of the convention.
On motion,
Resolved, That the proceedings of this convention besigned by the officers thereof and published in the Baltimore Republican.
Adjourned to 9 o'clock to-morrow morning.
Wednesday, May 23. 9 o'clock, A.M. The convention met, pursuant to adjournment — and was opened with prayer by the *rev. Mr. Burke.*
Mr. Archer, of Virginia, from the committee on the subject of an address to the people, made the following report:
The committee to whom was assigned the duty of preparing an address from this convention to the people of the United States, report,
That having interchanged opinions on the subject submitted to them, and agreeing fully in the principles and sentiments which they believe ought to be embodied in an address of this description, if such an address were to be made, nevertheless deem it advisable, under existing circumstance, to recommend the adoption of the following resolution:
Resolved, That it be recommended to the several delegations in this convention, in place of a general address from this body to the people of the United States, to make such explanations by address, report, or otherwise, to their respective constituents of the objects, proceedings and result of the meeting as they may deem expedient.
Which report and resolution were read and adopted unanimously.
Mr. Archer, of Virginia, offered the following resolution:
Resolved, That a general corresponding committee from each state, be appointed by the president of this convention.
Which resolution being adopted, the president made the appointments from each state.
Four were named for Maine — 3 for N. Hampshire, 6 for Vermont, 14 for Massachusetts, 5 for Rhode Island, 3 for N. York, 3 for Maryland, 18 for Virginia, 8 for N. Carolina, 6 for South Carolina, 10 for Georgia, 9 for Kentucky, 15 for Louisiana, 3 for Ohio, and 4 for the District of Columbia. Connecticut, Illinois and Missouri have no committee named for them.
The following proceedings then took place —
The committee appointed to confer with the committee of arrangement of the general committee of the Jackson republican party in Baltimore, to ascertain what expenses have been incurred, in order that they may be provided for, by the members of this convention — report that they have received a letter from the committee of arrangement, which is herewith presented, and which informs them that, under the direction of the general committee, all expenses have been provided for by them, and requesting that no further steps might be taken in the case.
The committee therefore recommend that the thanks of this convention be

given to the general committee of the Baltimore Jackson republican party, and to the Baltimore committee of arrangement, for their hospitable and liberal exertions for the accommodation of this body, in a manner worthy the patriotism and republican spirit, for which the citizens of Baltimore have been so long and eminently distinguished.

On motion of *Mr. Preston*, it was unanimously *resolved*, That the convention avail itself of the occasion now presented, to testify the sense of grateful respect entertained by this whole community for the venerable Charles Carroll of Carrollton, the last of the illustrious band of the signers of the Declaration of Independence, by waiting on him in a body at the termination of its session.

And Messrs. Preston, Waples and Stansbury were appointed a committee to wait upon Mr. Carroll and ascertain from him when it will be convenient for him to receive the convention.

Mr. Carter, of Virginia offered the following resolution:

Resolved, That this convention regard with unqualified respect, the prompt impartial, and dignified manner in which their president and vice presidents have presided over their deliberations, and that they make them an unanimous expression of their thanks.

Which resolution was unanimously adopted.

Mr. Carter, of Virginia, offered the following resolution:

Resolved, That the thanks of this convention are due to their several secretaries, for the efficient and satisfactory manner in which they have discharged the duties which devolved on them.

Which resolution was unanimously adopted.

The committee appointed to wait on Mr. Carroll, reported that they had performed that duty, and that Mr. Carroll would receive the members of the convention at any hour to-day.

Ordered, That the members of this convention will proceed to visit the venerable Charles Carroll immediately after the adjournment.

Ordered, That the secretaries cause the journals of the convention to be signed by the officers of the convention, and published in pamphlet form, for distribution among the members.

On motion of *Mr. Burke*, of Ohio,

Resolved, That the thanks of this convention be presented to the reverend clergy for their attendance upon the convention.

The rev. Mr. Wallace then closed the proceedings by an appropriate prayer, and on motion of George Kreemer, of Pennsylvania, the convention adjourned *sine die*.

> *Robert Lucas*, president.
> *Peter V. Daniel*, 1st vice president.
> *James Fenner*, 2d vice president.
> *John M. Barclay*, 3d vice president.
> *A. S. Clayton*, 4th vice president.

John A. Dix,
Stacy G. Potts, } secretaries.
Robert J. Ward,

THE VOTES IN THE 1832 ELECTION

| STATES | POPULAR VOTES FOR PRESIDENT | | ELECTORAL VOTES FOR | | | | | | | | |
| | Andrew Jackson, Democrat | Henry Clay,* Whig | PRESIDENT | | | | VICE-PRESIDENT | | | | |
			Andrew Jackson	Henry Clay	John Floyd	William Wirt	M. Van Buren	John Sergeant	W. Wilkins	Henry Lee	A. Ellmaker
Maine..........	33,291	27,204	10	—	—	—	10	—	—	—	—
New Hampshire..	25,486	19,010	7	—	—	—	7	—	—	—	—
Vermont........	7,870	11,152	—	—	—	7	—	—	—	—	7
Massachusetts....	14,545	33,003	—	14	—	—	—	14	—	—	—
Rhode Island.....	2,126	2,810	—	4	—	—	—	4	—	—	—
Connecticut......	11,269	17,755	—	8	—	—	—	8	—	—	—
New York.......	168,497	154,896	42	—	—	—	42	—	—	—	—
New Jersey.......	23,856	23,393	8	—	—	—	8	—	—	—	—
Pennsylvania.....	90,983	56,716	30	—	—	—	—	—	30	—	—
Delaware........	4,110	4,276	—	3	—	—	—	3	—	—	—
Maryland........	19,156	19,160	3	5	—	—	3	5	—	—	—
Virginia........	33,609	11,451	23	—	—	—	23	—	—	—	—
North Carolina...	24,862	4,563	15	—	—	—	15	—	—	—	—
South Carolina†..	—	—	—	—	11	—	—	—	—	11	—
Georgia.........	20,750	—	11	—	—	—	11	—	—	—	—
Alabama.........	—	—	7	—	—	—	7	—	—	—	—
Mississippi.......	5,919	No can.	4	—	—	—	4	—	—	—	—
Louisiana........	4,049	2,528	5	—	—	—	5	—	—	—	—
Kentucky........	36,247	43,396	—	15	—	—	—	15	—	—	—
Tennessee........	28,740	1,436	15	—	—	—	15	—	—	—	—
Ohio...........	81,246	76,539	21	—	—	—	21	—	—	—	—
Indiana.........	31,552	15,472	9	—	—	—	9	—	—	—	—
Illinois..........	14,147	5,429	5	—	—	—	5	—	—	—	—
Missouri........	5,192	—	4	—	—	—	4	—	—	—	—
	687,502	530,189	219	49	11	7	189	49	30	11	7

* The figures in the Henry Clay column include the votes for the Anti-masonic candidate William Wirt.

† Electors were appointed by the legislature.

Election of 1836

JOEL H. SILBEY is Professor of American History at Cornell University. He is the author of The Shrine of Party: Congressional Voting Behavior, 1841-1852 *and has edited* The Transformation of American Politics, 1840-1860 *and* National Development and Sectional Problems, 1815-1860. *He is currently at work on a study of the Democratic party in the mid-nineteenth century.*

Election of 1836

by *Joel H. Silbey*

The election of 1836 took place in the aftermath of the bitter partisanship that disrupted the second Jackson Administration. It crystallized formidable forces operating within American politics at the time and was, according to historian Richard McCormick, "of crucial importance in determining the ultimate outlines of the second [American] party system."

Although the popular voting trends in the three Jackson elections had been primarily sectional, a very different pattern emerged from the 1836 campaign. Support for the Whigs rose to impressive dimensions in states where that party had previously shown little or no visible popular strength. The Democrats also showed considerable gains in traditionally non-Democratic areas, as the American electorate shifted toward a national political system. Complementing and assisting this trend were the organizational advances made by the national parties in 1836. Politicians throughout the country increasingly accepted the necessity of party discipline, party loyalty, and party organization, concepts which they had by no means universally embraced up to that point.

None of these changes proved temporary. The underlying popular support for each party remained relatively stable during the two subsequent decades, and as a result parties and party organization took firm root. Thus the election was crucial in intensifying forces which shaped the ideological and institutional patterns of an entire era in American politics, a period which began with Jackson's first inauguration.

After its accession to power in 1829, the victorious Jackson coalition vigorously pursued a series of policies advocated by several of its component groups. The program, as it developed, generally was anti-national bank, anti-protective tariff, and anti-internal improvements. In the years of Jackson's first Administration, Secretary of State Martin Van Buren grew increasingly powerful, along with his associates and his lieutenants, particularly from the Middle Atlantic States, while at the same time the influence of Vice-President John C. Calhoun declined drastically. Van Buren's dominant position within the party as Jackson's heir apparent was formally confirmed by his elevation to the Vice-Presidency in 1832, and it was generally understood that four years later he would be the party's presidential candidate.

Concurrent with the rise of Van Buren, however, was the gradual shaking down of the Democratic coalition. The Jacksonians had begun as a miscellaneous group united primarily in opposition to John Quincy Adams. Van Buren had once been a supporter of William H. Crawford; others, such as Amos Kendall, were products of the western relief wars that followed the Panic of 1819; still others were southern planters and aristocrats who had backed Calhoun. Further support came from urban immigrant groups, western entrepreneurs, and large and small farmers throughout the country. During Jackson's first Administration, and especially after the break with the United States Bank, some of these supporters began falling by the wayside. Those who remained were usually men with principles in common, or at least not in sharp conflict with each other. Against them rose an opposition determined to overthrow the continued supremacy of the Jackson-Van Buren Democrats.

The Democrats often looked with public contempt upon the odd combination of "Federalists, nullifiers, and bank men" who were now emerging as the Whig party. "We have nothing to fear," wrote one Democrat to Van Buren late in 1834, "from the combined fragments we have to contend with." But these fragments could not be so lightly dismissed. The National Republicans, who had opposed Jackson from the beginning, were now receiving significant additions to their ranks. They had always been strong in New England and in areas such as northern Ohio and upper New York where people of New England origin predominated. Although some members shared economic interests, notably the protective tariff favored by manufacturers, the subsistence farmers who dominated those regions were probably attracted to the party by a traditional loyalty to fellow New Englanders such as John Quincy Adams. In 1828 the Jacksonians in the Northeast had received only one-third of the popular vote and 1 electoral vote.

The National Republicans had also shown some support in many areas of the South and West, mainly from people who believed in the American System of national development articulated by Henry Clay and Adams. Elsewhere, individuals and groups had supported Adams for local or personal reasons. He had received over 50 per cent of the vote in Maryland and New Jersey, almost that in New York and Ohio, and he did quite well in Indiana and Kentucky. All in all, the National Republicans in 1828 received about 44 per cent of the total national popular vote and 83 out of 211 electoral votes. In Congress approximately 75 of the 213 congressmen called themselves anti-Jackson men. At best this was a base for future action, but during Jackson's first Administration other groups began to join them in opposition to the Democrats.

The 1831 confrontation with South Carolina over the tariff and its nullification led many southern Democrats who resisted the President's "centralizing" tendencies to follow John C. Calhoun out of the party. In the North, the Anti-Masonic party was gaining strength. The movement, growing out of a spirit of religious fundamentalism, and fed by rapid changes in society, drew wide support for its bitter attack on secret orders in America. Led by Thurlow Weed in New York and Thaddeus Stevens in Pennsylvania, the Anti-Masons significantly threatened the more established Democratic leaders such as Van Buren and his supporters and eventually joined the nullifiers and National Republicans in opposition.

The greatest increase in the anti-Democratic forces occurred primarily as a result of the Bank War of 1832 – 34 when factional and ideological differences in formerly one-party states hardened into intense two-party rivalry. The Bank of the United States was popular in those areas where banking was undeveloped, or where the economy needed such an institution. As Charles Sellers has pointed out, this was especially true in some southern agricultural export areas where large staple producers and their economic colleagues, the merchants and lawyers living in the surrounding towns, needed banks to carry on their economic activities. The death of the Bank hampered western entrepreneurs as well. Both groups deeply resented Jackson's attack and his withdrawal of government deposits, and they therefore shifted their support away from the President.

"More important than the economic effects of the Bank War," Robert Remini has written, "was its significance in party development. . . .

> It is clear that in terms of party history the Bank War was the single most important event during the entire Middle period of American history. Not only did it give rise to the Whig party, but the clash between the opposing Bank forces established rigid lines that lasted practically to the Civil War. It exalted such things as party loyalty; it demonstrated that the President could be a politician of the masses; and it fashioned the character of the Democratic party in terms of leadership, organizational discipline, and popular following for nearly a generation."

In New York, for example, the Anti-Masons and the Whigs now subordinated their mutual antagonisms and worked together within the Whig party. In other states, too, similar anti-Jackson coalitions grew rapidly. The new group was more than an opposition movement, however. In spite of disparate origins and many differences of opinion the Whigs showed increasing agreement on policy as well as an ability to work together. In Congress, as Charles Sellers has shown, they united against the Jacksonians in debate and supported their policy positions with their votes. Even the southern Whigs for the most part favored rechartering the Bank of the United States, and disapproved of the removal of government deposits. They advocated Clay's land distribution bill, which Jackson opposed, and in general, took consistent anti-Administration and pro-"American System" positions. Some southern Whigs even supported a protective tariff.

The Democrats, of course, had not been idle. Party activists persistently and vigorously opposed the Whigs wherever they showed increasing strength, resisted any changes in government policies, and vigorously united their remaining forces behind the Jackson Administration. Most of all, the perfected their party organization and their sense of party loyalty and discipline. At the center of this new politics was Martin Van Buren, whose role was well described by Horace Greeley in his memoirs. Van Buren, he wrote,

> had none of that personal magnetism which made General Jackson and Mr. Clay respectively the idols of their contending parties. He was not even an orator, was far inferior to Silas Wright as a debater, and to William L. Marcy in executive ability. I believe his strength lay in his suavity. He was the reconciler of the estranged, the harmonizer of those who were at feud, among his fellow partisans. An adroit and subtle, rather than a great man, I judge that he owed his election . . . to the personal favor and imperious will of Andrew Jackson.

Van Buren's strength was in an efficient party organization, something the Vice-President believed to be absolutely necessary in an era of greater popular participation within an increasing geographical area. The party's function was to direct policy, mute internal differences, and develop a means of achieving the fullest measure of popular support. The Democrats accomplished these goals by building up their local and state organizations, founding newspapers, publishing hortatory pamphlets, and staging frequent meetings and rallies to reinforce unity and discipline. Local, state, and ultimately national party conventions were the capstone of their efforts, for representatives met there to discuss a program and leaders, and to prepare for future electoral battles.

By the mid-1830's, "the amorphous Jackson party of 1828 and 1832 had shrunk in size and had assumed disciplined form behind Van Buren," observed Richard McCormick. Though it was not yet comparable to a modern political machine, the group had a program, an organizational structure, candidates, and an agreed order of succession. To John Quincy Adams, an independent conservative it was an unfortunate time in American politics when men were "handcuffed with the manacles of party," but the virtues of the situation were not lost on Van Buren and his lieutenants who depended on their principles and their organization to overcome an increasingly forceful challenge from the Whig opposition. That challenge was to realign voting patterns in the United States.

No presidential election is unrelated to past behavior or attitudes for many individual voting decisions have been made before the campaign begins, the conventions take place, or the candidates make one speech. Thousands of voters continue to support the same party in election after election regardless of new conditions or campaign developments. The Democratic party had benefited from this kind of voting consistency up to 1836. They had received well over 50 per cent of the votes in presidential elections since 1828 and had usually controlled Congress as well as most of the state governments. In 1828 Jackson had gotten just over 56 per cent of the national popular vote and more than two-thirds of the electors; in 1832, his margin was almost as substantial. That year sectional and local issues greatly favored the Democrats and their totals in the South and West were incredibly high. They received 83 per cent of the popular vote in the South Atlantic States, and 63 per cent in the Southwest (68 per cent in the slave states), as well as 55 per cent of the vote in the Northwest. In some of the individual states the results were completely one-sided: Jackson earned 100 per cent of the electoral vote in Alabama, Georgia, Mississippi, and Missouri, and 95 per cent in Tennessee. He also carried an overwhelming proportion of the popular vote (over 60 per cent) in nine states with 91 electoral votes, and over 55 per cent in two more states, giving him an additional 37 electoral votes.

The elections of 1828 and 1832 demonstrated the basically one-party conditions which prevailed throughout most of the country. In both elections the national percentage difference between the parties was 36 per cent. (The smaller the percentage difference the more competitive is the situation.) The Middle Atlantic States were much closer — large fluctuations in Pennsylvania accounted for the change there from 13 per cent to 7 per cent. On the other hand, the South Atlantic States were heavily Democratic, showing percentage differences of 60 and 63 per cent. In 1828 there were eight states where one party carried over three-fourths of the popular vote, that is, the difference was more than 50 per cent. In 1832, the number of these states was six, and there were six others where one party received 60 per cent of the vote or more. In six South Atlantic and southwestern states the Democrats were unchallenged in presidential races. Illinois, Indiana, Missouri, and Louisiana gave them better than 65 per cent of the vote.

The opposition received over 60 per cent of the vote only in four New England States; these had 33 electoral votes divided between the National Republican and Anti-Masonic parties. In Kentucky, with 15 electoral votes, the opposition earned close to 55 per cent of the total. The vote was close only a very few places in the country — in New York, New Jersey, Maryland, Louisiana, Maine, New Hampshire, and Ohio in 1828, and in New York, New Jersey, and Delaware in 1832. Thus, the sectional and usually non-competitive political system generally favored the Democratic party, and that group entered the 1836 election with an enormous number of apparently "safe" states and what William H. Seward of New York referred to as an "immovable majority."

Actually the situation was slightly more hopeful for the Whigs. Their increasing popular support was demonstrated by post-1832 election returns. In the South, for example, in 1834 and 1835 the Whigs ran several successful campaigns leaving the Democrats often "disorganized and dispirited." In Virginia and Tennessee the Whigs gained control of the state legislatures; in both Tennessee, which had given Jackson 95 per cent of the popular vote in 1832, and Mississippi, Whigs won the governor's office. Richard McCormick has noted that with the 1834–35 elections "closely balanced" parties were emerging in many southern and western states, and in every state, whether the Whigs took office or not, they commanded an increasingly significant proportion of the vote.

McCormick has also noted another important fact about these Whig gains. In the early 1830's local and state political races had been conducted with little relationship to national politics, but in 1834–35 many of the campaigns dealt quite obviously with national issues, particularly the Bank and the presidential succession. What had once been an "unstable," confused, and often unrelated political opposition was growing into a significant voting bloc with a possible impact on the presidential election.

Whig strength was similarly increasing in Congress. Where there had been 139 Democrats and seventy-four National Republicans in the House of Representatives in 1829, the margin was 147–113 (forty-seven seats had been added) in 1833. Many of the Whig gains were made in formerly one-party Democratic states. In 1831 sixty-nine out of ninety southerners in the House of Representatives had been elected as Democrats, twenty-one as National Republicans. Two years later the Whigs held fifty-two of those seats, and in 1835 the number of their representatives dropped only slightly to forty-eight. They thus commanded half the congressional seats from a region which had previously been overwhelmingly pro-Democratic.

Of course, Democrats also made inroads in some areas since 1832, particularly in New England. Jackson's percentage of the popular vote in Rhode Island, for example, rose in each of his three presidential races, and by 1835 his party was strong enough to take both congressional seats and the governorship by close margins. Elsewhere in that region, the two-party system was also taking firm root. In Connecticut in the spring of 1835, Democrats won control of the legislature as well as all six congressional seats, and in New Hampshire they increased their share of the vote to 62 per cent in the campaign for governor. Even in Massachusetts, the weakest New England state for the Democrats, their strength grew. At the beginning of the decade Jackson's party captured only about 20 per cent of the vote for governor, placing third behind the National Republicans and Anti-Masons. In the next three years Democratic totals added up to almost one-fourth of the vote, and in 1835, when the Anti-Masons did not run any candidates, Democrats carried 38 per cent of the vote. All in all, the results of the 1828 election, when National Republicans carried two-thirds of New England's popular vote, and all but one elector, were not likely to be repeated.

Anti-Masonic forces in several northern states complicated the election, and both parties tried to win over those third party voters. In the election of

1832 the separate Anti-Masonic ticket received a substantial proportion of the vote in New York, Pennsylvania, and the New England States. It actually carried Vermont, outpolled Jackson in Massachusetts, and, as the only opposition party in Pennsylvania, earned 42 per cent of the vote. In some areas, such as New York, the Anti-Masonic organization and much of its support had since drifted to the Whigs, but in other areas this trend was not so clear. In several places Anti-Masonic leaders, unhappy with Whig attitudes, were leaning to the Democrats; as early as 1833 Anti-Masons and Democrats were cooperating in Rhode Island. Democrats also benefited from the withdrawal of the separate Anti-Masonic ticket in Connecticut in 1835, and in Massachusetts the coalition, which had been formed to help elect a governor, foundered, as the Anti-Masons "wisely" rejected "all further association with the Whigs." In Pennsylvania and Vermont the third party was so divided that there was little chance of uniting on any presidential candidate. An observer told Martin Van Buren in early 1836 that he and William Henry Harrison were "regarded . . . as the great competitors for Anti-Masonic votes" in New England, Pennsylvania, and Ohio. Both parties were eagerly and carefully seeking what may have been the only significant bloc of uncommitted votes left by the middle of 1836.

Little of the popular voting behavior of the American people in this period had revealed many signs of class cleavages within the general electorate despite the rhetoric of the Bank war and of the Jacksonians generally. "The rich and the poor," Professor Roy Nichols has summed up, "seemed to be distributed in equal proportions between Jacksonians and their opponents." This can be seen in Richard McCormick's study of North Carolina voting where neither party benefited from the removal of property qualifications for suffrage and the large scale intrusion of lower class voters into the electorate. Similarly, Lee Benson's study of New York voting and Ronald Formisano's analysis of popular voting in Michigan in the mid-thirties reflects a pattern of voting cutting vertically through the class structure. There were, to be sure, some people who did react to the politics of the period along class lines. In some eastern cities, for example, radical labor reform groups had become involved in politics in their fight against "the House of Have": banks and other examples of unequal opportunity. In New York City there was a sharp split between artisans and small shopkeepers and the Tammany Democracy, with many reformers deserting the Democratic party on class grounds. They were particularly unfriendly toward Martin Van Buren, although another leading national Democrat, Richard M. Johnson, had shown much sympathy to their goals. Some of these reformers worked with the Whigs in local races in the city in 1835 and 1836. But they appeared to be a relatively unusual class group within the American electorate at this time. In the mid-thirties, both parties apparently could count on some support from all areas of the American class structure.

The partisan divisions which had developed since the election of 1828 were aggravated in the last few years of Jackson's Presidency by his removal of government deposits from the Bank, by the Senate censure of that action, by Jackson's angry reaction, and by Biddle's manipulation of credit policy. All the political parties were obviously concentrating on the presidential succession and trying to maneuver for electoral advantage. The Democrats still seemed to dominate the political system with widespread popular support, but opposition was growing and recent Whig successes hinted at a promising future for that party.

The second Democratic national convention met on Wednesday, May 20, 1835 in the Fourth Presbyterian Church in Baltimore, Maryland, with over six hundred delegates attending. Four states, South Carolina, Alabama, Illinois, and Tennessee, were not represented although one Tennessee citizen did finally participate and cast that state's 15 votes. On the third day of the meetings, nominations for President and Vice-President were made; after only a brief discussion Martin Van Buren was unanimously named for the Presidency. Filling the second place proved to be more difficult. The major contender for the position was Senator Richard M. Johnson of Kentucky. An Indian fighter, and the supposed killer of Tecumseh, Johnson had huge political appeal in the West. If Johnson were nominated, a Kentuckian wrote to Jackson just before the convention, "we will carry this State and all the West." Other party leaders agreed wholeheartedly with this assessment, for Johnson also had strong support among labor groups and other Democrats.

On the other hand, southern Democrats were firmly opposed to Johnson. His "former domestic relations," that is, his longstanding involvement with a female mulatto slave, offended many delegates who also feared the possible impact of that relationship in several southern states. Johnson was "not only positively unpopular," wrote Justice Catron to Jackson, "with that class who give tone to a public man, but affirmatively odious . . . The idea of voting for him is loathed beyond anything that has occurred with us, since we have begun to act in concert with out sister states on national policy." From Tennessee, James K. Polk wrote to the President that Johnson would be "a dead weight" on the Democratic ticket there. These anti-Johnson forces supported Senator William Rives of Virginia in the hope of carrying the doubtful southern states. Johnson, however, won the nomination on the first ballot with the votes of the border states and the Southwest as well as those of most of the North and West.

The final important convention action was the appointment of a committee, chaired by a former Speaker of the House, Andrew Stevenson of Virginia, to draft a statement to the country, similar to the platform of a modern convention, setting forth Democratic principles, past accomplishments, and future policies.

The Whigs did not hold a national convention in 1836; they relied instead on legislative caucuses, local meetings, and state conventions to name their candidates. Thus, Hugh L. White, a former Jacksonian who succeeded Jackson in the Senate after the latter's resignation in 1825, was chosen by a caucus of Tennessee's opposition congressmen in December, 1834, and Senator Daniel Webster by a meeting of the Massachusetts legislature in early 1835. At the end of that year, the Whig state convention in Pennsylvania endorsed the hero of the Battle of Tippecanoe, William Henry Harrison. Fairly early in the campaign Whig members of the Ohio legislature nominated Judge John McLean, former Postmaster General under John Quincy Adams. The Whigs followed a similar process in the selection of vice-presidential candidates and proposed Francis Granger of New York, a prominent Anti-Mason, and John Tyler of Virginia, a former Democrat and now a bitter anti-Jacksonian.

A great deal was revealed about the two political parties by the means they used to choose their candidates in 1836. The Democrats by then had developed a significant party structure, stressing loyalty and unity against the opposition, in order to better concentrate popular support and elect their members to office. "Union, harmony, self-denial, concession, everything for the cause, nothing for men, should be the watchword and motto of the Democratic party," a Tennessee congressman told a party meeting at the outset of the campaign. More than anything else, division over candidates and issues had to be prevented, lest the party and its principles be defeated. The national convention afforded "the best means of concentrating the wishes and opinions of the Democratic Republican party, and of ensuring that union and concern of action so essential to success." Indeed, the party had met, consulted, compromised, and emerged united behind Van Buren, Johnson, Jackson's record, and Democratic principles.

The Whigs, on the other hand, bitterly attacked all aspects of party organization, particularly the national convention. For several years they had been checked, weakened, and frustrated by the Democrats, whose ability to deter people from their own best interests rested, according to the Whigs, on the circus atmosphere surrounding the Democratic party structure. They felt that showmanship had replaced reason in the Democratic campaign. "For eight years," John Minor Botts of Virginia noted, "a *'hurrah for Jackson'* was the only answer deemed necessary to the most potent arguments against the most lawless and unconstitutional acts of aggression and usurpation of power." Andrew Jackson considered the delegates to the Baltimore convention representatives "fresh from the people." The Whigs, however, thought them mere party hacks going to a "packed 'office-holders' convention" and whose "degrading subserviency . . . at the shrine of mere party idolatry" was repugnant to all American values of good government. Many were determined not to emulate in any way the behavior or example of the Democrats. "Only the spoilsmen are disciplined," one wrote, and the Whigs "are too independent to wear the collar of party discipline."

The Whigs, still in their "shaking down" phase as a party, were composed of several power blocs in an often uneasy alliance. These factions had not as yet developed any deep sense of party attachment or loyalty, and therefore the group lacked harmony and a spirit of compromise. Indeed, several of the Whig leaders were manifestly unhappy over the lack of coordination on candidates. "One is for Webster and for Webster only," John Jordan Crittenden complained, "and another equally, exclusively for Harrison. . . . We must run but one candidate lest we break up and divide when it is so necessary that we stay together and defeat Van Buren and Jacksonianism." Others were angry at the choice of particular nominees. "Some of Mr. Webster's friends in

Massachusetts are mad," the southern-oriented *United States Telegraph* wrote, "mad with man worship; mad with a slavish devotion to the 'god-like man.'" "With the thinking men of this state," an Ohio Whig complained, "it was a hard pill to swallow Harrison . . . it will choke thousands of us." Whig newspaper editorials were marked by pleas for harmony on a single ticket and the awareness that it probably could not be achieved. "We desire a candidate who will concentrate all our suffrage and we desire what is impossible," the *National Intelligencer* summed up their situation. A national convention would underscore these divisions, and without discipline and loyalty, that could blow up the party.

A second reason for the Whig refusal to emphasize party structure and loyalties in 1836 was recognition of their position as a minority party. Some leaders were quite pessimistic as the campaign opened. "Mark it," one wrote, *"no opposition man can be elected President."* Henry Clay agreed, "If I were the only Whig candidate in opposition to Mr. Van Buren," he noted, "I would receive a greater support than any other; but I apprehend it would fall short of securing my election." The Democrats had won two elections in a row by substantial margins and they appeared to be strong enough in certain places to be confident of success: New York with 42 electoral votes, the Northwest with 35, and the South with 94. These alone were enough for a national majority.

On the other hand, there was some rebellion within the Democratic ranks, particularly in the southern states. If the Whigs could break down Democratic party power and loyalty, they would be able to convert some former Jacksonian states to their side. Therefore, their campaign, indeed the campaign of any minority party, had to deemphasize party identification and appeal instead to dissident Democrats, while maintaining the commitment of their own supporters. The full-scale attack on blind party devotions advanced by Whig spokesman John Bell in Tennessee was echoed by his colleagues in other parts of the country as well. "Party division," the *Cincinnati Daily Gazette* wrote, "is an unhealthy and unsafe condition of things. Its tendency is to substitute mere party objects and coercive party discipline for the exercise of sound discretion in deciding upon measures." The Whigs felt that had happened under Jackson. The Government was now "administered for the Party—not for the People." But the watchword of every American," a group of Indiana Whigs resolved, "would be our country, not, our Party."

The Whigs carried out the strategy of appealing to normally Democratic voters by emphasizing in crucial areas that they too believed in Jacksonian principles, adding a sharp attack on those professing to enact those ideas. "We are for the admin[istration] and Van Buren," a Tennessee Democrat complained to Jackson in mid-1835. "Those opposed to us say they are for Jackson, the admin[istration] and White." In Illinois, the Whigs, who included young Abraham Lincoln, supported White and added their endorsement of original Democratic principles. They resolved, "that we approve of the democratic doctrines as laid down by Jefferson in 1801, and by Jackson in 1829, and that we disapprove of the convention system attempted to be forced upon the American people by the Van Buren party, and believe it to be destructive of the freedom of the elective franchise, opposed to republican institution and dangerous to the liberties of the poeple." Hugh White's response to Sherrod Williams developed this theme fully.

The particular Whig target was, of course, Martin Van Buren, the corrupter of Democratic principles, the organizer of party institutions, and the "little magician" of American politics. "The Vice-President thro' the Kitchen Cabinet has supplanted most of the early friends of the President, and has succeeded in establishing at Washington, the discipline of the New York school of politics." Now, however, there was an opportunity to be free of the "New York harness."

Jackson was not entirely ignored in the campaign attacks. "It is impossible for anyone, who has not been an eye witness," John C. Calhoun wrote in a public letter, "to realize the rapid corruption and degeneracy of the Government in the last few years." The general was portrayed as a man who had become power-mad and corrupt in his presidential years, using his "imperious will" to force the Democratic party to accept his hand-picked successor. Such action was both degrading and dangerous, according to the opposition. "Nothing could be more mischievous," the Whig members of the Virginia legislature wrote in their address to the people, "than to allow the President of the United States to indicate his successor, and employ the means of the government to elect him." They concluded, therefore, that "the Jackson dynasty ought to be exterminated root and branch."

The campaign was more than a matter of personalities to most Whigs. They often showed little hesitation to stand up against Democratic policies and pose their own alternatives. William Henry Harrison's reply to Sherrod Williams, for example, argued in favor of federal aid for internal improvements in order to better develop the United States economy and communication, a position passionately opposed by the Democrats. Money for such improvements, Harrison further noted, could be found in the surplus revenue of the United States Government which would be distributed to the states according to the proposals of Henry Clay. Harrison was willing to do without a national bank for a certain period of time to see what would happen to federal finances. However, he added that he would favor recharter if events demonstrated that the Bank were necessary. Harrison concluded with a strong statement of the general Whig charges against Jackson, denouncing the growth of executive power—evident in the move to expunge the Senate's resolution of censure against Jackson and in the increased use of the veto power—and the growth of the party, transforming the President from a representative of the people into the representative of a faction. Harrison's message was a clear call to those who supported traditional Jeffersonian policies as well as to newer anti-Van Buren converts. Old opposition and new discontents were rallying together.

As the Whig campaign developed throughout 1835, several party spokesmen began to find advantages in their multiplicity of candidates. Nicholas Biddle, hoping that local prejudices would bring out the highest possible opposition vote, favored White's candidacy in the South, Webster's in New England, and Harrison's in the West." I have said again and again to my friends," he wrote, "I have said it this very morning, 'this disease is to be treated as a local disorder — apply local remedies.'" Thus, what began as the result of party division was becoming, as the Whigs sought victory, deliberate and useful strategy.

The Democratic counter-strategy was clear and crisp: emphasize the party and its policies, not men. If the Democrats could hold on to their previous presidential vote, or at least limit defections to a minimum, all would be well. The obvious solution was to underline the traditional reasons for being a Democrat, and to minimize tensions and disagreements within the party. Van Buren's supporters felt that there were real differences between the parties and they tried to clarify these in the mind of the electorate. The Whigs, they said, wanted to re-establish the "train of measures introduced by the administration of John Quincy Adams": the Bank, a system of federal internal improvements, a corrupt land policy, and a high tariff—all of which would destroy the prosperity and freedom of the people of the United States who had enjoyed the virtues of Democratic policy for so long. The party's fifteen-thousand-word address to the people was an excellent statement of this strategy, and Richard M. Johnson summed it up well. This election, he said, was the "great and . . . final battle against thirty-five millions of money, against uncompromising nullification, against a scheme of protection and of its correlative, waste by internal improvements."

The Democrats denounced Whig support of the former Jacksonian Hugh White and the attempt to cloud the differences between parties. Beware of no party cries, Democratic spokesmen warned, because "the leaders of the most imbittered [sic] parties known to this country now make their approaches under . . . [that] watchword." "If Bankism, nullification, anti-instructionism, anti-Jacksonianism, and everything that is anti-republican," the Washington *Globe* concluded, "rallies under the White flag, and Van Burenism be the opposite, who should hesitate to give a preference to Van Buren? '*Principles are everything; men, nothing.*' If Van Buren be the rallying point of anti-bankism, anti-nullification, and the right of instruction, what republican will fail to rally around him? Is his mere name to frighten men from their principles . . . ? The Republican party will adhere to principle, regardless of names." Democrats argued that the Whigs, by running several candidates, were evidently trying to repeat the situation of 1824 which allowed the inequitable and undemocratic voting system of the House of Representatives to deprive Jackson of the Presidency and to deny the people their first-choice President. If the election went to the House in 1836, the Whigs would obviously unite on a single candidate, certainly not Hugh White, but a true Whig—Webster or Clay.

All of the Democratic campaign was designed to reinforce the traditional political divisions and emphasize the orderly transfer of power within the party from Andrew Jackson to Martin Van Buren, "the executor of . . . [Jacksonian] principles" whose election would "preserve the power of our party and secure the triumph of his [Jackson's] principles."

The strategy of each party—non-ideological and non-partisan on the part of the Whigs, sharply ideological, partisan, and defensive on the Democratic side, was evident in the bitter fight in the southern states between Hugh White and the Democrats. The Whigs, believing that "a small accession from the Jackson ranks might give us a majority" in the South, tried to benefit as much as possible from White's candidacy. They first promoted him as a loyal Jacksonian, pointing out his adherence to original Democratic principles. But they also underlined the necessity, at that moment, of voting for a native southerner, rather than the northern nominee Van Buren.

The sectional issue was a definite factor in the election. By the mid-1830's abolitionist activities had increased in intensity, and the publication and distribution of newspapers, pamphlets, and propaganda against slavery provoked a furor in the South. William Freehling has shown how the reaction of many South Carolinians in the nullification crisis had been particularly stimulated by their attitude towards the recent acceleration of the abolition movement. Little had changed in three years; petitions from abolitionist societies against slavery flowed into Congress, angering and frustrating southern congressmen. In 1835 the legislators moved to prevent the further reception of such petitions by the House of Representatives, and the ensuing fight over the "gag rule" was passionate and protracted. John C. Calhoun, seriously worried by this indication "of the progress of the Fanaticks," predicted that unless their activities ceased, there would soon "be a direct issue" between them and the South. Other southerners expressed similar concern; several slave state legislatures passed strong anti-abolitionist resolutions warning against further agitation, especially with implicit or explicit northern support. It was this mood that some Whigs tried to exploit against Van Buren.

"The geographic interests and impulses are coming to weigh down the scales of the election," John Quincy Adams wrote in early 1835, and he was right. The Democrats of the Jackson Administration, including Van Buren, had been quite hostile to the abolitionists, and the Postmaster General Amos Kendall, even permitted the banning of anti-slavery newspapers from southern mails. Nevertheless, a widespread movement against northern politicians in general, and Van Buren in particular, grew in the South during the campaign. The main argument was that in the North, "those who favor abolition outnumber those who do not." The northerners would therefore soon demand federal action against the South's "peculiar institution," and any northern politician, including the President, would have to submit to the pressure and ultimately advocate or enact some measures against slavery. "Vote for a Northern President from a free state," a Virginia newspaper warned, "and when the test comes, he will support the abolitionists."

The present Democratic candidates were deemed particularly dangerous. Van Buren, it was said, had been "uniformly against the South in every great and vital measure," and was now understandably "backed by the whole body of Northern fanatics." His record in the Missouri controversy of 1819 and in the New York constitutional convention of 1821, when the question of Negro suffrage was debated, clearly confirmed, in the eyes of his critics, that he had "always had a leaning toward putting the negroes on the same footing with the whites." Johnson's "practical amalgamation" experience with a black woman received its share of attention as well. "It may be a matter of no importance to mere political automatons whether Richard M. Johnson is a *white* or a *black* man," a Whig newspaper argued, "whether he is *free* or *slave* — or whether he is married to, or has been in connection with a jet-black thick lipped, odiferous negro wench," but to the South it did.

The Whigs specifically directed their arguments against the southern supporters of the Democratic ticket who, controlled by "a base party spirit," were playing down sectional differences and thus tremendously endangering the South. If such men would forget political parties, the South might still be saved, but the only hope was political unity. A newspaper emphasized that the South "must *organize*. The South must concentrate. Upon this subject there is no room for party." Finally, this necessitated a southern candidate. "I think our interests," the Louisiana Whig, Alexander Porter, summed up, "imperatively require a Slave holding President."

"The excitement in the whole South is very great," a party member reported to Van Buren in August, 1835, "the Whigs are endeavoring to bring it to bear on the presidential question and I fear their efforts may not be unavailing." Southern Democrats quickly responded to the challenge. They deprecated sectionalism as dangerous and inappropriate to the "total want of any real ground of dissension between the North and the South," and attacked the Whigs for raising the issue. One southern newspaper claimed that this was the only means the opposition had "of inflaming the passion of the people, so prosperous and happy are they under the administration of Andrew Jackson," and another particularly defended Van Buren from the assaults levelled against him. He was "emphatically a FIRM FRIEND OF THE SOUTH." His past record, particularly his voting record, is "no violation of the rights of the South, no interference with the interests of the South, no evidence of hostility to the welfare of the South."

The northern Democrats also worked hard to counteract the southern attacks. Democratic legislatures, including that of Van Buren's native New York, passed resolutions against abolition, reminding citizens that slavery was a domestic affair of the state where it existed, and no business of the North's. Van Buren's ally, Governor William Marcy of New York, strongly attacked the anti-slavery agitators in his annual message at the beginning of 1836, and elsewhere Democrats organized mass meetings and passed resolutions stressing their hostility to the abolition movement and their sympathy for the South. Van Buren's answer to a group of North Carolinians typifies his replies to questions on the subject. "God knows," he wrote at one point, "I have suffered enough for my Southern partialities. Since I have been a boy I have been stigmatized as the apologist of Southern institutions, and now your good people have it that I am an abolitionist." The party finally issued a long pamphlet detailing Van Buren's friendship to the South. This was frequently reprinted by Democratic newspapers and distributed to his southern supporters.

Hugh Lawson White's candidacy was a particular problem for the Democrats in the South. The combination of his political antecedents and his sectional popularity, they feared, would hurt them terribly. "Their great object,"

Jackson observed of the Whigs, "is to divide the Republican party and bring the election of President and Vice-President into Congress. There wielding the power of the Bank, the opposition are sure to succeed . . . . What could not be effected under the name of Mr. Calhoun" will be effected "under that of Hugh L. White." Throughout most of 1835 the Democrats therefore concentrated their attack on White's "apostacy," "ambition," and "hypocrisy," and his position as the leader of a "conspiracy against his [Jackson's] principles."

It was apparent, the Democrats claimed, that "in consenting to be used by the opposition, [White] *consents* to the prostration of the principles he had heretofore supported," while the election of Van Buren would perpetuate those principles. We have always "cherished a warm affection for Judge White," the editor of the *Federal Union* continued, and "we have felt a strong repugnance to Mr. Van Buren; but we tear from our hearts all these personal considerations, and cast them to the winds. We oppose the opposer of our principles; we support the supporter of our principles." "Is there anyone in Tennessee," Andrew Jackson asked. "but Bank men, Federalists and Nullifiers that can support him?" The answer plainly was no, for there was "no middle ground — there can be no *nullifying* Union party — no Federal Democrats — no *White* Jacksonians." The Democrats concluded their attack by arguing that White obviously could not win; indeed, no southerner running as a sectional candidate in only a few states could gain the Presidency. Therefore, "every vote withheld from Van Buren in the South, will benefit, not White, but Webster, or Clay or Harrison."

The impact of the anti-Van Buren, anti-abolitionist campaign is difficult to judge. It is true that Van Buren lost many votes that had previously gone to Jackson in the South. An Alabaman wrote Van Buren in early 1836 that "the derelection (sic) of Judge White . . . came very near creating an incurable leison (sic) in our ranks." How many voters would have deserted any Democratic candidate after Jackson, especially with the changes in politics of the preceding four years, is an open question, however. Certainly, many Van Buren supporters in the South thought they had kept the party members in line through legislative responses, public meetings, and personal disclaimers, but criticism of Richard Johnson continued throughout the campaign, and it was clear that some southern Democratic electors would definitely support someone else. At their state convention in mid-1836, Virginia Democrats dutifully nominated Van Buren but put William Smith of Alabama in Johnson's place. No other state took such an extreme position, however, and the real importance in the change in voting pattern lay in what it disclosed about political structure in 1836: The issue of sectionalism was strong enough that each party could benefit by playing up sensitivity to the issue.

The Whigs also tried to provoke anti-Catholic Democrats to defect to their party by unleashing a brief but intense flurry over Van Buren's relations with the Pope. As Secretary of State, Van Buren had had some official correspondence with the Vatican; this now came into question. "If you can lay your hands on any documents that will prove Mr. Van Burian [sic] has any leaning toward the Roman Catholics . . . I should be glad to get them," a

Whig wrote to North Carolina Senator Willie P. Mangum. "It is too palpable to be denied," Ohio Whigs wrote, "that Martin Van Buren has sought foreign aid to secure his election. His letter to the Pope of Rome is at once ridiculous and disgusting."

Van Buren was bombarded with complaints on the issue. "It is reported here," an Ohioan wrote, "and in a measure believed that you have strong Prejudice in favor of the Catholic religion." If so, the writer concluded, it could "prove a Barrier to your election in this part of *Ohio*." Others asked him about his knowledge of a "popish plot" on behalf of his election. Van Buren finally issued a strong denial of the charges, insisting that no plot existed, and pointing out that his correspondence with the Vatican had been in his capacity of Secretary of State and reflected nothing of his personal views. Most important, the claim that he was prejudiced in favor of Catholics was "without the slightest foundation in truth."

The Democrats responded to this charge as they had to Whig sectional appeals. They reminded their supporters of what, in their view, really lay behind the attack. "The federalists are reviving the old times of the alien law—of persecution and intolerance. . . . They will not only attack the Irish but the Catholic religion, believing that the time has arrived when toleration has ceased and we are to be governed by fanatics." William Henry Harrison was particularly identified as a supporter of the 1798 Alien and Sedition Acts, and it was argued that his victory, or indeed the victory of any Whig, would lead to "a religious test and an established Church in this country." All Democrats who wanted to prevent this, regardless of their particular attitudes toward Catholicism, obviously should vote for Van Buren, and for liberty for all religious groups.

"New questions of very grave and threatening aspect are starting up as if by evil enchantment," John Quincy Adams wrote in May, 1836, "which may yet have unexpected bearings upon the issue of the Election." Indeed, because of the intense political atmosphere of the presidential campaign the whole question of where the United States was going, and under whose leadership, became a very real issue. The session of Congress from December, 1835, through early July, 1836, included particularly stimulating debate, as well as a lot of electioneering. All of the presidential candidates except Harrison sat in the Senate and most actively participated in the discussions of the gag rule, the French crisis, the expunging resolution, and the distribution of the proceeds of public land sales. The discussion of expunging the Senate's censure of Andrew Jackson for his removal of government deposits from the Bank quickly divided the group along sharp political lines. "President Jackson has done more for the human race than the whole tribe of hack politicians put together," Thomas Hart Benton told the Senate in early 1836, "shall he remain stigmatized and condemned for the most glorious action [destroying the Bank] of his life?" The Whigs thought so. They violently opposed this "proposition to mar and mutilate the records of the Senate of the United States," in the interests of a power-mad President. The feelings grew so intense that several Whig senators, including vice-presidential candidate John Tyler, resigned their seats rather than obey the instructions of Democratic legislatures in their home states to vote to remove the censure of Jackson.

In the debate on foreign affairs, the Administration was charged with "impudence, folly," and "war spirit" because of threats to France over American citizens' claims of 1798. The Whigs, on the other hand, were accused of giving "foreign nations the impression that our country has not the spirit to vindicate her rights against a powerful aggressor." The conflict over distribution of the proceeds of public land sales concerned the Administration's alleged stupidity in allowing surplus revenue to rise to economically and politically threatening proportions, and Jackson's "*opposition to a fair, just, and equitable distribution among the people.*" The democrats claimed that the Whigs advocated a "universal bribery bill" which would lead to constant raids on the treasury and demands for more and more federal money for internal improvements — money available only if taxes and tariff duties were kept high.

The campaign developed momentum throughout 1835 and 1836 outside of Congress too, as both sides searched for all possible votes. In Massachusetts, Charles Francis Adams worked to bring the Anti-Masons into the Democratic ranks. In New York City, the Locofocos cooperated with the Whigs in several local elections. At a turbulent meeting at Tammany Hall, the radical Equal Rights Democrats opposed the nomination of some regular party candidates. The exasperated regulars burned out the lights in the hall, signifying the end of the meeting. The Equal Righters produced matches — called locofocos — from their packets, lit candles, and proceeded with the meeting; hence the name.

Most of the electioneering, however, was carried on by the two major parties. The Democrats set up local and state committees, raised funds, held conventions, established newspapers, and coordinated their activities through state central committees. Newspaper editorials from the party press, pamphlets, and campaign biographies set the tone; rallies, barbecues, dinners, stump speeches, and debates followed as part of the American campaign style. In Tennessee, Congressman James K. Polk toured his district and the rest of. the middle section of the state on behalf of his own reelection, as well as for the national democratic ticket. He organized speakers and people to get out the vote on Election Day. A new state newspaper, the *Nashville Union*, was established to counteract Whig domination of the Tennessee press. Party rallies in New York urged people to vote for Van Buren, and local addresses to the people, similar to the national message, were published. In Illinois Stephen A. Douglas helped to draft one such plea for votes for Van Buren, for Jackson's policies, and for the Democratic party.

The Whigs had not yet developed as full a sense of organization as the Democrats; and their refusal to hold a convention demonstrated a failure to grasp several essentials of the new politics of the period. On the other hand, campaign strategy and campaign organization were not lacking. The Whigs issued resolutions, addresses, and pamphlets, heard speeches at public rallies, and established newspapers, including some foreign language editions. Tippecanoe dinners took place in Indiana and Ohio, and reminded the celebrants of the virtues of William Henry Harrison. Chain letters also raised money for Harrison in Ohio. Despite their aversion to national conventions, the Whigs often gathered in local, district, and state conventions, where party coordination was developed. Harrison appeared on the ballot in fifteen states, Webster only in New England, and White in ten — mainly slaveholding — states. A good deal of political maneuvering had been needed to work out this arrangement of candidates. The Virginia convention which supported Harrison met and adopted the ticket of electors selected earlier by the White forces in that state so that the same electors would be chosen regardless of which nominee an individual Whig preferred. Nowhere was more than one set of Whig electors on the ballot so that despite the several Whig candidates, it was still a two-party race in every state.

The Whig campaign was never a passive one. If their efforts were imperfect and often haphazard, this reflected their late development as a party, rather than a lack of will. Even the presidential candidates themselves attended some of the dinners and rallies in their behalf, especially Harrison, who traveled to New York, Pennsylvania, and Virgina. "Parties have never been so thoroughly organized in Virginia as now," Senator Rives wrote to Van Buren toward the end of the campaign, "and I am happy to tell you that the Republicans are not outdone by their adversaries."

The question of sectionalism remained important until the end of the campaign. "The effort to make a southern sectional party out of the abolition question has been most eagerly pressed by the enemies of the administration," the *Globe* summed up. Whig supporters continued to call for southern unity, and Democrats still defended Van Buren's record. "Remember," one concluded, "next to Andrew Jackson, Martin Van Buren is the most powerful enemy of the abolitionists; and the safest president for the South." There were even signs that the Whig strength was increasing because of the issue. "We are beaten in N. Carolina," Francis Blair told Jackson in August, 1836, by the inertness of our friends and the vile falsehoods and panic got up on the negroe question." However, to the relief of the Democrats, Hugh White's candidacy was apparently not generating great support; he was now described as "so weak a candidate" that a high proportion of southern Democrats remained loyal to the national party nominee despite the fact that he was a northerner. The southern Whigs seemed to realize this as the campaign waned, and they slightly changed their tactic in response. They discussed, with increasing frequency, other issues between the parties: the baneful influence of the specie circular, Van Buren's improper attitudes on land policy, removal of government deposits from the Bank, Jackson's improper use of the veto power, his executive usurpation, and his general lust for power. Contrary to their earlier concentration on abolition and danger to the South, the Whigs now often drew sharp policy distinctions between themselves and the Democrats instead of minimizing them.

One of the most important aspects of the campaign was the emergence of William Henry Harrison as the most popular Whig candidate in many regions, including the South. He already had strong support in New York, Ohio, and

Pennsylvania; William H. Seward even then believed that Harrison had the qualities that four years later would win the first Whig presidential victory. "I do . . . see," he wrote Thurlow Weed in early 1836, "evidence that General Harrison is capable of being made, under any other circumstances than the present, an invincible candidate." Now voters in other regions of the country, particularly the South, rushed to endorse him. Although his views on sectional issues had been emphasized, Harrison had "taken high southern ground upon the abolition question," and was "entitled to Southern confidence" he could not easily be depicted as a Jacksonian seeking to restore a strayed party to its original principles. The Democrats endeavored to make their supporters see this clearly. They emphasized in their campaigning that Harrison was a Whig, "uniform and consistent; a friend of the protective tariff, and an advocate for internal improvements," as well as "a federalist of the black cockade school" who had always been "a thorough paced partisan of Mr. Clay."

Although different issues were emphasized at different points in the campaign — the White candidacy was important at the beginning, the French crisis early in 1836, the land policy in the fall of the year — they all remained important questions until the election. The campaign had a definite structure throughout; the Whigs primarily pursued a minority party strategy, attempting to split voters away from their normal loyalties by supporting an ex-Democrat, and stressing non-partisan matters. The Democrats countered by distinctly drawing party and policy lines and by reminding their supporters why they had become Democrats in the first place. Any attempts to blur the differences between themselves and the opposition were dismissed as subterfuge.

In 1836 there was no uniform national election day. Voters went to the polls on different days in different states, from November 4 in New Jersey, Pennsylvania, and Ohio, to November 23 in Rhode Island. (Actually, in most states the polls were open for several days.) The campaign continued in full force up to the very last minute. The Chicago *Democrat* warned Democrats on November 2, "your enemies are Nullifiers, Federalists, Anti-Masons, Political Apostates, Abolitionists and Aristocrats in every shape." The Richmond *Whig* concluded its electioneering with a final attack on Van Buren as an anti-slavery northerner, a Democrat and a political manipulator, "a man of many offices without any deeds of public usefulness." Nevertheless, despite the intensity and bitterness of the campaign, national voter turnout was not particularly high, averaging about 55.2 per cent of those eligible, an increase of only .2 per cent over 1832, and markedly lower than in many previous local and state elections. There were several profound changes, however, in the regional and local patterns of voter turnout since the last presidential election.

The number of voters rose in sixteen states between 1832 and 1836. In five of these, all in the South, the increase was over 20 per cent, ranging from 32 per cent in Georgia, and 31.7 per cent in Alabama to 30 per cent in Mississippi, 26.4 per cent in Tennessee, and 21.2 per cent in North Carolina. The only other increase above 10 per cent occurred in Maryland.

In Maine and New Hampshire voter turnout declined sharply from 1832, 28.8 per cent and 36 per cent respectively. In Kentucky and New York the drop was more moderate—about 12 per cent in each place. In five states changes were in the 4 to 8 per cent range, and in the other nine states, turnout remained relatively stable. In general, in the crucial South Atlantic and southwestern states, there was a huge increase in the number of people voting since the last presidential election, reflecting the involvement of this region in the campaign. Even in Virginia, where the voter turnout increased only slightly, it still reached its highest point in the state's history. Richard McCormick has observed that high voter turnout is a result of increased ideological and partisan division, greater opportunity to express attitudes, and a more widespread belief that the act of voting can change the nature of government. All these lead to more competitiveness between the parties. Indeed, the South had awakened during this period and was now coming into the mainstream of American two-party politics, just as national politics was itself becoming more competitive.

Certainly the closeness of the vote in many areas and the extent of the elections in time and space contributed to a period of uncertainty. As late as November 25, Van Buren wrote his son that it was still too early to be sure of the results. However, three days later the returns were clear enough to Thurlow Weed. "We are to be cursed with Van Buren for President," he lamented. The Democrats had held on to their majority and elected their candidate. Van Buren received 764,198 votes, 50.9 per cent of the total, while his combined opponents pulled 736,147 votes and 49.1 per cent. The Democrats carried fifteen states with 170 electoral votes, but the Whigs won 10, with 124 electors, and increased their total of 1832 by 49 votes. Both parties won states in all sections of the country, the Democrats taking 4 of the 6 states in New England, 2 of the 3 Middle Atlantic, 2 of 6 South Atlantic, 5 of 7 southwestern, and two of 4 western states.

The close popular vote contrasted quite sharply with Jackson's last two elections, but fitted in the pattern of most of the rest of the nineteenth century. Most important, the Democrats had maintained a bare national majority despite the loss of Jackson as a candidate and the rise of nationwide opposition. Only in the race for Vice-President did the Democrats' popularity and organization fail them. True to their promise, the Virginia Democratic electors cast their votes for Van Buren and William Smith, leaving Richard Johnson without a majority in the Electoral College. That election was forced into the Senate, where Johnson was subsequently chosen.

American political geography changed significantly in the election of 1836. Although the Democrats received 50.9 per cent of the national vote, only 3.6 per cent less than in 1832, there were noticeable swings from one party to the other on the regional and state level. Less than 5 per cent of the voters changed their party preference in only six states; elsewhere the shifts were much greater. In five states in the South Whig strength grew by more than 30 per cent. In two of those states, Tennessee and Georgia, the difference was over 50 per cent, and in Mississippi and Missouri the shift from one party to the other exceeded 40 per cent. The Democrats made moderate gains—between 15 and 25 per cent—in eight states, including five in New England. The usual state of continuity, stability, and sustained party identification was obviously shattered in 1836 by a major reshuffling of voter preference.

Political scientist Gerald Pomper has called this presidential election a "converting election," indicating that in 1836 "the Democrats were returned to power on the basis of a new voter coalition." Whigs, and areas of Whig support had become more Democratic, while many of the groups which had previously supported Jackson now joined the opposition. Pomper correlated the distribution of the popular vote in 1836 with that of earlier elections. If voting groups within each party remained stable, the correlation figure would be relatively high. For example, the voting patterns of 1828 and 1832 had a .93 correlation. However, the figure for 1836 and 1828 was .05, and for 1836 and 1832, only .22, both very low correlations.

In 1836 the strongest Democratic vote came from the Middle Atlantic States, and the lowest from the border and western states. Four years earlier the South Atlantic and the New England States had turned in the extreme votes. The greatest shift in voter sentiment occurred in the South Atlantic region, followed by the Southwest; the least change took place in the Middle Atlantic States. Table One documents these new regional patterns and compares them with the 1832 totals. The most significant blow to the Democrats was probably their 18 per cent drop in popularity in the slave states. On the other hand, they did retain control of almost all of the South Atlantic and southwestern states, where the White campaign had been concentrated. Despite the huge amount of Whig effort there, only Tennessee had been lost. In Virginia, Georgia, Alabama, and Mississippi there was now enormous Whig strength to be sure, but the Democrats had held on to enough support to remain the majority party there and throughout the country.

TABLE ONE
DEMOCRATIC VOTE BY SECTION

1832 – 1836

	1832	1836	Change
New England	39.8%	51.4%	+11.6%
Middle Atlantic	54.4	53.0	−1.4
Border	49.9	46.0	−3.9
South Atlantic	83.2	52.7	−30.5
Southwest	62.9	49.2	−13.7
/Slave South/	67.8	50.0	−17.8
Old Northwest	55.5	48.6	−6.9

Many aspects of the 1836 election can be more clearly seen by an examination of the Tennessee results. That state, which had been a Democratic leader in 1832, now showed the largest shift in popular vote to the Whigs. The issues that played a big role in the election were highlighted in that state. Throughout the spring and summer of 1836, Congressmen James K. Polk and

Cave Johnson tried to shift Jackson's popularity to the Democratic party and to Van Buren in particular. The Whigs were equally aggressive for Tennessee was Hugh White's home state; if their strategy of dividing the Democrats by appealing to personalities and issues could work anywhere, this was the logical place. National questions were also relevant here: there was significant support for the Bank of the United States; the high tariff and distribution policies was endorsed by some citizens; and there was sensitivity in the western plantation areas to the issue of slavery and abolitionist agitation.

Tennessee, of course, had given Jackson almost all of its popular vote four years before. Since then, however, the Whigs had increased in strength, particularly in the eastern and western sections of the state. The Democrats tended to keep their majority in the middle district, the home area of Polk, Johnson, and Jackson.

Voter turnout in Tennessee rose 26.2 per cent, from 28.8 per cent of those eligible in 1832, to 55 per cent in 1836. However, the Democrats carried just about the same number of votes as they had in 1832 — 26,120 compared to the earlier total of 28.740. The Whigs won just over 58 per cent of the 62,088 voters, carrying 46 of the state's 65 counties.

Thomas P. Abernethy has noted that the shift in Tennessee's voting "took place so suddenly that it would appear to have been due to temporary influences, but the permanence of the lines of political cleavage which were established . . . indicates that fundamental forces were at work." White's candidacy had had some effect, but as Charles Sellers has observed, "more fundamental geographic, economic and social bases of cleavage" were at work. Jackson tried hard to transfer his personal voter popularity to Van Buren, but issues proved too strong for the Democrats in Tennessee.

Elsewhere in the United States, similar combinations of local conditions, existing political structure, long-range changes, and the campaign itself shaped the final vote. In Massachusetts, where the Democrats had been making steady gains for several years, their strength now surged with Anti-Masonic support, to about 45 per cent of the presidential vote, despite the Whig favorite son candidate, Daniel Webster. In Illinois, the Whigs share of the vote increased 17 per cent, and that party filled some local offices for the first time. Abraham Lincoln was elected to the state legislature from a district where the Democratic vote had remained stable since 1832, while the Whig vote had doubled.

A new political era was obviously taking shape in 1836, despite local deviations; a second American party system was crystallizing. The sectional, local quality of voting had largely disappeared. Both parties were becoming national in scope, penetrating into the traditional strongholds of their opposition, and establishing new and enduring voting patterns. Almost everywhere the differences between the two parties were close, unlike the one-sided margins of previous elections. Professor McCormick has pointed out that the average national percentage difference between the Democrats and Whigs fell to 11 per cent in this election compared with 36 per cent four years before. In 1832, Jackson beat Clay by a 2 to 1 margin in eleven states; in 1836, only one state, New Hampshire, showed such a lopsided, non-competitive margin. In Connecticut, Mississippi, and New Jersey, with a total of twenty electors, the difference between the parties was less than 1 per cent; in five others, with 75 electoral votes, the difference was 5 per or less. In fourteen states, the minority party received at least 45 per cent of the vote, where in 1832 only seven states had been that competitive.

The voting patterns which appeared so dramatically in the 1836 election proved to be fairly stable. The problems and controversies of the 1820's and early 1830's were summed up and temporarily resolved in this campaign; new party alliances were firmly established and the electorate was intensely interested in the political process. In Tennessee, for example, party loyalties sprung up which were to last for over two decades. The Whigs retained control of the state even in the presidential election of 1844, when favorite son, James K. Polk, ran on the opposing ticket. The distribution percentage was to remain unchanged; the Whigs carried between 50 and 55 per cent of the vote until 1856, when the Democrats barely won a majority.

Within Tennessee, the internal voting patterns reached a similar stabilization. Thus in 1840, although the Democrats made slight gains in state elections, the vote distribution "bore a distinct resemblance to that by which Cannon [the Whig candidate] was first elected in 1835." White's influence on the vote was no longer felt, allowing the Democrats to recoup some of their losses, but the general partisan distribution did not change. Charles Sellers has traced the country votes in the state for subsequent presidential elections and noted that until 1952 53 of Tennessee's 65 countries continued to vote for the same party they had supported in 1836. Six of the remaining 12 remained consistently Democratic when White was no longer a candidate. Only six countries shifted their vote from election to election.

The same phenomenon was common throughout the South and, to a lesser extent, nationally. A southerner worte to Van Buren of his astonishment at the end of the campaign "at the declaration of many of the *White* wigs [sic], who have heretofore and still pretend to be the friends of Jackson and his administration, that they would vote for *any* man, no matter what his politics were, whether tariff or anti-tariff, Bank or anti, nullification or anti, or even Harrison the abolitionist before they would vote for the Democratic candidates."

The Era of Good Feelings had ended a long time before. In its wake, a deeply divided and highly competitive partisan electorate had emerged. Neither party could count on winning many safe states or regions; the one-party South which the Whigs hoped would materialize behind White did not develop in 1836. Looking back, Henry Clay wrote to White, "The disappointment was greatest in those States which were supposed to be friendly to you." Nor were the Whigs unchallenged in New England, or the Democrats in the West or the South. For the first time in our history a truly national two-party system was inaugurated. This era lasted about twenty years, or until strong regional attitudes and the death of the Whig party restored an essentially sectional political system to the United States. At that point one-party states and sections were to reemerge, but they would never again be as strong as before 1836.

The final chapter of the election of 1836 was completed on Capitol Hill early in February, 1837, when the Senate elected Richard M. Johnson Vice-President of the United States by a vote along party lines of 33 to 16. Less than a month later, Jackson and his protege rode together to Van Buren's inauguration. Just after the election, James Buchanan foresaw a rosy future, "We may anticipate," he wrote, "comparative peace and quiet in his [Van Buren's] day; for nearly all the exciting questions of the time have been happily settled by bold and commanding genius of General Jackson."

The Whigs, on the other hand, were dubious. "Van Buren goes in very weak," John C. Calhoun noted just after the inauguration, "and may be easily crushed with anything like a vigorous effort. There is a great and growing change in our favour." Others agreed with his observation. "There was a general waking up to the conviction," Horace Greeley remembered, that Van Buren "might have been beaten *by seasonable* concert and effort," which had not been forthcoming in 1836. Even Henry Clay, reviewing the election two years later, accepted this conclusion. "The condition of the opposition . . . at the last election, was unfortunate," he wrote to Hugh White. "No mode was devised and none seemed practicable to present a single candidate in opposition." The Whigs had learned something from the Democrats. From then on they would have a national convention, popular candidates, electioneering, and everything that was implied in the new politics of the mid-1830's. They had finally recognized, as Walter Dean Burnham has observed, "that effective opposition depended on acceptance of both the policy and organizational implications of democratization." A great stride had been taken in American politics. Within a year of the inauguration the economy had plunged into panic and depression. Within four, the President was unwillingly returned to private life.

Appendix

Letter from North Carolina Citizens
to Martin Van Buren
February 23, 1836

Southern sensitivity to abolitionist agitation became increasingly evident during the campaign. The Democratic candidate, a northerner, had to repeatedly defend himself as to his likely policies regarding the South's "peculiar institution." In his reply, Van Buren attempted to arrest southern apprehensions as he detailed his views on slavery.

NORTH CAROLINA CORRESPONDENCE.

His excellency Martin Van Buren:

Dear Sir: A portion of your fellow-citizens in this section, feeling a deep anxiety as to your views on a topic which most vitally affects our immediate welfare and happiness, have thought proper to propound to you the following interrogatory, to which we wish an explicit answer.

Do you, or do you not, believe that congress has the constitutional power, to interfere with or abolish slavery in the District of Columbia?

The conspicuous situation in which you are placed, and the importance of a thorough knowledge of your views on this interesting topic will, we hope, be sufficient apology for the liberty we have taken.

(Signed)

> *Junius Amis,*
> *Isaac Hall,*
> *John Wall,*
> *C. Yellowby,*
> *Saml. B. Spirrill,*
> *Jas. W. Puizinn,*

MARTIN VAN BUREN'S REPLY
MARCH 6, 1836

Gentlemen: I have the honor to acknowledge the receipt of your letter apprizing me of the deep anxiety which is felt by a portion of your fellow citizens, as to my views upon a topic vitally affecting their immediate welfare and happiness, and the importance of their being possessed of a thorough knowledge of them; and asking me to say, whether I do or do not believe that congress has the constitutional power to interfere with or abolish slavery in, the District of Columbia?

I am not only willing, but desirous, gentlemen, that you should have the most thorough knowledge of my views and feelings upon the delicate and interesting subject with which your question is connected; and I shall endeavor to acquaint you with them in the fullest manner in my power.

Not having, heretofore, had the honor of being in political communication with you I am not advised whether the sentiments relating to it, which have been avowed by myself and by my authority, within the last two years, have come to your knowledge. I deem it therefore proper, to furnish you with the substance of them, before I reply to your more specific inquiry. The avowals to which I refer, were—

1st. An opinion that congress has no right to interfere in any manner, or to any extent with the subject of slavery in the states;

2d. Against the propriety of their doing so in the District of Columbia; and

3dly. The statement of my full concurrence in the sentiments expressed by the citizens of Albany, in public meeting, the most important of which are as follows, viz: "That the constitution of the United States carries with it an adjustment of all questions involved in the deliberations which led to its adoption; and that the compromise of interests in which it was founded, binding in honor and good faith, independently of the force of agreement, on all who live under its protection and participate in the benefits of which it is the source" —"That the relation of master and slave is a matter exclusively belonging to the people of each state within its own boundary, and that any attempt by the government or people of any other state, or by the general government, to interfere with or disturb it, would violate the spirit of that compromise which lies at the basis of the federal compact"—"That we can only hope to maintain the union of the states by abstaining from all interference with the laws, domestic policy and peculiar interests of every other state"—"That all such interference, which tends to alienate one portion of our countrymen from the rest, deserves to be frowned upon with indignation by all who cherish the principles of our revolutionary fathers, and who desire to preserve the constitution by the exercise of that spirit of amity which animated its framers" —"That they deprecated the conduct of those who are attempting to coerce their brethren in other states into the abolition of slavery, by appeals to the fears of the master and to the passions of the slave; and that they could not but consider them as disturbers of the public peace, and would by all constitutional means, exert their influence to arrest the progress of such measures" —"That whilst they would maintain inviolate the liberty of speech and the freedom of the press, they considered discussions, which, from their nature, tend to inflame the public mind and put in jeopardy the lives and property of their fellow citizens, at war with every rule of moral duty, and every suggestion of humanity, and would be constrained, moreover, to regard those who, with a full knowledge of their pernicious tendency, persist in carrying them on, as disloyal to the union:"—That the people of the south would do great injustice if they allow themselves to believe, that the few who are interfering with the question of slavery, are acting in accordance with the sentiments of the north upon the subject;" and finally, "that they made these declarations to their southern brethren in the same spirit of amity which bound together their fathers and ours, during a long and eventful struggle for independence; and that they did, in full remembrance of that common association, plight to them their faith to maintain in practice as far as lies in their power, what they had solemnly declared."

These views, thus expressed and sanctioned by myself, appear to me to cover the whole ground, save the abstract question to which you have been pleased to call my attention, and I cheerfully embrace the opportunity you have felt it your duty to afford me, to explain myself fully on that also. As anxious as you can possibly be, to arrest all agitation upon this disturbing subject, I have considered the question you have propounded to me, with a sincere desire to arrive at the conclusion, that the subject, in respect to the District of Columbia, can be safely placed on the same ground on which it stands in regard to the states, viz: the want of constitutional power in congress to interfere in the matter. I owe it, however, to candor, to say to you, that I have not been able to satisfy myself that the grant to congress, in the constitution, of the power of *"exclusive legislation in all cases whatsoever"* over the federal district, does not confer on that body the same authority over the subject that would otherwise have been possessed by the states of Maryland and Virginia; or that congress might not, in virtue thereof, take such steps upon the subject in this District, as those states might themselves take within their own limits, and consistently with their rights of sovereignty.

Thus viewing the matter, I would not, from the lights now before me, feel myself safe in pronouncing that congress does not possess the power of interfering with or abolishing slavery in the District of Columbia. But, whilst such are my present impressions upon the abstract question of the legal power of congress—impressions which I shall at all times be not only ready, but disposed, to surrender upon conviction of error—I do not hesitate to give it to you as my deliberate and well-considered opinion, that there are objections to the exercise of this power, against the wishes of the slaveholding states, *as imperative in their nature and obligations*, in regulating the conduct of public men, *as the most palpable want of constitutional power would be.*

You have alluded in your letter to the conspicuous situation in which I have been placed before the public; and I take it for granted, that it is to that circumstance, rather than to any other, that I am to ascribe the solicitude felt by yourselves and your fellow citizens in respect to my views on the subject. I recognise, to the fullest extent, the propriety of this desire on your part, and although there is nothing in your letter making the avowal necessary, I prefer that not only you, but all the people of the United States shall now understand, that if the desire of that portion of them which is favorable to my elevation to the chief magistracy, should be gratified, I must go into the presidential chair the inflexible and uncompromising opponent of any attempt on the part of congress to abolish slavery in the District of Columbia, against the wishes of the slaveholding states; and also with the determination *equally decided*, to resist the slightest interference with the subject in the states where it exists. In saying this, I tender neither to them nor to you, any pledges, but declare only settled opinions and conviction of duty. Those who doubt that it will be carried into full and fair effect, are under no obligations to trust me. An opportunity is afforded them to exercise their free choice in the matter, and they may be assured, that there is no one less likely to complain of its exercise than myself.

The peculiar importance of the subject, and a desire (which you will allow me to feel) that my views of it should be correctly understood, make it proper that I should explain the grounds of the opinions above expressed. They are founded, amongst others, on the following considerations, viz:

1st. I believe that if it had been forseen, at the time of the adoption of the constitution, that the seat of the federal government would be fixed in a slave-holding region, that the subject of slavery would be there agitated to the prejudice of those holding this species of property, the right to do so, would, with the assent of the non-slaveholding states, have been made an exception to the unrestricted legislative power given to congress over the District to be ceded.

2dly. I cannot but regard the agitation of this subject in the District of Columbia, as a surprise upon the people of Maryland and Virginia, being very confident that if the state of things which now exists, had been at all apprehended by those states, the cession of the District would not have been made except upon the express condition that congress should exercise no such power; and that with such a condition the cession would, in the then state of public opinion, have been readily accepted.

3dly. I do therefore believe, that the abolition of slavery in the District of Columbia, against the wishes of the slaveholding states (assuming that congress has the power to effect it) would violate the spirit of that compromise of interests which lies at the basis of our social compact; and I am thoroughly convinced, that it could not be so done without imminent peril, if not certain destruction, to the union of the states. Viewing the matter in this light, it is my clear and settled opinion, that the federal government ought to abstain from doing so, and that it is the sacred duty of those whom the people of the United States entrust with the control of its action, so to use the constitutional power with which they are invested, as to prevent it.

I think it due to the occasion, and only a simple act of justice to my fellow citizens of the north, of all political parties; to add the expression of my belief, that the opinions above expressed, accord in substance, with those entertained by a larger majority of the people of the non-slaveholding states than has ever before existed in those states on a public question of equal magnitude. It is also due to them to say, that their sentiments on this subject spring out of considerations of too high a character, and look to consequences of too solemn an import, to be shaken by slight causes. With only a generous confidence on the part of the south in their brethern of the north, and a firm determination on the part of each, to visit with their severest displeasure any attempt to connect the subject with party politics, those sentiments cannot be overthrown. All future attempts on the part of the abolitionists to do so, will then only serve to accumulate and concentrate public odium on themselves. That there are persons at the north who are far from concurring in the prevailing sentiment I have described, is certainly true; but their numbers, when compared with the rest of the community, are very inconsiderable; and if the condition of things be not greatly aggravated by imprudence, many of them I have no doubt, will ultimately adopt sounder views of the subject; and the efforts of those who may persist in the work of agitation, may be overcome by reason, or rendered inoperative by constitutional remedies.

To one class of those who have hitherto petitioned congress for the abolition of slavery in the District of Columbia, I cannot forbear to refer: I allude to the society of Friends, or the people usually denominated Quakers. The uniformity of their course upon this subject, the temperate manner in which it has been manifested, and the marked excellence of their conduct and character, appear to have conciliated respect for their motives, even from those who differ with them in opinion. As far as my observation has enabled me to judge, it is due to them to say, that as there has been no indication of any change of opinion upon their part during the present excitement, so has there been no evidence of a disposition to lend themselves to the undue agitation of the public mind attempted by others. There is certainly no class of people in this country, who have a deeper interest in the preservation of the union and of the happy system of government which it upholds, than they; and it has now become very apparent to all reflecting and observing minds, that the question of slavery in the District of Columbia cannot be pressed to the result they desire, with safety to those paramount objects. Do not these considerations justify the hope that from them, at least, we may reasonably expect, for the future, a mode of dealing with the subject, which, whilst it does no injustice to their principles, shall repress instead of increasing agitation, and not endanger the great interests to which I have referred? To doubt it, would be to distrust the influence which industry, morality, intelligence and republican habits — qualities which all admit them to possess in a high degree — are calculated in great emergencies to exert upon the conduct of their possessors. And for the like reason, it may certainly be expected, that well disposed persons of other religious denominations, who, without a full consideration of the difficulties which surround this subject, and of the dangerous consequences to which the efforts of the abolitionists so evidently tend, have lent to those efforts the influence of their names and character, will be careful hereafter to avoid the repetition of an error so unfortunate and mischievous.

In every view of the subject, therefore, it does appear to me, that, although there certainly is in the present condition of the country, in relation to it, sufficient to excite the most serious attention, there is nothing in the state of public opinion in the United States, to justify that panic in the public mind which invariably disqualifies those who partake of it, from dealing wisely or successfully with the circumstances by which it is produced. From abroad we have, I think, some right to expect less interference than heretofore. We shall, I am confident, for some time at least, have no more foreign agents to enlighten us on the subject. Recent results here, and the discussions with which they have been attended, cannot fail to attract the attention of the reading and reflecting portion of the foreign public. By these means they will be made to understand our real condition in this respect, and they will know that the unchangeable law of that condition is, that the slave question must be left to the control of the slaveholding states themselves, without molestation or interference from any quarter; that foreign interference of every description, can only be injurious to the slave, without benefit to any interest, and will not be endured by any section of our country; and that any interference, coming from even the non-slaveholding portions of our territory, is calculated to endanger the perpetuity, and if sanctioned by the general government, would eventually occasion the dissolution of our happy union. Seeing the subject, in this, its true aspect, and conscious as they must be, that the downfall of this republic would be the severest blow that the cause of liberty and self-government could receive, and from which its recovery would be hopeless, the wise and the good among them—those who are really guided by the principles of justice and humanity—will pause and acknowledge, that they have misapprehended the true bearings of this question. Instead of accusing our countrymen who hold property in slaves, with disregarding the general principles of liberty and the dictates of a pure religion, they will recognize, in this class of our citizens, as sincere friends to the happiness of mankind as any others, and will become sensible that this species of property, the result of causes over which they had no control, is an inheritance, which *they* only know how to dispose of. Instead of charging the people of the non-slaveholding states, as has often been done, with hypocrisy in professing an ardent love of freedom, they will find that the free citizens of the north are only acting upon the principles of fidelity to their most solemn engagements; that if they were to attempt the accomplishment of what is desired of them by those who regard slavery as inconsistent with the equal rights on which our institutions are founded, they will involve themselves in the odium, either of seeking to evade a compact which was the means and the pledge of our national existence, or of availing themselves of their present power and unexampled prosperity, to dissolve a connection with their southern brethren, formed at a period of mutual adversity, for a cause which was then not only known to exist, but the continuance of which was expressly recognised in the bond of their union.

I have thus, gentleman, been compelled to extend my remarks considerably further than I intended, when I commenced to answer your inquiry. As, however, the subject was delicate and important, I feel that I have not trespassed more upon your time in its examination than was proper to enable you to comprehend the views I entertain of it, or than was respectful to the considerations which justified your call for those views. And I feel assured, whatever may be the difference of opinion, if any, which exists between myself and any other portions of my fellow citizens, that the issue of this matter as of all preceding questions which have agitated the public mind, and have been thought to be pregnant with danger, will, in their hands, be such as to strengthen the bonds of their union, and to increase those fraternal and patriotic affections which our past national history has so often and so honorably illustrated.

I am, very respectfully, your obedient servant.

M. Van Buren.

Messrs. Junius Amis, Isaac Hall, John Wall, C. Yellowby, Samuel B. Spirrill and James W. Puizinn

Letter from Sherrod Williams
to General William Henry Harrison
April 7, 1836

Because of the various warring factions within their party, the Whigs refrained from holding a national convention in 1836. The party thus was forced to fight Van Buren with a number of sectional candidates, the most popular being William Henry Harrison. Despite the absence of an official platform Harrison expressed several of his party's general attitudes in answering a letter from Kentucky Congressman Sherrod Williams. Also responding to Williams' letter was Judge Hugh White of Tennessee, who proceeded to outline his brand of "Whiggery." By adopting a middle stance between the more orthodox Whigs and the Democrats White attempted to portray himself as the sole candidate espousing true Jacksonian ideals.

To Gen. William H. Harrison:

Sir: I consider it the right of every citizen of the United States to ask and demand, and to be fully informed of the political principles and opinions of those who are candidates for the various offices in the gift of the people, and the imperious duty of the candidate to frankly and fully avow and declare the opinions which he entertains. I, therefore, as a voter, a citizen and an individual, feeling a deep and abiding interest in the welfare and prosperity of our common country, and an ardent desire to see the perpetuity of our free and happy form of government, take the liberty of asking you to give me your opinion and views on the following subjects:

1st. Will you (if elected president of the United States) sign and approve a bill distributing the surplus revenue of the United States to each state, according to the federal population of each, for internal improvements, education and to such other objects as the legislatures of the several states may see fit to apply the same?

2d. Will you sign and approve a bill distributing the proceeds of the sales of the public lands to each state, according to the federal population of each, for the purposes above specified?

3d. Will you sign and approve bills making appropriations to improve navigable streams above ports of entry?

4th. Will you sign and approve (if it becomes necessary to secure and save from depreciation the revenue and finances of the nation, and to afford a uniform sound currency to the people of the United States) a bill (with proper modifications and restrictions) chartering a bank of the United States?

5th. What is your opinion as to the constitutional power of the senate or the house of representatives of the congress of the United States, to expunge or obliterate from the journals the records and proceedings of a previous session?

607

A frank, plain and full answer to the foregoing inquiries is respectfully and earnestly solicited. — Your answer is desired as soon as possible. I intend this and your answer for publication.

I have the honor to be your humble and obedient servant,

GENERAL WILLIAM HENRY HARRISON'S REPLY
MAY 1, 1836

Sir: I have the honor to acknowledge the receipt of your letter of the 7th ultimo. . . .

*   *   *

From the manner in which the four first questions are stated, it appears that you do not ask my opinion as to the policy or propriety of the measures to which they respectively refer; but what would be my course, if they were presented to me (being in the presidential chair of the United States) in the shape of bills, that had been duly passed by the senate and house of representatives.

From the opinions which I have formed of the intention of the constitution, as to the cases in which the veto power should be exercised by the president, I would have contented myself with giving an affirmative answer to the four first questions; but, from the deep interest which has been, and indeed is now, felt in relation to all these subjects, I think it proper to express my views upon each one separately.

I answer, then, 1st. That the immediate return of all the surplus money which is or ought to be in the treasury of the United States, to the possession of the people, from whom it was taken, is called for by every principle of policy and indeed of safety to our institutions and I know of no mode of doing it better than that recommended by the present chief magistrate, in his first annual message to congress, in the following words: *"To avoid these evils, it appears to me that the most safe, just and federal disposition which could be made of the surplus revenue, would be its apportionment among the several states, according to the ratio of representation."*

This proposition has reference to a state of things which now actually exists, with the exception of the amount of money thus to be disposed of—for it could not have been anticipated by the president that the surplus above the real wants or convenient expenditures of the government would become so large, as that retaining it in the treasury would so much diminish the circulating medium as greatly to embarrass the business of the country.

What other disposition can be made of it with a view to get it into immediate circulation, but to place it in the hands of the state authorities? So great is the amount, and so rapidly is it increasing, that it could not be expended for a very considerable time on the comparatively few objects to which it could be appropriated by the general government; but the desired distribution amongst the people could be immediately effected by the states, from the infinite variety of ways in which it might be employed by them. By them it might be loaned to their own banking institutions, or even to individuals—a mode of distribution by the general government which, I sincerely hope, is in the contemplation of no friend to his country.

2d. Whilst I have always broadly admitted that the public lands were the common property of all the states, I have been the advocate of that mode of disposing of them which would create the greatest number of freeholders, and I conceived that in this way the interest of all would be as well secured as by any other disposition; but since, by the small size of the tracts in which the lands are laid out, and the reduction of the price, this desirable situation is easily attainable by any person of tolerable industry, I am perfectly reconciled to the distribution of the proceeds of the sales as provided for by the bill introduced into the senate by Mr. Clay; the interest of all seems to be well provided for by this bill; and as from the opposition which has hitherto been made to the disposition of the lands heretofore contemplated by the representatives of the new states, there is no probability of its being adopted, I think it ought no longer to be insisted on.

3d. As I believe that no money should be taken from the treasury of the United States to be expended on internal improvements but for those which are strictly national, the answer to this question would be easy but from the difficulty of determining which of those that are from time to time proposed would be of this description. This circumstance, the excitement which has already been produced by appropriations of this kind, and the jealousies which it will no doubt continue to produce if persisted in, give additional claims to the mode of appropriating all the surplus revenue of the United States in the manner above suggested. Each state will then have the means of accomplishing its own schemes of internal improvement. Still there will be particular cases when a contemplated improvement will be of greater advantage to the union generally, and some particular states, than to that in which it is to be made. In such cases, as well as those in the new states, where the value of the public domain will be greatly enhanced by an improvement in the means of communication, the general government should certainly largely contribute. To appropriations of the latter character there has never been any very warm opposition. Upon the whole, the distribution of the surplus revenue amongst the states seems likely to remove most if not all, the causes of dissention of which the internal improvement system has been the fruitful source. There is nothing, in my opinion, more sacredly incumbent upon those who are concerned in the administration of our government than that of preserving harmony between the states. From the construction of our system there has been, and probably ever will be, more or less jealously between the general and state governments; but there is nothing in the constitution — nothing in the character of the relation which the states bear to each other — which can create any unfriendly feeling, if the common guardian administers its favors with an even and impartial hand. That this may be the case, all those to whom any portion of this delicate power is entrusted should always act upon the principles of forbearance and conciliation; ever more ready to sacrifice the interest of their immediate constituents rather than violate the rights of the other members of the family. Those who pursue a different course, whose rule is never to stop short of the attainment of all which they may consider their due, will often be found to have trespassed upon the boundary they had themselves established. The observations with which I shall conclude this letter on the subject of the veto power by the president will apply to this as well as your other questions.

*   *   *

4th. I agree with Gen. Jackson in the opinion expressed in one of his messages to congress, from which I make the following extract: "*that a bank of the United States, competent to all the duties which may be required by the government, might be so organized as not to infringe on our delegated powers, or the reserved rights of the states, I do not entertain a doubt.*" But the period for rechartering the old institution has passed, as Pennsylvania has wisely taken care to appropriate to herself the benefits of its large capital. The question then, for me to answer, is, whether, under the circumstances you state, if elected to the office of president, I would, sign an act to charter another bank, to answer, I would, if it were *clearly ascertained* that the public interest, in relation to the collection and disbursement of the revenue would materially suffer without one, and there were unequivocal manifestations of public opinion in its favor. I think, however, the experiment should be fairly tried, to ascertain whether the financial operations of the government cannot be as well carried on without the aid of a national bank. If it is not necessary for that purpose, it does not appear to me that one can be constitutionally chartered. There is no construction which I can give the constitution which would authorise it, on the ground of affording facilities to commerce. The measure, if adopted, must have for its object the carrying into effect (facilitating at least the exercise of) some one of the powers positively granted to the general government. If others flow from it, producing equal advantages to the nation, so much the better; but these cannot be made the ground for justifying a recourse to it.

The excitement which has been produced by the bank question, the number and respectability of those who deny the right to congress to charter one, strongly recommend the course above suggested.

5th. I distinctly answer to this question, that, in my opinion, neither house of congress can constitutionally expunge the record of the proceedings of their predecessors. The power to rescind certainly belongs to them; and is, for every public legitimate purpose, all that is necessary. The attempt to expunge a part of their journal, now making in the senate of the United States, I am satisfied could never have been made but in a period of the highest party excitement, when the voice of reason and generous feeling is stifled by long protracted and bitter controversy.

In relation to the exercise of the veto power by the president, there is, I think, an important difference in opinion between the present chief magistrate and myself. I express this opinion with less diffidence, because I believe mine is in strict accordance with those of all the previous presidents to gen. Jackson.

The veto power, or the control of the executive over the enactment of laws by the legislative body, was not unknown in the United States previously to the formation of the present federal constitution. It does not appear, however, to have been in much favor. The principle was to be found in but three of the state constitutions; and in but one of them (Massachusetts) was the executive power lodged in the hands of a single chief magistrate. One other state (South

Carolina) had, indeed, not only adopted this principle, but had given its single executive magistrate an absolute negative upon the acts of the legislature. In all other instances it has been a qualified negative, like that of the U. States. The people of South Carolina seem, however, not to have been long pleased with this investment of power in their governor, as it lasted but two years; having been adopted in 1776 and repealed in 1778; from which time the acts of the legislature of that state have been entirely freed from executive control. Since the adoption of the constitution of the United States, the veto principle has been adopted by several states, and, until very lately, it seemed to be rapidly growing into favor.

Before we can form a correct opinion of the manner in which this power should be exercised, it is proper to understand the reasons which have induced its adoption. In its theory, it is manifestly an innovation upon the first principle of republican government—that the majority should rule. Why should a single individual control the will of that majority? It will not be said that there is more probability of finding greater wisdom in the executive chair than in the halls of the legislature. Nor can it possibly be supposed that an individual residing in the centre of an extensive country, can be as well acquainted with the wants and wishes of a numerous people, as those who come immediately from amongst them—the partakers, for a portion of the year, in their various labors and employments, and the witnesses of the effects of the laws in their more minute as well as general operations. As far, then, as it regards a knowledge of the wants and wishes of the people, wisdom to discover remedies for existing evils, and devising schemes for increasing the public prosperity, it would seem that the legislative bodies did not require the aid of an executive magistrate. But there is a principle, recognized by all the American constitutions, which was unknown to the ancient republics. They all acknowledge rights in the minority, which cannot rightfully be taken from them. Experience had shewn, that in large assemblies, these rights were not always respected. It would be in vain that they should be enumerated, and respect for them enjoined in the constitution. A popular assembly, under the influence of that spirit of party which is always discoverable in a greater or less degree in all republics, might, and would, as it was believed sometimes disregard them. To guard against this danger, and to secure the rights of each individual, the expedient of creating a department independent of the others, and amenable only to the laws, was adopted. Security was thus given against any palpable violation of the constitution, to the injury of individuals, or of a minority party. But it was still possible for a wilful and excited majority to enact laws of the greatest injustice and tyranny, without violating the letter of their charter.

And this I take to be the origin of the veto power, as well in the state governments as that of the United States. It appears to have been the intention to create an umpire between the contending factions which had existed, it was believed, and would continue to exist. If there was any propriety in adopting this principle in the government of a state, all the reasons in favor of it existed in a tenfold degree for incorporating it in that of the United States. The operations of the latter, extending over an immense tract of country, embracing the products of almost every clime, and that country divided too, into a number of separate governments, in many respects independent of each other, and of the common federal head, left but little hope that they could always be carried on in harmony. It could not be doubted that sectional interests would at times predominate in the bosoms of the immediate representatives of the people and the states, and combinations formed destructive of the public good, or unjust or oppressive to a minority. Where could a power to check these local feelings, and to destroy the effects of unjust combinations, be better placed than in the hands of that department whose authority, being derived from the same common sovereign, is co-ordinate with the rest, and which enjoys the great distinction of being at once the immediate representative of the whole people, as well as of each particular state?

In the former character, the interests of the whole community would be rigidly supported, and, in the latter, the rights of each member steadfastly maintained. The representation from the state authorities in the electoral colleges, I consider one of the most felicitous features in the constitution. It serves as an eternal momento to the chief magistrate that it is his duty to guard the interest of the weak against the unjust aggressions of the strong and powerful. From these premises, you will conclude that I consider the qualified veto upon the acts of the legislature, conferred by the constitution upon the president, as a *conservative* power, intended only to be used to secure the instrument itself from violation, or, in times of high party excitement, to protect the rights of the minority, and the interests of the weaker members of the union. Such, indeed, is my opinion, and such we must believe to be the opinion of nearly all the distinguished men who have filled the executive chair. If I were president of the United States, an act which did not involve either of the principles above enumerated, must have been passed under very peculiar circumstances of precipitancy for opposition to the known public will, to induce me to refuse to it my sanction.

If the opinion I have given of the motives of the framers of the constitution, in giving the veto power to the president, is correct, it follows that they never could have expected that he who was constituted the umpire between contending parties should ever identify himself with the interest of one of them, and voluntarily *raze* himself from the proud eminence of leader of a nation to that of chief of a party. I can easily conceive the existence of a state of things by which the chief magistrate of a state may be forced to act upon party principles; but such a course is entirely opposed to all the obligations which the constitution imposes on a president of the United States, The immense influence he possesses will always give to his party the preponderance, and the very circumstance of its being an executive party will be the cause of infusing more bitterness and vindictive feeling in these domestic contests. Under these circumstances, the qualified veto given by the constitution, may, if the president should think proper to change its character, become as absolute in practice as that possessed by the kings of England and France. From the great variety of local interests acting upon the members of the two houses of congress, and from the difficulty of keeping all the individuals of a large party under the control of party discipline, laws will often be passed by small majorities adverse to the interests of the dominant party; but if the president should think proper to use the veto power for the purpose of promoting the interests of his party, it will be in vain to expect that a majority so large as two-thirds in both houses would be found in opposition to his wishes. In the hands of such a president the qualified veto of the constitution would in practice become absolute.

I have, upon another occasion, expressed my views upon the danger of a dominant executive party. It may perhaps be said that the chief magistrate will find it impossible to avoid the influence of party spirit. Several of our chief magistrates, however, have been able to escape its influence; or what is the same thing, to act as if they did not feel it. As one mode of avoiding it, it would be my aim to interfere with the legislation of congress as little as possible. The clause in the constitution which makes it the duty of the president to give congress information of the state of the union, and to recommend to their consideration such measures as he shall judge necessary and expedient, could never be intended to make him the source of legislation. Information should always be frankly given, and recommendations upon such matters as come more immediately under his cognizance than theirs. But there it should end. If he should undertake to prepare the business of legislation for the action of congress, or to assume the character of code maker for the nation, the personal interest which he will take in the success of his measures will necessarily convert him into a partizan, and will totally incapacitate him from performing the part of that impartial umpire, which is the character that I have supposed the constitution intends him to assume when the acts passed by the legislature are submitted to his decision. I do not think it by any means necessary that he should take the lead as a reformer, even when reformation is, in his opinion, necessary. Reformers will never be wanting when it is well understood that the power which wields the whole patronage of the nation will not oppose the reformation.

I have the honor to be, with great consideration, sir, your humble servant,

JUDGE HUGH WHITE'S REPLY
JULY 2, 1836

I

*   *   *

Upon the powers of the federal government to charter a bank, my opinion has been so often expressed, publicly and privately, that I content myself with saying it remains unchanged. I do not believe congress has the power to charter one, to exercise its corporate powers *within the states*, and upon that opinion I must continue always to act, until I can be satisfied I am in error.

The only remaining question is, whether I would approve and sign a bill to improve a *navigable* river, or stream, *above* a port of entry.

I am one of those who deny that congress has the power to adopt and carry out a *system* of internal improvement, by constructing roads and canals *within the states*. In relation to navigable streams running *through them*, congress has the power to *regulate trade among the states*, and this, I think, confers the power to establish ports of entry upon those streams, wherever the *course of trade* may require, exactly to the same extent that it has the power to establish them on the sea coast, in virtue of the power *to regulate commerce with foreign nations.* Whenever the port of entry is established on a *navigable stream,* for the purpose of regulating trade, I cannot perceive any reason for a distinction in the power of congress over the stream, *above or below* the port of entry.

Although I admit the power of congress to establish ports of entry on our navigable streams for *such purpose,* yet I deny that, under the pretence of exercising that power, there is any right to commence, or carry on *a system of constructing harbors* or *clearing out rivers at pleasure.*

By its own *legislation* congress cannot *enlarge* its *own powers.* If, under the pretence of regulating trade among the states, we grant that congress may commence and carry on a system of clearing out streams, and of constructing harbors *within the states,* merely at *discretion,* it appears to me we sanction a fraud on the constitution; and that the exercise of such a power will soon operate so *partially* and *unjustly,* that the states cannot and will not long submit to its exercise.

Congress may do whatever the course of trade among the states requires, to regulate it fairly; but under a pretence of regulating it, is not at liberty to apply the funds of the nation to improvements in *some* states, to the *destruction* of the interests and the *annihilation* of the trade of others.

*   *   *

II

. . . "So far as I am capable of understanding my own political opinions, they conform to the true Jeffersonian creed.

"I am for limiting executive patronage, so that no officer holding his office at the will of the president can be displaced because he will not conform to the president's wishes in elections.

"It ought to be made a high offence in office holders to use their official station with a view to influence the votes of electors.

"It is, and ought to be, considered a high political offence in a chief magistrate to use any of the powers conferred upon him by his station, for the purpose of influencing public opinion in the choice of his *successor,* or in the choice of members to either house of congress.

"I am for such a construction of the constitution as will prevent congress and the president from exercising any power not *expressly* granted, or which is not necessary and proper to carry into effect some one of those powers which are expressly granted.

"I am against imposing or continuing any tax, direct or indirect, for the purpose of bringing money into the treasury; but when there is an accumulation beyond the wants of the federal government, I am for distributing such surplus. . . . among the states; and if the constitution does not now authorise such distribution, I am for so amending it that such power will be conferred.

"Now, sir, let the friends of the administration put down their creed, and if it differs from mine in any thing material, they, and not I, will be found on the federal side.

"On the principles I have ever avowed I have honestly endeavored to act; and if in any instance I have deviated, it was unintentional, and I am not aware of it. Those principles are the same on which the president came into power, and if we are not now together, *the change has not been with me.*"

Statement by the Democratic Republicans
of the United States
Washington, July 31, 1835

The Democratic Republicans did not issue a formal platform in 1836 but their national convention appointed a committee that drafted the following statement of party principles.

*　　*　　*

The interesting question of, "Who is to be our next President" is now fairly before the Nation, and considered in connection with all its probable consequences, may justly be regarded as one of the most important which has been agitated in our country. In its issue, are not only involved the fate of Democratic Republican principles, but the whole course of our national policy. Nay, more, it will comprehend in its result, not only the judgment of the present, but a direction of the future course of the administration of our National Government; and that, too, pronounced by the highest authority of the Republic, the sovereignty of the People. Such a contest, at such a time, cannot fail to produce the deepest political and party excitements; and the more attentively the subject shall be considered, the deeper will become the conviction of its importance, and the necessity of vigilance and caution on the part of the People. It must, moreover, Fellow Citizens, be now very apparent that in a country like ours, of such vast extent and diversified interests, it can seldom happen, in the course of human events, that any citizen will possess such pre-eminent qualifications and popularity, over all others, as to command the votes of a decided majority of the People; and consequently the best manner of concentrating the popular will, and giving it effect, in relation to the Candidates for those high offices, will not only attract a large share of public attention, but will be regarded by the whole Nation as a subject of absorbing interest. Such has already been the case, in relation to the approaching election. The People feel it the more sensibly too, inasmuch as the evils which must flow from filling offices so much sought after, and of such vast responsibility, with men who are neither the first nor second choice of a majority, are greatly aggravated by the defects of our Constitution, which devolves the election, in case no individual has received a majority of the electoral votes, upon the House of Representatives. It was to prevent the mischiefs which might result from having a Chief Magistrate thus imposed upon the Nation, contrary to its wishes, that the Democracy of the Union (following the example of their Republican fathers,) have lately united in a National Convention, and agreed to present to their country candidates for the two high Executive offices of the Government.

In the early history of our Confederation common dangers produced concert of action, and in the two first elections of a President the preeminent merits of Gen. Washington made harmless this defect in our political system. For long, meritorious, and well tried services, the Chief Magistracy was bestowed upon this illustrious citizen, unsought and unsolicited, by the unanimous voice of his country. So too, at the third election, which was, no doubt, essentially influenced by the opinions and administration of that great and good man, and his associates, it was not materially felt. At the fourth election, however, the defect was made evident, in the strongest colours. Then was displayed, one avenue at least, through which ambition and Party might successfully triumph over the People's will; and, although the particular point, from which the danger rose, was immediately seized on, and guarded by subsequent amendments of the Constitution, the radical defect which enabled a President to be elected (in case of no popular choice) by the Representatives of a small minority of the People, was left wholly untouched. The contest which then took place, as violent as it was alarming, was fruitful, however, of the soundest admonition to the leaders of the Republican Party, at the head of which stood the great apostle of Liberty, *Thomas Jefferson.* To avert the mischiefs and danger of an election by the House of Representatives, and to secure unity of action amongst the Republican Party, they undertook to devise means to concentrate, in all future elections the votes of that portion of the People who adopted their creed, upon a single candidate. For that purpose recourse was first had to *Congressional caucuses.* The system was then resorted to, and justified, as one of necessity. Its avowed, and real object was to secure the election of a Republican Chief Magistrate, and prevent such a collision as might transfer the choice to the House of Representatives. It was in this way, and through the agency of the Republican members of Congress, making nominations, in Caucus assembled, that *Mr. Jefferson, Mr. Madison, and Mr. Monroe,* were presented as Candidates to the American People, and were elected, and re-elected, by large majorities of the popular suffrages. Thus far, one of the great objects of the Constitution, (an election by the people in their primary colleges,) was believed to be guarded and secured. But this system was attacked and overthrown in the memorable contest of 1824-'5; and the failure by the Republican Party on that occasion to elect its candidate, was followed by the election of a Chief Magistrate by the House of Representatives, in utter disregard of the popular will, and under circumstances which produced the deepest excitement. Indeed, so strongly impressed was the distinguished individual who was the object of that choice, of the importance of an election by the People of their President, that, in his answer to the Joint Committee who announced to him his appointment, he declared, *"That could his refusal to accept the trust delegated to him, give an immediate opportunity to the People, to form and express, with a nearer approach to unanimity, the object of their preference, he should not hesitate to decline the acceptance of the eminent charge, and submit the momentous question again to their determination."* What less than the deepest conviction of the danger of an election by the House of Representatives, instead of the People, could have induced him, in the moment of triumph, to hold such language. What stronger avouchment, of the importance of a clear expression of the popular will, and this defect in our Constitution could have been given than this? This election, however, and the state of things to which it gave rise, soon roused the People, and the elements of the *Old Republican Party* rallied around General Jackson as the individual, in whose person popular rights and power were to be vindicated. After a very violent and embittered contest, they succeeded in placing him in the Presidential Chair. Of the election of 1824-5, and the scenes which then occurred, it is not needful, nor would it be proper, here to speak. They form a prominent and interesting part of the history of those times of our Republic, and will long be regarded by every friend of Representative Government, as a political *beacon*, rather than a *precedent?* This election, however, did more; it satisfied the friends of Popular Sovereignty, of the necessity of again resorting to some mode, for the purpose of securing this important election to the People, and preventing the recurrence of those scenes of intrigue and ambition, which were presented on that occasion, and may be expected invariably to be presented on an election of the President by the House of Representatives. In the case of General Jackson, owing to the peculiar circumstances, no step was deemed necessary to concentrate their power, and imbody the popular will, as it had been sufficiently indicated in the previous contest. Besides his great and signal military services, he had become so much endeared to the Republican Party, by the bold and determined manner in which he had resisted the principles and doctrines of the previous administration, that no measure of the sort was deemed necessary to insure his re-election. He accordingly came in, by an overwhelming vote of the American People. But the Republicans were not so fortunate, in relation to a candidate for the Vice Presidency, and danger was apprehended from the number of candidates, and at the conflicting claims and divisions of different sections of the Union. To obviate these, the Republicans of New Hampshire, with a disinterested patriotism worthy of themselves, came forward and proposed a *National Convention,* as the best means of healing divisions, and securing the triumph of Republicanism; and it was accordingly held with the happiest effect. This convention, no doubt, gave rise to that which has recently been held in Baltimore, and whose proceedings are now submitted for your approval.

Is there one liberal and disinterested Republican who considers the provisions of our Constitution in relation to this subject, the efforts that are making to carry the election to Congress, and who is opposed to such an election, that can fail to perceive the necessity of adopting some plan to unite the Democracy of the country, and give effect to its will in this all important election? We think not. The only alternative then presented, is a National Convention, springing immediately from the People, and representing the various parts of the Union, or an abandonment of the expedient for concentrating the national will, substituted for that of Congressional caucus nominations, and an election by the House of Representatives. Of the evils of such an election, you require, Fellow Citizens, at this day neither argument nor admonition from us. Few, it is to be hoped, if any, now doubt, that the wise men who framed our system, intended to secure to the People, the choice of the Executive branch of their Government, and to render it wholly independent of the Federal Legislature.

*   *   *

. . . It has been justly remarked, and it cannot be too strongly and often repeated, that one of the greatest evils which can threaten public liberty and our happy system, next to revolution and disunion, *is an election of President by the House of Representatives!* In this sentiment we are quite sure a large portion of the American People will concur, and it is therefore against the dangers and evils of such an election, that the liberal and enlightened of all parties should be most anxious to guard. Nor is this view weakened by the fact that such an election by Congress is authorized by the Constitution! It may be asked, we know, as it has been asked, why the sagacity of the wise framers of that instrument did not foresee these alarming consequences, and provide some other remedy? The answer is a plain one: they never imagined the occasion would arise when its exercise would be required. Indeed, so remote was believed to be the possibility of an election of President by the House of Representatives, that the celebrated triumvirate of '87, (with James Madison at their head,) in defending the various provisions of the Constitution and recommending it to their country, omitted to offer one reason in favor of this provision, or to defend such a mode of appointment. A negative argument, to be sure, but one entitled to great consideration. But, fellow citizens, whatever may be the mode or means of concentration which the Republican party shall adopt to avoid these evils, they must expect to be assailed by the enemies of their principles, with all the artifice of ambition and the ingenuity of party. Their motto is, *"Divide and conquer."* They know that, united, the Democracy of our country is, and ever will be, invincible. That to govern it, its opponents must distract and divide it. By destroying the means of union, they prevent that union by which only the Democracy can conquer. The opposition is a smaller body, and has more bonds of union. In their systems of corporations and exclusive privileges; in the partial legislation of the States, as well as of the United States, which enable the rich to become richer, and render the poor poorer, its members have a common interest, which will generally induce them to act together. If to the power of union of wealth and general intelligence, they are enabled to add the advantages of division among the Democracy, they are certain to govern the country, to mould all its laws, and direct their administration. It is against such division, therefore, that the Democracy should ever guard with sleepless vigilance. All the means of preserving union should be cherished by them with almost the same tenacity, as those principles which, without such union, can never have practical effect. To these advantages, which our political enemies expect from our divisions, are to be ascribed all the attacks which have been made, and will continue to be made, upon the Republican party and the Convention recently held by them in Baltimore. The objections to it are as various as the Protean shapes which the opposition themselves assume, who, having failed in their attempts to defeat the Convention with the People, will now assail it and its proceedings with renewed vigor. It becomes, then, not only proper, but a matter of duty in us, to examine some of the most prominent of these objections, and we shall proceed to do so in as brief a manner as possible.

The first is that against the character of the Convention itself. It is denounced in strong and unmeasured terms by the whole body of the opposition, not only as a mere instrument of party and a gross assumption of power, but as a system of dictation by self-organized and irresponsible individuals, intended to control and bias the popular will, and in violation of the true principles of our Constitution. That it is the will of the individuals only who compose these assemblies, and not that of the People, which gives the fiat.

Without yielding up for a moment what we conceive to be among the soundest Democratic doctrines, that in relation to public affairs any number of citizens, however assembled, have a right, in a respectful manner, to offer their opinions and express their wishes; and in so doing, are entitled to be respectfully heard, we insist that the late Convention held in Baltimore, was no voluntary and unauthorized assemblage of individuals; but that upon any fair and unprejudiced view, it consisted substantially of delegates from a very large portion of the Union, in whose candor a fair expression of the choice of the Democracy of their respectful portions of the country was made. That its members were supposed to speak, not their individual sentiments alone, but the opinions and wishes of those whom they represent. That they did not permit themselves to indulge individual and local preferences and partialities, but were bound by a sense of duty to collect and compare the sentiments of the people every where, and recommend those who possessed the largest share of public confidence. They acted in this as in a high representative character, and if it be true, that an Elector is bound to follow implicitly the will of his constituents, upon what ground can it be said that a Convention, thus constituted, would have any latitude of discretion, in the nomination of individuals, without regard to the opinions and wishes of the people? What then are the safeguards against misconduct in all such Conventions. Simply that care be taken that they emanate directly from the people, convene at some central point, and be separated as far as practicable from the influences of the existing administration. Would not such a mode of nomination be much more likely to imbody and give effect to the popular will, than any that has yet been adopted? Is it not preferable to the old mode of Congressional caucuses, sustained for more than twenty years by the established usages of the republican party, and which resulted in the election of *Mr. Jefferson, Mr. Madison, and Mr. Monroe.* If that mode was justified in the language of the Caucus of 1808 — *"From the necessity of the case, from a deep conviction of the importance of union to the republicans throughout all parts of the United States, and as the best mode of consulting and representing the interests and wishes of all upon a subject so interesting to the whole people of the United States,"* — how much more ought that of a *National Convention* to be justified by the same considerations, at the present moment? . . .

But all such modes are said to be liable to serious objections. Granted. But what are the evils which must arise without them? That is the question. It matters not, how strong the objections to a Convention may be, the enquiry still must be, is there not less danger to be apprehended from them, than a *Congressional Election?* Is it not a thousand times better that the evils even of a Convention, whatever they may be, should be borne, than that we should be exposed to the calamities of an election by the House of Representatives, the Pandora Box of our whole system? This is the only true issue. If, however, any better mode can be devised, gladly, we doubt not, would the nation bless the amending hand. But until some amendment of the Constitution shall be adopted to cut off the possibility of an election by the House of Representatives, and cause the will of the People to be respected in the choice of their Chief Magistrate, it should be the duty of the Republican party, either through National Conventions, or some other efficient mode, to concentrate their power, and produce harmony and union among their friends. It is in this way only, as experience has shown, and as all experience will show, that they can ever hope to maintain their ascendency, secure the triumph of their principles, and give effect to the popular will. . . .

The next objection against the Convention, and one recently urged by the opposition, is that the whole proceeding is purely of a party character; intended alone to preserve the power of party and perpetual party principles. Hence it is, that we hear the spirit of party so strongly deprecated by the very men who are invoking its aid, by their own ambitious and party purposes. — That this spirit, when carried to an extreme, may become injurious, we readily admit. But the man who expects to see free countries exempt from its influence, must be a very superficial observer of human affairs, and have but a slight acquaintance with the history of free governments. In a country like ours, it is not only the right but the duty of every citizen to make himself acquainted with the operations of the Government and the conduct of those intrusted with its administration — Every citizen here can aspire to the highest offices in the State; the only passports to which are the favor and confidence of his fellow men, acquired by the possession of talents and virtue. In such a state of society, that there should be collisions of sentiment and interests, and political parties, is not only a consequence natural, but irresistible. Nor is the existence of such parties destitute of public utility. They bring into action the greatest talents. They excite a jealousy and vigilance which insures fidelity in public functionaries. They check attempts at the usurpation of power, and thereby preserve the rights of the People. Such has been the effect, not only in our own free government, but in those much less so. In Great Britain has this not especially been the case? — There the great and overweening power of the monarchical and aristocratical branches of the government has been counteracted and kept in check by the boldness, talents, and popularity of the leaders of political party; nor is there any thing immoral or improper in men having the same object, co-operating as a party on honest principles, for its attainment. An individual in the political world taking his own course without consulting those of the same principles and opinions with himself, would become insignificant. His isolated exertions might become unavailing. He would be a unit, opposed to a strong phalanx, united by a common interest, and animated by a combined will. The only way that he could oppose with success the movements of his political opponents, would be to unite with those having the same views with himself. Nor would this imply a sacrifice of principle or independence on his part. A breach of political morality, the doing an act of injustice; or the trampling on the rights or liberties of a fellow citizen, can never be justified or excused, by regard or complaisance to a party. This is readily admitted. But the concession of subordinate questions; a compromise of views of policy; of the course to be pursued to attain a certain and laudable object; or the preference of particular individuals to fill certain stations are not only the dictates of wisdom, but are to be justified by the maxims of the severest and most inflexible morality. Men excited to preserve and maintain the liberties of the country; to oppose any attempt to sacrifice those liberties, and to bury them under the ruins of the Constitution, would not only be inexcusable, but highly criminal, to suffer those great and vital objects to be defeated; because, in the pride of opinion, they would not sacrifice, on a question of mere expediency, a cause which they might not have been the first themselves to suggest. The question which these political casuists ought to put to themselves, should be this: Would it be better that they should endanger the public happiness or the public liberty, than give up some favorite scheme of policy, or yield their assent to an individual's being placed in an office, whose opinions in general coincided with her own, though they might have a preference for another? When parties act on honorable principles, there is no danger from its existence. But this opinion is not meant to extend to the justification of that factious and envenomed spirit by which parties are sometimes influenced. Whenever an individual is ready to sacrifice the honor of the nation, the principles of the Constitution, or the rights of the People, to gratify his own ambition, or satiate his vengeance on political opponents, such a man deserves to be stigmatized as an enemy to his country! The great thing to be attended to in a free country, therefore, is not to pronounce an indiscriminate anathema against all political parties. The People should inquire into the motives by which parties are actuated, and into the tendency of their measures. If a particular party or set of individuals are united to preserve the public liberty, and to secure the Constitution on a firm basis, these men, by whatever epithets distinguished, deserve the public applause and gratitude. If the tendency of the measures of another party be to overturn that Constitution, or subvert the liberties of the People, such men, however imposing the name which they may have assumed, do not merit the public support, but should be firmly resisted by every friend of his country. It would be the duty of the good citizen to unite his efforts to those of one party, while he should avoid any connexion with the other. In a society constituted of such parties, and in a country like ours, who would be justified in standing aloof as an unconcerned spectator? Would he not be bound to choose between parties and measures, which might be beneficial or injurious to his country? Under the banners of the first described of these parties, would he not be impelled, by the strongest impulses of duty and patriotism, to enlist? Would he not be in a situation, where, next to the crime of uniting on measures hostile to the public happiness, would be that of remaining neutral? Miserable indeed would be the excuse of those who refrain from affording that aid which they owe to their country, under the pretext that they cannot agree upon any measure of policy, and upon any preference of individuals, with those whose main objects they admit to be similar to their own! Should these political opponents be successful, persons acting with such views would find it difficult either to justify their conduct to their country or their own consciences. They might discover too late that they had sacrificed the best of causes to that pride of opinion, which is not satisfied with success, but with nothing short of attaining it in its own way. These reflections ought, we think, to be seriously weighed by every citizen in a free country! . . .

We come now, fellow citizens, to another objection to the Convention, or rather to one of its nominations, and to another effort at division, of a very different character, and probably one of the most mischievous and wicked that has ever been made against the peace and happiness of any country! It is the attempt to create *sectional parties and divisions*, and to alienate one portion of our country from the rest, by charging upon the supposed defects of our complicated political system, the calamities which evil men are endeavoring themselves to bring about. This is a subject of transcendent and universal interest, and one that demands to be well weighed and considered, by all parties, and all men! And here we will take occasion to remark, that it is on this weak side of human nature, in appeals to the most degrading and dangerous passions of the human mind, that those who seek to betray nations to their purposes, and kindle the torch of discord, always resort. It is here that ambition as well as fanaticism (always prolific in the alurements and delusions necessary to accomplish their purposes,) direct their batteries. It is the point, moreover, in which not only all free Governments, but our own peculiar system can be most effectually assailed. Hence, it is, that in different parts of our country we see mischievous and misguided men attempting to weaken the bond of Union, and exciting the North against the South, and the South against the North. The peculiar differences in the social organization of these two sections of our country, is ever a ready and fruitful subject, to create these jealousies and dissensions. It has ever been a fundamental article in the Republican creed that these relations were not by our own Constitutional Charter, brought within the scope of Federal powers, and that Congress has as little right to interfere with the domestic relations and local institutions of the United States, with the relations of *master and apprentice* in Massachusetts, or *master and servant* in Virginia, as they have to meddle with similar social relations in Great Britain, France, or Spain. So deeply rooted is this conviction, not only in the minds of our brethern of the northern and middle States, but in the minds of the whole Republican party of the Union, that it is incorporated in the Democratic creed, and constitutes one of the broad lines of separation between the strict constructionists of the Jeffersonian school and the latitudinarians or consolidationists, under all their Protean colors. Republicanism is the safest guaranty of the stability of our Union. No man, nor set of men, can interfere, or even wish to interfere, with the reserved rights of the States, embracing their domestic institutions and social relations, and call himself a Democratic Republican, or a friend to Union. Republicanism, or Democracy, in the language of Mr. Jefferson, is *"the support of the State Governments in all their rights, as the most complete administration for our domestic concerns, and the safest bulwarks against anti republican tendencies, and the preservation of the General Government in all its constitutional vigor; as the sheet-anchor of our peace at home and prosperity abroad."* Those who would interfere with these reserved and vital rights of the States, cannot be Democrats; and on the other hand, those who would weaken the bonds of union, or wish to destroy its constitutional vigor, whatever they may call themselves, cannot be, in truth, Jeffersonian Republicans. The disposition to meddle with the just rights of the States, and especially those of a Democratic character, as well as the opposite disposition to arrest the constitutional and rightful action of the Federal Government, are alike inconsistent with the true spirit of Republicanism and the doctrines of the Republican party. Those who harbor either disposition, whatever may be their motives or professions, are anti-republican in principle, whether called Federal or National Republican, Whig or Tory, Abolitionist or Nullifyer. True Republicanism not only guarantees to each State the full enjoyment of its reserved rights, but it guarantees to each State protection from the molestation of other States. When we look, fellow citizens, upon the People of the large and the small States of this vast empire, all dwelling under the Republican system of our fathers in tranquillity and security; all under different local and State laws and domestic regulations; all pursuing happiness and prosperity in their own way; having no wall upon their borders, nor armies to defend them from one another; but each and all resting securely under the Republican banner of our Union, it would indeed seem as if the days had come, foretold of old, when the lion and the lamb should lie down in peace together. . . .

Those, then, who would urge the Government of our Union to trespass upon the rights of the States, or those who would force the States to dissolve the Union, are neither Republican nor the true friends of the States or the Union. They are not so, because they strike at the foundation and existence of our free institutions and Republican Government itself. They strike on different sides, to be sure, and with very different motives, but the effects are the same. It matters but little whether the harmony of these happy and prosperous States be destroyed by wrongs committed against their reserved rights, or whether it be by creating unjust disaffection to that Union to which they are all indebted, without exception, for their peace and prosperity at home and their respect abroad. Fellow citizens, there have always been two great political parties in our country. Names have changed, but the principle or grounds of difference between the two remain the same. The Republican party has always contended for a strict construction of the Constitution, the preservation of the rights of the States, and the integrity and supremacy of the Government of the Union, *when acting strictly within the letter and spirit of the constitutional conpact.* The Federal party or consolidationists, on the other hand, claimed a liberal or latitudinarian construction, and under the pretext of "general welfare" and "expediency," have not scrupled to exercise powers, not only of doubtful constitutional character, but in violation of many of the reserved rights of the States. Their principles have often led them not only to push the authority of the General Government to the most unwarrantable lengths, disregarding State rights and public sentiment, (as in the case of the Alien and Sedition Laws,) but to fly to the opposite extreme, and stoutly deny the authority of the General Government, when acting strictly within the line of its constitutional duty, as in the case of the Embargo proceedings during the late war, and the recent Bank question. The very same class of politicians, who had advocated the authority of the Federal Government to enact Alien and Sedition Laws, establish moneyed monopolies, create exhorbitant Tariffs, and tax the people of one section of the country to make roads and canals in another, denied the right of the same Government to protect the commerce of its citizens by an Embargo, defend the rights and liberties of its gallant seamen by a war, or remove even the public treasure from a soulless corporation, using its power for political and party purposes. All such extremes are alike inconsistent with the principles and doctrines of the Republican party. The consolidationists have twice had the Government in their hands, and both times their principles have been pushed to dangerous extremes. Names have changed, but the same party, with the same principles, leading to the same practices, are now striving for power.

It is true, and gratifying to believe, that a portion of this party are aiming at power, and in the conviction that their principles (although twice tried and failed) would be more conducive to the prosperity and happiness of this country, than the principles of Washington, Jefferson, Madison, Monroe, and Jackson. They, however, know that they are in the minority, and can never hope to gain the ascendancy except by dividing the Republican party. To this point all their energies are and will be directed. It cannot be concealed from you that many of our opponents, both in the North and the South, under different names and denominations, are playing into each others hands, by creating geographical parties, kindling sectional animosities, stirring up local jealousies, and arousing all the angry passions. It is in this way that they hope to divide the Republican party. Facts, however, will verify that all such proceedings are instituted by anti-republicans, and those who are opposed to us. This is more especially true as it regards the Eastern and Northern portions of our country. The Republicans have no lot or part in them, and all those who assume the name, and are now found engaged in them, if they ever belonged to the Democratic party, have since been alienated by ambitious or party views, or in the mists of party strife, have mistaken enemies for friends. True Republicans can never lend their aid and influence in creating geographical parties in the East, West, North, or South! They can never engage in such schemes, without violating their principles; principles which tell them that they are all brothers, each left a rich inheritance by their fathers, never to be cancelled, while they forbear to meddle with the local feeling and domestic relations of each other. Who then can doubt the virtue, the intelligence, and the patriostism of our brethren of the northern and middle States upon this subject? Have not the abolitionists and fanatics, in broaching their obnoxious plans in public in those quarters of our Union, been in danger even of mobs and violence? Within the last two years, while political incendiaries, with the view of creating sectional parties, have been proclaiming to the South, that the North were preparing to interfere with her domestic relations, have we not seen the preachers of such doctrines driven from public assemblies in the

North and Northwest, with mockery and scorn? It was but the other day that the abolitionists were refused permission, by an overwhelming vote of the Democratic legislature of New Hampshire, to hold meetings in either Legislative Hall, on the ground that the objects of the Society were incompatible with those Southern interests, secured by the Constitution, with which the Northern people had nothing to do, and which could never be agitated without danger and alarm. It is the power and influence of united Republicanism and patriotism, which ties the hands of the abolitionists and fanatics in the North, and scorns their doctrines. It is this power of united Republicanism which spell binds their deluded followers, and which they feel and dread. Indeed, so sure and safe a guarantee is Republicanism, for the peaceable possession of all the privileges resulting from this confederacy of States, that while there is a Republican in the North, the South will have a friend there. Let then the Republican party every where, stand firm and united, and trusting to her principles, fear not, all will be safe. And why shall not the Democracy of all quarters of our Union, and the several States, implicitly confide in each other? They entered into this Confederacy as independent States, with the express stipulation, that each State reserved to itself the right of managing its domestic concerns and social relations in its own way. The People of no State, therefore, can violate that compromise, on which this Union is based, and call themselves Republicans. It would be subversive of the fundamental principles on which the superstructure of Republicanism itself is based. They could not, as men of honor and truth, violate it, without being guilty of deception, treachery, and falsehood! They could not, as men of sense and true christians, violate it; because they know that, by so doing, the light of a great nation, now brightly shining on a benighted world, would be extinguished forever, and in blood! They know that the world affords ample fields for the exercise of the most boundless exertions of humanity, charity, and piety. They know that whatever may be the evils existing in any portion of the United States, and however they may be deplored by many in the north and northwest, that there are greater evils in other countries, where humanity, religion, and letters, may exert her empire over the human heart. Whenever religion leaves its proper home, the heart, to join in the noise and strife of the affairs of State, it is out of its province, and ever sullies its purity! Whatever movements may be made then in the North or the South, the East or the West, inconsistent with the domestic and social rights secured by the Constitution to the respective States of the Confederacy, will emanate from, and be confined to *anti Republicans*, and like all other evils, will be most effectually counteracted by the union, integrity, and resistance of the Republican party.

Under such circumstances, how wicked as well as unfounded, are these attempts to excite and inflame the South, and create sectional parties on such a basis. Who can look to such a state of things without dismay and horror? Was it not, fellow citizens, against the danger of indulging such feelings, and on the importance of discouraging them, and preserving harmony and union that our revolutionary fathers endeavored so deeply to impress their country? Will you pardon us while we ask you to read and listen to their eloquent and pathetic exhortation? *"But this detestable effort to alienate one portion of our country from the rest, and enfeeble the sacred ties which now link together its various parts, can never succeed. The People of America have too much good sense, to enter into the perilous and gloomy scenes, into which these advocates of disunion, would lead them. They will not hearken to the unnatural voice which tells them, that knit together as they are, by so many cords of affection, they can no longer live together, as members of the same great family; can no longer be mutual guardians of their mutual happiness; can no longer be fellow citizens of one great and flourishing empire. They will shut their ears against this unhallowed language. They will shut their hearts against the poison it contains. The kindred blood which flows in their veins; the mingled blood which they have shed in the defence of their sacred rights, consecrate their union and excite horror at the idea of their becoming aliens, rivals, enemies."* This was the admonition of a man of the soundest and most experienced head, and the purest and most patriotic heart. Need we say, it was that of James Madison, one of the most distinguished founders of our Constitution. Hence too the solemn warning of Washington, the great Virginian and saviour of his country, against the dangers of geographical discriminations, and these insidious and daring attempts at disunion and disaffection. In his valedictory and affectionate admonition, at the moment he was retiring forever from public life, he, too, warned his countrymen— *"Union which constitutes you one People is also now dear to you—it is justly so—it is the main pillar in the edifice of real independence; the support of your tranquillity at home; of your peace abroad; of your safety; of your prosperity; and of that very liberty which you so dearly prize. That it is the point of our political fortress against which the batteries of internal and external enemies will be most constantly and actively (though often covertly and insidiously) directed. Frown, therefore, indignantly frown,"* he continues, *"upon the first dawning of any attempt to alienate one portion of our country from the rest; or to enfeeble the sacred ties which now link together its various parts."* Who can turn a deaf ear to such counsel, and at a time so appropriate as this? Who does not feel and acknowledge the importance of this hallowed spirit speaking, as it were from the tomb, the prophetic and inspired language of truth and patriotism. Why then these attempts to alarm the Southern portion of our country and to assail the proceedings of the Convention on the score of geographical and sectional feeling? Why all this illiberality? Why this continued effort to excite unfriendly feelings between people who have always entertained such sincere respect for each other? Why shall we not regard (in national matters) all the States as one country; and the People which inhabit them as our brethren? Why shall any narrow and sordid and selfish spirit lead the people of one section, to view with envy, or jealousy, the prosperity and happiness of another. Why shall not the South rejoice in the prosperity of their Eastern brethren, in the greatness of Pennsylvania, and New York, and in the increasing power and population of those young and flourishing States, upon the waters of the mighty West; and why shall not these, in return, reciprocate the same kind feelings towards the patriotic South? When did the North, or the West, ever desert the South?

How long and nobly have they not stood by the South, and her distinguished men? Was it not in support of Southern men that the Democracy of the North, so often evinced a high degree of liberality? Was *General Washington, or Mr. Jefferson, or Mr. Madison, or Mr. Monroe,* ever objected to by them, because they were from the South? At the end of *General Jackson's* present term, the South will have enjoyed the honors of the Presidency for forty years out of forty-eight, since the adoption of the Constitution. As to the remaining eight years of our political existence under the Constitution, that high office has been in the hands of our political opponents, so that the Northern Democracy have never yet seen a man elevated from their own ranks, to that high station. Under these circumstances have they ever murmured, or complained? Never. And why? Because, in the spirit of true patriotism, they have believed that the interests of their Country would be better promoted, and their cherished principles best maintained, by their support of Southern men. And now, after so many years of disinterested conduct, would it not be illiberal and unjust, when they present one of themselves, for that high station, whose character and principles are every way unexceptionable, that they should be branded as enemies of the South, and hostile to the peculiar institutions of the Southern People. We are sure that such imputations, so groundless, and so wicked, can make no impression on the Southern Republicans. – They will not be induced by such means to refuse support to a Republican from the North – a man not selected as the Democratic Candidate, because he was a Northern man, but because he was an honest, enlightened, and trust-worthy American citizen; a Republican in principle and practice; and because these were the qualities which elected Jefferson, Madison, Monroe, and Jackson. They happened, it is true, to be Southern men, but it was not because they were so, that the destinies of this country were confided to their hands. Virginia, that has been honored with the Presidency for more than thirty years, will not be so unreasonable as to deny to the Northern Democracy, who secured to her the possession of that high honor, a boon of equal value. Such a spirit of selfishness and ingratitude, does not enter into her proud bosom, nor can it be found any where among the chivalry of the South. It dwells only in the hearts of the narrow minded and factious, who have in view the gratification of their own ambition, or harbor designs of more serious portent, to our beloved country. Under a just administration of the General Government, in all its departments, there is no conflict of interest between the different sections of our country, which can, or ought, to render their present union incompatible with their local freedom and prosperity. On the contrary, the interests embraced under the mantle of our Constitution, are common and pervading. All parts of the Union are interested in an equal and beneficial operation of the Federal Government. It is the interest of all to have peace, internal and external. It is the interests of all to preserve the freedom of intercourse and commerce with foreign nations, and among the several States. All have an interest in the management of the public revenue; in a common currency; in the inviolability of contracts; and in the establishments of mails. No power is delegated to the General Government, in the just exercise of which, the various States of the confederacy have not a common, if not, an equal interest; nor is there one which can be materially abused without injury to all. Even obstructions to trade, and the erection of monopolies are as injurious to the People of the North, as of the South, and may ever be overthrown by the diffusion of correct information among the People. Instead of building up sectional parties, estranging the People of one section from the People of another, and constantly talking of resort to revolution, and violence, to remedy real or imaginary evils; instead of this war against our *homes and our hearths*, the good man and the patriot will rather strive to diffuse through all sections, just views of our institutions, and national policy, and relief will certainly follow from the operations of the public mind, as certainly, as an effect is produced by an adequate cause.

*   *   *

We call upon all; upon the ambitious as well as the deluded, in their zeal of *fanaticism* and party, to look, if they dare, to the calamities which might rush in and deluge this fair land, if their efforts could succeed, and to pause, before it be too late—to remember that the progress of disaffection is often insensible and invisible; and that the mighty spirit which they are attempting to excite, if once roused, can neither be allayed by the cannon or the sword, by law or by blood. It is, fellow citizens, against this dangerous spirit of discontent and division, against these unhallowed attempts to weaken the bands of our glorious Confederacy, that it becomes the duty of every wise man, of every honest man, and of every American, to watch with sleepless vigilance. That watch can only be set in deep and abiding affection to our holy Union, upon the preservation of which depends not only our own liberty and happiness, but that of the world. . . .

We have said, fellow citizens, in a previous part of this Address, that the election of a successor to General Jackson ought to be regarded as one of the most important that had ever occurred in our country; that it involved not only the fate of the republican party and its principles, but the continuation of that wise course of national policy pursued by Gen. Jackson, and upon which his administration has been based. To prove this, will require a brief notice of some of its prominent and leading measures; and those especially which relate to our foreign intercourse, the tariff, internal improvement, and the Bank of the United States.

It will be borne in mind that Gen. Jackson came into the Presidential chair at a moment of deep political excitement, and under very peculiar circumstances. The previous Administration had come into power against the decided wishes of a majority of the American people, and its measures had been strongly reprobated and condemned by the great body of the Republican party. Under its policy, the doctrines of our political fathers had been forgotten or abandoned. Most of the landmarks to the exercise of unlimited power by the General Government had been disregarded or broken down. The doctrine of *expediency and the general welfare* had been openly proclaimed and revived, and under its broad wing power was asserted by its friends to pass laws as unconstitutional in their principles, as they were dangerous in their consequences. It was under such a state of things that the friends to limited Government became alarmed, and Gen. Jackson was called by the people to stay the spirit of innovation, and restore the purity and vigor of our free institutions. He accordingly came forward to devote himself to the service of his country, promote her happiness, and defend her rights. How faithfully did he fulfill the expectations and wishes of his friends, and accomplish the great objects of his election! What were the prominent trails that characterized his Administration both as to its external and internal policy? What its effects and benefits? Will you favor us with a brief review? Towards foreign nations, has it not been distinguished alike with ability, firmness, and moderation? Whilst its primary canon was to do justice to all, and suffer wrong from none, has it not, in the pursuit of a peaceful and liberal policy, studied the interest and regarded the sentiments of every portion of our extended country? Has it not given us peace with every foreign power, secured to us an unrestrained and flourishing and enriching commerce with the civilized nations of the world? Has it not placed our country abroad upon the most elevated and exalted ground, and caused its name to be respected in every quarter of the globe? So, too, in relation to our internal concerns. Has it not pursued a course equally distinguished by wisdom and moderation, and with like results? Has it not secured to all parts of our country internal prosperity, peace, and security? Has not the public debt been extinguished? Have not the great interests of the soil been exempted from unjust systems of taxation, in the shape of Tariffs, and the industry of the whole nation protected and cherished? Indulging no favor or fear, manifesting no preference towards any particular section of our country over another, cherishing no interest separate from the welfare of the whole, has not the Government been administered with a single eye to the benefit and prosperity of all? Has not one of the greatest objects of his civil Magistracy been the protection of the *rights of the States,* and the *integrity of the Union.* Has he not made the Constitution his guide, and brought back the Government to its true fundamental principles? Has he exercised any power not granted? Claimed any doubtful character? Has he not carried out the great principles which he laid down in his first Messages, and fulfilled his promises to the letter? Has he not in fact been true to his high trust, and faithful to his country? But, Fellow Citizens, notwithstanding these wise measures of the Administration, General Jackson, like his great prototype, Mr. Jefferson, was doomed to encounter all the evils and embarrassments of a powerful and talented coalition. From the moment he came into power, there sprung up one of the most determined, persevering, and concentrated oppositions that any country had ever witnessed, and which, in its final progress, became as formidable as it was alarming. For the three first years of the Administration, this opposition failed in its objects and efforts, and sank into a hopeless condition. They have tried all the means which opportunity and their own ingenuity could furnish, to regain their lost power and places; but in vain. Their assaults had fallen harmless upon the shield of the venerable Patriot. The nice measures of his administration, and the virtue and ability with which he had discharged his duty, the benefits secured to his country, and the increasing prosperity and happiness of the People, defeated their schemes and blasted all their hopes. He was too deeply seated in the affections of the People to be shaken. So far, however, the opposition had fought the battle upon political and party grounds, and by political men; but without success. But when parties in pursuit of their own ambitious views cannot obtain a favorite object by direct means, they will seek it through all the indirect experiments which the spirit of the times and chance may throw in their way. When fair and generous means will not avail such a party, they will employ every artifice which is calculated to reward ambition and secure success.

It was accordingly towards the termination of General Jackson's first term, when they had sunk into a desperate condition, that a new ray of hope burst upon them. Then it was that the Bank of the United States was looked to as the means by which to accomplish their ends, and secure their triumph. It was their last hope, and they instantly embraced it. Although the charter of the Bank was not to expire for four years, their policy was to get an application made for its renewal before the period for the re-election of General Jackson should arrive. By this means, the re-election of the President was to be defeated and their triumph secured. They regarded him as in a delicate and dangerous dilemma. His numerous friends were divided upon the subject of the Bank, both on grounds of constitutionality and expediency. Pennsylvania and the West had declared in favor of the Bank, and the entire South against it. If the bill for its re-charter should pass both Houses of Congress, (and the majority for it was believed to be certain,) the President would necessarily be obliged either to approve or to veto it. If he approved, the Bank would succeed in its object of a re-charter, and his friends in the South, (without whose support it was believed, he could not be re-elected,) would, upon principle, desert him. If he disapproved and vetoed, all eyes would be turned to Pennsylvania and the West; and his friends deserting him there, also, his re-election would be hazarded, if not defeated. This was the masterstroke of policy, and it was consequently adopted. They did not calculate, however, upon the application of the veto power. Although they knew the previous convictions of General Jackson as to the inexpediency and unconstitutionality of the Bank, and its dangerous tendencies, although he had expressed his opinions to Congress in the the years '29, '30, and '31, and his determination never to sanction it, yet they did not believe he would refuse to sign any bill that might finally pass for its re-charter; and, by doing so, hazard his re-election. Accordingly, the Bank came forward in 1831, with an application for re-charter. A bill for this purpose passed both Houses, and received the constitutional veto of the President. That these were the objects which influenced the opposition at that day, none, we think, acquainted with the history of those times, can doubt. Indeed, they were charged at the time, and universally believed. But how little did they know of *the individual with whom they were contending!* He met the crisis in a manner worthy of his principles, and vetoed the bill, both as unconstitutional and inexpedient; thus cutting off all hope as to its ever meeting his approbation.

It was then that the Bank took the field openly, and under the banners of a concentrated and powerful opposition, made every effort to defeat the re-election of General Jackson, but without success. The manly and fearless manner in which this duty had been performed, the Roman firmness and honesty of the President, so far from prejudicing him with the great body of the Democracy of Pennsylvania and the West, served only to endear him to them. It was regarded by them and the great majority of his friends, as one of the most important and glorious acts of his administration, and he was re-elected by an overwhelming majority. Of the means resorted to by the Bank to sustain itself, and to influence the Presidential election we shall forbear here to speak. They have long since been exposed to the nation, and must be familiar to all. But the contest did not stop here. There remained still another and severe struggle, which the President and his administration were doomed to encounter, in consequence of the course which he felt it his duty to pursue in relation to this institution. Having considered the fate of the Bank as settled by the decision of the People in his re-election, and that its charter would expire within four years, and seeing in its conduct good reason, as he believed, to justify the measure, the President deemed it his duty as the head of the Executive Department of the Government, to sanction the removal of the public deposites from the Bank of the United States, and their being placed elsewhere for safe keeping by the Secretary of the Treasury, whose duty it was to make such removal whenever in his opinion the public interests required it to be done.

Then was revived that bitter and vindictive war upon the President and his friends, and then commenced those scenes of panic and distress without any parallel in the history of our country, and which threatened, at one time, its peace and security. But to whom were they justly attributable? To whom, but to the opposition and their great ally, the Bank? Was not the object of these efforts and exertions, on the part of the Bank, to desturb and paralyze the ordinary avocations of our citizens, and to take from them the means of carrying them on? Did they not endeavor to arrest the whole course of business in almost every department of society, and to produce that individual ruin and distress which they had predicted would be the consequences of the measures of the President and his administration? Who is there that now doubts it? Did not these efforts not only embarass but expose the government and country to the most imminent perils? Was not the final issue even considered doubtful, and did not the friends of liberty and free government tremble for the result? From a state of things so pregnant with great evils, and forebodings still greater, was it not the firmness and virtue of the President, and those associated with him, that saved us. And how, fellow citizens, was this war against the Chief Magistrate of your country and his administration conducted? In what way did they not assail him? What charges was not made against him? What offence was not imputed to him? He was charged with a violation of the Constitution of his country, and a breach of almost all its laws. With having, in violation of these, assumed the purse as well as the sword. With the destruction of public and private credit. With bringing upon the nation a vitiated currency, and a load of public debt. With the loss of the agricultural products and individual industry of the People. With the decline of our commerce and manufactures, and the destruction of our trade; with having, in fact, disabled, dishonored, and oppressed his country. Indeed not only were the measures of the administration declared to be odious and corrupt, but it was said, that a species of tyranny had sprung up which was desolating the land, and threatened even the liberties of the People. The President was denounced in terms as another Tiberias or Caligula, ready to sacrifice his country at the shrine of his unholy ambition. Was not this the gloomy picture which our opponents gave of the venerable Chief Magistrate and his administration? Was he not moreover charged with having done this to gratify a vindictive and ruthless spirit against a moneyed institution, and in pursuit of a wild and frantic ambition, that knew no limits? Let the candid and liberal of all parties answer? And for what was this load of reproach heaped upon him and his friends? For what, but the firmness, independence, and vigor, with which they had resisted every attempt to recharter an institution against which the Republicans had warred from the moment of its existence, and which Mr. Jefferson, in the evening of his life, declared to be, *"One of the most deadly hostility existing against the principles and form of our Constitution; and which, penetrating by its branches, every part of our Union, and acting by command and in phalanx, might in a critical moment upset the Government."*

Who doubts but that it was because of his uncompromising hostility to this corporation, at a moment when it was waving its dreadful sceptre over the land, and his unshaken constancy in support of the People's cause, that this venerable and noble Patriot, and those associated with him, were arraigned and denounced, before their country and the world, in a manner, unparalleled in the history of any free Government. Yes, Fellow Citizens, it was for these things that an administration, which had secured to its country liberty, and union, and prosperity at home, and respect and peace abroad, was denounced as the most abandoned and profligate upon the earth. Posterity will look back with astonishment (and if possible with incredulity) upon the scenes which for the last three years distracted our country, and wonder how any one man could successfully have resisted the gigantic power of such an Institution, wielded under such circumstances. But what has become of this mass of mischief and ruin which was to proceed from the conduct of the President towards the Bank? Where is that universal bankruptcy which was to overwhelm the People? Where the suspension of the channels of their foreign connections? Where the loss of their trade; the annihilation of her manufactures? Where the deluge of debt; the ruin and divisions of our people? Where the fields without harvest; the merchants without customers? Where now are all these false prophets, with all their dreams of ruin and distress? Have they been fulfilled? Is it true, that we have no free Government to rally around; no country to love? Is our country humbled in the eyes of the world; dishonored and disgraced at home? Is all this true? No. There is not a liberal or candid man who does not and ought not to feel proud and exalted, at the spectacle which his country now presents, both at home and abroad. When was it ever more, if indeed so prosperous? When was public or private credit more stable? Prices so high? The People so happy? When did it ever progress so rapid in wealth, in arts, and useful knowledge, and public spirit, or national character? When so erect among the nations of the earth? Never. Have we not then a right to say, that these are the blessings of a President and Republican administration? These the generous triumphs of Democracy? And what else but the union of the Republican Party and confidence in the virtue and patriotism of Andrew Jackson, the Chief Magistrate of the People's choice, could have done this? And when the political and ambitious men of his day, who have assailed and calumniated him shall be mingled in the dust, with the thousands whose examples they have imitated; when no record shall be found of their memories, or any recollections of their services, this Patriot will be the admiration of every American, and the highest example of political virtue. But, Fellow Citizens, is this the time, happy and prosperous as we are, for the Democracy of the country to disarm? *"The danger is not yet over."* These last words of one of our political Patriarchs, soon after the adoption of the Constitution, may justly be regarded as peculiarly applicable at the present moment: although "Peace waves her hand over us, and Heaven is heaping upon us its blessings with a precious hand," do we not see ambition and party busy in every quarter of our land? If the wise and patriotic measures of the Administration have heretofore afforded our political enemies an opportunity for gross impositions, why shall we not expect them to be revived? What shall we have gained, and what will all our struggles avail, if we suffer ourselves to be divided, and sleep in seeming security, 'till the exertions of our opponents rouses us from our slumbers and convinces us of our mistake.

The Administration has taken ground which the Republicans cannot desert, without a surrender of their principles, and the destruction of themselves. The whole Democracy of the Union has sustained Gen. Jackson and his administration, and now demand that those who are to succeed him should carry out the principles and policy of his Administration. How is this to be done, but by united and harmonious councils and sleepless viglance?

The Democracy of the country must not rest too secure? The prosperity and safety of our country are essentially involved in the issue of the approaching election. We sincerely believe, that upon the preservation of the old Democratic Republican party the prosperity and happiness of our country greatly depend. To you, then, as Republicans, as friends of the Constitution, as supporters of Andrew Jackson and his Administration, and the advocates of union, we make this appeal. We make it not for ourselves alone, but for the Democracy of our country, and we hope not in vain. *Fellow citizens,* are not our opponents already in the field, prepared to battle with desperation? Have not three candidates already been presented to the nation, whose interests are as different as the interests of travellers in a great caravan? May not others soon be added to the list? Are you ignorant of the attempts that are making to get the friends of some of the opposing candidates to unite and co-operate for the purpose of preventing the election of the candidate supported by the Democratic party, or carrying the election to the House of Representatives? Are they not active and indefatigable in their exertions? Will a single vote be withheld, do you imagine, upon their side? Is there not something too, beyond the mere desire to defeat the Republican candidate, wished and expected.

Does not the Bank still exist, and consider the question of its recharter as one open and undecided? Who doubts that the contest is again in some shape to be revived? Is it not looked to as one of the strong holds of our political opponents, which they will never consent to abandon? Does not the Bank itself as undecided, although not openly in "battle array, with banners up?" Are not the sappers at work throughout the land? Why else, to propose extending its loans? Can we forget that its managers justified their curtailments two years ago, on the ground that her charter had but a short time to run, and prudence required them to draw in by degrees, their outstanding debts? Hence, in her application to Congress, in 1831, they say, "unless the question is decided by the present Congress, no definitive action upon it can be expected, until within two years of the expiration of the Charter, a period before which, in the opinion of your memorialists, it is highly expedient, not merely in reference to the institution itself, but to the more important interests of the nation, that the determination of Congress should be known." Again, they say — "If the wisdom of Congress shall determine that the Bank must cease to exist, it is still more important that the country should begin early to prepare for the expected change, and that the institution should have as much time as possible to execute the duty, always a very delicate and difficult one, of aiding the community to seek new channels of business, and by gradual and gentle movements, to press with the least inconvenience on the great interests connected with it." If in 1831 they justified their curtailments on the ground that the charter had but four years to run, how is it that with less than half the time, they are extending their accommodations? Why do those who then justified the curtailment, now justify the loans? Why but that both were intended for recharter? Farther attempts will be made to prolong its existence, if the People fail in the election of a Republican President. Will not the subject of the tariff in a few years, and that of internal improvement be again revived, if our opponents should succeed? Do you not again expect to have your views misrepresented; to hear the same wild denunciations; to witness the same disingenous means; the same artifices; the same stale conceits and misrepresentations resorted to to seduce you from the support of the Democratic candidates, and by division prevent an election by the People. Is not the project meditated to divide the friends of the Republican candidates and conquer under false colors? Are they not making every attempt to produce a schism in our ranks? And is such the time when the Democracy of the country should disarm? Is it not, on the contrary, the time and occasion for every one who would sustain the great principles that are in jeopardy to buckle on his armour and double his diligence and watchfulness? It is by political vigilance alone, that liberty and good government can ever be secured. Is not the alternative now presented either to abandon the principles and doctrines of the Republican party and the benefits of our present administration, or by vigilance and manly firmness maintain them? Was there ever a time in the history of our country since its independence, when vigilance and union on the part of Republicans were more important than the present? Who does not see the mischiefs that may arise from division and discord among ourselves? Shall we exhibit these

scenes of division and weakness for the benefit of our political enemies? If
you do not wish to see these things reacted, lay hold of the opportunity of
preventing it by union and concert. Perfection is in vain sought after in the
works of man. Every inconvenience cannot be avoided. A lesser evil should
sometimes be submitted to in order to avoid one greater and more durable. If
personal animosities or personal preferences exist, ought they not at such a
moment to be sacrificed for the public good? Will not he who refuses to make
such a sacrifice be justly regarded as a suspicious friend, if not a secret foe?
As members of the same great party, ought not our efforts to be directed to
the promotion of harmony and good feeling among ourselves? Let reason and
not denunciation, enlightened zeal and not intolerance, be our weapons, at
least with each other; and let our energies be employed to procure the election of individuals who will carry out the principles and maintain the policy of
the present Administration. It is incumbent, then, upon every Democrat, to
be upon the look out — every man to his post; and let no man slumber, while
the storm threatens, and the vessel is in danger. "Slavery is ever preceded by
sleep." The Republicans of America would be unworthy the high station of
freemen, if, at the call of patriotism, they did not fly to the post of danger, and
offer up, not only their faculties, but their feuds, upon the altar of their common country. Will they remain quiet and inactive amidst all these movements,
and at such a time? Will they, who have so often broken the ranks of their political enemies, suffer them now to erect her proud standard in the field of victory? Never! *Fellow citizens,* our enemies have set us a good example — they
have taught us that in "Union there is strength." Why should we not profit by
it? Why shall we, standing upon the broad and firm basis of the affections of
the People, let our opponents weaken and divide us? If we dislike to increase
and perpetuate the benefits and blessings we enjoy under a republican administration, if our republican institutions and liberties are dear to us, this is the
time to act — this is the time and occasion to meet with vigor and union our
opponents, and place the management of our affairs in the hands of those who
will secure to us these blessings, uninfluenced by ambitious or selfish motives.
Let us, then, discountenance contentions and jealousies between State and
State, and consider ourselves upon this subject, as well as all others of a national character, as citizens of one great and happy nation. Let us promote a
spirit of union among ourselves, without which democracy can never triumph.
Above all, let our councils be unmingled with personal preferences and local
partialities. In this way, and this only, can we expect to conquer. These were
the views with which the Democratic party called the Convention; and it was
to accomplish these desirable objects that that Convention presented to the
country the names of MARTIN VAN BUREN of New York, and RICHARD
M. JOHNSON of Kentucky, two of her distinguished and patriotic fellow
citizens, for the offices of President and Vice President of the United States.
We shall offer you no adulation of their characters, talents, or services. They
have both been long known to the country, and distinguished upon the theatre
of public life; and they have, moreover, declared, in advance, their political
principles, and the course which will govern them, should they be called by

their country to preside over its destinies. It rests with that country to decide. To the good sense of the People we confidently submit the decision; satisfied that whenever they shall be called to choose the sentinels who are to guard her rights and liberties, they will choose with propriety. We only ask them to be united and vigilant.

And now may we not, in conclusion, without giving offence, address ourselves to those Republicans in heart and sentiment, who have heretofore belonged to the Democratic party, and supported the measures of Gen. Jackson's administration, but who feel a personal preference for other individuals than those presented by the Democracy of the country, without any preference for the principles and measures of political opponents. May we not to these address ourselves, and in the spirit of friendship for political friends and associates, earnestly and solemnly propound to them the questions—What is the course you mean to pursue? What your situation? What your great duty on this occasion? Will you calmly and patriotically unite with the great body of your Democratic friends, or will you let your disappointed enthusiasm and personal friendships, or the artifices of designing and ambitious men, drive you into opposition to an Administration which you approve, and to a party with which you have so long acted? Are you prepared, on this trying emergency, to secede from the Republican ranks, and throw yourselves into the arms of your political enemies? These are serious questions, which it is now important you should consider well and appreciate. You must now take a bold and resolute stand in defence of your old principles and friends, or consent to abandon them forever. You have it now in your power to do great good or great mischief. You must now decide, (if your determination is not already formed,) and this decision may be as important to yourselves as your country.

Fellow Citizens, we do not use this language to excite your fear; far from it. The situation of our country, and the purposes and views of our opponents, might strike you with the danger hoped for by the latter, from discord and division among the Republican party. Of that you have heretofore composed an important part. Nothing, however, is more distant from our intention, than to offend, or to attempt to fasten blame upon any. We know that virtuous and enlightened men are often led away under the influence of the best feelings. Indeed, how often are many of those who spread delusion, themselves deluded. Our object is to harmonize and conciliate, not inflame. We feel it to be our duty to make this appeal, and we do it in the kindest spirit. To warn you of the possible dangers to which you are about to expose your country; to exhort you to forget the past in this crisis and moment of danger, and unite in the cause you profess to have so much at heart; above all, to remind you of what you ought now to be sensible, that your alliance is looked to and courted with the utmost solicitude by your enemies, and with the hope of making our political divisions the foundation of their success; not, however, by electing *your friends, but their own.* What, then, are you to gain by such an union? Avoid it, if you would not look back with bitter anguish to the overthrow and ruin of a party, which exists upon the principles which first bound them together, (in spite of difference of opinion, in matters concerning which good men may differ,) ought to be prevented. Ought such dangers to exist, and such a result be put within the reach of chance? Can there, or ought there to be but one answer? We know that among the portion of our Republican friends who have thus estranged themselves from us, and are becoming aliens to our cause, some have done so through *choice,* and many through mistake. To those who have sinned against conviction, we have nothing to say. They must answer that to their country. But to those who have no wish to desert the Republican standard, but who feel the influence of other considerations, (which induce them to consult individual wishes, rather than the concert and harmony of the Party,) we would freely extend the hand of fraternity. With them we hope the present is rather a misunderstanding than a schism; that time and reflection will soon heal it, and effect a perfect reconciliation, and that all collisions and heart burnings will perish in the blaze of better and more generous feelings. If they have been deluded by the artifices of enemies or misguided feeling, now is the time to look for the Republican banner, to see where it is planted, and who surround it. Let them return, then, to the Republican fold of their fathers. We invite them to do so, as brethren; as men united in a common cause for a common good. We invite them to let a common interest bind us together, and to let the only competition be, who shall render most service to the good old Democratic cause; who be most active in promoting the glory and happiness of our doubly blessed country.

A. STEVENSON, of Virginia.
SILAS WRIGHT, of New York.
UPTON S. HEATH, of Maryland.
GARET W. WILLIAMS, of N.
   Hampshire.
ROBT. STRANGE, of North Carolina.
SAML. A CARTWRIGHT, of Mississippi.

Excerpt from a Speech by John Bell
Nashville, July (n.d.), 1835

In their attempt to win over Democratic votes Whig spokesmen such as Tennessee Congressman John Bell violently attacked blind party loyalty, extensive party organization, and the existence of political parties themselves.

*   *   *

I have already said, that *party is* the only source whence destruction awaits our system. I am so fully and solemnly impressed with this truth, that were I asked, what I considered the first great duty of an American statesman, at this time, I would say, guard against the excesses of party. If I were asked what I considered the second, I would answer, guard the excesses of party—and were I asked the third, I would still say guard the excesses of party. Every thing else may be safely and confidently left to the free and natural action of our system. These are the dangers to be apprehended from the spirit of party, in its ordinary modes and forms. But when its spirit shall receive an organic existence—thus giving rise to a system within a system, not subordinate, but superior to and designed to control the natural operation of the regular, lawful and constitutional government of the country; when thus organized, and, I may say, personified spirit of party, no longer fed and sustained by the only safe and legitimate aliments of principle and a high souled emulation and competition for the honors of a free country, but, addressed to and relying for its support, upon the selfish and mercenary passion of our nature shall become the prime interest, and the country but a secondary one; when it shall be thought more perilous to a man's fame and prospects, to desert such a party, than to conspire against the interests, the glory and the liberties of the country; when a decent regard to consistency—when the first principles of a free government—when the sacred obligations of truth and justice are required to be yielded up a sacrifice to the *unity* of such a party, then, I proclaim to you, and to the world, that the spirit of evil which is in party is predominant. Those who would guard the public liberty and our free institutions from pollution and overthrow, must range themselves under a different standard. When *party* is the watchword and the ensign of those who fight for the spoils, the warning voice of patriotism says to every freeman, to every White man, inscribe your country upon your banner, and *"in hoc vince."*

THE VOTES IN THE 1836 ELECTION

| STATES | POPULAR VOTE | | | ELECTORAL VOTES FOR | | | | | | | | |
| | | | | PRESIDENT | | | | | VICE-PRESIDENT | | | |
	Martin Van Buren Democrat	Whig Candidate	Name of the Whig Candidate	Martin Van Buren	William H. Harrison	Hugh L. White	Daniel Webster	Willie P. Mangum	Richard M. Johnson	Francis Granger	John Tyler	William Smith
Maine..........	22,990	15,239	Harrison	10	—	—	—	—	10	—	—	—
New Hampshire..	18,722	6,228	Harrison	7	—	—	—	—	7	—	—	—
Vermont........	14,039	20,996	Harrison	—	7	—	—	—	—	7	—	—
Massachusetts...	33,542	41,287	Webster	—	—	—	14	—	—	14	—	—
Rhode Island....	2,964	2,710	Harrison	4	—	—	—	—	4	—	—	—
Connecticut.....	19,291	18,749	Harrison	8	—	—	—	—	8	—	—	—
New York......	166,815	138,543	Harrison	42	—	—	—	—	42	—	—	—
New Jersey......	25,592	26,137	Harrison	—	8	—	—	—	—	8	—	—
Pennsylvania....	91,475	87,111	Harrison	30	—	—	—	—	30	—	—	—
Delaware.......	4,153	4,733	Harrison	—	3	—	—	—	—	3	—	—
Maryland.......	22,168	25,852	Harrison	—	10	—	—	—	—	—	10	—
Virginia........	30,261	23,468	White	23	—	—	—	—	—	—	—	23
North Carolina..	26,910	23,626	White	15	—	—	—	—	15	—	—	—
South Carolina*.	—	—		—	—	—	—	11	—	—	11	—
Georgia........	22,104	24,876	White	—	—	11	—	—	—	—	11	—
Alabama........	20,506	15,612	White	7	—	—	—	—	7	—	—	—
Mississippi......	9,979	9,688	White	4	—	—	—	—	4	—	—	—
Louisiana.......	3,653	3,383	White	5	—	—	—	—	5	—	—	—
Arkansas........	2,400	1,238	White	3	—	—	—	—	3	—	—	—
Kentucky.......	33,435	36,955	Harrison	—	15	—	—	—	—	15	—	—
Tennessee.......	26,129	36,168	White	—	—	15	—	—	—	—	15	—
Missouri........	10,995	7,337	White	4	—	—	—	—	4	—	—	—
Ohio...........	96,948	105,404	Harrison	—	21	—	—	—	—	21	—	—
Indiana........	32,478	41,281	Harrison	—	9	—	—	—	—	9	—	—
Illinois..........	18,097	14,983	Harrison	5	—	—	—	—	5	—	—	—
Michigan.......	7,332	4,045	Harrison	3	—	—	—	—	3	—	—	—
	762,978	736,250		170	73	26	14	11	147	77	47	23

* Electors were appointed by the legislature.

Election of 1840

WILLIAM NISBET CHAMBERS is Professor of History at Washington University. He is the author of Political Parties in a New Nation: The American Experience, 1776-1809.

Election of 1840

by *William Nisbet Chambers*

Anyone who knows a smattering of American history can recall at least something of the passionate presidential contest of 1840. It has engrossed professional historians, although many of them have apparently underestimated its significance. Beyond its outward folderol, the campaign has an important place in the whole course of American political development.

Perhaps the candidates remain a little vague in popular recollection. Neither the incumbent Democratic President, Martin Van Buren, nor the Whig challenger, William Henry Harrison, were statesmen of the highest rank, despite Van Buren's real abilities. Yet the slogans, the nicknames, the general excitement still echo at least in sketchy memory —

> Van, Van, Van,
> Van is a used-up man.
>
> Tippecanoe and Tyler too,
> Tippecanoe and Tyler too!
>
> Farewell, dear Van,
> You're not our man;
> To guide the ship,
> We'll try old Tip.

If literate Americans cannot descry deep meaning in such rhetoric today, it was not much different in 1840 — even though, on examination, the rhetoric offers a key to the election and indeed to the times. The jingle-coiners, and the

643

managers and publicists of the Whig campaign in general, planned the slogans' obscurity. They were appealing to an unprecedented number of potential voters; indeed, the fact that more citizens went to the polls than ever before in a presidential election was a salient feature of the contest. The Whigs were also an underdog party, often on the unpopular side of issues, and now they wanted to win. Their directory avoided divisive questions of public policy as far as they could, and relied on a campaign of slogan, symbol, and shout, of "Huzzah!" When the Democrats, although they dispensed their nonsense too, tried to respond with something like cool reason, they failed to engage the hearts if not the minds of a sufficient number of the electorate.

For sheer excitement the nearest precedent to 1840 was the colorful campaign of Andrew ("Old Hickory") Jackson against John Quincy Adams in 1828. There are important similarities between the two elections. In a sense the Whigs of 1840 only elaborated and improved on techniques that had been explored in 1828, when the Jackson men or nascent Democrats had also devised a new style, "hurrah" appeal, but the Harrison men went much further. For vilification and vituperation—simply as an all-out, dirty campaign—the Whig onslaught of 1840 probably surpassed 1828, and may well stand unmatched except for 1884, when both Grover Cleveland and James G. Blaine were painted over with the tar brush.

More profoundly, the Harrison campaign plan of 1840 exhibits important parallels with certain modern, highly professional campaigns. For example, Dwight D. Eisenhower in 1952 and Richard M. Nixon in 1968 were, in large measure, sold to the electorate by sophisticated communications techniques, in what might be called a "merchandizing" style. All three undertakings relied heavily on adroit use of communications media, on "packaging," on shaping and disseminating a persona in the strict sense of "the social facade an individual assumes" on creating a public-relations image. Every politician of consequence has a public image, of course; the question is how nearly that image represents the real man. The Whig managers of 1840 were the new professionals of their party, and they made resourceful use of the proliferating mass media of the time. In the process they created a political persona for William Henry Harrison that had little to do with actuality. They called it "Old Tip," surrounded it with various trappings such as log cabins and cider barrels, offered it as packaged charisma, as the representative and savior of the common man, and sold it to the masses.

During the election of 1828 virtually every change was rung on the theme of Jackson as the man of the people, of Jackson the hero, of Jackson as savior. Yet "Old Hickory" was an authentic military hero and, as events proved, a highly competent political leader. By contrast Harrison was a minor military figure, and a folk hero only as the result of Whig campaign imagery. The Harrison crusade lacked television, but it "McLuhanized" the voters nonetheless. The Whig publicists also successfully created a marvelously ingenious negative image of Martin Van Buren. The Democrats cried fraud, but they were unable to stage an effective counter-movement.

In addition to its merchandizing aspects, the Whig endeavor of 1840 also exhibited a "militia" pattern of campaigning—a term put forth by Richard J. Jensen. Again and again thousands of voters were packed together in mass rallies; and thousands marched, marched, marched in endless parades. All of this was the product of genuine popular enthusiasm for "Old Tip," but it was also the result of careful organization and mobilization by local political party cadres. By 1840 party organization had reached previously unprecedented levels. If the party was not yet a machine, it could muster a political drill that matched or over-matched the uniformed militia of the time. To rally the faithful, win recruits, and mobilize the voters—such was the militia style which the Harrison men brought to near perfection.

The vacuousness of much of the Whig propaganda and the public response raise the question of voter rationality. The issue can best be considered in its total context, in terms not only of the campaign and election as a whole, but of their antecedents. At the moment it is enough to observe that there was at least a political rationale in the jingles, the log cabins, the marching political legions, the rhetoric; it worked. Long out of power, the varied politicians who shaped the new Whig party were determined to stage a breakthrough, and they planned accordingly.

Beneath the strategy was more than just political gamesmanship. The contest came as a part of, and was in large measure the product of, an emergent political democracy. It followed on a steady enlargement of the right to vote, a sharp rise in actual voting in national elections, long strides in political party development, and a trend toward closely contested elections in all parts of the nation. The Image Campaign of 1840 also set a number of precedents in party practices, many of which have endured to the present.

Political democracy did not spring full grown from the opening paragraphs of the Declaration of Independence, or even from the Revolution itself. Politics in early America were in effect a variant of the "Radical" Whig politics of England at the time, as Bernard Bailyn and others have shown. In the eyes of most informed men, sound government was epitomized in the so-called "balanced" Constitution, with its organic mixture of "monarchical," "aristocratical," and "democratical" elements. Even after 1776 what J. R. Pole has called a "rather attenuated and colonialized version of the English constitution" persisted as the ideal, despite the liberalization of constitutional forms in certain states. Social structure and political culture, meanwhile, sustained a politics of deference, of habits of subordination, in most parts of the new republic. Plain men looked to gentlemen of superior status, to established families, and to local notables as obvious candidates for office. Ordinary voters, the "democratical" element of the polity, certainly had to be taken into account, but they seldom expected to send one of their own to the state house. Despite Thomas Jefferson's bold, equalitarian formulations in the Declaration of 1776, democracy as the nineteenth century was to know it was simply not in the minds of men, or at least of influential men.

In the long run the new liberal ethos was to reshape old Whig politics. The creation by the Constitution in 1789 of the first truly national political arena, the rivalry of Federalist and Jeffersonian-Republican political parties, the liberal thrust of Jeffersonian appeals to the voters, the critical election of 1800 and the belated efforts of young Federalists to adapt Republican electioneering techniques thereafter, the admission of new western states, the political mobilization of reform movements that emerged in several states after the depression of 1819, advancing urbanization and improvements in transportation—these and other factors undercut deference patterns and promoted the rise of a liberal, increasingly democratic polity. What Louis Hartz has called the "liberal tradition" began to fall into place as the capstone of a distinctively American political culture. Its individualism, its emphasis on Lockean atomism rather than on social strata in an organic society, its equalitarian premises and promises, became the new order of the day.

Things moved more rapidly in the states than they did on the national scene. In effect, the advent of the new popular politics on the national level was announced by the election of Andrew Jackson to the Presidency in 1828, although he was not responsible for the phenomenon.

His humble origins, his frontier experience, and his democratic rhetoric made Jackson a ready symbol. It was easy to ignore the fact that as a master of the Hermitage, and of more than a hundred slaves and a stable of blooded horses, he was a regional nabob back in Tennessee. He expressed, and his managers expressed for him, the aggressive individualism that was part of the spirit of the time, and its bumptious, democratic equalitarianism as well. Students ranging from Tocqueville in the 1830's to Arthur Schlesinger, jr., Marvin Meyers, and Lee Benson in our own times have seen the decade Jackson dominated as an era of equalitarianism. The assertion that one man was as good as another, a notion that Richard Hofstadter maintains signalled "the decline of the gentleman," and the mystique of "the plain people," are common themes, although scholars are hardly agreed on all their implications and nuances. The thrust of equalitarianism, moreover, was not the peculiar property of Jackson and the Democrats. It was also expressed by many leaders of the anti-Masonic movement, for example, and by the nascent labor movement and miscellaneous reformers. Yet the figure of Jackson remained a focal point.

Equalitarianism in the Jacksonian perspective did not necessarily imply actual equality of condition. It was rather the assertive *claim* to equality that was the watchword. Indeed much of the politics of the era appears to have been as much symbolic and expressive as it was oriented to material interests. Often politics seemed to be a way of giving vent to hopes or hostilities, a kind of political displacement in the face of equalitarian promises which were not always fulfilled. Thus the attack on the "monopoly," "Monster" Bank of the United States, and the radical Jacksonian proposal for a specie or "Hard Money" currency, were great symbolic issues, although specific interests and policy questions were involved also. In a time of change, uncertainty, and stress in which old social bonds and assumptions had given way, men in an increasingly competitive society might be expected to look either backward to a simpler, presumably halcyon, Jeffersonian Arcadia, or forward to gain, capitalist enterprise, and advancement. To some men equality might mean at least a rough similarity of situation with that of their neighbors; to others it might mean opportunity to get ahead by trading or speculating in land, or going into business on their own. In many cases the same individual might look both ways, simultaneously indulging a nostalgia for the past and entertaining heady hopes for the future.

In any case, the equalitarian theme dominated in politics. Most elected and appointive officials, at the higher levels at least, were men of some substance and status, and of course men of ambition. Yet they could no longer count on established deference patterns to give them preferment, except for certain enclaves, mostly in the South. They had to run hard for office if they wanted it; and working politicians knew it was their business to curry votes. Even before the Image Campaign, nicknames bespoke the easy manners of plain citizens with statesmen or politicians. There was "Old Hickory," of course, "Old Bullion" Benton, "Old Tippecanoe," and even "Old Kinderhook" Van Buren, after the town in which he was born. (The initials of his nickname helped to establish "O.K." in the American language.) Who can imagine voters, in the days of deference, being urged to go all out for "Old Jack" Adams, or "Old Tom" Jefferson?

The long advance of democracy was marked by gradual liberalization of suffrage requirements. In keeping with English precedent and the old Whig emphasis on a demonstrable stake in the community, the colonies had generally required a man to own a freehold in land as a prerequisite to voting. The Revolution brought the first wave of suffrage extension when two states admitted owners of property other than land, and four accepted a taxpaying qualification. In the late 1700's and the first three decades of the nineteenth century, another wave of reform brought six more states to taxpaying-only as a requirement; and three states gave the vote to all adult white males. In all but two of the states that had established tax requirements, moreover, the tax was compulsory, or so small or so widely ignored that virtual adult male suffrage prevailed; and the two exceptions soon established adult male suffrage. Finally, of the thirteen new states that were admitted from 1791 through 1837 all but one (Louisiana) granted legal or virtual adult white male suffrage in their original constitutions, and by 1840 only three (Rhode Island, Virginia, and Louisiana) of the twenty-six states of the Union did not offer legal or actual white manhood suffrage.

The secular trend in voting was, in Chilton Williamson's language, "from property to democracy." Suffrage reforms expressed a new state of mind, the emergence of a liberal, democratic political culture that would base voting rights on individuals rather than on amounts or classes of property ownership. Nearly all of the important extensions of suffrage, moreover, were accomplished before the sway of Jacksonian democracy. What the Jacksonians did was to build on the enlarged suffrage and profit from it in 1828, as the Whigs were to do in 1840.

It was, to be sure, a white adult male democracy. Women, all but a few Negroes even in the free states, Indians, and minors were excluded. There was some agitation for votes for women and Negroes, but neither major party took it up and by the 1840's, blacks had the vote only in Maine, New Hampshire, Vermont, and Massachusetts. An estimated nine-tenths of the black men who lived in the North resided in states where they were barred from the polls. Even so, the extension of voting rights was unprecedented. A brief comparison with British experience is suggestive. The bitterly contested Reform Bill of 1832, virtually the last great achievement of English Whiggery, expanded the British electorate from about a half million to about 720,000 in a total population of some twenty-four million. In 1828 the United States held its first million-vote presidential election, in which 1,155,022 voters actually went to the polls. In 1832 the number of voters climbed to 1,217,691 out of a total population of about thirteen million. Britons who were *entitled* to vote constituted about 10 per cent of adult males before 1832, and about 14 per cent thereafter. Americans who *did* vote in the presidential contest of 1828 exceeded 57 per cent of all adult white males, and future years were to bring out even larger proportions.

Indeed, another feature of the age of equalitarianism was an unprecedented measure of participation in national elections. Even before the liberalization of suffrage, actual voting was determined more by interest or lack of interest than it was by legal qualifications. A sampling of participation levels from the 1790's to the 1830's, based on data gathered by J. R. Pole, is revealing (see Table 1). In five sample states—Massachusetts, New Hampshire, Pennsylvania, Virginia, and North Carolina—the trend of participation is generally upward, with some variation. Although two of the five states restricted the suffrage (Massachusetts until 1821 and Virginia throughout the period), substantial participation appears early in Massachusetts while the levels for Virginia remain low. The explanation probably lies not only in suffrage restrictions, but also in the fact that deference, low levels of political competition, and fragmentary political organization hung on longer in the Old Dominion than in the Bay State. The clear leaders in participation were New Hampshire and Pennsylvania. From the beginning these two states had ranked among the least deferential, most "liberal" commonwealths of the Union.

Notably, peak turnouts tended to come in state contests rather than in presidential elections everywhere except Virginia. The pattern was typical of other states. In a compilation of record turnouts before 1824 in all of the twenty-four states except South Carolina, Richard P. McCormick has shown that records were set in state contests in nineteen states and in presidential or congressional races in only four. Indeed, a variety of evidence makes it clear that the political involvements of most Americans in the early Republic were mainly local. From the founding years through the quarter-century of the Virginia dynasty of Jefferson, Madison, and Monroe, the Executive Mansion and Washington politics in general seemed remote to most men at the grass roots. Thus Pennsylvania achieved a turnout of 71 per cent in a gubernatorial contest in 1808, and Massachusetts a record of 67 per cent in a race for governor in 1812. Not until 1840, however, did either state match these figures in a presidential election.

Such comparisons make it clear that a profound change was wrought in the years from 1824 to 1840. Stimulated in part by Andrew Jackson's charisma, but furthered even more by competitive national political parties, a new concern with national political life emerged. On the wave of this growing sense of involvement, participation in presidential elections rose from about 27 per cent in 1824 to nearly 58 per cent in 1836; and in 1840 turnout was to reach 80 per cent. Another new element had appeared on the American political scene. From one point of view it was the popularization of national politics, the active engagement of the minds and hearts of men in national affairs, national candidates, national parties. Against the background of previous substantial participation in state and local elections, it was also the nationalization of popular politics, the focus of attention on the national as well as local political arenas. Popularization of national politics or nationalization of popular politics, this was the meaning of much that has been called Jacksonian democracy. Ironically, the campaign of 1840 was its apogee.

A major impetus for democratic participation, and vehicles for participation too, came with the advent of new, national political parties. The Federalists and Republicans of the 1790's had emerged in the face of disparagement of the idea of party; and they had fallen into desuetude during James Monroe's Presidency. Important as the first American party system was in virtually creating the forms of modern political parties, that system was national only in a limited sense. One or the other of the parties tended to be dominant in particular states; and competition was limited accordingly. By 1816 the Federalists were scarcely able to give the dominant Republicans a contest in the national arena; and soon the Republican phalanx broke up into local and personal fragments of the sort that characterized the presidential election of 1824. In the contest for the Presidency that followed, the movement toward new party formations was begun.

It was some time, however, before the second American party system took shape. Skilled managers like Martin Van Buren of New York, able wire-pullers and publicists like Amos Kendall and Francis Preston Blair of Kentucky, editor-organizers like Issac Hill of New Hampshire, a self-styled "efficient friend" in Pennsylvania named James Buchanan, the influential Thomas Ritchie of Virginia, bold leaders like Thomas H. Benton in far western Missouri—these and countless lesser workers brought the loose assemblage of Jackson men to the status of a national party. Yet progress was slow and erratic. Party development emerged out of a variety of state and local conditions, as McCormick has observed, as well as out of the contest for the Presidency. One can scarcely speak of a Democratic party before 1830 or 1832; and party formation came as late as 1836 or 1840 in several states. Forever after, the national Democracy was to show the federal, fragmented structure of its origins.

Party development was even slower among the opposition. The followers of Adams and Henry Clay joined in a National Republican proto-party in 1832; but in several states the Anti-Masonic party provided the chief opposition to Old Hickory. When the Whig party finally emerged, it too was federal in its structure and even more heterogeneous than the Jacksonian coalition. It was a melange of Adams men, old National Republicans like Clay and Daniel Webster and their followers, remnants of the anti-Masonic movement, and new leaders like Thurlow Weed and William H. Seward of New York and Thaddeus Stevens of Pennsylvania whose average age in 1840 was forty-three as compared to Clay's sixty-three. The Whig ranks were also swelled by renegade Jacksonians, and briefly by John C. Calhoun and his coterie. Not until the mid-1830's did a Whig party structure emerge, however, and in many areas it was not really effective until 1840. Yet the party announced its name in 1834, and by 1836 all but four of the twenty-six states exhibited some measure of rivalry between Whigs and Democrats.

Unlike its predecessor, the second party system was truly national in that it came to generate keen competition throughout the Union. Certainly by 1840 there was no captive section—no rockribbed New England, no monolithic East, no solid South, no united West. Uniquely in 175 years of party warfare, the battle for the Presidency and other offices was waged in close balance in every section and in nearly every state—a situation that may be about to recur only in our own times. This kind of competition stimulated voting turnout even further, and both competition and turnout set new records in 1840 (see Table 2). In all but four states, moreover, the presidential outpouring of 1840 surpassed or (in one) equalled previous high levels of participation in state contests.

The new parties were also channels for mass participation in themselves. Organization in the second party system far surpassed anything the Republicans or Federalists had achieved, although the early parties had had their organizational geniuses too; and organization meant people in action. The United States in 1840 was still overwhelmingly rural and agricultural: people who lived in "urban places" of twenty-five hundred or more constituted only 10.8 per cent of the total population. Yet, as Richard C. Wade and others have shown, it was the cities and towns that provided the major synapses of political leadership, as they also served as the centers of economic development. From New York or Harrisburg, Cincinnati or St. Louis, and a host of lesser towns, men and messages went out into the countryside, as did newspapers, pamphlets, and other propaganda. Local politicians played their part, but when a major party figure came to speak in a village or country grove, it was an event. Thus young Tom Sawyer (or young Sam Clemens) was disappointed when Senator Benton came up from St. Louis to speak in Hannibal, and he "was not twenty-five feet high, nor even anywhere in the neighborhood of it!" Yet as George Caleb Bingham's paintings have shown so vividly, countrymen also flocked to meetings and turned out at the polls; participation was general. In the absence of cinema, radio, television, chautauqua, or much in the way of theater, even in the cities, politics was antidote to rural isolation and tedium. It brought color and drama to often drab lives, a participatory form of communication and entertainment.

A sophisticated age can hardly imagine the degree to which party was a club, a militia, and a church. Untold thousands of the faithful followed the party press, attended mass rallies or local conventions, wore campaign emblems, argued with their neighbors, praised their favorite candidates, and joined in party life in other ways. Parties, their leaders, and even their platforms offered new loyalties. "Regularity" became the order of the day, as men proudly carried their Democratic or Whig allegiance to the grave. One of the costs of assertive individualism and equalitarianism, of breaking old social ties, was the threat of dislocation or anomie: no wonder men attached themselves to party standards and joined in party rituals. A piece of nineteenth-century doggerel suggests the mood surrounding the impulse to participate.

> Oh, they marches in parades and they gets up hurrahs,
> And they tramps through the mud for the good old cause.

To these forces encouraging high voter participation—an extended suffrage, the decline of the political culture of deference and the rise of a liberal-democratic ethos, close competition in elections—must be added party organization and party activity. Indeed, if one examines voting turnout state-by-state in the six presidential elections from 1824 to 1844, encompassing the two decades of the nationalization of popular politics (see Table 2), a crucial relationship appears. Although turnout is closely connected with competition in successive elections in each state, the association is by no means invariant. In all but three of the twenty-six states where presidential electors were chosen by popular vote in relevant elections, however, the establishment of national party structures within the state is marked by a spurt in voting participation. Declining competition and other factors could bring a decline in turnout thereafter, and local events and situations at particular times probably account for other variations in turnout. Even so, scrutiny of the data suggests not only the relevance of the conventional hypothesis that competition stimulated turnout, but also that party action and interaction as such was an important, independent factor. The role of party itself in promoting participation seems to be clear.

Nevertheless, 1840 was a banner year for voting everywhere, and there was still another element involved. This was the great Whig campaign and the events that preceded it.

If the Democrats constituted a broad, pluralistic, often-contradictory political combination typical of American major parties, the Whigs were an even more motley lot. Both parties were pragmatic formations aimed at attracting as many votes as possible in order to win office and power; both, if they were not "catch-all" parties, were "catch-much" parties. Early in 1839 a young Whig activist from Buffalo, Millard Fillmore, could well ask the question—

> Into what crucible can we throw this heterogeneous mass of old national republicans, and revolting Jackson men; Masons and anti-Masons; Abolitionists, and pro-Slavery men; Bank men & anti-Bank men with all the lesser fragments that have been, from time to time, thrown off from the great political wheel in its violent revolutions, so as to melt them down into one mass of pure Whigs of undoubted good metal?

It was the perdurable problem of the Whig party, and it was the particular problem of 1840 as well. In considerable part the campaign the Whigs prepared was designed to meet it.

If there was a Jacksonian persuasion, there was a general Whig persuasion also; the two parties were not cut from identical cloth. Men like Jackson, Nicholas Biddle of the Bank of the United States, Clay, Webster, Van Buren, Benton, Silas Wright of New York, Calhoun, and an array of lesser figures had defined a series of issues and given them partisan raiment. Editors at the national capital such as Joseph Gales and William W. Seaton of the *National Intelligencer* (Whig), and Frank Blair (Jackson called him Bl'ar) at the *Globe* (Democratic) gave the parties something like an ideological dress. Their utterances were copied and embroidered on by an array of local, partisan papers and carried to the people. Interminable partisan speeches in Congress, often lasting over three hours, were also spread interminably across the country in fat pamphlets, which presumably were read by the faithful.

However, it has proved difficult for scholars to determine just who wore what party colors, and why. Brahmin historians of the nineteenth century thought they knew the answer: all respectable men voted Whig, and Democrats were rabble. More carefully researched studies by progressive historians from Charles A. Beard to Arthur Schlesinger, jr. believed the distinction emerged from economic group interests or social class; and many of the issues of the era did involve different ideas of social and economic arrangements. More recent studies have tended to focus on broad outlooks or perspectives — on the nostalgia for Arcadia or the prospect of enterprise, or on ethnic, religious, and cultural identifications. There is as yet no scholarly consensus, and more research and analysis is needed. The problem is made more intricate by the different political positions men of similar economic interest or social status apparently took in different states or localities.

Even so, some patterns may be discerned. Nearly everywhere by the late 1830's at least, the wealthiest men appear to have been Whigs. Frank O. Gatell has shown that the thousand richest citizens of New York City were overwhelmingly of that persuasion, particularly after the controversy over the national Bank and the currency issue had shown where most leaders of either party stood. As Edward Pessen points out in a summary of recent research, however, it does not follow that the major parties were class parties. If the Whigs had the support of only the wealthy voters and their retinues, they would have been overwhelmed in every election; and there were wealthy men among the Democrats too. Several studies indicate that the Whigs had as much, and probably more, support among urban laborers than the Democrats did, although again the pattern appears to have varied from time to time or from city to city. In many communities, moreover, voters of modest means tended to divide their allegiances in about the same proportions as the more affluent.

There were, of course, other possible sources of division. In New York state, Lee Benson found ethnic background, religious affiliation, and place of birth to be the major correlates of voting preferences. Thus "Yankee," Huguenot, and Negro natives, and newly-arrived English, Scottish, Protestant-

Irish, and Welsh immigrants tended to vote Whig; by contrast, Catholic-Irish, French Canadian, and new German immigrants were generally Democratic. In addition, Benson argues, different outlooks and life-styles characterized voters for the competing parties. Whigs were inclined to hold "puritanical attitudes," and exalt piety, sobriety, steady habits, and thrift; the Democrats appealed more readily to men who liked to brag of affection for "hard liquor, fast women, and horses, and strong racy language." The distinction is suggestive even outside of urbanized New York, although not all Whigs were pure moralists, of course, or all Democrats from the Tenderloin.

Other common alignments appear to have emerged beyond New York. Donald B. Cole for New Hampshire, and John Vollmer Mering for Missouri, have found similar patterns for the two states. Generally, the older, well-established, commercially active, more prosperous, lowland communities, connected to the larger world by good roads, access to the sea, or major river routes, tended to be Whig. On the other hand, the poorer, more sparsely populated, and more isolated areas tended to be Democratic. Other variables were involved, at least in New Hampshire: whether a town had a Congregational (Whig) or a Baptist (Democratic) church, whether it had a lively newspaper (probably Whig), or whether it was growing fast (probably Democratic). By and large well-established centers took on a Whig coloration; areas that were out of the mainstream were likely to be Democratic. The pattern, with variations, seems to hold for a number of other states. Charles Sellers has found similar configurations in much of the South, where complexes of town bankers, merchants, and lawyers, linked with planters or "cotton capitalists," provided vital leadership for the powerful southern Whig party. Virginia and North Carolina were exceptions, however, and South Carolina was always a special case.

It remains uncertain whether the sources of such alignments are to be found in market connections or the lack of them, in predilections toward enterprise or Arcadia, in steady or looser habits, in ethnic or religious ties, or in other factors. Indeed the pattern may not hold up as research is pursued in other states. Yet the distinction between being closely related to the larger world or not, of what might be called cosmopolitan or provincial relationships, appears to be useful.

By the late 1830's party loyalties also appear to have been handed down for generations. In a study of presidential votes from the mid-1830's to the early 1850's, Walter Dean Burnham notes that throughout the era—

> [T]he Democrats tended to carry the upland, interior, watershed, and frontier counties, while the Whigs tended to carry—again with exceptions frequently depending upon local political situations—the tidewater, the lakeshore, the seacoast, the lowland, the riverbottom, and the well-settled counties.

Again Democratic counties were likely to be relatively underpopulated, with low income levels; and the big cities tended to divide evenly between Democrats and their opponents.

By and large, the voting patterns of the late 1830's corresponded at least roughly with the general persuasions of the different parties. The conflicts of issues that helped to form these policies are familiar. Many of them derived from the American System, which Henry Clay had proposed in the hope of promoting capitalist development. Its central features were a protective tariff; federal expenditures for roads, harbors, river-development, and other internal improvements; and a national bank to provide business capital and a stable common currency. When Jackson attacked Clay's conception, the battle was joined. When he went on to destroy the Bank of the United States, in which Clay, Webster, and many other Whigs had material as well as ideological interests, the great symbolic issue was made.

There were innumerable shadings. Men like Benton of Missouri, so-called "Democrats-in-principle," attacked Nicholas Biddle's "Monster" Bank because they opposed banks and paper currency in general. Others, perhaps "Democrats-by-trade," fought the "Monopoly of Chestnut Street" because they wanted state banks to provide easy currency and credit free of control by a central bank — "liberated capitalism," as Hofstadter has put it — and thereby extend entrepreneurial opportunities. Some Jacksonians managed to remain at least a little ambiguous, while most nascent Whigs supported the Bank and its recharter. Jackson, spurred and supported by "Hard Money" Democrats, nevertheless withdrew the federal deposits from the Bank, placed them in state banks instead, and then moved on to attack banks of issue and paper money generally. The conflict thereupon reached its practical and symbolic zenith. Many conservative Democrats, both in the North and South, broke with the Democrats, and formed the body of the "revolting Jackson men" who swelled the Whig ranks.

Filling out Jackson's "third term," Martin Van Buren took the issue further. In the face of economic depression and of Whig clamor for a restoration of the Bank, and for cancellation of the Specie Circular which required hard money in payment for the public lands, Van Buren called instead for a federal depository or "Independent Treasury" for the Government's funds. Reaction was sharp: Millard Fillmore's "political wheel" made another of its "violent revolutions," and spun off more conservative Democrats to join the Whigs.

Through it all the Jacksonian image took on a vaguely radical shade, despite the importance of *arriviste*, liberal capitalist elements. Democratic radicalism seemed to deepen when the party in New York City reached an accomodation with "Locofoco," so-called "Workingmen," and reform elements; and in 1840 Van Buren made an open bid to wage earners by shortening the working day for federal employees to ten hours. Beyond the cities, many Democrats appeared in the dress of agrarian friends of the plain countryman. Thus Benton spoke for much of the West when he pressed for reductions in the price of public lands and for pre-emption by settlers of occupied plots, proposals Van Buren was to endorse. Radicalism of the Jacksonian hue had far more in common with Jefferson or latter-day Populists than it did with Marx or even the impending Chartist movement in England. However, it was generally middle class rather than lower class or proletarian, and it tended to emphasize opportunity or even opportunism rather than fundamental change. Most Whigs, meanwhile, seemed to appear as prophets of gain, and of established rather than fledgling capitalism. They were seen as "selfish" by their enemies, although there were humanitarian reformers among them too, and as "responsible" by their friends. In the partisan arena, it was easy to damn all Whigs as a combination of nabobs and Scrooges, and all Democrats as Locofoco radicals.

Whether all this met the test of social reality is all but irrelevant. Men act in politics on what they perceive, and what they are persuaded of. The image and the general tendency of each party seemed to fit reasonably well with the kind of community where each found its readiest strength in many states. Each party's dress appears to have been broadly consistent with the company it kept.

Other events had contributed to the complex colorations the parties took on. In the confrontation with Calhoun on the tariff, nullification, and the Force Bill in 1832 and 1833, intensified as it was by South Carolina fears for its slave system, Jackson had emerged as a firm defender of the Union. Yet there was a strong states' rights tradition among the Democrats too. As Calhoun had broken with the party on the issues of slavery, minority interests against majority rule, presidential power, and state sovereignty, so he was able to return in 1837 on the basis of some understanding on states' rights and other issues. Meanwhile the Whigs were divided between their nationalist core and their states' rights minority. Even in the South many leading Whigs were not particularly vehement about state power, although few were self-conscious nationalists either.

In the rising tension that emerged in the 1830's between slavery and abolition, the moderate elements of each party followed a cautious course. There were abolitionists among the Whigs, or at least "abolitionized" Whigs, as one New York party worker put it, as well as pro-slavery men; and the generally pro-slavery Democrats had their nascent free-soilers. But in effect the second American party system lived by avoiding divisive sectional issues, and the most potentially disruptive issue was slavery. By going along with the rising racism of most whites in both sections of the country, and by preventing abolitionist petitions from being received in Congress, party leaders avoided possibly destructive conflict. The House maintained a "gag rule" against the petitions from 1836 to 1844, and the Senate simply tabled them. When the slavery conflict came to a head two decades later, it was to destroy the second party system.

Such were the two parties: broad, heterogeneous, vote-catching combinations, not profoundly different but divergent enough so that most men who cared could know their colors, their general persuasion. For three presidential elections the Jacksonians had maintained the ascendency, but 1837 brought an event that offered the Whigs their great chance.

Their opportunity was the result of a major economic depression. Distress stalked the cities as men lost jobs while the prices of many commodities remained high. In New York, the Locofocos posted placards about the city —

BREAD, MEAT, RENT, AND FUEL!

Their prices must come down!

The VOICE OF THE PEOPLE shall be heard and will prevail! The
people will meet in the park, rain or shine, at 4 o'clock, P.M.,
on Monday afternoon. . . . All friends of humanity determined
to resist monopolists and extortioners are invited to attend.

Yet according to Horace Greeley, a twenty-six year old editor who was to
play a major role in the Image Campaign, the "cry was, not for the bread
and fuel of charity, but for Work! . . . Work!" Banks suspended specie payments on their notes, and public land sales dropped from twenty million acres
in 1836 to only 3.5 million in 1838. The price of cotton and other agricultural
products fell, affecting the southern and western states most deeply.

The Whigs blamed the Democrats and reaped political profit accordingly.
Some blame indeed attached to Jacksonian policies, although the causes of
the downturn were complex. When Van Buren reiterated the then-conventional
view that it was not the Federal Government's job to relieve business distress,
and Silas Wright pressed Van Buren's independent "Sub-Treasury" in Congress, this issue was added to the Whig budget of complaints. The Democrats,
and Jackson, Van Buren, Benton, and Wright in particular, were denounced
as though they were the four horsemen of the apocalypse. The charge stuck,
and "Little Van" was to become the first victim of an aroused electorate in a
presidential contest that followed an economic collapse.

As they scented victory, the great question among the Whigs was – who
was to be the fortunate candidate? In 1836 the party had divided support
among William Henry Harrison and three other sectional candidates. The
game then was to deadlock the Electoral College, throw the choice into the
House of Representatives, and manage a Whig victory there. Indeed a shift
of 2,183 votes from Van Buren to Harrison in Pennsylvania would have
brought the issue to the House. Successes in local elections from 1837 to 1839,
however, and the fact that the Whigs almost won the House in 1837, persuaded
them that 1840 might give them a clear majority. They were ready to concentrate on a single entry and run with him.

How the candidate was to be selected was another matter. National delegate conventions had been called by the Anti-Masons and the National Republicans in 1831, and by the Democrats in 1832 and 1835; but the Whigs had
never employed one. Early conventions of the major parties, moreover, had
enjoyed no real ambit of decision: in effect their function was to ratify the
choice of already obvious candidates, and go home. As Roy F. Nichols has
pointed out, the national convention had not yet arrived at the working stage
of its development. A caucus of Whig members of Congress took the plunge
in May, 1838, however, and issued a call to meet in Harrisburg, Pennsylvania,
with the date finally set for December 4, 1839. Local conventions would
choose delegates from most of the states, although in some areas the Whig
members of the legislature made the selection. The immediate result was an

elaborate, protracted game of pre-convention maneuvering, the first appearance of the quadrennial game of picking delegates and making candidates.

The front runner was Henry Clay, who would be sixty-three in 1840. He had fought the good fight against the Jacksonians, and he had also devised the Tariff Compromise of 1833 which had mollified the proponents of nullification. Most of the measures Clay had sponsored appealed to disciples of capitalist development in the North, although they had a substantial following in the South too. Yet as a slaveholder whose views on slavery were "sound," Clay had courted states' rights southerners by assuring them that he no longer considered his American System to be an essential program; and he let the Bank issue lie quiet. He had also carefully abstained from voting on the Force Bill by which Jackson had planned to humble South Carolina. By following a compromise course, Clay could stand as a moderate in all sections, and by the late 1830's he had won strong backing in Virginia, where he was born. He was also the chief leader of the Whigs in Congress, and could count on his adopted state of Kentucky with its sizeable block of 15 electoral votes.

There were serious obstacles. Clay was a fixture on the national scene for almost thirty years and had been badly beaten in presidential bids in 1824 and 1832; he was tarnished by endless striving and was a bit shopworn. He had shown that he could be brilliant, charming, witty, and so had his wife Lucretia. Years earlier a Washington hostess had tried to discredit Mrs. Clay by asking if she didn't think it was terrible the way her husband gambled, but Mrs. Clay replied, "Oh, no, he most always wins." Yet Clay's brilliance had become mixed with a kind of personal and political presumption, and other politicians came to resent it. He was a legislator of an older style and not quite suited to modern, aggressively democratic ways. It was not exactly traditional deference that Clay expected. Rather he tended to assume that people would look up to him personally, and follow him accordingly.

There was also the question whether Clay could win in 1840 as readily as he might at the gaming table. He received support in Alabama, Mississippi, Louisiana, and North Carolina; the Whig convention in Virginia, the third-largest state with 23 electoral votes, was unanimously for him; and it appeared that he could count on Connecticut, Rhode Island, and Illinois. There was uncertainty elsewhere, however, and real trouble in New York. Touring the Empire State in the summer of 1839, Clay was greeted enthusiastically, and the New York City organization was for him. But there was also Thurlow Weed of Albany, the rising Whig star of the state. When Clay met Weed at Saratoga, the posh spa of the time, Weed told Clay bluntly that he lacked "availability," a neologism which was becoming popular. What Weed meant was that Clay could not win the election, and therefore should not be the nominee. Weed systematically ticked off three objections. First, Clay was associated in the minds of voters with the Bank of the United States, and there was too much anti-Bank sentiment to discount it. Second, rising anti-slavery forces might make the winning margin of votes in certain areas, and Clay was known as a slaveholder and a foe of emancipation. Finally Clay was a longtime Mason, and many Whig leaders and potential Whig voters were veterans of the anti-Masonic crusade. In short, Clay should withdraw. Naturally Clay rejected such advice from the upstart Weed, who was twenty years his junior; and he remained the front runner. However, after Saratoga, there was a shadow over his campaign.

Meanwhile another exemplar of the old style had put in his bid. Like Clay, the "godlike" Daniel Webster had fought the battles of National Republicans against Jacksonians. He had little support beyond Massachusetts with its 14 electoral votes, however, and had lost some of his old glamor even there; he seemed a bit seedy as well as shopworn. In the fall of 1838 the incisive Richard Hildreth, a young man of thirty-one, twenty-five years Webster's junior, wrote a series of editorials for the Boston *Atlas*. Aimed at exploding Webster's hopes and at demonstrating William Henry Harrison's superior "availability," the articles served their purpose: the "godlike Daniel" withdrew. He did not throw his support to Clay, though, but went for Harrison. His action inspired one of the innumerable dreadful puns of the campaign: "Now that we have got the *Clay* off our wheels," Webster's son-in-law wrote, "we shall get along."

The third candidate, "Old Tip" himself, seemed to score high on the magic availability gauge. A resident of Ohio, the fourth largest state, he could look toward a block of 21 electoral votes from his home bailiwick. In 1836 he had carried seven states with 73 electoral votes, at least one in every section except the Old South. He looked like a good prospect for a re-run.

The hero-to-be was also born in Virginia in 1773, not in a log cabin, but on the substantial estate maintained by his father, a signer of the Declaration of Independence and a local nabob. As a youth he attended Hampden-Sidney College, tried medical studies at the University of Pennsylvania, and gave it up. His attainments can be judged by his own statement that he became proficient "in Belles lettres information & particularly in History [*sic*]," and John Quincy Adams later noted that Harrison had "a lively and active, but shallow mind." After a seven-year hitch in the army, he became secretary of the Northwest Territory, its first delegate to Congress, and then governor of the Indiana Territory. He thus embarked on a long career of office holding in which he proved conscientious if not brilliant.

As settlers pushed steadily into the wilderness inhabited by Indian tribes, one of Governor Harrison's duties was to deal with the red men. In 1811 the Shawnee chief, Tecumseh, gathered an Indian league to resist the white advance, and Harrison was persuaded to attack near the joining of the Tippecanoe and Wabash rivers. It was the Indians who took the initiative, and in an all-day fight Harrison's troops suffered heavy casualties. But in the end they beat back the Indians and burned their village. The engagement was not particularly glorious or decisive; but for a presidential campaign nearly thirty years later, it sufficed. As a major general in the War of 1812, Harrison actually led troops to a decisive victory on the Thames River in Canada, but this battle did not have the mythic potential of the shield of humble pioneers.

When the time for image making came, it was to be "Old Tippecanoe," Indian fighter.

The next several years were anticlimactic. Benefitting from his military reputation as early as 1816, Harrison served without distinction as a congressman and senator from Ohio, and in 1828 was appointed minister to Colombia. Jackson recalled him the next year. Retiring to a comfortable farm at North Bend, Ohio, he found another, lesser office to hold, clerk of the common pleas court for the county. There the Whigs discovered him: in 1834 the Harrisburg *Intelligencer* proposed that "Old Buckeye" Harrison might be a Whig surrogate for the Democrats' "Old Hickory."

As 1840 approached, Harrison kept himself in readiness. In more or less overt appeals to what he called "the pioneers and old soldiers of the west," he presented himself as a potential rally-master for voters who had gone for Jackson, who was now out of the way. He was, he noted blandly, "the oldest and most extensively known of the Veteran Pioneers." Yet he was worried about a national convention: Clay, he thought, had no chance except "*by means of a packed convention one which will represent the politicians not the people* [sic]." Even so Harrison was put forward by successive Ohio state conventions in 1837 and 1838, and other endorsements followed. Late in 1838 a twenty-nine year old Whig legislator in Illinois, who was really born in a log cabin, regretfully broke with Clay, the favorite in the state, and came out for Harrison. He had turned to "the father of the Northwestern Territory" after "much reflection" and out of "gratitude," Abraham Lincoln wrote in an editorial for the *Sangamo Journal.* Perhaps it was for American youth too—

> When an individual's hairs have grown grey, and his eyes dim in the service of his country, it seems to us, if his country-men are wise, and polite, they will so reward him, as to encourage the youth of that country to follow his example.

Ultimately Harrison was to profit by the very characteristics of conventions he professed to fear, but he was no shoo-in.

One reason was that another soldier-hero had been discovered. Winfield Scott, also born in Virginia, was a career soldier who had reached the rank of major general. Later he was called "Old Fuss and Feathers," but he would be fifty-four in 1840 and was thus the youngest man in the race. His cachet of military glory also dated from the War of 1812, particularly the battle of Lundy's Lane near Niagara Falls. His immediate claim, however, came from his success in easing border tensions on the northeast boundary between the United States and Canada in the troubled winter of 1838 and 1839. The western counties of New York hailed Scott as the defender of the frontier and the "Hero of Bridgewater," and it was this that gave him his sudden availability. A Whig worker from western New York put the matter succinctly—

> Scott's name will bring out the hurra boys. The Whig party were broken down by the popularity and non-commital character of old Jackson [on political issues, presumably], and it is but fair to turn upon, and pros-

trate our opponents, with the. . . weapons, with which they beat us. We shall recruit from their ranks in mass. The General's lips must be hermetically sealed, and our shouts and hurras must be long and loud.

The advice fitted neatly into a broader, emergent strategy. This bluntly pragmatic conception was the device of young, new-style Whig stage managers who were tired of losing under old hands like Clay. They were also tired of the prominence of former Federalists like Chancellor James Kent, or "high-toned" socialites like the New York merchant Philip Hone—men who gave color to the persistent Democratic canard that the Whig party was only aristocratic Federalism in new dress. The first aim of the new strategy was to set Clay aside. Next the new directors wanted a protagonist who could win, almost anyone who would not evoke old animosities and old negative images. Finally, they were convinced that a potentially winning candidate must be someone who could be brought on stage as "a man of the people," who could relate to the popular-democratic ethos of the time. If he had availability and lacked ability, they would manage the Presidency for him. It would not be last time a military hero held the office and someone else ran the show.

The leading practitioners of the new Whig style came from neighboring New York and Pennsylvania. Both states had substantial urban populations, and both had generated a sophisticated if sometimes brutal politics. The largest and second-largest states, New York had 42 electoral votes and Pennsylvania 30. Together they could cast nearly one-fourth of the national total of 294.

In New York there were two dominant new leaders. One was the convivial but politically ruthless Thurlow Weed, whose editor's chair at the Albany *Evening Journal* was also a seat of party management. Called "the Jolly Drummer" by his foes, Weed was a wizard in the lobby or council room, always ready to hand out a cigar or clinch a deal. His chief colleague was William H. Seward of Auburn, whom Weed had helped to make governor in 1838; thereupon, Seward gave Weed the state printing. Small, given to easy talk and also to cigars, Seward's slouching manner hid a persuasive mind and strong abilities. The two men had gathered a cadre of lesser figures around them, local organizers or publicists like the eccentric but able Horace Greeley of Manhattan, whom Weed set up as a Whig editor. Both Weed and Seward had had training in the anti-Masonic movement, where they had learned the importance of the mass appeal and its technique.

In Pennsylvania the new wave was represented by Thaddeus Stevens of Gettysburg. Also an early anti-Masonic leader who had used his position as canal commissioner as a source of patronage to build the Whig party, the dour Stevens was a stentorian orator whose dark, vindictive manner could be intimidating, but there was no doubting his political savvy or his power. His chief ally was Joseph Ritner, a German farmer whom Stevens had helped to make governor on a coalition slate of Anti-Masons and Whigs in 1835; in turn, Ritner had named Stevens to the canal post.

There were other practitioners of the new politics elsewhere, of course. One was the intellectual Richard Hildreth of the Boston *Atlas*, who had blasted

Webster's hopes; another was Congressman "Tom" Corwin of Ohio, known as the "Wagon Boy" for his services as a youthful teamster in the War of 1812, and later as the "King of the Stump." But the great question was how the two big, bellwether states would go.

The situation in New York was complex. Fillmore had solicitously warned Governor Seward that he was in danger of becoming "*stuck in the Clay*;" and well before Saratoga, Weed had begun to undermine Clay as a candidate. Early in the game Seward had recommended Harrison; and in 1837 Weed had told Webster flatly that Harrison was then the strongest contender. Nonetheless, the "Jolly Drummer" had refrained from a final commitment: perhaps he wasn't altogether sure of "Old Tip's" sales appeal. It was this situation that made Winfield Scott's sudden appearance so opportune.

Weed's tactics pose a problem of interpretation. Thus Arthur Schlesinger, jr., suggests that Weed, along with other new managers, had already found his candidate when Harrison ran so well in 1836. In his invaluable, detailed monograph on the Log Cabin campaign, however, Robert Gray Gunderson says that Weed considered Scott seriously, although Seward later urged caution. According to Glyndon G. Van Deusen, the biographer of both Weed and Seward, Weed was at first favorable to Harrison but then turned gladly to Scott, as did Seward in the end. Still another view has been proposed by Roy F. Nichols, who argues that Weed "appeared" to favor Scott but was actually maneuvering to bring in Harrison. If so, Weed could be credited with the tactics that produced the ultimate result. In any case, caution prevailed at the New York state convention in Syracuse in November, 1839. Scott was not formally endorsed; and Clay's strength also manifested itself. Meanwhile James Gordon Bennett at the New York *Herald* urged the faithful to "Rouse, Rouse, Rouse," and "raise the banner of Scott." In the end more than half of the New York delegates to the national convention were for Scott, although there was a bloc for Clay too.

In Pennsylvania, where the Whigs were split into factions, Thaddeus Stevens saw Harrison as the candidate most likely to rally that state's voters. After an early gathering dominated by a Philadelphia contingent had chosen Clay, Stevens engineered a new "Union and Harmony" state convention in September, 1839. It praised Clay extravagantly but proposed Harrison for the national nomination: "no one but Harrison," the second Pennsylvania convention resolved, "could unite all the elements in the party." In Stevens' view, Clay could have the plaudits but Harrison was to have the votes. However, the "Harmony" meeting had not created union, and rival delegations from Pennsylvania were to appear at the national conclave.

The great national assembly met on December 4, 1839, at Harrisburg. It called itself the "Democratic Whig National Convention" (everybody had to bow to the symbolism of democratic faith). Harrisburg, the capital city of Pennsylvania, was of course home ground for Stevens, Ritner, and company, but it was also familiar territory for the New York operators; Weed arrived more than a week early to see what he might do. Neither he nor Stevens was an official delegate, but both were to play crucial roles at the convention.

The Whig national convention of 1839 set a number of precedents. It was the first such assemblage to be called by a central party group, the Whig members of Congress; not until 1848, when the Democrats established the first national committee, was there a continuing body to perform this function. It was the first to confine the number of delegates from each state to its quota of presidential electors, except for Pennsylvania where all members of the two contesting slates were seated as a combined delegation. In past national conventions each state could claim only as many votes as it had electors, but the number of actual bodies present might vary from one to as many as 181, a record set by Maryland at the Democratic gathering in Baltimore in 1835. The Whigs in 1839 were also the first to employ a version of the unit rule, by which each delegation cast its full vote as a block. Finally, and significantly, the Whig convention was apparently the earliest formally to resolve "that Reporters of the newspaper press be invited to occupy seats on the floor." After all, the communications media were to be of the essence in the coming campaign.

Besides procedures, the convention actually made decisions on the nominees. These came in part out of the long maneuvering that preceded the assembly, and in part from a strategic game that was played out at Harrisburg, but the result was not pre-ordained. It was an open convention, and as such it marked the beginning of the convention device as some kind of real central authority for the federal, sprawling form of American party structure.

The keynote address by former governor James Barbour of Virginia was scarcely a rouser. It did rake over the Jacksonians and the revolution that Jackson and Van Buren had allegedly wrought in exalting the executive — "his *sic volo sic jubeo* has been the law of the land for years past." It was an address in the old style, as perhaps fitted a Virginia gentleman who was a champion of Clay. Barbour noted the danger that the Whigs might not be able to unite — "I pray to God to avert such a catastrophy [*sic*]."

One form of unity was imposed early on the second day. A Harrison delegate from Massachusetts, Peleg Sprague, proposed a complicated procedure for nominating the candidates. Each state would name a committee of not more than three delegates who would canvass the state's wishes, and these committeemen would meet together as a general committee to discuss possible candidates. Then, "if it shall appear that a majority of the ballots are for any one man," they would report to the convention as a whole. These procedures would presumably minimize the chance that contention over nominees would break out on the floor. An amendment was immediately proposed by Charles B. Penrose of Pennsylvania, a Stevens ally whose surname was to mark a dynasty in the state's politics —

> That the vote of a majority of each delegation shall be reported as the vote of that State; and each State represented here shall vote its full electoral vote by such delegation in the committee.

After some resistance, "*so it was ordered.*" The Penrose Amendment added to the Sprague procedure constituted the Whigs' unit rule.

It proved to be one of the decisive elements of the convention. Even in the combined Pennsylvania delegation Stevens had a majority, as did Weed in the New York contingent. Thus Stevens could throw all of Pennsylvania's 30 votes for Harrison, and Weed all of New York's 42 for Scott, despite substantial minorities for Clay in each group. The rule also negated crucial minority strength for Clay in Ohio and other states. As the great decision neared, old-style Clay delegates tried to get the rule replaced by a procedure that would poll the delegates "*per capita*," as a Maryland spokesman put it. The new practitioners were in control, however, and the unit rule held.

For those who were convinced that Clay could not best Van Buren in 1840, it was well that it did. There were 254 authorized convention votes from twenty-two states, instead of the full 294 that would be cast in the Electoral College: South Carolina, Georgia, Tennessee, and Arkansas did not send delegations. Even with the cards stacked against him and each state voting as a unit, the Kentucky gambler showed remarkable strength in an early, informal canvass of the convention. With Michigan abstaining, Clay had a plurality of 103 while Harrison had 91 votes and Scott only 57. In a breakdown by sections (see Table 3) Clay carried all of the states voting from the South and the Southwest, and also won two states in each of the other three major sections of the country, for a total of twelve. Yet he commanded no delegation from states that had major urban centers, with the exception of Louisiana, or from states like New Hampshire, late-blooming Massachusetts, New York, Pennsylvania, New Jersey, and Ohio that were generating sophisticated, professionally developed political party structures and activity. In the larger game, moreover, delegations for Scott as well as for Harrison were delegations against Clay. Despite his strength, the way was open for the final, decisive maneuvers of the year.

They came in a period of uncertainty on the third day. Throughout, Weed and his minions kept reminding delegates that much of Clay's convention support came from states that he would probably lose to the Democrats in 1840. Meanwhile Weed pushed Scott to susceptible delegates as an "available," compromise candidate and managed to win over Connecticut (8) and Michigan (3), thereby bringing Scott's total to 68 while Clay fell to 95 votes. The grand committee still had no majority to report, and another informal canvass showed a continuing deadlock. The Virginia delegation considered switching to Scott, however; their "*adherence* to Clay," as another punster had put it, had begun to weaken. If Virginia switched, her 23 votes would have brought Scott neck-and-neck with Harrison.

Two events then followed in close succession. First, Stevens sauntered in among the Virginia delegates and dropped a letter on the floor. It was a letter Scott had written to Stevens' fellow-Pennsylvanian, Francis Granger, designed to curry the support of anti-slavery men: that was the end of "Old Bridgewater" in the Old Dominion. At this turn of events, Weed pivoted sharply and turned to "Old Tippecanoe." Added to Harrison's original strength of 91, Weed's 42 votes in New York alone would have made up a majority of 133: the magic figure was 128. "Old Tip" had the game. In the end the vote was Harrison 148, Clay 90, and Scott 16. The Buckeye candidate had gained New York (42), Vermont (7), and Michigan (3), all presumably under Weed's influence, and Illinois (5) for an increment of 57 votes, 20 more than he needed for a bare majority. The nominating committee could at last report, in the only official "ballot" of the convention. The nomination was promptly made unanimous, even though it was not.

In effect Stevens had won, and Weed too. Although Virginia did not switch to Harrison as Stevens had hoped, and lacked enough votes to put "Old Tip" over anyway, Stevens had thwarted an incipient Scott boom with his letter-drop and had seen his favorite nominated. In the larger view, Weed as well as Stevens had been primarily concerned with blocking Clay as a loser and with bringing on a winner, which Harrison proved to be; moreover, Weed had favored Harrison until he turned to Scott as another agent to foil Clay. It seems unlikely that Weed and Stevens had been playing some deep, collaborative game to advance Harrison: as far as the evidence shows, each was probably more or less on his own on the question of candidates despite their common basic strategy. In any case the result was a triumph for the new Whig politics.

Ensuring unity was another matter. Old friends and staunch allies of Clay were disappointed and angry. But Clay had anticipated the question with a long letter that was now read to the convention: he had left to the delegates "the free selection of candidates, as being the assembly to which, by common consent, that important duty has been referred." If the convention sought someone else who "would be more likely to be successful than any other, he ought to be nominated." Privately Clay is said to have exploded at the news —

> My friends are not worth the powder and shot it would take to kill them! . . . I am the most unfortunate man in the history of parties: always run by my friends when sure to be defeated, and now betrayed for a nomination when I, or any one, would be sure of an election.

His open letter to the convention was on the whole a generous one in the rising spirit of party loyalty, however, and it helped.

In a move to salve hurt feelings, the vice-presidential selection was offered to the Clay forces. They declined, and several possibilities were considered in night-watch conferences. Finally, on the fourth day, the nominating committee proposed John Tyler, a long-time personal friend of Clay. A "revolting" Jacksonian from Virginia who represented the states' rights wing of the Whig party, he was scarcely a major figure. More headstrong than strong, his views deviated sharply on many issues from those of the main Whig body. This fact was to give Clay and other Whig leaders endless anguish when Harrison died a month after his inauguration and Tyler took over. Commenting in 1841 on the nomination of "Tyler too," Philip Hone lamented that "there was rhyme, but no reason in it," and many others would have agreed.

This was hindsight, and in 1839 there was at least political reason. In every presidential election from 1789 except two, some sectional balance had been struck between President and Vice-President or between running-mates for the two offices, and the balance was almost invariably between North and South. With more than a million inhabitants, moreover, Virginia was by far the largest state in the South; with Ohio and Virginia represented, the Whig slate would draw on the third and fourth largest states. Finally, Tyler was an established spokesman for the planter elite in the Old Dominion, and he might appeal to this crucial source of influence in the previously-Democratic sections of the South. He was not the only southern possibility or even a first choice, but he had his quota of apparent availability.

In any case the stage was set, and soon the inevitable chorus would appear—

> Tippecanoe and Tyler too,
> Tippecanoe and Tyler too!

The final, ritual speeches rang the changes of solidarity. The long struggle of Clay, Harrison, and Scott was bound to be divisive, yet it had also brought some theatrical advantages. For almost two years it had thrust the ultimate Whig candidate before the public; it had stirred party workers and the faithful; it was a good show, with its climax at the convention. Publicity was not always favorable, but it was publicity; much later, Fanny Brice was to remark that they could print her name under a picture of a hippopotamus, just so they spelled the name right. Politics is not exactly show business, but the campaign of 1840 was to suggest that the two are not necessarily far apart.

There was no Whig platform. The conventional interpretation of this non-event is that the Whig managers wanted to avoid commitment on issues that might underscore divisions in the party. How, Millard Fillmore had asked, could disparate Whig elements be brought into "one mass of pure Whigs of undoubted good metal"; and part of the answer to Fillmore's problem was to avoid stirring up conflicting views on public questions. Beyond the conventional interpretation, however, there was the fact that no previous general convention had produced a platform either. An assembly of National Republican "young men" in 1832 had framed resolutions that amounted to a platform for the youth section of the party. By the late 1830's, state conventions had acquired the habit of issuing long, argumentative, platform-like "addresses to the people." However, writing a platform was by no means an established practice, and the omission at Harrisburg was not so glaring as it might seem. Not until the Democratic convention of 1840 was the first, official, national party platform composed.

In its last hour, the Whig convention planned another essay in public relations. It called upon "the Whig Young Men of the Several States" to meet at a "ratifying convention" in Baltimore in May, 1840, there to take measures to "aid the advancement of the Whig cause." The Democrats had already scheduled their national convention for the same time and place. An enthusiastic youth rally might well blanket the Democrats' publicity and advance the Whig cause in more ways than one. The great, merchandizing campaign was in the making, and astute party managers were planning ahead.

The expectant sense of triumph that had pervaded the Whig convention was notably absent at two other gatherings. One was the Democratic national convention; the other was a founding assembly for a new anti-slavery party.

There was no doubt that the Democrats would nominate Martin Van Buren again. Fifty-eight in 1840, nearly twenty years younger than Harrison, he had served his party well. He had also labored to maintain his position among the various blocs that constituted the party, and he could count on a national cadre of patronage officeholders. Short, round, and a bit dapper with his reddish side-whiskers, he was genial and urbane, a shrewd political manager who had been called the "Red Fox" and the "Little Magician." Yet he lacked flair, drama, the touch of charisma that makes for a strong popular image. It was all very well to dub him "Old Kinderhook," but his political persona was less than "O. K." for the times. In the face of depression and privation, the Whigs were nearer to the mark when they declared that "Matty Van" was "a used-up man."

The choice of a vice-presidential candidate was more troublesome. The incumbent was Richard M. Johnson of Kentucky, a genuinely common man with some uncommon habits. An old Indian fighter who had reputedly slain Tecumseh at the battle of the Thames—"Rumpsey, Dumpsey, Colonel Johnson Shot Tecumpsey"—and the sometime hero of Locofoco reformers, he also kept a crossroads tavern. In 1836 he had failed to win a majority of the electoral vote when Virginia refused to support him, and became the only Vice-President to be named by the Senate. The trouble was that he had taken to living openly with a Negro woman. As the convention of 1840 approached, according to one party agent, the Vice-President was residing at his Kentucky tavern with "a young Delilah of about the complexion of Shakespears [sic] Othello." "How can he expect friends to countenance and sustain him when he . . . openly and shamefully lives in adultery with a buxom young negro wench?" From foes there were even more salacious and overtly racist comments, and "Rumpsey Dumpsey's" availability was seriously impaired. Yet he retained much of his popular support, and Van Buren was not sure that he should be dropped.

Otherwise all was harmonious when the Democrats met on May 4 in the sedate hall of Baltimore's "Musical Association." In response to a call by the New Hampshire Democratic central committee, twenty-one states sent 248 delegates, with Connecticut, Delaware, Virginia, South Carolina, and Illinois absent. Each state could cast only its electoral vote total, but the number of delegates varied from one for Massachusetts to fifty-nine for New Jersey. The meeting was opened by Senator Felix Grundy of Tennessee, and Governor William Carroll, also from Andrew Jackson's home state, was the permanent president. Once hostile to Van Buren, the Tennessee Democrats were now making their support clear; but the symbolism may have been lost in the plethora of office holders. A long speech by Grundy called for "a clear, candid and true declaration of the sentiments of the republican party" (the old Jeffersonian name was still often used by the Democrats). Grundy went on to stigmatize any man who sought to "live on his wits alone," at the expense of "workingmen," as inevitably "a federalist, aristocrat, and modern whig besides." Indeed, the charge that Whigs were disguised Federalists was to be a major theme of Democratic propaganda.

The platform was substantial, as platforms go. In nine resolutions, the Democrats declared themselves for strict construction of the Constitution; against "a general system of internal improvements," federal assumption of state debts for local projects, and unequal protective tariffs; for economy in government; against a national bank and for "the separation of the moneys of the government from banking institutions;" against the efforts of abolitionists "to induce congress to interfere with questions of slavery;" and for the "liberal principles" of the Declaration of Independence as applied, presumably, to white citizens. There was reason to believe that the platform, particularly in its planks concerning limited government and slavery, was designed to seal the return of Calhoun and his followers to the Democratic ranks. Yet it was also in accord with positions the party had espoused over the years, and Van Buren had already denounced the "fell spirit" of abolition and promised to veto any act of Congress that would interfere with slavery. The resolutions were adopted unanimously, and were supplemented by an address to the people which Isaac Hill of New Hampshire prepared.

Like the Whigs, the Democrats set up a committee to propose candidates. The nomination of Van Buren followed without dissent: there was no occasion to employ the two-thirds rule the convention of 1832 had established, a procedure which was to trouble Democrats until it was finally eliminated in 1936. The committee was unable to find agreement on the nominee for Vice-President, however; instead, it proposed to leave the matter to the several states, in the hope that "opinions shall become so concentrated as to secure the choice of a vice president by the electoral colleges [sic]." Partisans of "Rumpsey Dumpsey" Johnson came out in full cry against this "expedient," but to no avail: the committee proposal was adopted. In the months to come, however, Johnson did become the effective Democratic candidate.

Despite its careful direction, there was something lugubrious about the meeting in the music hall. The chorus of agreement lacked sparkle and conviction; and there was an overtone of defeatism. Outside, moreover, the Whig "young men" were chanting, "With Tip and Tyler, We'll bust Van's biler." Such discords made it even harder for the Democrats to sound optimistic.

Although it dutifully endorsed "Tip" and "Ty," the young Whig "convention" at Baltimore was really a mobilization of political militia and a mass sales campaign. Participants began to assemble three days before the Democrats convened, but the tramp, tramp and chant, chant of the marchers was kept for the day the rival convention opened. The number of participants was estimated at anywhere from eight thousand to twenty-five thousand in the line of march and up to seventy-five thousand on the route, and the procession was three miles long. *"Every mountain sent its rill,"* the Baltimore *Patriot* exclaimed; "and lo! THE AVALANCHE OF THE PEOPLE IS HERE!" The avalanche was subdivided into state and (for some states) county units; and each platoon was greeted by shouts of applause, martial bands, and the roar of cannon.

Every delegation had its particular gimmick. Thus Allegany County, Maryland, "the frontier county of the state," contributed an immense ball twelve feet in diameter on which several verses were inscribed. At the culmination of his effort to get the Senate to expunge its resolution censuring Jackson for his withdrawal of federal funds from the Bank of the United States, Benton of Missouri had declared: "Solitary and alone, I put this ball in motion." Now the Whigs proclaimed, derisively —

> With heart and soul
> This ball we roll.
> May times improve
> As on we move.
>
> This democratic ball,
> Set rolling first by Benton,
> Is on another track
> From that it first was sent on.

There was more, much more, as the Allegany men in hunting dress pushed their ball on and on —

> Ye officeholders, fed with pap,
> Have very saucy grown;
> We tell ye, sirs, we don't like that,
> And mean to make it known. . .
>
> As rolls the ball,
> Van's reign does fall;
> And he may look
> To Kinderhook;
> His former friends
> To other ends.
>
> Take care your toes
> Ye loco fo's . . .
> Having no bell,
> We roll your knell.

Before the great Image Campaign was over, balls were to roll in state after state.

Less ambitious platoons employed less unwieldy symbols: anything to sell "Old Tip" would get a cheer. There were banners depicting honest, kindly, gentle, rustic Harrison at the plow. Other visual devices portrayed the sad state of the currency (a sinking ship with the legend, "hard up, Matty"), or the promise that as President Harrison would always have his latch string out. Some marchers settled for more or less meaningful slogans emblazoned on banners: "THE PEOPLE ARE COMING'" "NO REDUCTION IN WAGES;" "no subtreasury;" or even, "Tip, Tyler, and the tariff." There were, however, apparently no references to the Bank of the United States, to abolition, to slavery. The aim was mobilization and sales appeal, not debate over tricky policy issues.

The great symbols for these purposes were fast becoming the log cabin and the hard cider barrel. At Baltimore, specially-built log cabins were mounted on floats; and at least one barrel was filled with the genuine liquor. Late in 1839, a Democratic newspaper reporter had jested that if Harrison were given a pension of two thousand dollars a year and a barrel of hard cider, he would "sit the remainder of his days in his log cabin," and "study moral philosophy." Democratic editors had publicized the quip, only to have a Pennsylvania banker (Thomas Elder) and a Pennsylvania editor (Richard S. Elliott) pitch on it and built it into the central formula of the Whig campaign. A Pennsylvania ratifying convention in 1840 had exhibited a transparency showing a log cabin and a cider barrel, with a woodpile and a coonskin for good measure. The symbolism caught on; the "log-cabin and hard-cider candidate" was made.

All that remained for the Whig young men was a set of resolutions, all of them aimed at action and organization. The zeal of youth, they resolved, should go into forming Tippecanoe Clubs at the grass roots; to securing "the ablest and most efficient orators to address the people"; and to meeting regularly to "print and publish useful matter." Each delegation was also called on to raise a dollar a member, which would make a respectable sum. The mobilization of young men had set the pattern for the new Whig campaign. The task was to put it into operation everywhere, and the enthusiasm of youth could be invaluable.

No wonder the Democrats were hushed. Nothing to match the "great commotion" in the Baltimore streets had been seen before. The space devoted to the two assemblies in *Niles' National Register*, the weekly news journal of the time, was revealing. All told, the Democratic national convention got a little more than fourteen columns, while the doings of the young Whigs filled twenty-three. The Democrats had their own press, of course, but Whig editors had a bonanza of copy available to them.

No such publicity attended the other, founding convention of the year. When anti-slavery men met in Albany in April, 1840, to nominate James G. Birney of New York and Thomas Earle of Pennsylvania for President and Vice-President, they knew they were a small minority. Indeed, they had called upon Birney in an earlier meeting at Warsaw, New York, in November, 1839; but Birney, the executive secretary of the American Anti-Slavery Society, would not accept until he was convinced that neither major party would meet the slavery issue. Many abolitionists were not agreed that a third party would be efficacious, moreover, and the Liberty party that emerged from the Albany meeting was to muster only a tiny fraction of the popular vote. Even so, the Liberty movement of 1840 was the precursor of the more significant, if less militant, Free Soil and Republican parties of decades to come. Meanwhile the Democrats and Whigs would fight it out, each trying to catch a winner's share of the vote.

After the excitement at Baltimore, there were about six months before the election. Votes would be cast in various states from October 30 to November 18: not until 1845 did Congress set the first Tuesday after a Monday in November as a uniform election day.

The Democrats undertook a campaign in what had become a traditional style. They depended on organization, full use of their patronage platoons, and a conventional propaganda barrage. They deplored the "demagoguery" of the Whigs and tried to deal with issues, although they also heaped abuse on Harrison. The total effect was rather staid and prosaic.

The Whigs, on the other hand, elaborated their new-style campaign and made it as diverting as it was professional. They used organization to draw huge crowds—"*acres of men*," as one party worker put it. Everywhere there was movement and a heightened sense of participation, and Whig propaganda included a panoply of visual devices like Harrison "Liberty Poles" as well as mottoes, songs, and jokes, along with "efficient orators." Lures to the palate were not limited to cider: the word "*booze*" was established in the language by a Philadelphia distiller, E. G. Booz, who put his whiskey into cabin-shaped bottles for the campaign. It was all drama and popular commotion mixed with slander and smears designed to destroy "Martin Van Ruin." It was a combination of merchandizing and militia styles, with all the stops pulled out.

The chief Democratic manager was Amos Kendall, who resigned as Postmaster-General to do the job. He was slight and unimpressive in appearance, and often plagued by ill health; but he was a practiced political hand. A former editor of the Frankfort, Kentucky *Argus of Western America*, who was later to become business manager for Samuel F. B. Morse's telegraph, he presumably knew something about communications media, and he teamed with Blair to produce an *Extra Globe* as a campaign sheet. He was never able to match the new Whig publicists, however.

In silent partnership with Van Buren, Kendall drafted what today would be called a campaign plan or memorandum:

> Formation of Democratic associations to meet regularly in every town, and to "provide for the printing and distribution of correct information &c. &c. &c."

> Appointment of "committees of vigilance" to contact voters, "distribute information," and act as a kind of earlier-day truth squad to expose Whig propaganda.

> Establishment of committees to watch the polls and guard against fraud or violations of election laws.

On the publicity front, articles were to be prepared for publication by country editors so that the *Globe* could reprint them later; and patronage workers were to play a major role. Local postmasters were asked to sign up subscribers for the *Extra Globe*, and so also, Whigs charged, were the agents appointed to take the census of 1840. Indeed, the Whigs claimed, Kendall had a "perfect organization" of some hundred thousand officeholders who were also expected to contribute a portion of their salaries to the campaign. Special efforts were made to mobilize immigrants as instant voters in New York, allegedly with the aid of custom-house clerks; and special appeals were directed at Catholics generally.

Much of the Democratic effort foundered in the choppy seas of division and indifference. In New York, Pennsylvania, Virginia, North Carolina, and Georgia, the Grand Old Party of the 1830's was in trouble. In part it was a matter of intra-party factionalism, or of personal ill-feeling between party leaders. For example, relations were strained between Van Buren and Buchanan of Pennsylvania. In part it was a matter of leave-taking by conservative Democrats, alienated by radical-Jacksonian policies, who joined the Whigs, as did many from New York to Virginia, North Carolina, and Georgia. There was also still a strong undercurrent of popular antipathy to Van Buren in Tennessee, and in much of the South generally. Frantic efforts were made to turn the tide. "We are not to make a victory by rose water," Thomas Ritchie of Virginia proclaimed in his *Enquirer*: "Organize! Organize! Rally, and act — or the Philistines be upon you." But the party's plight called for a freshening breeze and waves of popular enthusiasm, and they were not forthcoming.

Indeed, the Democrats' propaganda campaign was on the whole flat and uninspired. They had newspapers: old standbys like the *Globe*, the Albany *Argus*, the *Ohio Statesman*, the *Enquirer*, or the Nashville *Union*, and special campaign sheets like the *Rough-Hewer*, distributed from Albany in imitation of the *Log Cabin* Horace Greeley put out for the Whigs. There were also mass rallies, but generally they fell short of Whig gatherings in generating a spirit of "Hurrah!" The aging Jackson was brought out of retirement to attend balls, receptions, and barbecues, stumping for "Little Van" as he had never done for himself in an effort to counter the persona of "Old Tip"; and Hickory Clubs were set up to match the Tippecanoe Clubs. Perhaps this only underscored the Whig charge that "Old Hickory" Jackson had been replaced by "Slippery Elm" Van Buren. Speakers included men as eminent as Felix Grundy, James K. Polk, Silas Wright, Buchanan, "Old Bullion" Benton, and Richard M. Johnson. Holding to tradition, Van Buren did not stump for himself. The Vice-President seemed to regain his old stature in the campaign and emerged as the party's best drawing card in state after state. The Democratic effort did not take fire, however, and a Louisville editor even remarked that he now believed that "Rumpsey-Dumpsey" *had* killed Tecumseh: "he must have gone at him with *twaddle*."

There was indeed twaddle in the Democrats' array of campaign themes, along with attempts to discuss issues. It was necessary, Kendall decided, to take the offensive against Harrison and the Whigs. Thus Whiggery was "Federalism and Abolition United," according to the *Globe*. Hard times and low wages were the work of "Federalist" business men who could "ESTABLISH WHAT RATES THEY PLEASE, AND STARVE THE LABORERS INTO ACQUIESCENCE." Meanwhile Harrison was attacked as a "*sham* hero," a "Granny," an addict of profanity, a lecher who had sired half-breed children on Winnebago squaws, an "Old Tip-ler;" when they went to the polls, voters should follow the injunction of his name spelled backward — "*Nosirrah*!" The Democrats also charged the Whigs with corrupting public morals by their hard cider and booze campaign. They even broke into verse, although Gunderson has noted "the dissonance of Democratic counterpoint" —

> Hush-a-bye-baby;
>   Daddy's a Whig,
> Before he comes home
>   Hard cider he'll swig;
> Then he'll be Tipsy
>
> And over he'll fall;
> Down will come Daddy,
>   Tip, Tyler and all.

More cogently, Democratic spokesmen attacked Harrison's silence or equivocation on national questions—his stands for the Bank, or against it; anti-abolitionist in the South, cautious emancipationist in the North; pro-tariff and anti-tariff—and called him *"General Mum."* They tried to force him to make commitments, and charged that he was the captive of a special "Conscience-Keeping Committee" at South Bend; he was an "Old Gentleman in Leading Strings." There was substance in the accusation, although the Democrats were not always able to dramatize it effectively—

> Another gourd for General *Mum*,
> Whose fame is like his fav'rite drum;
> Which when most empty makes most noise,
> Huzza for General Mum, my boys.

In contrast, the Democrats pointed to their record on issues like the national Bank, hard money against paper money, and the independent treasury. They also did what they could with the Baltimore platform and their presumed role as spokesman for the common man, and tried to portray Van Buren accordingly—

> Van's popularity fills the great West;
> His firmness and honesty none can contest;
> His measures considered, approved, and are sealed
> By the hard-fisted yeoman that toils in the field.

The claim was as weak as the prosody, however, especially by 1840. "Old Kinderhook" could never stir enthusiasm the way "Old Tippecanoe" did.

For the Whigs, drama seemed to come readily; their organization had "zip," their rhetoric had "zing." Abraham Lincoln was not alone when he remarked that "Old Tip" was taking "first rate." Popular enthusiasm blew up like an elemental storm. The Whig campaign was highly repetitious; but, as later practitioners and scholars would observe, reiteration was one of the touchstones of effective mass communication. Campaign songs made a substantial book, log cabins went up overnight, even such elegant politicians as Webster and Clay plugged the homespun theme, and a catalogue of mottoes and emblems would be tedious. It was Baltimore in May all over again, spread across the land.

Behind it all was careful management. Under Thurlow Weed's general direction, the Whigs also used the conventional organizational devices of the day, but with important additions. A special executive committee headed by Representatives Rice Garland of Louisiana and John C. Clark of New York took offices in Washington, assembled a staff, and, drawing on other Whig congressmen, compiled a master mailing-list of voters. Directives went out to central party committees in every county; state organization was mustered through state conventions and the establishment of state committees; patronage brigades were called out in Whig-controlled states like Weed's New York and Stevens' Pennsylvania. Organization was extended from the cities and the North into the countryside and the South, and was rounded out by specially devised "Harrison Reform Clubs," set up as havens for bolters from the Democratic ranks.

The themes of Whig propaganda and rhetoric were as varied as the electorate. The log-cabin, plain-folks, "Old-Tip" appeal was always central, but special bids were concocted for almost every conceivable block of voters. To the devout and the conservative: such Locofoco intellectuals as Orestes A. Brownson and Robert Dale Owen were labeled infidels and revolutionaries. To old soldiers, or the "veteran vote": the Hero of Tippecanoe was one of their own. To those who feared the enlargement of military forces in the face of border tensions with Canada: a plan by Van Buren was exposed to "take the crown and sceptre and announce to the world the high and sounding title of MARTIN *the 1st*, KING OF NORTH AMERICA." To German immigrants: campaign biographies of Harrison were printed in their own language. To other avid readers: scurrilous campaign biographies were published of "Sweet Sandy Whiskers," the allegedly perfumed and corseted occupant of the White House, who had opposed the war and escaped military service. To workingmen: "*Matty's policy, 12-1/2 cts. a day and French soup*, OUR *policy, 2 Dolls. a day and Roast Beef.*" To faithful Harrisonite farmers: an invitation was issued to name their horses *Tip* and *Ty*, which many did. To anyone else, or the voter about to climb on the bandwagon:

> Without a why or wherefore
> We'll go for Harrison therefore.

Meanwhile, an apparently unprecedented campaign chest was filled. Wealthy men like the merchants Philip Hone of New York or Abbott Lawrence of Boston were expected to stay in the background, but open their purses. Anxious to save themselves, Benton asserted, "the broken and suspended banks" were ready to supply the monetary "sinew of the contest." Rebates from canal contractors helped to support Stevens' Pennsylvania campaign, and candidates were expected to throw in their share. The genuine enthusiasm of the Whig onslaught was exhibited again and again, as contributions came from local organizations and ordinary voters too.

The Whig managers and publicists of 1840 were the working McLuhans of their time; and the medium was the message. Their major channels of communication were stump speakers, popular newspapers and other printed materials, and reinforcing visual symbols, all brought to an inventive peak of proficiency.

The emission of political bombast in town squares or in country groves was not new, but 1840 set records in "stumping." The Whigs not only drew on Clay and Webster, who traveled through eight states, or the ex-Jacksonian Nathaniel P. Tallmadge of New York, who spoke so assiduously from July through November that he was at home for only six nights. They also virtually created artists for the occasion like John W. Bear, the "Buckeye Blacksmith" of South Bloomfield, Ohio, who left the forge "to emit stirring blasts and strike hard blows" in 331 speeches. He usually appeared with a pair of blacksmith's tongs, which he declared to be necessary to deal with the dirty doings of the Democrats. "Only fancy," the *Globe* remarked—"a *Whig* blacksmith!" Johnny Bear was a first rate plain-folks symbol, and, aided by more literate Whig ghost writers, he reached the point where he could speak with confidence on the steps of the Washington city hall. Other more experienced "slangwhangers" also took on a plain-folks guise, among them the comical "Wagon Boy," Tom Corwin of Ohio. Before it was all over there were more than five thousand speakers "on the stump," according to a Washington journalist. In the absence of electronic amplification, many voters in the massive audiences could not hear them; but it was something just to be there.

In a land of few population centers and great distances, newspapers, broadsides, and campaign books constituted an even more important line of communication. Some 91 per cent of adult white Americans could read, according to the Census of 1840, although the data is shaky; in any case the overwhelming mass of voters were at least within the bounds of literacy. Printed matter was the staple of both parties, but the question was how it was used.

In the decade before the Image Campaign, the United States had experienced a media explosion if not a media revolution. In 1790, the new nation had had only ninety-two newspapers, of which only eight were dailies. For some time to come the usual sheet was a four-page publication of about twelve by eighteen inches. There were no headlines as we know them; type was tightly packed; and advertisements typically occupied the first page. Other columns were often filled with records of congressional proceedings, public notices, speeches, or letters, as well as with political polemics. Well into the 1800's most papers carried a price of six cents, and readership was limited accordingly. Most sheets had partisan attachments if they were not outright partisan organs, but their style was generally impersonal. The great day of newspaper communication was yet to come.

The newspaper explosion was brought on in part by technology, and in part by politics. A new wood-pulp process for making paper cut costs in half; steam-run presses took over from hand methods; cylinders were developed to carry paper swiftly across flat beds of type; and the whole process of production was speeded up. Sheets were greatly enlarged, and by the 1820's and 1830's they were substantially larger than the newspapers of today. Meanwhile the Jackson campaign of 1828 brought the emergence of something like a coordinated "party press," a collection of papers from Isaac Hill's *Patriot* in New Hampshire to Amos Kendall's *Argus of Western America* in Kentucky, all offering a common political fare and exchanging items among them. By

1828 there were some 861 newspapers across the country, and the number of dailies or semi-weeklies was gaining on the weeklies.

The great newspaper revolution came in the next decade, however. It built on technology and was stimulated by mass-oriented political parties, but it also drew on commercial impulses: editors of the new day wanted to be prosperous as well as influential and perhaps respected. The most significant innovation was the "penny press." The first successful venture was the New York *Sun*, launched in 1833 by Benjamin H. Day, who announced his intention to supply "the public with the news of the day at so cheap a rate as to lie within the means of all." The *Sun* was entertaining, scintillating, and readable as it went beyond legislative harangues and the chaff of politics to more sensational stories, one of which was the famous "Moon Hoax" of 1835, a circumstantial account of telescopic observations of life on the moon, including bat-like human beings. It wasn't so, as we know now, but it built circulation — and enlarged the opportunity to exert political influence. The New York *Herald* was founded in 1835 by James Gordon Bennett, who mixed Whig politics with a lively, personal style of journalism and other innovations, from coverage of crime, scandals, and sex to reports of "society." Other penny sheets followed, and soon journalists were going out to get the news instead of waiting for it to dribble in, looking for a "beat," joining the rush to be on the street first. Headlines and illustrations began to open up the heavy mass of type that had characterized older publications, and vigorous political editorials appeared.

Such developments, beginning in New York City, filtered out only slowly to lesser cities. Much of the provincial press was little affected and remained sleepy and old-fashioned in the small towns, as Pudd'nhead Wilson could testify. Yet Boston, Philadelphia, and Baltimore soon had their penny sheets, and newspapers as a whole probably became more lively and "up-to-date," as well as more copious in their coverage.

Another part of the newspaper explosion was purely quantitative, in the sheer increase in the number of publications. A tabulation derived from *Gregory's Guide to Newspapers* shows a total of 906 publications in 1830, of which only one hundred were dailies; comparable figures for 1840, only a decade later, reveal 1,577 newspapers, of which 209 were dailies. Increases were recorded between 1830 and 1840 in every state except South Carolina, which supported twenty presses in each year; and the number of dailies also rose in all but seven of the twenty-nine states and territories surveyed. The leaders in the total number of newspapers published in 1840 were New York (275), Pennsylvania (226), Ohio (157), Massachusetts (113), and Indiana (seventy-two). The four corners of the nation showed Maine with forty-one, Georgia with twenty-nine, Louisiana with forty-one, and Missouri with thirty-nine. The Mid-Atlantic region was the most prolific with a mean of 120 presses per state, although the numbers varied from New York's 275 to Delaware's eight. Means for other sections were the Northwest seventy, New England forty-six, the Southwest thirty-three, and the South thirty. Very broadly, these levels were consistent with the differential development of politics and parties in the various sections. Yet the striking fact is the explosion of presses nearly everywhere, and the resources of political intelligence and persuasion they could provide.

What the Whigs did was to seize upon such opportunities, by making creative, revolutionary use of newspapers and of printed media of their own. Like the Democrats they used established party organs: Weeds's *Journal*, the Washington *National Intelligencer*, Bennett's flamboyant *Herald*, the *Ohio State Journal*, or the staid *Missouri Republican* in St. Louis. But they utilized them imaginatively, filling their columns with lively copy, entertaining come-ons, and pointed appeals. Perhaps most important, they created special campaign sheets.

The great production in this line was the *Log Cabin*, which Horace Greeley set up at the beginning of May, 1840. He began with a printing of thirty thousand, but popular acceptance was so great that he was soon running off eighty thousand copies a week. The *Log Cabin* was filled with jokes and quips, illustrations like a woodcut of "HARRISON'S HUMANITY IN WAR" with accompanying short text, announcements of Tippecanoe Club meetings, campaign songs (many of which Greeley painstakingly wrote himself, borrowing the tune), and plugs for pamphlets like the "Harrison Almanac." The *Log Cabin* also offered routine news and reasoned arguments for the tariff, for a solidly-based bank currency that would be uniform across the nation, and for limitations on presidential power. It was, Henry Raymond of *The New York Times* commented later, the most effective campaign paper ever printed, and after the election Greeley reworked it into the brilliant New York *Tribune*, as a penny daily. Other campaign sheets fell into line elsewhere: the *Flail* (Brattleboro, Vermont), the Elyria *Old Tip's Broom* (to clean out corruption—one of seventeen Ohio ventures), the *Pilot* (Baltimore), the *Old Soldier* (under Abe Lincoln's direction, for the Illinois state committee), the *Snag Boat* (deep in Raymond, Mississippi), the *Hard Cider Press* (a Chicago pun), and many more—including, on Jackson's home ground of Nashville, the rebellious *Spirit of '76*. Nothing rivaled Greeley's *Cabin*, but many other sheets picked up his lively, inventive material.

Add to all this the reprints of speeches, the broadsides, the paper transparencies bearing portraits or emblems, five campaign biographies—the outlay of wood pulp, printers' ink, and ingenuity was immense.

There were also song-books and songs. In September the *Log Cabin* offered a new one in five verses to the tune of "Jefferson and Liberty," with music spread across a three-column width. One verse will suffice:

> From Mis-sis-sip-pi's utmost shore,
>   To cold New-Hampshire's piney hills;
> From broad At-lan-tic's sul-len roar
>   To where the Western ocean swells,—
> How loud the notes of joy a-rise
>   From eve-ry bosom warm and free!
> How strains tri-umphant fill the skies,
>   For HAR-RI-SON and LIB-ER-TY!

The prosody was usually insistent: anybody could grasp it and sing, and one of its aims was to convey a sense of movement bound for victory, even when *Little Pig's Tale* was the tune —

> What has caused the great commotion, motion, motion
>> All our country through?
>> It is the ball a rolling on, on.

> For Tippecanoe and Tyler too — Tippecanoe and Tyler too,
> And with them we'll beat little Van, Van, Van,
> Van is a used up man,
> And with them we'll beat little Van. . .

Finally, when previously Democratic Maine went Whig by a hairline margin in its early election:

> And have you heard the news from Maine,
>> And what old Maine can do?
> She went hell-bent for Governor Kent,
>> And Tippecanoe and Tyler too,
>> And Tippecanoe and Tyler too!

Such doggeral was sung or passed by word of mouth, of course, as well as printed and read, but its circulation in print was a major channel for Whig rhetoric.

Two other essays may be taken as a summary of Whig propaganda. One was a set of speeches by a previously obscure congressman, the other an address by the "gallant Harrison," himself; and both texts were widely reprinted.

The congressman was Charles Ogle, a scholar in Thad Stevens' rough Pennsylvania school. In a harangue spread across three days in mid-April, 1840, he treated the House to an unprecedented vilification of Martin Van Buren. His theme was that the pretended democrat was really a snob, a Frenchified dandy, a wastrel and loafer, an overbearing "*aristocrat!*" He had made the Executive Mansion a "PALACE *as splendid as that of the Caesars.*" He had caused a number of mounds to be constructed around the Mansion, "every pair of which . . . was designed to resemble . . . AN AMAZON'S BOSOM, with a miniature knoll or hillock on its apex, to denote the nipple." He used French bed-trappings and "ROYAL WILTON" carpets, while American craftsmen were all but starving. He ate from "*massive gold plate and French sterling silver services.*" His latch-string was pulled in to exclude "the *mobocracy* (democracy) from *intruding themselves* at his levees." He prided himself on his reception in aristocratic England, where he had served as the American minister. He proposed English, tyrannical methods of managing the public moneys: "the despots of Europe have these subtreasuries, and therefore we ought to adopt the scheme." He was President by "appointment of Andrew Jackson," not as the candidate of the Democratic party, "not by the election of the people." He plumed and perfumed himself, "strutting by the hour before golden-framed mirrors, NINE FEET HIGH and FOUR FEET and a HALF WIDE" — "behold a *democratic peacock!*" He had even installed a *bathtub* in his quarters. It all came, Ogle asserted, at a cost of "thousands of the People's dollars."

Democrats damned this non-stop vituperation as an "Omnibus of Lies," and even some Whigs thought it went too far. Like other Presidents before and after him, Van Buren had asked for an appropriation—of $3,665—to repair and renovate the White House. He had actually managed most frugally, but he got burned for the request. Ogle's omnibus made its way everywhere, on the front pages of Whig papers, in pamphlets, in translations; in a time of depression and financial straits, it undoubtedly had a profound effect. Whig jingle-makers, of course, drew the appropriate contrast—

> Let Van from his coolers of silver drink wine,
> And lounge on his cushioned setee,
> Our man on a buckeye bench can recline,
> Content with hard cider is he.

The address by "Old Tip" was in a different vein, and fulfilled a different purpose. Democratic accusations that Harrison shied from issues hurt; but in fact he was by no means wholly noncommittal. He had maintained an extensive political correspondence, including public letters setting out his views on at least some issues, as Jackson had done in breaking tradition in 1828; and he had also passed on what amounted to earlier-day press releases. But Harrison went further and engaged in a direct canvass of the voters. Thus, as Gunderson has pointed out, he broke another precedent by engaging in the first overt, speech-making campaign by a presidential candidate. All together he made twenty-three addresses, from one to three hours long; and press and pamphlets carried them to the country. Much of what Harrison said was chaff, such as the fact "that part of my dwelling is a log cabin," although he later omitted the "*part*." He was not an inspiring speaker, but his bearing was impressive and his very presence drew enthusiastic crowds. The climax of "Old Tip's" personal campaign came on September 10, 1840, in a broad valley near Dayton, Ohio. There, partisans calculated, one hundred thousand citizens turned out to hear Harrison's *summa politica*.

After duly modest references to his military career, he got on to "the various questions which now agitate our country." He would "carry out the doctrines of his party," although he would no more make "pledges" than Washington, Adams, or Jefferson would. He was never, ever a Federalist [tremendous cheering]. He was a true, simple Republican, aghast that "the *Government* [under "King Mat"] *is now a practical monarchy* [loud and long cheering]." As President he would reduce "the power and influence of the National Executive [sensation];" at the end of one term in office, he would "lay down . . . that high trust at the feet of the people [here the multitude was so excited as to defy description];" and he would not try to name his successor [nine cheers]. He cited his sponsorship of the liberal Public-Land Act of 1800—"Was I a Federalist then? [cries of no, no, no]." But, "methinks I hear a soft voice asking: Are you in favor of paper money? I AM [shouts of applause]," because it was the only means "by which a poor industrious man may become a rich man without bowing to collosal [sic] wealth [cheers]. But with all this, I am not a Bank man"—although I am "in favor of a correct banking system," undefined, but able to bring "the poor to a level with the rich." There was "tremendous cheering," presumably from rich and poor alike. Harrison abhorred "the violence of party spirit," and suggested that voters should support him for himself rather than follow party lines; in any case, the claims of the Democratic party were "the vilest imposture ever attempted [cheering]." Evocations of heroes from Patrick Henry and George Washington to Jefferson and Madison followed. With a final reference to "calumnies put forth against his military fame," the hero finished.

If it was all a bit ambiguous, it nevertheless amounted to a personal platform in accord with the Whig record and general persuasion. Indeed, Harrison said quite enough in his Dayton address and other statements to show that he was not always "General Mum." Yet like Weed and other new-style Whig politicians, the elderly candidate also had to grapple with the problem Millard Fillmore had posed so bluntly: how to get the incongruous mass of Whigs united as "undoubted good metal," alloyed together, active, moving toward victory. The demands of this problem helped to account for much of the Whig appeal, including Harrison's silences and equivocations.

The final step in the Whig campaign was to mobilize the electorate. The Whig managers knew that they had to lure voters from the Democratic standard, win a substantial number of new voters, and march their own faithful to the polls. Mobilization was accomplished at stump-speakings, by so-called mass "conventions," at great rallies, at vast encampments, "*acres of men!*" Fields were filled across the country, although Whig crowd-counts may have been more enthusiastic than accurate: some twenty-five thousand at Columbus, Ohio; "*fifteen acres*" including six thousand women at the site of the Battle of Tippecanoe; a "mighty army" of fifteen thousand at Springfield, Illinois; "thronging thousands" at Fort Meigs, Ohio; more than one hundred thousand at Nashville, Tennessee, enough to daunt even Andrew Jackson; a procession of sixty thousand from the Boston Common to Bunker Hill; even more, according to the local *Political Tornado*, at Cincinnati; and other throngs at Richmond and Wheeling in Virginia, at Utica, Auburn, and Syracuse in New York, and in newly-admitted Michigan and Arkansas. Nothing like it had ever been seen before: the Whigs had perfected the militia as well as the merchandizing aspects of campaigning. Even the dour John Quincy Adams credited "immense assemblages" of "fifty thousand souls": "Here is a revolution in the habits and manners of the people. Where will it end?" The "manifest tendency" of such populistic outpourings, he feared, "is to civil war." It wasn't really a call to the barricades, though, and the "*acres*" were carefully arranged by Whig managers and propagandists – "to the polls, to the polls!" It was, however, an omen for Van Buren and his cohorts.

Indeed the Democrats were never quite able to catch up, despite their legions of trained organizers and their attempts at rebuttal. In the din, moreover, the voice of anti-slavery could hardly be heard at all, and the Liberty party candidate was in England during the crucial months before the election.

The result was decisive, if not quite as dramatic as the super-heated Whig campaign might have led one to expect. In their public pronouncements dur-

ing the canvass, the Whigs were as cocksure as the Democrats were privately
gloomy; thus, the Harrison marchers had offered another jingle—

> Make way for Old Tip, turn out, turn out,
>   Make way for Old Tip, turn out!
> 'Tis the people's decree,
>   Their choice he shall be,
> So Martin Van Buren turn out, turn out,
>   So Martin Van Buren turn out!

In fact, however, the Whig managers knew that it would not be easy to van-
quish their seasoned, established rivals.

Throughout the life of the second party system the Whigs were number
two. They were a "moon" party to the dominant Democratic "sun," in Samuel
Lubell's metaphor (see Table 4). They and their predecessors had lost
every presidential contest since 1824, managing to amass only 44 per cent of
the popular vote in 1828 and 45 per cent in 1832, although the combined total
for the three Whig challengers in 1836 reached a substantial 49 per cent. In
1828 the opposition had carried only nine states to the Jacksonian's fifteen,
and in 1832 only eight to the Democrat's sixteen; but again, 1836 narrowed
the gap to eleven states for the Whigs and fifteen for the Democrats. Much of
the opposition strength lay in New England and the lesser Mid-Atlantic
states, although 1836 brought Whig inroads in other sections. Finally, the
Whig "moon" was to rise only once again in a presidential contest after
1840—in 1848, when the party ran another military hero against a sorely divided Democratic party. In the whole span of the second party system from
1828 to 1854, the Whigs and their forebears won majorities in the Senate only
in 1840 and 1842, and in the House only in 1840 and 1846.

In the battle against Van Buren, the new-style Whig managers saw their
chance, and strove desperately to catch up. Encouraged by the rising trend of
opposition in 1836 and in local elections thereafter, and by the political effects
of the Democratic depression of 1837, they had hope: a falling-off of support
as time passes and resentments build up has generally characterized the ca-
reers of dominant parties in American politics. The long-standing subordination of the Whigs to the Democrats, and the possibility of a breakthrough in
1840, are basic to an understanding of the whole character of the Whig
campaign. Together with the problem of uniting their heterogeneous following, the Whigs' status as a "moon" party all but dictated their strident rhetoric, as well as their assiduous organization and mobilization. Men like Weed
and Stevens were without illusions, determined on victory, and planning to
make sure they got it.

In the end they mobilized the masses and competed effectively in nearly
every state. The excitement of the contest brought some 2,412,698 voters to
the polls. Turnout in the nation as a whole rose from 57.8 per cent of adult
white males in 1836 to 80.2 per cent in 1840, according to Burnham's calculations—a record that was not to be equalled or surpassed except in 1860 and
1876. Every state in the Union reached new peaks of participation in presidential contests, and fifteen states exceeded the national average, with New

York recording a turnout of 91.9 per cent. Competition, moreover, had never been so close in every section and in nearly every state (see Tables 2 and 5). Even where the ticket lost, "Tippecanoe and Tyler Too" carried a respectable 45 per cent of the vote or better in every state but three. The competitive character of the second party system was clearly established nationwide; and 1844 was to exhibit even keener closer rivalry.

From the standpoint of the Whig directors, the salient fact was that they had won. Their "catch-much" appeal had succeeded. In the end Harrison had 52.9 per cent of the popular vote to 46.8 for Van Buren and 0.3 for Birney on the Liberty party ticket. There was no doubt about "the people's decree." Yet the margin between "Old Tip" and "Old Kinderhook" was only 6.1 percentage points, whereas in 1828 and 1832 Jackson had won over Adams and Clay by margins of 12 per cent. (The average spread between winners and their nearest rivals in all thirty-six presidential elections from 1828 through 1968, moreover, has been 9.3 per cent, and in twenty-one contests since 1828 the winner has enjoyed a wider popular-vote margin than Harrison did.) The result in the Electoral College in 1840 was decisive, indeed overwhelming (see Table 5). Harrison carried nineteen states with 234 electoral votes to Van Buren's seven states and 60 electoral votes. When it was all over, Van Buren had won only New Hampshire in New England, Virginia and South Carolina in the South, Illinois and Missouri in the Northwest, and Alabama and Arkansas in the Southwest. Meanwhile Harrison carried every large state except Virginia, and garnered 55 per cent or more of the popular vote in eleven states.

The results of the congressional elections were also clear. In the Senate, a previous Democratic advantage of 28 to 22 was turned into its exact opposite; and in the new House of Representatives the Whigs could claim 133 members to the Democrats' 102, a sharp reversal of the previous balance of 124 Democrats to 118 Whigs. It looked like Harrison was going to have an all-Whig government, until he died and Tyler upset everything.

In large part "Old Tip's" margin of victory came from once-stalwart Democratic states that were burdened with dissension or uncertainty by 1840. The Whigs snatched crucial blocks of electoral votes from a depleted Democratic party in New York (42), Pennsylvania (30), and North Carolina (15), as well as in Georgia (11) and Tennessee (15), which had also gone Whig in 1836, for a total of 113. Factionalism and personal antagonisms, desertions to the Whigs as the thrust of "Locofoco" Democratic policies became manifest, and feeling against Van Buren in Tennessee and elsewhere had all taken their toll—along, of course, with the effects of economic depression. The 113 electoral votes from these previously Jacksonian bastions, added to the 60 electoral votes Van Buren had managed to hold, would have given him a total of 173 to Harrison's 121 and a handy victory. The Whig margin was perilously close in New York and Pennsylvania, moreover. North Carolina and Tennessee were not to return to the Democratic column until 1852 and 1856 respectively; New York, Pennsylvania, and Georgia all recanted by 1844. Of all the states that had been most notably plagued by Democratic factionalism and desertions, only Virginia remained Democratic. Even there the vote for Van Buren fell sharply from 56.8 per cent in 1836 to 50.8 in 1840.

More broadly, the key to the Whig victory was image-making and rhetoric — or, sometimes, "buncombe," to use a contemporaneous term. From the outset the rhetoric was planned and sustained by clever managers; by solid, well-planned organization; and by mass mobilization. Throughout the campaign the persona of "Old Tippecanoe," the songs, the log-cabin symbolism and Greeley's *Log Cabin*, the attacks on "Sweet Sandy Whiskers", Ogle's slanders, and the cider barrels were crucial. The rhetoric was aimed at convincing the voters, but it was also an expression of the times, and a contribution in itself: popular democracy, popular appeals, and popular symbolism were fixed in American political culture. The whole campaign was in keeping with the rising spirit of assertive equalitarianism, or with a new kind of deference — a bow to The People and their ultimate political majesty rather than to a social elite. Much as they despised a Jackson and all his populistic sentiments and works, even the old-style Whigs had to go along, or go disguised accordingly.

It worked, as Weed and Stevens had thought it would. It got the Whig faithful to the polls. The record from 1828 to 1836, however, suggests that this would not have been enough. The campaign must also have recruited an undetermined number of disgruntled Democrats or first-time voters, enough to make the margin of victory. There was no Survey Research Center at work in 1840, and the proportions of Whigs, former Democrats, or new voters in the total for Harrison cannot be determined. Yet the extraordinary increase in voting turnout in 1840 suggests that the role of first-time voters may have been crucial.

Rejecting the notion that imitation is the sincerest form of flattery, the Democrats were outraged. The Whigs' "Hurrah" campaign was all too reminiscent of the successful canvass for "Old Hickory" in 1828. "They have at last learned from defeat the art of victory," the *Democratic Review* cried even before the results were in, "We have taught them how to conquer us!" The log-cabin symbolism was "unmeaning and ridiculously inappropriate," aimed only at "rousing the hurrah of popular enthusiasm," and the voters had bought it! Yet it appeared that the Democrats had become cynical *after* the election, and Greeley satirized them accordingly —

> *Blarney Before Election*: Dear People! nobody but *us* can imagine how pure, patriotic, shrewd, and sagacious you are. *You* can't be humbugged! You can't be misled! . . . You are always right as a book, and nobody can gum you. In short, you are O. K.

> *Raving After Election:* You miserable, despicable, know-nothing, good-for-nothing rascals! . . . Led away by Log Cabin fooleries! Gummed by coonskins! . . . Dead drunk on hard cider! Senseless, beastly, contemptible wretches! Go to the devil!

The diatribe was overdone, but Greeley had a point. Meanwhile, a number of Democrats including Van Buren waited more or less patiently for the sober second thought of the people to show itself.

The questions remain — what was the meaning or significance of the election of 1840, and how rational or irrational were the voters? The canvass was not a "critical election," in V. O. Key's term, or a "realigning election," in the language of the Survey Research Center. Unlike 1800, 1828, 1860, 1896, and 1932 – 1936, it did not mark a fall from dominance by one party and the rise to continuing power of another, with a lasting new direction in public policy as a result. Nor did it bring about a permanent readjustment of party identifications among voters, a lasting transfer of loyalties from Democrats to Whigs. It was rather a "deviating election," in the SRC's classification: the electorate returned to the Democratic standard four years later, though by a narrow margin, and the Democrats were to remain the dominant party until 1860. The triumph of Harrison was only temporary.

The issue of rationality is more complex, and may apply to virtually any election — to 1828 or 1840, to 1932 or 1952, or to 1968. But the question must be examined in the context of secular trends, of public policy and results, of party perspectives and performance, and of voting behavior. While 1844 may well have marked a sober reconsideration, 1840 may not have been as unsober as it has been painted.

There is no question that the rhetoric of the Whig campaign was often as empty as it was cynical; and a heavy emphasis on rhetoric and public-relations techniques may always present a threat to popular judgment and democratic choice. Modern students have pointed out, moreover, what a large part symbolism, emotion, sentiment, perceptions of and affections for candidates, and sheer ignorance have played in voting behavior even today, in an era of widespread access to information and considerable sophistication. However, V. O. Key has made a case for "the responsible electorate," offering evidence for patterns of voting behaviour through significant spans of time which indicate that most voters find ways to express their basic interests and concerns, or at least their real satisfactions or dissatisfactions. A substantial number of Americans had good reason to be dissatisfied with the Democrats by 1840. Some could complain of radical, Democratic policies and see greater opportunities for themselves in the Whig affinity for capitalist development and expansion. Some found it easy to distrust the "Little Magician" and the crew of office-holders that surrounded him, or at least question whether "Little Van" was big enough for "Old Hickory's" shoes. Others had suffered under the burdens of economic collapse and depression, knew from personal experience that times were hard, and logically blamed the President and party in power. Down, therefore, with "Martin Van Ruin" and the "Locofocos."

In the campaign the Whigs had stressed Democratic hard times almost as much as they had Harrison hard cider, and seemed to offer a way out. If it is difficult to believe that "Old Tip" could ever have been a popular savior in office, at least the persona his managers gave him was one of a sympathetic friend of the "plain people," of the "common man" of the day. Some voters will always be caught by hollow folderol. Many others in 1840 may have simply wanted a change from depression and distress. Perhaps they saw Harrison and the Whigs as the nearest way of bringing it about. Whether or not most of the voters behaved in the manner of "the responsible electorate," popular enthusiasm for William Henry Harrison was real. Undoubtedly the entertainment helped, but Gunderson has put the more significant point succinctly: "a vigorous frontier people rebelled against the harassments of depression by conducting a crusade against the party in office." They turned out and cheered "Old Tip" accordingly.

Meanwhile, the course of American political development had gone forward. More than any election since Jackson's first victory in 1828, the contest of 1840 served to set the Presidency and presidential elections as the focal point of American politics and popular attention. The year also brought the popularization of national politics to its zenith, and established its character in American life: never again could the Washington community go its way heedless of a national public. With various refinements after 1840, moreover, the structure of party politics was fixed in a form that was to last basically unaltered for generations to come. Only in our own century, and more recently as a result of the impact of television, the "multimedia," and new public relations techniques, have party structures and functions experienced significant change and indeed declined in force and weight. By the time of Harrison's triumph, the traditional features of party life were clear—continuing, professional organization; the convention system; adroit propaganda and mass appeals; the marching militia, "*acres of men*," and mass turnout at the polls; close, continuing two-party rivalry. No longer would voters follow after leaders who looked down on The People and dealt with a limited clientele in the electorate. Among Whigs as well as Democrats, party politics was concentrated more and more into the hands of a working political cadre who knew how to deal with the many, who assumed that mass participation was politics as usual. Often such men were little known to the nation, or to anyone except their immediate party superiors and their constituents: at both of the national conventions of 1840, most delegates including those who served on important committees stand faceless in the eyes of history. Political leaders and heroes remained, but the old politics of notables was all but gone. The new politics of *hoi polloi* was in.

During his travels in the American democracy, Alexis de Tocqueville observed with a touch of incredulity—

> The political activity which pervades the United States must be seen in order to be understood. No sooner do you set foot upon American ground, than you are stunned by a kind of tumult . . . almost the only pleasure which an American knows is to take a part in the government, and to discuss its measures.

The famous visit was made in 1831 and 1832. What would Tocqueville have thought if he had come after Weed and Stevens had perfected the art of national political management, after "Old Tippecanoe's" carefully contrived charisma had become manifest? The grand Image Campaign was in keeping with what Tocqueville observed, but it was larger than life and would surely have filled him with amazement.

TABLE 1

*VOTER PARTICIPATION; PEAK TURNOUTS FOR FIVE
STATES BY DECADE 1789–1839, 1840, PER CENT OF
WHITE ADULT MALES*

Sources—J. R. Pole, *Political Representation in England and the Origins of the American Republic* (London and New York, 1966), 544-564; Richard P. McCormick, "New Perspectives on Jacksonian Politics," *American Historical Review*, LXV (January 1960), 292; Turnout data compiled by Walter Dean Burnham, Washington University, St. Louis.

	MASS.	N.H.	PA.	VA.	N.C.
1789–99	28 G 1799	33 G 1798	56 G 1799	ND	ND
1800–09	64 G 1809	70 G 1809	71 G 1808	26 P 1800	ND
1810–19	67 G 1812	81 G 1814	61 G 1817	18 P 1812	12 ? 1816
1820–29	58 G 1824	74 P 1828	64 G 1820, 23	29 R 1829	70 C 1823
1830–39	55 G 1839	78 G 1838, 39	68 G 1838	35 P 1836	67 G 1836
1840	66 G 67 P	71 G 86 P	77 P	55 P	84 G 82 P

Key to type of election—G, election for governor of state; P, election for presidential electors; R, referendum; C, election for members of Congress; ?, unknown. ND, no data.

SOURCES—Turnout data compiled by Walter Dean Burnham, Washington University, St. Louis; also, Richard P. McCormick, "New Perspectives on Jacksonian Politics," *American Historical Review*, LXV (January 1960), 292. Index of competition calculated from data in Svend Petersen, ed., *A Statistical History of the American Presidential Elections* (New York, 1963), 18–27.

TABLE 2

TURNOUT AND COMPETITION IN PRESIDENTIAL ELECTIONS
PER CENT OF ADULT WHITE MALE VOTE / INDEX OF COMPETITION

		Previous High	1824	1828	1832	1836	1840	1844
New England								
N. H.	T	80.8	18.0	74.3P	70.1	38.2	86.3	68.9
	C		12.8	92.9	85.4	49.9	89.5	81.1
Vt.	T	79.9	L	54.5	50.0	52.5P	73.8	70.8
	C		L	51.2	93.9	80.2	71.6	82.1
Mass.	T	67.4	29.0S	25.7	39.4P	43.4	66.7	65.8
	C		35.5	33.6	71.7	89.6	83.9	88.9
Me.	T	62.0	19.1	42.7	66.2P	37.7	83.7	71.3
	C		37.0	80.3	88.9	79.9	99.5	86.7
Conn.	T	54.4	14.9	27.2	46.0P	52.3	75.7	80.0
	C		35.2	48.6	80.1	98.6	88.9	95.4
R. I.	T	49.4	12.0	17.1	26.3P	23.8	33.2	45.1S
	C		17.1	45.9	88.2	95.5	77.1	80.0
Mid-Atlantic								
Del.	T	81.9	L	LP	67.1	69.5	82.8	85.8
	C		L	L	99.0	93.5	90.0	97.7
N. J.	T	71.8	35.6	71.0P	68.8	69.2	80.4	87.2S
	C		91.2	96.0	99.0	99.0	96.4	98.9
Pa.	T	71.5	18.8	56.5	52.3	53.1	77.5P	77.3
	C		35.3	66.7	84.6	97.6	99.9	98.1
Md.	T	69.0	53.7	70.3P	55.7	67.6	84.5	81.4
	C		99.7	98.0	99.9	92.3	92.3	95.2
N. Y.	T	41.5	L	80.2S	84.2	70.5P	91.9	92.1
	C		L	98.1	95.8	90.8	97.0	98.9
Old South								
N. C.	T	70.0	41.8	56.9	31.3	53.0P	82.4	78.8
	C		86.7	53.8	31.0	93.5	84.3	95.2
Ga.	T	62.3	L	31.8	29.0	61.8	88.8P	92.6
	C		L	6.4	0.0	94.6	88.4	97.6
Va.	T	25.9	11.6	27.7	31.1S	35.2P	54.7	54.2
	C		64.6	62.3	50.8	86.3	98.4	93.8
S. C.			L	L	L	L	L	L

Continued

TABLE 2—Continued

		Previous High	1824	1828	1832	1836	1840	1844
Northwest								
Mo.	T	71.9	19.8	54.0	41.0	36.1	75.1P	77.8
	C		84.7	58.2	70.0	80.0	87.1	86.1
Ill.	T	55.8	24.3	52.4	46.0	43.5P	86.0	76.0
	C		92.4	65.6	55.5	90.6	97.8	88.0
Ind.	T	52.4	37.1	68.7	71.9	69.2	84.4P	84.7
	C		87.1	86.8	65.8	88.1	88.4	98.3
Ohio	T	46.5	34.8	75.9P	73.9	75.5	84.5	83.6
	C		98.5	96.8	97.0	95.8	91.5	98.1
Mich.	T		NA	NA	NA	35.0	84.9P	79.8
	C		NA	NA	NA	70.3	95.9	93.9
Southwest								
Ala.	T	96.7	49.1	54.6	33.3	64.9P	89.7	80.3
	C		48.4	20.3	0.0	86.4	91.2	81.7
Tenn.	T	80.0	28.3	55.0	31.3	57.3P	89.7	89.8
	C		4.1	9.6	9.5	83.9	88.9	99.9
Miss.	T	79.8	41.3	56.6	28.0S	64.4P	88.2	86.1
	C		69.5	37.9	0.0	98.5	93.1	86.6
Ky.	T	74.4	25.4	70.7P	74.0	61.1	74.3	80.7
	C		54.3	88.8	91.0	95.0	71.6	91.8
La.	T	34.2	L	36.2	22.3	19.2	39.4P	47.1
	C		L	94.2	76.9	96.2	80.6	97.4
Ark.	T		NA	NA	NA	28.9	67.6P	63.5
	C		NA	NA	NA	68.1	86.5	73.1
U. S.	T		26.9	57.6	55.4	57.8	80.2P	78.9
	C		89.7	88.0	88.3	85.7	93.9	98.6

T —Voting turnout, percentage of adult white males.

C —Index of competition in given presidential election: percentage of total popular vote for winning candidate minus percentage of popular vote for second-highest candidate, with remainder subtracted from 100.

Underline indicates turnout exceeds high for state previous to 1824.

P —Election coinciding with or immediately following year of establishment of second party system within state.

S —First election following an extension of suffrage in state.

L —Presidential electors chosen by legislature.

NA—Not yet admitted as a state.

TABLE 3

PREFERENCE VOTES FOR PRESIDENTIAL NOMINEE, BY SECTION: WHIG NATIONAL CONVENTION OF 1840

SOURCE—Adapted from Robert Gray Gunderson, *The Log-Cabin Campaign* (Lexington, Kentucky, 1957), 60.

New England

For Clay—Connecticut 8, Rhode Island 4; Total 12.
For Harrison—Maine 10, New Hampshire 7, Massachusetts 14; Total 31.
For Scott—Vermont 7; Total 7.

Mid-Atlantic

For Clay—Maryland 10, Delaware 3; Total 13.
For Harrison—Pennsylvania 30; Total 30.
For Scott—New York 42, New Jersey 8; Total 50.

Old South

For Clay—Virginia 23, North Carolina 15; Total 38.
For Harrison and Scott, 0.

Northwest

For Clay—Illinois 5, Missouri 4; Total 9.
For Harrison—Ohio 21, Indiana 9; Total 30.
For Scott 0.   Abstaining—Michigan 3.

Southwest

For Clay—Kentucky 15, Alabama 7, Mississippi 4, Louisiana 5; Total 31.
For Harrison and Scott, 0.

TOTALS—For Clay 103, for Harrison 91, for Scott 57.

TABLE 4

DEMOCRATIC DOMINANCE AND THE WHIG CHALLENGE, 1828–1844
WINNING PERCENTAGES OF THE PRESIDENTIAL VOTE BY STATE

SOURCE—Compiled from Svend Petersen, ed., *A Statistical History of the American Presidential Elections* (New York, 1963).

	1828		1832		1836		1840		1844	
	Ja	*Ad*	*Dm*	*NR*	*Dm*	*Wh*	*Dm*	*Wh*	*Dm*	*Wh*
New England										
Me.		60	55		60			50+	54	
N. H.		54	57		75		55		55	
Vt.		74		76[a]		60[H]		64		55
Mass.		83		77[a]		55[We]		57		51
Conn.		76		65[a]	51			55		51
R. I.		77		63[a]	52			61		60
Mid-Atlantic										
N. Y.	51		52		55			51	49[b]	
N. J.		52	50[b]			51[H]		52		51
Pa.	67		58		51			50[b]	51	
Del.		L		51		53[H]		55		51
Md.		51		50+		54[H]		54		52
Old South										
Va.	69		75		57		51		53	
N. C.	73		85		53			58		52
S. C.	L			L	L		L		L	
Ga.	97		100			53[Wh]		56	51	
Northwest										
Ohio	52		51			52[H]		54		50[b]
Ind.	57		67			56[H]		56	50+	
Ill.	67		72		55		51		54	
Mo.	71		65		60		56		57	
Mich.					65			52	50[b]	
Southwest										
Ky.	56			55		53[H]		64		54
Tenn.	95		95			58[Wh]		56		50+
Ala.	90		100		57		54		59	
Miss.	81		100		51			54	57	
La.	53		62		52			60	51	
Ark.					66		57		63	
U. S.	56		55		51			53	50[b]	

KEY—JA, vote for Andrew Jackson; AD, vote for John Quincy Adams; DM, Democratic; NR, National Republican; WH, Whig.

L Presidential electors chosen by legislature.

[a] Combined vote, National Republican and Anti-Masonic candidates in 1832.

[H] Vote for William Henry Harrison, [We]—for Daniel Webster, [Wh]—for Hugh Lawson White, Whig candidates in 1836.

[b] Liberty party vote in 1844 in New York (3.3%), Ohio (2.6%), Michigan (6.5%), and U.S. (2.3%), resulted in neither major-party candidate receiving a majority of the popular vote, as did votes for fractional candidates in New Jersey in 1832 and Pennsylvania in 1840.

TABLE 5

SUMMARY RESULTS OF THE PRESIDENTIAL ELECTION OF 1840 POPULAR AND ELECTORAL VOTE, AND STATES CARRIED BY SECTION

SOURCE—Adapted from Svend Petersen, ed., *A Statistical History of the American Presidential Elections* (New York, 1963).

	Popular Vote and Percent						Electoral Vote	
	HARRISON		VAN BUREN		BIRNEY		HA	VB
Ala.	28,471	45.6	33,991	54.4				7
Ark.	5,160	43.3	6,766	56.7				3
Conn.	31,601	55.4	25,296	44.3	174	.3	8	
Del.	5,967	55.0	4,884	45.0			3	
Ga.	40,349	55.8	31,989	44.2			11	
Ill.	45,574	48.8	47,625	51.0	159	.2		5
Ind.	65,308	55.8	51,695	44.2			9	
Ky.	58,489	64.2	32,616	35.8			15	
La.	11,297	59.7	7,617	40.3			5	
Me.	46,612	50.1	46,190	49.7	186	.2	10	
Md.	33,533	53.8	28,759	46.2			10	
Mass.	72,913	57.4	52,432	41.3	1,621	1.3	14	
Mich.	22,933	51.7	21,131	47.6	321	.7	3	
Miss.	19,518	53.5	16,995	46.5			4	
Mo.	22,972	43.6	29,760	56.4				4
N. H.	26,434	44.6	32,670	55.2	126	.2		7
N. J.	33,362	51.8	31,034	48.1	69	.1	8	
N. Y.	225,945	51.2	212,743	48.2	2,790	.6	42	
N. C.	46,379	57.9	33,782	42.1			15	
Ohio	148,157	54.1	124,782	45.6	903	.3	21	
Pa.	144,023	50.0	143,784	49.9	343	.1	30	
R. I.	5,278	61.2	3,301	38.3	42	.5	4	
S. C.								11
Tenn.	60,391	55.6	48,289	44.4			15	
Vt.	32,445	63.9	18,009	35.5	319	.6	7	
Va.	42,501	49.2	43,893	50.8				23
U.S.	1,275,612	52.9	1,130,033	46.8	7,053	.3	234	60

States Carried—New England, Harrison 5, Van Buren 1; Mid-Atlantic, Harrison 5, Van Buren 0; Old South, Harrison 2, Van Buren 2; Northwest, Harrison 3, Van Buren 2; Southwest, Harrison 4, Van Buren 2. Total States Carried, Harrison 19, Van Buren 7.

Appendix

Democratic Platform
1840

1. *Resolved*, That the federal government is one of limited powers, derived solely from the constitution, and the grants of power shown therein, ought to be strictly construed by all the departments and agents of the government, and that it is inexpedient and dangerous to exercise doubtful constitutional powers.

2. *Resolved*, That the constitution does not confer upon the general government the power to commence and carry on, a general system of internal improvements.

3. *Resolved*, That the constitution does not confer authority upon the federal government, directly or indirectly, to assume the debts of the several states, contracted for local internal improvements, or other state purposes; nor would such assumption be just or expedient.

4. *Resolved*, That justice and sound policy forbid the federal government to foster one branch of industry to the detriment of another, or to cherish the interests of one portion to the injury of another portion of our common country—that every citizen and every section of the country, has a right to demand and insist upon an equality of rights and privileges, and to complete and ample protection of person and property from domestic violence, or foreign aggression.

5. *Resolved*, That it is the duty of every branch of the government, to enforce and practice the most rigid economy, in conducting our public affairs, and that no more revenue ought to be raised, than is required to defray the necessary expenses of the government.

6. *Resolved*, That congress has no power to charter a national bank; that we believe such an institution one of deadly hostility to the best interests of the country, dangerous to our republican institutions and the liberties of the people, and calculated to place the business of the country within the control of a concentrated money power, and above the laws and the will of the people.

7. *Resolved*, That congress has no power, under the constitution, to interfere with or control the domestic institutions of the several states, and that such states are the sole and proper judges of everything appertaining to their own affairs, not prohibited by the constitution; that all efforts by abolitionists or others, made to induce congress to interfere with questions of slavery, or to take incipient steps in relation thereto, are calculated to lead to the most alarming and dangerous consequences, and that all such efforts have an inevitable tendency to diminish the happiness of the people, and endanger the

stability and permanency of the union, and ought not to be countenanced by any friend to our political institutions.

8. *Resolved*, That the separation of the moneys of the government from banking institutions, is indispensable for the safety of the funds of the government, and the rights of the people.

9. *Resolved*, That the liberal principles embodied by Jefferson in the Declaration of Independence, and sanctioned in the constitution, which makes ours the land of liberty, and the asylum of the oppressed of every nation, have ever been cardinal principles in the democratic faith; and every attempt to abridge the present privilege of becoming citizens, and the owners of soil among us, ought to be resisted with the same spirit which swept the alien and sedition laws from our statute-book.

Editorial by Abraham Lincoln
from the *Sangamo Journal*
November 3, 1838

Although Henry Clay was still the outstanding figure in Whig ranks, many leaders doubted his ability to unite the party's various factions. In this editorial, written more than a year before the Whigs held their "Union-and-Harmony" convention, a young Illinois lawyer foresees General William Henry Harrison as a prospective party healer and presidential candidate.

We, this week, raise the standard of Gen. Wm. H. Harrison, as a candidate for the Presidency. This stand, we have not taken without much reflection; but now, that we have taken it, we shall not be induced to abandon it unless we shall conceive that the harmony of our friends absolutely requires it.

We are aware that offices are not established in this country for the mere benefit and gratification of the individuals who may be called to fill them. — We are amongst the foremost to deny, that any man has just claims to office, unless the People, by recognizing those claims, can best advance their own interests. But while we say this, we insist, that so long as human nature remains as it is — so long as men continue ambitious of distinction — it is not the part of wisdom in any community, to let that ambition go ungratified, in an individual, who has rendered arduous and valuable services to that community; for what man will care to sacrifice his ease and comfort, and spend all the better part of his life in bearing the burdens and encountering the dangers of his country, if he shall know, that when he shall assert his claims to the gratitude of his country, another, who has toiled not, shall be preferred to him. — When an individual's hairs have grown grey, and his eyes dim in the service of his country, it seems to us, if his country-men are wise, and polite, they will so reward him, as to encourage the youth of that country to follow his example.

If such an individual can now be found in this country; if the policy we have been urging be sound, and that policy can be furthered in the person of any one man more than that of any other, that man, we insist, is Gen. Harrison. Near forty years ago, when the great North-Western Territory was but one extensive hunting ground of dusky savages, Gen. Harrison tore himself from all the comforts of civilized life and took up his abode among those savages, to lay the foundation for all that population, wealth and independence, that now find a home upon that fertile and, now, cultivated tract of country. He may, with great propriety, be called the father of the North Western Territory. There is not an important incident in its history, whether it conduce more to the glory of the past, or to the substantial advantages of the present and future, that does not bear the impress of his untiring hand. Go to the blood-drenched and bone-whitened field of every Indian battle; go to the records of every valuable Indian treaty; go to our most excellent public land system—that system which is so admirably calculated to guard the People of the country where it prevails, against the extremes of aristocratic wealth, and indigent poverty, and, in each and every of them, it will be seen that Harrison has been the man who has done most, suffered most, and profited least, by the respective results.

These services, with thousands of others of minor importance, constitute Gen. Harrison's claims to the gratitude of the American People, and particularly to that of the North Western portion of them. To these claims, there are no drawbacks—no deductions to be made for want of honesty or capability. All his acts bear, as well the marks of profound wisdom, and devoted patriotism, as those of much labor and toil. Unlike most men similarly circumstanced, he has not used the means placed in his power, in acquiring for himself a princely fortune. Though his intellectual powers are in full vigor, age, incessant toil, and long experience in the campaigns and other frontier services in the North West, have very much impaired his physical constitution; to which may be added, he is now poor, and dependent on his own hands for a living.

We repeat, that if the American People wish to honor a patriot and statesman; if they wish to reward a long-tried and faithful friend; if they wish to stimulate the youth of our country to emulation of noble examples; if they wish to proclaim to the world, that poverty shall never arrest virtue and intelligence on their march to distinction; they can, more effectually than in any other way, do all these, by elevating Gen. Wm. H. Harrison to the Presidency.

In expressing a preference for Gen. Harrison, we wish not to be understood, as having, to the smallest extent, lost confidence in the ability or patriotism of those other gentlemen, who are spoken of by our political friends, as candidates for the same high station. We consent to pass by such men as Henry Clay and Daniel Webster, only because their fame is already immortal—because they shine within themselves—because the sickly light reflected by office and power, can add nothing to their splendor—because, come weal or woe, their names will never be forgotten, so long as Cicero, Pitt and our own immortal Washington shall be remembered.

Letter from General William Henry Harrison
to Representative Harmar Denny
December 2, 1838

Henry Clay's Masonic affiliations precluded his winning the support of the remnants of the Anti-Masonic party. At an 1838 convention the Anti-Masons, who had actually become Whigs, groped for a likely candidate and finally settled on General Harrison. In this letter to former Whig Congressman Harmar Denny, Harrison explained the principles upon which the Anti-Masons should support him.

Dear Sir: As it is probable that you have by this time returned to Pittsburg, I do myself the honor to acknowledge the receipt of your letter from Philadelphia, containing the proceedings of the National Democratic Anti-Masonic Convention which lately convened in that city. With feelings of the deepest gratitude I read the resolution, unanimously adopted, nominating me as a candidate for the Presidency of the United States. This is the second time that I have received from that patriotic party, of which you yourself are a distinguished member, the highest evidence of confidence that can be given to a citizen of our Republic. I would attempt to describe my sense of the obligations I owe them, if I were not convinced that any language which I could command would fall far short of what I really feel. If, however, the wishes of the convention should be realized, and I should be the choice of those who are opposed to the present Administration, and success should attend their efforts, I shall have it in my power to manifest my gratitude in a manner more acceptable to those whom you represent than by any professions of it which I could at this time make. I mean, by exerting my utmost efforts to carry out the principles set forth in their resolutions, by arresting the progress of those measures "destructive to the prosperity of the People," and substituting for them those sound democratic republican doctrines upon which the Administrations of Jefferson and Madison were conducted.

Among the principles proper to be adopted by an Executive sincerely desirous to restore the Administration to its original simplicity and purity, I deem the following to be of prominent importance:

I. To confine his service to a single term.

II. To disclaim all right of control over the public treasure, with the exception of such part of it as may be appropriated by law, to carry out the public service, and that to be applied precisely as the law may direct, and drawn from the Treasury agreeably to the long established forms of that Department.

III. That he should never attempt to influence the elections, either by the People or the State Legislature, nor suffer the Federal officers under his control to take any other part in them, than by giving their own votes when they possess the right of voting.

IV. That, in the exercise of the veto power, he should limit his rejection of bills to, 1st. Such as are in his opinion unconstitutional. 2d. Such as tend to encroach on the rights of the States, or of individuals. 3d. Such as, involving deep interests, may in his opinion require more mature deliberation, or reference to the will of the People, to be ascertained at the succeeding elections.

V. That he should never suffer the influence of his office to be used for purposes of a purely party character.

VI. That in removals from office of those who hold their appointments during the pleasure of the Executive, the cause of such removal should always be communicated to the person removed, and, if he request it, to the Senate, at the time that the nomination of a successor is made.

And last but not least in importance,

VII. That he should not suffer the Executive Department of the Government to become the source of legislation, but leave the whole business of making the laws for the Union to be done by the department to which the Constitution has exclusively assigned it, until they have assumed that perfected shape where and when alone the opinions of the Executive may be heard. A community of power in the preparation of the laws between the Legislative and the Executive Departments must necessarily lead to dangerous commutations, and greatly to the advantage of a President desirous of extending his power. Such a construction of the Constitution could never have been contemplated by those who framed it, as they well knew that those who propose the bills will always take care of themselves, or the interests of their constituents; and hence the provision in the Constitution, borrowed from that of England, restricting the originating of revenue bills to the immediate Representatives of the People. So far from agreeing in opinion with the distinguished character who lately retired from the Presidency, that Congress should have applied to him for the project of a banking system, I think that such an application would have manifested not only great subserviency upon the part of that body, but an unpardonable ignorance of the chief danger to be apprehended from such an institution. That danger unquestionably consists in a union of interests between the Executive and the Bank. Would an ambitious incumbent of the Executive chair neglect so favorable an opportunity as the preparing of the law would give him to insert in it a provision to secure his influence over it? In the authority given to the President by the Constitution, "to recommend to Congress such measures as he shall judge necessary and expedient," it was certainly never intended that the measures he recommended should be presented in a shape suited for the immediate decision of the Legislature. The sages who made the Constitution too well knew the advantages which the Crown of England derived from the exercise of its power by its Ministers to have intended it to be used by our Chief Magistrate, or the Heads of Departments under his control. The boasted principle of the English Constitution, that the consent of the democratic branch of the Government was not only necessary to receive money from the People, but that it was its inviolable prerogative also to originate all the bills for that purpose, is true in theory as in the letter, but rendered utterly false and nugatory in effect by the participation of the Ministers of the Crown in the details of legislation. Indeed, the influence they derive from sitting as members of the House of Commons, and from wielding the immense patronage of the Crown, (constitutional or usurped,) gives them a power over that body that renders plausible at least the base flattery, or, as it is more probable, that intended sarcasm of Sir Walter Raleigh, in an address to James the First, that the demand of the Sovereign upon the Commons for pecuniary aid was intended only "that the tax might seem to come from themselves;" whereas, the inference is, it was really laid by the Sovereign himself.

Having thus given you my opinion of some things which might be done, and others which should not be done, by a President coming into power by the support of those of the People who are opposed to the principles upon which the present Administration is conducted, you will see that I have omitted one which is deemed by many of as much importance as any other. I allude to the appointment of members of Congress to office by the President. The Constitution contains no prohibition of such appointments, no doubt because its authors could not believe in its necessity, from the purity of character which was manifested by those who possessed the confidence of the People at that period. It is, however, an opinion very generally entertained by the Opposition party, that the country would have escaped much of the evil under which it has suffered some years past, if the Constitution had contained a provision of that kind. Having had no opportunity of personal observation on the conduct of the Administration for the last ten years, I am unable to decide upon the truth or error of this opinion. And I should be very willing that the known subserviency of the Legislature to the Executive, in several memorable instances, should be accounted for in a way somewhat less injurious to the character of our country and republicanism itself, than by the admission that the Fathers of the land, the trusted servants of a virtuous People, could be seduced from the path of duty and honor by the paltry trappings and emoluments of dependent offices. But if the evil really exists, and if there be good reason to believe that its source is to be found in the corruptibility of the members of the Legislature, an effectual remedy cannot be too soon applied. And it happens, in this case, that there is a choice of remedies. One of these, however, is, in my opinion, free from the objections which might be offered to the other. The one to which I object is, that which the late President has been so loudly called upon to adopt, in consequence of a promise made at the commencement of his Administration, viz. that the Executive, under no circumstance, should appoint to office a member of either branch of the Legislature. There are, in my mind, several weighty reasons against the adoption of this principle. I will detain you with a mention of two of them, because I believe you will agree with me that the alternative I shall present, while it would be equally effectual, contains no feature to which a reasonable objection could be made.

As the Constitution contains no provision to prevent the appointment of members of Congress to office by the Executive, could the Executive, with a due regard to delicacy and justice, without usurping power from the people, declare a disqualification which they had not thought necessary? And where is the American citizen, who regards the honor of his country, the character of its people, or who believes in the superiority of a republican form of government, who would be willing to proclaim to the world that the youthful nation which has attracted so much of its attention, which it has so much admired for its gigantic strength, its undaunted courage, its high attainments in literature and the arts, and the external beauty of its institutions, was, within, a mass of meanness and corruption? That even the chosen servants of the People were ever ready, for a paltry consideration, to abandon their allegiance to their lawful sovereigns, and to become the servants of a servant? The alternative to this degrading course is to be found in depriving the Executive of all motive for acquiring an improper influence over the Legislature. To effect this, nothing, in my opinion, is necessary but to re-establish the principles upon which the Administration was once conducted, with the single addition of limiting the service of the President to one term. A condensed enumeration of what I conceive these principles to have been is given above. And I think no one can doubt that, if faithfully carried out, they would be effectual in securing the independence of the Legislature, and confining the connexion between it and the Executive to that alone which is warranted by a fair construction of the Constitution.

I can conceive of but two motives which could induce a President of the United States to endeavor to perpetuate his power, by passing laws to increase his patronage, or gratify his vanity by obtaining their sanction to his schemes and projects for the government of the country, and thus assimilating his situation to that of the limited monarchs of Europe. The principles above suggested would effectually destroy any disposition of the person elected, by the combined votes of the Opposition, to place himself in either attitude. Retiring, at the end of four years, to private life, with no wish or prospect of "any son of his succeeding," legitimate or adopted, he would leave the Government as prosperous and pure in its administration as when it passed from the hands of the great "Apostle of Democracy" to those of the Father of our Constitution.

To the duties which I have enumerated as proper, in my opinion, to be performed by a President elected by the opposition to the present Administration, (and which are, as I believe, of constitutional obligation,) I will mention another, which I believe also to be of much importance; I mean the observance of the most conciliatory course of conduct towards our political opponents. After the censure which our friends have so freely and so justly bestowed upon the present Chief Magistrate, for having, in no inconsiderable degree, disfranchised the whole body of his political opponents, I am certain that no oppositionist, true to the principles he professes, would approve a similar course of conduct in the person whom his vote has contributed to elect. In a Republic, one of the surest tests of a healthy state of its institutions is the immunity with which every citizen may, upon all occasions, express his political opinions, and particularly his prejudices, in the discharge of his duty as an elector.

The question may perhaps be asked of me, what security I have in my power to offer, if the majority of the American People should select me for their Chief Magistrate, that I would adopt the principles which I have herein laid down as those upon which the Administration would be conducted. I could only answer, by referring to my conduct, and the disposition manifested in the discharge of the duties of several important offices which have heretofore been conferred upon me. If the power placed in my hands has, on even a single occasion, been used for any purpose other than that for which it was given, or retained longer than was necessary to accomplish the objects designated by those from whom the trusts were received, I will acknowledge that either will constitute a sufficient reason for discrediting any promise that I may make, under the circumstances in which I am now placed.

Proceedings of the Whig National Convention
Harrisburg, December 4, 1839

The Whig convention had a choice between Henry Clay and two appealing but politically inexperienced military heroes—General Winfield Scott and General William Henry Harrison. The following proceedings detail the party's decision.

In pursuance of a resolution adopted by the opposition members of Congress, for the assembling of a National Convention, composed of delegates from all the states, in proportion to their representation in both houses of Congress, for the purpose of recommending suitable persons as candidates for the offices of President and Vice President of the United States, at the next election;

The delegates from the respective states to the said National Convention, assembled at Harrisburg, in the commonwealth of Pennsylvania, at 12 o'clock, M. on the 4th of December, A. D. 1839; when,

On motion of Mr. Williamson, of Pennsylvania, Isaac C. Bates, of Massachusetts, was called to the Chair, and Charles B. Penrose and John Swift, of Pennsylvania, were appointed Secretaries.

On motion of Benjamin Watkins Leigh, of Virginia.

It was resolved, That the secretary call the respective states in the order in which they are called in the Congress of the United States, and that as they are so called, the delegations from each state present their credentials.

Which being ordered; the secretary proceeded to call the states.

THURSDAY, DECEMBER 5, 1839.

The Delegates met pursuant to adjournment, and the journal of yesterday was read.

When Mr. Burnet, of Ohio, announced the arrival of his colleague, Cyrus Falconer, and presented his credentials.

Mr. Leigh, of Virginia, of his colleagues William C. Moseley and Festus Dickinson.

Mr. Tupper, of Mississippi, of his colleague Anderson Miller.

Mr. Hill, of North Carolina, of J. C. Washington.

The said delegates appeared and took their seats.

Mr. Dickey, of Pennsylvania, informed the meeting that the question of the contested seats from that State had been amicably adjusted with the consent of the gentlemen claiming seats, and the approbation of the delegation, and that it was agreed that the following should take their seats as delegates, to wit:

Emmanuel C. Reigart, Thomas G. Henderson, James Colhoun, George Chambers, Moses J. Clark, Edward Overton.

Whereupon, on motion of Mr. Dickey, of Pennsylvania.

It was Resolved, That the said delegates be admitted to seats, and the journal of yesterday be amended accordingly.

Mr. Johnson, of Maryland, announced the arrival of his colleague William Price, District Delegate, and the substitution of John Bosman Kerr, as Senatorial delegate from that State.

The said delegates appeared and took their seats.

Mr. Sprague, of Massachusetts, from the committee appointed on yesterday to report officers for the permanent organization of this Convention, made the following report:

The Committee appointed to recommend officers for the permanent organization of this Convention, have attended to that duty, and

Report, That the officers shall consist of a President, thirteen Vice Presidents, and four Secretaries; and the following gentlemen are recommended to fill these offices, respectively.

PRESIDENT.

Gov. JAMES BARBOUR, of Virginia.

VICE PRESIDENTS.

Gov. John S. Peters, of Connecticut.
Gov. John Andrew Shulze, of Pennsylvania.
Gov. David Hazzard, of Delaware.
Gov. George Howard, of Maryland.
Gov. John Tyler, of Virginia.
Gov. John Owen, of North Carolina.
Gov. Thomas Metcalf, of Kentucky.
Hon. Peter R. Livingston, of New York.
Hon. Jacob Burnet, of Ohio.
Hon. Isaac C. Bates, of Massachusetts.
Hon. James Wilson, of New Hampshire.
Hon. Elisha M. Huntington, of Indiana.
Hon. Ephraim Marsh, of New Jersey.

SECRETARIES.

Charles B. Penrose, Esq. of Pennsylvania,
George W. Ralph, Esq. of Illinois,
Sylvanus R. Lyman, Esq. of Maine,
Charles Paine, Esq. of Vermont.

And the Chairman of this committee was instructed to recommend that a door-keeper and assistants be appointed by the first named Secretary.

On motion of Mr. Kirkland, of New York, the report of the committee was adopted.

Whereupon, Governor James Barbour, of Virginia, President of the Convention, was conducted to the Chair by Mr. Leigh, of Virginia, and Mr. Livingston, of New York.

Mr. Barbour, in an eloquent address, made his acknowledgments to the Convention for the honor conferred upon him; which, by order of the Convention, is inserted upon its Journal, as follows, to wit:

Gentlemen — I feel much obliged to you for the unexpected and distinguished mark of consideration you have so kindly vouchsafed to me, and in return I assure you that to the uttermost of my capacity, I will justify your confidence by discharging the duties assigned me with the most scrupulous fidelity — in which effort I anticipate the hearty co-operation of every member of this Convention.

The honor of presiding over such a Convention, under any circumstances, is great indeed — but is more highly appreciated by me, as I believe it was intended as a token of respect to the commonwealth of which I am a native citizen, and which, I am persuaded, she will feel and acknowledge with becoming sensibility.

Commissioned as we are, by a constituency never surpassed in intelligence and patriotism, to take charge of their interests in an affair of the gravest importance, every member of the Convention will feel the responsibility he has assumed corresponding with the honor conferred upon him in being a member of this Convention.

The American people have had but too much cause to complain of the disastrous effects of the mal-administration of their national affairs. A large portion of them are filled with inquietude and alarm at the still greater evils threatened them in the future. I would to God that those fears were without foundation — for myself, in the solemn place I now stand, I declare before my country, that I verily believe the present time as essentially in travail with the great problem of the capacity of man for self-government. When I cast my eye over the Convention, and see the many grey heads, most of whom may justly be called the conscript fathers of the Republic, a title won by long and illustrious services, alike in the State and federal Councils — having devoted their lives to the cause of liberty and free Government, and in better times to be hailed by their fellow citizens with the plaudit of well done; when I see such men, leaving their homes at this inclement season, and coming from the uttermost corners of the Republic, to aid by their counsels, it presents a fearful testimony to the awful solemnity of the crisis in which we are called to act. Nor can it be doubted that the voice of such men will be heard with respect — the malignity of faction will not dare to impeach their motives. They have run their political course — their grey hairs testify that the places which once knew them will shortly know them no more — they are here, not for themselves, but as Trustees for the rising generation, of which their own beloved children are a part — what motive can they have but the welfare of their country. When they speak, the little demagogue with his sinister purpose, the pest of society, will quail and stand rebuked, and the great body of the people, no matter with what party name they have been baptized, will be taught to feel that they have a country to love as well as a party to serve.

We are indeed in the midst of a revolution. Those walls of partition which our Fathers constructed between the different departments of the government, and which, judging from their own patriotic hearts, they thought would be impassable, have been insolently and audaciously broken down by Executive aggression, and he has assumed to himself a mass of power utterly incompatable with that equilibrum which all experience testifies is indispensible to the existence of free institutions. The forms of the Constitution are retained, but its spirit is gone—your President is a monarch almost absolute. It would be a waste of time to present to *this* assembly the facts which would make manifest the justness of this assertion. To the most incredulous beyond these walls let it be said, who troubles himself now to inquire what *Congress* will do—but all are alive as to the will or the wish of the President—his *sic volo sic jubeo* has been the law of the land for years past.

To avert the threatening evils, our constituents are convinced there is no remedy except by a change of our public agents, and especially of the Chief Magistrate;—and to effect this object, unanimity on the part of the opponents of the present mal-administration is indispensable—and to arrive at this result is the great object of the Convention. That in our extended confederacy, fortunate in the great number of distinguished citizens, differences of opinion should exist as to the best choice, is no matter of surprise—indeed, it is rather matter of pride, as it indicates that we have the independence to think for ourselves, and the firmness to express our opinions; to that extent personal predelictions may be justly indulged, but instantly to be surrendered as a ready sacrifice when that sacrifice is demanded by our country—unanimity, let it be impressed on every mind, is the only pivot on which our hopes can rest. We should poorly fulfil the wishes of our constituents were we to suffer any minor consideration to interfere with this all absorbing object. We are not here to promote any local object, to acquire the supremacy of this or that State, or to cater for the spoils of office. The horizon of our view should embrace the whole Republic. The object the reformation of our Government. Present me a man that promises success, and whose character guarantees this result, and I care not what letters of the alphabet make his name, I will sing hosannas to it as loud as any one.

Public expectation is waiting on tiptoe to learn the issue of your resolves. Not only the great portion of the American people we represent, but our rivals also. Division in our ranks is the foundation of their hopes—they have taunted us that we cannot unite.—If these prophesies be verified, then indeed our misfortunes will be speedily told in Gath and published in Askelon, and the Philistines will rejoice, while our friends will be clothed in sackcloth and ashes. I pray God to avert such a catastrophy.

In looking at the prospect before us, though candor requires us to admit that we see clouds as well as sunshine, yet a comparison of both presents no cause for despondency. We can redeem the country. Hang out your banner—let it be inscribed with your principles. One term for the Presidency—put down the horrible proscription for opinion's sake, which makes slaves of the thousands in office, and of the tens of thousands aspiring to office, who hope by their greater abasement to expel the incumbents—fit instruments to make slaves of us all—distribute equally the avails of the public domain among the old as well as the new States—dismiss the horde of useless officers. Bring to condign punishment the public swindler. Arrest the shameless waste of the people's money, but too much of which, it is charged, has been perverted to the wages of iniquity. With these principles, and with a candidate uniting wisdom and experience—presenting a long list of illustrious services to his country; with a liberality of spirit and a comprehensiveness of mind that will lift him far above the condition of a miserable tool of party—and who will become the President of the whole American people. A citizen presenting these qualities—standing on the broad platform of your principles—surely cannot fail of success, if we are true to ourselves.

Let us profit by the example of our opponents in vigilance and zeal. Defeat with them, instead of producing despondency, becomes a fresh stimulus to renewed exertions. Shall the friends of the constitution and liberty be less zealous and active than those whom we fear will impair both? Our rival has performed no act which addresses itself to the affection or pride of his country. Those who know him best tell us that he has devoted his whole life to an exaggerated egotism, in ministering to which he has been unscrupulous as to means. In such a conflict we are forbid to despair, alike by the genius of the Constitution, and the last hope of human liberty.

Let every man remember that no matter how small his influence, still he is an American citizen, and his country calls him to action, whether he belong to the tribe with ten talents, or the tribe with only half a talent. It is in the political as in the natural world—the whole is composed of atoms. Public sentiment is made up of individual opinion, and the great ocean itself would dry up if it were not for the drops that compose it.

Let us then, from this temple, send up a silent appeal to Heaven, under the most solemn sanctions of our religion, that nothing unworthy shall influence our deliberations, and pray to the Almighty, who has so often stretched out his protecting arm for our deliverance, still to have us in his holy keeping, and so direct our counsels that they may promote the happiness of our country, and especially to preserve our free institutions, so that in all coming time, so long as shall be spared, we may reflect with pride that we were members of this great National Convention.

The Vice Presidents and Secretaries then took their seats and the Convention was declared to be duly organized.

Mr. Graham, of Louisiana, asked leave to read a letter from F. W. Trapnall, of Arkansas.

Whereupon, on motion of Mr. Shaw, of Massachusetts, it was ordered that the letter be read by the Secretary; which being done, it was, on motion of Mr. Davies, of Connecticut, laid on the table.

On motion of Mr. Chambers, of Pennsylvania, it was

Resolved, That the Rules of order of the House of Representatives of the United States for its government, be adopted for the government of this convention, so far as the same may be applicable.

On motion of Mr. Johnson, of Ohio, the Convention proceeded to the consideration of the resolution inviting the Reverend Clergy of Harrisburg to officiate in succession during the sitting of the Convention.

Which resolution being under consideration, was agreed to.

On motion of Mr. Morris, of Pennsylvania.

Ordered, That Reporters of the newspaper press be invited to occupy seats on the floor of the Convention.

Mr. Chambers, of Pennsylvania, submitted a Letter accompanied by resolutions adopted at a Convention held at Chambersburg on the 13th and 14th of June, 1839, which, upon motion of Mr. King of New York, was laid upon the table.

Mr. Sprague, of Massachusetts, then submitted the following:

Ordered, That the Delegates from each State be requested to assemble as a Delegation, and appoint a committee, not exceeding three in number, to receive the views and opinions of such delegation, and communicate the same to the assembled committees of all the Delegations, to be by them respectively reported to their principals; and that thereupon the delegates from each State be requested to assemble as a Delegation, and ballot for candidates for of the offices of President and Vice President, and having done so, to commit the ballot to its committee; and thereupon all the committees shall assemble and compare the several ballots, and report the result of the same to their several Delegations, together with such facts as may bear upon the nomination, and said delegation shall forthwith re-assemble and ballot again for candidates for the above offices, and again commit the result to the above committees; and if it shall appear that a majority of ballots are for any one man for candidate for President or Vice President, said committee shall report the result to the Convention for its consideration; but if there shall be no such majority, then the delegations shall repeat the balloting until such a majority shall be obtained, and then report the same to the Convention for its consideration.

Which being under consideration,

Mr. Penrose, of Pennsylvania, moved to amend the same by adding the following to the end thereof.

"That the vote of a majority of each delegation shall be reported as the vote of that State; and each State represented here shall vote its full electoral vote by such delegation in the committee."

Mr. Newton, of Virginia, moved that the resolution, together with the amendment, be referred to a committee of one delegate from each state; which was not agreed to.

The question recurring on the amendment, it was agreed to.

The resolution as amended being under consideration,

Mr. Leigh, of Virginia, moved further to amend the same by inserting after the word "ballot," where it occurs the second time, the words "designating the votes of each candidate, and by whom given;" which was agreed to.

Mr. R. J. Bowie, of Maryland, then moved to strike out all after the word resolved and insert the following:

Resolved, That this Convention proceed at 12 o'clock, M. on Friday, to the nomination of a Candidate for the Presidency of the U. States; that the sense of the Convention be ascertained by yeas and nays, and after the votes of each member present have been cast, that the majority of each delegation cast the votes of the absent members of such delegation as they think proper, and the person having the majority of the whole number of votes, (after the first ballot,) be the nominee of this Convention.

Which motion being under consideration, Mr. Merril, of Pennsylvania, called for a division of the question, to end with striking out, which was ordered.

The first division being under consideration, it was disagreed to.

The question again recurring on the resolution as amended, it was agreed to.

So it was ordered, That the delegates from each State be requested to assemble as a delegation, and appoint a committee not exceeding three in number, to receive the views and opinions of such delegation, and communicate the same to the assembled committees of all the delegations, to be by them respectively reported to their principals; and that thereupon the Delegates from each State be requested to assemble as a delegation, and ballot for candidates for the offices of President and Vice President, and having done so, to commit the ballot designating the votes of each candidate, and by whom given, to its committee; and thereupon all the committees shall assemble and compare the several ballots, and report the result of the same to their several delegations, together with such facts as may bear upon the nomination, and said delegations shall forthwith re-assemble and ballot again for candidates for the above offices, and again commit the result to the above committees; and if it shall appear that a majority of the ballots are for any one man for candidate for President or Vice President, said committee shall report the result to the Convention for its consideration; but if there shall be no such majority, then the delegations shall repeat the balloting until such a majority shall be obtained, and then report the same to the Convention for its consideration.

That the vote of a majority of each Delegation shall be reported as the vote of that State, and each State represented here shall vote its full electoral vote by such delegation in the Committee.

On motion of Mr. Johnson, of Maryland, the Convention adjourned.

FRIDAY, DECEMBER 6, 1839.

The Convention met pursuant to adjournment, and the journal of yesterday was read.

The President laid before the Convention the proceedings of a Whig Convention of the State of Vermont; which were laid on the table.

Mr. Bates of Michigan, announced the arrival of his colleague Andrew T. McReynolds, who appeared and took his seat.

The President presented a letter from Samuel Pool, President of the Congregation of the Lutheran Church; which, on motion of Mr. Fisher of Pennsylvania, was read and laid on the table.

Mr. C. M. Clay of Kentucky, offered the following:

Ordered, That the Secretary shall proceed to call the names of all the members of this Convention in alphabetical order, and that each delegate shall designate viva voce, his choice of a candidate for President and Vice President; and where any delegation shall not be full, the majority of the delegates present shall cast the vote of the absent members; and when any one nominated shall have a majority of the electoral votes, he shall be the candidate for the Presidency, or for the Vice Presidency, as the case may be, of this Convention.

Ordered, That the committee appointed yesterday to ballot for President and Vice President, now report to this Convention the result of their ballot.

Which, on motion of Mr. Davies of Connecticut, was laid on the table.

Mr. Ralph of Illinois, announced the arrival of his colleague E. A. Whiple, who appeared and took his seat.

On motion of Mr. Horner of New Jersey, it was

Resolved, That the delegation from each State furnish to the Secretaries a list of the delegates of such State, together with their several post-offices.

On motion of Mr. Silliman of New York, it was ordered, that when the Convention adjourn it will adjourn to meet at three o'clock this afternoon.

Mr. M'Farland of New York, presented resolutions of a Whig Convention held in the county of Orange, New York; which, on motion of *Mr. Preston* of Kentucky, were laid on the table.

On motion of Mr. Williamson of Pennsylvania, it was

Resolved, That Mr. Fisher of Pennsylvania, Mr. King of New York, and Mr. Lee of Massachusetts, be a committee of Finance.

When, on motion, the Convention

Adjourned.

THREE O'CLOCK, P. M.

The Convention met pursuant to adjournment.

On motion of Mr. Williamson of Pennsylvania, it was ordered.

That when the Convention adjourn it will adjourn to meet at 7 o'clock, P. M.

And on motion, the Convention adjourned.

SEVEN O'CLOCK, P. M.

Convention met pursuant to adjournment.

Mr. Fleming of Alabama, announced the arrival of his colleague, John W. Swope of that State, who appeared and took his seat.

Mr. Wetmore of New York, presented the following:

The following resolutions were unanimously adopted by the General Committee of Whig young men of the city and county of New York, and ordered to be presented for the consideration of the Harrisburg Convention.

Resolved, That this committee recommend the assembling of a National Convention of Whig young men to respond to the Harrisburg nomination, and to deliberate on such other business as may come before them.

Resolved, That said convention assemble at   on   day of   1840.

Resolved. That this committee submit as the result of their judgment, that the

ratio for choosing delegates be double that of the Congressional representation.
    Ordered to lay on the table.
    Mr. Williamson of Pennsylvania, announced the substitution of Thomas E. Cochran of Pennsylvania in the room of W. R. Morris, called home.
    On motion, Convention adjourned to meet at 9 o'clock, P.M.

NINE O'CLOCK, P. M.

    The Convention met pursuant to adjournment.
    Mr. Johnson, of Maryland, offered the following:

Ordered, That the committee appointed by the resolution of the 5th instant, to confer in relation to the persons to be presented by this Convention as candidates for the offices of President and Vice President of the United States, be and they are hereby instructed forthwith to report progress, and that having done so, they be discharged from any farther action under said resolution.
    Laid on the table.
    Mr. Hoar, of Massachusetts, announced that the delegation from that State had substituted Richard Haughton to supply the vacancy occasioned by the absence of Mr. Colby.
    On motion, it was ordered that the Convention take a recess for one hour.

    After the recess the Convention again met; when
    Mr. Owen, of North Carolina, from the committee appointed by the several Delegations of the respective States, on the order of the 5th instant, Reported,
    That the whole number of ballots given for President were two hundred and fifty-four, one hundred and twenty-eight being a majority; that of these ballots—

WINFIELD SCOTT, of New Jersey, received	16
HENRY CLAY, of Kentucky, received	90
WILLIAM HENRY HARRISON, of Ohio, received	148

    Therefore, that WILLIAM HENRY HARRISON had received a majority of the whole number of the votes given for President.
    The committee further report that they had made progress, but not having completed the business committed to them, they asked leave to sit again.
    Which was agreed to; and
    On motion of Mr. Johnson, of Maryland, the Convention
    Adjourned.

SATURDAY, DECEMBER 7TH, 1839.

Convention met pursuant to adjournment.
    The Journal of yesterday being read,
    Mr. Kirkland, of New York, announced that the Delegation from that State had substituted Paraclite Potter in the place of Chandler Starr, who had been called home.
    Mr. Owen, of North Carolina, from the committee appointed under the order of the 5th instant, Reported,
    That two hundred and thirty one ballots had been cast for Vice President

of the United States, in said Committee, the State of Virginia declining, for reasons which would be stated by one of that delegation, to vote on the question; and that the whole number of ballots cast were given for

JOHN TYLER,
of Virginia

as the candidate for the Vice Presidency; who was therefore unanimously presented to the consideration of the convention as the candidate for that office.

Mr. Leigh, of Virginia, stated that the vote of that State had been withheld from Committee, from motives of delicacy towards Gov. Tyler, who was one of her delegation in this Convention; but the nomination made had the cordial approbation and concurrence of the colleagues of Mr. Tyler, as it would have of those whom they represented here.

Mr. Banks, of Kentucky, addressed the chair, and declared that however much the friends of the great Statesman of that State might regret that another distinguished patriot had been preferred, they were ready to yield up their preferences for the good of the country, and go for the nominations made by the committee.

Mr. Preston, of the same State, made a similar declaration, and informed the Convention that General Leslie Combs, one of the delegation, had in his possession a letter from the Hon. Henry Clay, which related to the question presented; and on his motion it was directed to be read: which being done, it was

On the motion of Mr. Boardman, of Connecticut,

Resolved, That the letter of the Honorable Henry Clay, just read, be, with the consent of the delegation from Kentucky, entered at large on the journals of the proceedings of this Convention.

Which is accordingly done, as follows:

Ashland
20th November, 1839.

Gentlemen: — The public use which has been made of my name, in connexion with the office of President of the United States, furnishes the motive, as I trust it will form the apology, for this note. I address it to you, because our common residence in the same State appears to me to render you the most appropriate repository and organ of what I wish now to say.

The Convention at Harrisburg to designate candidates of the Opposition to the present Federal Administration, for the offices of President and Vice-President of the United States, has been recommended, and the propriety of it has been generally concurred in by all who agree as to the necessity of a change in the General Administration. It appeared to me to be the best, if not the only practicable method of reconciling and uniting those who, coinciding in the general principle, entertained different views as to the most suitable candidates for those high offices, and I have accordingly frequently expressed, and now repeat the expression of my conviction of the expediency of an entire and cordial acquiescence in the recommendations of the Convention.

In the meantime, appeals directly and indirectly have been made to me by a highly respectable Convention holden in Pennsylvania, and by private individuals, to decline giving my consent to the use of my name, upon the ground that a distinguished citizen of the State of Ohio is the first choice of the Opposition in Pennsylvania, and in the opinion of that Convention would be more likely to conciliate general support than I should. I have been also addressed by various respectable and intelligent citizens of New York, directly and indirectly, recommending me to decline the contest in behalf of another eminent citizen, who has been distinguished in both the military and civil service of the United States.

Whilst I have been thus urgently but respectfully approached, numerous private citizens and public meetings and conventions in various parts of the United States (one of these conventions, indeed, in Pennsylvania itself) have done me the honor to express their confidence in me, and to intimate their wishes that I might be the candidate of the Opposition for the office of the Chief Magistrate.

It is perfectly manifest that I cannot comply with all these conflicting opinions and wishes, nor, I apprehend, with any one of them, without disobliging the others.

Under these embarrassing circumstances, I have thought it most advisable to leave to the Convention at Harrisburg the free selection of candidates, as being the assembly to which, by common consent, that important duty has been referred. Representing, as it probably will, all parts of the United States, bringing together the feelings and views of all, and comparing and weighing the local information which it will derive from every portion, it will be most competent to make a nomination acceptable to the great majority of its constituents. That it will be faithful to the high trust confided to its judgment and patriotism, cannot be doubted; and having a full view of the whole ground, it will be more likely to make a selection agreeable to the great body of the Opposition than any separate convention could do, however enlightened and patriotic it may be. If the Pennsylvania Convention, to which I have just alluded, be right in supposing that the distinguished citizen whom it prefers would be more likely to be successful than any other, he ought to be nominated, and undoubtedly, for that very reason, will be nominated by the Harrisburg Convention, should it entertain the same opinion.

With a just and proper sense of the high honor of being voluntarily called to the office of President of the United States by a great, free and enlightened people, and profoundly grateful to those of my fellow citizens who are desirous to see me placed in that exalted and responsible station, I must, nevertheless, say, in entire truth and sincerity, that if the deliberations of the Convention shall lead them to the choice of another as the candidate of the opposition, far from feeling any discontent, the nomination will have my best wishes, and receive my cordial support.

And, gentlemen, I hope that you, my friends and neighbors, will excuse the liberty I take in expressing to you my anxious desire that, discarding all attachment or partiality to me, and guided solely by the motive of rescuing our country from the dangers which now encompass it, you will heartily unite in the selection of that citizen although it should not be me, who may appear to be most likely, by his election, to bring about a salutary change in the administration of the General Government—a change without which we shall be mocked by the forms, and stript of the substantial benefits of free institutions.

From the tenor of this note, I scarcely need observe that you are at perfect liberty to make use of it as in your discretion may seem proper.

I am, with high respect, your friend, and obedient servant.

Henry Clay

To Gov. Thomas Metcalfe, Gen. Leslie Combs, and the other Delegates from Kentucky to the Harrisburg Convention.

Mr. Johnson, of Maryland, offered the following resolution:

Resolved, That this Convention unanimously recommend to the people of the United States, as a candidate for the office of President of the United States, WILLIAM HENRY HARRISON, of Ohio. And as a candidate for the office of Vice President of the United States, JOHN TYLER, of Virginia.

This resolution being under consideration, it was sustained with great animation and eloquence, by the mover, Mr. Johnson, of Maryland, and a delegate from each of the States represented in the Convention, in the course of which Judge Burnet, of Ohio, stated that it was the determination of Gen. Harrison, should he be elevated to the Presidency by the suffrages of his fellow citizens, not to consent to become a candidate for a second term. The interest of the discussion was greatly increased by the sketch given by Mr. Burnet of the private virtues, the ability, and eminent public services of the veteran patriot, Gen. Harrison, and the animated eulogy pronounced as well upon Henry Clay, as upon Gen. Harrison, by Governor Metcalfe, of Kentucky, who had been the associate of the latter in the public service, had witnessed his exploits, and bore generous and feeling testimony to his worth, to which, he said, his country had not yet done justice.

Mr. Leigh, of Virginia, also said, that in justice to an old, intimate, and personal friend, General Winfield Scott, he had to assure the Convention, that although another had been chosen as the candidate he would cordially acquiesce in the determination of the Convention.

The question being then taken on the resolution, it was carried by acclamation; so

WILLIAM HENRY HARRISON,
of Ohio,

was unanimously nominated as the candidate for the Presidency of the United States, and

JOHN TYLER,
of Virginia,

was unanimously nominated as the candidate for the Vice Presidency.

When, on motion of Mr. Boardman, of Connecticut, it was

Resolved, That we congratulate the Democratic Whig Party of the United States upon the unanimity and enthusiasm which have crowned the labors of this Convention, and we call upon our constituents to redeem the solemn pledges here given, and to consummate the *union* of the Whigs for the good of the union.

The following Resolution being then offered by Mr. Johnson, of Maryland, was considered and agreed to:

Resolved, That it be recommended to the several States to hold State Conventions on the twenty-second day of February, A. D. 1840, or on such other day as may in each State be agreed on, for the purpose of nominating electoral tickets, and for general organization, to ensure the success of the candidates recommended by this Convention.

On motion of Mr. Owen, of North Carolina, it was

Ordered, That a committee of one delegate from each State here represented, be appointed by the chair, to inform the nominees of this Convention of their nominations, respectively, and receive and publish their replies.

Whereupon the Chair appointed the following delegates that Committee.

> John Owen of North Carolina, Chairman.
> Elisha W. Allen of Maine.
> James Wilson of New Hampshire.
> Isaac C. Bates of Massachusetts.
> James F. Simmons of Rhode Island.
> William Henry of Vermont.
> Charles Davies of Connecticut.
> Robert C. Nicholas of New York.
> Ephraim Marsh of New Jersey.
> Richard Mansfield of Delaware.
> John Andrew Shulze of Pennsylvania.
> Reverdy Johnson of Maryland.
> James W. Pegram of Virginia.
> Thomas Metcalfe of Kentucky.
> Jacob Burnet of Ohio.
> Douglass M'Guire of Indiana.
> G. Mason Graham of Louisiana.
> T. C. Tupper of Mississippi.
> William H. Russell of Missouri.
> George W. Ralph of Illinois.
> Henry W. Hilliard of Alabama.
> George C. Bates of Michigan.

The following resolution, moved by Mr. Williamson of Pennsylvania, was adopted:

Resolved, That the Democratic Whig National Convention return their sincere thanks to the trustees of the Lutheran Church in the Borough of Harrisburg, for the use of their beautiful edifice, so handsomely accorded to them.

On motion of Mr. Horner, of New Jersey, it was

Resolved, That this Convention recommend to the Whig Young Men of the Several States to appoint delegates from their respective States, to assemble in Convention at the city of Baltimore, on the *First Monday of May next*, to take such measures as will most effectually aid the advancement of the Whig cause and sound principles.

On motion of Mr. Johnson, of Ohio, the following resolution was considered and agreed to:

Resolved, That the thanks of the Convention are tendered affectionately to the Reverend Clergy, who consented to officiate and officiated in opening the sessions of the Convention with prayer.

It was also, on motion of the same delegate, further

Resolved, That the Convention present its thanks to the Honorable James Barbour, President, and to the Vice Presidents and Secretaries, for the able and faithful manner in which they had discharged their duties.

Whereupon, The President returned his acknowledgements, and in an affectionate and impressive address, invoked a blessing upon the labors of the Convention and took leave of the members.

On motion of Mr. Penrose, of Pennsylvania, the President was requested to furnish a copy of his address, to be published with the proceedings of the Convention.

It was, on motion,

Ordered, That the proceedings of the Convention be published, under the direction of the Secretaries.

When, on motion of Mr. Newton, of Virginia, the Convention

Adjourned, Sine Die.

Proceedings of the Democratic National Convention
Baltimore, May 5, 6, 1840

In Baltimore the Democrats unanimously renominated Van Buren yet were unable to agree on a running mate, leaving that decision to the electorate.

In pursuance of the notice given, the delegates to this body met precisely at 12 o'clock on Tuesday morning, in the Hall of the Musical association. Felix Grundy, esq. called the convention to order, and then moved that governor Hill, of N. Hampshire, take the chair, and that general Dix, of N. York, be appointed secretary *pro tem.*; which was agreed to.

On motion, the rev. Mr. Burke offered up a prayer to the Throne of Grace.

On motion of Mr. Simpson, a committee consisting of one member from each state was appointed to nominate candidates for president, four vice presidents, and a secretary.

The secretary then proceeded to call the states, when

Mr. Smith, of Maine, suggested that it would be better to first ascertain whether all the delegates present were entitled to their seats, before making the appointments proposed.

Mr. Clay, of Alabama, was of the opinion that no question ought to be taken, as to the eligibility of any delegate, until the committees should have reported.

Mr. Bredin moved that a committee be appointed to receive the credentials of the delegates appointed. This he deemed to be the proper course, and thought that, if any other were adopted, it would lead to confusion.

Mr. Wishart opposed the motion, maintaining that the call of the roll should be continued, and that when it was gone through with, then a committee might be appointed to examine the credentials of delegates.

Mr. Clay, of Alabama, took a similar view of the question.

The president pro. tem. stated that the motion would be more properly in order when the gentlemen present should have taken their seats.

The secretary then proceeded in the call of states, and having completed it, it appeared there were delegates from 21 states in attendance.

Mr. Kauffman moved, as an amendment to the original motion, that a committee be appointed, consisting of one delegate from each state, to recommend the appointment of the officers in question, and that the name of each member be named, which was agreed to.

The following persons were appointed:

John G. Perkins, of Maine; Henry Y. Simpson, of New Hampshire; Phineas Allen, of Massachusetts; William Ennis, of Rhode Island; John Kellog, of Vermont; William M. Oliver, of N. York; Joseph Northup, of New Jersey; Joseph Engle, of Pennsylvania; John T. Stoddart, of Maryland; Wm. N. Edwards, of North Carolina; Joseph Sturgis, of Georgia; F. C. McCalla, of

Kentucky; Samuel H. Laughlin, of Tennessee; Samuel Medary, of Ohio; Clement C. Clay, of Alabama; Robert J. Walker, of Mississippi; R. C. Nicholas, of Louisiana; Nathan Jackson, of Indiana; John Jameson, of Missouri; Elijah B. Mitchell, of Michigan; Edward Cross, of Arkansas.

Mr. Smith, of Maine, moved the appointment of a committee, vesting the committee with power to ascertain who were entitled to seats in this convention, and also to report their names: agreed to.

On motion, it was ordered that the committee should consist of nine members, and that the president appoint it.

The president then named the following gentlemen to constitute the committee:

William T. Rogers, of Pennsylvania; Joel Terrell, of New York; John Cassidy, of New Jersey; Thomas Wilson, of Maryland; Jonas E. Thomas, of Tennessee; Albert Baker, of N. Hampshire; Peter Kauffman, of Ohio; James B. Peck, of Vermont; Jesse Bean, of Alabama.

Mr. Rodgers moved that when the convention adjourn, it adjourn to meet again at 4 o'clock this afternoon: agreed to.

Mr. Grundy then rose, and proceeded to make some remarks in favor of a strict scrutiny being instituted into the qualifications and rights of gentlemen presenting themselves here as delegates from the respective states, which they profess to represent. He argued that an investigation was necessary, in order to prevent injustice being done to the party, as had been the case four years ago, in regard to Tennessee. He said, that this convention ought to come out with a clear, candid and true declaration of the sentiments of the republican party as here represented. If they did so, and should be right in the principles avowed, there could be no doubt that an honest, free and independent people would sustain them. He repeated, that if this convention were frank with the people, they would be supported, if regarded as being in the right. But if they were wrong, they would at least go down under the conscientious conviction of having performed what they believed to be their duty. However, whether right or wrong, let us tell them what we think, and not beguile or deceive them by acting contrary to our sincere belief. (Loud cheering). Having said this much, he would now take his seat; but he would address the convention further on this subject on another occasion.

Mr. Frazer expressed his hope that the delegate from Tennessee, (Mr. Grundy), would proceed with his remarks. He referred to the number of delegates from the state of Pennsylvania, and remarked that it gave a majority of 50,000 for general Jackson, and asserted that at the coming presidential election, the democracy of the land of Penn, could not be beaten by tory federalism. The whole democracy of the state, were here represented, and they would speak trumpet tongued to the people. "We," (continued Mr. F.) "hanging our banner on the outer wall, we proclaim the eternal principle that man is fit for self-government, and by the aid of Almighty God, the people shall and will rule. They will triumph, and they shall triumph. And that party who are afraid of their principles, are unworthy of the suffrages and confidence of the people of this glorious republic."

Mr. Grundy rose amidst loud and enthusiastic cheering, and said: In one thing, fellow citizens, you are not mistaken. I am a veteran in the cause of democracy; I was born so and have lived so, even beyond my three score years. I have often met in political conflict men of the other party, and am still ready to meet them wherever and whenever they may present themselves, on proper and fit occasions. Yes, sir, an old and sound vessel, that has stood the quicksands, the shoals, and the sawyers of the Mississippi—that has met in the open sea, the proudest force of the enemy, and never struck her flag—has often been compelled to meet their little skiffs and bark canoes, is still as sound as ever, and prepared for a new contest. I stand here, fellow countrymen, as a Tennessean should stand here—as an old democrat; and not only that, but I bring with me one who has done his duty in the field (this allusion to general Carroll was received with an universal burst of applause). Here we present ourselves to the democracy of the union, not fearing to speak to them as boldly as we have done in the field and the cabinet, whatever it becomes patriotic citizens to say and do. This, however, has little to do with the present question. What, then, is our duty? What are the principles on which we stand? We say that we are the friends and advocates of equal rights, or, in other words, that every freeman shall stand on the broad platform of liberty and equality—we want an open field and a fair argument—we want no adventitious aid, either from exclusive privileges or banking corporations.

But let me admonish you, fellow citizens, that we must take care of this institution called a Bank of the United States. Do you say that you will put it under such restraints as will prevent it from usurping the liberties of the country? What you put restraints on this unshorn Sampson, that will rise up and snap the feeble bands you have put upon him? They want to rise up, my fellow countrymen, and set themselves above the constitution and the institutions of the country. Look to that instrument by which our liberties are secured, and where in it do you find any thing to authorise the belief that our wise forefathers intended that money should rule, where freemen only should do so. Is it money that makes the man, or honest industry? It is honest industry, aided by virtue; and let me tell you that it is the democracy who are the workingmen of the country. Show me the man who wants to live on his wits alone, or by the injuries he can inflict upon his neighbors, and I will tell you that that man is not one of us. He does not belong to our party at all. He is a federalist, aristocrat and modern whig besides. There was a time when the name of whig sounded delightfully and pleasantly to every patriot's ear, but that time has passed by. They were the whigs of the revolution—the friends of the country. There was no British gold diffused among them, for they would not take it. There was no British influence acting upon them, for they loved their country too well to be swayed by foreign influence. Now I do not charge this against the present whig party, for it is not safe or just to deal in such harsh denunciations; but this I must say, that when you do find such men, nineteen out of every twenty of them do not belong to our party, and that is not all. Men who do evil, shun the light—they do not want their deeds to be seen. Now, whether it is a consciousness or not that they are acting wrong, he would not say—but so it is, that the whigs are unwilling to disclose to their countrymen the principles which governed them, or indeed whether they have any principles at all. Is it not fair to infer that they well know that if they disclose their opinions and the objects for which they are contending, that the people will never put them in office? While casting my eyes around the room, I see my Ohio friends—and this reminds me of Cincinnati and the manner in which the whigs manage their affairs there. At the close of the late war with Great Britain, was there a man, woman or child, in that city, who ever thought of taking up the present whig candidate for the presidency? Now, I do not wish to detract from the merits of that individual, for I wish that he was wiser and better, and more meritorious than he is; but let us see how he is to be made president. It will be recollected by all of us that when the name of Andrew Jackson was announced for the presidency, the nomination, like a blaze, extended through the whole country, and never ceased to show its light till the illustrious hero and statesman was elevated to the chief magistracy. It is true that art, contrivances, &c. prevented his election at the first trial; but the next time all the devices of the federal party were ineffectual to prevent it.

But to return to the state of Ohio and the city of Cincinnati. The whigs there have a candidate whom they want to make president, and of whom four years ago very little was heard; but within the last few months no mortal man has ever grown so vastly as he. From a plain honest clerk of a county court, who interfered with nobody, and with whom nobody interfered, he has grown to be an astonishingly great man, destined in their opinions to carry all before him. But notwithstanding all this, no one can, by any possibility, come at his opinions on any of the great questions interesting to the country, nor obtain any information in regard to him, by which they can measure his fitness and capacity for the high station to which he aspires. What have his friends done in regard to him? Why, they won't let him be measured at all. They have shut him up, (I will not say in a cage, but he might as well be in one), and will not let him have the use of pen, ink and paper, while his conscience keepers say that he shall neither speak nor write, and they will not do it for him. Now I ask this convention, as sober, reflecting men, if this is the way to make the president for the people of the United States? I want to push this matter a little further.

Mr. Burke, the postmaster of Cincinnati, is here, and I intend, before we leave this place, to ask him to state whether this committee does not regularly attend their candidate to the post office, when he goes for letters, to see that he gets none that are not such as they are willing that he should receive. It is true that there are many wags in this country, and that some of them may probably write hoaxing letters to the old gentleman; and his whig advisers may wish to save him the mortification of reading them, or they may wish to save postage, which is always refunded on returning such letters to the post office. But they open all his letters for him, and where there is nothing to be said in reply, they answer them; though when there is, they will not answer them at all. Now, this is the way in which they want to make a president of the United States.

It was different in old times. When Andrew Jackson was put up for the presidency, I wonder if any man, or set of men opened and answered his letters for him. When he received a letter, he answered it himself; and whether his opinions were right or wrong, he expressed them openly and fearlessly, without being dictated to by a human being. This was the custom of all our former presidents, from Washington down to the present time; and it is the custom of our present chief magistrate. – When his opinions were asked on important questions of state policy, he gave them openly and distinctly. On the subject of abolition, which the whig committee will not let their candidate speak out upon, Mr. Van Buren has been most explicit. He has declared his opposition to that fell spirit, in the strongest terms; and stated in advance, that he would veto any bill passed by congress, interfering with the question of slavery, either in the states or in the District of Columbia. But how is it with the whig candidate? There are vast numbers of abolitionists at the north, and though they are a troublesome set of people, their votes count as well as those of others. Now the whig committee of Cincinnati have come to the conclusion that a letter written to the abolitionists, unfavorable to their views, would cause the loss of their votes, while a letter of a contrary character would cost them the votes of the south. Hence the necessity, on their part, for avoiding all correspondence on that subject; for whether they wrote one way or the other, they would be placed in an awful predicament.

After a few more remarks, Mr. G. concluded by pledging himself that the people of his state would never vote for any man whose principles and policy were not openly and fearlessly avowed to them; and that, well knowing and having the fullest confidence in the present democratic candidate for the chief magistracy, they would give him a hearty and efficient support.

Mr. Clay, of Alabama, from the committee of twenty-one, to recommend suitable persons for officers for the convention, reported:

For president – Gov. Wm. Carroll, of Tennessee.

For vice-presidents – Wm. T. Rogers, of Pennsylvania; governor C. P. Van Ness, of Vermont; Wm. N. Edwards, of North Carolina; Dr. Charles Parry, of Indiana; John Nelson, esq. of Maryland; honorable Alexander Mouton, of Louisiana.

For Secretaries – Geo. A. Starkweather, of New York; C. J. McNulty, of Ohio; G. B. Adran, of New Jersey; Albert F. Baker, of New Hampshire.

The report of the committee was unanimously concurred in, and the president was conducted to the chair.

Mr. Rogers moved that when the convention adjourn, it do so to meet again at 4 o'clock.

The president [Mr. Carroll] then took the chair; when,

On motion of Mr. Grundy, the convention adjourned.

AFTERNOON SESSION.

The convention met again at 4 o'clock, pursuant to adjournment.

The president then rose and addressed the convention to the following effect:

Fellow citizens:

I should do injustice to my feelings if I were to omit the expression of my gratitude on this occasion for the unexpected honor conferred on me, in calling upon me to preside over the deliberations of this body. I beg leave to remark, however, in justice to the convention and to myself, that I feel as if I was disqualified for the discharge of the duties of the station in which I am placed; for although I have spent twenty years of my life in the service of my country in peace and in war, yet it has so happened that I never belonged to a deliberative assembly. Of course, then, it is not to be expected that I should possess such a knowledge of the rules to govern their proceedings as is necessary to the discharge of the duties of the station I have been called to fill. I beg leave to remark, however, that I shall throw myself on your indulgence, and when I am at a loss, I shall ask the aid of those who have had more experience, and are able to guide me in that respect. And in truth, when I consider the cause which has brought us together, I can expect nothing but unanimity in our proceedings. There will, therefore, be very little demand for anything like talent in the presiding officer. When I came here, I did not expect to be elevated to this office, and I felt my incompetence; and I had a desire this morning that the committee would not present my name. However, as I came here resolved to do my duty in whatever station I might be placed, either as a soldier or an officer, I have submitted to them. With a single additional remark, I shall trouble you no further. The cause which has brought us together this day, is the cause of the American people, and it is one in which every republican feels a deep and abiding interest. It is a cause, if we succeed, to promote the happiness and prosperity of the yeomanry of the country—the great body of the people.

We have nothing, then, to do but that which intimately concerns all who belong to the republican party, and that is to take post in the ranks, wherever it be, and to fight the battle manfully till November next; and if we do that, the victory will be ours.—But, gentlemen, rely upon it, we must stand shoulder to shoulder—there must not be one single inch left in our ranks for the enemy to make an inroad. If we do, defeat may be the consequence. I say, again, let every republican in the United States, and more especially those now present, determine to do his duty, and victory will be the inevitable consequence. [Loud and reiterated cheers.]

Mr. Grundy here announced that he had discharged his duty on the committee on nominations, who had already made their report, and that the convention was now duly organized.

The reverend Mr. Hancock, at the suggestion of Mr. Grundy, came forward and offered up a prayer to the Throne of Grace.

Mr. Rogers, from the committee appointed to examine the credentials of delegates, made a report on that subject; which was laid on the table for the present.

On motion, the convention adjourned to meet again at 10 o'clock to-morrow morning.

The following gentlemen being loudly called for, severally addressed the meeting, in warm and enthusiastic speeches: Messrs. Howard, of Indiana, Duncan, Walker and Smith.

The following abstract of those speeches we extract from the Baltimore Republican.

Mr. Howard (being loudly called for) appeared, and began by expressing his thanks for the honor they had done him in calling upon him to address them. He regretted, however, that some more able advocate had not been called upon than himself. – Those before him had not come there with any badge about them, with a piece of blue ribbon and a pewter medal hung round their necks, like school boys. They had presented themselves here as plain and honest democrats, without any distinctive mark or badge to show to what party they belonged. They loved equality and simplicity, like true republicans, and detested any thing and every thing that was calculated to gull and deceive the people. This was an old device of the party, who now wore blue badges. He would to God that the farmers, and mechanics, and men of all other pursuits in the United States, could have seen what he had seen and what he now saw. Here he saw assembled the young, the middle aged, and the old men of the country, coming from every portion of the land to deliberate concerning the welfare of the republic. Mr. H. went on to say that the term "whig," as now used and applied, was perverted from its original meaning and use – that it was a glorious word in the days of our revolutionary ancestors, but then it was used in a different sense from what it is now. There was a time, when the term "whig" meant "sour milk," but now it means "hard cider." [Loud laughter]. It was a little acidulous at the commencement of the campaign and would be very, very sour at the end of it in November next. [Cheers]. If democracts did their duty from the present time until November, they would have nothing to fear as to the result. – This convention had assembled here for the purpose of representing those who were the advocates of liberty and equality – of liberty consistent with good order and sound government. This was why delegates were here, – not in order to drink hard cider or wine. They had come here for the purpose of sustaining those principles, which bound them together more closely than a name – those principles which lie at the foundation of our institutions, and to war against every thing, the design of which was to undermine and overthrow them.

He next adverted to the corrupt influence exercised by the banks, and argued that the parties to the present war, were the people on one side and the banking institutions on the other. It had been said that the loco focos wished to destroy the banks, therefore the whigs had selected a bank candidate. It was needless to say that the charge was without foundation; they did not wish to destroy them, but to put them on a more sound foundation than they are at present. He was for disconnecting the banks from the government, and in favor of the sub-treasury system. Mr. H. went on to remark—that he would not be guilty of the sin of preventing the multitude before him, from hearing from others present from all parts of the union. He himself, desired to visit every part of the *monumental city*, and see her improvements, and the monuments which she has raised to the valor of her own sons, and the fame of the great leader of the revolution. He would close his remarks by a few reminiscences. We, too, (said Mr. H.) have our heroes, who need no certificate of their valor. Kentucky can boast of one of the "bravest of the brave," now in our ranks—(alluding to Mr. Butler,) and I have seen a man who followed the fortunes of the hero of Orleans—who was ever in the thickest of the fight, at Enaeckfaw, Enotechopco, Talidiga, the Horse Shoe, and New Orleans. I saw him 20 years since. His locks were like the raven's wing—his cheek wore the bloom of health, and his step was the gallant warrior's tread.—Now, (said Mr. H. pointing to gen. Carroll's gray locks), I see him, his head is white with age, but his laurels will be green forever!

Amid loud and repeated cries of "Duncan," "Duncan."

Mr. Duncan rose, and was received with loud and repeated cheers. He said that he felt more flattered now than he had ever done in his life. At the outskirts of this city he had met an old man with a broad axe on his shoulder, and he asked him where he was going. He replied, "I am going out to hew wooden razors to shave the dead whigs with next fall." (Loud laughter). He asked him if he was not going for Harrison and the whigs, "No," said he, "not by a d—d sight," "Well," said I, "what is to become of us all, suffering as we are from distress of every kind? Who will come to our relief? "D—d the panic," he exclaimed, "if you would all work as I do you would have no panic." He then went off under the impression that he had given me a proper rebuke. And I pursued my way, well satisfied with his reply. It is our political misfortune, as the democratic party, to be beaten almost every day in the year, except one, and we generally succeed then, and we shall do so next year. (Reiterated cheering). He, (Mr. D.) would ask, what was the *animal* show we had yesterday? A friend of his, upon whose word and judgment he could rely, had occupied an eligible position for viewing the show as it passed down Market street, and he had counted the numbers which constituted it, and what, he would ask, did gentlemen suppose they were? Why, 7,604! Now, if we deducted all bank presidents, bank lounging loafers, and all the idle dogs that paraded the streets on the occasion, how many log cabin men would there be left? He had endeavored to get an introduction to some of these gentry for the purpose of feeling their soft, delicate hands. As soon as he had taken hold of them he was pretty careful to put his hand on his purse. (Laughter). They would rob you if they had an opportunity, of all your Benton mint drops, and every thing in the shape of money. You are contending with a foul faction under various claims and under various banners, but whose principal banner is that of federalism. The contest, then, is federalism against democracy. You have a party to contend with who have one set of principles at one time and another at another. Mr. D. concluded by expressing his conviction that Martin

Van Buren would be reelected president of the United States, notwithstanding all the clamor and efforts that were made by the federalists to elect general Harrison.

Mr. Walker addressed the convention at some length in which he reviewed the acts of the administration, and defended them against the attacks of its opponents. He contended that the democratic party were at present contending with the same party as at former different periods, though they had now exchanged the black for the blue cockade. He expressed his opinion that the democratic party would undoubtedly beat their federal opponents at the next election.

Mr. Smith, of New York, next spoke at considerable length, and showed that the democracy of the country had nothing to fear for the result of the presidential election.

The meeting then adjourned.

WEDNESDAY, MAY 6, 1840.

The convention met pursuant to adjournment, when Mr. Burke made an address to the Throne of Grace.

Mr. Bredin, of Pennsylvania, said he held in his hand the proceedings of a public meeting held in Hardy county, Virginia, at which meeting several gentlemen had been appointed to attend this convention. Two of that delegation, Mr. G. T. Barber and Dr. N. D. Parran, were then present. He observed that it was known that a state convention of Virginia had determined not to send delegates to this convention. This county was not represented in that convention. Under the circumstances of the case, he moved that the proceedings of this meeting, with the credentials of the delegates, he referred to the committee having charge of the credentials; which was agreed to: referred to the committee on credentials.

Mr. Gillet, of New York, from the committee appointed to draft resolutions, expressing the views and principles of the democratic party, reported that they had had that subject under consideration, and that they had instructed him to report the following resolutions. He was further instructed to say that the committee was entirely unanimous in favor of the proprositions they submitted to the convention. Mr. G. then read the resolutions in his place, as follows:

1. *Resolved*, That the federal government is one of limited powers, derived solely from the constitution, and the grants of power shown therein, ought to be strictly construed by all the departments and agents of the government, and that it is inexpedient and dangerous to exercise doubtful constitutional powers.

2. *Resolved*, That the constitution does not confer upon the general government the power to commence and carry on, a general system of internal improvements.

3. *Resolved*, That the constitution does not confer authority upon the federal government, directly or indirectly, to assume the debts of the several states, contracted for local internal improvements, or other state purposes; nor would such assumption be just or expedient.

4. *Resolved*, That justice and sound policy forbid the federal government to foster one branch of industry to the detriment of another, or to cherish the interests of one portion to the injury of another portion of our common country — that every citizen and every section of the country, has a right to demand and insist upon an equality of rights and privileges, and to complete an ample protection of persons and property from domestic violence, or foreign aggression.

5. *Resolved*, That it is the duty of every branch of the government, to enforce and practise the most rigid economy, in conducting our public affairs, and that no more revenue ought to be raised, than is required to defray the necessary expenses of the government.

6. *Resolved*, That congress has no power to charter a national bank; that we believe such an institution one of deadly hostility to the best interests of the country, dangerous to our republican institutions and the liberties of the people, and calculated to place the business of the country within the control of a concentrated money power, and above the laws and the will of the people.

7. *Resolved*, That congress has no power, under the constitution, to interfere with or control the domestic institutions of the several states, and that such states are the sole and proper judges of every thing appertaining to their own affairs, not prohibited by the constitution; that all efforts of the abolitionists or others, made to induce congress to interfere with questions of slavery, or to take incipient steps in relation thereto, are calculated to lead to the most alarming and dangerous consequences, and that all such efforts have an inevitable tendency to diminish the happiness of the people, and endanger the stability and permanency of the union, and ought not to be countenanced by any friend to our political institutions.

8. *Resolved*, That the separation of the moneys of the government from banking institutions, is indispensable for the safety of the funds of the government, and the rights of the people.

9. *Resolved*, That the liberal principles embodied by Jefferson in the Declaration of Independence, and sanctioned in the constitution, which makes ours the land of liberty, and the asylum of the oppressed of every nation, have ever been cardinal principles in the democratic faith; and every attempt to abridge the present privilege of becoming citizens, and the owners of soil among us, ought to be resisted with the same spirit which swept the alien and sedition laws from our statute book.

Mr. Grundy then moved that the question be taken on each resolution separately; which having been accordingly done, they were severally adopted unanimously.

The president inquired if the other committees were ready to report.

Mr. Hill, of New Hampshire, remarked that the committee on the address had met together and had agreed on one to present to the convention by a unanimous vote. The address however had a special reference to the nomination expected to be made, but as the committee had doubtless anticipated what that nomination would be, it might not be improper to report it at this time.

Mr. Grundy asked if the gentlemen meant that the address had any reference to the nomination for the vice presidency.

Mr. Hill replied that it had reference to the nomination of president only.

Mr. Bredin expressed the hope that the report on the address would not be made till after the report of the nominating committee.

The president observed, that the report of the nominating committee not being ready, it would perhaps save time to go on with reading of the address.

Mr. Henry Horn, after some few remarks, moved to dispense with the reading of the address, and to have it printed.

Mr. Grundy hoped that the convention would not agree to this proposition. We have come here, said he, some of us from a distance of 1,000 miles to deliberate on the important concerns of the nation. I have no doubt, said he, but that the address will please me and meet with my hearty approbation; but I never will vote for a paper till I hear it read. Let us hear what it is, and let me give it the sanction of my understanding as well as my heart.

Mr. Horn's motion having been negatived, the chairman of the committee [Mr. Hill], commenced reading the address, and had progressed for a short time, when

Mr. Cameron, of Pennsylvania, again moved to suspend the reading, and to have the report printed. Many of us, said he, are anxious to know what will be the report of the nominating committee in relation to a candidate for the vice presidency; and we are now unwilling to adopt any address until we are informed what that decision is.

Mr. Bredin seconded the motion. This committee, he understood, had come to a decision, and there surely could be no difficulty in letting the convention know what it was. He was opposed to any thing like management, and trusted and believed that there would be none, but as the delegation of Pennsylvania had come here instructed to support a certain candidate for the office of vice president, they wished to have every possible information on the subject.

Mr. Ennis here informed the delegate from Pennsylvania that there was one obstacle to the making the report of the nominating committee, and that was that the chairman was absent and engaged in writing it out.

Mr. Hill then proceeded with, and finished reading the address; after which,

Mr. Clay, of Alabama, having intimated that the committee on nominations were ready with their report.

Mr. Oneil, of Missouri, submitted a resolution, that in taking the votes on the nominations, the delegation of each state should give such vote as their states are entitled to in the election of president and vice president of the United States.

Mr. Kauffman moved to amend the resolution, so as to designate the manner in which each delegation shall announce its vote; which being agreed to, the resolution was, after some remarks from Messrs. Grundy and Clay, adopted without a division.

Mr. Clay, of Alabama, in behalf of the nominating committee, submitted the following report. — He would merely remark, he said, by way of explanation of his position in the committee, that he should present the result of their deliberations without comment. He would barely, however, remark that the conclusion to which the committee had arrived, was the result of harmony, concession, and self-denial, carrying out the democratic principle of every thing for measures, and nothing for men. Mr. C. then read the report and resolutions, as follows:

And whereas, in order to carry out the principles herein avowed, it is important that a chief magistrate should be chosen whose opinions are known to be in accordance with them; and, as many of the states have nominated Martin Van Buren as a candidate for re-election to the office he now holds, and which he has filled with distinguished honor to himself and advantage to the best interests of the country; and, as it is apparent from indications not to be doubted, that the undivided wishes of the republican party throughout the union point to him as the individual best calculated, at the present juncture, to execute the measures of policy which they deem essential to the public welfare, and as the members of this convention, unanimously concur in the opinion so generally entertained by their constituents; thereupon.

Resolved, That this convention do present the name of Martin Van Buren to the people as the democratic candidate for the office of president of the United States, and that we will spare no honorable efforts to secure his election.

And whereas several of the states, which have nominated Martin Van Buren as a candidate for the presidency, have put in nomination different individuals as candidates for the office of vice president, thus indicating a diversity of opinion as to the person best entitled to the nomination; and whereas some of the said states are not represented in this convention; and as all the individuals so nominated have filled the various public trusts confided to them, ably and faithfully, and have thereby secured for themselves the confidence of their republican fellow citizens; thereupon,

Resolved, That the convention deem it expedient at the present time not to choose between the individuals in nomination, but to leave the decision to their republican fellow citizens in the several states, trusting that before the election shall take place, their opinions shall become so concentrated as to secure the choice of a vice president by the electoral colleges.

Mr. Ashmead, of Pennsylvania, then observed, that there could be no objection to the adoption of the preamble and the first of the resolutions in relation to the nomination for president. On that question the convention was unanimous. There were objections to the second resolution, and he therefore moved that the question be divided so as to take it first on the preamble and first resolution, and afterwards on the second resolution.

This motion having been agreed to, the question was taken on the preamble and first resolution, and they were unanimously adopted.

Mr. Butler, of Kentucky, then rose and said, that by the instructions of the committee, he rose for the purpose of laying before the convention a letter, which he had received from the present vice president of the United States. He did not rise for the purpose of throwing the apple of discord before the convention, but for the opposite purpose. He well knew that there was no man so proper to present this offering for the public good as himself. If the failure to nominate Richard M. Johnson was to be felt in any one part of the United

States, it was in that neighborhood where he resided. He represented the very district which had been so long and so faithfully represented by that faithful public servant, in whose behalf he now addressed the convention. He acknowledged that he had been disappointed—he acknowledged that he felt some little sting of mortification, when the result of the committee's deliberations was known to him; that had passed off.

We have met here, said Mr. B. for the public good, and our own individual feelings must give way when that can be served. After offering the letter of his distinguished friend and fellow citizen, he would say that if there was one individual present, who, like him, felt disappointed, let him lay it aside. That man is not lost to his country. His whole life has been spent for its good, and he will not abandon the party to which he belongs, because they had not thought proper to make him their chief. He believed yet that that individual was the choice of the American people for the second high office in the government; and let his friends then go home, proclaim his worth, and, as he has beaten his political opponents before under similar circumstances, he can do it again. We know, said Mr. B. that he has strong claims on his countrymen. He has strong claims in the hearts of the American people—of the laboring class in which was to be found the democracy of the country. He was born in that class, raised among, and was literally among them. Born in Kentucky at the most eventful period of her history, in the midst of the Indian wars, he received at his birth that energy of character which has accompanied him through life—none but the brave went to that state at that period. It was then no place for cowards; it was the habitation only of the brave, and it was among them he caught that indomitable spirit and those generous feelings which have so much endeared him to his countrymen.

I know, said Mr. B. that he is but a man, and that, for a moment, he may feel the sting of disappointment; but I know him well, and know that nothing but the sting of death will separate him from the party with which he acted through life. I present, said he the letter of colonel Johnson, and in doing so, I am convinced that if there is an unkind feeling in this house it will disappear. We are engaged in a common cause for the good of the country; let not that cause be paralyzed by the slightest division among ourselves. Mr. B. then handed the letter to the chair, and it was read as follows:

City of Washington,
April 25, 1840.

Gentlemen: The near approach of the national democratic convention in Baltimore, on the 5th of May, induces me to address you. The object of that meeting is to nominate candidates for the next election of president and vice president of the United States. In relation to the presidency, I am happy to find it is universally understood, that there will be no division. The leading, and only point, in which any discussion is anticipated, is that of the vice presidency.

From the situation in which I am now placed, it seems to be proper that my sentiments and views should be definitively known. The first question will be, whether the convention will go into the nomination.

On this point, it is said, there will be a difference of opinion. Whether the convention shall make a nomination, or leave it to each state to make its own selection, I wish my friends to understand distinctly that that will be a matter with which I am not to interfere. I will be perfectly satisfied with the course the convention shall adopt; and, in any event, must beg of them not to suffer any feelings of partiality for me to endanger the principles which we are united in sustaining. My sentiments has ever been, that in a republic no citizen has any claims upon the people to election for any office, irrespective of the benefit and advantage resulting to themselves. All offices ought to be for the good of the people, and not for the incumbents. If special services ever merit special rewards, those rewards should be given in any other way than that which would endanger the great fundamental principles of liberty.

To regard a highly responsible elective office, as a reward for past services, is to regard the elective franchise as forestalled by the claim of justice; and it is therefore repugnant to republican principle. If such claim may be urged in favor of any other, on any occasion, I am conscious that my humble services merit nothing beyond what they have already received. So far as past services have elicited the principles of the man, they will be regarded as a pledge for his future course; and beyond this, they ought not to be considered; especially in relation to myself.

There rests no obligation on the part of my friends to me. The debt of gratitude, if it ever existed, has been more than paid. All the obligation that remains, is from me to them. The confidence which they have manifested, and the kindness shown to me, have imposed an obligation of gratitude in my bosom, which I can never cancel. There is at this time, a great interest at stake. It is the support of the principles in which we united, and upon which the government has long been administered. Those principles have been my guide for more than thirty-five years, during which time I have been continually afloat upon the tempestuous sea of political life. They are much more dear to me than my own elevation or that of any other person. I desire all of my friends in the convention to regard their preservation as infinitely more important than the qualification of any private friendship.

I have not solicited a re-nomination, nor shall I decline it. I am, as I ever have been in the hands of friends and fellow citizens. It is no less my pleasure than it is my duty to make the avowal, that I wish to be entirely at their disposal, and shall be perfectly content with their award. If, in their opinion, the great principles for which we contend, will be more likely to be secured by the use of my name, they will use it—if, in their opinion, another selection will be more likely to ensure success, they will make another selection.—If, in their opinion to make no nomination of a vice president, and leave the selection to the pleasure and preference of the republicans of the several states, will give most strength to our friends, the convention will take that course; and in either event, I shall continue to act with perfect integrity to those principles, and to the friends with whom I have hitherto acted in sustaining them. In assuming this position, I do not wish to be understood as declaring myself insensible to the honors which arise from public confidence. I can regard the man but a misanthrope, who is perfectly indifferent to the applause or the censure of his fellow men. — It is a quality to which I make no pretension. — Next to my own conscience, the many testimonials which I have received of the approbation of my fellow citizens, is the richest reward for my past services to which my ambition ever aspired; and this feeling has been the principal cause, for some years past, of my continuance in public life. It is also my greatest consolation, that in my present situation, while it has been my constant effort to discharge its responsible duties with fidelity, I have so far succeeded, at least, as to have avoided censure. I have heard of no disposition to make a different selection, on the ground that these duties are not satisfactorily performed. But, dearer than all these considerations, are the *principles* involved in the approaching election. They ought to be sustained, without regard to any individual partialities or feelings; and, under this conviction, I hope my friends will feel a perfect freedom of action in the convention.

It is with sentiments such as I have expressed and under an earnest desire that the labors of the convention may tend to the advancement and success of our cherished principles in the pending contest, that I have felt constrained to address to you this hasty letter. You will, of course, feel at perfect liberty to make such use of it as shall, in your judgments, be calculated to promote harmony in the convention, and give strength to our cause throughout our beloved country.

Most respectfully, your friend and fellow citizen.

RH. M. Johnson.

The hon. Linn Boyd and the hon. William O. Butler, members of congress from Kentucky, and delegate to the Baltimore convention.

The Baltimore republican says — the letter from colonel Richard M. Johnson having been read —

Mr. Medary, of Ohio, remarked that the political battle ground, as connected with the presidential contest, would be in Ohio. There it was that the great battle was to be fought. We had come here to support and carry out the cause of democracy, and not for the gratification of individual preference — (applause). — We went into convention on the 8th of January, a day glorious in the annals of American history, and nominated Martin Van Buren for the presidency, and we were instructed to urge the nomination of colonel Richard M. Johnson, for the vice presidency. He went on to say that Ohio would be the last that would shrink from her duty, and to cast a fire brand into this convention on the subject of such momentous importance. Her delegates here would do what they deemed best to promote unity and harmony in the democratic ranks. He much mistook the intelligence and character of the people of the west, if they would not feel themselves insulted by the exhibition which had been made in the streets of Baltimore of log cabins. He was sure when the day of election should arrive that the democrats would do their duty. As to their opponents coming here and saying that they (the whigs) would get a majority in Ohio of 25,000, they were asserting that which they knew not to be true. And if they did not know, then he would say they were ignorant of the public sentiment, and they might take which horn of the dilemma they chose. The contest which was about to ensue might be a bitter and a close one. He, however, never knew the democrats of his state to be in better spirits than they were at present, and felt sure that victory would crown their efforts. He spoke next of the governor of Ohio, being claimed by the whigs as a Harrison man, and argued that there was not the slightest foundation for the assertion. He was as good a democrat as could be found in Ohio or elsewhere.

Mr. Kauffman corroborated the statement of the last gentleman up to as the soundness and strength of Ohio in the democratic faith. He said the democrats there were now ready for the contest — that they knew their independence would be secured for ever by a glorious victory over the hard cider party. He eulogized colonel Richard M. Johnson as a man in every respect deserving of the confidence of his fellow citizens, and he expressed his fullest conviction that although he might not be nominated by this convention, he would be chosen by the voice of the people to re-occupy the eminent station he now fills.

Mr. Howard, of Indiana, remarked that colonel Johnson's character was universally known in Indiana, and it was as much appreciated. He was known as one, at least, of the heroes of the Thames, and was nominated by the state convention of Indiana, and he was the first, second, the last choice of Indiana. He would continue to be their choice, he (Mr. H.) trusted until the flag of democracy with his name inscribed on it, should float triumphantly in the breeze in November next. (Loud applause). Mr. H. next referred to the fact that in various states other candidates were preferred, and observed that the best course would be to fight the battle at home, and leave the issue to be tried at the fall elections.

Mr. Smith, of Maine, observed that the letter of colonel Johnson was just such a one as might be expected from him by every man who knew him. He was a democrat dyed in the wool. Mr. S. then alluded to the other distinguished individuals who had been spoken of to fill the station of vice president of the United States, and then argued that it was necessary to put on record a vote for the nomination of a vice president. This had been regarded heretofore as one of the most valuable usages of the democratic party, and a departure from which could not but be dangerous to say the least of it, to the future prosperity of the party.

Mr. Bredin felt quite sure that the delegates from Pennsylvania neither individually nor collectively would do any thing calculated to produce any divisions of sentiment among the great democratic party of the union. There never had been and he trusted there never would be a time when the people of Pennsylvania would refuse their support to democratic men and measures. There was not a state in the union that had stood so firm as Pennsylvania in defence of them. He had no wish that a nomination should be made, but he was in favor of putting on record the votes of the respective states, and if it was the desire of the convention not to go into a nomination of a vice president, he would cheerfully submit. He, however, thought it all important that the proceedings of the convention should be conducted as they usually had been.

Mr. Wishart cordially responded to what had fallen from the three or four gentlemen who preceded him. He had been in committee with one of these gentlemen, and he had then expressed himself warmly, perhaps, that Pennsylvania was in favor of the re-election of colonel Johnson. He (Mr. W.) venerated Richard M. Johnson as a soldier and a civilian. He had battled both for his military and civil reputation. He had heard in that part of the country in which he (Mr. W.) lived, the Sunday mail report spoken of as being odious in its character. He had, in consequence, asked them what part of the report it was they objected to, but when they come to enter into detail, nothing was found to be objectionable in it. (Applause). Warmly as he contended in behalf of colonel Johnson, both last night and this morning, he afterwards moved a reconsideration of the vote taken on the subject of the presidency in order that a vote might be taken in regard to the vice presidency. His object and desire was to produce harmony in this large, respectable and enthusiastic convention, whose measures and principles we all advocate. He was sorry to differ with his friend (Mr. Bredin), who last preceded him on that point, and that was to insist on recording the vote singly. He knew that some of his colleagues might differ from him; but he knew that Pennsylvania had spoken loudly by him at this time. He would suggest to those who entertained views different from his own, the propriety and policy of going in one unbroken phalanx to face the wily and insiduous enemy with whom we have to contend. He had a brother-in-law in this city, at this time, who officiated as one of the vice presidents of the whig convention. He had walked arm in arm with him to-day, and asked him when he intended leaving the city. He replied that he could not leave it until the democratic convention should adjourn. He keeps his own secrets, and he (Mr. Wishart) keeps his. Now, he inferred from this that the whigs were waiting to see whether there would not be some division in our ranks, which they might take advantage of. He would, therefore, on his own behalf and his respected colleagues who might differ with him on this occasion, suggest the propriety of taking the vote at once.

Mr. Clay explained the proposition before the convention, and expressed his hope that his Pennsylvania friends would understand that his object in offering it was to relieve this body from embarrassment. He contended that it was not necessary to vote by states, inasmuch as no man could be at a loss to know what was the opinion of each state on this important subject, as the record of it was before the convention. With regard to the chief magistrate there was but one opinion, but unfortunately this was not the case with regard to the other high officer. However, it was the duty of delegates to sacrifice every thing to the cause regardless of their individual preferences. He, for one, was ready to yield his opinion and acquiesce in whatever course the convention might think proper to take.

After a few words from Mr. Smith, of Maine, Mr. McCahen felt sure that his friends from the south who were in favor of the right of instruction could sympathise with the Pennsylvania delegation who had come here instructed to vote for R. M. Johnson, and he hoped that an opportunity would be offered him and his colleagues, of recording their votes. When they should have done that, they would agree with all unanimity, to the general course desired to be pursued by the convention at large — (Applause). He could assure this body that Pennsylvania would do nothing in the least calculated to produce division in the democratic family, or to give the federal party any advantage over them. It had been said that the democratic party were divided in Pennsylvania, and that the enemy entertained some hopes there. He would tell gentlemen around him that no cause existed for apprehension as to the unity of the democracy of the land of Penn. They had stood by old Hickory, and they would for the second time stand by Martin Van Buren. We promise to give him 15,000 majority. Now, he would go further and say he would not give him 15,000, but 25,000! *(Loud and reiterated cheers).* It will be for hard money against hard cider.

Mr. Grundy suggested the propriety and policy of gentlemen surrendering their individual preferences in regard to the nomination of a vice president, because he was decidedly of the opinion that no choice could be made at this time — that they could not unite upon any one man as the democracy of the country had done in regard to a candidate for the presidency. They had agreed on that point. — We had, then, got a commander-in-chief, and a brave one, too; and he thought if we could get the head along, the tail would not be far behind, *(laughter).* The question must and would be decided at the next election.

Mr. Butler remarked, that it would be better to leave the question as to the vice presidency, exactly where it stood, after taking the vote on it by states. And, then, let gentlemen go home and do their best to secure the election of their favorite candidates next November.

The question being taken on the second resolution of the committee, it was unanimously adopted.

On motion of Mr. Clay, the records of the nominating committee were ordered to be spread upon the journals of the convention, and to form part of its proceedings.

On motion of Mr. Grundy, the report of the nominating committee was unanimously adopted.

Mr. Smith, of Indiana, observed that he had been instructed to vote for Richard M. Johnson, and those whom he had the honor to represent, knew that he never had, in any instance, deviated from their instructions.

Mr. Kane remarked that the gentleman from Indiana, (Mr. Smith), was mistaken in saying that he was instructed. The convention, at first, concluded to do so, but afterwards resolved not to do it.

Mr. Smith accepted the explanation, and added that in what he had said he only expressed the feelings of those whom he represented.

Mr. Bean, of Alabama, said, that the democratic convention of his state, was organized for the purpose of appointing delegates to attend this convention to designate some person as a suitable candidate for vice president of the United States. — There was no conflict for the presidency. It was settled that Mr. Van Buren was the only democratic candidate. The committee of one from each state had determined that no nomination should be made of any candidate for the vice presidency, and as the proceedings then stood, it did not appear, but he accorded in this measure. He, as a delegate from Alabama, felt it his duty to say, that it was his decided opinion that it would be best for the democratic party to make the nomination, recommended by the convention of his state, and that he was unwilling the question should be decided without his giving to this convention his views upon this subject. It is true that Alabama had proposed a gentleman as candidate for the vice presidency; but, notwithstanding this choice, she was entirely willing to support any candidate which may be the choice of this convention. It was the wish of Alabama to preserve the union of the great democratic party.

Mr. Fisher, said that Pennsylvania, would support Martin Van Buren, and give him, not 15,000 but 25,000 majority. [Loud applause]. Such a vote as would wake gen. Harrison out of his reverie, and put an end to all his hopes and dreams of ever becoming the tenant of the white house.

Mr. Grundy moved that the report of the committee on the address be adopted; which was unanimously agreed to.

After some remarks from Mr. Thompson, of New Jersey, the convention took a recess until 4 o'clock.

AFTERNOON SESSION.

The convention met at four o'clock, pursuant to adjournment.

On motion of Mr. Clay, of Alabama, the records of the proceedings of the nominating committee was ordered to be spread upon the journals of the convention, and to form part of its proceedings; after which

On motion of Mr. Grundy, the address and the report of the nominating committee were unanimously adopted.

On motion of Mr. Gillet, it was

Resolved, That the thanks of this convention be tendered to the president and officers of this convention for the prompt and able manner in which they had performed their duty.

On motion of Mr. Gillet, of New York, it was

Resolved, That the thanks of this convention be tendered to the republican central committee of the city of Baltimore, for the commodious and appropriate arrangements made by them for the session of this convention.

Mr. Nelson, of Baltimore, then rose and addressed the convention in behalf of the committee, in a very able and eloquent manner.

The business of the convention having been thus gone through with, the convention was severally addressed by Mr. Thompson of New Jersey; Messrs. Nelson, Stoddard and Preston, of Maryland; Anderson, of Tennessee; Smith, of Maine; Kauffman, of Ohio; Brown and Thompson, of Mississippi.

After prayer by the reverend Mr. Burke, the convention adjourned *sine die*.

Letter from President Martin Van Buren
to the Democratic Citizens Committee
July 4, 1840

Late in the 1840 campaign President Van Buren, continuing Jacksonian policies, succeeded in getting through Congress a bill establishing an independent treasury, whereby government money would be deposited in subtreasuries in various parts of the country. Bitterly denounced by the Whig opposition as a blow against business, the bill was heralded by the President as a victory for the common man.

Gentlemen: I have had the honor to receive the invitation which you have been pleased to give me in behalf of the counties of Fayette, Woodford, and Scott, to be present as a guest at a public meeting and entertainment to be held by them at the White Sulphur Springs, in Scott county, Kentucky, on the 11th inst.

Truly grateful for this mark of their respect and kindness, I can but regret that my public duties will not permit me to express my gratefulness face to face.

That I have been so fortunate as to secure "the entire approbation of the democracy of Kentucky," that they look upon me as "true to the Constitution of the United States," "the representative and advocate of their principles in the Executive Department of our Government," cannot but afford me peculiar satisfaction, coming, as it does, from a highly respectable portion of the ancient and time-honored patriots of that noble State, and from the sons of those who, in their day, were the pillars of the republic. History, gentlemen, must be false to her duty when she ceases to inform mankind that it was by Kentucky that the first effectual blow was struck at the dangerous principles introduced into the administration of our Government soon after the adoption of the Constitution — principles which had already led to acts of fearful usurpation, and threatened speedily to destroy as well the rights of the States as the liberties of the People. It was the Kentucky resolutions, backed by those of her patriotic parent State, which changed the current of public opinion, and brought back the administration of the Government to the principles of the Revolution. For forty years the democracy of the Union have looked upon those resolutions as the creed of their political faith; political degeneracy has been marked by departure from that standard, and, like the original language of the Bible in matters of religion, they are the text book of every reformer.

Nothing could more effectually prove the purity of the principles then announced, than the progress they have since made in the minds of men. While even the name of the proud and powerful party which opposed them has come to be considered a term of reproach, if not of ignominy and insult, the principles of the Kentucky resolutions, in profession, if not in fact, now enter into the creed of every political sect, and the once derided name borne by their apostates and advocates is considered an essential passport to popularity and success. Nay, more, the People, almost with one voice, have recently recognised and consecrated the principles of those resolutions, by an act of impressive and emphatic as it is possible for a nation to perform. Since your letter has been laying before me waiting for a reply, it has become my agreeable duty to confirm the fiat of the nation settling forever the unconstitutionality of the sedition laws of 1798, by approving an act for the relief of the heirs of Matthew Lyon, refunding to them a fine collected of their ancestor under the law in question. Party prejudice, judicial authority, dread of the precedent, respect for that which has assumed the form of law for forty years, have successfully resisted this act of justice; but at length all are swept away by the irresistible current of public opinion, and the sedition act has been irreversibly decided to be unconstitutional by a tribunal higher than the courts of justice—the sovereign People of the United States. The Patriarchs of Kentucky and Virginia, the men who, in that day, midst obloquy and insult, voted for or sustained the Kentucky and Virginia resolutions of 1799, cannot but rejoice with joy unspeakable in witnessing the final triumph of the pure principles to which they then announced their allegiance. They and their descendants have a right to glory in seeing those principles recognised, even at this late day, by the acclamations of a nation, and one of the tyraninical acts against which they protested virtually expunged from the records of the country.

While to aged patriots it is a subject of congratulation and joy, it teaches the young that efforts at reform in the Government of their country ought never to be considered hopeless as long as there is any thing to improve, and that, if the fathers do not enjoy the fruits of their exertions in the cause of democratic principles, they are certain to fall in blessings upon the children.

I am most happy to inform you, gentlemen, that I have this day signed the bill for the establishment of an Independent Treasury, a measure of which you speak in decided commendation. By this measure, the management of an important branch of our national concerns, after a departure of nearly half a century, will be brought back to the letter, as well as to the obvious spirit and intention of the Constitution. The system now superseded was, in fact, one of those early measures devised by the friends and advocates of privileged orders for the purpose of perverting the Government from its pure principles and legitimate objects, vesting all power in the hands of the few, and enabling them to profit at the expense of the many. I need not inform you, gentlemen, that the effect of depositing the public money in banks was to lend it to those institutions, generally without interest, to be used as a part of their capital, and that they lent it out upon interest to their customers, thereby largely increasing the profits of the stockholders. Thus the few were enabled to enrich themselves by using the money which belonged to the many, and the public funds were in fact drawn from the Treasury, without an appropriation by Congress, in clear violation of the spirit of a constitutional prohibition.

The manner in which this abuse crept into the Government and fastened itself upon the country, with the acquiescence of the whole People, is an impressive lesson, teaching the necessity of perpetual vigilance and energy in detecting and resisting the first encroachments, however seemingly trifling, upon the principles of our Government. From the deposite of the public money in banks, it did not necessarily follow that the banks should use it. Its use was never, until lately, and then only to a limited extent, directly authorized by any act of the Government. But, as the banks were in the habit of using deposites, they silently treated those of the Government like those of private citizens, and the Government silently acquiesced in the practice. As for many years the revenues of the Government were moderate, and the surplus was wanted to pay the principal and interest of the public debt, the amount loaned out by the banks was comparatively small, and the profits of the stockholders less considerable. But in the progress of the Government its revenues increased, and the amount unexpended became greater, until it amounted to five, ten, and, after the extinguishment of the public debt, to nearly thirty millions.

The disastrous effects now became apparent. An extensive interest had sprung up, deriving wealth from the use of the People's money, and having powerful inducements so to act upon the Government as to increase the source of their income. Their influence was first directly felt in interferences to prevent the payment of the public debt; then in efforts, through the use of the public press, and in attempts to secure the influence of the leading politicians and of men in authority, to procure a prolongation of their chartered privileges; and, finally, in panic and pressure inflicted upon the country with the hope of controlling the action of the Government through the alarms and the sufferings of the People. By shifting the deposites from one great institution to many smaller ones, the unit of this interest was destroyed, but not its power. Though enfeebled, it still existed in a force which the boldest might fear, and had made itself felt in the contests of the last few years. But the intelligence and virtue of our People have triumphed over art, panic, and pressure, and the act of deliverance is this day consummated.

It is hoped that the business of the country will no longer be disturbed by the struggles of the banking interests to get possession of the money of the People that they may make a profit out of its use; but that they will settle down contented with the use of that which legitimately belongs to them, leaving the funds of the Government to be kept and expended according to the letter and spirit of the Constitution. But should it be otherwise, the intelligence and firmness of our People are equal to any emergency. They now understand the whole subject. They see no reason why the stockholders and debtors of banks should have an exclusive privilege to make themselves rich out of the use of the public money. They see no reason why they should be taxed to raise money for such a purpose. They see that its effect is to build up a rich privileged order at their expense to control the Government and destroy all equality among the People. Seeing all this, and that the plan for which that interest has so long struggled, to the derangement of the business of the country, is in palpable violation of the spirit of the Constitution, their firmness will be equal to every effort necessary to prevent its re-establishment.

In the progress of our Government the most gratifying evidences have been furnished that our People are, in intelligence, integrity, and determined resolution, equal to the task of self-government. In that Administration which has been appropriately named "the reign of terror," so appropriately that men of all parties now repudiate its acts and are prompt to redress, as far as they can, the wrongs it inflicted, the force of statute law and the arm of the Judiciary were called in to aid the influence of the Executive and the advocates of a strong Government in putting down the rising spirit of the People, and controlling the current of public opinion; but all these combined powers were exerted in vain.

The Samson of Democracy burst the cords which were already bound around its limbs, and in the election of Mr. Jefferson vindicated its principles, its firmness, and its power. A web more artfully contrived, composed of a high protective tariff, a system of internal improvements, and a National Bank, was then twined around the sleeping giant in the vain hopes of subjecting him forever to the dominion and will of the ambitious and grasping few, and you have seen how he has scattered the whole to the winds when roused by the warning voice of the honest and intrepid Jackson. Again, in the triumph of the Independent Treasury, we witness the triumph of the popular intelligence and firmness over the arts, arguments, appliances, and alarms of the interested few who desire to enrich themselves by the use of the public money—another and the most gratifying evidence that the People, when aroused, are competent to maintain any just principle, and correct any abuse, however sanctioned by precedent or sustained by wealth.

On these evidences of popular intelligence and firmness the Republican patriot rests with well-grounded faith that all means which may be used to mislead or intimidate the People, now or hereafter, into a surrender of their Constitution and their liberties, will, as they ever have done, meet with a signal and withering rebuke.

I am, gentlemen, with thanks for the friendly spirit in which you have individually performed the duty assigned to you, very respectfully, your friend and obedient servant,

M. Van Buren.

To Messrs. John M. McCalla, T. M. Hickey, B. Taylor, Esq. committee, and G. W. Johnson.

Speech by General William Henry Harrison
Dayton, September 10, 1840

During the campaign of 1840, for the first time, a presidential candidate engaged in face-to-face appeals to voters as William Henry Harrison addressed huge crowds. The nature of the Whig campaign often required Harrison to deal in careful ambiguities and some sheer buncombe. Even so, his speeches helped Whig propagandists to sell the public on the image of a poor, hardworking, cabin-dwelling frontiersman. In this Dayton speech, published by the Whig Republican Association, Harrison rises to a rhetorical elegance that characterizes and nearly parodies the Whig campaign effort.

I rise, fellow citizens, (the multitude was here agitated as the sea, when the wild wind blows upon it, and it was full five minutes before the tumult of joy, at seeing and hearing the next President of the United States, could be calmed) — I rise, fellow citizens, to express to you from the bottom of a grateful heart, my warmest thanks for the kind and flattering manner in which I have been received by the representatives of the valley of the Miami. I rise to say to you, that however magnificent my reception has been on this occasion, I am not so vain as to presume that it was intended for me; that this glorious triumphal entry was designed for one individual. No. I know too well that person's imperfections to believe that this vast assemblage has come up here to do him honor. It is the glorious cause of democratic rights that brought them here. [Immense cheering.] It is the proud anniversary of one of the brightest victories that glows on the pages of our country's history, which hath summoned this multitude together. [Tremendous cheering.]

Fellow citizens, it was about this time of the day, twenty-seven years ago, this very hour, this very minute, that your speaker, as commander-in-chief of the North-Western army, was plunged into an agony of feeling when the cannonading from our fleet announced an action with the enemy. His hopes, his fears, were destined to be soon quieted, for the tidings of victory were brought to him on the wings of the wind. With the eagle of triumph perching upon our banners on the lake, I moved on to complete the overthrow of the foreign foe. The anniversary of that day can never be forgotten, for every American has cause to rejoice at the triumph of our arms on that momentous occasion; but the brave and gallant hero of that victory is gone, gone to that home whither we are all hurrying, and to his memory let us do that reverence due to the deeds of so illustrious a patriot. From Heaven does his soul look down upon us, and gladden at the virtues which still animate his generous countrymen in recurring to his noble and glorious career while on earth. [Great sensation for several seconds.]

I am fully aware, my fellow citizens, that you expect from me some opinion upon the various questions which now agitate our country, from centre to circumference, with such fierce contention. Calumny, ever seeking to destroy all that is good in this world, hath proclaimed that I am averse from declaring my opinions on matters so interesting to you; but nothing can be more false [Cheers.]

Have I not, time out of mind, proclaimed my opposition to a citizen's going forward among the people and soliciting votes for the Presidency? Have I not, many a time and often, said, that in my opinion, no man ought to aspire to the Presidency of these United States, unless he is designated as a candidate for that high office by the unbought wishes of the people? [Cheering.] If the candidate for so high an office be designated by a portion or a majority of the people, they will have come to the determination of sustaining such a man from a review of his past actions and life, and they will not exact pledges from him of what he will do and what he will not do, for their selection of him is proof enough that he will carry out the doctrines of his party. This plan of choosing a candidate for the Presidency is a much surer bar against corruption than the system of requiring promises. If the pledging plan is pursued, the effect will be, to offer the Presidential chair to the man who will make the *most* promises. [Laughter.] He who would pledge most, he who would promise most, would be the man to be voted for, and I have no hesitation in declaring my belief, that he who would subject his course to be thus tied up by promises and pledges, would not stop to break them when once in office. [Cheering.] Are my views on this topic correct, or are they not? [With one voice the multitude indicated they were.]

If, fellow citizens, we examine the history of all Republics, we shall find as they receded from the purity of Representative Government, the condition of obtaining office was the making of promises. He who bid the highest in promises, was the favored candidate, and the higher the bids, the more marked and certain the corruption. Look at the progress of this thing in our own Republic. Were any pledges required of your Washington or your Adams? Adams was the candidate of the federal party, and as a statesman was bound to carry out the principles of his party. Was his successor, Thomas Jefferson, the high priest of constitutional democracy, called on for pledges? No. His whole life was a pledge of what he would do. And if we go back to this old system of selecting men for the Presidency, whose past career shall be a guarantee of their conduct when elected to the Chief Magistracy of the Republic, the nation would advance safely, rapidly, and surely in the path of prosperity. But of late years the corrupting system of requiring pledges hath been adopted. The Presidency has been put up to the highest bidder in promises, and we see the result. It remains for you, my fellow citizens, to arrest this course of things.

While then, fellow citizens, I have never hesitated to declare my opinions on proper occasions upon the great questions before the nation, I cannot consent to make mere *promises* the condition of obtaining the office which you kindly wish to bestow upon me. My opinions I am free to express, but you already have them, sustained and supported by the acts of a long and arduous life. That life is a pledge of my future course, if I am elevated by your suffrages to the highest office in your gift. [Immense cheering for several seconds.]

It has been charged against me, fellow citizens, that I am a Federalist.

While I acknowledge that the original Federal party of this country was actuated in its course by no improper motives, *I deny* that I ever belonged to that class of politicians. [Tremendous cheering.] How could I belong to that party? I was educated in the school of anti-federalism, and though too young to take an active part in the politics of the country, when at the erection of the Constitution, the nation was divided into two great parties, my honored father had inducted me into the principles of Constitutional Democracy, and my teachers were the Henrys and the Masons of that period. He who declared that the seeds of monarchy were sown in the soil of the Constitution, was a leader in my school of politics. He, who said that "if this government be not a monarchy, it has an awful squinting towards a monarchy," was my Mentor. [Immense applause. Some time elapsed before order could be restored, at hearing these emphatic declarations of the General.] If I know my own feelings, if I know my own judgment, I believe now, as I did then, with the patriarchs of the Jeffersonian school, that the seeds of monarchy were indeed sown in the fertile soil of our Federal Constitution; and that though for nearly fifty years they lay dormant, they at last sprouted and shot forth into strong and thriving plants, bearing blossoms and producing ripe fruit. *The Government is now a practical monarchy!* [Loud and long cheering indicating that the people felt the full force of his declaration] Power is power, it matters not by what name it is called. The head of the Government exercising monarchical power, may be named King, Emperor, President, or Imaum, [great laughter] still he is a monarch. But this is not all. The President of these United States exercises a power superior to that vested in the hands of nearly all the European Kings. It is a power far greater than that ever dreamed of by the old Federal party.

It is an ultra federal power, it is despotism! [Cheering.] And I may here advert to an objection that has been made against me. It has been said, that if I ever should arrive at the dignified station occupied by my opponent, I would be glad and eager to retain the power enjoyed by the President of the United States. *Never, never.* [Tremendous cheering.] Though averse from pledges of every sort, I here openly and before the world declare that I will use all the power and influence vested in the office of President of the Union to abridge the power and influence of the National Executive! [It is impossible to describe the sensation produced by this declaration.] Is this federalism? [Cries of no, no, for several seconds.] In the Constitution, that glorious charter of our liberties, there is a defect, and that defect is, the term of service of the President, — not limited. This omission is the source of all the evil under which the country is laboring. If the privilege of being President of the United States had been limited to one term, the incumbent would devote all his time to the public interest, and there would be no cause to misrule the country. I shall not animadvert on the conduct of the present administration, lest you may in that case, conceive that I am aiming for the Presidency, to use it for selfish purposes. I should be an interested witness, if I entered into the subject. *But I pledge myself before Heaven and earth, if elected President of these United States, to lay down at the end of the term faithfully that high trust at the feet of the people!* [Here the multitude was so excited as to defy description.]

I go farther. I here declare before this vast assembly of the Miami Tribe (great laughter) that if I am elected, no human being shall ever know upon whom I would prefer to see the people's mantle fall; but I shall surrender this glorious badge of their authority into their own hands to bestow it as they please!—(nine cheers.) Is this federalism? (no, no, no.) Again in relation to the charge of being a federalist, I can refer to the doings previous to, and during, the late war. The federal party took ground against that war, and as a party, there never existed a purer band of patriots, for when the note of strife was sounded, they rallied under the banner of their country. But patriotic as they were, I do know *that I was not one of them!* [cheering.] I was denounced in unmeasured terms as one of the authors of that war, and was held up by the federal papers of the day as the marked object of the party. I could here name the man who came to me, and a more worthy man never lived, to say that he was mistaken in his views of my policy, as Governor of Indiana, when I was charged by the federalists as uselessly involving the country in an Indian war. He told me that I acted rightly in that matter, and that the war was brought on by me as a matter of necessity. [Cries of name him, name him.] It was Mr. Gaston of North Carolina.—[Three cheers.] Is this a proof that I was a federalist?—[No, no, no.]

I have now got rid, my fellow citizens, of this baseless charge—no, I have not. There are a few more allegations to notice. I am not a professional speaker, nor a studied orator, but I am an old soldier and a farmer, and as my sole object is to speak what I think, you will excuse me if I do it in my own way. [Shouts of applause, and cries of—the old soldier and farmer for us.]

I have said that there were other allegations to notice.—To prove that I was a federalist, they assert that I supported the alien and sedition laws, and in doing so, violated the principles and express words of the Constitution. I did not, fellow citizens, ever participate in this measure—When these laws passed I was a soldier in the army of the United States! [Applause.]

Again, they censure me for my course in Congress, when I served you in that body as a representative of the North West Territory. And here I will advert to the fact that I represented, at the time, a territory comprising now the States of Indiana, Illinois and Michigan. I was the sole representative of that immense extent of country. [A voice here cried—"And you are going to be again!" Tremendous cheering.] As I understood federalism to be in its origin, so I understand it to be now. It was and is the accumulation of power in the Executive to be used and exercised for its own benefit. Was my conduct in Congress then such as to entitle me to the appellation of federalist?—[Cries of no, no, and cheering.]

I had the honor, as Chairman of a Committee in the year 1800, to devise a bill which had for its object to snatch from the grasp of speculators all this glorious country which now teems with rich harvests under the hands of the honest, industrious and virtuous husbandman. [Immense cheering.] Was I a federalist then? [Cries of no, no, no.] When I was Governor of Indiana, ask how unlimited power bestowed upon me was exercised—a power as high as that exercised by the present President of the United States! I was then sole monarch of the North West Territory! [Laughter.] Did I discharge my duties as Governor of that vast Territory in such a way as to show that I was in love with the tremendous powers invested in me? [Here some 4000 persons in one quarter of the crowd raised their hats in the air and rent it with shouts of—no, no, no. They were the delegation from Indiana. This prompt response from so many persons produced great sensation.] There is an essential difference between the President of the United States and me. When he was in the Convention which remodelled the Constitution of New York, he was for investing the Governor with the appointment of the Sheriffs.—When I was Governor of Indiana, and possessed the power of appointing all officers, I gave it up to the people! [Intense excitement and great cheering.] I never appointed any officer whatever, while Governor of Indiana, whether sheriff, coroner, judge, justice of the peace or aught else, without first consulting and obtaining the wishes of the people. [Shouts of applause.] Was this an evidence that I was a federalist? [No, no, no.]

I think I have now shown you, fellow citizens, conclusively, that my actions do not constitute me a federalist, and it is to them I proudly point as the shield against which the arrows of my calumniators will fall in vain. [Immense cheering.]

Methinks I hear a soft voice asking: Are you in favor of paper money? I AM. [Shouts of applause.] If you would know why I am in favor of the credit system, I can only say it is because I am a democrat. [Immense cheering.] The two systems are the only means, under Heaven, by which a poor industrious man may become a rich man without bowing to colossal wealth. [Cheers.] But with all this, I am not a Bank man. Once in my life I was, and then they cheated me out of every dollar I placed in their hands. [Shouts of laughter.] And I shall never indulge in this way again; for it is more than probable that I shall never again have money beyond the day's wants. But I am in favor of a correct banking system, for the simple reason, that the share of the precious metals, which, in the course of trade, falls to our lot, is much less than the circulating medium which our internal and external commerce demands, to raise our prices to a level with the prices of Europe, where the credit system does prevail. There must be some plan to multiply the gold and silver which our industry commands; and there is no other way to do this but by a safe banking system. [Great applause.] I do not pretend to say that a perfect system of banking can be devised. There is nothing in the offspring of the human mind that does not savor of imperfection. No plan of government or finance can be devised free from defect. After long deliberation, I have no hopes that this country can ever go on to prosper under a pure specie currency. Such a currency but makes the poor poorer, and the rich richer. A properly devised banking system alone, possesses the capability of bringing the poor to a level with the rich.—[Tremendous cheering.]

I have peculiar notions of government. Perhaps I may err. I am no statesman by profession, but as I have already said, I am a half soldier and a half farmer, and it may be, that, if I am elected to the first office in your gift, my fellow citizens will be deceived in me, but I can assure them, that if, in carrying out their wishes, the head shall err, the heart is true. [Great huzzaing.]

My opinion of the power of Congress to charter a national bank remains unchanged. There is not in the Constitution any express grant of power for such purpose, and it could never be constitutional to exercise, save in the event, the powers granted to congress could not be carried into effect, without resorting to such an institution. [Applause] Mr. Madison signed the law creating a national bank, because he thought that the revenue of the country could not be collected or disbursed to the best advantage without the interposition of such an establishment. I said in my letter to Sherrod Williams, that, if it was plain that the revenues of the Union could only be collected and disbursed in the most effectual way by means of a bank, and if I was clearly of opinion that the majority of the people of the United States desired such an institution, then, and then only would I sign a bill going to charter a bank. [Shouts of applause.] I have never regarded the office of Chief Magistrate as conferring upon the incumbent the power of mastery over the popular will, but as granting him the power to execute the properly expressed will of the people and not to resist it. With my mother's milk did I suck in the principles on which the Declaration of Independence was founded. [Cheering.] That declaration complained, that the King would not let the people make such laws as they wished. Shall a President or an executive officer undertake, at this late time of day, to control the people in the exercise of their supreme will? No. The people are the best guardians of their own rights, [applause,] and it is the duty of their Executive to abstain from interfering in or thwarting the sacred exercise of the law-making functions of their government.

In this view of the matter, I defend my having signed a well known bill which passed the legislature while I was Governor of Indiana. It is true, my opponents have attempted to cast odium upon me for having done so, but while they are engaged in such an effort, they impugn the honor and honesty of the inmates of the log cabins, who demanded the passage and signature of that bill. The men who now dare to arraign the people of Indiana for having exercised their rights as they pleased, were in their nurse's arms when that bill passed the legislature. What do they know of the pioneers of that vast wilderness? I tell them, that in the legislature which passed the bill exciting so much their horror, there were men as pure in heart, and as distinguished for their common sense and high integrity, as any who set themselves up for models in these days. [Immense cheering.] I glory in carrying out their views, for in doing so I submitted to the law-making power, in accordance with the declaration of independence, I did not prevent the people from making what laws they pleased. [Cheering.]

If the Augean stable is to be cleansed, it will be necessary to go back to the principles of Jefferson. [Cheers.] It has been said by the Henrys, the Madisons, the Graysons and others, that one of the great dangers in our government is, the powers vested in the general government would overshadow the government of the States. There is truth in this, and long since and often have I expressed the opinion that the interference of the general government with the elective franchise in the States would be the signal for the downfall of liberty. That interference has taken place, and while the mouths of professed democrats appeal to Jefferson, and declare they are governed by his principles, they are urging at the same time 100,000 office holders to meddle in the State elections! And if the rude hand of power be not removed from the elective franchise, there will soon be an end to the government of the Union. [Cries of assent.] It is a truth in government ethics, that when a larger power comes in contact with a smaller power, the latter is speedily destroyed or swallowed up by the former. So in regard to the general government and the State governments. Should I ever be placed in the Chief Magistrate's seat, I will carry out the principles of Jackson, and never permit the interference of office-holders in the elections. [Immense applause.] I will do more. While I will forbid their interference in elections, I will never do aught to prevent their going quietly to the polls and voting, even against me or my measures. No American citizen should be deprived of his power of voting as he pleases.

I have detained you, fellow-citizens, longer than I intended, but you now see that I am not the old man on crutches nor the imbecile they say I am — [cheering] — not the prey to disease — a voice cried here; nor the bear in a cage, nor the caged animal they wittily described me to be, [great laughter and cheering.]

But before I conclude, there are two or three other topics I must touch upon.

The violence of party spirit, as of late exhibited, is a serious mischief to the political welfare of the country. Party feeling is necessary in a certain degree to the health and stability of a Republic, but when pushed to too great an extent, it is detrimental to the body politic, it is the rock upon which many a Republic has been dashed to pieces. An old farmer told me the other day that he did not believe one of the stories circulated against me, and he would support me if I were only a Democrat. [Laughter.] But if I support and sustain democratic principles, what matters it how I am called? It matters a good deal, said he; you don't belong to the Democratic party! [Laughter] Can any thing be more ruinous in its tendency to our institutions, than this high party spirit, which looks to the shadow, and not to be the substance of things? Nothing, nothing. This running after names, after imaginings, is ominous of dangerous results. In the blessed Book we are told that the pretensions of false Christs shall be in future times so specious that even the elect will be deceived. And is it not so now with Democracy? The name does not constitute the Democrat. — It is the vilest imposture ever attempted upon the credulity of the public mind to array the poor of the country under the name of Democrats against the rich, and style them aristocrats. This is dealing in fables. The natural antagonist of Democracy is not aristocracy. It is monarchy. — There is no instance on record of a Republic like ours running into an aristocracy. It can hurry into a pure Democracy, and the confidence of that Democracy being once obtained by a Marius or Cæsar, by a Bolivar or a Bonaparte, he strides rapidly from professions of love for the people to usurpation of their rights, and steps from that high eminence to a throne! [Cheering.] And thus, in the name of Democracy, the boldest crimes are committed. Who forgets the square in Paris, where ran rivers of the people's blood, shed in the name of Democracy at the foot of the statue of liberty! Cherish not the man, then, who, under the guise and name of Democracy, tries to overthrow the principles of Republicanism, as professed and acted upon by Jefferson and Madison. [Immense cheering.]

Gen. Harrison here adverted to the calumnies put forth against his military fame by that noble pair of brothers, Allen and Duncan, and in severe but just terms exposed the falsehoods of these vilifiers. He proved that they were guilty of falsifying the records of the country, and in a brief and lucid manner vindicated himself and the honor of the nation from the aspersions of these and other reckless politicians. He showed that the received history of his brilliant career in the North West had been stamped by the impress of truth, and he will soon find that a generous and grateful people will testify their admiration of his glorious services in their cause by raising the brave old soldier to the highest office in their gift.

A precious inheritance, continued the General, has been handed down to you by your forefathers. In Rome, the sacred fire of fabled gods was kept alive by vestal virgins, and they watched over the gift with eager eyes. In America, a glorious fire has been lighted upon the altar of liberty, and to you, my fellow citizens, has been entrusted its safe-keeping, to be nourished with care and fostered forever. Keep it burning, and let the sparks that continually go up from it fall on other altars, and light up in distant lands the fire of freedom. The Turk busies himself no longer with his harem or his bow string. To licentiousness have succeeded the rights of man, and constitutions are given to the people by once despotic rulers. Whence came the light that now shines in the land of darkness? It was a brand snatched from your own proud altar, and thrust into the pyre of Turkish oppression.

Shall then the far seen light upon the shrine of American liberty ever be extinguished? [No, no, no.] It would not be your loss only—it would be the loss of the whole world. The enemies of freedom in Europe are watching you with intense anxiety, and your friends, like a few planets of heaven, are praying for your success. Deceive them not, but keep the sacred fire burning steadily upon your altars, and the Ohio farmer whom you design to make your Chief Magistrate will, at the end of four years, cheerfully lay down the authority which you may entrust him with, free from all ambition. It will have been glorious enough for me to be honored as those pure and honest republicans, Washington, Jefferson and Madison were honored—with the high confidence of a great, noble, just and generous people! [The excitement and cheering continued for several minutes, and the multitude were swayed to and fro, as the leaves of the forest in a storm of wind.]

[For 1840 Popular and Electoral Votes see p. 690.]

Election of 1844

CHARLES SELLERS is Professor of History at the University of California, Berkeley. His chief publications are James K. Polk (2 volumes), *and* Charles Willson Peale: Later Life (1790-1827).

Election of 1844

by *Charles Sellers*

The most notable feature of the presidential election of 1844 was its closeness. Out of the Jacksonian battles of the 1830's, a fully matured two-party system had emerged. Party organization and party newspapers had been carried to the town and county level throughout the country, impelling hosts of new voters into the electorate and imbuing them with firm allegiances as Democrats or Whigs. The press frequently highlighted the rigidity of partisan attachments by reporting such extreme examples as Westmoreland County, Pennsylvania, which the Democrats carried in 1840 and 1844 by identical votes of 4,704 to 2,778, or Davidson County, Tennessee, which the Whigs carried in the gubernatorial election of 1843, the presidential election of 1844, and the gubernatorial election of 1845 by identical majorities of 583 votes. This stability of partisan attachments meant that the great majority of votes in any election were determined less by the candidates and immediate issues than by the preexisting pattern of party identifications in the electorate.

In retrospect it is clear that the two-party system's inherent tendency toward equilibrium had produced by 1844 a situation where the two major parties commanded the loyalties of almost equal numbers of voters. This developing equilibrium of partisan attachments, obscured from contemporaries by the ephemeral electoral upheaval of 1840, had accompanied a waning of the high political emotions of the 1830's, particularly as they had centered around the symbolic issue of banking.

Andrew Jackson's Democratic party had gathered its original strength from a popular mood that was both egalitarian and conservative. Along with democracy, the major issue of the 1830's had been the country's adjustment to a newly dynamic economy, stimulated and governed by the mysterious workings of money and credit. Some—the entrepreneurially inclined or those whose advantages enabled them to perceive and exploit the new opportunities—accepted wholeheartedly the new gospel of entrepreneurial progress and insisted on public policies that would foster economic growth. The Whig party emerged in opposition to the Jacksonians as the great political instrument of such men and such attitudes.

Others, however, felt their old independence and security threatened by impersonal mechanisms of money and market, seemingly manipulated by a privileged elite. As on previous occasions, the democratic masses turned out to be the real conservatives; and the Jacksonian Democratic party succeeded the Jeffersonian Republican party as the political instrument of both their democratic and their conservative inclinations. Farmers and workingmen responded warmly to the Jacksonian promise that they would remain the central figures of the Republic, the peculiar exemplars of civic virtue; that wealth would be accumulated only out of honest toil and not filched away by dishonest speculators, manipulating the artificial mechanisms of credit; that government would, in the words of Jackson's Bank veto, "confine itself to equal protection, and, as Heaven does its rains, shower its favors alike on the high and the low, the rich and the poor."

Yet Jacksonian conservatism was ambiguous. For many Jacksonians, hostility to the speculative system masked an envious resentment at not sharing its largesse; and the Jacksonian "hard-money" program of stifling the speculative spirit by destroying the paper-money banking system that sustained it had produced results widely different from its avowed aims. By calling state banking interests to their aid in the war on the national bank, the Jacksonians not only heightened the speculative spirit but nurtured within their own ranks a discordant speculative-minded element.

Therefore the Whigs could only too plausibly blame the Democrats for the disastrous financial panic that fell upon the country in 1837, and for the protracted business depression that followed it. At the same time the Whigs finally managed to shake off the elitist overtones that had prevented them from bidding on equal terms for the support of an egalitarian electorate.

Meanwhile the depression had prompted a final struggle over financial policy. A sharpened consciousness of the evils of speculative banking had pushed the Democratic leadership toward a more uncompromising hard-money position. The Van Buren Administration insisted that the Government deal only in gold and silver coin, segregated in its own independent treasury system, while in the state legislatures, hard-money Democrats sought either to destroy the banking system or to surround it with stringent safeguards against overissue, excessive profits, and exclusive privileges. At the same time, however, the depression had prompted a louder outcry for an expansion of credit from Whigs and a minority of conservative Democrats who wanted the interrupted march of enterprise to resume.

At first, the two impulses fought to a stalemate. But as Americans gradually effected their psychological adjustment to the new economic order, the hard-money mood was bound to give way. If farmers and workingmen could not avoid the perils of the engrossing money-market nexus, neither in a fluid society could they long resist its allurements. Gradually, the gospel of entrepreneurial progress won more and more Jacksonian farmers and workingmen, converted by opportunities for petty entrepreneurship or speculation and by rising appetites for newly available conveniences and luxuries that only money could buy. Conversely, the boom-bust cycle was convincing more and more Whiggish and conservative Democratic entrepreneurs that some restraints should be placed on the banking system.

Gradually, as the political passions of the Jacksonian years cooled, a limited victory here and a compromise there began to produce a pragmatic consensus that the country, out of the exhaustion of its political emotions, was willing to accept. The National Bank was not to be revived, at least in its old untrammelled form; and the federal funds were to be deposited either in the state banks or in an independent treasury (most people no longer much cared), depending on which party was in power. The struggle over state banking was only reaching its climax in a few states like Ohio and Missouri; but in most of the country it had been pretty well decided that paper-money banking was to continue under various safeguards—free banking systems, specie reserve requirements, small note restrictions, extended liability of bank stockholders, or a state monopoly of the banking business. The great Whig victory of 1840 was not so much a mandate for orthodox Whig policies as it was a political binge that could be enjoyed because the serious issues of the 1830's were well on their way to settlement, while the serious issue of the future, slavery, had so far been kept pretty well off the political stage.

Under these circumstances the Democratic party emerged from the defeat of 1840 leaderless and mutinous. Its egalitarian insignia appropriated by the foe, the Democracy's war aims had become sadly ambiguous.

The growing consensus on banking in the country at large had been made possible by the retreat of many Democrats from the hard-money standard, and this in turn had deepened the schism in the Democratic party. The hard-money policy embodied the genuine, if quixotic, idealism of the party; and the faster the tide of Jacksonian idealism ran out, the more manfully Van Buren and the ideological wing of the party struggled to stem its ebbing. "What has democracy to do with compromise, with conciliation?" exclaimed a Van Buren partisan. "I say damn the idea of compromise." The line between the hard-money mood and the entrepreneurial mood was to the Van Burenites a moral line, and any Democrat who drifted across it was not just politically but also morally suspect.

The more entrepreneurial or pragmatic Democrats were just as irritated at the "undiscriminating radicals." "Our party was united & strong," complained Governor Enos T. Throop of New York, until the Van Buren radicals took up from "the tag rags of the party"—men full of "hostility to the people of better condition"—"the idea that all banks were evils." Actually, said

Throop, the banks were "operating very advantageously in the interests of industry & commerce, and our respectable & intelligent political friends were enjoying the benefits of them both as Stockholders and business men." Throop and men like him were baffled by the radicals' indifference to the interests of business and Democratic businessmen, irritated by their tone of moral superiority, and infuriated by their willingness to divide the party and court defeat in pursuit of an impracticable and an incomprehensible ideal.

The desertion of some of these "conservative" Democrats had frustrated Van Buren's efforts to get the independent treasury enacted until his last year in office; and the desertion or lukewarmness of many more had contributed to his ignominious defeat in the disgraceful "log cabin and hard cider" campaign of 1840. Emerged from defeat, the embittered Van Burenites resolved to purge the party of its corrupt and traitorous elements and to vindicate their leader by triumphantly renominating and reelecting him in 1844. The conservatives were no less determined to eliminate Van Buren and his "impracticables" once and for all.

In the contest that ensued Van Buren had certain great advantages. The hard-money mood had a considerable residual appeal to the whole generation of Democrats whose political attitudes had crystallized in the Jacksonian years of intense ideological commitment. Having once tasted the heady brew of ideological fervor, many were reluctant to shift to the flatter beverage of political practicality that was appropriate to a period of national consensus and relative placidity. Moreover, as President, Van Buren had been able to make the independent treasury and the hard-money mood it symbolized the official policy of the party and to commit the more zealous rank-and-file Democrats to it. Also, as President, Van Buren had used the extensive federal patronage to strengthen the politicians and newspapers that shared his views in the Democratic organizations of their respective states. "The old office holders who expect to be restored with Mr. Van Buren & the old editors who were liberally patronised by his Administration," observed James Buchanan, "are the regular troops in political warfare."

The regular troops got their marching orders from the national party organ, Francis P. Blair's Washington *Globe*. Frank Blair and his business partner John C. Rives had grown wealthy from Government printing contracts during the Jackson and Van Buren Administrations. Fanatically loyal to the two ex-Presidents, they made their slashing editorial columns a powerful weapon for Van Buren while claiming a purely technical neutrality that fooled no one. Also for Van Buren were such diverse but influential newspapers as William Cullen Bryant's *Evening Post* in New York, Samuel Medary's *Ohio Statesman* in Columbus, and that oracle of traditional Virginia Republicanism, the Richmond *Enquirer*, whose editor, Thomas Ritchie, doubled as party boss in the Old Dominion.

The old regulars supporting Van Buren included, too, a large share of the most prominent Democratic leaders, especially those distinguished for their ideological orientation toward politics and for their "republican" simplicity of style. The archetype was Van Buren's bosom friend Silas Wright, Democratic leader of the Senate. Able, self-effacing, and excruciatingly conscientious, Wright commanded from the most hostile a respect that enabled him to keep the rival Democratic prima donnas of the Senate working together. "It was not an easy task," said one observer, "for Calhoun would bolt, and Benton would bully, and Buchanan sneak; but he was the superior of all three." When Congress was not in session, visitors could find him working alongside the hired hands on his farm in upstate New York. The puzzled conservatives blamed Wright's influence for Van Buren's unaccountable lapse from his former pragmatic shrewdness, but a larger segment of the party would have agreed with the Van Burenite who called Wright "the Model Democrat of all men I have ever seen."

Wright's staunchest senatorial ally was the conceited, bombastic Thomas Hart Benton—"Old Bullion," the father of the new gold coins known as "Benton's mint drops," the very embodiment of the hard-money idea. Outside Congress was the foremost of the old regulars and Van Buren's weightiest champion, Old Hickory himself.

For all Van Buren's strong support, however, the fact remained that he simply was not very popular beyond the intransigent hard-money men. "He wont do at all," declared the shrewd and relatively disinterested Supreme Court Justice John Catron, being "unpopular with all classes—essentially so with the people at large . . . and what is more clearly so, with the rank & file of our political friends." Arkansas Democrats were reported to think Van Buren "rather cold blooded"; a Mississippian asserted that "the campaign of 1840 was so disastrous that our friends dread to fight another battle under his lead"; in Ohio it was said that "apart from party and political considerations Mr. Van Buren neither has or ever did have the feelings and sympathies of the western people"; and no less an authority than James Buchanan claimed that "he is not popular in Pennsylvania & never has been."

This conviction of the New Yorker's unavailability was not confined to conservative Democrats. Many others, heretofore faithful to Van Buren but interested above all in winning elections, were sufficiently apprehensive about a Van Buren ticket to be susceptible to any anti-Van Buren movement that seemed to have any chance of success. Such a movement would not lack for leaders. John C. Calhoun, James Buchanan, Richard M. Johnson, and Lewis Cass all saw that their chances for the Presidency might be blocked indefinitely if Van Buren were nominated a third time—and especially if he were elected and designated Benton or Wright as his successor. Nor would these older leaders lack for lieutenants. A whole new generation of Democratic politicians had come forward since the 1830's. Immune to the ideological viruses of the Jacksonian years, this pragmatic, ambitious "Young Democracy" chafed under the leadership of the old regulars. "Let the old dynasty be restored," complained one of these new men, and "the superannuated and broken down politicians will have full swing & we modern men must step into the rear rank of the political cohorts."

The basic weakness of the anti-Van Buren forces was their inability to rally behind a single leader. James Buchanan had volunteered early for the command, only to have his rivals at home, in characteristic Pennsylvania fashion, cripple his campaign by getting up a movement for another aspirant, Richard M. Johnson of Kentucky.

"Old Dick," still capitalizing on his fame as reputed slayer of Tecumseh at the battle of the Thames forty years before and on the popularity he had acquired with eastern workingmen's groups nearly twenty years before by his opposition to imprisonment for debt and his championing of church-state separation, really believed himself the people's choice. With an exhibitionistic egotism that was so transparent and innocent as to be almost attractive, "the Tecumseh-killer" defied the convention that forbade Presidential candidates to campaign. Traveling up and down the country, from New England to Missouri, in his old-fashioned brass-buttoned blue coat and waistcoat "of most 'unmitigated red,' " he visited churches, schools, and colleges, paraded the streets, made speeches, and rode in militia reviews "with hat off, and a very fierce look on." At an Irish Repeal meeting in Cincinnati, he expressed the wish that he "could speak only three minutes and fight the rest of the time," but only at the conclusion of a long speech in which "the never to be ended tale of the Battle of the Thames was once more repeated, the mutilated fingers exhibited, and the most violent love for Ireland and the Irish expressed in the most pathetic terms." Johnson's personal warmth convinced many ordinary Democrats that "his kind heart sympathizes deeply in the suffering interests of labor, " but the old regulars were disgusted and exasperated by his activities. "He has no fixed opinions; & he has not mind enough to frame fixed opinions," sneered George Bancroft; while Benton called Johnson "the damndest political wh—re in the country." These charges were given considerable substance by the welcome and support Johnson received from conservative Democrats everywhere.

When "Old Tecumseh's" candidacy failed to catch on as widely as his conservative backers hoped it might, many of them shifted their efforts to promoting the late-blooming candidacy of Michigan's Lewis Cass, who had won a sudden éclat by his anti-British demonstrations while American minister to France. Through a long public life this massive, dignified, stolid figure had carefully avoided or straddled every controversial issue. Now, it was observed, "He wraps himself in vague declarations of 'Jeffersonian Democracy,'" inducing his admirers to regard him as "the bow which spans and soothes the storms." "Perfectly free from the embittered associations of the last five years," Cass seemed the most available of all the conservative possibilities; and it was the effort to rally all anti-Van Buren opinion on him in the late summer and fall of 1843 that had given James Polk such trouble in Tennessee.

Yet one segment of the Democratic opposition—the one most feared and most hated by the Van Burenites—could never be rallied on Cass. It took its rise from other than "conservative" grounds and would follow no other leader than John C. Calhoun.

Let it be recognized at once that Calhoun was a man of extraordinary ability and magnetism. Otherwise, he could never have exerted such a potent force within the American political system while standing out so intransigently against the pragmatic, compromising mode that has ever been its genius. His great appeal was as a political thinker, but not in the sense commonly supposed. Calhoun's claim to distinction as a political philosopher is vitiated by the unreality of his much vaunted "realism," by his inexorable pushing of "realistic" premises to conclusions having no possible realistic application. Yet, his very devotion to formal logic, regardless of practical consequences, was powerfully attractive to some Americans, who were coming to feel themselves trapped in a situation which threatened their sense of security and moral worth and from which there seemed to be no practical escape. Calhoun would have been potentially disruptive to the American political process anywhere or any time; but a perverse fate had set him down at the very place where Americans had been under the severest social strain—not just in the South, but in that hotbed of southern sensitivity, South Carolina—and at the very time when the South's morbid sensitivity over its peculiar institution of human slavery was driving it toward irrationality.

For all the precision of movement and chiseled, emphatic speech through which Calhoun projected his own image of himself as a disinterested servant of great principles, the burning eyes set deep in his gaunt face told another story. The man seethed with a self-righteousness that was incredible and an egotism that made his principles and his personal fortunes indistinguishable. "The great 'I am,' " John Tyler called him after some intimate dealings; and even his admirers admitted that "He liked very much to talk of himself, and he always had the good fortune to make the subject exceedingly interesting and captivating to his hearers."

For years Calhoun had yearned for the Presidency, and his principles had shown a remarkable tendency to veer in whatever direction might advance his chances. In the early 1820's he had been the most conspicuous nationalist in the country; later he supported Jackson, expecting to be his successor; in the early 1830's he had broken with Jackson to become the prophet of nullification in South Carolina; a little later he had aspired to lead the great Whig coalition against Jacksonian tyranny. All these mores failing, Calhoun had at length embarked on his great crusade to persuade the South that slavery was a positive good and to unite all southerners in its defense—under the leadership of John C. Calhoun. Forgetting his former approval of the National Bank, and coming out vociferously for hard money, he had finally returned to the Democratic party, determined to win the Democratic presidential nomination with solid support from southern Democrats.

Most southerners remained suspicious of their self-appointed leader, and for a long time Calhoun's support was confined to a devoted little band of those whose chivalric hauteur or extreme sensitivity about slavery inclined them toward the doctrinaire intransigence that he preached. In South Carolina, such men were dominant, and here Calhoun's will was absolute. "All who sought promotion in the State had to follow and swear by him," complained Benjamin F. Perry. "He thought for the State and crushed out all independence of thought in those below him."

By the 1840's, however, Calhoun's support had begun to widen. Steady agitation by his fire-eating followers gradually heightened southern irritability over slavery, making southerners more susceptible to his preaching. By 1842, even Jackson's old crony, William M. Gwin of Mississippi, was ready to declare, "I want a slave-holder for President next time regardless of the man believing as I solemnly do that in the next Presidential term the Abolitionists must be put down or blood will be spilt." Meanwhile, Calhoun had been allaying distrust by his conciliatory behavior in the Senate, and his friends had begun constructing a conventional political organization which they thought extremely formidable.

It is instructive to note that the sordidness and crudities of practical politics were most apparent in the campaigns of the very candidates who thought themselves farthest above such things. In the South, the Calhounites operated on their principle of Greek democracy, relying on the leadership of high-minded gentlemen whom the people would be glad to follow. Outside the South, they resolved to fight fire with fire and — no sacrifice is too great for principle — to practice the political mendacity which they supposed to be characteristic of a democratic society. South Carolinians viewed the world through a prism that distorted North and South alike, a refraction that would be fateful indeed if ever imposed on the vision of other southerners.

Even in South Carolina, the ideal of political leadership by high-minded gentlemen did not hold up without a little practical reinforcement. The state's politics were adroitly managed for Calhoun by Franklin H. Elmore, president of that efficient Calhounite political machine, the Bank of South Carolina. Through loans to politicians, "the bank controlled the State, and Colonel Elmore controlled the bank." Where bank loans did not suffice, Elmore's superb talents for political maneuver — "one of the most adroit managing public men that I ever saw," Benjamin F. Perry called him — were usually more than adequate to the occasion. "If there were two ways of approaching any point, equally safe and secure, the one direct and the other circuitous," observed another South Carolinian, "Elmore would always take the latter."

To direct Calhoun's presidential campaign, Elmore had constituted a committee of high-minded gentlemen in Charleston. Similar gentlemen in the other southern states — except in North Carolina, where for a lack of authentic South Carolina types the Calhounites had to rely on loud, vulgar, and ambitious Romulus M. Saunders — coordinated their activities for Calhoun through correspondence with the Charleston committee. There was a similar directorate at Washington, where Robert M. T. Hunter of Virginia and the fiery South Carolina congressman Robert Barnwell Rhett supervised the national Calhoun newspaper, the *Spectator*, and managed the campaign in the North and West.

Outside the South, the Calhoun cause attracted a weird collection of the doctrinaire, the disaffected, the mercenary, and the opportunistic. In the great port cities, importing merchants desiring free trade joined forces with radical laborites like Orestes Brownson, who envisioned an anticapitalist alliance between northern workingmen and southern slaveholders, and with raucous demagogues like Mike Walsh, whose gang of "Bowery B'hoys" stood ready to brawl for Calhoun in order to strike at well-fed and well-groomed Tammany politicians.

In New England, Calhoun's fortunes were entrusted to the powerful conservative faction of the Democratic party, led by the gouty, choleric Boston banker, David Henshaw, who had bossed the Massachusetts Democracy until Marcus Morton and Bancroft led a successful rebellion against him. The Yankee Calhounites were counting, too, on the support of the "cool, cautious & selfish" Senator Levi Woodbury of New Hampshire, before whose nose the Calhoun managers were dangling the vice-presidential nomination.

The prim wantonness with which Calhoun and his gentlemanly managers yielded to the seductions of democratic politics was matched by the virginal ineptitude with which they played the game. The amateurs and adventurers who volunteered to conduct the Calhoun campaign in New York and New England had no trouble passing themselves off with Elmore and company as practical, influential politicians, or in convincing the gentlemen at Washington and Charleston that Calhoun was on the verge of a tremendous victory in the North. At any rate the Washington Calhoun committee permitted one of the New Yorkers to conduct the *Spectator* long enough to demonstrate his impracticality even to gentlemen, while the Charleston committee raised thousands of dollars from wealthy South Carolina planters for Calhoun newspapers and campaigning in the North.

The optimism of the Calhounites reached its peak in August and September of 1843. Their letters from the North exuded confidence; the party had agreed to their demand that the national convention at Baltimore be postponed until May 1844; the Georgia Democratic convention had given substance to their dream of a united South by instructing its delegates to support Calhoun at Baltimore; and James K. Polk's defeat for the governorship of Tennessee seemed to presage the collapse of Van Buren's candidacy by demonstrating his unpopularity and showing "that there are other spokes to the Democratic wheel besides the 'Old Hero.' "

From these rosy reveries they were wakened with dismaying suddenness. In rapid succession, the Democratic conventions of New York and most of the New England States declared for Van Buren, destroying any hopes of substantial Calhoun support from the North. Nearer home, the disillusionment was even more bitter. The Georgia endorsement of Calhoun had only stirred up the powerful currents of hostility and suspicion toward the South Carolinian that stemmed from the days of nullification; and as a result the Georgia Democrats suffered a stunning defeat in the fall elections. Promptly, a new state convention was called to revoke the endorsement of Calhoun, while indications multiplied that the anti-Calhounites would predominate in the Democratic conventions of the other southern states. "Our friends in New England have greviously [sic] misled us," one of Calhoun's advisers mournfully told him, "and . . . there is nothing left but to decide how you should be withdrawn so that you may be preserved for the country in future."

To this renewed disappointment, Calhoun reacted with a characteristic swing from excessive optimism to self-righteous despair. Just a year before, when he still expected to win the Presidency through the party system, he had "beheld with joy" the "truly republican and noble stand," the "rigid adherence to principle," of his fellow Democrats. Accordingly "I made up my mind to waive the objections which I have long entertained" to the convention nominating system. Now, however, with his hopes for a convention nomination blasted, he declared, "The whole affair is a gross fraud and I intend to wash my hands of it." "I am the last man that can be elected in the present condition of the country," he told his son. "I am too honest and patriotick to be the choice of anything like a majority." It was only from the perspective of Calhoun's almost pathological need to be justified and somehow victorious that the country, the party, and the convention system had so abruptly and so completely changed their character.

And so, as he had often done before, Calhoun struck a pose of principled intransigence. In a written address to his friends at Charleston and Washington, he withdrew his name from consideration as a candidate before the now contemptible Baltimore convention and called on his followers to defeat Van Buren by abandoning the Democrats and "standing fast and rallied on our own ground." What he clearly wished was to be run as an independent candidate, though even he recognized that such a movement had no chance of success. "The object now is, not victory," he explained, "but to preserve our position and principles; the only way, under [the] circumstances, by which we can preserve our influence and the safety of the South." It was also the only way to preserve Calhoun's image of himself as a heroic figure in the struggle between light and darkness that raged across his peculiar field of vision. His friends might follow if they wished: "if they shall have the spirit to raise the banner of free trade & the people," that is, the banner of Calhoun, "against monopoly and political managers, we shall have a glorious cause to rise or fall by." If not, "it will cause me no mortification or pain to stand alone, on the ground which I find it my duty to occupy."

Calhoun had reach his decision to withdraw at the beginning of December, 1843, just as his friends at Washington were joining the other anti-Van Buren forces in a last-ditch effort to stop the New Yorker. The Democratic politicians were streaming into the capital for a session of Congress at which they expected to settle finally on the candidates to be nominated by the Baltimore convention in May; and the anti-Van Burenites hoped to cripple the New Yorker's candidacy by electing anti-Van Buren Democrats over the regular nominees of the party caucus for officers of the House of Representatives.

This plan might have succeeded if the Whig minority had been willing to support the dissident Democrats. Normally, the Whigs would have exploited any opportunity to embarrass the Democratic majority, but this time the Whig leaders exerted "the most decisive & even violent action" to keep their followers from interfering in the Democratic quarrel. "If we cannot beat Mr. Van Buren," they had decided, "we can beat no one"; and they carefully avoided anything that might weaken Van Buren's chances of nomination. "A compromise candidate—Cass for instance," said one of the Whig strategists, "would have greatly endangered us in Penn. & Ohio, whereas as against Mr. V. B. these states are regarded as absolutely certain."

Rather than give up, however, the dissidents carried their fight into the Democratic caucus, where they hoped to succeed by imposing the two-thirds rule for nominating House officers. To their shocked surprise, the Van Buren-ites, secure in the possession of an overwhelming majority of the House Democrats, readily agreed to the two-thirds rule, and then proceeded to carry the Van Buren candidates for every House office with votes to spare.

This stunning demonstration of Van Buren's strength appeared to settle the question of the Democratic presidential nomination. Within a week the canny Buchanan had withdrawn as a candidate. "I waited," he said, "until I saw there was no earthly prospect of success . . . Mr. Van Buren is not my first choice among the other candidates; but it is now manifest that he will obtain the nomination by an overwhelming majority & it is our duty to sub-mit; though I know it will be a painful duty to many." Cass's friends likewise now had to confess that "the great popular movement in the democratic ranks is decidedly in favour of Mr. Van Buren"; and they promised to give the New Yorker "a most cordial and hearty support." Even Old Tecumseh scurried for cover, announcing that he would be glad to accept the vice-presidential nomi-nation if the convention preferred another for the Presidency.

Not until late January, however, did the Charleston committee finally publish Calhoun's address of withdrawal as a candidate before the Baltimore convention. Ignoring Calhoun's desire to stay in the race as an independent candidate, the Charleston *Mercury* at the same time removed his name from its masthead; and at the Virginia Democratic convention a few days later the Calhounites of that state further chagrined their chief by promising to support the Baltimore nominee. Thus deserted by his friends, even Calhoun could not endorse the project of his visionary supporter Duff Green for a convention of anti-Van Buren Democrats to meet at Philadelphia on the Fourth of July.

Meanwhile, eighteen state Democratic conventions had been held, five of them on January 8, the anniversary of Jackson's great victory at New Orleans. By the close of that Democratic day of jubilee, twelve of these eighteen states, including the southern states of Alabama, Arkansas, Louisiana, and Mississippi, had declared for Van Buren; four had been noncommittal; Geor-gia had withdrawn its endorsement of Calhoun; Kentucky adhered to its early nomination of Johnson; and no state had declared for any other candidate. There seemed to be no gainsaying Cave Johnson's report to Polk: "All the fragments of our party seem likely to unite upon Van Buren, make his nomi-nation unanimous & each party seek the succession by distinguished services in his behalf."

The Whigs had plunged from the pinnacle of their great victory into even greater distraction than the Democrats. Henry Clay, the "Great Embodi-ment" of Whig principles, was exceedingly bitter at having been passed over for the presidential nomination when a Whig victory seemed assured. Deter-mined to dominate the Harrison Administration from his position in the Senate, he had pressured the President into calling a special session of Congress to enact the orthodox Whig program — replacement of the independent treasury with a new national bank, distribution of public land revenues among the states, and a high protective tariff.

But before the special session could assemble, Harrison suddenly fell ill and died, and Vice-President John Tyler moved into the White House. It quickly developed that Tyler had constitutional scruples against the kind of national bank Clay wanted. The question could probably have been compromised if the new President's touchy pride — irritated by the Senator's imperious insistence on demonstrating mastery of the Whig party — had not driven him into vetoes of two successive bank charter bills that had some appearance of attempting to meet his objections.

Tyler's vetoes provoked a complete rupture between the President and his party. With Clay cracking the whip of party discipline, the Whig congressional caucus formally read the President out of the party, leaving him only a tiny handful of personal supporters in the legislative branch. His Cabinet resigned, except for Clay's rival Daniel Webster, who remained until it was apparent that further association with the doomed Administration meant political suicide.

Tyler's vanity now caused him to be persuaded that he could build a powerful new political force and win reelection as the candidate of either the Democrats or a third party. He filled his Cabinet with states rights doctrinaires and conservative Democrats, and, out of political innocence, turned the federal patronage over to as mercenary a band as has ever assembled in the history of American politics. Blinded by the sycophantic schemers who swarmed like flies around the federal honey pot he opened to them, and by a naive conviction that the public must recognize and reward the rectitude of his policies, poor Tyler never realized how futile his effort was and how ridiculous he seemed. Actually his appointees were smearing the federal honey about to catch flies not for Tyler but for Calhoun, Cass, or some other anti-Van Buren Democrat. One Indiana Democrat, after buzzing around the honey at Washington, warned his brother back home against coming out for Van Buren — and in his very next letter announced exultantly that he had received an Indian removal contract from which "I will make at least *ten thousand dollars.*"

The 1844 presidential nomination had been widely regarded as the prize that would go to the victor in the bitter struggle between Clay and Tyler at the special session of 1841. Clay's strategy proved overwhelmingly successful in establishing him as the foreordained candidate. Tyler's first veto evoked from Whig newspapers a chorus of demands that Clay be the party's standard bearer; the chorus swelled with the second veto; and by the time the special session adjourned public meetings all over the country were calling for Clay's nomination.

The Clay forces hoped at first to avoid a national convention and to run their man simply as the candidate selected by general acclamation. But enough dissatisfaction with the Kentucky statesman remained, particularly among antislavery Whigs, to generate movements for General Winfield Scott,

Supreme Court Justice John McLean, and Daniel Webster. While none of these movements got much support, they did persuade the Whig congressional caucus to call a national nominating convention to meet at Baltimore on May 1, 1844.

Already, by the middle of 1843, Clay had been nominated by Whig state conventions in Maine, Vermont, Massachusetts, New York, New Jersey, Pennsylvania, Delaware, Maryland, Virginia, North Carolina, Georgia, Mississippi, and Kentucky; and by early 1844, the additional states of Indiana, Illinois, Alabama, and Arkansas jumped on the bandwagon. Bowing to the inevitable, Webster declined a nomination from New Hampshire; and in February, 1844, he and Scott attended a dinner with leading Whig senators at which all agreed on the nomination of Clay.

Meanwhile, Clay had retired in early 1842 from the Senate to his estate, Ashland, at Lexington, Kentucky, where his supporters hoped he might be restrained from writing public letters, traveling, and making speeches. Two weeks after he got home he received a visit from none other than Martin Van Buren, then on an extended tour of the South and West. Both prospective candidates wanted the coming campaign to be waged on the traditional party issues, avoiding above all any sectionally divisive, slavery-tinctured questions like the annexation of Texas. Then, or upon some other occasion, Clay came to understand that Van Buren opposed annexation, and it may be wondered whether they did not at this time reach a tacit understanding that they would both take this position.

Since the 1820's, Van Buren had labored to mute sectional conflict, while seeking to build the Democratic party on the old Jeffersonian specifications as a union of southern planters and northern "plain republicans." Though his nomination seemed assured when Congress assembled for its winter session of 1843–44, the mounting distrust between northern and southern Democrats threatened to get out of hand and ruin his chances for election. The session saw rancorous intra-party disputes over tariff reform and the gag rule denying debate on anti-slavery petitions; and by early 1844, a growing anti-Van Buren sentiment was coalescing around the revived candidacy of Lewis Cass.

But Van Buren's friends were slow to recognize the real danger, which stemmed from the Tyler Administration. Repudiated by both parties and anxious for an issue that would redeem his Administration in the eyes of history while giving him some hope of reelection, Tyler had hit upon the idea of forcing the Texas question forward. At the previous session his supporters had enlisted the help of Mississippi Senator Robert J. Walker and several other Democratic enthusiasts for Texas in secretly preparing the ground. The Democratic members of the Texas coterie had been anxious to make annexation a Democratic measure; but Van Buren was sensitive to northern anti-Texas opinion and would probably try to evade the issue. This he could easily do if he succeeded in his plan to have the Democratic nominating convention meet in November, 1843, before the Texas issue could be broached at the 1843–44 session of Congress. The Calhounites, for reasons of their own, were anxious to postpone the convention until May, 1844, and the Texas men, joined them in urging a later convention. Van Buren was sure to be nominated anyhow, Senator Walker told Silas Wright in late February, 1843, and by insisting on an early convention the New Yorkers would only create bitterness that might hurt the ticket in the election. What Walker did not say was that Texas was meanwhile to be made an issue, that the latent pro-Texas sentiment in the party was to be whipped up, and that Van Buren was thus to be forced to declare for Texas in order to assure his nomination. Suspecting none of this — the movement for Texas was still secret and Walker was actually, as he professed to be, a supporter of Van Buren and not Calhoun or Tyler — Wright agreed to the fateful arrangement postponing the convention.

When Congress reassembled in December, 1843, the insiders were told that Tyler's Secretary of State, the Virginia Calhounite Abel P. Upshur, had secretly worked out the terms of an annexation treaty that would be signed as soon as a specially authorized Texan representative reached Washington. Upshur clearly viewed the matter as bearing on the presidential election. He sent word to Calhoun that so many southern Democrats were unreliable on the tariff "as to preclude the hope, that a rally can be made against Mr. V. B. on the antitariff protective principle alone." "Some more exciting topic" must be connected with it, said Upshur, and Texas "is the only matter, that will take sufficient hold of the feelings of the South to rally it on a southern candidate and weaken Clay & Van Buren so much there as to bring the election into the House." Tyler hoped to be the southern and pro-Texas candidate himself, Calhoun was told, but the President's chief secretary "considers you as the only one that can be taken up."

While the Administration was awaiting the arrival of the Texas envoy, fate took a hand. Secretary Upshur was killed in the explosion of a gun aboard a new naval vessel, and President Tyler was persuaded to appoint Calhoun his successor. Calhoun reached Washington to take up his duties on March 29, only a few days after the Texan envoy. The treaty was signed within two weeks and announced on April 12.

At this point the Administration learned that the Van Burenite Washington *Globe* was about to endorse annexation. Instead of sending the treaty promptly to the Senate, therefore, Calhoun held it up while he tried to drive a wedge between Van Buren and Texas. Digging out of the State Department files a long unanswered letter from the British minister Richard Pakenham, Calhoun spent a week drafting an elaborate reply.

Pakenham had acknowledged British interest in the abolition of slavery in Texas, but denied that this interest implied any thought of disturbing the institution in the United States. Calhoun's reply defended slavery as a positive good, citing elaborate statistics to prove that slaves were better off than free Negroes or even the white workers of Great Britain, and declaring almost without qualification that the United States had negotiated the treaty of annexation in order to protect American slavery against the threat of British interference through Texas. His reply completed, Calhoun bundled it up with the treaty and other supporting documents and tossed this "Texas bombshell," as Benton appropriately called it, into the Senate.

With the annexation treaty now officially labeled as a proslavery measure, it was instantly apparent that few northern men could support it. On April 27, while rumors from the angry debate in executive session of the Senate were floating through Washington, the morning *National Intelligencer* appeared with a letter from Henry Clay announcing his objections to immediate annexation. The evening *Globe* carried a letter from Martin Van Buren to the same effect.

Clay wrote from Raleigh, North Carolina, near the end of a tour that had taken him through most of the southern states. He had found, he told friends, little excitement on the subject of Texas, and little disposition among southern Whigs to differ with their northern allies on any other subject. In his public letter he declared unequivocally that annexation would mean war with Mexico, and he objected further to taking a step that would be strongly opposed by a substantial part of the United States.

Four days after the publication of Clay's letter the Whig convention met at Baltimore and nominated him by acclamation, choosing as his running mate Theodore Frelinghuysen of New Jersey. There was not a whisper of dissent about Texas, either in the convention or in the ebullient "ratifying convention" of Whig young men that followed the next day. To all appearances, the Whig party was going into the campaign enthusiastically united behind its magnetic chieftain.

Van Buren, on the other hand, had been under heavy pressure to endorse annexation, as he pondered the problem at his quiet retreat on the Hudson. Democratic opinion in the South and West was strongly pro-Texas; such sterling northern Democrats as George Bancroft called for annexation; and Old Hickory was sending out a stream of increasingly peremptory letters on the subject. But Van Buren had to consider the growing strength of the antislavery opposition to Texas in New York and other northeastern states. He also worried about both the morality and the danger of war in taking Texas when a weaker neighbor, Mexico, still claimed the territory. Most disturbing of all to Van Buren was the fear that annexation would inflame those dangerous passions of sectional enmity that he had labored throughout his long career to moderate and suppress.

In the end, the "Red Fox of Kinderhook," the very prototype of the scheming politician, made a conscientious decision that he knew would imperil and perhaps destroy his chances for the Presidency. Though support for annexation would have given him a political advantage over Clay, he said privately, "that was a consideration which I was not at liberty to embrace."

"We have a character among the nations of the earth to maintain," Van Buren told his fellow citizens, "and it has hitherto been our pride and our boast, that, whilst the lust of power, with fraud and violence in the train, has led other and differently constituted governments to aggression and conquest, our movements in these respects have always been regulated by reason and justice." Until Mexico acknowledged the Texans' independence, or until it became manifest that she could not subdue her rebellious province, annexation would be aggression against Mexico. Moreover, annexation was too important a step to take so suddenly and secretly, before the American people had had a chance to consider it. To be sure, Van Buren characteristically cloaked his sentiments in elaborate and ambiguous verbiage; and he promised that if the next Congress declared for annexation, he would carry out its wishes, whether Mexico consented or not. But one thing was unmistakably clear; the virtually designated candidate of the Democratic party was opposed to the Tyler-Calhoun treaty and to immediate annexation.

Coming on the heels of a severe Democratic defeat in the Virginia elections, Van Buren's letter "struck the democratic members of congress with panic." Excited discussions distracted church services on the Sunday morning the letter appeared and in Congress the next day "put an end to all business." The Calhounites, the Texas men, and all those who had harbored doubts about Van Buren as a candidate scurried about fomenting discontent, and even the loyal Van Burenites were "so perfectly frightened that they do as much harm as the indisposed." Calhoun himself, "in an extacy of delight," spent most of the day at the Capitol. "I can beat Clay and Van Buren put together upon this issue," he was reported as saying.

The next day anti-Van Buren circulars were passed around among congressmen for signatures, and the Texas men began writing back to their home states soliciting expressions of opinion in favor of annexation and against Van Buren. "Now we want Texas meetings in every town village & Hamlet in the South," wrote Alabama's mountainous Calhounite Senator Dixon H. Lewis. "I say hold meetings & agitate, agitate, agitate from the Potomac to the Sabine & make the question paramount to Presidents & every thing else."

Meanwhile Van Buren's letter was producing a similar uproar among local Democratic politicians throughout the country. Van Buren's earliest and most steadfast supporter in Tennessee told him, "The Breeders of Mules and horses and hogs cry out let us have Texas right or wrong. . . . 'If the British interfere we will give them New Orleans again. If those Mexicans come nigh we will eat them up.'"

Nowhere was the blow more staggering than in Virginia, where Van Buren's letter arrived at the very moment the Democrats were learning that his unpopularity had defeated them in the state election. Thomas Ritchie had just spent the morning trying to rally his demoralized associates back to the Van Buren standard when the mail brought his copy of the *Globe* containing Van Buren's views on Texas. "God knows what we are to do," he exclaimed. "But one month, one short month, to the Baltimore convention!"

For twenty years now Ritchie's Richmond Junto had cooperated with Van Buren's Albany Regency to maintain the New York-Virginia axis. Sanctified by Jeffersonian usage, this historic alignment had been the bulwark of neo-Jeffersonian politics. But sacred as it had become, Ritchie quickly discovered that in Virginia it could not withstand "this new and mighty question of Texian annexation." Letters poured in from the counties asserting that "the people seem literally to have taken fire on this subject of Texas, & nothing short of *immediate annexation* will serve them." Quickly the powerful Calhoun faction, only barely restrained in the recent state convention, pressed forward with demands that a new state convention be called to endorse Calhoun.

With genuine pain, Ritchie and his friends concluded that their old companion-at-arms would have to be abandoned. He must withdraw, they told Van Buren, to save the party from dissolution and to save the nation from Henry Clay, "the most profligate politician perhaps in our country." While the Virginians at Washington urged that Silas Wright replace Van Buren on the ticket, Ritchie struggled in heated party caucuses at Richmond to stave off the Calhounites. Finally a compromise was reached: the Calhounites would not demand an endorsement of their leader, but Ritchie must take the initiative in releasing the Virginia delegates to Baltimore from the state convention's endorsement of Van Buren and in urging them to support a candidate who favored annexation.

Van Buren was bitterly disappointed at Virginia's desertion, and a mood of self-sacrificing rectitude in an atmosphere of imminent peril quickly swept Van Buren's friends beyond the cool calculation that is normal to successful politicians. Filled with "smothered feelings that had no parallel in bitterness and indignation," they redoubled their efforts to save their leader from "the rotten portion of the party," and to eradicate "the noxious plants of expediency, speculation and availability" that had "taken such deep root in the ranks of the democracy."

The Van Burenites were especially bitter because, as they saw it, they had run political risks in the North for years in order to make concessions to the South on abolitionism, the tariff, and other questions, only to be deserted when they asked their southern allies to make a slight concession — to delay annexation — in deference to the opinions of northern voters. Wright grimly ran up the motto, "defeat rather than disgrace," and the whole Van Buren faction rallied to it.

By the eve of the convention it appeared that Van Buren was likely to have a clear majority, but the anti-Van Buren forces were insisting that the convention follow the precedent of previous Democratic conventions by requiring a two-thirds majority for nomination. Two-thirds Van Buren could not get, and some of the delegates instructed for Van Buren might be induced to vote for the two-thirds rule. If the rule were adopted, there seemed little chance that anyone else could get two-thirds either. The New York delegation, meeting in New York City, angrily resolved to insist to the bitter end on nomination by a simple majority; while Silas Wright was heatedly stiffening Van Burenite backs against any impulse to withdraw their candidate or to compromise in any way with "the rotton portion of the party." By sticking to Van Buren, his friends could prevent a two-thirds majority for any other candidate, and the convention would either have to acquiesce finally in nomination by simple majority or break up in confusion.

To break up the convention was precisely what some of the anti-Van Burenites wanted to do. Calhoun, hopeless now of his own nomination, seems to have preferred Tyler as the Texas candidate, and a Tyler convention had been called to meet simultaneously with the Democratic convention. If the two-thirds rule were rejected, and certainly if Van Buren were nominated, the Calhounites and some others as well would bolt the Democrats and join in nominating Tyler as a third candidate.

Walker was encouraging several of the anti-Van Buren aspirants for the nomination. Cass was the strongest by far, but Levi Woodbury hoped the lightning might strike in his direction, and Buchanan toyed with the idea of getting back into the race until he found the Pennsylvania delegation too deeply split to give him the united support of his own state. And Old Dick Johnson had come to Washington and was "going it" for either the presidential or vice-presidential nomination, "like a man electioneering for a clerkship before our Assembly." All of these presidential hopefuls had hastened to announce that they favored the immediate annexation of Texas.

This multiplicity of candidates seems to have increased rather than diminished the zeal of the Texas men. Directed by a "preparatory committee" in which Walker and the North Carolina Calhounite Romulus Saunders were prominent, Van Buren's foes labored night and day to insure his defeat by committing delegates to the two-thirds rule. If it were adopted, they told the Michigan delegation (instructed for Van Buren), Michigan's Cass would be the nominee. The New Hampshire men were similarly promised backing for Woodbury; the disunited Pennsylvanians had their various partialities played upon; and "the Tennesseeans were shown, in the same way, that Polk would be nominated for President," if they would only support the two-thirds rule. These blandishments were reinforced by threats, the Texas men loudly proclaiming that they would bolt the convention and join the Tylerites if their rule was not adopted. If Tennessee did not support the two-thirds rule, James K. Polk's friends were told, the Texas men would oppose Polk even for Vice-President.

The Pennsylvania and Tennessee delegations were under heavier pressure than any others. The Pennsylvanians had been instructed for Van Buren and included a strong contingent of staunch Van Burenites, mainly from the city and county of Philadelphia; but there were so many anti-Van Buren factions in the Keystone State that the ultimate course of the big delegation was highly uncertain.

Unlike the other aspirants, Buchanan was seeking to demonstrate a conspicuous loyalty to Van Buren, hoping that if Van Buren were to be defeated, the embittered Van Burenites might then turn to him in order to punish the overtly anti-Van Buren candidates. Until the very end, Buchanan insisted publicly that he would not allow himself to be considered for the nomination as long as Van Buren was in the running; but he refused to use his influence against the two-thirds rule, "his answer being that he has already made personal sacrifice enough in favor of V. B.—having a hope no doubt, that in the event of a failure to get Mr. V.B., he may be taken up." On Friday, May 24, a caucus of the anti-Van Buren leaders at Calhoun's house in Washington agreed to encourage Buchanan's presidential hopes if his friends would support the two-thirds rule. With this encouragement, Buchanan's friends threw themselves wholeheartedly into the anti-Van Buren operations; and one of them, Hendrick B. Wright, proved so adept at this undercover work that Walker's "preparatory committee" adopted him as its candidate for the highly strategic post of temporary chairman of the convention. Thus on the eve of the convention it seemed that "the destinies of the Union and of the democratic party hang on Pennsylvania"; while, as far as anyone could tell, Pennsylvania seemed to be hanging in the balance.

The Van Buren managers were slow to realize that Tennessee was an even more serious problem than Pennsylvania. Tennessee's favorite son, the twice-defeated former governor, James K. Polk, aspired to the vice-presidential nomination as a loyal Van Buren man, and the Tennesseeans were therefore counted as safe for the New Yorker. But Polk's reliable friends on the delegation, led by Gideon J. Pillow and Congressman Cave Johnson, were narrowly outnumbered by men hostile to Polk and Van Buren.

In addition Polk had written to Pillow and Johnson about a startling conversation he had had with Jackson after the delegation left for Baltimore. Old Hickory had suggested the possibility of a deadlocked convention, in which case who would be a more logical choice for the presidential nomination than the loyal Van Burenite and declared annexationist James K. Polk? Polk had cautiously granted his lieutenants permission to act upon this suggestion in the event Van Buren's nomination proved impossible, but meanwhile they must demonstrate unswerving loyalty to the New Yorker.

On Monday morning, May 27, an immense crowd collected before the Odd Fellows' Hall on Baltimore's Gay Street, while Democratic orators tuned up with the sidewalk harangues that were to continue all day. Toward noon the delegates began pushing through the noisy throng into the Egyptian Saloon, the largest hall in Baltimore. On the stroke of noon—or twenty minutes before, as some embittered Van Burenites claimed—the anti-Van Buren men carried off an audacious coup that gave them a substantial starting advantage. Marching to the platform, the loud-voiced, overbearing Romulus M. Saunders of North Carolina called the convention to order. Before the milling delegates knew what was happening, Saunders had nominated Hendrick B. Wright of Pennsylvania as President of the convention, had put the question to a vote, and had declared Wright unanimously elected.

The Van Buren men had planned to nominate Governor Henry Hubbard of New Hampshire as presiding officer. But while Walker's preparatory committee had been busily planning its coup on Sunday, Chairman Benjamin F. Butler of the New York delegation, a dignified elder in the Presbyterian church, had been piously observing the Lord's Day at a friend's house far from the profane business of caucuses; and the New Yorkers had come to the hall Monday completely unprepared to play Walker's kind of game. Throughout the struggle they were to suffer for lack of tactical planning and aggressive leadership.

Saunders had no sooner gotten Hendrick Wright elected than he moved adoption of the rules used by the Democratic conventions of 1832 and 1836, which included the rule requiring a two-thirds majority for nomination. Except for Cave Johnson's vigilance, this matter, too, decisive of the result, would have been railroaded through before a majority of the delegates were in their seats. Johnson demanded that a roster of official delegates be established before any further action was taken. Chairman Wright tried to gavel him down and proceed to Saunders' motion, but Walker wisely intervened, a credentials committee was appointed, and the convention adjourned until 4 p.m. to allow the committee time to prepare a roster of accredited delegates.

Following this respite the convention plunged directly into the showdown battle over the two-thirds rule. The New Yorkers, now better prepared, proposed a committee to report on the question, and Walker was disposed to agree. But the raucous Saunders, riding high with a majority at his back and a presiding officer under his thumb, forced an immediate debate that went on into the night. Amid cheers and hisses, Walker eloquently laid out the arguments for the rule, and Butler in reply "became white with excitement and actually . . . jumped up three or four times from the floor two or three feet high." Finally the exhausted delegates adjourned, and the struggle was continued in the streets, hotels, and barrooms. "I never saw such excitement in my life," exclaimed a spectator from South Carolina, "immense crowds every night & addresses in the streets &c. — of the most vulgar demagogism."

Tuesday morning, after further lengthy debate, Chairman Wright used his position as presiding officer to defeat a Van Burenite proposal that the states vote as units on the two-thirds resolution, thus enabling the anti-Van Buren forces to get the full benefit of their minority votes in split delegations where the Van Burenites had a majority. As a result, the two-thirds rule was passed by a vote of 148 to 116, whereas, with the states voting as units, it would have barely skimmed through, 120 to 119.

The outcome was a striking indication of the effectiveness of the anti-Van Buren agitation. Though sixteen of the twenty-six states had through conventions or otherwise declared a preference for Van Buren, only the delegations of Maine, New Hampshire, Ohio, and Missouri voted unanimously with New York against the two-thirds rule. Tennessee was among the thirteen states unanimously for the rule; while Pennsylvania, whose delegates were instructed to "vote for, and use all their influence to effect the nomination" of Van Buren, twelve voted for the rule making Van Buren's nomination impossible and thirteen voted against it. "The very atmosphere," exclaimed a New Yorker, "is burthened with the putrid odor of the corruption so rotten & rife in men's hearts." It is possible to understand this feeling, while at the same time recognizing that a real change in public sentiment in many states had rendered the instructions for Van Buren out of date.

After a recess for lunch, the presidential voting commenced at 3:30 in the afternoon. With a total of 266 votes, 134 constituted a majority, but 177 were needed to nominate under the two-thirds rule. With the twenty-six Pennsylvanians all honoring their instructions on the first ballot, Van Buren received 146 votes; Cass, with the solid support of Delaware, Virginia, Mississippi, and Tennessee, was second with 83; Old Dick garnered Kentucky and Arkansas, along with enough scattered votes elsewhere to total 24; and there were other scattered votes for Buchanan, Woodbury, Calhoun and Stewart.

Six more ballots were taken Tuesday afternoon and evening without reaching a decision. Throughout the voting a consistent pattern was maintained. Four states, Maine, New York, Ohio, and Missouri regularly gave all but 1 or 2 of their 75 votes to Van Buren. Ten other states, including Tennessee, just as regularly gave all but 1 or 2 of their 89 votes to Cass. Kentucky and Arkansas monotonously cast all their 15 votes for Old Dick Johnson. And nine states with 87 votes were badly split, shifting their anti-Van Buren votes from candidate to candidate in search of a winning trend.

Yet within this constant pattern there was a gradual but decisive tendency for Van Buren's vote to erode and Cass's to grow. Van Buren displayed his maximum strength of 146 on the first ballot, when many delegates felt obliged to honor their instructions by giving him at least their initial votes. His sharpest drop, down to 127, came on the second ballot, when he was deserted by most of his lukewarm or insincere supporters. This drop drew off virtually the entire delegations of Vermont and Connecticut; but the further fall to 121 on the third ballot resulted from small losses in different delegations. Not until the fourth ballot did the Pennsylvania delegation break open, and this accounted for most of the drop down to 111. Thereafter it was a matter of losing 1 or 2 votes in each of four or five states, as the Van Buren total fell to 103 on the fifth ballot and 101 on the sixth. The seventh ballot saw a further defection of 5 votes in Pennsylvania, bringing Van Buren down to 99.

Meanwhile Old Dick had made his bid on the second and third ballots, but could go no higher than 38; and the Buchanan rally followed on the second through the fifth ballots, peaking at 26 votes. As Johnson and Buchanan demonstrated their inability to attract major support, Cass began to surge ahead, building on the solid base of ten states amassed by the frantic activities of the previous weeks. From 83 on the first ballot, he climbed to 94 on the second; faltered back to 92 under the combined Johnson-Buchanan assault on the third; and from the fourth ballot on, moved steadily ahead. On the fifth ballot Cass overtook the declining Van Buren, 107 to 103, and by the seventh he had 123 votes to Van Buren's 99, with Buchanan holding on to 22 and Johnson to 21, and with a single delegate voting obstinately for Calhoun.

The crisis had come. The frightened Van Buren leaders realized that Pennsylvania was breaking wide open, that the less resolute Van Burenites in all delegations were faltering, and that the remaining Buchanan and Johnson supporters must soon go over to "the *damned rotten corrupt venal* Cass cliques." Unless the Cass bandwagon could be slowed, Cass would surely reach two-thirds in two more ballots, and as a result "every Van Buren man, every *pure* man in public life from Maine to Florida, as well as the true principles of democracy, would be politically *killed* and crushed." Their desperate cries for adjournment shouted down, the Ohio Van Burenites now "*stripped* for the fight, *determined at least*, that if Van Buren could not be saved, that the Jackson and Van Buren *policy* and its gallant body of supporters, should not be offered up on the altar of venality, corruption, and proscription."

In order to force adjournment, the Ohio men deliberately provoked "a *real western fight*—rough and tumble." It began with a motion by a strong-voiced Ohioan that Van Buren, having received a majority of the votes on the first ballot, should be declared the nominee. When this motion was ruled out of order, other Ohioans jumped into the mêlée, demanding an appeal from the decision of the chair. With several Ohio men shouting at once and with "defiances passing between the Ohio men and the Opposition," the uproar became "wholly ungovernable by the chair." The tension was broken momentarily by a stentorian voice moving to declare Andrew Jackson unanimously nominated, and Benjamin Butler nervously sought to quiet his boisterous western allies. But the Ohio men would not be quieted. Standing on chairs, one after another of them kept up fierce declamations amid "great anger and excitement" until at last the agitated and exhausted delegates acquiesced in a motion to adjourn for the night.

Despite the respite secured by adjournment, many of the Van Buren men gave way to despair. The seventh ballot had made it unmistakably clear that Van Buren could not be nominated. Sam Medary was having trouble keeping the Ohio men from deserting the convention in disgust, and most of the Van Burenites were too filled with "a deep and bitter wrath and sorrow" to think constructively about any alternative strategy for stopping the Cass bandwagon when the balloting resumed the next morning. Yet three men were hard at work, Gideon J. Pillow, George Bancroft, and Benjamin F. Butler, and on their midnight exertions was to turn the morrow's astonishing result.

All day long, Pillow had been quietly preparing for just such a crisis, talking with delegates about Polk as a vice-presidential candidate while ever so delicately suggesting his peculiar availability as the candidate of a united Democracy for the first office. Amid the "extraordinary excitement" created by the Ohio men at the end of the seventh ballot, some of the seeds he had planted began to bear fruit. A Massachusetts delegate and a Pennsylvania delegate approached Pillow separately, suggesting that Polk be proposed for the presidential nomination. Shrewdly, Pillow still declined to take the initiative, saying "that if it was the will of the Convention the name should be brought out by the North." "I do not think it prudent to move in *that* matter now," Pillow scribbled to Polk just before the tumultuous adjournment. "I want the North to bring you forward as a Compromise of all interests."

The Massachusetts delegate was George Bancroft, author of the celebrated *History of the United States*. Back in 1839, Bancroft had supplied his protégé J. George Harris to edit Polk's Nashville *Union*. The Bancroft-Morton group in the Massachusetts Democracy had been among Polk's strongest supporters for the vice-presidential nomination in 1840, and through Harris they had continued to follow his career with increasing respect. Bancroft and Morton had come to Baltimore intending to give Polk their support again for the vice-presidential nomination. Just before the convention they had discussed with Cave Johnson the possibility of substituting Silas Wright for Van Buren. This discussion had come to naught, but in the crisis following the seventh ballot, it apparently occurred to the Massachusetts men to try the same plan with Polk instead of Wright. "It flashed on my mind," Bancroft later told Polk, "that it would be alone safe to rally on you." Excitedly, Bancroft consulted Morton and several of the Van Burenites from New Hampshire, and it was after they approved the idea that he broached it to Pillow. Pillow thought that if New England would take the lead, Tennessee, Alabama, and Mississippi would follow. Now thoroughly aroused, Bancroft, Pillow, and Donelson hastened from the convention hall and spent the evening buttonholing delegates.

Bancroft took as his assignment the core of Van Burenism, the New York and Ohio delegations, and by midnight he had made such headway that he went to bed "tranquil and happy." Pillow concentrated mainly on the southern and southwestern delegations. He got little help from his fellow Tennesseeans but Pillow had enough confidence and energy to make up for them all. "I was fully convinced it would *work out right*," he said, "and I worked on until nearly day." The Mississippians he found hesitant, but Alabama and Louisiana seemed favorably disposed, and he doubtless made impressions elsewhere that helped insure the eventual result.

Meanwhile, Benjamin F. Butler had finally been galvanized into action by the crisis. With Van Buren's letter withdrawing in favor of Silas Wright in his pocket, he scurried about determining that all the Van Buren supporters were willing to follow New York's lead in shifting to Wright. In the process Butler, Bancroft, and Pillow crossed each others' trails, and the Polk and Wright projects must have become intertwined. At the same time, Bancroft was becoming confident that New York and Ohio were willing to support Polk, Butler was becoming "reasonably satisfied, that Tennessee might be induced to concur in" the movement for Wright; and in that event Butler "did not believe Virginia would *dare* to persist in supporting Lewis Cass, in preference to Silas Wright."

It seems reasonably certain that actually Butler, Bancroft, and Pillow joined forces in a joint movement for a "new man"; but whether the ticket would be Wright-Polk or Polk-Wright depended on Wright's willingness to accept first place. Butler knew that Wright had given Judge John Fine a letter absolutely declining to be considered; but nevertheless Butler decided to convene the New York delegation at eight the next morning and get their support for his plan to override Wright's objections. The rest of the sleepless night the pious Butler spent "in such meditations as the Occasion inspired, & seeking guidance & aid from a higher power."

But whatever aid his prayers elicited proved insufficient when the delegation met early Wednesday morning. Judge Fine was adamant against Butler's proposal and announced that if a single vote were cast for Wright, he would read to the convention Wright's entire letter, including the section declaring that Wright's views on Texas were identical with Van Buren's. There is no question but that Fine was faithfully representing Wright's wishes, and never before or since has an American politician so clearly thrown away a presidential nomination that was so certainly in his grasp. Butler pleaded with Fine until within five minutes of the time the convention met; but Fine would not give an inch, and the delegation unanimously decided that Wright's name could not be presented.

Meanwhile the rest of the Van Buren contingent was anxiously waiting in the convention hall to learn the outcome of New York's deliberations. Butler reluctantly informed them that Wright could not be run and urged them to adhere to Van Buren. Most of them agreed, but some, Butler told Van Buren, "did not consent, and then *to* them, *only* them, the name of Governor Polk was spoken of as a better one than any person then before the Convention." Polk, said Butler, "had not been a party to the conspiracies & plots by which we had been destroyed, and his nomination, it was most obvious would not only give us a *sound* democrat by whom we could make the *old* issues of *Bank* or no *Bank* &c. &c but flounders with a single blow, the whole posse by whom, or *for* whom, the plot had been set on foot — Tyler, Calhoun, Woodbury, Buchanan, Johnson, Stewart, & above all as most likely otherwise to get the benefit of them *Lewis Cass*."

By the time the voting started it was generally known among the Van Burenites around the hall that "the general idea appears to be to rally on Polk." The states were called in geographical order, beginning with New England. The eighth ballot began with Maine adhering to Van Buren, but previously divided New Hampshire, the second state called, gave all of its 6 votes for James K. Polk of Tennessee. "You should have heard the cheers," Bancroft told Polk, and they were repeated a state or two later when he cast the Van Burenite majority of the Massachusetts vote for Polk. Through the rest of the ballot, most of the Van Buren and Cass delegates stood by their favorites and the Johnson and Buchanan votes evaporated, while Tennessee, Alabama, Louisiana, and a few delegates from Pennsylvania and Maryland joined the New Hampshire and Massachusetts men for Polk. At the end of the ballot Polk had only 44 votes, compared to 104 for Van Buren and 114 for Cass, but these were enough to demonstrate that he was the only man on whom the convention could unite.

The ninth ballot began in a pandemonium of angry recriminations and ended in a delirium of joy and brotherly love. Desperate supporters of Buchanan and Johnson were calling out that their candidates were still available, the Pennsylvanians were accusing each other of treason to Buchanan on the one hand or Van Buren on the other, and the tension neared the breaking point during a passionate excoriation of Tyler's "mongrel administration" and its plot against Van Buren by the venerable Judge Samuel Spencer of New York. Meanwhile the excited convention had hissed down a request from the New York delegates to have the balloting held up while they withdrew for consultation; but after Spencer's philippic they withdrew anyhow, a Georgia Calhounite hurling a final angry insult at Spencer's retreating back.

A Pennsylvanian had gotten the floor to move that the balloting proceed and to deliver an effusive "man-who" eulogy of Polk, "the bosom friend of Old Hickory . . . the man who stood up in defence of the old hero during the panic session . . . the man who fought so bravely and so undauntingly the whigs of Tennessee—the pure, whole hog, Locofoco democrat, who goes against a bank of the United States, and all corrupting monopolies." The call of the states was ordered, but still the speeches went on, as filibustering Van Burenites sought to hold the floor until the New Yorkers could return. Before leaving the hall, Butler had advised some of his friends to go for Polk if this was the only way to hold their delegations together, and now from the downstairs room, where the New Yorkers were conferring, word came up that Van Buren would be withdrawn. The speeches took on a strong pro-Polk tone before finally dying away, and at last the voting began. The Maine Van Burenites led off for Polk, with New Hampshire and the Massachusetts Van Burenites chiming in. Virginia, seeing the handwriting on the wall, withdrew for consultation; and as the rollcall continued, other delegations, caucusing on the floor, asked to be passed.

For long minutes the proceedings bogged down in a hubbub of "much talk and agitation" until at last, not the New Yorkers, but the Virginians reappeared. Striding to the platform, their leader, William H. Roane, gave Polk Virginia's votes; and as the convention burst into a prolonged roar of frenzied cheering, he threatrically extended the "right hand of fellowship" to the New Hampshire Van Burenite Hubbard, who had cast the original votes for Polk.

Downstairs, Butler was having trouble persuading the embittered New Yorkers to go for Polk. Finally they agreed that Butler might withdraw Van Buren and announce his own vote for Polk, leaving the other delegates to vote as they wished. When the New Yorkers reentered the hall, Roane of Virginia still held the platform, and he turned to them, eulogizing Van Buren and speaking of the "bleeding heart of Virginia & himself in the course she had pursued." Butler immediately responded in kind with "deep & beautiful pathos," declaring that he "always knew that N.Y. & Va. would ultimately be found fighting side by side." Reluctantly, New York had concluded that Van Buren must be withdrawn, he announced. Each of her delegates would vote for himself, but his own vote was for Polk, who fully met the old Jeffersonian test; "honest, capable, faithful to the Constitution." Promptly the rest of New York's votes—except Spencer's, who held out until the end of the ballot—were cast for Polk. This was the signal for a mad rush to the Polk bandwagon, as other states cast or "corrected" their votes to produce a unanimous result.

The excitement reached its peak when a Maryland delegate, spying in the gallery Elmore and Pickens of South Carolina, the only unrepresented state, shouted that "nothing now was wanting but one absent sister to complete the harmony of the party." The South Carolinians rose and announced that, as far as was in their power, they could promise the support of their state for the nomination. "South Carolina *seconds* the nation," declared Elmore, and instantly, said a reporter, "every person in the room, I believe, rose from his seat: and such waving of handkerchiefs and cheering I never saw or heard before."

By now, the convention was in a "state of sublime enthusiasm." The heartbroken Butler "wept like a child" over Van Buren's defeat, and some Van Burenites were "weeping with one eye while we smile with the other at the overthrow of the intriguers and traitors." But most of the delegates were simply overwhelmed with ecstatic astonishment at their miraculous deliverance from the fatal deadlock which until the last few moments had seemed to doom their party to certain defeat and possible dismemberment. Forgetting the bitterness of recent days, they allowed themselves to be swept away on a tide of delirious celebration. As the unanimous vote for Polk was announced at 2 p.m., one man stopped cheering long enough to scribble the news to the party's new nominee for President. "The Convn. is shouting," he wrote. "The people in the Streets are Shouting. The news went to Washington and back by Telegraph whilst the votes were counting and the Congress is shouting. There is one general Shout throughout the whole land, and I cant write any more for Shouting. . . . I am yours shouting." And so, James Knox Polk, now forty-nine years old, became his party's nominee. Polk had a long career in politics — a Tennessee legislator (1823–25); congressman (1825–39); Speaker of the House of Representatives (1835–39); governor of Tennessee (1839–41). The ninth ballot now brought to him his party's highest honor.

Late Wednesday afternoon, the exhausted delegates, or some of them, reassembled to nominate a vice-presidential candidate. Without hesitation, Walker and Ritchie accepted Butler's suggestion that Wright's nomination would insure harmony and a big Democratic vote in New York. Walker made the nominating speech, and Wright was chosen almost unanimously, with only eight Georgians obstinately voting for Woodbury.

Unfortunately, Butler had underestimated the extent of Wright's bitterness. To accept would be to condone the "insult" the convention had offered New York by rejecting Van Buren, Wright complained; and the instant the newly installed telegraph line between Baltimore and Washington brought word of his nomination, he flashed back his refusal. But the New Yorkers at Baltimore had "lost their judgements in the excitement," as Wright put it; and despite four telegraphic declinations, Butler continued to assure the other delegates that Wright would be persuaded to accept. The nettled senator finally had to send two New York congressmen to Baltimore in a wagon — the trains did not run at night — carrying letters making his refusal positive and unmistakable. At the same time, he warned Butler against nominating "Woodbury, or any one else, who has been engaged, as he has, in the Conspiracy here." Instead the convention should take "a true, strong and good man, and one of the true States ought to furnish him," but not New York.

Thus when the convention met again at 7:30 Thursday morning, supposedly only to approve a report of the Resolutions Committee, it found that the vice-presidential job had to be done all over again. With the convention running overtime, attendance was so sparse that only one Ohioan was present to cast that state's 23 votes. The southern and Texas men were pushing hard for Woodbury or Cass, while the Van Burenites insisted on Senator John Fairfield of Maine; and the first ballot ended in a deadlock that reproduced the pattern of the presidential voting. But the technique for breaking such a deadlock had now been mastered, and on the second ballot Walker ingeniously proposed his kinsman George M. Dallas of Pennsylvania, who had kept his

pre-convention activities against Van Buren so quiet that he was still acceptable to both sides, and who might give the ticket additional strength in his large
and crucial state. The southern plus the Pennsylvania votes assured his nomination, and in the new spirit of harmony it was accordingly made unanimous.

Almost as an afterthought the convention ended its labors by endorsing
the "platform" which Walker had proposed to the Resolutions Committee the
night before and which had been accepted with certain revisions by Butler.
the committee chairman. For the most part the resolutions simply incorporated
the Democratic resolutions of 1840, reciting the party's historic addiction
to the principle of strict construction and its opposition to a national bank, to
an excessive tariff, to a federal system of internal improvements, to federal
assumption of state debts, and to federal interference with "the domestic institutions of the several States."

One new resolution was to have some momentous consequences: "That
our title to the whole of the Territory of Oregon is clear and unquestionable;
that no portion of the same ought to be ceded to England or any other power,
and that the reoccupation of Oregon and the reannexation of Texas, at the
earliest practicable period, are great American measures, which this convention recommends to the cordial support of the democracy of the Union." Two
things are notable about this resolution. One is that Butler apparently had little difficulty getting the party to take an official position on Texas far weaker
than that demanded during the "immediate annexation" hue and cry of a few
weeks before. The other is that the strong position on Oregon seems to have
been adopted almost accidentally, without any unusual demand, as a means of
camouflaging and subordinating the Texas provision. In fact, it is questionable
whether the whole set of resolutions got any very careful consideration from
the jaded members of the Resolutions Committee, much less from the sparse
rump session of delegates who gave it final approval.

The Democracy's miraculous deliverance from self-destruction at Baltimore had interrupted only briefly the mounting intraparty tension at Washington. With Congress moving toward adjournment in the days following the
convention, Tyler's Texas treaty was decisively rejected in the Senate by a
coalition of Whigs and northern Van Burenites. Everyone realized that the
issue was only postponed, and it was producing ever angrier exchanges between the Democratic factions. These developments had intensified the bitterness of the northern Van Burenites against the southern "traitors."

The South Carolinians were even more bitter than the Van Burenites,
and Cave Johnson had stumbled into the line of fire of the warring factions by
a project to promote his friend's presidential candidacy. At his urging, the
Democrats in Tennessee had begun preparations for a great national Democratic mass meeting and jubilee to be held at Nashville in July. This was no
sooner announced than Johnson learned that some of the Carolinians were
agitating for "a *Southern Convention*, a sort of rally upon Southern principles," also to be held at Nashville.

For several years now cotton prices had been at an all-time low, and
combustible South Carolina was again drifting into a revolutionary mood. The

British interest in abolishing slavery in Texas was making the Carolinians as hypersensitive over annexation as they had long been over the tariff; and the failure of the Texas treaty intensified their rage at the failure of Congress to reform the tariff. "If the Union is to break there could not be a better pretext" than the failure to annex Texas, declared Governor James H. Hammond to Calhoun in May.

Hammond's sentiments were presently being echoed at public meetings in various parts of South Carolina, particularly in Robert Barnwell Rhett's lowcountry district. "The safety, if not the very existence of the institution of slavery is dependent upon" annexation, proclaimed the speaker on one of these occasions. "THE ONLY TRUE ISSUE BEFORE THE SOUTH SHOULD BE TEXAS OR DISUNION." Most of these meetings adopted resolutions calling for a Nashville convention of the slave states to demand that the President call a special session of Congress, "when, the final issue shall be made up, and the alternative distinctly presented to the free states, either to admit Texas into the Union, or to proceed peaceably and calmly to arrange the terms of a dissolution of the Union."

News of these demonstrations reached Washington after the Tyler Administration was known to be considering a special congressional session on Texas for late in the presidential campaign, and after Cave Johnson had innocently broached his plan for a great Democratic meeting at Nashville. The alarmed Van Burenites at once suspected that all of these things were part of a single plot. The *Globe* warned against any effort "to identify Governor Polk and annexation with nullification"; and Benton devoted one of his jeremiads to "the South Carolina procession at Nashville."

By June 11, when Polk received the official announcement of his nomination, his table was piled high with letters making plain the party's perilous situation; and he had already decided on one step to alleviate it. Most party workers would be taking their cues from the established leaders, Buchanan, Wright, Cass, Van Buren, Benton, Calhoun, and Richard M. Johnson—men who could not help feeling that they had stronger claims on the Presidency than Polk. The outcome at Baltimore had already postponed for four years the presidential aspirations of these party chieftains; and Polk saw that if he were elected, he could claim renomination in 1848, further postponing and in many cases probably destroying their hopes of reaching the White House. Could all these powerful party leaders be expected to give hearty support to a candidacy that might prove fatal to their own future chances?

The Calhounites had been the first to raise this question. When they lost hope of nominating their own leader at Baltimore, they had resolved to ";go for no one but for *one* term, as we mean to run him [Calhoun] in 1848, if alive, in spite of Conventions." The convention's Resolutions Committee had smothered their efforts to secure a declaration in favor of the one-term principle, but the subject doubtless figured in the hectic negotiations by which Pillow and his associates swung the delegates to Polk. The moment the nomination was accomplished, Aaron Brown advised Polk that "you must some way or other express your self in favor of the one term system." It was "all important," said Brown, and "I need not say who & how many of our friends expect it." Along with Brown's letter came a number of others expressing the same wish.

At any rate, on the day after Polk received official notice of his nomination, he wrote a letter of acceptance declaring his "settled purpose," if elected, "of not being a candidate for re-election." The enthusiasm with which this statement was received—not only by the Calhounites, but by the supporters of Van Buren and the other potential presidential candidates—suggests that it may have been politically necessary.

The same day that Polk drafted his one-term pledge, he also wrote to Silas Wright in a more direct effort to reconcile the Van Burenites to his candidacy. Sensing the depth of Wright's bitterness, Polk made haste to assure him, saying "Certainly nothing was further from my thoughts, than that any state of circumstances could arise, by which the nomination would fall on me." Somewhat more accurately, he recited his long record of unbroken support for Van Buren, and protested that he was "never consulted by any human being in regard to the 2/3 rule or any other movement which led to" Van Buren's rejection. As for his letter endorsing annexation, he reminded Wright that he had written it before Van Buren's Texas letter appeared, believing that Van Buren's opinions "would accord with my own."

These assurances served to restrain the New Yorkers from any public expressions of doubt about the party's candidate. At a rally in New York City shortly afterward, Wright declared that he had known Polk since 1827 and that he could "cheerfully and proudly say to you, that when Mr. Van Buren's nomination ceased to be a question, no man's name had been used, no man's name could be used for that purpose more consonant to my feelings, than that of James K. Polk."

Yet privately the New Yorkers were not altogether reassured, and the agitation for a southern convention at Nashville revived their suspicions. "Our democracy will support faithfully the Baltimore ticket," wrote Wright to a confidant at the end of June, but only "if there be no more Southern bad faith, no sectional issues raised, to produce further suspicions." Yet, he continued, there was all too much evidence that Calhoun would deliberately try to raise such questions "unless he finds Gov. Polk willing to throw himself into his hands." "If Polk does that," Wright warned grimly, "or brings himself under just suspicion of having done it, he will be lost."

About the time Wright was expressing these ominous sentiments, Polk first learned of the agitation for a southern convention at Nashville. Perceiving at once its probable effect on the Van Burenites, he was determined that "the idea of a Southern convention or sectional meeting to be held at Nashville or elsewhere *must not for a moment be entertained*."

One other major problem faced Polk in the first weeks of the campaign. He had no sooner been nominated than the Democrats from pro-tariff areas discovered with consternation his strong anti-protectionist record. Within a few days the Whigs were labeling him a free-trader, and soon worried letters were pouring into Columbia from Democratic leaders in New York, New Jersey, Pennsylvania, and Louisiana.

The heaviest pressure came from the electorally powerful state of Pennsylvania, which the Democrats had narrowly lost in 1840 and without which they could not hope to succeed in 1844. Pennsylvania had long been a center of protectionist sentiment, and the depression of the late 1830's had intensified the zeal for high duties as a means of economic salvation. Most persuasive of all was a letter from Robert J. Walker, who strongly opposed protection. His political realism and connections in Philadelphia had made him a shrewd judge of what was necessary. The Democrats had to win Pennsylvania to succeed, he cautioned Polk, and the tariff was the one issue that could cause defeat. The Texas issue would be sufficient to carry the South, leaving Polk free to "go as far as your principles will permit for incidental protection." Anticipating troublesome scruples on Polk's part, Walker reminded him that he now belonged "not to *one* State, but to the *Union*."

During the first days of becoming accustomed to the idea of himself as a presidential candidate, Polk was inclined to think it his duty to answer interrogations on all the major issues "frankly and with proper independence." But as the flood of mail revealed the full complexity of the political situation, he grew more circumspect. He would declare his opinions "prudently," he promised his anxious advisers, "and in a manner which I trust will not injuriously affect our cause."

The tariff question was particularly difficult because people on both sides saw it not only as deeply affecting their material interests, but also as a matter of principle and equity. Everyone agreed that the tariff must be the basic source of federal revenue. Even the Calhounites had no objection to whatever "incidental" protection might be afforded by duties designed purely for revenue; but they were vehement against the slightest appearance of "discrimination," that is, adjusting the rates on different articles at different levels with an eye to protecting them against foreign competition. They insisted on a uniform percentage (or "ad valorem") rate for all imported articles, including articles not produced in the United States, such as tea and coffee.

Polk's record showed unmistakably that he had always fought for the lowest possible duties, and he had said some harsh things about the protective policy in general. Yet he had always stayed within the marvelous Jacksonian formula of a "judicious" tariff and had deliberately avoided—perhaps with an eye to the contingency that now arose—committing himself absolutely against any degree of protection.

Thus Polk was in a position to give the Pennsylvanians some reassurance, if necessary, and the only problem was to decide how necessary such reassurance was and how far he ought to go, as weighed against the necessity of preventing a rebellion against him on the tariff issue in the South. On June 19 he addressed his famous letter to John K. Kane, a Philadelphia Van Burenite who had been among the first to appeal to him on the subject.

The Kane letter was far more forthright than it would have been if Polk had followed the advice then on its way from Washington. Walker and company, in outlining what they thought he ought to say, carefully avoided the crucial issue of "discrimination," both the word and the idea, and further manifested their nervousness over words by urging Polk to use " 'aid' " as "a better word than 'protection.' " Polk, on the other hand, declared carefully but clearly, "In adjusting the details of a revenue tariff, I have heretofore sanctioned such moderate discriminating duties, as would produce the amount of revenue needed, and at the same time afford reasonable incidental protection to our home industry." He opposed, he said, "a tariff for protection *merely*, and not for revenue." Only toward the conclusion of his letter did Polk resort to the kind of resounding evasion Walker had been recommending. Adopting almost verbatim a passage from Walker's first letter on the subject, he declared that he thought it "the duty of the Government to extend as far as it may be practicable to do so by its revenue laws & all other means within its power, fair and just protection to all the great interests of the whole Union, embracing agriculture, manufactures, the mechanic arts, commerce, and navigation."

Historians, accepting too readily the Whig charges that Polk's Kane letter was evasive and insincere, have generally characterized it a masterly straddle. It was anything but. It clearly faced up to the real issues in dispute, endorsing both "protection" and "discrimination," and actually using both of these dangerous words several times. In fact the danger was that he had spoken less "prudently" than "frankly and with proper independence."

Polk was well aware that this declaration might decide the outcome of the election—as indeed it may have done—and in a covering letter he asked Kane to consult with Dallas and his old Philadelphia friend Henry Horn and to withhold the tariff letter from publication "unless it be deemed absolutely necessary." At the same time he reminded Kane that the Whigs would probably interrogate him on the subject; "and in that event," he said, "I *must* answer."

Polk was struggling with the conviction, growing out of his democratic ideology, that a candidate was obligated to declare his position whenever responsible voters demanded it. But he was also shrewdly aware—and this was where his political insight proved notably superior to Clay's—of the dangers of frequent public declarations. The tariff problem had forced him to rethink the whole matter; and the Kane letter was no sooner dispatched than he wrote to Dallas that he would issue no more public letters and make no public appearances whatever, believing that "it will comport best with propriety, and the dignity of my position to remain quietly at home." Further reflection convinced him that even the Kane letter had been a mistake, and on July 2 Pillow wrote for him to Kane and Horn asking that it be withheld if it had not yet been published.

But the Pennsylvanians, understandably delighted, had published the letter instantly, printing alongside it a recent tariff statement of Clay's taking a similar position and using almost the same language. Polk's declaration, rejoiced Buchanan, "removes all difficulties from his way in Pennsylvania"; and for the remainder of the campaign, the Pennsylvania Democrats exaggerated what Polk had said to argue that he was a better protectionist than Clay. All over the state, on flagpoles, across streets and highways, and at country road junctions, they mounted banners reading,

POLK, DALLAS, SHUNK

and the

DEMOCRATIC TARIFF OF 1842

And sometimes, "as if determined to show how far impudence and audacity could go," they added to the inscription,

WE DARE THE WHIGS TO REPEAL IT

Furious at this all too successful imposture, the Whigs demanded that he say whether he favored the Tariff of 1842, but he refused to answer. Meanwhile Polk's old antagonist Governor Lean Jimmy Jones of Tennessee was able to supply the Pennsylvania Whigs with an arsenal of Polk's past antitariff statements—for example, "I have at all times been *opposed to the protective policy.*" These were published by the National Clay Club of Philadelphia with an offer of one thousand dollars to any man who could prove that Polk had not made them. Jones himself publicly charged Polk with being "a free trade man, in the same sense in which Mr. Calhoun is." The efforts of the Pennsylvania Democrats to call Polk a friend of protection were, said Jones, "an outrage which, for impudence and falsehood, is unparalleled in the history of party warfare." He particularly denounced Polk's refusal to respond to demands for a specific statement about the Tariff of 1842. "Why does he not speak out like a man?" he challenged. "Why are his lips sealed as with the stillness of death?"

The Pennsylvania Democrats were satisfied that Polk had done all he could for them, but still Buchanan was worried enough to give up his cherished plan of staying home during the campaign. On a tour through northern Pennsylvania he tried countering the dangerous tariff issue by fulminating against the long dead national bank. This produced such a fine response that against the long dead National Bank. This produced such a fine response that anti-Bankism became the staple of Democratic oratory, and the Democrats ized the Whig advantage on the tariff question to make a Democratic victory possible.

In the South the Whigs were only lukewarm defenders of protectionism, while most Democrats interpreted Polk's Kane letter as leaving room for substantial reductions in the Tariff of 1842. Only in South Carolina did the issue cause trouble.

Calhoun himself was surprisingly well disposed toward Polk. The Baltimore nomination had suddenly presented to his vision once more the prospect that he might win the Presidency. Suddenly the national Democratic party did not seem so corrupt after all. As in 1828, Calhoun again pictured himself as the dominant figure in the Administration of an inexperienced Democratic President, and this time Polk's one-term pledge seemed to make his chances of advancing to the Presidency after four years even better than they had seemed to him during the first Jackson campaign.

But Calhoun's state and many of his lieutenants had learned too well his politics of intransigence to recognize at once the cogency of the new party line. South Carolina was seething with disunionism over the inaction of the Democratic Congress on tariff reform and Texas; and as Congress approached adjournment Rhett had the state's delegation at work on a call for immediate state action.

Calhoun had to assemble the delegation and exercise all his persuasive powers to stop Rhett's project. But Rhett was not persuaded for a minute by Calhoun's arguments and was soon agitating on his own for the program of state action which Calhoun had dissuaded the other congressmen from endorsing. In a printed address to his constituents and later in a series of fiery speeches through his lowcountry district he demanded that the upcoming legislature call a state convention to meet shortly after the new President was inaugurated and to nullify the tariff if the incoming Administration had not committed itself to thoroughgoing reform. Polk's Kane letter added fuel to the fire lit by Rhett, and soon Congressmen Holmes and Burt, Governor Hammond, and Senator McDuffie were joining the clamor for radical action, McDuffie declaring that he would raise the "banner of Disunion if only three men follow him." The Charleston *Mercury*, long Calhoun's semiofficial mouthpiece, broke from the traces to announce that Polk had deserted South Carolina by "going over to the protectionists after she had hailed his nomination as that of a free trade man," and declared that "passive submission to tyranny is too costly a price to be paid for a worthless and barren share in his election triumph."

Rhett's agitation was a serious threat to Calhoun's strategy and to his hopes for a prominent role in a Polk Administration, and he promptly moved "with great delicacy, but at the same time firmness" to stamp out the disaffection. The reliable Elmore promptly took charge and organized a meeting of the leading men in Charleston, which adopted resolutions expressing confidence in the national Democratic party and in Polk — "a southern man — a friend of free trade and identified with us and our institutions, and an enemy of the protective policy and abolition" — and denouncing "any action of our State, to embarrass or lessen the chances of his election . . . whereby we shall draw on ourselves the blame of our friends in other States . . . thus increasing the numbers and spirit of our enemies and adding to our difficulties in obtaining justice."

Rhett remained incorrigible. "I am sick and disgusted with the meanness and falsehood of the Democratic Party," he wrote to a friend; and as for Polk, his "equivocating" Kane letter had "rendered him too dispicable [*sic*] in my estimation to regard him in the least." Alluding to Calhoun, he bluntly declared that he had no faith in "those who go on shouting at the tail of the Democratic Party, only to . . . have the august privilege of placing a tool in power like Polk, who they can appropriate and wield for their own ends." Instead, "despairing of all their reasoning I turn to this little State, and am striving at least to save her honour. She has declared she will resist the tariff policy. . . . I say let her go on. I have no doubt of the result, if this cursed spirit of President-making does not prostrate her."

But for all this rhetorical extravagance, Calhoun's potent influence prevailed in the state. Legislative candidates spoke up against Rhett's proposals even at the meetings he addressed, and though Rhett himself was running unopposed, there was a noticeable lack of enthusiasm for his reelection to Congress.

Polk had played an important part in strengthening Calhoun in his course. While the Rhett agitation was at its height, prominent Democrats from all over the country had been traveling to Nashville for the great Democratic mass meeting on August 15. Calhoun ordered Francis Pickens to go as his representative, mainly in order to confer with Polk. Pickens did not reach Nashville in time for the mass meeting, but he spent two days at Polk's house in Columbia and a day with Jackson at the Hermitage.

The South Carolinians wanted to know whether Polk would nominally preside over a Calhoun Administration or a Van Buren-Wright Administration. Specifically they wanted assurances that he would dispense with Frank Blair's *Globe* as his Administration organ and, especially in view of the Kane letter, that he would push thoroughgoing tariff reform. Overwhelming Pickens with cordiality, Polk left him utterly convinced. *"Every thing* is *completely satisfactory,"* Calhoun's emissary reported. Polk was having *"no correspondence even"* with the Van Burenites. Nor was there any need to worry about the Kane letter, for Polk "is determined to do all he can to reform the gov. and the 1st thing is to reduce the Tariff of 1842 to a revenue measure entirely & upon the principles of the compromise act, 2d, to introduce strict economy, 3d. acquire Texas at all hazards."

At any rate Pickens left Columbia so thoroughly committed to Polk that he afterward made himself unpopular in South Carolina, while Calhoun immediately began to radiate optimism and confidence in the Democratic nominee. "I cannot but think," he wrote after receiving Pickens' report, "that the prospect is now fairer to return to the good old Republican doctrines of '98, to reform the Government, restore the Constitution, and throw off the burthen, which has been weighing down the South, exhausting her means & debasing her spirit, than it has been since 1828." At once his friends began pressing his claims to be retained as Secretary of State if Polk were elected, and talking confidently about his presidential chances in 1848.

As Robert Barnwell Rhett fomented disaffection at one end of the Democratic spectrum, Thomas Hart Benton did so at the other. While most of the Van Burenites swallowed their bitterness and tried to do their best for the Polk ticket, Benton carried his rage against the Tyler-Calhoun project for annexing Texas into the campaign. "Yes! He would say that he was in favor of the annexation," he told his Missouri constituents in a speech in July, "but for none of the negro reasons — or, as it ought to be pronounced on this occasion, *nigger* reasons" contained in Calhoun's Pakenham letter. "He was in favor of annexation, but not by a treaty carefully and artfully contrived to dissolve the Union, and to make unjust and unconstitutional war upon a peaceful neighbor, and which incorporated two thousand miles of undisputed Mexican territory within the United States."

Benton's anti-Texas agitation was echoed by the more ideological segment of the Democratic party in New York, where William Cullen Bryant's New York *Evening Post* had kept up a steady fire of criticism against the Tyler-Calhoun project. In August, Bryant and some associates, including the attorney general of the state, sent a circular letter to leading New York Democrats declaring that annexation was "abhorrent to the opinions and feelings of a great majority of northern freemen." The circular proposed a public declaration by prominent Democrats that they would support Polk while rejecting the Texas plank in the party platform, and that they would try to get anti-Texas Democrats elected to Congress.

This movement was the more dangerous because it coincided with a widening rift in the New York Democratic party. Democratic Governor William C. Bouck, supported by former Governor William L. Marcy and Edwin Croswell, editor of the powerful party organ the Albany *Argus*, had alienated a growing number of Democrats by his friendliness to banks and state-financed improvement projects and by his distribution of the state patronage. The Democrats who were most vociferous against Bouck's "conservatism" were now agitating against Bouck's renomination for governor at the September state convention. Since it was the anti-Bouck men who were most bitter about Van Buren's rejection at Baltimore, the schism threatened to commit one whole wing, probably a majority, of the New York Democracy not only against conservatism at home but against Texas and against Polk in national politics.

It had quickly become apparent that the only way to patch up the rift was to prevail on Silas Wright to resign from the Senate and replace Bouck as the gubernatorial nominee. Only he was sufficiently popular with all factions — even Marcy called him "the most perfect specimen of a democrat in the nation" — to force Bouck to retire gracefully.

Polk had been following the developments in New York with growing concern. Very early he had warned Marcy about the dangers of disunity, and he allowed the Nashville *Union* to carry an editorial cautiously canvassing the merits of nominating Wright for governor. But this latter demonstration provoked a prompt rebuke from the New York conservatives, and Polk wisely concluded that further "neither I, nor my friends *out of the State*, can interfere."

Wright was finally forced to accept the nomination, though he complained that he would regard his election to the governorship as "personally the severest misfortune of my life." Bouck, Marcy, and Croswell, though harboring resentments for the future, promised Polk cordial support for the ticket; and Wright's popularity with the Democratic rank and file augured a maximum party vote. The Texas circular men were mollified by the nomination, while Wright brought the New York party more into harmony with the national

Democratic position by conceding the advantages of annexation and predicting that "but a few years will pass over until we shall see the Union indisputably, and, I believe, peacefully and honorably, embracing both Oregon and Texas."

Actually annexation was popular with many New York Democrats, especially in New York City and along the northern frontier, where anti-British feeling growing out of the Caroline incident was still strong. Many staunch Van Burenites were annexationists; and long before Wright's nomination Marcy had claimed that the Van Buren-Wright objections to immediate annexation were "viewed rather as a speculative question among us" and that the Democrats would "be very little disturbed by the issue."

Indeed in most of the country annexation was still much more a party question than a sectional one. In Pennsylvania, Buchanan reported annexation to be "decidedly popular." In New England, the Van Burenite Senator Fairfield of Maine spoke for Texas "as strongly and ardently as I could" and reported that the issue "has not excited much feeling"; the New Hampshire Democrats were "united on the annexation question" and "go for immediate annexation"; and George Bancroft, in accepting the Democratic gubernatorial nomination in Massachusetts, made a powerful argument for Texas, "not on sectional but on national grounds." In the Old Northwest, "there is but one voice among the Indiana democrats, North, South, east or west, & that is for annexation now, let Mexico take it as she will," and the question "has made very considerable encroachments on the Whig ranks"; and the same was true in Illinois, where the opposition of the Whig press was "half-hearted and halting." The question was equally strong in the South, where several leading Whigs broke with their party to support Polk and immediate annexation.

Thus by the middle of the campaign, Polk had every reason to feel satisfied with the state of the Texas question, and he had the Nashville *Union* deal gently with Benton's aberrations.

There was one other matter relating to Texas that had required careful handling by the Democratic nominee. A convention of John Tyler's friends, meeting simultaneously with the Baltimore convention, had placed the President in nomination as an independent candidate for reelection. In spite of his capacity for self-delusion, Tyler recognized as soon as the Democrats nominated a pro-Texas candidate that he had no chance. But he refused to withdraw under fire or until the Democrats should recognize his supporters "as entitled to trust and confidence," or in other words as acceptable officeholders.

Tyler's following was composed mainly of business-minded and/or office-hungry Democrats. Though not very numerous in most states, their control of the federal patronage and a network of Tylerite newspapers made them dangerous, and in the evenly divided condition of the country the Democrats needed all the support they could get.

Many of the more respectable of these men had flocked back to the Democratic banner as soon as the Van Burenites were defeated at Baltimore. But others, knowing that they were despised by the party regulars, demanded assurances that "the democrats who have fallen off from men & a few Radical measures (and not principle)" would not be proscribed. In the first days of the campaign Walker passed along to Polk such a request, with a prediction that "unless many of the wanderers of 1840 return to our party, we are again beaten." Polk replied in a carefully drafted private letter that he would welcome with joy "the re-union of all the old Jackson Democrats of '28 and '32"; but as to future appointments he would only say that, if elected, he would assume his duties "certainly with no prejudices or unkind feelings toward any portion of the party."

Meanwhile Polk was trying to induce Tyler to withdraw by having Jackson write through various intermediaries, particularly the general's old crony Major Lewis, who held office under Tyler in Washington, and Polk's former college mate, Tyler's Secretary of the Navy John Y. Mason. Through these intermediaries Jackson was telling the President that all true Democrats applauded him for his Bank vetoes and his efforts for Texas, and that he must serve his country and save his reputation by withdrawing. Polk also had the President and his Cabinet cordially invited to the Democratic mass meeting at Nashville.

Unfortunately, not all Democrats were applauding Tyler. The *Globe* and many other newspapers of the Van Buren-Benton persuasion were flaying the President unmercifully, saying that "we always wanted him to keep away from the Democratic party, the mass of whom hold him in as much contempt as the Whigs do"; and Van Burenite orators were charging, "His administration originated in dissoluteness and fraud, and has ended in bare-faced corruption." Smarting from these attacks, the proud Tyler was determined to "make these men feel the great necessity of my cooperation." The *Madisonian* and Calhoun's *Spectator* gave blow for blow against the "Jacobins" of the Benton-Van Buren persuasion, and the three hundred newspapers holding federal contracts for publishing the laws were ordered to follow the *Madisonian's* lead, and more particularly to make "attacks on Benton."

The President "expects, if Polk is defeated, that the Democracy will rally on him," reported his confidant Duff Green; and accordingly the pressure was increased on the Democrats for an arrangement that would guarantee the retention of a corps of loyal Tylerites in the federal offices. On July 4 the Tyler men in Philadelphia announced that they would run independent tickets throughout the country, for local and congressional offices as well as for presidential electors. On July 15 a Tylerite caucus in New York made plans to nominate a slate for every elective office in the state, and announced a public meeting for July 23. About the same time Tyler removed the collector of customs in New York, whom he had inherited from his predecessor, replacing him with the more pliable Cornelius P. Van Ness; and Van Ness promptly began removing subordinates in batches of sixty to make way for faithful Tylerites.

The Democrats in the most threatened states took immediate alarm, and Walker hastened to seek an interview with the President. In a conversation of several hours, Tyler said that he was anxious for Polk's election, but that he could not withdraw until the Democratic newspapers stopped assailing him, and until he received assurances "on reliable authority" that his friends would be "treated as brethren & equals" by the Democratic party. Walker promptly suggested to Polk that he write a private letter and Jackson a public one giving the required assurances, and that Jackson induce Blair to adopt a conciliatory tone toward the President.

The moment Polk received Walker's account of the interview, he sent General Pillow to the Hermitage to enlist Jackson's aid. Polk was sure that "I ought not to write to him or his friends, or to make any pledges to any one," and he also doubted the propriety of a public letter by Jackson. But Jackson could write a private letter to be shown to Tyler, and to Jackson, Polk was willing to say, in the exact language of his earlier letter of reassurance to conservatives, that, if elected, he would assume office "certainly with no prejudices or unkind feelings towards any portion of the party." Jackson promptly embodied this intimation in a letter to Major Lewis. If Tyler withdrew, the general wrote, his friends would be "received as brethren, . . . all former differences forgotten."

But Polk was convinced that the *Globe's* attacks were an even more serious obstacle to Tyler's withdrawal. He was already urging Jackson to use his influence with Blair when the Tyler situation developed; and Jackson's intervention was apparently effectual, for within a few weeks Polk was satisfied that the *Globe* was "giving a fair support to the nomination."

Meanwhile, throughout the country both parties were outdoing each other at the kind of billingsgate that had worked so well for the Whigs in 1840. Starting with the gibe "Who is James K. Polk?" the Whigs harped throughout the campaign on Polk's mediocrity. "He is destitute of the commanding talent—the stern political integrity—the high moral fitness—the Union should possess at this crisis," declared one Whig circular, "and having been twice rejected for the Office of Governor in his own State—having no hold upon the confidence or affections of his countrymen at home, and no talent to command respect for us abroad he is not the man for the times or for the Union." To this kind of argument Ritchie replied in the *Enquirer* that the country could not afford a spectacular but dangerous personality. Clay "may be a more brilliant orator—but we do not want splendid eloquence to conduct the executive department—neither Washington nor Jefferson was an orator. He may be a more dashing politician than Mr. Polk—but we do not want any high flying and daring politician, who soars even beyond the constitution, and disdains all its restrictions, in order to carry out some extravagant object of his towering ambition. We want not the arrogant temper of a dictator. . . . We want no aspiring, 'moon-reaching' president." With "inflexible firmness" Polk would "carry out the true principles of the constitution"; and "no man would be more anxious to walk in the footsteps of Thomas Jefferson himself, than this much reviled citizen of Tennessee."

Polk's most grandiloquent traducer was his old foe Sargeant S. Prentiss of Mississippi, one of whose speeches was reported as follows: "Suddenly he paused, and with the voice of a trumpet asked, 'Who is the opponent of Henry

Clay?' His eyes flashed unwonted fire . . . he fairly heaved with emotion. The foam dashed from his lips, and he repeated in defiant notes, 'Who is the opponent of Mr. Clay?' and then hissed the answer, "A blighted burr that has fallen from the mane of the warhorse of the Hermitage.' " But to this theme also the Democrats had their response, equally grandiloquent. Gansevoort Melville's eulogy of Polk in New York City was reported as follows: "Hereafter he shall be known by the name that we now give him—it is Young Hickory. (Here the cheering was deafening, and continued for some moments. . . .) We have had one old hickory tree. . . . Sixteen millions of Americans have reposed under its shade in peace and happiness. It is yet vigorous—but it cannot live forever. And now, to take its place, is springing up at its very side a tall and noble sapling. It imbibes its nourishment from the same soil. It flourishes in the same atmosphere. It springs from the same staunch old democratic stock. It is heart of oak and sound to the core. It grew originally upon the same Carolinian ground. Like it, it was early transplanted to the West. There it has struck its roots wide and deep. It will yet be cradled in the tempest and rocked by the storm. Storm and tempest will alike beat against it in vain. Its growth cannot be checked. It is destined to reach a correspondent elevation with the parent stem. We and our children will yet live in prosperity under the broad branches of this new young hickory tree. On the 4th day of March next, that young hickory tree will be transplanted by the people to the people's house at Washington; and you and I, and all of us, will assist in that transplanting."

The Democrats also continually echoed a resolution by an Ohio Democratic meeting comparing the moral characters of Polk and Clay, "the former, distinguished for all the moral attributes which adorn the private man and make the good citizen—the latter, notorious for his fiendish and vindictive spirit, for his disregard of the most important moral obligations, for his blasphemy, for his gambling propensities, and for his frequent and blood-thirsty attempts upon the lives of his fellow-men." These general charges against Clay were soon particularized in a shocking piece of Democratic propaganda, "Henry Clay's Moral Fitness for the Presidency. Texted by the Decalogue." The Whig candidate transgressed the first of the Ten Commandments because his God was Mammon; the second because he encouraged idolatry of monied corporations. To prove his violation of the third commandment Democrats cited the incident when he came into the House of Representatives just as Speaker Polk rendered a decision against the Whigs and exclaimed, "Go home, G-d damn you!" He was charged with violating the fifth and sixth commandments by campaigning on the Sabbath and being involved in duels. As to the seventh commandment, "Thou shalt not commit adultery," "The history of Mr. Clay's debaucheries and midnight revelries in Washington is too shocking, too disgusting to appear in public print." And the remainder of the Decalogue had been transgressed by a technical violation of his oath to support the Constitution, and by his winning as much as forty thousand dollars in a single night at the gambling table.

But the most effective propaganda was probably that which related the candidates to the gross polemical party images through which the voters formed their partisan identifications. An Ohio paper followed up the standard Democratic comparison of Polk's morals with Clay's by claiming that "The one is emphatically the candidate of the PEOPLE, the other that of the ARISTOCRACY." Every "crowned head" in Europe "desires the election of HENRY CLAY, as the efficient means of subverting our Republican governments. The tendency of the principles advocated by the Whigs is to concentrate the wealth and power of the country into the hands of the few, and to impoverish the many. The tendency of the Democratic principles is to enlarge the powers and privileges of the mass of the people, and curtail those of the few." Democratic orators continually asserted that "There never was a question started yet for enlarging the privileges of the people, but that it was done by a Democrat."

A few days before the election the New York *Courier and Enquirer* summarized the various elements in the counter-image of the Democratic party which the Whigs sought to convey. Let every citizen, said the editor "put it to his *conscience* whether he can vote for a man pledged to the 'immediate annexation' of Texas . . . *a step conceived by traitors and base conspirators against the Union.* . . . Let him remember that if he votes for Polk he votes to *turn out of employment* EIGHT HUNDRED THOUSAND American citizens, now engaged in manufacturing. . . . Let him remember that if he votes for James K. Polk he votes for a man who . . . owes his selection to the fact that he is the pliant tool of Southern disunionists . . . who would instantly plunge us into a disgraceful war, which he has not the ability to conduct—who would set in motion causes which could not fail to result in disunion and civil war."

The gross polemical images of both parties were convincing to one sophisticated observer who was too conservative for either. The elegant New York lawyer George Templeton Strong had difficulty deciding whether "the jacobinical spirit and the antipathy to law and order and the overthrow of everything worth preserving" of the Democrats was worse than the "speculating bank-swindling, money-worshipping *primum mobile*" of the Whigs. "Certainly since the downfall of Federalism there has been no conservative party in the country which has ventured to avow any higher aim than the cultivation of tariffs and credit systems, trade and manufactures," he concluded sadly. "Its unchecked development would make us a commercial aristocracy which is mean enough everywhere, but here 'twould be a fluctuating mushroom aristocracy and the meanest the world has seen yet."

Amid the partisan vituperation, the political excitement, according to *Niles' Register*, soon caught up even more people than in 1840. "Standards are erected not only at places for holding elections—places of party meetings, and before public hotels, but hundreds are to be seen in every county at private residences towering far above the forest trees and decorated with the names, ensigns or flags of the partisans. Processions—standards—transparencies—bands of music—thundering artillery—burning tar barrels—and all the other paraphernalia of electioneering warfare are in active requisition." Niles was awed by the moral sublimity of this political spectacle. "Imagine twenty millions of people – for men, women, and children partake of the enthusiasm of the moment, – each one contributing his quota towards the success of his favorite party or favorite candidate, and each influenced with the persuasion that the destinies of the country largely depend upon the result, and some idea may be conceived, though a faint one, of what is actually now going on in the U. States."

In promoting all this activity the Whigs had the advantage of superior financial resources. While there were wealthy Democrats, the bulk of the well-to-do business class gave its loyalties to the Whigs. The ironmasters of Pennsylvania closed their establishments in order to transport their workers to Whig meetings; the turnout of leading businessmen for a Whig procession in New York City caused a complete suspension of business; while a leading dealer in stocks and bonds testified that "the respectable ones are for Clay and Tariff and a conservative sound Govt." but "the lower orders," "myriads of Irish and miserable poor and ignorant devils who are led away by the rank Democracy," are "for upsetting every thing good and breaking down men of property to their own level." This man devoutly hoped that "Whig rule and law and order will triumph"; and men like him gave money gladly to that end.

Groups like the Whig "Commercial Committee" in Philadelphia needed only gentle hints from Clay to furnish the means whereby Whig tracts were "poured out by the acre." Half a million of them were distributed from New York City alone, and another stream flooded the country from a Whig central committee at Washington. At a Whig meeting of thirty "gentlemen" at New York's Astor House, "the first ten men who took pen in hand subscribed $8,100," six of them giving $1,000 each, "and they have all been giving to the same object every day for months past." The Democrats, on the other hand, were constantly hard pressed for funds, and a fund-raising agent sent out by Polk to canvass middle Tennessee collected promises of only $165.

The Whigs sought to exploit their financial advantage by offering to bet large sums on the election, which, if not met, would dispirit the Democrats and lessen their efforts. When the Whig newspapers claimed that no takers had been found for thirty thousand dollars offered at Nashville on Clay at two-to-one odds, the Nashville *Union* replied that all the bets offered by Whigs had been taken, and that Democrats were "too well acquainted with the turf . . . to ask or expect odds when running against A NAG THAT NEVER DID WIN." The heaviest Democratic bettor was Frank Blair, who felt an obligation to use for the party some of the wealth he had acquired as public printer under Jackson and Van Buren. Blair sent out his partner to call the bluff of the Whig bettors, took all bets offered, and then challenged the Whigs by offering to give fifty dollars to anyone who would return him fifty dollars for every electoral vote over 50 that Polk beat Clay, and to give one hundred to anyone who would return him any one of the following: ten dollars for every electoral vote that Polk beat Clay, one hundred for every electoral vote over 100 that Polk beat Clay, one hundred for every 10,000 popular votes that Polk beat Clay, and one mill doubled for every electoral vote over 60 that Polk beat Clay. By these means Blair "at last silenced their Brays," but not until he had put up more than $22,000.

Frank Blair was not the only man trying to calculate the electoral results. There were 275 electoral votes, with 138 needed to elect. From the beginning of the contest, most politicians conceded to the Whigs Kentucky and the four New England states of Connecticut, Rhode Island, Massachusetts, and Vermont for a total of 40 electoral votes. The Democrats seemed equally sure of the 80 electoral votes of Maine and New Hampshire in New England; Virginia, South Carolina, Alabama, Mississippi, Arkansas, and Missouri in the South; and Michigan and Illinois in the Northwest. State elections in July seemed to assign Louisiana and Indiana to the Democrats and North Carolina to the Whigs, giving the Democrats a lead of 98 to 51 in electoral votes. This lead did not mean much, for it left eight states undetermined, including the three great states of New York, Pennsylvania, and Ohio, with 85 electoral votes. To win, the Democrats would need only two of these large states, or one of the large states together with two of the closely contested smaller states of Georgia, Maryland, New Jersey, and Tennessee. Five of these states, Pennsylvania, Ohio, Georgia, Maryland, and New Jersey, were to elect governors or congressmen early in October.

At this point Polk felt that Democratic prospects were better than they had ever been before, while the Whigs became increasingly discouraged, especially in the crucial state of New York. Their discouragement was related to the abolitionist vote, a factor in the campaign that had become more and more important as the votes of Ohio and New York had become more crucial. The abolitionist Liberty party had won only a tiny vote in its first presidential venture in 1840, but in several closely divided and now probably decisive states, its vote had risen steadily and sharply in state elections since that time. In New York the abolitionists had risen from 2,808 votes in 1840 to 16,275 in 1843, and in Ohio during the same period from 903 to 7,480. The Liberty party had now nominated for the Presidency James G. Birney of Michigan, a former Alabama slaveholder and Democrat but a fervent opponent of slavery.

The abolitionists made their greatest appeal to the strongly religious people in the rural and small town areas of the North, who were both antislavery and Whig. The important question was how many of them would be drawn from the Whig ticket to waste their votes on Birney and thus aid Polk. Early in the campaign the Liberty men joined the Democrats in denouncing Clay's moral character, but the Texas issue was aiding the efforts of Whigs in antislavery areas to represent Clay as "*the* Abolition Candidate of the North." In upstate New York, the Whigs displayed banners on which Polk was portrayed as dragging a Negro in chains behind him; and the state's former Whig Governor William H. Seward exulted, "It would be marvelous if Abolition should carry the country at the first effort." The New York Democrats told Polk that "This in a Free State is a sharp sword," while Seward was confident that taking the abolition and tariff issues together, "we are safe and right."

But Clay had little stomach for being "*the* Abolition Candidate of the North." Identifying himself with the whole nation, he was peculiarly vulnera-

ble to the cries of southern Whigs that they were being destroyed by his opposition to Texas. Certainly he did not want to throw away his excellent prospects for victory in the slaveholding states of Delaware, Maryland, North
Carolina, Georgia, Louisiana, Tennessee, and Kentucky. And so he embarked on his disastrous course of trying to make his position on Texas and
slavery equally acceptable to northern and southern voters. On July 1, he
addressed a public letter to the editor of a Whig newspaper in Alabama explaining that personally he had no objection to annexation, but that in view of
the strong opposition in the North, he feared it might result in the dissolution
of the Union. But this was not enough for the southern Whigs. In order to
combat the Democratic attacks, they needed at least a definite statement in
favor of eventual annexation. Accordingly, on July 27, Clay wrote again to
Alabama. After reviewing the difficulties in the way of immediate annexation,
he declared, "I have, however, no hesitation in saying that, far from having
any personal objection to the annexation of Texas, I should be glad to see it,
without dishonor, without war, with the common consent of the union, and
upon just and fair terms." He protested further that "It would be unwise to
refuse a permanent acquisition which will exist as long as the globe remains,
on account of a temporary institution," slavery, which was "destined to become extinct, at some distant day, in my opinion by the operation of the inevitable laws of population."

Now the northern Whigs cried out in alarm. "*That* horrid letter has given
us a dreadful shock," wrote Thurlow Weed from Albany. Seward, who was
doing missionary work in the antislavery areas of western New York, "met
that letter at Geneva, and there, here, and until now every body droops, de-
spairs. . . . It jeopards, perhaps loses this State."

Similar alarms were sounded from Ohio, but worse was yet to come.
Clay's kinsman Cassius M. Clay, who had waged a brave battle against
slavery in Kentucky, had published a letter appealing to antislavery men to
support the Whig candidate. "I do not mean to say that Mr. Clay is an emancipationist," he had written, "but I believe his feelings are with the cause. I
know that those most immediately within his influence approximate to myself
in sentiment upon the subject of slavery." The great issue in the campaign, he
insisted, was "*Polk, slavery, and Texas*" versus "*Clay, Union, and liberty.*"
The Whig candidate concluded that this letter might ruin his chances in Tennessee, North Carolina, and Georgia, and might even endanger Kentucky. So,
on September 2 he published a letter in the Lexington newspaper repudiating
the antislavery opinions attributed to him and his friends and declaring that
Congress could not interfere with slavery, either in the states or in the District of Columbia. Shortly afterward, the Democrats intercepted and published a private letter from Clay to Cassius declaring that he was neither "an
ultra supporter" of slavery nor an abolitionist.

The northern Whigs were thunderstruck. A former Whig congressman
who was a strong antislavery man announced his intention of voting for Birney. Clay "is as rotten as a stagnant fish pond, on the subject of Slavery &
always has been," he declared. "Confound him and all his compromises

from first to last—he is just the man to make some diabolical compromise by which the lone star shall have a place in our galaxy." The Democrats were correspondingly jubilant. A New Yorker informed Polk that Clay's letters had put "an impassable gulf" between him and the abolitionists, and as a result "the State is ours beyond a question."

The unnerved Whig candidate was thrown into a state of fretful indecision about how the damage might be repaired before the crucial state election in Ohio on October 8. First he wrote a letter to mollify the antislavery men, but the recipients he addressed did not publish it. Then, though hoping publication would not be thought necessary, he sent a similar letter to another antislavery correspondent. Two days later he changed his mind again and wrote yet another letter, dated September 23, to be published in the *National Intelligencer*. Declaring flatly, "I am decidedly opposed to the immediate annexation of Texas to the United States," he denied that any of his statements on the subject were inconsistent with each other and stated that he would write no further letters for publication on any public question. The Democratic press had a field day contrasting Clay's various statements, and a Missouri editor was even moved to versify:

> He wires in and wires out,
> And leaves the people still in doubt,
> Whether the snake that made the track,
> Was going South, or coming back.

Clay's nervous and disastrous handling of the Texas question was in notable contrast to Polk's cool and astute course on the tariff. In fact, Polk was an incomparably superior strategist throughout the campaign. Sanguine by nature and made overconfident by his ability to persuade men at close range, Clay was not a good judge of the elements at work in a national campaign or of the means by which they might be influenced. His estimates of the outcome were naively and extravagantly overoptimistic by contrast with Polk's shrewd and realistic assessments. And he was constantly writing letters on every other conceivable subject, including the old "bargain and corruption" charges of 1828, so that "The Whig papers are busy half their time in explaining Clay's letters."

Clay's letters would have been even more disastrous to his cause if the Liberty candidate had not likewise proved to be politically incautious and addicted to letter writing. In two letters published during August, Birney argued against any tariff that went beyond the revenue level, a national bank, and distribution of public land proceeds. He followed up this endorsement of Democratic principles by allowing himself to be nominated for the Michigan legislature by a Democratic convention in his home county of Saginaw. He then made matters worse, in attempting to justify himself, by saying that while he opposed Polk, "I more deprecate the election of Mr. Clay—because, possessing abilities superior to Mr. Polk's, he would proportionally weaken the influence" of the great truths of the Declaration of Independence.

These events produced "a great sensation in the Abolition ranks." One leader of the Liberty party complained that he was being "told a dozen times a day, that Mr. B. *has* come out in favor of the loco focos" and that the Liberty men were "positively used up in this town." Polk was informed by a New York politician that Birney's Democratic nomination had "alarmed a portion of that large section of the Abolitionists who were originally Whigs, and . . . paves the way for an unexpected accession to Clay's strength from that quarter." The news was especially disastrous in Ohio, where the Whigs, not content with the facts, circulated on the eve of the state election thousands of copies of a fabricated letter in which Birney was made to say, "I AM NOW and EVER HAVE BEEN, a Democrat of the 'Jeffersonian School.' The Democracy of the county must be well satisfied that I am rendering them more effectual service by advocating abolition principles, than if I WERE OPENLY A DEMOCRAT."

The Ohio election was also influenced by the even more flagrant "Roorback forgery." On August 21, there appeared in an abolitionist newspaper at Ithaca, New York, a purported extract from *Roorback's Tour through the Southern and Western States in the Year 1836*. The writer told of encountering on the Duck River in Tennessee an encampment of a slave trader who was taking two hundred slaves to a southern market. "Forty of these unfortunate beings had been purchased, I was informed, of the Hon. J. K. Polk, the present speaker of the house of representatives: the mark of the branding iron, with the initials of the same on their shoulders distinguishing them from the rest." This extract was picked up and given wide circulation by Thurlow Weed's Albany *Evening Journal*, and began appearing in the Ohio Whig press two weeks before the election. Fortunately the Democrats discovered promptly that it was a complete fabrication, based on a similar passage, having nothing to do with Polk, in G. W. Featherstonhaugh's recently published book on his American travels.

The forgery was merely an elaboration of current Whig charges that Polk treated his slaves cruelly. In reply, the Nashville *Union* had fatuously asserted that "he now owns no slave, who is of the years of discretion, who would, on any persuasion, consent to be emancipated and turned loose into the world, deprived of his constant guardianship and protection." When the ineffectiveness of this bit of southern sentimentality became apparent, General Pillow issued an unadorned statement of the actual facts: that Polk's slaves had come down to him through his family; that he had bought and sold one or two wholly for the purpose of preventing slave families from being separated; and that he was known throughout his area as a "kind & humane master." Still, Abbott Lawrence could go on telling the voters that "Mr. Polk was an *ultra* slaveholder, that he had recently, say within six years, purchased a large plantation in the State of Mississippi, and *stocked* it with negroes, that he had gone into it *up to his ears* &c." Lawrence knew whereof he spoke, for Polk had tried to borrow money from him for the venture.

For all the exposures of Whig fabrications, the fact that Polk was a slaveholder could not be blinked before the antislavery voters of the North; and they were made even more uneasy about his party by a Democratic blunder on the eve of the Ohio election. At the end of September, Walker issued through the Democratic Association at Washington a pamphlet entitled "THE SOUTH IN DANGER! READ BEFORE YOU VOTE." This document, composed of statements showing the antislavery leanings of northern Whigs, was designed to be circulated quietly among Whigs in Georgia, where congressmen were to be elected the day before the Ohio election. Unfortunately the Whig campaign committee at Washington got hold of the pamphlet and distributed many thousands of copies through Ohio and other northern states, where it was read as advocating annexation of Texas as a measure to preserve and extend slavery. This pamphlet and Birney's indiscretions did much to neutralize Clay's vacillations and to keep many antislavery men in the Whig ranks.

The Walker pamphlet was the final straw in Ohio, and the Democratic gubernatorial candidate lost the state by the narrowest of margins. Also by the thinnest of margins the Democrats were defeated during the same week in New Jersey and Maryland; but in previously Whig Georgia they carried the congressional races by a sufficient majority to enable them to count on the state in November.

Also voting that week was the great state of Pennsylvania, and although the Democrats elected their governor, a new and unexpectedly potent political element cut the margin of victory so thin that Democratic hopes for the Presidential election were seriously dampened. The sharp rise in foreign immigration during the early 1840's, particularly from Ireland and Germany, had caused an upsurge of antiforeign, anti-Catholic prejudices. Nowhere was this truer than in New York City and Philadelphia, where the native-born resented the little offices and perquisites which the local Democratic organizations were distributing to the "adopted citizens" in the process of garnering the growing foreign-born vote. By 1843, an American Republican party had been organized in New York City to advocate severe restrictions on naturalization, and it grew so rapidly that it carried the city elections in the spring of 1844. This success inspired imitation in Philadelphia, where the activities of the American Republicans provoked a series of bloody riots in July.

The American Republicans or "Natives" were drawn from both major parties, and the politicians hesitated to attack them for fear of confirming them in their deviation from the regular party ranks. The Democrats had historically been friendly to immigrants, but so many Democrats had gone into the Native movement that Democratic politicians implored Polk to refuse demands that he denounce the Nativist agitation and let the party's record speak for itself. This advice Polk heartily accepted.

The Whigs, on the other hand, had been traditionally hostile to the foreigners who enlisted so solidly against them, and Henry Clay was strongly tempted to declare for tighter naturalization requirements. But in New York, the shrewd Whig leaders Seward and Weed had been competing with the Democrats for support from the foreign-born. While they had not been spectacularly successful with the rank and file, they had established such a close working relationship with Catholic Bishop John Hughes that he was said to be a "violent whig"; and they hoped through his influence "to persuade the Irish that they should vote for 'Patrick O'Clay.' " The New Yorkers dissuaded Clay from making a public statement, but late in the campaign he sent a private letter favoring the Nativists' proposed changes in the naturalization laws to be shown around extensively in Philadelphia. At the same time he sent a personal representative to New York to seek the support of Bishop Hughes. The bishop obviously did not know about the private letter to Philadelphia, for he told Clay's emissary that he was impressed by the difference between Clay's sentiments and "the sentiments and conduct of the intolerant Whigs . . . in the City of New York." While he "hoped for their defeat on the legislative ticket," he would use his influence for Clay's election "& believed his brethren would be divided on the Presidential vote."

Meanwhile in Pennsylvania the Democratic politicians had conceded that "there may . . . be some falling off in the City & County of Philadelphia, both on account of the Native American feeling & for other causes"; but obviously they did not recognize the seriousness of the threat until almost the day of the election. Suddenly it became clear that the Whigs and Natives had agreed to join forces in the city, the Native candidates to get united support for three of the four congressional seats, most of the legislative seats, and some local offices, and the Whig candidates to get united support for the governorship, the remaining congressional seat, some legislative seats, and most local offices. The Natives attacked the Democratic gubernatorial candidate Francis Shunk for having participated in the dedication of a Catholic church and for saying that the Protestant Bible should not be required in schools where it offended the religious convictions of parents. The coalition was astonishingly successful. The Democrats lost the city by 6,000 votes, cutting Shunk to 50.7 per cent of the statewide vote, with a hazardous margin of 4,000. In addition the Natives elected two congressmen and nine members of the legislature.

The Pennsylvania result was not so alarming in itself, for the Pennsylvania Democrats could reasonably expect to hold their narrow October margin in November, and even to increase it with returning Natives. What shook Democratic politicians was the prospect that the devastating strategy of Whig-Native coalition would now be applied to the more evenly divided and absolutely crucial state of New York.

Despite the narrow margins of the October elections, they seemed to realistic politicians to assign Georgia and Pennsylvania to the Democrats and Maryland, New Jersey, and Ohio to the Whigs. This brought the Democrats to 132 probable electoral votes of the 138 needed for a majority, and the Whigs to 89. Still uncertain were New York (36 electoral votes), Tennessee (13), and Delaware (3). The Democrats could win by carrying either Tennessee or New York, while the Whigs would need both.

New York quickly felt the effect of the Philadelphia returns. Silas Wright told Polk that the Democrats "were driving the Whigs out of the field of argument and into despair, when the Pa. election came off. The moment the news from the City and County of Philadelphia spread over our State, the . . . sweep of the coalition with the natives in Philadelphia awakened new hope and new life in the whole party, and from that moment coalitions form their only hope, and they are openly and shamelessly attempted with every faction, every interest, every prejudice, and even every fanaticism to be found within our wide limits." In New York City the Whigs prepared to support the Native congressional and legislative tickets, while the Natives were expected to vote Whig for governor and President. The Democrats lost all hope of their anticipated majority of several thousand in the city and redoubled their efforts to hold enough of a majority elsewhere to save the state. "Political excitement in this state has reached a new and almost fearful point," they reported to Polk. "It is unexampled in the history of New York politics." In the city, the Democrats were naturalizing more than sixty new voters a day—"every man of them Democrats"—and trying to control Mike Walsh's Empire Democratic Club, "one of those fighting and bullying political clubs," which was endangering the cause by beating up respectable Whig citizens, including a son of Alexander Hamilton. Upstate in Silas Wright's home town, the Democrats and Whigs who would have to be away from hone on Election Day were pairing off against each other, and Democrats who could not find pairs were hiring Whigs to leave town with them. The way things looked, a single vote might decide the state, and with it the Presidency.

As the tension of the struggle for New York mounted, Polk realized that if New York were lost, "the vote of Tennessee may and probably will decide the contest of the Union." "We *can* and *must* save her," he kept telling his Tennessee friends, "but to do it will require our whole energy, and the unceasing labour of every man whether he is a debater or not, every hour until the election is over." He took special care to have Democrats stationed at the polls on the Kentucky border to prevent Kentuckians from crossing over and voting illegally in Whig precincts. "Let our friends ride on Saturday and Monday through every [illegible word] District," he exhorted several days before the election, "see every Democratic voter, and urge him to attend the polls. Let no Democrat, not one, remain at home on the day of the election."

In the final moments of his struggle to carry the state, he resorted to the kind of sectional appeal he had always been loath to use. Dallas had written recently from Philadelphia that only the resistance of northern Democrats kept abolitionism from growing more rapidly in the North. But if in the face of Clay's flirtation with the abolitionists the Whigs should win enough southern support to carry the election, "it would be impossible to keep the northern democrats battling on that point" and "abolition will become irresistible." If, on the contrary, he said, "the South stands manfully and unitedly by the cause, the abolitionists will rapidly retrograde and disappear." The Tennessee Democrats incorporated these sentiments in "an authentic and *authoritative* exposure" of Clay's "offer to *sell the South* for the abolition votes of New York," which was broadcast by the Nashville *Union* with careful timing "to do good here and south, but *not* in time, as we calculate it, to do harm north."

The Whigs, too, resorted to last-minute desperation tactics, especially in

the two states they had to carry, Pennsylvania and New York. Spurious tickets were issued, with the names of Whig electoral candidates interspersed
among the legitimate Democrats. Forged letters, purporting to be from a
prominent Philadelphia Democrat, were sent out desponding of Democratic
success in Pennsylvania, and even Silas Wright was depressed by one of
them. A fund of $100,000 was said to have been raised in Boston for use in
New York, where Wright reported that Whig money "flows like water."
Similarly, the Philadelphia Whigs put together a last-minute fund of twenty
thousand and dispatched agents through the state to disburse it. In this case,
however, the Democrats intercepted a letter concerning distribution of the
money and were able to follow the Whig agents warning the voters of this
attempt to buy them up.

The voting was scheduled for different days in different states. Pennsylvania and Ohio voted on November 1, followed by most of the states on the
fourth, but New York did not vote until the following day, and the balloting
was not wound up until Delaware and Vermont voted on the twelfth. This
scheduling proved advantageous for Polk. On the first day of voting the Pennsylvania Democrats reduced the Whig-Native October majority in Philadelphia by some 1,400 votes. This "glorious news," guaranteeing Pennsylvania
to the Democrats, was rushed to New York, where the city Democrats dispatched a "locomotive printing office" on board a steamboat up the Hudson
to scatter the glad tidings throughout the state.

By the eve of the election, New York City was in a hubbub: "Little knots
of men at every corner. The political head quarters of the different parties
thronged. Tammany Hall a perfect jam from 8 AM till after midnight." That
day the Democrats took 497 new voters to the city court to be naturalized,
creating such a crush that the courtroom windows had to be opened to let
people in and out. Providence seemed to be smiling on the Democratic cause.
A rainstorm in the morning had forced postponement of a Nativist demonstration which the Democrats had feared would provoke a riot and damage their
cause.

By now, the desperate Whigs were hoping for "salvation through a miracle, to be worked by the Native Americans." The miracle did not occur. The
Natives elected three of the four congressmen from the city, but the Philadelphia returns influenced many of the Democratic Nativists to stick with Polk
in the presidential voting, and he carried the city by nearly 2,000. On the
other hand the Nativist agitation provoked an immense and unanimously
Democratic turnout of foreign-born voters, while the abolitionists in western
New York failed to support Clay as strongly as the Whigs had hoped. Still the
state was extremely close. Down in Baltimore the night after the New York
election five thousand people waited on the wharves for the midnight boat
bringing the first New York returns. The city results cheered the Democrats,
but upstate returns the next day revived Whig hopes. Another day passed,
and more New York returns left the state trembling in the balance. Friday
night, the eighth, Baltimore's streets remained crowded as at midday, and
again thousands were waiting on the wharves when the midnight boat brought

the definitive New York returns. Polk had carried the state by slightly over 5,000 votes, with Birney garnering 16,000 antislavery voters who might otherwise have gone to the Whigs. The other states had voted as expected, and Polk was elected.

It was six days later, on the fourteenth, when the New York news reached distant Tennessee. The booming of the Democrats' cannon in Nashville conveyed the news to the nearby Hermitage, and no one was more overjoyed than Andrew Jackson. "I thank my god that the Republic is safe, & that he had permitted me to live to see it, & rejoice," he wrote, "and I can say in the language of Simeon of old 'Now let thy servant depart in peace.'" Another former President was less willing to credit the result to Divine Providence. "The partial associations of Native Americans, Irish Catholics, abolition societies, liberty party, the Pope of Rome, the Democracy of the sword, and the dotage of a ruffian," wrote John Quincy Adams, "are sealing the fate of this nation, which nothing less than the interposition of Omnipotence can save." Adams' bitter judgment was echoed by the far-off *Times* of London. Polk's election, declared this august journal, "is the triumph of every thing that is worst over every thing that is best in the United States of America. It is a victory gained by the South over the North—by the slave States over the free —by the repudiating States over the honest ones—by the partisans of the annexation of Texas over its opponents—by the adventurous and unscrupulous democracy of the new States, and the foreign population in those States, over the more austere and dignified republicanism of New England."

From Mississippi to New York the Whigs echoed the *Times* in interpreting the outcome as the defeat of the respectable classes. "The Whigs embrace three-fourths of the intelligence, moral character, and property of the United States," said Sergeant Prentiss. A New Yorker raised the proportion to nine-tenths. "All such as live by their skill and the labor of their honest hands, who have wives whom they cherish and children whom they strive to educate and make good citizens, men who go to church on Sundays, respect the laws and love their country . . . but alas! the numerical strength lies not in these classes." Clay was defeated by "the Sovereigns without 'brick habitations,'" according to Thurlow Weed. "Too many of our fellow-citizens do not want prosperity. They hate to see their thrifty neighbors go ahead." A New York stockbroker concluded that "nothing can withstand the Democracy of this Country, back'd by the rabble who hate the rich."

The Whigs particularly emphasized the foreign-born vote as the cause of their defeat. "Foreigners who have 'no lot or inheritance' in the matter have robbed us of our birth-right, the 'scepter has departed from Israel,'" mourned one man. "Ireland has re-conquered the country which England lost." Weed and Seward lamented that the Whig press had yielded so readily to the seductions of Nativism, negating all their previous work to keep the foreign-born vote divided; and the Democrats agreed in telling Polk that "the true-hearted Adopted Citizens abandoned the Whig Party almost *en masse* and supported you with the same zeal and devotedness they did General Jackson. It was an avalanche they could not resist." Clay, who seems to have been totally surprised by his defeat, likewise attributed it in large measure to the foreign-born vote and had "no doubt of the greatness of the evil of this constant manufacture of American citizens out of foreign emigrants." He thought that "Some day or other this evil will doubtless be corrected," but was so far persuaded by the Seward-Weed arguments that he still opposed any avowal of Nativist principles by the Whigs.

There was argument at the time, and there has been since, as to whether the election was a mandate for the annexation of Texas. The New York *Evening Post* claimed that it spoke for many Democrats who had supported Polk in spite of his position on Texas rather than because of it. On the other hand it seems clear that the issue had much to do with the shrinkage of normal Whig strength throughout the South. One prominent southern Whig told Clay after the election that, "For the present the Whig party in the South is dispersed"; while another had no doubt that only the Texas question could have caused the people to elect "a mere *Tom Tit* over the old Eagle." John Quincy Adams was hardly correct in calling the election a "victory of the slavery element"; but those who viewed it in that light were right in sensing a portent of sectional polarization in the returns. A Vermont Whig looked out a window in Washington on the morning after the result was known to see a Democratic victory banner floating over the slave market. "That flag means *Texas*," he exclaimed, "and *Texas* means *civil war*, before we have done with it."

Yet for all the presumed effect of the Texas question in weakening the Whigs throughout the South, it enabled the Democrats to carry, of states they could not have expected otherwise, only Georgia and possibly Indiana, or perhaps also, with the aid of fraudulent voting, Louisiana, having a total of 28 electoral votes; while it may have lost them Ohio with 23.

Even in these states the Texas question and other issues did not determine the bulk of the votes. Probably more voters favored annexation because they were Democrats than voted Democratic because they favored annexation. People voted for the party with which they identified, forming their identifications mainly in terms of the party image's appeal for the social group to which they belonged. Thus the Whigs were nearest the truth when they emphasized the political solidarity of the respectable classes on the one hand and the foreign-born on the other.

Because the social groupings and criteria relevant to party identification — religious, class, ethnic, economic, regional — were so numerous in American society, the parties were coalitions of a variety of social groups with cross-cutting inclinations on the issues. A New York editor illustrated this when he posed the question, "Who elected James K. Polk?" "I," says the free trade man of South Carolina, "I did it; hurrah for free trade!" "No," says the Annexationist of Mississippi, Alabama and Louisiana, "It was I that did it; I went for the enlargement of the territory of slavery." "Not so fast," respond the Annexationists of the North, "It was we who did it — we who went for getting rid of slavery by taking Texas and thus enlarging the bounds of freedom." "No, no"; declare the tariff men of Pennsylvania, "we did it, and did it by shouting for the tariff of 1842" . . . . "Don't boast too much," say the Tyler men, "we did it; the post-office and custom house did it; we did it by giving you public offices and public money"; and these are not all who say they did it. The friends of Silas Wright and Mr. Van Buren in New York declare that it was their work. The Irish say they did it—the Germans that they did it; and the Abolitionists of the locofoco creed exult by proclaiming, "We did it."

What is most striking about the election of 1844 is the closeness of the vote throughout the country. Not only did Polk's percentage of the popular vote lead Clay's by a mere 1.4 percentage points, but in fifteen of the twenty-six states the winning party had a lead of less than 8 percentage points. This parity of party strength testified to the skill with which the politicians of both parties had learned to manipulate their parties' images so as to attract enough social groups to bring them toward a majority.

This party parity having been achieved, large blocks of electoral votes turned on handfuls of popular votes, the 113-vote margin in Tennessee being only the most extreme manifestation of a general situation. Under these circumstances Texas, abolition, Nativism, and the tariff had little to do with most of the votes cast, but everything to do with the result of the election. In these marginal but decisive effects the embittered Clay could see only "a most extraordinary combination of adverse circumstances." "If there had been no Native party," he wrote, "or if all its members had been truer to their principles; or if the recent foreigners had not been all united against us; or if the foreign Catholics had not been arrayed on the other side; or if the Abolitionists had been true to their avowed principles; or if there had been no frauds, we should have triumphed."

Actually the candidates had a great deal to do with these effects, and the decisive factors seem to have been: first, Polk's astute handling of the tariff issue, which saved Pennsylvania; second, Clay's contrastingly maladroit handling of the Texas issue, which kept too many antislavery men out of the Whig ranks in New York; and third, the Whigs' too conspicuous sympathy for Nativism, which brought a host of foreign-born voters into the Democratic ranks.

Appendix

Democratic Platform

1. *Resolved*, That the American Democracy place their trust, not in factitious symbols, not in displays and appeals insulting to the judgment and subversive of the intellect of the people, but in a clear reliance upon the intelligence, patriotism, and the discriminating justice of the American masses.

Resolved, That we regard this as a distinctive feature of our political creed, which we are proud to maintain before the world, as the great moral element in a form of government springing from and upheld by the popular will; and we contrast it with the creed and practice of Federalism, under whatever name or form, which seeks to palsy the will of the constituent, and which conceives no imposture too monstrous for the popular credulity.

Resolved, therefore, That, entertaining these views, the Democratic party of this Union, through their delegates assembled in general convention of the States, coming together in a spirit of concord, of devotion to the doctrines and faith of a free representative government, and appealing to their fellow-citizens for the rectitude of their intentions, renew and reassert before the American people the declaration of principles avowed by them on a former occasion, when, in general convention, they presented their candidates for the popular suffrages.

1. That the Federal Government is one of limited powers, derived solely from the Constitution, and the grants of power shown therein ought to be strictly construed by all the departments and agents of the government, and that it is inexpedient and dangerous to exercise doubtful constitutional powers.

2. That the Constitution does not confer upon the General Government the power to commence or carry on a general system of internal improvements.

3. That the Constitution does not confer authority upon the Federal Government, directly or indirectly, to assume the debts of the several States, contracted for local internal improvements or other State purposes; nor would such assumption be just or expedient.

4. That justice and sound policy forbid the Federal Government to foster one branch of industry to the detriment of another, or to cherish the interests of one portion to the injury of another portion of our common country—that every citizen and every section of the country has a right to demand and insist upon an equality of rights and privileges, and to complete and ample protection of person and property from domestic violence or foreign aggression.

5. That it is the duty of every branch of the government to enforce and practice the most rigid economy in conducting our public affairs, and that no more revenue ought to be raised than is required to defray the necessary expenses of the government.

6. That Congress has no power to charter a United States Bank, that we believe such an institution one of deadly hostility to the best interests of the country, dangerous to our republican institutions and the liberties of the people, and calculated to place the business of the country within the control of a concentrated money power, and above the laws and the will of the people.

7. That Congress has no power, under the Constitution, to interfere with or control the domestic institutions of the several States; and that such States are the sole and proper judges of everything pertaining to their own affairs, not prohibited by the Constitution; that all efforts, by abolitionists or others, made to induce Congress to interfere with questions of slavery, or to take incipient steps in relation thereto, are calculated to lead to the most alarming and dangerous consequences, and that all such efforts have an inevitable tendency to diminish the happiness of the people and endanger the stability and permanency of the Union, and ought not to be countenanced by any friend to our Political Institutions.

8. That the separation of the money of the government from banking institutions is indispensable for the safety of the funds of the government and the rights of the people.

9. That the liberal principles embodied by Jefferson in the Declaration of Independence, and sanctioned in the Constitution, which makes ours the land of liberty and the asylum of the oppressed of every nation, have ever been cardinal principles in the Democratic faith; and every attempt to abridge the present privilege of becoming citizens, and the owners of soil among us, ought to be resisted with the same spirit which swept the alien and sedition laws from our statutebook.

Resolved, That the proceeds of the Public Lands ought to be sacredly applied to the national objects specified in the Constitution, and that we are opposed to the laws lately adopted, and to any law for the Distribution of such proceeds among the States, as alike inexpedient in policy and repugnant to the Constitution.

Resolved, That we are decidedly opposed to taking from the President the qualified veto power by which he is enabled, under restrictions and responsibilities amply sufficient to guard the public interest, to suspend the passage of a bill, whose merits cannot secure the approval of two-thirds of the Senate and House of Representatives, until the judgment of the people can be obtained thereon, and which has thrice saved the American People from the corrupt and tyrannical domination of the Bank of the United States.

Resolved, That our title to the whole of the Territory of Oregon is clear and unquestionable; that no portion of the same ought to be ceded to England or any other power, and that the reoccupation of Oregon and the re-annexation of Texas at the earliest practicable period are great American measures, which this Convention recommends to the cordial support of the Democracy of the Union.

Liberty Platform

PREAMBLE

Being assembled in general Convention, as the representatives of the Liberty party in the United States, and feeling it incumbent on us to set forth, clearly and fully, the principles which govern us, and the purposes which we seek to accomplish, and this, the rather because these principles and purposes have been much misunderstood, and either ignorantly or maliciously much misrepresented: be it therefore

1. *Resolved,* That human brotherhood is a cardinal doctrine of true Democracy, as well as of pure Christianity, which spurns all inconsistent limitations; and neither the political party which repudiates it, nor the political system which is not based upon it, nor controlled in its practical workings, by it, can be truly Democratic or permanent.

2. *Resolved,* That the Liberty party, placing itself upon this broad principle, will demand the absolute and unqualified divorce of the General Government from Slavery, and also the restoration of equality of rights, among men, in every State where the party exists, or may exist.

3. *Resolved,* That the Liberty party has not been organized for any temporary purpose, by interested politicians, but has arisen from among the people, in consequence of a conviction, hourly gaining ground, that no other party in the country represents the true principles of American Liberty, or the true spirit of the Constitution of the United States.

4. *Resolved,* That the Liberty party has not been organized merely for the overthrow of Slavery. Its first decided effort must indeed be directed against slaveholding, as the grossest form and most revolting manifestation of Despotism; but it will also carry out the principles of Equal Rights, into all their practical consequences and applications, and support every just measure conducive to individual and social freedom.

5. *Resolved,* That the Liberty party is not a Sectional party, but a National party—has not originated in a desire to accomplish a single object, but in a comprehensive regard to the great interests of the whole country—is not a new party, or a third party, but is the party of 1776, reviving the principles of that memorable era, and striving to carry them into practical application.

6. *Resolved,* That it was understood in the time of the Declaration and the Constitution, that the existence of slavery in some of the States, was in derogation of the principles of American Liberty, and a deep stain upon the character of the country, and the implied faith of the States and the Nation was pledged, that slavery should never be extended beyond its then existing limits;

but should be gradually, and, yet, at no distant day, wholly abolished by State authority.

7. *Resolved*, That the faith of the States, and the nation they pledged, was most nobly redeemed by the voluntary abolition of slavery in several of the States, and by the adoption of the ordinance of 1787, for the government of the Territory North West of the river Ohio, then the only Territory in the United States, and consequently the only Territory subject in this respect to the control of Congress, by which ordinance slavery was forever excluded from the vast regions which now compose the States of Ohio, Indiana, Illinois, Michigan, and the Territory of Wiskonsan, and an incapacity to bear up any other than freemen, was impressed on the soil itself.

8. *Resolved*, That the faith of the States and Nation thus pledged, has been shamefully violated by the omission, on the part of many of the States, to take any measures whatever for the abolition of slavery within their respective limits; by the continuance of slavery in the District of Columbia, and in the Territories of Louisiana and Florida; by the legislation of Congress; by the protection afforded by national legislation and negotiation to slaveholding in American vessels, on the high seas, employed in the coastwise slave traffic; and by the extension of slavery far beyond its original limits, by acts of Congress, admitting new slave States into the Union.

9. *Resolved*, That the fundamental truths of the Declaration of Independence, that all men are endowed by their Creator with certain inalienable rights, among which are life, liberty, and the pursuit of happiness, was made the fundamental law of our National Government, by that amendment of the constitution which declares that no person shall be deprived of life, liberty or property, without due process of law.

10. *Resolved*, That we recognize as sound, the doctrine maintained by slaveholding Jurists, that slavery is against natural rights, and strictly local, and that its existence and continuance rest on no other support than State legislation, and not on any Authority of Congress.

11. *Resolved*, That the General Government has, under the Constitution, no power to establish or continue slavery any where, and therefore that all treaties and acts of Congress establishing, continuing or favoring slavery in the District of Columbia, in the Territory of Florida, or on the high seas, are unconstitutional, and all attempts to hold men as property within the limits of exclusive national jurisdiction, ought to be prohibited by law.

12. *Resolved*, That the plea sometimes urged, in behalf of the constitutionality of slaveholding under the sanction of national legislation, that the continuance of slavery was secured in the District of Columbia, by stipulations in the Deeds of cession by Virginia and Maryland, and in Florida by the provisions of the Treaty with Spain is false in fact; and the other plea, sometimes urged to the same purpose, that Congress might constitutionally authorize slaveholding in the District, under the power to legislate for the same in all cases whatsoever, and in Florida under the power to make needful rules and regulations for the government of national territories, and in American vessels

on the seas under the power to regulate commerce, cannot be sound in law, so long as the great Interdict of the People against depriving *any person* of life, liberty, or property, without due process of law, remains unaltered.

13. *Resolved*, That the provision of the Constitution of the United States, which confers extraordinary political powers on the owners of slaves, and thereby constituting the two hundred and fifty thousand slaveholders in the slave States a privileged aristocracy; and the provision for the reclamation of fugitive slaves from service, are anti-republican in their character, dangerous to the liberties of the people, and ought to be abrogated.

14. *Resolved*, That the operation of the first of these provisions is seen in the growth of a power in the country, hostile to free institutions, to free labor, and to freedom itself, which is appropriately denominated the slave power; this power has maintained slavery in the original States, has secured its continuance in the District and in the Territories, has created seven new slave States, has caused disastrous fluctuations in our national policy, foreign and domestic, has gradually usurped the control of our home legislation, has waged unrelenting war against the most sacred rights of freedom, has violated and set at naught the right of petition, has dictated the action of political parties, has filled almost all the offices of the National Government with slaveholders, and the abettors of slaveholders, and threatens, if not arrested in its career, the total overthrow of popular freedom.

15. *Resolved*, That the practical operation of the second of these provisions, is seen in the enactment of the act of Congress respecting persons escaped from their masters, which act, if the construction given to it by the Supreme Court of the United States in the case of Prigg *vs.* Pennsylvania be correct, nullifies the habeas corpus acts of all the States, takes away the whole legal security of personal freedom, and ought therefore to be immediately repealed.

16. *Resolved*, That the peculiar patronage and support hitherto extended to slavery and slaveholding, by the General Government, ought to be immediately withdrawn, and the example and influence of national authority ought to be arrayed on the side of Liberty and free labor.

17. *Resolved*, That we cherish no harsh or unkind feelings towards any of our brethren of the slave States, while we express unmitigated abhorrence of that system of slaveholding which has stripped a large portion of their population of every right, and which has established an aristocracy worse than feudal in the midst of Republican States, and which denies to the poor non-slaveholder and his children the benefits of education, and crushes them in the dust, or drives them out as exiles from the land of their birth.

18. *Resolved*, That the impoverished and embarrassed condition of the slave States, so much deplored by their own statesmen, may be clearly traced to the fact that the coerced, reluctant, and ill-directed labor of slaves will not supply their own scanty subsistence, and also support their masters in the habits of wasteful extravagance which slavery generates.

19. *Resolved*, That the withering and impoverishing effect of slavery on the free States, is seen in the fact, among many others, that these States are taxed

to the amount of about half a million of dollars a year, to pay the deficits of the slave States, and that the slave States have received, for years past, to the amount, as it is estimated, of more than ten millions of dollars a year, for which no payment has ever been, or ever will be made.

20. *Resolved*, That we behold with sorrow and shame, and indignation, the dishonor brought upon the name of the country by the influence of the slave power upon our National Government—corrupting its administration at home—paralyzing all generous action and utterance in behalf of right and freedom abroad, and exhibiting the American people to the world in the ridiculous and contemptible character of patrons of the slave trade.

21. *Resolved*, That we are inflexibly opposed to that policy of the General Government, which plies every art, and strains every effort of negotiation, to secure the markets of the world for the products of slave labor, while the products of free labor are to a great extent, confined to the nonpaying market of the slave States; and we insist that it is the duty of the Government, in its intercourse with foreign nations, to employ all its influence, and to exert its utmost energies to extend the markets for the products of free labor, and we do not doubt that if this duty be performed in good faith, the result will be most auspicious to the general and permanent prosperity of the country.

22. *Resolved*, That we are fully persuaded that it is indispensably necessary to the salvation of the union of the States, to the preservation of the liberties of the people, and to the permanent restoration of prosperity in every department of business, that the National Government be rescued from the grasp of the slave power; that the spirit and practice of slaveholding be expelled from our National Legislature, and that the administration of the Government be conducted henceforth in conformity with the principles of the Constitution, and for the benefit of the whole population.

23. *Resolved*, That the practice of the General Government, which prevails in the slave States, of employing slaves upon the public works, instead of free laborers, and paying aristocratic masters, with a view to secure or reward political services, is utterly indefensible, and ought to be abandoned.

24. *Resolved*, That we believe intelligence, religion, and morality, to be the indispensable supports of good government, and are therefore in favor of general education; we believe, also, that good government itself is necessary to the welfare of society, and are therefore in favor of rigid public economy, and strict adherence to the principles of justice in every department of its administration.

25. *Resolved*, That freedom of speech and of the press, and the right of petition, and the right of trial by jury, are sacred and inviolable; and that all rules, regulations and laws, in derogation of either are oppressive, unconstitutional, and not to be endured by a free people.

26. *Resolved*, That we regard voting in an eminent degree, as a moral and religious duty, which when exercised, should be by voting for those who will do all in their power for immediate emancipation.

27. *Resolved*, That we can never lose our vote, although in ever so small a minority, when cast for the slave's redemption; as each vote for the slave,

whether in minority or majority, is a part of that great mass of means which will work out his final deliverance.

28. *Resolved*, That the Whig and Democratic parties always throw away their votes, whether in a majority or minority, and do worse than throw them away, as long as they cast them for binding the slave with fetters, and loading him with chains, and for depriving him of himself, his wife and his children, which these parties always have done, in bowing down to the slaveholding portions of said parties.

29. *Resolved*, That we especially entreat the friends of Liberty in the slave States to reflect on the vast importance of voting openly for Liberty, and Liberty men; and to remember and adopt the words of the illustrious Washington, who said, "There is but one proper and effectual mode by which the abolition of slavery can be accomplished, and that is by legislative authority; and this, as far as my suffrage will go, shall not be wanting."

30. *Resolved*, That we earnestly exhort the Liberty men everywhere, to organize for efficient action in their respective States, counties, cities, towns, and districts, and not to turn to the right side or to the left, until despotism shall have been driven from its last entrenchment, and thanksgivings for victory in the second great struggle for Liberty and Independence shall be heard throughout the land.

31. *Resolved*, That we most earnestly recommend that the Liberty party make efforts to secure the control of the town power, so that every officer shall be a Liberty party man; and that our friends should not fail to nominate a Liberty ticket annually in their towns, and sustain the same, never yielding to a compromise with the other parties.

32. *Resolved*, That a county and State organization of the Liberty party should be faithfully maintained; and we also recommend that our friends employ some proper person to lecture, organize, and distribute tracts in each Congressional district, in the several States, for the space of at least three months in a year.

33. *Resolved*, That the friends of Liberty in each town form tract organizations, of men and women, to distribute tracts in every family in such towns, by directing the labors of said tract distribution, so that no neighborhood or family be overlooked or unsupplied.

34. *Resolved*, That it be recommended that said tract distributors circulate petitions through the several towns, praying Congress to abolish the abominable act of Congress, of the 12th of February, 1793, so that we may be delivered from the unconstitutional obligation to become kidnappers on our own soil.

35. *Resolved*, That this Convention recommend to the friends of Liberty in all those free States where any inequality of rights and privileges exists on account of color, to employ their utmost energies to remove all such remnants and effects of the slave system.

36. *Resolved*, That we cordially welcome our colored fellow citizens to fraternity with us in the *Liberty party*, in its great contest to secure the rights of mankind, and the religion of our common country.

37. *Whereas,* The Constitution of these United States is a series of agree-ments, covenants, or contracts between the people of the United States, each with all, and all with each; and

Whereas, It is a principle of universal morality, that the moral laws of the Creator are paramount to all human laws; or, in the language of an apostle, that "we ought to obey God, rather than men;"—and

Whereas, The principle of Common Law—that any contract, covenant, or agreement, to do an act derogatory to natural right, is vitiated and annulled by its inherent immorality—has been recognized by one of the Justices of the Supreme Court of the United States, who, in a recent case, expressly holds that "*any* contract that rests upon such a basis, is *void*";—and

Whereas, The third clause of the second section of the fourth article of the Constitution of the United States—when construed as providing for the surrender of a fugitive slave—*does* "rest upon such a basis," in that it is a contract to rob a man of a natural right—namely, his natural right to his own liberty; and is, therefore, absolutely *void.*

Therefore, Resolved, That we hereby give it to be distinctly understood, by this nation and the world, that, as abolitionists, considering that the strength of our cause lies in its righteousness—and our hope for it in our conformity to the LAWS OF GOD, and our respect for the RIGHTS OF MAN, we owe it to the Sovereign Ruler of the Universe, as a proof of our allegiance to Him, in all our civil relations and offices, whether as private citizens, or as public functionaries sworn to support the Constitution of the United States, to re-gard and to treat the third clause of the second section of the fourth article of that instrument, whenever applied to the case of a fugitive slave, as utterly null and void, and consequently as forming no part of the Constitution of the United States, whenever we are called upon, or sworn, to support it.

38. *Resolved,* That the power given to Congress by the Constitution, to provide for calling out the militia to suppress insurrection, does not make it the duty of the Government to maintain slavery, by military force, much less does it make it the duty of the citizens to form a part of such military force. When freemen unsheath the sword it should be to strike for *Liberty*, not for Despotism.

39. *Resolved,* That to preserve the peace of the citizens, and secure the blessings of freedom, the Legislature of each of the free States, ought to keep in force suitable statutes rendering it penal for any of its inhabitants to trans-port, or aid in transporting from such State, any person sought, to be thus transported, merely because subject to the slave laws of any other States; this remnant of independence being accorded to the free States, by the decision of the Supreme Court, in the case of Prigg, *vs.* the State of Pennsylvania.

40. *Resolved,* That we recognize in Daniel O'Connell, a true Patriot of the Liberty school, and admire his consistent devotion to freedom throughout the world. We thank him and the Irish people whom he represents, for their sympathy with us in our great struggle.

41. *Resolved,* That the thanks of this Convention are hereby tendered to Professor Taylor, for his kindness in furnishing the spacious tent, belonging

to the Oberlin Collegiate Institute, which has been occupied by the Convention during its sittings.

42. *Resolved*, That the doings of the Convention be published, under the direction of the Secretaries.

43. *Resolved*, That the thanks of this Convention be tendered to the authorities of the County of Erie, and of the city of Buffalo, for the use of the Court House and the Park for its sittings.

44. *Resolved*, That the thanks of this Convention be presented to the President, Vice-Presidents, and Secretaries, for their services during its session.

Whig Platform

Resolved, That, in presenting to the country the names of Henry Clay for president, and of Theodore Frelinghuysen for vice-president of the United States, this Convention is actuated by the conviction that all the great principles of the Whig party — principles inseparable from the public honor and prosperity — will be maintained and advanced by these candidates.

Resolved, That these principles may be summed as comprising, a well-regulated currency; a tariff for revenue to defray the necessary expenses of the government, and discriminating with special reference to the protection of the domestic labor of the country; the distribution of the proceeds of the sales of the public lands; a single term for the presidency; a reform of executive usurpations; — and, generally — such an administration of the affairs of the country as shall impart to every branch of the public service the greatest practicable efficiency, controlled by a well regulated and wise economy.

Resolved, That the name of Henry Clay needs no eulogy; the history of the country since his first appearance in public life is his history; its brightest pages of prosperity and success are identified with the principles which he has upheld, as its darkest and more disastrous pages are with every material departure in our public policy from those principles.

Resolved, That in Theodore Frelinghuysen we present a man pledged alike by his revolutionary ancestry and his own public course to every measure calculated to sustain the honor and interest of the country. Inheriting the principles as well as the name of a father who, with Washington, on the fields of Trenton and of Monmouth, perilled life in the contest for liberty, and afterwards, as a senator of the United States, acted with Washington in establishing and perpetuating that liberty, Theodore Frelinghuysen, by his course as Attorney-General of the State of New Jersey for twelve years, and subsequently as a senator of the United States for several years, was always strenuous on the side of law, order, and the constitution, while as a private man, his head, his hand, and his heart have been given without stint to the cause of morals, education, philanthropy, and religion.

Address by John C. Calhoun
Fort Hill, South Carolina, December 21, 1843

Nearly a half year before the Democrats convened in Baltimore, John C. Calhoun withdrew on ideological grounds as a candidate for his party's presidential nomination.

I have left it to you, my friends and supporters, through whose favorable estimate of my qualifications my name has been presented to the people of the United States for the office of chief magistrate, to conduct the canvass on such principles, and in such manner, as you may think best. But in so doing, I did not waive my right to determine, on my individual responsibility, what course my duty might compel me to pursue ultimately, nor have I been an inattentive observer of the canvass and the course you have taken.

It affords me pleasure to be enabled to say, that on all leading questions, growing out of the canvass, I heartily concurred with you, in the grounds you took, and especially in those relating to the mode in which the delegates to the proposed convention to be held in Baltimore should be appointed, and how they should vote. You have, in my opinion, conclusively shown, that they should be appointed by districts, and vote *per capita;* but your reasons, as conclusive as they are, have proved in vain. Already New York and some other States have appointed delegates *en masse* by State conventions, and one State (Virginia) has resolved that the votes of her delegates should be given by the majority, and be counted *per capita.* Their course would necessarily overrule that which you have so ably supported, should you go into convention, and would leave you no alternative, but to yield yours and adopt theirs, however much you may be opposed to it on principle, or to meet them on the most unequal terms, with divided against united and concentrated forces.

The question, then, is, what course, under such circumstances, should be adopted? And that question you will be compelled speedily to decide. The near approach of the time for the meeting of the proposed convention will not admit of much longer delay. But as your course may depend, in some degree, on that which I have decided to take, I deem it due to the relation subsisting between us, to make mine known to you without further delay.

I, then, after the most careful and deliberate survey of the whole ground, have decided that I cannot permit my name to go before the proposed convention, constituted as it must now be, consistently with the principles which have ever guided my public conduct. My objections are insuperable. As it must be constituted, it is repugnant to all the principles on which, in my opinion, such a convention should be formed. What those principles are, I shall now proceed briefly to state.

I hold, then, with you, that the convention should be so constituted as to utter fully and clearly the voice of the people, and not that of political managers, or office-holders, and office-seekers; and for that purpose, I hold it indispensable that the delegates should be appointed directly by the people, or, to use the language of General Jackson, should be "fresh from the people." I also hold, that the only possible mode to effect this, is for the people to choose the delegates by districts, and that they should vote *per capita*. Every other mode of appointing would be controlled by political machinery, and place the appointments in the hands of the few who work it.

I object, then, to the proposed convention, because it will not be constituted in conformity with this fundamental article of the republican creed. The delegates to it will be appointed from some of the States, not by the people in districts, but, as has been stated, by State Conventions, *en masse*, composed of delegates, appointed in all cases, as far as I am informed, by county or district conventions; and, in some cases, if not misinformed, these again composed of delegates appointed by still smaller divisions, or a few interested individuals. Instead, then, of being directly, or fresh from the people, the delegates to the Baltimore convention will be the delegates of delegates; and of course removed, in all cases, at least three, if not four, degrees from the people. At each successive remove, the voice of the people will become less full and distinct, until, at last, it will be so faint and imperfect as not to be audible. To drop metaphor, I hold it impossible to form a scheme more perfectly calculated to annihilate the control of the people over the presidential election, and vest it in those who make politics a trade, and who live, or expect to live, on the government.

In this connexion, I object not less strongly to the mode in which Virginia has resolved her delegates shall vote. . . . There is, indeed, something monstrous in the idea of giving the majority the right of impressing the vote of the minority into its service, and counting them as its own. The plain rule —that which has ever prevailed, and which conforms to the dictates of common sense, is, that where a State votes as a State, by a majority of its delegates, the votes count one, be they few or many, or the State large or small. On the contrary, where the votes of all the delegates are counted they vote individually and independently each for himself counting one. . . . The course which Virginia has resolved to take, is in violation of this plain and fundamental rule; and, if it should become a settled practice, would be destructive of the foundation on which the whole structure of the State-right doctrine is reared.

I hold it, in the next place, to be an indispensable principle, that the convention should be so constituted as to give each State, in the nomination of a candidate, the same relative weight which the constitution secures to it in the election of the President, making allowance for its relative party strength. By the election, I mean the whole, the eventual choice, when it goes into the House of Representatives, as well as the primary vote in the electoral college. The one is as much a part of the election as the other. The two make the whole. The adoption of the one, in the convention which framed the constitution, depended on the adoption of the other. Neither could possibly be adopted alone. The two were the result of compromise between the larger and smaller States, after a long and doubtful struggle, which threatened the loss of the constitution itself. The object of giving to the smaller States an equality with

the larger, in the eventual choice by the House, was to counterpoise the preponderance of the larger in the electoral college. Without this, the smaller
would have voted against the whole provision, and its rejection would have
been the consequence. Even as it stands, Delaware voted against it. In confirmation of what I state, I refer to Mr. Madison's report on the proceedings
of the convention.

Having stated what I mean by the election, it will require but a few words
to explain my reasons for the principles I have laid down. They are few and
simple, and rest on the ground that the nomination is in reality the election, if
concurred in, as far as the party is concerned. It is so intended to be. The leading reason assigned for making it, is to prevent a division of the party, and
thereby prevent the election from going into the House, where the smaller
States would have the advantage intended to be secured to them by the constitution, by being placed on an equality with the larger.

Such being the intended object and effect, I now submit to every candid
mind, whether the convention ought not to be so constituted as to compensate,
in the nomination for the important advantage in the election, which the smaller
States surrender by going into a convention. . . .

I object, then, to the proposed convention, in this connexion, because it
makes no compensation to the smaller States for the surrender of this unquestionable and important constitutional right. . . . I regard the adjustment of the
relative weight of the States in the government to be the fundamental compromise of the constitution, and that on which our whole political system
depends. . . .

*   *   *

The preservation of the relative weight of the States, as established by the
constitution in all the departments, is necessary to the success and duration of
our system of government; but it may be doubted, whether the provision
adopted to effect it in the executive department, is not too refined for the strong,
and I may add, corrupt passions, which the presidential election will ever
exeite. Certain it is, that if the practice of nominating candidates for the presidency, by conventions constituted as they proposed, shall become the established usage, it will utterly defeat the intention of the framers of the constitution, and would be followed by a radical and dangerous change, not only in
the executive department, but in the government itself.

*   *   *

I have laid down the principle, on which I rest the objection in question,
with the limitation that the relative weight of the States should be maintained,
making due allowing for their relative party strength. The propriety of the
limitation is so apparent, that but a few words, in illustration, will be required.
The convention is a party convention, and professedly intended to take the
sense of the party, which cannot be done fairly, if States having but little party
strength are put on an equality with those which have much. If that were
done, the result might be that a small portion of the party from States the least
sound politically, and which could give but little support in Congress, might
select the candidate, and make the President, against a great majority of the
soundest, and on which the President and his administration would have to

rely for support. All this is clearly too unfair and improper to be denied. There may be a great difficulty in applying a remedy in a convention; but I do not feel myself called upon to say how it can be done, or by what standard the relative party strength of the respective States should be determined. Perhaps the best would be their relative strength in Congress at the time. . . .

But, in order to realize how the convention will operate, it will be necessary to view the combined effects of the objections which I have made. Thus viewed it will be found, that a convention so constituted, tends irresistibly to centralization—centralization of the control over the presidential election in the hands of a few of the central, large States, at first, and finally, in political managers, office holders and office seekers; or to express it differently, in that portion of the community who live, or expect to live, on the government, in contradistinction to the great mass, who expect to live on their own means or their honest industry, and who maintain the government, and, politically speaking, emphatically the people.

That such would be the case, may be inferred from the fact, that it would afford the means to some six or seven States lying contiguous and not far from the centre of the Union, to control the nomination, and through that the election, by concentrating their united votes in the convention. . . .

But the tendency to centralization will not stop there. The appointment of delegates *en masse* by State convention, would tend, at the same time and even with greater force, to centralize this control in the hands of the few, who make politics a trade. The farther the convention is removed from the people, the more certainly the control over it will be placed in the hands of the interested few; and when removed three or four degrees, as has been shown it will be, where the appointment is by State conventions, the power of the people will cease, and the seekers of executive favor will become supreme. At that stage, an active, trained, and combined corps will be formed in the party, whose whole time and attention will be directed to politics. It will be their sole business. Into their hands the appointment of delegates in all the stages will fall, and they will take special care that none but themselves or their humble and obedient dependants shall be appointed. The central and State conventions will be filled by the most experienced and cunning, and after nominating the President, they will take good care to divide the patronage and offices, both of the general and State governments, among themselves and their dependants. But why say *will*? It is not *already the case*? Have there not been many instances of State conventions being filled by office-holders and office-seekers, who, after making the nomination, have divided the offices in the State among themselves and their partisans, and joined in recommending to the candidate whom they have just nominated to appoint them to the offices to which they have been respectively allotted? If such be the case in the infancy of the system, it must end, if such conventions should become the established usage, in the President nominating his successor. When it comes to that, it will not be long before the sword will take the place of the constitution.

*   *   *

That which they have urged with the greatest confidence is, that each State has a right to appoint delegates as she pleases. . . . I have, I also trust, shown more—that the supposed right is perfectly deceptive; for while it claims for each State the right to appoint delegates as it pleases, it in reality gives the larger States the right to dictate how the others shall appoint. If, for example, the Empire State (as it is called) adopts the mode of appointing (as she has) which will concentrate her whole strength, what discretion would she leave to others, if they go into convention, but to appoint as she has appointed, or to be ruled by her. It is, then, neither more nor less than a claim to dictate, under the garb of a right, and such its exercise has proved in the present case. It has left no option, but to conform to her course, or be overruled, or refuse to go into the convention.

I regret this, because I sincerely desire to preserve the harmony of the party. I had strong hope that the rally after the defeat of 1840 would be exclusively on principles. This hope was greatly strengthened by the truly republican and noble stand taken at the extra session, and the earlier portion of the succeeding regular session. During that period of rigid adherence to principle, perfect harmony pervaded the ranks of the party. I beheld it with joy. I believed the moments highly favorable for the thorough reformation of the government and the restoration of the constitution. To the republican party I looked for the accomplishment of this great work; and I accordingly felt the deepest solicitude that the stand taken, and the harmony which existed, should be preserved. In order that it should, I made up my mind to waive the objection, which I have long entertained to any intermediate body, unknown to the constitution, between the people and the election of the President, in the hope that the proposed convention would be so constituted that I might consistently, with my principles, give it my support. In this I have been disappointed, and being so, I am compelled to decide as I have done. The same motives which impelled me to separate from the administration of Gen. Jackson, in the plentitude of its power, and to come to the rescue of Mr. Van Buren's at its greatest depression, compels me now to withhold my name from the proposed convention.

Having now assigned my reasons for refusing to permit my name to go before the Baltimore convention, it rests with you, who have placed it before the people, and assented to abide by a convention fairly constituted, to determine what course you will pursue.

Be your decision what it may, I shall be content. But I regarded it as due to the occasion, to you and myself, to declare, that under no circumstances whatever shall I support any candidate who is opposed to free trade, and in favor of the protective policy, or whose prominent and influential friends and supporters are. . . .

                                        *   *   *

Much less, still, can I give my support to any candidate who shall give his aid or countenance to the agitation of abolition in Congress or elsewhere; or whose prominent and influential friends and supporters shall. . . . I regard the deluded fanatic far less guilty and dangerous than he who, for political or party purposes, aids or countenances him in what he knows is intended to do that which he acknowledges to be forbidden by the constitution.

It is time that an end should be put to this system of plunder and agitation. They have been borne long enough. They are kindred measures, and hostile, as far, at least, as one portion of the Union is concerned. While the tariff takes from us the proceeds of our labor, abolition strikes at the labor itself. The one robs us of our income, while the other aims at destroying the source from which that income is derived. It is impossible for us to stand patiently much longer, under their double operation, without being impoverished and ruined.

Letter from Henry Clay to the Washington *National Intelligencer*
April 17, 1844

Henry Clay, the leading Whig presidential candidate, opposed the annexation of Texas, claiming that it would be tantamount to a declaration of war on Mexico — a position he would soon regret.

Gentlemen: Subsequent to my departure from Ashland, in December last, I received various communications from popular assemblages and private individuals, requesting an expression of my opinion upon the question of the annexation of Texas to the United States. . . . During my sojourn in New Orleans, I had, indeed, been greatly surprised, by information which I received from Texas, that, in the course of last fall, a voluntary overture had proceeded from the executive of the United States to the authorities of Texas to conclude a treaty of annexation; and that, in order to overcome the repugnance felt by any of them to a negotiation upon the subject, strong and, as I believed, erroneous representations had been made to them of a state of opinion in the Senate of the U. States favorable to the ratification of such a treaty. According to these representations, it had been ascertained that a number of senators, varying from thirty-five to forty-two, were ready to sanction such a treaty. I was aware, too, that holders of Texas lands and Texas scrip, and speculators in them, were actively engaged in promoting the object of annexation. Still, I did not believe that any executive of the United States would venture upon so grave and momentous a proceeding, not only without any general manifestation of public opinion in favor of it, but in direct opposition to strong and decided expressions of public disapprobation. But it appears that I was mistaken. To the astonishment of the whole nation, we are now informed that a treaty of annexation has been actually concluded, and is to be submitted to the senate for its consideration.

If, without the loss of national character, without the hazard of foreign war, with the general concurrence of the nation, without any danger to the integrity of the Union, and without giving an unreasonable price for Texas, the question of annexation were presented, it would appear in quite a different light from that in which, I apprehend, it is now to be regarded.

*　　*　　*

After the battle of San Jacinto, the U. States recognised the independence of Texas, in conformity with the principle and practice which have always prevailed in their councils of recognising the government "*de facto*," without regarding the question *de jure*. That recognition did not affect or impair the rights of Mexico, or change the relations which existed between her and Texas. She, on the contrary, has preserved all her rights, and has continued to assert, and so far as I know yet asserts, her right to reduce Texas to obedience, as a part of the republic of Mexico. — . . . Under these circumstances, if the government of the United States were to acquire Texas, it would acquire along

814

with it all the incumbrances which Texas is under, and among them the actual or suspended war between Mexico and Texas. Of that consequence there cannot be a doubt. Annexation and war with Mexico are identical. Now, for one, I certainly am not willing to involve this country in a foreign war for the object of acquiring Texas. I know there are those who regard such a war with indifference and as a trifling affair, on account of the weakness of Mexico, and her inability to inflict serious injury upon this country. But I do not look upon it thus lightly. I regard all wars as great calamities, to be avoided, if possible, and honorable peace as the wisest and truest policy of this country. What the United States most need are union, peace, and patience. Nor do I think that the weakness of a power should form a motive, in any case, for inducing us to engage in or to depreciate the evils of war. — Honor and good faith and justice are equally due from this country towards the weak as towards the strong. And, if an act of injustice were to be perpetrated towards any power, it would be more compatible with the dignity of the nation, and, in my judgment, less dishonorable, to inflict it upon a powerful instead of a weak foreign nation. But are we perfectly sure that we should be free from injury in a state of war with Mexico? Have we any security that countless numbers of foreign vessels, under the authority and flag of Mexico, would not prey upon our defenceless commerce in the Mexican gulf, on the Pacific ocean, and on every other sea and ocean? What commerce, on the other hand, does Mexico offer, as an indemnity for our losses, to the gallantry and enterprise of our countrymen? This view of the subject supposes that the war would be confined to the United States and Mexico as the only belligerents. But have we any certain guaranty that Mexico would obtain no allies among the great European powers? Suppose any such powers, jealous of our increasing greatness, and disposed to check our growth and cripple us, were to take part in behalf of Mexico in the war, how would the different belligerents present themselves to Christendom and the enlightened world? We have been seriously charged with an inordinate spirit of territorial aggrandizement; and, without admitting the justice of the charge, it must be owned that we have made vast acquisitions of territory within the last forty years. Suppose Great Britain and France, or one of them, were to take part with Mexico, and, by a manifesto, were to proclaim that their objects were to assist a weak and helpless ally to check the spirit of encroachment and ambition of an already overgrown republic, seeking still further acquisitions of territory, to maintain the independence of Texas, disconnected with the United States and to prevent the further propagation of slavery from the United States, what would be the effect of such allegations upon the judgment of an impartial and enlightened world?

Assuming that the annexation of Texas is war with Mexico, is it competent to the treaty-making power to plunge this country into war, not only without the concurrence of, but without deigning to consult congress, to which, by the constitution, belongs exclusively the power of declaring war?

I have hitherto considered the question upon the supposition that the annexation is attempted without the assent of Mexico. If she yields her consent, that would materially affect the foreign aspect of the question, if it did not remove all foreign difficulties. On the assumption of that assent; the question would be confined to the domestic considerations which belong to it, embracing the terms and conditions upon which annexation is proposed. I do not think that Texas ought to be received into the Union, as an integral part of it, in decided opposition to the wishes of a considerable and respectable portion of the confederacy. I think it far more wise and important to compose and harmonize the present confederacy, as it now exists, than to introduce a new element of discord and distraction into it.

*   *   *

It is useless to disguise that there are those who espouse and those who oppose the annexation of Texas upon the ground of the influence which it would exert, in the balance of political power, between two great sections of the Union. I conceive that no motive for the acquisition of foreign territory would be more unfortunate, or pregnant with more fatal consequences, than that of obtaining it for the purpose of strengthening one part against another part of the common confederacy. Such a principle, put into practical operation, would menace the existence, if it did not certainly sow the seeds of a dissolution of the Union. . . . For if today Texas be acquired to strengthen one part of the confederacy, to-morrow Canada may be required to add strength to another. . . . Finally, in the progress of this spirit of universal dominion, the part of the confederacy which is now weakest, would find itself still weaker from the impossibility of securing new theatres for those peculiar institutions which it is charged with being desirous to extend.

But would Texas, ultimately, really add strength to that which is now considered the weakest part of the confederacy? If my information be correct, it would not. According to that, the territory of Texas is susceptible of a division into five states of convenient size and form. Of these, two only would be adapted to those peculiar institutions to which I have referred, and the other three, lying west and north of San Antonio, being only adapted to farming and grazing purposes, from the nature of their soil, climate, and productions, would not admit of those institutions. In the end, therefore, there would be two slave and three free states probably added to the Union. If this view of the soil and geography of Texas be correct, it might serve to diminish the zeal both of those who oppose and those who are urging annexation.

Should Texas be annexed to the Union, the United States will assume and become responsible for the debt of Texas, be its amount what it may. What it is, I do not know certainly; but the least I have seen it stated at is thirteen millions of dollars.

*   *   *

If any European nation entertains any ambitious designs upon Texas, such as that of colonizing her, or in any way subjugating her, I should regard it as the imperative duty of the government of the United States to oppose to such designs the most firm and determined resistance, to the extent, if necessary, of appealing to arms to prevent the accomplishment of any such designs.

*   *   *

From what I have seen and heard, I believe that Great Britain has recently formally and solemnly disavowed any such aims or purposes—has declared that she is desirous only of the independence of Texas, and that she has no intention to interfere in her domestic institutions. If she has made such disavowal and declaration, I presume they are in the possession of the executive.

In the future progress of events, it is probable that there will be a voluntary or forcible separation of the British North American possessions from the parent country. I am strongly inclined to think that it will be best for the happiness of all parties that, in that event, they should be erected into a separate and independent republic. With the Canadian republic on one side, that of Texas on the other, and the United States, the friend of both, between them, each could advance its own happiness by such constitutions, laws, and measures, as were best adapted to its peculiar condition. They would be natural allies, ready, by co-operation, to repel any European or foreign attack upon either. . . . Although I have felt compelled, from the nature of the inquiries addressed to me, to extend this communication to a much greater length than I could have wished, I could not do justice to the subject, and fairly and fully expose my own opinions in a shorter space. In conclusion, they may be stated in a few words to be, that I consider the annexation of Texas, at this time, without the assent of Mexico, as a measure compromising the national character, involving us certainly in war with Mexico, probably with other foreign powers, dangerous to the integrity of the Union, inexpedient in the present financial condition of the country, and not called for by any general expression of public opinion.

I am, respectfully, your obedient servant.

Letter from Secretary of State John C. Calhoun
to British Minister Richard Pakenham
April 18, 1844

At the time the Senate was debating the annexation of Texas, John C. Calhoun was lecturing British Minister Pakenham on the blessings of slavery and the desirability of procuring Texas as a new slave territory.

The undersigned, Secretary of State of the United States, has laid before the President the note of the Right Honorable Mr. Pakenham, envoy extraordinary and minister plenipotentiary of Her Britannic Majesty, addressed to this department on the 26th of February last, together with the accompanying copy of a despatch of Her Majesty's Principal Secretary of State for Foreign Affairs to Mr. Pakenham. In reply, the undersigned is directed by the President to inform the Right Honorable Mr. Pakenham, that, while he regards with pleasure the disavowal of Lord Aberdeen of any intention on the part of Her Majesty's Government "to resort to any measures, either openly or secretly, which can tend to disturb the internal tranquillity of the slave-holding States, and thereby affect the tranquillity of this Union," he at the same time regards with deep concern the avowal, for the first time made to this Government, "that Great Britain desires and is constantly exerting herself to procure the general abolition of slavery throughout the world."

So long as Great Britain confined her policy to the abolition of slavery in her own possessions and colonies, no other country had a right to complain. It belonged to her exclusively to determine, according to her own views of policy, whether it should be done or not. But when she goes beyond, and avows it as her settled policy, and the object of her constant exertions, to abolish it throughout the world, she makes it the duty of all other countries, whose safety or prosperity may be endangered by her policy, to adopt such measures as they may deem necessary for their protection.

It is with still deeper concern the President regards the avowal of Lord Aberdeen of the desire of Great Britain to see slavery abolished in Texas, and, as he infers, is endeavoring, through her diplomacy, to accomplish it, by making the abolition of slavery one of the conditions on which Mexico should acknowledge her independence. It has confirmed his previous impressions as to the policy of Great Britain in reference to Texas . . .

. . . the consummation of the avowed object of her wishes in reference to Texas would be followed by hostile feelings and relations between that country and the United States, which could not fail to place her under the influence and control of Great Britain. This, from the geographical position of Texas, would expose the weakest and most vulnerable portion of our frontier to inroads, and place in the power of Great Britain the most efficient means of effecting in the neighboring States of this Union what she avows to be her

818

desire to do in all countries where slavery exists. To hazard consequences which would be so dangerous to the prosperity and safety of this Union, without resorting to the most effective measures to prevent them, would be, on the part of the Federal Government, an abandonment of the most solemn obligation imposed by the guarantee which the States, in adopting the Constitution, entered into to protect each other against whatever might endanger their safety, whether from without or within. Acting in obedience to this obligation, on which our federal system of Government rests, the President directs me to inform you that a treaty has been concluded between the United States and Texas, for the annexation of the latter to the former as a part of its territory, which will be submitted without delay to the Senate, for its approval. This step has been taken as the most effectual, if not the only means of guarding against the threatened danger, and securing their permanent peace and welfare.

It is well known that Texas has long desired to be annexed to this Union; that her people, at the time of the adoption of her Constitution, expressed, by an almost unanimous vote, her desire to that effect: and that she has never ceased to desire it, as the most certain means of promoting her safety and prosperity. The United States have heretofore declined to meet her wishes; but the time has now arrived when they can no longer refuse, consistently with their own security and peace, and the sacred obligation imposed by their constitutional compact for mutual defence and protection. Nor are they any way responsible for the circumstances which have imposed this obligation on them. They had no agency in bringing about the state of things which has terminated in the separation of Texas from Mexico. . . .

They are equally without responsibility for that state of things, already adverted to as the immediate cause of imposing on them, in self-defence, the obligation of adopting the measure they have. They remained passive so long as the policy on the part of Great Britain, which has led to its adoption, had no immediate bearing on their peace and safety. While they conceded to Great Britain the right of adopting whatever policy she might deem best, in reference to the African race, within her own possessions, they on their part claim the same right for themselves. The policy she has adopted in reference to the portion of that race in her dominions may be humane and wise; but it does not follow, if it prove so with her, that it would be so in reference to the United States and other countries, whose situation differs from hers. But, whether it would be or not, it belongs to each to judge and determine for itself. With us it is a question to be decided, not by the Federal Government, but by each member of this Union, for itself, according to its own views of its domestic policy, and without any right on the part of the Federal Government to interfere in any manner whatever. Its rights and duties are limited to protecting, under the guarantees of the Constitution, each member of this Union, in whatever policy it may adopt in reference to the portion within its respective limits. A large number of the States has decided, that it is neither wise nor humane to change the relation which has existed, from their first settlement, between the two races; while others, where the African is less numerous, have adopted the opposite policy.

It belongs not to the Government to question whether the former have decided wisely or not; and if it did, the undersigned would not regard this as the proper occasion to discuss the subject. He does not, however, deem it irrelevant to state that, if the experience of more than half a century is to decide, it would be neither humane nor wise in them to change their policy. The census and other authentic documents show that, in all instances in which the States have changed the former relation between the two races, the condition of the African, instead of being improved, has become worse. They have been invariably sunk into vice and pauperism, accompanied by the bodily and mental inflictions incident thereto—deafness, blindness, insanity, and idiocy —to a degree without example; while, in all other States which have retained the ancient relation between them, they have improved greatly in every respect —in number, comfort, intelligence, and morals—as the following facts, taken from such sources, will serve to illustrate:

The number of deaf and dumb, blind, idiots, and insane, of the negroes in the States that have changed the ancient relation between the races, is one out of every ninety-six; while in the States adhering to it, it is one out of every six hundred and seventy-two—that is, seven to one in favor of the latter, as compared with the former.

The number of whites, deaf and dumb, blind, idiots, and insane, in the States that have changed the relation, is one in every five hundred and sixty-one; being nearly six to one against the free blacks in the same States.

The number of negroes who are deaf and dumb, blind, idiots, and insane, paupers, and in prison in the States that have changed, is one out of every six; and in the States that have not, one out of every one hundred and fifty-four; or twenty-two to one against the former, as compared with the latter.

Taking the two extremes of North and South—in the State of Maine, the number of negroes returned as deaf and dumb, blind, insane, and idiots, by the census of 1840, is one out of every twelve; and in Florida, by the same returns, is one out of every eleven hundred and five; or ninety-two to one in favor of the slaves of Florida, as compared with the free blacks of Maine.

In addition, it deserves to be remarked, that in Massachusetts, where the change in the ancient relation of the two races was first made (now more than sixty years since), where the greatest zeal has been exhibited in their behalf, and where their number is comparatively few (but little more than 8,000 in a population of upwards of 730,000), the condition of the African is amongst the most wretched. By the latest authentic accounts, there was one out of every twenty-one of the black population in jails or houses of correction; and one out of every thirteen was either deaf and dumb, blind, idiot, insane, or in prison. On the other hand, the census and other authentic sources of information establish the fact that the condition of the African race throughout all the States, where the ancient relation between the two has been retained, enjoys a degree of health and comfort which may well compare with that of the laboring population of any country in Christendom; and it may be added, that in no other condition, or in any other age or country, has the negro race ever attained so high an elevation in morals, intelligence, or civilization.

If such be the wretched condition of the race in their changed relation, where their number is comparatively few, and where so much interest is manifested for their improvement, what would it be in those States where the two races are nearly equal in numbers, and where, in consequence, would necessarily spring up mutual fear, jealousy, and hatred, between them? It may, in truth, be assumed as a maxim, that two races differing so greatly and in so many respects, cannot possibly exist together in the same country, where their numbers are nearly equal, without the one being subjected to the other. Experience has proved that the existing relation, in which the one is subjected to the other, in the slaveholding States, is consistent with the peace and safety of both, with great improvement to the inferior; while the same experience proves that the relation which it is the desire and object of Great Britain to substitute in its stead in this and all other countries, under the plausible name of the abolition of slavery, would (if it did not destroy the inferior by conflicts, to which it would lead) reduce it to the extremes of vice and wretchedness. In this view of the subject it may be asserted, that what is called slavery is in reality a political institution, essential to the peace, safety, and prosperity of those States of the Union in which it exists. Without, then, controverting the wisdom and humanity of the policy of Great Britain, so far as her own possessions are concerned, it may be safely affirmed, without reference to the means by which it would be affected, that, could she succeed in accomplishing, in the United States, what she avows to be her desire and the object of her constant exertions to effect throughout the world, so far from being wise or humane, she would involve in the greatest calamity the whole country, and especially the race which it is the avowed object of her exertions to benefit.

*   *   *

Letter from Martin Van Buren to W. H. Hammet
April 20, 1844

Martin Van Buren went against the thinking of his own party and opposed the annexation of Texas on moral grounds. His conscience in this matter cost him the Democratic nomination.

My dear sir: Your letter of the 28th of March last, was duly received.

Acting as an unpledged delegate to the Baltimore convention you ask my opinion in regard to the constitutionality and expediency of an immediate annexation of Texas to the United States, or as soon as the assent of Texas may be had to such annexation. . . .

*   *   *

. . . There is no express power giving to any department of the government to purchase territory except for the objects specified in the constitution, viz: for arsenals, &c.; but the power has, on several very important occasions, been regarded as embraced in the treaty-making power; and territories have been so annexed with a view and under engagements for their ultimate admission into the Union as states.

If there be nothing in the situation or condition of the territory of Texas, which would render its admission hereafter into the Union as a new state improper, I cannot perceive any objection, on constitutional grounds, to its annexation as a territory. In speaking of the right to admit new states, I must, of course, be understood as referring to the power of congress. The executive and senate may, as I have already observed, by the exercise of the treaty-making power, acquire territory; but new states can only be admitted by congress; and the sole authority over the subject, which is given to it by the constitution, is contained in the following provision, viz: "new states may be admitted by the congress into this Union." . . . That these words, taken by themselves, are broad enough to authorize the admission of the territory of Texas, cannot, I think, be well doubted; nor do I perceive upon what principle we can set up limitations to a power so unqualifiedly recognized by the constitution in the plain simple words I have quoted, and with which no other provision of that instrument conflicts in the slightest degree. But if, with no other guides than our own discretion, we assume limitations upon a power so general, we are at least bound to give to them some intelligible and definite character. The most natural, and indeed the only one of that nature which has been suggested, and which was presented by Mr. Jefferson whilst he entertained doubts in respect to the constitutional power to admit Louisiana, is, that the new states to be admitted must be formed out of territory, not foreign, but which constituted a part of the United States, at the declaration of independence, or the adoption of the constitution. So far from there being any thing in the language of the constitution, or to be found in the extraneous and cotemporaneous circumstances which preceded and attended its adoption, to show that such was the intentions of its framers, they are, in my judgment, all strongly the other way. . . .

*   *   *

The proposition to restrict the power to admit new states to the territory without the original limits of the United States, was distinctly before the convention, once adopted by it, and finally rejected in favor of a clause making the power in this respect general. . . .

*   *   *

— Having thus given you my views upon the constitutional question, I will, with the same frankness, answer the remaining portion of your inquiries, viz: the expediency of immediately annexing Texas to the United States, or so soon as her consent to such annexation may be obtained.

*   *   *

. . . Many persons who enter upon the consideration of the subject with the purest intention and are incapable of knowingly giving a false interpretation to anything connected with it, take it for granted that the United States, in recognising the independence of Texas, declared to the world, not only that she was independent *in fact*, but also that she was such *of right*. Acting upon this erroneous construction, they very naturally conclude, that having gone thus far, having examined into and passed not only upon the existence of her independence, but also upon her right to its enjoyment, it is now (and more especially after the lapse of several years) too late to hesitate upon the question of annexation on the ground of any existing controversy upon those points. The fallacy of this reasoning will be apparent when it is considered that the usage of nations to acknowledge the government, *de facto*, of every country, was established for the express purpose of avoiding all inquiry into, or the expression of any opinion upon, the question of *right* between the contending parties. . . .

In respect to all beyond this, the laws and usages of nations require the observance of a strict neutrality between the contending parties, as long as the war lasts. . . .

I return now to the question. Has the condition of the contest between Texas and Mexico, for the sovereignty of the former, so far changed as to render these principles now inapplicable? What is the attitude which these two states at this moment occupy towards each other? Are they at war, or are they not? We cannot evade this question if we would. — To enumerate all the circumstances bearing upon it, in a communication like this, would be impracticable, nor is it necessary. In respect to the parties themselves, there would seem to be no misunderstanding upon the subject. Mexico has been incessant in her avowal, as well to our government as to others, of the continuance of the war, and of her determination to prosecute it. How does Texas regard her position in respect to the war with Mexico? Three years subsequent to our recognition of her independence, we find her entering into a stipulation with a foreign power to accept of her mediation to bring about a cession of hostilities between her and Mexico, engaging to assume a million sterling of the debt due from

Mexico to the subjects of that power, if she, through her influence, obtained from Mexico an unlimited truce in respect to the war then raging between her and Texas within one month and 'a treaty of peace in six. As late as last June, we see a proclamation of the president of Texas, declaring a suspension of hostilities between the two powers during the pendency of negotiations to be entered upon between them, issued on the supposition that a similar proclamation would be issued by Mexico; and actual hostilities are now only suspended by an armistice to be continued for a specified and short period, for the sake of negotiation. . . . The government of the United States should be at all times ready to interpose its good offices to bring about a speedy, and, as far as practicable a satisfactory adjustment of this long pending controversy. Its whole influence should be exerted constantly zealously and in good faith, to advance so desirable an object, and in the process of time it can, without doubt, be accomplished. But what, my dear sir, is the true and undisguised character of the remedy for those evils, which would be applied by the "immediate annexation of Texas to the United States?" Is it more or less than saying to Mexico, we feel ourselves aggrieved by the continuance of this war between you and Texas; we have an interest in seeing it terminated; we will accomplish that object by taking the disputed territory to ourselves; we will make Texas a part of the United States, so that those plans of reconquest which we know you are maturing, to be successful, must be made so against the power that we can bring into the contest; if the war is to be continued as we understand to be your design, the United States are henceforth to be regarded as one of the belligerents?

We must look at this matter as it really stands. — We shall act under the eye of an intelligent, observing world; and the affair cannot be made to wear a different aspect from what it deserves if even we had the disposition (which we have not) to throw over it disguises of any kind. We should consider whether there is any way in which the peace of the country can be preserved, should an immediate annexation take place, save one — and that is, according to present appearances, the improbible event that Mexico will be deterred from the farther prosecution of the war by the apprehension of our power. How does that matter stand? She has caused us to be informed, both at Mexico and here, in a manner the most formal and solemn, that she will feel herself constrained, by every consideration that can influence the conduct of a nation, to regard the fact of annexation as an act of war on the part of the United States and that she will, notwithstanding, prosecute her attempts to regain Texas, regardless of consequences. . . .

*   *   *

. . . The question then recurs, if, as sensible men, we cannot avoid the conclusion that the immediate annexation of Texas would, in all human probability, draw after it a war with Mexico, can it be expedient to attempt it? Of the consequences of such a war, the character it might be made to assume, the entanglements with other nations which the position of a belligerent almost unavoidably draws after it, and the undoubted injuries which might be inflicted upon each, — notwithstanding the great disparity of their respective forces, I will not say a word. God forbid that an American citizen should ever count the cost of any appeal to what is appropriately denominated the last resort of nations, whenever that resort becomes necessary either for the safety or to vindicate the honor of his country. There is, I trust, not one so base as not to regard himself and all he has to be forever and at all times subject to such a requisition. But would a war with Mexico, brought on under such circumstances, be a contest of that character? Could we hope to stand justified in the eyes of mankind for entering into it; more especially if its commencement is to be preceded by the appropriation to our own uses of the territory, the sovereignty of which is in dispute between two nations one of which we are to join in the struggle? This sir, is a matter of the very gravest import, one in respect to which no American statesman or citizen can possibly be indifferent. We have a character among the nations of the earth to maintain. – All our public functionaries, as well those who advocate this measure as those who oppose it, however much they may differ as to its effects, will I am sure, be equally solicitous for the performance of this first of duties. It has hitherto been our pride and our boast, that whilst the lust of power, with fraud and violence in its train, has led other and differently constituted governments to aggression and conquest, our movements in these respects have always been regulated by reason and justice. A disposition to detract from our pretensions in this respect, will in the nature of things be always prevalent elsewhere; and has, at this very moment, – and from special causes assumed, in some quarters, the most rabid character. Should not every one, then who sincerely loves his country – who venerates its time-honored and glorious institutions – who dwells with pride and delight on associations connected with our rise, progress and present condition – on the steady step with which we have advanced to our present eminence, in despite of the hostility, and in contempt of the bitter revilings of the enemies of freedom in all parts of the globe, – consider and that deeply whether we would not by the immediate annexation of Texas, place a weapon in the hands of those who now look upon us and our institutions with distrustful and envious eyes, that would do us more real, lasting injury as a nation, than the acquisition of such a territory, valuable as it undoubtedly is, could possibly repair? . . .

In regard to the performance by us of that duty, so difficult for any government to perform, – the observance of an honest neutrality between nations at war – we can now look through our whole career, since our first admission into the family of nations, not only without a blush, but with feelings of honest pride and satisfaction. The way was opened by President Washington himself, under circumstances of the most difficult character, and at no less a hazard than that of exposing ourselves to plausible, yet unjust, imputations of infidelity to treaty stipulations. The path he trod with such unfaltering steps – and which led to such beneficial results, has hitherto been pursued with unvarying fidelity by every one of his successors of whom it becomes me to speak.

If our sympathies could induce a departure from a policy which has so much in its commencement to consecrate it, and such advantages to recommend its continuance, they would doubtless draw us to the side of Texas. That the happiness of her people would be promoted by the maintenance of her independence, I have no doubt. Few, if any, efforts for the extension of the blessings of free government in any part of the world have been made since the establishment of our own independence, that have failed to excite our earnest and sincere wishes for their success. But they have never been permitted to withdraw us from the faithful performance of our duty as a neutral nation. They were excited, and deeply too, at the commencement of the French revolution; they were revived in the struggle of the South American states for the establishment of their independence; they have been put to their severest trial in this very contest between Texas and Mexico. Yet, in that whole period of time, amidst the convulsions of empires and the lawlessness of power by which many of its possessors have been distinguished, it has been a cardinal point in the administration of the affairs of this republic to adhere with the strictest fidelity to the rule which was laid down by Washington, enforced by Jefferson and respected with unabated sincerity by their successors.

*   *   *

. . . I by no means contend that a formal recognition of the independence of Texas by Mexico is necessary to justify us in assenting to her annexation to the United States. Time and circumstances may work such a change in the relations between those two countries, as to render an act of that character, on the part of Mexico, unnecessary and unimportant. What I mean to say, is, that from all the information I have been able to acquire upon the subject, no change has yet taken place in those relations that would make the objections, which I have here detailed, inapplicable.

*   *   *

It is also apprehended by many, that the British authorities, will attempt to make Texas a British colony or dependency. I find it difficult to credit the existence of such infatuation on the part of any European power. I cannot bring myself to believe that any European government which has not already made up its mind to provoke a war with this country, will ever attempt to colonize Texas, either in form or in substance. If there be any such power, the considerations to which I have adverted, would soon lose most of their importance; for opportunities would not then be slow in presenting themselves for the conquest of whatever territory might, in that event, be deemed necessary to our security, in legitimate self defence. Commercial favors Texas has, to the same extent as other independent powers, the right to dispose of as she thinks proper; subject only to the penalties which are certain, sooner or later, to follow in the wake of national injustice. But European colonization of Texas is another and a very different matter—a matter in respect to the ultimate consequence of which no European nation can possibly deceive either herself or us. I have no access to the sources of true information in respect to the degree of credit which may be due to these rumors; but our government ought, without doubt, to exercise a most jealous vigilance against the extension of British influence, and indeed foreign influence, or dominion of any kind, or from any quarter, either in Texas, or in any portions of the continent bordering on the Gulf of Mexico. If the time ever comes when the question resolves itself into whether

Texas shall become a British dependency or colony, or a constitutional portion
of this union, the great principle or self-defence, applicable as well to nations
as to individuals, would, without doubt, produce as great a unanimity amongst
us in favor of the latter alternative, as can ever be expected on any great question of foreign or domestic policy.

*   *   *

. . . The present condition of the relations between Mexico and Texas may
soon be so far changed as to weaken, and perhaps to obviate entirely, the
objections against the immediate annexation of the latter to the United States,
which I have here set forth, and to place the question on different grounds.
Should such a state of things arise, and I be found in charge of the responsible
duties of president, you may be assured that I would meet the question, if
then presented to me, with a sincere desire to promote the result which I
believed best calculated to advance the permanent welfare of the whole
country. In the discharge of this, the common duty of all our public functionaries, I would not allow myself to be influenced by local or sectional feelings.
I am not, I need hardly say to you, an untried man in respect to my disposition
or ability to disregard any feeling of that character in the discharge of official
duties. You, as well as all others, have therefore at least some grounds on
which to form an opinion as to the probable fidelity with which these assurances would be observed.

I shall add a few words on another aspect of the question, and then dismiss
the subject. Mexico may carry her persistance in refusing to acknowledge the
independence of Texas, and in destructive but fruitless efforts to reconquer
that state, so far as to produce, in connexion with other circumstances, a decided conviction on the part of a majority of the people of the United States,
that the permanent welfare, if not absolute safety to all, make it necessary that
the proposed annexation should be effected, be the consequences what they
may. . . .

. . . If any application for annexation, under such circumstances, were made
to me, I would feel it to be my duty to submit the same to congress for a public
expression of their opinion, as well upon the propriety of annexation, as in
regard to the terms upon which it should take place. If, after the whole subject
had been brought before the country, and fully discussed, as it now will be,
the senate and house of representatives, a large portion of the former, and the
whole of the latter having been chosen by the people, after the question of
annexation had been brought before the country for its mature consideration,
should express an opinion in favor of annexation, I would hold it to be my
farther duty to employ the executive power to carry into full and fair effect
the wishes of a majority of the people of the existing states, thus constitutionally
and solemnly expressed.

There may, notwithstanding, be those, on both sides of this great question,
who are unwilling to confer their suffrages on one who is not prepared to give
them specific pledges in regard to the course he would, if elected, pursue in
respect to the various aspects in which this matter may hereafter be presented.

I have expressed a willingness to discharge, to the best of my abilities, the responsible duties of the high office in question, should the democracy of the U. States be able and willing to re-elect me to the same. But I can take no steps to obtain it by which my ability to discharge its duties impartially and usefully to every portion of our common country would be impaired; nor can I in any extremity, be induced to cast a shade over the motives of my past life, by changes or concealments of opinions maturely formed upon a great national question, for the unworthy purpose of increasing my chances for political promotion.

I am, sir, very respectfully, your friend and obedient servant,

Proceedings of the Democratic National Convention
Baltimore, May 27-30, 1844

The following proceedings outline the drama of the 1844 Democratic convention. After 8 ballots it became apparent that the delegates would not be able to overcome their sectional differences and agree on a presidential nominee. Only after the courageous withdrawal of candidate Van Buren was the convention able to produce a compromise standard-bearer.

TUESDAY, MAY 28, 1844.

The convention reassembled this morning pursuant to adjournment, and was called to order by the president, (Mr. Wright, of Pennsylvania) . . . .

* * *

Mr. Clifford, of Maine, explained that the proposition was to strike out and insert; therefore, all those who were in favor of the two-thirds rule would vote "ay," and those against it would vote "no."

The vote was accordingly taken, each State voting either for or against, or dividing, as they themselves determined. The States being called, the chairman of the several delegations answered as follows:

	For the rule.	Against it.
Maine,	0	9
New Hampshire,	0	6
Massachusetts,	5	7
Vermont,	3	3
Rhode Island,	2	2
Connecticut,	3	3
New York,	0	36
New Jersey,	7	0
Pennsylvania, (1 absent,)	12	13
Delaware,	3	0
Maryland,	6	2
Virginia,	17	0
North Carolina, (1 absent,)	5	5
Georgia,	10	0
Alabama,	9	0
Mississippi,	6	0
Louisiana,	6	0
Tennessee,	13	0
Kentucky,	12	0
Ohio,	0	23
Indiana,	12	0
Illinois,	9	0
Michigan,	5	0
Missouri,	0	7
Arkansas,	3	0
	116	148

So the two-thirds rule was adopted.

* * *

Mr. Tibbatts, of Kentucky, moved that the convention take a recess until half-past 3 o'clock; which motion was agreed to.

AFTERNOON SESSION.

The convention met at half past three o'clock, pursuant to adjournment; when it was called to order by the president.

A motion was made, seconded, and agreed to, that the vote on the nominations should be taken viva voce.

*   *   *

The convention then proceeded to vote, each State voting as it was respectively called. The following was the result:

FIRST VOTE.

	Van Buren.	Cass.	Buchanan.	Johnson.	Woodbury.	Calhoun.	Stewart.
Maine,	8	0	0	0	1	0	0
New Hampshire,	6	0	0	0	0	0	0
Vermont,	5	1	0	0	0	0	0
Rhode Island,	4	0	0	0	0	0	0
Massachusetts,	8	1	3	0	0	0	0
Connecticut,	6	0	0	0	0	0	0
New York,	36	0	0	0	0	0	0
New Jersey,	3	2	0	2	0	0	0
Pennsylvania,	26	0	0	0	0	0	0
Delaware,	0	3	0	0	0	0	0
Maryland,	2	4	0	0	1	0	1
Virginia,	0	17	0	0	0	0	0
North Carolina,	2	4	0	5	0	0	0
Georgia,	0	9	0	0	0	1	0
Alabama,	1	8	0	0	0	0	0
Mississippi,	0	6	0	0	0	0	0
Louisiana,	0	0	1	0	0	5	0
Tennessee,	0	13	0	0	0	0	0
Kentucky,	0	0	0	12	0	0	0
Ohio,	23	0	0	0	0	0	0
Indiana,	3	9	0	0	0	0	0
Illinois,	5	2	0	2	0	0	0
Michigan,	1	4	0	0	0	0	0
Missouri,	7	0	0	0	0	0	0
Arkansas,	0	9	0	3	0	0	0
	146	83	4	24	2	6	1

Whole number of votes 266. Necessary to a choice 177.

Mr. Miller, of Ohio, said he perceived by the result that Martin Van Buren had received a majority of all the votes cast. He therefore moved that it be declared as the sense of the convention that Mr. Van Buren received the nomination.

Objected to by several; and the president declared the motion to be out of order.

And, on motion by Mr. Bredin, of Pennsylvania, the convention proceeded to a

SECOND VOTE.

	Van Buren.	Cass.	Buchanan.	Johnson.	Calhoun.	Stewart.
Maine,	8	1	0	0	0	0
New Hampshire,	6	0	0	0	0	0
Vermont,	0	6	0	0	0	0
Rhode Island,	3	1	0	0	0	0
Massachusetts,	7	3	2	0	0	0
Connecticut,	0	0	0	6	0	0
New York,	36	0	0	0	0	0
New Jersey,	2	2	1	2	0	0
Pennsylvania,	26	0	0	0	0	0
Delaware,	0	3	0	0	0	0
Maryland,	2	5	0	0	0	1
Virginia,	0	17	0	0	0	0
North Carolina,	0	5	0	5	0	0
Georgia,	0	9	0	0	1	0
Alabama,	1	8	0	0	0	0
Mississippi,	0	6	0	0	0	0
Louisiana,	0	0	6	0	0	0
Tennessee,	0	13	0	0	0	0
Kentucky,	0	0	0	12	0	0
Ohio,	28	0	0	0	0	0
Michigan,	1	4	0	0	0	0
Indiana,	3	9	0	0	0	0
Illinois,	2	2	0	5	0	0
Missouri,	7	0	0	0	0	0
Arkansas,	0	0	0	3	0	0
	127	94	33	33	1	1

Whole number of votes, 265. Necessary to a choice, 176.

There being no choice, the convention proceeded to a

THIRD VOTE.

	Van Buren.	Cass.	Buchanan.	Johnson.	Calhoun.	Woodbury.
Maine,	8	1	0	0	0	0
New Hampshire,	3	0	1	0	0	2
Vermont,	0	6	0	0	0	0
Massachusetts,	7	3	2	0	0	0
Connecticut,	0	0	0	6	0	0
Rhode Island,	2	1	1	0	0	0
New York,	36	0	0	0	0	0
New Jersey,	1	4	1	1	0	0
Pennsylvania,	26	0	0	0	0	0
Delaware,	0	3	0	0	0	0
Maryland,	2	6	0	0	0	0
Virginia,	0	17	0	0	0	0
North Carolina,	0	0	0	11	0	0
Georgia,	0	8	0	0	2	0
Alabama,	1	8	0	0	0	0
Mississippi,	0	6	0	0	0	0
Louisiana,	0	0	6	0	0	0
Tennessee,	0	13	0	0	0	0
Kentucky,	0	0	0	12	0	0
Ohio,	23	0	0	0	0	0
Michigan,	0	5	0	0	0	0
Indiana,	3	9	0	0	0	0
Illinois,	2	2	0	5	0	0
Missouri,	7	0	0	0	0	0
Arkansas,	0	0	0	3	0	0
	121	92	11	38	2	2

Whole number of votes 266. Necessary to a choice 177.

After the third ballot, a motion was offered by Mr. Bredin, of Pennsylvania, that the convention adjourn; which was rejected. The convention then proceeded to the

FOURTH VOTE.

	Van Buren.	Cass.	Buchanan.	Johnson.	Calhoun.
Maine,	8	1	0	0	0
New Hampshire,	2	0	4	0	0
Vermont,	0	6	0	0	0
Massachusetts,	7	3	2	0	0
Connecticut,	0	0	0	6	0
Rhode Island,	2	1	1	0	0
New York,	36	0	0	0	0
New Jersey,	1	4	1	1	0
Pennsylvania,	18	0	8	0	0
Delaware,	0	3	0	0	0
Maryland,	2	6	0	0	0
Virginia,	0	17	0	0	0
North Carolina,	0	11	0	0	0
Georgia,	0	9	0	0	1
Alabama,	1	8	0	0	0
Mississippi,	0	6	0	0	0
Louisiana,	0	0	1	5	0
Tennessee,	0	13	0	0	0
Kentucky,	0	0	0	12	0
Ohio,	22	1	0	0	0
Michigan,	0	5	0	0	0
Indiana,	3	9	0	0	0
Illinois,	2	2	0	5	0
Missouri,	7	0	0	0	0
Arkansas,	0	0	0	3	0
	111	105	17	32	1

Whole number of votes, 266. Necessary to a choice 177.

FIFTH VOTE.

	Van Buren.	Cass.	Buchanan.	Johnson.	Calhoun.
Maine,	8	1	0	0	0
New Hampshire,	2	0	4	0	0
Vermont,	0	6	0	0	0
Massachusetts,	7	3	2	0	0
Connecticut,	0	0	0	6	0
Rhode Island,	1	1	2	0	0
New York,	36	0	0	0	0
New Jersey,	0	4	2	1	0
Pennsylvania,	16	0	10	0	0
Delaware,	0	3	0	0	0
Maryland,	2	6	0	0	0
Virginia,	0	17	0	0	0
North Carolina,	0	7	0	4	0
Georgia,	0	9	0	0	1
Alabama	1	8	0	0	0
Mississippi,	0	6	0	0	0
Louisiana	0	0	6	0	0
Tennessee,	0	13	0	0	0
Kentucky,	0	0	0	12	0
Ohio,	20	3	0	0	0
Michigan,	0	5	0	0	0
Indiana,	1	11	0	0	0
Illinois,	2	4	0	3	0
Missouri,	7	0	0	0	0
Arkansas,	0	0	0	3	0
	103	107	26	29	1

Whole number of votes 266. Necessary to a choice 177.

Mr. Dawson, of Pennsylvania, moved that the convention adjourn to meet to-morrow morning at 9 o'clock.

A delegate proposed to adjourn to meet at 7 o'clock.

Mr. Dawson accepted the modification; when the question was put on the motion to adjourn, and negatived.

On motion of Mr. Thompson, of Mississippi, the convention proceeded to a

SIXTH VOTE.

	Van Buren.	Cass.	Buchanan.	Johnson.	Calhoun.
Maine - -	8	1	0	0	0
New Hampshire	2	0	4	0	0
Vermont - -	0	6	0	0	0
Massachusetts -	6	4	2	0	0
Connecticut -	0	6	0	0	0
Rhode Island -	1	1	2	0	0
New York - -	36	0	0	0	0
New Jersey -	0	5	2	0	0
Pennsylvania -	17	0	9	0	0
Delaware - -	0	3	0	0	0
Maryland - -	2	6	0	0	0
Virginia - -	0	17	0	0	0
North Carolina -	0	7	0	4	0
Georgia - -	0	9	0	0	1
Alabama - -	1	8	0	0	0
Mississippi - -	0	6	0	0	0
Louisiana - -	0	0	6	0	0
Tennessee - -	0	13	0	0	0
Kentucky - -	0	0	0	12	0
Ohio - -	20	3	0	0	0
Michigan - -	0	5	0	0	0
Indiana - -	1	11	0	0	0
Illinois - -	0	5	0	4	0
Arkansas - -	0	0	0	3	0
Missouri - -	7	0	0	0	0
	101	116	25	23	1

Whole number of votes 266. Necessary to choice 177.

SEVENTH VOTE.

	Van Buren.	Cass.	Buchanan.	Johnson.	Calhoun.
Maine - -	8	1	0	0	0
New Hampshire	3	0	3	0	0
Vermont - -	0	6	0	0	0
Massachusetts -	6	5	1	0	0
Connecticut -	0	6	0	0	0
Rhode Island -	2	1	1	0	0
New York - -	36	0	0	0	0
New Jersey -	0	5	2	0	0
Delaware - -	0	3	0	0	0
Pennsylvania -	12	4	9	1	0
Maryland - -	0	8	0	0	0
Virginia - -	0	17	0	0	0
North Carolina -	2	7	0	2	0
Georgia - -	0	9	0	0	1
Alabama - -	1	8	0	0	0
Mississippi - -	0	6	0	0	0
Louisiana - -	0	0	6	0	0
Tennessee - -	0	13	0	0	0
Kentucky - -	0	0	0	12	0
Ohio - -	20	3	0	0	0
Michigan - -	0	5	0	0	0
Indiana - -	1	11	0	0	0
Illinois - -	1	5	0	3	0
Missouri - -	7	0	0	0	0
Arkansas - -	0	0	0	3	0
	99	123	22	21	1

Whole number of votes 266. Necessary to a choice 177.

After the result of the seventh ballot had been declared,

Mr. John K. Miller, of Ohio, rose and asked to be permitted to submit a motion to the convention, on which, in view of the position which he occupied, he should demand the yeas and nays; and if decided in the negative, it would probably dissolve his connection with the convention. Some objection having been manifested, Mr. Miller declared, with much vehemence, that he was entitled to, and would demand as his right, a respectful hearing. He represented 10,000 of the democracy of Ohio; and in the name of that 10,000 he demanded it. He would read his motion. It was as follows:

"*Resolved*, That Martin Van Buren, having received the vote of a majority of the delegates in this convention on the first ballot, is elected as the nominee for the office of President of the United States."

A number of gentlemen instantly rose to a point of order, when

Mr. Miller continued, amidst the general din, to speak with much animation, though it was impossible to hear what he said.

Mr. Hickman, of Pennsylvania, who occupied a front seat, rose, and above the confusion suddenly proposed a resolution that General Andrew Jackson, of Tennessee, receive the unanimous vote of this convention as a candidate for the office of President of the United States. This was received with mingled applause and good-humored laughter.

A delegate moved to proceed to another ballot.

Mr. Steenrod. I demand that, before you put that question, you put the question on the motion of the gentleman from Ohio.

The chair [Mr. Hubbard, of New Hampshire,] decided that the resolution was not in order, because it conflicted with one of the standing rules adopted by the convention for the government of its proceedings. The resolution went to declare that Mr. Van Buren, having received a majority of the votes given, was the nominee of the convention, when the rule required a vote of two-thirds of the members present to make a nomination.

Mr. Butler, of New York, offered a motion to adjourn; which was lost by acclamation.

In the mean time the confusion increased, several of the Ohio delegation being upon their feet, in an effort to sustain their colleague.

Mr. Medary at length commanded the attention of the convention, and by a strenuous effort made himself heard. He said he could explain the matter instantly. All that was desired was an appeal from the decision of the chair to the convention.

The Chair said the appeal must be reduced to writing, or it could not be entertained.

Mr. Medary was than permitted, by consent, to speak to the appeal. He then proceeded to a discussion of the right of the convention to rescind an imperative rule, and continued in a desultory argument to speak against the decision of the chair, contending that the resolution would be of itself a repeal of the rule, if adopted.

Some confusion still prevailing,

Mr. Butler asked permission (when Mr. Medary took his seat) to address a few remarks to the gentleman from Ohio; and proceeded with a few sentences, when he was interrupted by a call to order, and a denial that he had the unanimous consent of the convention.

Mr. Bartley, of Ohio, took the floor, and demanded to be heard.

The Chair said the gentleman could not be heard but by unanimous consent. Objections being made,

Mr. Cave Johnson desired leave of the convention for the gentleman to be heard.

Mr. Jacob Thompson appealed to gentlemen to withdraw their objections, and let the gentleman from Ohio proceed.

Mr. Bartley, of Ohio, then took the floor, and inquired of the chair what his decision was.

The Chair repeated his decision.

Mr. Bartley then said that the resolution submitted by his colleague was one in substance, though not in so many words, to rescind the rule. He inquired whether it was not in order in the House of Representatives, whose rules had been adopted for the government of this convention, to pass a resolution rescinding a rule adopted for its government. He asked those gentlemen present connected with that body whether it was not in order there to propose to rescind any rule by a majority vote. The resolution just offered was to rescind a rule of this convention; and there was great necessity and propriety for its adoption. Mr. B. insisted that the convention could make no nomination unless it was rescinded. Would not those gentlemen who had been instrumental in placing such an anti democratic rule upon them have cause to blush, if no nomination was made in consequence of its adoption? What, he asked, was their intention? Did they intend to prevent the convention from making a nomination? . . .

*   *   *

. . . Let me tell you, Mr. President, that more than twenty-two States out of the twenty-six have, if not positively instructed, at least formally declared the instruction in favor of the man who received the majority vote of the convention. I ask, is this not a rule, then, by which we can determine who it is that is represented by a majority of the people in this convention? We find that twenty-two out of the twenty-six States directly or indirectly instructed their delegates to vote for the majority man; and yet it is insisted that a majority are incompetent to determine the candidate of the convention. I insist, sir, in conclusion, that the rescinding that rule of this convention is essentially necessary to accomplish the object for which we were convened—to carry out the views of the majority of the convention, and the views of twenty-two out of the twenty-six States. Mr. B. concluded by appealing from the decision of the Chair.

The President, having resumed the chair, said the gentleman must reduce his appeal to writing.

*   *   *

Mr. McNulty handed up his appeal to the Chair; which was read as follows:

"The president having decided that it requires a vote of two-thirds to suspend or rescind a rule for the government of this convention, I appeal from that decision."

He then spoke on the question, but was frequently called to order. He investigated the usage of Parliament, and contended in favor of his appeal. He continued speaking up to about 7 o'clock, when a motion was made to adjourn until 9 o'clock to-morrow morning; which, after a division, prevailed.

*   *   *

WEDNESDAY, MAY 29, 1844.

The convention assembled at 9 o'clock, pursuant to adjournment, and was called to order by the president, the question pending being the appeal from the decision of the Chair, taken by Mr. McNulty, of Ohio.

*   *   *

Mr. McNulty, of Ohio, then withdrew his appeal, on the decision of the Chair, stating that his opinion had undergone no change, but that he acted for the sake of harmony. This was received with tremendous cheers.

Mr. Dawson, of Pennsylvania, moved that the convention proceed to another ballot: agreed to.

Mr. Tibbatts, of Kentucky, observed that the whig party had, with a unanimity unparalleled in the history of that party, nominated a candidate for the Presidency, who was a distinguished citizen of the State of Kentucky. . . .

. . . We had (said he) hopes that the whig party, having concentrated their strength on one distinguished citizen of Kentucky, the democratic party would have concentrated theirs in another distinguished citizen of that State – a war worn veteran; one who had served his country in the council chamber, as well as in the battle field, with fidelity and ability unsurpassed by any. . . .

. . . He pledged himself yesterday, for the Kentucky delegation, that if the time should arrive when it would be necessary for the harmony of the democratic party to give up their candidate, they would offer him up as a ready and willing sacrifice. That time had now arrived, and he was, therefore, unanimously instructed by his colleagues, for the purpose of securing a nomination, no matter of whom it might be, to say to the convention that they would not now press the claims of Colonel Johnson as a candidate before the convention, but would cast their vote, on the ballot about to be taken, in favor of some other gentleman.

Mr. Brewster, of Pennsylvania, spoke at some length, in relation to the peculiar position which the Pennsylvania delegation occupied in the present crisis, reviewing the history of the proceedings of the party in that State, and deprecating the division which, for its last three ballots, had existed in the delegation. Pennsylvania's first choice was James Buchanan; but, after the withdrawal of that pure patriot and high-minded man, she had, in her last 4th of March convention, instructed her delegates to vote for Martin Van Buren. Every delegate had been pledged to carry out those instructions, and wo to that man who dared to disobey them.

He had been asked to explain the position of the Pennsylvania delegation, and why a part voted for Mr. Van Buren and a part for Mr. Buchanan, and what their ultimate course would be. In reply to the inquiry, all he had to say was that the Pennsylvania delegation dare not vote for any other man but Martin Van Buren or James Buchanan, until the friends of Mr. Van Buren deserted him. (Cheers.) Until the friends of Mr. Van Buren withdrew him, the Pennsylvania delegation ought not to budge an inch. (Tremendous cheering.)

Mr. Hickman, of Pennsylvania, said the delegation from that State were instructed to vote for Mr. Van Buren and Col. R. M. Johnson, and they had been required to give a pledge to that support, otherwise their places would have been supplied by others; and yet, in the face of all this, he regretted to say, a portion of that delegation had disobeyed their instructions, and a portion of them had also voted in favor of an unjust resolution, by which the chances of Mr. Van Buren were sacrificed.

* * *

Several gentlemen here desired to address the convention.

Mr. Thompson, of Mississippi, proposed that, by universal consent, they be heard; but objection having been made, the convention proceeded to the 8th vote; which resulted as follows:

EIGHTH VOTE.

	Van Buren.	Polk.	Cass.	Buchanan.	Calhoun.
Maine,	8	1	0	0	0
New Hampshire,	0	0	6	0	0
Vermont,	0	6	0	0	0
Massachusetts,	0	5	7	0	0
Connecticut,	0	6	0	0	0
Rhode Island,	4	0	0	0	0
New York,	36	0	0	0	0
New Jersey,	1	5	0	1	0
Pennsylvania,	22	1	2	1	0
Delaware,	0	3	0	0	0
Maryland,	1	6	1	0	0
Virginia,	0	17	0	0	0
North Carolina,	2	8	0	0	1
Georgia,	0	9	0	0	1
Alabama,	0	0	9	0	0
Mississippi,	0	6	0	0	0
Louisiana,	0	0	6	0	0
Tennessee,	0	0	13	0	0
Kentucky,	0	12	0	0	0
Ohio,	21	2	0	0	0
Michigan,	0	5	0	0	0
Indiana,	1	11	0	0	0
Illinois,	1	8	0	0	0
Missouri,	7	0	0	0	0
Arkansas,	0	3	0	0	0
	104	114	44	2	2

Whole number of votes 266. Necessary to a choice 177.

When the State of Tennessee was called,

Mr. Cave Johnson desired to say that the delegation of the State of Tennessee came not there for the purpose of presenting the name of James K. Polk for any other nomination than that for the second office in the government; and, as such, it had been their desire and intention to cast the vote of their State for him. Yet the Tennessee delegation felt for James K. Polk the same warmth of feeling that the delegations of the other States felt for the distinguished candidates they supported; and, though their votes had hitherto been cast for another man, they felt it to be their duty, when other States came forward to support him, to give him their votes also. Under instructions, therefore, from the Tennessee delegation, he with much pleasure cast the 13 votes of that State for James K. Polk. [Cheering.]

No candidate having received a two-thirds vote,

Mr. Frazer, of Pennsylvania, moved to proceed to a ninth ballot, and remarked that, on the last ballot, he had voted for James K. Polk, and would do so on the next, despite the threat that had been thrown out, that those who had violated their instructions would hang their heads with shame in the presence of their constituents. . . . Mr. F. said he had, in accordance with his instructions, voted three times for Mr. Van Buren, and he found that he had been sinking every vote. He then voted for Mr. Buchanan. His constituents decided that Mr. Buchanan was their first choice. But that eminent man was not available before the convention. He then took Polk. Even their own son was willingly sacrificed. Who are we going for now? (said Mr. F.) The bosom friend of Old Hickory, the illustrious patriot, and hero of the Hermitage — the man who stood up in defence of the old hero during the panic session, when all the lightnings of whigery were playing at him, in a vain attempt to blast him. We are going for the man who fought so bravely and so undauntingly the whigs of Tennessee — the pure, whole hog, locofoco democrat, who goes against a bank of the United States, and all corrupting monopolies; against the distribution of the proceeds of the public lands; against the assumption of the debts of the States by the federal government; against the tory whigs of this country and tyrannizing England; — in a word, a man who goes against the ring-streaked and speckled whig party, with all its odious, abominable measures. . . .

*   *   *

Mr. Samuel Young, of New York, said he rose for the purpose of submitting a resolution. Other gentlemen were permitted to define their position in this assembly, and the position their States occupy. In the course of the debate, it was more than intimated that New York showed a pertinacious disposition to obtrude a candidate on this convention. Now, sir, I ask leave to define the position of N. York in this respect. The State of N. York was perfectly mute on the subject of a new democratic candidate in 1841 and in 1842; and not until 1843 did she speak out upon the subject. What was the course of other States? There were sixteen States in the Union which had distinctly named Mr. Van Buren as the next candidate for the presidency before New York opened her mouth; . . . It was under these circumstances, sir, that, in the fall of 1843, New York held her convention, appointed delegates, and instructed them to follow the lead given by 16 States, and go for Mr. Van Buren. Sir, what is the obligation which instructions impose on a man? Sir, if any state of things occurs which deprives him of the power concientiously to fulfil the instructions, he is bound to resign. He has his choice, either to obey the will of his constituents or resign, and give them timely notice to appoint another who will express their wises. Has anything occurred in the great body of the democracy indicating an alteration of the will of the democracy? So far as he was informed, nothing had occurred, if the country had the same sentiment which pervaded New York. . . . If the democracy of the Union had been consulted six weeks ago, such would have been the response in every State. But a new issue has been made up. The mongrel administration at Washington threw a firebrand among us—threw in the fire-brand of Texas—to drive us from the old platform of democracy.

. . . The excitement is purely artificial. It was concocted for the occasion. It is said in history that Nero fiddled whilst Rome, fired by his orders, was burning; and no doubt the political Nero of this country, who had contributed, by collusion, to enkindle the flame now raging in the democratic citadel, was looking on, and rejoicing, with feelings overflowing with delight.

Mr. Cohen, of Georgia. Who is that Nero? (Cries of "order, order.")

The President said that the gentleman must not be interrupted; the gentleman from Georgia would have an opportunity of replying when he had done.

Mr. Young refused to answer, and continued; . . .

What, sir, is the extraordinary state of things which exists at this moment? We come together, and it is proposed to introduce a rule by which two-thirds of the convention will be requisite to make a nomination. Before the rule was adopted, sir, a gentleman on this floor gives us the information that a member of the convention had taken every possible measure to canvass the opinion of the convention; and he had arrived at the result that there could not be two-thirds procured for any candidate, and that gentleman called upon the convention to contradict the assertion. Every one assented. Notwithstanding, the rule was adopted, and the result showed that the assertion was true. . . . He hoped, after its wasting so much time, and exciting so much warmth, he could now induce the convention to abandon this extraordinary rule; and for that purpose he rose to offer the following resolution.

Several gentlemen rising, the Chair gave the floor to

Mr. Cohen, of Georgia, who said: I now beg leave to inquire of the gentleman from New York [Mr. Young] who the Nero is to whom he referred.

Mr. Young's reply was not heard, but the reporter understood it to be a refusal to answer the question.

Mr. Butler asked the gentleman to give him the floor for a moment.

Mr. Cohen declined to yield the floor. As much want of courtesy had been shown him on the part of a gentleman of the New York delegation, he must refuse to give way to the gentleman. . . .

*   *   *

Mr. Saunders, of North Carolina, hoped that his friend from Georgia [Mr. Cohen] would forbear for a single moment, to see if an explanation would be given him.

Mr. Dickinson, of New York (addressing the Chair) said that the New York delegation would retire for a short time, but would soon return.

[The New York delegation accordingly left the room.]

Mr. Cohen said that he should not suspend his remarks, because the gentleman chose to retire. The gentleman might retire or not, as he pleased. He was proceeding to express the hope that nothing but what was consistent with good temper, would have come from the lips of the venerable man, whose head was whitened with the snows of age, and in whose heart he had hoped there dwelt better and kinder feelings. He found, however, that he was mistaken in the gentleman; and that, after having cast the apple of discord in our ranks, he had meanly skulked out of the room. (Cries of "order," and hisses.) He was not, (Mr. C. said,) speaking of others. He was only referring to one who had done him personal and political wrong, and had refused to give him an explanation, though respectfully called on to do so.

Mr. Hammet, of Mississippi, hoped that nothing would come from Georgia — that nothing would come from any portion of the southern delegation — calculated to interrupt the harmony of the convention. Nothing had as yet been said by any portion of the southern delegation that was harsh or intemperate. He implored the gentleman from Georgia — he implored the whole South — that, if anything unpleasant should occur, it should not come from the south of Mason and Dixon's line.

Mr. Cohen said that nothing was further from his intention than to disturb the harmony of the convention. He came there with a disposition to conciliate and harmonize with his fellow-delegates from the other States. He came there to vote for the nomination of an individual who would be the strongest in the support of the democracy of the country. He heard a gentleman make a remark reflecting on a distinguished citizen of the South, as being one of the mongrel administration. He applied to him for an explanation, which was refused under the parliamentary rule; he applied to him again, and, at the instance of the gentleman from North Carolina, waited for a reply; and being again refused, he repelled, in what he thought a proper spirit, the exceptionable language that was used. If the gentleman had abandoned the controversy, he left him where he was.

Mr. Hubbard, of New Hampshire, then rose and said:

Mr. President: I feel deeply solicitous in common, I doubt not, with every other member of this convention, that the result of our deliberations should be that result, of all others, which will be most beneficial to the democratic party, and consequently to the true interest of the American people. . . . I came here as one of the delegation from my native State with the strongest preposessions in favor of Martin Van Buren; and my colleagues came here with like feelings. It was the known and expressed will of the democracy of our little Commonwealth that the distinguished statesman, the pure patriot, the honest citizen to whom I have referred, should be designated as the democratic candidate for the presidency. We heartily and sincerely concurred in the known principles of Mr. Van Buren. He was their choice. And myself and colleagues would have experienced great gladness of heart if we could but have accomplished the will and the wish of our constituency — a democracy as pure, as unwavering, as firm as their own granite hills. But, Mr. President, we had balloted seven times without effecting a nomination, and without even the prospect of effecting a nomination. Under these circumstances, what was our duty? To go on, with no better hopes, when it was manifest that the result of every ballot tended to increase the irritation and distraction of the party? We paused. We conferred. As much as we value our favorite candidate—as much as we were disposed to follow out the desire of our own people, we felt it to be our bounden duty to present another candidate to the consideration of the convention. We have, with entire unanimity, brought to your notice the Hon. James K. Polk, of Tennessee. It is my good fortune to know that man well. I have served with him in public life. I can bear testimony to his fidelity to the constitution and to his devotion to the honor and welfare of our beloved country. In one of the most perilous periods of our political history, we were both members of the popular branch of our government, and acted together on that committee which divises the ways and means for the support of the republic. He was always most faithful found among the faithful. His opinions upon matters of public policy, his sentiments upon all the great questions which at that time agitated the country, commanded the full approbation of the people of New Hampshire; and her delegation have seen fit to announce him as our candidate for the presidency. We present him as a man well worthy of the confidence of the democracy of our land; and we earnestly hope that he may receive the individual support of this convention. In presenting to the convention this distinguished fellow-citizen, no man must say that it was produced by bargain, or by any improper management. One controlling motive induced our delegation to nominate Mr. Polk; and that was, to secure the harmony and the union of the great democratic party. . . .

*   *   *

Mr. Medary, the editor of the Ohio Statesman, rose for the purpose of stating to the convention that, if a feeling was raised in the breasts of any one during their deliberations, having a tendency towards an alienation of that good feeling which should characterize that body, he would be the first to come forward and yield every thing but honor and principle to eradicate that feeling. Throw out the flag of peace (he said) before we separate, and harmony will prevail in the ranks of the democracy abroad. Wherever it could be done, there should be a sacrifice of personal preferences and personal feelings. He spoke as one of the Ohio delegation, and was ready to make the sacrifice. He appealed to his southern brethren, and to the north, to sacrifice all their personal preferences on the altar of their party's and their country's good. He wished to leave that convention with no feeling but that of brotherly affection, such as ought to exist with democrats. If there was an individual proposed to the convention, upon whom they could go to their constituents with feelings of harmony, he, for one, felt ready for the movement. When he spoke before, it was under the ardor of feeling with which they of the West sometimes might differ. The delegates from Ohio wanted but to carry out the great principles of the party. He had no personal preferences further than the interests and honor of the country were concerned. Give them, he said, a candidate who was right on the Oregon question, and who would carry forward the interests of the democracy, and the victory in Ohio was certain. He repeated that he was ready to sacrifice personal preferences for the sake of union and harmony. (Tremendous cheers.)

He declared that he was a friend to the annexation of Texas; and should they give Ohio a candidate in favor of that object, and of extending the protecting ægis of our flag over the Oregon, he would pledge that the "lone star" of Texas should be blazoned on the democratic standard in Ohio, and that under it they would lead on to certain victory.

The convention then proceeded to a ninth vote, and after the first four States had cast their votes, it became evident that this was to be the last trial. The enthusiasm and perfect harmony that now prevailed in the convention, was in striking contrast with the proceedings of an hour previous. The delegation from each State appeared to be firm and undivided in their support of Mr. Polk; and although about forty votes were cast in the first portion of the ballot for other candidates, before the States were all called these were changed for Col. Polk, and he was declared to be unanimously chosen as the nominee of the convention—two hundred and sixty-six votes having been cast, to which was subsequently added the ratification of South Carolina.

The State of Virginia being called on to vote,

Mr. Roane, of Virginia, then rose, and said he had requested the venerable chairman of his delegation to allow him the privilege of announcing the vote of Virginia, because he meant to request of that august assembly to allow him to address them a few words prior to announcing that vote. He thanked his honorable friend from New Hampshire [Mr. Hubbard] for the patriotic sentiments he had just expressed, and extended to him the right hand of fellowship. [Loud and continued applause; and, before it had subsided, the New York delegation was observed entering the room.] Mr. R. then observed that he would suspend his remarks until the New York delegation had taken their seats. [Continued cheering.] Mr. R. resumed. It was with the most heartfelt gratification that he had extended the right hand of fellowship to his friend from New Hampshire; but his chief object in wishing to be the organ of his State on this occasion was to address a few remarks to the delegation from New York. He would say to New York that Virginia had resigned Mr. Van Buren with a bleeding heart, and that she had felt on this occasion the most trying emotions. He did but reflect the feelings of ninety-nine out of every hundred democrats in Virginia, when he said that, until very recently, they felt that the triumph of their principles could be best secured by the restoration of that pure patriot, enlightened statesman, and unbending democrat, to the seat which he had so nobly filled, and which he had been deprived of by such unworthy means. Though Virginia loved and admired Mr. Van Buren as a patriot and statesman, and fully appreciated his public and private worth, yet she had a higher duty to perform than that of showing her sense of his distinguished services in the manner she could have wished. She saw the arch apostate Henry Clay, who, for twenty years, had been endeavoring to overthrow her most cherished and time-honored principles, with thousands of hungry expectants hanging on in his train, and stimulating every vindictive feeling of his heart against the democracy of the country,—she saw this chieftain and his followers eagerly preparing for the approaching conflict, and confident of success; and it was to defeat him that Virginia yielded up the man of her choice, and placed her heart on the altar of her country and her principles. It was to arrest the progress of that man to the supreme chair of the Union, that she called up her first principles — "everything for the cause, nothing for men." She came there in the spirit of harmony and conciliation, to make a nomination that would be most conducive to the success of the democratic party of the whole Union; and in that spirit she called upon that convention — the most talented and the most respectable he had ever been in, not even excepting the great free-trade convention of Philadelphia — to meet her in a corresponding spirit. To that able and patriotic convention he would say that, in the approaching contest, Virginia would be found where she always had been — in the van of the democracy of the Union. It was in that spirit he felt anxious to respond yesterday to the gentleman from New York, [Mr. Dickinson,] when he asked what State it was that had not, at some time, been overwhelmed with whigery, and to tell him that Virginia had never given a vote to a federal candidate. In that spirit, he would now (as he was instructed to do by his colleagues) cast the seventeen votes of Virginia for James K. Polk, of Tennessee. [Thunders of applause.]

Mr. Benjamin F. Butler, of New York, in behalf of the delegation from Mr. Van Buren's native State, responded with all his heart to the remarks which had just fallen from the gentleman from Virginia. The citizens of New York never doubted that Virginia would stand by her, and now he was authorized to say they were still together, and would be found fighting side by side. During the discussion which had just taken place in the committee room among the New York delegation, the question was whether they had yet fulfilled their pledge, and were at liberty to withdraw the name of their distinguished fellow-citizen. . . .

. . . He therefore told them that if they did not advise him against it, he should feel it his duty to take the responsibility of withdrawing that honored name in view of the best interests of the democratic party. He therefore declared his intention to vote for James K. Polk, who fully came up to the Jeffersonian standard of qualification, being both capable, honest, and faithful to all his trusts. He felt satisfied that he would receive from 15 to 20,000 majority in New York, and that his nomination would heal all those difficulties over which the whigs had built all their hopes of success.

*   *   *

Mr. Walker said he rose to perform the agreeable duty of casting the entire electoral vote of the State of Mississippi for James K. Polk, as the democratic candidate for the presidency of the United States. Heretofore, the delegation from the State (twelve in number) were greatly divided, but now they were, one and all, cordially united in the support of James K. Polk; and he was directed, by the whole delegation, to assure the convention that the vote of Mississippi would be given to the patriot statesman of Tennessee, by a majority of thousands upon thousands. In truth, the State would now be carried almost without a contest, or if contest there should be, it would resemble that at San Jacinto, and the defeat of the anti-Texas allies of Mexico and Britain would be complete and overwhelming.

North Carolina being called,

Mr. Saunders said he came as a delegate from that county in North Carolina (Mecklenburg) which, on the 20th of May, 1775, put in motion the ball of the revolution which led to the declaration of independence; and in that county was James K. Polk born. He was instructed by the delegation from North Carolina to announce the vote of that State for the statesman and patriot, James K. Polk, A single word more. . . .

The State of Kentucky being called,

Mr. Tibbatts inquired if all *mistakes* had been corrected.

The President replied that there was one more correction to be made — that a mistake still existed in the vote of Vermont.

Mr. Tibbatts said then that he would wait until the mistake had been corrected; for as to the vote of Kentucky, there *could be no mistake.*

The vote of Vermont having been corrected, and the State of Kentucky again called,

Mr. Tibbatts rose and . . . cast the unanimous vote of the State of Kentucky in favor of James K. Polk, of Tennessee.

Connecticut being called,

Mr. Toucey said the delegates from Connecticut had been, from the beginning to the end, for union, concession, and compromise; ready to go for any man who was true to the interests of the democratic party — a man who was opposed to a national bank, to a high tariff, the distribution of the proceeds of the public lands, and the assumption of the debts of the States: they were all, therefore, for James K. Polk.

Michigan being called,

Mr. Bodely, of Michigan, said the delegates from his State came there with a heavy heart. They saw clouds lowering; but now how brightly breaks the morning. Every discord is healed. Every bitter feeling is gone. He rose to say that, of all men in the nation, Mr. Cass was the first choice of Michigan; but of all men out of that State, James K. Polk was the most acceptable. He appealed to the friends of Mr. Cass, from other States, to do as he was instructed to do by the delegates of Michigan — to withdraw the name of Mr. Cass, and to cast their votes for James K. Polk.

Mr. Kettlewell, of Baltimore rose, (amidst the enthusiasm which pervaded the hall,) and remarked that, in this great national jubilee, there was but one thing wanting to perfect the happiness of the occasion. He found that, of this family of States represented here, one sister was absent. Where, he asked, is that lost sister? Are there none here to represent the Palmetto State — the noble, the chivalric South Carolina? The presence of that sister is required to complete the national family. I wish to make the inquiry. My heart, which is almost too full for expression, desires to see that sister present. I do want to see the name of the Palmetto State upon the record. Who knows any thing of of our lost sister? [A voice: the Palmetto State is here. Loud bursts of enthusiasm.] . . .

A member here announced that Messrs. Pickens and Elmore, of South Carolina were in attendance.

Messrs. Pickens and Elmore were then conducted to the stand by Messrs.

Roane, of Virginia, and Hubbard, of New Hampshire, two of the vice presidents; and as they advanced up the hall, were greeted with the liveliest acclamations, and with the waving of hats and handkerchiefs. Order being restored —

Mr. Pickens addressed the convention for about half an hour in the most eloquent and enthusiastic manner. He stated that although he was not authorized technically to appear in the convention, or an authenticated and legally appointed delegate from South Carolina to cast her vote on this important occasion, yet as a democrat, as a republican — [applause,] knowing the man this convention nominated — standing by him, as he had in many a hard-fought battle — he would say, individually, that he was ready to respond with his whole heart and soul to the glorious nomination. [Enthusiastic applause.] Mr. P. adverted to the powerful and wily enemy the democratic party had to encounter in Mr. Clay; extolled the character, talents, and opinions, of Colonel Polk, and said South Carolina would give her most cordial and hearty support to him.

Loud calls were then heard from all parts of the house for Elmore! Elmore! which was increased and prolonged until

Mr. Elmore rose and remarked that he should, as his colleague had said, be cold indeed if he could be insensible to the kindness manifested, not only to himself but to his State, on this occasion. . . . We are ready and willing to fight under the banner which will be borne by the glorious son of Tennessee. . . . On this occasion I lay before him the tribute of South Carolina's gratitude for the many great services he rendered her; and, though we have not the right of voting for the nomination, yet we confirm and ratify it with all our hearts. . . . South Carolina records the motion, and ratifies, with all her heart, the nomination.

*   *   *

The President then announced the whole number of votes given to be 266; 177 necessary to a choice, consequently, Col. Polk, having received the entire vote of the convention, was declared unanimously nominated as the candidate of the democratic party for the presidency.

On this announcement being made, the whole assembly rose as one man, and gave three deafening and enthusiastic cheers, and nine cheers more for Col. Polk, amidst the waving of hats and handkerchiefs.

On motion of Mr. McCahen, of Philadelphia county, "three cheers were also given for Texas."

And afterwards, three cheers were also given for Mr. Van Buren.

On motion of Mr. McNulty, three cheers were likewise given for Colonel R. M. Johnson; and three for every gentleman that had been spoken of as a candidate for President of the United States.

The following table exhibits the ninth vote as first cast, and as afterwards corrected:

NINTH VOTE.

	As first cast.			As corrected.
	Van Buren.	Cass.	Polk.	Polk.
Maine,	0	1	8	9
New Hampshire,	0	0	6	6
Vermont,	0	6	0	6
Massachusetts,	0	2	10	12
Connecticut,	0	0	6	6
Rhode Island,	0	0	4	4
New York,	0	0	36	36
New Jersey,	0	5	2	7
Pennsylvania,	0	7	19	26
Delaware,	0	0	3	3
Maryland,	0	1	7	8
Virginia,	0	0	17	17
North Carolina,	0	0	11	11
Georgia,	0	0	9	9
Alabama,	0	0	9	9
Louisiana,	0	0	6	6
Tennessee,	0	0	13	13
Kentucky,	0	0	12	12
Ohio,*	2	2	18	23
Michigan,	0	5	0	5
Indiana,	0	0	12	12
Illinois,	0	0	9	9
Missouri,	0	0	7	7
Arkansas,	0	0	3	3
Mississippi,	0	0	6	6
	2	29	243	275

*Ohio cast 1 vote for Morton.

The enthusiasm which now filled the convention was indescribable, and continued to increase up to the hour of adjournment.

*   *   *

THURSDAY, MAY 30, 1844

The convention was called to order at 7½ o'clock, when . . .

Mr. Butler of New York, chairman of the committee to prepare an address to the people of the United States, reported the following resolutions, which were unanimously adopted; and, on motion, leave was granted to the committee to prepare the address at their leisure:

Resolved, That the American democracy place their trust not in factitious symbols, not in displays and appeals insulting to the judgments and subversive of the intellect of the people, but in a clear reliance upon the intelligence, the patriotism, and the discriminating justice of the American masses.

Resolved, That we regard this as a distinctive feature of our political creed, which we are proud to maintain before the world as the great moral element in a form of government, springing from and upheld by the popular will; and we contrast it with the creed and practice of federalism, under whatever name or form, which seeks to palsy the will of the constituent, and which conceives no imposture too monstrous for the popular credulity.

Resolved, therefore, That, entertaining these views, the democratic party of this Union, through their delegates assembled in a general convention of the States, coming together in a spirit of concord, of devotion to the doctrines and faith of a free representative government, and appealing to their fellow-citizens for the rectitude of their intentions, renew and re-assert before the American people, the declaration of principles avowed by them when, on a former occasion, in general convention, they presented their candidates for the popular suffrages: —

1. That the federal government is one of limited powers, derived solely from the constitution, and the grants of power shown therein, ought to be strictly constructed by all the departments and agents of the government, and that it is inexpedient and dangerous to exercise doubtful constitutional powers.

2. That the constitution does not confer upon the general government the power to commence and carry on a general system of internal improvements.

3. That the constitution does not confer authority upon the federal government, directly or indirectly, to assume the debts of the several States, contracted for local internal improvements, or other State purposes; nor would such assumption be just and expedient.

4. That justice and sound policy forbid the federal government to foster one branch of industry to the detriment of another, or to cherish the interests of one portion to the injury of another portion of our common country; that every citizen and every section of the country has a right to demand and insist upon an equality of rights and privileges, and to complete and ample protection of persons and property for domestic violence or foreign aggression.

5. That it is the duty of every branch of the government to inforce and practise the most rigid economy in conducting our public affairs, and that no more revenue ought to be raised than is required to defray the necessary expenses of the government.

6. That Congress has no power to charter a national bank; that we believe such an institution one of deadly hostility to the best interests of the country, dangerous to our republican institutions and the liberties of the people, and calculated to place the business of the country within the control of a concentrated money power, and above the laws and the will of the people.

7. That Congress has no power, under the constitution, to interfere with or control the domestic institutions of the several States; and that such States are the sole and proper judges of everything appertaining to their own affairs, not prohibited by the constitution: that all efforts of the abolitionists, or others, made to induce Congress to interfere with questions of slavery, or to take incipient steps in relation thereto, are calculated to lead to the most alarming and dangerous consequences; and that all such efforts have an inevitable tendency to diminish the happiness of the people, and endanger the stability

and permanency of the Union, and ought not to be countenanced by any friend to our political institutions.

8. That the separation of the moneys of the government from banking institutions, is indispensable for the safety of the funds of the government and the rights of the people.

9. That the liberal principles embodied by Jefferson in the declaration of independence, and sanctioned in the constitution, which makes ours the land of liberty, and the asylum of the oppressed of every nation, have ever been cardinal principles in the democratic faith; and every attempt to abridge the present privilege of becoming citizens and the owners of soil among us, ought to be resisted with the same spirit which swept the alien and sedition laws from our statute book.

Resolved, That the proceeds of the public lands ought to be sacredly applied to the national objects specified in the constitution; and that we are opposed to the law lately adopted, and to any law for the distribution of such proceeds among the States, as alike inexpedient in policy and repugnant to the constitution.

Resolved, That we are decidedly opposed to taking from the President the qualified veto power by which he is enabled, under restrictions and responsibilities, amply sufficient to guard the public interest, to suspend the passage of a bill, whose merits cannot secure the approval of two-thirds of the Senate and House of Representatives, until the judgment of the people can be obtained thereon, and which has thrice saved the American people from the corrupt and tyrannical domination of the Bank of the United States.

Resolved, That our title to the whole of the Territory of Oregon is clear and unquestionable; that no portion of the same ought to be ceded to England or any other power; and that the reoccupation of Oregon and the reannexation of Texas, at the earliest practicable period, are great American measures, which this convention recommends to the cordial support of the democracy of the Union.

Resolved, That this convention hereby presents to the people of the United States James K. Polk, of Tennessee, as the candidate of the democratic party for the office of President, and George M. Dallas, of Pennsylvania, as the candidate of the democratic party for the office of Vice President of the United States.

Resolved, That this convention hold in the highest estimation and regard their illustrious fellow-citizen, Martin Van Buren of New York: that we cherish the most grateful and abiding sense of the ability, integrity, and firmness with which he discharged the duties of the high office of President of the United States, and especially of the inflexible fidelity with which he maintained the true doctrines of the constitution, and the measures of the democratic party during his trying and nobly arduous administration; that in the memorable struggle of 1840 he fell a martyr to the great principles of which he was the worthy representative, and we revere him as such; and that we hereby tender to him, in his honorable retirement, the assurance of the deeply seated confidence, affection, and respect of the American democracy.

Resolved, That an address to the people of the United States, in support of the principles of the democratic party, and of the candidates presented, as their representatives, by this convention, be prepared by the committee on resolutions, and be published by them.

Resolved, That the proceedings of this convention be signed by its officers, and published in the democratic republican newspapers of the United States.

* * *

Letter from James K. Polk to John K. Kane
June 9, 1844

During the campaign Polk wooed the "protectionist" vote.

Dear Sir: I have received recently several letters in reference to my opinions on the subject of the tariff, and among others yours of the 30th ultimo.—My opinions on this subject have been often given to the public. They are to be found in my public acts, and in the public discussions in which I have participated.

I am in favor of a tariff for revenue, such a one as will yield a sufficient amount to the treasury to defray the expenses of the government economically administered. In adjusting the details of a revenue tariff, I have heretofore sanctioned such moderate discriminating duties, as would produce the amount of revenue needed, and at the same time afford reasonable incidental protection to our home industry. I am opposed to a tariff for protection *merely* and not for revenue.

Acting upon these general principles, it is well known that I gave my support to the policy of General Jackson's administration on this subject. I voted against the tariff act of 1828. I voted for the act of 1832, which contained modifications of some of the objectionable provisions of the act of 1828. As a member of the committee of ways and means of the house of representatives, I gave my assent to a bill reported to that committee in December, 1832, making further modifications of the act of 1828, and making also discriminations in the imposition of the duties which it proposed. That bill did not pass, but was superseded by the bill commonly called the compromise bill, for which I voted.

In my judgment, it is the duty of the government, to extend, as far as it may be practicable to do so, by its revenue laws and all other means within its power, fair and just protection to all the great interests of the whole Union, embracing agriculture, manufactures, the mechanic arts, commerce, and navigation. I heartily approve the resolutions upon this subject, passed by the democratic national convention, lately assembled at Baltimore.

I am, with great respect, dear sir, your ob't serv't,

Acceptance Letter of James K. Polk
June 12, 1844

In accepting the Democratic nomination Polk pledged that if elected President he would not seek a second term.

Gentlemen: I have had the honor to receive your letter of the 29th ultimo, informing me that the democratic national convention, then assembled at Baltimore, had designated me to be the candidate of the democratic party for president of the United States, and that I had been unanimously nominated for that office.

It has been well observed that the office of president of the United States should neither be sought nor declined. I have never sought it, nor shall I feel at liberty to decline it, if conferred upon me by the voluntary suffrages of my fellow citizens. In accepting the nomination I am deeply impressed with the distinguished honor which has been conferred upon me by my republican friends, and am duly sensible of the great and mighty responsibilities which must ever devolve on any citizen who may be called to fill the high station of president of the United States.

I deem the present to be a proper occasion to declare, that if the nomination made by the convention shall be confirmed by the people and result in my election, I shall enter upon the discharge of the high and solemn duties of the office with the settled purpose of not being a candidate for re-election. In the event of my election it shall be my constant aim, by a strict adherence to the old republican land marks, to maintain and preserve the public prosperity, and at the end of four years I am resolved to retire to private life. In assuming this position I feel that I not only impose on myself a salutary restraint, but that I take the most effective means in my power of enabling the democratic party to make a free selection of a successor who may be best calculated to give effect to their will, and guard all the interests of our beloved country.

With great respect, I have the honor to be your ob't servant,

James K. Polk

To Messrs. Henry Hubbard, William H. Ross, Benjamin H. Brewster, Romulus M. Saunders, Robert Rantoul, jr., committee of the Democratic National Convention at Baltimore.

Letter from Henry Clay to Messieurs
Thomas M. Peters and John M. Jackson
July 27, 1844

As the campaign wore on, Clay realized that his opposition to the annexation of Texas was seriously jeopardizing his chances; thus by mid-summer expediency demanded that he soften his position.

Gentlemen: I have received your favor informing me that my views, as disclosed in my letter from Raleigh, on the question of the annexation of Texas, are misconceived, if not misrepresented in your quarter; . . .

* * *

. . . How totally different are all the circumstances under which, with Mr. Adams' authority, I authorized the overture to Mexico, from those which attended the recent treaty of Mr. Tyler! So far from Mexico being silent, she repeatedly and solemnly declared that she would consider annexation as war with her. Texas was no longer an uninhabited country. It had been wrested from the dominion of Mexico by citizens, many of whom went armed from the United States. The war between Mexico and Texas had not been terminated by any treaty of peace. Mr. Tyler not only did not consult Mexico, but he announced that her assent to the annexation was altogether unnecessary. And he proceeded to conclude a treaty, embracing a large extent of territory, and a numerous population, not comprehended in the Texas which the United States ceded to Spain in 1819.

In the mean time, too, a powerful opposition had arisen in the United States against the annexation of Texas to them. Several States had declared, through their Legislatures, against it, and others, if not whole sections of the Union, were believed to be adverse to it. This was the opposition to the measure, to which, in my Raleigh letter, I alluded, when I spoke of a 'considerable and respectable portion of the *confederacy*.' I did not refer to persons but to States or sections.

Under such circumstances I could not but regard the annexation of Texas, at this time, as compromising the honor of my country, involving it in a war, in which the sympathies of all Christendom would be against us, and endangering the integrity of the Union. I thought then, and still believe, that national dishonor, foreign war, and distraction and division at home were too great sacrifices to make for the acquisition of Texas.

But, gentlemen, you are desirous of knowing by what policy I would be guided, in the event of my election as Chief Magistrate of the United States, in reference to the question of the annexation of Texas. I do not think it right to announce in advance what will be the course of a future Administration in respect to a question with a foreign power. I have, however, no hesitation in

855

saying that, far from having any personal objection to the annexation of Texas, I should be glad to see it, without dishonor, without war, with the common consent of the Union, and upon just and fair terms. I do not think that the subject of slavery ought to affect the question, one way or the other. Whether Texas be independent, or incorporated in the United States, I do not believe it will prolong or shorten the duration of that institution. It is destined to become extinct, at some distant day, in my opinion by the operation of the inevitable laws of population. It would be unwise to refuse a permanent acquisition, which will exist as long as the globe remains, on account of a temporary institution.

In the contingency of my election, to which you have adverted, if the affair of acquiring Texas should become a subject of consideration, I should be governed by the state of fact, and the state of public opinion existing at the time I might be called upon to act. Above all, I should be governed by the paramount duty of preserving this Union entire, and in harmony, regarding it as I do as the great guaranty of every political and public blessing, under Providence, which, as a free people, as we are permitted to enjoy.

I am, gentlemen, respectfully, Your obedient servant,

Letter from Henry Clay to the Washington *National Intelligencer*
September 23, 1844

Clay's growing embarrassment over the public ridicule over his fence-straddling position on Texas prompted this clarifying statement, which was, in essence, a return to his initial view.

Gentlemen: Since my nomination at Baltimore in May last, by the whig convention, as a candidate for the office of president of the United States, I have received many letters propounding to me questions on public affairs, and others may have been addressed to me which I never received. To most of those which have reached me I have replied; but to some I have not, because either the subjects of which they treated were such as that, in respect of them, my opinions, I thought, had been sufficiently promulgated, or that they did not possess, in my judgment, sufficient importance to require an answer from me. I desire now to say to the public, through you, that, considering the near approach of the presidential election, I shall henceforward respectfully decline to transmit for publication any letters from me in answer to inquiries upon public matters.

* * *

In announcing my determination to permit no other letters to be drawn from me on public affairs, I think it right to avail myself of the occasion to correct the erroneous interpretation of one or two of those which I had previously written. In April last I addressed to you, from Raleigh, a letter in respect to the proposed treaty annexing Texas to the United States, and I have since addressed two letters to Alabama upon the same subject. Most unwarranted allegations have been made that those letters are inconsistent with each other, and, to make it out, particular phrases or expressions have been torn from their context, and a meaning attributed to me which I never entertained.

I wish now distinctly to say that there is not a feeling, a sentiment, or an opinion expressed in my Raleigh letter to which I do not adhere. I am decidedly opposed to the immediate annexation of Texas to the United States. I think it would be dishonorable, might involve them in war, would be dangerous to the integrity and harmony of the Union, and, if all these objections were removed, could not be effected, according to any information I possess, upon just and admissible conditions.

It was not my intention, in either of the two letters which I addressed to Alabama, to express any contrary opinion. Representations had been made to me that I was considered as inflexibly opposed to the annexation of Texas under any circumstances; and that my opposition was so extreme that I would not waive it, even if there were a general consent to the measure by all the states of the Union. I replied, in my first letter to Alabama, that personally I had no objection to annexation. I thought that my meaning was sufficiently obvious, that I had no personal, private or individual motives for opposing, as I have none for espousing the measure, my judgment being altogether influenced by general and political considerations, which have ever been the guide of my public conduct.

In my second letter to Alabama, assuming that the annexation of Texas might be accomplished without national dishonor, without war, with the general consent of the states of the Union, and upon fair and reasonable terms, I stated that I should be glad to see it. I did not suppose that it was possible I could be misunderstood. I imagined every body would comprehend me as intending that, whatever might be my particular views and opinions, I should be happy to see what the whole nation might concur in desiring under the conditions stated. Nothing was further from my purpose than to intimate any change of opinion as long as any considerable and respectable portion of the confederacy should continue to stand out in opposition to the annexation of Texas.

In all three of my letters upon the subject of Texas, I stated that annexation was inadmissible except upon fair and reasonable terms, if every other objection were removed. In a speech which I addressed to the senate of the United States more than three years ago, I avowed my opposition, for the reasons there stated, to the assumption, by the general government, of the debts of the several states. It was hardly, therefore, to be presumed that I could be in favor of assuming the unascertained debt of a foreign state, with which we have no fraternal ties, and whose bad faith or violation of its engagements can bring no reproaches upon us.

"The Roerback Forgery"
Niles' Register, October 5, 1844

For the purpose of injuring Polk in the North, the Whigs widely circulated the Roerback letter which purported that Polk once was a slave trader. The following is a report of the incident in Niles' Register.

As the elections approach, not only the voters, but the editors of public journals have to be exceedingly vigilant, not to be imposed upon by the un-principled portion which mix in with, and form an ingredient in the contro-versies of all parties, ever ready to resort to any expedient for success, without regard to the character or other consequence of their movement. Just before an election, the evil one is certainly kept busy inventing expediencies and lies to supply the demand of the market. . . . One of the most flagrant cases of im-position upon the public press of this kind was perpetuated a few days ago and has already become notorious as the Koorback or as some have it, the Roer-back forgery. On tracing the article, it appears that a communication over the signature of "an abolitionist" was originally published in the *Ithaca Journal*, an abolitionist paper in the state of New York, professing to give an extract from a respectable volume published by a foreign traveler entitled *Koorback's Tour Through Southern and Western States in the Year 1836.* The correspondent observes: "This work has received the approbation of every American critic, not only for its graphic description of scenery, but for its candid and impartial remarks on men and manners. The Niles account then relates the "Roerback Story" of how a slave trader observed that "Forty of these unfortunate beings had been purchased, I was informed, by the Hon. J. K. Polk, the present spea-ker of the house of representatives; the mark of the branding iron, with the initials of his name on their shoulders distinguishing them from the rest."

The publication was copied from the *Ithaca Journal* by the *Albany Patriot,* another abolitionist paper, and from that it found its way into the *Albany Evening Journal,* a Whig paper, and thence into a number of other Whig papers.

Mr. Weed, editor of the *Albany Evening Journal,* may have been wanting in discretion in allowing himself to be imposed upon, but the moment he dis-covered the article to be forgery, made all the atonement an editor has in his power in such a case by stating it to be a forgery as publicly as he had con-tributed to its dissemination. The other responsible papers that had copied the article did so also and immediately. . . . The real author of the forgery has been found out in the meanwhile and now stands exposed. . . . The forgery and fraud is placed where it belongs, and consequences, if unpleasant, must re-coil, upon the Locofoco Party. [We] were imposed upon by a vile hoax, or something worse. Our agency in its circulation was wholly unsuspicious of its real character.

The affidavit of Mr. McKinney, showing the origin of this "Roerback's Tour," follows.

This is to verify, that on or about the 19th day of August, 1844 Mr. Wm. Lynn, esq. called on me with an article purporting to be an extract from Roerback's Tour through the Western and Southern States, requesting me to copy the same and hand it to the editor of the Chronicle for publication, stating as a reason for this request, that there was a loco foco printer in that office who was acquainted with his chirography. I complied with his request, without the slightest suspicion that it was not a genuine extract from a veritable book.

DANIEL MCKINNEY

Subscribed and sworn the 27th day of September, 1844, before me,

C. G. HEATH, J.P.

THE VOTES IN THE 1844 ELECTION

STATES	POPULAR VOTE			ELECTORAL VOTE	
	James K. Polk Democrat	Henry Clay Whig	James G. Birney Abolitionis	Polk and Dallas	Clay and Frelinghuysen
Maine..........	45,719	34,378	4,836	9	—
New Hampshire..	27,160	17,866	4,161	6	—
Vermont........	18,041	26,770	3,954	—	6
Massachusetts....	52,846	67,418	10,860	—	12
Rhode Island....	4,867	7,322	107	—	4
Connecticut......	29,841	32,832	1,943	—	6
New York.......	237,588	232,482	15,812	36	—
New Jersey......	37,495	38,318	131	—	7
Pennsylvania.....	167,535	161,203	3,138	26	—
Delaware........	5,996	6,278	—	—	3
Maryland........	32,676	35,984	—	—	8
Virginia.........	49,570	43,677	—	17	—
North Carolina...	39,287	43,232	—	—	11
South Carolina*..	—	—	—	9	—
Georgia.........	44,177	42,100	—	10	—
Alabama........	37,740	26,084	—	9	—
Mississippi.......	25,126	19,206	—	6	—
Louisiana........	13,782	13,083	—	6	—
Kentucky........	51,988	61,255	—	—	12
Tennessee........	59,917	60,030	—	—	13
Missouri.........	41,369	31,251	—	7	—
Arkansas........	9,546	5,504	—	3	—
Ohio............	149,117	155,057	8,050	—	23
Michigan........	27,759	24,337	3,632	5	—
Indiana.........	70,181	67,867	2,106	12	—
Illinois..........	57,920	45,528	3,570	9	—
	1,337,243	1,299,062	62,300	170	105

* Electors were appointed by the legislature.